A Frequency Dictionary c Arabic

A Frequency Dictionary of Arabic is an invaluable tool for all learners of Arabic, providing a list of the 5,000 most frequently used words in Modern Standard Arabic (MSA) as well as several of the most widely spoken Arabic dialects.

Based on a 30-million-word corpus of Arabic which includes written and spoken material from the entire Arab world, this dictionary provides the user with detailed information for each of the 5,000 entries, including English equivalents, a sample sentence, its English translation, usage statistics, an indication of genre variation, and usage distribution over several major Arabic dialects.

Users can access the top 5,000 words either through the main frequency listing or through an alphabetical index arranged by Arabic roots. Throughout the frequency listing there are thematically-organized lists of the top words from a variety of key topics such as sports, weather, clothing, and family terms.

An engaging and highly useful resource, *A Frequency Dictionary of Arabic* will enable students of all levels to get the most out of their study of modern Arabic vocabulary.

Tim Buckwalter is Research Associate at the University of Maryland.
Dilworth Parkinson is Professor of Arabic at Brigham Young University (Provo, Utah).

Routledge Frequency Dictionaries

Other books in the series

A Frequency Dictionary of American English
A Frequency Dictionary of Mandarin Chinese
A Frequency Dictionary of French
A Frequency Dictionary of German
A Frequency Dictionary of Portuguese
A Frequency Dictionary of Spanish
A Frequency Dictionary of Czech (forthcoming)

A Frequency Dictionary of Arabic

Core vocabulary for learners

Tim Buckwalter and Dilworth Parkinson

Routledge
Taylor & Francis Group

LONDON AND NEW YORK

First edition published 2011
by Routledge
2 Park Square, Milton Park, Abingdon, OX14 4RN

Simultaneously published in the USA and Canada
by Routledge
711 Third Ave, New York, NY 10017

Routledge is an imprint of the Taylor & Francis Group, an informa business

Typeset in Parisine by Graphicraft Limited, Hong Kong
Printed and bound in Great Britain by CPI Antony Rowe, Chippenham, Wiltshire

British Library Cataloguing in Publication Data
A catalogue record for this book is available from the British Library

Library of Congress Cataloging in Publication Data
A catalog record for this book has been requested

ISBN 13: 978-0-415-59543-8 (hbk)
ISBN 13: 978-0-415-44434-7 (pbk)
ISBN 13: 978-0-203-88328-0 (ebk)

Contents

Thematic vocabulary list

* includes countries where Arabic is co-official: Israel, Chad, and Somalia

Series preface

Frequency information has a central role to play in learning a language. Nation (1990) showed that the 4,000–5,000 most frequent words account for up to 95 percent of a written text and the 1,000 most frequent words account for 85 percent of speech. Although Nation's results were only for English, they do provide clear evidence that, when employing frequency as a general guide for vocabulary learning, it is possible to acquire a lexicon which will serve a learner well most of the time. There are two caveats to bear in mind here. First, counting words is not as straightforward as it might seem. Gardner (2007) highlights the problems that multiple word meanings, the presence of multiword items, and grouping words into families or lemmas, have on counting and analyzing words. Second, frequency data contained in frequency dictionaries should never act as the only information source to guide a learner. Frequency information is nonetheless a very good starting point, and one which may produce rapid benefits. It therefore seems rational to prioritize learning the words that you are likely to hear and read most often. That is the philosophy behind this series of dictionaries.

Lists of words and their frequencies have long been available for teachers and learners of language. For example, Thorndike (1921, 1932) and Thorndike and Lorge (1944) produced word frequency books with counts of word occurrences in texts used in the education of American children. Michael West's *General Service List of English Words* (1953) was primarily aimed at foreign learners of English. More recently, with the aid of efficient computer software and very large bodies of language data (called corpora), researchers have been able to provide more sophisticated frequency counts from both written text and transcribed speech. One important feature of the resulting frequencies presented in this series is that they are derived from recently collected language data. The earlier lists for English included samples from, for example, Austen's *Pride and Prejudice* and Defoe's *Robinson Crusoe*, thus they could no longer represent present-day language in any sense.

Frequency data derived from a large representative corpus of a language brings students closer to language as it is used in real life as opposed to textbook language (which often distorts the frequencies of features in a language, see Ljung, 1990). The information in these dictionaries is presented in a number of formats to allow users to access the data in different ways. So, if you would prefer not to simply drill down through the word frequency list, but would rather focus on verbs for example, the part of speech index will allow you to focus on just the most frequent verbs. Given that verbs typically account for 20 percent of all words in a language, this may be a good strategy. Also, a focus on function words may be equally rewarding – 60 percent of speech in English is composed of a mere 50 function words. The series also provides information of use to the language teacher. The idea that frequency information may have a role to play in syllabus design is not new (see, for example, Sinclair and Renouf, 1988). However, to date it has been difficult for those teaching languages other than English to use frequency information in syllabus design because of a lack of data.

Frequency information should not be studied to the exclusion of other contextual and situational knowledge about language use and we may even doubt the validity of frequency information derived from large corpora. It is interesting to note that Alderson (2007) found that corpus frequencies may not match a native speaker's intuition about estimates of word frequency and that a set of estimates of word frequencies collected from language experts varied widely. Thus corpus-derived frequencies are still the best current estimate of a word's importance that a learner will come across. Around the time of the construction of the first machine-readable corpora, Halliday (1971: 344) stated that "a rough indication of frequencies is often just what is needed". Our aim in this series is to provide as accurate as possible estimates of word frequencies.

Paul Rayson and Mark Davies
Lancaster and Provo, 2008

References

Alderson, J.C. (2008) Judging the frequency of English words. *Applied Linguistics*, 28 (3): 383–409.

Gardner, D. (2007) Validating the construct of Word in applied corpus-based vocabulary research: a critical survey. *Applied Linguistics*, 28, pp. 241–265.

Halliday, M.A.K. (1971) Linguistic functions and literary style. In S. Chatman (ed.) *Style: A Symposium*. Oxford University Press, pp. 330–65.

Ljung, M. (1990) *A Study of TEFL Vocabulary*. Almqvist & Wiksell International, Stokholm.

Nation, I.S.P. (1990) *Teaching and Learning Vocabulary*. Heinle & Heinle, Boston.

Sinclair, J.M. and Renouf, A. (1988) 'A lexical syllabus for language learning', in R. Carter and M. McCarthy (eds) *Vocabulary and Language Teaching*. Longman, London, pp. 140–158.

Thorndike, E.L. (1921) *Teacher's Word Book.* Columbia Teachers College, New York.

Thorndike, E.L. (1932) *A Teacher's Word Book of 20,000 Words*. Columbia University Press, New York.

Thorndike, E.L., and Lorge, I. (1944) *The Teacher's Word Book of 30,000 Words*. Columbia University Press, New York.

West, M. (1953) *A General Service List of English Words*. Longman, London.

Acknowledgments

We are indebted to a number of research assistants who put in countless hours on this project, most notably Bashar Sadr, Muhammed Barakat, Amany Ezzat, and Najwa Ezzat. We are also indebted to a number of students from Brigham Young University who helped with this project: Jeff Smith, David Tensmeyer, Laila Lamani, Shereen Salah, Rana Derwy, Mira Ansari, Falah Alsiekh, and Mais Yahya.

We are particularly indebted to Julie Vonwiller, Director of Appen Pty Limited, for providing us with the transcripts of an Algerian speech corpus compiled by Appen.

The first author is indebted to Arabic language experts Elizabeth M. Bergman from Miami University (Ohio) and Jonathan Owens from the University of Bayreuth, who provided assistance in interpreting data from the Algerian speech corpus. He would also like to express his gratitude to the University of Maryland Center for Advanced Study of Language (CASL) staff for their encouragement and support, especially during the analysis of Arabic dialect data. He also wishes to acknowledge the valuable assistance he received from Arabic dialect experts associated with research at CASL: Peter Schultz provided advice on vocabulary items from numerous dialects and proofread an early draft, and Sana Smith helped with difficult Algerian and Levantine lexical items. And finally, the first author is extremely grateful to his supportive wife Crissie who also provided research and editing in the final and critical stages of this work. He dedicates this dictionary to his parents, Albert and Lois, former missionaries, Bible translators, and lexicographers among the Toba Indians of the Argentine Chaco.

The second author would like to thank Brigham Young University and Dean John Rosenberg of the College of Humanities, as well as Prof. Kirk Belnap of the National Middle East Language Resource Center, for significant financial support for this project. He dedicates this book to his wife, Laura Beth, who is always up for another 'adventure' in the Arab World, and to his students, from whom he derives continual inspiration and admiration from their intense desire to reach across cultures and connect with people.

Abbreviations

a.p.	active participle	قادِم *adj.* next, following; *a.p.* arriving, coming
acc.	accusative	أخ brother; *acc.* أخا
adv.	adverb	هُنا *adv.* here
coll.n.	collective noun	سَمَك *coll.n.* fish, *un.n.* سَمَكَة
dem.pron.	demonstrative pronoun	ذٰلِكَ *dem.pron.* that (masc.sg.)
du.	dual	اللَّذانِ *rel.pron.* (masc.du.) who, whom; which
elat.	elative	أَفْضَل *elat.* better/best
fem.	feminine	كِلا *fem.* كِلْتا both of
fig.	figurative	شارع pl. شَوارِع street; (fig.) الشارع the public
gen.	genitive	ذُو having; *gen.* ذِي
imperat.	imperative	أَخَذَ *v. I (u)* to take sth; (imperat.) خُذْ
imperf.	imperfect	كادَ *I (a)* (with imperf.) to almost do sth
interrog.	interrogative	كَيْفَ *interrog.* how
invar.	invariable	غَلَط (Dia.) *adj.* (invar.) wrong
masc.	masculine	هٰذا *dem.pron.* this (masc.)
n.	noun	يَوْم *n.* pl. أيّام day
neg.	negative	لا *neg.part.* no
nom.	nominative	أب *n.* father; nom. أبُو
num.	number	أَلْف *num.* pl. آلاف thousand
part.	particle	قَدْ *part.* (with imperf.) may, might
pass.	passive	اِسْتَشْهَدَ *v. X pass.* اُسْتُشْهِدَ to be martyred
perf.	perfect	قَدْ *part.* (with perf.) has/have already
pers.	person	إيّا *part.* (with 2nd pers. *pron.*) إيّاكَ و/مِن be careful with, watch out for!
poss.adj.	possessive adjective	بِتاع *poss.adj.* (Egy.) belonging to; of
prep.	preposition	عَلى *prep.* on, above
prep.phr.	prepositional phrase	بِسْم *prep.phr.* بِسْمِ الله in the Name of God

pl.	plural	أَمْرِيكِيّ *n./adj.* pl. -uun, أَمْرِيكان American
p.p.	passive participle	مُشار *p.p.* المُشار إليه/إليها the aforementioned
pron.	pronoun	أَنْتَ *pron.* you (masc.sg.)
rel.	relative	الَّتِي *rel.pron.* (*fem.*sg.) who, whom; which
sg.	singular	نِساء *pl.n.* women (sg. اِمْرَأة)
un.n.	unit noun	بَيْض *coll.n.* eggs, *un.n.* بَيْضَة
vn.	verbal noun	وَضْع *vn.* laying down
voc.	vocative	*voc.part.* (you) O...!

Dialect and Regional Labels

Alg.	Algeria
Bah.	Bahrain
Dia.	Dialect
Egy.	Egypt
Gul.	Gulf
Irq.	Iraq
Jor.	Jordan
Kuw.	Kuwait
Leb.	Lebanon
Lev.	Levant
Lib.	Libya
MSA	Modern Standard Arabic
Magh.	Maghreb
Mor.	Morocco
Pal.	Palestine
Qat.	Qatar
Sau.	Saudi Arabia
Sud.	Sudan
Syr.	Syria
Tun.	Tunisia
UAE	United Arab Emirates
Yem.	Yemen

Introduction

A frequency dictionary of Arabic

Enrollments in university-level Arabic language programs in the United States have more than doubled in the past decade and in many cases rival enrollments in what used to be considered more commonly taught languages like German. High school Arabic programs are starting in almost every state. There is no question that the study of Arabic has become increasingly popular and widespread. Because this change has happened so quickly, the field of Arabic language teaching has been working hard to provide high quality materials and resources. This book is a contribution to that effort.

What is the value of a frequency dictionary for Arabic language teachers and learners? Isn't it enough to rely on the vocabulary lists in course text books and on regular dictionaries? The short answer is that although text books provide vocabulary in each chapter, there is almost never any indication of which of these words the student is most likely to encounter in actual conversations or texts. For independent learners the situation is even more frustrating. They may pick up a work of fiction or a newspaper and begin to work through the text looking up unfamiliar words in a dictionary. But they often have an uncomfortable suspicion that their time could be maximized if they could begin with the most common words in Arabic, using them as a core vocabulary on which more extensive reading could be based. Finally, frequency dictionaries can be a valuable tool for language teachers and materials developers. It is often the case that students enter into an intermediate language course with deficiencies in terms of their vocabulary. In these cases the teacher often feels frustrated because there doesn't seem to be any systematic way to bring less advanced students up to speed. With a frequency dictionary, however, the teacher could assign students to work through the list to fill in the gaps in their vocabulary in a way that makes most effective use of their time. And when they develop materials for their students, the frequency dictionary can be a guide to the difficulty and usefulness of any proposed text or exercise that involves vocabulary.

Arabic is reputed to have a remarkably rich vocabulary. Various statistical techniques have been devised to test this, all of which have major problems, but most scholars of Arabic still agree that Arabic seems to value the maintenance in the system of large numbers of synonyms, and that the overall vocabulary of the language is relatively large. This, in addition to the fact that Arabic has far fewer cognate forms for English speaking learners than most European languages do, makes the above-mentioned arguments for the value of a frequency dictionary even more salient in the Arabic case. The vocabulary acquisition task for students is both more extensive and more difficult, making techniques to maximize time spent learning vocabulary all the more important.

As stated, the purpose of this book is to prepare students of Arabic for the words they are most likely to encounter in the real world. In the case of Arabic, this brings up the issue not only of how frequently words are used, but what variety of Arabic those words come from. Students often complain that Arabs do not speak the way they do "in the textbook." Today one could add that when Arabs communicate by email or post messages on forums, blogs, and other social media, they do so in a language that is not entirely Modern Standard Arabic (MSA) or entirely dialect, but contains a mixture of both, often corresponding to the register, formal or informal, that the writer wishes to convey. It is often noted that even in highly formal social situations few educated native speakers of Arabic are able to make exclusively and sustained use of MSA, without resorting to the vocabulary, especially the function words, of their native dialect. Furthermore, due to the popularity of satellite television in the Arab world, many Arabs are now exposed daily to speakers of dialects other than their own, thereby increasing their comprehension of the more frequently occurring vocabulary items of these dialects. Therefore, one of the purposes of this book is to identify those

highly-frequent dialect words that often pop up in the middle of a conversation, written or spoken, that is otherwise in MSA, or a simplified form of MSA, or a combination of MSA and dialect. At the same time, it is noted that for communication to take place between Arabic-speakers from different dialect regions, usage of a considerable amount of MSA vocabulary is absolutely necessary. Furthermore, the dominance of MSA in formal written media and literature is undisputed, and it is certain that MSA will continue to occupy the center of most Arabic language curricula. In response to this sociolinguistic reality, this dictionary takes into account the current usage status of both MSA and the dialects, and attempts to provide an accurate record of the frequency of vocabulary used in both varieties.

What is in this dictionary?

The principal part of this book is the frequency dictionary proper, that is, the list of 5,000 most frequently used Arabic lemmas, as determined by the process described below. This information is arranged in four different formats: (i) a main frequency listing, which lists the lemmas (with their associated information) in order of descending frequency; (ii) an alphabetical index of these words; (iii) a frequency listing of the words organized by part of speech; and (iv) thematic lists, or "call-out" boxes, listing groupings of these words into related semantic classes.

For pedagogical reasons we have chosen to use the traditional system of arranging entries by root, which highlights important aspects of Arabic derivational morphology that play an important role in vocabulary development.

Each of the entries in the main listing contains the word itself (its headword or citation form), its part(s) of speech (verb, noun, adjective, etc.), a sample sentence or context reflecting actual usage, an English translation of that context, and summary statistical information about the usage of that word. The dictionary is focused on single words, so the treatment of collocations and multiword expressions falls outside its scope.

Previous frequency dictionaries of Arabic

Previously published frequency counts of Arabic have focused exclusively on the formal written language, Modern Standard Arabic (MSA), and have ignored spoken and dialectal Arabic. To be fair, these

frequency counts conformed to the language attitudes and pedagogical expectations of their day. The situation today, however, is quite different, as the use of colloquial Arabic in the media, both written and spoken, is widespread and growing, and Arabic textbooks for language learners have adjusted to this reality by including some vocabulary and phraseology from the major dialects.

Currently available frequency dictionaries of Arabic are seriously outdated and are based on corpora that are considered very small by today's standards. The following is a brief summary and description of previous frequency dictionaries of Arabic, in order of publication:

- Brill's (1940) *The Basic Word List of the Arabic Daily Press*, was based on a corpus of 136,000 words from the newspapers of Egypt and Palestine in the late 1930s;
- Aqil's (1953) *al-Mufradat al-Asasiyyyah lil-Qira'ah al-Ibtida'iyyah* (Basic vocabulary for elementary reading) was based on a corpus of 180,000 words taken from 18 elementary-level school readers used in six Arab countries;
- Landau's (1959) *A Word Count of Modern Arabic Prose*, incorporated Brill's frequency count of newspaper prose, and added a frequency count obtained from a comparable corpus of 136,000 words consisting of essays and learned prose;
- Abduh's (1979) *al-Mufradat al-Sha'i'ah fi al-Lughah al-Arabiyyah* (Frequently used Arabic vocabulary) included the surveys of Brill, Aqil, and Landau, to which he added the results of a survey he made earlier (1955–1957) of 255,000 words from Jordanian newspapers and elementary school readers;
- Fromm's (1982) *Häufigkeitswörterbuch der modernen arabischen Zeitungspache* (Frequency dictionary of modern newspaper Arabic), was based on a corpus of 79,561 words derived mainly from the editorial content of the leading government newspaper of Egypt, Syria, and Iraq;
- Kouloughli's (1991) *Lexique fondamental de l'arabe standard moderne* was based on a corpus of 200,000 words taken from newspapers and magazines from all parts of the Arab world, and includes extracts from plays and short stories of modern writers.

In addition the above publications, there are two surveys that focused exclusively on Arabic verb frequencies:

- Bobzin's (1980) "Zur Häufigkeit von Verben in Neuhocharabischen," *Zeitschrift für arabische Linguistik* (5:35–69) computed the frequencies of 43,543 verbs occuring in literature, cultural magazines, and scholarly publications in seven Arab countries;
- Bobzin's (1983) "On the Frequency of Verbs in Modern Newspaper Arabic," *al-Abhath* (31:45–63) surveyed 21,055 verb tokens from twelve different newspapers published from Baghdad to Algiers.

Of the above frequency dictionaries only Kouloughli (1991) is currently in print. Since the 1990s considerable progress has been made in corpus-based computational linguistics, making it possible to survey much larger amounts of data. In fact, computational corpus-based lexicography of MSA was introduced some years ago by lexicographers van Mol (2001) and Hoogland, Versteegh, and Woidich (2003), but corpus-based lexical statistics has not received adequate attention. In the meantime, the amount of Arabic data published on the Web has increased dramatically. Because this new electronic medium provides great freedom for self-expression, published material today covers not only MSA but also various forms of written Arabic dialect that are undergoing a process of orthographic standardization though widespread use.

In order to identify the most frequent 5,000 lexical items of Arabic one must develop a balanced corpus that includes not only the familiar MSA of newswire reports, newspaper editorials, academic and scientific publications, short stories, novels and other works of literature, but also the informal written Arabic and dialectal Arabic that abounds today on Internet discussion forums and the personal websites of social media. A frequency dictionary of Arabic would not be complete without a statistical survey of the daily spoken language as well, most of which is also in dialect. We addressed all these issues in selecting the corpus we would use for this frequency dictionary.

The corpus

Our dictionary was compiled from a corpus of 30 million words of which 10 percent was made up of spontaneous (unscripted) speech data, consisting mostly of informal conversations between individuals from the same country or region in the Arab world. These conversations were conducted primarily in a single dialect, although in some cases there was some use of simplified MSA when the register or tone of the conversations was more formal. The dialects and dialect groups represented in this collection were Egyptian, Levantine, Iraqi, Gulf and Algerian.

The remaining 90 percent of the corpus came from written sources, divided into five different text or genre types of equal size, i.e. about 5.4 million words each: (i) daily newswire; (ii) newspaper editorials, opinion essays, regular columns; (iii) learned prose, consisting mostly of articles in academic and scientific journals, including "Islamic guidance" essays, and popular but formal magazines and publications; (iv) postings on Internet discussion forums; and (v) literature and fiction, made up of short stories, novels, and plays. Several aspects of the written corpus are worth pointing out:

With the exception of the literature section, each of the five text types contained material originating from all regions of the Arabic-speaking world, from Morocco to Oman, and from Syria to Yemen, from a total of 90 different sources. Practically all of the texts were published in 2006–2007, with the exception of some academic, scientific and popular publications from the late 1990s, and some well-known works of fiction from the 1950s.

The daily newswire section of the corpus was obtained from the official news agency of each country, and was supplemented by front page (headline) news items from one of the leading newspapers in the same country. In order to avoid duplicate news items we limited selections to different years: e.g. 2006 for the country's official news agency, and 2007 for headline news from the leading newspaper of that country. The corpus section of newspaper editorials, opinion essays, and regular columns came primarily from long-standing and well-known newspapers of major Arab capital cities, as well as the leading pan-Arab newspapers in London and Paris. Samples of academic, scientific, religious, and popular formal writing was obtained primarily from weekly magazines and monthly journals, although in-depth articles from newspaper publications, especially from the "Friday supplement," were also found to fit in well with this genre or text type.

The corpus section containing postings on Internet discussion forums was our primary source for samples of informal written Arabic as well as written dialect. The discussion forums are dominated by the interests of youth culture (e.g. sports, technology, videos, music, and pop stars) and the concerns of women (e.g. child rearing, marital relations, soap operas, and cooking), and have become an important venue for obtaining religious guidance and medical advice, and for discussing personal and family issues. Although many of these topics have received coverage over the years in newspapers and magazines, in the forums they are covered more informally, directly, and personally. The language of the forums is unedited, unevenly censored, and often quickly produced. It abounds in first and second person discourse, and imperative verb forms, and proved to be an excellent source for the written forms of vocabulary associated primarily with spoken colloquial Arabic. In fact, many of the most frequent words in the spoken corpus also appeared in the forums section of the corpus, often with considerable orthographic variation. Recording this orthographic variation is an important part of the lexicographic description of these words.

The literature section of the corpus contained a solid core of works by recognized authors such as Naguib Mahfouz, Tawfiq al-Hakim, Ali Salim, Edwar al-Kharrat, Tayeb Salih, Ghassan Kanafani, Elias Khoury, Khalil Gibran, Ahlam Mosteghanemi, Tahar Ouettar, Najwa Barakat, as well as authors of more recent fame such as Rajaa Alsanea and Alaa Al Aswany. Supplementary works of fiction, especially short stories and poems, were obtained from the literary section of magazines and newspapers.

The first four sections of the written corpus (i.e. newswire, editorials, learned prose, and forums) were subdivided into document units of 200,000 words each, so that we had a total of 27 documents of equal size in each of these four sections (200,000 × 27 = 5.4 million words). The literature section of the corpus consisted of 72 documents of varying sizes, and the spoken corpus consisted of eleven subsections, also of varying sizes.

Annotating the data from the corpus

The first step in annotating the data was to generate a frequency count of all surface forms (i.e. Arabic words as they are actually written, with prefixes and suffixes) taking into account not only the raw frequency of these surface forms but also their distribution over the corpus. This was done in two separate processes, one for the written corpus and one for the spoken corpus. The purpose of this was to determine the optimum number of unique surface forms or types to analyze, disambiguate in context, and tag for lemmatization. We determined that we would begin by processing the top 20,000 word forms of the written corpus, after which we would examine the yield of disambiguated and tagged lemmas to determine if a larger selection of word forms was necessary. We used a similar approach with the spoken corpus, in which we tagged the most frequent 10,000 word forms, and then assessed the results in terms of lemmas covered. As it turned out, the combination of both processes yielded some 9,900 unique lemmas, with sufficient statistical evidence to identify with confidence the top 5,000 lemmas for this frequency dictionary. Lemmas at the very end of the frequency ranking display absolute frequency figures of around 200 occurrences, with a distribution over 50 percent of the corpus.

The top 20,000 word forms of the written corpus were processed using the Buckwalter (2004) morphological analyzer in order to assign one or more possible lemma tags to each word form, as well as to identify all prefixes and suffixes that would be listed in the frequency dictionary. The disambiguation and final tagging of each word form was done in an online interactive concordance and annotation tool developed at BYU and customized for this task. The core idea of the tool was that by allowing the annotator to sort all the concordance lines related to a single word form, either by the word before or the word after the word form, large numbers of similar items could quickly be coded at the same time, saving hundreds of hours of coding time. In this tool, the annotator selected from a menu of possible morphological analyses, applied the selection to the appropriate lines in the concordance, then clicked on a button to store that selection in a database. In other words, the process of disambiguation and tagging of the written corpus involved the examination of 20,000 individual concordance lines. The same process was followed for tagging the 10,000 most frequent word forms in the spoken corpus. Items for which no acceptable morphological analysis was available were tagged for separate processing. Much of the dialectal data, both

spoken and written, required manual analysis and tagging before storing the results in the database.

Organizing and categorizing the data

For determining the lemma status of words and for the general organization of lemmas we were guided by the content and arrangement of entries in the leading comprehensive dictionaries of MSA, namely Wehr (1985), Kropfitsch (1996), and Hoogland, Versteegh, and Woidich (2003), although some differences among these were duly noted. For guidance in integrating dialectal lemmas within the larger predominantly MSA lexicon we followed Bergman (2005) for Algerian, Hinds and Badawi (1986) for Egyptian, Woodhead and Beene (1967) for Iraqi, and Qafisheh (1997) and Holes (2001) for Gulf Arabic.

In addition to making use of standard part of speech labels such as "noun" and "adjective," we also used the sub-categories "verbal noun" as well as "active participle" and "passive participle" when it was felt that the lexicographic description warranted such distinctions. Active and passive participles were lemmatized with their adjectival counterparts, rather than counted as instances of the corresponding verb lemma. (A few exceptions were made for dialectal active participles that had no adjectival counterpart). However, these lexical items were labeled as active or passive participles in order to differentiate them from adjectival uses of the same lemma, in cases where this usage was attested. It was also observed that in many cases, items that carry the primary label "adjective" could also function syntactically as nouns. When such behavior was noted in the corpus data, it was also noted in the description, including any attested inflectional properties. It is important to note that the plural forms listed in this frequency dictionary, both regular and irregular ("broken"), are only those that were attested in the analyzed and tagged corpus. Similarly, dialectal labels within MSA lexical entries were applied only when such usage was attested in the data.

The morphology analysis and tagging process provided detailed statistics on bound morphemes. We have included in this dictionary only those bound morphemes that are traditionally listed in Arabic lexicons, such as the definite article *al-*, the conjunctions *wa-* and *fa-*, the prepositions *bi-*, *li-*, and *ka-*, etc. These bound morphemes as listed along with all the other entries in the alphabetical index.

Although suffixes are normally not listed in Arabic dictionaries, we decided that the dialectal negative marker −*sh* was sufficiently important for inclusion.

Frequency, range, and adjusted frequency ("Selecting the top 5,000 words")

Obtaining the raw or absolute frequency of each lemma was a fairly straightforward computational process. However, for selecting the most frequent 5,000 lemmas we needed to compute an adjusted frequency figure that took into consideration the dispersion characteristics of each lemma, that is, how each lemma was distributed over the different sections and document units of the entire corpus. A dispersion figure of 1.00 meant a perfect distribution over all sections of the corpus. We identified 191 corpus sections, of which 108 were of regular and equal size (200,000 words each from the first four sections of the written corpus: i.e. newswire, editorials, learned prose, and forums) and 83 sections of uneven size (from the literature and spoken corpus data), and adjustments were made to account for the relative size differences. The final adjusted frequency was obtained by multiplying the raw frequency by the dispersion figure. For example, the dialectal word كمان had a raw frequency of 8,928, but because its usage was restricted to 54.28 percent of the corpus, its adjusted frequency was 4,846 (8,928 × 0.5428), which placed it in rank position 768. Notice the raw frequency and range count (distribution) of the lemmas ranked directly before and after كمان (Table 1).

Because the spoken corpus accounted for only 10 percent of the data, much of the high-frequency vocabulary of spoken colloquial Arabic did not make it into the top 5,000 list. Those words that did make it, however, were dialect vocabulary items that are now also widely used in written media, and were observed to have relatively high frequencies and good distribution especially in the "forums" section of the corpus. In order to "rescue" some of these high-frequency dialect words that are primarily spoken, but not written, we experimented briefly with adding weights to the spoken corpus. However, it quickly became obvious that this process actually "promoted" many more MSA words that it did dialect words. Also, a comparison of the lists of words "lost" and words "gained" showed that there was nothing intrinsically "spoken" about the MSA words in the words "gained" list.

Table 1 Frequency and dispersion

Rank	Lemma	PoS	Gloss	Dispersion	Raw Frequency	Adjusted Frequency
767	قَرَّرَ	v. II	to decide	0.9660	5019	4848.6
768	كمان (Egy.Lev.)	adv.	also	0.5428	8928	4845.8
769	حَدِيث	adj.	new; modern	0.9660	5014	4843.5

The main frequency index

The main frequency index presents a rank-order listing of the top 5,000 lemmas in Arabic, from the highest-scoring lemma to the lowest-scoring one. Each entry contains the following information:

> rank frequency (1, 2, 3, ...), **headword**, *part(s) of speech*, English glosses (including any additional part of speech tags and relevant dialect labels), sample sentence or context, English translation of sample sentence or context, range count (dispersion), raw frequency total, indication of register variation

For example, here is the entry for the word مِلْعَقَة :

> **3495** مِلْعَقَة *n. pl.* مَلاعِق spoon; (also Egy.Lev.) مَعْلَقَة تشرب الشاي في كوب مع ثلاث ملاعق من السكر وبدون حليب — She drinks tea from a cup with three spoonfuls of sugar and without milk
>
> 41 | 873 | +for

This entry shows that the word in rank position 3495 is مِلْعَقَة, which is glossed as "spoon," and that its plural form is مَلاعِق (and by listing the plural we also imply that it was attested in the corpus). The entry goes on to say that in Egyptian and Levantine data the interesting variant form مَعْلَقَة occurred. An Arabic sentence from the corpus illustrates usage of the word—in this case the plural form—and is followed by an English translation. The last line in the entry presents the range count figure of 41, meaning that usage of this word was distributed over 41 percent of the corpus; the raw frequency figure of 873, which is the total number of occurrences for the singular and plural forms combined; and the "genre bias" tag +*for*, which indicates that a significant majority of uses were attested in the "forums"

section of the corpus. (Although we have computed the individual raw frequencies of all inflected forms, providing these additional statistical details in the current presentation format was not feasible).

The part of speech

Verbs were labeled with a part of speech code accompanied by the traditional Roman numeral designation for the derived form measures, namely I through X for triliteral roots, and QI and QII for quadrilateral roots. (Quadriliterals of form III and IV were not attested in the corpus). The part of speech tags of triliteral form I verbs also make note of the stem vowel of the Imperfect. All verbal nouns were lemmatized and counted separately from their respective verbs, and are often listed with their corresponding nominalized forms. The distinction between noun and verbal noun was made explicit primarily when the data provided ready evidence of the noun's inflection for number, which was also noted in the entry. Gender labels were provided for unmarked feminine nouns (e.g. حرب *fem.n.*) as well as masculine nouns with feminine suffixes (e.g. خليفة *masc.n.*). Collective nouns were labeled as such (e.g. ورق *coll.n.*) and their unit nouns were also identified (e.g. ورقة *u.n.*), provided that they had been attested in the corpus.

The English gloss

The English glosses are not comprehensive, but attempt to capture the most important or frequent meanings of the lemma. (In the alphabetical index, the glosses were further reduced to what could fit on one line of text). When concordance data showed a specific high-frequency collocation or idiomatic use whose meaning might not be deduced from the meaning of the lemma in isolation, an attempt was made to include the collocation and its gloss within the entry. Dialectal use was also noted in the English

gloss field, as well as any relevant pronunciation information.

Dialect information

Dialect labels were applied to lemmas that were exclusively dialectal, as well as lemmas that were primarily MSA but also manifested certain dialect-influenced uses that showed up in the data. Sometimes it was simply a frequent dialectal or regional spelling, like چان (and جان) for the verb كان, multiple pronunciations and spelling variations of what can essentially be considered the same word (e.g. هم /hum/ "they," which in the various dialects can be pronounced /humma/, /humme/ and /ham/, and written همه, هما, and همي), or specific dialectal meanings, such as عيش, ("life") which is "bread" in Egyptian, and "rice" in Gulf dialects. We applied dialectal labels only to describe what was observed and attested in the corpus.

Phrase in context and translation

The sample sentences and usage contexts came from the corpus itself. It should also be noted that for the sake of authenticity some common inconsistencies in Arabic spelling regarding the use of *hamza*, particularly, and *yaa'* without the two dots at the end of words, were left unchanged in the examples. These sample sentences also reflect real-world usage and certain ideological biases, and may not always be factual or politically correct. Their use in this dictionary does not imply any editorial endorsement of the ideas conveyed in these examples.

Statistical and register information

The last line of each entry contains two numbers separated by a vertical bar. The number on the left is the range count or dispersion figure discussed above. The number on the right is the raw frequency total of all the variant and inflected forms of the lemma represented by this entry. Some entries will contain additional register variation codes which record the observed "genre bias" of the lemma. These codes indicate whether the lemma occurred primarily in spoken data (+spo), in newspaper material (+news), in literature (+lit), or in informal written Arabic, i.e. the postings on Internet forums (+for). Note that by definition, data marked as +spo is almost all dialectal. Data marked as +for, however, contains a good balance of written dialect (e.g. عشان, كده, خالص, ياريت, and عقبال) and MSA that is

specific to informal on-line written discourse (e.g. انشالله, and جزيلا, مبروك, جزاك, مشكور) as well as the computer-oriented vocabulary of Arab Internet citizens (e.g. رابط, تحميل, حذف, زرّ, and إيميل).

Thematic vocabulary ("call-out boxes")

Some 30 tables of thematically-related words have been placed throughout the frequency index. Some of these tables include lists of words related to specific semantic classes, such as food, clothing, sports, colors, nationalities, and professions. Other tables focus more on grammatical aspects of Arabic, such as the derivational morphology system of base and augmented verbs, or the vocabulary of the regional varieties or different dialects of Arabic. In order to be more complete, some of these tables list vocabulary beyond the set of 5,000 described in the frequency index. Finally, although proper names are often excluded from frequency dictionaries, names in Arabic are especially challenging for the learner because of the absence of capitalization in Arabic, and because many names are also used as common nouns and adjectives. Our tables show, for example, that the most frequent female given name is زهرة ("flower"). Although names were not included in the list of top 5,000 lemmas, we obtained their individual frequencies and separate ranking in the process of disambiguating and tagging the data used for selecting the top 5,000 lemmas.

Alphabetical and part of speech indexes

The alphabetical index lists all 5,000 lemmas alphabetically according to the root system that is followed in most dictionaries and which facilitates internalizing the root and pattern morphology system of Arabic. The entries in the index are considerably abbreviated in order to fit on one line of text. Each entry provides the headword citation form, the part of speech, a basic English gloss, and the lemma's score (rank frequency) in the dictionary. The full description of the lemma can be found by looking up the rank frequency number in the main frequency listing.

The part of speech index provides two sections: one listing Function words (conjunctions, interjections, interrogatives, numbers, particles, prepositions, and pronouns) and the other listing Lexical words (adjectives, adverbs, elatives, nouns, and verbs). Each part of speech category is listed in descending rank frequency order.

References

Abduh, D. (1979)
al-Mufradat al-Sha'i'ah fi al-Lughah al-Arabiyyah. [Frequently used Arabic vocabulary]. Riyadh: University of Riyadh.

Bergman, E. (2005)
Spoken Algerian Arabic. Springfield, VA: Dunwoody Press.

Bobzin, H. (1980)
"Zur Häufigkeit von Verben in Neuhocharabischen." *Zeitschrift für arabische Linguistik* 5: 35–69.

Bobzin, H. (1983)
"On the Frequency of Verbs in Modern Newspaper Arabic." *Al-Abhath* 31: 45–63.

Brill, M. (1940)
The Basic Word List of the Arabic Daily Press. Jerusalem: Hebrew University Press.

Buckwalter, T. (2004)
Buckwalter Arabic Morphological Analyzer. Philadelphia: Linguistic Data Consortium.

Fromm, W-D. (1982)
Häufigkeitswörterbuch der modernen arabischen Zeitungspache: ein Mindestwortschatz: arabisch, deutsch, englisch. Leipzig: Verlag Enzyklopädie.

Hinds, M. and Badawi, S. (1986)
A Dictionary of Egyptian Arabic: Arabic-English. Beirut: Librairie du Liban.

Holes, C. (2001)
Dialect, Culture, and Society in Eastern Arabia: Vol. I, Glossary. Leiden: Brill.

Hoogland, J., Versteegh, K., and Woidich, M. eds (2003)
Woordenboek Arabisch-Nederlands. Amsterdam: Bulaaq.

Kouloughli, D. (1991)
Lexique fondamental de l'arabe standard moderne. Paris: L'Harmattan.

Kropfitsch, L. (1996)
Langenscheidt Handwörterbuch Arabisch-Deutsch. Berlin: Langenscheidt.

Landau, J.M. (1959)
A Word Count of Modern Arabic Prose. New York: ACLS.

No author (c. 1979)
Qa'imat Makkah lil-Mufradat al-Sha'i'ah. Mecca: Al-Wahda.

Qafisheh, H. (1997)
NTC's Gulf Arabic-English dictionary. Lincolnwood, Ill.: NTC Pub. Group.

van Mol, M. (2001)
Leerwoordenboek Arabisch-Nederlands. Amsterdam: Bulaaq.

Wehr, H. (1985)
Arabisches Wörterbuch für die Schriftsprache der Gegenwart. 5th ed. Wiesbaden: Harrassowitz.

Woodhead, D.R. and Beene, W. eds (1967)
A Dictionary of Iraqi Arabic: Arabic-English. Washington, DC: Georgetown University Press.

Frequency index

Format of entries

---

rank frequency, **headword**, *part of speech*, English equivalent

sample sentence — English translation

range count | raw frequency total | genre bias tag

---

1 الـ *part.* (definite article) the; (written لـ after *prep.*) لِلْكِتاب — أمضى البائع حياته في البحث عن الألماس — The seller spent his life searching for diamonds
100 | 5004793 |

2 وَ *conj.* and; *prep.* with
نعم، هناك مسؤولية عربية وهناك مسؤولية فلسطينية — Yes, there is an Arab responsibility and there is a Palestinian responsibility
99 | 1110144 |

3 في *prep.* in, inside; on (a date); at (a time); about (a topic); among (with pl. pron.) فِيكُم among you; could (in requests) هَل فِينا أَنْ could we...?
ربنا يكون في عون المسلمين في فرنسا وفي جميع الدول الإسلامية — May our Lord help the Muslims in France and in all Muslim countries
99 | 924823 |

4 مِن *prep.* from; (with foll. verb or vn.) since
الفن عبارة عن كأس، إما أن نشرب منه ماء عذبا وإما أن نتجرع منه ما يغضب الله — Art is just a cup, we can either use it to drink fresh water or we can use it to gulp down that which angers God (i.e. alcohol)
100 | 745190 |

5 لـ *prep.* for, to; (with pron.) لي/لِّي but لَـ for all others: لها, لَهُ, etc.
كيف تعاملت الحكومة الإيرانية معكم بعد وصول الإمام الخميني للحكم خلفا للشاه في ١٩٧٩؟ — How did the Iranian government deal with you after Imam Khomeini assumed power in succession to the Shah in 1979?
100 | 584786 |

---

1 Animals

1233	طير	bird	3860	عصفور	bird	6175	بوم	owl
1267	كلب	dog	3969	جمل	camel	6246	حمل	lamb
1916	سمك	fish	3998	نحل	bees	6256	دبّ	bear
2403	طائر	bird	4207	حمام	dove	6283	صقر	falcon, hawk
2456	خيل	horse	4354	داجن	chicken	6447	نمر	tiger
2665	دجاج	chickens	4575	حشرة	insect	6658	فراش	butterflies
2730	حمار	donkey	5042	فأر	mouse	7106	يراع	firefly
2884	ذئب	wolf	5145	غنم	sheep	7155	حيّة	snake
3103	قطّ	cat	5231	عنكبوت	spider	7297	ريم	white antelope, addax
3148	أسد	lion	5372	فيل	elephant			
3174	وحش	beast	5414	جواد	steed, horse	7563	فهد	lynx
3307	حصان	horse	5663	فرس	horse	7607	جدي	goat
3339	بقر	cows	5980	ديك	rooster	7869	بكر	young camel

6 بِـ *prep.* with, by; (with pron.) بِي، بِهِ، بِهَا, etc.;
بِسَبَب because of, due to
إذا كانت الحكومة الإسرائيلية تريد أن يعيش شعبها
بأمان فإن عليها أن تلتزم بقرارات الأمم المتحدة — If
the Israeli government wants its people to live in
security, then it has to adhere to the United
Nations resolutions
100 | 553234 |

7 عَلَى *prep.* on, above; (with pron.) عَلَيْـ;
عَلَيَّ (Lev.) عَلَيَّا (Dia.) on/above me
سقط الحاج محمود على الأرض من شدة وقع الخبر على
نفسه — Hajj Mahmud fell on the ground due to
the strong impact of the news on him
99 | 518692 |

8 أَنَّ *conj.* that (with foll. noun in acc.);
(with pron.) أَنَّنِي and أَنِّي that I; أَنَّنَا and
أَنَّا (less frequently) that we
هل هذا يعني أنكم ستدعمون موقف سوريا؟ — Does
this mean that you will support Syria's position?
99 | 303942 |

9 إِلَى *prep.* to, towards; till, until; (with pron.) إِلَيْهِ
to him/it, إِلَيَّ to me
يأتي إلينا السواح من مختلف دول العالم، إلا أن أعلى
نسبة منهم تأتي من أوروبا — Tourists come to us
from all countries of the world, but the highest
percentage of them comes from Europe
99 | 299648 |

10 كَانَ *v. I (u)* to be; (Irq.Gul.) جان /chaan/
ألم تكوني المرأة التي قلبت حياتي رأسا على عقب؟
— Weren't you the woman who turned my life
upside down?
100 | 281097 |

11 لا *neg.part.* no; not, non-; وَلَا...وَلَا neither...nor;
أَلَا doesn't/didn't...?; (Dia.) لأ /la'/ no
إنه لا يعرف إن كان ما يقرأ مقالا للرأي أو خبرا
— He doesn't know whether what he is reading is
an opinion article or a piece of news
99 | 247225 |

12 الله *n.* God, Allah; (with *prep.* لِـ) لله /li-l-laah/;
وَالله (I swear) by God; (in names) عبد الله Abdallah,
نصر الله Nasrallah
إن الحمد لله نحمده ونستعينه ونستغفره — Praise God.
We praise Him and seek His help and forgiveness
99 | 211480 |

13 أَنْ *conj.* (with subjunctive) to; لِأَنْ in order to;
بَعْدَ أَنْ (with perf. or imperf.): بَعْدَ أَنْ ذَهَبَ after
he went, بَعْدَ أَنْ يَذْهَبَ after he goes
يمكن أن يؤدي ذلك إلى صراع شامل — That could
lead to a wide-ranging conflict
94 | 192807 |

14 عَنْ *prep.* from, about; (with pron.) عَنِّي from/about
me; عَنَّا from/about us; عَنْ طَرِيقِ by way of, via
لم تصدر نشرات جديدة عنكم؛ ما سبب هذا النقص
الإعلامي؟ — No new bulletins have been issued
about you; what is the reason for this lack of
publicity?
100 | 180308 |

15 قَالَ *v. I (u)* to say إِنَّ that, to tell ل sb إِنَّ that
لا بد أن أقول إنني لا أختار مواضيع كتبي وإنما هي
التي تختارني — I must say that I don't choose
the topics of my books, they choose me
100 | 170778 |

16 هٰذَا *dem.pron.* this (masc.sg.); هاذا (non-standard
spelling); هدا (substandard or dialect spelling)
هذا ما ينتظره العالم — This is what the world is
waiting for
99 | 155507 |

17 مَعَ *prep.* with; مَعَ هٰذَا/ذٰلِكَ nevertheless; مَعاً
together; (Dia.) مَعَ (with pron.) مَعاي، مَعاك،
مَعايا, etc.; مَعَ السَّلَامَة goodbye!
ذهبت عندهما وبقت معها حتى ناما — She went to
(both of) them and stayed with (both of) them
till they fell asleep
99 | 152096 |

18 الَّتِي *rel.pron.* (fem.sg.) who, whom; which
عين في قسم الهيستولوجي بدلا من الجراحة العامة التي
كان يحلم بها — He was appointed in the Histology
Department instead of General Surgery which he
had been dreaming of
95 | 155316 |

19 كُلّ *n.* each; every; all (of); الكُلّ everyone;
كُلُّ مَنْ everyone that; كُلُّ مَا everything that;
كُلُّ شَيْء everything; كُلٌّ مِن each one of (the
following); عَكُلٌّ عَلَى كُلٍّ in any case, anyhow;
(Lev.) *adv.* anyways
لم تتكلم بكل ما تعلم — She didn't say everything
she knows
100 | 145875 |

20 هُوَ *pron.* he, it; (Dia.) /huwwa/, (Lev.) /huwwe/

لم أفعل شيئًا غير لائق.. بل هو الذي هبط علينا دون موعد — I didn't do anything inappropriate. In fact, he is the one who dropped in on us without an appointment

99 | 115797 |

21 فَـ *conj.* and, so; (Dia.) sometimes written separately as فا

لم تصل الرسالة، فاستفسرت عن السبب، فوجدت أن رجال البريد أرسلوها للمحافظة وليس للمدينة — The letter was not received, so I inquired about the reason and found out that the post office sent it to the district (building), not the city (building)

95 | 117124 |

22 هٰذِهِ *dem.pron.* this (fem.sg.), these (things)

مهمة هذه المصحة أن تساعد المرضى الميؤوس من شفائهم — The mission of this hospice is to help the incurably ill

99 | 110618 |

23 أَو *conj.* or

العناق العلني في الضيعة قد يكون بين أب وابنه أو بين رجل ورجل ولكن أبدًا ليس بين أب وابنته — Public hugging in the village can take place between a father and his son or a man and another man, but never between a father and his daughter

99 | 108848 |

24 الَّذِي *rel.pron.* (masc.sg.) who, whom; which

لم يبق سوى تلك الحقيبة التي قد تشهد على مروره من هنا — There is nothing left but that bag which may testify to his passing through here

96 | 108664 |

25 أَنا *pron.* I

أرجوكم ساعدوني فأنا لا أطيق ما حصل وما سيحصل — Please help me as I can't endure what happened and what will happen

99 | 104898 |

26 يَوْم *n.* pl. أَيّام day; اليَوْمَ today; (ما) يَوْماً some day; يَوْمَها that day; يَوْماً ever; (with neg.) never

شهدت محافظة عجلون خلال اليومين الماضيين تساقطًا كثيفًا للأمطار — Ajloun district witnessed heavy rainfall during the past two days

100 | 93393 |

27 لَمْ *neg.part.* (with jussive) did not; أَلَمْ didn't...?

اللافت أن هذا البطل السلبي لم يشعر يومًا بأي ندم إزاء ما ارتكب من أفعال شنيعة — What is intriguing is that this anti-hero never felt any remorse for the heinous actions he committed

96 | 94821 |

28 ما *neg.part.* not; أَما don't/doesn't/didn't...?

اللي بيدخن وما بيعمل رياضة نهائيًا بيتعب بربع ساعة — A person who smokes and doesn't exercise at all gets tired in a quarter of an hour

69 | 127514 |

29 إنَّ *conj.* (after the verb قالَ and the vn. قَوْل) that; (with pron.) إنَّني and (less frequently) إنِّي that I; إنَّا and إنّا that we

قال إن المحافظة استعدت جيدًا لهذه المناسبة — He said that the district prepared well for this occasion

99 | 86705 |

30 ما *rel.pron.* what, whatever, that which

أصبح بمقدور المستعمرين أن يقتلوا ما شاءوا من الهنود بلا أدنى ظل من الندم أو الشعور بالذنب — The colonists were able to kill whatever Indians they wanted to, without the slightest shadow of regret or feelings of guilt

87 | 95564 |

31 بِـ /bi-/ (Egy.Lev.) *part.* (with imperf., indicates continuous or habitual action; Lev. also /mi-/ with 1st pers. pl.); بيقول /bii'uul/ he says, he's saying; بتحب...؟ /bitHibb/ would you like...?

قول بسم الله الرحمن الرحيم وانت بتفتح — Say "in the name of God, the Merciful, the Compassionate" as you open (the door)

97 | 84571 | +spo +for

32 بَيْنَ and ما بَيْنَ *prep.* between; among; (with pron.) بَيْني وَبَيْنَكَ between (just) me and you; بَيْنَنا وَبَيْنَهُم between us and them; فِيما بَيْنَنا among ourselves

ربما كنت أريد أن أضع حاجزًا بيني وبينك — Maybe I wanted to put a barrier between me and you

99 | 81509 |

33 هِيَ *pron.* she; it (fem.sg.); they (non-human pl.);
هي and هيه (Egy.Irq.Gul.) /hiyya/, (Lev.) /hiyye/
هي تعرف أن الولد يسرق — She knows that the
boy steals

99 | 79477 |

34 بَعْدَ *prep.* after; (with pron.) بَعْدَهُ after him/it,
بَعْدِي after me
اكتشف بعد ثلاثين عاما أنه أخطأ بالهجرة إلى أمريكا
— He realized after thirty years that he made
a mistake by immigrating to America

99 | 76319 |

35 يا *voc.part.* (you) O...!; يا أُسْتاذا Sir!; *interj.* oh!
how (wonderful, horrible, etc.) يا سَلام! wow!;
(Dia.) يا..يا *conj.* either...or; (Irq.) *interrog.* which
هل أنت شيوعي يا صديقي؟ — Are you a
communist my friend?

78 | 96575 |

36 ذلِكَ *dem.pron.* that (masc.sg.)
كان ذلك في العام ١٩٨٠ م عندما كنت في زيارة
للعاصمة الإيطالية — That was in the year 1980 AD
while I was on a visit to the Italian capital

99 | 75488 |

37 قَدْ *part.* (with perf.) has/have already; كانَ قَدْ
had already; يَكُونُ قَدْ will have already
كان ذلك الاستقبال العدائي قد خلف في نفسها شعورا
مقبضا — This hostile reception left a tight
feeling in her soul

91 | 73404 |

38 آخَر *adj.* pl. -uun, أُخَر fem. أُخْرَى pl. أُخْرَيات
other, another; one more, additional; هُوَ الآخَر
he also, هِيَ الأُخْرَى she also
يجب أن نحترم الرأي الآخر ولو كان مخالفا أو حتى
متصادما مع قناعتنا — We must respect others'
opinion even if it is in disagreement with or
even in contradiction to our convictions

99 | 63343 |

39 شَيْء *n.* pl. أَشْياء thing, something; (Lev.Irq.Yem.)
شي /shii/, (Gul.) شي /shayy, shey/, (Lev.)
اشي /'ishi/, شي /shi/ (Mor.) *indef.art.* a, one
طلب مني أن أخرج كل ما معي من أشياء وأن أضعها
على الطاولة أمامه — He asked me to get out all
the things I had and to put them on the table in
front of him

100 | 63264 |

40 عِنْدَ *prep.* with, next to; at (time, location); (with
pron. often indicating possession = "to have")
عِنْدِي I have, ما عِنْدِي I don't have
هي في الواقع ابنة عمي الذي كنت أقيم عنده أيام
دراستي — Actually she is the daughter of my
uncle whom I used to live with back in the days
when I was a student

99 | 60994 |

41 أَوَّل *adj.* fem. أُولَى, pl. أَوائِل first; best,
top-most; *n.* أَوَّل beginning; أَوائِل forefathers;
أَوَّلًا first of all, primarily
أول ما نلاحظه هو تزايد نسبة الذكور مقارنة بنسبة
الإناث — The first thing we notice is the growing
percentage of males compared to that of
females

100 | 59417 |

42 غَيْر *n.* other (than), different (than); *neg.part*
not; غَيْرَ أَنَّ however, but; بِغَيْر without
ذبح الأعرابي ناقته التي لا يملك غيرها طعاما وقدمها
لضيفه تقديرا واحتراما — The Bedouin (man)
slaughtered the only (female) camel he owned
and offered it as food to his guest in respect
and appreciation

99 | 56329 |

43 إذا *conj.* when, if, whenever; (in indirect
questions) (ما) إذا if, whether; وَإِذا بِ and (then)
suddenly
إنها مجنونة ولا تصلح له أبدا، وإذا تزوجها سيتحول
بيتها إلى ساحة معارك — She is crazy and not good
for him at all, and if he marries her, their house
will turn into a battlefield

99 | 52854 |

44 نَفْس *n.* pl. أَنْفُس (with pron.) same, self
وجد نفسه واقفا وسط عشرات المنكوبين المذهولين —
He found himself standing among dozens of
confused victims

100 | 52702 |

45 عَرَبِيّ *n./adj.* pl. عَرَب Arab; Arabian; Arabic;
عَرَبِي (Dia.) *n.* Arabic (language)
إنهم ليسوا عربا في الأصل، وإنما استوطنوا في هذه البلاد
منذ مئات السنين — They are not of Arab origin,
but they have settled in this country for
hundreds of years

98 | 53325 |

46 أيّ *n.* fem. أيّة (in idafa) any; *interrog.* what, which; *rel.pron.* whatever, whoever

منعها من الخروج من المنزل أو إقامة أي صلة مع الناس — He forbade her from leaving the house or having any contact with (other) people

99 | 51568 |

47 رَئيس *n.* pl. رُؤَساء president, leader; chief, head, chairman; *adj.* main, chief, principal

رئيس الوزراء نوري المالكي التقى عقب وصوله أمريكا أمس الثلاثاء بالرئيس الأمريكي جورج بوش في البيت الأبيض — After his arrival in America yesterday (Tuesday), Prime Minister Nouri Al-Maliki met with the American President George Bush in the White House

97 | 52478 |

48 عَمَل *vn.* working; *n.* pl. أعْمال work, activity, action

كيف تصفين عملك كمراسلة صحافية في زمن الحرب؟ — How do you describe your job as a media correspondent in time of war?

99 | 50613 |

49 عَرَف *v.* I (i) to know sth/sb or أنّ that; (perf.) to learn, find out أنّ that; (Lev.) عَرَفْت كِيف؟ you see (what I mean, what I'm saying)?

أنا لا أقبل الإشراف على أي طالب إلا بعد أن أعرف، إلى حد ما، طريقة تفكيره — I don't agree to supervise any student until after I know, to some extent, his way of thinking

100 | 50348 |

50 بَعْض *n.* some, several; بَعْض الشَّيْء a little, to some extent; مَع بَعْض together; بَعْضُهُم بَعْضاً each other; عَلى بَعْض on top of each other; وَراءَ بَعْض in line, in a row (one behind the other)

حُرم من دخول بعض الأندية بسبب لون بشرته الأسمر وأصله العربي — He was banned from entering some clubs because of his dark skin color and Arab origin

99 | 49902 |

51 دَوْلَة *n.* pl. دُوَل state, country

لم يعد واضحا ما إذا كان حل الدولتين للصراع الإسرائيلي الفلسطيني مازال ممكنا — It is not clear any more whether the two-state solution to the Israeli-Palestinian conflict is still possible

98 | 49360 |

52 كَما *conj.* and, also, as well

أتوقع أنني لن ألقاك ما دمت رئيسا للوزراء، تماما كما حصل مع سلفك — I expect that I will not meet you as long as you are a Prime Minister, just like what happened with your predecessor

96 | 48078 |

53 إلّا *part.* (exception) except (for), but (for), save; إلّا أنّ however, except that; وَإلّا otherwise

أحس بأني عرفتك من قبل في أزمان قديمة، وإلا فكيف تفسرين هذا الانجذاب بيننا منذ اللحظة الأولى؟ — I feel that I have known you since ancient times, otherwise how can you explain this attraction between us from the moment we first met?

99 | 46733 |

54 أنْتَ *pron.* you (masc.sg.); (Dia.) انته , إنت and انتا /'inta/

أنا مجرد مساعد وأنت جراح كبير — I am just an assistant, and you are a great surgeon

98 | 45267 |

55 كَثير *adj.* pl. -uun many, much, numerous; كَثيراً very much; كَثيراً ما frequently, often; (Egy.) /kitiir/, (Lev.) /ktiir/ *adj./adv.* كتير

رأيت الكثير في حياتي وسمعت أمورا كثيرة ولكني لم أهتم بالتفاصيل — I've seen a lot in my life, and I've heard many things, but I haven't cared about the details

99 | 44541 |

56 واحِد *num.* one; *adj.* one, single; (Dia.) *n.* fem. واحدة, وحدة /waHda/ a person, someone

هؤلاء يكذبون ويقولون إننا شعب واحد — These (persons) are lying and saying that we are one people

99 | 43466 |

57 لأنَّ *conj.* because (with foll. noun in acc.); (with pron.) لأنِّي because I; لأنَّنا and لأنَّني because we

كان يجب أن أصل قبل حلول الظلام لأنني إن تأخرت فسأضل الطريق — I had to arrive before nightfall because if I were late I would lose my way

99 | 43701 |

58 لٰكِنَّ *conj.* (with pron. or following noun in acc.) however, but; لٰكِنِّي and لٰكِنَّنِي however I, but I
هو في الأربعين لكنه في صورة ابن العشرين — He is forty, but he looks twenty

90 | 45859 |

59 لَيْسَ *v. I* (perf. only) لَيْسَت he/it is not, she/it is not, لَسْنا we are not; أَلَيْسَ isn't...?
لو استطعت أن أوظفكم جميعا عندي لفعلت، ولكن ذلك ليس في وسعي — If I could employ all of you I would have done it, but that isn't within my reach

90 | 45416 |

60 جَدِيد *adj.* pl. جُدُد new, modern; مِن جَدِيد again, anew
هل هناك نية لضم لاعبين جدد لفريق النجف؟ — Is there any intention to add new players to the Najaf team?

99 | 40375 |

61 إِنْ *conj.* if; whether; وَإِنْ even if, although; ما إِنْ..حَتَّى no sooner had...than, had just...when
هذا فعلا ما تريده المرأة وإن تظاهرت بالعكس — This is what the woman really wants, even if she pretends the opposite

99 | 40464 |

62 عام *n.* pl. أَعْوام year
أعمل مدرسا للغة العربية في مدارس المحافظة منذ عام ١٩٩٥ — I have worked as an Arabic language teacher in the district's schools since the year 1995

99 | 38637 |

63 أَحَد *n.* fem. إِحْدَى one (of), someone; anyone; (neg.) nobody, no one; *num.* (in compounds) eleven أَحَدَ عَشَر, fem. إِحْدَى عَشْرَة
إنك لا تثق بأحد! لا تثق إلا بطائفتك — You don't trust anyone! You only trust (the people of) your sect

100 | 37897 |

64 أَكْثَر *elat.* more/most, greater/greatest in number
نام ليلته الأولى في هذه القرية قبل أكثر من عام — He slept his first night in this village more than a year ago

99 | 37538 |

65 كَبِير *adj.* pl. كِبار large; great, important, major; adult, senior; pl.n. الكِبار adults
يلبس عمامة كبيرة تميل قليلا إلى الأمام — He is wearing a large turban that is tilted slightly forward

99 | 37236 |

66 أَخ *n.* pl. إِخْوَة ,إِخْوان brother; (in idafa) nom. أَخُو, gen. أَخِي, acc. أَخا; (with pron.) أَخُوهُ ,أَخُو his brother; أَخِي my brother, (Lev.Gul.) أَخُوي ,ياخي (Dia.) ,أَخُويا (Egy.Irq.) ,ياخُوي يا أَخِي my friend; (hey) buddy ياخُويا = يا أَخِي
هذا البيت ليس بيتك ولا أم لك فيه ولا أخ — This house is not your house, and you have neither a mother nor a brother in it

99 | 36766 |

67 كَيْفَ *interrog.* how; (Lev.) /kiif, keef/, (Gul.) چيف /cheef/; (with pron.) كيفك (Lev.) /kiif-ak, keef-ak/ how are you?
سوف اعلمه كيف يعتمد على نفسه وكيف يتوقف عن الاعتماد علي — I will teach him how to depend on himself and how to stop depending on me

99 | 36412 |

68 قَبْلَ *prep.* before; مِن قَبْل before, prior to; *adv.* (also مِن قَبْلُ) previously, earlier
قبل انتهاء العام بيومين حدث زلزال رهيب دمر قرى عديدة في تركيا — Two days before the end of the year a terrible earthquake happened and destroyed many villages in Turkey

99 | 35711 |

69 سَنَة *n.* pl. سِنُون ,سَنَوات (gen./acc. سِنِين) year
لم أره منذ خمس سنوات — I have not seen him in (the past) five years

99 | 34782 |

70 أَمْر *n.* pl. أُمُور matter, issue, concern, affair
أريده لأمر مهم لا يقبل التأجيل — I need him for an important matter which cannot be postponed

99 | 34681 |

71 قُوَّة *n.* pl. -aat وقُوَىً قِوَىً and power, strength, force; قُوّات (armed) forces
أصيب فتيان بنيران قوات الاحتلال الإسرائيلي في قطاع غزة — Two boys were injured by the fire of the Israeli occupation forces in the Gaza Strip

99 | 34642 |

72 هَل *interrog.* هَل هُناك is there any...?
هل يمكن للواحدة منا أن تنسى أحلام وأحاسيس
المراهقة؟ — Is it possible for (any) one of us to
forget the dreams and emotions of adolescence?

98 | 34854 |

73 خِلال *prep.* during, through; في خِلالِ in the
course of; في خِلالِ ذلِكَ meanwhile; مِن خِلالِ by
means of, through; across, via; on the basis of,
based on
نحو ستة آلاف عامل مناجم لقوا حتفهم خلال العام
الماضي بسبب حوادث في الصين — About six
thousand mine workers met their death during
the past year because of accidents in China

87 | 39028 | +news

74 مَرَّة *n. pl.* -aat, مِرار time, moment, occasion;
مَرَّةً once; مَرَّتَيْنِ twice; مِراراً repeatedly; مَرّاتٍ
several times, repeatedly; بالمَرَّة totally,
completely; (with neg.) never, not at all
كان مجد الدين حريصا على أن يزوره مرة أو مرتين كل
عام — Magd Al-Din made sure to visit him once
or twice a year

99 | 33861 |

75 رَأَى *v. I* يَرَى to see sth/sb; to think, believe أَنَّ
that
هل تصدقين أنني لم أر خالي منذ أكثر من ستة أشهر؟ —
Do you believe that I haven't seen my (maternal)
uncle for more than six months?

99 | 34062 | +lit

76 أَب *n. pl.* آباء father; الأَبَوانِ the parents;
(in idafa) nom. أَبُو, gen. أَبِي, acc. أَبا; (with
pron.) أَباهُ، أَبِيهِ، أَبُوهُ his father; أَبِي my father,
(Lev.Gul.) أَبُويَ، (Egy.Irq.) أَبُّويَ
وجد فيه الأب الذي حرم منه — He found in him
the father (figure) that he had been deprived of

99 | 33766 |

77 هُناكَ *adv.* there, over there; there is, there are;
مناك /minnaak/ (Irq.Gul.) from there, from that
place; لهُناك /la-hunaak/ (Dia.) to there, to that
place
عندما لا يجد مالا يشتري به الخمر، يضطر للسرقة من
هنا وهناك — When he doesn't find money to
buy alcohol, he is forced to steal from here and
there

99 | 33870 |

78 تَمَّ *v. I* (i) to finish, conclude, come to an end;
to take place, be held (event)
تمت محاكمتنا في حزيران أمام محكمة عسكرية —
Our trial took place in June before a military
court

97 | 34557 |

79 حَيْثُ *adv.* where, in which; *conj.* and
بِحَيْثُ، حَيْثُ أَنَّ so that, in order to; أَنَّ since,
because, given that; مِن حَيْثُ الـ in terms of,
based on
قررت أن آخذهما معا إلى بيتي حيث أصبح لهما مكان
ثابت في مكتبي — I decided to take both of them
to my house where they came to have a stable
place in my office

97 | 34098 |

80 ثان (def. الثاني) *adj.* second, additional; next,
following; ثانِياً secondly, furthermore; ثانِيَةً
again, once more; تاني (Egy.) *adv.* again,
more, also
وجدت نفسها وحيدة في غرفة الجلوس، فصعدت إلى
الدور الثاني — She found herself alone in
the sitting room, so she went up to the
second floor

99 | 33321 |

81 حَتَّى *prep.* until, up to; لحتى (Lev.) /la-Hatta/
prep. until, up to
عليك أن تغذي حبك حتى ينمو ويزدهر — You
have to nourish your love until it grows and
prospers

99 | 33051 |

82 جَميع *n.* all (of); every one (of); الجَميع
everyone; جَميعاً altogether; all, entirely
تحياتي لجميع العاملين بالمجلة لجهودهم من أجل إعداد
جيل واع مثقف — My greetings to all the
magazine staff for their efforts in preparing
a perceptive and educated generation

100 | 32553 |

83 مِنْطَقَة (often مَنْطَقَة or مَنْطِقَة) *n. pl.* مَناطِق region,
area, zone, territory
تطمح إلى تعزيز حضورها وتوسعة نطاق أعمالها في
منطقة الخليج — (The company) aspires to
enhance its presence and expand the range
of its businesses in the Gulf region

98 | 32675 |

84 حَقّ *n.* truth; pl. حُقُوق (legal) right; law; *adj.* true, right; حَقّاً really, truly

يَجِب أن نعطي المرأة حقوقها ونترك لها حريتها — We must give the woman her rights and leave her her freedom (referring to women in general)

99 | 32127 |

85 أَمِيرِكِيّ and أَمْرِيكِيّ /'ameeriki/ *n./adj.* pl. -uun, أَمِيرِكان, أَمْرِيكان /'ameerikaan/ American

قال إن هناك حاجة ملحة لآلاف من القوات الأمريكية هناك لصد التمرد — He said that there is an urgent need for thousands of American troops to repel the insurgency there

96 | 33325 |

86 مِثْل *n.* pl. أَمْثال (somebody, something) like, similar; (in idafa) مِثْلَ like, such as; أَمْثالَ like, such as, the likes of

هل كل واحدة تحب زوجها مثلك يا ست زهرة؟ — Does every woman love her husband like you do, Mrs. Zahra?

99 | 31527 |

87 لَوْ *conj.* if; وَلَوْ even if; لَوْلا if not, if it weren't for

لو كنت تزوجت في فترة مبكرة من عمري لكان لدي أبناء — If I had married at an early stage of my life, I would have had children

99 | 31350 |

88 عامّ *adj.* general, common, public

هذه أمور لا يجدر بإنسان أن يناقشها في أماكن عامة — These are matters which people should not discuss in public places

98 | 30916 |

89 اِسْم *n.* pl. أَسْماء, أسام (def. أسامي) name

تظهر المرأة على التليفزيون بجِوار اسمها الحقيقي ومهنتها — (This) woman appears on television with her real name and profession

99 | 30452 |

90 أَمْكَنَ *v. IV* to be possible (ل for sb) to do sth; يُمْكِنُكَ أَنْ it's possible to (do sth); you can (do sth)

2 Body

110	قلب	heart	2441	سِنّ	tooth	3859	رقبة	neck
130	عين	eye	2476	كفّ	palm	4351	جوف	belly
148	يد	hand	2548	عظم	bone	4356	رجل	leg
170	وجه	face	2619	إصبع	finger	4373	كلية	kidney
215	رأس	head	2686	أيسر	left hand	4388	عصب	nerve
363	دم	blood	2844	مرارة	gall bladder	4524	رئة	lung
627	قدم	foot			(also bitterness)	4672	ثدي	breast
786	صدر	chest	3082	كبد	liver	4846	حلق	throat (also
947	شعر	hair	3122	عنق	neck			chasm, gorge)
1026	لسان	tongue	3151	أنف	nose	4897	عاتق	shoulder
1327	يمين	right hand	3247	عضلة	muscle	5183	معى	intestine
1373	ظهر	back	3262	حضن	bosom	5248	كاهل	nape of neck
1423	عقب	heel (also	3278	كتف	shoulder	5945	أنملة	fingertip
		after)	3286	ذراع	arm	6053	خدّ	cheek
1476	راحة	palm (also	3323	فؤاد	heart	6479	كعب	heel, ankle
		rest)	3327	جبين	forehead	6556	ساعد	forearm
1525	فم	mouth	3376	هيكل	skeleton (also	6772	حنك	jaw
1853	أذن	ear			framework)	6780	ركبة	knee
2080	بطن	stomach	3479	دماغ	brain	7250	مرفق	elbow
2089	شفة	lip	3629	معدة	stomach	7330	جمع	fist
2178	جلد	skin	3642	شريان	artery	7744	ثمّ	mouth
2322	أيمن	right hand	3786	بشرة	skin			
2372	رحم	womb	3818	مخّ	brain			

كان هناك فندق اسمه ويلورد مشهور وهو لا يزال موجودا ويمكن أن تزوره — There was a famous hotel named Wilword, and it is still there and you can visit it

99 | 30678 |

91 لٰكِن *conj.* however, but; (also لاكِن in informal or sub-standard spelling)

وتساءلت: أين هيئة الرقابة على الدواء والغذاء؟ لكن أحدا لم يرد — And I asked: Where is the food and drug control administration? But nobody answered

90 | 33727 |

92 رَجُل *n.* pl. رجال *n.* man

هل المرأة أكثر صبرا من الرجل؟ — Is the woman more patient than the man?

99 | 30264 |

93 عالَم *n.* pl. -uun, عَوالِم world; رَبّ العالَمِين Lord of the Universe (God)

كان عالمنا الصغير يتسع كل يوم ونحن نكتشف الجديد — Our small world was getting bigger every day as we discovered new things

99 | 30204 |

94 حَياة *n.* life

— لماذا لا تتكلم؟ لماذا لا تحدثني عن ماضي حياتك؟ Why don't you speak? Why don't you tell me about your past life?

99 | 30100 |

95 مَوْضُوع *n.* pl. مَواضِيع subject, topic, issue, theme; *adj.* placed, laid down; located, situated; spurious (Hadith)

أحب أن ألفت انتباهك إلى أن كلامك خارج عن موضوع الدرس تماما — I would like to draw to your attention to the fact that your talk is completely outside the subject matter of the study

97 | 30657 |

96 وَزير *n.* pl. وُزَراء minister

تضم هذه الوزارة ٢٤ وزيرا بينهم امرأة واحدة — This government includes 24 ministers only one of whom is a woman

97 | 30636 |

97 نَحْنُ *pron.* we; حنا, إحنا /iHna/ (Dia.); نحنا /niHna/ (Lev.)

لماذا يعاقبنا الله نحن المسلمين عندما نقترف الذنوب فى حين يتساهل مع الأمريكيين؟ — Why is God punishing us, the Muslims, when we commit sins while he is going easy on the Americans?

99 | 29658 |

98 وَقْت *n.* pl. أوْقات time, moment, period; فِي الوَقْت الذي while

هو — صديقي. من حقي أن أستقبله في أي وقت He is my friend. I have the right to receive him any time

99 | 29493 |

99 بَلَد *n.* (rarely fem.; Dia. masc./fem.) pl. بُلْدان, بِلاد country, nation; البِلاد the country; بَلَد (Egy.Lev.) fem.n. town, village

أمضيت كثيرا من السنين في بلدان مثل المغرب وإيران وأفغانستان — I spent many years in countries like Morocco, Iran, and Afghanistan

99 | 29658 |

100 مَن *rel.pron.* who, whom

كل من يقرأ التاريخ الأمريكي لابد أن يتوقف أمام هذه المفارقة — Whoever reads American history has to be struck by this paradox

92 | 31648 |

101 مَجْلِس *n.* pl. مَجالِس council, board; مَجْلِس الشَّعْب parliament; مَجْلِس الشُّيُوخ (US) Senate

كذلك اطلع المجلس على التقارير الخاصة بالإصلاح البيئي — The Council also took a look at the reports concerning environmental reform

96 | 30206 |

102 قامَ *v. I* (u) to rise, stand up; to undertake, carry out بـ (task, activity); to play بـ (a role); to be based على on; (with imperf.) to start to do sth

قمنا بهذا العمل منذ زمن طويل — We carried out that work a long time ago

99 | 29003 |

103 حُكُومَة *n.* pl. -aat government, administration

لا أريد للمطعم أن يكبر فيلفت نظر الحكومة — I don't want the restaurant to get bigger and attract the attention of the government

95 | 29332 |

104 بَيْت *n.* pl. بُيُوت house; family; pl. أَبْيَات verse (poetry)

في النهاية يجب أن يكون لديها بيت وأسرة وأطفال — In the end she must have a house, a family, and children

99 | 27875 |

105 دُونَ *prep.* without; under, below; مِن دُونِ and بِدُونِ without

المشكلة العراقية تحل من قبل العراقيين بدون تدخل أطراف أخرى — The Iraqi problem will be solved by the Iraqis without the interference of other parties

99 | 27400 |

106 سِياسِيّ *adj.* political; *n.* pl. -uun, سَاسَة politician, statesman

يحدد زعيم القبيلة أو شيخ القرية الاتجاه السياسي لسكان القرى والأرياف الخاضعة لسيطرته — The leader of the tribe or the Sheikh of the village determines the political direction of the inhabitants of the villages and the countryside that is subject to his control

95 | 28526 |

107 فِلَسْطِينِيّ *n./adj.* Palestinian

في مقهى في عمان عرفه رفيقه فائز بمجموعة من الفلسطينيين — In a coffee house in Amman, his companion Fayiz introduced him to a group of Palestinians

94 | 28613 |

108 ثُمَّ *conj.* then, afterwards; besides, furthermore

أذهب إلى مكتبي كل صباح ثم أعود آخر النهار — I go to my office every morning then I come back at the end of the day

80 | 33045 |

109 جاء *v. I (i)* to come (إلى to); to come to sb: e.g. جاءَتْني صَدِيق a friend came to (see) me; جاءني رِسالَة I received a letter; to appear, show up (في in sth written or spoken)

أوضحوا أن الارتفاعات في الاسعار جاءت كنتيجة حتمية لارتفاع أسعار الأعلاف والمياه وأجور النقل — They clarified that the rise in prices came as an inevitable result of the rise in the prices of feed and water and transportation costs

99 | 26234 |

110 قَلْب *n.* pl. قُلُوب heart; center, essence; *vn.* overthrowing, toppling (a regime); turning over (pages)

دق قلبه بسرعة مع مجيء القطار — His heart beat quickly with the coming of the train

99 | 26075 |

111 أَلْف *num.* pl. آلاف thousand; (du.) أَلْفانِ (gen./acc. أَلْفَيْ/أَلْفا) two thousand, أَلْفَيْ كِتاب two thousand books

عدد العراقيين المتواجدين في الأردن من خمسمائة ألف إلى سبعمائة ألف عراقي وهذا عدد هائل — The number of Iraqis present in Jordan is from five hundred thousand to seven hundred thousand Iraqis, and this is a huge number

99 | 26022 |

112 اللي /illi/ (Dia.) *rel.pron.* that, which, who; whoever, whichever; (Lev. also) يللي /yalli/; (Lev.Gul.) هاللي /ha-lli/ (this, the one) that

فين الشقة اللي مفروض نقعد احنا فيها؟ — Where's the apartment we are supposed to stay in?

81 | 31362 |

113 راح *v. I (u)* (Dia.) to go; راح (Dia.) future marker (with imperf.) will (do sth), (is/are) going (to do sth); (MSA) راحَ ضَحِيَّة to be the victim of; (Dia.) to pass على sb by (opportunity), leave على sb behind (time)

سكانها الدروز وين راحوا؟ ليش راحوا؟ ليش باعوها؟ — Where did its Druze inhabitants go? Why did they go? Why did they sell them?

98 | 25643 | +spo

114 ناس *pl.n.* (also fem.sg.) people, humans; persons

أحب أن أكون محاطة بالناس في كل لحظة وحتى اللحظة الأخيرة التي تسبق نومي أكون فيها مع أهلي — I like to be surrounded by people at every moment, even the last moment before I go to sleep I am with my family

100 | 25207 |

115 طَرِيق *fem./masc.n.* (MSA rarely fem.; Lev. mostly fem.) pl. طُرُقات, طُرُق road, course; way, method; عَن طَرِيق via, by way of; by means of, by using

التاريخ الآن على مفترق الطرق فلا القديم قد انتهى تماما ولا الحديث قد بدأ بعد — History now is at a crossroads, since the old has not completely ended, and the new has not yet started

99 | 24751 |

116 أَرْض *fem.n.* pl. أَراضٍ (أَراضِي .def) earth, ground; land, territory

لمن أصابه الزهايمر أو فقد الذاكرة الفلسطينيون يقاومون احتلال أرضهم والصهاينة هم المحتلون — For anyone who has been struck by Alzheimers or memory loss, the Palestinians are resisting the occupation of their lands, and the Zionists are the occupiers

99 | 24627 |

117 سَبَب *n.* pl. أَسْباب reason, cause; بِسَبَبِ because of

المسيح لا يحل لرجل أن يطلق امرأته لأي سبب إلا لعلة الزنا — Christ does not permit a man to divorce his wife for any reason except perhaps adultery

99 | 24502 |

118 شِرَكَة *n.* pl. -aat company, corporation

قد خصصت الشركة ٦ ملايين جنيه للتوسعات والإحلال والتجديد بالشبكة ولاستقرار التغذية الكهربائية — The company designated 6 million pounds for widening, setting up and renewing the network, and for the stability of the power supply

97 | 24875 |

119 عَدَد *n.* pl. أَعْداد number, quantity; (periodical) issue, edition; بَيْنَ أَعْدادِ الـ among those who

هل يستطيع أن يحصى أوقاته السعيدة؟ كم عددها؟ — بضعة أشهر؟ عدة أيام؟ Can he count his happy times? How many are they? A few days? A few months?

98 | 24721 |

120 صُورَة *n.* pl. صُوَر picture, image, photo; manner, way, form

هل جورج واشنطن الذي حقق استقلال اميركا من الاحتلال البريطاني كان ارهابيا؟ بالعكس، يضعون صورته اليوم على العملة، لأنه وقف في وجه الغزاة وحرر ارضه — Was George Washington, who achieved the independence of America from British occupation, a terrorist? On the contrary, they put his picture today on the currency, because he stood in the face of the invaders and liberated his land

99 | 24052 |

121 دَوْلِيّ and دُوَلِيّ *adj.* international, world, global; دُوَلِيّاً internationally, worldwide, globally; دَوْلِيّ *adj.* (rare) state, national

اكد قبل النهائيات انه سيعتزل اللعب دوليا بعد المونديال — He confirmed before the finals that he will retire from international play after the World Cup

96 | 24817 |

122 شَعْب *n.* pl. شُعُوب people, nation

على الغرب عدم الإساءة إلى الشعوب بإطلاق تسميات كمحور الشر ولصق تهمة الإرهاب بالإسلام — The West should not insult people by calling them names like "Axis of Evil" and accusing Islam of terrorism

98 | 24222 |

123 عاد *v. I (u)* to return, go back إلى to sth; to be attributed إلى to sth/sb; (with imperf.) عادَ يَفْعَلُ to repeat sth, do sth again; (neg.) لَمْ يَعُدْ (Dia. ما عاد) to no longer do sth or be sth

أعزائي المشاهدين فاصل قصير ونعود لنواصل هذا الحوار نعود إليكم بعد لحظات نحن معكم ابقوا معنا — My dear viewers, a short break and we will return to continue this dialog. We will return to you. After a few moments we will be with you. Stay with us

99 | 23911 |

124 شاء *v. I (a)* to want, desire sth; كَما شِئْتَ as you wish; إن شاء الله and انشاء الله (informally) hopefully, God willing (انشاله)

نحن مستعدون لسماع كل وجهات النظر المعارضة لكن أن يصبح لكل شخص إذاعة وتلفزيون ويقول ما يشاء — فهذه فوضى وليست حريات We are prepared to listen to all opposing points of view but for every person to have their own radio and television program and say whatever he wants, well that is chaos, and not freedom

98 | 24097 | +for

125 آن *n.* time, moment; الآنَ now

البلد الآن يواجه حالة خطيرة جدا، وهي أن الأمن مفقود إلى حدود كبيرة — The country now faces a very dangerous situation, namely that security is lacking to a large extent

98 | 23885 |

126 أَرَادَ *v. IV* to want, desire sth or أَنْ to do sth
المواطن العراقي يريد حياته ويريد أمه ويريد أطفاله ويريد أكله وخبزه وكهرباءه وصحته — The Iraqi citizen wants his life and he wants his mother and he wants his children and he wants his food and his bread and his electricity and his health
97 | 23965 |

127 إِنَّ *part.* indeed
إن مكة حرمها الله، ولم يحرمها الناس — God is the one who made Mecca a sacred place, not people
72 | 32395 |

128 أَهْل *coll.n.* pl. أَهالٍ (def. الأَهالي) family, relatives, folks; people, inhabitants; أَهْلًا welcome! hello! /'ahleen/ أهلين (Lev.)
نواجه مشاكل حينما يرسب الطلاب في التوجيهي فيأتي الأهل ويسألون لماذا رسب ابني أو ابنتي وقد كان معدله في الأول الثانوي ٩٥٪ — We face problems when students fail in final secondary school exam, since the family comes and asks why did my son or daughter fail when his average for the first year secondary exams was 95%
99 | 23479 | +spo

129 تِلْكَ *dem.pron.* that (fem.sg.); those (non-human pl.)
أحست في تلك اللحظة بأنها غريبة ووحيدة وضائعة — She felt, at that moment, that she was a stranger, alone and lost
89 | 25722 |

130 عَيْن *fem.n.* pl. أَعْيُن, عُيُون eye; water spring, water source; spy, secret agent; eye (needle)
ظل يغمز لها بعينه — He kept winking at her with his eye
100 | 22982 |

131 الَّذِينَ *rel.pron.* (masc.pl.) who, whom; (with prep. لِـ) لِلَّذِينَ
هذه اللقاءات تسهم في خلق علاقات مباشرة بين الممثلين الذين سيعملون في السفارات المصرية — These meetings help create direct relationships between the representatives who will be working in Egyptian embassies
98 | 23446 |

132 شَكْل *n.* pl. أَشْكال manner; form, shape; appearance, look; (Gul.Lev.) شكلي /shakl-i/ it seems to me, شكلك /shakl-ak/ it seem that you
لابد أن يتعلم أبناؤنا كيف ينتمون إلى بلدهم وبشكل عملي حقيقي، وليس من خلال شعارات تعبوا وتعبنا كلنا منها — Our children need to learn how to belong to their country in a real practical way, and not through slogans which they and we are all tired of
99 | 23021 |

133 عَمَلِيَّة *n.* pl. -aat operation, process
في اعتقادي سنفرغ من العملية في ظرف يومين — In my opinion we will be finished with the operation in about two days
98 | 22811 |

134 أَمَّا *part.* (focus) أَمَّا .. فَـ as for..., concerning...; أَمَّا بَعْدُ approx. and now, to our main point
فأنا يخيل لي اني لم اتغير جسمانيا منذ ربع قرن.. اما هو فلم يتغير فيه شيء كأنه لم يفارقنا الا لأمسية واحدة — It seems to me that I have not changed physically in a quarter century. As for him, nothing has changed in him, as if he had only left us for an evening
99 | 22527 |

135 خاصّ *adj.* special, specific; private, personal; exclusive, elite
كان السلطان يثق فى طبيبه الخاص اليهودي ربما أكثر من أولاده وزوجاته — The Sultan trusted his private Jewish doctor perhaps more than his children or his wives
99 | 22528 |

136 حَوْلَ *prep.* around; about, concerning
استقبلتني غيمة كبيرة من دخان الغليون المعطر.. تلفت حولي لأرى إن كانت هناك نافذة — A big cloud of perfumed pipe smoke greeted me. I looked around me to see if there was a window
99 | 22294 |

137 عَمِلَ *v. I (a)* to work, function; to make, prepare, build sth
أمها تعمل اختصاصية اجتماعية، وأبوها طبيب أسنان — Her mother works as a social specialist, and her father is a dentist
99 | 22316 |

138 عَنَى *v. I (i)* to mean, imply sth or أَنَّ that; (pass.) عُنِيَ يُعْنَى to be concerned ب with, take an interest ب in

تعرفين جيدا ماذا تعنين بالنسبة إليّ، لكني أمر بأزمة لن أخرج منها قريبا — You know well what you mean to me, but I am passing through a crisis which I am not going to be able to get out of soon

99 | 22428 |

139 وَجَدَ *v. I (i)* to find sth/sb; (pass.imperf.) يُوجَدُ to exist (there is, there are)

شرحت له نوع الاغاني التي في حيازتنا ولم أجد المصطلح الملائم له في الانكليزية — I explained to him the type of songs which are in our possession, and I couldn't find the appropriate term for it in English

90 | 24528 |

140 خَيْر *n.* goodness, good; *adj.* better (مِن than), best; نَحْنُ بِخَيْر we're fine; صَباح الخَيْر good morning!; الوِقايَة خَيْرٌ مِن العِلاج prevention is better than cure

وجدته خير زوج يمكن أن تحلم به امرأة — I found him to be the best husband a woman could dream of

99 | 22099 |

141 شو /shu/ (Lev.Kuw.UAE) *interrog.* what

شو رأيك بالوضع السياسي في البلد؟ — What is your opinion regarding the political situation in the country?

59 | 36869 |

142 آه (Dia.) *interj.* yes, right, ah, yeah

زوجي لم يقل لي لا آه ولا لأ قال لي إن شاء الله — My husband neither said "yes" nor "no" to me, he said "if God's willing"

38 | 57277 | +spo

143 وَطَنِيّ *adj.* national; nationalistic; *n.* pl. -uun nationalist

مصر تحتاج الآن إلى العمل الوطني المباشر أكثر بكثير من احتياجها إلى مدرسين ومحاسبين — Egypt now needs direct national action a lot more than it needs teachers and accountants

95 | 22704 |

144 مَدِينَة *n.* pl. مُدُن city

يحتاج إلى أحد يأخذ بيده في هذه المدينة — He needs someone to take him by the hand in this city

99 | 21718 |

145 اِبْن *n.* pl. أَبْناء son; أَبْناء البِلاد children; the native population; (shortened to بن after personal name) عمر بن الخطاب

كل أب في الدنيا يكن كراهية عميقة لزوج ابنته مهما تظاهر بالعكس — Every father in the world harbors a deep hatred for the husband of his daughter, no matter how much he pretends the opposite

99 | 21714 |

146 أَيْض *n.* أَيْضاً also, as well; besides

قيل إنه مختل عقليا، وقيل أيضا إنه الرجل الثالث في الحزب النازي بعد هتلر وجورنج — It was said that he was mentally retarded, and it was also said that he was the third man in the Nazi Party after Hitler and Goering

96 | 22381 |

147 طَيِّب *adj.* good, nice; pleasant; delicious; *interj.* good, fine, OK; (Egy.Lev. shortened to طَب; Lev. shortened also to طا)

أليس هناك حل يقي الرجل الطيب من الهلاك دون أن يهدد سعادتها؟ — Isn't there a solution that saves the good man from annihilation without threatening her (woman's) happiness?

99 | 21587 |

148 يَد *fem.n.* pl. أَيْدِ (def. الأَيْدِي) hand; (Dia.) إيديك /'iideek/ your (two) hands; إيد

كثير من النازحين وضعوا مصيرهم بين أيدي عصابات المهربين لاجتياز خليج عدن وصولا إلى اليمن — Many refugees put their fate in the hands of gangs of smugglers to cross the Gulf of Aden to arrive in Yemen

100 | 21407 |

149 سَـ *part.* (future marker, short form of سَوْفَ) will

مكتب البعثات سيتكفل بمصاريف الدراسة — The office of (overseas student) delegations will cover educational expenses

90 | 23562 |

150 مَشْرُوع *n.* pl. -aat, مَشَارِيع project, enterprise; *adj.* lawful, legal; مشروع قانون bill, draft law
هناك مشروع آخر لمكافحة عمل الأطفال ولكن المشكلة أكبر من المشروع — There is another project to fight children working, but the problem is bigger than the project
99 | 21424 | +news

151 ثَلَاثَة *num.* fem. ثَلَاث three; ثَلَاثَةَ عَشَر thirteen; تلاتة /talaata/ (Egy.), /tlaate/ (Lev.), تلاثة /tlaatha/ (Irq.)
ظهرت فجأة ثلاث عربات جيب يقودها جنود عراة الصدر قادمة من الشمال مسرعة — Three jeeps suddenly appeared driven by bare-chested soldiers coming quickly from the north
99 | 21101 |

152 صَوْت *n.* pl. أَصْوات voice, sound; vote
ولما انفض الاجتماع سمعت صوتا يناديني وأنا ماض نحو الباب الخارجي — When the meeting ended I heard a voice calling me as I was heading toward the outside door
100 | 20881 |

153 أَمَام *n.* front, front part; أَمَامَ in front of, facing; إلى الأَمَام forward
وجه إليه بقدمه ركلة قوية دفعته إلى الأمام وكادت تسقطه — He aimed a strong kick at him which sent him reeling forward and almost knocked him over
90 | 22799 |

154 سَمِعَ *v.* I (a) to hear sb, إلى listen to sb
مشى رأفت مبتعدا وسمع خلفه ماكس يتحدث إلى شخص آخر — Ra'fat walked away and he heard Max behind him talking to someone else
99 | 20116 |

155 نِسْبَة *n.* pl. نِسَب ratio, rate, percentage figure; بالنِّسْبَة إلى concerning, regarding, in relation to
قاس الطبيب وزن الطفل وطوله وحسب نسبة الوزن الى الطول — The doctor measured the baby's weight and height, and he calculated the weight to height ratio
96 | 20802 |

156 بَس (Egy.Lev.Irq.Gul.) *adv.* only, just; *conj.* however, but; (Lev.Irq.Gul.) *interj.* enough! stop! (Lev.) (with imperf.) as soon as
مش كده وبس، بعت شكوى للسياحة من عشرين صفحة — Not only that, but I sent a twenty-page complaint to the (Ministry of) Tourism
43 | 46255 |

157 حال *n.* (rare as fem.) pl. أَحْوال situation, condition, case; كَيْفَ حالُكَ how are you?; حالاً immediately, right now; لَحَال (Lev.) *adv.* (with pron.) لحَالَك alone, by yourself
لو استمر على هذه الحال فلن يجددوا عقده مهما يكن تعاطفهم — If he continues in this condition, they will not renew his contract no matter how much sympathy they have
99 | 20003 |

158 شَهْر *n.* pl. شُهُور, أَشْهُر month
جلسنا منذ شهر لساعة كاملة كان يحدثني فيها عن آماله وأحلامه — We sat a month ago for a whole hour in which he talked to me about his hopes and dreams
99 | 19967 |

159 هُنا *adv.* here
إنني عازم أن لا أموت هنا — I am determined not to die here
99 | 19821 |

160 بَل *conj.* but, rather; in fact
لا يوجد لدينا جمهور يعشق ناديه بل يعشقون فلان وعلان — We don't have fans who love their club (i.e. club's team), but they love this person (i.e. player) or that
89 | 22123 |

161 بَرْنامِج *n.* pl. بَرامِج program
إذا نجح فريق المحبة فإن المدمن يكون جاهزا لبدء برنامج علاجي مكون من ١٢ خطوة — If the "love team" succeeds, the addict will be ready to begin a 12-step treatment program
97 | 20293 |

162 لَن *neg.part.* (with subjunctive) will not, will never
هذه الأم لن تستطيع أن توفر الرعاية الكاملة لتوائمها الثلاث — This mother will not be able to provide full care to her triplets
95 | 20626 |

163 أُم n. pl. أُمَّهات mother; بِأُمِّ العَيْن/عَيْنَيْهِ with one's own eyes; the best, greatest, finest; أُم الدُّنْيا Egypt

أخذ مكانه جوار أمه وزوجته.. كانت أمه نائمة — He took his place near his mother and his wife. His mother was sleeping

99 | 19626 |

164 إيه /'iih/ and إي /'ii/ (Dia.) interj. yes, OK, uh-huh; إي نَعَم yes, that's right; إيه وَالله /'iih waLLa/ yes indeed

كنت أُحبك وأحبك ايه نعم أحبك لكن الفراق ماكان اختياري — I used to love you, yes, love you, but our separation was not my choice

39 | 49435 | +spo

---

3 Food

This list includes foods, drinks and other ingestible substances, as well as other words related to serving and obtaining food.

236	ماء	water	3797	عصير	juice	5947	سلطة	salad
1408	عيش	bread; rice	3827	ثمرة	fruit	6151	تغدّى	to have lunch
1683	سكّر	sugar	3835	وصفة	recipe	6198	حمّص	hummus
1840	قهوة	coffee	3965	خضار	vegetables	6217	لحمة	meat
1916	سمك	fish	3994	دهن	fat	6225	خلّ	vinegar
2051	عسل	honey	4015	أرزّ	rice	6239	تعشّى	to have dinner
2070	شاي	tea	4114	حلوى	dessert			
2153	خبز	bread	4134	عنب	grapes	6277	فطر	mushrooms
2187	جوع	hunger	4146	فنجان	cup	6279	طيب	delicious
2239	عشاء	dinner	4181	كريم	cream	6354	خيار	cucumber
2471	زيتون	olives	4201	حلاوة	sweets,	6449	بيتزا	pizza
2660	بابا غنوج	baba ghannouj (بابا: papa, pope)	4300	بصل	candy onions	6450	بصلة	onion
			4335	إفطار	iftar; breakfast	6452	كبّة	kibbeh
						6516	طبخة	meal, dish
						6523	منسف	mansaf
2665	دجاج	chicken	4336	شوكة	fork	6539	فطور	breakfast
2692	بيض	eggs	4364	ليمون	lemon	6625	سادة	plain (coffee,
2774	غداء	lunch	4490	زجاجة	bottle			tea)
2801	ملح	salt	4518	صحن	bowl, plate	6637	شيشة	sheesha
2856	ثمر	fruit	4567	شهيّة	appetite	6638	بطاطا	sweet potato,
2858	تغذية	nutrition	4601	تفّاح	apples			potato
2982	خمر	wine	4663	تمر	date	6640	كيك	cake
3010	فاكهة	fruit	4794	سكّين	knife	6768	فلفل	pepper
3082	كبد	liver	4807	برتقال	oranges	6787	بندورة	tomatoes
3085	لبن	milk; yoghurt	4909	حلويّات	sweets	6802	ملوخيّة	mulukhiyah
			4970	دقيق	flour	6823	مرق	broth, stock
3225	عرق	araq	5366	جبن	cheese	6890	باميا	okra
3354	لقمة	morsel	5404	لوز	almonds	6938	كبسة	kabsa
3442	شراب	drink	5431	ذرة	sorghum	6953	كحول	alcohol
3489	قمح	wheat	5584	مأدبة	banquet	7022	فطر	have
3495	ملعقة	spoon	5633	قوت	food			breakfast
3696	مقوّم	ingredient	5770	شهيّ	delicious	7073	مقلوبة	makloubeh
3795	عشب	herb, plant	5871	جزر	carrots	7260	تمّن	rice

165 حَرْب *fem.n.* pl. حُرُوب war, warfare

رومیل هو بطل حروب الصحراء بلا منازع — Rommel is the undisputed hero of desert wars

98 | 19739 |

166 عِنْدَما *conj.* when, as soon as

عندما سقطت الأندلس فى أيدى المسيحيين الإسبان، اضطهدوا المسلمين واليهود — When Andalusia fell into the hands of the Christian Spaniards, they persecuted the Muslims and the Jews

88 | 21928 |

167 وَضْع *vn.* laying down, putting, placing; drafting (document); *n.* pl. أَوْضَاع situation, state of affairs, status, condition

لو تزوجا لكان الوضع أفضل للجميع — If they had married, the situation would have been better for everyone

98 | 19640 |

168 هُم *pron.* they (masc.); همه and هما /humma/ (Egy.Irq.Gul.), همه and همي /humme/ (Lev.), هم /ham/ (Alg.)

هناك اناس مختصون بمثل هذه الاشياء وهم اطباء نفسيون يدرسون كيفية وضع الاعلانات لكي يتأثر بها الزبون — There are people who specialize in such things, and they are psychologists who study how to come up with ads to influence the customer

98 | 19420 |

169 دَوْر *n.* pl. أَدْوَار role, part; task, function; floor (building level); round, stage, set (sports tournament); turn (chance to act, play a role)

وقفوا كل اليوم في البرد القاسي بانتظار دورهم للدخول — They stood all day in the bitter cold waiting for their turn to enter

99 | 19242 |

170 وَجْه *n.* pl. وُجُوه face, front; side; way, manner; aspect, facet; بِوَجْهٍ عامّ/خاصّ generally, specifically; pl. أَوْجُه persons, individuals; وجوه and ويه /weeh/ (Gul.) face

بالكاد ظهرت على وجهها ابتسامة مكسوفة — A shy smile barely appeared on her face

99 | 19108 |

171 جِدّ *n.* seriousness, earnestness; جِدًّا very, much; جَيِّدٌ جِدًّا very good; بِجِدٍّ seriously, in earnest

الياس كان فرحا جدا بأخيه بسام.. يعامله وكأنه ابنه — Elias was very pleased with his brother Bassam. He was treating him as if he were his son

99 | 19258 |

172 بَدَأ *v. I (a)* to start, begin (في) sth or (with imperf.) to do sth; (Dia.) بَدَى ،يَبْدَى بديت /badeet/

فجأة بدأت أمي تصرخ بأعلى صوتها وتنعتني بأبشع الشتائم — Suddenly my mother started yelling in her loudest voice and calling me the ugliest of insults

99 | 19025 |

173 كَلِمَة *n.* pl. -aat word; remark; speech

فكرت للحظة كي تنتقي كلماتها ثم قالت بطء: «هل أنتما أصحاب فقط»؟ — She thought for a moment in order to choose her words and then she slowly said: "Are you just friends"?

100 | 18787 |

174 طِفْل *n.* child, infant; boy, baby boy; fem. طِفْلَة girl, baby girl, pl. أَطْفَال *n.* children, infants; babies

تسري شهرتي بين أطفال الحارة، وربما في المدينة كلها — My reputation is spreading through the children of the neighborhood, and perhaps (through) the whole city

99 | 18707 |

175 مُنْذُ *prep.* since, ago; *conj.* (ever) since, starting from

تكلما ما يقرب من ساعتين.. ومنذ تلك الليلة تغيرت حياته — The two of them spoke for close to two hours...and since that night his life has changed

88 | 21011 |

176 لَدَى *prep.* with, by, at; (with pron.) لَدَيْهِ he/it has, لَدَيَّ I have

لم أنم منذ الأمس، ولدي عملية غدا فى السابعة صباحا — I haven't slept since yesterday, and I have an operation tomorrow at seven in the morning

89 | 20719 |

177 عِراقيّ *n./adj.* Iraqi

قتل ١٣ عراقيا في هجمات في بغداد ومناطق أخرى من العراق — Thirteen Iraqis were killed in attacks in Baghdad and other areas of Iraq

93 | 19794 |

178 أَصْبَحَ *v. IV* to become sth; to begin, start (to do sth)

زوجي مجنون في هذه اللعبة ويصبح عصبيا جدا إذا ما هزم فريقه — My husband is crazy about this game, and he becomes very nervous if his team is defeated

97 | 18931 |

179 مَكان *n. pl.* أَمْكِنَة, أَماكِن place, location; position, role, post

كانت أمه قد جاءت إلى القرية من مكان مجهول، ولم تكن تملك شيئا غير ملابسها — His mother had come to the village from an unknown place, and she didn't own anything but her clothes

100 | 18520 |

180 صارَ *v. I (i)* to become; to happen; (with imperf.) to begin to do

وصار يتصل بها بواسطة البطاقات المسبقة الدفع حتى لا يكتشف أهل خطيبته ما بينه وبينها — And he began to call her using prepaid cards so that the family of his fiancee would not discover what's between him and her

97 | 18833 |

181 مُشْكِلَة *n. pl.* -aat, مَشاكِل problem, issue

نم جيدا يا صديقي وسوف تكتشف في الصباح أن المشكلة بسيطة — Sleep well my friend and you'll find out in the morning that the problem is simple

99 | 18438 |

182 عَشَرَة *num. fem.* عَشْر ten; *n.* عَشَرات tens, scores, dozens; (used in the numbers 11–19)

عشرات الرجال سهروا الليالي في جهد متواصل حتى ثبتت لهم براءتك — Dozens of men stayed up nights in a prolonged effort until your innocence was proven

99 | 18273 |

183 وَصَلَ *v. I (i)* to arrive إلى at; to connect, link, join بَيْنَ between; (Egy.Lev.) /wiSil, yiwSal/ (Lev. also /yuuSal/), (Irq.Gul.) /wuSal, yooSal/

حتى الأحلام الجميلة تصل إلى نهاياتها — Even beautiful dreams reach their end

99 | 18236 |

184 إسْلاميّ *adj.* Islamic; *n./adj.* Islamist

سياستنا الخارجية يجب أن تعكس الثقافة الإسلامية العميقة — Our foreign policy should reflect profound Islamic culture

95 | 18613 |

185 ساعَة *n. pl.* -aat hour, time, o'clock; clock, watch, timepiece

بعد نحو نصف ساعة وصلنا إلى مبنى منعزل — After about half an hour we reached a secluded building

99 | 17755 |

186 شَيْخ *n. pl.* مَشايِخ, شُيُوخ sheikh, leader; *pl.* شُيُوخ old man; (pol.) senator

بدأ كثير منهم يفسرون عبارة الشيخ الأخيرة، كل حسب معلوماته — Many of them started to interpret the Sheikh's last sentence, each according to their information

99 | 17884 |

187 أكَّدَ *v. II* to confirm sth or أنَّ that; to underscore, emphasize (على) sth or أنَّ (على) that

تقرير الطبيب الشرعي يؤكد أن الوفاة نتجت عن قطع شرايين رسغ اليد اليسرى — The medical examiner's report confirms that the death resulted from severing the arteries of the left wrist

89 | 19464 |

188 السَّلامُ *n.* peace; *pl.* -aat greeting, salute; السَّلامُ الوَطَنيّ the national anthem عَلَيْكُمُ hello;

هذا ما يميزنا عن باقي الأحزاب التي تتحدث عن السلام ولا تفعله — This is what distinguishes us from the rest of the parties that talk about peace but don't make it

92 | 18801 | +spo

189 سَيِّد *n. pl.* سادَة Sir, Mr; lord, master, boss

خلاص يا سيدي.. انت السيد وأنا العبد، عاوزني أعمل لك إيه تاني؟ — Ok sir....you are the master and I am the slave, what else do you want me to do for you? (Said in ridicule)

99 | 17543 |

190 صاحِب *n. pl.* أُصْحاب owner, possessor;
originator; friend, companion; *pl.* صَحْب
companion (esp. of the Prophet); صاحِبَة *n.*
-aat (female) friend, girlfriend

من هم أصحاب المصلحة في الفصل بين الدين
والسياسة، وبين الدين والعلم؟ — Who are those
who possess an interest in the separation
between religion and politics, and between
religion and science?

99 | 17450 |

191 عَدَم *n.* (in idafa) absence of, lack of; non-, not

أعتذر بشدة على رداءة خطي وعدم وضوحه
— I apologize strongly for my horrible script and
its illegibility

98 | 17472 |

192 ها *interj.* look! here (he/she is, they are,
I am, we are); (with pron.) هاكَ here, take!;
(Dia.) *interrog.* huh?

سيشرب ويتطلع إلى الصور القديمة.. ها هى أيام
السعادة تبدى أمام عينيه — He will drink and look
at old pictures...the days of happiness appear
before his eyes

98 | 17352 | +lit +spo

193 حَرَكَة *n. pl.* -aat movement, motion, activity;
organization, (political) movement

اعتبرته المؤسسة الحاكمة مثلا لحركة حماس في الاخوان
المسلمين الاردنيين — The ruling establishment
considered him to be a representative of the
Hamas movement in the Jordanian Muslim
Brothers

99 | 16997 |

194 رَبّ *n. pl.* أَرْباب lord, master; Lord (God);
owner, proprietor

ربنا يحفظك وينصرك ويخليك — May our
Lord protect you and grant you victory and
keep you

99 | 17092 | +for

195 أَكْبَر *elat.* fem. كُبْرَى larger/largest, greater/
greatest; *adj.* senior, elder; important,
significant; great, major

إندونيسيا هي أكبر دولة إسلامية فى العالم
— Indonesia is the largest Muslim country
in the world

100 | 16943 |

196 كِتاب *n. pl.* كُتُب book

عندما جاء أخذت كتبها وتظاهرت بالدراسة
— When he came she took her books and
pretended to be studying

99 | 16965 |

197 حَدّ *n. pl.* حُدُود extent, limit, level; edge,
corner; حُدُود border, frontier; range, scope;
لَحَدّ (Lev.) *prep.* up until

عاشت عمرها ملتزمة ولم تسمح لأحد فى الكلية بأن
يتجاوز حدود الزمالة — She lived her life strictly,
and did not permit anyone in the college to go
beyond the limits of simply being colleagues

99 | 16894 |

198 أَخَذَ *v. I (u)* to take sth; (with imperf.) to begin
to do sth; (imperat.) خُذ, (Irq.) أُخُذ take!

خذ راحتك.. سأنتظرك فى الاستقبال — Take your
time...I'll wait for you in the reception (hall)

99 | 16858 |

199 نِظام *n. pl.* نُظُم, أَنْظِمَة regime, government;
system; نِظام orderliness

اختلطت أصواتهم بغير نظام — Their voices
jumbled together in disarray

95 | 17514 |

200 ذات *fem.n. pl.* ذَوات ego, self; ذات same, -self
(himself, herself, etc.); (in idafa) a certain,
a given (day, time, occasion, person, thing);
بالذّات exactly, precisely

لم أعد أشعر بذات الرعب الذي كنت أشعر به في
البداية — I no longer feel the same fear that
I used to feel in the beginning

99 | 16679 |

201 نَعَم *interj.* yes

هل تعيش في سكن الطلبة؟ – نعم — Do you live
in the student housing? – Yes

98 | 16762 | +spo

202 قَضِيَّة *n. pl.* قَضايا problem, issue; lawsuit,
legal case

الصحف الأميركية ركزت على عدد من القضايا، طبعا
كان من أهمها جنازة البابا — The American
newspapers focused on a number of issues,
the most important of which, of course, was
the Pope's funeral

99 | 16601 |

203 ماضٍ (def. الماضِي) *adj.* past; previous, last; *n.* الماضِي the past
ألم أقل لك في المرة الماضية إني لا أريد أَنْ أرى وجهك مرة أخرى؟ — Didn't I tell you last time that I don't want to see your face again?
98 | 16829 |

204 إنْسان *n. fem.* إِنْسانَة pl. أُناس human being
لا يستطيع الإنسان أن يُخفي دينه — A man cannot hide his religion
99 | 16596 |

205 حالَة *n. pl.* -aat condition, state, situation; case, instance
يصعب علي أن أراه في هذه الحالة — It is difficult for me to see him in this condition
99 | 16488 |

206 أخِير *adj.* last; latest, recent; الأَخِير the latter; أَخِيراً finally; recently, lately
لم تظن قط أن يوما كهذا سيأتي، لكنه أتى أخيرا — She never thought a day like this would come, but it finally came
99 | 16524 |

207 رَغْم *n.* رَغْمَ, and عَلَى الرَّغْمِ مِنْ, and بِالرَّغْمِ مِنْ in spite of, despite
أهنئك لأنك تفوقت بالرغم من التعليم البائس الذى تلقيته — I congratulate you because you excelled despite the wretched education you received
98 | 16548 |

208 جانِب *n. pl.* جَوانِب side, aspect, part; إلى جانِبِ and بجانِبِ next to, beside
كان الرجل يقف في جانب المكان يراقب ما يدور حوله في دهشة — The man was standing to the side of the place watching in amazement what was happening around him
90 | 18004 |

209 حُبّ *n.* love, affection; حُبّاً لِ out of affection for, for love of
لو فقدنا إيماننا بالحب، فستفقد كل الأشياء في هذه الدنيا لذتها — If we lose our faith in love, everything in this world will lose its pleasure
99 | 16244 |

210 جامِعَة *n. pl.* -aat university; league
دعوتها يوم الجمعة الى القهوة فى كافيتريا الجامعة — I invited her on Friday for coffee in the university cafeteria
98 | 16373 |

211 قَرار *n. pl.* -aat decision, resolution
أتمنى أن أعيد حياتي مرة أخرى لأتخذ قرارات مختلفة — I hope to redo my life again so I can make different decisions
98 | 16341 |

212 لُبْنانِيّ *n./adj.* Lebanese
كيف يمكن أن تسوى هذه الخلافات بين الأطراف اللبنانية المعارضة؟ — How can these differences between the opposing Lebanese parties be settled?
92 | 17309 |

213 لَقَدْ *part.* (with perf.) has/have already
لقد انتهى من لوحته الجديدة هذا المساء وقرر أن نكون أول من يشاهدها — He finished his new painting this evening, and he decided that we will be the first to see it
88 | 18150 |

214 زالَ *v. I (a)* to cease; (with neg.) ما زالَ, لا يَزالُ and لا زالَ and ما يَزالُ to continue to be or do sth (lit. to not cease being or doing sth)
لا يزال هناك أفراد يأتون عبر هذه الحدود، والسوريون يستطيعون أن يمنعوهم — There are still individuals who come through these borders, and the Syrians could prevent them
99 | 16026 |

215 رَأْس (Dia. راسي /raas/) *n. pl.* رُؤُوس head; tip, top; (fin.) capital; رَأْس مال pl. رُؤُوس أَمْوال (geo.) cape; رَأْساً immediately
رفعت زهرة رأسها أكثر من مرة إلى شرفات البيوت — Zahra raised her head more than once to (see) the houses' balconies
99 | 15864 |

216 تَحْت *n.* bottom part; تَحْتَ *prep.* below, under; لتحت /la-taHt, la-taHit/ (Lev.) *adv.* down, downward
كلما أخرج الرجال شخصا حيا من تحت الأنقاض ارتفعت الصيحات الله أكبر الله أكبر — Whenever the men pulled a living person from under the rubble, cries of "God is great, God is great" arose
99 | 15655 |

217 وِزَارَة *n.* pl. -aat ministry

تم اجراء الاتصالات والتنسيق مع وزارات الأشغال
العامة والصحة — Communications and
coordination have been established with the
Ministries of Public Works and Health

96 | 16143 |

218 هَدَف *n.* pl. أَهْداف goal, target; intention,
objective; (in sports) goal, point

ان هدفنا هو تجويع الشعب الفلسطيني، ولكن ليس
الى درجة الموت — Our goal is to starve out
the Palestinian people, but not to the point
of death

98 | 15682 |

219 عَلاقَة *n.* pl. -aat relation, link, tie,
connection

ما علاقة الدين بالاقتصاد؟ — What is the
relationship between religion and the
economy?

99 | 15425 |

220 شُكْر *n.* thankfulness, thanks; شُكْراً *interj.*
thank you, thanks

شكرا على تهنئتك بالعيد السعيد — Thank you for
your congratulations on a happy holiday

99 | 15492 | +for

221 مُتَّحِد *adj.* united

رأت هيئة الأمم المتحدة أن التقسيم هو خير الحلول
— The United Nations Organization felt
that partitioning (Palestine) was the best
solution

92 | 16529 |

222 مُجْتَمَع *n.* pl. -aat society

المدينة الجامعية تسهم في خلق مجتمع أشبه ببستان
متنوع الأشجار والأزهار — The University City
contributes to the creation of a society that is
more like a grove with various (types of) trees
and flowers

96 | 15867 |

223 مَرْكَز *n.* pl. مَراكِز center; station; (sports)
ranking, position

لينينجراد هى المركز الصناعى والثقافى لروسيا ولن
تسقط — Leningrad is the industrial and cultural
center of Russia, and it will never fall

98 | 15483 |

224 حَكَى *v. I (i)* to tell, relate, report; (Lev.)
/Haka, tiHki/, (Irq.) /Hicha, tiHchi/ to speak,
talk; say; tell

كيف سيقنعها بأن تحكي له كل الأمور ليفهم ما يجري؟
— How is he going to convince her to tell him
everything so that he understands what is
happening?

86 | 17673 | +spo

225 نَتِيجَة *n.* pl. نَتائِج result, outcome; consequence;
نَتِيجَةً لِـ as a result of

شفاؤه من الأزمة لم يأت نتيجة الأدوية، وإنما بفضل
صلابة داخلية — His recovery from the crisis did
not come as a result of medications, but thanks
to (his) inner strength

98 | 15357 |

226 أُخْت *n.* pl. أَخَوات (خَوات Lev.Irq.Gul.) sister;
mate, counterpart (in a pair); إِخْوات (Egy.)
sisters; siblings

لا أفهم كيف استطاعت أختك العيش مع هذا
الرجل وكيف لم تطلب الطلاق منه — I don't
understand how your sister could live with
this man and how she didn't seek a divorce
from him

91 | 16432 | +for

227 رَأْي *n.* pl. آراء opinion, view; idea

أشكرك على الصور التي بعثت بها إلي، وإذا أردت
رأيي فإني أقول لك إن بلدك جميل — Thank you for
the pictures you sent me, and if you want my
opinion, I'll tell you that your country is
beautiful

99 | 15012 |

228 إدارَة *n.* pl. -aat administration, management;
bureau, office, directorate

نسبة كبيرة من الأميركيين يؤيدون قرارات الإدارة
الحالية — A large percentage of the Americans
support the decisions of the current
administration

96 | 15434 |

229 مُسْلِم *n./adj.* pl. -uun Muslim

المذهب الوهابى يحرم الخروج على الحاكم المسلم حتى
لو ظلم الناس — The Wahhabi sect forbids
rebellion against a Muslim ruler, even if
he oppresses the people

97 | 15307 |

230 صَغير *adj.* pl. صِغار small; young; الصغار children, youths; (Lev.Irq.) زغير /zghiir/, زغار /zghaar/

ستعمل على تنفيذ مشروع القروض الصغيرة الذي سيسهم في الحد من مشكلة الفقر والبطالة — She will work on implementing the small loan project which will contribute to curbing the problem of poverty and unemployment

99 | 14834 |

231 ما *interrog.* what, which

ما رأيك يا رأفت؟ هل نبدأ بالعشاء أم نشاهد اللوحة أولاً؟ — What is your opinion, Ra'fat? Should we begin with dinner or should we see the painting first?

96 | 15396 |

232 قانُون *n.* pl. قَوانين law, statutes, regulations

كان على كل منهما، حسب القانون، ألا يعمل في شيء غير قراءة القرآن — According to the law, each one of (the two of) them cannot take any career except in reciting the Qur'an

98 | 14954 |

233 إسْرائيليّ *n./adj.* pl. -uun Israeli

عملية السلام الإسرائيلية الفلسطينية لم تشهد أي تطور ملموس على أرض الواقع — The Israeli-Palestinian peace process hasn't witnessed any tangible progress in reality

84 | 17343 |

234 بِما *part.* with what, with which; بِما أنَّ because, in view of the fact that, considering that; بِما في ذلِكَ including

وبما أن الانتخابات مقررة في يناير فإنه من الضروري تحقيق نوع من السلام لكي يتم الاقتراع في جميع أنحاء البلاد — Since the elections are scheduled for January, it is necessary to accomplish a kind of peace so that voting in all parts of the country can be carried out

99 | 14771 |

235 إسْتَطاعَ *v. X* أنْ/*vn.* to be able to do sth, to be capable أنْ/*vn.* of doing sth

رغم كل هذا، لم تستطع ميشيل أن تحبه، أو أنها لم تسمح لنفسها بالمحاولة — Despite all this, Michelle was not able to love him, or she didn't allow herself to try

90 | 16240 |

236 ماء *n.* pl. مِياه water; liquid; juice; (body of) water; waters; (Dia.) ماي /maay/, مي /mayy/ and مية /mayya/: (Egy.) /mayya/; (Lev.) /mayy(a)/; (Irq.) /mayy(a), maay/; (Gul.) /maay, mayy(a)/

شطف البراد وملأه بالماء ووضعه على النار ليصنع الشاي — He washed the kettle and filled it with water and put it on the fire to make tea

99 | 14641 |

237 أمْس *adv.* yesterday; الأمْس and بالأمْس yesterday

علمت بخبر الافراج عنك اول امس وفرحتى لا يحدها حدود — I learned of your release the day before yesterday, and my joy knew no bounds

92 | 15763 | +news

238 أمْن *n.* safety, security, protection; order, control, discipline

العلاقة بين أمراض ضعف المناعة والإيدز من ناحية، والأمن الغذائي من ناحية أخرى ، علاقة مهمة — The relationship between immune deficiency illnesses and AIDS on the one hand, and food security on the other hand, is significant

97 | 14715 |

239 مِش and مُش (Egy.Lev.Gul.) *neg.part.* not

أيه اللي حصل؟ – لأ، حاصدق — What happened? – You won't believe it. – No, I will believe it

65 | 21911 |

240 قَدَّمَ *v. II* to offer, present sth; to submit (request, complaint); to apply على for (position)

قدمت له هدية بسيطة: طبق مرصع بالصدف من خان الخليلي — I offered him a simple gift: a plate inlaid with mother-of-pearl from Khan Al-Khalili

99 | 14411 |

241 شَخْص *n.* pl. أشْخاص person, individual

الشارع خال إلا من ثلاثة أشخاص — The street is empty except for three people

99 | 14382 |

242 كَلام *n.* speech, talk; statement, remark; saying, quote

جلست تفكر بعمق في كلام مها، لكن التليفون رن من جديد وفوجئت بصوت أبيها — She sat thinking deeply about what Maha said, but the telephone rang again and she was surprised by the voice of her father

99 | 14240 |

243 مَوْقِع *n. pl.* مَواقِع position, location, site; website
أطلب منكم وضع موقع خاص للعربي الصغير على
شبكة الإنترنت — I'm asking you to put up a
special site for the "Young Arab" on the Internet
98 | 14428 |

244 مِائَة and مِائَة *num.* (one) hundred, pl. مِئات
hundreds; مِئَتانِ two hundred; بِالمِئَة and في المِئَة in the
percent; مية (Egy.Irq.) /miyya/, (Lev.) /miyye/,
(Gul.) /miya, 'imya/; مية (in idafa)
(Egy.Lev.Irq.) /miit/, (Gul.) /miyat, 'imyat/
كان المئات من سكان منطقة السليمانية قد تظاهروا
خلال اليومين الماضيين احتجاجا على القصف الإيراني
— Hundreds of inhabitants of the Sulaimaniyya
area demonstrated during the last two days
protesting the Iranian bombing
99 | 14276 |

245 حِينَ *prep.* when
وحين حاولنا معرفة أصل هذه اللغة وخصائصها
دهشنا حين اكتشفنا أن الغجر أنفسهم لا يعرفون ماهية
هذه اللغة ولا أصلها — When we tried to find out
the origins of this language and its characteristics,
we were surprised when we discovered that the
gypsies themselves do not know the identity of
the language and its origins
94 | 15052 |

246 داخِل *n.* interior, inside; داخِلَ *prep.* inside (of);
a.p. entering, coming in
أين يذهب بهذه الأرانب التي تعلقت داخل سرواله؟
— Where is he going with these rabbits which
are hanging inside his pants?
99 | 14216 |

247 وَحْدَة *n.* unity; solitude, loneliness; pl. -aat
unit, item; portion, section
كانت أجمل الجميلات لكن الوحدة اصابتها بشيخوخة
باكرة — She was the most beautiful of all the
beauties, but her isolation struck her with early
old age
94 | 14958 |

248 أُمَّة *n. pl.* أُمَم nation; people, community;
الأُمَّة الإِسْلامِيَّة the Islamic community;
الأُمَم المُتَّحِدَة the United Nations
لقد تحولنا إلى أمة من النمل، تبحث عن قوتها وجحر
تختبئ فيه — We have been transformed into
a nation of ants, searching for their food and
a burrow to hide in
95 | 14824 |

249 مُهِمّ *adj.* important, serious; المُهِمّ the main
thing, what's important

4 Clothing

669	حوايج	clothing (حاجة: need, thing)	3840	غسيل	dirty clothes	6602	بدلة	suit
			3921	لباس	clothes, dress	6604	حلق	ring, earring
1213	حلقة	ring (also circle, class)	3999	نقاب	veil	6684	تنّورة	skirt
			4126	ارتداء	wearing, putting on	6819	أواعي	clothes
1433	ثوب	robe; pl clothes	4312	لبس	clothing, dress	6973	جينز	jeans
1709	ملبس	pl clothes	4353	زر	button	7017	كمّ	sleeve
2068	مخطط	patterned (also plan)	4630	قميص	shirt	7248	قبّة	collar
2373	حجاب	hijab, veil	4763	خاتم	ring	7361	لبّس	to dress
2705	ارتدى	to wear, put on	4812	حزام	belt	7526	أكسى	to clothe
3224	ستر	to veil	5090	طوق	collar	7528	طرحة	headcloth, veil
3371	ستار	veil	5189	حلّة	suit of clothes	7582	شرّاب	sock
3396	زيّ	uniform, dress	6167	فستان	dress	7611	سترة	jacket
			6373	بنطلون	pants	7663	خمار	veil
3637	حذاء	shoe	6462	محجّب	wearing hijab	7927	بلغة	slipper
			6592	عصابة	headband		تي شيرت	T-shirt (تي: T.)

آسف لأني جئت بهذه الطريقة، لكني فعلا أريدك لأمر مهم — I'm sorry to have come this way, but I really want you for an important matter

99 | 14105 |

250 مِلْيُون *num.* pl. مَلايِين million; (Alg.) pl. ملايين /mlaayin/

تم تطويق قرابة نصف المليون جندي فرنسي خلف خط ماجينو — About a half million French soldiers were encircled behind the Maginot line

98 | 14317 |

251 سَيَّارَة *n.* pl. -aat car, automobile, vehicle

نعم جرت حادثا اعتداء على منزلي وتم تحطيم زجاج سيارتي من قبل مجهولين — Yes, my house was broken into twice, and the window of my car was broken by unknown assailants

98 | 14274 |

252 بِنْت *n.* pl. بَنات daughter, girl; بِتّ; (Egy., short form of بِنْت)

عمل الأم خارج المنزل يستلزم قيام البَنات بالأعمال المنزلية عوضا عنها — The mother's working outside of the home required the daughters to do the housework instead of her

99 | 14110 |

253 دُكْتُور *n.* pl. دَكاتِرَة doctor (physician or holder of a doctorate); (title) Dr

بدا واضحا أنها صديقة للدكتور صلاح لأنه سألها عن أسرتها — It seemed clear that she was a friend of Dr Salah, because he asked her about her family

96 | 14494 |

254 فِعْل *vn.* doing; *n.* pl. أَفْعال deed, act, action; (ling.) verb; فِعْلًا and بِالفِعْل really, actually, in fact; بِفِعْل because of, owing to

ابتسمت فانكشفت أسنانها الكبيرة المعوجة المتسخة بفعل النيكوتين — She smiled, and revealed her big, crooked teeth stained from the effects of nicotine

98 | 14189 |

255 حُلْو *adj.* sweet, nice, pleasant; (Dia.) /Hilu/, fem. /Hilwa/, pl. /Hilwiin/

شكله حلو وكلامه حلو وروحه حلوة — His figure is attractive, his words are pleasant and his soul is sweet

89 | 15620 |

256 فَرِيق *n.* team, group, band; faction, party; pl. فُرَقاء lieutenant general

اللقاء هو الثالث بين الفريقين في المسابقة هذا الموسم — The meeting is the third between the two teams in this season's competition

95 | 14555 |

257 بَقِيَ *v. I (a)* to remain, stay (على in a state); to last, endure; to remain, be left over; to continue doing sth or being sth; (with neg.) to no longer do sth or be sth

لقد بقيت على شاطئ البحر شهرين — I stayed on the ocean beach for two months

99 | 13980 |

258 لَجْنَة *n.* pl. لِجان committee, council, commission

شكلنا لجنة تتحدث باسم الحي أمام الجهات الرسمية — We have formed a committee to speak on behalf of the neighborhood before the authorities

86 | 16153 |

259 مُخْتَلِف *adj.* different, divergent; various; in disagreement (في/على about sth)

لا يرى أي فرق بين الأجناس المختلفة فالبشر كلهم في عقيدته أبناء الله — He doesn't see any difference between the various races, since all humans, in his belief, are the children of God

98 | 14095 |

260 وَجَبَ *v. I (i)* to be necessary على for sb أنْ to do sth; to be incumbent على upon sb أنْ to do sth

يجب معاملة السجناء باحترام عوضا عن إهانتهم — The prisoners must be treated with respect instead of abuse

92 | 15042 |

261 نَظَر *vn.* looking إلى at; examining, looking في into; *n.* pl. أَنْظار view, look, glance; opinion; نَظَرًا لِـ in view of the fact that

ظلت صامتة، تحاشت النظر إليه، مما ضاعف جزعه — She remained silent, and avoided looking at him, which doubled her sense of alarm

99 | 13973 |

262 مَجَال *n.* pl. -aat area, space; field,
domain, sphere; sector; arena; مَجَال جَوِّيّ
air space

— نحن في هذا المجال خبراتنا أفضل منهم بكثير
Our experience in this field is better than
theirs by a lot

98 | 14094 |

263 فَتْرَة *n.* pl. فَتَرَات time period, phase,
interval

ظللنا صامتين لفترة.. كانت سحابة من الكآبة تظللنا
— We remained silent for a while. Clouds of
depression overshadowed us

98 | 13943 |

264 شَبّ *n./adj.* young man, شَبَّة young woman,
pl. شَباب youths

يواجه شبابنا جملة قضايا في حياتهم تحد من منسوب
طموحاتهم — Our young people are facing
issues in their lives which limit the level of
their ambitions

99 | 13854 |

265 شَأْن *n.* pl. شُؤُون matter, affair, case; situation,
condition

لا تتدخل في شؤون غيرك — Don't interfere in the
affairs of others

94 | 14518 |

266 ذَكَر *v. I (u)* to mention sth/sb; to remember
sth/sb; يُذْكَر it's worth mentioning (أنَّ that)

لا بد كما ذكرت أن نبدأ الحوار لن نحل هذه المشكلة
إلا إذا ما جلسنا مع الدول الكبرى — As I
mentioned, we need to begin the dialog; we will
never solve this problem unless we sit down
with the big powers

98 | 13960 |

267 سُؤَال *n.* pl. أَسْئِلَة question, inquiry

هذه الأسئلة ليست ابدا في مستوى الطالب المتوسط أو
الأهبل وإنما هي أسئلة يعجز المدرسون أنفسهم عن
الإجابة عليها — These questions are never
at the level of the average student or the
stupid one, but rather they are questions
which the teachers themselves are unable to
answer

99 | 13720 |

268 وُجُود *n.* existence; presence, being present

أشتاق إليه وإلى وجوده اليومي معي.. أريد أن أراه كما
كنت أراه — I miss him and I miss his daily
presence in the house with me...I want to see
him just as I used to see him

97 | 13951 |

269 حَلّ *vn.* solving (a problem); *n.* pl. حُلُول
solution; dissolution, annulment; cancellation

يجب أن نجد حلا آخر، حلا أكثر تمشيا مع منطق
الأشياء — We need to find another solution, a
solution that is more in line with the logic of
the things

99 | 13635 |

270 طالِب *n.* pl. طَلَبَة, طُلَّاب student, طالبات female
students; الطلاب/الطلبة والطالبات male and
female students; pl. -uun applicant; (person)
seeking, requesting

ترك المدرسة مع طلاب صفه بعد الدرس الثالث، لعدم
وجود مدرس — He left school with his
classmates after the third period because there
was no teacher present

98 | 13692 |

271 مُسْتَوًى *n.* pl. مُسْتَوِيات level, standard

استمر سعر النفط العالمي بالارتفاع نحو مستويات
جديدة ليصل الى سعر ٦٦ دولارا للبرميل الواحد —
The price of oil continued rising toward new
levels to the price of 66 dollars for a single barrel

98 | 13696 |

272 وَ *part.* (oath) وَاللهِ by God! (I swear!); وحياتك
I swear (by your life)

وحياتك عيشتنا تقرف الصراصير — I swear, our
living conditions would disgust the cockroaches

82 | 16314 | +for +spo

273 أَمْ *conj.* or (in questions) أَمْ..؟ ...or not?

هل يعيشان بعد الزواج في القاهرة أم طنطا؟ — Will
they live in Cairo or Tanta after the marriage?

97 | 13775 |

274 فَقَط *part.* only, just, solely; (with neg.)
لَيْسَ..فَقَطْ بَلْ.. not just...but (also)...

صار لي تقريبا ثلاث شهور متزوج فقط — I've been
married only three months, approximately

89 | 14945 |

275 ماذا *interrog.* what

ماذا سيقول لها عندما يطرق الباب ويوقظها فى الثانية
صباحا؟ — What will he say to her when he
knocks on the door and wakes her at two in the
morning?

93 | 14181 |

276 وِلاَيَة *n.* mandate, term of office; pl. -aat state,
province; الوِلاَيات المُتَّحِدَة the United States
الكثير من هذه الشركات موجودة في ولاية كاليفورنيا
ولها مصالح كثيرة في هذه الولاية — Many of these
companies are present in the state of California,
and they have many interests in this state

94 | 14150 |

277 قَدْ *part.* (with imperf.) may, might; قَدْ لا may
not, might not
يقاوم أي إحساس قد يعطله عن العمل — He resists
any feeling that would interrupt his work

90 | 14795 |

278 عُضْو *n.* pl. أَعْضاء member, associate; (anat.)
organ, member, limb
تخونني يداي، رجلاي، كل عضو في جسدي المتعب
يتآمر ضدي — My hands betray me, my legs, every
member in my tired body conspires against me

89 | 14748 |

279 حَتَّى *conj.* (with foll. subjunctive) in order to,
so that
بقوم بتمارين معينة عندي مثلا أخفف حتى الكرش —
I'm doing specific exercises so that I can lose
weight, around my waist for example

96 | 13792 |

280 عَـ، عَ (Dia.) *prep.* (short form of عَلَى) on;
عَفِكْرَة (Lev.) by the way; عَكُل حال (Lev.) in any
case
انتي هلق رايحة عالبيت؟ — You are going home
now?

99 | 13211 |

281 عُمْر *n.* pl. أَعْمار age (of a person); life, lifetime;
يا عُمْري my dear, my darling (Dia.)
لو كنت نمت طول عمرك على سرير واحد انت
وإخواتك الخمسة.. كنت فهمتني — If you had slept
your whole life on a single bed, you and your
five brothers, you would have understood me

99 | 13094 |

282 شاف *v. I (u)* (Dia.) to see, look at sth/sb;
a.p. شايف /shaayif/, fem. شايفة /shayfa/,
pl. شايفين /shayfiin/
الليلة دي أول مرة أشوف فيها المسرح الانجليزي —
Tonight is the first time I see English theater

79 | 16493 | +spo

283 دائم *adj.* lasting, enduring; permanent,
constant; دائمًا always
هناك فرصة تاريخية لتحقيق تسوية عادلة شاملة دائمة
في هذا العام قبل أن تثقل المعاناة كاهل أجيال
أخرى — There is a historic opportunity to
accomplish a lasting, just, comprehensive
settlement this year before burdening the
next generations

99 | 13082 |

284 سابق *adj.* pl. -uun former, previous, preceding;
سابقًا formerly, previously
نفهم من حديثك أن الحكومات السابقة أخطأت في
مبدأ التعيين في البلديات — We understand from
what you are saying that the previous
governments made a mistake in the principle
of appointments in the towns

94 | 13759 |

285 خَبَر *n.* أَخْبار news, report; (gram.) predicate;
الأَخْبار the news; (Egy.) أَخْبارَك إيه؟ (Irq.)
شَاخْبارَك؟ What's new with you? How are
you?
هل تعلم شيئا عن أخبار أحمد؟ هل هو في صحة
جيدة؟ — Do you have any news of Ahmad?
Is he in good health?

99 | 13016 |

286 تاريخ *n.* date; history
ذلك لم يحدث قط على طول تاريخ القرية — That
had not ever happened in the whole history of
the village

99 | 13012 |

287 دِراسَة *n.* pl. -aat study, research, examination
القبول في التخصصات قد لا يرضي كل من تقدم
بطلب للدراسة في الجامعات — The assignment
into the specialties might not please everyone
who submitted an application to study at the
universities

99 | 13037 |

288 مَوْقِف *n.* pl. مَواقِف position
كم حاولت أن تجتذبه إلى موقفها، لكنه كان فى واد آخر
— She tried so hard to get him to see things her way, but he was in another world
99 | 12978 |

289 حِزْب *n.* pl. أَحْزاب (political) party
هناك أحزاب أخرى مدنية بين الإخوان المسلمين وبين الحزب الحاكم — There are other civilian (political) parties among the Muslim Brothers and the ruling party
93 | 13699 |

290 مُؤَسَّسَة *n.* pl. -aat institution, organization; foundation
نجد مؤسسات فردية بأسماء تجارية لكنها قادرة دوما على تجنب الضريبة — We find individual associations with trade names but they are always able to avoid taxes
96 | 13224 |

291 أَضافَ *v. IV* to add sth
قال «انتظريني هناك» ثم أضاف: «اختاري لنا طاولة أخرى» — He said: "Wait for me here" and then added: "Choose another table for us"
89 | 14215 |

292 قِطاع *n.* pl. -aat sector, section; قِطاع غَزَّة Gaza Strip
نسعى بالتأكيد إلى بناء شراكة بين القطاع العام والقطاع الخاص — We are trying to make certain the building of a partnership between the public and private sectors
90 | 14028 |

293 مَجْموعَة *n.* pl. -aat collection, group; squad; bloc
ارتدى نظارته ذات الإطار الذهبي وأخرج مجموعة أوراق — He put on his glasses with the golden frames and took out a stack of paper
98 | 12856 |

294 سَلَّمَ *v. II* to turn over, surrender sth إلى to sb; to greet, salute sb; سَلِّم لي على give my regards to; يسلموه and يِسلمُوه /yislamuh/ (mostly Gul.) *interj.* thanks!
كعادته فى الأزمات سلم أمره لله — As usual in crises, he turned his affairs over to God
99 | 12735 | +for +spo

295 سُوق *fem.n.* (rarely masc.) pl. أَسْواق market
تغزو المنتجات الصينية كل أسواق الدول العربية وإفريقيا — Chinese products are invading all the markets of the Arab World and Africa
99 | 12718 |

296 حَمْد *n.* praise; commendation; الحَمْدُ لله praise God, thanks be to God; (Dia.) حمدلله /Hamdilla 9-s-salaama/ عالسلامة praise God for your safety! (said to sb returning from a trip)
الموضوع انتهى على خير والحمد لله — The matter was concluded well, praise God
94 | 13315 | +for +spo

297 دَخَلَ *v. I (u)* to enter sth
بعد ذلك انحرفت إلى اليسار ودخلت إلى ممر آخر — After that she turned to the left and entered another passageway
99 | 12590 |

298 باب *n.* pl. أَبْواب door, gate; category, rubric; section, chapter
دخلت وتركت الباب مفتوحا — She entered and left the door open
99 | 12585 |

299 مِمَّا (من ما) *rel.pron.* which; a fact that
أطلقوا الرصاص بغزارة مما أدى إلى إصابة الكثيرين — They shot a lot of bullets, which led to the wounding of many
90 | 13967 |

300 أَجْل *n.* sake; لِأَجْل and مِن أَجْل because of, for the sake of; لِأَجْل أَنْ in order to
نعتز بالجهود المباركة التي تبذلونها جلالتكم من أجل الشعب العراقي الشقيق كي تزول عنه الغمة ويجتاز المحنة — We are proud of the praiseworthy efforts which Your Majesty has been making on behalf of our Iraqi brothers, in order to rid them of their distress and overcome hardship
96 | 13027 |

301 اتِّحاد *vn.* unification, unifying; *n.* pl. -aat union
لست طالبا عاديا.. أنا رئيس اتحاد الدارسين المصريين في أمريكا كلها — I am not a regular student. I am the president of the Egyptian Student Union for all of America
93 | 13364 |

302 تَحْقِيق *vn.* and *n. pl.* -aat achievement, realization; investigation; interrogation (مع of sb)

نعلن عن ارتياحنا للجهود المقدرة للأمين العام لجامعة الدول العربية لتحقيق الوفاق الوطني في العراق — We announce our satisfaction with the esteemed efforts of the Secretary General of the Arab League to accomplish national harmony in Iraq

88 | 13875 |

303 مَدْرَسَة *n. pl.* مَدارِس school

كل مدرسة ثانوية خاصة لها كرافتة خاصة به — Every private secondary school has its own special tie

99 | 12353 |

304 جَمِيل *adj.* beautiful, nice; الفُنُون الجَمِيلَة fine arts

هل ضاع بعض من قيمنا الجميلة؟ أم ضاعت كلها أم أكثرها تأثيرا؟ — Have some of our beautiful values gotten lost? Or have they all gotten lost, or the most influential of them?

99 | 12198 |

305 نَوْع *n. pl.* أَنْواع type, kind, form; نَوْعاً ما somewhat, more or less

استخدم الألمان نوعا جديدا من القنابل فوق لندن — The Germans used a new kind of bomb over London

98 | 12318 |

306 طَلَع *v. I (u)* to appear, emerge, rise; to go out, come out, get out; (Dia.) طِلَع *(a)* to appear, seem; to turn out, end up, amount to

صار يقضي الليل في الاتصال حتى يطلع الصبح فيأخذ حماما ويحتسي عدة أقداح من القهوة ويتوجه إلى العمل — He began to spend the night calling until dawn, then he would take a shower, sip several cups of coffee, and head for work

96 | 12562 | +spo

307 خِدْمَة *n. pl.* خَدَمات service, assistance; خَدَمات services, assistance, aid; خِدْمَة (Magh.) work, employment; job, task

في الأيام القادمة سيصل أكثر من عامل إلى نهاية الخدمة — In the coming days more than one worker will reach the end of his service

98 | 12380 |

308 عالَمِيّ *adj.* international, global, worldwide, world

هذا الخطر موجود من عام ١٩١٨ عندما حدث الوباء العالمي لأول مرة بين البشر — This danger has been present since the year 1918 when the first world epidemic happened among humans

96 | 12522 |

309 فِيما *conj.* while, meanwhile; فِيما بَعْدُ later

وفيما كان عمرو في طريقه إلى المدينة المنورة، التقى بصديقيه خالد بن الوليد وعثمان بن طلحة — While Amr was on his way to Medina, he met his two friends Khalid Ibn Al-Walid and Uthman Ibn Talha

89 | 13495 |

310 حالِيّ *adj.* present, current; حالِيّاً presently, currently

إن عدد العراقيين المتواجدين في الأردن بلغ حاليا سبعمائة ألف عراقي وفي سوريا ستمائة ألف — The number of Iraqis present in Jordan currently reaches 700,000 Iraqis, and in Syria 600,000

96 | 12597 |

311 حُكْم *n.* rule, government; *pl.* أَحْكام judgment, decision, verdict; أَحْكام statutes, laws; بِحُكْم by virtue of, because of

رجال الدين في العراق أثناء حكم الدولة العباسية أباحوا شرب النبيذ — Religious leaders in Iraq during the rule of the Abbassid state permitted the drinking of wine

98 | 12301 |

312 أَشارَ *v. IV* to indicate, mention, cite, refer to إلى sth

للمقارنة نشير إلى أن القيادات الكردية العراقية منعت الاحتفالات الشعبية — For the sake of comparison, we point out that the Iraqi Kurdish leadership forbade popular celebrations

90 | 13362 |

313 جِهَة *n. pl.* -aat side; direction; part, party; sector, office, institution; جِهات entities, parties, individuals, "players"

ومن جهته حاول الصوراني أن يطلع وزير التعليم د. خالد طوقان على الأوضاع السيئة للمدارس الخاصة — For his part, Surani tried to inform the Minister of Education, Dr Khalid Tuqan about the terrible conditions in private schools

99 | 12124 |

5 Transportation

115	طريق	road	1674	انطلاق	start, departure	3333	عبر	to cross
223	مركز	center; station	1706	غادر	to leave, depart	3344	مركبة	vehicle; cart
251	سيّارة	car				3417	حافلة	bus
298	باب	door	1760	هجرة	emigration	3482	عبور	crossing
467	شارع	street	1781	سفينة	ship	3483	شحن	cargo; shipment
487	وقف	to stop	1891	مسار	path, route			
504	عودة	return (trip)	1959	سائق	driver	3640	منفذ	exit, way out
510	مرّ	to pass by	2015	رحيل	departure	3651	سدّد	to obstruct
528	مرور	traffic	2082	مسافر	traveler, passenger	3652	هدى	to lead, guide
536	نقل	transportation				3663	سيارة	ambulance
541	قيادة	driving, piloting	2203	رحل	to depart, travel		إسعاف (سيّارة: car)	
543	سبيل	way, road	2379	حارة	quarter	3675	نفق	tunnel; underpass, subway
638	وصول	arrival	2395	طار	to fly			
819	سار	to go, walk	2408	قطار	train	3694	متن	deck
872	خروج	departure, exit	2435	بوّابة	door, gate	3846	شاحنة	truck
879	ساحة	field, arena	2447	راكب	rider, passenger	3873	حلّق	to fly, hover
936	توقّف	to stop, halt				3889	إسراع	speeding up
941	محطّة	station	2509	عربيّة	car (also Arabic)	3991	شقّ	to make one's way
973	طائرة	aircraft						
1009	رحلة	trip	2516	صعود	ascent; take-off	3996	اختراق	traversing
1027	سفر	traveling; trip				4048	زحمة	(traffic) jam
1030	قطع	to cover (a distance) (also to cut)	2543	فات	to pass by	4090	مروريّ	traffic-related
			2571	ميناء	port, harbor	4371	مركب	ship, boat
1069	صندوق	box; trunk (car)	2637	وقّف	to park (also to stop)	4421	زحام	crowd; congestion
1175	انطلق	to depart, take off	2647	عابر	passing by	4708	مفترق	intersection, junction
1248	مشى	to walk, go	2736	مغادرة	departure	5013	مجيء	arrival
1289	قاد	to lead; drive, pilot	2815	وداع	farewell; departure	5085	محطّ	stopping place; station
1349	مطار	airport	2862	مجرى	course, path	5128	تخطّي	crossing
1373	ظهر	back; deck				5157	مسير	journey, march
1456	جسر	bridge	2914	عربة	cart, vehicle			
1463	طيران	aviation; airline	3024	مخرج	exit, way out	5348	شحنة	freight, cargo
1489	صاروخ	missile, rocket	3076	ركب	to get in, board	5384	سدّة	gate
1515	آليّة	machine; vehicle	3132	مشوار	walk, stroll	5399	تسريع	acceleration
			3146	معبر	crossing point	5417	جيب	jeep
1590	درب	path, road				5437	ملاحة	navigation
1594	ذهاب	going; departure	3159	هبط	to drop; to land	5516	خطا	to step, walk
1661	ميدان	city square, plaza	3222	هبوط	descent, landing	5866	نزّل	to lower, unload
1672	سافر	to travel				5887	مرق	to go by
						5989	فارق	to depart from
						6113	باص	bus

6226	سلك	take (a road)	6454	سيرة	march, walk	6798	باخرة	steamship
6254	عود	return	6455	روحة	errand	6858	مفرق	intersection, junction
6262	طيّارة	airplane	6486	سوّاق	driver	6871	حوّس	to take a walk
6269	أمشى	to make walk	6519	كرنيش	corniche	6929	تمشّى	to walk, stroll
6303	تاكسي	taxi	6626	شوفير	chauffeur	6944	قطر	train
6355	عجقة	congestion	6632	بسكليت	bicycle	7023	سكّة	road, way
6374	مقدم	arrival	6718	نزلة	stop	7046	كبري	bridge, overpass
6388	فلك	ark	6778	صفّ	to park (also to arrange)	7146	توموبيل	automobile
6428	سفرة	journey						

314 نَحْوَ *prep.* towards; approximately

المجلس الدولي للحبوب يتوقع انتاجا عالميا هذا العام من القمح يقدر بنحو ٥٩٣ مليون طن مقابل ٦١٨ مليون طن في العام الماضي — The International Seeds Council expects a worldwide production of wheat that is estimated at approximately 593 million tons compared with 618 million tons last year

89 | 13340 |

315 فيه /fii-h, fii/ *part.* (Egy.Lev.Gul.) there is, there are; (Lev.Gul.) مافيه /ma-fii-h/, (Egy.) /ma-fii-sh/, (Lev.) مافش /ma-fi-sh/, and (Lev.) فش /fi-sh/ there isn't, there aren't

نعم ياخويا؟ عاوز مين يا سيدي؟ مفيش حد هنا... اتفضل مع السلامة — Yes, (what do you want) brother? Whom do you want sir? There is nobody here....go ahead, good bye ("brother" and "sir" are used here for ridicule)

62 | 19037 |

316 طَويل *adj.* pl. طِوال long; tall; طَويلًا for a long time; extensively

لا يزال الطريق طويلا فتركيا لن تنضم فعليا لعضوية الاتحاد الأوروبي قبل مرور ١٠ سنوات — There is a long road ahead, and Turkey will not actually join the European Union for another ten years

99 | 11914 |

317 كَذٰلِكَ *adv.* likewise, also

نحن لدينا أناس متعلمون من أطباء ومثقفين وموسيقيين كذلك — We have educated people, doctors, intellectuals, and musicians also

96 | 12279 |

318 كَأَنَّ and وَكَأَنَّ *conj.* as if; (with pron.) كَأَنِّي and كَأَنَّا as if I; كَأَنَّني and (less frequently) as if we

كن في الدنيا كأنك غريب أو عابر سبيل — Be in the world as if you were a stranger, or a passerby

99 | 11773 |

319 حاوَلَ *v. III* to attempt, try to do sth

حاولنا أن نعيد البنت إلى صوابها وفشلنا — We tried to get the girl to come to her senses, but we failed

99 | 11772 |

320 قَوْل *n.* pl. أَقْوال statement, remark; saying, utterance

يذكر التقرير السري بعض أقوال الخبراء أن كوريا الشمالية قد تستعد للقيام باختبارها الأول للسلاح النووي — The confidential report mentions some statements from experts that North Korea might be preparing its first test of nuclear weapons

97 | 12036 |

321 مَرْأَة *n.* woman, wife; (without def. article) إمْرَأَة : (Lev.Irq.; Egy. derog.) مرة /mara/ woman, wife; (in idafa) مرات /miraat/ (Egy.), (Lev.Irq.) /mart/; (with pron.) مراتي /miraat-i/ (Egy.) my wife, مرتي /mart-i/, (Irq.Lev.) (Lev.) /marat-i/

لا توجد مساواة مطلقة بين الرجل والمرأة، ولا يدل هذا على نقص — There is no full equality between men and women, and this does not imply any shortcoming

99 | 11747 |

322 حَقِيقَة *n.* pl. حَقائِق truth, reality; fact
ومن خلال قراءة كتاب كارتر، نستطيع القول
انه لا جديد فيه على صعيد الحقائق والوقائع
المعروفة جيدا في المنطقة العربية، لكنه صدم
الاسرائيليين — Through reading Carter's
book, we can say that there is nothing new
in it in terms of facts and very well-known
events in the Arab region, but it shocked
the Israelis
99 | 11773 |

323 جَعَلَ *v. I (a)* to make sb/sth do sth
(with imperf.); to cause sb/sth to be sth;
to appoint sb (minister, etc.); to begin to do
sth (with imperf.)
لا أظن أن ثمة رجلا أو شيئا يستطيع الآن أن يجعلني
أرتعش أو أرتبك — I don't think there is a man
or a thing that can make me tremble or be
confused now
90 | 12881 |

324 لَمّا *conj.* when, after
لما سأل عنهم قيل له إنهم على وشك دخول النار —
When he asked about them, he was told that
they are about to enter hell
99 | 11598 |

325 سَأَلَ *v. I (a)* to ask sb (إن/إذا ;في/عن about;
whether); to request from sb (أن to do sth);
to pray to (God)
دخل الزوج متجرا ليشتري ثوبا لزوجته، فسأله
البائع. أي مقاس وأي لون تريد؟ — The husband
entered a store to buy a dress for his wife,
so the seller asked him: What size and color
do you want?
95 | 12075 |

326 عاشَ *v. I (i)* to live, be alive; to experience sth
عاشوا أكثر من خمسة وثلاثين سنة من كبت النظام
السابق — They lived more than thirty-five years
under the repression of the former regime
99 | 11475 |

327 مُواطِن *n.* pl. -uun citizen; fellow citizen,
compatriot
أصبح المواطن لا يستطيع الحصول على مياه الشرب
ولا على وقود السيارات — Citizens are no longer
able to obtain drinking water or car fuel
97 | 11765 |

328 سُلْطَة *n.* pl. سُلُطات power, rule, authority;
سُلُطات authorities, people in power
يجب ان يكون النقل السلمي للسلطة على اساس
انتخابات تتسم بالحرية والشفافية اساسا للحكومة
الديمقراطية — The peaceful transfer of power
on the basis of elections characterized by
freedom and transparency must be a basis for
democratic government
95 | 11978 |

329 بَدا *v. I (u)* to appear, seem (ل to sb, أنَّ that);
to look, seem (big, small, happy, sad, etc.);
كَما يَبْدُو and عَلى ما يَبْدُو evidently, apparently,
it seems
بدا واضحا أنها لم تعد تخشى شيئا الآن — It seemed
clear that she no longer feared anything now
98 | 11547 |

330 خَمْسَة *num. fem.* خَمْس five; خَمْسَةَ عَشَرَ
fifteen
وقد اصيب في الحادث خمسة من رجال الامن غادر
بعضهم المستشفى — Five security men were
wounded in the incident, some of whom have
left the hospital
99 | 11406 |

331 اِقْتِصاديّ *adj.* economic, economical;
(Lev.) thrifty
نحن نريد أن نحقق نموا اقتصاديا في حدود ١, ٧٪ —
We want to accomplish economic growth in the
range of 7.1%
88 | 12838 |

332 بَحْث *n.* pl. بُحُوث , أبحاث search (عن for);
discussion (في of); research, examination
(في of)
يجب أن أقرأ هذا البحث لأني سأشرحه غدا للطلبة —
I need to read this research because I will
explain it tomorrow to the students
99 | 11374 |

333 دِين *n.* pl. أَدْيان religion
قتل الابرياء لا يقبله عقل ولا دين ولا مبدأ —
Neither mind, nor religion, nor principle can
accept the killing of innocent people
99 | 11346 |

334 حَمَلَ *v. I (i)* to carry, bear sth; to transport
(cargo); to become pregnant (حامِل); to attack
على sth, campaign على against

فتح مكتبا كبيرا فى الشارع الذى حمل اسم سعد زغلول فيما بعد — He opened a big office on the street that bore the name of Saad Zaghloul later on

97 | 11514 |

335 عَسْكَرِيّ *adj.* pl. -uun military, army; *n.* soldier, private

للكثير من الطيارين وظائف مدنية إلى جانب عملهم العسكري في الطيران — Many pilots have civilian jobs along with their military jobs in aviation

94 | 11770 |

336 كَم *interrog.* how many/much; (Egy.) كام /kaam/, (Irq.Gul.) چم /cham/

كم أتمنى هذه النهاية وأنتظرها بفارغ الصبر — How I hope for this end, and I await it impatiently

99 | 11171 |

337 جَيْش *n.* pl. جُيُوش army; armed forces; troops

غاندى ليس لديه جيش لكن لديه شعب كامل — Gandhi does not have an army, but he has a whole people

96 | 11497 |

338 جهاز *n.* pl. أَجْهِزَة apparatus, machine; device, appliance; organization; agency, bureau, office

إن الناس يريدون العودة إلى ما كانت عليه الأمور قبل اختراع الهواتف الخلوية وأجهزة الكمبيوتر — People want to go back to the way things were before the invention of the cell phone and the computer

97 | 11379 |

339 مُشَارَكَة *n.* pl. -aat participation, association

وصل الى القاهرة عصر امس على رأس وفد رفيع المستوى للمشاركة في اجتماعات اللجنة — He arrived in Cairo yesterday afternoon at the head of a high level delegation to participate in the meetings of the committee

94 | 11721 |

340 طَبْع *n.* nature, character; بِالطَّبْع and طَبْعاً naturally, of course; *vn.* printing

هل تشعر بالأمان أم لا؟ - لا، طبعا لا نشعر بالأمان — Do you feel secure or not? – No, of course we don't feel secure

98 | 11291 |

341 اِعْتَبَر *v. VIII* to consider sth/sb to be; to regard sb/sth as; to believe أَنَّ that

شغلت هذا المنصب لسنوات عديدة وأنا أعتبر نفسي تلميذة لها وسوف أسير على نفس الطريق للنهوض بالمرأة — She occupied this position for many years, and I consider myself a student of hers and I will take the same road to bettering women's (lives)

98 | 11281 |

342 أَحَبَّ *v. IV* to love, like sb; to want, like sth or to do sth

إنه يحبها ويفتقدها بشدة طوال النهار — He loves her and misses her a lot during the day

95 | 11536 | +lit +for

343 أَتَى *v. I (i)* to come إلى to sth; to come to sb; to bring ب sth

بهذا مشاهدينا الكرام نأتي إلى ختام حلقة اليوم من السلطة الرابعة — With this, dear viewers, we come to the conclusion of today's episode of "The Fourth Estate"

90 | 12231 |

344 بدّ and بَدّ (Lev.) *part.* (verbal) to wish, want, need; (with pron.) بِدّي I want, مابِدِّي and (ما) بِدِّيش I don't want

ما بدي إعمل رجيم — I don't want to go on a diet

52 | 21052 | +spo +for

345 خَرَجَ *v. I (u)* to exit, go out من/عن from; to leave من (a place); to deviate عن from; (Alg.) to appear, show up, be visible

استعاروا الذهب المصري ثم ذهبوا بدون عودة عندما خرجوا من مصر — They borrowed Egyptian gold then left never to return, when they went out of Egypt

99 | 11082 |

346 أَعْطَى *v. IV* to give, provide sth to sb, or ل to sb

قرر أن يعطي لنفسه فرصة للتفكير، فاستدار وبدأ يطوف على مهل حول المنزل — He decided to give himself the opportunity to think, so he turned around and started to circle slowly around the house

99 | 11077 |

347 حَبِيب *n./adj.* pl. أُحْباب, أَحِبَّة (Dia.) حَبايِب dear, beloved, sweetheart, darling

تبغي الخلود لكن الحب يا حبيبي لا يعيش سوي عمر الورود — You want it to last forever, but love, my dear, only lives the life span of roses

97 | 11167 |

348 فَوْق *n.* top, upper part; فَوْقَ above, over

يركع أمام الصليب الذي يحتفظ به فوق فراشه — He kneels in front of the cross which he keeps over his bed

99 | 10908 |

349 خارِج *n.* outside, outer part, exterior; خارِجَ outside (of); في الخارِج and بالخارِج overseas, abroad; خارِجاً outside

نحن نتسول كل شيء من الخارج حتى الأسلحة التي ندافع بها عن أنفسنا — We beg for everything from abroad, even the weapons with which we defend ourselves

99 | 10903 |

350 مَثَل *n.* pl. أَمْثال example; proverb; مَثَلاً for example

شيكاجو أكثر أمنا من نيويورك مثلا — Chicago is safer than New York, for example

97 | 11170 |

351 رَقْم *n.* number, numeral, figure; rate; record

كيف يستطيع الوصول اليها لانها لم تعطه رقم هاتفها النقال ولا يملك سوى الحيلة الوحيدة وهي ايميلها — How can he reach her, since she didn't give him her cell phone number and he only has one strategy (left), and that is to email her

98 | 11013 |

352 ضِدّ *n.* opposite; ضِدَّ *prep.* against

سيكون بجواره حتى لو وقف العالم كله ضده — He will be beside him even if the whole world stands against him

89 | 12137 |

353 جَرَى *v. I (i)* to occur, take place; to happen لِ to sb; to flow, run (liquid); to run (person) وَراءَ after sb

هناك مأساة تجري في الأحواز لا تغطيها وسائل الإعلام العربية — There is a tragedy happening in Ahwaz which the Arab media are not covering

95 | 11306 |

354 مَسْؤُول and مَسْئُول *n.* pl. -uun official, functionary; employer, boss, supervisor; *adj.* responsible, dependable

أدين قبل فترة أحد المسؤولين العراقيين الكبار بالتجسس — After a time, one of the high Iraqi officials was convicted of spying

96 | 11182 |

355 بَعِيد *adj.* pl. بِعاد distant, far, remote; بَعِيداً عَن far away from

بعد دقائق قليلة اقترب منه بخطوات سريعة شخص بملابس بعيدة كل البعد عن الذوق — A few minutes later a person wearing clothes that were as far as one could possibly get from being tasteful approached him

99 | 10807 |

356 أَرْبَعَة *num. fem.* أَرْبَع four; أَرْبَعَةَ عَشَر fourteen

بعد أربع سنوات أصبح العالم أكثر خطورة مما كان عليه — After four years, the world became more dangerous than it had been

99 | 10823 |

357 كَتَبَ *v. I (u)* to write sth; (pass.) كُتِبَ لَهُ to be granted (success); كُتِبَ عَلَيْهِ أَنْ to be destined (by God) to

جلس أمام الكمبيوتر ووجد نفسه يمحو ما كتبه ويبدأ بصيغة أخرى — He sat in front of the computer and found himself erasing what he had written and beginning with a different approach

99 | 10747 |

358 حِين *n.* pl. أَحْيان time, moment, opportunity; أَحْياناً sometimes, occasionally

استسلمت هي لنوم هادئ على حين ظل هو غارقا في خواطره — She surrendered herself to a calm sleep while he remained immersed in his thoughts

99 | 10724 |

359 وَضَعَ *v. I (a)* to put, place sth في/على/تحت inside/on/under; to lay down (rules, conditions); to lay (an egg); to give birth to (a child); to write, compile, draft, compose sth

وضعنا شروطا جديدة للاستثمار في سوريا لم تكن موجودة سابقا — We put new conditions in place for investment in Syria which were not present previously

94 | 11331 |

360 نائِب *n.* pl. نُوّاب deputy, delegate; vice-
التقيت رئيس مجلس النواب وتبادلنا الرأي حول
الوضع في لبنان — I met the president of the
Council of Deputies and we exchanged opinions
concerning the situation in Lebanon
85 | 12514 |

361 خاصَّة *n.* خاصَّة especially, particularly; الخاصَّة
the elite, the upper class
سأكبر وأكون شاعرا متميزا ، ويحبني الناس وخاصة
النساء كما تحب الشاعر الرومانسي نزار قباني — I will
grow up and become a notable poet, and
people will love me, particularly the women,
as they love the romantic poet Nizar Qabbani
94 | 11333 |

362 وَلَد *n.* pl. أوْلاد، وِلاد (Egy.) child, son, boy
هذا الأمر جعلني أفكر بعد أن ينتهي أولادي من
دراستهم الجامعية في التطوع في إحدى هيئات الإغاثة
— This matter made me think, after my
children finish their university studies, of
volunteering in one of the aid organizations
99 | 10683 |

363 دَم *n.* pl. دِماء blood; (Dia.) دَمّ
ما لبثت أن انهمرت الدموع من عينيها حينما تذكرت
الدماء في فلسطين، والعراق، وأفغانستان، تهدر ظلما في
حرب — It was not long before tears began to
flow from her eyes when she remembered the
blood in Palestine, Iraq, and Afghanistan, wasted
unjustly in war
99 | 10621 |

364 صَحِيح *adj.* true, correct; sound, healthy;
authentic (Hadith): صَحِيح البُخاري Sahih
Al-Bukhari (Hadith collection); *interj.* yes,
right; صَحِيحاً really, truly
إن كانت أرقام وزارة الدفاع صحيحة فإن المشكلة في
الجيش يمكن أن تكون عشرة أضعاف ذلك — If the
numbers of the Ministry of Defense are correct,
the problem in the army could be ten times that
99 | 10605 |

365 إسْلام *n.* Islam
اختلط العرب الأصليون بالاسبانيين الذين تعربوا
واعتنقوا الاسلام واتخذوه لهم دينا جديدا — The
original Arabs mixed with the Spaniards, who
were Arabized and embraced Islam and adopted
it as their new religion
95 | 11031 |

366 مَرْحَلَة *n.* pl. مَراحِل phase, stage, step; (sports)
round
يبدو أن مرحلة جديدة من حبس الأنفاس والقلق
تجتاح حاليا الحياة اليومية للبنانيين — It seems that
a new stage of holding one's breath and worrying
is currently pervading the daily life of the Lebanese
97 | 10806 |

367 ثالِث *adj.* third (ordinal); ثالثاً thirdly, in third
place
مصر مثل بلاد كثيرة في العالم الثالث تعاني من مشاكل
عميقة وكثيرة تراكمت على مدى قرون — Egypt, like
many countries of the third world, suffers from
many deep problems which have piled up over
centuries
99 | 10560 |

368 اِجْتِماعِيّ *adj.* social; الحالَة الاِجْتِماعِيَّة personal
status
نتطلع الى مبادرة الحكومة بتنفيذ حزم أمان اجتماعي
لتفادي سلبيات السوق — We are looking forward
to the government's initiative to carry out
social security packages to avoid the negatives
of the market
94 | 11095 |

369 حَدِيث *n.* pl. أحادِيث discussion, conversation,
talk; story, interview; Hadith (narratives based
on the words and deeds of the Prophet
Muhammad)
يجب أن يجري هذا الحديث على أكثر من صعيد —
This discussion needs to take place on more
than one level
97 | 10667 |

370 سِياسَة *n.* politics; pl. -aat policy
٥٪ الذين لا يرغبون بالمشاركة في الاستفتاء ليسوا
مهتمين بالسياسة، و ٢٦٪ منهم لا يهتمون بالدستور
— Five percent of those who want to participate
in the election are not interested in politics, and
26% of them are not interested in the constitution
95 | 10867 |

371 طَرَف *n.* pl. أطْراف edge, side; tip, end; extremity
(body limb); participant, player, party, team
جميع الأطراف اللبنانية موافقة على ما يحصل وتدعم
المقاومة — All the Lebanese factions are agreed
on what is happening and they support the
opposition
99 | 10407 |

372 أَ *part.* (interrog., often with neg.part.) أَلَا doesn't, don't; أَلَمْ didn't, أَلَيْسَ isn't, aren't نحن بحاجة لأناس يفهمون لا لأناس أغبياء، أليست فضيحة أبو غريب نتيجة لجهل هؤلاء الناس بالآخرين؟ — We need people who understand, not stupid people; wasn't the Abu Ghreib scandal a result of the ignorance of these people towards others?

94 | 11013 |

373 وَطَن *n.* pl. أَوْطان nation, homeland نشكركم من أعماق قلوبنا على ما قدمتموه للوطن من إنجازات تاريخية — We thank you from the depths of our hearts for what you have offered to the nation in the way of historical accomplishments

96 | 10693 |

374 رُبَّمَا and رُبَّا *adv.* perhaps, maybe نذهب إلى الزميلة سميرة ربما لديها المزيد من المعلومات — We will go to our colleague Samira, perhaps she has more information

98 | 10486 |

375 لِماذا *interrog.* why يعرف لماذا تركوا القرية إلى الإسكندرية، أى فضائح ارتكبوها قبل رحيلهم — He knows why they left the village for Alexandria, what scandals they committed before they left

90 | 11470 |

376 قَليل *adj.* few, small amount; قَليلًا *adv.* a little, somewhat; briefly, shortly كيف تقيم أداء الاقتصاد الوطني خلال السنوات القليلة الماضية؟ — How do you evaluate the performance of the national economy during the last few years?

99 | 10329 |

377 عَلِمَ *v. I* (a) to know sth or أَنَّ that; to find out أَنَّ that نحن الآن نعلم أن هناك حوارات بين عدد كبير من المجموعات المسلحة — We now know that there are conversations between a large number of armed groups

99 | 10266 |

378 حَتَّى *adv.* even, including; although, even though يعمل حتى في اجازة الصيف — He even works during summer vacation

87 | 11707 |

379 مُدِير *n.* director, manager; (office) boss, chief لو رآك من لا يعرفك لظن أنك مدير لشركات كبرى — If someone sees you who doesn't know you, he would think that you are a director of some big companies

97 | 10445 |

380 نِهاية *n.* end, finish; termination, ending هذا أمر سيئ بالطبع، لكنه ليس نهاية العالم — This is a bad thing, of course, but it is not the end of the world

99 | 10187 |

381 مِصْرِيّ *n./adj.* pl. -uun Egyptian; (Egy.Lev.Gul.) /maSri/ ينقسم الاقتصاديون المصريون حول مدى الحاجة إلى اتفاق جديد مع صندوق النقد الدولي — Egyptian economists are divided over the extent of the need for a new agreement with the International Monetary Fund

97 | 10434 |

382 إِضافة *n.* addition; بالإضافة إلى in addition to بالإضافة إلى الحرب والعنف والدم هناك أيضا حرب كلامية — In addition to the war and the violence and the blood, there is also the war of words

94 | 10665 |

383 واقِع *n.* reality, fact; actual situation; *adj.* falling (date), occurring (time); located, found, situated (place) هل توافق دكتور محمود في الواقع على أن منظمة التحرير الفلسطينية هي الممثلة للفلسطينيين — Do you agree with Dr Mahmoud in fact that the PLO is the representative of the Palestinians?

98 | 10193 |

384 كامِل *adj.* complete, full; integral, perfect; بالكامِل completely المدعي العام يعمل بحرية كاملة وباستقلال كامل بالنسبة لي — The public prosecutor works with complete freedom and complete independence as far as I am concerned

99 | 10092 |

385 عَبْر *prep.* across, over, via; through,
be means of
أمسكت بيديها عبر المائدة، رفعتها ببطء إلى شفتى
وقبلتها — I took hold of her hands across the
table, and raised them slowing to my lips and
kissed them
95 | 10358 |

386 شَرْق *n.* east; شَرْقاً eastward, in the east
ذلك سوف يفتح الباب أمام دول كثيرة فى الشرق
الاوسط لتمتلك هذه التكنولوجيا — That will open
the door for many countries in the Middle East
to possess this technology
98 | 10112 |

387 ظَلَّ *v. I (a)* to stay, remain; to continue to be;
(with imperf.) to keep on doing
لم تعد بحاجة إلى فراس كي تظل على قيد الحياة.. لم
يعد فراس الماء والهواء — She no longer needs
Firas to stay alive...Firas is no longer water and air
98 | 10006 |

388 تَعْليم *n.* pl. -aat, تَعاليم education, teaching;
instruction; تَعْليمات instructions, guidelines;
تَعاليم precepts
كان أبى رحمه الله رجلا مستنيرا يؤيد تعليم المرأة
وعملها — My father, God rest his soul, was an
enlightened man who supported the education
of women, and women working
97 | 10122 |

389 رُوح *fem./masc.n.* pl. أَرْواح spirit, soul; life;
يا رُوحي! my love!; (Gul. with ب and pron.)
by oneself; بروحي /b-ruuHi/ by myself
الحق أنه يمارس عمله بروح الفنان — The fact is that
he carries out his work with the spirit of an artist
99 | 9915 |

390 أَفْضَل *elat.* better/best
يجب أن تكون عادلا.. الفريق الأفضل هو الذي فاز
— You must be fair. The best team is the one
that won
98 | 9989 |

391 مال *n.* pl. أَمْوال money, capital; رَأْس مال and
رَأْسِمال capital; أَمْوال assets, funds, monies
لا مجد في الدنيا لمن قل ماله — There is no glory in
the world for him who has little money
98 | 9951 |

392 لَيْل *n.* night, night-time; لَيْلاً by night;
(وَ)نَهاراً day and night
كان الخواجة ديمترى يعمل ليلا فى جراج البلدية هذا
الأسبوع فهو يعمل بنظام الورديات — Mr Dimitri
was working at night in the municipal garage
this week, since he works shifts
99 | 9832 |

393 أُسْبُوع *n.* pl. أَسابِيع week
فى الأسبوع القادم سأطلب إليك فى الفصل تلخيص
البحث والتعليق عليه — Next week I will ask you
in class to summarize the study and comment
on it
98 | 9972 |

394 مُؤْتَمَر *n.* pl. -aat conference, congress,
convention
قام الملك الحسين بدور رئيس في عقد مؤتمر مدريد
للسلام من خلال توفير مظلة للفلسطينيين للتفاوض
حول مستقبلهم — King Hussein played a major
role at the Madrid Peace Conference by
providing an umbrella for the Palestinians to
negotiate about their future
92 | 10549 |

395 لِقاء *n.* pl. -aat meeting, encounter; interview
مشاهدينا الكرام أهلا وسهلا بكم معنا في هذا اللقاء
الخاص مع السيد محمود عباس رئيس منظمة التحرير
الفلسطينية — Esteemed viewers, we welcome
you among us in this special meeting with
Mr Mahmoud Abbas, the head of the PLO
95 | 10174 |

396 رَدَّ *v. I (u)* to answer على sb, to respond to
sth/sb; to return, reciprocate (a favor)
هو قال بأنك عضو في حكومة محلية بأنه هو وزير
خارجية لكل فلسطين، كيف ترد على هذا الكلام؟
He said that you are a member of a local
government, and that he is the foreign minister
of all of Palestine, how do you respond to these
statements?
99 | 9732 |

397 لِكَي and كَي *conj.* (with foll. subjunctive) in
order to, so that
أردت أن أخرج كي لا أضايقه، فناداني — I wanted
to go out so I wouldn't bother him, and then
he called to me
90 | 10724 |

6 Family

66	أخ	brother	1700	تزوّج	to get married	4638	حام	guardian
76	أب	father				4766	جوز	husband
104	بيت	house; family	1731	مرتبط	linked to	4829	عيلة	family
			1767	شقيق	full brother	4832	حريم	women, harem
128	أهل	family, relatives	1914	آل	family, clan	4935	متجوّز	married
145	ابن	son	1964	تربوي	child-rearing (adj)	5011	ربّة بيت	homemaker, housewife
163	أمّ	mother	2120	عرس	wedding	5069	رزق	to be blessed with (a child)
174	طفل	child	2407	ماما	mama			
226	أخت	sister	2453	صبيّ	young boy	5379	رضيع	breast-feeding infant
252	بنت	daughter, girl	2590	عروس	bride			
			2616	طلاق	divorce	5398	نجل	son
264	شبّ	young man	2660	بابا	papa	5662	عرق	ancestry; ethnicity
321	مرأة	woman, wife	2776	شابّة	young woman			
362	ولد	child, son, boy				5711	غلام	boy, youth
			2926	خالة	maternal aunt	5756	يا	mom
464	زوج	husband				5811	تجوّز	to get married
476	قريب	relative	2951	عيال	child			
496	زوجة	wife	3140	تبنٍّ	adoption	5857	عمّة	paternal aunt
547	أصل	lineage (also origin)	3188	خال	maternal uncle	5899	يابا	papa
			3197	عائليّ	domestic	5913	مجوّز	married
559	والد	father	3205	خيّ	brother	5940	ربّى	to raise
594	دار	home; family	3226	متزوّج	married	5944	قرابة	kinship, relationship
			3229	راعي	guardian			
664	أسرة	family	3232	تبنّى	to adopt	6021	تكفّل	to be legal guardian
764	زواج	marriage; wedding	3236	يتيم	orphan			
			3581	حرمة	married woman, wife	6038	واد	boy
770	عمّ	paternal uncle				6096	بنيّة	little girl
791	فتاة	girl	3666	شقيقة	sister	6114	أخوّة	brotherhood
829	تربية	child-rearing	3838	عريس	bridegroom	6156	أعزب	bachelor
850	عائلة	family	3879	نسب	lineage; kinship	6162	وليد	little child
1046	جاب	give birth to (also to bring)	3901	منزليّ	domestic, household	6170	بيّ	daddy
						6173	طنط	aunt
1052	امرأة	woman	4040	شيخة	elderly woman	6200	زوجيّة	matrimony
1151	بنو	sons	4066	صبيّة	girl, young girl	6253	وليد	child, newborn
1226	جدّ	grandfather						
1354	أقرب	pl. relatives	4128	أسريّ	domestic	6272	عزّابيّ	single, unmarried
1386	ابنة	daughter	4236	جاهل	child (also ignorant)	6280	قران	marriage
1394	ولي الأمر	legal guardian				6362	بيبي	baby
1410	أهليّ	domestic	4281	خلّف	to give birth	6376	مخطوب	engaged
1612	ولد	to give birth to	4298	انفصال	separation	6378	حم	father-in-law
			4599	زفاف	wedding	6387	بني	little son

6429	زوّج	to marry off	6659	يبا	dad	6963	جوّز	to marry off
6430	مزوّج	married	6665	حضانة	child custody,	6996	صهر	brother-in-law,
6515	ودّ	boy, son			nursery, daycare			son-in-law
6636	طلّق	to divorce	6764	يمّ	mom	7342	طاطا	aunt
6645	كريمة	daughter	6766	بو	father			
6656	أخويّ	brotherly	6812	توم	twin			

398 صَدِيق *n. pl.* أَصْدِقاء friend
يبدأ الكاتب مقاله بالحديث عن أصدقائه ومعارفه من العرب الذين قال انهم نجحوا في التقريب بين المجتمعات العربية الإسلامية والأمريكيين — The author begins his article by talking about his Arab friends and acquaintances who he said have succeeded in bringing together Americans and Arab-Islamic societies
99 | 9751 |

399 دُولار *n. pl.* -aat dollar
وصل سعر البرميل الى ٧٥ دولارا، فاضطررنا الى رفع اسعار المشتقات النفطية مرة اخرى — The price of oil reached seventy-five dollars, so we were forced to raise the prices of oil derivatives once again
94 | 10209 |

400 بِناء *vn.* building, constructing, erecting; *n.* building, structure, edifice; بِناءً على based on, according to
هل ستؤيد صدور قانون موحد لبناء المساجد والكنائس؟ — Would you support a unified law for building mosques and churches?
97 | 9894 |

401 طَرِيقَة *n.* method, procedure, way
ليس من اللياقة أن تتعامل مع صديقى بهذه الطريقة — It is not appropriate for you to deal with my friend in that manner
99 | 9727 |

402 أَعْلَى *elat. fem.* عُلْيا higher/highest; *adj.* advanced, superior; أَعْلاهُ above (mentioned), aforementioned
دفعه دميان إلى أعلى أكثر واستطاع مجد الدين أن يجلس فى النهاية فوق السور — Dumyan pushed him even higher and Magd Al-Din was able to sit, in the end, on top of the wall
97 | 9854 |

403 مُمْكِن *adj.* possible
هل كان من الممكن أن تصمت الولايات المتحدة الأميركية عن هذا الموضوع؟ — Was it possible for the United States of America to stay silent about this subject?
98 | 9784 |

404 دَعْم *n.* support, assistance, bolstering, promotion
ألا يمكن أن يتحول هذا الدعم لمصلحة إيرانية وليس لمصلحة عراقية؟ — Couldn't this support end up benefiting Iran and not Iraq?
93 | 10286 |

405 إيه /'ee/ (Egy.) *interrog.* what; *n.* الإيه /il-'ee/ the thing; so-and-so
أيه الجمال ده والله مسمعتش حاجة قبل كده زي الجملة دي — What is all this beauty, by God I've never heard anything like this sentence before
90 | 10586 |

406 وين /ween/ (Lev.Irq.Gul.) *interrog.* where; (Lev. /la-ween/, Irq. /li-ween/) to what place, to where; (with pron.) وينك /ween-ak/ where have you been?
بيقول لك البنزين زاد عليكم، فالمواطن من وين بده يجيب؟ طيب ارفعوا لنا الرواتب شوي — He's telling you that gas has gone up on you, where is the regular guy going to get it from? OK, so raise our salaries for us a bit
65 | 14746 |

407 مَصْدَر *n. pl.* مَصادِر source
علمت البيان من مصادر مطلعة أن تحرير سعر وقود السيارات سيتم تنفيذه نهاية العام — The Al-Bayan newspaper learned from informed sources that floating the price of car fuel will be implemented at the end of the year
89 | 10701 |

408 حَدَثَ *v. I (u)* to happen, occur, take place

كانت تحس بأن روحها مسحوبة وبأن كل ما يحدث
غير حقيقي — She felt that her soul was being
dragged out of her, and that everything that was
happening was not real

90 | 10546 |

409 لَحْظَة *n. pl.* لَحَظات moment, instant

— كانت تحبه فى تلك اللحظة أكثر من أى وقت مضى
She loved him at that moment more than any
time in the past

99 | 9522 |

410 فُرْصَة *n. pl.* فُرَص chance, opportunity

اكدوا اهمية حق الشباب فى الحصول على فرص التعليم
الاساسي — They stressed the importance of the
right of young people to obtain basic
educational opportunities

99 | 9470 |

411 نادي *n. pl.* أَنْدِيَة club, association

هذه الأعلام الحمراء تحتفل بفوز النادي الأهلي
في مباراة لكرة القدم — These red flags
celebrate the victory of the Ahli Club in
a soccer match

95 | 9733 |

412 مَعْلُومَة *n.* item of information, piece of data;
pl. مَعْلُومات information, data

هذه معلومة جديدة ما كنت أعرفها — This is a
new piece of information I didn't know

97 | 9494 |

413 هَيْئَة *n. pl.* -aat agency, organization; outward
appearance, look

العرب في الهيئة ست دول فقط من سبع وخمسين دولة
— The Arabs in the organization are six states
only, out of fifty-seven states

95 | 9595 |

414 قِصَّة *n. pl.* قِصَص story, tale

ذلك بسبب نقص المعلومات، ولكن يجب تكملة
القصة طبقا للمعلومات المتاحة — That is because
of a lack of information, but the story needs to
be completed according to the information
available

99 | 9186 |

415 بِدَايَة *n. pl.* -aat beginning, start; starting
point; بدايات origins, early history

كانت خطوتها ثقيلة مترددة فى البداية، ثم
انتظمت واكتسبت إيقاعا رصينا مفعما بالمعانى —
Her steps were heavy and hesitant in the
beginning, and then they became more
regular and took on a steady rhythm full
of purpose

99 | 9185 |

416 جَنُوب *n.* south, southern part; جَنُوباً
southward

القوات البريطانية تطارد ميليشيات عدة في
جنوب العراق مدعومة من قبل قوات الحرس
الثوري الإيراني — The British forces are
pursuing several militias in the south of
Iraq, supported by forces of the Iranian
Revolutionary Guard

96 | 9470 |

417 دَرَى *v. I (i)* to know, be aware of sth or ب sth
or أَنَّ that; مادري and مدري /ma-dri/ (Gul.Irq.)
I don't know

لذلك حتى قطر التي دعت لعقد الجلسة تدري أكثر
من غيرها أنه لا جدوى من ذلك — Therefore even
Qatar, which called for holding the session,
knows more than others that there is no use
in that

97 | 9258 | +spo

418 دَعا *v. I (u)* to call إلى for sth; to call (upon)
sb إلى to do sth; to invite sb إلى to or to
do sth

كان المسلمون من بيشاور ولاهور يؤيدون محمد على
جناح الذى يدعو لانفصال باكستان عن الهند —
The Muslims from Peshawar and Lahore
support Muhammad Ali Janah who calls for
the separation of Pakistan from India

89 | 10054 |

419 مُبارَاة *n. pl.* مُبارَيات game, match, bout;
competition

لا تتخيلي فرحتي عندما علمت ان زوجي لن يشاهد
مباريات كأس العالم — You can't imagine my joy
when I found out that my husband would not
watch the World Cup matches

90 | 9985 |

420 تَعالَى *v. VI* to be exalted (God); قالَ تَعالَى approx.
God said (used when quoting the Qur'an);
(imperat.) تَعالَ (fem. تَعالِي, pl. تَعالُوا);
let's...; (Lev. shortened to تَعْ, fem. تَعِي)
— لا يوجد من يساعدني غير الله سبحانه وتعالى
There is no one to help me except God, may
He be praised and exalted
99 | 9087 |

421 إذ *conj.* as, since, seeing that; while,
when; إذ أَنَّ since, given that
قد تواجه الدورة البرلمانية الجديدة ازمات سياسية ممكنة
إذ يصر عدد من النواب على مساءلة وزراء — The
new Parliamentary session may face possible
political crises, since a number of deputies
insist on questioning ministers
89 | 10000 |

422 اِعْتَقَد *v. VIII* to believe في in sth, or أَنَّ/بأَنَّ
that
نعتقد أنه بحاجة إلى قانون أو تشريع يمنع التعذيب في
السجون — We believe that it is in need of a
law or legislation that forbids torture in the
prisons
97 | 9201 |

423 حَسَب *n.* حَسَبَ, بِحَسَبِ, and عَلَى حَسَبِ
according to
يجب أن يضع الرئيس استراتيجية الخروج من العراق
بحسب رأي الصحيفة — The president must put
in place an exit strategy from Iraq according to
the opinion of the newspaper
98 | 9079 |

424 دَقِيقَة *n.* pl. دَقائِق minute
وما هي الا دقائق حتى تعود الأمور الى وضعها
الطبيعي — It was only a few minutes before
matters returned to their natural state
99 | 8932 |

425 مَلِك *n.* pl. مُلُوك king; المَلِك (title) King
اشاد الرفاعي بالجهود الدؤوبة التي يبذلها جلالة الملك
دفاعا عن قضايا الامة العربية العادلة وفي طليعتها
القضية الفلسطينية — Al-Rafai praised the tireless
efforts which His Majesty the King is exerting in
defense of the just issues of the Arab nation,
and at their forefront, the Palestinian issue
97 | 9153 |

426 أَعْلَنَ *v. IV* to announce, declare, proclaim (عن)
sth or أَنَّ that
هناك بلاد عربية أعلنت حالة طوارئ منذ أكثر من
ثلاثين سنة — There are Arab countries which
announced a state of emergency more than
thirty years ago
89 | 9920 |

427 قِيمَة *n.* pl. قِيَم value, worth; importance; قِيَم
values, morals, ethics
الاعمال الارهابية الاجرامية لا تمثل القيم الاردنية
فالاردن يقف أبناؤه متراصين صفا واحدا خلف
القيادة الهاشمية — Criminal terrorist acts do
not represent Jordanian values, since Jordan's
people stand tightly in a single rank behind the
Hashemite leadership
98 | 9002 |

428 لاعِب *n.* pl. -uun player, athlete; *a.p.* playing
لعب اشبيلية بتسعة لاعبين بعد طرد خافي نافارو (٢٤)
وماريسكا (٨٦) — Seville played with nine
players after the expulsion of Javi Navarro (24)
and Maresca (86)
91 | 9647 |

429 أَدَّى *v. II* to cause, produce إلى sth; to lead,
direct, guide ب sb إلى to; to perform
(function), to carry out (duty, mission); to take
(test, oath)
كان لهذه الدار ثلاثة أبواب تؤدي إلى شوارع وأسواق
مختلفة — This house had three doors which lead
to various streets and markets
92 | 9519 |

430 مادَّة *n.* pl. مَوادّ substance, material; subject
matter, topic; (school) course, subject; article,
paragraph; material things, money
احتفظت بتقدير ممتاز في كل المواد التي درستها —
I maintained excellent grades in every subject
I studied
97 | 9026 |

431 خَطّ *n.* pl. خُطُوط line; phone line; air route;
airline (company); handwriting; script,
calligraphy
يعملون في خطوط السكك الحديدية جنوب المدينة —
They work in the railroad lines south of the city
99 | 8830 |

432 عَرْض *n.* pl. عُرُوض show, display, presentation; offer, tender; width, breadth
وصمتت خافضة رأسها إذ لم تتوقع عرضا كهذا إطلاقا — وتابع حديثه دون أي اعتبار لردة فعلها She was silent, lowering her head, since she had not expected an exhibition like this at all, and he continued talking without any consideration of her reaction
99 | 8798 |

433 رسالة *n.* pl. رَسائِل letter, missive; message, communication; dissertation, thesis; pl. -aat mission, task
أشرف على عشرات الرسائل للماجستير والدكتوراه، — وكان بين تلاميذه العديد من المصريين He supervised dozens of MA and PhD theses, and there were a number of Egyptians among his students
98 | 8844 |

434 اِنْتِخاب *n.* pl. -aat election; selection
بعد مرور عام على انتخابه لا تزال شعبية أحمدي نجاد في صعود مستمر — After the passage of a year since his election, the popularity of Ahmadinejad is still continually rising
85 | 10144 |

435 هؤُلاءِ *dem.pron.* these (people)
أما الذين يعملون من أجل مصالحهم فحسب، فهؤلاء لا يريدون بالمجتمع خيرا — As for those who work only for their own interests, they do not desire good for society
96 | 9044 |

436 مَعْنًى *n.* pl. مَعانٍ (def. مَعاني) sense, meaning, significance; concept, nuance; (Lev.) مَعْناة (with pron.) مَعْناتِها, مَعْناتُه its meaning
إن إكرام الأقليات معناه الصعود في سلم الحضارة أمام العالم — Honoring minorities means rising on the cultural ladder in front of the world
99 | 8629 |

437 نُقْطَة *n.* pl. نِقاط point, dot; location, position
أول من وضع النقاط فوق الحروف العربية هو نصر بن عاصم — The first person to put dots over the Arabic letters was Nasr bin Asim
98 | 8743 |

438 قَوِيّ *adj.* strong, powerful; great; (Gul.Irq.) serious, major, intense; قوى and اوى /'awi/ (Egy.) *adv.* a lot, very much, very
انتهى شهر أبريل بغارة قوية قتلت ستين شخصا وجرحت أكثر من مائة — April ended with a heavy raid which killed sixty people and wounded more than a hundred
99 | 8637 |

439 حِوار *n.* pl. -aat discussion, conversation, dialog, talk
بإمكاننا أن نقول أننا مستعدين للحوار فور أن تقوم حماس بالعودة عن الانقلاب العسكري — We can say that we are ready for dialog immediately after Hamas abandons the military coup
97 | 8792 |

440 رَدّ *n.* pl. رُدُود response, reply; رَدّ فِعْل reaction
قالت انها لا تحب الخوض في السياسة الا ان ردودَ الافعال الشعبية كانت واضحة — She said she did not want to get into politics, but that the popular reactions were clear
96 | 8870 |

441 لُغَة *n.* pl. -aat language
الرياضة أصبحت هي اللغة التي تربط العالم — Sports became the language that links the world
99 | 8559 |

442 لِـ *conj.* (with foll. subjunctive) in order to, so that; لِيَكُونَ for him/it to be...
وقد وقع اختياري على أخيكم أدهم ليدير الوقف تحت إشرافي — My choice has fallen on your brother, Adham, to direct the Endowment under my supervision
97 | 8710 |

443 بَلَغَ *v. I (u)* to reach, arrive at, attain sth; to come to sb (i.e. to hear) أَنَّ that
لقد بلغت السادسة والثلاثين ولم تعش قط كما أرادت — She had reached thirty-six years old, and she had not lived at all like she had wanted
89 | 9476 |

444 سِعْر *n. pl.* أَسْعار price, cost, rate
كان الكثير منهم قد توقع أن تستمر أسعار النفط في
الانخفاض لتصل إلى حدود ٥٠ دولارا للبرميل —
Many of them had expected that the price
of oil would continue to fall to reach around
50 dollars a barrel
96 | 8806 |

445 حَصَلَ *v. I (u)* to get, obtain, acquire على sth
لما كبر وتخرج من الجامعة كان يحلم بأن يحصل على
عمل ويتزوج وتأتيه بنت صغيرة — When he grew
up and graduated from the university, he
dreamed that he would get a job and marry
and have a small girl
96 | 8769 |

446 أَقَلّ *elat.* less/least, smaller/smallest, lower/
lowest; *n.* minimum
على الأقل أريده أن يتصل بي تليفونيا مرة كل يوم —
At least I want him to contact me by telephone
once a day
99 | 8481 |

447 قَلّ *v. I (i)* to be less (عن than), decrease, diminish
السفينة كانت بعيدة عن تلك المنطقة بما لا يقل عن ١٠
أميال بحرية — The ship was far from this area,
not less than 10 nautical miles
91 | 9296 |

448 تَمام *adj.* exact; complete; good, fine; تَماماً
exactly; completely, totally
كانت أنوار المدرسة تطفأ في تمام الساعة التاسعة بالليل،
وتصمت الأصوات القليلة المضطربة بعد ذلك — The
lights of the school were turned off at exactly
nine at night, and the few troubled voices went
silent after that
99 | 8523 |

449 صَباح *n.* morning; صَباحاً in the morning
لم أنم منذ الأمس، ولدي عملية غدا في السابعة صباحا
— I haven't slept since yesterday, and I have an
operation tomorrow at seven in the morning
98 | 8524 |

450 مَوْجُود *adj.* existing, found, located; present
ما الفيتامينات الموجودة في البصل؟ — What are the
vitamins which are present in onions?
98 | 8547 |

451 تَمَنَّى *v. V* to wish ل sb (happiness, success);
to hope أَنْ that
نفتخر بالسد العالي ونتمنى له طول العمر — We are
proud of the High Dam and we hope it will
have a long life
98 | 8580 |

452 مَرَض *n. pl.* أَمْراض illness, disease
اكتشف والداها أعراض المرض نتيجة زرقة جلدها
وصعوبة تنفسها — Her parents discovered the
symptoms of the illness as a result of the
blueness of her skin and her difficulty breathing
99 | 8490 |

453 تَحَدَّثَ *v. V* to speak إلى/مع to/with sb; to
discuss عن (a topic)
يحضرون لهم رجال دين ومختصين نفسيين يتحدثون
معهم حتى يزول خوفهم من مواجهة الموت — They
bring them men of religion and psychology
experts to speak with them so that their fear of
facing death will dissipate
95 | 8852 |

454 أَهَمّ *elat.* more/most important
مدينة القدس تعتبر من أهم المدن في العالم بحكم
الاهمية العقائدية للديانات السماوية الثلاث — The
city of Jerusalem is considered to be one of the
most important cities in the world on account
of its creedal importance to the three heavenly
religions
98 | 8546 |

455 بُدّ *n.* avoidance, escape; لا بُدَّ مِن there is
no avoiding, escaping (it's necessary, it's
inevitable)
الحياة لا تتوقف أبدا أمام شيء.. لا بد لها أن تستمر —
Life does not stop for anything...it has to
go on
98 | 8543 |

456 فَعَلَ *v. I (a)* to do sth
هل يعتبر أن لهذه الحكومة إنجازات أم كل ما فعلته
هذه الحكومة حتى اليوم هي إخفاقات متتالية؟ —
Does he consider that this government
has accomplishments, or is everything this
government has done until today consecutive
failures?
90 | 9309 |

457 طَلَبَ *v. I (u)* to request, ask for sth (مِن from sb); to apply for sth; to order, place an order for sth; to seek, look for sth; to dial, press (number on a phone)

هذا القانون يطلب من كل مواطن أن يتجسس على المواطن الآخر — This law asks each citizen to spy on other citizens

99 | 8391 |

458 صِحَّة *n.* health, wellness; authenticity, truth; صحتين /SaHteen/ (Lev.) *interj.* bon appétit!

هناك مؤشرات تدل على صحة موقف الاقتصاد المصري ومنها على سبيل المثال ارتفاع معدل النمو — There are indications which point to the health of the Egyptian economy, and among them, for example, is the rise in the rate of growth

99 | 8421 |

459 وَقَعَ *v. I (a)* to fall down; to take place; to be located

هل تعرفين أين يقع بيته؟ — Do you know where his house is located?

99 | 8415 |

460 سَوْفَ *part.* (future) will, shall

رسائلكم على الإيميل سوف تذهب مباشرة إلى الزميلة سميرة في غرفة الاتصالات — You email letters will go directly to our colleague Samira in the communications room

88 | 9471 |

461 أَيْنَ *interrog.* where

لم أرك منذ زمن بعيد، فأين كنت؟ — I haven't seen you for a long time, where have you been?

89 | 9321 |

462 لازم *adj.* necessary, required; needed; (Dia.) (modal verb) must, should; لازِمْنِي I need, have to, should

الكهرباء انقطعت، والكوبرى مفتوح للمراكب، يعني لازم ننتظر — The electricity was cut off while the bridge was open for ships, meaning we have to wait

97 | 8549 |

463 تَعاوُن *n.* cooperation

يجب أن يكون هناك تعاون بين الدول العربية — There has to be cooperation among the Arab states

85 | 9755 |

464 زَوْج *n. pl.* أَزْواج spouse; husband; زَوْجان married couple

تجربة زوجي في مثل تلك الأوضاع ساعدتنا كثيرا — My husband's experience in circumstances such as these helped me a lot

98 | 8453 |

465 لِذلِكَ *conj.* therefore

أبوها لم يستقر في البلد سوى من سنوات قليلة، ولذلك فإن اسمه غير معروف للكثيرين من أهل الرياض — Her father only settled in the country a few years ago, and therefore his name is not known to many of the people of Riyadh

97 | 8472 |

466 تالٍ (تالي .def) *adj.* following, subsequent; بالتالي therefore, consequently

في أول أيام الأسبوع التالي، سألت سديم طاهر عن صديقه فراس — On the first days of the following week, I asked Sadim Tahir about his friend Firas

97 | 8475 |

467 شارع *n. pl.* شَوارع street; (fig.) الشارع the public, public opinion

لا يزال يذكر الفتى هيس وهو في الخامسة عشرة يمشى في شوارع البلدة قبل الحرب الأولى — He still remembers the boy Hess when he was fifteen years old walking in the streets of the town before World War I

98 | 8360 |

468 نار *fem.n. pl.* نِيران fire; gunfire; hellfire

تعرض فندق يقيم فيه مسئولون من الحكومة الانتقالية إلى إطلاق نار دون وقوع إصابات — A hotel in which officials of the transitional government were residing was exposed to gunfire that did not result in any injuries

98 | 8346 |

469 عَديد *n.* large number, large quantity; *adj.* numerous, many

قام برحلات عديدة للارض المقدسة آخرها اشراف ومراقبته للانتخابات الفلسطينية — He made numerous trips to the Holy Land, the last of which was (for) his supervision and monitoring of the Palestinian elections

88 | 9291 |

470 صَلَّى *v. II* to pray; to worship; to say a prayer عَلى for sb

قمت وتوضّأت وصليت — I got up, did my ablutions, and prayed

97 | 8403 |

471 فِكْرَة *n.* idea, concept, notion (عن about); عَلَى فِكْرَة (Dia. عَفِكْرَة) by the way, now that you mention it

في البداية لم أكن متحمسا لفكرة البيان، لكنني بعد ذلك وجدتها ممتازة — At the beginning I wasn't enthusiastic about the idea of the communiqué, but after that I found it to be excellent

99 | 8227 |

472 تَرَكَ *v. I (u)* to leave (behind), quit, abandon sth

طبيعة المكان كانت لا تترك لروميل فرصة المناورة — The nature of the place did not leave Romell the opportunity to maneuver

98 | 8295 |

473 دَرَجَة *n.* pl. -aat degree, grade, level; class, rank

التصق القميص بجسده لدرجة كادت تؤلمه — The shirt clung to his body so much that it started to hurt him

98 | 8282 |

474 آخِر *adj.* pl. أواخِر last, final, concluding; *n.* end, tail, conclusion; bottom, foot; أَخيراً وَلَيْسَ آخِراً إلى آخِرِه et cetera; last but not least

لم أحاول بعد ذلك أن ألتفت خلفي لأشاهد لآخر مرة ذلك المنظر الذي لن يتكرر بعد ذلك أبدا — I didn't try after that to turn behind me to see for the last time that scene which will never again be repeated

98 | 8267 |

475 اِجْتِماع *n.* pl. -aat meeting, gathering; عِلْم الاِجْتِماع sociology

تمت مناقشة القضية في اجتماعات المجلس الاعلى لاتحاد الصيادلة العرب التي عقدت في عمان — The issue was discussed in the meetings of the Higher Council of the Arab Pharmacists Union which was held in Amman

92 | 8843 |

7 Materials

558	ورق	paper; leaves	3269	سائل	liquid	5283	بلاستيك	plastic
948	نفط	petroleum	3358	مائيّ	watery, liquid	5359	محروق	fuel
1363	حجر	stone	3471	رماد	ashes, cinders	5494	إسمنت	cement
1720	حديد	iron	3508	قماش	fabric, cloth	5644	سلك	wire, thread
1745	زيت	oil	3512	معدنيّ	metallic	5652	صينيّة	porcelain
1904	ذهب	gold	3556	عيّنة	sample,	5837	نحاس	copper
1946	رصاص	lead			specimen	6043	بلاطة	floor tile
2095	رمل	sand	3658	خام	raw; crude	6401	زفت	asphalt
2264	بترول	petroleum	3780	خليط	mixture, blend	6408	مذهّب	gilded, golden
2323	صلب	steel (also	3815	خشبيّ	wooden	6847	معبّد	asphalted,
		hard)	3994	دهن	grease, fat			paved
2755	خيط	string, thread	4165	خشب	wood	6901	لبن	adobe bricks
3039	حبل	rope, cord	4295	مزيج	mixture	6902	ماس	diamonds
3050	زجاج	glass	4532	قطن	cotton	7235	خلط	to mix, blend
3086	خشبة	wood; board	4622	خلط	mixture, blend	7286	صفر	brass, copper
3138	حديديّ	iron (adj)	4709	معدن	metal	7422	جاز	gasoline,
3206	عود	stick	4769	حرير	silk			kerosene
3210	جوهر	gem, jewel	4785	فحم	coal	7574	فيروز	turquoise
3242	نسيج	fabric, textile	4883	فضّيّ	silver	7785	بنّور	crystal, glass
3265	طين	clay; mud	4904	بتروليّ	oil-based			

476 قَرِيب *adj.* near, close; related; pl. (Lev.) قُراب
related; قَرِيباً recently; soon; *n.* pl. قَرائِب
relative, near relation
هز الطبيب رأسه واستدار متوجها ببطء نحو المقعد
القريب — The doctor shook his head, and
turned slowly toward the nearby chair
99 | 8185 |

477 وَسَط *n.* pl. أوْساط middle, center; environment;
وَسْطَ amid, among, in the middle of; أوْساط
(diplomatic) circles, quarters
شعره مثير للجدل في الاوساط الثقافية خصوصا بعد
نشره مجموعتين من الشعر الحداثي — His poetry is
controversial in cultural circles particularly after
two collections of modernist poetry were
published
99 | 8164 |

478 نَظَر *v. I (u)* to look إلى at; to examine, look في
into
استمر في السير.. لا تنظر خلفك ولا تتحدث مع أحد
— Continue walking...Don't look behind you
and don't speak to anyone
91 | 8856 |

479 سَعُودِيّ *n./adj.* pl. -uun Saudi
هل أنت تميل إلى هذه النظرية: أن الإعلام السعودي
إعلام غير مستقل؟ — Do you lean toward to
this theory: that the Saudi media is not an
independent media?
89 | 9006 |

480 واضِح *adj.* clear, explicit; obvious, visible
كان واضحا أيضا أنها تستعد للخروج — It was
clear that she was also getting ready to leave
99 | 8125 |

481 مَوْت *n.* death
راح في غيبوبة وأصبح معلقا بين الحياة والموت —
He went into a coma, and began to hang between
life and death
98 | 8147 |

482 خُصُوص *n.* (as to this) matter, issue; (in this)
regard, respect; خُصُوصاً especially, particularly
صباح الخير.. أنا أتصل بخصوص الوظيفة التي أعلنتم
عنها — Good morning...I am calling regarding
the job which you announced
95 | 8455 |

483 إنَّما *conj.* but rather, on the contrary; (not just)
but (also)
قال إن اللحم ليس مخصصا للبيع، وإنما هو للعرض
فقط، وأحس الزبون أنه يسخر منه — He said that
the meat was not designated for sale, but rather
it was for display only, and the customer felt
that he was making fun of him
98 | 8192 |

484 مَصْلَحَة *n.* pl. مَصالِح interest, advantage, favor;
department, agency
لا نحتاج إلى مثل هذه العمليات لو كانوا هم يريدون
مصلحة العراق — We do not need such
operations if they indeed desire the good of
Iraq
97 | 8227 |

485 أساس *n.* pl. أُسُس foundation, base; basis,
principle; أساساً basically, fundamentally; عَلَى
أساس on the basis of; في الأساس in principle;
عساس انه and عاساس /9asaas 'innu/ (Egy.Lev.)
so that; with the understanding that; on
condition that
القنبلة الذرية الاساس فيها هو يورانيوم عالي
التخصيب — The basis of the atomic bomb is
highly enriched uranium
98 | 8141 |

486 صَحِيفَة *n.* pl. صُحُف newspaper
ما هي أهم العناوين التي استقطبت اهتمامك من
الصحف الأميركية؟ — What are the most
important headlines that attracted your interest
from the American newspapers?
93 | 8543 |

487 وَقَفَ *v. I (i)* to stop, cease (doing sth); to
stand, rise; وَقَفَ جَنْبَهُ to stand by, support sb;
قِفْ! stop!
هل تعتقد أن هناك جهات أخرى غير بن لادن وقفت
وراء هجمات الحادي عشر من سبتمبر؟ — Do you
believe that there are other parties besides Bin
Laden who stand behind the attacks of
September 11th?
99 | 7924 |

488 جَيِّد *adj.* good; جَيِّداً *adv.* well
هكذا قلت مبتسما بأدب محاولا أن أعطي له انطباعا
جيدا — I said this smiling and politely, trying to
give him a good impression
98 | 8006 |

489 ذَهَبَ *v. I (a)* to go, leave, depart
لماذا لا تذهب إلى التحقيق وتخبرهم بالحقيقة؟ — Why don't you go to the investigator's office and tell them the truth
90 | 8703 |

490 زِيارَة *vn.* visiting; *n.* pl. -aat visit
ذهبت لزيارة صديق يسكن بيتا بعيداً عن ضجة الاجتماع — I went to visit a friend who lives in a house far from the clamor of society
97 | 8046 |

491 رائع *adj.* fantastic, amazing, marvelous, magnificent, awesome
عشت قصة حب واحدة حقيقية رائعة.. لكنها انتهت للأسف في الصيف الماضي — I experienced a single, wonderful true love story...but it ended, unfortunately, last summer
97 | 8028 | +for

492 إِجْراء *vn.* conducting, carrying out, undertaking; *n.* pl. -aat procedure, process; step, measure; move, action
أعلن أرميتاج دعمه الكامل لإجراء الانتخابات العراقية في الثلاثين من الشهر الحالي — Armitage announced his complete support for holding the Iraqi elections on the thirtieth of the current month
85 | 9084 |

493 اِتِّصال *n.* pl. -aat contact, communication; connection, relation, relationship
تستطيعين الاتصال بى في أى وقت إذا أردت الاستفسار عن أى شيء — You can get in touch with me at any time if you want to consult about anything
97 | 7989 |

494 دُنْيا *n.* world
إن زوجها لديه مزايا وعيوب مثل أى شخص في الدنيا، وعليها أن تذكر مزاياه كما تذكر عيوبه — Her husband has good traits and faults like any person in the world, and she needs to remember his good traits as much as she remembers his faults
98 | 7872 |

495 حَبَّ *v. I (i)* to love, like sb; to want, like sth or to do sth; *a.p.* حابّ and (Lev.) حابب wanting, desiring; loving, liking
حبيت أقدم هدية بسيطة لمشرفنا الغالي — I wanted to offer a small gift to our dear supervisor
92 | 8371 | +spo

496 زَوْجَة *n.* pl. -aat wife
لحظات ووصل العمدة إلى بيته، وقف أمام زوجته يرتعش بالغضب، يكاد يتناثر إلى آلاف من القطع الصغيرة — In a few moments the mayor arrived at his house. He stood in front of his wife shaking with anger. He was on the verge of breaking apart into thousands of tiny pieces
98 | 7840 |

497 تَنْفِيذ *n.* execution, implementation, carrying out
من الواضح أن كثيرا من الأمور كان يمكن تنفيذها بشكل مختلف، ما من شك في ذلك — It is clear that many things could have been carried out in a different manner, there is no doubt about that
88 | 8675 |

498 لَوْن *n.* pl. ألْوان color, tint, hue; type, sort, kind
اندفع شعرها الذي له لون الليل إلى الخلف وراء أذنين مزينتين بأقراط ذهبية — Her hair, which had the color of the night, was pushed to the back behind her ears which were decorated with gold earrings
99 | 7668 |

499 قَدِيم *adj.* pl. قُدَماء، قُدامَى old, ancient; *n.* قُدامَى old timers, veterans
بدأ يرتدى ثيابه القديمة، قطعة قطعة — He began to put on his old clothes, piece by piece
99 | 7669 |

500 قادِم *adj.* next, following, future; *a.p.* arriving, coming, proceeding
خيل إليه فجأة أنه يستمع إلى أصوات قادمة من الدور الأرضي، صوت باب يفتح ويغلق — It seemed to him suddenly that he was listening to sounds coming from the ground floor, the sound of a door opening and closing
88 | 8633 |

501 كُرَة *n.* pl. -aat ball, globe, sphere; كورة (Dia.)
/kuura/, (Egy.) /koora/ football (soccer);
(shortened in idafa) كرة قدم /kurat qadam/
هو اللاعب الأمريكي الوحيد الذي أحرز هدفا في
بطولة العالم لكرة القدم عام ٢٠٠٢ — He is the
only American player who got a goal in the World
championships for soccer in the year 2002
97 | 7866 |

502 زادَ *v. I (i)* to grow, increase; to exceed, go
beyond عن/على sth; to increase, add to (مِن) sth
اشتد غضبها حين علمت بالحقيقة، وزاد غضبها حين
خاطبها الخنزير من داخل بيته — Her anger grew
when she found out the truth, and her anger
increased when the pig talked to her from
inside his house
99 | 7657 |

503 عِدَّة *n.* (in idafa) a number of; *adj.* (invar.)
several, numerous
عمل بالتدريس في عدة جامعات أمريكية في نيويورك
وبوسطن — He worked in education in a
number of American universities in New York
and Boston
97 | 7758 |

504 عَوْدَة *n.* return, going back; return trip
كان الرجل المسكين لا ينتظره ما يعرف عند عودته
لمنزله — The poor man didn't know what was
awaiting him when he got back to the house
94 | 7992 |

505 عال (def. عالي) *adj.* high, elevated
أتمنى يا جدي أن أنال شهادة علمية عاليةً، وأن أسافر
— I hope, grandfather, to get a higher scientific
degree, and to travel
99 | 7576 |

506 سِوَى *neg.part.* other than, except for
في الختام لا يسعني سوى أن أشكر ضيوفي الكرام
الذين شاركوا معي في حلقة اليوم — In conclusion,
I can only thank our generous guests who
participated with me in this episode today
90 | 8312 |

507 بَحْر *n.* pl. بحار sea
جاءت من طنطا إلى شيكاجو هكذا، مرة واحدة، دون
استعداد أو تمهيد، كمن قفز في البحر بملابسه الكاملة
وهو لا يعرف السباحة — She came from Tanta to

Chicago in this way, all at once, without
preparation, like someone jumping into the ocean
fully dressed and not knowing how to swim
99 | 7560 |

508 شَعَرَ *v. I (u)* to feel, be aware of ب sth
في كل يوم كنت تجعلينني أشعر بأنني أقل منك في كل
شيء — Every day you made me feel that I was
less than you in everything
97 | 7748 |

509 تَقْرِير *n.* pl. تَقَارِير report, account
حكى لها كأنه يقدم تقريرا عن وضعهم هناك — He
spoke to her as if he were submitting a report
about their situation there
94 | 7919 |

510 مَرَّ *v. I (u)* to pass by, go by (time, event); to
pass by, go past ب/على sth/sb; to visit, stop by
على (sb's place)
مرت دقيقة كاملة ولم يفتح أحد، فضغطت الجرس من
جديد — A full minute passed and no one
opened the door, so I pressed the bell again
99 | 7524 |

511 نِساء *pl.n.* women (sg. اِمْرَأَة)
روت لي حكايات لا تنتهي عن رجال ونساء عرفتهم
وأحببتهم — She told me never-ending stories
about men and women she knew and loved
95 | 7826 |

512 فَتَحَ *v. I (a)* to open sth; to open, start
(a business); to turn on (lights, radio, TV);
to conquer (city, land)
يغلق الدكتور محمد صلاح جهاز التسجيل ويرتدي
نظارته الطبية ويفتح أجندة التليفونات ويبدأ في
الاتصال بمعارفه وأصدقائه القدامى — Dr
Muhammad Salah closes the recorder, puts on
his medical glasses, opens the phone book and
begins to call his acquaintances and old friends
99 | 7487 |

513 شَهِدَ *v. I (a)* to witness, observe, see sth/sb;
to testify, bear witness: أَشْهَدُ أَنْ لا إِلَهَ إِلَّا الله
I testify that there is no god but God
وقد شهدت تلك الفترة ازدهار النظرية الأنثوية —
This period has seen the flourishing of feminist
theory
89 | 8378 |

514 سِلاح *n.* pl. أَسْلِحَة weapon; branch of the armed forces; سِلاح الجَوّ air force
جلس الجندي على ركبته اليمنى وقد صوب سلاحه نحوي — The soldier crouched on his right knee and aimed his weapon at me
97 | 7684 |

515 عِلْم *vn.* knowing; عِلْمًا أَنَّ knowing that, in view of the fact that; *n.* knowledge, information; pl.n. عُلُوم (Gul.) news; وِيش علومك /weesh cluumak/ what's new? (what news do you have?)
يجاهد بصمت ليؤدي رسالته في بناء الإنسان المسلح بالعلم والمعرفة وغرس قيم الانتماء وحب الوطن والتضحية من أجله — He strives quietly to carry out his mission to build people armed with knowledge and to graft in the values of belonging and love of the nation and sacrificing for its sake
99 | 7502 |

516 إعادة *n.* repeating, doing sth again; returning, giving sth back
جاء بكؤوس الشاي، فألقى التحية العسكرية، وتلقى المهمة بإعادة حسان إلى زنزانته — He brought the teacups, saluted, and was given the duty of taking Hassan back to his cell
96 | 7694 |

517 عَم *part.* (Lev.) (with imperf., to indicate present continuous) عَم بَمْزَح مَعَك I'm (just) kidding you
عم يضايقك هلق كتفك؟ — Is your shoulder bothering you now?
41 | 17658 |

518 لَيْلَة *n.* pl. لَيالِ (def. اللَّيْلَة) night, evening; اللَّيْلَة tonight
سأنتظرك الليلة في السادسة — I will wait for you tonight at six
99 | 7411 |

519 ثَقافَة *n.* pl. -aat culture, civilization
يقدم الكتاب بحثا ووصفا عاما للثقافة التقليدية في المجتمع الكويتي — The book presents a piece of research and a general description of traditional culture in Kuwaiti society
96 | 7674 |

520 داخِلِيّ *adj.* internal; domestic; الرَّقَم الدّاخِلِيّ telephone extension, direct number
خرج خالي يونان من غرفة داخلية أقفل بابها وراءه، وجاء إلى الفسحة وهو بالقميص الحرير — My uncle Yunan came out of an inner room and locked the door behind him, and came to the open area in a silk shirt
99 | 7466 |

521 مُنَظَّمَة *n.* pl. -aat organization
كان عضوا في اللجنة التنفيذية لمنظمة التحرير الفلسطينية — He was a member of the executive committee of the PLO
85 | 8647 |

522 فِكْر *n.* pl. أَفْكار thinking, thought; idea, concept, notion
ان الانسان تكون لديه افكار لا يتجرأ ان يبوح بها كما يبوح بها عبر الانترنت — People have thoughts they don't dare reveal the way they reveal them over the Internet
99 | 7397 |

523 رَسُول *n.* messenger (Muhammad); pl. رُسُل messenger, apostle
أنسيت أنك زوجي على سنة الله ورسوله؟ — Did you forget that you are my husband, married according to the Sunna of God and his Prophet?
93 | 7845 |

524 جُزْء *n.* pl. أَجْزاء part, section, piece; portion, fraction
شدى الجزمة من قدمي وغطيني.. لا تتركى جزءا فى جسمى إلا وتغطيه — Fasten the shoes on my feet and cover me...don't leave any part of my body uncovered
98 | 7495 |

525 انْتَهَى *v. VIII* to end, finish, conclude sth
لماذا تهتمين به إذا كانت علاقتكما انتهت؟ — Why are you interested in him if your relationship ended?
99 | 7390 |

526 غَرِيب *adj.* strange; *n.* pl. غُرَباء stranger, foreigner
كان يلهث من فرط الانفعال.. بدا صوته غريبا على سمعه وكأنه يصدر من شخص آخر — He was panting from excitement...his voice seemed strange to his ears, as if it was coming out of some other person
99 | 7346 |

527 غُرْفَة *n. pl.* غُرَف room, chamber

قال لها البهى أيضا إنه سيتركهما ينامان فى غرفتها الليلة، وسيخرج لينام فى مدخل البيت — Bahiy told her also that he would leave them to sleep in the room tonight, and he would go sleep in the entrance to the house

99 | 7358 |

528 مُرُور *vn.* passing (of time); going through; passing by; stopping by (to visit); كَلِمَة المُرُور password; مُرُوراً بِـ passing, crossing, going through, via; *n.* traffic

حصلت على محام بعد مرور سبعة أشهر على احتجازي، لكنه كان عاجزا عن فعل شيء — I got a lawyer seven months after my detention, but he was unable to do anything

88 | 8201 | +for

529 حُرِّيَّة *n. pl.* -aat freedom

إذا لم نطالب بحقوق الناس فى العدل والحرية، فلا خير فى أى علم نتعلمه — If we don't demand people's rights for justice and freedom, then there will be no good in any knowledge we learn

98 | 7416 |

530 هٰكَذَا *adv.* like this, this way, thus

لا تحب الاختلاط بالناس، هكذا هي منذ طفولتها — She doesn't like mixing with people; she has been like that since her childhood

98 | 7408 |

531 سَلِمَ *v. I (a)* to be safe; to be faultless; تَسْلَم، تَسْلُمِين *fem.sg.* thanks!

تسلم يدك — Thank you (May your hand be kept safe)

91 | 7888 | +for

532 هيك /heek/ (Lev.), هيج /hiich/ (Irq.) *adv.* like this, like that, thus

شوف الهندسة المعمارية هلق، الأوتوكاد وهيك عالكمبيوتر — Look, architecture now is basically just Autocad and the like on the computer

45 | 15832 |

533 زيادة *n.* increase, rise, growth; addition, supplement

ربما نحن هنا لنلتقى بك ونعرفك، وهذا وحده يسعدنا وزيادة — Perhaps we are here to meet you and get to know you, and this alone makes us happy and more

97 | 7424 |

534 قائِد *n. pl.* قادة leader, commander

ثار المصريون ضد الحملة الفرنسية مرتين خلال ثلاثة أعوام وقتلوا قائد الحملة — The Egyptians revolted against the French campaign twice during three years, and they killed the leader of the campaign

87 | 8278 |

535 وَسِيلَة *n. pl.* وَسائِل device, instrument, medium, means

إنه واقع فاسد لابد من تغييره بكل الأساليب الممكنة والوسائل المتاحة — It is a corrupt reality which must be changed with every possible style and means available

98 | 7325 |

536 نَقْل *n.* transportation, transfer; transmission, relaying (of news); نَقْلاً عَن quoting, as reported by

لقد ازدهرت الإسكندرية بحركة النقل بين الميناء والدلتا والصعيد — Alexandria flourished through its involvement in the activity of transporting goods between the port and the Delta and Upper Egypt

96 | 7415 |

537 حَقِيقيّ *adj.* true, real, factual, authentic

تحولت الحدائق إلى ميادين قتال حقيقية، كانت الشرطة تضرب المتظاهرين بكل الطرق المتاحة وبمنتهى القسوة — The gardens were transformed into actual fields of battle; the police were beating the demonstrators with every means they had, and with the utmost of harshness

98 | 7272 |

538 اِحْتاجَ *v. VIII* to need, want إلى sth/sb

أعلنا صراحة أن الولايات المتحدة تحتاج إلى الإبقاء على وجود عسكري ضخم في بلاد الرافدين ولسنوات كثيرة — We announced frankly that the United States needs to keep a huge military presence in Iraq for many years

98 | 7243 |

539 مُسْتَقْبَل *n.* future; مُسْتَقْبَلًا in the future

علاقتنا رائعة، لكنها بلا مستقبل — Our relationship is wonderful, but it has no future

98 | 7237 |

540 مَحْكَمَة *n.* pl. مَحَاكِم court, tribunal

تم القبض على جزار ومحاكمته أمام المحكمة العسكرية لأنه امتنع عن بيع اللحم — A butcher was arrested and convicted before the military court because he refused to sell meat

95 | 7435 |

541 قِيَادَة *n.* leadership, command; driving (a vehicle), piloting (an aircraft); قِيَادات leaders, commanders

قال إن قائدا جديدا اسمه مونتجمري تولى قيادة الجيش الثامن وهو قائد شديد في التعامل مع الجنود — He said that a new leader, named Montgomery, would take over the leadership of the eighth Army, and he is a strong leader in dealing with soldiers

87 | 8047 |

542 دِفَاع *n.* defense (military, legal, sports); protection

أعلن روزفلت عزم أمريكا على الدفاع عن حرية البحار — Roosevelt announced America's intention to defend the freedom of the seas

96 | 7233 |

543 سَبِيل *n.* pl. سُبُل way, road; means

إن الرب لا يصنع شيئا على سبيل الصدفة.. ما يحدث الآن عادل ومنطقي تماما — The Lord does not make anything by way of chance... whatever happens now is just and perfectly logical

97 | 7153 |

544 إِنْتِي and أَنْتِي (Dia.) *pron.* you (fem.sg.); (Tun.) you (masc./fem.sg.)

عزيزتي أم علي والله اني حاسة باللي انتي حاسة فيه لأني مريت بها التجربة — Dear Um Ali, really, I feel what you are feeling because I (also) went through this experience

43 | 15970 | +spo +for

545 عِلْمِيّ *adj.* scientific, scholarly, academic; خَيال عِلْمِيّ science fiction

جداولهم مشغولة لأسابيع قادمة، وأمامهم أبحاث علمية لا بد من إنجازها — Their schedules are busy for the next weeks, and they have scientific research that they need to get done

97 | 7188 |

546 بَيْنَا *conj.* while

تمشى الست مريم على الرصيف بثقة، بينا لا ترفع زهرة عينيها عن الأرض غير المرصوفة — Mrs Mariam walks on the street with confidence, while Zahra does not raise her eyes from the unpaved ground

96 | 7250 |

547 أَصْل *n.* pl. أُصُول source, origin; descent, lineage; original, master copy; أَصْلًا originally, primarily; أُصُول principles, basic rules; funds, assets, capital

عين ساركوزي أول امرأة من أصل عربي وزيرة في الحكومة الفرنسية — Sarkozy appointed the first women of Arab origin to be a minister in the French government

99 | 7020 |

548 عِلْم *n.* pl. عُلُوم science, the study of; عِلْم النَفْس psychology

تعرفا اثناء دراستها للعلوم السياسية في الجامعة — They got to know each other while studying political science at the university

99 | 7014 |

549 أَمْنِيّ *adj.* safety, security, protection

أريد أن أقول إن سوريا تطالب بتوقيع اتفاق أمني منذ سنوات مع العراقيين — I want to say that Syria has been calling for the signing of a security agreement with the Iraqis for years

87 | 7967 |

550 مَنْزِل *n.* pl. مَنَازِل house, residence

أصرت سديم على إقامته في منزل أبيها بالرياض — Sadim insisted on his staying in her father's house in Riyadh

96 | 7183 |

551 زَمَن *n.* time, period, duration

المنطقة آمنة ولم يحدث فيها شيء مكروه منذ زمن طويل — The area is secure and nothing bad has happened in it for a long time

99 | 6996 |

552 بَيَان *n.* statement, declaration; bulletin, communiqué; (press) release; بَيَانات data, information; غَنِيّ عَن البَيَان needless to say, it goes without saying

8 Time

General Terms

74	مرّة	(one) time
98	وقت	time
263	فترة	time period
283	دائم	lasting
286	تاريخ	date; history
358	حين	time
409	لحظة	moment
415	بداية	beginning
476	قريب	near, close
499	قديم	old, ancient
551	زمن	time
586	مدى	range, extent
590	مدّة	time period
737	زمان	time
769	حديث	new; modern
1005	موعد	appointment
1424	مبكّر	early
1652	أجل	period, term
1761	دوام	business hours
1864	حصّة	class period
1912	فراغ	free time
1944	مؤقّت	temporary
2069	لسّة	yet, still
2114	إجازة	vacation
2229	توقيت	(standard) time
2539	شوط	half (sports)
2770	أوان	time
2800	تأخير	delay
2947	عطلة	vacation
3315	ميعاد	appointment
3336	سهرة	soiree
3505	باكر	early
3559	تقويم	calendar (also rating)
3584	مهلة	extension
3748	إبّان	during
3817	أمد	duration; extent
4117	مولد	birthday
4255	برهة	moment
4305	طور	stage, phase
4536	مراهقة	adolescence
4886	استراحة	intermission

5175	ميلاديّ	AD
5264	تزامن	simultaneity
5305	صباحيّ	morning
5411	فينة	time, moment
5876	لمح	instant (also glance)
5973	غرّة	beginning
6072	بكّير	early
7167	نوبة	time, occasion

Abbreviations (ranking is from list of names and abbreviations)

14	م	AD, CE
80	هـ	hijrah year
320	ت	date; time
472	جمت	GMT
966	ور	After Prophet's Death (Libya)

Relative Time

125	آن	time; (الآن: now)
203	ماضٍ	past
237	أمس	yesterday
500	قادم	next, coming
539	مستقبل	future
598	مقبل	next, coming
775	غد	tomorrow
1088	جارٍ	current
1094	حاضر	present
1703	هلق	now
1776	راهن	current
1783	لاحق	later, next
1810	بكرة	tomorrow
2245	آتٍ	coming, next
2370	معاصر	contemporary
2480	آنذاك	at that time
2849	الحين	now
2850	عشيّة	eve, night before
3017	بارحة	yesterday
3794	عصريّ	contemporary

3871	هسّة	now
3952	منصرم	gone by
4481	امبارح	yesterday
4590	دلوقتي	now
4902	باكر	tomorrow
4962	بارح	yesterday
4969	النهارده	today
5119	غداة	morning, tomorrow
5170	سالف	previous
5840	درك	now
6065	بدري	early
6072	بكّير	early
6178	غدوة	tomorrow
6801	دوك	now
7198	بكري	early
7245	مبارحة	yesterday
7655	آجل	future

Units of Time (from small to large)

2303	ثانية	second
424	دقيقة	minute
185	ساعة	hour, o'clock
26	يوم	day
393	أسبوع	week
7226	سمانا	week
158	شهر	month
1856	فصل	season (also section, class)
978	موسم	season
62	عام	year
69	سنة	year
2253	عقد	decade
1103	جيل	generation
366	مرحلة	stage
4305	طور	stage
892	عهد	age
883	قرن	century
880	عصر	age
3631	حقبة	era
584	أبد	eternity
5140	خلد	eternity

Parts of the day (from morning to night)		
1048	فجر	dawn
6588	سحر	dawn
5137	صبيحة	early morning
1967	صبح	morning
449	صباح	morning
980	نهار	daytime
4898	ضحى	forenoon
1425	ظهر	noon
	(بعد الظهر:	afternoon)
4925	ظهيرة	noon
2443	عصر	afternoon
3416	غروب	sunset
4816	مغرب	sunset
4644	عشاء	evening
642	مساء	evening
392	ليل	night
518	ليلة	night

Days of the week (in order)		
1174	أحد	Sunday
1347	اثنين	Monday
1504	ثلاثاء	Tuesday
1291	أربعاء	Wednesday
1115	خميس	Thursday
955	جمعة	Friday
1148	سبت	Saturday

Months (ranking is from list of names and abbreviations)		
Eastern Calendar (Lev.Ir.)		
196	كانون	December, January
306	شباط	February
120	آذار	March
258	نيسان	April
278	أيّار	May
226	حزيران	June
174	تمّوز	July
285	آب	August
214	أيلول	September
191	تشرين	October, November

Western Calendar (Egy. and some Magh.)		
158	يناير	January
167	فبراير	February
116	مارس	March
143	أبريل	April
134	مايو	May
137	يونيو	June
907	جوان	June
136	يوليو	July
175	أغسطس	August
83	سبتمبر	September
124	أكتوبر	October
144	نوفمبر	November
162	ديسمبر	December

Islamic calendar		
796	محرّم	Muharram
1250	صفر	Safar
335	ربيع	Rabi' (1&2)
1006	جمادى	Jumada (1&2)
420	رجب	Rajab
437	شعبان	Sha'ban
60	رمضان	Ramadan
1377	قعدة	Dhul Qa'dah
714	حجّة	Dhul Hijjah

Libyan calendar (since 1994)		
1521	أي	Ai (January)
987	نار	Nar (January)
335	ربيع	Rabi' (March)
900	طير	Tair (April)
1053	ماء	Maa (May)
1372	صيف	Saif (June)
61	ناصر	Nasir (July)
374	فاتح	Fatih (September)

Seasons		
1121	صيف	summer
1722	شتاء	winter
1943	ربيع	spring
3034	خريف	autumn, fall

— تم الاتفاق على اصدار بيان رسمي بهذا الشأن

Issuing an official communiqué on this matter was agreed upon

86 | 8020 |

553 غَرْبِيّ *adj.* Western; *n.* pl. -uun Westerner; *prep.* west of

بالرغم من مرافعاته المطولة دفاعا عن الثقافة الغربية فهو ما زال يحمل عقلية الرجل الشرقي — Despite his lengthy arguments in defense of Western culture, he still has the mentality of an Eastern man

96 | 7217 |

554 أَثَر *n.* pl. آثار record, trace; sign, mark; effect, influence; على/في أَثَر immediately after; عِلْم الآثار antiquities; archeology آثار

هل ترك عليها الزمن الرديء أثره؟ — Did evil time leave its trace on her?

97 | 7125 |

555 ضَرُورَة *n.* necessity, need; بالضرورة necessarily

في الحقيقية - يا أبي - إني لا أشعر بضرورة المشاركة في هذا الحفل — In truth, my father, I don't feel the necessity of participating in this ceremony

93 | 7401 |

556 كَرِيم *adj.* pl. كِرام noble, distinguished;
decent, dignified; generous, magnanimous;
dear, precious; القُرْآن الكَرِيم the Holy
Qur'an
يجب أن أوفر لابني حياة كريمة — I must provide
a dignified life for my son
98 | 6989 |

557 أَساسِيّ *adj.* basic, fundamental
هو فصل مهم لأنه يقدم للباحث المبادئ الأساسية التى
سيتبعها فى رسالته — It is an important class
because it offers the researcher the basic
principles which he will follow in his
dissertation
95 | 7216 |

558 وَرَق *coll.n.* paper; leaves; cards; وَرَقَة *un.n.* pl.
أَوْراق sheet of paper; leaf; playing card
انحنى وسجل على الورق كل ما قلته.. ثم بان على
وجهه التفكير — He leaned over and recorded on
the paper everything I said...then he appeared
to be thinking
99 | 6916 |

559 والِد *n.* father; fem. والِدَة mother; الوالِدان
parents
التدخين بين الطلبة يكون اكثر ما يكون اذا كان
احد الوالدين او كلاهما مدخنين وخاصة في
البيت — Smoking among students is at its
highest when one of the parents or both
of them are smokers, and particularly in the
home
99 | 6914 |

560 جَمْعِيَّة *n.* pl. -aat association, society
انضم ماتي إلى مجموعة المشاركين بصفته رئيس جمعية
أصدقاء الطبيعة في الجامعة — Matti joined the
group of participants in his role as president of
the Friends of Nature organization in the
university
95 | 7203 |

561 رَسْمِيّ *adj.* official, formal; رَسْمِيّاً officially,
formally
لقيها خادم وقور بملابس رسمية سوداء وقادها إلى
قاعة كبيرة — A staid servant met her in official
black clothing and led her to a big hall
97 | 7019 |

562 أُسْتاذ *n.* fem. أُسْتاذَة, pl. أَساتِذَة professor,
teacher; (title) Prof, Mr; (polite form of
address) Sir!; يا أستاذ (Egy.) /'ustaaz/,
(Lev.) /'istaaz, 'ustaaz/
أنا الآن أستاذ فى كلية الطب — I now am
a professor in the College of Medicine
97 | 6991 |

563 اِحْتِلال *vn.* occupation (of land or property);
filling (a post, a position)
من المنطق أن نقول إن هناك قوة احتلال في العراق
معادية لسوريا ولا ترغب بتحسن العلاقات السورية
العراقية — It is logical for us to say that
there is an anti-Syrian occupation force in
Iraq and it doesn't want to improve Iraqi-Syrian
relations
85 | 7979 |

564 أَبْيَض *adj.* fem. بَيْضاء, pl. بِيض white; البِيض
n./adj. whites, Caucasians
كان الطبيب فى الأربعينيات.. أصلع ويرتدى معطفا
أبيض ونظارة طبية بإطار فضي — The doctor was
in his 40s...bald, wearing a white coat, and
medical glasses with a silver frame
99 | 6824 |

565 مَكْتَب *n.* pl. مَكاتِب office, bureau,
department
كان يستعد لمغادرة مكتبه بعد يوم شاق عندما سمع
فجأة صوت جهاز الفاكس — He was preparing to
leave his office after a difficult day when he
suddenly heard the sound of the fax machine
98 | 6924 |

566 مُنْتَدىً *n.* pl. مُنْتَدَيات assembly room, gathering
place; (Internet) forum
أنا عضو مشارك في منتدى المثقف العربي بالقاهرة منذ
تأسيسه عام ٢٠٠١ م — I have been a
participating member in the Arab Intellectual
Forum in Cairo since its inception in 2001
81 | 8390 | +for

567 مُقاوَمَة *n.* resistance, opposition
تفتح الباب أمام القوميات الأخرى للمطالبة بإحياء
لغاتها ومقاومة اللغة العربية في السودان — It opens
the door for other nationalities to demand the
revival of their languages and to resist the
Arabic language in the Sudan
87 | 7766 |

568 شِعْر *n.* poetry

قد اخترت الشعر موضوعا لمحاولتي لأن الشعر هو الفن الذي تضرب جذوره بشدة في القديم — I chose poetry as a subject for my attempt, because poetry is the art whose roots go way back to ancient times

98 | 6856 |

569 مَحَلِّيّ *adj.* local; مَحَلِّيّاً locally

الجهاز يستفيد من علاقاته الدولية والاقليمية والمحلية لتوفير الاحصاءات اللازمة للحكومة وللقطاع الخاص — The agency benefits from its international, regional, and local relationships to provide the necessary statistics to the government and the private sector

95 | 7121 |

570 عَظِيم *adj.* pl. عِظام great, mighty, powerful

أمامك فرصة عظيمة للتعلم فلا تضيعها — You have a great opportunity to get an education, so don't waste it

99 | 6811 |

571 إعْلام *n.* information, media; *vn.* informing, notifying

العرب محقون في شكواهم من أن إعلام الغرب يعطي قيمة أكبر للقتل الإسرائيليين — The Arabs are right in their complaint that Western media places greater value on the Israeli dead

95 | 7023 | +news

572 فَرَنْسِيّ *n./adj.* pl. -uun French

إنها مغربية الاصل كندية الجنسية بثلاث لغات هي العربية والانجليزية والفرنسية — She is of Moroccan origin, Canadian of nationality, with three languages: Arabic, English and French

95 | 6976 |

573 فِيلم film/ *n.* pl. أفْلام film, movie

يرتدى ثيابه القديمة ويشاهد فيلما أبيض وأسود من الستينيات ويستمع إلى أغنيات أم كلثوم — He puts on his old clothes and watches a black and white film from the 60s and listens to Um Kalthoum songs

96 | 6929 |

574 طَبِيعيّ *adj.* natural, normal

يئست تماما من استئناف حياتها الطبيعية — She completely despaired of resuming her normal life

97 | 6829 |

575 طَلَب *n.* pl. -aat request; demand; application; (purchase) order

إذا أردت أية مساعدة لا تتردد فى طلبها مني — If you want any help, don't hesitate to ask me

99 | 6681 |

576 شابّ *n.* pl. شُبّان young man; *adj.* youthful, fresh

كان هناك ألف شاب مصرى يتمنون مكانك فى كلية الطب — There were a thousand Egyptian young men who would have liked your spot in the College of Medicine

99 | 6663 |

577 وَراء *n.* behind, past, beyond; إلى الوَراءِ backward, in reverse; وَراءُ *adv.* behind; مِنْ وَراءُ from behind

أغلق صلاح الباب وراءه، ثم صعد ببطء على الدرج المفضى إلى حجرة النوم — Salah shut the door behind him, and then slowly went up the stairs leading to the bedroom

90 | 7372 |

578 سُوريّ *n./adj.* Syrian

يحمل لقيس مئة وخمسين ليرة سورية — He is carrying one hundred and fifty Syrian Lira to Qais

94 | 7026 |

579 وَحْد *n.* (with pron.) وَحْدَها, وَحْدَهُ alone, by itself/himself/herself; only it/he/she

أداء الامتحان لا يكفي وحده للنجاح — Test performance is not enough, by itself, for success

99 | 6640 |

580 فَهِمَ *v.* I (a) to understand sth/sb or في sth or أنّ that; (Dia.) to understand على sb

لا أفهم لماذا تكرهه إلى هذا الحد — I don't understand why you hate him so much

99 | 6620 |

581 بِلا *prep.* without; (Lev.) /bala/, (Alg.) /bla/

الأساليب التي يستخدمها الشين بيت في الاستجواب مدعومة بلا شك من قبل محكمة العدل العليا الاسرائيلية — The methods which Shin Bet use to interrogate are supported, without a doubt, by the Israeli High Court of Justice

99 | 6635 |

582 دَعْوَة *n. pl.* دَعَوات call; invitation; propaganda; (Islamic) missionary work, (دَعْوَة (إِسْلامِيَّة) Da'wah

منذ ذلك الحين تتدفق عليه الدعوات للمشاركة في المهرجانات الشعرية في مختلف ارجاء هولندا — Since that time invitations to participate in poetry festivals have poured in from various parts of Holland

98 | 6683 |

583 خَطْوَة and خُطْوَة *n. pl.* خَطَوات, خُطُوات, خُطىً step, stride; measure

تقدم خطوة الى وسط الصالة، متمهلا كأنما يؤكد سيطرته على الموقف — He moved forward a step into the center of the hall, hesitating as if to make sure of his control over the situation

98 | 6719 |

584 أَبَد *n.* eternity, forever; أَبَداً never; not at all; (Irq.Gul.) أَبَد never; not at all

لماذا يكون علي أن أحرم من ابنتي إلى الأبد يا شيخ مجد؟ — Why should I have to be deprived of my daughter forever, Sheikh Magd?

92 | 7129 |

585 تَقْدِيم *n.* offering, presenting, submitting

نحن إخوة ومستعدون لتقديم الدعم متى احتجتم — We are brothers and we are prepared to offer support when you need it

88 | 7457 |

586 مَدىً *n.* range, extent, reach; time period, duration

هل يدركون مدى بشاعة الجرائم التي تقترفها حكوماتهم في حق الإنسانية؟ — Do they realize the extent of the monstrosity of the crimes their governments are committing against human rights?

95 | 6917 |

587 تَجْرِبَة *n. pl.* تَجارِب experiment, test; experience, encounter; trial, ordeal

ألا تعتقد أن الولايات المتحدة قد تعلمت من التجربة العراقية؟ — Don't you believe that the United States has learned from the Iraqi experience?

98 | 6687 |

588 وَحِيد *adj.* only, sole, exclusive; alone

لقد مات ابني الوحيد من الإدمان — My only son died of addiction

99 | 6577 |

589 أَمِير *n.* prince, commander; (title) Emir, Prince; *fem.* أَمِيرَة princess; (title) Emira, Princess

قد ولد صاحب السمو أمير دولة الكويت الشيخ جابر الاحمد الجابر الصباح سنة ١٩٢٨ — His Majesty, Sheikh Jabir Al-Ahmad Al-Jabir Al-Sabah, the Emir of Kuwait, was born in the year 1928

95 | 6843 |

590 مُدَّة *n.* time period, length of time, interval

إذا أردت الاستفسار عن أي شيء.. الاستشارة مجانية لمدة شهر — If you want to inquire about anything, consultation is free for a month

98 | 6655 |

591 سِتَّة *num. fem.* سِتّ six; سِتَّة عَشَر sixteen

لقد مرت حتى الآن ست سنوات على أسرهم، وما زلنا جميعا في الانتظار — Up to now six years have passed since they were imprisoned, and we are still waiting

99 | 6601 |

592 تَغْيِير *n. pl.* -aat change, modification; replacement, switch

إذا كنا نحب مصر فعلينا أن نبذل أقصى جهدنا لتغيير هذا النظام — If we love Egypt, we must exert our utmost efforts to change this regime

98 | 6605 |

593 ماتَ *v. I (u)* to die, pass away; (Lev.) to love sth/sb to death في

تحولت الإسكندرية إلى محرقة لأهلها ومات كثير من العائلات ولم يتبق من بعضها غير طفل واحد — Alexandria was transformed into a Holocaust for its people, and many families perished, some leaving behind only a single child

98 | 6614 |

594 دار *fem.n. pl.* دُور, دِيار house, home, abode; family, household

استأذنت اصحابي بحجة العودة الى دار الحاج فريح للاطمئنان عليه — I begged leave of my friends with the excuse of returning to the home of Hajj Furaih to check up on him

99 | 6566 |

595 دُخُول *n.* entering, entrance

صار باب حجرة الست مريم لا يفتح إلا لدخول أحد أو خروجه — Mrs Miryam's room door now did not open except for someone to go in or come out

96 | 6772 |

596 أَهَمِّيَّة *n.* importance, significance

قال لي إن شخصية الطالب عنده لا تقل أهمية عن مستواه العلمي — He told me that the personality of the student, for him, was not less important than his educational level

93 | 6963 |

597 صَعْب *adj.* difficult, hard

طالما سألت نفسي هذا السؤال، لكن الاجابة صعبة للغاية — I have often asked myself this questions, but the answer is very hard

98 | 6619 |

598 مُقْبِل *adj.* next, coming, approaching, nearing

أنا إن شاء الله سأكون بينكم في الأسبوع المقبل — Hopefully I will be among you next week

87 | 7399 |

599 حَدَث *n.* pl. أَحْداث event, incident

راحت تسترجع في ذهنها جميع الأحداث التي جرت — She started to review in her mind everything that had happened

97 | 6675 |

600 دَوْرَة *n.* pl. -aat (sports) championship, tournament; cycle, turn, rotation, lap; circulation; round (elections); session (meeting); tour, patrol, round; (school) course, class; دَوْرَة مِياه bathroom, toilet

التنظيم الرائع لمسيرة الشعلة يبشر بتنظيم اروع لدورة الالعاب الآسيوية باعتبارها الحدث الاهم الذي تترقبه جميع دول العالم — The splendid organization of the torch relay bodes well for an even more splendid organization of the Asian Games tournament, in consideration of the fact that it is the most important event that all countries of the world are waiting for

96 | 6738 |

601 نَشاط *n.* pl. -aat, أَنْشِطَة activity, movement, action

بدأت تنهمك في الدراسة والأنشطة الجامعية علها — She began to immerse herself in her studies and in university activities, so that perhaps she might forget what had happened

98 | 6586 |

602 ضِمْنَ *prep.* within, inside; among

حصل اتفاق على أن تحل الميليشيات وتدمج ضمن قوات الأمن — An agreement took place over dissolving the militias and integrating them into the security forces

97 | 6646 |

603 أُورُبِّيّ and أُورُوبِّيّ /'urubbi/ *n./adj.* pl. -uun European

— بتابع أخبار الرياضة خاصة الرياضة الاوروبية I follow sports news, especially European sports news

91 | 7003 |

604 فَنِّيّ *adj.* artistic; technical; *n.* technician

بالنسبة لمراقبة الشركات فهي ليس لديها الأجهزة الفنية والقدرات الفنية والموارد القادرة على أن تذهب لكل موقع يقوم بمثل هذه النشاطات — In regard to watching over the companies, it does not have the technical apparatus and the technical abilities nor the resources which would enable it to go to each site which carries out these activities

87 | 7291 |

605 أَوْضَحَ *v. IV* to clarify, explain (ل to sb) (أَنَّ that

وأوضح نافع أن أفضل الاستثمارات في مدينة العقبة هو بناء الشقق — Nafie clarified that the best investments in the city of Aqaba were in the building of apartments

86 | 7400 | +news

606 قُدْرَة *n.* pl. -aat, قُدُرات capacity, ability, potential, power

اشتهر أيضا بالصبر والقدرة على معايشة الألم والانغماس في الكآبة — He also became famous for patience and the ability to live with pain and to immerse himself in depression

95 | 6671 |

607 نِصْف *n.* half, middle, semi-
ظل صامتا يحدق في السقف ما يقرب من نصف ساعة، ثم قام وخرج من شقته — He remained silent, staring at the ceiling for about a half hour, then he got up and left the apartment
96 | 6574 |

608 صَرَاحَة *n.* sincerity, candor, frankness; بِصَرَاحَة and صَرَاحَةً frankly
اسمع يا طارق، سأسألك سؤالا وأرجو أن تجيب بصراحة — Listen, Tariq, I will ask you a question and I want you to answer frankly
95 | 6651 |

609 جَمَاعَة *n. pl.* -aat group, party; gang
خلاص يا جماعة.. مش عاوزين نفسد المناسبة الجميلة دي — Cool it, guys, we don't want to spoil this lovely occasion
98 | 6437 |

610 مَعْرِفَة *vn.* knowing sth/sb; meeting sb, becoming acquainted with sb; *n. pl.* مَعَارِف knowledge, information; culture, education
التفكير والمعرفة والتأمل هي ما يميز الانسان عن الكائنات الاخرى — Thinking and knowledge and contemplation are what distinguish man from the other creatures
99 | 6380 |

611 ظَهَرَ *v. I (a)* to appear; seem كَأَنْ as if
وقفت أمام المحل مترددة لحظات حتى فوجئت بالباب يفتح وتظهر فتاة في العشرينيات — She stood in front of the shop hesitantly for a few moments, until she was surprised when the door opened and a girl in her 20s appeared
99 | 6363 |

612 مُوَاجَهَة *vn.* facing, confronting, encountering; *n. pl.* -aat confrontation, encounter
الوضع سيء، وقد تحدث مواجهات في الساعات القليلة القادمة بين المتظاهرين والجيش — The situation is bad, and there could be confrontations in the next few hours between the demonstrators and the army
88 | 7117 |

613 رَجَعَ *v. I (i)* to return, go back, come back إلى to; to be traced back إلى to; to reverse عن (one's decision); to go back بِكَلامِهِ on one's word)
لقد تركت العمل في البار ولن ارجع إليه — I quit working at the bar and will not return to it
98 | 6428 |

614 إِيَّا *part.* (with object pron.) إِيَّاها (to/of) her; (مَعَها =) وَإِيَّاها (وَاو الْمَعِيَّة with)
جاءت إحدى الساعيات إلى فصل لميس مخبرة إياها بأن مديرة القسم الثانوي بالمدرسة قد طلبت رؤيتها — One of the messengers came to Lamis' class informing her that the director of the secondary department had requested to see her
97 | 6471 | +spo

615 عِشْرُون *num.* twenty; twentieth
ارتبطت بهذا البيت.. عشت فيه عشرين عاما.. كل ركن فيه يذكرني بجزء من حياتي — I am connected with this house...I lived in it for twenty years...every corner in it reminds me of a part of me life
99 | 6296 |

616 بُطُولَة *n.* heroism; starring role; *pl.* -aat championship, tournament
وتترقب المدينة حاليا بدء فعاليات بطولة كأس العالم حيث يستضيف استاد المدينة بعض مباريات كأس العالم ٢٠٠٦ — The city is currently waiting for the opening events of the World Cup championships, since the city stadium will host some of the 2006 World Cup matches
92 | 6755 |

617 نَجَاح *n. pl.* -aat success
حقق الأسلوب الجديد نجاحا باهرا جعل أقسام الشرطة الأخرى تأخذ به — The new style achieved a notable success which made the other police departments take notice of it
97 | 6377 |

618 شُرْطَة *n.* police
قيل إن الشرطة قد داهمت الحي واعتقلت سمير المريني موجهة له تهمة الاعتداء على المختار — It was said that the police raided the quarter and arrested Samir Al-Marnini, accusing him of assaulting the mayor
94 | 6594 |

619 لَعِبَ *v. I (a)* to play (game, role)
كان يلعب الدومينو مع أحد الأشخاص
وحولهما ثلاثة آخرون — He was playing
dominoes with one of his friends, with
three others around them
99 | 6236 |

620 تَنْمِيَة *n.* development, growth; progress
البلديات تحتاج إلى تنمية شمولية على كافة
المستويات — The towns need comprehensive
development on all levels
80 | 7662 |

621 حاجَة *n. pl.* -aat need, want (for what one
lacks); desire, wish; objective, purpose, goal;
بحاجَة إلى in need of
أصدر مجلس الوزراء قرارا باستيراد مائتي ألف جهاز
كمبيوتر لتلبية حاجات الجامعات والمعاهد والمدارس
— The Council of Ministers issued a decision to
import two hundred thousand computers to
cover the needs of the universities, institutes
and schools
98 | 6242 |

622 فَكَّرَ *v. II* to think في/ب about sth/sb; to
consider في أنْ doing sth; to think, believe
أنَّ that
مشى فى شارع البان يفكر فى هذا الشخص
السعيد الذى أطلق هذا الاسم على الشارع
He walked down Al-Ban Street thinking about
this happy person that the street had been
named after
99 | 6168 |

623 تَطْوِير *n.* development, advancement;
promotion, encouragement
أنا لدي رؤية واضحة بأهمية التطوير والتحديث
والاصلاح بالنسبة لمستقبل شعبنا — I have a clear
vision of the importance of development and
modernization and reform for the future of our
people
82 | 7422 |

624 شَمال *n.* north; *adj.* northern
المخيم بحد ذاته يقع شمال النهر الذي يصب في البحر
المتوسط — The camp itself is located to the
north of the river which flows into the
Mediterranean Sea
98 | 6260 |

625 بَنْك *n. pl.* بُنُوك bank (financial institution)
البنك يعتزم زيادة رأسماله من ٣٠٠ مليون درهم الى
مليار درهم — The bank intends to increase its
capital from 300 million dirhams to a billion
dirhams
95 | 6456 |

626 فَرْد *n. pl.* أفْراد individual, person; فَرْداً فَرْداً
separately, individually, one by one
كان أفراد العائلة المقربون الوحيدون الذين علموا
بمرض أمي — Close family members were the
only ones who knew about my mother's illness
97 | 6261 |

627 قَدَم *fem.n. pl.* أقْدام foot (also as unit of measure)
هي طبعا أحد الأندية المعروفة جدا في كرة القدم — It
is, of course, one of the very well-known soccer clubs
99 | 6167 |

628 عامِل *n. pl.* -uun employee; العامِلُون staff,
workforce, personnel; *pl.* عُمّال worker, laborer;
operator; regent, prefect; حِزْب العُمّال Labor Party
أغلقوا باب الاستقدام فانه يوجد الكثير من العمال
الاجانب العاطلين عن العمل — They closed the
door of acceptance, because there are a lot of
foreign workers who are unemployed
97 | 6247 |

629 ثَقافيّ *adj.* cultural, intellectual, educational
مدينة الناظور تفتقر إلى المعاهد الثقافية والدرامية
وقاعات التمثيل — The city of Nazur lacks
cultural and dramatic institutes and halls for
putting on plays
86 | 7056 |

630 قاعِدَة *n. pl.* قَواعِد rule, principle, basis;
(military) base; القاعدة Al-Qaeda
يجهلون أصول الدين وقواعد الدين — They are
ignorant of the fundamentals and basic
principles of religion
88 | 6878 |

631 عاديّ *adj.* regular, normal; ordinary
ألا زلت تحتفظين بأفكارك الثورية أم أنك تحولت إلى
امرأة عادية، موظفة حكومة توقع فى كشف الحضور؟
— Are you still holding on to your revolutionary
ideas, or have you become a normal woman,
a government employee who signs in on the
attendance sheet?
99 | 6124 |

9 Sports

218	هدف	goal	1417	حارس	goalie (also guard)	4122	رامي	rifleman; archer (also aiming)
256	فريق	team						
419	مباراة	game, match	1594	ذهاب	first half (also going)	4197	تمرين	drill, practice
428	لاعب	player				4264	بدنيّ	bodily, physical
501	كرة	ball; soccer	1762	خسر	to fail, lose	4347	قوس	bow, arch
542	دفاع	defense	1818	مقابلة	match, game (also meeting)	4477	قفز	jumping, leaping
600	دورة	tournament; round	1825	نال	to attain, achieve (prize)	4584	ركل	kick
616	بطولة	championship, tournament	1857	تنس الطاولة	table tennis (طاولة: table)	4626	حلبة	arena, ring, track
619	لعب	to play				4688	تعادل	to tie (each other)
652	منتخب	national team	1884	سباق	race			
704	رياضة	sports	1890	منافسة	competition, rivalry	4691	كرويّ	football (soccer) (adj)
721	رياضيّ	sportive						
816	إصابة	point, goal (also striking)	1956	مضيف	home team (also host)	4697	إستاد	stadium
						4732	رمي	throwing; shooting
819	سار	to march, walk	2000	جناح	wing			
			2438	مرتبة	level, rank	4913	بركة	pool
840	كأس	cup	2539	شوط	half period	4928	فوتبول	football, soccer
843	لعب	playing; game	2591	مرمى	goal	5245	غوص	diving
871	بطل	hero; champion	2623	تدريبيّ	training, coaching	5459	طفرة	leap, jump
			2716	فائز	winner, victor	5495	خاسر	loser
877	سجّل	to score (point) (also to register)	2805	مسجّل	scoring (point) (also recording)	5789	طرد	to expel, kick out
882	فرقة	group, team	2911	مهاجم	attacker; striker	5929	تنس	tennis
922	تدريب	training; exercise	2920	سباحة	swimming	6098	ركض	running, jogging
988	ممارسة	playing (sport) (also practicing)	2990	مدافع	defender	6438	خسران	loser
			3013	تعادل	tie (also balance)	6442	مسبح	swimming pool
1018	دوريّ	league, tournament	3018	عادل	to tie (also to be equal to)	6612	بول	ball
1040	مسابقة	competition; race	3026	قفز	to jump, leap	6788	شدّة	a card game; deck of cards
1046	جاب	to score (a goal) (also to bring)	3246	تنافس	competition	6866	جري	running
			3343	خطف	snatch (weightlifting) (also kidnapping)	7255	وثب	to jump, leap
1086	جائزة	prize, reward				7600	جون	goal
1196	لعبة	match, game	3356	تشكيلة	line-up (also assortment)	7833	لعّب	to make or let play
1255	مدرّب	trainer, coach	3396	زيّ	uniform, dress			
1304	ملعب	playing field, court	3651	سدّد	to aim, shoot (also block)	7931	عدو	racing, running
1393	مارس	to play (sport) (also practice)	4042	لعبة	game, sport		سبّاح	swimmer
							مونديال	Mondial (World Cup)
1398	غالب	winner, victor	4081	حكم	referee		الفيفا	the FIFA (Fédération Internationale de Football Association)

632 أَكِيد *adj.* sure, certain, definite; أَكِيداً definitely, for sure

استغربت إزاي البدوي يعرف ألماني وقلت أكيد أنه جاسوس لابس بدوي — I was amazed at how a Bedouin could know German, and I said: I'm sure he is a spy wearing Bedouin clothing

77 | 7875 | +spo

633 سَواء *conj.* except, whether (or not), regardless, either (or); *n.* equality

الموت حق علينا، سواء جاء من حرق أو غرق أو عفريت أو نبوت — Death has a right to claim us, whether it comes from a fire, or drowning, or a devil, or a beating stick (violence)

97 | 6208 |

634 يَوْمِيّ *adj.* daily; يَوْمِيّاً *adv.* every day, on a daily basis; per diem

أثناء إجازته في القاهرة يلتقى يوميا كبار رجال الدولة.. ماذا يعيبه إذن كعريس؟ — During his vacation in Cairo he is meeting daily with senior state officials. What could possibly be wrong with him as a groom?

97 | 6214 |

635 صَلاة *n. pl.* صَلَوات prayer

أنصحك بحمام ساخن ثم الصلاة ركعتين بنية انفراج الهم — I advise you to take a hot shower and then pray a couple of prostrations with the intention of letting go of your worries

99 | 6100 |

636 شاعِر *n. pl.* شُعَراء poet

أليس أبو نواس هو الشاعر الذي اشتهر بالخمر في العصر العباسي؟ — Isn't Abu Nuwas the poet who became famous for wine in the Abbasid era?

94 | 6364 |

637 حُلْم *n. pl.* أَحْلام dream

لقد التحق بكلية الطب واجتهد سنوات من أجل حلم واحد ملأ حياته: أن يكون جراحا — He joined the college of medicine and worked hard for years on behalf of a single dream which filled his life: to become a surgeon

97 | 6192 |

638 وُصُول *n.* arrival; attainment, achievement

لقد تعذر عليه الحضور اليوم بسبب وصول وفد من الجزائر البارحة — It was difficult for him to come today because of the arrival of a delegation from Algeria yesterday

89 | 6728 |

639 قَتَل *v. I (u)* to kill sb; (often pass.) قُتِلَ to be killed

انتهى شهر أبريل بغارة قوية قتلت ستين شخصا وجرحت أكثر من مائة — The month of April ended with a heavy raid that killed sixty people and wounded more than a hundred

95 | 6311 |

640 سُرْعَة *n.* speed; بسرعة quickly

سأدخل الحمام وأعود بسرعة — I will go to the bathroom and return quickly

99 | 6061 |

641 عَزيز *adj. pl.* أَعِزّاء dear, precious

انا آسف يا عزيزي.. آسف.. لن اكون دبلوماسيا معك — I am sorry, dear...sorry...I won't be diplomatic with you

97 | 6161 | +for

642 مَساء *n.* evening

ستتصل بهما يوم الجمعة القادم في السابعة مساء — She will call them next Friday at seven o'clock in the evening

99 | 6066 |

643 عُنْوان *n. pl.* عَناوين address; title, headline; (website) URL

في النهاية يخرج ورقة ويكتب عنوان شقته الخاصة في شارع الشواربي — Finally, he takes out a piece of paper and writes the address of his private apartment on Shawarbi Street

95 | 6247 |

644 طَبيب *n. pl.* أَطِبّاء physician, doctor

يقول الطبيب إنه في مثل هذه الأحوال يجب أن ننقله إلى المستشفى — The doctor says that in cases like these we must transfer him to the hospital

97 | 6108 |

645 اِسْتِخْدام *n.* usage, using, utilization

قضت قمرة أشهرا في التعليم على استخدام الكمبيوتر
— Qamara spent months in learning how to use the computer

88 | 6785 |

646 عَقْل *n. pl.* عُقُول mind, intellect; بالعقل (Alg.) /bi-l-9qal/ slowly

الفن لا يفهم بالعقل، لكننا ندركه بالإحساس —
Art is not understood with the mind, but we comprehend it with feelings

99 | 6004 |

647 عيد *n. pl.* أَعْياد holiday, festival, feast

في عيد رأس السنة كسرت طبقا وفنجان شاي —
During the New Year holiday, I broke a plate and a tea cup

98 | 6068 |

648 أَمَل *n. pl.* آمال hope, wish; أَمَلًا hoping, wishing, in the hope (أَنْ في) that)

جاء في زيارة قصيرة أملا في أن يعود مصطحبا
زوجة من بنات وطنه — He came on a short visit hoping to return accompanied by a wife from among the daughters of his homeland

98 | 6059 |

649 خارجيَّة *n.* foreign ministry, foreign office

الإدارة الأميركية المقبلة يجب أن تدخل تغييرات على
سياستها الخارجية لحل المشاكل العالقة — The next American administration must make changes to its foreign policy to solve outstanding problems

86 | 6914 |

650 دَفَعَ *v. I (a)* to push sth; to pay (a sum of money); to compel, move sb إلى to do sth

هل تعتقدين أن هناك من سيدفع دولارا واحدا
ليشتري هذا الهراء الذي يلطخ به اللوحات؟ — Do you believe that there is someone who will pay a single dollar to buy this nonsense with which he tarnishes the canvases?

99 | 5963 |

651 قِيام *vn.* undertaking, carrying out ب (task, activity); playing ب (a role); rising, standing up

الغجر أيضا يعيشون هناك، ولكن منذ قيام الحرب لا
أحد يراهم في الشوارع — Gypsies also live there,

but since the beginning of the war no one sees them in the streets

89 | 6658 |

652 مُنْتَخَب *adj.* elected; *n.* -aat (spo.) national team

قبل كل شيء، تلعب الفرق – لا سيما المنتخبات
الوطنية – بهدف عدم الخسارة — Before anything else, teams play, especially national teams, with the goal of not losing

86 | 6828 |

653 اِثْنان *num. fem.* اِثْنَتان two; اِثْنا عَشَر *fem.* اِثْنَتا عَشْرَة twelve

اثنان موافقان واثنان معترضان.. سأحتفظ برأيي
للنهاية — Two in favor and two opposed...I will keep my opinion till the end

98 | 6001 |

654 جُنْدِيّ *n. pl.* جُنُود soldier

بدأت الطائرات الألمانية غاراتها على مواقع الجنود
المتقدمة والخلفية في وقت واحد لإرباكها وإحداث
الفوضى بينها — The German airplanes began their raids on the soldier's forward and rear positions simultaneously, to confuse them and cause chaos among them

87 | 6781 |

655 إِذَن and إذاً *adv.* therefore, consequently

لماذا إذن لم تقرأ البحث؟ — Why, then, don't you read the study?

96 | 6119 |

656 اِتِّفاق *n. pl.* -aat agreement; accord, treaty

خلال السنوات الأخيرة وقعت الصين اتفاقات تجارية
وعقود استثمار بمئات مليارات الدولارات مع عدد
كبير من دول المنطقة — During recent years China has signed commercial agreements and investment contracts for hundreds of billions of dollars with a large number of states of the region

87 | 6737 |

657 نُور *n. pl.* أَنْوار light; lamp

كانت الأنوار مضاءة مع أنني أذكر جيدا أنني أغلقتها
قبل خروجي — The lights were lit despite the fact that I remember well that I turned them off before I left

99 | 5892 |

658 شَدِيد *adj.* intense, strong, severe

هبت ريح شديدة خيل إلي أنها ستقتلع الأشجار —
A strong wind blew; it occurred to me that it was going to uproot the trees

| 94 | 6170 |

659 شَعْبِيّ *adj.* popular; national, of the people

الغارة لم تصب السفن بسوء بقدر ما أصابت الأحياء الشعبية — The raid did not harm the ships as much as it harmed the popular quarters

| 95 | 6114 |

660 مُحَافَظَة *n.* pl. -aat province, governorate

أنا عملت ضابط بوليس عشرة أعوام في محافظات مختلفة، طفت بالقرى والنجوع والحارات، وعرفت قاع المجتمع — I worked as a police officer for ten years in various governorates, and I wandered around villages, hamlets and alleyways, and I got to know the dregs of society

| 91 | 6386 |

661 اِنْتَظَرَ *v. VIII* to expect, wait for sth/sb

سأنصرف لأني لو انتظرت لحظة واحدة سأضربه — I will leave because if I wait a single moment, I'll beat him

| 98 | 5903 |

662 مَثَّل *v. II* to represent, speak for sb; to play, act as sb (film); to exemplify, illustrate sth

أكد أن الأردن بما يمثله من سياسة معتدلة سيكون نموذجا في استخدام الطاقة النووية — He confirmed that Jordan, with what it represents in terms of moderate policy, would be a model in the use of nuclear energy

| 96 | 6003 |

663 ظَرْف *n.* pl. ظُرُوف circumstance, condition, situation

علينا التصرف بحكمة في مثل هذه الظروف المعقدة — We need to act wisely in complicated circumstances such as these

| 99 | 5834 |

664 أُسْرَة *n.* pl. أُسَر family, community

اشترى سيارة جديدة لم تعلم عنها أسرته شيئا — He bought a new car which his family did not know anything about

| 94 | 6043 |

665 قَرْيَة *n.* pl. قُرىً village

يسافرون إلى القرى القريبة لإحياء موالد المشاهير من الأولياء — They travel to nearby villages to celebrate the birthdays of the famous saints

| 98 | 5843 |

666 مُقابِل *n.* opposite (to), corresponding (to), vis-à-vis

جلس فواز على الكرسي مقابل الضابط — Fawaz sat on the chair facing the officer

| 97 | 5905 |

667 جَوّ *n.* pl. أَجْواء air, atmosphere; weather, climate; جَوّاً by air, by plane; سِلاح الجَوّ air force

أغلقت الباب خلفي وخلعت ثيابي.. كان الجو دافئا فظللت بملابسي الداخلي — I closed the door behind me and took off my clothes. The air was warm so I stayed in my underclothes

| 99 | 5758 |

668 وَكالة and وِكالة *n.* pl. -aat agency; office; dealership; proxy, deputation, power of attorney

طلبت الوكالة الدولية للطاقة الذرية مرارا من ايران تعليق انشطتها النووية الحساسة — The International Atomic Energy Agency repeatedly asked Iran to suspend its sensitive nuclear activities

| 90 | 6274 |

669 حاجَة *n.* (Egy. /Haaga/ pl. -aat, Magh. /Hazha/ pl. حَوايج /Hwayizh/) thing, something, object; حَوايج (Magh.) clothes; belongings

بقى حاقعد مع مامتك قعدة أعرف منها كل حاجة — Well, then, I'll sit with your mother until I find out everything from her

| 98 | 5784 |

670 خِطَّة and خُطَّة *n.* pl. خِطَط, خُطَط plan, project

أعدكما بأننا سننجح.. إذا طبقت الخطة كما أتصورها — I promise you that we will succeed...if the plan is carried out as I imagine it

| 88 | 6433 |

671 مَدَنِيّ *adj.* civil, civilian; *n.* pl. -uun civilian

قبل ذلك لقي خمسة مدنيين حتفهم وأصيب سبعة آخرون بجروح بانفجار سيارة مفخخة — Prior to that, five civilians were killed and seven others were wounded in a booby-trapped car explosion

90 | 6252 |

672 شارَكَ *v. III* to participate, share (with sb) في in sth

استمر رفع الأنقاض ثلاثة أيام، وشارك في ذلك ناس من كل الإسكندرية — They continued to sift through the rubble for three days, and people from all over Alexandria participated in that

96 | 5880 |

673 نَزَلَ *v. I (i)* and نَزَّلَ *(a)* to descend; stay في at

نزل درجات السلم ببطء وكأنه منوم، وكأنه محمول — He went down the stairs slowly, as if he were drugged, as if he were being carried

98 | 5743 |

674 صَحّ *adj.* right, correct; true

كل شي في هالدنيا فيه صح وفيه غلط — Everything in this world has good and bad in it

72 | 7762 | +spo

675 أَزْمَة *n.* pl. أَزَمات crisis, crunch

لسنا في أزمة.. بعد أيام قليلة سيتسلم جيف عمله الجديد — We are not in crisis...after a few days Jeff will get a new job

93 | 6034 |

676 بَحَثَ *v. I (a)* to look, search عن for; to discuss, debate (في) sth; to research, examine, look into في sth

أنا فعلا لا أفهمك.. لماذا تبحث عن المتاعب؟ — I really don't understand you...why are you looking for trouble?

99 | 5653 |

677 مَمْلَكَة *n.* kingdom

جاء الرئيس بوش واجتمع مع ولي عهد المملكة العربية السعودية وملك البحرين وملك الأردن وفخامة الرئيس مبارك — President Bush came and met with the Saudi Crown Prince and the King of Bahrain and the King of Jordan and President Mubarak

90 | 6184 |

678 إِطْلاق *n.* releasing, launching; (النّار) firing, shooting; على الإطْلاق and إِطْلاقاً (yes) absolutely, definitely; (no) not at all; على وَجْهِ الإِطْلاق for sure

إنه بخيل أناني لا يفكر إطلاقا إلا في نفسه — He is stingy and selfish, not thinking at all about anything except himself

88 | 6322 |

679 أَوْسَط *adj.* fem. وُسْطَى middle, central; الشَّرْق الأَوْسَط the Middle East

ظاهرة بن لادن نتيجة الأحوال في الشرق الأوسط وسيطرة أميركا على المنطقة — The Bin Laden phenomenon is a result of conditions in the Middle East and the control of America over the area

86 | 6448 |

680 مُحاوَلَة *n.* pl. -aat attempt, effort

نجى من عدة محاولات اغتيال بأعجوبة — He miraculously escaped numerous assassination attempts

88 | 6239 |

681 قَدَرَ *v. I (i)* and قَدِرَ *(a)* to be able to, be capable of (doing sth)

لا يقدر على ان يفهم لماذا انتخب الشعب الاميركي الرئيس بوش للمرة الثانية — He is not able to understand why the American people elected President Bush for the second time

98 | 5602 |

682 أَسْوَد *adj.* fem. سَوْداء, pl. سُود black; السود *n./adj.* blacks

ارتدت النساء جميعا ملابس سوداء وتنورة طويلة سوداء وسترة سوداء وحجابا أسود — The women all wore black clothing and a long black skirt and a black jacket and a black headscarf

99 | 5560 |

683 قِسْم *n.* pl. أَقْسام section, portion; department, division

لقد تم قبولك في القسم بمعركة — You have been accepted into the department with a battle

97 | 5602 |

684 تَحْدِيد *n.* specification; definition; تَحْدِيداً and بِالتَّحْدِيد specifically

هذه المرة نأتيكم من مدينة جدة وبالتحديد من المنتدى الاقتصادي السابع المنعقد حاليا بها — This time we are coming to you from the city of Jeddah, and specifically from the Seventh Economic Forum which is currently being held here

93 | 5839 |

685 خَلْف *n.* back, rear part; خَلْفَ (*prep.*) and مِن behind (of) sth/sb; مِن الخَلْف from the back, from the rear; خَلْفُ (*adv.*) and مِن خَلْفُ at the back, in the rear

اتخذ مكانه خلف الكاميرا وحدق فى العدسة بعناية He took his place behind the camera and stared into the lens with care

97 | 5628 |

686 شَمْس *fem.n.* sun

اليوم تشرق شمس الحرية من أقصى المغرب العربي على بلاد العرب المظلمة بالاستبداد — Today the sun of freedom is dawning from the furthest Arab west on the countries of the Arabs which are dark with despotism

99 | 5481 |

687 مَزِيد *n.* addition, added amount, greater number (مِن of); more, additional, increased (من)

لا أريد أن أسبب لك المزيد من الآلام.. أقترح أن ننفصل ولو مؤقتا — I don't want to cause you any more pain. I suggest that we separate, even if only temporarily

88 | 6154 |

688 تَعَرَّض *v. V* to be exposed إلى to sth; to encounter, run into, have to deal with إلى sth

ماذا يحدث لو مرضت أو تعرضت لحادث؟ — What would happen if you got sick or had an accident?

95 | 5689 |

689 سَبْعَة *num. fem.* سَبْع seven; سَبْعَةَ عَشَر seventeen

هي بالفعل من عجائب الدنيا السبع — It, in fact, is one of the seven wonders of the world

98 | 5505 |

690 اِهْتِمام *n.* interest, attention; care, concern

وما إن رد حتى تغير وجهه من الترحيب العادى إلى الاهتمام البالغ، وسرعان ما أنهى المكالمة وانتفض واقفا — Hardly had he answered the phone when his face changed from normal welcome to extreme interest, and he quickly ended the call and stood up

88 | 6117 |

691 دِينيّ *adj.* religious; spiritual

إن التعصب الديني نتيجة مباشرة للكبت السياسى — Religious intolerance is a direct result of political repression

96 | 5598 |

692 مُساعَدَة *n. pl.* -aat help, support; مساعدات aid

اتصلت بأبيها وطلبت منه مساعدة مالية — I contacted her father and asked him for monetary help

86 | 6221 |

693 كافَّة *n.* (in idafa) all of, the entirety of; كافَّةً all together

هنا معتقلون من كافة الفصائل الفلسطينية — There are prisoners here from all the Palestinian factions

85 | 6301 |

694 عَبْد *n. pl.* عَبِيد servant, slave; *pl.* عِباد servant (of God); العَبْد لله العِباد humanity, humankind; I, myself

الله في عون العبد ما كان العبد في عون اخيه — God helps the servant as long as the servant helps his brother

92 | 5795 |

695 غَرْب *n.* west; West; غَرْباً westward, in the west

كان حي الحرية شمال غرب العاصمة مسرحا لمعظم هذه الهجمات — The Hurriyya district north-west of the capital was the scene of most of these attacks

98 | 5465 |

696 عاصِمَة *n. pl.* عَواصِم capital city

صدر قرار بمنع ركوب الدراجات ببعض شوارع العاصمة — A decision was issued to forbid riding bicycles in some of the streets of the capital

92 | 5764 |

697 إطار *n.* framework, context

في النهاية السياسة هي فن الواقع وفن الممكن في إطار المعطيات الموجودة — In the end, politics is the art of the real and the art of the possible in the framework of the present givens

88 | 6079 |

698 صِحِّيّ *adj.* health-related, sanitary

انهمرت التبرعات من أجل توفير الطعام والثياب والرعاية الصحية لآلاف الأسر المشردة — Donations poured in to provide food and clothing and health care for thousands of homeless families

92 | 5759 |

699 مَشْكُور *adj.* thankful, grateful; *interj.* thanks!

حكومتنا مشكورة تسعى جاهدة لتوطين التقنيات وعدم هجرة العلماء — Our government, thankfully, is trying diligently to nationalize technologies and keep scientists from emigrating

62 | 8543 | +for

700 حُضُور *vn.* arrival, coming; attending, being present at (meeting, party, concert); viewing (film, TV show)

سافرنا إلى مدينة بابل لحضور إحدى فعاليات مهرجان بابل الدولي — We travelled to the city of Babel to attend one of the events of the International Babel festival

89 | 5974 |

701 مَحَلّ *n.* pl. -aat, مَحَالّ place, location; shop, store

وجدت المحل على بعد خطوات من فتحة المترو — I found the place a few steps away from the entrance to the metro

98 | 5373 |

702 يَهُودِيّ *n./adj.* pl. يَهُود Jew, Jewish

بن أليعازر ولد في مدينة البصرة عام ١٩٣٦ لأسرة يهودية كانت تمتلك كثيرا من المحال التجارية — Bin Eleazer was born in the city of Basra in the year 1936 to a Jewish family that owned many commercial shops

86 | 6093 |

703 تَنْظِيم *vn.* organizing, planning; regulating, controlling; *n.* pl. -aat organization, network

فتح هي التنظيم الأكبر في الساحة الفلسطينية — Fatah is the largest organization in the Palestinian arena

89 | 5914 |

704 رِياضَة *n.* sports; physical exercise; physical education; mathematics

يقال إن الدراجة وسيلة نقل سهلة، ومفيدة للعمل وممارسة الرياضة — It is said that the bicycle is an easy means of transportation, and beneficial for work and sports

91 | 5746 |

705 فَضْل *n.* favor, grace; kindness, goodwill; distinction, merit, credit; surplus; بِفَضْل due to, thanks to; فَضْلًا عَن aside from, not to mention; فَضْلًا عَن ذلِكَ furthermore, moreover

عبد الله بن أحمد محارب له الفضل في تثبيت حكم أسرة آل خليفة في البحرين — Abd Allah Ibn Ahmad is a warrior who is credited with establishing the rule of the Al-Khalifa family in Bahrain

93 | 5613 |

706 أَثْناء *prep.* during; في تِلْك/هذِه during; في أثْناء during; في الأَثْناء meanwhile

قتل ما لا يقل عن ٩ نساء رميا بالرصاص، أثناء هجوم الجنجويد على القرية — At least nine women were shot dead during the Janjaweed attack on the village

89 | 5868 |

707 حَقَّقَ *v. II* to achieve, realize (success, goals); to serve, promote (interests); to investigate في sth; to interrogate مع sb

يبدو أنك سعيد بما حققته من أرباح — It appears that you are happy with what you have achieved in the way of profits

88 | 5946 |

708 رَفَضَ *v. I (u)* to reject, refuse sth

لماذا ترفض قيام أحزاب على أساس ديني كما في بعض البرلمانات الغربية؟ — Why do you reject the founding of parties on a religious basis, as in some Western parliaments?

89 | 5802 |

709 شَخْصِيَّة *n. pl.* -aat personality, identity; person, individual

تنبأ له معلموه بمستقبل باهر بسبب قوة شخصيته — وانضباطه وكفاءته الذهنية والجسمانية His teachers predicted a glorious future for him because of the strength of his personality and his self-control and his intellectual and physical capabilities

97 | 5340 |

710 أَمِين *n. pl.* أُمَنَاء trustee, keeper; secretary; *adj.* loyal, faithful, reliable; أَمِين الصَّنْدُوق treasurer

يشارك في الافتتاح هاني سيف النصر الأمين العام للصندوق الاجتماعي للتنمية — Hani Saif al-Nasr, the secretary general of the Social Development Fund, participated in the grand opening

87 | 5939 |

711 مُسْتَشْفَى *n. pl.* مُسْتَشْفَيات hospital

يعتقد الوزير أن كل شيء عظيم، في حين كان المستشفى يعاني من إهمال شنيع — The minister believes that everything is great, while the hospital was suffering from terrible neglect

96 | 5386 |

10 Nature

116	أرض	earth; land	1624	حديقة	garden	3965	خضار	vegetables
130	عين	water spring (also eye)	1693	صحراء	desert	4021	نخيل	date palms
			1733	جزيرة	island	4044	قطر	region, district
507	بحر	sea	1806	حقل	field	4074	هوّة	abyss, chasm
686	شمس	sun	1833	تراب	dirt, soil	4322	بادية	wilderness
728	سماء	sky, heaven	1874	بحريّ	maritime; naval	4389	كهف	cave
798	قمّة	summit				4408	ذروة	peak
830	جبل	mountain	2095	رمل	sand	4455	مشرف	view; heights
844	قناة	canal; channel	2144	غابة	forest	4520	فيض	flood
902	طبيعة	nature	2155	صخر	rocks	4556	هاوية	cliff; abyss
984	جنّة	garden; paradise	2172	موجة	wave	4860	بركان	volcano
			2199	ساحل	coast, seashore	5012	هلال	crescent, new moon
993	خليج	gulf	2220	شاطئ	shore, beach			
1001	شجر	trees	2405	موج	waves	5091	غرس	plant
1019	نجم	star	2493	أطلّ	to overlook; to look out of	5118	ثرى	soil, earth
1039	بيئة	environment				5199	خضرة	vegetable
1081	قمر	moon	2571	ميناء	port, harbor	5211	جبليّ	mountainous
1127	مشهد	scene, view	2596	منظر	view, scenery	5242	بستان	orchard
1137	مساحة	surface	2681	برّيّ	land (adj)	5549	تيه	desert
1184	نهر	river	2733	كوكب	planet	5557	برّيّة	wilderness
1298	تيّار	current, stream	2793	برّ	land; dry land	5714	بدر	full moon
			2795	نبات	plants	5831	ضيعة	village; estate
1319	ربع	quarter	3115	روضة	garden	6153	بسيطة	planet earth
1361	ضفّة	bank, shore	3230	بئر	well	6297	ربوة	hill
1396	واد	wadi, valley	3535	بحيرة	lake	6366	معين	water spring
1435	محيط	periphery; ocean	3553	تربة	dust, dirt	6505	تلّ	hill
			3639	واحة	oasis	7061	غدير	brook
1478	فضاء	space; vacant	3795	عشب	grass; herb	7192	منخفض	low ground
1481	أفق	horizon	3804	ريف	countryside	7301	شعب	reef
1590	درب	path, trail	3919	صحراويّ	desert	7302	بيد	wilderness
1596	هادئ	calm, Pacific	3928	ساحليّ	coastal	7410	شهاب	shooting star

712 ولا and الا *conj.* or; otherwise, or else; (Egy.) /walla/, (Lev.Irq.Gul.) /willa/, (Magh.) /wella, wala/

يعني ماشتغلتش ولا أجرتش أوضة ولا أي حاجة —
In other words you haven't worked, or rented a room, or anything

23 | 21684 |

713 طُول *n.* length; height; طُولَ throughout, during (the entire); عَلى طُول (Egy.) straight ahead; directly; (Lev., also عطول /9a-Tuul/) immediately; always; completely; for good

لها أحسن تربية.. الحمد لله.. طول عمرها فى مدارس لغات.. من الحضانة حتى الثانوية — She has the best education, thank God...her whole life she has been in language schools...from kindergarten till secondary

99 | 5194 |

714 رابع *adj.* fourth (ordinal)

فى الساعة الرابعة والدقيقة الخامسة والأربعين، أعلنت إيطاليا الحرب على إنجلترا وفرنسا — At 4:45, Italy declared war on England and France

99 | 5202 |

715 كَذا *adv.* thus, like that, in this way; كَذا وَكَذا such-and-such, so-and-so; كَذا وَكَيْتَ this and that

والحين ما ادري ايش اسوي؟ كذا مرة احاول ابتعد وانهي الموضوع لكن ما اقدر — Now I don't know what to do; several times I've tried to distance myself and close the matter but I can't

92 | 5614 |

716 طاقة *n.* energy, power; potential, ability

هذا فوق طاقة البشر على الاحتمال — This is beyond man's ability to bear

96 | 5368 |

717 مين (Egy.Lev.) *interrog.* who; لَمين (Lev.) to/for whom; whose

انت عارف مين بيدفع بقشيش كويس.. الياباني والعربي — You know who pays really good tips? The Japanese and the Arabs

66 | 7717 | +spo

718 قائل *a.p.* saying; *n.* (person) saying

بادرها قائلا بابتسامة: السلام عليكم — He initiated a conversation with her saying with a smile: hello!

89 | 5777 |

719 كاتِب *n.* pl. كُتّاب writer, author; pl. كَتَبَة office worker, clerk; *a.p.* pl. -uun writing

فرح محمد فرحا لن يستطيع أي كاتب حكايات في العالم أن يصفه — Muhammad was really so happy that no story writer in the world could describe his happiness

96 | 5344 |

720 مَعْرُوف *adj.* known, well-known; *n.* favor, kind gesture, good deed; what is right (opposite of مُنْكَر)

هناك قاعدة فقهية معروفة أن الضرورات تبيح المحظورات — There is a well-known legal rule that "Necessity knows no law" (necessities make forbidden things permissible)

98 | 5252 |

721 رِياضِيّ *adj.* sports, sportive; mathematical; *n.* pl. -uun mathematician; رِياضيّات mathematics; تَرْبِيَة رِياضِيَّة physical education

يجلس فى المدرج وقد ارتدى قبعته الرياضية بالمقلوب، يتابع اللعب بشغف وحماس — He is sitting in the stadium, having put his sports cap on backwards, following the game with passion and enthusiasm

94 | 5453 |

722 اِتَّصَلَ *v. VIII* to contact ب sb, get in touch with sb; to be connected or related الى to sth

سوف يتصل بها لا لكي يصالحها، وإنما ليوبخها — He is going to call her, not to make up with her, but to scold her

97 | 5289 | +spo

723 أَجْنَبِيّ *n./adj.* pl. أجانِب foreign, foreigner

تبين لي أن شخصا يجلس قريبا منا يطالع مجلة أجنبية وكأنه يتصنت علينا — It became obvious to me that someone sitting near us reading a foreign magazine appeared to be eavesdropping on us

96 | 5360 |

724 جُمْهُور *n.* pl. الجَماهِير جَماهِير multitude, public; the masses

إذا أنكرت هذا الكلام تكون قد خالفت إجماع جمهور الفقهاء وأنكرت ما هو معلوم من الدين بالضرورة — If you reject this statement, then you have gone against the consensus of the main body of religious scholars, and denied what is necessarily known about religion

94 | 5401 |

725 هاي (Lev.Irq.Gul.) *dem.pron.* this (fem.sg.), these (non-human pl. and fem.pl.)

لأ إحنا بنهتم بهاي الشغلات خصوصا عندنا بالبيت — كثير كثير بنهتم بهاي الشغلات — No, we take an interest in those things, especially at home, we really take a big interest in those things

45 | 11287 | +for +spo

726 اِسْتَمَرّ *v. X* to last, go on (for a certain amount of time); to continue في doing sth

يستمر التعذيب حتى يستسلم المتهم ويعترف بما هو منسوب إليه — The torture continues until the accused surrenders and confesses to whatever has been attributed to him

89 | 5737 |

727 قَرَأ *v. I (a)* and (Dia.) قَرَى *(a)* to read sth

يبدو أنك لم تقرأ التاريخ جيدا — It appears that you haven't read history well

97 | 5267 |

728 سَماء *n.* pl. سَمَوات, سَماوات sky, heaven

آدم عليه السلام حين هبط من السماء، نزل في مكان شبيه بهذا المكان — Adam, may peace be upon him, when he fell from the sky, came down in a place like this place

98 | 5198 |

729 هٰذي (often written هادي) *dem.pron.* this (fem. sg.), these (MSA: non-human pl.; Dia. also fem.pl.)

انا هادي التكنولوجيا ما بعرفها — I don't know this technology

99 | 5112 | +for

730 نَسِيَ *v. I (a)* to forget sth/sb

إن أسرته وأهله حوله الآن حقا لكنه لا ينسى رمضان الماضي، وخلاء الصحراء وخشوع غروبه — His family is really around him now but he will not forget last Ramadan, and the emptiness of the desert and the humiliation of separation

96 | 5270 |

731 جَهْد and جُهْد *n.* pl. جُهُود effort, exertion; endeavor

الأحداث الضخمة تحتاج إلى جهود ضخمة، إلى تحضير، إلى تخطيط — Big events require big efforts, to prepare, to plan

85 | 5918 |

732 شَهيد *n.* pl. شُهَداء martyr

حدث الانفجار ولم اصب باغماء فرأيت جثث الشهداء وهي تتطاير وسقف الصالة وقع على الارض بالكامل — The explosion occurred and I did not lose consciousness, and I saw the bodies of martyrs flying in all directions, and the ceiling of the hall fell completely to the ground

88 | 5762 |

733 رَفَعَ *v. I (a)* to lift, raise sth; to increase, boost sth; to lodge على against sb (a complaint)

من يوافق يرفع يده من فضلكم — Whoever agrees, raise his hand please

98 | 5104 |

734 عادَة *n.* pl. -aat habit, custom, practice; usually, generally, typically

انتهى طارق من مراجعة عينات البحث كعادته وأغلق مكتبه واستعد للانصراف — Tariq finished reviewing the research samples as usual and locked his desk and prepared to leave

99 | 5056 |

735 ضَغْط *vn.* pressing, exerting pressure; *n.* pl. ضُغُوط pressure, stress; voltage

استخرج تقريرا يفيد أنه كان يعاني من ضغط مرتفع أدى إلى جلطة في المخ — He extracted a report that stated that he was suffering from high blood pressure which lead to clot in the brain

95 | 5269 |

736 سَهْم *n.* pl. أَسْهُم (econ.) share, stock; pl. سِهام arrow

واصلت معظم اسعار الاسهم في اسواق المال والبورصات العربية ارتفاعها — Most of the prices of the stocks in the Arab stock exchanges and money markets continued their rise

85 | 5902 |

737 زَمان *n.* time, period, duration; مِن زَمانٍ (it has been) for some time; (it was) a long time ago; بالزَّمانات (Lev.) a long time ago

هذه خطوة تأخرت وكان يجب اتخاذها من زمان — This step is late, it should have been taken a long time ago

98 | 5131 |

738 مَسْأَلَة *n. pl.* مَسائِل issue, affair; matter, question
أخبرني أنه سيتجه إلى الشيخ ابن عثيمين ليسأله في بعض مسائل الجهاد — He told me that he would go to Sheikh Ibn Uthimin to ask him about some issues of jihad
97 | 5136 |

739 كَوْن *vn.* لِكَوْنِ being, by virtue of being; because; *n.* الكَوْن the universe, existence
لا يمنع كون الأسئلة صعبة من أن تبحث عن الاجابة — The fact that the questions are hard does not prevent one from searching for the answers
97 | 5136 |

740 جَريمَة *n. pl.* جَرائِم crime
سأل القاضي المتهم: هل ارتكبت هذه الجريمة من دون شريك؟ — The judge asked the accused: Did you commit this crime without a partner?
96 | 5204 |

741 إرْهاب *n.* terror, terrorism; *vn.* terrorizing, frightening
طالما هناك ظلم بحق بعض الشعوب كفلسطين والعراق، فإن الإرهاب سيظل مبررا — As long as there is injustice against people such as (those in) Palestine and Iraq, terrorism will continue to be justified
90 | 5556 |

742 شوي /shway/ (Lev.Gul.Irq.) *adv.* a little bit; شوية /shwayya/ (Egy.Lev.Gul.Irq.Yem.) *n.* some, a few; *adv.* a little bit
عصمت.. لازم نفكر شويه.. أنا حانزل مصر دلوقت اعمل ايه؟ — Ismat...we have to think a bit. What am I going to do when I go to Egypt now?
60 | 8225 | +spo

743 قَدْر *n.* extent, degree; amount, value; ability, capability, capacity
قرر أن يتجنب المواجهة بقدر الإمكان — He decided to avoid the confrontation as much as possible
98 | 5050 |

744 نهائِيّ *adj.* final, definitive, conclusive; *n. pl.* -aat final (in sports); نِهائِيّاً finally, in the end
لا أفهمهم.. طوال عمري أحصل على الدرجة النهائية في اللغة الإنجليزية، لكنهم يتكلمون إنجليزية أخرى — I don't understand them...My whole life I've received the top grade in English language, but they speak another English
94 | 5285 |

745 جِسْم *n. pl.* أجْسام body; form, mass; organism
يجلس على المقعد وهو يحدق في جسم عبده الممدد على الأرض — He sits on the chair staring at the body of Abdu stretched out on the floor
98 | 5040 |

746 حِساب *n. pl.* -aat calculation, appraisal; account, invoice; expense
إنني على يقين بان الأموال التي تسلمها ذهبت إلى حسابه وحساب أصدقائه — I am sure that the money he received went into his account and the accounts of his friends
98 | 5004 |

747 إنْسانِيّ *adj.* human; humane, humanitarian
أعلن وزير خارجية أمريكا أن دخول إيطاليا الحرب كارثة إنسانية كبرى، وقطعت مصر علاقاتها بإيطاليا على الفور — The US Secretary of State announced that Italy's entering the war was a major human catastrophe, and Egypt cut off its relations with Italy immediately
88 | 5603 |

748 ساكِن *n. pl.* سُكّان resident, inhabitant; *a.p.* ساكِن see under verb سَكَنَ (u)
تسرق المياه وتبيعها لسكان القطاع — She steals the water and sells it to the inhabitants of the Strip
97 | 5093 |

749 شُغْل *n. pl.* أشْغال work, labor; occupation, business
هو شيطان انجليزي فاهم شغله كويس.. مش زي الشيطان المصري اللي كنت باعرف أقاومه — He is an English devil who understands his work very well, not like the Egyptian devil whom I used to know how to resist
96 | 5144 | +spo

750 عِلاج *n.* treatment, therapy
العلاج بالجينات سيفتح باب الأمل لمرضى القلب خلال السنوات العشر المقبلة — Gene therapy will open the door of hope to heart patients during the next ten years
97 | 5073 |

751 يَعْني *part.* (used as a filler) I mean, y'know, like, uh; (as a response) sort of, more or less

أنا خبرتي في الطيران مش كبيرة قوي.. يعني يادوب هم الخمس ساعات اللي ركبتهم من مصر لهنا — My experience in the airline industry is not very big...it's, well, barely the five hours during which I took the plane from Egypt to here

10 | 49368 |

752 إقامَة *n.* residency; setting up, establishing; erecting

خاصة ان الشباب يلجأ الى الزواج العرفي والسري بهدف إقامة علاقة جنسية فقط — Especially since young people resort to civil and secret marriages with the sole purpose of establishing a sexual relationship

96 | 5135 |

753 سَعادَة *n.* happiness; (honorific) His Excellency

لا يحول بيننا وبين السعادة إلا العفاريت الكامنة في أعماقنا — The only things keeping us from happiness are the devils hiding inside ourselves

89 | 5499 |

754 مُو (Irq.Gul.Lev.) *neg.part.* not; مُو مُشْكِلَة no problem; (Lev.) مو هيك؟ /muu heek/, (Irq.) مو هيچي؟ /muu hiichi/ isn't that so? innit?

هو مو مبسوط — He is not happy

55 | 8913 | +spo

755 أَصابَ *v. IV* (usu. pass.) أُصِيبَ to suffer (injuries); to be struck, afflicted ب by (illness)

يجب دائما أن نخفض توقعاتنا حتى لا نصاب بخيبة أمل — We have to always lower our expectations so that we are not hit with disappointment

99 | 4927 |

756 تَعَلَّقَ *v. V* to be connected ب with, have to do with sth/sb ب

هل هناك أسئلة تتعلق بالمحاضرة؟ — Are there questions related to the lecture?

91 | 5362 |

757 حِمايَة *n.* protection, protecting

اتحاد الصحافيين العرب يطالب الامم المتحدة بحماية الصحافيين العراقيين — The Arab journalists' union is demanding that the United Nations protect Iraqi journalists

95 | 5112 |

758 اعْتِبار *vn.* considering, regarding; *n. pl.* -aat consideration, regard, belief; اعْتِباراً مِن beginning on, starting from (date)

لماذا توقفت شعوب العالم بحسب رأيك عن اعتبار أنفسها أميركية أي متضامنة مع أميركا؟ — Why, in your opinion, have the world's people stopped considering themselves American, that is, in solidarity with America?

88 | 5516 |

759 تَقَدُّم *n.* progress, advancement; *vn.* coming forward

الإبداع أساس التقدم سواء في الفن أو العلم أو الفكر — Creativity is the basis of progress, whether in art, science, or thought

95 | 5117 |

760 شَخْصِيّ *adj.* personal, private; شَخْصِيّاً personally, in person

قام فضيلة شيخ الأزهر شخصيا بعقد القرآن في جامع سيدنا الحسين — His eminence, the Sheikh of Al-Azhar, personally performed the marriage in the Mosque of Sayyidna Al-Hussein

98 | 4953 |

761 مُثِير *a.p.* pointing out, indicating; *adj.* indicative

تحدث عن انشاء شبكات توزيع الغاز الطبيعي، مشيرا الى ان الخطط كانت تقضي بان يصل الى عمان والزرقاء — He spoke about building a network for the distribution of natural gas, pointing to the plans that stipulate that it reach Amman and Zarqa

83 | 5830 | +news

762 شَبَكَة *n. pl.* -aat, شِباك net; web, network; grid, system

الجيل الثالث سيصبح افضل الشبكات المتوفرة — Third Generation (3G) will become the best available network

96 | 5022 |

763 خَلَّى *v. II* (Dia.) to preserve, keep sb safe (of God): الله يَخَلِّيك God keep you safe! (used to express thanks for a service); to let sb do sth: خَلِّيني أَرُوح let me go!; (aux. verb, with 2nd pers. pron.) stay: خَلِّيك مَعِي stay with me; خَلِّيك قاعِد remain seated; خَلِّيك بِالمَوْضُوع stick with the subject

ربنا يخليك يابني ويديك الصحة أنت واللي زيك يا كريم يا رب يا كريم — God keep you, my son, and give you health, you and all those like you, O Generous Lord

66 | 7277 | +spo

764 زَواج *n.* marriage; wedding

لديه مبلغ معتبر مكنه في العام الماضي من الزواج بابنة تاجر ثري يمتلك محلا كبيرا للأدوات الصحية في الرويعي — He has a considerable amount (of money) which enabled him last year to marry the daughter of a rich merchant who owns a big health supplies shop in Al-Ruwayi

96 | 5033 |

765 خارِجِيّ *adj.* foreign; outer, exterior, outside

من المعروف أن الحيوان يمتلك شعورا مباشرا بالعالم الخارجي، لكنه بالتأكيد لا يمتلك شعورا بذاته — It is known that animals possess direct consciousness about the outside world, but they certainly do not possess self-consciousness

96 | 5049 |

766 مُجَرَّد *adj.* bare, naked; free (من/عن from); pure, absolute (truth); *n.* mere, nothing but; بِمُجَرَّدِ as soon as, the instant; لِمُجَرَّدِ for no other reason but, for the sole reason that

فقدت وظيفتها ليس لأنها مهملة او غير كفء ولكن لمجرد أنها سوداء — She lost her job not because she was neglectful or not qualified, but merely because she was black

97 | 4961 |

767 قَرَّرَ *v. II* to decide, resolve أن to do sth

ظل رأفت يراقبها من نافذة مكتبه، ثم قرر فجأة أن يتجاهل ابنته تماما، فلتذهب إلى الجحيم — Ra'fat kept watching from the window of his office, then he suddenly decided to ignore his daughter completely, let her go to hell

96 | 5019 |

768 كَمان (Egy.Lev.) *adv.* also; كَمان مَرّة again, once more; أنا كَمان me too; كَمانَه (Lev.) *adv.* also

حلو الموضوع كتير وكمان في فائدة — The subject is very nice, and it also has some use

54 | 8928 |

769 حَدِيث *adj.* new, recent; modern; *pl.* -uun أَطْفال حَدِيثُو الوِلادَة newborn babies (mostly in idafa); حَدِيثاً recently, lately

كانت الشقة متسعة وقد أُثثت بطريقة حديثة فخمة — The apartment was roomy, and it was furnished in a luxurious, modern way

96 | 5014 |

770 عَمّ *n. pl.* عُمُوم paternal uncle; (يا) عَمُّو/عَمُّه /9ammo/ (Lev.Irq.Gul.) friendly term of address: (hey) buddy, pal, man

لا أحب أن يراني عمي صالح سكران — I don't want my uncle Salih to see me drunk

95 | 5063 |

771 بال *n.* mind, attention; خَطَرَ عَلى بالي it occurred to me; راح عَن بالي it slipped my mind; ما على باليش (Alg.) I don't know

خد بالك من اللصوص في الزحام — Watch out for thieves in the crowd

98 | 4864 |

772 كَشَفَ *v. I* (i) to reveal, disclose عن sth; to expose, uncover النِّقابَ عَن sth; to examine على sb (medically)

بدت متألقة في ثوب سهرة أنيق كشف عن كتفيها وصدرها — She looked exquisite in a stylish evening gown that revealed her shoulders and cleavage

95 | 5018 |

773 ذُو *n.* (gen. ذِي, acc. ذا) *pl.* ذَوُو (gen./acc. ذَوِي), fem. ذات, *pl.* أُولُو (gen./acc. أُولِي), ذَوات having, possessing; (pl.) those who

أمامها قصر الملك الأبيض ذو النوافذ العديدة، والنخيل السلطاني العالمي يتمايل تحت الريح — In front of her was the white palace of the king, with the many windows, and the royal palms swaying in the wind

89 | 5336 |

774 طالَبَ *v. III* to demand, call for ـب sth (from sb); to require ـب sth (from sb)

يخاف إذا زار فرنسا أن يطالب أقارب بعض الضحايا السلطات الفرنسية بمنعه من العودة إلى الجزائر — He is afraid if he visits France that the relatives of some of the victims would demand the French authorities to prevent him from returning to Algeria

94 | 5063 |

775 غَد *n.* tomorrow; غَداً tomorrow

تذكرت أن لدي امتحانا غدا — I remembered that I have a test tomorrow

91 | 5254 |

776 أَحْسَن *elat.* better/best

سأعمل لك بيتسا أحسن من المطعم مائة مرة.. ما رأيك؟ — I will make a pizza for you that is one hundred times better than the restaurant (one)...What do you think?

96 | 4942 |

777 مِلَفّ *n.* pl. -aat and مَلَفّ file, folder; dossier; (computer) document, file

يمكن لنا بعد ذلك أن ننقل الملف إلى الكمبيوتر بواسطة كابل خاص — We can transfer the file after that to the computer by means of a special cable

84 | 5643 |

778 حَجْم *n.* volume, size

ما زال مشدوها يحدق بالغريب فهو لم ير رجلا بهذا الحجم ابدا — He was still amazed, staring at the stranger, since he had never seen a man of that size before

89 | 5334 |

779 شَرْط *n.* pl. شُرُوط precondition, stipulation

حين تم تعيينه، كان هناك شرط أن يمحو أميته قبل مرور عام — When he was appointed, there was a condition that he become literate within a year

98 | 4834 |

780 شَكَّلَ *v. II* to constitute, form, compose sth

الماء يشكل أكثر من ثلثي الأرض.. واليابسة ليست سوى جزيرة تشكل الثلث فقط او أقل — Water makes up over two thirds of the earth. Dry land is only an island that constitutes only one third or less

88 | 5374 |

781 وَفْق *n.* وَفْقَ and وِفْقاً لـ according to, in accordance with, pursuant to

لم يسأل نفسه عما إذا كان ما يفعله وفق رغبته، أم أنه مكره عليه — He didn't ask himself about whether he was doing what he was doing according to his desires, or whether he was being forced

87 | 5446 |

782 عُنْصُر *n.* pl. عَناصِر factor, element; component, ingredient; race, ethnicity; member, agent; (pl.) individuals

إن من أهم عناصر نجاح خطتنا هو أن نقطع صلتنا نهائيا مع صديقنا أحمد — Among the most important elements in the success of our plan is that we cut off contact, finally, with our friend Ahmad

86 | 5500 |

783 مُناسَبَة *n.* pl. -aat occasion, opportunity; مُناسَبات special occasions (feasts, holidays); بالمُناسَبَة incidentally, by the way

كان والد العروس، كما يحدث في تلك المناسبات، يتحدث عن ابنته بحب وإعجاب — The father of the bride, as happens on these occasions, is speaking about his daughter with love and admiration

99 | 4785 |

784 اللَّهُمَّ *interj.* oh God! dear God!; اللَّهُمَّ إلّا apart from (the fact that)

اللهم أسلمت نفسي إليك، ووجهت وجهي إليك — God, I submit myself to you, and turn my face toward you

87 | 5404 | +for

785 غالٍ (def. غالي) *adj.* expensive, costly; dear, precious, beloved; (Gul.) غالياً dearly; يا غالي buddy, pal; يا غالية darling, love

كم ستطول التضحية بالأرواح الغالية، في مجهود فاشل لفرض إدارة كبيرة وباهظة الثمن على الجماهير العربية التي لم تطلبها ولم تردها؟ — How long do we have to sacrifice costly lives in a failed effort to impose a big and extremely costly administration on the Arab

masses who did not request it and don't
want it?

98 | 4811 | +for

786 صَدْر *n. pl.* صُدُور chest; bosom

تحسست صدرها فوجدت النقود تحت ثيابها —
She felt her breast and found the money under
her clothes

96 | 4847 |

787 سَمَحَ *v. I (a)* to allow, permit لِ sb (to do sth);
لَوْ سَمَحْت اِسْمَح لِي excuse me (allow me);
please (if you don't mind)

طلبت من أمها أن تسمح لها بدراسة اللغة الفرنسية في
مدارس برليتز بشارع سعد زغلول — She asked her
mother to permit her to study French in the
Berlitz school on Saad Zaghloul Street

99 | 4704 |

788 فَوْز *n.* victory

تل أبيب لن تعترف بنتائج الانتخابات الفلسطينية
إذا حققت حماس فوزا ملحوظا — Tel Aviv
will never recognize the results of the
Palestinian elections if Hamas achieves
a notable victory

86 | 5387 |

789 بَعْدُ *adv.* afterward, later; still; (not) yet;
أمّا بَعْدُ approx. and now, to our main
point (the reason for this speech, letter,
etc.)

تم إنشاء الجامعة اللبنانية في العالم، التي سميت فيما بعد
الجامعة اللبنانية الثقافية في العالم — The World
Lebanese University was established, which was
called thereafter The World Lebanese Cultural
Union

72 | 6475 |

11 Weather

667	جوّ	air; weather, climate	2657	طقس	weather, climate	4520	فيض	flood
978	موسم	season	2702	زلزال	earthquake	4548	غيمة	cloud
1219	هواء	air	2997	هدأ	to subside (storm)	4658	جليد	ice
1235	ريح	wind				4791	رطوبة	humidity
1370	حرارة	temperature, heat	3102	دافئ	warm	5152	طوفان	typhoon
			3237	حرّ	heat	5386	مهبّ	wind direction
1380	بارد	cold	3500	ثلج	snow; ice	5543	مناخيّ	weather-related
1447	جبهة	front	3558	جفاف	drought	5544	نسمة	breeze
1468	مطر	rain	3587	جافّ	dry	5590	هطول	downpour
1492	جوّيّ	air (adj)	3641	طاغ	oppressive (also tyrant)	5928	شوب	hot
1722	شتاء	winter				6024	عاصف	tempestuous
1856	فصل	season (also section)	3667	دفء	warmth	6243	شتويّ	wintry
			3841	عصف	to be stormy	6368	رعد	thunder
1943	ربيع	spring	3863	معتدل	moderate	6807	ريّح	windy
2242	برد	cold	3910	رصد	to track, monitor (weather)	6818	سخن	hot, warm
2298	صبّ	to fall (rain, snow) (also to pour)				6940	براد	cold
			4018	غمرة	flood	6970	شتّى	to rain
			4035	ندى	dew	6974	ديمة	continuous rain
2355	ساخن	hot	4041	حراريّ	thermal	7081	هبّة	breeze, gust
2459	حارّ	hot	4170	نسيم	breeze	7082	سقعة	cold
2525	عاصفة	storm	4362	تكثيف	condensation	7147	سموم	hot wind
2553	مناخ	climate	4392	برق	lightning	7177	صبا	east wind
2575	هبّ	to blow (wind)	4465	ضباب	fog; vapor	7345	برد	hail, hailstone
2599	سحاب	clouds	4485	جفّ	to become dry	7625	محل	drought

790 سِجْن *n. pl.* سُجُون prison

قبض عليه عدة مرات، وحوكم وقضى فى السجن
فترات مختلفة وصلت إحداها إلى ستة أشهر كاملة
— He was arrested several times, and he was
found guilty and he spent various periods in
prison, one of which reached a full six-months

88 | 5246 |

791 فَتَاة *n. pl.* فَتَيَات young woman, girl

لا يستطيع أحد أن يعرف أن تلك الفتاة نامت أم لم
تنم.. إنها أشياء بعيدة عن إدراكنا — No one can
know whether that girl went to sleep or not...
these are things that are far from our
understanding

89 | 5229 |

792 سِّر *n. pl.* أَسْرار secret; سِرّاً secretly, privately;
السِّر المُقَدَّس sacrament; أَمِين/كَاتِب السِّرّ secretary;

لا وجود للأسرار بين أهل الأخوية.. لكن يبقى سرا
بيننا، أعدك بذلك — There are no secrets among
the family of the brotherhood...but it will
remain a secret between us, I promise you
that

99 | 4699 |

793 حُرّ *adj. pl.* أَحْرار free, independent; *n.* أَحْرار
liberals; independents

إن لبنان ليس ملفا، إن لبنان دولة مستقلة حرة ذات
سيادة يجب أن تتعامل سوريا معها على هذا الأساس
— Lebanon is not a file, Lebanon is an
independent, free state, with sovereignty,
which Syria must deal with on this basis

99 | 4684 |

794 مَسْؤُولِيَّة *n. pl.* -aat and مَسْؤُولِيَّة responsibility,
duty

كنت اطمئنه وأخبره أن المسؤولية ليست كاملة على
عاتقه — I reassured him and informed him
that the responsibility was not all on his
shoulders

93 | 4941 |

795 مَن *interrog.* who, whom; المن /'il-man/
(Irq.Gul.) *interrog.* to/for whom; whose

هل تعرفين من هو صفوت شاكر؟ — Do you know
who Safwat Shakir is?

88 | 5271 |

796 نَشْر *n.* spreading, propagation; publication,
announcement

هذا النوع من القصائد لا يصلح للنشر في العربي
الصغير — This type of ode is not appropriate
for publication in "The Young Arab"

87 | 5291 |

797 صِنَاعَة *n.* manufacture, industry; *pl.* -aat trade,
craft

هنالك ضرورة لاعطاء الصناعة المحلية حقها في
التعامل على أسس عادلة — There is a need to
give local industry its due in trading, on fair
principles

87 | 5316 |

798 قِمَّة *n. pl.* قِمَم summit

أنا الآن في قمة حياتي العملية.. قد يتم اختياري وزيرا
فى أى وقت — I am now at the peak of my
working life...I might be chosen as a minister
at any time

89 | 5186 |

799 عَدُوّ *n./adj. pl.* أَعْداء enemy

من يتخلى عن بلاده فى محنتها ويضع نفسه فى خدمة
الأعداء؟ — Who abandons his country during
its trial and puts himself in the service of the
enemies?

88 | 5189 |

800 مَلَكَ *v. I (i)* to own, possess sth; to control sth

ملايين من الناس يملكون هذا النوع من السيارات —
Millions of people own this type of car

89 | 5118 |

801 ناحِيَة *n. pl.* نَواح (def. نَواحِي) side, perspective,
aspect; area, region

الوضع الأمني معروف طبعا، من الناحية السياسية ما
هي مصادر قلقك أنت كمراقب للوضع العراقي؟ —
The security situation is known, of course; from
the political standpoint what are the sources of
your worry as an observer of the Iraqi situation?

98 | 4693 |

802 مَطْلُوب *adj.* wanted, needed; demanded,
required, necessary

بعد أن دفع أهله الرشوة المطلوبة أطلق سراح طفلهم
بعد يومين — After his family paid the required
bribes, their child was released after two days

97 | 4730 |

803 اِسْتِثْمَار *vn.* investing; *n.* pl. -aat investment
وضعنا شروطا جديدة للاستثمار في سوريا لم تكن
موجودة سابقا — We laid down new conditions
for investment in Syria which were not there
before
76 | 6008 |

804 تَوَقَّعَ *v. V* to expect, anticipate sth; to look
forward to sth
استغرب لأن زوجته لم تخبره بأنها تتوقع أحدا على
العشاء — He was amazed because his wife had
not told him that she expected anyone for
dinner
98 | 4678 |

805 نَفْس *fem.n.* pl. نُفُوس soul, spirit; عِلْم النَّفْس
psychology
النفس تتعلق بالمكان الذي تطرد منه، أليس كذلك؟
— The soul becomes attached to the place it is
driven out of, isn't that true?
95 | 4822 |

806 اِسْتِمْرَار *n.* continuation, continuity; بِاسْتِمْرَار
constantly
أكد أن هذا القرار امتداد واستمرار للنهج الديكتاتوري
الذي يتبعه النظام الحاكم في البلاد — He stressed
that this decision was an extension and
continuation of the dictatorial program which
the ruling regime was following in the country
95 | 4816 |

807 مُنَاسِب *adj.* suitable, appropriate
هل اتصلت بك في وقت مناسب؟ لا أريد أن أعطلك
عن العمل — Did I call you at an appropriate
time? I don't want to delay you at work
98 | 4681 |

808 حَوَالَيْ (Dia. حَوَالِي) and حَوَالَيْ *prep.*
approximately, around, about
كم نسبة النجاح؟ - حوالي خمسين في المائة — What is
the percentage of success? – About fifty percent
96 | 4772 |

809 حَضَرَ *v. I (u)* to come, show up; to attend, be
present at (meeting, party, concert); to view
(film, TV show)
ذياب لم يحضر إلى الفندق منذ شهرين تقريبا ولعله لن
يعود — Diyab has not come to the hotel for
about two months; and maybe he will not return
99 | 4598 |

810 إِمَارَة *n.* pl. -aat Emirate
سافرت إلى الإمارات لزيارة أختي — I traveled to
the Emirates to visit my sister
92 | 4969 |

811 خَطَأ *n.* pl. أَخْطَاء mistake, blunder, error;
adj. (invar.) wrong, mistaken
الوقت أمامنا ضيق، وأي خطأ من ناحيتنا يعمل مصيبة
— The time available to us is limited, and any
error on our part would create a catastrophe
95 | 4767 |

812 تَحِيَّة *n.* pl. -aat, تَحَايا greeting, salute,
salutation
كان هناك حراس قدموا التحية العسكرية
There were guards who saluted the soldiers
87 | 5215 | +for

813 نَبِيّ *n.* pl. أَنْبِياء prophet; النَّبِيّ the Prophet
Muhammad
تزوج النبي الكريم عليه الصلاة والسلام من
عربيات وغير عربيات — The noble Prophet,
peace be upon him, married Arab and
non-Arab women
96 | 4728 |

814 تَطَوُّر *n.* pl. -aat progress, development,
growth; تَطَوُّرات events, developments
هذا بطبيعة الحال يستدعي التطور السياسي
الديمقراطي من أجل تحرير الشعب البحريني من
القيود التقليدية — This, naturally, requires
democratic political development in order to
free the Bahraini people from the traditional
bonds
85 | 5334 |

815 مَتَى *interrog.* when
لا أرى أيا من البنتين.. لا أعرف متى تخرجان
في الصباح.. إنهما تتسللان بلا صوت فيما
يبدو — I don't see either of the two girls...
I don't know when they go out in the
morning...They creep out without a sound,
as it appears
86 | 5240 |

816 إِصَابَة *n.* affliction, illness; pl. -aat casualty,
injury; pl. -aat point, score, goal
ربطت دراسة أمريكية عام ١٩٩١ بين التدخين
قبل الحمل وإصابة الأولاد بالسرطان

An American study in the year 1991 linked smoking before pregnancy and children getting cancer

85 | 5301 |

817 فَنّ *n.* pl. فُنُون art; specialty; type, variety

أما الرسم على طريقة الفن الحديث فأنا بصراحة لا أفهمه — As for drawing in the way of modern art, I frankly don't understand it

93 | 4834 |

818 قَتْل *n.* murder, killing

رومیل لا یمکن هزیمته.. لا یمکن قتله — Rommel cannot be defeated...he cannot be killed

94 | 4789 |

819 سار *v.* I (i) to move, march; (Gul.) to go, walk

الأمور تسير نحو الأفضل دائما، بالرغم من أننا نعید اكتشاف العجلة — Things are getting better always, despite the fact that we keep reinventing the wheel

97 | 4666 | +spo

820 مُهِمَّة and مَهَمَّة *n.* pl. -aat, مَهامّ task, assignment, mission; مُهِمّات equipment, material, supplies

أما صالح مهمته متابعة الأستاذ عادل المحاسب، وتحين الفرصة لمحادثته — As for Salih, his duty will be to follow Prof Adil, the accountant, and to wait for an opportunity to talk to him

91 | 4947 |

821 حُزْن *n.* pl. أَحْزان sadness, grief, sorrow, anguish

كان رشدی شاحبا شحوب الموت، سكن الحزن العميق عينيه وترك ذقنه لكنها لم تطل كثيرا — Rushdi was pale as death; a deep sadness was in his eyes, and he let his beard grow, but it didn't get very long

89 | 5054 | +lit +for

822 مَریض *n.* pl. مَرْضَى patient, sick person; *adj.* ill, sick

مهمة هذه المصحة أن تساعد المرضى الميئوس من شفائهم.. الذین ینتظرون الموت — The mission of

this hospice is to help patients who can't be cured, who are awaiting death

98 | 4575 |

823 مُشْتَرَك *adj.* shared, common, joint, collective

طلبت منا خالتي أن نأتي بالماء من الحنفية المشتركة — التي أقیمت خصیصا وسط المخیمات My aunt asked us to bring water from the shared faucet that was especially set up in the middle of the camp

92 | 4868 |

824 جُمْهُورِیَّة *n.* republic

— تعرض رئیس الجمهوریة لمحاولة اغتیال The president of the republic was exposed to an assassination attempt

83 | 5372 |

825 واسِع *adj.* wide, broad, extensive, widespread

— ظلت هي فى الشقة الواسعة مع الولد She remained in the wide apartment with the child

98 | 4568 |

826 ده and دا /da/ (Egy.) *dem.pron.* this (masc.sg.)

حاسة برضه إنها حالمة جدا وده مع الاحساس العالي بتاعها ممكن یسبب لها مشاكل في الحیاة — I also feel that she is very day-dreamy, and that, along with her high level of sensitivity, could cause her problems in life

71 | 6304 |

827 قادِر *adj.* pl. -uun capable, able

لم یعد باستطاعته أن ینام بدون منوم، ولم یعد — قادرا على عمل أى شيء، لا باللیل ولا بالنهار He is no longer able to sleep without a sleeping pill, and he is no longer able to do anything, neither at night nor during the day

99 | 4522 |

828 حاكِم *n.* pl. حُكّام ruler, governor; *adj.* ruling, in power

نحن لا نرید من هؤلاء الحكام شیئا أكثر من أن یترکونا نعیش في وطننا — We don't want anything from those rulers more than to let us live in our homeland

96 | 4646 |

829 تَرْبِيَة *n.* education, pedagogy; raising,
child-rearing; breeding

قد عملنا ما بوسعنا لنوفر لها أحسن تربية —
We did what we could to provide her with
the best education

94 | 4731 |

830 جَبَل *n.* pl. جِبال mountain

بدأ الجليد يذوب من فوق الجبال واندلاح الضباب من
فوق الأرض — The snow on top of the
mountains started to melt, and the clouds
spread out over the earth

99 | 4501 |

831 أَطْلَقَ *v. IV* to let go, let out sth; to release, set
free سَراح sb; to fire, shoot النّار/الرَّصاص على at
sb; to call على sth/sb (ب a name)

أطلق فرناندو ضحكة عالية واحتضنها بقوة ورفعها
من على الأرض — Fernando let out a loud laugh
and embraced her strongly and lifted her off
the ground

89 | 4988 |

832 جَلْسَة *n.* pl. جَلَسات session, meeting; (court)
hearing

مجلس النواب الأردني أقر مشروع قانون منع الإرهاب
بعد جلسة استمرت ثلاث ساعات من النقاش —
The Jordanian Parliament passed a bill outlawing
terrorism following a debate session that lasted
three hours

95 | 4691 |

833 حَيّ *n.* pl. أَحْياء quarter, district

يطلعنا الكاتب على مجموعة الكنائس التي تحويها حي
القاهرة القديمة — The author informs us about
the group of churches which are in the Old
Cairo neighborhood

98 | 4532 |

834 عَدَّ *v. I (u)* to count, enumerate sth;
to consider, regard sth/sb as; لا يُعَدُّ
countless

عدد مقاهي الإنترنت يزيد على مائتي مقهى في
مدينة لا تعد كبيرة بمعايير المساحة — The
number of Internet cafés is more than two
hundred in a city which is not considered large
in surface area

91 | 4879 |

835 عافِيَة *n.* good health, vigor; يُعْطِيكُم العافِيَة (الله)
(lit.: may God give you good health) well
done! nice job!

عند الانتهاء من عمله يشكرونه ب «الله يعطيك العافية
يا معلم» — At the end of his work, they thank
him with "God give you health, teacher"

83 | 5312 | +for +spo

836 تِجارِيّ *adj.* commercial, business

السعودية تتجه إلى شراكة تجارية استراتيجية مع الصين
— Saudi Arabia is headed for a strategic
commercial partnership with China

91 | 4819 |

837 القُرْآن *n.* the Qur'an

أخذ يقرأ في سره شيئا من قصار السور بالقرآن علها
تريح أعصابه — He started to read to himself
some of the shorter chapters in the Qur'an so
that perhaps he could calm his nerves

94 | 4667 |

838 أُغْنِيَّة and أُغْنِيَة *n.* pl. أَغانٍ (def. أَغاني), (أُغْنِيات)
song, melody

استمعت خلال تلك الأسابيع القليلة لعدد من الأغاني
الحزينة يفوق ما استمعت إليه طوال حياتها —
During those few weeks she listened to
a number of sad songs, more of them than
she had listened to her whole life

95 | 4645 |

839 رَئِيسِيّ *adj.* main, chief, principal

التفت يمينا نحو الشارع الرئيسي.. كان نور القمر
يضيء كل شيء — He turned right toward the
main street; the light of the moon was lighting
everything

93 | 4715 |

840 كَأْس and كاس *n.* pl. كُؤُوس cup; Cup (in prize
names)

يحصل الفريق الفائز ببطولة كأس العالم على كأس ذهبية
— The team that wins the World Cup
championship gets a golden cup

93 | 4718 | +for

841 مُعْظَم *n.* (in idafa) most of, the majority of

تشتت ذهنه أكثر وأكثر حتى إنه لم يسمع معظم ما قالته
— His mind was scattered more and more until
he did not hear most of what she said

95 | 4617 |

842 شَكَّ *n.* pl. شُكُوك doubt; لا شَكَّ and بِلا شَكَّ without a doubt

كان رئيس جمهورية تونس.. الحبيب بورقيبة.. لا شك — أنكم جميعا تعرفونه It was the president of the Republic of Tunis, Habib Bourqiba. No doubt you all know of him

98 | 4487 |

843 لَعِب (also لِعْب or لَعِب) *vn.* playing; *n.* pl. ألْعاب game, sport

كانت الألعاب الأولمبية أبصرت النور في دورة أثينا العام ١٨٩٦ — The Olympic games first saw the light of day in the Athens tournament in the year 1896

97 | 4501 |

844 قَناة *n.* pl. قَنَوات canal; channel (broadcasting)

أوضح التقرير ان ايرادات قناة السويس خلال الفترة من يناير وحتى يوليو من العام الحالي بلغت ٢١٢١ مليار دولار — The report clarified that the income from the Suez Canal during the period from January to July of the current year reached 2121 billion dollars

94 | 4655 |

845 إنْتاج *n.* production, output

تعتزم شركة السيارات اليابانية «نيسان موتور» إقامة مصنع لإنتاج سيارات الركاب في الهند — The Japanese car company Nissan Motors intends to set up a factory to produce passenger cars in India

90 | 4817 |

846 حُصُول *vn.* obtaining, getting, acquiring; occurring, happening

هل تستمرون بالحصول على السلاح بعد الحرب لزيادة ترساناتكم؟ — Are you continuing to obtain weapons after the war to increase your arsenals?

87 | 4989 |

847 مُعَيَّن *adj.* specific, determined; fixed, set, prescribed; appointed, designated

هناك مذاهب معينة والسائل قد يكون من مذهب والمفتي من مذهب آخر — There are specific sects, and the requester might be from one sect and the mufti from another

97 | 4469 |

848 رَفْع *n.* raising, lifting, elevating; increasing, augmenting, boosting

اكتفيت برفع حاجبي ويدي إلى الأعلى — I contented myself with raising my eyebrows and my hand high

95 | 4577 |

849 بَسيط *adj.* pl. بُسَطاء simple, plain; naive, unsophisticated; easy, uncomplicated; insignificant (amount), trifle, pinch; (Lev.) *interj.* بَسيطَة no problem! no big deal!

قدم لنا الطعام القروي البسيط: زيتون ولبنة وجبن مع الشاي وخبز — He offered us simple village food: olives, drained yoghurt, cheese, with tea and bread

98 | 4418 |

850 عائلَة *n.* pl. -aat family, household, clan

لم تصدق العائلة أنه كان كل ذلك الوقت في جيش السلطة — The family did not believe that he was all that time in the army of the Authority

96 | 4514 |

851 عارف (Egy.Lev.Gul.) *a.p.* knowing (to know); (to be) familiar, acquainted (with sb)

قعدت أفتش في المعسكر إزاي أهرب لاقيت؟ نفسي مش عارف الشرق من الغرب — I kept searching in the camp; how could I flee? I found myself not knowing East from West

77 | 5577 | +spo

852 مَسْجِد *n.* pl. مَساجِد mosque

خلال شهرين على الأكثر سنصلي معا بإذن الله في المسجد الجديد — In two months, at the most, we will pray together with God's permission in the new mosque

88 | 4912 |

853 أيُّها *voc.part.* fem. أيَّتُها oh!

ضيفنا اليوم أيها الإخوة والأخوات هو الناطق الرسمي باسم حزب الأمة الكويتي — Our guest today, brothers and sisters, is the official spokesman for the Kuwaiti Al-Umma Party

84 | 5122 |

854 سَريع *adj.* quick, prompt; سَريعاً quickly, promptly

كان القطار سريعا أكثر مما ينبغي، ورفع العمال أيديهم بالتحية للجنود — The train was faster than necessary, and the workers raised their hands in greeting to the soldiers

98 | 4375 |

855 سَلامَة *n.* security, safety; integrity; مَعَ السَّلامَة goodbye!

قبلت زهرة قبلتين على خديها وتمنت لها السلامة فى السفر والسلامة فى الوضع — She kissed Zahra two kisses on her cheek and wished her safety on her trip and safety in giving birth

98 | 4387 |

856 ماليَّة *n.* finance

وقد بلغت كمية الأسهم المتداولة فى سوق البحرين للأوراق المالية خلال الأسبوع الماضى ٢٠,٧١ مليون سهم — The quantity of shares traded in the Bahrain Money Market during the last week was 20.71 million shares

80 | 5342 |

857 اتِّجاه *n.* pl. -aat direction; course; trend, movement

اندفعت بأقصى سرعة باتجاه محطة المترو.. تعمدت ألا تنظر حولها — She started off as fast as possible in the direction of the Metro station...She deliberately did not look around her

89 | 4800 |

858 نَقَلَ *v. I (u)* to transfer, transport sth; to transmit (news); to translate sth; نَقَلَتِ (الصَّحيفَةُ) عَنِ (الرَّئيسِ) قَوْلَهُ إنَّ (the newspaper) quoted (the President) as saying that

تم اعتقاله ونقل إلى جبل الطور مع المجرمين الذين يهددون الأمن وسلامة البلاد — He was arrested and transferred to Jabal Al-Tur with the criminals who threaten the security and safety of the country

97 | 4421 |

859 صَمْت *n.* silence

هكذا قال بحدة، فساد صمت ثقيل لم يقطعه سوى خرير المياه المتدفقة من النافورة — He said this sharply, and then a heavy silence reigned which

was only broken by the trickling water flowing from the fountain

89 | 4809 | +lit

860 سَعَى *v. I (a)* to strive إلى for sth; to pursue, chase وَراءَ after (a goal)

هل تسعى للحصول على مخالفة سرعة؟ — Are you trying to get a speeding ticket?

88 | 4841 |

861 أقامَ *v. IV* to install, establish, set up sth; to hold, host (event, party); to reside, live, set up residence فى at

ان المتحف يقام على مساحة ٤ آلاف متر مربع عند مدخل مدينة العريش — The museum is being erected on an area of 4 thousand square meters at the entrance to the city of Al-Arish

89 | 4800 |

862 خَوْف *n.* fear; خَوْفاً for fear (مِن of), fearing (على for)

لاحظ علامات الخوف والدهشة فى وجه صديقه — He noticed signs of fear and surprise on the face of his friend

99 | 4297 |

863 ضَوْء *n.* pl. أضْواء light, lamp; دَوْرِيّ الأضْواء Premier League

مع تزايد الضوء ظهرت أشكال جديدة، اختلطت فى البداية، لكنها لم تلبث أن انفصلت واتضحت شيئا فشيئا — With the increasing light, new forms appeared, all mixed together at first, but it was not long before they broke up, and became clear bit by bit

96 | 4426 |

864 بَدَل *n.* substitute; بَدَلاً مِن instead of, in lieu of

قاموا بإنزال العلم الأمريكى ورفعوا بدلا منه قميصا ملطخا بالدماء — They took down the American flag and raised in its place a shirt spotted with blood

99 | 4315 |

865 طِبِّيّ *adj.* medical

إنها بالرغم من دراستها الطبية لا تعرف شيئا عن أحاسيس الرجل — Despite her medical studies, she doesn't know anything about the feelings of men

95 | 4497 |

866 دائِرَة *n.* pl. دَوائِر office, bureau; district, circuit; circle, ring

ألم أقل لك إنه قد أوقعك في دائرة سحره.. وأبدل قلبك بقلب دجاجة؟ — Didn't I tell you that he has entrapped you in his circle of magic...and exchanged your heart with the heart of a chicken?

90 | 4742 |

867 رِئاسَة *n.* presidency, leadership, direction, chairmanship

منذ أن توليت رئاسة القسم تحمست دائما لقبول الطلبة المصريين لأنهم أذكياء ومجتهدون — Since I took over the leadership of the department, I have always been enthusiastic about accepting Egyptian students because they are smart and diligent

79 | 5379 |

868 اِرْتِفاع *n.* rise, increase; height, elevation

حذرت لجنة الصحة بمجلس الشعب من استمرار ارتفاع أسعار الدواء وعدم قدرة المرضى من محدودي الدخل على شرائها — The Health Committee warned in the People's Assembly against continuing to raise the prices of medicine, and about the lack of ability of patients of limited income to buy them

85 | 5004 |

869 عالِم *n.* pl. عُلَماء scientist, scholar; عُلَماء ulama (Muslim legal scholars); *a.p.* knowing, knowledgeable of

كان التلفزيون جهازا منكرا عند العلماء — The television was a device disapproved of by the religious scholars

91 | 4624 |

870 كَـ *prep.* as, like; كَالتّالي as follows; (occasionally written separately as كا in informal media)

بدت شاحبة كالأموات، ظلت ترتجف وتتنفس بعمق وتحاول استجماع نفسها — She looked pale, like the dead, and kept trembling and breathing deeply and trying to get control of herself

90 | 4708 | +lit

871 بَطَل *n.* pl. أَبْطال hero; (sports) champion; (film) star

يلعب لنادي الوحدات الاردني وتوج معه بطلا للدوري المحلي الموسم الفائت — He plays for the Jordanian Al-Wahdat Club, and along with it he was crowned champion of the local tournament last season

96 | 4386 |

872 خُرُوج *n.* departure, leaving; getting out, exit; deviation (عن from)

التقطت حقيبتها من فوق المقعد واتجهت إلى باب الخروج — She grabbed her bag from off the chair and headed for the exit door

90 | 4688 |

873 إعْلان *vn.* announcing, declaring; *n.* pl. -aat announcement, declaration, statement; advertisement, billboard

بعضها يقول إن الواجب هو قتال الأميركان والاصطفاف ضدهم وإعلان الجهاد عليهم — Some of them say that the duty is to fight the Americans and to line up against them and announce Holy War against them

88 | 4765 |

874 عَقَدَ *v. I (i)* to hold, conclude, convene (meeting)

عقدت سوريا اتفاقية تجارية مع الصين، واتفاقية مع ألمانيا الديمقراطية — Syria concluded a commercial agreement with China, and an agreement with Democratic Germany (East Germany)

88 | 4748 |

875 ثَمانِيَة *num. fem.* ثَمانِ (def.) ثَمانِيَةَ عَشَرَ eight; eighteen; ثمانية /tamaaniya/ (Egy.Lev.)

قامت وزارة الشئون الاجتماعية بتوزيع ثمانية آلاف زوج من الأحذية على الفلاحين بالقرى — The Ministry of Social Affairs distributed eight thousand pairs of shoes to the farmers in the villages

97 | 4296 |

876 ظِلّ *n.* pl. ظِلال shade; patronage; ظِلال auspices; ثَقيل الظِلّ unpleasant, disagreeable (person)

حاولت أن تؤدي دورها في ظل غياب السلطة — She tried to perform her role in light of the absence of authority

89 | 4710 |

877 سَجَّلَ *v. II* to register; to record (audio); to score (point)

لاذ الطبيب بالصمت.. وسجل بضع كلمات في الأوراق — The doctor remained silent, and recorded some words on the papers

97 | 4277 |

12 Professions

47	رئيس	president
96	وزير	minister
106	سياسيّ	politician
194	ربّ	owner, proprietor (also lord)
253	دكتور	doctor
270	طالب	student
335	عسكريّ	soldier
354	مسؤول	official
360	نائب	deputy, vice-
379	مدير	director
425	ملك	king
428	لاعب	player
534	قائد	leader
562	أستاذ	professor
589	أمير	prince, commander
604	فنّيّ	artist; technician
628	عامل	worker
636	شاعر	poet
644	طبيب	doctor
654	جنديّ	soldier
710	أمين	trustee; secretary
719	كاتب	writer; clerk
828	حاكم	ruler, governor
869	عالم	scientist, scholar
884	حكوميّ	government officer
899	معلّم	teacher
903	ممثّل	representative; actor
915	موظّف	employee
925	فنّان	artist
939	صحفيّ	journalist
1008	ضابط	officer
1015	سفير	ambassador
1075	إعلاميّ	media worker
1102	إمام	Imam
1134	مهندس	engineer
1173	زعيم	leader
1221	قاضٍ	judge

1247	خبير	expert
1255	مدرّب	coach
1282	باحث	researcher
1417	حارس	guard, goalie
1487	ركن	chief of staff (also corner)
1514	وكيل	agent
1519	متخصّص	specialist
1615	محافظ	governor
1658	مساعد	assistant
1662	تاجر	businessman
1751	صحافيّ	journalist
1771	رائد	pioneer; major
1805	لواء	major general
1817	حامل	bearer, porter
1826	محام	lawyer
1842	مشرّف	supervisor
1926	فاعل	doer
1948	حكيم	wise man; doctor
1956	مضيف	host, steward
1959	سائق	driver
1978	مستشار	counselor, adviser
2026	مختصّ	specialist
2039	مجاهد	fighter
2048	كهربائيّ	electrician
2049	عميل	agent; operative, spy; client
2062	مؤلّف	author, composer
2129	خادم	servant
2147	دبلوماسيّ	diplomat
2160	جنرال	general
2165	منتج	manufacturer
2196	مدرّس	teacher
2225	مولى	master, patron
2263	مستثمر	investor
2319	مخرج	director
2383	عميد	dean; brigadier general

2401	مراقب	inspector; censor
2416	تلميذ	student
2482	حرس	guard
2570	موسيقيّ	musician
2707	فارس	horseman; knight
2751	خليفة	successor; caliph
2840	كادر	cadre, staff
2872	محترف	professional
2972	مندوب	delegate; agent
2990	مدافع	defender
3029	عقيد	colonel
3073	محقّق	investigator; editor
3074	قياديّ	leader
3204	أديب	author
3284	منظّم	organizer
3345	فلّاح	farmer
3350	معلّق	commentator
3373	مفتي	mufti
3389	شرطيّ	policeman
3400	ساحر	magician
3409	عماد	major general
3484	مطرب	musician, singer
3499	صانع	manufacturer
3529	ناقد	critic
3857	مقاتل	combatant
3877	نقيب	union boss; captain
3932	مزارع	farmer
3951	محلّل	analyst
3959	استشاريّ	consultant
4059	روائيّ	novelist
4081	حكم	referee
4103	مبعوث	envoy
4132	مراسل	reporter
4189	مساهم	shareholder
4265	مصوّر	photographer
4294	مدّع	prosecutor
4304	مذيع	announcer
4308	لصّ	thief
4507	مختار	village chief

4534	بروفسور	professor	5786	مطران	archbishop	7101	دهّان	painter
4547	كابتن	captain	5956	معين	assistant; supporter	7131	مسيّر	director
4568	مرشد	guide				7191	حبر	pontiff
4638	حامٍ	guardian; patron	6041	حافظ	guardian; knows Qurʾan	7210	معدّ	preparer, editor
4699	ناشر	publisher	6147	ساحرة	witch	7231	قوّاد	procurer, pimp
4716	ممرّض	nurse	6183	نجّار	carpenter			
4737	رقيب	inspector; censor; sergeant	6186	بحّار	sailor	7276	ساقي	water carrier
			6274	خطيب	orator	7466	مشغّل	operator
			6295	حدّاد	blacksmith	7517	منظّر	theoretician; critic
4798	ملّا	Muslim cleric	6316	علّام	expert			
4813	متطوّع	volunteer	6342	طيّار	pilot	7570	مقرّر	reporter
4867	والٍ	ruler	6475	قابلة	midwife	7636	عمدة	mayor
5121	فيلسوف	philosopher	6486	سوّاق	driver	7717	محسّن	beautician
5200	سكرتير	secretary	6487	حلّاق	barber	7728	محضّر	technician
5409	مغنّي	singer	6498	راهبة	nun	7758	نقّاش	sculptor
5468	مؤرّخ	historian	6542	هادي	leader, guide	7761	أراجوز	puppeteer
5481	جهاديّ	Jihadist	6626	شوفير	chauffeur	7765	حذّاء	shoemaker
5555	ملحق	attaché	6706	محاسب	accountant	7768	سارق	thief
5612	منفّذ	executor	6708	رئيس	chief, boss	7812	محصّل	cashier
5640	هدّاف	sharpshooter	6736	كوافيرة	hairdresser	7816	جمّال	camel driver
5675	منتدب	deputized	6754	مراجع	reviewer	7826	محاضر	lecturer
5678	محرّر	editor; liberator	6775	ميكانيكيّ	mechanic	7896	مفصّل	commentator
			6838	متعهّد	contractor	7928	خوريّ	priest
5713	جارية	housemaid	6852	صيدليّ	pharmacist	7950	قمّاش	cloth merchant
5724	جرّاح	surgeon	6920	دلّال	auctioneer; real estate agent	7955	بوّاب	doorman
5737	فرّاش	janitor				7956	ملّاح	sailor
5754	داعية	missionary; propagandist	7074	خدّام	worker			

878 أُرْدُنّيّ (Dia. /ʾurduni/) *n./adj.* Jordanian
لا يحق لأحد أن يتحدث باسم الشعب الأردني إلا البرلمان الأردني — No one has the right to speak in the name of the Jordanian people except the Jordanian parliament
86 | 4853 |

879 ساحَة *n.* pl. -aat scene; field, arena
إذا تزوجها سيتحول بيتها إلى ساحة معارك — If he marries her, their home will be transformed into a battle field
89 | 4652 |

880 عَصْر *n.* pl. عُصُور age, period, time, epoch
انتهى عصر البطولات والشهادة، هذا عصر الكولا والهمبرغر والأمراء الوطاويط — The age of heroism and martyrdom has ended; this is the age of cola, hamburgers and (comic book) superheroes (lit. "bat princes")
97 | 4253 |

881 نَوَويّ *adj.* nuclear, atomic; nucleic
إن الأسلحة النووية التي بحوزة أميركا اليوم لا تتماشى ومتطلبات العالم الحديث — The nuclear weapons which America has today are not consistent with the requirements of the modern world
79 | 5190 |

882 فِرْقَة *n.* pl. فِرَق group, team, troupe; (music) band, ensemble; (mil.) division, squad
من هم أعضاء الفرقة الذين يعزفون معك؟ — Who are the members of the ensemble that play with you?
96 | 4274 |

883 قَرْن *n.* pl. قُرُون century, age; horn
كيف ظلت هذه الأعمال النادرة بعيدة عن الأضواء قرابة قرن من الزمان؟ — How did these rare works stay far from the limelight for almost a century?

88 | 4700 |

884 حُكُومِيّ *adj.* governmental, state; official; *n.* state or government officer
من الذي يقاتل التكفيريين أم قوات الاحتلال أم القوات الحكومية العراقية؟ — Who is fighting the Takfiris? The occupation forces or the Iraqi government forces?

88 | 4659 |

885 رُؤْيَة *n.* vision, sight; view, viewing; perspective, view, opinion
لا بد أن نحل مشكلة الرؤية العربية أن هناك عدم توازن نووي — It is necessary that we solve the problem of the Arab viewpoint that there is no nuclear balance

89 | 4610 |

886 تِجَارَة *n.* commerce, business
يميل معظمهم إلى التجارة ويحبون جمع المال الجم بكل السبل المشروعة وغير المشروعة — Most of them are leaning toward business and they love to make lots of money by all means, legal and illegal

96 | 4265 |

887 تَابَعَ *v. III* to continue, follow sth/sb; to monitor, keep an eye on sth/sb
هو يحب مصر لدرجة أنه يتابع كل ما يجري فيها باهتمام بالغ — He loves Egypt so much that he follows everything that happens in it with extreme interest

98 | 4186 |

888 تَصْرِيح *n.* pl. -aat declaration, statement
ماذا تريد أكثر من هذا؟ لقد أعلن في تصريح رسمي أن إسرائيل سرطان — What do you want more than this? He announced in an official statement that Israel is a cancer

83 | 4918 |

889 وَقْف *vn.* stopping, ceasing; *n.* pl. أَوْقاف waqf (Islamic religious endowment)
إن السبيل الوحيد لوقف كل ذلك أن تغادرنا فورا وتعود إلى روما — The only way to stop all this is for you to leave us immediately and return to Rome

93 | 4417 |

890 صِرَاع *n.* pl. -aat struggle, conflict, fight
حدث صراع شفوي أول الأمر، تحول إلى عراك وضرب بالأيدي — A verbal conflict occurred at first, then changed to a battle and blows with fists

88 | 4642 |

891 تَعَامُل *n.* pl. -aat working, doing business (مع with); relations, (business) dealings
استبعد ـ في تصريحات له ـ امكان تعامل الولايات المتحدة مع حكومة الوحدة الوطنية الفلسطينية المقترحة — In his statements he thought the possibility of the United States dealing with the suggested Palestinian Unity Government unlikely

89 | 4559 |

892 عَهْد *n.* pl. عُهُود age, period; tenure, administration, reign; treaty, pact, promise, oath; وَلِّي العَهْد crown prince
هناك تشريعات ثقيلة اصدرها صدام في عهده حيث تم تأسيس اسس الفساد والتمييز الطائفي والعنصري — There were heavy regulations which Saddam issued in his era such that the bases of corruption and sectarian and racial discrimination were established

88 | 4637 |

893 كُلِّيَّة *n.* pl. -aat college, institute, faculty; entirety, totality
التحق بكلية الهندسة لتفوقه ودرس التمثيل بمعهد الفنون المسرحية — He joined the College of Engineering because of his superior standing, and he studied acting in the Institute of Theatrical Arts

96 | 4225 |

894 ثِقَة *n.* confidence, trust
المهم أصبحت أكثر ثقة بنفسي — The important thing is that I became more self-confident

99 | 4126 |

895 ضَبْط *n.* adjusting; regulating; seizure, confiscation; بالضبط (at) exactly; /bi-z-zabT/ (Egy.Lev.) *interj./adv.* exactly

وفى صباح تلك الليلة الاخيرة لمجد الدين، بالضبط فى الساعة الرابعة وخمس وأربعين دقيقة، بدأ الهجوم الكبير — In the morning of that last night for Magd Al-Din, at exactly 4:45, the big attack began

98 | 4157 |

896 سَمَّى *v. II* to name, designate, call

قد عالج ابن خلدون فى كتابه ما نسميه الآن «الظواهر الاجتماعية» — Ibn Khaldoun treated this in his book what we now call "the social phenomena"

97 | 4171 |

897 زَيّ (Egy.Lev.) *prep.* like, as, similar to; (with pron.) زَيِّي like me; زي ما as much as

انت تعترف ثقافة وحضارة زي ما انت عاوز.. بس بعيد عني — You can consume culture as much as you want...just far away from me

81 | 4991 | +spo

898 عانَى *v. III* to suffer sth or من from sth

الشعب الموريتاني عانى الكثير من نظام ولد الطايع — The Mauritanian people have suffered a lot from the regime of Wuld Al-Tayi

89 | 4558 |

899 مُعَلِّم *n.* pl. -uun teacher, instructor; master (of a trade); foreman, boss, chief

وقف المعلم أمام طلابه شارحا لهم طبيعة المهمة التي تنتظرهم — The teacher stood in front of his students explaining to them the nature of the task which awaited them

98 | 4143 |

900 هَلا /hala/ and ياهلا /ya-hala/ (Lev.Irq.Gul.) *interj.* welcome! hello!

هلا فيج ويا مرحبا وحياج الله — Welcome to you, welcome, God greet you

62 | 6553 |

901 عُنْف *n.* violence, force

انطلق بسرعة نحو الباب.. دق الجرس بعنف وبلا انقطاع، وأخذ يخبط الباب بكفيه وقدميه بأقصى ما يستطيع — He headed quickly for the door...He rang the doorbell violently and without ceasing, and he began to pound on the door with his palms and his feet with everything he had in him

89 | 4537 |

902 طَبِيعَة *n.* nature, character; normal, natural (state)

هل تعرف طبيعة أهل الفتاة؟ هناك مسيحيون — طيبون وهناك مسيحيون غير طيبين Do you know the nature of the family of the girl? There are good Christians and there are bad Christians

99 | 4090 |

903 مُمَثِّل *adj.* representing, acting on behalf of; *n.* pl. -uun representative, delegate; actor; مُمَثِّلَة pl. -aat actress

قرر قادة الحلف الأطلسي، بإجماع أعضائها، باستثناء ممثل الولايات المتحدة الأمريكية، قرروا تجميد عضوية أمريكا — The leadership of NATO decided unanimously, with the exception of the delegate of the United States of America, to suspend America's membership

86 | 4670 |

904 عِبارَة *n.* pl. -aat expression; phrase, word; بِعِبارَةٍ أُخْرَى in other words

هي عبارة عن منازل مبنية من الطين وتشتمل على ساعة شمسية — They are a kind of house built of adobe and they contain sun clocks

96 | 4174 |

905 صَفّ *n.* pl. صُفُوف line, row, rank; class, classroom

نزلت من الطائرة ووقفت فى صف طويل حتى وصلت إلى ضابط الجوازات الذى فحص أوراقى مرتين — I got off the plane and stood in a long line until I arrived at the passport officer who examined my papers twice

97 | 4139 |

906 تَحْرِير *n.* liberation; editorship, editing

شغل منصب رئيس تحرير لأكثر من مجلة سياسية واجتماعية عربية — He occupied the position of editor in chief for more than one Arab social and political magazine

87 | 4588 |

907 بريطانيّ *n./adj.* pl. -uun British

بعد الاحتلال البريطاني استأنف الشيخ الصالح مع أصدقائه تأسيس مدرسة وطنية — After the British occupation, Sheikh Salih resumed founding a nationalist school with his friends

82 | 4863 |

908 مَضَى *v. I (i)* to pass, go by, elapse (time); to continue (في) doing sth; to proceed, go إلى/نحو to/towards

— مضى إلى النافذة ينظر إلى الحارة في الليل
He went to the window looking at the alley at night

89 | 4502 | +lit

909 سُمُوّ *n.* loftiness, nobility; (in titles) His/Her Highness

ياله من موقف رجولي يدل على الثقة بالنفس وسمو الأخلاق.. كانت خطبة مميزة — What a manly stance, which is a sign of self-confidence and high moral standards...It was a distinguished sermon

77 | 5183 |

910 فَتْح *n.* opening; beginning; conquest (esp. in Islamic history)

سمحوا له بفتح ملهى صغير في الغابة جنوب المدينة — They permitted the opening of a small night club in the forest south of the city

88 | 4517 |

911 خَطَر *n. pl.* أَخْطار danger, threat; risk, hazard; alarm (signal), warning (sign)

نقترب من بغداد أعلى نقطة خطر في المشوار كله — We are approaching Baghdad, the most dangerous point in the whole journey

96 | 4179 |

912 مُباشِر *adj.* direct, immediate; live (broadcast)

مصر تحتاج الآن إلى العمل الوطني المباشر أكثر بكثير من احتياجها إلى مدرسين ومحاسبين — Egypt now needs direct national work a lot more than it needs teachers and accountants

95 | 4192 |

913 تَقْريب *n.* approximation; تَقْريباً approximately, around; almost, not quite

إنها يعرفانه جيدا، يقابلانه كل يوم تقريبا يعطيانه شيئًا مما أعطاها الجنود — They know him well, they meet him almost every day and give him something from what the soldiers gave them

96 | 4137 |

914 نَصّ *n. pl.* نُصُوص text; wording; نَصّاً وَرُوحاً in letter and spirit

ينبغي أن يكون مضمون النص قادرا على كسب ثقة الأطفال واحترامهم وإيمانهم بفائدتها — The contents of the text must gain the trust and respect of the children, as well as their faith in its benefits

88 | 4548 |

915 مُوَظَّف *n. pl.* -uun employee

ركاب المترو في تلك الساعة خليط من عمال نظافة يذهبون لتنظيف أماكن العمل قبل حضور الموظفين، وسكارى متشردين قضوا ليل في العربة — The metro riders at that hour were a mixture of janitors going to clean work places before the arrival of the employees, and drunk homeless people who had spent the night revelling

97 | 4098 |

916 صَفْحَة *n. pl.* صَفَحات page; leaf

قرأ عدة صفحات من القرآن وبدأ صوته يرتفع قليلا وهو يختم سورة «المؤمنون» — He read a number of pages from the Qurʾan and his voice began to rise a little as he finished the Surah "Al-Muʾminuun"

94 | 4220 |

917 مُسَلَّح *n. pl.* -uun gunman; *adj.* armed, bearing arms; armored, reinforced

اكد مصدر في الشرطة ان مسلحين مجهولين خطفوا صباح امس سائقين ايرانيين لشاحنات تنقل الغاز السائل — A police source confirmed that unknown gunmen kidnapped two Iranian truck drivers transporting liquid gas yesterday morning

77 | 5138 | +news

918 حَمْلَة *n. pl.* حَمَلات campaign, expedition; attack, raid

أصبح على المرشح أن يتحدث عن مدى تدينه في الحملة الانتخابية — Candidates now feel the need to speak about their level of religiosity during election campaigns

87 | 4553 |

919 باقٍ (الباقي) *adj. pl.* باقُون remaining, lasting; *n.* remainder, remnant

ثلاث دول صوتت معه والباقي امتنع عن التصويت — Three countries voted with it, and the rest abstained

98 | 4053 |

920 شَكَرَ *v. I (u)* to thank, give thanks to sb;
كُلْ وَاشْكُرْ Kul Wa-Ishkur (a type of baklava
pastry; lit. eat and be thankful)
في نهاية الحديث أحب أشكر ضيوفي من
جدة ومن الأردن ومن القاهرة — In closing
our conversation, I would like to thank our
guests from Jidda and from Jordan and
from Cairo
94 | 4188 | +for

921 لَعَلَّ *conj.* perhaps, maybe; (with pron.) لَعَلِّي
perhaps I, maybe I
الرنين استمر حتى انقطع، لم ترد، لعلها
تنام بعد الظهر كعادتها — The ringing
continued until he hung up. She did not
answer. Perhaps she was sleeping in the
afternoon as usual
95 | 4167 |

922 تَدْرِيب *vn.* training, coaching; practicing;
n. pl. -aat exercise, drill, practice session
المياه أفضل وسط لتدريب الرياضيين ولعلاج
إصابات الملاعب — Water is the best
medium to train athletes and to treat
sports injuries
91 | 4334 |

923 قِرَاءَة *n.* reading; recitation; interpretation;
قراية /qraya/ (Alg.) education, studying
أليس من الأجدى أن نركز جهودنا لتعليمهم
القراءة والكتابة؟ — Isn't it better that we
concentrate our efforts on teaching them
to read and write?
98 | 4015 |

924 جَلَسَ *v. I (i)* to sit (down); to sit إلى at
(a table); to sit على on/upon sth
جلس أمام الكمبيوتر ووجد نفسه يمحو ما كتبه
ويبدأ صيغة أخرى — He sat down in front
of the computer and found himself erasing
what he had written and beginning in another
way
88 | 4487 | +lit

925 فَنَّان *n.* fem. -a, pl. -uun artist
بماذا يحس الفنان عندما ينجز عملا جديدا؟ — What
does the artist feel when he accomplishes a
new work?
92 | 4297 |

926 تَكَلَّمَ *v. V* to speak (a language); to speak مع
with sb (على/حول/عن about)
اندفع يتكلم بسرعة وحرارة كأنما يلقى بحمل ثقيل
He started speaking quickly and passionately as
if throwing off a heavy burden
97 | 4053 |

927 أَحْمَر *adj.* fem. حَمْراء, pl. حُمْر red
رأت أمامها دكانا ذا واجهة حمراء، عليه كتابة سوداء
كبيرة — She saw in front of her a shop with a
red façade, on which was a large black sign
99 | 3966 |

928 بَقِيَّة *n. pl.* بَقَايا remainder, left over, remnant;
end, ending, conclusion (article or story)
كان مثل بقية العمال، يحب الغداء والراحة في البيت
He was like the rest of the workers, he liked to
eat lunch and rest at home
99 | 3986 |

929 أَلَم *n. pl.* آلام pain, hurt; suffering
التمعت عيناها متناسية ما بها من تعب وألم —
Her eyes glowed, oblivious to her fatigue and
pain
90 | 4385 |

930 نَوْم *n.* sleep
راح يصدر شخيرا مزعجا، لكنه كان ينهض فجأة من
نومه فزعا يمسح لعابه الذى سال على جانبى فمه ثم
ينام مرة أخرى — He started to snore noisily, but
he woke suddenly from his sleep in a panic,
wiping the saliva that had spilled out of the
sides of his mouth, and then he went to sleep
again
97 | 4064 |

931 ضَمَّ *v. I (u)* to include, incorporate sth
ويضم المتحف مخطوطات قرآنية تعود إلى الأندلس —
The museum includes Qur'anic manuscripts
which go back to Andalusia
89 | 4427 |

932 ما *part.* (durative) ما دامَ as long as, provided
that; ما لَمْ as long as...(do/does) not
قال إنه ملتزم بهذه التوجيهات ما لم تصدر تعليمات
أخرى غير ذلك — He said he would adhere to
these guidelines as long as different instructions
were not issued
72 | 5477 |

933 عَشان and عِشان (Egy.Lev.Gul.) *conj.* because, in
order to; *prep.* for the sake of; (from على شأن)
ده أنا عاوزه ربع ساعة على الأقل عشان أعمل مكياج
— I need a quarter hour, at least, to put on my
make-up

49 | 7933 | +for +spo

934 دَليل *n.* pl. دَلائل, أَدِلَّة sign, clue, indication,
evidence, proof (على of); pl. أَدِلَّة guide,
handbook
الحفاظ على المواعيد دليل الإيمان والمروءة، أليس كذلك
يا أبا مروان؟ — Keeping appointments is an
evidence of faith and honor, isn't that so, Abu
Marwan?

96 | 4078 |

935 رَغْبَة *n.* pl. رَغَبات wish, desire
حدث منذ أيام معدودة أن شعرت برغبة في المشي
وحدي على رغم البرد والظلام، فخرجت — It
happened a few days ago that I felt a desire to
walk by myself despite the cold and darkness,
so I went out

98 | 3997 |

936 تَوَقَّف *v.* V to stop, halt; to be dependent,
conditional على on (sb's will)
طلبت من زميلي ان نتوقف في وسط المركز لعل احد
الموظفين ينتبه لوجودنا — I requested from my
colleague that we stand still in the middle of
the center so perhaps one of the (center)
employees would become aware of our existence

95 | 4121 |

937 قائم *a.p.* carrying out ب (task, activity); playing
ب (a role); *adj.* ongoing, present; standing
كتبت هذه القصة بناء على التصور القائم في ذهني
لميدان رمسيس — I wrote this story based on
the image of Ramses Square that exists in
my mind

86 | 4520 |

938 لِمَ *prep.phr.* to what, for what
عندئذ انتبه جيف لما يحدث واندفع نحو رأفت ليمسك
به — At that point Jeff paid attention to what
was happening and he rushed toward Ra'fat to
grab him

89 | 4361 |

939 صُحُفِيّ *adj.* journalistic, press; *n.* journalist,
reporter
نشر عشرات المقالات الصحفية في الادب والفن

والنقد — He published scores of newspaper
articles on literature, art, and criticism

84 | 4642 |

940 صَهْيُونِيّ *n./adj.* Zionist
وبدأت الحركات الدينية والحركات الاجتماعية في
الكيان الصهيوني تصطدم مع الأكاديميين حول تراث
الصهيونية — The religious movements and the
social movements in the Zionist entity began
to clash with the academics about the Zionist
heritage

79 | 4882 |

941 مَحَطَّة *n.* pl. -aat station (gas, electrical power,
broadcasting); stop, layover
أخذ القطار طريقه إلى الصحراء في المساء فلم يتوقف
في المحطات ولم يصادف عمالا حتى وصل إلى مرسى
مطروح بعد يومين — The train made its way to
the desert in the evening and didn't stop at
the stations and didn't encounter any workers
until it arrived at Marsa Matruh two days later

97 | 3999 |

942 مِلْيار *num.* pl. -aat billion (Fr. milliard)
وضعت أمريكا أكبر ميزانية للحرب، خمسين مليار
دولار للصناعات الحربية والعمليات العسكرية —
America passed the biggest budget for the war,
fifty billion dollars for war industries and
military operations

80 | 4803 |

943 دِيمُوقراطِيّ and دِيمُقراطِيّ *adj.* democratic; *n.* pl.
-uun democrat; Democrat
يعيش في سلام، متمتعا بمزايا الحياة الديموقراطية —
He lives in peace, enjoying the privileges of
democratic life

78 | 4961 |

944 إيرانِيّ *n./adj.* pl. -uun Iranian
قالوا ان الحرب الامريكيه على العراق منحت الايرانيين
واتباعهم فرصه تاريخيه لتحقيق تلك الاهداف —
They said that the American war on Iraq gave
the Iranians and their followers a historic
opportunity to accomplish these goals

71 | 5424 |

945 إِصْلاح *n.* pl. -aat reform, restoration; إصلاحات
corrections, amendments
خليك في حالك ولا تحاول إصلاح الكون — Stay as
you are and don't try to reform the world

87 | 4424 |

946 أَداء *n.* performance, execution; rendering, carrying out; fulfillment, satisfaction

لم أستطع أداء واجبي المادي تجاههم كتأمين الدواء والخبز والتعليم — I wasn't able to perform my material duty towards them, like guaranteeing medicine, bread, and education

88 | 4402 |

947 شَعْر *coll.n.* hair, *un.n.* شَعْرَة, pl. شُعُور (rare)

كانت الاختصاصية النفسية عجوزا أشبه بجدة طيبة، شعرها أبيض تماما وقصير ينساب على جانبي رأسها الصغير — The psychological specialist was an older woman, something like a kind grandmother; her hair was completely white and short, flowing down the sides of her small head

93 | 4154 |

948 نَفْط and نِفْط *n.* petroleum, (mineral) oil

هي تنتج في حدود ٤ مليون برميل من النفط الخام يوميا — It produces in the range of 4 million barrels of crude oil a day

82 | 4684 |

949 صالح *n.* advantage, interest; *adj.* suitable, applicable; pious, upright, righteous

بعد هذه العملية يصبح العصير صالحا للاستهلاك والحفظ — After this operation the juice becomes suitable for consumption and preservation

90 | 4284 |

950 سُلْطان *n.* Sultan; power, authority (على over)

أعيد فتح الجامع للعبادة في عهد السلطان سليم الثالث — The mosque was reopened for worship during the era of Sultan Selim III

95 | 4015 |

951 ما *rel.pron.* (in apposition, after indef. noun) a certain, some, any; إلى حَدٍّ ما to a certain extent; نَوْعاً ما somewhat

مدت ذراعيها جانبا وكأنها تتأهب لاحتضان شخص ما — She stretched out her arms to the sides as if she were about to embrace some person

72 | 5345 |

952 تَغَيَّر *v. V* to change, be modified

كان وجهها الجميل تتغير تعبيراته أحيانا على نحو غامض — The expressions of her beautiful face changed occasionally in a mysterious way

99 | 3855 |

953 شامِل *adj.* comprehensive, thorough; extensive, sweeping, global; full, complete

أدركت إدارة البنك مدى الحاجة إلى تقديم مجموعة شاملة ومتكاملة من الخدمات المصرفية للأفراد والشركات والمؤسسات وفقا لأحكام الشريعة — The bank administration realized the extent of the need to offer a complete and comprehensive group of banking services to individuals and companies and establishments according to Islamic rulings

94 | 4050 |

954 نَجَحَ *v. I (a)* to succeed

لقد انتهى القتال مع نهاية نوفمبر ولم ينجح روميل في الاستيلاء على طبرق لكنه أوقع بالحلفاء خسائر كبيرة — The fighting ended at the end of November and Rommel did not succeed in taking control of Tabruk, but he did cause huge losses for the Allies

98 | 3891 |

955 جُمْعَة *n.* الجُمْعَة (يَوْم) Friday

اليوم صلى الملك فاروق صلاة الجمعة في مسجد مصطفى أودة باشا بشارع الفتوح بالجمرك — Today King Farouq prayed Friday prayer in the mosque of Mustafa Odah Pasha in Al-Futuh Street in Al-Gumruk

98 | 3911 |

956 شَهادَة *n.* pl. -aat certificate, degree; testimony, witness

أكدت له أنني عملت سكرتيرة تنفيذية لسنوات وأن معي شهادات خبرة.. لكنه صرفني بإشارة من يده وكأنني خادمة — I assured him that I worked as an executive secretary for years and that I had (professional) experience certificates...but he dismissed me with a flick of his hand, as if I were a servant

98 | 3904 |

957 تابِع *adj.* belonging ل to; attached ل to, associated ل with; *n.* pl. -uun adherent, follower; التابعون contemporaries of the Prophet Muhammad

صادرت الحكومة البن من الأسواق، معلنة ان تجارته ستكون تابعة للحكومة نفسها لتزويد الجيوش — The government seized the coffee beans from the market, announcing that trade in coffee beans would be handled by the government itself, in order to supply the armies

94 | 4036 |

958 خِلاف *n.* pl. -aat dispute, conflict; disagreement, difference (في الرَّأْي of opinion) لم تعد تتذكر الخلاف بينهما، نسيت مشاكلهما واتفاقهما على الطلاق — She no longer remembered the disagreement between them, she forgot their problems and their agreement to divorce

96 | 3966 |

959 اِخْتِيار *n.* choice, selection; election; preference المجتمع الأمريكي يعتمد على التلفزيون في تكوين آرائه بدءا من اختياره للطعام، وصولا إلى اختياره للرأي — American society relies on television to form its opinions, all the way from choosing foods to choosing opinions

89 | 4296 |

960 ذِكْرَى *n.* pl. ذِكْرَيات remembrance, memory; anniversary; ذِكْرَيات memoirs, diary طارت بها الذكريات إلى منزلها في الرياض — Memories took her back to her house in Riyadh

95 | 4001 |

961 زَيْن *adj.* beautiful, lovely, pretty, charming; (Irq.Gul.) /zeen/ *adj.* pl. -iin good, fine, okay ألو، كيف حالكم؟ - الحمد لله، زنين. شنو علومكم؟ زنين، الله يسلمك، زنين — Hello, how are you? – Praise God, (we're) doing fine. What's new? – (We're) fine, thanks, fine

71 | 5343 | +spo

962 مَبْلَغ *n.* pl. مَبالِغ amount, sum (of money); extent, degree; scope, range استطاع أن يهرب بمبلغ مالي كبير بدأ به حياته الجديدة — He was able to escape with a large amount of money with which he began his new life

97 | 3913 |

963 جَسَد *n.* pl. أَجْساد body وقف وسط الحجرة رجل مصري يناهز الستين، جسده رياضي فارع ممشوق، وشعره أبيض مفروق من منتصف الرأس — In the middle of the room stood an Egyptian man, around sixty, of athletic build, tall and lean, with white hair, parted in the middle

89 | 4224 |

964 رَجا *v. I* (u) to hope for sth; to request sth من from sb; يُرْجَى الاتِّصال بـ (would you) please contact; أَرْجُوكَ please! — أرجو ألا تستغرب إجابتي.. أنا في الحقيقة شاعر I hope that my answer will not surprise you... I am, in fact, a poet

86 | 4383 | +for

965 ـش *part.* (Dia. suffix, negative marker) not; ما كانش he/it wasn't; بَعْرَفِش/ماعْرَفْش I don't know; ما بانامش.. مانامتش.. مانمتش من ساعة ما نزلت من الطيارة — I can't sleep...I haven't slept... I haven't slept since the moment I got off the plane

67 | 5610 | +spo

---

13 Colors

498	لون	color	3522	ملوّن	colored	7075	بيج	beige
564	أبيض	white	3703	بياض	whiteness	7116	خضر	green
682	أسود	black	4164	بنّي	brown	7286	صفر	brass
927	أحمر	red	4452	أسمر	brown-skinned	7392	حائل	dusky, pale
987	أخضر	green	5010	خافت	light	7571	أشقر	blond
1692	ذهبيّ	golden	5353	رماديّ	ashen, gray	7574	فيروز	turquoise
1754	أزرق	blue	5782	تألّق	to sparkle	7682	صفار	yellowness
2099	أصفر	yellow	6518	لوّن	to colorize	7759	أبلق	black and white
2577	فاتح	clear	6629	احمرّ	to turn red			
3322	سواد	blackness	6834	حالك	dark	7967	اسودّ	to become black
3515	ورديّ	rose-colored	6962	شقر	blond			

966 كِتابَة *n.* pl. -aat writing; script; essay, piece of writing

كان همنجواي أهم روائي فى عصره، ولما عجز عن الكتابة انتحر — Hemingway was the most important novelist of his age, and when he became incapable of writing, he committed suicide

88 | 4267 |

967 إنْشاء *vn.* establishing, setting up, founding; إنْشاء الله substandard spelling of إن شاء الله

— تعمدت السلطات إنشاء المساكن الرخيصة للفقراء The authorities were determined to build houses for the poor

84 | 4444 |

968 سَيِّدَة *n.* pl. -aat lady

قدمت السيدة عزيزة أمير الشكر للشعب المصرى على صفحات الصحف لتشجيعه لفيلمها الجديد — Mrs Aziza Amir offered thanks to the Egyptian people on the pages of newspapers for their encouragement of her new film

89 | 4204 |

969 اِقْتِصاد *n.* economy; saving

لماذا لا نبني اقتصاد الأمة ونعيد مجدها الغابر؟ — Why don't we build the economy of the nation and restore its past glory?

88 | 4227 |

970 مَعْرَكَة *n.* pl. مَعارك battle, campaign

حل موعد نوم مونتجمرى فدخل إلى مكمنه مطمئنا ونام بينها ظل العالم كله يقظا ينتظر المعركة الفاصلة — Montgomery's time to sleep had come, so he entered into his chamber confidently and went to sleep while the whole world stayed awake waiting for the decisive battle

92 | 4030 |

971 بارَكَ *v. III* to bless فى sb (of God); to send blessings على upon (of God, usu. on the Prophet)

الله يبارك فيج ويحفظج إن شاء الله — May God bless you and protect you, I hope

90 | 4141 | +for

972 رَحْمَة *n.* mercy, compassion

الدين نعمة البشرية وهو يدعو للحب والرحمة — Religion is a blessing for mankind, calling for love and mercy

98 | 3796 |

973 طائِرَة *n.* pl. -aat aircraft, airplane

هدد هتلر إنجلترا بأنه سيقضى عليها بألف طائرة كل يوم — Hitler threatened England (by saying) that he would annihilate it with a thousand planes a day

88 | 4225 |

974 كُلَّما *conj.* (with perf. verb) whenever; the more (this)...the more (that)

كلما زادت فترة الرضاعة الطبيعية كانت الفائدة اكبر — The longer natural nursing lasts, the greater the benefit

89 | 4144 |

975 دَمْع *coll.n.* tears, *un.n.* دَمْعَة teardrop, pl. دُمُوع tears, teardrops

تطلعت إليه بعينين مغرورقتين بالدموع فغمره الإشفاق عليها — She looked at him with eyes drowning in tears, and he was overcome by sympathy for her

84 | 4377 | +lit

976 كَفَى *v. I (i)* to be enough, be sufficient (for sth/sb)

لقد خلق الله لنا الأرزاق في هذه الأرض قدر ما يكفينا جميعا فنعيش جميعا سعداء كما خلق الهواء والنور بالضبط — God created sustenance for us on this earth to the extent that suffices us all, so we all live happily just as He created the air and light exactly

96 | 3827 |

977 قُرْب *n.* proximity, nearness; قُرْب and بِالقُرْب مِن and بِالقُرْب مِن near, near to

راح يدفع به بعيدا عنه، و أوصله الى مكانه قرب الباب، واجلسه — He started to push him away from him, and he got him to his place near the door, and sat him down

94 | 3891 |

978 مَوْسِم *n.* pl. مَواسِم season, festival

كنا في بداية الموسم الدراسي — We were at the beginning of the academic season

94 | 3914 |

979 مالِيّ *adj.* financial, monetary, fiscal

هو مسؤول عن أكبر فضيحة مالية في تاريخ الولايات المتحدة — He is responsible for the biggest financial scandal in the history of the United States

92 | 3972 |

980 نَهار *n.* daytime, day; نَهاراً by day, during the day

كان شكل الحي مختلفا أثناء النهار، الشوارع خاوية وكأنها مهجورة — The shape of the neighborhood was different during the day, the streets were empty as if they were deserted

99 | 3717 |

981 تَمَكَّنَ *v. V* to be able مِن to do sth

ستظل حبيبته مدى الحياة ولن تتمكن امرأة أيا كانت من احتلال مكانها في قلبه — She will remain his beloved throughout life, and no woman, no matter who she is, shall be able to occupy her place in his heart

88 | 4171 |

982 دام *v. I (u)* to last, continue; to endure, persevere; ما دَام as long as

ما دام يعمل في صمت فكل شيء على ما يرام — As long as he is working in silence, everything is as it should be

98 | 3752 |

983 وَجَّهَ *v. II* to send, direct sth إلى to

في نهاية حديثي كنت أوجه لكل واحد منهم سؤالا مباشرا: هل تريد أن تفعل شيئا من أجل بلادك؟ — At the end of my talk I directed to each of them a direct question: Do you want to do something for your country?

90 | 4075 |

984 جَنَّة *n.* pl. جَنّات, جِنان paradise; garden

إذن فأنت لا تؤمن بوجود الجنة والنار — Therefore you don't believe in the existence of heaven or hell

94 | 3847 |

985 كاد *v. I (a)* to almost (with imperf.) do sth or أَنْ do sth; (with neg.) ما كاد...حَتَّى and لَمْ يَكَدْ...حَتَّى as soon as (this happened)...(that happened); no sooner had (this happened)...than (that happened)

شربت كوب العصير دفعة واحدة، إذ كدت أموت من العطش في تلك اللحظة — I drank the cup of juice in one gulp, since I was about to die of thirst at that moment

89 | 4069 |

986 تَطْبيق *n.* implementation (plan, project, decision, strategy); application, enforcement (law, regulation, standards)

لكي نستطيع تطبيق خططنا بدقة، لا بد لنا من التنظيم — So we can carry out our plan in detail, we need to be organized

86 | 4213 |

987 أَخْضَر *adj.* fem. خَضْراء, pl. خُضْر green; المِنْطَقَة الخَضْراء the Green Zone

نمشي في ممرات الخط الأخضر الذي كان يفصل بيروت عن بيروت — We are walking in the passageways of the Green Line that used to divide (East) Beirut from (West) Beirut

98 | 3670 |

988 مُمارَسَة *vn.* practice, pursuit (profession, hobby); practicing, playing (sport); exercising, carrying out (policy); exerting (pressure); *n.* pl. -aat activity, practice, action

ليس هنا من يمنع الشيخ محفوظ من ممارسة حرفته — There is no one here who is keeping Sheikh Mahfouz from practicing his profession

85 | 4246 |

989 صَدَّقَ *v. II* to believe sb/sth; to confirm, ratify على sth

لم يصدق أحد أن الدنيا يمكن ان تكون صغيرة إلى هذا الحد — No one believed that the world could be that small

95 | 3768 |

990 وَفْد *n.* pl. وُفود delegation

استقبل المفتي قباني وفدا من اتحاد الجمعيات والهيئات والفاعليات الاجتماعية — The Mufti Qabbani welcomed a delegation from the Federation of Social Associations, Organizations and Activities

82 | 4355 | +news

991 نَفْسِيّ *adj.* mental, spiritual; psychological

إنها – والعياذ بالله – مريضة نفسيا وتتناول حبوبا مهدئة — She is, God forbid, mentally ill and is taking tranquilizers

97 | 3715 |

992 تَقْدير *vn.* appreciation, gratitude; تَقْديراً in appreciation (ل for); *n.* pl. -aat estimate, calculation; appraisal; (academic) level, performance

نظرت أنا إليها بكثير من الإعجاب والتقدير — I looked at her with a lot of admiration and esteem

87 | 4111 |

993 خَلِيج *n.* gulf

كانت أميرة قد اشتغلت مع زوجها في الخليج، وتفرق أولادها في البلاد التي قبلت أن يدرسوا فيها — Amira had worked with her husband in the Gulf, and her children were scattered throughout countries where they had been admitted for study

94 | 3795 |

994 نَظْرَة *n.* pl. -aat look, glance, view

رأى فى نظرة أمها لؤما وشراهة — In his mother's gaze he saw miserliness and greed

97 | 3687 |

995 عَكْس *n.* opposite, reverse, contrary

قرر أن يصل إلى النيل ويمشى عكس سريانه حتى يصل إلى أسيوط — He decided to get to the Nile and walk upstream until he got to Assiut

98 | 3626 |

996 قَصِيدَة *n.* pl. قَصائِد poem, ode

تم تقديم قصيدة واحدة لكل شاعر من الشعراء المختارين — One ode from each of the chosen poets was presented

85 | 4188 |

997 اِسْتِقْرار *n.* stability; setting down

لماذا لم تفكر في الاستقرار في بريطانيا؟ — Why didn't you think about settling down in Britain?

89 | 3976 |

998 تَشْكِيل *n.* formation, composition, constitution

منذ اليوم الاول لتشكيل الحكومة كان من اهم اهدافها مكافحة الفقر وزيادة فرص التشغيل — From the first day of the formation of the government, one of its most important goals was to fight poverty and increase employment opportunities

81 | 4379 |

999 مُسْتَمِرّ *adj.* continuous, incessant; continuing

هذا المطر المستمر منذ أيام سينقطع مع بداية العام الجديد — This rain that has continued for days will end with the beginning of the new year

96 | 3673 |

1000 كدا and كده /kida/ (Egy.) *adv.* thus, this way, like this

نفسى كل الزوجات يكونوا كده مع ازواجهم — I wish all wives could be like that with their husbands

84 | 4188 | +for +spo

1001 شَجَر *coll.n.* trees, *un.n.* شَجَرَة, pl. أَشْجار

لعب الكرة الشراب وتسلق أشجار الجنينة الممنوعة في بيت الناظر — He played "sock soccer" and climbed the trees of the forbidden garden in the house of the supervisor

95 | 3691 |

1002 ذِكْر *n.* mention, citation; memory

شاركت في التعليق على محاضرة السفير التي اقتصرت على ذكر الأحداث والتطورات السياسية — I participated in commenting on the ambassador's lecture which had limited itself to mentioning events and political developments

92 | 3824 |

1003 دِيمُوقراطِيَّة and دِيمُقراطِيَّة *n.* democracy

نتحدث عن الديموقراطية ولكننا نعيش القمع ونمارسه — We talk about democracy, but we live and practice repression

83 | 4193 |

1004 ذاكَ *dem.pron.* that, that (other) one; (Egy.) ذِيج, fem. (Irq.) داك; دِيك, fem. (Irq.Gul.) ذاك, /dhiich/, (Gul.) ذِيك

ما هي الطريقة التي تجعل ابنتي بعد زواجها ابنتي أيضا؟ إما أن يتنصر هو وإما أن ندخل كلنا في الإسلام، وهذا وذاك مستحيل — What is the way to keep my daughter as my daughter even after her marriage? Either he converts to Christianity, or we all enter into Islam; both of these are impossible

91 | 3833 |

1005 مَوْعِد *n.* pl. مَواعِد appointed time or date; deadline; appointment, engagement, commitment, rendezvous

الساعة بلغت الواحدة صباحا.. أمامه ساعات قليلة على موعد الاستيقاظ.. دخل تحت الغطاء لينام — It was now one o'clock in the morning...He had a few hours ahead of him before it was time to get up...He went under the covers to sleep

97 | 3593 |

1006 بَغَى *v. I (i)* to pursue, strive for sth; (Gul.) بَغَى, يِبِي/يَبِي (frequent variant يِبْغِي) to want, need sth or to do sth

يلا عن أذنكم أبغى اروح اكمل البودي كير — Excuse me, I want to go finish my "body care" (pedicure, manicure)

73 | 4786 |

1007 واجَهَ *v. III* to face, be opposite sth; to confront sb

أمامه عامان كاملان حتى يواجه لحظة اتخاذ القرار.. فلينهل الآن من السعادة — He has two full years until he faces the moment he must make the decision...so let him now drink from happiness

89 | 3934 |

1008 ضابِط *n. pl.* ضُبّاط officer; *pl.* ضَوابِط controller, controlling device

أصدر وزير الدفاع الوطني قرارا بحظر الزواج على ضباط الجيش المصري الذين هم في رتبة الملازم ثان، حتى لا تشغلهم الأعباء العائلية عن الشئون العسكرية — The Minister of National Defense issued a decree banning the marriage of Egyptian army officers who are of the rank of 2nd Lieutenant, so that family burdens would not distract them from military matters

91 | 3796 |

1009 رِحلَة *n. pl.* -aat trip, excursion; journey, voyage; career

غيرت المترو وقطعت المرحلة الثانية من الرحلة، وعندما خرجت من المحطة كان عليها أن تمشي قليلا — She changed metros, and got through the second stage of the trip, and when she left the station, she had to walk a little

99 | 3507 |

1010 مَعرِض *n. pl.* مَعارِض exhibit, exhibition, show

عيناه واسعتان مستديرتان مفعمتان بالذكاء والحزن وكأنه خرج لتوه من إحدى لوحات معرض «وجوه الفيوم» — His eyes were wide and round, filled with intelligence and sadness, as if he just came out of one of the Fayoum Portraits Exhibition paintings

95 | 3629 |

1011 جُرح *n. pl.* جِراح ,جُرُوح wound, injury

أكدت المصادر سقوط ٤ قتلى في حادث مماثل ادى الى اصابة ١٧ شخصا بجروح مختلفة — The sources confirmed four dead in a similar incident which led to 17 injured with various wounds

89 | 3874 |

1012 خامِس *adj.* fifth (ordinal)

غدا.. الساعة الخامسة مساء سأنتظرك في هذا العنوان — Tomorrow, at five o'clock in the evening, I will wait for you at this address

99 | 3477 |

1013 تارِيخيّ *adj.* historical

تصدرت القضية الفلسطينية جدول أعمال الزيارة التاريخية لجلالة الملك عبد الله الثاني إلى اليابان — The Palestinian issue headed the agenda of the historic visit of His Majesty King Abdallah II to Japan

85 | 4053 |

1014 تَوفِير *n.* providing, furnishing; fulfillment (conditions, requirements); saving (time, money)

تم إنشاء عشرات الملاجئ الأهلية، وانهمرت التبرعات من أجل توفير الطعام والثياب والرعاية الصحية لآلاف الأسر المشردة — Dozens of domestic shelters were built, and contributions flowed in to provide food and clothing and health care for the thousands of homeless families

83 | 4160 |

1015 سَفِير *n. pl.* سُفَراء ambassador

الفلسطينيون أينما هم يعتبرون عمارا سفيرا لهم — The Palestinians wherever they are consider Amar to be their ambassador

86 | 4009 |

1016 كمبيوتر and كومبيوتر /kumbyuutar/ *n.* computer

ما زالت موسيقى البوب محظورة لكن الأسرة التي تملك جهاز كمبيوتر تحمل الموسيقى من الإنترنت، لا سيها موسيقى البوب الفارسية — Pop music is still banned but the family that owns a computer gets music from the Internet, particularly Persian pop music

88 | 3888 |

1017 أُسلُوب *n. pl.* أسالِيب style, manner, way; method, device

الجمعية تبحث امكانية تطبيق أسلوب الشباك الواحد لاصدار تصاريح المزارع السمكية تيسيرا على المستثمرين — The association is discussing the possibility of putting into effect the "single window" style to issue its fish farm permits, to facilitate matters for investors

93 | 3701 |

1018 دَوريّ *n. pl.* -aat (sports) league, tournament; *adj.* regular, periodic, intermittent, cyclical; circulatory

اقوم بتفقد محالي دوري بشكل — I visit my shops on a regular basis

83 | 4115 |

1019 نَجْم *n. pl.* نُجُوم star, constellation; celebrity
وترقى ويسلي كلارك في الجيش الأميركي حتى بلغ
رتبة جنرال بأربعة نجوم — Wesley Clark
advanced in the American army until he
reached the rank of four-star general

88 | 3877 |

1020 تَأْثِير *n. pl.* -aat effect, impact, influence,
impression (في/على) on)
أسألك عن تأثير الحرب على الإرهاب على الحريات
المدنية في الولايات المتحدة — I am asking you
about the influence of the war on terror on
civil liberties in the United States

93 | 3676 |

1021 قَلَم *n. pl.* أَقْلام pencil, pen; بِقَلَم written by
سحب الدكتور كرم ورقة من على المائدة وأخرج من
جيبه قلما ذهبيا — Dr Karam picked up a paper
from off the table and took a gold pen out of
his pocket

96 | 3559 |

1022 مَقال and مَقالَة *n. pl.* -aat article, essay
يمدني بجريدة مقربة منه، ويدلني على مقال
سياسي يحمل توقيع خالد بن طوبال — He hands
me a newspaper that is near him, and points
me to a political article which bears the
signature of Khalid Ibn Tubal

87 | 3911 |

1023 بَدْء *n.* start, beginning; بَدْءاً مِن starting from
بلغ قتلاهم وأسراهم مائة وخمسين ألفا منذ بدء الهجوم
البريطاني — Their dead and captured reached
150,000 since the beginning of the British attack

89 | 3839 |

1024 أَظْهَرَ *v. IV* to show, manifest, demonstrate
إذا كانت هناك جريمة حقا فسوف تظهر — If there
really is a crime, it will appear

99 | 3453 |

1025 سَبَقَ *v. I (i,u)* to precede, come before sb/sth;
سَبَقَ لَهُ أَن to have done sth previously
انقطع الهمس فورا وساد سكون عميق قطعته النحنحة
التي تسبق كلامه، والتي غالبا ما تنتهي بنوبة سعال
— The whispering was cut off immediately
and a deep silence reigned, cut by the
coughing that (usually) precedes his talk, and
which usually would end with a coughing fit

89 | 3819 |

1026 لِسان *n. pl.* أَلْسِنَة tongue; language;
spokesperson; (publication) mouthpiece
مات أبوك يا بهي وليس على لسانه إلا اسمك —
Your father died, Bahiy, and the only thing on
his tongue (the last thing he said) was your
name

97 | 3508 |

1027 سَفَر *vn.* traveling; *n.* journey, trip
لا شك أنت متعب من السفر.. يجب أن تستريح —
You are no doubt tired from the trip, you need
to rest

98 | 3461 |

1028 غايَة *n.* utmost, extreme; لِلغايَة extremely,
greatly; غايَة pl. -aat goal, objective, purpose;
لِغايَة until
يرتل القرآن في المساء بصوت خفيض للغاية —
He chants the Qur'an in the evening with
a very low voice

90 | 3743 |

1029 شَمِلَ *v. I (a)* and شَمَلَ (u) to include,
comprise, contain sth
مشروعي الجديد لا يخصك وحدك بل يشمل
الدول العربية كلها — My new project does
not concern you alone, but it includes all
the Arab countries

85 | 3985 |

1030 قَطَعَ *v. I (a)* to cut off, sever sth;
to interrupt, stop (flow); to block
(street); to cover, travel (a distance);
to pledge (a vow)
كيف أنجب ابنتي وأربيها ثم بعد ذلك يأخذها شاب
يقطع كل طريق بيننا وبينها — How can I bear
my daughter and raise her and then a young
man takes her, severing all paths between us
and her?

99 | 3403 |

1031 ثَوْرَة *n.* revolution, uprising
كانوا على يقين من أن العالم يتغير، وسوف تنتصر
الثورة في أمريكا كما انتصرت في أماكن أخرى كثيرة
— They were certain that the world was
changing, and that the revolution would be
victorious in America as it had been victorious
in many other places

87 | 3893 |

1032 بعدين /ba9deen/ (Egy.Lev.) *adv.* later, afterwards; then, after that; besides; وبعدين and then; كانت زميلتي في المطبخ جوه.. وبعدين اشتغلت جرسونة — My colleague was in the kitchen, inside...and then she started working as a waitress
55 | 6052 | +spo

1033 تَأْكِيد *n.* confirmation; affirmation; certainty; بالتَأْكِيد certainly; تَأْكِيداً لِـ in confirmation of; underscoring, emphasizing
من أين حصل عليها؟ بالتأكيد يوجد تعاون بين المخابرات المصرية وإدارة الجامعة — Where did he get it? For sure there is some cooperation between the Egyptian intelligence agency and the administration of the university
93 | 3627 |

1034 دَارَ *v. I (u)* to revolve, turn; to circle, go around حَوْلَ sth
كانت منفعلة وسعيدة.. دارت حول نفسها عدة مرات — She was excited and happy...She turned around in a circle several times
99 | 3384 |

1035 نَشَر *v. I (u)* to publish sth; to announce sth; to propagate sth
صدرت عشرات الكتب ونشرت مئات المقالات والأبحاث عن شخصية كولبس — Dozens of books were issued and hundreds of articles and studies were published about the personality of Columbus
88 | 3812 |

1036 دِينار *n.* pl. دَنَانِير dinar
كتب رسالة إلى الله سبحانه طالباً منه مائة دينار — He wrote a letter to God, may He be praised, asking him for a hundred dinar
85 | 3968 |

1037 إِشَارَة *vn.* mentioning, pointing out; *n.* pl. -aat indication, sign, signal
لابد من وضع إشارات ضوئية هنا من أجل تنظيم المرور — Traffic lights need to be put up here to regulate the traffic
97 | 3465 |

1038 ظَنَّ *v. I (u)* to think, believe, presume أنَّ that
ظلت صامتة حتى ظننت أنها لم تسمعني — She remained silent until I thought that she wasn't listening to me
95 | 3526 |

1039 بِيئَة *n.* environment; milieu
وهذا يؤدي الى حالة من الاحباط والاحتقان، وقد يستغل لخلق بيئة ينمو فيها الارهاب — This leads to a state of depression and anger, and might be exploited to create an environment in which terrorism grows
90 | 3696 |

1040 مُسابَقَة *n.* pl. -aat contest, competition; race
فاز بالجائزة الأولى فى مسابقة محمود مهدى الأدبية لشعر الفصحى عن عدد من القصائد — He won first prize in the Mahmoud Mahdi literary contest for Standard Arabic poetry, for a number of odes
91 | 3659 |

1041 رِعايَة *n.* custody, protection; patronage, sponsorship; (social) welfare, (health) care
شهدت المملكة تطورا كبيرا في المجال الصحي والرعاية الصحية إذ يتم تقديم الخدمات الصحية على امتداد مساحة الوطن — The kingdom witnessed a big development in the health and health care arenas, since health services are being offered over the whole breadth of the nation
92 | 3617 |

1042 خافَ *v. I (a)* to fear sth/sb; to be afraid مِن of sth/sb; to be worried على about sth/sb; to fear على for (sb's safety)
فكرت هذا الصباح فى الانتحار.. لكنى أخاف من ربنا سبحانه وتعالى — This morning I thought about suicide, but I am afraid of our Lord, may He be praised and exalted
96 | 3463 |

1043 ألْقَى *v. IV* to throw, toss; to deliver, give (a speech); ألْقَى القَبْضَ على to arrest sb
دخلا العربة وعلى أقرب مقعد ألقى كل منها بنفسه — وعادت أصوات المدافع تزداد — They entered the car and each one threw himself onto the nearest seat, and the sound of cannons kept getting louder
89 | 3711 |

14 Opposites

Note that in most cases the positive term is ranked higher than the negative one.

Word 1	#	#	Word 2	Def 1	Def 2
بعد	34	68	قبل	after	before
أوّل	41	206	أخير	first	last
كثير	55	376	قليل	many	few
جديد	60	499	قديم	new	old
أكثر	64	446	أقلّ	more/most	less/least
كبير	65	230	صغير	large	small
عامّ	88	135	خاصّ	general, public	special, private
حياة	94	481	موت	life	death
دون	105	348	فوق	below	above
أمام	153	577	وراء	front	behind
حرب	165	188	سلام	war	peace
أكبر	195	1860	أصغر	larger/largest	smaller/smallest
ماضٍ	203	539	مستقبل	past	future
تحت	216	348	فوق	below	above
داخل	246	349	خارج	inside	outside
سابق	284	500	قادم	preceding	next
سؤال	267	1391	جواب	question	answer
طويل	316	1061	قصير	long; tall	short; small
أخذ	198	346	أعطى	to take	to give
بعيد	355	476	قريب	far	near
صحيح	364	811	خطأ	correct	wrong
نهاية	380	415	بداية	end	beginning
شرق	386	695	غرب	east	west
أفضل	390	2265	أسوأ	better/best	worse/worst
ممكن	403	1614	مستحيل	possible	impossible
صديق	398	799	عدوّ	friend	enemy
جنوب	416	624	شمال	south	north
قويّ	438	1285	ضعيف	strong	weak
واضح	480	2685	غامض	clear	obscure
جيّد	488	1493	سيّء	good	bad
دنيا	494	2992	آخرة	world	the hereafter
داخليّ	520	765	خارجيّ	internal; domestic	external; foreign
غربيّ	553	1114	شرقيّ	Western	Eastern
خارجيّة	649	1548	داخليّة	foreign ministry	ministry of the interior
أبيض	564	682	أسود	white	black
دخول	595	872	خروج	entering	leaving
صعب	597	1147	سهل	difficult	easy
شديد	658	1420	خفيف	intense	slight
صباح	449	642	مساء	morning	evening
نور	657	1587	ظلام	light; lamp	darkness; injustice
رفض	708	1097	قبل	to reject	to accept
معروف	720	1741	مجهول	known	unknown
قادر	827	2946	عاجز	capable	incapable
سريع	854	4648	بطيء	quick	slow

1044 اِحْتِرام *n.* respect, honor; اِحْتِراماً لِـ out of respect for, in honor of

أنا عندي احترام للدستور، يجب أن يكون أعلى من كل شيء — I have respect for the constitution; it has to be above everything

93 | 3551 |

1045 مَفْتُوح *adj.* open, opened

لا يبدو أن الضوء المنسكب من الباب المفتوح كافٍ لطرد الرطوبة — It doesn't appear that light streaming in from the open door is enough to get rid of the humidity

99 | 3365 |

1046 جاب *v. I (i)* (Dia.) to bring, fetch sth (لـ for sb); to get, earn (school grade); to score (goal); to have, give birth to (baby boy, girl)

لازم يشتري لها شيء.. المهم نزل الأخ يجيب لها ببسي — He has to buy her something...The important thing is that the brother went down to get her a Pepsi

62 | 5273 | +spo

1047 تَحَوَّل *v. V* to be changed, be converted, be transformed

حدثت مواجهات عنيفة مع البوليس، تحولت الحدائق إلى ميادين قتال حقيقية، كانت الشرطة تضرب المتظاهرين — Violent confrontations took place with the police; the gardens were transformed into actual battlefields; the police were beating the demonstrators

89 | 3697 |

1048 فَجْر *n.* dawn

عجز عن النوم.. أخذ يتقلب حتى سمع أذان الفجر، نهض وأخذ حماما وارتدى ثيابه وعاد إلى الجامعة — He was unable to sleep; he started to toss and turn until he heard the dawn call to prayer; he got up and took a shower and put on his clothing and returned to the university

97 | 3368 |

1049 اِلْتَقَى *v. VIII* to meet, encounter sb بـ/مع

تريد شقيقتي أن تتعرف عليك، متى نستطيع أن نلتقي — My sister wants to get to know you; when can we meet?

98 | 3356 |

1050 صَدَرَ *v. I (u)* to be published, be issued; to emerge, come forth, appear

لقد صدرت لي أول رواية منذ سنتين — My first novel was published two years ago

89 | 3682 |

1051 طَعام *n.* pl. أَطْعِمَة food

أنا لا أعرف أنواع الطعام التي تأكلونها في بلدكم.. لكني أنصحك أن تغيري طعامك المفضل لأنه كاد أن يتسبب في إحراق الجامعة — I don't know the types of food which you eat in your country... but I advise you to change your preferred food because it almost burned down the university

89 | 3681 |

1052 اِمْرَأَة *n.* woman (pl. نساء is listed separately); (with def. article) المَرْأة

تقدمت امرأة فقيرة إلى النائب العام تشكو اختفاء ابنتها — A poor woman came to the prosecutor complaining about the disappearance of her daughter

89 | 3649 |

1053 أيْش /'eesh/ (Lev.Gul.) *interrog.* what

إشرح لي ايش قصة هالتلفون — Explain to me what's the story with that phone

46 | 6976 | +spo

1054 ضَحِكَ *v. I (a)* to laugh (على at)

انطلق مجد الدين يضحك من غيظ دميان وطريقته في الكلام — Magd Al-Din started to laugh at Dumyan's anger and his manner of speaking

89 | 3667 |

1055 اِسْتَخْدَمَ *v. X* to use, employ, utilize sth

حسب خبرتي كصانع احذية ان الجنود الرومان كانوا يستخدمون هذا النوع الثقيل من الاحذية اثناء المعارك — According to my experience as a shoemaker, the Roman soldiers were using this heavy type of shoe during battles

85 | 3825 |

1056 ساعَدَ *v. III* to help, assist, support sb

إن صوت أم كلثوم يساعده على الاحتفاظ بهدوء أعصابه وهو يعمل — Um Kalthoum's voice helps him keep his nerves calm while he is working

97 | 3354 |

1057 ظاهِرَة *n.* pl. ظَواهِر phenomenon
وكان من أهم ما قام به المحافظ الجديد إنهاء ظاهرة الدقيق المغشوش فى الخبز — One of the most important things the new governor did was to end the phenomenon of fake flour in the bread
92 | 3511 |

1058 سَقَطَ *v. I (u)* to fall; drop, decline
عندما سقطت الأندلس فى أيدى المسيحيين الإسبان، اضطهدوا المسلمين واليهود معا — When Andalusia fell into the hands of the Spanish Christians, they persecuted the Muslims and the Jews together
90 | 3600 |

1059 سُبْحان *n.* praise; سُبْحانَ الله praise God!
سبحان الله الذى جعل للجمال مائة شكل — Praise be to God who made a hundred kinds of beauty
90 | 3571 |

1060 مُؤَكَّد *adj.* confirming; underscoring, emphasizing
ثم أنهى كلمته بخطاب إلى المبعوثين مؤكدا أن كل واحد فيهم سفير لمصر — He ended his speech with a message to the delegates, stressing that each one of them is an ambassador for Egypt
87 | 3718 |

1061 قَصِير *adj.* short, small (of stature)
أوصله إلى الباب ودار بينها حديث قصير جدى عما يجب عمله فى الأيام التالية — He accompanied him to the door and a short, serious conversation took place between them about what needed to be done in the coming days
99 | 3248 |

1062 تَعْبِير *vn.* expressing عن (opinion, feeling), stating عن (position, policy); *n.* expression, word, phrase
يقوم بإجراءات إضافية تزيد فى يمينه اليمين إذا صح التعبير — He is taking additional steps to make the right even more right, so to speak (if the expression is correct)
88 | 3645 |

1063 كُوَيْتِيّ *n./adj.* Kuwaiti
التقى سمو رئيس مجلس الوزراء بالطلبة الكويتيين فى الاردن فى حفل العشاء الذى اقامه السيد يوسف عبدالله — His excellency the prime minister met with the Kuwaiti students in Jordan in a dinner party which Mr Yusuf Abdallah gave
84 | 3833 |

1064 عامِل *adj.* working, operating; active; (Dia.) *a.p.* doing, making
فى نفس الوقت تؤكد الدراسة أن الجهد البدني الذي تبذله المرأة العاملة فى عملها سيساعد على تجنبها ضغط الدم وأمراض القلب — At the same time the study confirms that the physical effort that the working woman exerts at work will help her avoid (high) blood pressure and heart disease
96 | 3329 |

1065 تَفْكِير *n.* thinking, pondering; reflection, meditation
كان تتابع الأحداث أسرع من قدرتى على التفكير — Things were happening faster than my ability to think
98 | 3265 |

1066 دَرَسَ *v. I (u)* to study, learn sth
قرر أن يدرس القانون ليصبح قاضيا، وعاد بعد ذلك إلى بلدته عام ١٦٤٧ — He decided to study law to become a judge, and he returned after that to his home town in the year 1647
97 | 3312 |

1067 تليفزيون /tilfizyoon, tilivizyoon/ and تلفزيون *n.* television
جلس يتفرج على التليفزيون حتى انتهت شيماء من الطهى — He sat watching television until Shima finished cooking
93 | 3461 |

1068 بَشَر *coll.n.* humankind, humans
يا فندم سيادتك تبذل مجهودا فوق طاقة البشر فى عملك.. ومن حقك أن ترفه عن نفسك — Sir, your excellency exerts superhuman efforts in your work; you have a right to entertain yourself
97 | 3311 |

1069 صَنْدُوق *n. pl.* صَنَادِيق (often صُنْدُوق) box, bin; treasury, fund; trunk (of a car)
طلب منه أن يضعه فى أقرب صندوق بريد بالإسكندرية — He asked him to put it in the nearest post office box in Alexandria
88 | 3648 |

1070 سَوَّى *v. II* (Lev.Irq.Gul.) to do, make; *a.p.* مسوي /msawwi/ doing, making
لا إيران ولا غير إيران ممكن أن تسوي شي بالعراق — Neither Iran nor anyone else can do anything in Iraq
60 | 5295 | +spo

1071 حَيّ *adj. pl.* أَحْياء alive, living; active, lively; live (fire); *n. pl.* أَحْياء creature, living thing
ترجم الكتاب من الإنجليزية إلى عدد كبير من اللغات الحية — The book was translated from English to a large number of living languages
98 | 3254 |

1072 مَرْحَباً *interj.* (usu. مَرْحَبا) hello! welcome! مرحبتين (Gul.) hello!; /marHabteen/ مَرْحَب (Lev.) hello! (in response to مَرْحَبا)
اهلا ومرحبا بكم، شرفتموني — Hello, welcome, you have honored me
80 | 3987 |

1073 أَقْصَى *adj. fem.* قُصْوَى farthest, most remote; المَسْجِد الأَقْصَى Al-Aqsa Mosque
الظروف والتحديات التي تواجه الوطن تتطلب من ابنائه مزيدا من الجهد والعمل وبذل اقصى الطاقات لمواصلة مسيرة البناء والتنمية — The circumstances and challenges which face the nation demand of its citizens more effort and work and the exertion of the utmost energy to continue the march of building and growth
86 | 3713 |

1074 ريال *n.* riyal (currency)
العقوبة كلها لا تتجاوز ألف ريال — The entire punishment does not exceed a thousand riyals
72 | 4440 |

1075 إعْلامِيّ *adj.* media, information; *n.* journalist, person from the media, media worker
طموحها أن تستمر في العمل الإعلامي وأن تحصد المزيد من النجاح والشهرة — Her ambition is to

continue media work and get more success and fame
81 | 3929 |

1076 مُشارك *n.* participant; *adj.* participating
كل مشارك، أثناء عرض السلع عليه، يجلس داخل الجهاز — Each participant, during the presentation of the goods to him, will sit inside the machine
91 | 3495 |

1077 مُتابَعَة *n.* pursuing, following; continuation
لكن مستواه الحقيقي انكشف وعجز عن متابعة الدراسة — But his actual level had been revealed, and he was incapable of continuing his studies
86 | 3712 |

1078 بَيْع *n.* sale; selling
بيتنا ارتفع ثمنه بعد التجديد.. إذا عرضناه للبيع الآن سيدر علينا مبلغا معقولا — The price of our house went up after the renovation...if we offer it for sale now, it will bring us a reasonable sum
97 | 3252 |

1079 باتَ *v. I (i)* to become (known, certain); to start, begin to do sth; to spend the night, stay overnight (في/عند at)
آمن بأن الفتونة باتت فى متناول يديه — He believed that the leadership of the gang was within reach
88 | 3601 |

1080 نَحْو *n.* way, manner, method; (ling.) grammar; *pl.* أَنْحاء areas, regions
أخذ يبحث عنها فى أنحاء البيت، وأحس بقلق لأنها خرجت دون أن تخبره كعادتها — He started to look for her all over the house, and he felt worried that she had left without informing him as was her custom
88 | 3590 |

1081 قَمَر *n. pl.* أَقْمار moon; قَمَر صِناعِيّ satellite
حتى أضواء القنابل ابتعدت وعاد ضوء القمر يدخل إلى العربة — Even the lights of the bombs receded and the light of the moon once more entered the car
97 | 3270 | +lit +for

1082 أعادَ *v. IV* to repeat sth, do sth again; to give back, return sth

ضغط رقمها بعد ترد، ولما أعاد المحاولة أغلقت عليه الخط — He dialed her number, but she didn't answer, and when he tried again, she hung up on him

99 | 3190 |

1083 سِنّ *n.* age (of a person)

ينبه الدكتور محمود إلى أن المرأة بعد سن الأربعين قد تحدث لها مشكلات في الكبد — Dr Mahmoud warns that women after the age of forty might get kidney problems

96 | 3282 |

1084 أدْرَكَ *v. IV* to grasp, understand, comprehend sth or أنَّ that; to reach, attain sth

كان يدرك أن مقابلة الرئيس قد تغير حياته — He realized that meeting with the president could change his life

97 | 3240 |

1085 قَوْميّ *adj.* national, state; nationalist

إن المسألة لا تتعلق هنا ـ في رأيي ـ بخصائص قومية أو ثقافية بقدر ما تتعلق بمنطق نظام لا يكترث بأخطائه — The issue here is not related – in my opinion – to the national or cultural characteristics as much as it is related to the logic of a regime which doesn't care about its errors

78 | 4019 |

1086 جائِزَة *n. pl.* جَوائِز prize, award, reward

قال انها عبقرية وقد فازت بعدد كبير من الجوائز وصممت الكثير من المباني في امريكا واليابان وبريطانيا وهولندا — He said that she was brilliant and that she won a large number of prizes and designed a lot of buildings in America and Japan and Britain and Holland

93 | 3386 |

1087 أفريقيّ *n./adj. pl.* أفارِقَة and إفْريقيّ African

حصل على جائزة الجارديان للقصة الإفريقية القصيرة — He got the Guardian Prize for African Short Stories

76 | 4118 |

1088 جارٍ (def. جاري) *adj.* current, present (time); occurring, taking place, in progress; flowing, running (liquid)

وحسب تقارير الأطباء فإنه في نهاية الشهر الجاري — According يكون سماحة الشيخ قد أنهى فترة النقاهة to the doctors' reports, by the end of the current month his excellency the Sheikh will have completed his period of convalescence

88 | 3576 |

1089 ضَرَبَ *v. I (i)* to strike, hit; ضَرَبَ مَثَلًا to give an example (ل of)

هجم عليه أحد الشبان وضرب يده لتسقط السيجارة على الأرض — One of the young men attacked him and beat his hand to make the cigarette fall on the floor

99 | 3180 |

1090 قَضاء *n.* justice, judiciary; court, court system; district, province; judgment, ruling, decision; fate, destiny

القضاء العسكري في العالم المتقدم هو لمحاكمة العسكريين دون غيرهم — The military courts in the developed world are for military trials only

88 | 3557 |

1091 حَضْرَة *n.* (with pron., polite term of address) حضرتك (Egy.) /HaDritak/, (Lev.Irq.) /HaDirtak/ you (masc.sg.); حَضْرَة صاحِب الجَلالَة His Majesty

قرأ أن حضرة صاحب السعادة مراد سيد أحمد باشا عين وزيرا مفوضا لمصر — He read that His Eminence, Mr Murad Sayyed Ahmad Pasha was appointed minister plenipotentiary to Egypt

82 | 3812 | +spo

1092 اشْتَغَلَ *v. VIII* to work, be employed

الواحد لو نظم وقته، ممكن يشتغل خمستاشر ساعة في اليوم — A person, if he organizes his time, can work fifteen hours a day

67 | 4697 | +spo

1093 صِفْر *n. pl.* أصْفار، (Lev. صفورة /Sfuura/ zero; *adj.* empty: صفر اليَدَيْن empty-handed

حقق العراق انجازا تاريخيا بتأهله الى المباراة النهائية بعد ان اقصى كوريا الجنوبية بفوزه عليها ٤-٣ بركلات الترجيح بعد انتهاء الوقتين الاصلي والاضافي صفر - صفر — Iraq has made a historic achievement by qualifying for the final match after excluding South Korea by beating them 4–3 on penalty kicks after the end of the original and additional periods 0–0

97 | 3252 |

1094 حاضِر *adj.* present (time); (person) present, attending; *n. pl.* -uun, حُضُور person present, participant; الحُضُور audience; (Dia.) حاضِر *interj.* ok, yes

ساد صمت متوتر، وراح يتفحص الحاضرين بنظراته القوية، ثم أعلن الانتقال إلى جدول الأعمال — A tense silence prevailed, and he began to scan those present with his searching look, and then he announced (his) moving on to the agenda

97 | 3215 |

1095 اِرْتَفَعَ *v. VIII* to rise, ascend; to increase, grow

لقد ارتفعت أسعار كثير من السلع — The prices of a lot of goods rose

89 | 3510 |

1096 خَلْق *vn.* creating, forming; *n.* creation; creatures, humankind

قالت جلالتها ان العالم العربي بحاجة لخلق ٣٠ مليون وظيفة خلال السنوات العشر القادمة — Her Majesty said that the Arab World needs to create 30 million jobs within the coming ten years

91 | 3434 |

1097 قَبِلَ *v. I (a)* to accept, receive; approve

أريد أن أعرف رأيكم.. هل نقبل هذا الطالب؟.. أماكن الدراسات العليا عندنا محدودة كما تعرفون — I want to know your opinion...Do we accept this student? Graduate study slots here are very limited as you know

99 | 3151 |

1098 قائِمَة *n. pl.* قَوائِم list, index; قَوائِم legs (chair)

أي رقم سيكون رقمي في قائمة الاغتيالات حسب رأيك؟ — What will be my number in the list of assassinations in your opinion?

88 | 3550 |

1099 مَبْدَأ *n. pl.* مَبادِئ principle, basis; fundamental concept

البابا لم يقد جيوشا بل نشر المبادئ — The Pope did not lead armies, but rather he spread principles

94 | 3303 |

1100 تَقَدَّمَ *v. V* to present, submit (request), offer (suggestion); to advance, be ahead (in age, experience)

الفلسطينيون تقدموا بطلب أمس لنقل لواء بدر من الأردن إلى الضفة الغربية — The Palestinians submitted a request yesterday to transfer General Badr from Jordan to the West Bank

89 | 3471 |

1101 ثَمَن *n.* price, cost; value, worth

على أن أدفع وحدي كل شيء: مصاريف المدرسة وثمن الطعام والملابس وفواتير الغاز والكهرباء — I have to pay everything by myself: school expenses, the cost of food and clothing, and the gas and electric bills

96 | 3219 |

1102 إمام *n. pl.* أَئِمَّة imam (person who leads prayers at the mosque); (used as a title) Imam

قال أحد أئمة المسجد إن ظهورها من علامات اقتراب الساعة — One of the Imams of the mosque said that its appearance was one of the signs of the nearness of the hour (Day of Judgement)

90 | 3450 |

1103 جِيل *n. pl.* أَجْيال generation, age

الجيل القديم كان يرفض مشاركة الصغار جلساتهم ويعتبرونه عيبا — The old generation refused to let young people participate in its sessions, considering it to be shameful

97 | 3185 |

1104 مَشْعَر *n. pl.* مَشاعِر feeling, sense, emotion

كانت متأكدة أنه يحمل لها في قلبه من المشاعر أكثر مما تحمله هي له في قلبها — She was certain that he was carrying more feelings for her in his heart than she was carrying for him in her heart

88 | 3489 |

1105 مُبادَرَة *n. pl.* -aat initiative; proposal

قالت إن بعض عناصر مبادرة السلام العربية تناقض مبدأ الدولتين الفلسطينية والإسرائيلية — She said that some elements of the Arab peace initiative contradict the principle of two states, a Palestinian and an Israeli one

83 | 3719 |

1106 أَنْتُم *pron.* you (masc.pl.)

أنتم محظوظون.. يوما ما سيكون بمقدوركم أن تقولوا لأولادكم إنكم قابلتم الزعيم العظيم وجها لوجه — You are lucky...one day you will be able to tell your children that you met the great leader face to face

93 | 3308 |

1107 جَمَعَ *v. I (a)* to bring together, gather, assemble (things, people)

اختار ربوة عالية أقام فوقها قصرا ضخما جمع فيه ألوانا من التحف وأحاطه بحديقة جميلة — He chose a high hill on which he built a huge palace in which he gathered various types of artwork, and he surrounded it with a beautiful garden

94 | 3254 |

1108 ثَلاثُون *num.* thirty; thirtieth

أعرف أنك قابلته حين زار مصر سنة ستة وثلاثين — I know that you met him when he visited Egypt in 1936

98 | 3095 |

1109 اِخْتَلَفَ *v. VIII* to be different عن from sth/sb; to disagree على/في (about) مع with sb

من العبث أن نختلف الآن حول ما حدث منذ ثلاثين عاما — It is useless to argue now about what happened thirty years ago

97 | 3129 |

1110 أَجابَ *v. IV* to respond, reply إلى to sb or a question) عن/على about; to answer, reply أنَّ that or ب with (a yes, a no); to comply إلى with (sb's request)

اسمع يا طارق، سأسألك سؤالا وأرجو أن تجيب بصراحة — Listen, Tariq, I will ask you a question and I beg you to answer frankly

89 | 3397 |

1111 شُعُور *n.* feeling, sentiment, awareness

لفظة «يا ولدي» قد أيقظت في داخلها شعورا جديدا عذبا — The phrase "my boy" awoke within her sweet new feelings

96 | 3147 |

1112 تَفْصِيل *n.* pl. تَفاصِيل detail, elaboration; بالتَّفْصِيل in detail

لا تسألني عن كل التفاصيل ولا تكلمني في فلسفة الحب هذه — Don't ask me about all the details and don't speak to me about this philosophy of love

97 | 3114 |

1113 إعْداد *vn.* preparation

رفع رأسه ببطء، كان منهمكا في الاعداد لمحاضرة سيلقيها بعد قليل — He raised his head slowly. He was engrossed in preparing for a lecture he was giving in a while

87 | 3477 |

1114 شَرْقيّ *adj.* Eastern, oriental; *n.* East, eastern region

من أهم مدنها كلباء وخورفكان وتقع على الساحل الشرقي لخليج عمان — Two of its most important cities are Kalba and Khor Fakkan, and they are located on the eastern coast of the Gulf of Oman

96 | 3140 |

1115 خَمِيس *n.* (يَوْم) الخَمِيس) Thursday

سأنتظر الى ما بعد يوم الخميس لابدأ العمل — I will wait until after Thursday to begin work

92 | 3265 |

1116 أَسَف *n.* sorry, regret, remorse; pity, sympathy; لِلْأَسَفِ unfortunately; يا لَلْأَسَفِ how unfortunate!

متى خطبها؟ - والله ما أعرف، وللأسف ما أقدر أسأل نزار عن حاجة زي كده — When did he ask for her hand in marriage? – Really, I don't know, and unfortunately I can't ask Nizar about something like this

96 | 3147 |

1117 أَفادَ *v. IV* to report أنَّ/بأنَّ that; to provide ب (information); to be useful, be effective (for sb)

افاد شهود عيان ان مجهولا هاجم ليل الاحد فندقا في مقديشو يقيم فيه مشاركون في مؤتمر المصالحة الوطنية بقنبلة يدوية — Eyewitnesses stated that an unknown assailant on Sunday night attacked with a hand grenade a hotel in Mogadishu in which participants in the National Reconciliation Conference are staying

95 | 3174 | +news

1118 عَقْد *vn.* holding, concluding, convening (meeting)

أصدر بيانا استنكر فيه الجريمة الاسرائيلية في بيت حانون مطالبا بعقد اجتماع فوري لجامعة الدول العربية — He issued a communiqué in which he condemned the Israeli crime in Bet Hanun, calling for an immediate meeting of the League of Arab States

88 | 3412 |

1119 ليش /leesh/ (Lev.Irq.Gul.) *interrog.* why

ليش ما قلتي لي من أول؟ — Why didn't you tell me in the first place?

51 | 5870 | +spo

1120 بَشَرِيّ *adj.* human

إن هذا سيقود الجنس البشري نحو الدمار — This will lead the human race to ruin

88 | 3413 |

1121 صَيْف *n.* summer

اكتفت إيفون بما تعلمته في الصيف من فرنسية — Yvonne was satisfied with what she had learned of French in the summer

99 | 3032 |

1122 مُعَدَّل *n. pl.* -aat average, rate, mean figure; *adj.* modified, altered, amended

معدلات الفقر في قطاع غزة تفوق معدلات الفقر في الضفة الغربية بحوالي الضعف — The poverty rate in the Gaza Strip is twice as high as the poverty rate in the West Bank

87 | 3433 |

1123 خَسَارَة *n. pl.* خَسائِر loss, failure; casualty, damage

قالت إن وفاته خسارة كبيرة للعراق وأستراليا — She said that his death was a big loss to Iraq and Australia

97 | 3068 |

15 Nationalities

Arab			Non-Arab					
45	عربي	Arab	85	أمريكي	American	4331	هولاندي	Dutch
107	فلسطيني	Palestinian	233	إسرائيليّ	Israeli	4410	كنديّ	Canadian
177	عراقيّ	Iraqi	572	فرنسيّ	French	4665	كردستانيّ	Kurdistani
212	لبنانيّ	Lebanese	603	أوروبيّ	European	4728	صوماليّ	Somali
381	مصريّ	Egyptian	907	بريطانيّ	British	4981	برتغاليّ	Portuguese
479	سعوديّ	Saudi	944	إيرانيّ	Iranian	5139	دنماركيّ	Danish
578	سوريّ	Syrian	1087	إفريقي	African	5311	سويديّ	Swedish
878	أردنيّ	Jordanian	1166	ألمانيّ	German	5469	سويسريّ	Swiss
1063	كويتيّ	Kuwaiti	1462	إنجليزي	English	5619	أفغانيّ	Afghan
1266	سودانيّ	Sudanese	1480	تركيّ	Turkish	5783	إندونيسيّ	Indonesian
1371	خليجيّ	from Gulf	1491	روسيّ	Russian	6994	كوبيّ	Cuban
1405	مغربيّ	Moroccan	1640	هنديّ	Indian	7047	ماليّ	Malian
1663	جزائريّ	Algerian	1763	صينيّ	Chinese	7968	بندقيّ	Venetian
1689	يمنيّ	Yemeni	1954	إيطاليّ	Italian	**Groups in Arab countries**		
1739	ليبيّ	Libyan	2346	يابانيّ	Japanese	229	مسلم	Muslim
1847	قطريّ	Qatari	2479	آسيويّ	Asian	702	يهوديّ	Jew
2017	عمانيّ	Omani	2746	إسبانيّ	Spanish	1561	مسيحيّ	Christian
2052	تونسيّ	Tunisian	3096	سوفيتي	Soviet	1811	سنيّ	Sunni
2642	إماراتيّ	Emirati	3173	باكستانيّ	Pakistani	1872	شيعيّ	Shiite
3264	بحرينيّ	Bahraini	3670	يونانيّ	Greek	2296	كرديّ	Kurd
7189	كوفيّ	from Kufa	3723	برازيليّ	Brazilian	4804	نصرانيّ	Christian
7364	بصريّ	from Basra	3726	كوريّ	Korean	5844	مارونيّ	Maronite
7538	حجازيّ	from Hijaz	3771	فارسيّ	Persian	6729	مالكيّ	Malikite
7629	مكيّ	Meccan	4320	عثمانيّ	Ottoman			

1124 فائِدَة *n.* pl. فَوائِد benefit, use, usefulness; (fin.) interest

المال لا فائدة منه إذا لم يخدم الناس — There is no use for money if it doesn't serve the people

96 | 3113 |

1125 خِبْرَة *n.* pl. -aat, خِبْرَات experience, expertise

أكدت له أنني عملت سكرتيرة تنفيذية لسنوات وأن معي شهادات خبرة — I assured him that I worked as an executive secretary for years and that I have certificates of experience

96 | 3090 |

1126 صِفَة *n.* pl. -aat feature, characteristic, attribute; trait

انها فتاة ساذجة، ولقد أحببتها لهذه الصفة بالذات — She is an innocent girl, and I loved her specifically for that characteristic

88 | 3378 |

1127 مَشْهَد *n.* pl. مَشاهِد scene, view, spectacle, sight

وما إن فتحت الباب حتى تبدى أمامها المشهد الذى لن يفارق ذهنها بعد ذلك أبدا — Hardly had she opened the door when a scene that will never be erased from her memory appeared before her

88 | 3365 |

1128 لَقِيَ *v.* I (a) to find; meet, encounter sb/sth

بعد ذلك بشهور لقي مصرعه برصاص المتعصبين — A few months after that he was killed by bullets from fanatics

98 | 3049 |

1129 تَحَدٍّ *n.* pl. -aat (تَحَدِّي def.) challenge

كيف استطعتم سيادتكم أن تجتازوا بمصر كل التحديات الكبرى؟ — How were you, Your Excellency, able to get Egypt through all the major challenges?

89 | 3349 |

1130 عَمَّا *prep.phr.* (عَنْ ما) about what, from what; concerning, regarding; عَمَّا قَرِيبٍ shortly, soon; عَمَّا إذا (about) whether

أنا أعتذر عما قلته لك يا سيدتي.. أرجو أن تغفري لى — I apologize for what I said to you, ma'am. I beg you to forgive me

89 | 3313 |

1131 جِدار *n.* pl. جُدْران wall; الجِدار العازل/الفاصِل the Wall of Separation, the West Bank Wall

كان بالصالة الخارجية الملحقة بالغرفة يتأمل الجدران شديدة القذارة ويندهش من الرائحة التى تصعد من دورة المياه — He was in the outer hall that is attached to the room, considering the extremely dirty walls and being surprised at the smell coming out of the bathroom

89 | 3316 |

1132 مَجَلَّة *n.* pl. -aat magazine, journal

أجرت معه أسرة تحرير المجلة حوارا تحدث فيه عن سيرته ومسيرته الثقافية والفنية — The editorial staff of the magazine held an interview with him in which he spoke about his life story and his cultural and artistic journey

95 | 3115 |

1133 هُجُوم *n.* attack, assault; charge, raid

بدأت أمستردام فى غمر أجزاء من حدودها بالمياه لعرقلة أى هجوم ألماني — Amsterdam began to flood parts of its outlying areas with water to prevent any German attack

87 | 3376 |

1134 مُهَنْدِس *n.* engineer, technician

شغل فيصل وهو شاب وظيفة مهندس احصاء لدى احدى المؤسسات الخاصة — As a young man Faisal worked as a statistical engineer with one of the private establishments

92 | 3209 |

1135 تَجاوَزَ *v.* VI to surmount, overcome sth; to exceed, go beyond, overstep sth; to disregard, bypass sth

عاشت عمرها ملتزمة ولم تسمح لأحد فى الكلية بأن يتجاوز حدود الزمالة — She lived her life in accordance with the rules, and she did not allow anyone in the college to go beyond the line of being merely colleagues

89 | 3316 |

1136 صِناعِيّ *adj.* industrial, industrialized; manufacturing; artificial

ضع فيها بعض الورود والزهور الطبيعية، وإذا لم تتوافر فيمكنك وضع الزهور الصناعية — Put some natural roses and flowers in it, and if there aren't any, then you can put in artificial flowers

91 | 3228 |

1137 مِسَاحَة *n.* pl. -aat surface; space; land, terrain
يمتلك شقة فاخرة من مستويين، تطل على شارع
فيصل بالهرم — He owns a luxurious apartment
with two levels, which looks out on Faisal
Street in the Pyramids area
96 | 3077 |

1138 قَضَى *v. I (i)* to eliminate على sth/sb; to pass,
spend (time, holiday); to stipulate, decree ب
sth; to fulfill, complete (a duty); (pass.) قُضِيَ
عَلَيْه to be sentenced
ثيابها متسخة وكأنها قضت ليلتها على الرصيف —
Her clothes are dirty as if she spent the night
on the sidewalk
99 | 2985 |

1139 مُحَدَّد *adj.* defined, determined, set
ليس لديه تعليمات محددة فى حالة دخول الألمان إلى
المدينة — He does not have specific instructions
in case the German's enter the city
95 | 3086 |

1140 تِسْعَة *num. fem.* تِسْع nine; تِسْعَةَ عَشَرَ nineteen
وبلغ عدد الجنود المتقاتلين من الناحيتين على الجبهة
الروسية تسعة ملايين جندى فى حرب لم تعرفها
البشرية ضراوة — The number of fighting
soldiers from the two sides on the Russian
front was nine million soldiers in a war of
a ferocity that mankind had never known
96 | 3049 |

1141 تَعْدِيل *n.* pl. -aat change, modification;
adjustment; amendment; reshuffle (cabinet)
توجهت الحكومة مؤخرا لوضع تعديلات على قانون
المطبوعات والنشر بموجبها تلغى عقوبة حبس
الصحافيين — The government has recently
gone in the direction of instituting changes
in the law of publications and publishing,
according to which the punishment of
imprisoning journalists will be cancelled
85 | 3441 |

1142 نُمُوّ *n.* development, growth; progress
مادام التدخين يؤثر في نمو دماغ الجنين فمن الطبيعي
أن يكون مستقبلي على القدرة العقلية لدى
الوليد — As long as smoking influences the
growth of the brain of the fetus, it is natural
that it would have a future effect on the
intellectual capabilities of the child
85 | 3447 |

1143 حَرْف *n.* pl. حُرُوف letter (of the alphabet)
لقد كره البهى مبكرا كل محاولة لأن يتعلم حرفا فى
الكتاب أو الزاوية أو البيت — Bahiy hated early
on all attempts to have him learn even a
single letter either at the Qurʾan school or at
the mosque or at home
94 | 3111 |

1144 مُؤْمِن *adj.* believing, faithful; *n.* pl. -uun
believer; Muslim
أرجوك.. أنا مسيحية مؤمنة.. هل يمكن أن تحترم
مشاعرى قليلا؟ — I beg you...I am a believing
Christian...Can you respect my feelings
somewhat?
87 | 3361 |

1145 اِعْتَمَد *v. VIII* to depend, rely على on sth/sb; to
adopt, authorize, accredit (plan, method,
curriculum)
عرفت سر الكرنك الاقتصادى فهو لا يعتمد
أساسا على زبائنه المحدودين ولكن على أصحاب
الحوانيت بشارع المهدى — I found out the
economic secret of Al-Karnak, for it does not
rely at base on its limited customers, but
rather on the owners of the shops in Al-Mahdi
Street
94 | 3088 |

1146 فَجْأَة *n.* surprise; فَجْأَةً and فُجْأَة suddenly
تكون هادئة ولطيفة للغاية، وفجأة تنتابها حالة
من الهياج بلا سبب — She will be calm
and very nice, and then suddenly a state
of agitation will sweep over her without
a reason
95 | 3052 | +lit

1147 سَهْل *adj.* easy, simple
تذكر أن علاج الإدمان ليس سهلا.. يجب دائما
أن نخفض توقعاتنا — Remember that the
treatment for addiction is not easy...we must
always lower our expectations
99 | 2922 |

1148 سَبْت *n.* السَّبْت (يَوْم) Saturday
دعا زوجته إلى العشاء يوم السبت فى المطعم المكسيكي
المفضل لديها — He invited his wife to dinner
on Saturday at her favorite Mexican restaurant
94 | 3060 |

1149 لَوْ *part.* (conditional) لَوْ ... لَـ if...then (would have)...; لَوْلَا ... لَمَا ... if not for...then (wouldn't have)

جزاه الله كل خير، لولا أمره هذا لكنت من الهالكين! — May God reward him greatly: had it not been for that order of his, I would be doomed!

89 | 3220 |

1150 مُبَاشَرَة *n.* pursuit, practice; performance, execution, implementation; مُبَاشَرَةً directly, immediately

لم يحب أن يذهب إلى المحطة من داره مباشرة — He didn't like going to the station from his house directly

97 | 2961 |

1151 بَنُو *pl.n.* (gen./acc. بَنِي; sg. بن cf. ابْن) sons, children (tribe, people); (Dia.) بَنِي آدَم human being (fem. بَنِي آدْمَة, pl. بَنِي آدْمِين)

هو من الحيوانات التي أمر الله بني إسرائيل بألا يأكلوها لأنها نجسة — It is one of the animals that God commanded the children of Israel not to eat, because they are unclean

95 | 3011 |

1152 مَنْع *n.* prevention, prohibition; depriving, withholding

لا أستطيع منع نفسي من التفكير فيه — I cannot keep myself from thinking about it

88 | 3244 |

1153 خَطِير *adj.* significant, important; serious, grave; dangerous, risky

لا تخافي.. العملية ليست خطيرة — Don't be afraid...the operation is not dangerous

93 | 3056 |

1154 رَحِمَ *v. I (a)* to have mercy (God) on sb; رَحِمَهُ الله God rest his soul

الله يرحم رفيق الحريري راح وراح معاه الشرف والاخلاص — God have mercy on Rafiq Al-Hariri; he passed away, and with him passed away nobility and loyalty

96 | 2967 |

1155 حَاجّ *n.* fem. حَاجَّة pl. حُجَاج pilgrim (esp. to Mecca); حَاجّ Hajj, fem. حَاجَّة Hajja (title of respect for a person who has made the pilgrimage to Mecca; also, polite form of address to an older person)

قد أعدت «السعودية» خطتها لنقل الحجاج في مرحلتي القدوم والعودة بعد دراسة مستفيضة للمواسم السابقة — Saudi Arabia prepared its plan for transferring the pilgrims during the stages of arrival and return after a thorough study of the previous seasons

96 | 2956 |

1156 لِذا *conj.* therefore, that's why, because of that

لا أرغب أن أتعلق بأذيال الأوهام.. لذا سأسألك وأريد الجواب فورا — I do not wish to cling to illusions...Therefore, I shall ask you and I want an immediate answer

88 | 3235 |

1157 وَظِيفَة *n.* pl. وَظائِف job, position; work, employment; function, task

أحب أن أكون صريحة معك.. لا أعتقد أن الوظيفة تناسبك — I want to be frank with you...I don't believe that the job is suitable for you

97 | 2939 |

1158 قَانُونِيّ *adj.* legal, law-related, statutory; legitimate, licit, legal; قَانُونِيّاً legally, from a legal standpoint

مستقبله العلمي مهدد.. اليوم وجهوا له إنذارا قانونيا، وغدا يفصلونه — His scientific future is threatened...Today they sent him a legal warning, and tomorrow they might expel him

82 | 3475 |

1159 هُما *pron.* they both

لقد ناما وهما يشاهدان التلفزيون — They slept while they were watching TV

91 | 3107 |

1160 عامِل *n.* pl. عَوامِل factor, element, agent; (math.) coefficient

يعد التعليم عاملا مهما في حياة اي مجتمع من المجتمعات — Education is considered to be an important factor in any society

92 | 3072 |

1161 إِدارِيّ *adj.* administrative, management, departmental

هناك توجهات ما تزال قيد الدراسة لتتولى وزارة
العدل الاشراف الإداري على السجون بدل وزارة
الداخلية — There is a suggestion still being
studied to have the Ministry of Justice
take over the administrative supervision
of the prisons instead of the Ministry of the
Interior

91 | 3114 |

1162 إِرْهابيّ *n./adj.* terrorist
نتفق أن ما حصل في ١١ من سبتمبر هو عملية
إرهابية ما زالت حتى منطقتنا تعاني منها — We
agree that what happened on the 11th of
September is a terrorist operation which even
our region is still suffering from

83 | 3388 |

1163 صَبْر *n.* patience, endurance
— لم يعد لي صبر.. كان لابد أن أخبر مصطفى
I no longer had any patience...I had to tell
Mustafa

98 | 2875 |

1164 ضَحِيَّة *n. pl.* ضَحايا victim
القوات الإسرائيلية لاحقتهم وارتكبت مذبحة بشعة
راح ضحيتها أكثر من ٢٠ شخصا — The Israeli
forces chased them and committed a terrible
massacre that left more than twenty people
dead

88 | 3199 |

1165 غَضَب *n.* anger, rage; غَضَباً in anger, angrily
سمع من الجيران كلاما عن ابنه اشتاط له غضبا
فدخل على ابنه في حجرته وانهال عليه بالضرب بيديه
ورجليه — He heard from the neighbors
something about his son which inflamed him
with anger, so he went to his son in his room
and started beating him with his hands and
feet

90 | 3145 |

1166 أَلْمانيّ *n./adj. pl.* أَلْمان German
هذه أول مرة يشاهدون الألمان الذين ظلوا لغزا منذ
اندلاع الحرب — This was the first time they
saw Germans, who had remained a riddle
since the beginning of the war

93 | 3041 |

1167 إِنْجاز *vn.* implementation, carrying out
(project); *n. pl.* -aat accomplishment,
achievement, success
يتوقع لهم تحقيق إنجازات باهرة — He expects
them to achieve remarkable things

86 | 3274 |

1168 عَبَّر *v. II* to express عن (opinion, feeling),
state عن (position, policy)
تتكهرب الأجواء كالعادة كلما عبرت ميشيل عن
آرائها الحادة — The air was electrified, as usual,
whenever Michelle expressed her sharp
opinions

91 | 3084 |

1169 جَمال *n.* beauty
كانت تدرك أنها جميلة ، وأن جمالها من النوع
الذى يثير شهوة الرجال — She knew she was
beautiful, and that her beauty was of the type
that incited the desires of men

98 | 2880 |

1170 صادِر *adj.* issued, published; exported; *n.*
صادِرات exports
قدرت دراسة صادرة عن جامعة نايف العربية
أعداد المدمنين في السعودية حتى العام قبل
الماضي بـ ٢٥٢٦٠ مدمنا — A study
published by the Arabic University of Nayf
estimated the number of addicts in Saudi
Arabia the year before last to be 25,260
addicts

84 | 3334 |

1171 فِئَة *n. pl.* -aat faction, party; group, sector;
type, kind, class
— فى حوزتها ثلاثون ألف ورقة من فئة الجنيه
She has in her possession thirty thousand
one pound notes

86 | 3267 |

1172 مُتَوَسِّط *adj.* middle, central; medium,
average
أغلبية هؤلاء هم من الطبقة المتوسطة وجاؤوا
تحت ضغط الحالة الأمنية — Most of those are
from the middle class, and came due to
pressure from the security situation

95 | 2957 |

1173 زَعِيم *n.* pl. زُعَمَاء leader, head of state
يسلط الكتاب الضوء على حياة زعيم حزب العمل الإسرائيلي إيهود باراك وعلى سياسته ومواقفه وخداعه للعرب — The book shines a light on the life of the leader of the Israeli Labor Party, Ehud Barak, and on his policy and his positions and his deceiving the Arabs
84 | 3346 |

1174 أَحَد *n.* الأَحَد (يَوْم) Sunday; (Egy.) الحَدّ (يوم), الأَحَد (يوم) (Irq.)
— كان من عادته يوم الأحد أن يصحو متأخرا
It was his custom on Sundays to get up late
93 | 3004 |

1175 اِنْطَلَقَ *v. VII* to depart, take off; to begin, get started; to be fired (bullet)
أصر على أن الرصاص انطلق من بندقيته دون قصد — He insisted that the bullets had been shot from the rifle unintentionally
89 | 3135 |

1176 دَقَّ *v. I (u)* to beat (heart); to strike, hit sth; to knock on (door) or على (door); to ring (bell); to call لـ sb (on the phone)
أحست بقلبها يدق بعنف، واجتاحتها هواجس مرعبة — She felt her heart beating violently, and frightening anxieties swept over her
88 | 3178 | +spo

1177 اِسْتِعْداد *vn.* preparation; *n.* readiness, willingness; عَلَى اِسْتِعْداد ready; اِسْتِعْدادات preparations, arrangements
كانت على استعداد للمساهمة في نفقات البيت بأكثر من ذلك — She was ready to participate in the household expenses with more than that
88 | 3158 |

1178 دَفْع *vn.* pushing; compelling, moving, driving; payment; pushing back, repelling
نجحت في دفعه إلى التقدم لخطبتها رسميا من أهلها قبل نهاية المهلة المحددة — She succeeded in pushing him to officially ask her family for her hand in marriage before the end of the specified period
88 | 3166 |

1179 تَعَلَّمَ *v. V* to learn, study sth
— يجب أن تتعلم كيف تعامل النساء في أمريكا
You must learn how to deal with women in America
98 | 2851 |

1180 مِثال *n.* pl. مُثُل, أَمْثِلَة example, model, ideal
لدينا الكثير من الأمثلة عن المدارس التي تعاني من وضع صعب جدا — We have many examples of schools which are suffering from very difficult circumstances
92 | 3008 |

1181 فَرَح *n.* joy, happiness; pl. أَفْراح party, celebration, festivity; فَرَحاً with joy, joyfully
وجد رجل محفظة نقود فكاد أن يطير من شدة الفرح، وعندما فتحها وجد فيها فاتورة كهرباء، فذهب دفع ثمنها — A man found a wallet with money, and was almost beside himself with joy, and when he opened it he found an electric bill, so he went and paid it
98 | 2841 |

1182 رِواية *n.* pl. -aat novel, story; narration; report, account
يتنقل باسكوال – بطل الرواية – من جريمة إلى جريمة وينتهي بقتل أمه — Pasquale, the hero of the novel, goes from crime to crime and ends up killing his mother
86 | 3233 |

1183 أَجْمَل *elat.* more/most beautiful
أجمل أيام عمري تلك التي قضيتها متشردا في الشوارع — The most beautiful days of my life were those I spent homeless in the streets
95 | 2919 |

1184 نَهْر *n.* pl. أنْهار river
تحدث عن اهمية المياه خاصة نهر النيل في حياة المصريين — He spoke about the importance of water, especially the Nile River, in the life of Egyptians
96 | 2886 |

1185 كَهْرُباء and كَهْرَباء *n.* electricity
الكهرباء انقطعت، والكوبري مفتوح للمراكب، يعني لازم ننتظر — The electricity was cut off while the bridge was open for ships, which means we have to wait
95 | 2915 |

1186 وَصَفَ *v. I (i)* to describe, characterize sth/sb ب/بِأَنَّهُ as; (doctor) to prescribe sth ل to sb

كانت فرحتها لا توصف وهي تراقب أمها تكويها قطعة بعد قطعة بمكواة قديمة — Her joy could not be described as she watched her mother iron for her one piece of clothing after another with an old iron

89 | 3111 |

1187 ما *part.* (nominalizing, with foll. perf.)

بَعْدَ ما ذَهَبُوا = بَعْدَ ذَهَابِهِم بعدما قام أهل القرية بترميم المدرسة، تم هدمها — After the people of the village had built the school, it was torn down

95 | 2915 |

1188 مِهْرَجان and مَهْرَجان *n. pl.* -aat festival

أكثر من ١٠٠٠ شخص تابعوا مهرجان الرقص الشرقي السابع في القاهرة — More than 1,000 people followed the Seventh Eastern Dance Festival in Cairo

88 | 3129 | +news

1189 أَلَّا *conj.* (= أَنْ لا) not to

صعد ببطء على الدرج المفضي إلى حجرة النوم محاولا ألَّا يحدث صوتا لئلا يوقظ زوجته — He went slowly up the stairs leading to the bedroom, trying not to make a sound so as not to wake up his wife

89 | 3080 |

1190 اِنْتِظار *vn.* waiting, anticipating

أوقف السيارة في مكان الانتظار وأغلقها أوتوماتيكيا — He stopped the car in the parking place and locked it automatically

89 | 3078 |

1191 رَضِيَ *v. I (a)* to be pleased, satisfied ب/عن/على with sth; رَضِيَ اللهُ عَنْهُ may God be pleased with him

وهل يرضى شاب ذكي مثل قيس أن يترك المدرسة ليغلق مستقبله بيده؟ — Would a smart young man like Qais be satisfied with leaving school to shut off his future with his own hand?

93 | 2944 |

1192 سَنَوِيّ *adj.* annual, yearly; سَنَوِيّاً annually, yearly

كثير من الأمهات يخلدن الذكرى السنوية لموت عزيز عليهن — Many mothers mark the anniversary of the death of one of their loved ones

84 | 3275 |

1193 نَصْر *n.* victory, triumph

النصر من عند الله آت لا ريب فيه — Victory from God is coming, no doubt

88 | 3112 |

1194 تَعْزِيز *vn.* strengthening, bolstering, reinforcing; *n.* reinforcement

ستعمل الحكومة ايضا على ربط الانتاج الزراعي بمتطلبات السوق وتعزيز الصادرات كما ونوعا — The government will also work on linking agricultural production with the requirements of the market, and on strengthening exports, in quantity and quality

74 | 3713 |

1195 أَدَب *n. pl.* آداب literature; good manners, etiquette

دخل الجامعة ليدرس آداب.. وقع في شباك حب زميلة له — He entered the university to study literature...He fell into the love trap of one of his colleagues

96 | 2860 |

1196 لَعْبَة *n.* contest, competition, game; *un.n.* (one) match, game; (fig.) trick, fast one

لا بد أن يلتزم بقوانين اللعبة — He needs to adhere to the rules of the game

96 | 2832 |

1197 عَقْد *n. pl.* عُقُود contract, agreement

نادي النجمة وقع عقدا لزراعة ملعب المنارة بالعشب الاصطناعي — The Star Club signed a contract to plant artificial turf in the Al-Manara Stadium

95 | 2874 |

1198 أَثَارَ *v. IV* to raise, provoke, stir up sth; to bring up (a subject)

كل شيء في هذه المدينة يثير دهشتي — Everything in this city surprises me

90 | 3015 |

16 Emotions

Adjectives

Positive

699	مشكور	thankful
1295	سعيد	happy
3043	راضي	pleased
3874	مرتاح	relaxed
4523	مقتنع	satisfied; convinced
4594	شاكر	thankful
4654	مبسوط	happy
4736	سالم	safe
4792	واعي	alert
5092	مصدّق	convinced
5133	فاخر	proud
5901	حازم	resolute
6204	صاحي	vigilant
6343	سهران	awake
6686	فرح	cheerful
7045	فرحان	cheerful
7203	يقظ	awake
7505	رضيّ	satisfied
7745	معتزّ	proud

Neutral

1596	هادئ	calm
1673	بريء	innocent
1808	جادّ	serious
2437	صامت	silent
2494	مشغول	busy
2505	جدّيّ	serious
2507	فارغ	free, idle
2906	واثق	confident
3123	مهتمّ	interested
3192	حريص	mindful
3619	متأكّد	certain
3789	فاضي	available, free
4076	مطمئنّ	relieved, reassured
4118	آسف	sorry
5031	مستغرب	surprised
6301	ساكت	silent
6383	رايق	calm
6744	خجل	embarrassed

Negative

1285	ضعيف	weak
1766	حزين	sad
2308	مجنون	crazy
2335	عصبيّ	nervous
2808	غاضب	angry
2946	عاجز	incapable
3507	ضائع	lost
3626	قلق	worried
4008	مظلوم	oppressed, threatened
4287	مهدّد	threatened
4370	غارق	immersed
4827	زعلان	angry
4954	غلطان	mistaken
5257	حائر	confused
5537	باهت	pale; startled
5691	تعبان	tired
6066	واهم	deluded
6317	تعب	tired
6353	متضايق	annoyed
6377	زهقان	disgusted
6488	عيّان	sick
6676	ضايج	bored
6816	طائح	lost

Verbs

Positive

1191	رضي	to be satisfied with
3200	فرح	to rejoice
3561	تشرّف	to be honored
4086	عجب	to please
4144	عشق	to love, be fond of
4327	ارتاح	to relax
4503	سعد	to be happy
5554	سرّ	to delight, make happy
5588	هوي	to love/like
6192	انبسط	to have fun
7338	هام	to be in love

Neutral

1625	اهتمّ	to be interested in
2475	تأثّر	to be affected by
2893	اكتفى	to be content with
2935	همّ	to concern; to worry
2964	تعوّد	to become accustomed to
2975	سكت	to be quiet
2997	هدأ	to calm down
4111	استغرب	to be surprised at
6176	درج	to get used to
6411	تفاجأ	to be surprised

Negative

1042	خاف	to be afraid of
1679	خشي	to fear
2607	عجز	to be incapable
2621	تعب	to be tired
4154	غضب	to become angry
4480	حزن	to be sad
4803	أسف	to be sorry
5167	زعل	to be angry
5402	جنّ	to go crazy
5631	قلق	to be worried
6302	حار	to be confused
6687	تخوّف	to be afraid
6693	طاح	to be lost
6725	خجل	to be shy, embarrassed
6889	تضايق	to be annoyed
7096	خبل	to be confused
7358	تاه	to get lost
7569	رعب	to be alarmed

1199 شَرّ *n.* evil, malice

كل ما يفعله شر مطلق — Everything he does is absolute evil

95 | 2876 |

1200 مُعارَضَة *n.* opposition (esp. in politics), resistance

لا يبدو أن فتح فعلا قادرة على استيعاب أنها في المعارضة — It doesn't appear that Fatah is actually capable of recognizing that it is in the opposition

79 | 3442 |

1201 نَبَأ *n.* news item, report; pl. أنْباء news

كانت هناك أنباء عن وصول قوات ألمانية كبيرة إلى ليبيا — There was news of the arrival of large German forces to Libya

87 | 3128 |

1202 عُدْوان *n.* aggression, hostility; enmity, animosity

سنخسر عطف العالم إذا سجل علينا هذا العدوان الصارخ — We will lose the sympathy of the world if this blatant hostility is attributed to us

88 | 3064 |

1203 خِطاب *n.* speech; message, letter

بدأ يكتب الخطاب على الكمبيوتر، لكنه فجأة نهض من مكانه وكأنما تذكر شيئا ما — He began to write the letter on the computer, but suddenly he got up from his place as if he remembered something

88 | 3084 |

1204 عُمُوم *n.* generality, totality, whole; people, masses, public; عُمُوماً in general, generally; مَجْلِس العُمُوم House of Commons

الثقافة الاقتصادية عموما في مجتمعنا تكاد تكون زيرو إن لم تتخطى هذا — Economic culture in general in our society is almost nothing if it doesn't go beyond this

92 | 2958 |

1205 اِخْتارَ *v. VIII* to select, pick, choose sth/sb; to prefer, choose sth على over sth else

يجب أن نختار شخصا لا يتوقعه صفوت شاكر إطلاقا — We must choose a person who Safwat Shakir will not at all expect

99 | 2736 |

1206 إيجابيّ *adj.* good, positive; affirmative

موسكو لا زالت تؤيد معظم قضايانا الرئيسية، وتلعب دورا إيجابيا في أزماتنا الملتهبة — Moscow still supports most of our principle issues, and it plays a positive role in our burning crises

81 | 3322 |

1207 جَوْلَة *n.* pl. -aat tour; round; session; patrol

ورفعت اليابان رصيدها الى ست نقاط بعد فوزها في الجولة الاولى على باكستان ٣ – ٢ — Japan increased its total to six points after its victory in the first round over Pakistan, 3–2

93 | 2891 |

1208 رَفْض *n.* rejection, refusal

أشار بيده علامة الرفض ومضى بعيدا — He signaled his refusal with his hand, and went off

88 | 3048 |

1209 أعْظَم *elat.* fem. عُظْمَى greater/greatest, mightier/mightiest; *adj.* major, supreme

إني أعرفك جيدا، ألست فيلسوف اليونان الأعظم إلى جانب تلميذك أرسطو؟ — I know you well, aren't you the greatest philosopher of Greece next to your student Aristotle?

89 | 3035 |

1210 شِراء *n.* buying, purchasing; purchase, acquisition

كان يقف على المخبز يتزاحم مع الناس عله يفوز بشراء كيلوغرام من الخبز — He was standing near the bakery, crowding with the people so he might succeed in buying a kilo of bread

88 | 3033 |

1211 مَسْرَح *n.* theater, stage

عادت فيروز أكثر من أربع مرات الى المسرح — Fairuz returned more than four times to the stage

84 | 3167 |

1212 غِياب *n.* absence; disappearance

لقد عرف إن أخواته بعن أرضه لأنفسهن فى غيابه — He found out his sisters had sold his land for themselves in his absence

88 | 3023 |

1213 حَلْقَة *n.* pl. حَلَقَات and حَلْقَة ring, circle; link; program, show; (student) class, course

أهلا بكم إلى برنامج عبر المحيط من واشنطن.. في هذه الحلقة: إلى أي مدى تؤثر الاعتبارات الدينية على صياغة سياسة الرئيس بوش؟ — Welcome to the program "Across the Ocean" from Washington...In this episode: To what extent do religious considerations influence the formation of President Bush's policies?

97 | 2764 |

1214 ضَرُورِيّ *adj.* necessary, required

خضرا أرجوك ردي على الهاتف الأمر ضروري — Khadra, I beg you, answer the phone, the matter is urgent

94 | 2834 |

1215 فَساد *n.* corruption; deterioration, decomposition

هذا التفكير يعود إلى فساد النظام الحاكم في مصر وليس إلى المصريين أنفسهم — This thinking can be attributed to the corruption of the ruling regime in Egypt, and not to the Egyptians themselves

87 | 3074 |

1216 اِتِّفاقِيَّة *n.* pl. -aat treaty, accord

هذه الدول الثلاثة لم تنضم إلى اتفاقية منع انتشار السلاح النووي — These three countries did not join the Nuclear Non-proliferation Agreement

76 | 3491 |

1217 تَذَكَّرَ *v. V* to remember sth

بعد ثلاثين عاما لا يزال يتذكر تلك الليلة بوضوح — After thirty years he still remembers that night clearly

97 | 2742 |

1218 تَناوَلَ *v. VI* to deal with, treat (a subject, an issue); to eat (a meal); to take, ingest (medicine)

قدم له سيجارة، تناولها الرجل بأصابع مرتعشة.. أشعلها له دميان — He offered him a cigarette; the man took it from him with shaking fingers...Dumyan lit it for him

88 | 3027 |

1219 هَواء *n.* air, atmosphere; climate; عَلى الهَواء live (broadcast)

كان وجه أبيها الغاضب يظهر ويده ترتفع في الهواء — وتصفعها المرة تلو الأخرى The angry face of her father appeared, raising his hand in the air, striking her again and again

99 | 2694 |

1220 شَريف *adj.* pl. شُرَفاء noble, honorable, respectable; الحرمين الشريفين the Two Holy Mosques (of Mecca and Medina)

يقع الحرم الإبراهيمي الشريف في الخليل — The Ibrahimi Mosque is located in Hebron

90 | 2947 |

1221 قاض (قاضِي .def) *n.* pl. قُضاة judge, magistrate

لا يجوز لي أن أفتي لأن القاضي لا يجوز له أن يفتي — I should not give religious rulings since judges are not supposed to do that

84 | 3165 |

1222 داع (داعِي .def) *n.* reason, cause, motive; *a.p.* calling for sth, calling on sb, inviting sb; *n.* pl. دُعاة person (or voice) calling

لا داعي لجدل جانبي وهامشي لا قيمة له — There is no call for marginal arguments of no value

94 | 2837 |

1223 عَدْل *n.* justice, fairness; وَزير العَدْلِ Minister of Justice

هل من العدل أن تتحمل المرأة وحدها مسئولية الحمل غير المرغوب فيه؟ — Is it fair for woman alone to bear the responsibility of an unwanted pregnancy?

90 | 2939 |

1224 طَرَحَ *v. I (a)* to throw, cast sth; to pose, present, suggest (question, issue); على to sb (for discussion); to offer (gesture, greeting); to offer sth (for sale); to invite (bids, tenders); to float, put into circulation (shares)

طرحت عليه جميع الأسئلة عن أصل العائلة والعمل وكل شيء — She asked him all the questions about the origins of the family, and work, and everything

92 | 2857 |

1225 شَمالِيّ *adj.* northern, north
الصين تنتزع وعدا من كوريا الشمالية بعدم إجراء
تجربة نووية أخرى — China extracted a promise
from North Korea not to carry out another
nuclear test
92 | 2875 |

1226 جَدّ *n.* grandfather, fem. جَدَّة grandmother
بابا هل سيذهب جدي معنا إلى البحر؟ — Papa,
will Grandpa go with us to the sea?
93 | 2834 | +lit

1227 هاتِف *n. pl.* هَواتِف telephone
أرسلت رسالة قصيرة من هاتفها الجوال إلى هاتف
فيصل تقول له فيها: مبروك يا عريس — She sent
a short message from her cell phone to Faisal's
phone telling him: Congratulations, Bridegroom!
95 | 2764 |

1228 حَفِظَ *v. I (a)* to save, preserve, maintain; to
protect, guard; to memorize; الله يَحْفَظَك
(Irq./yHufDHak/) God preserve you!
(in response to praise or kind gesture)
كان من الصعب عليه أن يحفظ كل شيء بدقة لينقله،
فأصبحت الكتابة وسيلته لنقل المعلومات — It was
difficult for him to memorize everything
precisely to quote it, so writing became his
means of transferring information
97 | 2717 |

1229 ضُعْف *n.* weakness
الحب حالة ضعف وليس حالة قوة — Love is
a condition of weakness, not a condition of
strength
97 | 2708 |

1230 إِقْلِيمِيّ *adj.* regional, territorial, area;
provincial, district
لا أدري ما معنى قوة إقليمية؟ فإسرائيل اليوم قوة
إقليمية بمعنى من المعاني، فهي موجودة — I don't
know what the meaning of "regional power" is.
Israel today is a regional power in one sense,
since it exists
73 | 3577 |

1231 مَعْهَد *n. pl.* مَعاهِد institute, academy, school
بعدما تخرجت من معهد الموسيقى حاولت إنتاج
شريط — After I graduated from the Music
Institute I tried to produce a tape
96 | 2725 |

1232 دِي (Egy.) *dem.pron.* this (fem.sg.), these
(non-human pl. and fem.pl.)
دي مش ولية! دي مراتي! — This isn't some
woman! This is my wife!
73 | 3576 |

1233 طَيْر *n. pl.* طُيُور bird
تستطيع الطيور ان ترى مسافة واسعة من
الفضاء — Birds can see wide distances
from the air
86 | 3014 |

1234 إِمّا *conj.* إِمّا .. أَوْ/إِمّا either...or
قد علمتني الحياة أن الفرصة تأتي مرة واحدة، إما
أن نستغلها أو نضيعها إلى الأبد — Life has
taught me that opportunity comes only once;
either we take advantage of it or we lose
it forever
99 | 2647 |

1235 رِيح *n. pl.* رِياح wind; odor
انجلت الغيوم عن المدينة اليوم وخفت الرياح —
The clouds cleared from the city today, and
the winds calmed down
90 | 2883 |

1236 سَلْبِيّ *adj.* negative, passive; *n.* سَلْبِيّات
negative points
كنت أخاف أن يكون لتلك القصة تأثير سلبي
على علاقتنا، أو على نظرتك لي — I was afraid that
this story would have a negative effect on our
relationship, or on your view
of me
91 | 2851 |

1237 سادِس *adj.* sixth (ordinal)
تفكر في حياتها.. لقد بلغت السادسة والثلاثين ولم
تعش قط كما أرادت — She is thinking about her
life...she has reached thirty-six and has not at
all lived as she wanted
96 | 2697 |

1238 بَكَى *v. I (i)* to cry, weep (على over sth/sb);
to mourn, weep for sb
كلما قامت بتخريط البصل بكى الجيران —
Whenever she chopped onions, the neighbors
cried
89 | 2907 |

1239 دَواء *n.* pl. أَدْوِيَة remedy, medicine, medication
لكن شفاءه من الأزمة لم يأت نتيجة الأدوية ولا جلسات العلاج، وإنما بفضل صلابة داخلية — But his recovery from the health crisis did not come as a result of the medicine nor of the therapy sessions, but rather thanks to an inner toughness
96 | 2716 |

1240 وِجْهَة and وُجْهَة *n.* pl. -aat direction, angle; وجهة نظر point of view
اللي حصل من وجهة نظر القانون، يعتبر حادثة سرقة — What happened from the point of view of the law would be considered theft
97 | 2676 |

1241 عُمْق *n.* pl. أَعْماق depth, deep, bottom
جلست تفكر بعمق في كلام أمها ، لكن التليفون رن من جديد — She sat thinking deeply about her mother's words, but the telephone rang again
89 | 2904 |

1242 عَميق *adj.* deep, profound
وما إن وضعت رأسها على الوسادة حتى راحت فورا في نوم عميق — Hardly had she put her head on the pillow when she fell into a deep sleep
90 | 2885 |

1243 بَلَدِيَّة *n.* pl. -aat municipality, community, township; city council
اجتمعت لجنة الأسعار بالإسكندرية بدار البلدية لتحديد أسعار السلع — The prices committee in Alexandria met in the municipal building to set the prices of the goods
87 | 2965 |

1244 خَلاص (Egy.Gul.Alg.) *interj.* OK, that's it, it's over, that's enough
خلاص بقى حايسيب العسكرية ويبقى أفندي، لا يطلع دوريات — That's it, then, he will leave the military and become an Efendi, not going out on patrols
73 | 3546 | +spo

1245 سِيَّا (لاسِيَّا) (usu.) *adv.* especially
نقل عدد من أعماله البارزة إلى لغات متعددة، ولا سيما الفرنسية والإنكليزية — A number of his prominent works were translated into several languages, especially French and English
84 | 3060 |

1246 ضَمان *n.* pl. -aat guarantee, insurance
القانون في صيغته النهائية لم يقدم أية ضمانات جديدة تدعم حرية الإعلام — The law in its final form did not offer any new guarantees which support the freedom of the media
91 | 2834 |

1247 خَبير *n./adj.* pl. خُبَراء expert, specialist
يذكر التقرير السري بعض أقوال الخبراء أن كوريا الشمالية قد تستعد للقيام باختبارها الأول للسلاح النووي — The secret report mentions some quotes from experts that North Korea might be preparing to do its first testing of nuclear weapons
87 | 2963 |

1248 مَشَى *v.* I (i) to walk, go; to leave, go away; امْشِي! (Dia.) go away!
جه قعد شوية ومشى — He came and sat a while, and then left
76 | 3357 | +spo

1249 مُخَيَّم *n.* pl. -aat camp; refugee camp
أعاده البريطانيون إلى قبرص، قضى ستة أشهر في مخيم «فاماغوستا»، ثم وصل أخيرا إلى مخيم المهاجرين — The British returned him to Cyprus, he spent six months in the Famagusta Camp, and then he finally reached the Emigrants' camp
84 | 3053 |

1250 مادّيّ *adj.* material, physical; materialistic; financial; مادّيّاً materially, physically; financially
أحوال والدي المادية جيدة ثم إن صرف الدينار بالنسبة لليرة السورية عال جدا — My father's material condition is fine, and the exchange rate of the dinar for the Syrian lira is very high
95 | 2691 |

1251 تَوْفيق *n.* success; reconciliation, mediation
أتمنى لك التوفيق وكسب الكثير من الأصدقاء الجدد — I wish you success and (gaining) lots of new friends
92 | 2789 | +for

1252 صَعيد *n.* pl. أَصْعِدَة level, plane; الصعيد Upper Egypt

— يجب أن يجري هذا الحديث على أكثر من صعيد This conversation needs to take place on more than one level

81 | 3138 |

1253 فَوْر *n.* عَلى الفَوْر and فَوْراً immediately, at once; فَوْرَ immediately after

إذا لاحظ أدنى ارتباك أو تناقض في الإجابة يصطحبهم فورا إلى مكتب جانبي لاستجوابهم بشكل موسع — If he notices the slightest confusion or contradiction in the answer, he accompanies them immediately to a side office to interrogate them more extensively

93 | 2736 |

1254 فَرْض *vn.* imposing, levying; *n.* (religious) duty

لقد حاولت فرض منطقها علينا، وكل ما فعلناه أننا تجنبناها — She tried to impose her logic on us, and all we did was avoid her

95 | 2666 |

1255 مُدَرِّب *n.* trainer, coach; instructor

وقفوا جميعا أمام الاختصاصية كاترين وكأنهم لاعبون يتلقون توجيهات المدرب قبل المباراة — They all stood up in front of the specialist Catherine as if they were players receiving instructions from the coach before the match

80 | 3189 |

1256 حَمْل *n.* carrying; pregnancy

حاول أن يساعدني في حمل الحقيبة إلى السيارة، لكني رفضت شاكرا — He tried to help me carry the suitcase to the car, but I refused, thanking him

95 | 2668 |

1257 يالله (also يلا and يللا) /yaLLa/ (Dia.) *interj.* c'mon! hurry up! let's...!

يالله يا سيدي انت وهو.. ابقوا تعالوا — Come on, guy, you and him...come on!

41 | 6096 | +spo

1258 كَمِّيَّة *n.* pl. -aat quantity, amount

تركها وأخذ طريقه إلى المنزل وحمل لها أكبر كمية ممكنة من الهدايا — He left her and made his way to the house and brought her the largest possible number of gifts

93 | 2721 |

1259 أَيْ *part.* or, in other words, that is to say, i.e.

من يوم الأربعاء الماضي، اي قبل يومين، كنت حائرا، قلقا، دون سبب — Since last Wednesday, i.e. two days ago, I've been confused, worried, for no reason

73 | 3436 |

1260 قَدَّر *v. II* to estimate, calculated, appraise sth; to appreciate, value sth; to allow, make possible (of God); to respect sth, take sth into consideration

من ميزات هذه المبادرة التي لا تقدر بثمن انها لن تكلف الدولة فلسا واحدا — Among the characteristics of this priceless initiative is that it will not cost the state a single penny

91 | 2770 |

1261 حَرام *adj.* forbidden, out of bounds; sacred, holy; يا حَرام! what a shame!

— إن ما تفعلينه حرام شرعا بإجماع جمهور العلماء What you are doing is forbidden by religious law, with the consensus of all the religious scholars

95 | 2652 |

1262 مِتْر *n.* pl. أَمْتار meter

كان منزله يبعد نحو مائة متر عن موقف السيارات — His house was about a hundred meters from the parking lot

97 | 2611 |

1263 سُوء *n.* offense; bad, ill; miss-

ستتهمني بالجهل وسوء التصرف — She will accuse me of ignorance and bad behavior

89 | 2839 |

1264 فَقَد *v. I (i)* to lose sth; to lack, be missing sth

أخشى أن يفقد صلاح وظيفته — I am afraid that Salah will lose his job

90 | 2804 |

1265 اِشْتَرَى *v. VIII* to buy, purchase sth

لم يستطع بماله أن يشتري ضمائرنا — He wasn't able to buy our consciences with his money

94 | 2677 |

1266 سُودانِيّ *n./adj.* Sudanese

تقوم السلطات السودانية بالقبض على الفتيات الحاملات جراء تعرضهن للاغتصاب على يد عناصر ميليشيا الجنجويد — The Sudanese authorities are arresting the girls who became pregnant as a result of their being raped by members of the Janjaweed militia

76 | 3291 |

1267 كَلْب *n.* pl. كِلاب dog

كان الوقت ظهرا حين أعلن نباح الكلب عن قدوم السيد الذي هبط من سيارته البيجو — It was noontime when the barking of the dog announced the arrival of the man who got out of his Peugeot

91 | 2743 |

1268 نامَ *v. I (a)* to sleep; lie down

صفا ذهنها وتحررت عضلاتها من التوتر وكأنها نامت بعمق يوما كاملا — Her mind became clear and her muscles freed themselves of stress, as if she had gone into a deep sleep for an entire day

92 | 2727 |

1269 قَصْر *n.* pl. قُصُور castle, palace

لقد كان يسمح لكل من في القصر بالذهاب إلى المكتبة للقراءة والاطلاع — He allowed everyone in the palace to go to the library to read and browse

97 | 2572 |

1270 حادِثَة *n.* pl. حَوادِث accident, mishap; event, incident

أكدت الدراسة ان ظاهرة تزايد حوادث النقل في مصر اتخذت في الآونة الأخيرة بعدا دوليا — The study confirmed that the phenomenon of traffic accidents in Egypt has taken, in recent times, an international dimension

97 | 2566 |

1271 ليه /leeh/ *(Egy.Lev.Gul.) interrog.* why

أنت مش مبسوط ليه، مع إن الكلام دا في الأصل إقتراحك؟ — Why aren't you happy, even though this was your idea in the first place?

56 | 4434 | +spo

1272 دَرْس *vn.* studying; examining, checking; *n.* pl. دُرُوس lesson, course, study

لقد أضعت وقت الدرس في كلام بلا معنى — You have wasted the class's time with meaningless words

97 | 2579 |

1273 اِنْتِهاء *n.* finish, completion, conclusion

نشرت الصحف قصيدة شوقي التي كتبها عن باريس بعد انتهاء الحرب الأولى — The newspapers published Shawqi's ode which he wrote about Paris after the end of World War I

88 | 2831 |

1274 تَضَمَّنَ *v. V* to guarantee; comprise, include

لقد أعددت وثيقة تضمنت أربعة عشر فصلا وغطت كل هذه القضايا — I have prepared a document that included fourteen chapters and covered all these issues

82 | 3048 |

1275 حَدَّدَ *v. II* to specify, determine sth; to set, define sth

ظل يحدثني طويلا دون أن يحدد مبتغاه — He kept talking to me for a long time without making his desires clear

97 | 2561 |

1276 لَوْحَة *n.* pl. -aat painting, picture; panel, board; لَوْحَة مَفاتيح keyboard

إن أجمل لحظة في حياتي عندما أضع الفرشاة الأخيرة على اللوحة — The most beautiful moment of my life is when I put the last brush stroke on the canvas

88 | 2816 |

1277 (مِن مَن) مِمَّن *prep.phr.* from whom

عدد الطلبة ممن هم فوق معدل ٧٩ يقدر ب ١٦٨٤٠ طالبا وطالبة — The number of students who are above a 79 average is estimated at 16,840 male and female students

87 | 2840 |

1278 طَرْح *n.* suggestion, proposal (topic, idea); offering (gesture, greeting); offering (for sale); inviting (bids, tenders); floating, putting into circulation (shares)

لم يعد بإمكان الصحفي طرح سؤال آخر.. فسؤاله الوحيد كان جوابه محاضرة كافية وشاملة — The journalist was not able to submit another question...since the answer to his only question was a comprehensive and sufficient lecture

86 | 2858 |

17 Movement

109	جاء	to come	2332	ابتعد	to move away from	5634	روّح	to go home
113	راح	to go				5667	هجر	to emigrate
123	عاد	to return	2374	توجّه	to head towards	5708	اتّبع	to follow
183	وصل	to arrive				5747	ضلّ	to go astray
297	دخل	to enter	2395	طار	to fly	5793	دبّ	to crawl
343	أتى	to come	2412	صعد	to rise	5827	ساق	to drive, pilot
345	خرج	to go out	2543	فات	to pass by	5853	تجوّل	to roam
472	ترك	to leave	3025	سال	to flow	5887	مرق	to pass
489	ذهب	to go	3026	قفز	to jump	5920	تخلّف	to be late
510	مرّ	to pass by	3069	انقلب	to turn over	5949	تعثّر	to crawl, move slowly
613	رجع	to return	3095	غرق	to sink, drown			
673	نزل	to descend	3121	قدم	to arrive, come	5979	جاوز	to pass, exceed
809	حضر	to come; attend	3159	هبط	to drop; land	6007	زحف	to crawl, march
819	سار	to walk	3167	قرب	to approach			
860	سعى	to pursue	3263	أقبل	to approach	6109	عدّى	to cross
887	تابع	to follow	3288	أقدم	to undertake, approach	6191	نفذ	to penetrate
908	مضى	to go by				6232	توغّل	to make an incursion
1025	سبق	to precede	3333	عبر	to cross			
1030	قطع	to cover (a distance) (also cut)	3573	انخفض	to drop, fall	6242	تسرّب	to infiltrate
			3652	هدى	to guide	6299	أسرى	to travel by night
1034	دار	to revolve	3816	ركض	to run			
1100	تقدّم	to submit; advance	3856	نبع	to emanate	6417	تعاقب	to follow consecutively
			3873	حلّق	to hover;			
1135	تجاوز	to go beyond	3912	اخترق	to traverse, cross	6581	بعد	to go away
1175	انطلق	to depart				6677	عجل	to hurry
1248	مشى	to walk	3935	سارع	to hurry to	6835	عقب	to follow
1289	قاد	to drive, pilot	3974	تسلّل	to infiltrate	6871	حوّس	to take a walk
1381	تحرّك	to move	3991	شقّ	to cut through	6876	أوغل	to penetrate
1383	اقترب	to get close to	4079	تدفّق	to flow	6919	راج	to circulate
1512	انتقل	to transfer	4138	سبح	to swim	6929	تمشّى	to walk, stroll
1672	سافر	to travel	4145	حطّ	to descend, land	6960	خشّ	to enter
1699	تبع	to follow				7009	سرّع	to accelerate
1706	غادر	to leave	4360	جال	to wander about	7137	تهرّب	to escape
1869	تراجع	to retreat	4426	جرّ	to drag	7197	عام	to float, swim
1870	ورد	to arrive	4491	اقتحم	to invade	7206	غرب	to depart
1901	علا	to rise	4624	عدا	to run	7255	وثب	to jump, leap
1953	فاق	to surpass	4747	تصاعد	to climb	7358	تاه	to get lost
2009	اتّجه	to face towards	4844	فرّ	to escape	7464	تسرّع	to hurry
			5059	رقي	to ascend	7504	مار	to move from side to side
2033	لحق	to be attached	5122	قلّب	to turn upside down			
2200	هرب	to flee				7511	تقارب	to approach
2203	رحل	to travel	5291	حام	to hover, circle	7557	نهج	to pursue, follow
2221	تأخّر	to be late	5516	خطا	to step, walk			
2299	توصّل	to arrive at	5550	أتبع	to follow	7767	جوّل	to travel
						7852	وشك	to hurry

1279 جَنُوبِيّ *adj.* southern, south

المسلحون الآن محاصرون في الجهة الجنوبية للمخيم في مساحة تبلغ ١٠٠٠ متر مربع — The armed men are now surrounded in the south of the camp in an area of 1,000 square meters

92 | 2683 |

1280 عَرَضَ *v. I (i)* to show, exhibit, present sth; to review, inspect sth

استعان بزوجة أحد أصدقائه العرب التي عرضت تعليمها القيادة لقاء مبلغ مالي — He asked the help of the wife of one of his Arab friends who offered to teach her to drive in exchange for an amount of money

94 | 2624 |

1281 مَقَرّ *n.* center, headquarters, main residence

كان العنوان مطبوعا بالتفصيل مع خريطة توضيحية، فوصلت إلى مقر الرابطة بسهولة — The address was printed in detail with an explanatory map, so I arrived at the headquarters of the union easily

87 | 2844 |

1282 باحِث *adj.* searching (عن for); discussing (في sth); researching (في sth); *n.* pl. -uun researcher, scholar

لاحظ أن معظم الباحثين عن عمل مؤقت ممزقو الثياب — He noticed that most of the temporary job seekers had torn clothing

88 | 2815 |

1283 صُعُوبَة *n.* pl. -aat difficulty

— آسف للتأخير.. وجدت مكانا لسيارتي بصعوبة I am sorry for being late...I had difficulty finding a spot for my car

95 | 2586 |

1284 طالَ *v. I (u)* to be long or lengthy; to take a while ـب for sb

البهى يظهر بين وقت وآخر مهما طال الوقت بين ظهوره — Bahiy appears from time to time no matter how long the time between his appearances

98 | 2517 |

1285 ضَعِيف *adj.* pl. ضُعَفاء weak; powerless

بصفتي قديم في لندن، عاوز أوعيك.. الضعيف هنا يموت.. وماحدش بيستحمل حد — In my role as an old-timer in London, I want to warn you: the weak here die; no one puts up with anyone

98 | 2495 |

1286 مَفْهُوم *adj.* understood; *n.* pl. مَفاهِيم concept, notion; meaning, sense, definition

في ظل هذه اللوحة المعقدة لابد لنا من البحث عن المفهوم الأمريكي للشرق الأوسط الجديد — In view of this complicated picture, it is necessary for us to search for the American conception of the new Middle East

87 | 2833 |

1287 دُسْتُور *n.* constitution

ما أراد أن يقوم به الإخوة في الحقيقة خروج على الدستور اليمني — What the brothers wanted to do is in fact a departure from the Yemeni constitution

77 | 3176 |

1288 سَيْطَرَة *n.* control, dominion

إذا انفعل يفقد صوابه تماما ولا يمكنه السيطرة على تصرفاته — If he gets emotional, he completely loses his good judgment and he cannot control his behavior

86 | 2856 |

1289 قادَ *v. I (u)* to lead, guide sb إلى to; to drive (a vehicle), pilot (an aircraft)

قاد سيارته إلى البيت وهو يبذل مجهودا كبيرا ليحتفظ بتركيزه — He drove his car to the house, exerting great efforts to maintain his concentration

87 | 2810 |

1290 إذْن *n.* permission, authorization; بإذْنِ الله God willing

— سنصلي معا بإذن الله في المسجد الجديد We will pray together, with God's permission, in the new mosque

96 | 2552 |

1291 أَرْبِعاء *n.* الأَرْبِعاء (يَوْم) Wednesday

— مهرجان الفيلم الأوروبي في اليمن يبدأ الأربعاء The European Film Festival in Yemen opens on Wednesday

87 | 2817 |

1292 أَسِير *n.* pl. أَسْرَى prisoner, captive

المشكلة في المثقفين أمثالك أنهم يعيشون أسرى الكتب والنظريات.. أنتم لا تعرفون شيئا عن حقيقة ما يحدث في بلادكم — The problem with educated people like you is that they live as

prisoners to books and theories...You don't know anything about what really happens in your country

87 | 2827 |

1293 تُجاهَ and تِجاهَ *prep.* towards; facing

كان ديمي حساسا جدا ودوما أحس بالمسؤولية الكبيرة تجاه اخوته — Dimi was very sensitive and always felt a big responsibility towards his brothers

87 | 2800 |

1294 حَسَّ *v. I (i,a)* to feel, sense ب sth or أنَّ that; *a.p.* حاسِس (Egy.Lev.) حاسّ,

لم ترد، لم تلتفت إليه، كأنها لا تحس بوجوده.. — She didn't respond, she didn't pay any attention to him, as if she didn't feel his presence...She kept on opening drawers and closing them violently

85 | 2887 |

1295 سَعيد *adj.* pl. سُعَداء happy, content

لو وجدت ما تريده ستكون سعيدة، ولو حدث العكس فلن تكون نهاية العالم — If she finds what she wants she will be happy, and if the opposite happens, it won't be the end of the world

99 | 2466 |

1296 حِكايَة *n.* pl. -aat story, tale, account, narrative

كان خبيرا بأم كلثوم، يعرف حكاية كل أغنية ومى أذيعت لأول مرة — He was an expert on Um Kalthoum; he knows the story of each song and when it was broadcast for the first time

95 | 2569 |

1297 تَسْجيل *n.* registration; recording; documentation

غادر القبو بسرعة وعاد وهو يحمل جهاز تسجيل، أدار أغنية الأطلال وجلس يستمع إليها — He left the cellar quickly and returned carrying a tape recorder, he put on the song "The Ruins" and sat listening to it

93 | 2623 |

1298 تَيّار *n.* pl. -aat current, stream

كانا قد توقفا عن التجديف ووقفت الفلوكة وسط المحمودية وحملها تيار خفيف منحرفا بها حتى

— They stopped rowing and the falucca stopped in the middle of the Mahmudiyya Canal, and a light current carried it until it ran into the bank and stayed there

86 | 2834 |

1299 جازَ *v. I (u)* to be allowed, be possible ل for sb; (Lev.) بجُوز, بيجُوز maybe, perhaps; (as modal verb) might, may, could

لا يجوز الدخول إلى هذه الغرفة إلا من قبل مولاي الملك والأمراء — No one should enter this room except His Highness the King and the princes

93 | 2623 |

1300 قَبُول *n.* reception; acceptance, approval

يستحيل علينا قبول الفقر إلى الأبد — It is impossible for us to accept poverty forever

88 | 2760 |

1301 كافٍ (def. كافي) *adj.* sufficient, adequate; competent

القمر يتضاءل ليكون هلالا لكن كان ضوؤه كافيا للناس — The moon is waning, on its way to becoming a crescent, but its light was enough for the people

96 | 2536 |

1302 إيمان *n.* faith, belief (ب in, بأنَّ that)

الحياة بلا إيمان يا سليم جحيم لا يطاق — Life without faith, Salim, is an unbearable hell

90 | 2703 |

1303 حَفْل *n.* ceremony, celebration

تم الزفاف فى حفل أسطورى كلف الحاج نوفل ربع مليون جنيه — The marriage took place in a fabulous party which cost Hajj Nofal a quarter million pounds

87 | 2793 |

1304 مَلْعَب *n.* pl. مَلاعِب playground; stadium, sports field

حاول بعض المتفرجين النزول إلى أرض الملعب والتدخل من أجل فك النزاع بين الفريقين — Some of the fans tried to go down onto the playing field and intervene in order to break up the fight between the two teams

89 | 2722 |

1305 بَعْدَما *conj.* after

لقد رأيت الشمس بعدما حرمت منها قرونا — I saw the sun after being denied it for centuries

87 | 2779 |

1306 ذاكِرَة *n.* memory (human and computer)

إنه مخلوق ضعيف الذاكرة، ألا يعرف أنني لا ألمس الخضراوات مطلقا؟ — He is a creature of weak memory, doesn't he know that I don't touch vegetables ever?

88 | 2728 |

1307 غاز *n.* pl. -aat natural gas

وأدت زيادة مبيعات الغاز وارتفاع أسعار النفط إلى دفع الاقتصاد القطري إلى أعلى مستوياته — The increase in the sales of gas and the rise in the price of oil have lead to pushing the Qatari economy to its highest levels

93 | 2602 |

1308 شَرْعِيّ *adj.* legitimate, lawful; legislative

اللحم في المحلات العادية مذبوح بطريقة غير شرعية — The meat in the regular shops is butchered in a non-Islamic manner

86 | 2785 |

1309 أَحْلَى *elat.* sweeter/sweetest

أيش الحلاوة هادي؟ أحلى عروسة شفتها في حياتي! — What is this loveliness? The most lovely bride I've ever seen in my life!

76 | 3150 |

1310 ثَمَّ *adv.* there (is/are); مِن ثَمَّ therefore, because of that, that is why; (Alg.) ثَمّا and ثَمّا (*adv.*) there, over there

من ثم فقد رأى الجانب الأمريكي الانتظار لبعض الوقت قبل تحريك الموضوع للكونجرس ضمانا لوجود مناخ سياسي إيجابي — Therefore, the American side felt it better to wait a while before putting the matter before Congress to guarantee a positive political climate

80 | 3018 |

1311 مَرْكَزِيّ *adj.* central

حال وصوله محطة القطارات المركزية قطع تذكرته في قطار الحادية عشرة والربع ليلا — Immediately after his arrival at the central train station, he bought his ticket for the 11:15 pm train

80 | 2981 |

1312 هُدُوء *n.* calmness, quiet, peace

أغلق باب الشقة بهدوء وألقى بنفسه على السرير بملابسه الكاملة — He shut the door of the apartment quietly and threw himself onto the bed fully dressed

90 | 2677 |

1313 تَحَقَّقَ *v.* V to become reality (dreams); to be achieved (peace, goals); to verify مِن sth

لم يتحقق هدف واحد مما ناضلت من أجله — Not a single one of the goals I struggled for has been achieved

88 | 2731 |

1314 حَيَوان *n.* pl. -aat animal, creature

فكرت القطة أن تذهب إلى إنجلترا لأنهم هناك يعاملون الحيوانات كأفراد من الأسرة، وتوجد هناك مؤسسة لحماية الحيوانات — The cat thought about going to England because there they treat animals like members of the family, and there is an establishment to protect animals

96 | 2495 |

1315 خَلَصَ *v.* I (u) to conclude إلى أنَّ that; to arrive إلى at (a place, a result); (Dia.) to be finished, be over; to be all gone

حكت لنا انها لما خلصت الثانويه كانت عايزة تدخل كلية آثار ووالدها رفض لأنها بعيدة — She told us that when she finished secondary school she wanted to enter the College of Archeology, and her father refused because it was far away

88 | 2715 | +spo

1316 مُناقَشَة *n.* pl. -aat argument, debate

لا أتفق مع منطق الحرب ولا بد من الحوار ومناقشة أمورنا المصيرية هذه بجدية — I don't agree with the logic of war, there needs to be a dialog and a serious discussion of these crucial affairs of ours

83 | 2863 |

1317 تَوْزِيع *n.* distribution, handing out (على among)

قامت وزارة الشئون الاجتماعية بتوزيع ثمانية آلاف زوج من الأحذية على الفلاحين بالقرى — The Ministry of Social Affairs distributed eight thousand pairs of shoes to the farmers in the villages

87 | 2757 |

1318 بالغ *adj.* extreme, intense, profound; serious, critical; *a.p.* reaching, attaining; *n.* adult

تغير وجهه من الترحيب العادي إلى الاهتمام البالغ — His face changed from normal welcome to extreme interest

88 | 2710 |

1319 رُبْع *n.* pl. أَرْباع quarter, fourth; الرُّبْع الخالِي the Empty Quarter

دخل السجن قبل أكثر من ربع قرن عندما اعتقل من داخل كليته — He went to prison more than a quarter century ago, when he was arrested from inside the college

98 | 2441 |

1320 تَأْمِين *n.* securing, safeguarding, protecting; insuring, insurance

اعترفوا بفضله في تأمين فرص الدراسة لأبنائهم — They acknowledged his merit in insuring study opportunities for their children

89 | 2673 |

1321 خِيار *n.* pl. -aat option, choice; selection, preference

بعد مقتل رسولنا زايد لا خيار أمامنا إلا الحرب — After the killing of our messenger Zayid, there is no other option in front of us except war

87 | 2724 |

1322 مُعالَجة *vn.* treatment (disease, sick person); dealing with (topic, problem, issue); processing (data)

يا أمي أبو سعيد ختان من أين له المعرفة في معالجة مثل هذا الجرح — Mother, Abu Saeed is a circumciser, where would he have gotten the knowledge to treat this kind of wound?

82 | 2885 |

1323 نُسْخة *n.* pl. نُسَخ copy, replica

المسئولون في أمن الدولة أرسلوا إلي نسخة كاملة من ملفه.. انتبه إليه لأنه عنصر مشاغب — The officials in state security sent me a complete copy of his file...Watch out for him because he is a hooligan

91 | 2601 |

1324 تَعْلِيق *vn.* commenting; suspending; *n.* pl. -aat comment, remark, commentary

سكت الرجل القصير مندهشا من تعليق زميله — The short man went quiet, amazed at his colleague's comment

96 | 2477 |

1325 تَصْمِيم *n.* determination, perseverance; pl. تَصامِيم design, sketch, plan

قرعت الباب بقوة وتصميم ربما للتخلص من ارتباكي وترددي — I knocked on the door with strength and determination, perhaps to rid myself of my bewilderment and hesitation

83 | 2859 |

1326 إله *n.* god, deity; God; يا إلهِي my God!

هل كانت الأم وابنتها ابنتين لبوسايدون إله البحر أم كانتا إلهتين بحريتين؟ — Were the mother and her daughter both daughters of Poseidon the God of the Sea, or were they sea goddesses themselves?

88 | 2681 |

1327 يَمِين *n.* right side; *fem.n.* right hand; *fem.n.* pl. أَيْمان oath

لاحظت أن البعير لم يرع من العشب سوى القائم على يمين الطريق، فعرفت أنه لا يرى بعينه اليسرى — She noticed that the camel only grazed on grass on the right side of the road, so she realized that he couldn't see out of his left eye

98 | 2397 |

1328 سَكَنَ *v. I* (u) to live, reside, dwell في at/in; *a.p.* ساكِن residing, living في at/in

في بيتنا يسكن رجل يعمل بالسكة الحديد — A man who works on the railroad lives in our house

94 | 2504 |

1329 شِعار *n.* pl. -aat slogan, motto; emblem, symbol

كل واشرب ولا تهتم فهذا خير شعار في الحياة — Eat, drink, and don't worry; this is the best slogan of life

87 | 2699 |

1330 قَصْد *n.* intent, purpose, goal

بعدين اشتغلت جرسونة.. قصدي مش جرسونة.. مساعدة جرسونة — After that I worked as a waitress...I mean not as a waitress, as an assistant waitress

97 | 2419 |

1331 اِنْبَغَى *v. VII* (mostly imperf.) to be necessary to do sth; to be incumbent على upon sb أنْ to do sth (he should do sth)
هل ينبغي أن ننتظر معجزة؟ لم احصل في حياتي كلها على الألم والظلم سوى — Do we need to wait for a miracle? My whole life I've only received pain and injustice
84 | 2779 |

1332 اِتَّفَقَ *v. VIII* to agree (مع with sb, على on/about sth)
اتفقنا يا أمي وانتهى الأمر — We agreed, my mother, and that's it
97 | 2412 |

1333 سابع *adj.* seventh (ordinal)
قام وخرج من شقته واستقل المصعد إلى الدور السابع — He got up and left his apartment and rode the elevator to the seventh floor
97 | 2399 |

1334 واصَلَ *v. III* to continue doing sth
حسام — Husam يجب أن يواصل تعليمه أولا must continue his education first
89 | 2620 |

1335 اِعْتَرَفَ *v. VIII* to admit, confess ب (having done) sth; to acknowledge, recognize, accept ب sth
حكى لها كل شيء عن سارة، كأنه يعترف من وراء الستار لقس رحيم — He told her everything about Sarah, as if he were confessing to a merciful priest from behind a veil
88 | 2636 |

1336 أَثَّرَ *v. II* to affect, influence على sth/sb
أنت تعلمين جيدا أن الانفعال يؤثر على ضغط الدم لديك، أرجوك اهدئي — You know very well that being upset affects your blood pressure; I beg you to calm down
93 | 2509 |

1337 قَصَدَ *v. I (i)* to intend, mean sth; to pursue sth
لا تؤاخذني.. أنا لا أقصد الإهانة — Don't take offense...I didn't mean to insult you
92 | 2515 |

1338 أَكَلَ *v. I (u)* to eat sth; to corrode sth; (fig.) to consume, gnaw at sth/sb; (imperat.) كُلْ eat! (Lev. كول /kool/); (imperf.) (Dia.) ياكل /yaakul/, (Lev.) also يوكل /yookol, yookel/
لقد أكلت فى مصر كميات من الفول تكفيني إلى قيام الساعة — In Egypt I ate large quantities of beans which should suffice me till Judgment Day
93 | 2486 |

1339 جَريدَة *n. pl.* جَرائِد newspaper, periodical, journal
يمر أسبوع من دون أن أقرأ موضوعا يتناولني في جريدة أو مجلة أو منتدى على الإنترنت — A week goes by without me reading an article that deals with me in a newspaper or magazine or an Internet forum
97 | 2392 |

1340 آه *interj.* ah!; ouch!
في بطني ألم شديد جدا..آه.. بطني بيوجعني كثير — There is a sharp pain in my stomach...ouch... my stomach hurts a lot
72 | 3182 |

1341 مُتَوَقَّع *adj.* expected, anticipated
كانت ردة فعله غير متوقعة — His reaction was unexpected
86 | 2676 |

1342 اِلْتِزام *vn.* following, adhering to ب (rules, laws, plans); *n. pl.* -aat commitment, obligation
قرر الالتزام بتعاليم الدين الحنيف، والسير على منهج الله سبحانه وتعالى — He decided to adhere to the teachings of Islam, and to walk in the path of God, may He be exalted
86 | 2685 |

1343 طِوال and طَوالَ and طَوالَ *n.* throughout, during (the entire)
رفض بإصرار طوال حياته الإعارة لدول الخليج أو إعطاء الدروس الخصوصية — Throughout his life he rejected determinedly being seconded to the Gulf or giving private lessons
93 | 2470 |

1344 مُمَيَّز *adj.* distinguished, outstanding, prominent; special
تستمتع كثيرا بمكتبته المميزة وبقراءة بعض كتبها — She really enjoys his distinguished library and reading some of its books
95 | 2403 |

1345 بِيه (Dia.) *prep.* with, by; (with pron.) بِيها, بِيه,
بِيكِي (Irq.Gul. بِيچ), بِيك (Lev. also بِيهن), بِيهُم
بِينا (Lev. also بِيكُن), بِيّا/بِي, بِيكُم
الراجل اللي باحلم بيه لازم يكون أقوى مني.. أذكى
مني — The man I am dreaming of must be
stronger than me, and smarter than me

70 | 3287 | +spo

1346 مَنْصِب *n.* pl. مَناصِب post, position, office
مهما يكن منصبه فليس من حقه أن يدخل بيتك وأنت
غائب — Whatever his position, he has no right
to enter your house when you are not there

86 | 2663 |

1347 الاثْنَيْن (يَوْم) *n.* اثْنَيْن Monday
قالت منظمة الاغذية و الزراعة (الفاو) يوم الاثنين
ان النيجر يشهد أزمة غذائية حادة بسبب القحط —
The World Food and Agriculture Organization
(FAO) said Monday that Niger was witnessing
a severe food crisis because of the drought

92 | 2480 |

1348 مَعْقُول *adj.* reasonable, plausible, logical
الفقير بحاجة إلى دخل معقول وقدرة على تعليم أبنائه
وقدرة على العلاج وتأمين لشيخوخته — The poor
person is in need of a reasonable income and an
ability to educate his children and an ability to
get medical care and insurance for his old age

96 | 2363 |

1349 مَطار *n.* pl. -aat airport, airfield
مانمناش من يومين.. قعدنا عشرين ساعة في المطار
— We haven't slept for two days...we stayed in
the airport for twenty hours

92 | 2466 |

1350 ثَمَّةَ *adv.* there (is/are)
سينتهى الأمر بدفنها فى مدافن الصدقة إذ لا يبدو أن
ثمة أهلا لها — The matter will end with her
being buried in the paupers' graveyard, since
she doesn't appear to have any family

85 | 2675 |

1351 مُشْتَرَك *n.* participant; subscriber; *adj.*
participating; subscribing
أجريت مناورات مشتركة بين الجيش المصرى
والبريطانى فى الصحراء الغربية — Joint
maneuvers were held between the Egyptian
army and the British in the Western Desert

94 | 2426 |

1352 فُنْدُق *n.* pl. فَنادِق hotel
وكان أول ما فعله فى أسيوط أن دخل أحد الفنادق
الرخيصة، يستحم وينام طويلا وينام أن حلق ذقنه —
The first thing he did in Asyut was to go to
one of the cheap hotels, take a shower, and
sleep for a long time, after he shaved his
beard

95 | 2391 |

1353 لاحَظَ *v. III* to notice, observe sth or أنَّ that
كان فواز قد قضى اليوم كله في البيت، ولاحظ ضابط
الشرطة ومعاونيه في سيارة زرقاء يعبرون المنطقة
مرارا — Fawaz had spent the whole day in the
house and he noticed the police officer and
his aides in a blue car passing by the area
repeatedly

95 | 2383 |

1354 أَقْرَب *elat.* nearer/nearest, sooner/soonest;
n. pl. أقارِب relatives, extended family
لا بد أن أغير هذا السكن فى أقرب فرصة — I need
to change this residence at the earliest
opportunity

98 | 2307 |

1355 اتِّخاذ *n.* taking; adopting, passing (a
resolution)
هذه خطوة تأخرت وكان يجب اتخاذها من زمان —
This is a step which has been delayed, and it
should have been taken a long time ago

85 | 2652 |

1356 فِكْرِيّ *adj.* intellectual, mental
المعول الحقيقي على التطور هي الحرية العلمية
والفكرية في ظل مناخ يتسم بالعدالة التي هي أساس
لكل تقدم — The true sustainer of
development is scientific and intellectual
freedom under the auspices of a climate
characterized by justice which is the basis
of all advancement

90 | 2512 |

1357 فَقير *adj.* poor; destitute; *n.* poor (person),
pauper
الغني يحتقر الفقير والفقير يحقد على الغني وابناء
الطبقة الوسطى اختفوا — The rich despise the
poor, and the poor hate the rich, and the sons
of the middle class have disappeared

94 | 2413 |

1358 بُعْد *n.* pl. أَبعاد dimension; distance

بدأت حكايتي معها تأخذ بعدا إنسانيا لطيفا —
My story with her began to take on a nice, humanistic dimension

90 | 2504 |

1359 أَصْدَرَ *v. IV* to publish (book), release (film); to issue (decree, ruling, decision); to pass (sentence); to emit (sound)

أصدرت أمرا بتغيير السياسة المتبعة في المعتقل والسماح للمعتقلين بمقابلة أقربائهم — It issued an order to change the policy followed in the prison, and to allow the prisoners to meet their relatives

91 | 2481 |

1360 نَظَّم *v. II* to organize, arrange; regulate

نختار من بيننا رئيسا لجلستنا ينظم اجتماعنا ويتولى إدارة الحوار والنقاش — We choose from among us a president of our session who organizes our meeting and takes the responsibility for directing the discussion

85 | 2666 |

1361 ضِفَّة *n.* pl. ضِفاف bank, shore; الضفة الغَرْبِيَّة the West Bank

تركب القارب وحيدة قاطعة النهر إلى الضفة الأخرى حيث اسرتها — She is riding the boat alone, crossing the river to the other side where her family is

72 | 3130 |

18 Communication

15	قال	to say	1923	نادى	to call	3249	حدّث	to speak to
187	أكّد	to confirm	1994	روى	to narrate	3261	زعم	to claim
224	حكى	to tell, talk	2018	أعرب	to express	3321	حثّ	to urge
266	ذكر	to mention	2025	حذّر	to warn	3461	همس	to whisper
312	أشار	to indicate	2091	أبدى	to show	3506	أدان	to condemn
325	سأل	to ask	2092	ناقش	to debate	3575	نصح	to advise
396	ردّ	to answer	2096	علّق	to comment on	3610	أبلغ	to inform
418	دعا	to call on				3894	خبّر	to tell
426	أعلن	to announce	2101	نفى	to deny	4058	نوّه	to point out
453	تحدّث	to speak	2107	ادّعى	to claim	4239	نمّ	to slander
457	طلب	to request	2205	أمر	to order	4544	خاطب	to address
605	أوضح	to clarify	2301	صدق	to be sincere	4589	أنّ	to complain
676	بحث	to discuss (also search, research)	2413	أشاد	to praise	4631	حمد	to praise
			2425	أصرّ	to insist on	4650	أدلى	to express
772	كشف	to reveal	2426	اقترح	to suggest	4668	عيّط	to scream
774	طالب	to demand	2654	وضّح	to clarify	4686	أوصى	to advise
858	نقل	to transmit; quote	2682	وعد	to promise	5168	جاوب	to respond to
			2683	أخبر	to inform	5426	هتف	to shout, cheer
920	شكر	to thank	2703	شرح	to explain	5427	مزح	to joke
926	تكلّم	to speak	2725	استدعى	to summon	5641	خابر	to phone
1110	أجاب	to answer	2816	نطق	to speak	5671	هدر	to talk
1117	أفاد	to report, state	2823	صاح	to scream	5674	ناشد	to implore
1168	عبّر	to express	2980	اعتذر	to apologize for	5938	كذّب	to deny
1224	طرح	to offer	2986	كلّم	to speak with	5984	عقّب	to criticize
1335	اعترف	to admit	3003	اعترض	to object	6090	تلفن	to call (on phone)
1616	بيّن	to clarify	3020	انتقد	to criticize			
1671	صرّح	to declare	3032	شجّع	to encourage	6182	فهّم	to explain
1764	تساءل	to wonder	3131	أنكر	to deny	6869	دردش	to chat
1894	صرخ	to shout	3170	فسّر	to explain	7121	سقسى	to ask
1918	ردّد	to repeat	3172	شكا	to complain	7368	قبّر	to chat

1362 اِعْتِماد *vn.* reliance, dependence على on; recognition (of)

— لم تكن ثمة رواية مؤكدة يمكن الاعتماد عليها
There was not a reliable account that could be depended on

85 | 2642 |

1363 حَجَر *n.* pl. حِجارَة stone

— الإيطاليون على مرمى حجر من الإسكندرية
The Italians were a stone's throw from Alexandria

96 | 2350 |

1364 ـشـ /sh-/ *interrog.* (prefix, mostly Irq.; shortened form of شُو) what; شَاخْبارَك؟ what's new with you?

— هلا هلا وشو أخبارك انت Hello, hello.
So, what's new with you?

54 | 4173 | +spo

1365 قَلَق *n.* unrest, unease; concern, anxiety

الذين عملوا معه يعرفون جيدا ذلك القلق الذى ينتابه قبل المحاضرة، كالممثلين قبل العرض — Those who worked with him know very well this worry which overcomes him before a lecture, like actors before a presentation

89 | 2521 |

1366 مَسيرَة *n.* march, parade; movement, course

وواصل العمل الدبلوماسي مسيرته وراء أستار السرية
— The diplomatic work went on behind secret curtains

84 | 2668 |

1367 اِزْداد *v. VIII* to grow, increase, rise

ازدادت حوادث السرقة بسبب الظلام الذى شمل البلاد — Robberies increased because of the darkness which enveloped the country

89 | 2508 |

1368 هامّ *adj.* important, significant

لديه أسئلة هامة حول معنى الحياة والموت والبعث والوجود — He has important questions about the meaning of life and death and resurrection and existence

85 | 2606 |

1369 عاد (Lev.Gul.) *adv.* so, then, therefore; (Irq.) *adv.* already, now; *conj.* but, even though

مشكورة على مرورك الطيب اختي ولا تنسيني عاد
—Thanks for your nice visit (to the forum), sister, and don't you forget me now

85 | 2621 |

1370 حَرارَة *n.* temperature, heat; fever; passion

أليس غريبا أن تدافع عن الإسلام بهذه الحرارة وأنت سكران؟ — Isn't it strange for you to defend Islam with such passion while you are drunk?

97 | 2295 |

1371 خَليجيّ *adj.* of or relating to the Persian Gulf (الخَليج العَرَبيّ)

كانت الكويت من أكبر وأول الدول الخليجية التى استوعبت الكثير من الشباب ومنحتهم فرص العمل المختلفة — Kuwait was one of the biggest and first Gulf states which absorbed a lot of young men and gave them various work opportunities

83 | 2680 |

1372 سَير *n.* course, motion, march; going, walking

استمر فى السير.. لا تنظر خلفك ولا تتحدث مع أحد — Keep walking...don't look behind you and don't speak with anyone

97 | 2295 |

1373 ظَهْر *n.* back; rear; deck (ship); عَن ظَهْرِ قَلْب by heart

— أسند ظهره إلى المقعد وتطلع بعيدا كأنه يتذكر
He leaned his back against the chair and looked out into the distance as if he was remembering

99 | 2238 |

1374 هَدَفَ *v. I* (i) to target, aim at إلى sth; to be intended, be designated إلى for sth (as a goal)

إن هذه الإجراءات الصارمة التى تنال من الحريات العامة تهدف بالأساس إلى زرع الخوف في نفوس المواطنين — These harsh measures which undermine civil liberties are intended primarily to instill fear in the hearts of the citizens

83 | 2690 |

1375 مُتَعَدِّد *adj.* diverse, numerous, multi-, poly-
هم من اتجاهات ثقافية ودينية وعرقية واجتماعية متعددة
— They are from numerous cultural, religious, ethnic, and social orientations
86 | 2569 |

1376 إيجاد *n.* discovery, finding
فى الليل استلقى مفتوح العينين مجهدا عقلي في سبيل إيجاد مخرج لجنودى المساكين من هذه المحنة — At night I lay with my eyes wide open searching my mind to find an escape for my poor soldiers from this trial
84 | 2646 |

1377 فَصْل *vn.* detaching, separating; firing, laying off; rendering a judgment, reaching a decision (في قضية in a case)
دعم المساعي الكندية لإرسال قوات من الأمم المتحدة للفصل بين الطرفين — He supported the Canadian efforts to send United Nations troops to separate the two sides
97 | 2297 |

1378 ألو /'aloo/ (Dia.) *interj.* hello! (also آلو /'aaloo/, هالو /haaloo, haalaw/, and هلو /haloo, halaw/)
الو نعم عيني تفضل الو — Hello, yes, with pleasure, go ahead, hello
9 | 23028 |

1379 عَفْو *n.* pardon, amnesty; العَفو and عَفواً excuse me!; (response to شُكراً) you're welcome!
— عفوا يا مولاي.. نسيت والله أعطني فرصة أخرى Excuse me, sir...By God I forgot, please give me another chance
93 | 2388 |

1380 بارد *adj.* cold, frigid; (food) dull, flat, bland
قد أحس بانتعاش رائع وهو يلقى بجسده فى المياه الباردة، وظل يسبح ما يقرب من ساعة — He felt wonderfully refreshed as he threw his body into the cold water, and he went on swimming for about an hour
98 | 2270 |

1381 تَحَرَّكَ *v. V* to move, get moving
ظل واقفا فى مكانه ونظر إلى أعلى وكأنه يرقب شيئا يتحرك على السقف — He stayed standing in his place, and looked up as if he were watching something moving on the ceiling
99 | 2245 |

1382 واجِب *adj.* necesssary, obligatory (على for); *n.* pl. -aat duty, obligation, requirement
أليس من واجب الزوجة مساندة زوجها؟ — Isn't it the wife's responsibility to support her husband?
96 | 2295 |

1383 اِقْتَرَب *v. VIII* to get close من to sth, approach sth من
حياتي تقترب من النهاية، على أفضل تقدير قد أعيش عشرة أعوام — My life is nearing an end, the best estimate is that I could live ten years
89 | 2475 | +lit

1384 شِدَّة *n.* intensity, forcefulness; بِشِدَّة strongly, forcefully
إنه يحبها ويفتقدها بشدة طوال النهار، ولكن هل يعنى كل ذلك أنه سيتزوجها؟ — He loves her and misses her greatly throughout the day, but does all this mean that he will marry her?
95 | 2302 |

1385 مُفِيد *adj.* useful, beneficial
الطب الحديث يقرر أن صعود السلم مفيد للقلب — Modern medicine has established that walking up stairs is beneficial for the heart
95 | 2312 |

1386 اِبْنَة *n.* daughter (pl. بَنات, cf. بِنْت)
إنها تعيش وحدها بعد وفاة زوجها وزواج ابنتها الوحيدة — She has been living by herself since the death of her husband and the marriage of her only daughter
85 | 2593 |

1387 رَسَمَ *v. I (u)* to draw, sketch (picture); to outline, describe sth; to design, plan sth; to chart (a course)
أعاد ترتيب شتات ذاته ورسم على شفتيه ابتسامة صفراء باهتة — He put the shattered pieces of his self back together, and painted a pale yellow smile on his face
89 | 2458 |

1388 فَهْم *n.* understanding, comprehension
ارتبك طارق وتشتت ذهنه تماما حتى إنه فشل فى فهم درس الكيمياء العضوية الجديد — Tariq was bewildered and his mind was so completely scattered that he failed to understand the new Organic Chemistry lesson
93 | 2363 |

1389 مَعْنِيّ *adj.* concerned, affected; interested ب in, concerned ب with

هزت سلاف رأسها وكأنها غير معنية بما قالته أمها — Salaf shook her head as if she was not concerned about what her mother had said

82 | 2653 |

1390 شنو (Gul.Irq.) /shinu/, (Magh.) /shnu/ *interrog.* what

والله ما اعرف شنو اقول بالضبط.. تعلمت اشياء كثيرة لا استطيع حصرها — I don't know what to say exactly...I learned many things which I cannot enumerate

37 | 5836 | +spo

1391 جَواب *n.* answer, response; (Egy.) pl. -aat letter

سأله عن منزل معلم المدرسة وكان الجواب أنه مجاور لمنزل المختار — He asked him about the house of the school teacher and the answer was that it was next to the house of the mayor

96 | 2264 |

1392 صادِق *adj.* truthful, veracious

هذا الأسف ليس صادقا، إنها سعيدة بما حدث — This sorrow is not sincere, she is happy with what happened

97 | 2243 |

1393 مارَسَ *v. III* to practice, pursue (profession, hobby); to practice, play (sport); to exercise, carry out (policy), to exert (pressure)

لماذا تمارس السرقة والتخريب طالما أنك تخشى العواقب؟ — Why do you practice thievery and sabotage (even) while you fear the consequences?

95 | 2298 |

1394 وَلِيّ *n.* pl. أَوْلِياء patron, protector; وَلِيّ العَهْد heir, crown prince; وَلِيّ الأَمْر pl. أَوْلِياء الأُمُور legal guardian, parent

غالبية الأسر تعاني قهرا اجتماعيا واقتصاديا بل وهناك من أولياء الأمور من ينتحرون لأنهم لا يجدون ما ينفقونه على أبنائهم — Most families suffer from social and economic hardship; in fact, there are legal guardians (parents) who commit suicide because they can't find enough money to cover their children's expenses

92 | 2362 |

1395 مَيِّت *n./adj.* pl. مَوْتَى, أُمْوات dead, deceased

كانت تؤمن بأن الموتى يعيشون معنا لكننا لا نراهم — She believed that the dead live with us but we don't see them

99 | 2199 |

1396 وادٍ (def. الوادِي) *n.* wadi (dry riverbed), valley

المسافة من الوادي إلى قمة الجبل صعودا تساوي تقريبا المسافة من قمة الجبل إلى الوادي وراء هذا الجبل هبوطا — The distance from the valley to the top of the mountain going up is approximately equal to the distance from the top of the mountain to the valley behind the mountain going down

96 | 2276 |

1397 أَجْرَى *v. IV* to conduct, carry out, perform sth

أجرى لها عدة بروفات حتى فهمت دورها وأتقنته — He conducted a number of rehearsals for her until she understood her role and got good at it

87 | 2485 |

1398 غالِب *n.* winner, victor; majority, most of; غالِباً mostly, largely

إنهم في الغالب يفهمون الدين على أنه صلاة وصوم وحجاب — Mostly they understand religion as prayer, fasting and head scarf

93 | 2334 |

1399 إلِكْتُرونِيّ *adj.* electronic; البَريد الإلِكْتُرونِيّ email

هذه نافذة مفتوحة للرد على أي تساؤل يخطر على بالك وتريد له إجابة، ارسل سؤالك على البريد الالكتروني للصفحة — This is an open window to respond to any question that might occur to you and for which you want an answer; send your question by email to the page

82 | 2644 |

1400 تَعْليمِيّ *adj.* educational, instructional, pedagogical

رحت أشرح أصول اللعبة، غير أن جهودنا التعليمية فشلت فشلا ذريعا — I started to explain the rules of the game, but our educational efforts failed completely

90 | 2404 |

1401 مُقارَنَة *n.* comparison
هل توصلتم الى قراءة اولية لخريطة المعدلات مقارنة بالعام الماضي؟ — Did you get to a preliminary reading of the rate map compared to last year?
89 | 2413 |

1402 قَوْم *n.* people, nation
أجبتها بأنني أدافع عن قومي وتاريخهم ولم أتجاوز حدود الأدب — I answered her that I was defending my people and their history and that I did not go beyond the bounds of politeness
87 | 2484 |

1403 ضَخْم *adj.* large, voluminous
يحملون أجهزة تسجيل ضخمة تنبعث منها موسيقى صاخبة يرقصون على نغماتها — They carry huge recording devices, out of which comes loud music to whose tunes they dance
94 | 2297 |

1404 ظُلْم *n.* injustice; ظُلْمًا wrongly, unjustly
ألا يشعر بظل من تأنيب الضمير عندما يقترف هذا الظلم؟ — Doesn't he feel a hint of remorse when he commits this injustice?
87 | 2469 |

1405 مَغْرِبِيّ *n./adj.* pl. مَغارِبَة Moroccan; Maghrebi
لذا فإننا نجد أن العمارة المغربية مختلفة عن مثيلتها في شرق العالم الإسلامي — Therefore we find that Moroccan architecture is different from its counterpart in the east of the Islamic World
77 | 2798 |

1406 اِحْتِمال *n.* probability, likelihood; اِحْتِمالات possibilities
بدأت المخاوف فى بلجيكا وهولندا من احتمال خرق ألمانيا لحيادها — Fears that Germany would break its neutrality began in Belgium and Holland
98 | 2193 |

1407 نافِذَة *n.* pl. نَوافِذ window
جلست شيماء فى مقعد بعيد بجوار النافذة وتعمدت ألا تنظر حولها — Shima sat on a far chair next to the window and deliberately did not look around her
88 | 2427 |

1408 عَيْش *n.* life, living; (Egy.) bread; (Gul.) rice
لم يسبق له العيش فى الصحراء، لكنها بلاد الله فى النهاية — He had never lived in the desert before, but it was the country of God in the end
91 | 2341 |

1409 إمْكانِيَّة *n.* pl. -aat possibility; capability
شعرت أن أمي خسرت إمكانية النظر إلى دمشق كما في السابق — I felt that my mother lost the ability to look at Damascus as before
89 | 2400 |

1410 أَهْلِيّ *adj.* civil, domestic; family, home; private (school)
ليست الحرب القائمة في فلسطين حربا أهلية كما ذكرتم — The current war in Palestine is not a civil war, as you mentioned
86 | 2487 |

1411 آمَنَ *v. IV* to believe ب in sth or بأَنَّ/أَنَّ
نحن نؤمن بأن بلادنا تستحق نظاما سياسيا ديمقراطيا — We believe our country deserves a democratic political system
88 | 2417 |

1412 حَضارَة *n.* pl. -aat civilization; culture
العلم والمنهج العلمي هو ما يجب أن نتقبله من الحضارة الغربية دون مناقشة — Science and the scientific method are what we must accept from Western culture, without discussion
84 | 2528 |

1413 بَرْلَمان *n.* parliament
البرلمان أخذ قرارا بالإجماع بإقرار هذا القانون — The Parliament made a unanimous decision to pass this law
76 | 2793 |

1414 تَقْنِيَّة *n.* pl. -aat technology, technique
أود أن أستخدم هذه التقنية في الأغراض السلمية — I want to use this technology for peaceful purposes
83 | 2553 |

1415 جُهْد *n.* effort, exertion, strain
تساند زوجها بكل ما تملك من جهد ومال — She supports her husband with everything she has in the way of effort and money
89 | 2390 |

1416 وَعْي *n.* consciousness; awareness, attention
لقد أثبت الزعيمان أنهما على مستوى عال من الوعي
والمسؤولية — The two leaders confirmed that
they were on a high level of awareness and
responsibility
95 | 2231 |

1417 حارِس *n.* pl. حُرّاس guard, sentry; guardian,
keeper; (sports) goalie, goal-keeper
وقف طارق متحفزا يحدق فى شيء وكأنه حارس
مرمى يترقب وصول الكرة من أى اتجاه ليصدها فورا
— Tariq stood up all ready, staring at Shima as
if he were a goalie watching for the ball from
any direction to block it immediately
82 | 2565 |

1418 صَحافة *n.* journalism, press
الصحف العربية بدأت تركب الموجة التي خلقتها
الصحافة الإسرائيلية حول هذا الموضوع — The
Arab newspapers began to ride the wave
created by the Israeli press regarding this
subject
87 | 2423 |

1419 طالَما and لَطالَما *conj.* as long as; how often!
طالَما أَنَّ provided (that)
سأظل على حالى طالما يحملني جسدى — I will keep
doing what I'm doing as long as my body will
carry me
96 | 2187 |

1420 خَفيف *adj.* light; slight, minor; sparse
إنا لن نبيع لها غير الأسلحة الخفيفة وبأثمان باهظة
— We will only sell it light arms, and at
prohibitive prices
99 | 2127 |

1421 مَنَعَ *v. I (a)* to prevent, forbid sth; to prevent
sb من/عن from doing sth; to deprive sb
من/عن of sth
من حق الولايات المتحدة أن تمنع أى شخص عربي
من دخول أراضيها حتى تتأكد من أنه شخص
متحضر — It is the right of the United States
to prevent any Arab person from entering its
lands so that it can be sure that he is a
cultured person
89 | 2363 |

1422 جُمْلة *n.* pl. جُمَل sentence, clause; group, bunch,
handful; بالجُمْلة on the whole, altogether;
جُمْلَةً وَتَفْصيلًا completely, through and
through
قال المعلم للتلميذ: ضع جملة «أنا رجل» في صيغة
الماضي — The teacher said to the student:
Put the sentence "I am a man" into the past
tense
98 | 2138 |

1423 عَقِبَ *fem.n.* pl. أَعْقاب heel; عَقِب and عَقْب
prep. immediately after; (Gul.) عقب /9ugub/
adv. afterwards (also *prep.* after)
قبض عليه وصوله مباشرة عقب من قبل الشرطة
وتم تسفيره — He was arrested directly
after his arrival by the police, and he was
deported
83 | 2508 |

1424 مُبَكِّر *adj.* early; مُبَكِّراً early (*adv.*)
استيقظت مبكرا فى الصباح وطبعت البيان، ثم
صورت منه عشرين نسخة — I woke up early in
the morning and printed the report, then I
made twenty copies of it
87 | 2390 |

1425 ظُهْر *n.* noon, afternoon; ظُهْراً in the
afternoon, at noon
استغرقت فى نوم عميق ولم أستيقظ إلا بعد الظهر —
I was in a deep sleep and didn't wake up till
afternoon
97 | 2147 |

1426 وافَقَ *v. III* to agree with sb على on sth;
to approve, authorize على sth
لو كان الأمر بيدى لما وافقت على تعيينك — If the
matter were in my hands, I would not have
agreed to your being appointed
95 | 2182 |

1427 مُتَعَلِّق *adj.* attached, connected (ب to sth/sb);
concerning (ب sth/sb)
يقوم بأعمال البحث والتطوير في المجالات المتعلقة
بمصادر المياه — He is engaged in research and
development in the fields related to water
resources
82 | 2544 |

1428 زَمِيل *n.* pl. زُمَلاء colleague, associate, companion

عليه أن يبذل مجهودا مضاعفا ليكون أفضل من أى زميل أمريكى مرتين على الأقل — He needs to redouble his efforts to be at least twice as good as any American colleague

95 | 2175 |

1429 كَيْفِيَّة *n.* manner, mode; way; how

تعلمت تدريجيا كيفية الاعتماد على النفس — I learned gradually how to rely on myself

84 | 2471 |

1430 نَمُوذَج *n.* pl. نَاذِج sample; model, example

الفاتحة على روحك يا أمى.. كنت نموذجا للزوجة الصالحة — (I recite) The Fatiha over your soul, mother... You were an example of the good-hearted wife

85 | 2450 |

1431 حادِث *n.* pl. حَوادِث event, occurrence; incident, accident

تسبب هذا السائق في حادث اصطدام بين ثلاث سيارات — This driver caused a collision between three cars

91 | 2273 |

1432 فازَ *v. I (u)* to win (ب) sth; to defeat على sb

إن الحلم الأمريكى وهم، سباق بلا نهاية لا يفوز فيه أحد — The American Dream is a phantom, a race without an end in which no one wins

92 | 2258 |

1433 ثَوْب *n.* pl. ثِياب garment, robe, tunic; clothes, clothing

ثيابه بسيطة نظيفة ودائما مجعدة قليلا ربما لأنه لا يجد الوقت الكافي لكيها بإتقان — His clothes are clean and simple, and always a little wrinkled, perhaps because he can't find enough time to iron them skillfully

92 | 2235 | +lit

1434 بَدِيل *n.* pl. بَدائِل alternative; replacement, substitute; *adj.* alternate, substitute; equivalent

الهدف من المؤتمر نشر التوعية بأهمية لبن الأم والحد من استخدام بدائل لبن الأم — The goal of the conference is to spread awareness of the importance of mother's milk and to curb the use of substitutes for mother's milk

85 | 2419 |

1435 مُحِيط *adj.* peripheral, surrounding; *n.* periphery, surrounding area; milieu, environment; ocean; المُحِيط الهادِئ Pacific Ocean

كل همه الاستماع بما يدور في محيطه — His only concern is to enjoy that which happens around him

88 | 2351 |

1436 آيَة *n.* pl. -aat verse (in the Qurʾan); sign, wonder, miracle

اقرأ بعض آيات القرآن لتساعدك على النوم هادئ البال — Read some verses of the Qurʾan to help you sleep with peace of mind

84 | 2467 |

1437 تَهْدِيد *vn.* threatening, menacing; *n.* pl. -aat threat, menace; danger, risk

أتهدد.. أتظن أن التهديد يخيفني.. لن تفعل أكثر مما فعلت — Are you threatening? Do you think that threatening scares me? You won't do anything more than you have done

86 | 2403 |

1438 هَدِيَّة *n.* pl. هَدايا gift, present; هَدِيَّة as a gift

كانت الهدية عبارة عن سلة كبيرة تناثرت فيها الورود المجففة والشموع الحمراء — The gift was a kind of large basket in which dried roses and red candles were strewn

97 | 2134 |

1439 قاعِد *a.p.* sitting; (Dia.) staying, remaining; (with imperf.) in the process of doing sth

طول الاسبوع بابقى انا و هو قاعدين في البيت الصبح — The whole week he and I will be staying home in the morning

49 | 4229 | +spo

1440 مُوسِيقَى *fem.n.* music

لا أفهم الكلمات، لكن الموسيقى تحرك قلبى — I don't understand the words, but the music moves my heart

94 | 2199 |

1441 بَعَثَ *v. I (a)* to send, mail sth or ب sth إلى to sb

كان مارتن لوثر كينج يريد أن يبعث برسالة حب وإخاء مسيحية — Martin Luther King wanted to send a message of Christian love and brotherhood

99 | 2087 |

1442 نَدْوَة *n. pl.* -aat seminar, symposium, colloquium

نرحب بكم ترحيبا حارا في ندوة نعقدها لمناقشة آخر التطورات المتعلقة بالمدينة المقدسة — We welcome you warmly to this panel we are holding to discuss the latest developments related to the Holy City

79 | 2616 |

1443 جِهاد *n.* jihad (struggle, from the phrase الجِهاد في سَبيلِ اللهِ struggle in the way of God)

ينسى كل ما قدمناه من الجهاد الطويل في سبيلِ حرية سوريا ومجد العروبة أجمع — He forgets

everything that we have offered in terms of lengthy struggle for the freedom of Syria and the glory of all of Arabism

88 | 2321 |

1444 قاعَة *n. pl.* -aat hall, large room

في أقصى القاعة رجل أسود يرتدى بدلة سهرة ويعزف على البيانو — At the far end of the hall is a black man wearing an evening suit and playing the piano

93 | 2194 |

19 Health

253	دكتور	doctor	3428	جراحي	surgical
452	مرض	illness	3443	التهاب	inflammation
458	صحة	health	3490	جراحة	surgery
644	طبيب	doctor	3517	تشخيص	diagnosis
698	صحي	healthy	3578	انفلونزا	influenza
711	مستشفى	hospital	3588	نزيف	bleeding
750	علاج	treatment	3663	إسعاف	first aid; ambulance
755	أصاب	to strike (of an illness)	3683	وباء	epidemic, disease
816	إصابة	being struck with	3700	عدوى	infection
822	مريض	sick	3706	حمى	fever
835	عافية	health	3713	إيدز	AIDS
865	طبي	medical	3741	سكري	diabetes
929	ألم	pain	3768	مزمن	chronic
1011	جرح	wound	3835	وصفة	prescription
1041	رعاية	care	3845	شلل	paralysis
1322	معالجة	care	3933	مرضي	pathological
1340	آه	ouch	3995	فيتامين	vitamin
1488	مصاب	wounded, stricken	4017	نزف	to bleed, hemorrhage
1529	طب	medicine	4053	حامل	pregnant
1902	عناية	care	4153	عقّار	drug, medicine
1934	معاناة	suffering	4369	عيادة	clinic
2012	ولادة	birth	4403	وجع	ache, pain
2100	حيوي	biological مضاد حيوي: anti-biotic	4461	عافى	to heal, cure
			4612	غيبوبة	unconsciousness, trance
2134	سرطان	cancer	4632	سمنة	fat, obese
2211	فيروس	virus	4716	ممرض	nurse
2291	مخدر	drug	4764	وراثي	hereditary, genetic, congenital
2791	داء	sickness			
2814	شفاء	cure	4802	جرعة	dose, vaccine; gulp
2847	مؤلم	painful	4936	جنازة	funeral
2863	عالج	to treat	4945	علاجي	therapeutic

1445 فَرْق *n.* difference, distinction; discrepancy
لن أتخاذل عن المحاولة كالجميع، وهذا هو الفرق بيني وبين الآخرين — I won't get tired of trying like everyone else, and that is the difference between me and the others
98 | 2092 |

1446 حِفاظ *vn.* guarding, preserving; memorization; *n.* diaper; حِفاظ الحَيْض sanitary napkin
لقد استشهد الشريف أمزيان من أجل الحفاظ على بلادنا وكياننا وكنوزنا — Al-Sharif Amziyan has suffered martyrdom in order to protect our country and our being and our treasures
86 | 2368 |

1447 جَبْهَة *n.* (military, political, weather) front; front line; الجَبْهَة الشَّعْبِيَّة Popular Front
لماذا يجب أن يبقى لبنان الجبهة الوحيدة المفتوحة مع إسرائيل؟ — Why should Lebanon remain the only open front with Israel?
82 | 2465 |

1448 تَوْقِيع *n.* signing; signature
الولايات المتحدة الأمريكية رفضت التوقيع على اتفاقية كيوتو التي تحد من انبعاث الغازات — The United States of America refused to sign the Kyoto Agreement which limits gas emissions
86 | 2361 |

1449 مُمْتاز *adj.* excellent, superior, first-class; privileged, favored
لقد وجد وظيفة ممتازة في مكتب سمسرة — He found an excellent job in a brokerage office
93 | 2175 |

1450 هَمّ *n.* pl. هُموم worry, concern; anxiety, distress; care, interest
صحيفة عكاظ خصصت مساحة لمناقشة بعض هموم الفتاة السعودية — The Ukaz newspaper designated some space for the discussion of some concerns of Saudi young women
96 | 2118 |

1451 مُكافَحَة *n.* fight, battle, confrontation
إن الاعلان عن اليوم العالمي لمكافحة المخدرات يشكل مناسبة لدعوة الآباء والأهالي لمراقبة سلوك الابناء — The announcement of the International Day against Drug Abuse (World Day for Fighting Drugs) represents an

opportunity to call on parents and families to monitor their children's behavior
80 | 2541 |

1452 فَشِلَ *v. I (a)* to fail, be unsuccessful في in sth
المطلقة هى المرأة التى فشلت فى الاحتفاظ بزوجها — The divorced woman is the woman who failed to keep her husband
87 | 2332 |

1453 حَظّ *n.* luck, fortune
هذا الجيل أسعد حظا من غيره بسبب هذه البركة الإلهية — This generation is luckier than others because of this divine blessing
97 | 2082 |

1454 ضَيْف *n. pl.* ضُيُوف guest, visitor
نأسف لعدم تمكن الضيف من الإجابة نظرا لانتهاء زمن البرنامج — We are sorry the guest will not be able to respond since the time for the program has ended
97 | 2097 |

1455 ثانَوِيّ *adj.* secondary; lower-ranking, subordinate
إنه مجرد تلميذ فاشل ترك المدرسة الثانوية وهرب من أهله، حتى محطة البنزين التى كان يعمل فيها طردوه منها — He is merely a failing student who left secondary school and ran away from his family; even the gas station he used to work in fired him
94 | 2144 |

1456 جِسْر *n. pl.* جُسُور bridge; (reinforcement) beam or bar; (dental) bridge
سار خلفه متتبعا خطواته، فرآه يعبر الجسر ويدخل السوق — He walked after him following his footsteps, so he saw him crossing the bridge and entering the market
94 | 2143 |

1457 مُتَمَيِّز *adj.* distinguished, outstanding, prominent; different (عن from)
أكاد أتمزق ألما وأنا أرى طبيبة متميزة مثلها تقبع بين أربعة جدران ضحية حرب على الحجاب — I am almost being torn apart in pain when I see an excellent doctor like her languishing between four walls, a victim of the war on the head scarf
84 | 2396 |

1458 بَلْدَة *n.* town, township, community

كان الطريق الذي يمر من المحطة إلى البلدة كما هو،
رفيعا مترّبا، قليل التعرجات — The road that led
from the station to the town was the same:
narrow, dusty, its curves few

78 | 2586 |

1459 اِسْتَحَقَّ *v. X* to deserve, merit sth

نؤمن بأن بلادنا تستحق نظاما سياسيا ديمقراطيا
— We believe that our country deserves a
democratic political system

89 | 2265 |

1460 تَنْفِيذِيّ *adj.* executive, implementing

يشعر بأن السلطات التنفيذية داخل الدولة تتعامل مع
قضاياه بنوع من اللامبالاة — He feels that the
executive authorities inside the state are dealing
with his problems with a kind of unconcern

75 | 2664 |

1461 وَزْن *vn.* weighing, measuring the weight of;
n. pl. أَوْزان weight

الأكراد اليوم لهم وزن كبير في الحياة السياسية العراقية
الحالية — The Kurds today carry a lot of weight
in current Iraqi political life

94 | 2140 |

1462 إنجليزي and إنكليزي /'ingliizi/ *n./adj. pl.* إنجليز,
إنكليز English; (Dia.) English (language)

يضحك العمال على طريقة حمزة في نطق اللغة
الإنجليزية — The workers are making fun of
Hamza's way of pronouncing English

82 | 2454 |

1463 طَيَران *n.* aviation, flying; airline

وصل صوت المدافع إلى الإسكندرية، ورأى الناس
حركة الطيران فوقها، فارتعدت القاهرة وسهرت
سائر البلاد — The sound of cannons reached
Alexandria, and the people saw the activity of
airplanes above it, so Cairo trembled and the
rest of the country couldn't sleep

92 | 2176 |

1464 عُقُوبَة *n. pl.* -aat punishment, penalty, sanction

ميثاق الأمم المتحدة هو الذي يجيز فرض كل أنواع
العقوبات وبما فيها استخدام السلاح — The United
Nations Charter is the thing which permits the
imposition of all kinds of sanctions, including
the use of weapons

85 | 2342 |

1465 هون /hoon/ (Lev.) *adv.* here; لهون /la-hoon/
to here

عن جد الدنيا حر هون ما عاد فيه الواحد يستحمل
أبدا — The weather is really hot here, a person
can't bear it at all any more

49 | 4089 | +spo

1466 ثابِت *adj.* firm, established, constant; stable,
steady

لم يستطع الوقوف في مكان ثابت — He couldn't
stop in a fixed place

97 | 2053 |

1467 مُؤَشِّر *n. pl.* -aat indicator, index; measure,
gage; مُؤَشِّرات clues, indications, pointers

الحمد لله هناك كثير من المؤشرات التي تقول أن وضع
المرأة في البحرين على ما يرام — Praise God, there
are a lot of indicators which say that the
situation of women in Bahrain is going well

78 | 2537 |

1468 مَطَر *n. pl.* أَمْطار rain

أحست زهرة بالفعل بالخوف من صوت الرعد وقوة
الأمطار، وكثيرا ما أظلمت الدنيا نهارا كاملا —
Zahra indeed felt afraid of the sound of the
thunder and the strength of the rain, and many
times the world was dark for a complete day

93 | 2153 |

1469 مَفْرُوض *adj.* necessary, required; imposed,
prescribed; *n.* obligation, duty

المفروض انكم تكونون مع بعض على الحلوة والمرة
— You were supposed to be with each other
through good times and hard times

93 | 2152 |

1470 فَضَّلَ *v. II* to prefer sth (على to sth else)

اللصوص يفضلون الظلام، حتى أنتما ليس من
مصلحتكما أن تريا وجهيكما — Thieves prefer
darkness; even you two, it is not in your
interest to show your faces

96 | 2080 |

1471 جَمْع *n.* bringing together, gathering,
assembling; joining together

لا يعرف من هدف في الحياة إلا جمع المال ولو كان
على حساب كل شيء — The only goal he knows
for life is gathering money, even at the
expense of everything else

89 | 2236 |

1472 مَقْعَد *n.* pl. مَقاعِد seat; place

أعادته ومضة إلى الوعى، فوجد نفسه ممددا على المقعد الطويل فى عيادة الطبيب النفسى — A flash brought him back to consciousness, and he found himself lying on the long chair in the psychiatrist's office

88 | 2242 |

1473 مَقْتَل *n.* murder, killing

كانت له يد في مقتل عدد من الجنود الفرنسيين، فاقتيد إلى السجن — He had a hand in the killing of a number of French soldiers, so he was led to prison

84 | 2355 | +news

1474 ساهَمَ *v. III* to participate in, contribute to

هل ساهم الإخوان المسلمون في نشر الفكر التكفيري؟ — Did the Muslim Brothers participate in spreading Takfiri thought?

86 | 2291 |

1475 اتَّخَذَ *v. VIII* to take sth; to adopt, pass (a resolution)

اتخذت مقعدها بين مقاعد الدرجة الأولى ووضعت سماعات الووكمان في أذنيها — She took her seat among the first class seats and put her Walkman earphones on her ears

87 | 2265 |

1476 راحَة *n.* rest, relaxation, repose, leisure; راحَة اليَد palm of the hand

احتاجت لساعة من الراحة قبل أن تستطيع الوقوف والعودة معه إلى البيت — She needed an hour of rest before she was able to stand and return with him to the house

97 | 2039 |

1477 أَحَسَّ *v. IV* to feel, sense ب sth or أنَّ that

أحسست بأنني المسئولة الأولى عن موته — I felt that I was primarily responsible for his death

84 | 2350 | +lit

1478 فَضاء *n.* space; (outer) space, cosmos; vacant (plot of land)

لقد دخلت كاميليا البيت ذلك اليوم كعصفور طليق فى الفضاء — Camelia entered the house that day like a bird flying in the air

87 | 2269 |

1479 مُسْتَقِلّ *adj.* independent, autonomous

قرر أن يسكن في غرفة مستقلة داخل المأوى — He decided to live in a separate room inside the shelter

85 | 2308 |

1480 تُرْك، أَتْراك *n./adj.* pl. تُرْكِيّ Turk; Turkish

قد يرى العرب السنة في الأتراك نوعا جديدا من الإمبريالية العثمانية — The Sunni Arabs might see in the Turks a new kind of Ottoman Imperialism

91 | 2170 |

1481 أُفْق *n.* pl. آفاق and أُفُق horizon; آفاق view, perspectives; outlook, prospects

رفعت سلمى رأسها ونظرت نحو الأفق البعيد — Salma raised her head and looked out towards the far horizons

87 | 2245 |

1482 جُثَّة *n.* pl. جُثَث corpse, body

بدأ الجميع يرفعون الجثث من تحت الأنقاض — Everyone started to bring out the bodies from under the ruins

88 | 2240 |

1483 شِبْه *n.* semi-, almost, like

كانت الموافقة على إقامة مسجد فى هذا المكان شبه مستحيلة، لكن ربنا سبحانه وتعالى أراد لنا التوفيق — Agreement on building a mosque in this place was almost impossible, but our Lord, may He be praised and exalted, wanted us to have success

98 | 2003 |

1484 شَرَف *n.* honor, distinction

النتائج التى قدمتها مغشوشة.. أنت شخص بلا شرف.. سألغى رسالتك وأفصلك من القسم فورا — The results which you presented were faked...You are a person without honor...I will cancel your dissertation and have you dismissed from the department immediately

97 | 2016 |

1485 هُوِيَّة *n.* identity; identity card

حضر الجميع أوراق إثبات الهوية.. وبدأنا العبور — Everyone prepared their identity papers...and we began to pass through

86 | 2274 |

1486 بِطاقَة *n.* pl. -aat card; tag; ticket; ballot
أدخلوا بطاقات دعواتهم فى جهاز الليزر للتأكّد من
أنها ليست مزورة — They put their invitation
cards into the laser machine to make sure that
they weren't counterfeit
94 | 2074 |

1487 رُكْن *n.* pl. أَرْكان pillar, foundation, support;
(mil.) chief of staff; corner, nook; section
(newspaper)
تأمّل شكله فى المرآة الموضوعة فى ركن القبو
واستغرق فى الضحك — He contemplated his
form in the mirror that was placed in the
corner of the cellar, and he laughed
uproariously
88 | 2217 |

1488 مُصاب *n./adj.* injured, wounded; afflicted
تأخّرت عملية نقل المصابين بسبب عدم وجود
سيارات إسعاف مهيأة وصالحة — The operation
of transporting the wounded was delayed
because of the unavailability of prepared, valid
ambulances
88 | 2220 |

1489 صارُوخ *n.* pl. صَوارِيخ missile, rocket
يصرّ سكان المنطقة على أن الصواريخ قتلت أساتذة
وتلامذة أبرياء — The inhabitants of the area
insist that the rockets killed some innocent
teachers and students
84 | 2328 |

1490 تَحَوُّل *n.* pl. -aat change, transformation,
conversion
كانت نقطة التحوّل في حياته عندما شاهد شجاعة
أحد المتظاهرين الشباب أثناء مظاهرة في تل أبيب عام
٢٠٠٢ — The turning point in his life was
when he saw the courage of one of the young
demonstrators during a demonstration in Tel
Aviv in the year 2002
87 | 2248 |

1491 رُوسِيّ *n./adj.* pl. رُوس Russian
أفغانستان لم تكن فيتنام الروسية، بل كانت حربا
بعيدة لم تؤثر سوى سطحيا على الرأي العام
السوفيتي — Afghanistan was not the Russian
Vietnam, rather it was a distant war which
only influenced Soviet public opinion in a
superficial manner
80 | 2425 |

1492 جَوِّيّ *adj.* air, aerial; atmospheric; climatic,
weather-related
كانت الرحلة متعبة جدا لسوء الأحوال الجوية
— The trip was very tiring because of the bad
weather
82 | 2367 |

1493 سَيِّء *adj.* bad
ابتعد عن هذا الطريق لأن نهايته سيّئة — Get off
that road, since its end is bad
97 | 1995 |

1494 أَمان *n.* safety, security, protection
كل سيادتك لقمة سريعة ثم انصرف فى أمان الله إلى
موعدك — Eat a quick bite, Your Excellency,
and then leave in peace to your appointment
97 | 1991 |

1495 أَكْل *vn.* eating; consuming; *n.* food, meal
تغدوا أنتم، فلا رغبة لي في الأكل الآن — Go ahead
and eat lunch, I have no desire to eat now
91 | 2134 |

1496 مُرَشَّح *adj.* nominated, selected; expected,
prepared, slated; (most) likely; *n.* pl. -uun
candidate, nominee
تجري الانتخابات ليختار الشعب أحد المرشحين
الثلاثة — The elections are taking place
for the people to choose one of the three
candidates
79 | 2452 |

1497 وَصْف *n.* description, portrayal,
characterization; *n.* pl. أَوْصاف characteristic,
trait; بِوَصْفِهِ in his capacity as (chairman,
minister, etc.)
جلست متهالكا على أقرب مقعد.. لا أستطيع
وصف مشاعري تلك اللحظة.. خليط من الذهول
والغضب والمهانة — I sat exhausted on the
closest chair; I can't describe my feelings at
that moment; a mixture of confusion, anger
and humiliation
88 | 2198 |

1498 مُلاحَظَة *vn.* observing, noticing; *n.* pl. -aat
note, remark, observation
اسمحي لي أن أقدم ملاحظة: — Permit me to
offer an observation:
90 | 2141 |

1499 لَقَب *n.* title; nickname

الحقيقة اسمي رضوان أحمد لكن البدو أعطوني لقب الفلاح لتمييزي، وفي الغالب يسمونني رضوان — إكسبريس — The truth is that my name is Radwan Ahmad, but the Bedouin gave me the nickname "The Farmer" to distinguish me, and usually they call me Radwan Express

85 | 2263 |

1500 مَسافة *n.* pl. -aat distance, interval

عندما نسافر حتى إلى مسافة قريبة، نحب أن يكون أحد في انتظارنا — When we travel even a short distance, we like there to be someone waiting for us

98 | 1960 |

1501 فَقْر *n.* poverty, lack of; فَقْر الدَم anemia

الواقع أن أكثر من نصف المصريين يعيشون تحت خط الفقر — The fact is that more than half of all Egyptians live beneath the poverty line

93 | 2056 |

1502 اِنْتِشار *n.* spreading, diffusion

أمريكا تحث منظمة الأمن على منع انتشار أسلحة الدمار الشامل — America urges the Security Organization to prevent the spread of weapons of mass destruction

85 | 2241 |

1503 خائِف *adj.* afraid, fearful, frightened

بدأ توتر والدتها يتدرج إلى خوف حقيقي وهي تراقب انهيار صحة ابنتها وإصرارها على محاربة الطعام — Her mother's tension began to step up to actual fear as she watched her daughter's health collapse and her insistence on fighting food

95 | 2023 |

1504 ثُلاثاء *n.* (يَوْم) الثُلاثاء Tuesday

يعتبر ما حدث يوم الثلاثاء الماضي شيئا استثنائيا — He considers what happened on last Tuesday to be something exceptional

84 | 2280 |

1505 ما *part.* (exclamatory, with foll. elat.) how...!

ما أَحْلاها how pretty she is!

ها هو جرس الباب.. حبيبتي منضبطة في مواعيدها.. — ما أجمل هذا كله!.. سأنهض لأفتح الباب There's the doorbell...My girlfriend always keeps her appointments on time...How beautiful all of this is!...I'm going to get up and open the door

54 | 3557 |

1506 تَواصُل *n.* continuation, maintaining; interconnection, mutual contact; intercommunication

أتمنى أن يزداد التواصل بيننا في المستقبل وسأكون دائما سعيدا بالتواصل معكم — I hope our interaction with each other will increase in the future and I will always be happy to be in touch with you

85 | 2243 |

1507 ظُهُور *n.* appearance, emergence; advent

هكذا صار الناس يتوقعون ظهور الأسود والنمور في أي وقت — Thus the people were expecting the appearance of lions and tigers at any moment

88 | 2161 |

1508 زِراعَة *n.* agriculture, cultivation; implanting, transplanting (organ)

في هذه الجزيرة أنشىء مركز عالمي لأبحاث الزراعة في الأراضي القاحلة — On this island was build an international center for agricultural research in dry lands

83 | 2287 |

1509 غَرَض *n.* pl. أغْراض goal, purpose, intent; أغْراض (Lev.Irq.Gul.) things, items, personal effects

يغادرون الأردن ويأتون لأغراض تجارية — They are leaving Jordan and coming for commercial purposes

94 | 2024 |

1510 إمْكان *n.* pl. -aat capability, ability, power; possibility, (what is) possible

قرر أن يتجنب المواجهة بقدر الإمكان — He decided to avoid the confrontation as much as possible

90 | 2120 |

1511 أثْبَتَ *v.* IV to prove, ascertain, establish sth

هذا يعني ان الفنان ان فيروز أثبتت ان تستطيع ان لا يكون سجين نفسه وماضيه — This means that Fairuz has proven that an artist doesn't have to be a prisoner of himself and his past

87 | 2189 |

20 Dialect Words

This is a list of the most frequent words from the dialects. Note that dialect words that have a Standard Arabic counterpart are not listed here. Dia. means all or most of the dialects.

Word	Rank	Dialects	Definition
بـ	31	Egy. Lev.	(verb marker)
اللي	112	Dia.	which
راح	113	Dia.	to go; (future marker)
شو	141	Lev. Kuw. Alg.	what
بسّ	156	Egy. Lev. Irq. Gul.	only; but
مِش / مُش	239	Egy. Lev. Gul.	not
عـ / ع	280	Dia.	on
شاف	282	Dia.	to see
فيه	315	Egy. Lev. Gul.	there is
بِدّ / بَدّ	344	Lev.	to wish, want
إيه	405	Egy.	what
وين	406	Lev. Irq. Gul.	where
عم	517	Lev.	(verb marker)
هيك / هيچ	532	Lev. Irq.	like this
مين	717	Egy. Lev.	who
هاي	725	Lev. Irq. Gul.	this
شوي	742	Lev. Gul. Irq.	a little bit
مو	754	Irq. Gul. Lev.	not
كمان	768	Egy. Lev.	also
ده / دا	826	Egy.	this
زيّ	897	Egy. Lev.	like
عشان / علشان	933	Egy. Lev. Gul.	because
ـش	965	Dia.	not
كده / كدا	1000	Egy.	thus
بغى، يبغي، / يبي	1006	Gul.	to want, need
بعدين	1032	Egy. Lev.	afterwards
جاب	1046	Dia.	to bring
أيش	1053	Lev. Gul.	what
سوّى	1070	Lev. Irq. Gul.	to do
ليش	1119	Lev. Irq. Gul.	why
دي	1232	Egy.	this (fem)
خلاص	1244	Egy., Gul., Alg.	OK, that's it
يالله / يللا / يلا	1257	Dia.	c'mon!, let's...!
ليه	1271	Egy., Lev., Gul.	why
شـ	1364	Irq.	what
شنو	1390	Gul. Irq. Magh.	what
عيش	1408	Egy., Gul.	life, living; bread; rice
هون	1465	Lev.	here
دار	1629	Magh	to do, make
وشّ / ويش	1695	Gul.	what
هلق	1703	Lev.	now
بكرة / بكرا	1810	Egy., Lev., Gul.	tomorrow

Word	Rank	Dialects	Definition
كويّس	1888	Egy., Lev.	good
إنتو / إنتوا	1906	Dia.	you (pl)
هـ	1909	Lev., Irq., Gul.	this
أيوا / أيوه	1927	Dia.	yes
آني	1972	Irq., Alg.	I
حدّ	2042	Egy., Lev.	someone
برا / بره	2054	Dia.	outside
لسه/ لسة	2069	Egy., Lev., Gul.	yet, still
فين	2177	Egy., Lev.	where
نصّ	2195	Dia.	half
شلون	2277	Bah., Irq., Qat.	how
عايز / عاوز	2567	Egy.	to want
برضو / برده	2715	Egy., Lev.	also
حدا	2732	Lev.	anyone, someone
ياريت	2775	Dia.	if only, I wish
واجد	2845	Gul.	very, a lot
الحين	2849	Gul.	now, right now
عيّل	2951	Egy., Gul.	child
ويّا	3054	Irq.	with
سالفة	3119	Irq., Gul.	chat, talk
بتاع	3238	Egy.	belonging to
بقى	3458	Egy.	then, so
ماكو	3591	Irq., Kuw.	there is not, there are not
معليش / معلش	3601	Egy., Lev.	never mind
تبع	3627	Lev.	belonging to
زلمه / زلمي	3668	Lev.	guy, man
منيح	3669	Lev.	good
عقبال	3688	Egy., Lev.	may it be the same for
بلاش	3733	Egy., Lev., Irq., Gul.	don't; for nothing
منو	3747	Gul., Irq., Sud.	who
هسة / هسه / هسا / هسع	3871	Irq., Lev., Gul.	now, right away
قديش/ قديه	3884	Lev.	how many, how much
أوف / أفّ	4037	Lev., Irq., Gul.	ugh!
حـ	4072	Egy.	(future marker)
هذاك / هداك / هديك/ هديج	4131	Lev., Irq., Gul., Magh.	that (m, f)
را	4196	Alg.	(verbal particle)
مال	4230	Irq., Gul.	of, for, belonging to
متاع / تاع	4283	Magh.	belonging to
كلّش / كلّش	4311	Irq., Gul.	very, very much
لين	4462	Gul.	when, whenever; until
راجل	4471	Egy.	man
مبارح / امبارح	4481	Lev.	yesterday
سكّر	4498	Lev., Gul.	to close, shut
دلوقتي	4590	Egy.	now
مب / موب	4606	Gul.	not
هول	4609	Lev.	these
إزّاي	4615	Egy.	how

Word	Rank	Dialects	Definition
خوش	4660	Irq.	good
هيدي	4784	Lev.	this (fem)
هذول / هدول	4831	Lev., Irq., Gul.	these
واش	4835	Magh., Alg.	what, which
ايمتى / ايمتا / امتى	4849	Lev., Egy.	when
مشان / منشان	4863	Lev.	for the sake of; so that
شكون	4864	Magh.	who
انزين / نزين	4893	Gul.	good
علاش	4905	Magh.	why
هيدا	4907	Lev.	this (mas)
مليح	4921	Lev., Alg.	good
فدّ	4929	Irq.	one
كيفاش / كيفاه	4941	Magh.	how, how come
شكو / شاكو	4953	Irq., Kuw.	what? what is there?
جوّا / جوه	4957	Lev., Irq., Egy.	inside
هوايا	4963	Irq.	a lot, very much
النّهارده	4969	Egy.	today
استنّى يستنّى	4973	Dia.	to wait for
نطى	4974	Irq.	to give
شقد	4979	Irq.	how many, how much
أكو	4980	Irq., Kuw., Bah.	there is, there are
بلكي	4986	Lev., Irq.	maybe, perhaps
مصاري	4990	Lev.	money
لكان	5080	Lev.	then, so
مبلى	5214	Lev.	yes
دول / ذول	5395	Egy., Lev., Irq., Gul.	these, those
ولـ	5616	Lev.	hey
كي	5666	Alg.	when; like, as
هدر	5671	Alg.	to talk, speak
دِغري / دُغري	5718	Lev.	straight
يمّ	5722	Irq., Gul.	next to, near
بلّش	5753	Lev.	to start, begin
برك	5764	Alg.	only, just
شون	5773	Irq., Kuw.	how
لعد / لعاد	5807	Irq., Lev.	so, then, well; but, otherwise
درك / ذرك / ضرك	5840	Alg.	now
نمرة	5852	Egy., Lev.	number
همّ	5886	Irq., Gul.	also
مرّة	5921	Sau., Yem.	very, a lot
أبصر / إيصر	5925	Lev.	maybe, perhaps; I wonder
لول	5931	Dia.	LOL (laughing out loud)
كليات	5963	Lev.	all of; in its entirety
مالة	6033	Alg.	so, therefore, then
بكّير	6072	Lev.	early
اثنينات / اتنينات	6085	Irq., Lev.	both of
كيا	6111	Alg.	as, like
قاع	6129	Alg.	all, every

Word	Rank	Dialects	Definition
أشو	6346	Irq.	it seems, it appears that; OK
آش / أش	6382	Magh.	what
موش / ميش	6491	Alg.	not
زعما / زعمة	6527	Alg.	so then; really?; uh
والو / ولو	6558	Magh.	nothing
باش	6560	Magh.	so, so that; in order to
ماعليش / ماعليهش	6655	Alg.	he's OK
كوبي	6657	Alg.	to hang up (the phone)
هكّة	6685	Alg., Tn	like this, thus
زاف / بزاف	6763	Magh.	very, a lot, many
دوك	6801	Alg.	now
قدّاه / قدّاش	6854	Alg.	how many, how much

1512 اِنْتَقَلَ *v. VIII* to move, transfer; اِنْتَقَلَ إلى رَحْمَةِ الله تَعالَى to die

لقد ترك دميان مكانه أمام مجد الدين على يسار العربة وانتقل إلى اليمين يطل من النافذة مخلوب الرشد — Dumyan left his place in front of Magd Al-Din on the left of the car and moved to the right looking out the window, enchanted

89 | 2125 |

1513 دَلَّ *v. I (u)* to point على at sth; to indicate, serve as proof على أنَّ that

إن حمرة وجوه الجنود، وبياض بشرة أذرعهم وسيقانهم، تدل على أنهم جنود لم يروا الصحراء من قبل — The redness of the faces of the soldiers, and the whiteness of the skin of their arms and legs, indicate that they are soldiers who have not seen the desert before

88 | 2156 |

1514 وَكِيل *n.* representative, agent

وكيل وزارة السياحة في كندا حتى وقت قريب هو عربي الأصل — The assistant minister of tourism in Canada until just recently was of Arab origin

93 | 2041 |

1515 آلِيَّة *n.* pl. -aat mechanism, machine; vehicle, vessel

يبقى هناك ضرورة ملحة لوضع آلية فاعلة ودائمة لتنفيذ بنود هذا القانون — There is a pressing need to put in place an effective and permanent mechanism to carry out the provisions of this law

77 | 2446 |

1516 حِرْص *n.* desire, keenness, eagerness; حِرْصاً على out of concern for, for the sake of

أكد في مؤتمر صحفي حرص الملك والحكومة على تحسين المستوى المعيشي للأردنيين — He emphasized in a press conference the King's and the government's determination to improve the Jordanians' standard of living

87 | 2166 |

1517 حِينَما *conj.* when, while

العراقي لا يشعر حينما يأتي ويزور الأردن انه غريب عن هذا البلد — The Iraqi, when he comes and visits Jordan, does not feel that he is a stranger to this country

87 | 2171 |

1518 لَحْم *n.* pl. لُحُوم meat, flesh

أنا من لحم ودم أمامك لكن روحي محبوسة كأنها في قبر — I am of flesh and blood before you but my soul is trapped as if it were in a tomb

94 | 1999 |

1519 مُتَخَصِّص *adj.* specialized; *n.* pl. -uun specialist

عقد دورات وورش عمل متخصصة في مجال إدارة الأزمات بالتعاون مع القوات المسلحة — He held sessions and specialized workshops in the area of crisis management in cooperation with the armed forces

83 | 2258 |

1520 تَلَقَّى *v. V* to receive, get

أنا أيضا فى مشكلة كبرى.. تلقيت إنذارا قانونيا من الجامعة.. متوسط درجاتى انخفض بشدة — I also have a big problem...I received a legal warning from the university...my average grades have fallen drastically

88 | 2134 |

1521 جَلالَة *n.* majesty; (in titles) جَلالَة المَلِك His Majesty, the King

وصل السيد مايلز لامبسون السفير البريطانى قادما من لندن لمقابلة جلالة الملك بقصر المنتزه — Mr Miles Lambson, British ambassador, arrived, coming from London, to meet His Majesty the King in the Muntazah Palace

64 | 2944 |

1522 بِنْيَة *n. pl.* بِنىً , بُنىً and بُنْيَة structure; make-up, physique; بِنْيَة تَحْتِيَّة infrastructure

الإرهاب يحاول ضرب العملية السياسية وضرب البنية التحتية وإرباك جهاز الدولة — Terrorism tries to hit the political operation and to hit the infrastructure, and to confuse the state apparatus

91 | 2058 |

1523 تَحْسِين *vn.* improving, enhancing, bettering; *n.* improvement, enhancement

يعمل على تطوير نفسه بنفسه وتحسين ظروفه قدر المستطاع — He is working on developing himself by himself and improving his circumstances as much as possible

83 | 2250 |

1524 مَبْنىً *n. pl.* مَبانٍ (def. مَبانِي) building, edifice; structure

يكفى أن تعرف رقم أى مبنى لتصل إليه بسهولة — It is enough that you know the number of any building to be able to reach it easily

86 | 2195 |

1525 فَم *n. pl.* أفواه mouth

وفتح فمه دون أن يقول شيئا — And he opened his mouth without saying a thing

83 | 2264 |

1526 خَمْسُون *num.* fifty; fiftieth

من هنا يستدير يمنة، ثم يتقدم نحو خمسين خطوة ينبغي أن يقع بعدها على حجر كبير — From here he turns right, and then goes forward about fifty steps, after which he should find a big rock

97 | 1925 |

1527 أَهَمَّ *v. IV* to concern sb; to be important to sb

ماذا لو مات؟ هل يهم ذلك أحدا؟ — What if he died? Does that concern anyone?

97 | 1941 |

1528 اِمْتِحان *n. pl.* -aat examination, test; trial

الأب لابنه: إذا نجحت في الامتحانات سأعطيك ٥٠ دينارا — The father to his son: if you succeed in the exams I'll give you 50 dinar

95 | 1970 |

1529 طِبّ *n.* medicine, medical treatment

والأهم من ذلك أنه مدرس مساعد فى كلية الطب، ويتعلم فى أمريكا، وسوف يحصل على الدكتوراه — More important than that is that he is a teaching assistant in the College of Medicine, and is studying in America, and he will obtain a doctorate

94 | 2001 |

1530 مُقَدِّمَة *n. pl.* -aat preface, introduction; front part

قرروا أن يعودوا ليحصدوا قمحهم.. تجمع الرجال في المقدمة وخلفهم النساء — They decided to return to harvest their wheat...the men gathered at the front, and behind them the women

92 | 2031 |

1531 فَرْع *n. pl.* فُرُوع branch, department, subdivision, section

عائلة العقاد لها فروع هاجرت إلى السودان واستقرت بها ولا تزال تعيش فيها إلى اليوم — Aqqad's family has branches that emigrated to the Sudan and settled in it, and still live there today

95 | 1977 |

1532 مَصِير *n.* path, destiny, fate

كنت قلقة على مصير والدي.. أما الآن، فقلقة على صحته فقط — I was worried about my father's fate...but now I am worried only about his health

88 | 2117 |

1533 سَليم *adj.* correct, sound; flawless; safe
أهم ما يجب فعله الآن هو الاستراحة لنتمكن من التفكير السليم — The most important thing that must be done now is to rest, so we will be able to think clearly
93 | 2013 |

1534 تَرْتيب *n. pl.* -aat preparation, arrangement, putting in order; organization, planning
عصمت يعيد ترتيب الشقة في سرعة، سعيد يساعده — Ismat rearranges the apartment quickly, and Said helps him
93 | 1993 |

1535 مَبْرُوك *adj.* blessed, happy; *interj.* !مَبْرُوك
!أَلْف مَبْرُوك (على on/for); congratulations! many congratulations!
مبروك، لقد استطعت القراءة! — Congratulations, you were able to read!
66 | 2831 | +for

1536 مُطْلَق *adj.* absolute, unlimited; مُطْلَقاً absolutely
في أميركا لك الحق المطلق في ألا تدلي بشهادتك — In America you have the full right not to be a witness against yourself
88 | 2114 |

1537 نَفَّذَ *v. II* to implement, carry out, execute
أرجو أن تنفذ وعدك وتمنحني مكافأتي — I hope you will fulfill your promise and grant me my reward
88 | 2106 |

1538 حَسْب *n.* sufficiency, enough; فَحَسْب and حَسْب *adv.* only; حَسْبُنا الله God is sufficient for us
هل تقتصر الدعوة على احترام عقائد الديانات السماوية الثلاث فحسب؟ أم تشمل العقائد الدينية جميعا؟ — Is the call limited to respecting the doctrines of the three heavenly (revealed) religions only? Or does it include all religious doctrines?
89 | 2088 |

1539 قَبيلة *n. pl.* قَبائل tribe
حمل البطيخة وفى عودته فكر أن يهديها إلى شيخ القبيلة ففى ذلك فائدة أكثر من أكلها — He carried the watermelon, and while he was going back he thought about giving it to the Sheikh of the tribe, since there would be more benefit in that than in eating it
86 | 2150 |

1540 أوكي and أوكيه /'okey/ (Dia.) *interj.* OK
أوكي يلا نبدأ — OK, let's start
28 | 6505 | +spo

1541 تَوَفَّرَ *v. V* to be plentiful; to be available ل for sb; to be met, fulfilled (conditions, requirements) في in sth/sb
نرغب في شراء كل المعادن التي تتوفر في المنطقة — We want to buy all the metal that is available in the region
84 | 2198 |

1542 تَمَتَّعَ *v. V* to enjoy ب sth, be blessed ب with sth; to possess, be endowed ب with (qualities)
يتمتع بثقافة واسعة ومعلومات غزيرة — He's a broadly cultured man who possesses a wealth of information
87 | 2117 |

1543 قَطْع *vn.* breaking off, interruption; قَطْعاً absolutely; *vn.* traversing (a distance); issuing (a ticket)
عليها أن يتعاونا على قطع هذا الخيط — They need to cooperate in cutting this thread
90 | 2046 |

1544 وَفاة *n. pl.* وَفَيات death; الوفايات obituaries (newspaper section)
احتفلت تركيا بذكرى وفاة أتاتورك — Turkey celebrated the anniversary of the death of Ataturk
87 | 2112 |

1545 سُقُوط *n.* fall, downfall, collapse; crash (aircraft)
أدى سقوط صواريخ في الكريوت إلى إصابة سبعة إسرائيليين — Rockets falling on Krayot led to the wounding of seven Israelis
86 | 2123 |

1546 رائِحة *n. pl.* رَوائِح scent, odor, perfume
كان أنيقا كالعادة تفوح منه رائحة عطر فاخر — He was elegant, as usual, the smell of luxurious perfume coming from him
83 | 2204 |

1547 فَعَّالِيَّة *n.* effectiveness, efficiency; فَعَّالِيّات events, activities

تترقب المدينة حاليا بدء فعاليات بطولة كأس العالم — The city is currently waiting for the beginning of the activities for the World Cup Championship

76 | 2399 |

1548 داخِلِيَّة *n.* (ministry) interior, of state

انا اناشد السيد وزير الداخلية على اعدام المسؤولين عن هذه الجريمة حتى يكونوا عبره لغيرهم — I exhort you, Mr Minister of the Interior, to execute those responsible for this crime so that they will be a lesson to others

73 | 2496 |

1549 عَدالَة *n.* justice, fairness

لن يكون هناك بعد الآن من أحد فوق العدالة، العدالة ستطول الجميع — No one will be above justice, after today, justice will reach everyone

81 | 2249 |

1550 جار *n.* pl. جِيران neighbor

كان الوقت غروبا ومر من أمام جيرانه وأهله دون أن يحيي أحدا ودون أن يشعر بهم — The time was sunset, and he passed in front of his neighbors and family without greeting anyone and without being aware of them

96 | 1903 |

1551 وَثِيقَة *n.* pl. وَثائِق document; certificate; title, deed; paper, record

من يعمل معه سيطلع على وثائق خطيرة.. إنه يريدك لأنه يثق بك — Whoever works with him will become familiar with dangerous documents... he wants you because he trusts you

84 | 2184 |

1552 عَلامَة *n.* pl. -aat mark, indication, sign; point

قد بدت على ملامحه علامات التعب والمرض — Signs of tiredness and illness appeared upon his features

96 | 1897 |

1553 تَنْسِيق *n.* coordination, collaboration

هل هناك تنسيق بين سلطات الأمن في بلادنا وسلطات ألمانية الشرقية؟ — Is there any coordination between the security authorities in our country and the East German authorities?

81 | 2263 |

1554 فَرَض *v. I (i)* to impose sth على on sb; to assume أنَّ that

لا يجوز لك أن تفرض أي ضريبة على الشعب You should not impose any tax on the people

88 | 2080 |

1555 بَقاء *n.* survival; *vn.* remaining, staying

أحس أن جسده يشاركه الفرح فلم يستطع البقاء فى مكانه — He felt that his body shared his joy, and he couldn't stand still

89 | 2049 |

1556 اِحْتِفال *vn.* celebrating; *n.* pl. -aat celebration, ceremony

هذه البدلة السوداء المخططة اشتراها خصيصا للاحتفال بعيد ميلاد زينب — He bought this striped black suit especially for celebrating Zaynab's birthday

86 | 2113 |

1557 أبْرَز *elat.* more/most prominent

هي من أبرز المتفوقين فى كلية طب طنطا، وهى تتمتع بذكاء خارق — She is one of the most prominent outstanding students in the College of Medicine in Tanta, and she has a superb intelligence

81 | 2238 |

1558 قَيْد *n.* pl. قُيُود restriction, condition, stipulation; fetter, chain, shackle; قَيْدَ undergoing, in the process of; قَيْدِ الإنْشاء under construction; على قَيْدِ الحَياة alive; لا قَيْدَ أنْمُلَة not one iota, not an inch; (leg.) register, record

تقدم نحوى ووضع القيد الحديدى فى يدى.. الغريب أننى استسلمت له تماما — He advanced towards me and placed the iron fetter on my hand... The strange thing is that I surrendered completely to him

86 | 2114 |

1559 حِكْمَة *n.* wisdom; pl. حِكَم wise saying, proverb, moral

بقليل من الحكمة يعود كل شىء إلى مكانه With a little wisdom, everything will return to its place

92 | 1963 |

1560 فِتْنَة *n.* pl. فِتَن charm, allure, enchantment; dissent, unrest; riot, rebellion

أنا أعرف أنك رجل صالح لا تفرق بين مسلم وقبطي، لكن أولاد الحرام يحبون أن يشعلوا نار الفتنة — وخصوصا في الأحياء الفقيرة مثل حينا I know that you are a good man who does not distinguish between a Muslim and a Copt, but those bad guys love to set the fire of conflict, especially in the poor areas like our neighborhood

86 | 2104 |

1561 مَسِيحِيّ *n./adj.* Christian

أنا أعرف أنك مسيحية.. صليب في عنقك.. أنا مسلم — I know that you are a Christian...a cross around your neck...I am a Muslim

85 | 2124 |

1562 تليفون and تلفون /talifoon, tilifoon/ *n.* pl. -aat telephone

انا حاديكى نمرة تلفون ايفون دلوقتى — I will give you Yvonne's telephone number now

41 | 4380 | +spo

1563 زارَ *v. I (u)* to visit sb or a place

قام الرئيس القبرصي تاسوس بابا دوبلوس الذي يزور مصر حاليا وقرينته السيدة بزيارة منطقة الأهرام ومراكب الشمس — The Cypriot president Tassos Papadopoulos who is visiting Egypt currently, and his wife, visited the Pyramids area and the Sun Boat

97 | 1857 |

1564 هائِل *adj.* great, huge, formidable; frightful, appalling

شعبنا يمتلك إمكانات هائلة.. لو تحققت الديمقراطية ستصبح مصر بلدا قويا متقدما — Our people possess amazing resources...if democracy is achieved Egypt will become a strong, advanced country

88 | 2044 |

1565 مُؤَخَّر *n.* rear, end, back; balance (of a payment); مُؤَخَّراً recently, lately; finally, in the end

لم يمت إلا مؤخرا في عامه الواحد والثمانين — He died only recently in his eighty-first year

81 | 2228 |

1566 سِياحَة *n.* tourism

بالنسبة للسياحة الاجنبية تعتبر هذه الفترة هي بداية موسم السياحة الاوروبية والامريكية — As far as foreign tourism goes, this period is considered the beginning of the European and American tourist seasons

87 | 2071 |

1567 وُقُوف *n.* standing, stopping, halting

البيوت تنهار في كرموز وتهتز هنا، أفضل لكم الخروج والوقوف في الشارع — The houses are falling in Karmouz and are shaking here, it is better for you to go out and stand in the street

88 | 2043 |

1568 ثَقِيل *adj.* heavy, cumbersome

سمعت صوت وقع أقدام ثقيلة، ثم صوت باب حديدي ضخم يفتح محدثا صريرا — I heard the sound of heavy footsteps, then the sound of a huge iron door opening, causing a creaking sound

98 | 1838 |

1569 رَسْم *vn.* drawing, sketching, illustrating; *n.* pl. رُسُوم picture, drawing; tax, fee

حسب الجدول لدي فان رسوم العام الدراسي ستكون ألفا و سبعمائة دولار — According to my schedule, the fees for the academic year will be one thousand seven hundred dollars

85 | 2112 |

1570 جامِعِيّ *adj.* university

تخلى عن دراسته الجامعية وهو يكتشف عبثية تكديس الشهادات — He abandoned his university studies when he discovered the absurdity of accumulating degrees

89 | 2009 |

1571 أَشْبَهَ *v. IV* to resemble, look like, be similar to sth/sb

تطبخ بطريقة ممتازة تشبه طريقة أمي تماما — She cooks in an excellent way that resembles my mother's way exactly

85 | 2102 |

1572 تَطَلَّبَ *v. V* to require, demand sth (مِن from sb)

لم يكن الأمر يتطلب الكثير من التفكير — The matter did not require a great deal of thought

85 | 2116 |

1573 تَوْجِيه *vn.* directing, guiding, sending; *n. pl.*
-aat instruction, guideline, directive

حذر جلالته من ان توجيه ضربة الى ايران سوف
يفجر الوضع الاقليمي برمته — His majesty
warned that directing a strike at Iran would
explode the entire regional situation

86 | 2083 |

1574 حَطَّ *v. I (u)* to put, place, set down; *a.p.* (Dia.)
حاطِط, حاطّ (.Lev)

بكره بقى حاروح أصرف الشيك، أحط فلوس فى
البنك وأدى لمامتك المتين — Tomorrow, then,
I will go cash the check; I'll put money in the
bank and give your mother the two hundred

58 | 3065 | +spo

1575 حَبّ *coll.n.* grain, seed(s); *un.n.* حَبَّة *n. pl.*
حَبّات , حُبُوب grain, seed; pill; bead

نهض ببطء وابتلع حبة المنوم — He got up slowly
and swallowed a sleeping pill

94 | 1894 |

1576 شَوْق *n.* desire, yearning

لا يبدو عليه شوق لشيء سوى كأسه — He doesn't
seem to have passion for anything but his cup

79 | 2248 |

1577 دَقِيق *adj.* precise, accurate; minute, micro-;
delicate

يحاول توصيل المعلومة الدقيقة إلى تلاميذه —
He is trying to get precise information over
to his students

87 | 2049 |

1578 مُتَقَدِّم *adj.* advanced, developed; *n.* applicant
(person submitting an application); *a.p.*
applying, seeking (job position or admission)

أريد أن أساعد المرضى الفقراء وأنقل إلى مصر تقنيات
الجراحة المتقدمة — I want to help the poor sick,
and bring to Egypt advanced surgical
techniques

86 | 2063 |

1579 زِراعِيّ *adj.* agricultural, farming

نحن في الأردن من أفقر دول العالم في الأرض
الزراعية، فهي لا تشكل ١٪ من مجموع مساحاتها —
We in Jordan are among the poorest countries
in the world in agricultural land, since it
represents less than 1% of the total area

79 | 2265 |

1580 شَيْطان *n. pl.* شَياطِين devil; الشيطان the Devil,
Satan

هو شيطان انجليزي فاهم شغله كويس . مش زي
الشيطان المصري اللي كنت باعرف أقاومه — He is
an English devil who understands his work
very well, not like the Egyptian devil who
I knew how to resist

87 | 2044 | +lit +for

1581 قَتِيل *n. pl.* قَتْلَى casualty, dead/killed person

ذكرت الوكالة في وقت سابق ان ٥٧ شخصا سقطوا
قتلى في ثلاثة تفجيرات وقعت بالعاصمة الاردنية
مساء أمس — The agency previously mentioned
that fifty-seven persons were killed in three
explosions which took place in the Jordanian
capital yesterday evening

84 | 2122 |

1582 اِسْتِفادَة *n.* benefiting مِن from, making
use مِن of

تكلمت حول إمكانية الاستفادة من تجربتهما،
والوقوف إلى جانبهما في هذه المحنة الموسمية — She
talked about the possibility of benefiting from
their experience, and standing beside them in
this seasonal ordeal

83 | 2150 |

1583 اِسْتِقْبال *n.* reception; receiving, welcoming

تذكرت أن لديه فى مكتب الاستقبال شاشة
تكشف أمامه المبنى كله من الداخل — I
remembered that he had in the reception
office a screen that shows right in front of
him the whole building from the inside

87 | 2034 |

1584 وَرْد *coll.n.* roses, flowers; *un.n.* وَرْدَة, *pl.* وُرُود,
وَرْدات

صاروا يجولون في سياراتهم في الشوارع متوقفين كل
فتاة جميلة ليقدموا لها وردة حمراء — They started
to drive around in their cars in the streets,
stopping every pretty girl to offer her a red
rose

88 | 2022 |

1585 ثامِن *adj.* eighth (ordinal)

هذه التحاليل تتم مابين الأسبوع الخامس عشر
والأسبوع الثامن عشر من الحمل — These tests
take place between the fifteenth and
eighteenth weeks of pregnancy

95 | 1870 |

1586 مَدَّ *v. I (u)* to extend, stretch sth; to spread out, stretch out sth

ابتسم ومد يده مصافحا — He smiled and stretched out his hand in greeting

98 | 1809 | +lit

1587 ظَلام *n.* darkness; injustice

أغلقت نور الحجرة ودلفت فى الظلام إلى فراشها — Noor closed the room and slipped in the dark to her bed

86 | 2055 | +lit

1588 مُوافَقَة *n.* agreement; approval

إننا لا نستطيع أن نبرم أمرا بدون موافقة جلالته — We cannot conclude anything without the agreement of his majesty

84 | 2094 |

1589 سِياق *n.* context, course

وفي سياق الحديث أخبرها كيف رآها لأول مرة — In the course of the conversation he informed her how he saw her for the first time

78 | 2264 |

1590 دَرْب *n. pl.* دُرُوب path, pathway, trail, road

سارا في درب ضيق.. وبعد دقائق قليلة استطاعا أن يتبينا مدينة الناصرة التي تهجع بين التلال — They walked along a narrow road...and after a few minutes they were able to make out the city of Nazareth which slumbered among the hills

86 | 2043 | +lit

1591 دُعاء *n.* call, appeal, request; invocation

ولقد كان ـ صلى الله عليه وسلم ـ يكثر من الدعاء الى الله ـ تعالى ـ أن يديم على أمته نعمه — He, may peace be upon him, used to pray a lot to God, may He be exalted, that He would continue to show grace to his nation

79 | 2229 | +for

1592 أَرْسَلَ *v. IV* to send, transmit (ب) sth إلى to sb

كانت المدرسة قد أرسلت خطابا إلى والدها تخبره بغيابها المتكرر — The school sent a letter to her father informing him of her repeated absences

89 | 1976 |

1593 هَوىً *n.* love, affection; inclination, preference; desire, wish; على هَواهُ as he likes, according to his preference

يغرقان في بحر الهوى، ولا يصغيان إلى همس الناس ونقدهم وأقوالهم — They are drowning in the sea of love, and they are not listening to the whispers of the people or their criticism or talk

83 | 2103 | +lit

1594 ذَهاب *n.* going; leaving, departure; first half (game, match)

لقد قرر فى الصباح الذهاب إلى الدير الذى عرف الطريق إليه — He decided in the morning to go to the monastery that he knew the way to

89 | 1970 |

1595 كَثْرَة *n.* abundance, large amount, great number

لا يستطيع البقاء فى الإسكندرية أكثر من ليلة على كثرة شوقه لزوجته — He can't stay in Alexandria more than one night in spite of his great longing for his wife

95 | 1843 |

1596 هادِئ *adj.* calm, quiet, peaceful; المُحِيط الهادئ/الهادي the Pacific Ocean

يخرج من كابينة القيادة، يختار مكانا هادئا، وتحت ظل شجرة يتمدد — He comes out of the steering cabin, chooses a calm place, and stretches out under the shade of a tree

97 | 1798 |

1597 حِفْظ *vn.* saving, preserving, maintaining; protecting, guarding; memorizing

شاركوا في قوات حفظ السلام بقيادة حلف الأطلسي في البوسنة وكوسوفو — They participated in the peacekeeping forces under the leadership of the Atlantic Alliance in Bosnia and Kosovo

86 | 2017 |

1598 شاشَة *n. pl.* -aat screen; computer monitor

ضغطت اسمي على شاشة الكمبيوتر فظهرت البيانات — I clicked on my name on the computer screen, and the information appeared

94 | 1860 |

1599 شَرِيك *n.* pl. شُرَكاء partner, associate
باع الشركة للشيخ شاهين المراغي ودخل معه شريكا بالعمل بثلث الأرباح — He sold the company to Sheikh Shahin Al-Muraghi and entered into a partnership with him to work for a third of the profits
96 | 1813 |

1600 مَحْدُود *adj.* limited; determined
— أماكن الدراسات العليا عندنا محدودة كما تعرفون Slots for graduate study at this institution are limited, as you know
94 | 1848 |

1601 أَدْخَلَ *v. IV* to insert, introduce, include sth in إلى/في
أدخل ذراعيه في الجاكت بصعوبة ولم يعد بمقدوره أن يحركها — He put his arms in the jacket with difficulty, and was no longer able to move them
99 | 1760 |

1602 تَبادُل *n.* exchange, interchange
يسهم في تبادل الرأي بين القادة والمسؤولين حول القضايا العربية الراهنة — He participates in the exchange of opinions among leaders and officials about the current Arab problems
85 | 2038 |

1603 سِيادة *n.* sovereignty, supremacy; سيادته His Excellency
سيادة وزير السجون يقوم بجولة تفتيشية، وسوف يمر عليكم — His Excellency the Minister of Prisons is making an inspection tour, and he will pass by you
81 | 2133 |

1604 رَمْز *n.* pl. رُمُوز symbol, sign, emblem; symbolic figure; (computer) icon; (telephone, postal) code; indicator; *vn.* symbolizing, indicating, pointing (إلى to); dialing (phone number)
هذه المقبرة رمز للموت والنضال والمعاناة والمستقبل — This graveyard is a symbol of death and struggle and suffering and of the future
88 | 1973 |

1605 ضَرْبَة *n.* pl. -aat blow, strike; shot
— لم يبد مقاومة، لم يحتج، لم يرد الضربة لمجد الدين He did not exhibit any resistance, he did not protest, he did not return Magd Al-Din's blow
97 | 1775 |

1606 مَلامِح *n.* pl. features, characteristics
لا تبدو على أي منهن ملامح الحزن، بعضهن جئن بكامل الزينة والأناقة — Features of sadness are not showing on any of them; some of them came with all their make-up and elegance
89 | 1952 |

1607 غابَ *v. I (i)* to be absent (عن from); to set (sun) عن on
المطر لا ينقطع لعدة أيام، ثم يغيب أياما ليعود متصلا — The rain does not stop for several days, then it goes away for a few days to come back continuously
87 | 1984 |

1608 مُفاوَضة *n.* pl. -aat negotiation, discussion, talk
أحيانا كان يبدو لنا من متابعة تقارير المفاوضات التي تجري أن الحركات داخل دارفور نفسها غير متفقة فيما بينها — Sometimes it seemed to us from following the reports of the negotiations which were taking place that the movements inside Darfur itself are not agreed among themselves
71 | 2418 |

1609 تَدْمِير *n.* destruction, demolition; wrecking, ruining, damaging
— انهم يريدون تدميرك وتدمير سمعتك They want to destroy you and destroy your reputation
84 | 2059 |

1610 تَحْلِيل *vn.* dissolution, dissolving; legalizing (making sth حَلال Halal); *n.* pl. تَحالِيل analysis, (laboratory) test
— تسلمت اليوم نتيجة تحليل دمي Today I received the results of my blood test
86 | 1998 |

1611 دَوْم *n.* continuance, continuation; دَوْماً always
لاحظت أن عينيه تعكسان دوما تعبيرا ساخرا وكأنه يشاهد شيئا مسليا — I noticed that his eyes always reflect a sarcastic expression as if he were looking at something funny
89 | 1934 |

1612 وَلَدَ *v. I (i)* to bear, give birth to (child); (pass.) وُلِدَ to be born

هناك التقى بزوجته، وهي فتاة روسية الأصل ولدت في فلسطين، وبقي معها — There he met his wife, and she was a young girl of Russian origin who was born in Palestine, and he stayed with her

96 | 1795 |

1613 شَريط *n.* tape, strip, ribbon

وضعت له الشريط واستمع اليه كاملا من دونَ أن ينبس بكلمة — She put in the tape for him, and he listened to the whole thing without saying a word

97 | 1777 |

1614 مُسْتَحيل *adj.* impossible

ليس من المستحيل أن يقع في الغد ما وقع بالأمس — It is not impossible for what happened yesterday to happen tomorrow

97 | 1766 |

1615 مُحافِظ *n.* governor; *adj.* conservative; *a.p.* preserving, protecting

اجتمعت لجنة الوقاية من الغارات برئاسة محافظ المدينة، وقررت زيادة مراكز الإطفاء إلى ثلاثة — The committee for protection from raids under the leadership of the governor of the city met and decided to increase the number of fire stations to three

81 | 2122 |

1616 بَيَّن *v. II* to clarify, explain sth; to show, demonstrate sth; (Lev.Irq.Gul.) to appear, be visible; to seem, look, appear to be

بين ان عدد المدارس التابعة للمديرية (١٥٧) مدرسة — He made it clear that the number of schools belonging to the directorate was 157 schools

94 | 1820 |

1617 مُراقَبة *n.* surveillance, monitoring; censorship; observation, inspection; supervision, oversight

أمضيت سنة تحت المراقبة التامة، وقد ابتعد عني الأصدقاء المقربون حفاظا على سلامتهم I spent a year under total supervision; close friends distanced themselves from me out of fear for their safety

89 | 1927 |

21 Female Names

Ranking is from list of names and abbreviations.

99	زهرة	Zahra	403	هبة	Hiba	592	نورا / نورة	Noura
111	فاطمة	Fatima	408	حنان	Hanan	621	آمال	Amal
126	مريم	Maryam	410	إيمان	Iman	637	عزيزة	Aziza
131	ليلى	Layla	414	فيروز	Fairuz	647	سحر	Sahar
178	صباح	Sabah	417	منال	Manal	654	وفاء	Wafa'
195	نور	Nour	428	ميّ	Mayy	661	حوّاء	Eve
201	زينب	Zaynab	452	مها	Maha	666	سامية	Samia
252	سارة	Sarah	467	وردة	Warda	680	لينا	Lina
254	عائشة	Ayesha	480	سوزان	Suzanne	687	سمر	Samar
290	أحلام	Ahlam	486	نانسي	Nancy	691	فرح	Farah
345	سناء	Sanaa	515	نوال	Nawal	695	روز	Rose
355	ريم	Reem	521	هيفاء	Haifa	723	هناء	Hanaa
359	أمل	Amal	525	هالة	Hala	725	زينة	Zeina
371	سلمى	Salma	526	هدى	Huda	734	سهام	Siham
384	خديجة	Khadija	527	سميرة	Samira	743	خلود	Khuloud
387	ندى	Nada	533	شروق	Shurouq	747	ماريا	Maria
393	سعاد	Suad	541	عبير	Abeer	803	دينا	Dina
396	منى	Muna	546	غادة	Ghada	821	نهى	Nuha
397	أمينة	Amina	547	سرور	Surour			

1618 تَفَضَّلَ *v. V* (usu. imperat. with foll. imperat.) please (come in, sit down, help yourself, go ahead, you first, etc.); لَوْ تَفَضَّلْت if you would be so kind

تفضلي كلمي تفضلي تفضلي كلمي — Go ahead, speak, go ahead, go ahead, speak

83 | 2067 | +spo

1619 كُتْلَة *n. pl.* كُتَل bloc, group; mass, bulk

شهد الشهر الماضي لقاءات بين رئيس الوزراء مع الكتل النيابية للتشاور معهم في التعديل الوزاري — Last month witnessed meetings between the prime minister and the blocs of deputies to consult with them on the ministerial change

80 | 2132 |

1620 بَاعَ *v. I (i)* (ب for a price) to sell sth

من الولد الصغير الذي يبيع الصحف أمام المقهى فوق صندوق خشبي صغير؟ — Who is the small boy who is selling newspapers in front of the coffee house from the top of a small wooden box?

97 | 1766 |

1621 مَاشِي *adj.* (Dia. pl. مَاشِين, مَاشِيِين) (going, walking; مَاشِي (Dia.) *interj.* OK, all right (I agree, accept); *adj.* good, fine; أنا ماشي الحال I'm doing fine

فيه كذا بنت شافته هنا وهو ماشي في الشارع لوحده كده — There's a girl that saw him here as he was walking alone in the street like this

36 | 4671 | +spo

1622 إِحْسَاس *n.* feeling, sensation; sensitivity

الخوف إحساس طبيعي، لكنني أتغلب عليه — Fear is a natural feeling, but I have overcome it

86 | 1968 |

1623 انْفِجَار *n. pl.* -aat explosion, detonation

حينما ابتعدا كثيرا عن المحطة حدث انفجار جبار اهتز له الهواء، وفقدا اتزانها وسقطا — When they got quite far from the station, a huge explosion happened which shook the air, and they lost their balance and fell

84 | 2021 |

1624 حَدِيقَة *n. pl.* حَدَائِق garden; حَدِيقَة حَيَوَانَات zoo

جلسا في أول مقعد قابلهما في الحديقة، الشمس طالعة والجو منعش — They sat on the first chair they encountered in the garden, the sun shining, the air refreshing

93 | 1836 |

1625 اِهْتَمَّ *v. VIII* to be interested ب in sth; to care, be concerned ب about sth

المصري لا يهتم في الدنيا إلا بثلاثة أشياء: دينه ورزقه وأولاده — Egyptians are only interested in three things in the world: their religion, their living, and their children

97 | 1759 |

1626 اِعْتِرَاف *vn.* admission, confession (ب of sth); acknowledgment, recognition, acceptance (ب of sth)

قررت الاعتراف بخطئي.. وها أنذا أعلن توبتي — I decided to admit my error...and I hereby announce my repentance

87 | 1954 |

1627 مَنْطِق *n.* logic, mentality

كنت تخاطبينها بمنتهى المنطق والرزانة وتقنعينها — You were addressing her with the utmost logic and sobriety, and you were convincing her

94 | 1807 |

1628 مُتَّهَم *adj.* accused ب of, charged ب with, indicted ب for; *n. pl.* -uun accused, suspect

يستمر التعذيب حتى يستسلم المتهم ويعترف بما هو منسوب إليه — The torture continues until the accused surrenders and confesses what is attributed to him

84 | 2009 |

1629 دَار *v. I (i)* (Magh.) /dar, ydir/ to do, make sth; to prepare (food); (Egy.Lev.Irq.Gul.) /daar, ydiir/ to turn (one's face, head, back); دِير بَالَك! (Lev.) watch out!

لازم يديروا لها حل — They need to make a solution for it

92 | 1843 | +spo

1630 أَصْلِيّ *adj.* original, master; real, true; genuine, authentic

فقدوا السمة القومية لهم، وضعفت لغتهم التتارية الأصلية، وسرعان ما ذابوا داخل المجتمع البولندي — They lost their national characteristics, their original Tatar language weakened, and they quickly melted into Polish society

91 | 1854 |

1631 مِثْلَما *conj.* like, as, just as

يظهرون فجأة ويختفون مثلما ظهروا — They appear suddenly, then disappear as suddenly as they appeared

86 | 1959 |

1632 صَفْقَة *n.* pl. صَفَقَات deal, transaction

أعرب حمدان عن أمله في حصول صفقة تبادل أسرى واسعة مع الصهاينة — Hamdan expressed his hope that a wide-ranging prisoner exchange deal with the Zionists would happen

82 | 2058 |

1633 مَنْهَج *n.* pl. مَناهِج method, approach; program, curriculum

لا يكون ذلك اطارا عاما لتقديم المنهج الدراسي بالكامل بلغة أجنبية — That is not a general framework for offering the whole curriculum in a foreign language

90 | 1876 |

1634 تَعَرَّفَ *v. V* to get to know على sb, become acquainted على with sb; to identify على sb

لقد تعرفت على صديق بولندي مهذب يعمل معي في المطعم — I got to know a polite Polish friend who works with me in the restaurant

90 | 1884 | +spo

1635 جِنْسِيَّة *n.* nationality, citizenship

تركها بعد ما حصل على الجنسية الأمريكية — He left her after he obtained American citizenship

94 | 1788 |

1636 اِتِّهام *n.* pl. -aat accusation, charge, indictment

يلجأ الكذاب إلى اتهام الآخرين بالكذب، أو اللص إلى اتهام سواه باللصوصية — The liar resorts to accusing others of lying, or the thief to accusing others of thievery

85 | 1982 |

1637 صِدْق *n.* sincerity, candor

أنتظر عودتك لنتحدث أخيرا بصدق مطلق. ماذا تريدين مني بالتحديد؟ — I await your return so we can finally speak with utter candor. What do you want from me exactly?

96 | 1755 |

1638 عاشِق *n.* pl. -uun, عُشّاق lover, person in love; admirer, fan; enthusiast, aficionado

لا أعرف من منا العاشق والمعشوق — I don't know which one of us is the lover, and who the beloved

79 | 2116 |

1639 مُقَدَّس *adj.* holy, sacred; *n.* مُقَدَّسات sacred sites; sacred things

كان المشهد أسطوريا مرعبا أشبه بوصف الجحيم في الكتب المقدسة — The scene was legendarily scary, close to the description of Hell in the holy books

87 | 1929 |

1640 هِنْدِيّ *n./adj.* pl. هُنُود Indian; الهُنُود الحُمْر Native Americans; تَمْر هِنْدِيّ tamarind

أنت لا تعترف بوحدة الأمة الهندية؟ — You don't recognize the unity of the Indian nation?

93 | 1800 |

1641 تُهْمَة *n.* pl. تُهَم accusation, charge

قبض على سيدة تسمى بدرية بتهمة تعدد الأزواج — A woman named Badraya was arrested with the accusation of having more than one husband

87 | 1927 |

1642 إِبْداع *n.* creativity, originality

ألم يصرح للعالم أن تونس قد عانقت الإبداع في التنظيم — Did he not declare to the world that Tunis had embraced creativity in organizing

84 | 2003 |

1643 حادّ *adj.* sharp, intense

جرعة المخدر الزائدة أدت إلى هبوط حاد في وظائف المخ.. أرجو ان تتقبل تعازي الصادقة — The extra dose of the drug led to a sharp drop in the functioning of the brain; I hope that you will accept my most sincere condolences

89 | 1885 |

1644 اِمْتَدَّ *v. VIII* to extend, reach, spread إلى to

إنه ساحل مهجور تمتد خلفه الصحراء إلى ما لا نهاية — It is a deserted coast behind which stretches the desert more or less forever

88 | 1894 |

1645 مِحْوَر *n. pl.* مَحَاوِر axle; axis, pivot

كانت قضية فلسطين محور اهتمام لكثير من الكتاب والشعراء ومادة دسمة لأغاني المطربين والمطربات — The Palestinian issue was a focus of concern for many authors and poets, and a rich subject matter for the songs of male and female performers

83 | 2007 |

1646 طائِفِيّ *adj.* sectarian, factional

لا يوجد عندنا اضطهاد ولكن يوجد عندنا مشكلة طائفية، وفيه فرق بين مشكلة طائفية وبين اضطهاد — There is no persecution among us, but we do have a sectarian problem, and there is a difference between a sectarian problem and persecution

70 | 2389 |

1647 إصْدار *n.* exporting; issuing, publication

لم يوافق الأمن على إصدار جواز سفري لي، رغم كل ما دفعت من رشوة — Security did not agree to issue a passport to me, despite everything I paid in the way of bribes

80 | 2076 |

1648 غَيَّر *v. II* to change, modify sth; to replace, switch sth

ما رأيك لو غيرنا هذه المرة الدرس ومشينا معا بعض الوقت؟ — What do you think about changing the lesson this time, and us going for a walk together for a while?

96 | 1727 |

1649 مُنْتَصَف *n.* middle, halfway

تعود أن يعمل منذ الصباح الباكر وحتى منتصف الليل بغير أن يشكو أو يتذمر — He was used to working from early morning until midnight without complaining or murmuring

88 | 1887 |

1650 أَرْبَعُون *num.* forty; fortieth

قضى العقاد في الخرطوم نحو أربعين يوما — Aqqad spent about forty days in Khartoum

94 | 1759 |

1651 حَلَّ *v. I (u)* to dissolve, split up, untie sth; مَحَلَّهُ to replace, take the place of sb/sth; to solve (problem)

حتى التفكير في إجراء عملية جراحية لن يحل مشكلتك الوهمية — Even thinking about a surgical operation will not solve your imaginary problem

89 | 1851 |

1652 أَجَل *n.* time, period, term; final moment, death

منح القروض الميسرة طويلة الأجل وبفوائد مدعومة للمؤسسات الصغيرة والمتوسطة لتحريك العجلة الاقتصادية — He granted easy, long-term loans, with subsidized interest rates, to the small and medium-sized firms to turn the economic wheels

86 | 1926 | +lit

1653 شاهِد *n. pl.* شُهُود witness; spectator; *adj.* witnessing, viewing

أنا شاهد عيان على جرائمه.. تعاملت معه بإخلاص كسائق خاص — I am an eyewitness of his crimes...I have dealt with him sincerely as a private chauffeur

88 | 1858 |

1654 جَماعِيّ *adj.* group, collective; common

بدأت عمليات الهجرة الجماعية من الإسكندرية، وتبرع الملك والأمراء بالأموال للضحايا — Mass emigration operations have begun from Alexandria, and the king and princes have donated money to the victims

86 | 1902 |

1655 تاسِع *adj.* ninth (ordinal)

في التاسع من أبريل ١٩٤٠ قام هتلر بغزو الدانمارك — On the 9th of April, 1940, Hitler invaded Denmark

93 | 1765 |

1656 زاوِيَة *n. pl.* زَوايا corner, nook; section (newspaper); angle

أمرتني أن أجلس على كرسي في زاوية الغرفة. امتثلت لأمرها وعلى الفور سقطت علي اشعة — She ordered me to sit on a chair in the corner of the room. I obeyed her order, and immediately rays fell upon me

88 | 1855 |

1657 تَصَرُّف *n. pl.* -aat behavior, conduct; تَصَرُّفات actions

لا بد من التصرف بعقلانية قبل أن تنتشر الفضيحة بين الناس — We must act intelligently before the scandal becomes known among the people

91 | 1795 |

1658 مُساعِد *n.* assistant, aide, supporter; *adj.* helping, assisting, supporting

شيماء جاوزت الثلاثين بغير زواج؛ لأن وضعها كمدرس مساعد فى كلية الطب قلل كثيرا من فرصتها — Shima had passed thirty without marriage; because her situation as a teaching assistant in the College of Medicine decreased her opportunities

93 | 1760 |

1659 اِغْتِيال *n. pl.* -aat assassination

منذ تعرض ذياب لعملية اغتيال وهو يعيش مختبئا ولم أستطع حتى أن أقابله — Since Diyab was subjected to an assassination attempt, he has been living in hiding, and I haven't been able even to meet him

76 | 2141 |

1660 اِعْتِداء *n. pl.* -aat assault, attack, aggression

يجب وقف هذا الاعتداء الشنيع على سمعتنا وكرامة بلادنا — This horrible attack on our reputation and the dignity of our country must stop

81 | 2009 |

1661 مَيْدان *n. pl.* مَيادين arena, field, domain; city square, plaza

اقتحمت المرأة العديد من ميادين العمل وحققت نجاحا وتفوقا — Women have moved into many fields of work and have achieved success and excellence

84 | 1938 |

1662 تاجِر *n. pl.* تُجَّار merchant, businessman, trader; *adj.* trading, dealing

كان لديه مبلغ معتبر مكنه فى العام الماضي من الزواج بابنة تاجر ثرى يمتلك محلا كبيرا للأدوات الصحية فى الرويعى — He had a considerable amount of money that enabled him last year to marry the daughter of a rich businessman who owns a large shop for sanitary ware in Al-Ruwayi

97 | 1685 |

1663 جَزائِريّ *n./adj.* Algerian

اتجهت العلاقات المغربية الجزائرية نحو مزيد من الاضطراب — Moroccan-Algerian relations were headed towards more disturbances

75 | 2156 | +news

1664 هَجْمَة *n. pl.* -aat attack, assault; raid, strike

هل تعتقد أن هناك جهات أخرى غير بن لادن وقفت وراء هجمات الحادي عشر من سبتمبر؟ — Do you think that there are parties, other than Bin Laden, who stand behind the attacks of September 11?

81 | 2004 |

1665 أداة *n. pl.* أدَوات tool, utensil, instrument; appliance, apparatus; (ling.) particle

انها تتميز بسهولة الاستخدام كأي أداة منزلية إلكترونية — It is characterized by ease of use, like any electronic household appliance

93 | 1743 |

1666 تَدَخُّل *n.* intervention, interference

نرفض التدخل في شؤوننا الداخلية وعلاقاتنا بين شعوبنا وبين حكامنا — We reject interference in our internal affairs and our relationships between our people and our rulers

85 | 1910 |

1667 أمْر *n. pl.* أوامِر order, command

كانت الأوامر قد صدرت بالتشديد على سائقي السيارات بطلاء مصابيحهم بالأزرق القاتم — Strict orders were issued for the drivers of cars to paint their headlights dark blue

96 | 1684 |

1668 سَبَّبَ *v. II* to cause, produce, provoke sth

لا حق لك يا مستر دالاس أن تسبب لها هذه الصدمة العصبية — You have no right, Mr Dallas, to cause her this nervous shock

91 | 1783 |

1669 بِواسِطَة *n.* واسِطَة by means of, by using, by making use of; (Dia.) /wasTa/ intermediary, (person with) influence, pull, connections

لصق الصورة على ورق مقوى بواسطة اللاصق — He stuck the picture onto cardboard with tape

92 | 1755 |

1670 عَيْب *n.* pl. عُيُوب fault, weakness; shame, disgrace, shameful behavior
الحياة في أمريكا لها عيوب، لكن ميزتها الكبرى أنها تمنح الفرصة لكل إنسان — Life in America has its faults, but its major positive feature is that it provides opportunity to every person
96 | 1692 |

1671 صَرَّحَ *v. II* to declare, announce بأنَّ that
وفي غضون ذلك صرحت مصادر دبلوماسية غربية بأن ايران بدأت بالفعل في معالجة كمية محدودة من اليورانيوم في منشآتها النووية — In the meantime, Western diplomatic sources explained that Iran had actually begun to process limited quantities of uranium in their nuclear establishments
86 | 1884 |

1672 سافَرَ *v. III* to travel إلى to; to depart (on a trip)
قالت كاميليا إن حلم حياتها كان أن تسافر إلى باريس يوما — Camelia said that her life dream was to travel to Paris some day
93 | 1727 |

1673 بَرِيء *adj.* pl. أَبْرِياء innocent, blameless; naive, unsuspecting; exempt, free (مِن of); *n.* innocent person
يبيعون أسلحة تقتل عشرات الألوف من الأبرياء حتى تنهمر عليهم الأرباح بالملايين — They sell weapons which kill tens of thousands of innocent people so that millions in profits will rain down on them
89 | 1821 |

1674 اِنْطِلاق *n.* start, departure; اِنْطِلاقاً مِن proceeding from; on the basis of
تردد صوت قائد الطائرة يعلن مراسيم انطلاق الرحلة — The voice of the captain of the plane came on announcing the trip departure regulations
85 | 1886 |

1675 تامّ *adj.* complete, concluded
حرك رأسه وهو يعرج على ساقه السليمة، بهدوء تام، وكأنه لا يريد ان ينبه الظلام الذي حوله — He shook his head, limping on his good leg, in complete calm, as if he did not want to alert the darkness around him
88 | 1823 |

1676 جُنَيْه *n.* pl. -aat pound (currency); (Egy.) جنيه /gineeh/ pl. -aat
لو أعطيتك مائة جنيه ماذا تفعل؟ — If I gave you a hundred pounds, what would you do?
72 | 2245 |

1677 مِعْيار *n.* pl. مَعايير standard, criterion, norm; standard measure, gauge
ازدواجية المعايير في مكافحة الإرهاب أمر يساعد على توليد الإرهاب — Double standards in fighting terrorism is something that helps breed terrorism
79 | 2033 |

1678 تَمْويل *n.* financing, funding, backing, underwriting
بقية المنظمات تعمل وحدها وتعتمد على التمويل الذاتي — The rest of the organizations are working by themselves and rely on self-funding
73 | 2213 |

1679 خَشِيَ *v. I (a)* to fear sth/sb or مِن sth/sb; to fear, anticipate أنْ that; to be afraid, anxious على for (sb's safety)
لم يتعود الغياب الطويل، أخشى أن يكون سوء قد لحق به — He wasn't used to being gone long, I'm afraid something bad has happened to him
88 | 1822 |

1680 تَقْليدِيّ *adj.* traditional, conventional
هذا ما نسميه قوى حفظ السلام التقليدية المعروفة بالقبعات الزرقاء، إذا هي تعمل تحت راية الأمم المتحدة — This is what we call traditional peacekeeping forces, who are known as the Blue Berets, if they work under the flag of the United Nations
83 | 1945 |

1681 أَمانَة *n.* loyalty, reliability; honesty, integrity; deposit, safekeeping; secretariat; office of mayor; أَمانَة الصَّنْدُوق office of treasurer; في أَمانَة الله God keep you safe (goodbye)
وفي محافظة العاصمة عمان بلغ عدد المرشحين لعضوية مجلس أمانة عمان الكبرى ١٦٧ مرشحا في اليوم الاول — In the governorate of the capital, Amman, the number of candidates for membership in the Greater Amman City Council reach 167 on the first day
80 | 2013 | +news

1682 اِخْتِلاف *n.* variance, difference, disagreement; conflict, controversy

العنصرية هى الاعتقاد بأن اختلاف العنصر يؤدى — إلى اختلاف السلوك والقدرات الإنسانية Racism is the belief that a difference in race leads to a difference in human behaviors and abilities

89 | 1807 |

1683 سُكَّر *n.* sugar; مَرَض السكر diabetes

يشترون من إربد الطحين والرز والسكر، يحملونها على البغال ويهربونها إلى بلادهم المحتل — They buy flour, rice and sugar from Irbid, carrying it on donkeys and smuggling it to the occupied lands

90 | 1771 |

1684 تَرْكيز *n.* emphasis, focus, concentration (على)

فقد قدرته على التركيز فبدا معظم الوقت وكأنه يحدق فى الفراغ — He lost his ability to concentrate, and he appeared most of the time as if he were staring into space

84 | 1893 |

1685 أَقْوى *elat.* stronger/strongest, more/most powerful

لقد هزمنا وانتهى الأمر.. إنهم أقوى منا بكثير، ويستطيعون سحقنا فى أى لحظة — We were defeated, and it's over...They are a lot stronger than us, and they can crush us at any moment

94 | 1704 |

1686 تَناوُل *vn.* dealing with (subject, issue); eating (meal); taking, ingesting (medicine)

بعد الانتهاء من تناول الطعام، وضع أحد الجنود كمية من البرتقال في جيبه — After finishing eating, one of the soldiers put a bunch of oranges in his pocket

85 | 1878 |

1687 تَحْويل *n.* conversion, transfer

قرر محمود غالب باشا، وزير المواصلات، تحويل بعض عربات السكك الحديدية إلى مستشفى ميدان — Mahmoud Ghalib Pasha, the Minister of Transportation, decided to transform some of the railway cars into a field hospital

82 | 1936 |

1688 حَرَم *n.* holy site; (university) campus; الحَرَمان الشَّريفان the Two Holy Sites (Mecca and Medina); ثالِث الحَرَمَيْن Jerusalem

حفظك الله يا خادم الحرمين الشريفين وترجع للمملكه سالما غانما إلى وسط شعبك الوفي — May God keep you, O servant of the two sacred sites, and may you return to the Kingdom healthy and happy amidst your loyal people

84 | 1903 |

1689 يَمَنيّ *n./adj.* Yemeni

تضطر الدولة اليمنية إلى مواجهة تمرد جديد في منطقة صعدة — The Yemeni state is forced to face a new rebellion in the Saada area

73 | 2174 | +news

1690 اِنْتِخابيّ *adj.* electoral, election; selection

على المرشح أن يتحدث عن مدى تدينه في الحملة الانتخابية — The candidate must speak about his level of religiosity in the election campaign

68 | 2341 |

1691 إِسْتراتيجيّ *adj.* strategic; *n.* strategist

قيمتها الدفاعية حيوية من الناحية الاستراتيجية كما سيتضح بعد ذلك — Its defensive value is vital from the strategic viewpoint, as will become clear afterwards

70 | 2258 |

1692 ذَهَبيّ *adj.* golden, gilded

تعتبر قارة افريقيا في نظر هذه الشركات بمثابة الفرصة الذهبية للتوسع والاستثمار — The African continent, in the view of these companies, is considered to be a golden opportunity to expand and invest

88 | 1797 |

1693 صَحْراء *n.* desert

يمضون بها جميعا إلى الصحراء الواسعة التى يبدو أنها تبتلع كل شىء — They all take it to the vast desert which looks like it can swallow everything

86 | 1838 |

1694 حَكَمَ *v.* I (u) to rule, govern (people, country); to judge, sentence على sb

لكن مصر حكمها الطغاة أكثر من أى بلد آخر فى التاريخ — But tyrants ruled Egypt more than any other country in history

94 | 1695 |

22　Male Names

Ranking is from list of names and abbreviations.

2	محمّد	Muhammad	96	إسماعيل	Ismail; Ishmael	195	نور	Nour; Nureddine;
3	عبد الله، عبد	Abdullah, Abd	97	صلاح	Salah		عبد النور	Abd Al-Nur
	العزيز Abd	Al-Aziz, etc.	101	وليد	Walid			
			107	بدر	Badr	197	محسن	Muhsin
6	بن	bin	108	عادل	Adil	199	كمال	Kamal
7	عليّ	Ali	110	راشد	Rashid	204	سيف	Saif
8	أحمد	Ahmad	114	سمير	Samir	205	عمّار أبو	Abu Ammar = Yasir
15	حسن	Hassan	118	منصور	Mansour			Arafat
18	حسين	Hussein	119	طارق	Tariq			
24	خالد	Khalid	123	قاسم	Qasim	207	أسامة	Usama
27	عمر	Omar	125	مهديّ	Mahdi	209	فراس	Firas
29	محمود	Mahmoud	127	سعود	Saud	215	ميشيل	Michael; Michel; Michelle
32	إبراهيم	Ibrahim	128	جابر	Jabir			
33	صالح	Salih	129	رشيد	Rashid	216	علاء	Alaa
35	عزيز	Aziz; Abd Al-Aziz	133	زيد	Zaid	219	آدم	Adam
	عبد العزيز		139	فؤاد	Fuad	220	حسني	Hosny
37	كريم	Karim; Abd Al-Karim	140	خليل	Khalil	222	مازن	Mazin
	عبد الكريم		147	زايد	Zayid	228	ياسين	Yaseen
			151	عيسى	Eissa; Jesus	229	عدنان	Adnan
38	سعيد	Said	152	عثمان	Uthman	230	زياد	Ziad
41	محي الدين دين	Muhi Al-Din, Izz Al-Din, etc.	156	حمدان	Hamdan	231	عامر	Amer/Amir
	عز الدين		159	سامي	Sami	236	عماد	Imad
			160	جعفر	Jaafar	238	ماجد	Majid
			161	رفيق	Rafiq	239	نبيل	Nabil
43	عمرو	Amr	163	ياسر	Yasir	240	عبده	Abduh
45	عبّاس	Abbas	164	يحيى	Yahya	242	شريف	Sharif
47	يوسف	Yusif	165	حامد	Hamid	243	طه	Taha
50	عبد الرحمن رحمن	Abd Al-Rahman	166	حميد، عبد الحميد	Hameed; Abd Al-Hameed	244	هشام	Hisham
						247	إلياس	Elias
52	صدّام	Saddam				253	مالك	Malik
59	مبارك	Mubarak	168	بشير	Bashir	255	بشّار	Bashar
63	موسى	Mousa; Moses	172	سليم	Salim	256	أيمن	Ayman
65	مصطفى	Mustafa	177	حبيب	Habib	260	نهيان	Nahyan
66	جمال	Jamal, Gamal	179	حسّان	Hassan	263	هاني	Hani
67	سعد	Saad	180	زين	Zein; Zineddine	264	طاهر	Tahir
72	أبو مازن أبو	Abu Mazen		زين الدين		266	حمزة	Hamza
						267	داوود	Daoud; David
84	سالم	Salim	181	قيس	Qays	271	مجد الدين مجد	Majd; Majd Al-Din
85	سليمان	Sulayman; Solomon	184	عبد الهادي	Abd Al-Hadi			
86	حمد	Hamad	187	أمين	Amin	274	حكيم	Hakeem
87	جورج	George	189	سلمان	Salman	277	عبيد	Obaid
91	فيصل	Faisal	192	جاسم	Jasim	279	جهاد	Jihad
95	فهد	Fahd	193	فارس	Faris	280	طلال	Talal
						283	تركيّ	Turki

1695 وِشّ and وِيش /weesh/ (Gul.Sau.) *interrog.* what تخبرني عن ويش — What are you going to tell me about?

60 | 2650 | +for

1696 إِسْتراتِيجِيّة *n.* pl. -aat strategy استراتيجية البيت الأبيض في العراق ستبقى على ما هي عليه — The White House strategy in Iraq will remain what it has been

71 | 2232 |

1697 مُقَرَّر *adj.* decided upon, stipulated; scheduled; *n.* agenda, plan; curriculum يقفون مصطفين في طابور طويل لاستلام موادهم التموينية المقررة رسميا من صاحب المتجر — They stand lined up in a long line to receive their officially determined rations from the owner of the shop

80 | 1964 |

1698 اِنْسِحاب *n.* withdrawal, evacuation; pulling out, removing بدلا من الانسحاب أمام الإيطاليين صبوا عليهم مدفعيتهم فأصابوا منهم الكثير — Instead of withdrawing in front of the Italians, they poured out their heavy guns against them, and wounded a lot of them

80 | 1962 |

1699 تَبِعَ *v. I (a)* to follow, pursue sth/sb أحب أن يتبع المرء مزاجه السري، ويستسلم لأول فكرة تخطر بذهنه — I like people to follow their secret passion, and to give in to the first idea that comes into their heads

97 | 1635 |

1700 تَزَوَّجَ *v. V* to marry sb; to get married (مِن to sb) قد جاوز الستين ولم يتزوج لأنه ببساطة لم يجد وقتا لذلك — He has passed sixty and he didn't marry because, quite simply, he didn't find time for it

89 | 1781 |

1701 لَفَتَ *v. I (i)* to draw, turn (نَظَر/اِنْتِباه) sb's attention to; لَفَتَ نَظَرَهُ/اِنْتِباهَهُ إلى to catch sb's attention to: كان عنترة في هذه المعارك الفارس الذي لفت الأنظار ، وعرف بعد ذلك بالشجاعة والكرم — Antara, in this battle, was the knight who turned eyes, and he was known after that for his courage and generosity

87 | 1821 |

1702 ذاتِيّ *adj.* autonomous, self-, auto-; personal, individual لا أقول لك أن نترك الأمور للفوضى وللرغبات الذاتية.. إذ لابد من التنظيم والتحديد — I'm not telling you to leave matters to chaos, and to individual desires...since there has to be organization and definition

86 | 1831 |

1703 هلق /halla'/ (Lev.) *adv.* now الموبايلات اللي نازلة هلق بتجنن — The cell phones that are coming out now are unbelievable

12 | 13210 | +spo

1704 مُسَلْسَل *n.* pl. -aat serial show (esp. soap opera) حصلت على جائزة احسن ممثلة عن دورها في مسلسل «الوتد» في مهرجان القاهرة الرابع للإذاعة والتليفزيون — She obtained the prize for Best Actress for her role in the series "The Stake" in the fourth Cairo Festival for Radio and Television

88 | 1795 |

1705 وَلِيَ *v. I (i)* to follow, come after (sth/sb); to govern, rule sth or على over sth فيما يلي النص الكامل للقاء — What follows is the full text of the interview

87 | 1813 |

1706 غادَرَ *v. III* to leave (a place), depart (on a trip) كانت نوارة قد غادرت البيت مع أولادها بمجرد إدانة كريم والحكم عليه بعشرين سنة — Norah had left the house with her children as soon as Karim was found guilty and sentenced to twenty years

86 | 1826 |

1707 كارِثة *n.* pl. كَوارِث catastrophe, tragedy حذرت منظمة أطباء بلا حدود من كارثة إنسانية في لبنان بسبب قرب نفاد المواد الأساسية من المستشفيات — The Doctors Without Borders organization warned of a humanitarian catastrophe in Lebanon because of the near exhaustion of basic commodities in the hospitals

92 | 1706 |

1708 اِسْتَهْدَفَ *v. X* to target, aim at sth/sb
هذه التفجيرات الارهابية تستهدف الامن المصري،
وتسعى الى تقويض الاستقرار الوطني — These
terrorist explosions are targeting Egyptian
security, and are attempting to undermine
national stability

76 | 2060 |

1709 مَلْبَس *n. pl.* مَلابِس clothes, dress, attire
قامت الست مريم ودخلت الغرفة الداخلية لترتدي
ملابس الخروج — Mrs Mariam got up and
entered the interior room to put on her
clothes for going out

89 | 1764 |

1710 قاتِل *n. pl.* قَتَلَة murderer, assassin; *adj.* deadly,
lethal; fatal
اليوم بعد اقرار المحكمة لم يعد مهما تحديد هوية
القاتل، بل بات الاهم محاكمته وانزال العقوبة التي
يستحقها به — Today, after the decision of
the court, it is no longer important to
determine the identity of the killer, rather
it has become more important to bring
him to trial and bring down on him the
punishment he deserves

86 | 1820 |

1711 سِياحِيّ *adj.* tourist, tourism
تأشيرة الدخول اللي معاكم، تأشيرة سياحية.. بتسمح
لكم بالاقامة في لندن شهر واحد — The entrance
visas you have, are tourist visas...they allow
you to stay in London for one month

79 | 1991 |

1712 نِيَّة *n. pl.* نَوايا intention, purpose; desire
كان يفتقر إلى القدرة على تتبع سياق القصة وعلى فهم
نوايا ودوافع شخصياتها — He lacked the ability
to follow the context of the story and to
understand the intentions and motivations of
its characters

97 | 1620 |

1713 شِيعَة *n.* Shiites; partisans, followers
أكد الرئيس المصري ان ولاء أغلب الشيعة في المنطقة
هو لايران وليس لدولهم — The Egyptian
president affirmed that the loyalty of most of
the Shiites in the area was to Iran and not to
their countries

67 | 2328 |

1714 نَقْص *n.* lack, loss; decrease, diminution;
deficit; deficiency; inferiority
عاش طفولته يعاني من نقص التغذية — He lived
his childhood suffering from malnutrition

94 | 1664 |

1715 تَدَخَّلَ *v. V* to intervene, interfere, meddle
نحن حقيقة نتمنى ان لا أحد يتدخل بشؤوننا
الداخلية نهائيا — We really hope that no one
will interfere in our internal affairs, at all

87 | 1790 |

1716 إِجابَة *n. pl.* -aat answer, reply, response
كل البدو هنا يتحدثون بسرعة ويمشون بسرعة..
قضيت عمري كله أسأل نفسي عن سبب ذلك ولم
أصل إلى إجابة — All of the bedouins here
speak quickly and walk quickly...I have spent
my whole life asking myself about the reason
for that, and I have not reached an answer

87 | 1799 |

1717 خَلَقَ *v. I (u)* to create, form sth
ترعة المحمودية هي التي خلقت الإسكندرية في
العصور الحديثة — The Mahmoudiya Canal is
the thing that created Alexandria in the
modern era

95 | 1636 |

1718 دِراسِيّ *adj.* study-, school-related;
instructional, pedagogical
سألته عن المرحلة الدراسية التي وصل لها —
I asked him about the educational level he
had reached

83 | 1872 |

1719 سِلْسِلَة *n.* chain, series
فترة الاعداد تم تقسيمها إلى فترة اولى للاعداد البدني
ثم سلسلة من المباريات الودية — The preparatory
period is divided into a first period of physical
preparation and then a series of friendly
matches

87 | 1794 |

1720 حَدِيد *n.* iron; steel
ليس في هذه السيارة قطعتان من بلد واحد.. كل
قطعة حديد فيها من بلد — This car doesn't have
two parts from the same country...Each steel
part in it is from a (different) country

97 | 1601 |

1721 جِوار *n.* proximity, vicinity; بِجِوارِ near, next to; حُسْن الجِوار good neighbor (relations)

نعم نقف بحزم ضد تدخل دول الجوار وغير دول العراقية — الجوار في الشؤون العراقية Yes, we stand with determination against the interference of neighboring countries, and other countries, in Iraqi affairs

87 | 1781 |

1722 شِتاء *n.* winter

المسافة من العصر إلى المغرب في الشتاء تمر كلمح البصر — The time span from afternoon till evening in the winter passes like the blinking of an eye

96 | 1620 |

1723 حُسْن *n.* good, goodness; beauty

كنا ننطلق انطلاقات قوية وجديدة بتأييده ودعمه لنا وحسن تفهمه لعملنا ونشاطاتنا — We set out anew strongly, with his support for us and his good understanding of our work and activities

92 | 1693 |

1724 ضَرَر *n.* pl. أَضْرار damage; injury, harm; *n.* evil, sin

يناشد مواطن وزيري المياه والبيئة التحقق من اضرار مشروع الصرف الصحي على السكان والمياه الجوفية — A citizen calls on the Ministers of Water and the Environment to investigate the damages caused by the sewer project to the citizens and the ground water

86 | 1810 |

1725 سُنَّة *n.* Sunna (orthodox Islam; body of Islamic law; customary procedure)

لا يمكن أخذ الأحكام الشرعية إلا من الكتاب والسنة — It is only possible to take legal rulings from the Qur'an and the Sunna

82 | 1896 |

1726 اِسْتَقْبَلَ *v.* X to meet, welcome, greet sb; to receive sth

كان ناظر المحطة قد خرج يستقبل القطار وتحدث قليلا مع السائق — The station master had left to meet the train, and he spoke a little with the driver

87 | 1787 |

1727 سُلوك *n.* behavior, conduct

تلوم نفسها بشدة لأنها لم تر إشارات واضحة في سلوك زوجها من البداية — She blames herself a lot because she didn't see the obvious signs in her husband's behavior from the beginning

87 | 1775 |

1728 أَهْلًا وَسَهْلًا *n.* *interj.* hello! welcome!

مشاهدينا الكرام أهلا وسهلا بكم معنا في هذا اللقاء الخاص مع السيد محمود عباس — Dear viewers, we welcome you to this special interview with Mr Mahmoud Abbass

64 | 2403 | +spo

1729 حَسَن *adj.* good; حَسَناً *adv.* well; *interj.* good, fine, OK

الطريق إلى الجحيم مليء بذوي النوايا الحسنة — The road to hell is full of people with good intentions

88 | 1761 |

1730 سِينَما *n.* cinema

الحياة في الواقع مختلفة عنها في السينما — Life in fact is different than it is in the cinema

83 | 1854 |

1731 مُرْتَبِط *adj.* connected, linked ب to; in a relationship ب with

أنسيتم أن مصيرنا مرتبط بمصيرهم؟ إن باد هؤلاء فستحل بنا الهزيمة — Did you forget that our fate is connected to their fate? If they are annihilated, we will be defeated

92 | 1679 |

1732 حَفْلَة *n.* pl. حَفَلات party, ceremony, celebration

رأته أكثر من مرة في حفلات القنصلية ولم تسترح له قط — She saw him more than once in Consular parties, and she was not comfortable with him at all

93 | 1661 |

1733 جَزيرَة *n.* pl. جُزُر island; شِبْه جَزيرَة peninsula; (شِبْه) الجَزيرَة العَرَبِيَّة and جَزيرَة العَرَب the Arabian Peninsula

كانت السفن راسية بالقرب من جزيرة أرواد — The ships were anchored near Arwad Island

93 | 1669 |

1734 اِسْتَفَادَ *v. X* to benefit, profit مِن from, to make use مِن of
أرادت الدولة أن تستفيد بنبوغه في مجال جديد، فتم نقله إلى المخابرات العامة — The state wanted to benefit from his genius in a new area, so he was transferred to general intelligence
93 | 1664 |

1735 صِلَة *n. pl.* -aat link, connection; contact
زين العابدين وغد ولكن لا صلة له بالسلطة فضلا عن أنه يخشاها لانحرافه — Zain Al-Abdin is a scoundrel but he has no connection to the authorities based on the fact that he fears them because of his illegal activities
88 | 1752 |

1736 تَرَاجُع *n.* retreat, backing down/off عن from; decrease, decline
لا يعرف الوهن او التراجع، فرأيه نافذ و كلمته مطاعة — He doesn't know weakness or retreat, since his opinion is carried out, and his word is obeyed
84 | 1818 |

1737 اِكْتَشَفَ *v. VIII* to discover sth; to detect, uncover sth
اكتشف بعد الستين أنه أخطأ لما ترك بلاده — He discovered after sixty that he made a mistake when he left his country
88 | 1751 |

1738 تَرَدَّدَ *v. V* to hesitate في to do sth; to pause, wait (an instant); to frequent على (a place); to be repeated, occur repeatedly; to be widely discussed
مافيش داعي تتعب نفسك يا (يتردد قليلا) يا أبيه عصمت — There is no need to wear yourself out (he hesitates a little), big brother Ismat
89 | 1717 |

1739 لِيبِيّ *n./adj. pl.* -uun Libyan
مطر كاتب من أصل ليبي، ولد في مدينة نيويورك ١٩٧٠ من أبوين ليبيين — Matar is an author of Libyan origin; he was born in the city of New York in 1970 to Libyan parents
67 | 2279 |

1740 نَقْد *n.* criticism, critique
الذين هربوا من بلادهم مثلك يجب أن يكفوا عن توجيه النقد إليها — Those who fled from

their countries like you must stop criticizing them
86 | 1778 |

1741 مَجْهُول *adj.* unknown, unidentified; *n. pl.* -uun unknown person, unidentified person
لقد عثرنا في قبو المقهى على جثة مجهولة.. نحن في انتظار الشرطة — We found in the cellar of the coffee house an unidentified corpse...we are waiting for the police
89 | 1715 |

1742 صَنَعَ *v. I (a)* to design, build; fabricate
إن الرب لا يصنع شيئا على سبيل الصدقة — The Lord does not do anything by chance
88 | 1732 |

1743 ثَرْوَة *n. pl.* ثَرَوات wealth, fortune; abundance
قال لنفسه: إن الله أعطاه ثروة طائلة، فعليه أن ينفق بما يوازى قدرته — He said to himself: God gave him immense wealth, so he needs to spend equal to his ability
88 | 1737 |

1744 حِصار *n.* siege, blockade
أتكلم باسم الشعوب التي فرضتم عليها الحصار فجاعت، والمدن التي حملتم إليها الدمار فبادت — I speak on behalf of the people upon whom you have imposed a siege, so that they have starved, and the cities to which you have brought destruction, so they were annihilated
81 | 1882 |

1745 زَيْت *n.* oil (food, mineral)
تطش قرون الفلفل واحدا بعد الآخر في الزيت المغلي لتطهو أكلتها المحببة — She plops the peppercorns one after the other into the bubbling oil to cook her favorite food
89 | 1695 |

1746 سَحَبَ *v. I (a)* to withdraw (support); to take out, pull sth عن from)
فتح الدرج وسحب منه مسدسه العتيق من نوع "بيرتا" الذى اشتراه أول ما جاء إلى المدينة — He opened the drawer and pulled out of it his old Beretta revolver which he had bought when he first came to the city
89 | 1694 |

1747 قِبَل *n.* مِن قِبَل on the part of; by
— لا أبالغ إن تصورت احتمالات قتلك مِن قبلهم
I don't exaggerate if I imagine the chances
of you being murdered by them
22 | 6731 |

1748 إرْسال *vn.* sending; deploying (troops);
n. transmission, broadcast; signal (cell phone)
بعد ذلك يتم إرسال صورة من وثيقة الزواج إلى
السجل المدني فى القاهرة — After that, a copy of
the marriage certificate should be sent to the
civil records office in Cairo
94 | 1613 |

1749 كُرْسِيّ *n.* pl. كَراسي (def. كَراسي) chair, seat
دعاها فرناندو إلى الجلوس على الأريكة، وجلس
أمامها على الكرسي — Fernando invited them to
sit on the couch, and he sat in front of them
on the chair
92 | 1639 |

1750 طَبَقَة *n.* pl. -aat class, category, rank; level,
layer
إن الأرض مؤلفة من طبقات عديدة ونحن نسير على
القشرة منها — The earth is made up of several
layers, and we walk on its skin
90 | 1675 |

1751 صَحافِيّ *adj.* journalistic, press; *n.* journalist,
reporter
عقد الوزير حداد مؤتمرا صحافيا مشتركا مع رئيس
وفد المفوضية الأوروبية — Minister Haddad held
a joint news conference with the head of the
European Commission's delegation
65 | 2329 |

1752 أكْمَلَ *v. IV* to complete, finish sth
سوف تكمل دراستها في قسم الاتصالات المرئية في
الجامعة الأمريكية بدبي — She will finish
her studies in the Department of Visual
Communication at the American University
of Dubai
93 | 1621 |

1753 تَجاوُز *vn.* surmounting, overcoming;
exceeding, going beyond, overstepping;
disregarding, bypassing; *n.* تَجاوُزات abuses,
violations

الحقيقة التي لا نستطيع تجاوزها أن لكل بلد عربي أو
أجنبي عصابة تنتفع من خيرات البلد — The truth
that we can't get around is that every Arab or
foreign country has a gang that benefits from
the good things the country has
85 | 1764 |

1754 أزْرَق *adj.* fem. زَرْقاء blue
كان يرتدي بدلة زرقاء ماركة كريستيان ديور اشتراها
خصيصا للمناسبة — He was wearing a blue
suit, Christian Dior brand, which he bought
specifically for the occasion
93 | 1621 |

1755 تَبَيَّنَ *v. V* to become clear or evident (أنَّ that);
to appear, become visible
تبين أن جوابي كان أقرب الإجابات إلى الحقيقة — It
became clear that my answer was the closest
answer to the truth
92 | 1630 |

1756 تَخْطيط *n.* planning, preparation; plan, sketch,
diagram
يجري التخطيط لانشاء فصل لتأهيل المكفوفين
وضعاف البصر وآخر لذوي الاحتياجات الخاصة —
Planning is currently being carried out to
create a class to qualify blind people and
weak-sighted people, and another for those
with special needs
85 | 1763 |

1757 إرادَة *n.* desire, will
الحكومة الفلسطينية تمثل ارادة الشعب الفلسطيني في
ظل انتخابات نزيهة شهد العالم بنزاهتها — The
Palestinian government represents the will
of the Palestinian people in light of the fair
elections whose fairness the world witnessed
93 | 1614 |

1758 نقاش *n.* argument, debate
كان الواحد منهم يعود ويطلق زوجته بلا نقاش.. فى
ثلاثة أعوام تم طلاق عشرين امرأة — One of
them would go back and divorce his wife
without discussion...in three years 20 women
were divorced
94 | 1600 |

1759 مُتَحَدِّث *n. fem. -a,* spokesperson, speaker

وقالت المتحدثة إنه لم تقع خسائر بين قوات التحالف والقوات الحكومية الأفغانية — The spokeswoman said that losses did not occur among the allied forces and the Afghan government troops

77 | 1943 | +news

1760 هِجْرَة *n.* migration; emigration, exodus, flight; هِجْرَة العُقُول brain drain; the Hijrah

توجه إلى السفارة الأمريكية حيث قدم طلبا للهجرة — He went to the American Embassy where he submitted a request for emigration

83 | 1812 |

1761 دَوَام *n.* office or business hours, work schedule; duration, time period; constancy, permanence

وجودك هنا اسعدنا كثيرا متمنين لكم دوام الصحة والتوفيق — Your presence here has made us very happy, and we wish you continued health and success

93 | 1610 |

1762 خَسِرَ *v. I (a)* to fail, lose, suffer a loss; to lose (a game, one's life, time)

سوف تخسر البنت سنة دراسية ولكن هذا أفضل من أن تخسر عمرها — The girl will lose an academic year but that is better than losing her life

97 | 1533 |

1763 صِينِيّ *n./adj.* Chinese

وجدت دراسة استرالية صينية ان ممارسة نشاط بدني معتدل مثل الأعمال المنزلية تقيك مخاطر الإصابة بسرطان المبيض — An Australian-Chinese study found that doing moderate physical exercise like housework protects you from the dangers of being stricken with ovarian cancer

91 | 1635 |

1764 تَسَاءَلَ *v. VI* to ask oneself, wonder, ponder

لا بد أنه تساءل: ما الذى أتى بهذه الفتاة الريفية إلى أمريكا؟ — He must have wondered: What is it that brought this farm-girl to America?

86 | 1730 |

1765 ناجِح *adj.* successful, winning; *n.* winner

الروائي الناجح هو رجل يكذب بصدق مدهش، أو هو كاذب يقول أشياء حقيقية — The successful novelist is a man who lies with a surprising truth, or he is a liar who says true things

93 | 1602 |

1766 حَزِين *adj.* sad, unhappy, sorrowful

عاد رأفت حزينا إلى البيت، فوجد زوجته ممددة على الأريكة — Ra'fat returned sadly to the house, and found his wife lying on the couch

80 | 1855 |

1767 شَقِيق *n. pl.* أَشِقَّاء brother, full brother

تجادلا حتى انتهى الأمر بأن ضربه شقيقه وتدخل الجيران للتفريق بينهما وأدخل المستشفى بسبب نوبة عصبية — They argued until the matter ended up with him hitting his brother; the neighbors intervened to separate them, and he was put in the hospital because of a nervous attack

85 | 1750 |

1768 خَدَمَ *v. I (i,u)* to serve, assist sb; to serve one's country, في الجَيْش in the army)

إن أباه أيضا كان يخدم فى الجيش البريطانى فى فرقة الخيالة أثناء الحرب العالمية الماضية — His father also was serving in the British Army Cavalry Division during the last World War

91 | 1631 |

1769 مَزْرَع *n. pl.* مَزارع farm, plantation

كنت ابحث عن قطعة ارض لانشاء مزرعة صغيرة عليها — I was searching for a plot of land to establish a small farm on it

89 | 1667 |

1770 جَرّاء *n.* جَرّاء and مِن جَرّاءِ because of, as a result of

فقد ابن عمي عنز نصف أرضه العام الماضي جراء عجزه عن دفع استحقاقه لابن جزمة النضيري — My cousin Anz lost half his land last year as a result of his inability to pay his mortgage to Ibn Jazma Al-Nadiri

85 | 1746 |

1771 رائِد *n.* pl. رُوَّاد pioneer, explorer; leader; (mil.) major, commandant; رائِد الفَضاء astronaut; *adj.* pioneering, leading

صلاح أبو سيف من رواد السينما العربية الذين ساهموا في بناء السينما الواقعية — Salah Abu Saif is one of the pioneers of Arab cinema who participated in building realistic cinema

86 | 1721 |

1772 قِلَّة *n.* scarcity, lack of; small number or amount of

يعيشون في ظروف اعتقالية قاسية بسبب قلة الطعام المقدم من إدارة السجون They live in harsh detention circumstances because of the lack of food offered from the prison administration

95 | 1555 |

1773 مَلَكِيّ *adj.* royal; of or relating to a kingdom

عين أستاذا للفلسفة الاسلامية في المكتب الملكي ومدرسا للآداب العربية في دار الفنون — He was appointed a professor of Islamic Philosophy in the Royal Office, and a teacher of Arabic Literature in Dar Al-Funun

80 | 1849 |

23 Electronics, Computers, Phones, Web

161	برنامج	program	2112	فضائي	satellite
243	موقع	(web) site	2129	خادم	(web) server
338	جهاز	device	2226	مكالمة	phone call
351	رقم	number	2258	رابط	link
431	خط	(phone) line	2311	ضغط	to click
457	طلب	to dial (a phone number)	2396	جوّال	mobile phone
			2435	بوّابة	portal
643	عنوان	URL	2503	مخابرة	phone conversation
762	شبكة	network	2552	تحديث	update (website)
777	ملفّ	file, document	2556	هاتفيّ	telephone (adj.)
1016	كمبيوتر / كومبيوتر	computer	3071	فضائية	satellite station
1067	تلفزيون	television	3182	تواصل	to get in touch with
1176	دقّ	to ring; to call	3469	محمول	mobile phone
1227	هاتف	telephone	3628	راديو	radio
1228	حفظ	to save	3640	منفذ	port
1276	لوحة	board;	3808	تلفاز	television
		لوحة المفاتيح: keyboard	3912	اخترق	to hack into
1297	تسجيل	recording;	4047	كليب	(video clip)
		جهاز تسجيل: recorder	4141	خانة	field, cell, box for answers
1306	ذاكرة	memory	4179	حاسوب	computer
1399	إلكتروني	electronic	4219	حاسب	calculator;
1562	تلفون	telephone			الحاسب الآليّ: computer
1598	شاشة	screen	4274	رنّ	to ring; to call
1748	إرسال	signal (cell phone)	4668	عيّط	to call (Alg.)
1812	بريد	البريد الإلكتروني: email	4788	نقّال	mobile phone
1845	مفتاح	key	4809	إيميل	email
1893	خلية	cell	4944	قرص	disk; القرص الصلب: hard drive
1915	فصل	to hang up			
1919	إذاعة	radio; broadcasting	4947	موبايل	mobile phone
2096	علّق	to hang up	4960	كبس	to press (key); to dial; to click
2111	فيديو	video			

1774 مُوَحَّد *adj.* united, unified; standardized, normalized

هل ستؤيد صدور قانون موحد لبناء المساجد والكنائس؟ — Will you support the issuance of a unified law for the building of mosques and churches?

85 | 1747 |

1775 جَاهِز *adj.* ready, prepared; equipped, outfitted

لماذا هربوا وكان العشاء جاهزا؟ — Why did they run away, when dinner was ready?

97 | 1524 |

1776 رَاهِن *adj.* present, current

نحن في زمن يتكاثر فيه الاكتئاب والقلق بسبب الأوضاع الراهنة — We are in a time in which depression and despair are prevalent because of the current conditions

80 | 1840 |

1777 دُسْتُورِيّ *adj.* constitutional

مطلوب مني الموافقة على التعديلات الدستورية لقانون الارهاب وأنا لا أعرف مضمونه؟ — I have been asked to agree to the constitutional amendments for the law of terrorism, and I don't know its contents?

66 | 2233 |

1778 رَاتِب *n. pl.* رَوَاتِب salary, wage, pay

ما الذي جعلها تسرف هذا الإسراف، وهى تعلم أن راتب زوجها لا يتجاوز ثلاثة جنيهات كل شهر؟ — What made her overspend like that, when she knows that her husband's salary does not exceed three pounds a month?

91 | 1606 |

1779 أَمَلَ *v. I (u)* to hope في أَنْ or أَنْ that; to hope for, expect (ب/في) من sth, from sth/sb

نحن أيضا يا صديقي أحمد سعداء برسالتك ونأمل أن يتسنى لك دائما مراسلتنا والمشاركة في مسابقاتنا الثقافية — My friend Ahmad, we are also happy with your letter and hope that you will be able to always write us and participate in our cultural competitions

85 | 1716 |

1780 اِفْتِتَاح *n.* opening, inauguration

سيتم خلال الشهر الحالي افتتاح معهد للغات بمركز المعلومات — During the current month, an institute for languages will be opened in the Information Center

79 | 1846 |

1781 سَفِينَة *n. pl.* سُفُن ship, vessel

ولن يلبث صوته الأجش أن يجلجل في الحجرة بنبرة درامية منذرة ، وكأنه قبطان سفينة على وشك الغرق — And it was not long before his gravelly voice was reverberating in the room with a scary, dramatic tone, as if he were the captain of a ship that was about to sink

87 | 1683 |

1782 اِعْتِقَال *n. pl.* -aat arrest, detention

قلت لأذهب الى بيت المخرج علي أجده فأعرف منه أسباب اعتقال الكاتب فوجدته معتقلا هو الآخر — I said I'll go to the house of the director so that perhaps I might find him and find out from him the reasons for the arrest of the author, and I found that he had also been arrested

78 | 1886 |

1783 لَاحِق *adj.* later, subsequent; next, following; لَاحِقاً shortly, soon

اذهبي أنت الآن لتستحمي وتغيري ملابسك.. سنتحدث بالأمر لاحقا — Go shower now and change your clothes...We will speak of the matter later

85 | 1721 |

1784 ضَيِّق *adj.* narrow, restricted, tight

المكان ضيق لكنه نظيف، ويحمل، بسبب ورق الحائط المنقوش ومصابيح الإضاءة غير المباشرة، طباعا غريبا أنيقا كذلك الذي نراه في الأفلام الأجنبية — The place is narrow but it is clean, and it carries, because of the engraved wallpaper and the indirect lighting lamps, an elegant, Western character

95 | 1534 |

1785 أَخْذ *n.* taking; seizure

أنت قادرة على العطاء أكثر من قدرتك على الأخذ — You are able to give more than you are able to take

86 | 1692 |

1786 قَبْر *n. pl.* قُبُور tomb, sepulcher
أوصاه مجد الدين بأن لا يكلف أمه مشقة الحضور — لزيارة قبر ابنها Magd Al-Din advised him to not make his mother go through the trouble of coming to visit the grave of her son
80 | 1811 |

1787 عَجِيب *adj.* wonderful, amazing; astonishing, strange
لست أدري كيف أقص هذه الحكاية العجيبة — I don't know how to tell you this amazing story
88 | 1647 |

1788 تَمَثَّل *v. V* to be represented, be incorporated في in sth; to appear, be seen في in sth
التحديات الاقتصادية تتمثل في قلة الاقبال على العمل في القطاع الخاص بسبب قلة المزايا وقلة نسبة عمل المرأة في القطاع المصرفي والاستثماري والصناعي والمهني — The economic challenges are represented by a lack of willingness to work in the private sector because of the lack of benefits and the small ratio of women working in the banking, investment, industrial, and professional sectors
85 | 1701 |

1789 شاهَد *v. III* to see, watch, observe sth/sb
لا يمكن أن ينام قبل أن يشاهد على القناة الرياضية مباراة كاملة في مصارعة المحترفين — He can't go to bed until he watches a complete match of professional wrestling on the sports channel
87 | 1662 |

1790 اِنْتِصار *n. pl.* -aat victory, triumph
مجرد جلوس كل هذه الأطراف على هذه الطاولة يعتبر انتصارا لمن نادى بالدبلوماسية وبالحلول السياسية وليس بالحلول العسكرية منذ البداية — Just having all these parties sitting around this table is considered a victory for those who called for diplomacy and political solutions, and not military solutions from the beginning
83 | 1750 |

1791 هُنالِكَ *adv.* there, over there; there is, there are
اتصلت بمدير المشفى وهو يؤكد أنه ليس هنالك ما يدعو إلى القلق — I contacted the director of the hospital and he confirmed that there is nothing that calls for despair
82 | 1772 |

1792 أَدْنَى *elat.* lower/lowest, nearer/nearest; *adj.* inferior, low, near; *n./adj.* minimum
أريد أن أعيد البيت القديم كما كان أول مرة دون أدنى تغيير — I want to make the old house as it was the first time without the slightest change
85 | 1695 |

1793 مُجاوِر *adj.* neighboring, adjacent
سرعان ما احترق البيت ثم البيوت المجاورة — The house quickly burned, and then the neighboring houses
87 | 1664 |

1794 نِعْمَة *n. pl.* نِعَم blessing, grace
لقد حرمنا أشياء كثيرة ، فلا تحرمنا نعمة الحب! — We were denied many things, so don't deny us the blessing of love!
94 | 1549 |

1795 بَأْس *n.* لا بَأْسَ بِه not a bad...at all; لاباس /la-bas/ (Magh.) *adj.* fine, good (lit. not bad)
وجدته – بحسابات العقل – زوجا لا بأس به.. لو استطاعت فقط أن تنسى ملامحه الغليظة — She found him, intellectually speaking, not to be a bad husband...if only she could forget his ungainly features
88 | 1648 |

1796 سَطْح *n.* surface
موسيقاها أثارت مشاعرنا كحركة ريح على سطح الماء — Her music stirred up our feelings like a breeze over the water
88 | 1642 |

1797 اِحْتَوَى *v. VIII* to contain, include على sth
يحتوي الموقع على عدد كبير من البطاقات الرائعة المصممة ببرنامج فلاش — The site contains a large number of exquisite cards designed with the Flash program
85 | 1705 |

1798 أَشَدّ *elat.* stronger/strongest; more/most intense
إن الناس تخشى قيام حرب جديدة تكون أشد فتكا من الحرب السابقة — People are afraid of a new war arising that would be more deadly than the previous war
88 | 1638 |

1799 غَنِيّ *adj.* pl. أَغْنِيا rich, wealthy

أنت الآن غنية، وباستطاعتك أن تعثري على سكن
بسهولة — You are now rich, and you can find
housing easily

93 | 1540 |

1800 رَوْعَة *n.* magnificence, splendor, beauty;
(Gul.) *adj.* (invar.) beautiful, great, fantastic,
awesome

كنت لا أرى فيها، من قبل، إلا روعة جمالها وسحرها،
الخارجيين — I only saw in her, previously,
the outward splendor of her beauty and her
magic

65 | 2217 | +for

1801 خَصَّ *v. I (u)* to concern, affect, relate to
sb/sth; (often with neg.) to be sb's
business or concern; to choose, select,
single out sth/sb; فِيَا يُخَصُّ in regard to,
with respect to

أنا طبعا لا أعرف هل الموضوع يخص أسرة ديمتري
أم غيرها، لكن على أي حال ديمتري في أزمة ستتضح
مع الأيام — Of course, I don't know whether
the subject relates to Dimitri's family or some
other family, but in any case Dimitri is having
a crisis which will become clear as the days
go by

95 | 1513 |

1802 اِبْتَسَم *v. VIII* to smile (ل at sb)

لم يملك في النهاية غير أن يبتسم فزال الرعب من
على وجهي هلال وعامر — The only thing
he could do in the end was smile, and the
terror disappeared from the faces of Hilal
and Amer

74 | 1951 | +lit

1803 مُبارَك *adj.* blessed; lucky, fortunate

كانت الأسرة في مكة لأداء شعائر العمرة في شهر
رمضان المبارك — The family was in Mecca to
perform the rites of the Minor Pilgrimage in
the blessed month of Ramadan

87 | 1659 |

1804 أَغْلَب *elat.* most, majority

لا أدري لماذا تكون أغلب حالات الولادة في منتصف
الليل — I don't know why most cases of birth
happen in the middle of the night

93 | 1545 |

1805 لِواء *n.* (mil.) major general; district, province;
flag, banner; (mil.) brigade

تدرج في الرتب العسكرية من رتبة ملازم حتى رتبة
لواء ركن شغل خلالها عديدا من الوظائف مثل قائد
فصيل — He advanced in military rank from
the rank of lieutenant to the rank of major
general, during which he occupied a number
of jobs like platoon leader

74 | 1940 |

1806 حَقْل *n.* pl. حُقُول field

أقام حقول الألغام الكثيفة بينه وبين الجيش الثامن،
حقول الشيطان الجبارة — He set up thick mine
fields between him and the eighth Army, the
mighty fields of Satan

84 | 1706 |

1807 خُلُق *n.* أَخْلاق character, personality,
temperament; أَخْلاق morals, ethics

يسلط الكتاب الضوء على الرابط بين الأخلاق والدين
وعلى بعض مظاهر الحداثة — The book shines a
light on the link between morals and religion
and on some modernist phenomena

94 | 1537 |

1808 جادّ *adj.* earnest, serious

لاحظت أن عينيه تعكسان دوما تعبيرا ساخرا، لكنه
ما إن يبدأ في الحديث حتى يكتسب وجهه طابعا جادا
— I noticed that his eyes always reflect a
sarcastic expression, but as soon as he begins
to talk his face takes on a serious look

91 | 1585 |

1809 وَعْد *n.* pl. وُعُود promise, pledge

الصين تنتزع وعدا من كوريا الشمالية بعدم إجراء
تجربة نووية أخرى — China extracted a promise
from North Korea to not carry out another
nuclear test

95 | 1509 |

1810 بُكْرَة (بُكْرا and) (Egy.Lev.Gul.) *adv.* tomorrow

عيد ميلادي بكره — My birthday is tomorrow

60 | 2382 | +spo

1811 سُنِّيّ *n./adj.* pl. سُنَّة Sunni

انني سني متزوج من شيعية وقد تركت منطقتي
الدورة الى الزعفرانية لأسكن وسط أهل زوجتي —
I am a Sunni married to a Shiite, and I have

left my area, Al-Dora, Al-Zafraniya to live among my wife's family

82 | 1752 |

1812 بَريد *n.* mail, postal service; post office; البَريد الإلِكْتُرونّي email
أصدرت مصلحة البريد طابعا تذكاريا يحمل صورة الأميرة فريال — The Post Office issued a commemorative stamp bearing the image of Princess Faryal

91 | 1569 |

1813 إقْليم *n.* pl. أَقاليم region, district; province
اقترح هتلر على الحكومة البريطانية تسوية النزاع بتسليم إقليم دانزج إلى ألمانيا — Hitler suggested to the British government to resolve the conflict by handing over the Danzig region to Germany

72 | 1988 |

1814 مُنْتَج *adj.* produced; *n.* pl. -aat product; مُنْتَجات products, manufactured goods
قدموا له مائدة كبيرة من منتجات البيت دون أن يشتروا أي شيء — They offered him a large table of household products without them buying anything

78 | 1820 |

1815 رابطَة *n.* pl. رَوابِط association, union, league; tie, connection, link
إن هناك بعض الأدلة عن وجود روابط بين عبدالله والقاعدة — There are some indications of the presence of links between Abdallah and Al-Qaeda

83 | 1726 |

1816 دَمار *n.* destruction, devastation, ruin
لا يصدق أن الإنسان يمكن ان يصنع كل هذا الدمار، ويسأله دميان هل في أوروبا ناس مثلنا أم شياطين؟ — He doesn't believe that man could create such destruction, and Dumyan asks him if there are people in Europe like us, or are they devils?

86 | 1661 |

1817 حامِل *adj.* bearing, carrying; *n.* pl. حَمَلَة bearer, carrier; porter
عاد إلى وطنه حاملا طفلا بوسنيا جريحا اسمه سعيد — He returned to his country carrying a wounded Bosnian child named Said

88 | 1619 |

1818 مُقابَلَة *n.* pl. -aat encounter, meeting; interview; (sports) match, game
اضاف جلالته في مقابلة نشرتها صحيفة اللوموند الفرنسية امس ان اسرائيل تخطىء اذا ظنت ان بامكانها غسل يديها من المشكلة الفلسطينية ورميها على الاردن — His Majesty added, in an interview published by the French newspaper "Le Monde" yesterday, that Israel is making a mistake if it thinks that it is able to wash its hands of the Palestinian problem and throw it onto Jordan

94 | 1512 |

1819 إنْقاذ *n.* rescue, saving; relief, bailout
لا يمتلكون الخبرة الكافية لإنقاذ البلد من الانهيار — They do not possess sufficient experience to save the country from collapse

85 | 1670 |

1820 تَفْجير *vn.* blowing up, detonating; *n.* pl. -aat explosion
نفذ أحد عناصرها سلسلة تفجيرات في إسرائيل أدت إلى مقتل شخص وجرح آخرين — One of its elements carried out a series of explosions in Israel which led to the killing of one person and the wounding of two others

79 | 1788 |

1821 تُراث *n.* heritage; inheritance
هو معروف بسعة اطلاعه ليس على التراث العربي وحسب، بل على تراث الأمم الأخرى — He is known for the breadth of his knowledge, not only about the Arab heritage, but also about the heritage of other nations

85 | 1661 |

1822 قُنْبُلَة *n.* pl. قَنابِل bomb, shell; grenade
استخدم الألمان نوعا جديدا من القنابل فوق لندن، قنابل حارقة تشعل النار الجهنمية في كل مكان — The Germans used a new type of bomb over London, a fire bomb that would ignite a hellish fire everywhere

85 | 1666 |

1823 مَطْعَم *n.* pl. مَطاعِم restaurant
ذهبا إلى السينما ثم تناولا العشاء في مطعم إيطالي على البحيرة — They went to the cinema, and then had dinner in an Italian restaurant on the lake

95 | 1487 |

1824 سُهُولَة *n.* ease, facility

أنت الآن غنية، وباستطاعتك أن تعثرى على سكن بسهولة — You are now rich, you can find housing easily

94 | 1488 |

1825 نَالَ *v. I (a)* to attain, achieve (prize); to acquire, gain (distinction)

كل شعب فى العالم ينال الحكومة التى يستحقها.. — هكذا قال ونستون تشرشل Every nation in the world gets the government it deserves; this is what Winston Churchill said

88 | 1599 |

1826 مُحَام (*def.* مُحَامِي) *n. pl.* مُحَامُون lawyer, defense counsel

لم أهتم بهذه التفاصيل الدقيقة، سوف يهتم بها محامي — I didn't take an interest in these fine details; my lawyer will take a look at them

88 | 1594 |

1827 غِذَائِيّ *adj.* nutritional, food-related

قد أقبلوا على شراء المواد الغذائية المستوردة من البلاد العربية — They have started to buy food imported from Arab countries

80 | 1749 |

1828 مِسْكِين *n. pl.* مَساكِين poor soul, wretch; *adj.* poor, humble, miserable

بسرعة يا أمي.. اعطني نقودا، هناك رجل مسكين يصرخ في الشارع وأريد أن أهدئه — Hurry, mom, give me money, there is a poor man yelling in the street and I want to calm him down

82 | 1702 |

1829 مِهْنَة *n. pl.* مِهَن vocation, trade, profession, occupation

لا بد أن يكون لى مهنة أعيش منها — I have to have a profession from which I can live

92 | 1518 |

1830 مَكْتَبَة *n. pl.* -aat library; bookstore

ليس بالضرورة شراء الكتاب، فسيستطيعون قراءته في المكتبات أو استعارته لقراءته — Buying the book is not necessary, they will be able to read it in the libraries or borrow it to read it

94 | 1488 |

1831 مَظْهَر *n. pl.* مَظاهِر view; appearance, looks

لماذا لم يخرج أبي لمواجهتهم وقد كان دائما يظهر أمامي بمظهر الرجل الشجاع الذي لا يخاف؟ — Why didn't my father go out to face them, when he had always appeared before me as a brave man who doesn't fear anything?

88 | 1587 |

1832 ظاهِر *adj.* evident, apparent; *n.* obvious

عصمت أنا آسف جدا.. الظاهر مش حانعرف نواصل مع بعض — Ismat, I'm really sorry...It seems that we won't be able to continue with each other

94 | 1492 |

1833 تُراب *n.* dirt, soil

أسرع مجد الدين بإغلاق النوافذ لكن التراب كان يدخل إليهم مع الريح من الأبواب المفتوحة — Magd Al-Din hurried to close the windows but the dust was coming in on them with the wind from the open doors

87 | 1597 |

1834 وُضُوح *n.* clarity; بِوُضُوح clearly, plainly, explicitly

يفضل الظلام على النور والغموض على الوضوح — He prefers darkness to light, and mystery to clarity

88 | 1588 |

1835 مَكْتُوب *adj.* written; predestined; *n. pl.* مَكاتِيب message, letter

بدأ يقرأ كلمته من ورقة أمامه على المنصة مكتوبة بحروف كبيرة (لأنه لا يستعمل نظارة القراءة أبدا) — He began to read his words from the paper in front of him on the table, written with large letters (since he never uses reading glasses)

96 | 1451 |

1836 حاجِز *n. pl.* حَواجِز obstacle, hurdle; *adj.* blocking, blockading

علمتني مهنتي أن أجتاز الحواجز التي تفصلني عن الآخرين وأعبر إلى عوالمهم وخوافي وعيهم — My profession has taught me to get beyond the barriers that separate me from others and pass through to their worlds and the hidden parts of their consciousness

89 | 1572 |

1837 ما *part.* (redundant, in indirect questions)

ما إذا if, whether

تستطيع ان تكتشف ما إذا كان الشخص المتحدث كاذباً — You can detect whether the person speaking is lying

72 | 1944 |

1838 رَغِبَ *v. I (a)* to wish for, desire, want في sth

هل من العدل أن نأتي إلى العالم بطفل لا يرغب فيه أحد؟ — Is it fair that we bring into the world a child that no one wants?

88 | 1585 |

1839 مَوْرِد *n. pl.* مَوَارِد source, resource

نجحوا في رفع كفاءة الموارد البشرية السنغافورية وتوطين التقنية — They succeeded in raising the proficiency of Singaporean human resources, and in nationalizing technology

76 | 1819 |

1840 قَهْوَة *n.* coffee; café, coffeehouse

أخذت حماما ساخنا واحتسيت كوبا كبيرا من القهوة — I took a hot shower and sipped a big cup of coffee

87 | 1601 |

1841 مَطْلَب *n. pl.* مَطَالِب request; demand, claim; desired goal, objective

ساهم بقسط كبير في توحيد المغاربة حول مطلب الاستقلال — He contributed to a large extent in uniting the Moroccans around the demand for independence

86 | 1607 |

1842 مُشْرِف *n.* supervisor, director; *adj.* supervising, directing

إنه مدير المطعم وصاحبه المشرف على تصريف شؤونه في الترتيب والنظافة والتموين والضيافة He is the manager of the restaurant and its owner, who oversees the conducting of its affairs: its organization, cleaning, supply, and hospitality

86 | 1621 |

1843 ضَرْب *vn.* beating, hitting, striking; *n.* strike, attack; *n.* type, kind, variety

ألم يسمح الشرع الحنيف للرجل بضرب زوجته بغرض التأديب؟ — Doesn't Islamic Law allow

the man to hit his wife for the purpose of discipline?

92 | 1513 |

1844 تَحَمَّلَ *v. V* to bear, carry (burden); to shoulder (responsibility)

لم يتزوج لأنه لا يؤمن بمؤسسة الزواج وليس بمقدوره أن يتحمل مسئولية إحضار أطفال إلى هذا العالم الفاسد — He did not marry because he does not believe in the institution of marriage, and he is not able to bear the responsibility of bringing children into this corrupt world

97 | 1433 |

1845 مِفْتاح *n. pl.* مَفَاتِيح key (door, lock, computer keyboard); switch; wrench

أضعت مفاتيح سيارتي وأنا ألعب الكرة ولم أعثر عليها أبدا — I lost the keys of my car, while I was playing soccer, and I never found them

97 | 1421 |

1846 جَزَى *v. I (i)* to repay, reward sb; جزاك الله خَيْراً may God reward you! (used to express thanks for a service)

لا أعرف ماذا أقول يا دكتور طارق.. جزاك الله خيرا بما فعلته معي — I don't know what to say, Dr Tariq...May God reward you well for what you have done for me

43 | 3222 | +for

1847 قَطَرِيّ *n./adj.* Qatari

الدوري القطري مع بداية الموسم القادم سيكون له شأن عظيم جدا — The Qatari tournament at the beginning of the coming season will be a really big deal

68 | 2044 |

1848 سِرِّيّ *adj.* secret; private

كان الشيخ سليمان يستخدم جيشه السري من العميان في إيصال تعليماته وأوامره إلى الوجهاء والمشايخ — Sheikh Sulaiman was using his secret army of blind people to get his teachings and orders out to the dignitaries and sheikhs

88 | 1567 |

1849 تَشْغِيل *n.* operation, activation; employment, hiring

يحاول السائق ثانية وثالثة تشغيل سيارته الواقفة في طريق عام — The driver tries again a second

and third time to operate his car which is stopped on a public road

79 | 1746 |

1850 وَدَعَ *v. I (a)* to let, allow sb to do sth; دَعْني allow me

دعنا نتكلم فى العمل، فهذا ما يهمني أكثر — Let's talk about work, this is what concerns me more

83 | 1660 |

1851 حُجَّة *n.* pretext, excuse; proof, evidence; بِحُجَّةِ أنْ under the pretext that

رفض صاحب مطعم استقبالهما بحجة أن المطبخ مغلق، مع أن زبائن آخرين كانوا فى نفس اللحظة ينتظرون الوجبات التي طلبوها — The owner of the restaurant refused to accept them under the pretext that the kitchen was closed, despite the fact that other customers were at the same moment waiting for the meals they had ordered

91 | 1509 |

1852 مُسْتَعِدّ *a.p.* getting ready, preparing لـ for; *adj.* ready, prepared

كنت متعبا.. لم أكن مستعدا للمزيد من الجدل والمشاكل — I was tired...I wasn't ready for more argument and problems

96 | 1442 |

1853 أُذُنِّي *my* ear; أُذُن and آذان *pl. fem.n.* أُذُن and أُذُن (two) ears

حين دق التليفون تردد فى تناول سماعته.. رفعها إلى أذنه واستمع إلى صوت وزير خارجيته — When the telephone rang he hesitated to pick up the receiver...he raised it to his ear and listened to the voice of his foreign minister

82 | 1688 |

1854 مُفاجَأَة *n. pl.* مُفاجَآت surprise

عندى لك مفاجأة مدهشة.. أتُحب أن تعرفها؟ — I have a surprise for you...Do you want to know (what it is)?

92 | 1504 |

1855 عاجِل *adj.* urgent, speedy; عاجِلًا أَوْ آجِلًا sooner or later

نعتقد أن وقفا لاطلاق النار أمر عاجل — We believe that a cease fire is urgent

87 | 1578 |

1856 فَصْل *n. pl.* فُصُول section, chapter; season; class, classroom; semester, term

ربيع باريس ليس مجرد فصل من فصول العام، ولكنه طاقة تتجدد بلا انقطاع — A Paris spring is not just one of the seasons of the year, but rather it is an energy that is constantly renewing itself

94 | 1461 |

24 Arabic Speaking Countries/Regions

Ranking is from list of names and abbreviations.

5	لبنان	Lebanon	58	المغرب	Morocco	411	رأس	Ras (Cape)
4	العراق	Iraq	68	البحرين	Bahrain	424	سيناء	Sinai
9	إسرائيل	Israel	70	إفريقيا	Africa	426	شبعا	Shabaa
10	مصر	Egypt	76	تونس	Tunisia	429	متوسّط	Mediterranean
13	سوريا	Syria	82	اليمن	Yemen	443	عمان	Oman
19	الكويت	Kuwait	89	ليبيا	Libya	501	الجولان	the Golan
20	فلسطين	Palestine	186	الشّام	Syria; the Levant	554	الفرات	Euphrates
28	الأردن	Jordan	194	النيل	Nile	556	تشاد	Chad
30	السودان	Sudan	208	الصومال	Somalia	567	سويس	Suez
40	الجزائر	Algeria	217	البحر الأحمر	the Red Sea	602	دجلة	Tigris
49	قطر	Qatar	218	البقاع	Bekaa/Biqa (Leb.)	613	موريتانيا	Mauritania
55	السّعوديّة	Saudi Arabia	273	الخليج	the Persian Gulf			

1857 طاوِلَة *n.* table (It. tavola); لَعِبَة الطّاوِلَة and طاوِلَة الزَّهْر backgammon; تِنِس الطّاوِلَة table tennis

دخل المطبخ، وجلس إلى طاولة الطعام يتأمل قوام زوجته نوارة، وهي تعد له الإفطار — He entered the kitchen, and sat at the food table contemplating his wife Nura's stature, as she prepared breakfast for him

92 | 1495 |

1858 مُعْتَقَل *n.* prison camp; *n. pl.* -uun prisoner, detainee; *adj.* detained, held prisoner

يروي معتقلون في غوانتانامو معاناتهم في هذا المعتقل في مجموعة قصائد قاموا بتسليمها الى محاميهم — Prisoners in Guantanamo tell of their suffering in prison in a collection of poems they handed to their lawyers

78 | 1744 |

1859 مَصْنَع *n. pl.* مَصانِع factory, industrial plant

يذكر أن هذه المنطقة الأردنية تضم العديد من المصانع الإسرائيلية التي تشغل عمالا أردنيين — He mentions that this Jordanian area includes a number of Israeli factories which employ Jordanian workers

93 | 1468 |

1860 أَصْغَر *elat.* fem. صُغْرَى smaller/smallest; younger/youngest; *adj.* lesser, minor

في الحرب الثانية قتل أخي الأصغر وفي الثالثة سقط الشاه فوق أكوام من الجثث — In the second war, my younger brother was killed, and in the third, the Shah fell on a pile of bodies

97 | 1405 |

1861 نادِر *adj.* rare, unusual, infrequent; نادِراً rarely, seldom

أصدقاؤه قليلون نادرا ما يتسع وقته لرؤيتهم — His friends are few, and rarely does his time permit him to see them

93 | 1469 |

1862 مِقْدار *n.* extent, amount; value; degree, level, dosage

انخفض سعر البرميل بمقدار ١,٢٧ دولار ليبلغ ٧٠,٣٦ دولار —The price of a barrel fell by 1.27 dollars to reach 70.36 dollars

87 | 1575 |

1863 مِهْنِيّ *adj.* professional, vocational, occupational, trade

تستهدف النشاطات تعزيز القدرات المهنية من خلال الدمج بين البعد النظري والبعد العملي — The activities aim at strengthening the professional capabilities through integrating the practical with the theoretical aspects

87 | 1563 |

1864 حِصَّة *n. pl.* حِصَص share, quota, portion; (school) class period

من الجدير ذكره هنا أن حصة أوروبا في إجمالي واردات الكويت تبلغ حوالي الثلث — It is worth mentioning here that Europe's share in the total imports of Kuwait reaches about one third

91 | 1501 |

1865 عاشِر *adj.* tenth (ordinal)

الساعة العاشرة صباحا بتوقيت القاهرة.. موعد مناسب للاتصال — Ten o'clock in the morning Cairo time...a good time to call

97 | 1405 |

1866 نَصِيحَة *n. pl.* نَصائِح advice, word of advice, counsel

يجب عليها أن تحترم نصيحة أبويها لأنهما أكثر خبرة منها ولا يريدان إلا خيرها وسعادتها — She needs to respect the advice of her parents because they have more experience than she does, and they only want her well-being and happiness

94 | 1436 |

1867 هَدَّد *v. II* to threaten sb ب with (murder, blackmail); to threaten, intimidate sb ب with (a weapon)

استنجدت بزوجها الذي اتصل بالعامل والأمن وأخبرهم بأن هناك من يهدد حياته وحياة زوجته — She called on her husband for help, who got in touch with the worker and security and informed them that there was someone threatening his life and the life of his wife

85 | 1602 |

1868 تِكْنُولُوجِيا *n.* technology

شدد على حق بلاده في امتلاك التكنولوجيا النووية مؤكدا ان طهران ليست مهتمة بامتلاك سلاح نووي — He stressed the right of his country to own nuclear technology, affirming that Teheran was not interested in owning nuclear weapons

89 | 1521 |

1869 تَرَاجَعَ *v. VI* to retreat, back down/off عن from (a position); to lag behind, fall back, decrease

هممت أن أستطلع الأمر من خلال النافذة لكني تراجعت في آخر لحظة وعجلت أنزل السلم — I was about to investigate the matter by looking through the window, but I retreated at the last moment and hurried down the stairs

88 | 1539 |

1870 وَرَدَ *v. I (i)* to arrive, show up; to appear, be mentioned في in (a text)

أضاف النائب بومجيد أن التوصيات التي وردت في التقرير تستحق النظر فيها بكل عناية واهتمام — The deputy Bumajid added that the advice which came in the report need to be looked into very carefully

91 | 1490 |

1871 مُسَاهَمَة *vn.* participation, contribution

يجب علينا جميعا المساهمة ولو بجزء بسيط في التخفيف من الحصار المفروض على إخواننا — We all have to participate, even if only with a small part, in lightening the blockade imposed upon our brothers

79 | 1700 |

1872 شِيعِيّ *n./adj.* Shiite

عملت على الحد من التغلغل الإيراني في المناطق الشيعية الأفغانية — I worked to limit Iranian penetration into the Afghan Shiite areas

62 | 2175 |

1873 تَعَامَلَ *v. VI* to deal with (ب مع) sth/sb with); to work together, do business مع with sb

يتعاملون مع غيرهم وفق المنظور الطائفي — They deal with others according to a sectarian viewpoint

91 | 1486 |

1874 بَحْرِيّ *adj.* maritime, sea; naval, navy

يؤكد العالمان أن أربع وجبات أسبوعيا من أسماك هونج كونج كفيلة برفع مستوى الزئبق لدى الآكلين، أعلى بكثير منه لدى الذين لا يقبلون على المأكولات البحرية — The two scholars stress that four meals weekly of Hong Kong fish is enough to raise the level of mercury in those who eat it,

much higher than for those who do not eat seafood

77 | 1761 |

1875 ذِهْن *n. pl.* أَذْهَان mind, thought, intellect

لم يستطع للحظة واحدة أن يبعد زينب عن ذهنه — He was not able for a single moment to get Zaynab out of his mind

87 | 1553 |

1876 أُولَائِكَ and أُولَئِكَ *dem.pron.* those (human)

ان لم يقتنع بي فما هو رأيهم بالشيخ ابن باز؟ — If they aren't convinced of me, what is their opinion about Sheikh Ibn Baz?

88 | 1532 |

1877 رِبْح *vn.* winning, gaining; *n. pl.* أَرْبَاح profit, gain; dividend, revenue; interest

معظم الذين ذهبوا للإمارات هم الأفراد الذين يبحثون عن الربح السريع — Most of those who went to the Emirates are the individuals who are looking for a quick profit

89 | 1507 |

1878 مُرَاجَعَة *n.* review, inspection; checking, consulting

لا بد من مراجعة المواقف كلها، ومراجعة تفاصيل المعركة — All the positions must be reviewed, as well as the details of the battle

83 | 1611 |

1879 زَهْر *coll.n. pl.* أَزْهَار, زُهُور flowers

صافحتها وناولتها الزهور، فشكرتني بحرارة وهى تشمها — I shook her hand and handed her the flowers, and she thanked me warmly as she smelled them

89 | 1514 |

1880 تَصْوِير *n.* photography, filming; illustration; depiction, characterization, description

اندفع بعض الحاضرين وطلبوا التصوير مع سيادة الرئيس فاستجاب وأشار للحرس فأفسحوا لهم — Some of those present rushed forward and requested a picture with His Excellency the President, and he responded and signaled to the guards, so they made room for them

86 | 1562 |

1881 بَنَى *v. I (i)* to build, construct, erect sth

يقولون إن الذى بنى الإسكندرية واحد مجنون اسمه الإسكندر، وملأها مصانع خمور — They say that the one who had built Alexandria was a crazy guy named Alexander, and (that) he filled it with wineries

95 | 1413 |

1882 كَرامَة *n.* dignity, honor; generosity, magnanimity

المرأة هنا مواطنة محترمة وليست مخلوقا بلا كرامة كما تعتبرونها فى الصحراء التى أتيت منها — The woman, here, is a respected citizen, and not a creature without dignity as you consider her to be in the desert you came from

87 | 1537 |

1883 تَقَبَّلَ *v. V* to receive, accept

وفرض إدريس نفسه على الجنازة فاشترك فى تشييعها، بل وقف يتقبل العزاء بصفته عم الفقيد — Idriss imposed himself on the funeral, participating in the holding it, indeed he stood accepting condolences in his role as uncle of the deceased person

90 | 1493 |

1884 سِباق *n.* pl. -aat race; competition

كنت أحلم وأنا طفل بأن أكون قائدا لسيارات السباق — I used to dream, when I was a child, that I was a race car driver

85 | 1569 |

1885 مُحافَظَة *vn.* protection, preservation; guarding, safeguarding; *n.* conservatism, modesty

نعرف أنك قادر على مساعدتنا فى المحافظة على مصدر رزقنا.. لن نطلب منك الكثير — We know you are able to help us maintain our source of livelihood...we won't ask much of you

90 | 1483 |

1886 دِرْهَم *n.* pl. دَراهِم dirham

صاحب الشركة يأخذ من كل موظف جديد تسعة آلاف درهم مقابل تعيينه — The owner of the company takes nine thousand dirhams from every new employee in exchange for appointing him

64 | 2097 |

1887 مُقَدَّم *adj.* offered, submitted; advanced, ahead of schedule; مُقَدَّماً in advance, beforehand; *n.* lieutenant colonel

واشتد هول الناس حين تبين أن الطعام المقدم إليهم معونات من الدول الغربية ومن الصليب الأحمر الدولى — The terror of the people increased when it became clear the food coming to them was aid from the Western states and from the International Red Cross

81 | 1655 |

1888 كُوَّيِّس /kwayyis/ (Egy.Lev.) *adj.* pl. -iin good, nice; *adv.* well

لما يكون حد بيكلمك، لازم تحترم كلامه، وتسمعه كويس — When someone is talking to you, you have to respect his words, and listen to him well

39 | 3360 | +spo

1889 جَدْوَل *n.* pl. جَداوِل table, chart; schedule; stream, rivulet

وحتى إذا ما عقدت الانتخابات وفق الجدول المقرر لها، فهناك الكثير من رجال الدين السنة يحثون أتباعهم على مقاطعتها — Even if the elections were held according to the schedule set for them, still there are many Sunni men of religion who are urging their followers to boycott them

86 | 1546 |

1890 مُنافَسَة *n.* pl. -aat competition, rivalry

المستفيد الأول هو المواطن عن طريق مزيد من المنافسة، وهو أيضا المستفيد فى المرتبة الثانية عن طريق فرص العمل — The first beneficiary is the citizen, through more competition, and he is also the beneficiary secondly through job opportunities

75 | 1779 |

1891 مَسار *n.* pl. -aat path, route; *n.* trajectory, orbit

تجري الدنيا فى مسار لا نريده، لا نوافق عليه، كأنها مقدرة علينا — The world goes on a path which we don't want, which we don't agree to, as if it were fated for us

84 | 1587 |

1892 سَفارَة and سِفارَة *n.* pl. -aat embassy

حتى لو كنت مسئولا فى السفارة المصرية، فليس من حقك أن تقتحم بيتى — Even if you were an official in the Egyptian Embassy, it would not be your right to invade my home

87 | 1524 |

1893 خَلِيَّة *n.* pl. خَلايا (biological, political) cell; beehive

يتنسم روائح الطهي بكل خلية من خلايا رئتيه، ويستنشق رائحة تقلية الثوم المشتهاة بفتحتي انفه — He smells the aromas of cooking in every cell of his lungs, and he inhales the smell of fragrant fried garlic in his nostrils

86 | 1546 |

1894 صَرَخَ *v. I (u)* to shout, scream

أصابها رعب شديد، واستمرت تصرخ وتصرخ لكن دائماً بلا صوت — She was struck by a strong terror, and she continued to scream and shout but always without sound

79 | 1671 | +lit

1895 حَلَمَ *v. I (u)* to dream ب of sth/sb

خطر لى أنى أحلم وأن كل ما يحدث غير حقيقى — It occurred to me that I was dreaming and that everything that was happening was not real

85 | 1569 |

1896 تَغَيُّر *n.* pl. -aat change, variation

لقد شاهد تشرشل بنفسه التغير الذى أحدثه مونتى فى الجنود — Churchill saw for himself the changes which Monty had implemented in the soldiers

92 | 1443 |

1897 فَوْضَى *n.* chaos, anarchy

ألا تعتقد أن المظاهرات والإضرابات ستفضى بالبلد إلى الفوضى؟ — Don't you believe that demonstrations and strikes will throw the country into chaos?

88 | 1513 |

1898 اِسْتِقْلال *n.* independence

لقد كنت بعد الاستقلال أهرب من المناصب السياسية التى عرضت علي — After independence I avoided political positions which were offered me

79 | 1680 |

1899 وَدَّ *v. I (a)* to want, like sth or أَنْ to do sth; أَوَدُّ I would like

إيران تؤكد أنها لا تود الحصول على سلاح نووي — Iran stresses that it does not want to obtain nuclear arms

87 | 1520 |

1900 ضَريبة *n.* pl. ضَرائِب tax, levy

عندما أراد ملك مصر مقاتلة جيوش التتار، فرض ضرائب باهظة على الشعب المصري — When the King of Egypt wanted to fight the armies of the Tatars, he imposed heavy taxes on the Egyptian people

90 | 1477 |

1901 عَلا *v. I (u)* to rise, ascend, loom; to be elevated

استدار وهرع إلى الخارج، وسرعان ما علا صوت سيارته وهى تبتعد — He turned and hurried out, and soon the sound of his car grew louder as it pulled away

89 | 1492 | +lit

1902 عِناية *n.* care, concern, attention, regard

كان يتكلم معى فى حين كان الاثنان الآخران يفتشان البيت بعناية — He was talking with me while the two others were searching the house carefully

88 | 1494 |

1903 مُوَجَّه *adj.* directed, aimed

أريد أن أعرف التهمة الموجهة إلي — I want to know the accusation that is being brought against me

87 | 1514 |

1904 ذَهَب *n.* gold

كانت حول رقبته سلسلة سميكة من الذهب — Around his neck was a thick chain of gold

95 | 1395 |

1905 قاس (def. قاسِي) *adj.* harsh, cruel, severe

بدأ يوجه اللوم لنفسه، لماذا كنت قاسياً معها؟ كانَّ على أن أعطيها الكتاب الذي طلبته — He started to blame himself, why was I so harsh with her? I should have given her the book she asked for

88 | 1499 |

1906 إنتو /'intu/ and إنتوا (Dia.) *pron.* you (pl.)

الواحد عايز يرضى ضميره لو انتو مش موافقين خلاص — A person needs to satisfy his conscience, and if you all don't agree, well that's it

41 | 3197 | +spo

1907 طائِفَة *n.* pl. طَوائِف faction, sect
الفتنة موجودة فى كل وقت وبين كل طائفة وأختها،
— بلدنا محسودة يا خواجة ديمتري Conflict is
present at all times and between every
faction and its sister; our country is envied,
Mr Dimitri
78 | 1692 |

1908 صَرْف *n.* spending, changing (money);
بِصَرْفِ النَظَرِ عن diverting (attention);
regardless of; الصرف الصِحّي wastewater/
sewage treatment
اعلنت ادارة النادي عن صرف مكافآت للاعبين
— تقديرا للأداء الذي قدموه اثناء المواجه The
administration of the club announced the
payment of bonuses to the players in
recognition of the performance they showed
during the match
80 | 1649 |

1909 هَـ *dem.pron.* (prefix, with def. art.)
هالموضوع /ha-l-/ (Lev.Irq.Gul.) this; هالـ
this topic
— ما قدرت أتكلم واياه بهالموضوع I wasn't able
to speak with him about this subject
28 | 4712 | +spo

1910 مُواصَلَة *vn.* continuation, continuing; *n.* pl.
مُواصَلات -aat communication, connection;
(public) transportation
كرر حداد عادل إعلان استعداد بلاده لمواصلة الحوار
بشأن رزمة المقترحات الأوروبية وتسوية موضوع
البرنامج النووي السلمي — Haddad Adil reiterated
his country's readiness to continue the dialog
regarding the package of European proposals
and settling the matter of the peaceful nuclear
program
82 | 1590 |

1911 إنْهاء *n.* termination, completion, ending
يؤكد الملك أن العام الحالي فرصة لإنهاء العَنف
وتحقيق السلام وبناء المستقبل الاقتصادي —
The king stresses that the current year is
an opportunity to end the violence and
achieve peace and build the economic
future
83 | 1573 |

1912 فَراغ *n.* vacuum, empty space; free time,
leisure
قالت ان الغول يستطيع أن يضع رجلا ضخما في الفراغ
الذي بين أسنانه — She said that the ogre can
put a large man in the space between his
teeth
89 | 1467 |

1913 تَشْريعيّ *adj.* legislative
مجلس النواب هو السلطة التشريعية يمارس الرقابة
الشاملة على سياسة الحكومة وأعمالها — The
Council of Deputies is the legislative authority,
exercising full supervision over the policies
and actions of the government
64 | 2030 |

1914 آل *n.* family, clan
— لم يكن أحد من آله يهتم بهم None of his family
was concerned with them
79 | 1654 |

1915 فَصَلَ *v. I (i)* to separate, detach, disconnect
sth; to dismiss, fire sb; to lay sb off, let sb
go; to hang up (phone), get off (the line);
to get disconnected, get cut off; to render
a judgment, reach a decision (في قضية in
a case)
والمدهش أكثر أنها أحبته بالرغم من عمر كامل يفصل
بينهما — The more surprising thing was that
she loved him despite a full year age
difference between them
97 | 1344 |

1916 سَمَك *coll.n.* fish, *un.n.* سَمَكَة, pl. أَسْماك
هما يومان للصوم المقدس لا نأكل فيهما السمك مثل
الصوم الكبير تماما — They are two days of holy
fasting during which we don't eat fish, just like
the big fast
91 | 1426 |

1917 تَوَجُّه *n.* pl. -aat attitude, orientation,
approach
تم تحذير الناس من التوجه إلى ضاحية سيدي بشر
ليلا خارج نطاق شريط الترام — People were
warned from going to the suburb Sidi Bishr
at night outside the area of the tram line
83 | 1576 |

1918 رَدَّدَ *v. II* to repeat, reiterate sth

قام سمير من سريره وخرج من غرفته وهو يردد في نفسه: عمتي وراء كل المشاكل — Samir got up from his bed and left his room repeating to himself: My aunt is behind all the problems

89 | 1465 |

1919 إِذَاعَة *vn.* broadcasting; *n.* pl. -aat broadcast, transmission

ارتفع صوت من الإذاعة الداخلية يحذر من أن المبنى يتعرض إلى حريق ويطلب من السكان مغادرة شققهم بأقصى سرعة — A voice came over the internal speakers, warning that the building was on fire, and requesting all the residents to leave their apartments as fast as possible

95 | 1370 |

1920 تَأْسِيس *n.* establishment, foundation; creation; installation

ساهمت في تأسيس جمعية لحقوق الإنسان — I participated in founding a human rights organization

79 | 1639 |

1921 تَحَرُّك *n.* pl. -aat movement, activity, motion

لم يجرؤ أحد على التحرك في المنطقة — No one dared to move in the area

82 | 1575 |

1922 تَشْجِيع *vn.* encouragement, promotion, support

تسعى بشتى الطرق لتشجيع السياحة الداخلية وتوفير بنيتها الأساسية والتعريف بمعالم المملكة المختلفة — It is trying by every means to encourage internal tourism and to provide its basic infrastructure and an introduction to the various features of the kingdom

80 | 1619 |

1923 نادَى *v. III* to call بـ for sth/sb; to call على for sb; to call out, announce (بـ) sth

انصرفت أنا عائدا إلى الأولاد، لكن بعد دقائق، نادى ماجد علي من النافذة الخشبية لغرفته — I left, going back to my children; but minutes later, Majid called me from the wooden window of his room

88 | 1468 |

1924 مَنَحَ *v. I (a)* to grant, bestow, award sb sth or sth لـ to sb

خلال فترة الخمسينيات منحت الحكومة الكويتية امتيازا جديدا لشركة النفط الأمريكية المستقلة للتنقيب — During the period of the Fifties, the Kuwaiti government granted a new concession to the independent American oil company to drill

87 | 1481 |

1925 كَبُر *v. I (u)* to grow up, grow older; to get bigger

لقد كبرت، وأستطيع أن أتدبر أموري بنفسي — I've grown up, and I can manage my own affairs by myself

92 | 1395 |

1926 فاعِل *adj.* effective, efficient; active; *n.* pl. -uun doer, agent; فاعِل خَيْر philanthropist

ألا يستطيع أحد أن يتكهن ماذا هو فاعل؟ — Can't anyone predict what he is going to do?

84 | 1536 |

1927 أيوا /'aywa/ and أيوه /'aywah/ *interj.* (Dia.) yes

يعني انت عارف الحاجات اللى زى دى؟ – ايوه — You know the things that are like this? – Yes

9 | 13327 | +spo

1928 بَرَكَة *n.* pl. -aat blessing; حَبَّة البَرَكَة black cumin, fennel-flower

انتهى شهر وابتدينا في الشهر الجديد على بركة الله — A month ended and we began the new month with God's blessing

91 | 1412 | +for

1929 خالِص *adj.* sincere; pure, clear; (Lev.) finished (with), (having) completed; ready; done, over, ended; depleted; (Egy.) *adv.* very, totally

أنا خائف من العلمين ياشيخ محمد.. خايف خالص — I am afraid of Alamein, Sheikh Magd, I'm really afraid

76 | 1684 | +for +spo

1930 مِيلاد *n.* birthday; birth; عِيد المِيلاد (المَجِيد) Christmas

تحب صاحباتها في المدرسة وتتبادل معهن هدايا عيد الميلاد — She loves her girlfriends in school, and she exchanges birthday gifts with them

96 | 1340 |

1931 إِجْمالِيّ *adj.* comprehensive, full; total, gross

يتوقع ان يزداد الناتج المحلي الاجمالي بنسبة ٨ — في المائه في العام — It is expected that the gross domestic product will increase by 8 percent per year

69 | 1870 |

1932 شِعْرِيّ *adj.* poetic

أنجزت بحوث جامعية حول إنتاجه الشعري في جامعة ابن زهر بأغادير — University research was carried out concerning his poetic output at the Ibn Zohr University in Agadir

77 | 1671 |

25 Arabic Speaking Cities

Ranking is from list of names and abbreviations.

23	بغداد	Baghdad	287	صنعاء	San'a	560	رمثا	Ramtha
25	غزّة	Gaza	297	جنين	Jenin	563	بعقوبة	Ba'quba
26	بيروت	Beirut	324	خليل	Hebron	570	الريّان	Al-Rayyan
36	عمّان	Amman	331	بارد	نهر البارد	577	عدن	Aden
39	القاهرة	Cairo			Nahr Al-Barid	603	جبيل	Jubayl
40	الجزائر	Algiers	336	تل أبيب أبيب	Tel Aviv	604	حانون	بيت حنون
46	رياض	Riyadh	338	حلب	Aleppo			Beit Hanoun
48	دبيّ	Dubai	340	طائف	Ta'if	638	زرقاء	Zarqa
51	القدس	Jerusalem	349	كركوك	Kirkuk	643	جبل	جبل موسى
62	دمشق	Damascus	364	زمالك	Zamalek			Mt. Sinai
76	تونس	Tunis	377	عقبة	Aqaba	650	مقديشو	Mogadishu
92	ظبي	Abu Dhabi	381	رفح	Rafah	669	دمّام	Dammam
94	عين	Ain Shams;	388	الفالوجة	Fallujah	678	سامرّاء	Samara
		Al-Ain	419	رباط	Rabat	700	بابل	Babylon; Babil
115	الخرطوم	Khartoum	421	إربد	Irbid	707	كفر	كفر الشيخ
117	طرابلس	Tripoli	422	شرم	شرم الشيخ			Kafr Al-Shaykh
122	مكّة	Mecca			Sharm El-Sheikh	702	متن	Matn
142	جدّة	Jeddah	431	قادسيّة	Qadisiyya	712	ظفار	Dhofar
150	صيدا	Sidon	436	نجف	Najaf	717	حمص	Homs
169	الدوحة	Doha	446	كربلاء	Karbala	718	طولكرم	Tulkarem
173	مسقط	Muscat	465	موصل	Mosul	722	محرّق	Muharraq
188	صور	Tyre	466	حيفا	Haifa	729	سرت	Sirte
202	شارقة	Sharjah	474	مدينة	Medina	742	حماة	Hama
206	الإسكندريّة	Alexandria	493	دير	Deir	758	صهيون	جبل صهيون
225	طيّبة	Taibeh			Al-Balah, دير يسين			Mt. Zion;
232	رام	Ramallah			Deir Yassin, etc.)			Sahyoun
246	البصرة	Basra	499	يرموك	Yarmouk	763	بنغازيّ	Benghazi
251	بعلبك	Baalbek	509	خان	خان يونس	775	الرماديّ	Ramadi
262	تلّ	Tel; Tel Aviv			Khan Yunis;	792	قصيم	Qussaim
268	بيت لحم بيت	بيت لحم		الخليلي خان	خان الخليلي	801	حائل	Hayil
		Bethlehem;			Khan Al-Khalili	808	الجيزة	Giza
	حنون بيت	بيت حنون	516	أبو غريب غريب	Abu	809	منامة	Manama
		Beit Hanoun			Ghraib	816	زحلة	Zahle
281	نابلس	Nablus	520	قانا	Qana			

1933 نِطاق *n.* scope, range, extent

تحدث عن مستقبل افضل يستعمل فيه الايثانول على نطاق اوسع لتقليل اعتماد الولايات المتحدة على النفط المستورد — He spoke about a better future in which ethanol would be widely used to lessen the reliance of the United Sates on imported oil

82 | 1559 |

1934 مُعاناة *n.* effort; hardship, suffering

عاش عبد الستار سنوات أخرى في معاناة مستمرة مع المرض — Abd Al-Sattar lived a few more years in constant suffering with the disease

85 | 1503 |

1935 تَأَكُّد *n.* assurance, confirmation (من of); certainty, conviction

أمرت بعض رجالنا بتقصي أخباره، والتأكد من هويته أكثر — I ordered some of our men to investigate his news (report), and to further confirm his identity

85 | 1504 |

1936 تَكْوين *vn.* creating, forming; educating, training (specialists); *n.* structure; education, formation

قد ساعدني ذلك على تكوين شخصيتي — That helped me form my personality

86 | 1497 |

1937 راد *v. I (i)* /raad, yriid/ (Irq.Gul.) to want, need sth, or (with imperf.) to want to do sth

اعطيني رقمك إذا بتريد — Give me your number, if you want

89 | 1442 | +spo

1938 تَمَيَّزَ *v. V* to stand out, distinguish oneself ب by, due to (على compared with, above); to be different عن from

كانت البيوت في عصر صدر الإسلام تتميز بالبساطة والتواضع — Houses in the early Islamic period were characterized by simplicity and modesty

85 | 1505 |

1939 قَدَر *n.* fate, destiny

يتحمل ذلك في كثير من الصبر والاستسلام والخضوع لحكم الأقدار — He is bearing this with a lot of patience, resignation and submission to the rule of fate

90 | 1424 |

1940 تَوَتُّر *n.* pl. -aat tension, strain, unrest; (electrical) tension

أتذكر أيضا بوضوح وصفاء وجه أمي الشديد التوتر والاكفهرار ساعة انتقالنا إلى المسكن الجديد — I remember clearly the very tense, gloomy face of my mother at the time of our moving to the new home

85 | 1493 |

1941 دِقَّة *n.* accuracy, precision; minuteness

— مع توافد المدعوين بدأ فحصهم بمنتهى الدقة As the invitees started coming, he began to scrutinize them with the utmost care

86 | 1470 |

1942 كِيان *n.* entity; essence, being; structure

كانت تحاول وبكل السبل حماية امن الكيان الصهيوني من خلال احتلال افغانستان بحجة مكافحة الارهاب — It was trying by every means to protect the security of the Zionist entity by occupying Afghanistan on the excuse of fighting terrorism

81 | 1566 |

1943 رَبيع *n.* spring (season)

— استمتعت بعطلة أخرى من عطل الربيع الهادئة I enjoyed another one of those calm spring vacations

93 | 1365 |

1944 مُؤَقَّت *adj.* temporary, interim, provisional; مُؤَقَّتاً temporarily

أستطيع أن أؤجل القضية أو أوقف تنفيذ الحكم بشكل مؤقت — I can postpone the case or stop the execution of the punishment temporarily

84 | 1512 |

1945 بُكاء *n.* crying, weeping

لاحظت إميلي ذلك، وما إن سألتها حتى أجهشت بالبكاء وحكت لها كل شيء — Emily noticed that, and hardly had she asked her when she broke out crying and told her everything

79 | 1603 | +lit

1946 رَصاص *n.* lead (metal); *coll.n.* bullets

إن الفدائيين الذين لا يرهبون الموت من رصاص أعدائهم لا ينبغي أن يخافوا من حكم العدالة

حكومة بلادهم — Freedom fighters who don't fear death from the bullet of their enemies should not fear the verdict of justice from the government of their country

86 | 1466 |

1947 تَفَاهُم *n.* mutual understanding, mutual comprehension

إنجليزيتها الضعيفة لا تمكنها حتى من التفاهم مع الناس فى الشارع — Her weak English doesn't even enable her to communicate with people in the street

92 | 1367 |

1948 حَكِيم *adj.* wise; *n.* wise man, sage; philosopher; (Lev.) physician, doctor; (Lev.) حَكِيم أَسْنان dentist

نتذكر معا قول الرجل الحكيم للأمير ناصحا: «ضع الألفاظ في مواضعها» — We remember together the saying of the wise man in advising to the prince: "Put the phrases in their proper places"

86 | 1466 |

1949 طُفُولَة *n.* childhood, infancy; youth

كنت أحلم منذ الطفولة بأن ألتقى يوما شاعرا حقيقيا — Since childhood I have dreamed that I would one day meet a real poet

88 | 1432 |

1950 جَلَّ *v. I (i)* to be majestic, exalted, lofty الله جَلَّ جَلالُهُ (of God); approx. Almighty God

شهر رمضان هو شهر عبادة وتقرب إلى الله عز وجل وليس بشهر الموائد والإسراف في تناول الطعام — The month of Ramadan is a month of worship and getting close to God, may He be exalted and glorified, and not a month of tables and eating too much food

77 | 1630 |

1951 سَرِير *n.* pl. أَسِرَّة bed, couch

استلقت جوار طفلتها فوق السرير، ورفعت عينيها إلى السقف الخشبى الأبيض — She lay down next to her child on the bed, and raised her eyes to the white wooden ceiling

84 | 1502 | +lit

1952 عَجُوز *n./adj.* old person, elderly

سمحت لها بتحية أمها العجوز بسرعة ثم جذبتها من يدها إلى حجرتها وأغلقت عليهما الباب — She permitted her to greet her aged mother quickly, and then she led her by the hand to her room and locked the door on them

75 | 1661 | +lit

1953 فاقَ *v. I (u)* to surpass, excel sth/sb; to wake up, regain one's senses

سرعة الإنسان مهما كانت لن تفوق سرعة الطائرة — The speed of a man, no matter how fast, will never exceed the speed of an airplane

87 | 1439 |

1954 إيطالِيّ *n./adj.* Italian

موضوع واحد لم يختلف عليه البيت الأبيض والحكومة الإيطالية وهو وصف مقتل نيكولا كايباري بالحادث المؤسف — One thing the White House and the Italian government didn't disagree about, was describing Nicola Calipari's murder as an unfortunate incident

76 | 1633 |

1955 أَرْضِيّ *adj.* ground, land; ground-based, land-based

تعرضت تايوان الى هزة أرضية بلغت شدتها ٤ , ٥ درجة بمقياس ريختر — Taiwan was hit by an earthquake that reached 5.4 degrees on the Richter scale

94 | 1330 |

1956 مُضِيف *n.* host, steward; fem. مُضِيفَة stewardess, hostess; *a.p.* adding; *adj.* (in sports) home (team), hosting (club)

قال: لقد زاد وزني ١٣ كيلو، مضيفا ان العمل النيابي مرهق — He said: My weight has increased 13 kg, adding that parliamentary work is exhausting

79 | 1584 |

1957 اسْتِغْلال *n.* utilization; exploitation, taking advantage (of an opportunity)

يجب استغلال هذه الفرصة لتسويق المحافظة ولفت الانظار اليها من قبل المستثمرين — This opportunity must be exploited to market the province and attract the gaze of investors to it

84 | 1484 |

1958 مِيزان n. pl. مَوازِين weight scales, balance; measure, standard

— كل شيء سيوضع في الميزان وفي الحساب Everything will be put on the balance, and taken into consideration

80 | 1542 |

1959 سائِق n. pl. -uun chauffeur, driver

طلب من السائق أن يوصله الى حي من أحياء البدو في الصحراء — He asked the driver to take him to one of the Bedouin living areas in the desert

83 | 1486 |

1960 مَدْخَل n. pl. مَداخِل entrance; introduction, beginning

— ظل الباب الخارجى مفتوحا وأنوار المدخل مضاءة The outside door remained open, and the lights of the entrance were lit

88 | 1404 |

1961 مُحاضَرة n. pl. -aat lecture

أما الهيئة التدريسية التي تقوم بإلقاء المحاضرات والتدريس فتبلغ نحو ١٥٠٠ أستاذ وكلهم من الجنسية الجزائرية — The faculty which gives the lectures and teaches reaches 1,500 teachers and all of them are of Algerian nationality

92 | 1341 |

1962 هَيّا interj. let's...! let's go!

هيا نتكَلم قليلا — Let's talk a little

72 | 1706 | +lit

1963 مَقْبُول adj. acceptable; welcome

هدف المصحة أن تجعل فكرة الموت مقبولة وغير مؤلمة بالنسبة للمرضى المحتضرين — The goal of the hospice is to make the idea of death acceptable and not painful for the dying patients

94 | 1308 |

1964 تَرْبَوِيّ adj. pedagogical, educational; related to child-rearing or breeding

علينا أن نستمر بدروسنا التربوية للأطفال، فضلا عن دروس القرآن الكريم — We must continue our educational lessons for the children, not to mention Qurʾan lessons

78 | 1578 |

1965 مُحْتَلّ adj. occupied (land); filled (post, position)

البنية التحتية والمرافق هي من مسئولية بلدية القدس المحتلة حاليا — The infrastructure and services are the responsibility of the municipality of Jerusalem, which is currently under occupation

74 | 1674 |

1966 تَعَرُّف vn. getting to know على sb, becoming acquainted على with sb

مراسلة إخوتكم العرب هي أفضل وأمتع طريقة للتعرف على أناس من بلدان مختلفة، وحضارات متنوعة — Corresponding with your brother Arabs is the best and most enjoyable way to get to know people from different countries and various cultures

92 | 1342 |

1967 صُبْح n. morning, daybreak

— أحمد وعبده ومعاهم مجموعة حايسافروا الصبح Ahmad and Abdu, along with a group, will travel in the morning

71 | 1723 |

1968 اِنْتَشَر v. VIII to spread out, extend; to be diffused, be publicized

انتشر رجال الإطفاء في أنحاء المبنى وأخذوا يتأكدون من إخلاء كل دور على حدة — The firemen spread to all parts of the building and began to make sure that all the floors were evacuated separately

88 | 1392 |

1969 حَضارِيّ adj. cultural; civilized

ان المواطنة بجوهرها هي قيم وممارسات حضارية ورقي في المفاهيم المجتمعية الحديثة — Citizenship, at its core, is cultural values and practices, and an advance in modern societal concepts

78 | 1567 |

1970 خاطِر n. pl. خَواطِر idea, thought; mind, feeling; wish, volition; inclination; عَشان/عَلَشان خاطِر (Egy.) for the sake of; so that, in order to; على خاطِر (Alg.) because of, on account of

عجبا لك كيف يخطر ببالك مثل هذا الخاطر السخيف — It's amazing how such a silly thought would occur to you

90 | 1367 |

1971 خِتام *n.* conclusion, closure, end
انفرد فريق اليرموك وحيدا بصدارة دوري اندية الدرجة الاولى في ختام الجولة الثانية بعد فوزه الصعب والمستحق امس على عين كارم — The Yarmouk team is alone at the top of the tournament of first class clubs at the end of the second round after its difficult and deserving victory yesterday over Ain Karam
87 | 1402 |

1972 آني (Irq.Alg.) *pron.* I
مشكورة اختي الكريمه واني فعلا سعيد بكلامك — Thanks a lot, my dear sister, I'm really happy with your words (with what you said)
48 | 2525 | +spo

1973 مُثَقَّف *n.* pl. -uun intellectual; *adj.* cultured, educated, cultivated
انت احد شباب القرية المثقف، والشعب يعتمد عليكم — You are one of the educated youth of the village, and the people depend on you
82 | 1498 |

1974 اِجْتَمَعَ مع/ب *v. VIII* to meet, hold a meeting with
في فناء المنزل كانت تجتمع العائلة لشرب القهوة — In the courtyard of the house, the family would meet to drink coffee
88 | 1393 |

1975 خَيال *n.* imagination, fantasy; الخَيال العِلْميّ science fiction
كان العدوان شاملا والدمار يتعدى حدود الخيال — The attack was comprehensive, and the destruction went beyond the bounds of the imagination
85 | 1445 |

1976 مُتَواصِل *adj.* continuous, constant, unceasing; connected
لا تستطيع النوم لأكثر من ثلاث ساعات متواصلة — She can't sleep for more than three hours in a row
86 | 1430 |

1977 جَريح *n./adj.* pl. جَرْحَى wounded, injured
من بين الجرحى الثلاثين، خمسة بحالة الخطر — Among the thirty wounded, five were in serious condition
83 | 1470 |

1978 مُسْتَشار *n.* counselor, adviser
يبدأ المستشار الشخصي للامين العام للامم المتحدة مايكل ويليامز غدا زيارة للبنان — The personal counselor to the Secretary General of the United Nations Michael Williams began a visit to Lebanon yesterday
78 | 1571 |

1979 اِمْتَلَكَ *v. VIII* to possess, own sth
الجامعة تركز على تكوين طلاب يمتلكون مهارات ذهنية واجتماعية عالية — The university is concentrating on creating students who have high intellectual and social skills
86 | 1419 |

1980 جِنْس *n.* gender, sex; sexual intercourse; type, kind
لا أكتمك القول أني أصبت بعقدة تجاه الجنس الآخر ، جعلتني شديد النفور منهن — I won't hide from you the statement that I have been struck by a complex toward the opposite sex, which has made me feel an aversion for them
87 | 1405 |

1981 غِذاء *n.* pl. أَغْذِيَة food, nourishment
كان يتناول الغذاء الصحي المفيد ولم يتوقف يوما عن تناول عسل النحل — He was eating healthy, beneficial food, and he didn't stop eating bee's honey for a single day
84 | 1450 |

1982 جاي (Dia.) *a.p.* (fem. جايَة, pl. جايِين) coming, arriving; *adj.* next; (with object pron.) جايَك coming to (see) you
أنا هنا في لندن بقالي سبع شهور.. كنت جاي أحضر للماجستير — I have been here in London for seven months...I came to prepare my masters degree
42 | 2862 | +spo

1983 سِلْميّ *adj.* peaceful
خرجوا بانتظام في مظاهرة سلمية احتجاجا على غلاء الوقود — They went out in an orderly fashion in a peaceful demonstration protesting the high price of fuel
77 | 1576 |

1984 جَنْب *n.* side; جَنْباً إلى جَنْب next to; side by side; جمب (Egy.) /gamb/, (Lev.) /jamb/; (for Irq.Gul. see يم /yamm/)
ضحكتا معا وراحتا تمشيان جنبا الى جنبها وكأنهما فراشتان — They laughed together and started to walk side by side as if they were butterflies
94 | 1300 |

1985 تَجَمُّع *n.* pl. -aat gathering, assembly; grouping
المسلمون والسيخ والهندوس يميلون إلى التجمع في الأحياء نفسها — The Muslims, Sikhs, and Hindus tend to gather in the same quarters
93 | 1313 |

1986 فَحْص *n.* pl. فُحُوص, فُحُوصات examination, check-up (medical), test (blood, IQ)
ينبغي الوقاية بعمل الفحص الطبي قبل الزواج ومعرفة فصيلة الدم للأفراد المقبلين على الزواج — It is necessary to take the precaution of having a medical exam before marriage, and to know the blood type of the individuals approaching marriage
92 | 1320 |

1987 سَعْي *n.* endeavor, pursuit; striving, endeavoring
هاجروا إلى فرنسا سعيا وراء الرزق — They emigrated to France, searching for a living
85 | 1436 |

1988 آلَة *n.* pl. -aat instrument, device; apparatus, appliance, machine
إنه يستعمل الكلام كما يستعمل قائد السيارة آلة التنبيه، فقط عندما لا يكون هناك مفر من ذلك — He uses words like a car driver uses his horn, only when there is no way to get out of it
92 | 1317 |

1989 عَريض *adj.* wide, broad; bold (line)
تنظر له بابتسامة عريضة — She is looking at him with a broad smile
96 | 1266 |

1990 رَفيق *n.* pl. رفاق companion, partner, colleague; comrade; رِفْقات (Lev.) friends, buddies, companions
في احدى المعارك حوصر مع رفاقه فوق قمة جبل وكاد يموت من العطش — In one of the battles he was surrounded, with his companions, on top of a mountain, and he almost died of thirst
89 | 1368 |

1991 تَسْليم *n.* delivery, handing over; surrender
بكل هدوء تم تسليم الطعام وصب الشاي وإغلاق باب الزنزانة — The food was delivered in complete calm, and tea was poured, and the door of the cell was shut
85 | 1429 |

1992 إسْتِعْمال *n.* use, usage; handling; application
يقال إن المرأة تحب استعمال عطر الرجل الذي تحبه — It is said that women love using the perfume of the man they love
85 | 1430 |

1993 عَكَسَ *v. I* (i) to reflect, mirror (light, image); to contradict or oppose sb
ان كلام أمها لا يعكس الحقيقة كلها — The words of her mother do not reflect the whole truth
83 | 1452 |

1994 رَوَى *v. I* (i) to tell, narrate sth; to report, provide an account of sth
أخذ نفسا طويلا من سيجارة اشعلها، واستمر يروي وكأنه يواصل حديثا لم ينقطع — He took a long drag on a cigarette he lit, and continued to tell his story as if he was continuing talking without a break
80 | 1503 |

1995 كَشْف *n.* revelation, disclosure, report; النِّقاب عن exposing, uncovering sth; examination, detection
نقل مسؤول اسرائيلي رفيع المستوى طلب عدم الكشف عن اسمه عن الوزير افي ديشتر ان الحكومة يجب ان تراجع سياستها في قطاع غزة بسبب استمرار اطلاق صواريخ منها — A highly placed Israeli official who asked that his name not be revealed quoted the minister Avi Dichter saying that the government must review its policy in the Gaza Strip because of the continuation of the launching of rockets from it
84 | 1430 |

1996 خُطُورَة *n.* significance, importance; seriousness, gravity; danger
قال ديمتري آسفا إنه يتمنى لو أدرك الفتى خطورة المسألة وتركها تمر بسلام — Dimitri said sorrowfully that he hoped the boy would realize the seriousness of the issue and let her go in peace
84 | 1441 |

1997 عِشْرِين *n.* twentieth year; العِشْرِينات the Twenties

— كان المقاتلون في معظمهم شبابا تحت العشرين

The fighters, for the most part, were kids under the age of twenty

88 | 1367 |

1998 ذَنْب *n.* pl. ذُنُوب fault, offense, misdeed

الأسوأ من هذا كله شعوري بالذنب لأني أفسدت السهرة وتسببت في مشكلة للدكتور جراهام —

Worse than all that was my feeling of guilt because I wrecked the evening and caused a problem for Dr Graham

83 | 1448 |

1999 تَفْسِير *n.* explanation, commentary; Tafsir (Qur'anic exegesis)

وقفت أمامه إحسان ذاهلة لا تقوي على تفسير ما حدث وكيف حدث — Ihsan stood in front of him confused, unable to explain what happened and how it happened

86 | 1396 |

2000 جَناح *n.* pl. أَجْنِحَة wing (of a bird, airplane, building; army wing; political wing; wing position (in soccer and basketball); flank

لا تريد منه أكثر من رحلة تستعير بها أجنحة البلابل وتطير — She doesn't want anything more from him than a trip with which to borrow the wings of a nightingale and fly

87 | 1379 |

2001 قُطْعَة *n.* parcel (of land), plot, lot

جاءت المعلمة وفي يدها قطعة شوكولاتة وعلبة عصير — The teacher came with a piece of chocolate and a can of juice in her hand

87 | 1382 |

2002 فِعْلِيّ *adj.* actual, real; de facto; فِعْلِيّاً really, actually

لا يزال الطريق طويلا فتركيا لن تنضم فعليا لعضوية الاتحاد الأوروبي قبل مرور ١٠ سنوات على الأقل — The road is still long, since Turkey will not in actuality join the European Union before the passing of 10 years at least

82 | 1468 |

2003 مَذْكُور *adj.* mentioned, cited

أكد رئيس اللجنة المذكورة أنه لا توجد حتى الآن أية إصابة بشرية بهذا المرض — The head of the mentioned committee stressed that till now there have been no human casualties from this illness

82 | 1456 |

2004 كُلِّيّ *adj.* complete, total, full, entire; كُلِّيّاً completely, entirely

أفاد مسئولون فلسطينيون أن الجيش الصهيوني انسحب كليا فجر اليوم الخميس من بيت حانون — Palestinian officials said that the Zionist army withdrew completely at dawn today, Thursday, from Bet Hanun

92 | 1303 |

2005 قَضائِيّ *adj.* judicial, legal

قد رفعت بعض الموظفات دعاوى قضائية على شركة بلومبيرغ وفي إحداها اتهمن بلومبيرغ شخصيا بالتحرش الجنسي في مكان العمل — Some of the employees filed a lawsuit against the Bloomberg Company, and in one of them they accused Bloomberg, personally, of sexual harassment in the workplace

76 | 1581 |

2006 مُعامَلَة *n.* pl. -aat treatment, procedure; dealing with

لا أستطيع أن أحتمل هذه المعاملة.. (تنهمر عيناها بالدمع) هذا لا يطاق! — I can't bear this treatment...(her eyes fill with tears). This is unbearable!

91 | 1307 |

2007 ضاعَ *v.* I (i) to disappear, vanish

يجب أن يتصرف بسرعة وإلا ضاع كل شيء — He must act quickly, or else everything would be lost

94 | 1263 |

2008 مَنْح *n.* granting, bestowing, awarding

في قسم الشرطة اعترفت بجريمتها وعزت تصرفها لعدم منحها إجازة أسبوعية وعدم السماح لها بالخروج مع أحد أبناء بلدتها — In the police station she confessed her crime, and attributed her behavior to her not being granted a weekly vacation, and her not being allowed to go out with one of her compatriots

82 | 1444 |

26 Religion

11	الله	God	1580	شيطان	Satan, the devil	2802	فتوى	religious ruling
184	إسلامي	Islamic	1591	دعاء	invocation, request, calling upon God	2812	جامع	mosque
194	ربّ	Lord				2922	شرع	law
229	مسلم	Muslim				2992	آخرة	the hereafter
296	حمد	praise				3044	كفر	unbelief, apostasy
333	دين	religion	1639	مقدس	holy	3059	خطبة	sermon
364	صحيح	authentic (Hadith)	1688	حرم	holy site; campus	3067	جحيم	hell
365	إسلام	Islam	1713	شيعة	Shiites	3143	فضيلة	eminence
420	تعالى	to be exalted	1725	سنّة	the Sunna, Sunnis	3147	أخطأ	to make a mistake
470	صلّى	to pray	1803	مبارك	blessed	3183	إنشالله	if God wills
494	دنيا	world	1811	سنّي	Sunni	3223	مسيح	messiah
523	رسول	messenger	1872	شيعي	Shiite	3290	نبوي	prophetic
582	دعوة	missionary work	1907	طائفة	sect	3292	ارتكاب	committing, perpetrating
635	صلاة	prayer	1928	بركة	blessing	3300	بسم	in the name of
691	ديني	religious	1998	ذنب	sin, fault	3373	مفتي	mufti (Muslim legal scholar)
702	يهودي	Jewish	1999	تفسير	Qur'anic exegesis			
784	اللهم	O God	2039	مجاهد	(Muslim) warrior	3376	هيكل	temple
811	خطأ	mistake				3470	صيام	fasting
813	نبي	prophet	2056	كنيسة	church	3475	فقه	Islamic jurisprudence
837	القرآن	the Qur'an	2141	ارتكب	to commit (error)			
852	مسجد	mosque	2201	قارئ	Qur'anic reciter	3480	خلاص	salvation
869	عالم	(religious) scholar	2225	مولى	master, lord	3530	تضحية	sacrifice
889	وقف	religious endowment	2238	سورة	Surah	3580	محرّم	forbidden
			2292	ملاك	angel	3581	حرمة	taboo; married woman
971	بارك	to bless	2317	شريعة	Islamic law	3646	كافر	infidel
984	جنّة	heaven	2341	هدى	guidance	3652	هدى	to lead, guide
1059	سبحان	praise	2373	حجاب	veil, head scarf	3655	خالق	creator
1102	إمام	person who leads prayers	2380	خاطئ	mistaken	3680	جهنّم	hell
1144	مؤمن	believer	2397	حلال	permissible	3770	فطر	end of Ramadan fast
1155	حجّ	pilgrim	2463	حجّ	pilgrimage	3782	فقيه	expert in Islamic jurisprudence
1261	حرام	forbidden	2488	مذهب	sect			
1302	إيمان	faith	2578	آمين	amen			
1308	شرعي	lawful	2588	عقيدة	doctrine	3799	وحي	inspiration
1411	آمن	to believe	2660	بابا	pope	3826	صليب	cross
1436	آية	verse of Qur'an	2678	قيامة	resurrection (Judgement Day)	3898	صحابة	companions of the Prophet
1443	جهاد	struggle (for God)				3934	حنيف	orthodox
1560	فتنة	unrest, disturbance				3966	حرّم	to forbid
						3976	مصل	praying
1561	مسيحي	Christian	2719	عبادة	worship	3999	نقاب	full veil

4006	زكاة	zakat alms	4335	إفطار	meal breaking Ramadan fast for the day	4797	معشر	assembly (يا معشر المسلمين)
4049	فداء	sacrifice				4798	ملا	mullah (Muslim cleric)
4052	برّ	righteousness	4349	فاتحة	opening Surah	4804	نصراني	Christian
4105	رحمن	merciful	4395	فردوس	paradise	4820	أسلم	to become a Muslim
4130	إلهي	divine	4457	أذان	call to prayer			
4194	قبلة	prayer direction	4461	عافى	to heal, cure	4823	نبوّة	prophecy, prophethood
4200	توبة	repentance	4550	مسيحية	Christianity			
4217	معجزة	miracle	4551	ديانة	religion	4852	عمرة	lesser pilgrimage
4223	صوم	fasting	4607	أضحى	sacrifice	4866	مغفور	the late, deceased
4238	تبارك	to be blessed, praised	4608	إمساك	start of Ramadan fast			
4240	عاذ	to seek refuge (in God)	4644	عشاء	evening prayer	4890	استغفر	to beg God for forgiveness
4288	علماني	secular	4647	عذراء	virgin	4942	مستقيم	righteous
4292	سماوي	heavenly	4656	قرآني	Qur'anic	4955	صليبي	cross-shaped; Crusader
4299	جاهلية	pre-Islamic period, age of ignorance	4684	فريضة	religious duty	4975	مصحف	copy of Quran
			4724	اجتهاد	reinterpreting the Qur'an			
4309	تقوى	piety	4731	بطريرك	Patriarch			

2009 اتَّجَهَ *v. VIII* to turn, face إلى/نحو towards; to go, proceed إلى to/towards; to be directed, be aimed إلى at

اتجها وحدهما يسارا باتجاه السينما بينما اتجهت هي يمينا نحو شقتها — They went by themselves to the left in the direction of the cinema, while she went to the right towards her apartment

88 | 1349 |

2010 وارد *adj.* arriving, coming; imported; recently arrived; apparent, showing; appearing, mentioned; *n.* الواردات imports

التغير وارد بل ضروري كما ان دوام الحال من المحال — Change is possible, in fact it is necessary, and staying in the same situation is impossible

84 | 1420 |

2011 رَقابَة *n.* censorship; surveillance; supervision, oversight

منعت الرقابة لمدة طويلة مسرحيته «إفرايم يعود إلى الجيش» — The censors banned his play "Ephraim Returns to the Army" for a long time

85 | 1404 |

2012 وِلادَة *n.* birth; childbearing, parturition

قال التقرير إن السويد هي الدولة التي تؤمن أفضل الخدمات الصحية أثناء الولادة وبعدها — The report said that Sweden was the country which guarantees the best health services during birth and after it

86 | 1385 |

2013 رَصيد *n.* balance; funds; stock, inventory

يكتشف احمد أن لديه في رصيده البنكي مليون دينار — Ahmad discovers that he has in his bank account a million dinars

83 | 1430 |

2014 تَوَلَّى *v. V* to take charge of sth, to be in charge of sth; to seize control of sth; to go by, pass, be gone; to turn away عن from

أعلنت في صفحاتها الأولى اسم القائد الألماني الذي يتولى قوات المحور في ليبيا الآن.. إنه إيروين روميل — It announced in its first pages the name of the German leader who would take over the Axis forces in Libya now...he is Erwin Rommel

85 | 1392 |

2015 رَحيل *n.* departure; death, demise
اعرف انك لن ترحلي بدوني ولكن الرحيل ليس
حلا.. الحل هو أن نتخلص من سبب مشكلاتنا —
I know that you will not travel without me,
but traveling is not the solution...The
solution is that we get rid of the cause of
our problems
87 | 1366 |

2016 مُتَأَخِّر *adj.* pl. -uun late, delayed; مُتَأَخِّراً late,
too late
عاد عتريس إلى أصدقائه، يسهر لوقت متأخر من
الليل دون فائدة، ويعود إلى عمله متعبا — Atris
returned to his friends, staying up late at
night to no avail, and returning to work
tired
96 | 1230 |

2017 عُمانِيّ *n./adj.* Omani
قد نتج عن الحادث ستة إصابات ووفاة واحدة من
الجنسية العمانية — The accident left six wounded
and one Omani national dead
48 | 2475 | +news

2018 أَعْرَبَ *v. IV* to express, indicate, manifest
عن (opinion, sentiment)
أردت أن أعرب لك عن مشاعرى — I wanted to
express my feelings to you
69 | 1716 | +news

2019 مَخاطِر *pl.n.* dangers, perils; adventures
رددت عليه كل ما تلقته فى المدرسة عن مخاطر
المخدرات، لكنه ضحك وقال ببساطة: من لم يجرب
المزاج ليس من حقه أن يتحدث عنه — She
repeated to him everything that she received
at school about the danger of drugs, but he
laughed and said simply: he who has not
experienced the mood does not have the right
to talk about it
82 | 1440 |

2020 أَخْرَجَ *v. IV* to take out sth; to expel, oust sb;
to emit, send out sth; to direct (film); to
stage (play); to produce, publish sth
مد رأفت يده ببطء إلى جيبه وأخرج محفظة نقوده
— Ra'fat put his hand slowly into his pocket and
pulled out his wallet
84 | 1394 |

2021 ههه *interj.* (laughter) ha-ha-ha, he-he-he
(written in varying lengths: ههههه, هه, etc.)
يعنى اذا دخلتى هنا مش حتخرجى الا اخر اليوم
ههه — Well, if you enter here you won't leave
until the end of the day, ha ha ha
35 | 3366 | +for

2022 رَحَّبَ *v. II* to welcome, receive ب sth/sb
إذا رفضت المرأة إعطاءك تليفونها أو اعتذرت عن
دعوتك للعشاء يكون معنى ذلك أنها لا ترحب
بالعلاقة معك — If the woman refuses to give
you her telephone number, or if she excuses
herself from an invitation to dinner, that would
mean that she does not welcome a relationship
with you
87 | 1347 |

2023 تَقْليد *n.* pl. تَقاليد tradition, custom
معظم هؤلاء المتعلمين ما استطاعوا أن يعصموا
أنفسهم من سيطرة التقاليد الطائفية على مشاعرهم
— Most of these educated people were not
able to defend themselves from the control of
sectarian traditions over their feelings
90 | 1312 |

2024 تَخَلُّص *n.* escape, freedom (مِن from); getting
rid (مِن of)
تسعى الوزارة للتخلص تدريجيا من هذه الابنية التي
لا توفر البيئة التعليمية المناسبة — The ministry is
striving gradually to get rid of the buildings
which don't provide an appropriate
educational environment
86 | 1367 |

2025 حَذَّرَ *v. II* to warn, caution sb من of
تحذر دراسة أمريكية من تناول الأطفال للبطاطس
المحمرة — An American study warns against
children eating fried potatoes
84 | 1390 |

2026 مُخْتَصّ *adj.* responsible; competent,
specialized; *n.* pl. -uun specialist, expert
عملت وزارة الصحة واليونيسيف على بناء قدرات
المختصين في المجال الصحي في عدة مستشفيات
ومراكز لتعزيز الرضاعة الطبيعية — The Ministry
of Health and UNICEF worked on building the
capabilities of specialists in the health field in
several hospitals and centers in order to
promote natural nursing
77 | 1520 |

2027 تَفْعِيل *n.* putting into effect, activating
أكد سموه على أهمية تفعيل الاتفاقيات المبرمة بين البلدين في المجالات المختلفة — His highness stressed the importance of putting the agreements concluded between the two countries in various fields into effect

67 | 1756 |

2028 كِيلُو *n.* kilo, kilogram; (Dia.) kilometer
هذا الكيس فيه خمسة كيلو سكر — This sack has five kilos of sugar in it

88 | 1335 |

2029 اِقْتِراح *n.* proposal, suggestion
حث الرأي العام وأعضاء الكونغرس على تبني الاقتراح الذي تقدم به دونالد رامسفيلد في هذا الشأن — He urged public opinion and the members of Congress to adopt the suggestion which Donald Rumsfeld submitted on this matter

83 | 1412 |

2030 أَدَبِيّ *adj.* literary; ethical, moral
هذا هو أول مؤتمر ينعقد حول إبداع نجيب محفوظ الأدبي، ويشارك فيه عدد كبير من الباحثين والنقاد — This is the first conference to be held concerning the literary creativity of Naguib Mahfouz, and a large number of researchers and critics are participating in it

89 | 1311 |

2031 اِبْتِسامَة *n.* smile
تطلعت إليه بابتسامة باهتة، ثم طبعت على خده قبلة سريعة — She looked at him with a ravishing smile, and then planted a quick kiss on his cheek

80 | 1470 | +lit

2032 اِخْتِبار *vn.* testing, experimenting, probing; *n.* pl. -aat test, experiment, probe
ينظر بعين واحدة داخل أنبوبة اختبار زجاجية وكأنه يفحص ماسورة بندقية — He looks with one eye inside a glass test tube as if he were investigating the barrel of a rifle

79 | 1477 |

2033 لَحِقَ *v. I (a)* to follow, be attached to; to befall, afflict, hit, strike بـ sb (calamity, tragedy, damages, losses)

إننا شهود عيان على الخراب والدمار الذي يلحق بوطننا — We are eyewitnesses to the destruction and devastation which are afflicting our country

97 | 1206 |

2034 واقِف *adj.* standing; stopped
ظل رأفت واقفا وسط الصالة وكأنه لا يدري ماذا يصنع بعد ذلك — Ra'fat stayed standing in the middle of the hall as if he did not know what to do after that

85 | 1372 |

2035 أَعْجَبَ *v. IV* to delight, please sb (يُعْجِبُنِي it pleases me = I like it); (pass.) أُعْجِبَ بـ to admire, be amazed at sth
ما الذى يعجبك فى الممثل أبو اسم صعب هذا؟ — What do you like about this actor with the hard name?

78 | 1486 |

2036 قَعَدَ *v. I (u)* to sit down, be seated; (Dia.) stay, remain; (with imperf.) continue to do sth
لطاف بشكل ماقولكش وانا حبيتهم جدا جدا يعنى و نفسى يقعدوا معانا كتير بس هم مش حيقدروا يقعدوا اكتر من يوم السبت — They are so nice, I can't tell you, I really really liked them, and I want them to stay with us a lot but they aren't able to stay more than Saturday

53 | 2170 | +spo

2037 مُقِيم *n.* resident; *a.p.* residing في at (a location)
كان من المقيمين في الكويت آنذاك لعمل والده في السفارة السعودية هناك — He was among those living in Kuwait at the time because of his father's working in the Saudi Embassy there

90 | 1285 |

2038 تَوَصُّل *n.* arrival; attainment, achievement
إذا لم نتمكن من التوصل إلى هذا الحل القائم على وجود الدولتين، لن نتمكن من تحقيق السلام بين الإسرائيليين والعرب — If we can't achieve this solution based on two states, we won't be able to achieve peace between the Israelis and Arabs

74 | 1556 |

2039 مُجاهِد *adj.* fighting; *n.* pl. -uun fighter, warrior; (pl.) mujahideen (Muslim warriors)

قد التحق بصفوف المجاهدين وعمره لم يتجاوز السابعة عشرة — He joined the ranks of the Mujahideen when he was not yet seventeen years old

72 | 1597 |

2040 دَخْل *n.* income, revenue; (with pron.) دَخْلَك! (Lev.) Please! I'm begging you!

إن الحكومة بصدد الإعلان عن إجراءات جديدة لتشجيع محدودي الدخل على الاستفادة من نظام التمويل العقاري للحصول على مسكن — The government is in the process of announcing new measures to encourage those of limited income to take advantage of the real estate funding system to obtain housing

85 | 1365 |

2041 شَدَّدَ *v. II* to strengthen, intensify, emphasize sth

شدد دنانه من حصار زوجته والتحريض بها، وهو ينتظر اللحظة التي تنهار فيها وتقدم له الاعتذار اللائق — Danana strengthened the siege and incitement around his wife, waiting for the moment in which she would collapse and offer him an appropriate apology

71 | 1630 | +news

2042 حَدّ (Egy.Lev.) *n.* someone, anyone; ماحد /ma-Hadd/ and ماحدش /ma-Hadd-ish/ nobody; محد and محمد /maHHad/ (Irq.Gul.) nobody

الظاهر مفيش حد إلا احنا — It looks like there's no one here but us

28 | 4144 |

2043 تَداوُل *n.* circulation, dissemination; alternation; consultation, deliberation

تضاعف حجم التداول وزاد صافي الاستثمارات الأجنبية إلى ٣٠٩ مليار دولار — The volume of trading doubled, and net foreign investments increased to 309 billion dollars

74 | 1545 |

2044 تَسَبَّبَ *v. V* to cause, result in في/ب sth

صدر قرار من مجلس المدينة بمنع تشييد البيوت الخشبية لأنها تسببت في انتشار النار — A decree was issued by the city council to forbid building wooden houses because they caused the spread of the fire

82 | 1405 |

2045 مُخَصَّص *adj.* designated, singled out; allocated, set aside

كان عليكم أن تسلكوا الطريق المخصص للأجانب، فهذه السيدة كما أرى أجنبية — You needed to go on the road designated for foreigners, since this woman, as I see, is a foreigner

84 | 1376 |

2046 عادِل *adj.* fair, just, honest, equitable

إن كل شخص يعتقد نفسه الوحيد العادل على الأرض — Every person believes himself to be the only just person on earth

84 | 1372 |

2047 وَفاء *n.* loyalty, allegiance, faithfulness; *vn.* fulfillment (promise, obligation)

هو الصديق الوفي لسوريا كان يعلم معنى الصداقة والوفاء ومستلزماتها واولها النصح والنصيحة الاخوية الصادقة لا المداهنة والنفاق — He is a loyal friend of Syria, he knew the meaning of friendship and loyalty and their requirements, the first of them being advice, brotherly, honest, friendly advice, not flattery and hypocrisy

87 | 1313 |

2048 كَهْرُبائيّ and كَهْرَبائيّ *adj.* electrical; *n.* pl. -uun electrician

دخلنا إلى مبنى أنيق من دورين عليه لافتة كهربائية مضيئة مكتوب عليها «بيانو بار» — We entered an elegant building, two stories high, with an electric lit sign on which was written "Piano Bar"

82 | 1402 |

2049 عَميل *n.* pl. عُمَلاء agent, representative; lackey, stooge; operative, spy; client, customer

كل خريجي قصر العيني يعرفونه لأنه عميل للمباحث — All the graduates of Qasr Al-Aini know him because he is an agent of state security

84 | 1360 |

2050 خالي *adj.* empty, devoid, free (مِن of)

تحسس مفتاح النور وضغط عليه.. كان القبو خالِيًا إلا من بعض الأشياء التي خزنتها كريس تمهيدا للتخلص منها — He groped around for the flashlight, and pushed on it...The hall was empty except for some things which Chris had stored in preparation for getting rid of them

88 | 1302 |

2051 عَسَل *n.* honey

— سافر العروسان لقضاء شهر العسل في تركيا

The couple travelled to spend their honeymoon in Turkey

83 | 1383 | +for

2052 تُونِسِيّ *n./adj.* Tunisian

على الجانب الآخر فإن المعارضة التونسية الفعالة في الخارج تواجه مشكلة عدم توحيد الكلمة أو الرأي

— On the other hand, the effective Tunisian opposition abroad faces the problem of disunity in both word and opinion

68 | 1667 |

2053 قَبْض *n.* arrest, seizure, capture

— الشرطة جادة في إلقاء القبض على هذه العصابة

The police are diligently arresting this gang

85 | 1340 |

2054 برا and بره /barra/ (Dia.) *prep.* outside; *adv.* out, outside, outdoors

وعلى فكرة ممكن انك تعملي أقراص القطايف في البيت أو إنك تشتريها جاهزة من بره — By the way, you can make the Atayif crepes at home or you can buy them ready-made from outside

55 | 2069 | +spo

2055 عَزَّ *v. I (i)* to be strong, be dear; الله عَزَّ وَجَلَّ God Almighty

ابتدأ الحفل بآيات من كتاب الله عز وجل، تلتها كلمة ترحيبية مؤثرة — The ceremony began with verses from the Qurʾan, followed by a touching welcome speech

85 | 1345 |

2056 كَنِيسَة *n.* pl. كَنَائِس church; temple

أمر تشرشل أن تدق أجراس الكنائس في لندن لأول مرة منذ اندلاع الحرب — Churchill ordered that the church bells be rung in London for the first time since the outbreak of the war

79 | 1430 |

2057 اِخْتَفَى *v. VIII* to disappear, vanish; to hide; to be absent

ا — ظللت أتابعه بنظري حتى اختفى عبر باب البار continued to follow him with my gaze until he disappeared through the door of the bar

86 | 1321 |

2058 صَدَد *n.* في صَدَدِ in/with regard to; في هذا الصَّدَد in this respect, in this regard

كما يشير الكاتب إلى نقطة أخرى في هذا الصدد وهي أن الاقتصاد الأوكراني يعتمد على تحويلات ملايين الأوكرانيين الذين يعملون في روسيا — The author points out something else in this regard and that is that the Ukrainian economy relies on the remittances of millions of Ukrainians who work in Russia

80 | 1426 |

2059 كَمَنَ *v. I (u)* and كَمِنَ *(a)* to lie, be hidden in (said of an answer or solution); to consist of (said of a problem or issue) في

أغلب المشكلات الزوجية تكمن أسبابها في عدم الإصغاء — The causes of most marital problems are to be found in not listening

82 | 1380 |

2060 لَيْتَ and يا لَيْتَ *part.* if only, would that; (with pron.) لَيْتَنِي I wish; لَيْتَ شِعْرِي I wish I knew

ليت صوتها يباع في الصيدليات لأشتريه.. إنني أحتاج صوتها لأعيش — I wish her voice could be sold at pharmacies, so I could buy it...I need her voice to be able to live

63 | 1791 |

2061 عائد *a.p.* returning إلى to, being attributed to; *n.* pl. -aat revenue, profit; royalty

سوف يضعها في البنك الأهلي كوديعة تدر عليه عائدا سنويا لا بأس به — He will put it in the National Bank as a deposit which will get a reasonable yearly return

88 | 1291 |

2062 مُؤَلِّف *n.* author, composer

في هذا الكتاب يقوم المؤلف برصد وتحليل استراتيجية أمريكا في الحرب على الإرهاب — In this book the author examines and analyzes America's strategy in the War on Terrorism

74 | 1536 |

2063 ناتِج *a.p.* resulting, ensuing عن/من from; *n.* الناتِج المَحَلِّي الإجْمالِي the gross domestic product

لجأت بعض الدول النامية إلى الإجراءات التعويضية لتقليل الآثار السلبية الناتجة عن تخفيض الدعم بالنسبة لهذه الفئة — Some developing countries

resorted to compensatory measures to lessen the negative effects resulting from a reduction in support regarding this sector

81 | 1390 |

2064 قَصْف *n.* bombardment, shelling

قررت الخروج من مكاني رغم القصف المستمر ووميض الانفجارات — I decided to go out of my place despite the continual bombing and the flash of explosions

77 | 1457 |

2065 فَتَىً *n.* pl. فِتْيَة young man, adolescent, youth

كان متحيرا للغاية فى أمر ذلك الفتى الصغير شبه المجنون الذى يفاجأ به دائما يقف جواره — He was extremely confused about the matter of this young, half-crazy boy who always surprised him by showing up standing next to him

81 | 1397 | +lit

2066 اِنْتَمَى *v. VIII* to belong إلى to, be affiliated with

لقد كانت تنتمي لجيل من النساء نذرن حياتهن للمطبخ — She belonged to a generation of women who devoted their lives to the kitchen

86 | 1319 |

2067 مَلَأَ *v. I (a)* to fill sth up بـ with; to fill out (form); to occupy (place); to fill (gap)

كانت رائحة البصل تملأ المكان خارج وداخل الكنيسة الصغيرة — The smell of onions filled the place outside and inside the small church

82 | 1383 | +lit

2068 مُخَطَّط *n.* pl. -aat plan, sketch; *adj.* planned; patterned (material, fabric, dress)

الام العاملة يجب ان يكون لديها مخطط واضح لحياتها وحياة اولادها — The working mother needs to have a clear plan for her life and the life of her children

81 | 1382 |

2069 لسه (also لسا and لسة)/lissa/ (Egy.Lev.Gul.) *adv.* yet, still; (with pron.; Lev.) لساتك /lissaat-ak/ you are still, لساتني /lissaat-ni/ I am still

لسه الطيارة ما وصلتش — The plane didn't arrive yet

42 | 2667 | +spo

2070 شاي *n.* tea

باكون شاكر قوي لو عملت لي شاي — I would be really grateful if you would make me some tea

84 | 1327 |

2071 هَزِيمَة *n.* defeat

وهرع العالم كي يفرض الهدنة على العرب كلما لمح هزيمة اليهود — The world hurried to impose a truce on the Arabs whenever it glimpsed the defeat of the Jews

84 | 1330 |

2072 قِطْعَة *n.* pl. قِطَع piece, portion, segment; قِطَع غِيار spare parts

ذهبت وحيدا إلى غرفتي وأنا أحمل تلك القطعة اليابسة من الخبز — I went by myself to my room carrying that dry piece of bread

97 | 1154 |

2073 اللَّذانِ *rel.pron.* (masc.du.; gen./acc. اللَّذَيْنِ) who, whom; which

هل سيبقى للوطنية التحديد والمفهوم ذاتها اللذان كانا لها في الماضي القريب والماضي البعيد؟ — Will "nationalism" keep the same definition and concept it had in the recent and distant past?

85 | 1322 |

2074 مُجَدَّد *adj.* renewed, renovated; مُجَدَّداً again, anew

عادت إلى مخيلته مجددا صورة منال، لم يكن قد نسيها طيلة هاته الأيام — The image of Manal came back to his imagination, he hadn't forgotten her throughout those days

81 | 1381 |

2075 جَزاء *n.* reward; punishment; penalty

هذا جزاء من يعصي أمري ويحاول الهروب من قبضتي — This is the reward of those who disobey my command, and try to escape my grasp

83 | 1338 |

2076 تَجْدِيد *n.* renovation, renewal

وضع نظام جديد لصرف مياه الامطار وتجديد أعمدة الانارة وتغيير الكشافات التالفة وتركيب العلامات الارشادية لكل كوبري — He set up a system for storm water drainage, upgrading lamp-posts, changing broken lights, and setting up road signs for all bridges

86 | 1300 |

2077 عَمَلِيّ *adj.* practical, pragmatic; عَمَلِيّاً in practice

الهجرة هي التطبيق العملي لهذه الرسالة الخالدة — Emigration is the pragmatic application of this eternal message

89 | 1250 |

2078 قِتال *n.* fighting, combat

اشتد القتال أمام لينينجراد، وبالطبع توقفت الغارات على لندن — The fighting intensified outside Leningrad, and naturally the raids on London stopped

82 | 1352 |

2079 سِيرة *n.* pl. سِيَر biography; epic

إن قراءة السيرة الذاتية للثوري الروسي ليون تروتسكي أثناء دراسته أقنعته بحتمية خوض غمار السياسة — Reading the autobiography of the Russian revolutionary Leon Trotsky during his studies convinced him of the certainty of his plunging into the fray of politics

94 | 1176 |

2080 بَطْن *n.* stomach, abdomen; inside, interior; depth, core

لم يستطع أن يغلق حزام البنطلون على بطنه، والتصق القميص بجسده لدرجة كادت تؤلمه — He was not able to close the belt of his pants over his belly, and his shirt stuck to his body to the point that it almost hurt him

87 | 1273 |

2081 شَرِبَ *v. I (a)* to drink (sth); (Dia.) to smoke (tobacco)

استيقظ في الصباح فاغتسل وتوضأ وصلى ثم جلس في الصالة يشرب الشاي ويدخن — He woke up in the morning, washed up, did his ablutions, prayed, and then sat in the hall drinking tea and smoking

86 | 1283 |

2082 مُسافِر *n.* pl. -uun traveler, passenger; *a.p.* traveling, away (on a trip)

بعد ذلك سيطلب منك ادخال بياناتك الشخصية وبيانات كل مسافر معك بالرحلة — After that it will ask you to enter your personal information and the information of each person traveling with you on the trip

94 | 1176 |

2083 تَعْريف *vn.* defining, identifying; introducing, presenting; *n.* definition; notification

سيكون هذا اللقاء فرصة للتعريف بدور و مسؤولية شركات النقل البحرية في المجال الأمني — This meeting will be an opportunity to get to know the role and responsibility of the sea transport companies in the security area

89 | 1251 |

2084 تَبَقَّى *v. V* to remain, be left over; to remain, stay (على in a state)

باستخدام ما تبقي من التمر ويامش رمضان يمكنك إعداد عصائر وحلويات شهية لاسرتك — By using what is left from the dates and dried fruits of Ramadan, you can prepare delicious juices and sweets for your family

93 | 1189 |

2085 كَفاءة *n.* pl. -aat qualification, competence; talent, ability, proficiency; كَفاءات talent, talented people

يتحول قطاع الكهرباء إلى قطاع على درجة أعلى من الكفاءة والإنتاجية — The electricity sector is being transformed into a more efficient and productive sector

80 | 1382 |

2086 لَهْجة *n.* tone, voice; pl. لَهَجات dialect

أنصحك بمشاهدة التليفزيون كثيرا حتى تتدربى على فهم اللهجة الأمريكية — I advise you to watch television a lot so that you can practice understanding the American dialect

93 | 1188 |

2087 نَظَرِيَّة *n.* pl. -aat theory

قال ان تلك الفترة شهدت انتشار نظريات جديدة في الأكاديميا الأميركية تركز على القواعد الألسنية — He said that this period witnessed the spread of new theories in American academia, which focused on linguistic rules

80 | 1374 |

2088 نَهَضَ *v. I (a)* to rise, awaken; to stand, be based على upon; to assume, take charge of ب sth

جرس التليفون ألح مرة بعد أخرى حتى نهضت في النهاية لترد — The telephone rang persistently time after time until she got up finally to answer it

78 | 1423 | +lit

27 Verb Form I

A list of up to the 10 most frequent of each category of verb listed below.

Sound a/u

266	ذَكَرَ	to mention
297	دَخَلَ	to enter
306	طَلَعَ	to appear, emerge
345	خَرَجَ	to exit
357	كَتَبَ	to write
408	حَدَثَ	to happen
443	بَلَغَ	to reach
445	حَصَلَ	to obtain
457	طَلَبَ	to request
478	نَظَرَ	to look at

Sound a/i

49	عَرَفَ	to know
334	حَمَلَ	to carry
613	رَجَعَ	to return
673	نَزَلَ	to descend; stay
681	قَدَرَ	to be able
772	كَشَفَ	to reveal
800	مَلَكَ	to own
874	عَقَدَ	to hold (meeting)
924	جَلَسَ	to sit
1025	سَبَقَ	to precede

Sound a/a

323	جَعَلَ	to make sb/sth do sth
456	فَعَلَ	to do
489	ذَهَبَ	to go
512	فَتَحَ	to open
611	ظَهَرَ	to appear
650	دَفَعَ	to push; pay
676	بَحَثَ	to search for; discuss
733	رَفَعَ	to lift, raise
787	سَمَحَ	to permit
954	نَجَحَ	to succeed

Sound i/a

137	عَمِلَ	to work
154	سَمِعَ	to hear, listen
377	عَلِمَ	to know
513	شَهِدَ	to witness
531	سَلِمَ	to be safe
580	فَهِمَ	to understand
619	لَعِبَ	to play

Sound a/u

1029	شَمِلَ	to include
1054	ضَحِكَ	to laugh
1097	قَبِلَ	to accept

Sound u/u

1925	كَبُرَ	to grow up; get bigger
2522	صَلُحَ	to be suitable
2544	صَعُبَ	to be difficult
2554	ثَبُتَ	to be confirmed
2729	كَثُرَ	to be numerous
2786	بَعُدَ	to be located
3167	قَرُبَ	to approach, draw near
3370	جَدُرَ	to be worth
3803	سَهُلَ	to be easy

Doubled a/u

396	رَدَّ	to answer, respond to
510	مَرَّ	to pass by
834	عَدَّ	to count
931	ضَمَّ	to include
1038	ظَنَّ	to think
1176	دَقَّ	to knock; strike; call
1513	دَلَّ	to point at
1574	حَطَّ	to put, place
1586	مَدَّ	to extend
1651	حَلَّ	to dissolve

Doubled a/i

78	تَمَّ	to be concluded
447	قَلَّ	to be less
495	حَبَّ	to love; want
1294	حَسَّ	to feel, sense
1950	جَلَّ	to be majestic
2055	عَزَّ	to be strong
2227	شَدَّ	to make sth strong
2728	حَقَّ	to be right
2942	صَحَّ	to be correct
3384	حَلَّ	to befall, strike

Doubled i/a

387	ظَلَّ	to stay, remain
1899	وَدَّ	to want, like
2819	مَسَّ	to touch
4768	مَلَّ	to get bored

Hamzated Initial

198	أَخَذَ	to take
1338	أَكَلَ	to eat
1779	أَمَلَ	to hope
2205	أَمَرَ	to order
4803	أَسِفَ	to feel

Hamzated Medial

325	سَأَلَ	to ask
4034	رَأَسَ	to head

Hamzated Final a/a

172	بَدَأَ	to begin
727	قَرَأَ	to read
2067	مَلَأَ	to fill
2398	لَجَأَ	to resort to
2634	نَشَأَ	to grow up
2997	هَدَأَ	to subside
4036	طَرَأَ	to happen; occur to

Hamzated Final u/a

4143	جَرُؤَ	to dare

Hamzated Double

4589	أَنَّ	to complain, moan
5282	أَمَّ	to visit
6306	أَبَّ	to desire

Assimilated a/i

139	وَجَدَ	to find
183	وَصَلَ	to arrive
260	وَجَبَ	to be necessary
487	وَقَفَ	to stop, stand
1186	وَصَفَ	to describe
1612	وَلَدَ	to give birth
1870	وَرَدَ	to arrive, show up
2682	وَعَدَ	to promise

Assimilated a/a

359	وَضَعَ	to put, place
459	وَقَعَ	to fall; take place; be located
1850	وَدَعَ	to allow
4449	وَهَبَ	to donate

Hollow a/u

10	كَانَ	to be
15	قَالَ	to say

102	قَامَ	to stand up; carry out
113	رَاحَ	to go
123	عَادَ	to return
282	شَافَ	to see
593	مَاتَ	to die
982	دَامَ	to last
1034	دَارَ	to turn; go around
1289	قَادَ	to lead; drive, pilot

Hollow a/i

180	صَارَ	to become
326	عَاشَ	to live
502	زَادَ	to increase
819	سَارَ	to walk
1046	جَابَ	to bring
1079	بَاتَ	to become; start; spend the night
1607	غَابَ	to be absent
1620	بَاعَ	to sell
1629	دَارَ	to do, make
1937	رَادَ	to want

Hollow a/a

214	زَالَ	to cease
985	كَادَ	to almost
1042	خَافَ	to fear
1268	نَامَ	to sleep
1825	نَالَ	to attain

Defective -aa/-uu

329	بَدا	to appear, seem
418	دَعا	to call; invite
964	رَجا	to hope
1901	عَلا	to rise, ascend
2136	خَلا	to be free of
2330	نَما	to grow, develop
3172	شَكا	to complain
3463	غَدا	to become
4056	تَلا	to follow; recite
4624	عَدا	to run, race

Defective -aa/-ii

138	عَنَى	to mean
224	حَكَى	to tell; speak
353	جَرَى	to occur, take place; run
417	دَرَى	to know
908	مَضَى	to pass, go by
976	كَفَى	to be enough

1006	بَغَى	to pursue; want, need
1138	قَضَى	to eliminate
1248	مَشَى	to walk, go
1846	جَزَى	to repay, reward

Defective -iya/-aa

257	بَقِيَ	to remain, stay
730	نَسِيَ	to forget
1128	لَقِيَ	to find; meet
1191	رَضِيَ	to be pleased, satisfied with
1679	خَشِيَ	to fear
2246	حَظِيَ	to enjoy; acquire
3525	خَفِيَ	to be hidden
3862	قَوِيَ	to be strong

Defective -aa/-aa

860	سَعَى	to strive for; pursue
3051	رَعَى	to graze, take to pasture; look after
3620	بَقَى	to become; to begin to do sth; to remain, stay

Defective -iya/-ii

1705	وَلِيَ	to follow; govern

Doubly Weak or "Mixed"

Hollow and Hamzated

109	جاء	to come
124	شاء	to want

Hamzated and Hollow

3009	آنَ	to come (of time)
4645	آلَ	to arrive
6848	آهَ	to moan, sigh

Hamzated and Defective

343	أَتَى	to come
3351	أَبَى	to refuse
5609	أَلَا	to neglect
7165	أَوَى	to retire, seek shelter

Assimilated and Defective

1705	وَلِيَ	to follow, come after; govern
3510	وَعَى	to be aware of
5661	وَفَى	to fulfill
6168	وَسُعَ	to be spacious

Assimilated, Hamzated and Defective

7666	وَأَدَ	to bury alive

Irregular Verbs

75	رَأَى	to see, believe
2644	حَيَّ	to live; experience
6237	إدَّى	to give

2089 شَفَة *n.* pl. شِفاه lip; edge, ridge, margin
حاول أن يتكلم، لكنها وضعت يدها على شفتيه برفق
— He tried to speak, but she put her hand on his lips gently
73 | 1515 | +lit

2090 مُشاهَدَة *n.* observation, viewing; inspection
أعلنت الحكومة نصف يوم عمل لإتاحة الفرصة
للمواطنين لمشاهدة المباراة — The government announced a half work day to give citizens the opportunity to watch the match
81 | 1366 | +for

2091 أَبْدَى *v. IV* to show, demonstrate sth; to express sth
بدأ كل واحد يبدي رأيه في كيفية الهرب — Everyone began to express his opinion about how to flee
90 | 1222 |

2092 ناقَشَ *v. III* to debate, argue (an issue, topic)
في هذه الصفحات سوف يناقش مع أصدقائه
موضوع الكتاب الذي قرأوه مسبقا — In these pages he will discuss with his friends the subject of the book that they had previously read
75 | 1468 |

2093 اِسْتِثْناء *n.* exception, exclusion; بِاسْتِثْناء with the exception (of)
وفي هذه الفترة توسع الزحف العمراني في كافة
اتجاهات المدينة باستثناء الغرب لوجود المنطقة الاثرية
التي يحظر البناء فيها — In this period urban sprawl expanded in all directions from the city except in the west because of the existence of an archeological area on which building is forbidden
84 | 1313 |

2094 غَزْو *n.* invasion, raid

ان إيران وقفت في السابق مع الكويت ضد الغزو العراقي وخصصت كل إمكاناتها لصالح الكويت — Iran previously stood with Kuwait against the Iraqi invasion and set aside all its capabilities for the benefit of Kuwait

84 | 1312 |

2095 رَمْل *n.* pl. رمال sand

وجد نفسه فجأة يقف وسط رمال مترامية من كل جهة ولم يعد يعرف الشمال من الجنوب — He suddenly found himself standing in the middle of a vast sea of sand on every side, and he didn't know north from south

86 | 1276 |

2096 عَلَّق *v. II* to comment على on sth; to hang, suspend sth; to postpone sth; to hang up (the phone) على on sb

كان يتكلم بطريقة عادية وكأنه يعلق على سوء الجو أو ازدحام الطريق — He spoke in a normal way, as if he were commenting on the bad weather or the congestion in the streets

93 | 1183 |

2097 نَفَعَ *v. I (a)* to be useful ل to/for sb

تناولت الأم أدويتها التي إن لم تكن تنفع فهي لا تضر — The mother took her medicine which, although it didn't do any good, didn't do any harm either

92 | 1193 |

2098 بِضْعَة *n.* fem. بِضْع (as numbers 3–10) some, several; بِضْعَة أَيَّام several days, بِضْع ساعاتٍ several hours

دكتور أرجوك اسمح لي أن أرى ماما ولو بضع دقائق.. أريد أن ألمس يدها.. أريد أن أقبلها.. — Doctor, I beg you, permit me to see mother even if only for a few minutes...I want to touch her hand...I want to kiss her

86 | 1266 |

2099 أَصْفَر *adj.* fem. صَفْراء, pl. صُفْر yellow

أما حمزة، فقد تحول وجهه الأحمر إلى الأصفر المائل إلى الزرقة — As for Hamza, his red face changed to bluish-yellow

92 | 1194 |

2100 حَيَوِيّ *adj.* vital; lively; biological; مُضاد حَيَوِيّ antibiotic

البعض يقترح أن يشمل التخصيص قطاع النفط حتى يتمكن القطاع الخاص من لعب دور حيوي وفعال في النشاط الاقتصادي — Some suggest that privatization should include the oil sector so that the private sector could play a vital and effective role in economic activity

80 | 1371 |

2101 نَفَى *v. I (i)* to deny, disavow; reject

نفى المتهم أية علاقة له بالجريمة — The suspect denied any relation to the crime

83 | 1318 |

2102 رَكَّزَ *v. II* to focus, concentrate على sth; to emphasize على sth

ركز بصره على الصندوق وعلى اليد السوداء التي تحمله — He concentrated his gaze on the box, and on the black hand that was carrying it

84 | 1297 |

2103 دَعَمَ *v. I (a)* to support, back, bolster, promote sth/sb

جددت سوريا تأكيدها أنها تدعم لبنان، وايمانها بوحدة شعبه وسلامة أرضه وسيادته — Syria once again affirmed that it supports Lebanon, and stressed its faith in the unity of its people and the integrity of its land and sovereignty

80 | 1371 |

2104 شَغَلَ *v. I (a)* to occupy sth (a post or position); to preoccupy sb; to keep sb busy

بدا لها مجد الدين دائما في حالة صمت؛ ماذا يشغل باله هذه الأيام؟ — Magd Al-Din always appeared to her to be silent; what was occupying his mind these days?

97 | 1121 |

2105 كَلَّا *interj.* not at all, definitely not

سنصرخ في وجه الغزاة وبصوت واحد كلا وألف كلا.. لن نعيش عبيدا تحت أحذيتكم — We will scream in the face of the invaders, with one voice: No, and a thousand noes! We will not live as slaves under your shoes

70 | 1547 | +lit

2106 تَقْيِيم *n.* evaluation, assessment; rating

نبدأ بأمانة في إعادة تقييم ما الذي لا يزال بإمكاننا تحقيقه هناك — We are honestly starting to re-evaluate what we can still accomplish there

74 | 1456 |

2107 اِدَّعَى *v. VIII* to allege, claim أَنْ/بأَنَّ that

إذا كنت عاجزا عن قتل من تدعي كراهيته، فلا تقل إنك تكرهه — If you are incapable of killing someone you claim to hate, then don't say you hate him

86 | 1264 |

2108 إِلْغَاء *vn.* cancellation; abrogation, repeal

أضفنا بعض المطالب عن الإفراج عن المعتقلين وإلغاء المحاكم الاستثنائية ومنع التعذيب — We added some demands about freeing the prisoners, canceling the exceptional courts, and preventing torture

81 | 1342 |

2109 فَرْحَة *n.* joy, happiness

كادت الفرحة ترفع دميان من فوق الأرض — Joy almost lifted Dumyan off the ground

93 | 1166 |

2110 نِزَاع *n.* conflict, struggle

اشتد الجدل بين الإخوة الثلاثة وصاحب الجمل ودخلوا في نزاع حاد، ولكنهم اتفقوا أخيرا على اللجوء إلى القضاء — The argument between the three brothers and the owner of the camel grew intense, and they entered into a sharp conflict, but they finally agreed to resort to the courts

76 | 1415 |

2111 فيديو /viidiyo, vidyo/ *n.* video

يوفر الموقع افلام فيديو وتسجيلات صوتية، بالاضافة إلى تجول افتراضي في المسجد الاقصى — The site provides video films and sound recordings, in addition to a virtual tour of the Al-Aqsa Mosque

87 | 1238 |

2112 تَحَالُف *n.* alliance

الإرهاب يؤدي إلى بقاء قوات التحالف الدولي، الإرهاب يؤدي إلى فشل سياسي — Terrorism leads to the international allied forces remaining; terrorism leads to political failure

69 | 1573 |

2113 حُدُوث *n.* occurrence, happening, taking place

تضغط الدول حول العالم من أجل حدوث تغييرات في سلوك النظامين الايراني والكوري الشمالي — Countries around the world are pressuring for changes to take place in the behavior of the Iranian and North Korean regimes

81 | 1327 |

2114 إِجَازَة *n.* vacation, holiday, furlough, time off; permit, license, permission; pass, admission; certificate, degree, diploma

سنرفع تقريرنا بعد العودة من إجازة العطلة الصيفية، سواء قدم الجهاز تقريره او لم يقدمه — We will send in our report after returning from summer vacation, whether the agency submits its report or not

87 | 1244 |

2115 تَسْهِيل *n.* pl. -aat facilitation, assistance

تم الكشف عن عدد من الأفراد قدموا تسهيلات لوجستية مدفوعة الأجر للمجموعة التي نفذت العملية — A number of individuals were discovered who had offered paid logistical support to the group which carried out the operation

79 | 1355 |

2116 مَكَانَة *n.* position, standing, status, reputation

احتلت الأهرام مكانة عالية في الحياة العامة المصرية والعربية والعالمية — "The Ahram" has occupied a high position in the Egyptian, Arab and international public life

87 | 1242 |

2117 عَجَب *n.* pl. أَعْجاب admiration, amazement; appreciation

لا غرابة أن يحبها هذا الحب ولا عجب أن يبحث عنها بين ركام الحجارة المتناثرة هنا وهناك — It is not strange that he loves her that much, and it is no wonder that he is searching for her among the rubble of the scattered stones here and there

80 | 1334 |

2118 صَنْع *n.* making, building

تبدأ رحلة اليوم الجميلة من تحضير العجين لصنع الخبز، وغسل الملابس بالأيدي، وتحضير اللبن الزبادي — Today's lovely trip begins with preparing dough to make bread, washing the clothes by hand, and making yogurt

88 | 1225 |

2119 فارِق *n.* difference; distinctive feature
لم يكن فارق السن بيننا مانعا لكلينا من اللعب معا — أيام الطفولة The difference in age between us did not prevent either of us from playing together in the days of childhood
85 | 1263 |

2120 عُرْس *n.* pl. أَعْراس wedding
كان العرس كبيرا اجتمع إليه الأقارب والأصدقاء من كل مكان — The wedding was big, with friends and relatives coming from everywhere
85 | 1268 |

2121 شَرْح *n.* explanation, commentary
أخذت تشرح درس العلوم شرحا عمليا ، وأثناء الشرح أخذ تلميذ يأكل من الفاكهة — She started to explain the science lesson scientifically, and during the explanation a student started eating some fruit
87 | 1233 |

2122 فَضائيّ *adj.* (outer) space, satellite (esp. communications)
أكد المدير العام لشبكة الجزيرة الفضائية أن منتدى الجزيرة الإعلامي الثالث يركز هذا العام على إشكالية التغطية الإعلامية العالمية للوضع في الشرق الأوسط — The general director of the Al-Jazeera satellite company stressed the third Al-Jazeera Media Forum will concentrate this year on the problem of global media coverage of the situation in the Middle East
83 | 1296 |

2123 زائِر *n.* pl. زُوّار visitor, guest; tourist
بلعت ريقها.. ارتبكت.. لم تتوقع هذا الزائر الغريب — She swallowed her saliva...she was confused... she didn't expect this strange visitor
85 | 1253 |

2124 عَدا *part.* (ما) عَدا and فِيما عَدا except for; فِيما عَدا ذلِكَ apart from that, other than that; عَدا عَن with the exception of
تتغير كل أعضاء الإنسان أثناء نموه، ما عدا بصمة الأذن، التي لا تتغير منذ ولادته وحتى مماته — All the body parts of a person change during growth, except for the shape of the ear, which does not change from birth through until death
96 | 1120 |

2125 تَعْيِين *n.* appointing, designating
حاول اللورد كرومر ممثل الاحتلال الانجليزي تعطيل المشروع، وقام بتعيين سعد زغلول وزيرا للمعارف — Lord Cromer, the representative of the English occupation, tried to cripple the project, and he appointed Saad Zaghloul as Minister of Information
80 | 1344 |

2126 اِتَّهَمَ *v. VIII* to accuse sb ب of
لا يسمح لأحد منكم أن يتهم الآخر دون أن يقدم الدليل على الاتهام — None of you are permitted to accuse the other without offering evidence for the accusation
82 | 1305 |

2127 عَذاب *n.* punishment, torture; pain, suffering
يخضع لكثير من العذاب والألم، ويتحمل ذلك في كثير من الصبر والاستسلام والخضوع لحكم الله — He is subjected to a lot of torture and pain, and he bears it with a lot of patience and resignation and obedience to God's judgement
76 | 1402 |

2128 هَزَّ *v. I (u)* to shake, jolt, rock sth; هَزَّ رَأْسَهُ to nod (in agreement); هَزَّ ذَيْلَهُ to wag its tail
هل تفهمني؟ - هز الطبيب رأسه وأشار إليه أن يستمر — Do you understand me? – The doctor shook his head and motioned for him to continue
84 | 1268 | +lit

2129 خادِم *adj.* serving, waiting on, assisting; *n.* servant, attendant; (computer) (web) server
أنا أم متفرغة لأولادي فقط.. ولا أعتمد على الخادمة — I am a mother who devotes all her time to her children...I don't rely on the servant
81 | 1315 |

2130 بارِز *adj.* outstanding, prominent, distinguished
جسده البدين اللين الذي يخلو من أية عضلة بارزة، وطريقته في رفع حاجبيه إذا اندهش، كل هذه العلامات تجعله أشبه بامرأة متنمرة منه برجل صارم — His soft, fat body which is devoid of any prominent muscle, and his way of raising his eyebrows when he is surprised, all of these features make him more like a bullying woman than a tough man
85 | 1258 |

2131 شَتَّى *n.* all, many, diverse
وقد ركبت على الجدران رفوف حملت بأنواع شتى من الأوعية والآنية والأكياس — Some shelves had been fastened to the wall that carried various types of pots, vessels and bags
83 | 1277 |

2132 وُقُوع *n.* occurrence, happening; falling
أشاروا إلى أن قوات الشرطة ارتابت في السيارة وحاولت سد الطرق المؤدية إلى الجسر وإبعاد المارة قبل وقوع الانفجار — They indicated that the police forces suspected the car and tried to block the road leading to the bridge and get the pedestrians away before the explosion happened
79 | 1341 |

2133 طَابَع *n.* pl. طَوَابِع and طَبْع postage stamp; stamp, mark, impression; feature, characteristic, personality
ان هذه المعاهد غلب عليها الطابع التجاري فهي بالغة التكاليف وقد لا يتمكن الكثير من الشباب الالتحاق بها نظرا للتكلفة الباهظة — These institutions came to be dominated by a commercial nature, for they are very expensive, and many young people are not able to sign up for them in view of the high costs
84 | 1260 |

2134 سَرْطان *n.* cancer
لا أستطيع أن أحكم على عدد حالات السرطان في اليمن إلا بعد مرور سنتين من إنشاء المركز — I cannot judge the number of cancer cases in Yemen until two years have passed since the founding of the center
81 | 1304 |

2135 مَثَابَة *n.* بِمَثَابَة virtually, tantamount to
كان يقول إن الحكيم بمثابة ضمير الأمة — He was saying that Al-Hakim was like the conscience of the nation
83 | 1285 |

2136 خَلا *v. I (u)* to be free, devoid مِن of sth; to withdraw, be alone لِ for sth; to be alone مع with sb; to elapse, run out, be over (time, period)

بدأ غفارة يهجر غيط العنب وكرموز بعد أن خلت معظم البيوت من سكانها — Ghafara started to leave Ghait Al-Inab and Karmuz after most of the houses became empty of their inhabitants
87 | 1216 |

2137 مَرْء *n.* man; person; المَرْء one (people in general)
يمكنك أن تحكم على المرء من خلال أعدائه، كما تحكم عليه من خلال أصدقائه — You can judge a man by his enemies, as much as you can judge him by his friends
85 | 1239 |

2138 عَنِيف *adj.* violent, forceful, fierce
دخل مع طارق في جدل عنيف حول الفرق بين المدارس التجريبية ومدارس اللغات — He and Tareq got into a violent argument about the difference between the experimental schools and language schools
88 | 1206 |

2139 إِعْدام *n.* execution, capital punishment
الحكم قد صدر عليه بالإعدام، وقد عين موعد تنفيذه — He was condemned to death, and a date for the execution was set
83 | 1280 |

2140 تَسْوِيَة *n.* settlement, solution
أما في مجال الكفر والإيمان فلا تسوية بين المؤمن والكافر — In the area of apostasy and faith, there is no settlement between a believer and an apostate
71 | 1492 |

2141 إِرْتَكَبَ *v. VIII* to commit, perpetrate (crime, error)
لم يحدث أن ارتكبت حتى مخالفة سير بسيطة — I never even committed a simple traffic violation
85 | 1246 |

2142 شَهِير *adj.* famous, well-known
تزوجت من ابن المليونير فرج البهتيمي صاحب مصانع الحلويات الشهيرة — She married Tamir, the son of the millionaire Faraj Al-Bahtimi, the owner of the famous sweets factories
83 | 1266 |

2143 اِسْتَمَعَ *v. VIII* to listen إلى to
بعد الهجوم على روسيا استمع العالم إلى خطبة تشرشل في الإذاعة البريطانية — After the attack on Russia, the world listened to Churchill's speech on British radio
88 | 1203 |

2144 غابَة *n. pl.* -aat forest, jungle; (fig.) haze, fog, confusion
قررت حيوانات الغابة إقامة حفل حضره الجميع — The animals of the forest decided to have a party which everyone would attend
84 | 1245 |

2145 شَرِيحَة *n. pl.* شَرائِح slice, cross-section; slide
من الظواهر الإيجابية التي يفرزها الحوار الوطني في السعودية أن جميع الشرائح الاجتماعية أصبحت أكثر قدرة على الحديث بصوت عال عن مشاكلها — Among the positive phenomena which the national dialog in Saudi Arabia is bringing is that all social classes have become more able to speak out about their problems
81 | 1301 |

2146 رَبْط *vn.* connecting, linking, coupling; *n.* bond, connection
يحاول الربط بين أفكار متقطعة في خياله — He is trying to link disparate ideas in his imagination
85 | 1240 |

2147 دِبلُوماسِيّ *adj.* diplomatic; *n.* diplomat
نقلت الصحيفة عن مصادر دبلوماسية أمريكية قولها إن أي تمثيل لحماس في الحكومة بعد الانتخابات سيكون له عواقب — The newspaper quoted American diplomatic sources that any representation from Hamas in the government after the elections would have consequences
70 | 1495 |

2148 كَلَّفَ *v. II* to cost (money, time, effort); to charge, entrust, commission sb ب with (a task); to assign, appoint sb ب/أَنْ to do sth
كلف الرئيس الفلسطيني محمود عباس اليوم سلام فياض الشخصية المستقلة بتشكيل حكومة الطوارئ الفلسطينية — The Palestinian president Mahmoud Abbas today commissioned Salam Fayad, the independent (politically unaffiliated) figure, to form an emergency Palestinian government
97 | 1080 |

2149 عَطاء *vn.* giving, offering, contributing; *n.* gift, present; (econ.) offer, bid
قد خلقنا لنواصل العمل والعطاء — We were created to continue working and giving
84 | 1247 |

2150 نِقابَة *n. pl.* -aat union, syndicate
نحن الآن في النقابة نعمل باتجاه ضم كل العاملين بالصحافة إلى هذه المظلة — We are now at the union working towards including all the workers in journalism under this umbrella
71 | 1474 |

2151 مُخالَفَة *n. pl.* -aat violation, infraction; (sports) foul
خبر تغريم رئيس وزراء ماليزيا بسبب ارتكابه مخالفات مرورية متعددة يثير حفيظتنا تجاه ما يجري عندنا من مخالفات مرورية وعلى جميع المستويات — News of the fines (issued to) the Prime Minister of Malaysia because of his numerous traffic violations raises our indignation about traffic violations occurring among us, and at all levels
82 | 1272 |

2152 ثُنائِيّ *adj.* dual, bilateral
يجري خلال الزيارة مباحثات تتناول العلاقات الثنائية التي تربط البلدين — During the visit, discussions will take place which will deal with the bilateral relations which bind the two countries
75 | 1391 |

2153 خُبْز *n.* bread
أمام مخبز فاجأتني رائحة الخبز الطازج فدخلت مستسلمة لجوع مفاجئ — In front of the bakery, I was surprised by the smell of fresh bread, so I entered, surrendering to sudden hunger
92 | 1139 |

2154 شَرْعِيَّة *n.* legitimacy, legality
دول أفريقية صغيرة مثل بنين وتوجو أصبحت أداة للحصول على شرعية زائفة ولإلهاء الجماهير عن القضايا الحقيقية في العالم العربي — Small African states like Benin and Togo have become a tool to obtain a false legitimacy and to distract the masses in the Arab World from the real issues
74 | 1403 |

2155 صَخْر coll.n. rocks, un.n. صَخْرَة, pl. صُخُور
عندما رأت الوالدة قبة الصخرة أمامها، هلّلت
وكبرت بخشوع — When the mother saw the
Dome of the Rock in front of her, she humbly
exclaimed "la ilaha illa Allaah" and "Allahu akbar"
84 | 1241 |

2156 مُوَضِّح adj. clarifying, explaining; indicating,
pointing out
أصدر البنك الدولي تقريرا موضحا فيه التزام
الاقتصاد المصري بالقواعد والمعايير الدولية — The
International Bank issued a report in which it
clarified that the Egyptian economy is in
compliance with the international rules and
standards
70 | 1482 |

2157 صَدًى n. pl. أَصْداء echo; effect; repercussion
كان حامد وأسرته يسمعون أصداء القصف من بعيد،
وأخبارها في أجهزة المذياع — Hamid and his
family were listening to the echoes of the
bombing from far away, and to news of it on
the radio
89 | 1168 |

2158 جَمْع n. pl. جُمُوع crowd, gathering, assembly;
collection, accumulation
وقفت بين الجموع أتأمل مهارة هذا الإنسان البسيط
في صناعة الأمل — I stood among the crowd
contemplating the skill of this simple person
in creating hope
87 | 1197 |

2159 عَجْز n. weakness, deficiency, inability; (econ.)
deficit
دخل الشيخ مسعود متكئا على عصاه بسبب العجز
الذي أصاب رجله منذ سنوات — Sheikh
Mahmoud entered leaning on his cane
because of the weakness which has afflicted
his leg for many years
86 | 1208 |

2160 جِنِرال n. (mil.) general; (in titles) الجِنِرال
General
هو جنرال اميركي متقاعد والأمين العام السابق
لحلف شمال الاطلسي — He is a retired
American general and former secretary
general of NATO
73 | 1411 |

2161 أَسْعَدَ v. IV to make happy; يُسْعِدُنا أن we're
delighted to (do sth)
يسعدني أن مجلة العربي الصغير تعجبك، وأنك تحبين
القراءة — It makes me happy that the magazine
"The Young Arab" pleases you, and that you
like reading
80 | 1293 | +for

2162 لَـ part. (emphatic) indeed, truly; لَطالَما how
often!
ما هو إلا الابن الذي لطالما حلم به في حياته المديدة
— He is none other than the son he had so
often dreamt of during his lengthy life.
88 | 1183 |

2163 كَسَرَ v. I (i) to break sth; to violate, defy
(tradition, the law)
لذلك لا يصاب الممثل الذي نشاهده يكسر الزجاج
بقبضة يده، لأنه يكسر لوحا من السكر — Therefore
the actor whom we see breaking the glass with
the fist of his hand is not hurt, because he is
breaking a sheet of sugar
89 | 1164 |

2164 نَفَس n. pl. أَنْفاس breath
يحدق في السقف ويجذب نفسا عميقا من السيجارة
وتبين على وجهه علامات التفكير — He stares at the
ceiling and takes a deep breath from his cigarette
and signs of thinking appear on his face
86 | 1202 | +lit

2165 مُنْتِج adj. productive, producing; n.
manufacturer, maker, producer
كلما قابلت منتج سينما طلبت منه أن يجد لها دورا في
فيلم — Whenever she met a movie producer
she asked him to find her a role in a film
76 | 1351 |

2166 كِذْب n. lying; deceit
لن يضطر بعد اليوم للتظاهر والكذب.. لقد انتهت
علاقتهما.. هذه الحقيقة — He won't be forced,
after today, to pretend and lie...their
relationship has ended...this is the truth
90 | 1150 |

2167 مُسْتَقْبَلِي adj. future
بحيرة البردويل في سيناء، تصدر أسماكها الطازجة
مباشرة من البحيرة للعديد من عواصم العالم وهي
بذلك تمثل أحد مصادر الثروة المستقبلية في سيناء —

The fish from the Bardawil Lake in Sinai are exported fresh from the lake to a number of world capitals and it thus represents one of the sources of future wealth in Sinai

82 | 1258 |

2168 خَلَّصَ *v. II* (Dia.) to finish, complete sth; (MSA) to purify, refine, clarify sth; to save, rescue sb; to extricate, set free, disentangle sb

بتذكري مفرش الصينية اللي كنت بتطرزي فيه؟ — خلص والا لسة؟ — Do you remember that plate cover you were sewing? Is it finished or not yet?

63 | 1615 | +spo

2169 إزالة *n.* removal, elimination; uninstalling (software)

يأمل الاتحاد الأوروبي في مساعدة الحكومة المصرية في ازالة العقبات والوصول لنتائج ملموسة ومؤثرة في مستوى المعيشة للمواطن المصري — The European Union hopes to help the Egyptian government to eliminate the obstructions and reach tangible and effective results in the standard of living of the Egyptian citizen

82 | 1257 |

2170 اِنْقَطَعَ *v. VII* to break, snap; to be severed, be cut off; to be interrupted

الكل ينتحب وأصوات الطائرات لا تنقطع من فوق المدينة والمدافع المضادة تطاردها — Everyone was in mourning, and the sounds of airplanes never stopped over the city with the anti-aircraft fire following them

90 | 1135 |

2171 سادَ *v. I (u)* to prevail, be predominant; to rule, govern

ساد السكون الحجرة حتى قطعه صوت سكرتيره حسن عبر جهاز الاتصال — Silence reigned in the room until the voice of his secretary Hassan broke it, coming over the intercom

87 | 1173 |

2172 مَوْجَة *n.* pl. -aat wave

تعاني دارفور من موجات الجفاف — Darfur is suffering from waves of drought

84 | 1217 |

2173 خَلْفِيَّة *n.* background, history; (computer) wallpaper

تكشف هذه الدراسة عن خلفية العلاقة الفلسطينية – الكويتية قبل وبعد الغزو — This study reveals the background of the Palestinian-Kuwaiti relationship before and after the invasion

84 | 1223 |

2174 تَوْسِيع *n.* expanding, widening, augmenting

قال الدكتور احمد نظيف أن محافظة دمياط ستشهد مشروعا ضخما لتوسيع ميناء دمياط وزيادة قدراته لاستيعاب حركة الاستثمار والتصدير — Dr. Ahmad Nazif said that the Governorate of Dumyat would witness a huge project to widen the port of Dumyat and increase its capacity to accommodate investment and export activities

76 | 1349 |

2175 دَوْرِيَّة *n.* pl. -aat patrol, squad; journal, periodical

عند أبواب العاصمة كانت الدوريات المسلحة تستوقف جميع السيارات القادمة — At the gates of the capital, armed patrols are stopping all incoming cars

81 | 1266 |

2176 تَسَاؤُل *n.* pl. -aat questions, doubts

عاد التساؤل إلى ذهني، متى نستطيع حكم أنفسنا — The question returned to my mind: when will we be able to rule ourselves

84 | 1213 |

2177 فين /feen/ (Egy.Lev.) *interrog.* where; (with pron.) فينك /feen-ak/ where have you been?

ساكن فين يا أستاذ محفوظ؟ — Where do you live, Prof. Mahfouz?

65 | 1565 |

2178 جِلْد *n.* skin; leather

تبدأ البثور أو الدمامل بشكل احمرار مؤلم يظهر بصفة مفاجئة على الجلد، وفي خلال ٢٤ ساعة سرعان ما تمتلئ بالصديد — Pimples or boils start in the form of painful redness which appears suddenly on the skin, and within 24 hours it quickly fills with puss

83 | 1229 |

2179 تَعْذِيب *n.* torture; punishment

قضى سنتين في السجن والتعذيب — He spent two years in prison and under torture

85 | 1205 |

28 Verb Forms II-X

A list of up to the 10 most frequent of each category of verb listed below.

Form II

Sound

187	أَكَّدَ	to confirm
240	قَدَّمَ	to offer
294	سَلَّمَ	to greet
622	فَكَّرَ	to think about; consider
662	مَثَّلَ	to represent
707	حَقَّقَ	to achieve
767	قَرَّرَ	to decide
780	شَكَّلَ	to form
877	سَجَّلَ	to register, record
983	وَجَّهَ	to send, direct sth to

Defective

429	أَدَّى	to lead to
470	صَلَّى	to pray
763	خَلَّى	to preserve, keep
896	سَمَّى	to name
1070	سَوَّى	to do, make
2207	غَطَّى	to cover; conceal
2328	غَنَّى	to sing
3033	حَيَّا	to greet
3383	لَبَّى	to meet, fulfill
5098	وَلَّى	to entrust, commission

Form III

Sound

319	حاوَلَ	to try
672	شارَكَ	to participate in
774	طالَبَ	to demand
887	تابَعَ	to follow
971	بارَكَ	to bless
1007	واجَهَ	to face; confront
1056	ساعَدَ	to help
1334	واصَلَ	to continue
1353	لاحَظَ	to notice
1393	مارَسَ	to practice, pursue

Defective

898	عانَى	to suffer
1923	نادَى	to call
2534	لاقَى	to meet
2585	ساوَى	to equalize
3778	راعَى	to heed, observe
4461	عافَى	to heal, cure

Form IV

Sound

90	أَمْكَنَ	to be possible
178	أَصْبَحَ	to become
426	أَعْلَنَ	to announce
831	أَطْلَقَ	to release
1024	أَظْهَرَ	to show
1084	أَدْرَكَ	to comprehend
1359	أَصْدَرَ	to publish
1511	أَثْبَتَ	to prove
1571	أَشْبَهَ	to resemble
1592	أَرْسَلَ	to send

Doubled

342	أَحَبَّ	to love
1477	أَحَسَّ	to feel
1527	أَهَمَّ	to concern
2425	أَصَرَّ	to insist on
2493	أَطَلَّ	to overlook
2565	أَقَرَّ	to ratify
2765	أَعَدَّ	to prepare
3241	أَتَمَّ	to complete

Hamzated

1411	آمَنَ	to believe
3147	أَخْطَأَ	to be wrong
4464	أَنْشَأَ	to establish
5759	آسَفَ	to sadden

Assimilated

605	أَوْضَحَ	to clarify
2983	أَوْقَفَ	to detain sb
6012	أَوْقَعَ	to inflict

Hollow

126	أرادَ	to want
291	أضافَ	to add
312	أشارَ	to indicate
755	أصابَ	to stike, afflict
861	أقامَ	to set up; reside
1082	أعادَ	to repeat
1110	أجابَ	to respond
1117	أفادَ	to report
1198	أثارَ	to provoke; bring up
2413	أشادَ	to praise

Defective				Form VI			
				Sound			
346	أَعْطَى	to give		1135	تَجَاوَزَ	to exceed, go beyond	
1043	أَلْقَى	to throw; deliver		1218	تَنَاوَلَ	to deal with; partake of	
1397	أَجْرَى	to conduct		1764	تَسَاءَلَ	to wonder	
2091	أَبْدَى	to show		1869	تَرَاجَعَ	to retreat	
2273	أَنْهَى	to complete		1873	تَعَامَلَ	to work together,	
2714	أَخْفَى	to hide, conceal				do business with	
3636	أَرْضَى	to satisfy		2428	تَرَاوَحَ	to vary	
3913	أَلْغَى	to cancel		2790	تَنَاسَبَ	to be compatible with	
3956	أَضْحَى	to become; begin		3182	تَوَاصَلَ	to maintain, pursue (efforts)	
3989	أَجْدَى	to be useful		3613	تَعَارَضَ	to clash, conflict with	
				4238	تَبَارَكَ	to be blessed	

Doubly Weak			
3136	أَوْحَى	to suggest, imply	
3359	أَسَاءَ	to harm, offend, insult	
4214	أَضَاءَ	to illuminate	
4686	أَوْصَى	to advise	

Defective			
420	تَعَالَى	to be exalted; come!	
3964	تَوَالَى	to follow in succession	
5627	تَمَاشَى	to conform with	
6091	تَلاقَى	to meet each other	

Form V			
Sound			
453	تَحَدَّثَ	to speak	
688	تَعَرَّضَ	to be exposed to	
756	تَعَلَّقَ	to be connected with	
804	تَوَقَّعَ	to expect, anticipate	
926	تَكَلَّمَ	to speak	
936	تَوَقَّفَ	to stop	
952	تَغَيَّرَ	to change, be modified	
981	تَمَكَّنَ	to be able	
1047	تَحَوَّلَ	to be changed, transformed	
1100	تَقَدَّمَ	to present, submit	

Form VII			
Sound			
1175	اِنْطَلَقَ	to depart; begin	
2170	اِنْقَطَعَ	to break	
2358	اِنْفَجَرَ	to explode	
2737	اِنْطَبَقَ	to be applicable	
2739	اِنْسَحَبَ	to withdraw	
2811	اِنْعَكَسَ	to be reflected	
3069	اِنْقَلَبَ	to turn around, turn over	
3573	اِنْخَفَضَ	to drop; be lowered	
3920	اِنْدَرَجَ	to be inserted, included	
4494	اِنْدَلَعَ	to break out	

Defective			
451	تَمَنَّى	to wish	
1520	تَلَقَّى	to receive	
2014	تَوَلَّى	to take charge of	
2084	تَبَقَّى	to remain,	
2523	تَوَفَّى	(pass.) to die	
2778	تَخَلَّى	to give up, abandon	
3113	تَعَدَّى	to exceed, go beyond	
3232	تَبَنَّى	to adopt, claim	
		responsibility for	
3314	تَجَلَّى	to become clear	
5964	تَسَلَّى	to have fun	

Doubled			
3586	اِنْضَمَّ	to join	
5698	اِنْصَبَّ	to be poured out	
6579	اِنْحَلَّ	to be dissolved	

Hollow			
4190	اِنْهَارَ	to collapse	
6727	اِنْرَادَ	to be wanted	
7940	اِنْصَابَ	to fall ill	

Defective			
1331	اِنْبَغَى	to be necessary	
3773	اِنْطَوَى	to contain	

Form VIII

Sound

341	اعْتَبَرَ	to consider
422	اعْتَقَدَ	to believe
661	انْتَظَرَ	to expect, wait
1092	اشْتَغَلَ	to work
1095	ارْتَفَعَ	to rise
1109	اخْتَلَفَ	to be different
1145	اعْتَمَدَ	to depend on
1335	اعْتَرَفَ	to admit, confess
1383	اقْتَرَبَ	to get close to
1512	انْتَقَلَ	to transfer

Doubled

1625	اهْتَمَّ	to be interested in
1644	امْتَدَّ	to extend
2261	احْتَلَّ	to occupy
2700	اضْطَرَّ	to compel, force
3766	اشْتَدَّ	to intensify
5110	اخْتَصَّ	to dedicate
5418	اهْتَزَّ	to tremble

Hamzated

4896	امْتَلَأَ	to be filled
7064	ابْتَدَأَ	to begin

Assimilated

722	اتَّصَلَ	to contact
1332	اتَّفَقَ	to agree
1367	ازْدادَ	to grow
1475	اتَّخَذَ	to take, adopt
2009	اتَّجَهَ	to turn, face towards
2107	ادَّعَى	to claim
2126	اتَّهَم	to accuse of
2519	اطَّلَعَ	to review
2675	اتَّضَحَ	to become clear
2700	اضْطَرَّ	to compel, force

Hollow

538	احْتاجَ	to need
1205	اخْتارَ	to choose
1367	ازْدادَ	to increase
3527	اعْتادَ	to become accustomed to
4136	اجْتاحَ	to invade
4327	ارْتاحَ	to relax
5067	اشْتاقَ	to long for
5393	امْتازَ	to be distinguished

Defective

525	انْتَهَى	to end
1049	الْتَقَى	to meet
1265	اشْتَرَى	to buy
1797	احْتَوَى	to contain
2057	اخْتَفَى	to disappear
2066	انْتَمَى	to belong to
2107	ادَّعَى	to allege, claim
2705	ارْتَدَى	to wear, put on
2893	اكْتَفَى	to be content with
3445	اقْتَضَى	to demand, require

Form IX

6629	احْمَرَّ	to turn red
7967	اسْوَدَّ	to become black

Form X

Sound

1055	اسْتَخْدَمَ	to use
1708	اسْتَهْدَفَ	to target
1726	اسْتَقْبَلَ	to meet
2446	اسْتَغْرَقَ	to last
2867	اسْتَعْمَلَ	to use
3133	اسْتَعْرَضَ	to review
3175	اسْتَيْقَظَ	to wake up
3476	اسْتَشْهَدَ	to quote; be martyred
3638	اسْتَوْعَبَ	to comprehend
3885	اسْتَأْهَلَ	to deserve

Doubled

726	اسْتَمَرَّ	to last
1459	اسْتَحَقَّ	to deserve
2527	اسْتَقَرَّ	to settle down
2952	اسْتَغَلَّ	to exploit
2994	اسْتَعَدَّ	to get ready for

Hollow

235	اسْتَطاعَ	to be able
1734	اسْتَفادَ	to benefit from
3164	اسْتَجابَ	to accept; comply with
3213	اسْتَعادَ	to recover
3942	اسْتَضافَ	to host
4680	اسْتَحالَ	to be impossible

Defective

2725	اسْتَدْعَى	to summon, call

Quadriliteral I				Quadriliteral II		
2259	سَيْطَرَ	to control		6308	تَعَلْمَنَ	to be secularized
4856	طَمْأَنَ	to pacify		6943	تَمَسْخَرَ	to mock
5192	تَرْجَمَ	to translate		7099	تَدَهْوَرَ	to deteriorate
6090	تَلْفَنَ	to call on the phone		7970	تَسَيْطَرَ	to dominate
6869	دَرْدَشَ	to chat		**Irregular Derived Verb**		
7121	سَقْسَى	to ask		4973	إِسْتَنَّى	to wait
7408	مَسْخَرَ	to ridicule				

2180 اِنْتِقال *n.* transfer; transition

الموت لا يُخيف المؤمنين لأنه انتقال إلى حياة أخرى وليس نهاية — Death does not frighten believers because it is a transfer to another life, not the end

83 | 1229 |

2181 وَفَّرَ *v. II* to provide sth لـ to sb; to fulfill (conditions, requirements); to save (time, money, space)

توفر الدار الإقامة الآمنة للمرأة التي تتعرض للعنف مع أو بدون أطفالها — The home provides a secure residence for the woman who is exposed to violence either with or without her children

87 | 1165 |

2182 نِيابَة *n.* representation; proxy; النِّيابة العامّة (public) prosecutor's office; نِيابةً عَن in lieu of; on behalf of; بالنِّيابة by proxy, acting

طعن شاب صديقه الحلاق بسكين فكاد يقتله، واعترف أمام النيابة أنه متعطل من زمان وأن الحلاق صديقه من زمان أيضا — The young man stabbed his friend the barber, and almost killed him, and he confessed in front of the prosecutor that he was unemployed for a long time and that the barber had been his friend for a long time as well

71 | 1419 |

2183 اِكْتِشاف *n.* discovery; detection, uncovering

ذكر الباحثون أن هذا الاكتشاف هو مجرد الخطوة الأولى على الطريق — The researchers mentioned that this discovery was merely the first step on the road

85 | 1195 |

2184 دافِع *n.* pl. دَوافِع incentive, motive, reason; *adj.* pushing; paying; *n.* payer (person or entity); دافِع الضَّرائِب taxpayer

أشارت مصادر الشرطة إلى أن دوافع القتل سياسية — Police sources indicated that the motivations for the killing were political

92 | 1097 |

2185 سِتُّون *num.* sixty; sixtieth

بعد أسابيع قليلة سأتم ستين عاما.. حياتي تقترب من النهاية — In a few weeks I will turn 60...my life is nearing the end

95 | 1067 |

2186 جَدَل *n.* controversy, dispute; argument, debate

أثار الفيلم جدلا كبيرا أثناء المهرجان لأنه يقدم معالجة تدور حول التطرف الديني — The film incited a big argument during the festival because it presents a treatment which revolves around religious extremism

82 | 1234 |

2187 جُوع *n.* hunger; starvation; المَوْت جُوعاً starving to death

يقال إن هدى هانم هي التي أنقذتنا من الموت جوعا — It is said that Huda Hanim is the one who saved us from death by starvation

84 | 1201 |

2188 سَلَّة *n.* basket

مزقت الأوراق ورمتها في سلة المهملات — She tore up the papers and threw them into the waste basket

91 | 1111 |

2189 مَقام *n.* place, position, rank

تساعده بأملاكها الواسعة على إيجاد مقام رفيع بين الخاصة والأشراف — She helps him with her extensive property to find a high position among the rich and noble

87 | 1163 |

2190 حَسِبَ *v. I (a,i)* to regard, consider sb/sth to be; to think, believe أَنَّ that; حَسَبَ *(u)* to calculate, compute; حَسُبَ *(u)* to be esteemed, be valued

هو يعرف أن كل شيء يحسب عند أمه بحساب المصلحة، ولا أثر عندها لشيء يسمى العواطف — He knows for his mother, everything is judged in terms of personal benefit; she has no room for anything called emotion

90 | 1121 |

2191 تَحَكُّم *vn.* control (في of)

ضغط على زر التحكم فتم إغلاق السيارة أوتوماتيكيا، ثم أغلق باب الجراج — He pushed the control button and the car locked automatically, then he locked the door of the garage

87 | 1151 |

2192 رَهِيب *adj.* awful, horrible, dreadful, gruesome

وظللت أعاني من هبوط وحموضة في معدتي بالإضافة ا — إلى صداع فظيع وكأن مطارق رهيبة تدق رأسي continued to suffer from depression and from acidity in my stomach in addition to a terrible headache, as if dreadful hammers were pounding my head

92 | 1094 |

2193 مُثِير *adj.* influential, provocative; *a.p.* provoking, agitating, stirring up, raising

اتهامي بالجنون مثير للضحك — Accusing me of insanity is funny

87 | 1150 |

2194 رَفِيع *adj.* elevated, high; lofty, sublime; high-ranking, top-level; thin, slim, delicate; fine, exquisite, refined

لا يختلف اثنان على أخلاقه الراقية وسلوكياته الرفيعة التي جعلته محبوبا من جماهير الكرة المصرية — No one disagrees about his refined morals and his lofty behavior which have made him beloved of Egyptian soccer fans

87 | 1156 |

2195 نُصّ (Dia.) *n.* half, middle, semi-

ما أنت عارف، البلد مابقالهاش صحاب.. النص سافر ونص قاعد على القهوة يستنى — But you know, the country no longer has any friends... Half of them left and half are sitting at the coffee house waiting

45 | 2213 | +spo

2196 مُدَرِّس *n.* teacher, instructor

سارت حياتي بشكل طبيعي ونسيت الأستاذ إبراهيم وغيره من المدرسين الذين أحضرهم والدي من وحدته العسكرية لتعليمنا — My life went on in a natural way, and I forgot professor Ibrahim and the other teachers who my father brought from his military unit to educate us

86 | 1169 |

2197 بَذَلَ *v. I (u,i)* to exert, expend (effort)

قاد سيارته إلى البيت وهو يبذل مجهودا كبيرا ليحتفظ بتركيزه — He drove his car to the house, making a huge effort to maintain his concentration

85 | 1176 |

2198 وَفَّقَ *v. II* to grant success (God) to sb; to reconcile بَيْنَ..وَبَيْنَ between...and

نسأل الله أن يوفق الجميع و يوفقكم لما يحبه و يرضاه — We ask God to grant success to all and to grant success to you for that which he loves and which pleases him

71 | 1401 | +for

2199 سَاحِل *n.* pl. سَوَاحِل coast, seashore, beach

عرفت أوربا الحديثة طريقها إلى سواحل إريتريا في مستهل القرن السادس عشر — Modern Europe found its way to the Eritrean coasts at the beginning of the sixteenth century

83 | 1202 |

2200 هَرَبَ *v. I (u)* to flee, escape مِن from sth/sb; to desert مِن (the army)

انها بحاجة لفرملة لسانها بعد ذلك وإلا فإن العريس سوف يهرب من طول لسانها — She needs to put brakes on her tongue after that, otherwise the bridegroom will flee because of her abusive words

89 | 1120 |

2201 قَارِئ *n.* pl. قُرّاء reader; Qurʾanic reciter

أكثر الكتب التي يقبل عليها القارئ في كافة البلدان المذكورة هي القرآن الكريم باستثناء لبنان — The book most accepted by readers in all the mentioned countries is the Holy Qurʾan, with the exception of Lebanon

79 | 1257 |

2202 اِعْتَقَل *v. VIII* to arrest, detain sb

السعودية تعتقل ٢٠٨ بتهمة التخطيط لهجمات إرهابي — Saudi Arabia imprisons 208 accused of planning terrorist attacks

76 | 1314 | +news

2203 رَحَل *v. I (a)* to depart; to pass away; to travel

— رحلت سامية إلى صيدا، ولم ألتق بها بعد ذلك Samiya had left for Sidon, and I haven't seen her since

81 | 1230 |

2204 رِئاسيّ *adj.* presidential; executive

أعتقد أن الانتخابات الرئاسية الفلسطينية ستشهد منافسة حقيقية بالرغم من مقاطعة حركتي حماس والجهاد الإسلامي — I believe that the Palestinian presidential elections will witness a real competition despite the boycott of the Hamas and Islamic Jihad movements

63 | 1576 |

2205 أَمَر *v. I (u)* to order, command sb ب to do sth

لكن الإسلام يأمر أتباعه باحترام عقائد الآخرين.. لا يمكن أن تكون مسلما إلا إذا اعترفت بالأديان الأخرى — However Islam commands its followers to respect the beliefs of others...You can't be a Muslim unless you recognize other religions

86 | 1159 |

2206 صَداقَة *n.* friendship

أعمالكم هذه ليست أعمال محترمة ولن تكون هناك أي صداقة بيننا وبينكم — These acts of yours are not respected acts and there will not be any friendship between us and you

92 | 1074 |

2207 غَطّى *v. II* to cover; conceal

كان الثلج الذى هطل أثناء الليل قد غطى كل شيء — The snow which fell during the night covered everything

87 | 1133 |

2208 مَسْرَحِيّة *n.* play (theater)

وتنتقل الإضاءة في المسرحية من الإشعاع الكلي إلى الخفوت قصد الانتقال من حركة مشهدية إلى أخرى — The lighting in the play changes from total illumination to dimming, indicating the change from one scene to another

75 | 1314 |

2209 تَكْليف *vn.* charging, entrusting, commissioning sb ب with (a task); assigning, appointing sb ب/أَنْ to do sth; *n.* pl. تَكاليف (usu. pl.) costs, expenses, charges

قرر المحافظ تكليف رؤساء الاحياء بقطع التيار الكهربائي عن المحلات والورش التي أقيمت دون تراخيص — The governor decided to commission the heads of the neighborhoods to cut off the electric current from the shops and workshops which were set up without permits

82 | 1198 |

2210 بَساطَة *n.* sincerity, frankness; simplicity; simply, plainly, without further ado

كيف يسمح لنفسه بأن يقضي على مستقبل الآخرين بهذه البساطة؟ — How can he permit himself to destroy the future of others with such ease?

87 | 1131 |

2211 فَيْروس and فِيْروس *n.* pl. -aat also /vayruus, viiruus, vayrus, viiris/ (medical, computer) virus

هنالك دلائل وإثباتات أن هذا الفيروس ما زال فيروس حيواني وليس فيروس بشري — There are evidences and proofs that this virus is still an animal virus and not a human virus

66 | 1494 |

2212 غِناء *n.* singing

لم يكن ممكنا تحمل مشاق العمل دون غناء — It was not possible to bear the difficulty of the work without singing

80 | 1227 |

2213 رَبَط *v. I (i,u)* to tie, connect sth ب to sth else; to make a connection بَيْنَ..وَبَيْنَ between sth and sth else

العلاقة التي تربط القارئ بالكتاب، ليست علاقة إنسان بجماد — The relationship that binds the reader to a book, is not the relationship of a human being to an inanimate object

88 | 1124 |

2214 نائِم (Dia. نايِم) *a.p.* sleeping, asleep

هرعت لتطمئن على مارك، فوجدته نائما بسلام كما تركته — She hurried to check on Mark, and she found him sleeping as peacefully as she had left him

97 | 1020 |

2215 إعْطاء *vn.* giving, donating; *n.* offer, donation, concession

اطلب منهم عدم إعطاء أية معلومات دون إذن مني
— I ask them not to give any information without permission from me

83 | 1190 |

2216 غالِبِيَّة *n.* majority

أظهر استطلاع جديد للرأي أن الغالبية الساحقة من البريطانيين تعتقد أنه يتعين على الجالية المسلمة في المملكة المتحدة بذل المزيد للاندماج في الثقافة البريطانية — A new opinion survey showed that the overwhelming majority of British people believe that the Muslim community in the United Kingdom should exert more effort to integrate into British culture

77 | 1277 |

2217 مُوافِق *adj.* agreeing, consenting; corresponding to, coinciding with (date)

أنا موافق على اقتراح زوجتي — I agree with my wife's suggestion

87 | 1130 |

2218 مَقْهىً *n. pl.* (مَقاهٍ) مَقاهِي (def.) café, coffeehouse

نحتاج إلى كوب من الشاي في أى مقهى، ما رأيك؟
— We need a cup of tea from any coffee house, what do you think?

81 | 1216 |

2219 مُحادَثَة *n. pl.* -aat discussion, talk; negotiation

لقد اجريت محادثات مباشرة وصريحة مع الرئيس —
Frank and direct talks were held with the president

72 | 1365 | +news

2220 شاطِئ *n. pl.* شَواطِئ shore, coast, beach

الأطفال على الشاطئ يبنون قصورا وأهرامات من الرمال ثم يرفسونها بأرجلهم فتنهار — The children on the beach are building castles and pyramids of sand and then kicking them with their feet so they collapse

82 | 1193 |

2221 تَأَخَّرَ *v. V* to be late, to arrive late; to fall behind; to get late (of time); to be delayed or postponed

لقد تأخرت في البحث نتيجة المهمات التى كلفتنى بها سيادتك — I got behind in my research as

a result of the duties Your Excellency assigned to me

93 | 1049 |

2222 واقِعَة *n. pl.* وَقائِع incident, event; development

يضحك الدكتور كرم من قلبه كلما حكى هذه الواقع
— Dr Karam laughs his heart out whenever he recounts this event

79 | 1244 |

2223 مُغْلَق *adj.* closed, locked

دكان أبي حامد مغلق لكنه سيفتح من جديد في وقت ما — Abu Hamid's shop is locked but it will open again some time

94 | 1042 |

2224 قابل *adj.* capable, able

يدرك أن ما فعله غير قابل للنسيان — He realizes that what he did is not capable of being forgotten

87 | 1120 |

2225 مَوْلىً *n.* master, lord, patron

قل لن يصيبنا إلا ما كتب الله لنا هو مولانا وعلى الله فليتوكل المؤمنون — Say: the only thing that will happen to us is what God has decreed for us; he is our master, and let the believers rely on him

58 | 1692 | +lit

2226 مُكالَمَة *n. pl.* -aat conversation, discussion; (phone) call

ستبقى أنت في البيت بانتظار مكالمة هاتفية مني
You will stay at home waiting for a phone call from me

80 | 1214 | +spo

2227 شَدَّ *v. I (i,u)* to make sth tight or strong; to pull, draw sth/sb near; (Dia.) شد حيلك /shidd Heelak/ be strong!

انها اكثر المواضيع اللي تشد انتباهي — It is the subject that attracts my attention the most

93 | 1047 |

2228 تَرْجَمة *n.* translation, interpretation; biography

هل فكرت في ترجمة بعض الكتب المفيدة؟
Have you thought of translating some useful books?

92 | 1066 |

2229 تَوْقيت *n.* (standard) time; timing
الساعة العاشرة صباحا بتوقيت القاهرة.. موعد مناسب للاتصال — Ten in the morning Cairo time...a good time to call
82 | 1191 |

2230 أَسْرَع *elat.* faster/fastest; sooner/soonest
كان متلهفا على الزواج بأسرع وقت — He was anxious to get married as soon as possible
94 | 1040 |

2231 فَعّال *adj.* effective, efficient; active
إن فرنسا ستتخذ إجراءات فعالة ضد الدولة التي ستبدأ بشن الحرب — France will take effective measures against the state that begins to launch the war
84 | 1159 |

2232 نِيابِيّ *adj.* representative; parliamentary
على مدى الستة عشر عاما الماضية شهدت اليمن ثلاث انتخابات نيابية وواحدة رئاسية وأخرى محلية — Over the last sixteen years, Yemen has witnessed three parliamentary elections and one presidential election, and other local ones
62 | 1558 |

2233 إِحْتِياج *n.* pl. -aat need, requirement
حفر المزارعون بئرا لتأمين احتياجات عائلاتهم اليومية من المياه — The farmers dug a well to insure their families' daily needs for water
72 | 1340 |

2234 حَذَر and حِذْر *n.* care, caution, prudence, vigilance
يدخل الواحد منهم إلى العربة فيجده جالسا ينظر إليه بحذر ثم يترك العربة كلها إلى أخرى — One of them enters the railway car and finds him sitting looking at him warily, and then he leaves the entire car for another
87 | 1109 |

2235 مُسْبَقاً *adj.* previous, preceding; مُسْبَقاً in advance
بادرني بالاعتذار عن حضوره بلا موعد مسبق — He offered me an apology for coming without a prior appointment
83 | 1166 |

2236 بَلَدِيّ *adj.* indigenous, native; popular, folk; local, communal; municipal
أحتاج إلى ذكر بط بلدي وصينية رقاق بالشوربة والسمن البلدي — I need a male country duck and a tray of biscuits with soup and ghee
84 | 1157 |

2237 تَعْويض *n.* pl. -aat compensation, restitution; تَعْويضات reparations; substitutes
الخطة الجديدة في أفغانستان، دفع تعويض للمزارعين لاستبدال زراعة الأفيون بزراعات بديلة — The new plan in Afghanistan is to pay recompense to farmers for switching away from growing opium to alternate plants
83 | 1164 |

2238 سُورَة *n.* pl. سُوَر Surah (Qurʾanic chapter)
توضأت وفتحت المصحف وقرأت سورة يس، ثم أدت صلاة الاستخارة وأعقبتها بالدعاء — She did her ablutions and opened the Qurʾan and read the Surah "Ya sin", and then performed the prayer of asking for guidance, and followed it up with a Duʾaa prayer
70 | 1383 |

2239 عَشاء *n.* dinner, supper, evening meal
كانت عائلته الكبيرة تقضي الكثير من الليالي بدون عشاء، وكانت وجبة الطعام هي الخبز بدون أدام — His large family spends many evenings without dinner, and a meal would be bread without butter
93 | 1040 |

2240 قَضاء *vn.* extermination, annihilation على of sb/sth; spending (time, holiday); performing, fulfilling (a duty); قَضاء الحاجَة (euph.) going to the bathroom
سيتم تكثيف الحملات الرقابية على الأسواق للقضاء على التجارة العشوائية وضبط عمليات الغش والتدليس التجاري والصناعي — Market observation will be increased to do away with random commerce and to control cheating operations, and commercial and industrial fraud
78 | 1245 |

2241 آمِن *adj.* secure, safe
كل الحدود الإسرائيلية آمنة وبالقوات العربية — All the Israeli borders are secure, and with Arab forces
86 | 1128 |

2242 بَرْد *n.* cold, coldness

كان البرد قارسا والجليد يغطي كل شيء — The cold was severe, and ice covered everything

80 | 1213 |

2243 مُلْتَقَىً *n.* meeting; meeting place, juncture; forum, conference

تركيا ملتقى قارتين ، ومصر ملتقى ثلاث قارات — Turkey is at the juncture of two continents, and Egypt is at the juncture of three continents

74 | 1299 |

2244 صِيغَة *n. pl.* صِيَغ form, shape; formula

أمكن التوصل الى الصيغة النهائية لعقد تزويد ليبيا صواريخ "ميلان" المضادة للدبابات بعد ١٨ شهرا من المفاوضات — A final version of the contract to provide Libya with MILAN anti-tank missiles was reached after 18 months of negotiations

81 | 1193 |

2245 آتٍ (def. آتِي) *adj.* coming, future; following, next

إلى أي حد يمكننا أن نتنبأ بها هو آت في المستقبل؟ — To what extent can we predict what is coming in the future?

83 | 1156 |

2246 حَظِيَ *v. I (a)* to enjoy ب (respect, confidence, support, popularity); to acquire, gain ب sth

نال أكثر من جائزة عن كتبه التي حظيت بشعبية ضخمة — He received more than one prize for his books which attained a huge popularity

83 | 1164 |

2247 فَشَل *n.* failure

لقد تزوج مرتين، لكن المحاولتين انتهتا بالفشل — He married twice, but the two attempts ended in failure

87 | 1113 |

2248 بَنْد *n. pl.* بُنُود article, clause

ما نريد هو خلق الظروف المناسبة لتنفيذ كافة بنود خارطة الطريق — What we want is to create situations appropriate for carrying out all the stipulations of the Road Map

81 | 1193 |

2249 حادِي *adj.* first (in compounds) الحادِي عَشَر, الحادِي وَالعِشْرُون eleventh; *fem.* الحادِيَة عَشْرَة twenty-first

كانت الساعة تشير إلى الحادية عشرة وسبع وعشرين دقيقة — The clock indicated eleven o'clock and twenty-seven minutes

84 | 1149 |

2250 مُجْرِم *n./adj.* criminal

أضاف: «نناشد الحكومة انقاذنا وقتل هؤلاء المجرمين (القاعدة)» — He added: "We call on the government to save us and kill these criminals (Al-Qaeda)"

84 | 1147 |

2251 فَرْدِيّ *adj.* personal, private; individual, single

لا وقت للتفكير بالمشكلات الفردية إن كانت هناك مشكلات — There is no time to think about individual problems, if there are problems

77 | 1243 |

2252 سَلْطَنَة *n.* sultanate

سأحاول البحث عن هذه الكتب في سلطنة عمان — I will try to search for these books in the Sultanate of Oman

54 | 1776 | +news

2253 عَقْد *n. pl.* عُقُود decade

الذين ولدوا في طفرة الزيادة السكانية قبل عقدين، باتوا الآن شبابا — Those who were born in the period of rapid population growth (the baby boom) two decades ago have now become youths

80 | 1195 |

2254 يَأْس *n.* despair, hopelessness

يعاني المعتقلون شعورا بالمرارة واليأس بسبب الاعتقال — The prisoners are suffering from feelings of bitterness and despair because of being imprisoned

85 | 1120 |

2255 مَصْرِف *n. pl.* مَصارِف bank

المصرف مغلق والطابور على ماكينة السحب طويل — The bank is closed and the line for the withdrawal machine is long

67 | 1416 |

2256 خَيْرِيّ *adj.* charitable, philanthropic

أقيمت حفلة خيرية بسينما أستوديو مصر لتدعيم — الهلال الأحمر والصليب الأحمر المصريين A charity party was held in the movie house Studio Misr to support the Egyptian Red Crescent and Red Cross

78 | 1226 |

2257 إِثْر prep. and فِي إِثْرِ right after, immediately after

انتقل نظرها إلى وردة زرقاء، كلون السماء إثر الغروب — Her gaze moved onto a blue rose like the color of the sky after sunset

84 | 1139 |

2258 رابط *adj.* tying, connecting, linking; *n.* tie, connection; link (website)

لم تكن قمرة تريد أن يكون الأطفال هم الرابط الوحيد لراشد للاستمرار معها — Qamara did not want the children to be the only link for Rashid to continue with her

71 | 1329 | +for

2259 سَيْطَرَ *v. QI* to control, dominate over, seize على

— قضى عدة أيام حتى استطاع أن يسيطر على أحزانه It was several days before he was able control his grief

86 | 1106 |

2260 كِلا *part.* fem. كِلْتا (in idafa) both of; (with pron.) كِلاهُما both of them

نظر كلاهما للآخر بالحال راضيا وسقطا معا فى نوم عميق — Both of them looked at the other in a satisfied way, and they fell together into a deep sleep

91 | 1046 |

2261 اِحْتَلَّ *v. VIII* to occupy (land); to fill (post, position)

طول عمرى أعرف أن إنجلترا تحتل مصر والسودان، — أول مرة أعرف أن مصر تحتل السودان My whole life I have known that England occupies Egypt and the Sudan; (but) this is the first time I find out that Egypt occupies the Sudan

82 | 1149 |

2262 مَأْساة *n. pl.* مَآسٍ (def. مَآسِي) tragedy, calamity

— الحياة حلوة رغم كل المآسي والاحزان Life is sweet despite all the tragedies and sorrows

87 | 1082 |

2263 مُسْتَثْمِر *n. pl.* -uun investor; *adj.* investing

بطبيعة الحال سيكون العمل الأساسي للشركة هو جذب المستثمرين لهذا المكان — Naturally the basic task of the company is to attract investors to this place

62 | 1522 |

2264 بِتْرُول *n.* petroleum, oil

قد جاء في الأخبار الآن أن سعر البترول بلغ الأَلْف دولار للبرميل الواحد — It just came on the news that the price of petroleum reached a thousand dollars for one barrel

74 | 1265 |

2265 أَسْوَأ *elat.* worse/worst

بعد الغروب تغير الجو نحو الأسوأ وهطل مطر خفيف — After sunset the weather changed for the worse, and light rain fell

92 | 1023 |

2266 جَدْوَى *n.* benefit, advantage, utility

لم تجد مروة جدوى من الاستمرار فى الحديث، فأنهت المكالمة بعبارات غائمة — Marwa didn't see any advantage in continuing the conversation, so she ended the call with some mumbled expressions

84 | 1121 |

2267 أَسْفَل *elat.* lower/lowest; *n.* bottom or lower part

أخرج الثعبان من جيب سترته الأسفل — He took the snake out of the bottom pocket of his jacket

85 | 1108 |

2268 أَسْر *n.* capture, captivity; بِأَسْرِهِ/بِأَسْرِها in its entirety, completely

تبين أن حى الجرابيع بأسرها قد غادر الحارة خوفا من الانتقام فخلت الدور والدكاكين — It appeared the entire Al-Jarabi quarter had left the alleyway in fear of revenge, so the homes and the shops were empty

85 | 1103 |

2269 دُخان *n.* smoke; smoking

استغرق لحظات حتى أشعل غليونه ونفث سحابة دخان كثيفة — He was absorbed for a few moments until he lit his pipe, and exhaled a thick cloud of smoke

91 | 1027 |

29 War and Security

71	قوة	force	1193	نصر	victory	2064	قصف	bombardment
133	عمليّة	operation	1202	عدوان	aggression,	2071	هزيمة	defeat
165	حرب	war			hostility	2078	قتال	fighting,
188	سلام	peace	1292	أسير	prisoner			combat
238	أمن	security	1417	حارس	guard	2094	غزو	invasion; raid
335	عسكري	military	1443	جهاد	struggle, jihad	2110	نزاع	conflict
337	جيش	army	1447	جبهة	front	2138	عنيف	violent
468	نار	fire, gunfire	1451	مكافحة	fight, battle,	2139	اعدام	execution
514	سلاح	weapon			confrontation	2160	جنرال	general
534	قائد	leader	1473	مقتل	killing, murder	2182	نيابة	prosecutor's
541	قيادة	leadership	1488	مصاب	wounded			office
542	دفاع	defense	1489	صاروخ	rocket, missile	2202	اعتقل	to arrest,
549	أمني	security (adj)	1581	قتيل	casualty, killed			detain
563	احتلال	occupation			person	2205	أمر	to order,
567	مقاومة	resistance	1605	ضربة	blow, strike			command
612	مواجهة	confrontation	1609	تدمير	destruction	2241	آمن	secure, safe
618	شرطة	police	1623	انفجار	explosion	2250	مجرم	criminal
630	قاعدة	base	1659	اغتيال	assassination	2261	احتلّ	to occupy
639	قتل	to kill	1660	اعتداء	aggression	2268	أسر	capture,
654	جندي	soldier	1664	هجمة	assault, raid			captivity
671	مدني	civilian	1667	أمر	order, command	2284	مضاد	counter-
678	إطلاق	launching,	1691	استراتيجي	strategic	2287	معسكر	camp
		firing	1696	استراتيجية	strategy	2312	لاجئ	refugee
741	إرهاب	terrorism	1698	انسحاب	withdrawal	2345	سيف	sword
755	أصاب	to wound	1701	قاتل	killer	2347	مجزرة	massacre,
788	فوز	victory	1708	استهدف	to target			blood bath
790	سجن	prison	1744	حصار	siege, blockade	2358	انفجر	to explode
799	عدوّ	enemy	1771	رائد	major;	2470	سجين	prisoner
816	إصابة	wounding			commandant	2482	حرس	guard
818	قتل	murder,	1782	اعتقال	arrest	2503	مخابرة	intelligence
		killing	1790	انتصار	victory			service
820	مهمة	mission	1805	لواء	major general	2542	محاربة	making war
881	نووي	nuclear	1816	دمار	destruction			on
882	فرقة	division;	1820	تفجير	blowing up	2704	انتفاضة	uprising
		squad	1822	قنبلة	bomb	2711	كتيبة	squadron;
890	صراع	conflict	1843	ضرب	beating; striking			Phalangists
901	عنف	violence	1858	معتقل	prison, jail	2739	انسحب	to withdraw
906	تحرير	liberating	1887	مقدم	lieutenant	2824	اشتباك	clash
917	مسلح	gunman,			colonel	2826	ناري	gunfire (adj)
		armed person	1897	فوضى	chaos, anarchy	2832	انقلاب	coup
970	معركة	battle	1946	رصاص	bullets	2911	مهاجم	attacker
1008	ضابط	officer	1977	جريح	wounded	2976	قذيفة	shell, bomb
1031	ثورة	revolution	1983	سلمي	peaceful	3029	عقيد	colonel
1133	هجوم	attack	2039	مجاهد	warrior;	3073	محقق	investigator
1162	إرهابي	terrorist (adj)			mujahid	3107	محتل	occupier;
1164	ضحية	victim	2049	عميل	spy; operative			occupied

3112	خاض	to wage (war), embark on	3842	مدمر	destructive	4290	تسلل	infiltration
3114	دبابة	tank	3848	عبوة	package (bomb)	4294	مدع	prosecutor
3150	عداء	aggression, hostility	3849	أمّن	to secure	4318	جمرك	customs
3202	نضال	struggle, battle	3866	خصم	adversary	4345	فرار	fleeing
3208	ميليشيا	militia	3905	تعبئة	mobilization	4346	متمرد	rebel, insurgent
3217	تمرد	rebellion	3918	مستهدف	targeted	4400	نهب	looting
3254	غارة	raid	3937	ناسف	explosive, exploding	4437	هاون	mortar
3311	جنائي	criminal; penal	3943	مصرع	death, fatality	4474	كفاح	struggle, fight
3334	استخبار	pl. intelligence service	3974	تسلّل	to infiltrate	4482	عدواني	hostile
3337	إسقاط	shooting down	3977	هاجم	to attack	4491	اقتحم	to invade
3343	خطف	kidnapping, abduction	3982	تهريب	smuggling	4494	اندلع	to break out
3379	ثوري	revolutionary	4016	مقاوم	adversary; opposing	4495	مشتبه	suspicious
3389	شرطي	policeman	4030	قاتل	to fight	4571	رصاصة	bullet, shot
3406	إفراج	releasing	4032	بحرية	navy	4586	صلح	peace, reconciliation
3432	حارب	to fight, wage war against	4050	اجتياح	incursion, invasion	4588	سرية	(military) company
3472	دفاعي	defensive	4055	اقتحام	incursion, assault; storming into	4597	ملاحقة	pursuit, chase
3476	استشهد	to die in battle, a martyr				4605	مهاجمة	attack
3523	حراسة	guard	4136	اجتاح	to invade	4681	عسكر	army, troops
3609	استشهاد	martyrdom	4157	استجواب	interrogation	4737	رقيب	sergeant
3615	هدنة	truce	4191	اختطاف	abduction, kidnapping	4761	قصف	to bomb, shell
3624	درع	shield, armor	4204	حدودي	frontier, border (adj)	4774	تخريب	destruction
3625	شن	to launch	4210	استهداف	targeting	4780	قتالي	fighting (adj)
3651	سدد	to obstruct; to shoot	4245	بندقية	rifle, gun	4783	ملجأ	shelter, refuge
3687	شن	launching	4247	اقتتال	fighting	4786	فريسة	victim, prey
3691	قلعة	stronghold	4249	احتياطي	reserves	4800	مرصاد	lookout; ambush
3708	قاوم	to resist	4250	استسلام	surrender	4844	فر	to flee; to defect
3722	ذري	atomic	4251	ثار	to revolt, arise	4918	تجسس	espionage; spying
3743	مفخخ	booby-trapped	4259	اندلاع	breaking out, flaring up	4967	معتِد	aggressor
3809	انتصر	to be victorious				4996	ملحمة	fierce battle

2270 مُذَكِّرَة n. pl. -aat note, memorandum; notebook; مُذَكِّرات memoirs, diary
الحكومة تعاقدت مع أربع شركات عبر مذكرات تفاهم ودون كلفة على الخزينة لاستخراج الصخر الزيتي — The government contracted with four companies through memoranda of understanding, and without cost to the treasury, to extract the oil rock
78 | 1200 |

2271 راحِل adj. deceased, late
أعمال الأديب الراحل نجيب محفوظ حظيت — بمكانة مرموقة وبارزة على الصعيد العالمي
The works of the deceased author Naguib Mahfouz hold a high and prominent position on the world level
80 | 1168 |

2272 حَليب *n.* milk

لا تأسف على حليب انسكب على التراب — Don't worry about milk that has been spilled on the dirt

80 | 1166 |

2273 أَنْهَى *v. IV* to complete, finish

قال لها ما رآه وكيف أحس، ثم أنهى حكايته وهو يبذل مجهودا خارقا للسيطرة على مشاعره — He told her what he saw and how he felt, then he brought his story to an end, exerting miraculous efforts to control his feelings

92 | 1017 |

2274 ناطِق *n.* speaker, spokesperson; (fig.) voice

قالت زوجتي بلهجة ناطق عسكري يلقي بيان هام: سنكتفي بوجبتين خفيفتين — My wife said in the voice of a military spokesman delivering an important communiqué: We will make do with two light meals

78 | 1197 |

2275 زَمَنِيّ *adj.* temporal, time; chronological; transitory

يطرق الباب ثلاث مرات ويكون بين كل مرة ومرة فاصل زمني ليعطي فرصة لإجابة من يسمعه — He knocks on the door three times and between each time there is a time break to give the opportunity for whoever hears him to answer

80 | 1162 |

2276 انْخِفاض *n.* reduction, decrease, drop

شهدت أسعار الخضر والفواكه منذ عدة اسابيع انخفاضا ملموسا عبر كامل ربوع الوطن مما أثار ارتياح العائلات ضعيفة الدخل — The prices of fruit and vegetables have witnessed a noticeable decrease in the last several weeks in all parts of the nation which has made low-income families happy

74 | 1258 |

2277 شلون /shloon/ (Bah.Irq.Qat.) *interrog.* how

اتركونا ابحالنا احنا نعرف شلون نحل مشاكلنا ما نريد مساعدتكم — Leave us alone, we know how to solve our problems, we don't want your help

34 | 2721 | +spo +for

2278 ارْتَبَطَ *v. VIII* to be tied, be connected ب to sth

قد ارتبط الإسلام فى ذهنه بالإرهاب والقتل — Islam was connected in his mind to terrorism and killing

83 | 1115 |

2279 حَرَّكَ *v. II* to make move, activate, stimulate sth/sb

الطائر الطنان يحرك أجنحته أسرع من أي طائر آخر، أحيانا يحرك أجنحته على حوالي ٤ آلاف حركة في الدقيقة الواحدة — The hummingbird moves its wings faster than any other bird, sometimes flapping his wings at approximately 4,000 beats a minute

96 | 969 |

2280 إشْراف *n.* supervision, direction

أنا حصتي بين إخواني الإشراف على حقل القمح والشعير — My share among my brothers is to look after the wheat and barley field

83 | 1125 |

2281 صَيْد *n.* hunting, fishing

صار واحد منهم.. يخرج معهم إلى رحلات الصيد، ويأكل ما يأكلونه من كائنات الوديان العجيبة — He became one of them…He goes out with them on hunting trips, and he eats what they eat in the way of strange creatures of the wadis

87 | 1065 |

2282 مَعْلاة *n. pl.* مَعالِ greatness, nobility; glory, loftiness; مَعالِي (in titles) Highness, Excellency

الطعام جاهز يا معالي الوزير — The food is ready, Your Excellency (the Minister)

53 | 1755 | +news

2283 أَسْفَرَ *v. IV* to result عن in, cause sth

داهمت السلطات الأمنية مخبأه لاعتقاله ودار اشتباك طويل أسفر عن استشهاد أحمد واثنين من المجاهدين — The security authorities raided his hideout to arrest him, and a long battle took place which resulted in the death of Ahmad and two of the mujahidin

79 | 1172 | +news

2284 مُضادّ *adj.* anti-, counter-; *n. pl.* -aat anti(biotic), anti(depressant)

لقد كلفتني شركة دبل إكس بتنظيم حملة إعلانية مضادة — The Double-X company has enlisted me to organize a counter media campaign

80 | 1153 |

2285 يَقِين *n.* certainty; conviction

لم تخف أبدا عليه.. كانت على يقين بنجاته ووصوله إليها — She never feared for him...she was sure he would be saved and come back to her

85 | 1085 |

2286 مَقْبَرة *n.* pl. مَقابِر grave, tomb; graveyard

ما زالت تذهب الى المقبرة أسبوعيا لزيارة قبر زوجها الذى توفي قبل عشرين سنة — She still goes to the graveyard every week to visit the grave of her husband who died twenty years ago

80 | 1166 |

2287 مُعَسْكَر *n.* pl. -aat camp, encampment

تم إنشاء معسكرات جديدة لتدريب الجيش المرابط الذى استعرض قواته وزير الأوقاف — New camps were built to train the attached army, whose troops the Minister of Islamic Endowments reviewed

78 | 1183 |

2288 مَعْلَم *n.* pl. مَعالِم sign, mark, marking; feature; مَعالِم features, contours; landmarks, sights

ا — كنت سعيدا لأن المعالم الرئيسية في بغداد لم تتغيّر was happy because the principle features in Baghdad have not changed

86 | 1079 |

2289 أَوَّلِيّ *adj.* first, primary, chief, foremost

تشير التقديرات الأولية إلى زيادة في معدلات البطالة — Initial estimations point to an increase in the rate of unemployment

81 | 1146 |

2290 جِنْسِيّ *adj.* sexual

لن يبدي أي تسامح عندما يتعلق الموضوع بالاعتداء الجنسي في الجيش — He will not show any tolerance at all when the matter has to do with sexual assault in the army

81 | 1132 |

2291 مُخَدِّر *n.* anesthetic: مُخَدِّرات narcotics, drugs

يصادف السادس والعشرين من شهر يونيو اليوم العالمي لمكافحة المخدرات هذا الخطر الذي يقلق المجتمعات الإنسانية — The 26th of June is International Day against Drug Abuse (World Day for Fighting Drugs), a menace that troubles human societies

85 | 1084 |

2292 مَلاك *n.* pl. مَلائِكَة angel

ورد في بعض الآثار أن الله عز وجل أرسل ملك الموت ليقبض روح امرأة من الناس — In some old sources it says that God, may He be glorified, sent the angel of death to take the spirit of a woman from the people

76 | 1205 |

2293 واقِعيّ *adj.* realistic; actual

الإسلام دين واقعي.. لذلك أباح التعدد وحدده ووضع له قيدا — Islam is a realistic religion... therefore it permitted polygamy and limited it and put restrictions on it

84 | 1089 |

2294 نَصَّ *v. I (u)* to stipulate, specify على sth

مواثيق الأمم المتحدة تنص على أن للمواطن حقا في التعليم بلغته القومية — The United Nations Charter stipulates that citizens have the right to education in their national language

76 | 1211 |

2295 دَعْوَى *n.* lawsuit, legal action; claim, allegation; (Egy.Lev.) right, business; (Egy.) مالكش دعوى /ma-lak-sh da9wa/ you have no right; it's none of your business

جاء من يقنعها بأن ترفع دعوى على المصور الذي صنع «مجده» وثراءه بفجيعتها — Someone came to convince her to sue the photographer who made his "glory" and his wealth from her disaster

85 | 1075 |

2296 كُرْدِيّ *n./adj.* pl. أَكْراد Kurd, Kurdish

دخلتها مع مرور الزمن بعض المفردات من اللغة الكردية وقليل من العربية والتركية أيضا — With the passage of time, some vocabulary items from the Kurdish language entered it, as well as a little Arabic and Turkish

61 | 1499 |

2297 تَوْحِيد *n.* unification, unity; standardization, oneness; monotheism

شددوا على توحيد كل الجهود لمعالجة الحالة الناشئة في مخيم نهر البارد — They stressed uniting all efforts to deal with the developing situation in the Nahr Al-Brad camp

75 | 1217 |

2298 صَبَّ *v. I (u)* to flow; to fall (rain, snow); to pour, serve (tea or similar beverage)

جلست المرأة إلى جانب زوجها من الناحية الأخرى، وراحت تصب القهوة فى الفناجيل — The woman sat beside her husband on the other side, and began to pour coffee into the cups

88 | 1046 |

2299 تَوَصَّلَ *v. V* to arrive at, reach ب (agreement); to receive ب sth

لقد فكرت طويلا حتى توصلت إلى فكرة مبتكرة تماما — I thought a long time until I arrived at a completely innovative idea

85 | 1086 |

2300 عِصَابَة *n. pl.* -aat gang, band, group

كثير من النازحين وضعوا مصيرهم بين أيدي العصابات المهربين لاجتياز خليج عدن وصولا إلى اليمن — Many of the displaced persons put their fate into the hands of smuggling gangs to cross the Gulf of Aden to reach Yemen

81 | 1137 |

2301 صَدَقَ *v. I (u)* to be sincere, be truthful, tell the truth; to be correct

لا ألومك، ولكن ألوم نفسى التى صدقت فى لحظة من اللحظات كلامك المعسول والذى طار فى الهواء — I am not blaming you, but I blame myself for believing for a moment your honey words which flew into the air

80 | 1143 |

2302 مُحَاكَمَة *n.* trial, legal proceeding

وضعت تحت الإقامة الجبرية في منزلها، ريثما تقدم إلى المحاكمة لمعرفة مصير الأموال الهائلة التي سرقتها من أموال الشعب — She was placed under house arrest, until she was taken to court to find out the fate of the large amount of the people's money she stole

78 | 1169 |

2303 ثَانِيَة *n. pl.* ثَوانٍ (def. ثَوانِي) second (time span)

الليل يطول وتتباعد دقائقه لتصبح كل ثانية ساعة كاملة — Night lengthens and its minutes grow far apart so that each second becomes a whole hour

89 | 1028 |

2304 أَجْر *n. pl.* أُجُور wage, pay; fee; recompense, remuneration

من حق العامل على الدولة والمجتمع أن ينال الأجر الذي يناسب عمله ويجزي إنتاجه ويوفر له حياة كريمة — It is the right of the worker, owed him by the state and by society, that he obtain a wage which is appropriate to his work and which rewards his productivity and provides him a dignified life

84 | 1091 |

2305 خَلَل *n.* malfunction, breakdown; defect, flaw; deficiency, impairment; crack, gap

الخلل القائم في تطبيق العدالة الدولية لن يزول إلا بزوال الخلل الراهن القائم في واقع النظام السياسي العالمي — The outstanding problems in applying international justice will not disappear unless the current problems that exist in the world political regime disappear as well

89 | 1024 |

2306 حَوَّلَ *v. II* to change, convert sth (إلى into); to divert sth عن away from

بدلا من أن تسعده حولت حياته إلى معاناة — Instead of making him happy, you changed his life into suffering

93 | 982 |

2307 غَضّ *n.* lowering (one's gaze); بِغَضّ النَّظَر عن while ignoring, turning a blind eye to

وبعض النظر عمن يحكم تركيا، فإن الأحلام هي نفسها — No matter who rules Turkey, the dreams are the same

90 | 1019 |

2308 مَجْنُون *n./adj. pl.* مَجَانِين crazy, insane (person)

انصرف غاضبا وقال لنفسه إنها مجنونة ولا تصلح له أبدا — He left angrily and said to himself that she is crazy and is not suitable for him at all

84 | 1085 |

2309 حَمّام *n.* bath, bathroom

أضعت نظارتي الشمسية في حمام السباحة ولم أجدها — I lost my sunglasses at the swimming pool and didn't find them

85 | 1069 |

2310 سِلْم *n.* peace

أثبت هذا النوع من الطائرات فعالية ملحوظة في الحرب والسلم على حد سواء — This type of airplane proved to be noticeably effective equally in war and peace

84 | 1091 |

2311 ضَغَطَ *v. I (u)* to press, push على sth; (computer) to click على sth

كان يضغط على الكلمات بحيث تبتعد الكلمة عن الأخرى وتتوضح تماما — He would stress the words so that each word would be separated from the other and would be completely clear

84 | 1078 |

2312 لاجئ *n.* refugee; *adj.* seeking refuge

انتقلت إلى ذلك البيت المتهدم ١٥ عائلة من اللاجئين المسيحيين — Fifteen families of Christian refugees moved into that dilapidated house

65 | 1397 |

2313 بَرَزَ *v. I (u)* to emerge, appear; to stand out, be prominent

بينما كان المسلمون يحفرون الخندق، برزت لهم صخرة ضخمة، حاولوا تكسيرها فلم يستطيعوا — While the Muslims were digging the trench, they came to a huge rock; they tried to break it but they were not able to

84 | 1080 |

2314 فاضِل *adj.* honorable, eminent, distinguished; left over, remaining; *n.* rest, leftover, remainder

يساهم في بناء جيل صالح ينشأ على الأخلاق الفاضلة — He is helping build a worthy generation brought up on honorable morals

65 | 1387 | +for

2315 عِطْر *n. pl.* عُطُور perfume

سرت في الجو رائحة العطور الرخيصة من المارة، ومن الذاهبين إلى الكنيسة — The smell of the cheap perfume of the passers-by and the church-goers filled the air

74 | 1227 |

2316 تَغْطِية *n.* covering; (news) coverage

استخدمت أشجار النخيل لتغطية سقفه، وخصص قسم من المسجد لإيواء الضعفاء والفقراء — Palm trees were used to cover the roof, and a part of the mosque was set aside for the accommodation of the weak and the poor

83 | 1099 |

2317 شَرِيعَة *n.* law; Sharia (Islamic law); شريعة الغاب law of the jungle

ذهبت للدراسة بالأزهر الشريف وأنا عمري عشر سنوات، وتعلمت فيه الشريعة والفقه حتى صرت قاضيا — I went to study at Al-Azhar when I was ten years old, and I studied Islamic Law and jurisprudence until I became a judge

79 | 1155 |

2318 نِداء *n.* call, appeal; invitation, summons

هذا يعني أنه لم يسمع النداء ولا يدري ما يدور حوله — This means that he did not hear the call, and he doesn't know what is happening around him

86 | 1056 |

2319 مُخْرِج *n.* (screen, stage) director; *adj.* directing (movie, play)

لا يعد النص نقطة انطلاق للعرض المسرحي ولا هدفا له وقد يستغني المخرج عن النص المكتوب بالمرة — The text is not considered a starting point of the theatrical presentation, nor a goal of it, and the director can do without the written text completely

77 | 1168 |

2320 سَماح *n.* permission; magnanimity; indulgence

وزير الداخلية أذاع بلاغا على الناس بعدم السماح لأحد بدخول البيوت وتفتيشها إلا بإذن موقع من الوزير نفسه — The Minister of the Interior broadcast an announcement to the people about not permitting anyone to enter homes and search them without permission signed by the Minister himself

86 | 1054 |

2321 شَقَّة *n.* apartment

ينتقل بين قاعات المحاضرات والمعامل والمكتبة، ثم يعود إلى الشقة لتناول غدائه أمام التليفزيون وينام القيلولة ساعتين كاملتين — He moves between the lecture halls and the labs and the library, then he returns to the apartment to take his lunch in front of the television, and to take a full two-hour nap

84 | 1075 |

2322 أَيْمَن *adj.* fem. يُمْنَى right, right hand; lucky (person)

إنه إبني وساعدي الأيمن في إدارة المصنع — He is my son and my right arm in directing the factory

78 | 1152 |

2323 صُلْب *adj.* hard, solid; stiff, inflexible; steel; *n.* core, crux, essence; steel

عرضنا لكم سابقا أن القرص الصلب بالكمبيوتر هو الوسيط الأساسي لتخزين البرامج والملفات — We previously demonstrated to you that the hard disk of the computer is the basic means for storing programs and files

85 | 1059 |

2324 مُطالَبَة *n.* demand; requirement

من لا يقوى على المطالبة بحقه لا يمكنه أن ينوب عن الآخرين — He who is not able to demand his right is not able to represent others

75 | 1200 |

2325 بَعْثَة and بِعْثَة *n.* pl. بَعَثات delegation; mission

كما تعرفون، فإن مكتب البعثات سيتكفل بمصاريف الدراسة — As you know, the office of delegations will be responsible for the study fees

74 | 1226 |

2326 مَجْد *n.* glory, magnificence, splendor

ها هي فرصتنا التاريخية كي نعيد مجد الآباء — This is our historic opportunity to restore the glory of the ancestors

78 | 1154 | +lit

2327 مَحَبَّة *n.* love, affection

سأحارب الظلم وأنشر الخير والمحبة والفضيلة — I will fight oppression and spread goodness and love and virtue

92 | 979 |

2328 غَنَّى *v. II* to sing (sth)

كان صاحب البقالة يغني مع أم كلثوم بطرب واضح — The owner of the grocery store was singing along with Um Kalthoum with evident joy

86 | 1051 |

2329 تَوازُن *n.* balance, equilibrium; balancing

يجب خلق توازن بين منافع التكنولوجيا ومخاطرها المحتملة — A balance needs to be created between the benefits of technology and its possible dangers

81 | 1113 |

2330 نَا *v. I (u)* to grow, develop; rise, increase

علاقات التجارة بين البلدين تنمو بصورة جيدة — Business relations between the two countries are growing well

74 | 1208 |

2331 نَوْعِيَّة *n.* peculiarity, characteristic

إن هذه النوعية من التعليقات ليست مفيدة وغير مقبولة — This type of commentary is not useful, and not acceptable

81 | 1116 |

2332 اِبْتَعَدَ *v. VIII* to move away, distance oneself عن from sth/sb

نصيحة لوجه الله.. ابتعد عن هذا الطريق لأن نهايته سيئة — Some free advice: stay away from that road, because its end is bad

84 | 1067 |

2333 تَدْخِين *n.* smoking; fumigating

كانت قلقة متوترة الأعصاب فأكثرت من التدخين، ولم أكن على حال أحسن — She was worried and nervous, so she smoked a lot, and I wasn't in any better shape

76 | 1175 |

2334 سُرْعانَ ما *n.* how quickly, it didn't take long for

إذا لم تشعر بالنوم استفيد من الوقت بالقراءة وسرعان ما تخلد إلى النوم بهدوء دون التفكير بأمور الحياة اليومية — If you don't feel sleepy, use the time in reading and soon you will fall into a peaceful sleep without thinking of the affairs of daily life

82 | 1098 |

2335 عَصَبِيّ *adj.* nervous, irritable; (med.) nervous, neural

كان وجهه مرهقا وحركاته عصبية ويدخن بشراهة — His face was exhausted and his movements were nervous, and he smoked greedily

88 | 1026 |

2336 نَظيف *adj.* clean, tidy

رأيت الأطفال يلبسون ثيابا نظيفة ويقطفون
الأزهار — I saw the children wearing clean clothes
and picking flowers

95 | 951 |

2337 تَصَوَّرَ *v. V* to imagine, envision, ponder sth

أخشى أن تكون كاذبا.. أتصور أنك لا تعرف الحب
ولكنك تطلب اللذة — I am afraid you are lying...
I imagine that you don't know love but that
you are seeking pleasure

90 | 1001 |

2338 تَمْثيل *n.* representation, exemplification;
acting

أعضاء البرلمان نجحوا في تمثيل المواطنين خير تمثيل
— The members of parliament succeeded in
representing the citizens as well as possible

85 | 1059 |

2339 شَعْبِيَّة *n.* popularity, mass appeal

من المعروف أنه يحظى بشعبية هائلة في بلاده —
It is known that he attained great popularity
in his country

70 | 1272 |

2340 وَجَبة *n.* pl. وَجَبات meal; menu

لا استطيع مقابلته الا خلال وجبات الطعام وفترة
النوم — I can't meet him except during meals
and sleep time

89 | 999 |

2341 هُدًى *n.* guidance; الهُدَى the right path

تعبت اليوم من السير الذي كان على غير هدى في
كثير من الأحيان — I got tired today from
walking, mostly going nowhere in particular

72 | 1237 |

2342 سَكَن *n.* housing

يعمل موظف استقبال هنا فى سكن الطلبة — He
works as a receptionist here in student housing

91 | 981 |

2343 شَهْرِيّ *adj.* monthly; شَهْرِيّاً *adv.* monthly

سيقضي عطلته الشهرية بين الاهل والاصدقاء — He
will spend his monthly vacation among family
and friends

82 | 1084 |

2344 أَمْسَكَ *v. IV* to grab, hold sth/sb or ب sth/sb;
to refrain عن from

أمسك بذراعها وسألها عن اسمها — He grabbed
her arm and asked her what her name was

77 | 1161 | +lit

2345 سَيْف *n.* sword

يا قابيل إن قابيل قادم على فرسه، وهو يحمل سيفا
مهندا ربما يريد به رقبتك — O Cain, Cain, coming
on his horse, carrying a sword of Indian steel,
perhaps he wants to use it on your neck

81 | 1098 |

2346 يابانيّ *n./adj.* Japanese

يبحث مع السفير الياباني إقامة جامعة تكنولوجيا
يابانية — He is discussing with the Japanese
ambassador the establishment of a Japanese
technological university

77 | 1157 |

2347 مَجْزَرة *n.* pl. مَجازِر massacre, blood bath,
slaughter

تلاعبت في ذهني صور المجزرة الرهيبة.. دخان ونار
وجثث متهالكة فوق بعضها — Images of the
terrifying massacre were playing in my head...
smoke and fire and corpses decaying on top
of each other

79 | 1128 |

2348 حَرَصَ *v. I (a)* to desire, be eager على for sth

فلأن المصريين أجسادهم مترهلة وحياتهم غير صحية،
يحرص هو على رشاقته ولياقته — Because Egyptian's
bodies are bloated and their lives are unhealthy,
he is insistent on fitness and being thin

86 | 1033 |

2349 تَصَوُّر *n.* depiction, conception, imagination;
concept, notion, view, idea

ويرى أصحاب هذا التصور أن هذه هي الطريقة
الفعّالة لإعادة بناء منظمة التحرير — Those who
espouse this view believe that this is the
effective way to rebuild the (Palestinian)
Liberation Organization

88 | 1008 |

2350 مُرْتَفِع *adj.* high, elevated; rising, climbing,
soaring

أشار إلى المبنى الأبيض الفخم، ذى النوافذ الطويلة
المرتفعة، والشرفة الفسيحة، الذى يتوسط الميدان

30 Politics

47	رئيس	president	552	بيان	report; communiqué	1548	داخلية	internal affairs
51	دولة	state				1549	عدالة	justice, fairness
96	وزير	minister	561	رسمي	official			
99	بلد	country	569	محلّي	local	1603	سيادة	sovereignty
101	مجلس	council	589	أمير	prince; commander	1608	مفاوضة	negotiation
103	حكومة	government				1615	محافظ	governor
106	سياسي	political; politician	649	خارجية	foreign affairs	1619	كتلة	bloc
121	دولي	international	659	شعبي	popular	1635	جنسية	nationality
122	شعب	people	660	محافظة	governorate	1690	انتخابي	electoral
143	وطني	national	677	مملكة	kingdom	1694	حكم	to rule, govern
188	سلام	peace	696	عاصمة	capital			
193	حركة	movement	703	تنظيم	organization	1759	متحدث	spokesman
199	نظام	regime	723	أجنبي	foreign; foreigner	1773	ملكي	royal
202	قضية	issue; lawsuit				1777	دستوري	constitutional
211	قرار	decision; resolution	765	خارجي	external, foreign	1782	اعتقال	arrest
						1813	اقليم	region
217	وزارة	ministry	810	إمارة	emirate	1892	سفارة	embassy
228	إدارة	administration	824	جمهوريّة	republic	1898	استقلال	independence
232	قانون	law	828	حاكم	governor, ruler	1913	تشريعي	legislative
248	أمة	nation				1983	سلمي	peaceful
258	لجنة	committee	867	رئاسة	presidency	2071	هزيمة	defeat
276	ولاية	state; term of office	884	حكومي	govenmental	2110	نزاع	conflict
			888	تصريح	statement	2112	تحالف	alliance
278	عضو	member	918	حملة	campaign	2125	تعيين	appointing
289	حزب	party	940	صهيوني	Zionist	2147	دبلوماسي	diplomatic
301	اتحاد	union	943	ديمقراطي	democratic	2150	نقابة	union
308	عالمي	international	950	سلطان	Sultan	2152	ثنائي	bilateral
311	حكم	rule, government	958	خلاف	dispute	2154	شرعيّة	legitimacy
			986	تطبيق	implementation	2171	ساد	to prevail; rule, govern
327	مواطن	citizen		وفد	delegation			
328	سلطة	authority	990	استقرار	stability	2182	نيابة	prosecutor's office
354	مسؤول	official	997	ديمقراطيّة	democracy			
360	نائب	deputy; vice-	1003	سفير	ambassador	2204	رئاسي	presidential
370	سياسة	politics; policy	1015	قومي	national, state	2216	غالبيّة	majority
373	وطن	nation; homeland	1085	زعيم	leader	2232	نيابي	parliamentary
			1173	معارضة	opposition	2248	بند	article, clause
394	مؤتمر	conference	1200	اتفاقية	agreement	2252	سلطنة	Sultanate
425	ملك	king	1216	إقليمي	regional	2274	ناطق	spokesman
434	انتخاب	election	1230	بلديّة	municipality	2310	سلم	peace
521	منظمة	organization	1243	دستور	constitution	2312	لاجئ	refugee
529	حرّية	freedom	1287	برلمان	parliament	2415	تصويت	voting
534	قائد	leader	1413	تنفيذي	executive	2461	برلماني	parliamentary
540	محكمة	court, tribunal	1460	عقوبة	penalty, sanction	2464	عرش	throne
541	قيادة	leadership	1464		sanction	2483	معارض	opposing; opponent
542	دفاع	defense	1479	مستقلّ	independent			

2533	ملكة	queen	3403	مباحثة	discussion, dialog	4318	جمرك	customs duties
2537	أغلبية	majority	3423	معاهدة	treaty	4326	قومية	nationalism
2713	متطرف	extremist	3435	جماهيرية	Jamahiriya	4380	علمانية	secularism
2718	مديرية	administration; district; department	3453	مفوضية	delegation	4414	استبداد	despotism
			3467	علم	flag	4419	عاهل	king, monarch
2723	مظاهرة	demonstration	3547	وطنيّة	nationalism	4446	وساطة	mediation
2782	تفاوض	negotiation	3549	اقتراع	voting	4473	صهيونيّة	Zionism
2807	شفافيّة	transparency	3596	تظاهرة	demonstration	4488	أجندة	agenda, schedule; roadmap, blueprint
2838	مؤامرة	conspiracy	3641	طاغ	tyrant			
2840	كادر	cadre	3709	ائتلاف	coalition			
2843	مصالحة	conciliation	3714	ناخب	voter			
2900	وزاري	ministerial	3793	قمع	oppression, repression	4505	تعصب	fanaticism
2929	شورى	consultative				4540	عنصرية	racism
2972	مندوب	delegate	3806	طاغية	tyrant	4561	استعماري	colonialist; settlement (adj)
2974	تطرف	extremism	3821	متشدد	extremist			
3035	جمهوري	Republican	3863	معتدل	moderate			
3038	حزبي	partisan	3866	خصم	adversary	4562	تعددية	pluralism
3041	ترشيح	nomination	3877	نقيب	union boss	4586	صلح	reconciliation
3055	استعمار	colonialism	3911	جالية	expatriate community	4597	ملاحقة	pursuit; legal prosecution
3074	قيادي	leading; leader						
3149	اشتراكي	socialist	3944	متظاهر	demonstrator	4670	بعثي	Baathist
3157	حلف	alliance, treaty	3959	استشاري	advisory; advisor	4679	اعتدال	moderation
3220	ميثاق	treaty, pact, charter	3980	طائفيّة	sectarianism	4777	زعامة	leadership
3234	حشد	build-up, mobilization; crowd	3993	دبلوماسيّة	diplomacy	4862	تحريض	incitement
			4044	قطر	region, district	4867	والٍ	ruler, governor
			4075	مشاورة	consultation	4873	عبوديّة	slavery
3310	وفاق	agreement, accord	4103	مبعوث	envoy, delegate	4875	تمرير	passing (including passing a law)
3313	اتحادي	unionist	4178	خصخصة	privatization			
3324	حليف	ally	4188	عاقب	to punish sb for a crime	4888	معاقبة	punishment, sanction
3328	شيوعي	communist						
3365	عروبة	Arabism	4225	نفاق	hypocrisy	4910	وصاية	trusteeship, guardianship
3367	أكثريّة	majority	4241	أقلّيّة	minority			
3380	مرسوم	decree, edict	4288	علماني	secular	4955	صليبي	Crusader

He pointed to the luxurious white building, with long, high windows, and broad balconies, which lay near the center of the square

88 | 1005 |

2351 مُحِبّ *adj.* affectionate, loving, desiring; *n.* aficionado, fan, enthusiast

هل يمكن للإنسان الجامعي المثقف المحب للموسيقى أن يكون مجرما؟ — Is it possible for a cultured,

university-educated person who loves music to be a criminal?

80 | 1112 |

2352 تأهيل *n.* certification, qualification; training, education

إن محو الامية يساعد على تأهيل اعداد كبيرة ومساعدتهم على ايجاد وظائف مناسبة والعيش حياة كريمة منتجة — Eradicating illiteracy helps

rehabilitate large numbers (of people), and helps them find suitable jobs and to live a decent, productive life

71 | 1253 |

2353 نِسائِيّ *adj.* women-related, women's; feminine

هي طبيبة نسائية وداعية إسلامية في الموصل — She is a gynecologist and an Islamic preacher in Mosul

79 | 1121 |

2354 تَمْييز *n.* distinction, differentiation; discrimination

لم أتمكن من تمييز الفريقين كونهما يلعبان بلباس متشابه ومتقارب اللون — I am not able to distinguish the two teams since they both play with similar clothing and close colors

86 | 1032 |

2355 ساخِن *adj.* hot, heated

الواضح أن أعصابك تعبت.. أنصحك بحمام ساخن ثم صلاة ركعتين بنية انفراج الهم — It is clear that your nerves are tired...I advise you to take a hot shower and then do a couple of prostrations with the purpose of letting go of your worries

86 | 1022 |

2356 عِزّ *n.* prime, peak, height

لقد تعودوا على حياة الرفاهية وحياة العز — They got used to the life of luxury and the life of renown

86 | 1023 |

2357 بَطالَة and بِطالَة *n.* unemployment; inactivity, idleness

من المسؤول عن الفقر والبطالة والمرض؟ — Who is responsible for poverty and unemployment and illness?

81 | 1091 |

2358 اِنْفَجَرَ *v. VII* to explode, detonate; to burst, erupt

بدأ القطار يهتز وصوت الانفجارات يقترب والخوف ينفجر في عيونها — The train began to shake, and the sound of the explosions drew near, and fear exploded in their eyes

84 | 1045 |

2359 ثُلْث *n.* one third; du. (in idafa) ثُلْثَيْ two thirds (of)

بعد ثلث ساعة، في العاشرة تماما، حل موعد نومه — After twenty minutes, at exactly ten o'clock, the time for going to bed had come

93 | 949 |

2360 مُؤَثِّر *adj.* influential, effective; moving, touching; *n.* effect, impact

إنها مجرد خطوة، لكنها ستكون مؤثرة.. أليس من واجبنا أن نفعل شيئا من أجل هؤلاء؟ — It is merely a step, but it will be influential...Isn't it our duty to do something for these people?

87 | 1008 |

2361 لائِحَة *n. pl.* لَوائِح list, table; schedule

كان المنتخب العراقي ارغم حسب اللوائح الى خوض التصفيات ضمن المجموعة الثانية — The Iraqi national team was forced, according to the regulations, to enter the elimination tournament as part of the second group

75 | 1165 |

2362 دَمَوِيّ *adj.* bloody; blood-

الرمان يقلل أكسدة الكوليسترول السيء ويمنع ترسبه على جدران الأوعية الدموية فيساعد في الوقاية من أمراض القلب — Pomegranates reduce the oxidation of bad cholesterol and prevents its being deposited on the walls of the blood vessels, and thus it helps prevent heart diseases

87 | 1015 |

2363 مُبَرِّر *adj.* excusing, justifying; *n. pl.* -aat excuse, justification

ما المرأة دون أمومة؟ أليست الأمومة مبرر لوجودها وعنوانًا لمعنى أن تكون امرأة؟ — What is a woman without motherhood? Isn't motherhood the reason for her existence and the epitome of the meaning of being a woman?

85 | 1039 |

2364 مَطْروح *adj.* submitted, proposed, suggested; presented, offered; thrown, cast; prostrate

ترى الولايات المتحدة أن ايران تبدو عازمة على إنتاج قنبلة نووية وتقول إن جميع الخيارات مطروحة لمحاولة منعها من ذلك — The United States is of the opinion that Iran appears determined to produce a nuclear bomb, and it says that all options are on the table to attempt to prevent them from doing that

78 | 1120 |

2365 فَلْسَفَة *n.* philosophy

فلسفة هذا الجيل – إن كانت ثمة فلسفة – هي
فلسفة براجماتية من نوع «هنا والآن» The —
philosophy of this generation – if there is
a philosophy – is a pragmatic philosophy
of the type "here and now"

90 | 980 |

2366 الْتَفَتَ *v. VIII* to turn around; to pay
attention إلى to sb/sth; to heed, consider
إلى sb/sth

هكذا اندفع يسألها، لكنها لم ترد، لم تلتفت إليه، كأنها
لا تحس بوجوده In this way he hurried and —
asked her, but she didn't respond, she didn't
turn towards him, as if she was not aware of
his presence

74 | 1178 | +lit

2367 تَفْتِيش *n.* search, inspection; (security) check

تم القبض على المتهمين كما تم تفتيش سيارتهما
The — وعثرت الشرطة بداخلها على مواد مخدرة
two accused were arrested, and their car was
searched and the police found addictive
substances inside it

87 | 1004 |

2368 مَجَّانِيّ *adj.* free, free of charge

نشاط الجمعية يتركز في المجال الطبي بتقديم العلاج
المجاني لغير القادرين The activity of the —
association is focused in the medical arena
on offering free treatment for those unable
to pay

89 | 982 |

2369 شُرْب *vn.* drinking

مازالوا يحصلون على مياه الشرب من الآبار الملوثة —
They still get drinking water from polluted
wells

95 | 922 |

2370 مُعاصِر *adj.* contemporary, contemporaneous;
modern

نجيب محفوظ قد أثرى أدب الرواية والقصة العربية
المعاصرة بعشرات الروايات والقصص القصيرة،
متفوقًا على أقرانه Naguib Mahfouz enriched —
the literature of the contemporary Arab novel
and story with scores of novels and short
stories, excelling over his peers

80 | 1099 |

2371 وَرْشَة *n. pl.* وِرَش workshop

إن ما يجري داخل هذه الورشة عبارة عن حوار لا
يعبر عن رأي مسبق What happens inside this —
workshop is a kind of discussion which doesn't
express a previous opinion

72 | 1212 | +news

2372 رَحِم *n.* uterus, womb; bosom; inside; kin,
kinfolk

أحيانا أشعر أننا خرجنا من الرحم نفسه —
Sometimes I feel that we came out of the
same womb

80 | 1090 | +for

2373 حِجاب *n.* hijab (Islamic head scarf), veil

الحرب على الحجاب بدأت في فرنسا، ثم انتقلت
إلى بريطانيا The war on the head scarf —
began in France, and then it moved to
Britain

79 | 1105 |

2374 تَوَجَّهَ *v. V* to go, head إلى towards; to turn,
face إلى/نحو towards; to direct ب (a question)
إلى at

يقف بقرب الصورة الأولى ثم يتوجه الى اليسار
ويقف بقرب الصورة الثانية متبسمًا He stands —
close to the first picture and then moves to
the left and stands next to the second picture
smiling

85 | 1024 |

2375 مُتَنَوِّع *adj.* diverse; sundry, various

الحياة هي مجموعة من الخبرات المتنوعة —
Life is a group of varied experiences

81 | 1075 |

2376 صَريح *adj.* candid, frank, sincere

أحب أن أكون صريحة معك.. لا أعتقد أن الوظيفة
تناسبك I want to be frank with you…I don't —
believe the job is suitable for you

91 | 958 |

2377 صَيْفِيّ *adj.* summer, summery

استمرت في تلك الوظيفة حتى بعد انقضاء العطلة
الصيفية وبدء الدراسة She continued with this —
job even after the summer vacation period
ended and the school year began

81 | 1076 |

2378 جَوْدَة *n.* excellence, good quality

أشار إلى نجاح قطاع البترول في تصدير منتجات — بترولية عالية الجودة He pointed to the success of the petroleum sector in exporting high quality petroleum products

78 | 1113 |

2379 حارَة *n.* quarter, district; neighborhood; alley, lane

إنهم بؤساء يا سيدتي على الرغم من أنهم أكرم أهل الحارة أصلا — They are wretched, Ma'am, despite the fact that they are the most noble family in the alleyway, originally

62 | 1400 | +lit

2380 خاطِئ *adj.* mistaken, at fault

قال دبلوماسي في السفارة إن هذه معلومات خاطئة وغير صحيحة وايران لم تقدم هذه الاسلحة — A diplomat in the embassy said that this information is false and not true and Iran did not offer those weapons

83 | 1038 |

2381 سِلْعَة *n. pl.* سِلَع commodity, commercial item, product; *pl.* سِلَع goods

الحب ليس سلعة رخيصة نساوم بها كما نريد — Love is not a cheap product that we can bargain over as much as we want

80 | 1081 |

2382 مَطْلَع *n.* beginning, dawn (of an era)

المدارس الخاصة غير الحكومية بدأت تنتشر في الأردن مع مطلع التسعينات — The non-governmental private schools began to become widespread in Jordan at the beginning of the Nineties

82 | 1058 |

2383 عَمِيد *n.* dean; chief; (mil.) brigadier general

طه حسين هو «عميد الأدب العربي» — Taha Hussein was the "Dean of Arabic Literature"

77 | 1124 |

2384 حَنان *n.* affection, love; sympathy, empathy, compassion

يَخطف قبلة على خدها، فتوجه له نظرة بين اللوم والحنان — He steals a kiss on her cheek, and she shoots him a glance somewhere between reproach and compassion

77 | 1116 |

2385 بَصَر *n.* vision, perception; sight, seeing; view, glance

لم يمنعه فقدان بصره من أن يكون عنصرًا فعالًا في مجتمعه القروي الصغير — The loss of his eyesight did not prevent him from being an effective element in his small village society

78 | 1102 |

2386 قَرْض *n. pl.* قُرُوض (bank) loan

لا حاجة بنا إلى قرض فعندنا مال كثير — We have no need for a loan, since we have a lot of money

76 | 1130 |

2387 صافٍ (*def.* صافِي) *adj.* pure, clear; sincere; (econ.) net (profit)

كان وجهه رائقا بلا تجاعيد، ونظرته صافية متلألئة، وشعره غزيرا أسود فاحما بلا شعرة بيضاء واحدة — His face was clear with no wrinkles, and his gaze was pure and sparkling, and his hair was thick and coal black without a single white hair

85 | 1016 |

2388 رَجاء *n.* hope, expectation; رَجاءً please, if you please

اذا مات القلب فلا عزاء له ولا رجاء منه — If the heart dies, there is no comfort for it and no hope from it

75 | 1138 |

2389 ذا *dem.pron. fem.* ذِي this, that

من ذا الذي ذات مرة بنى هذا البيت الوحيد؟ — Who is it that once built this single house?

66 | 1297 |

2390 قارَّة *n. pl.* -aat continent

سافر الى او عمل في حوالي ١٠٠ دولة منتشرة في القارات الخمس خلال السنوات الخمس والعشرين الماضية — He traveled to or worked in about 100 countries spread over the five continents during the last twenty-five years

73 | 1176 |

2391 حَرِيق *n. pl.* حَرائِق fire

ظل الحريق مشتعلا، بلا هوادة ولا رحمة، على مدى يومين — The fire kept on burning, relentlessly and without mercy, for the period of two days

80 | 1065 |

2392 تَكْلِفَة *n.* cost, expense, charge

تسهم التجارة الالكترونية في تخفيض تكلفة الاستثمار بسبب توافر المعلومات بأقل التكاليف — Electronic commerce contributes to lowering the cost of investment because of the availability of information at a minimal cost

67 | 1268 |

2393 مُرَبَّع *adj.* quadruple; square; *n.* square; رَمْز المُرَبَّع number sign, pound sign, hash mark

سيقام المشروع على مساحة تبلغ ٢١٠٠٠ متر مربع في قلب منطقة السيف، مقابل المركز التجاري الجديد — The project will be built on an area reaching 21,000 square meters in the heart of the Al-Saif district, opposite the new business center

82 | 1045 |

2394 مُتَكامِل *adj.* integral, comprehensive

أكدت الحكومة اللبنانية أنها ستقوم بإعداد برنامج عمل متكامل لمشروعات التنمية وإعادة الإنهاء والإعمار في لبنان — The Lebanese government stressed that it would prepare a comprehensive work program of development and rebuilding projects in Lebanon

79 | 1079 |

2395 طارَ *v. I (i)* to fly; to hurry; to travel by air; طارَ عَقْلُهُ to lose one's mind

ما إن شمت المسحوق حتى أحست أنها تطير، تحلق بين السحاب، لا أحزان ولا قلق ولا خوف من المستقبل — Hardly had she smelled the powder then she felt that she was flying, soaring between he clouds, no sadness and no fear of the future

81 | 1052 |

2396 جَوّال *n.* mobile (phone); *adj.* itinerant, wandering

أرسلت رسالة قصيرة من هاتفها الجوال إلى هاتف فيصل تقول له فيها: مبروك يا عريس — She sent a short text from her mobile phone to Faisal's phone in which she said: Congratulations, Bridegroom!

66 | 1293 |

2397 حَلال *adj.* permissible, legitimate; Halal (acceptable to Muslims)

الجزار الفلسطيني الذى نشترى منه اللحم الحلال.. أغلق محله للأسف وترك شيكاجو — The Palestinian butcher we buy Halal meat from closed his shop, unfortunately, and left Chicago

88 | 971 |

2398 لَجَأَ *v. I (a)* to resort إلى to, take refuge إلى in

أحس روميل بالخذلان بعد فشله وقرر ألا يهاجم مرة ثانية، وأن يلجأ إلى الحرب الدفاعية لأول مرة منذ تولى القيادة في الصحراء — Rommel felt betrayed after his failure and he decided that he would not attack again, and that he would resort to a defensive war for the first time since he took over the leadership in the desert

85 | 1002 |

2399 جالِس *adj.* seated, sitting

كنت جالسة مع احدى الطالبات نضحك معا ونتحدث في فناء المدرسة — I was sitting with one of the students, laughing together and talking in the courtyard of the school

79 | 1085 |

2400 سَكَنِيّ *adj.* housing, residential

تقوم الحكومة بتحويل هذه العشوائيات إلى أحياء سكنية حقيقية فيها الشوارع وفيها الملاعب وفيها الحدائق — The government is transforming these random neighborhoods into actual residential quarters with streets, playgrounds and parks

67 | 1264 |

2401 مُراقِب *n.* observer, inspector; supervisor, monitor; censor

تناول الطعام في غرف النوم، خوفا من أعين المراقبين — He took his food in the bedrooms, for fear of the eyes of observers

82 | 1043 |

2402 مَوْلُود *n.* pl. مَواليد newborn infant; *adj.* born in/on; هِيَ مِن مَوالِد she was born in/on

تقافزت شهلاء وسديم فرحا خارج الغرفة وهما بانتظار معرفة جنس المولود الذي أخبرتهم الممرضة الهندية بعد دقائق أنه صبي — Shuhala and Sadim flew out of the room in joy, waiting to know the gender of the newborn, about which the Indian nurse told them a few minutes later that it was a boy

84 | 1015 |

2403 طائِر n. bird; adj. flying, airborne; الكُرَة الطّائِرَة volleyball

تم حتى الآن اعدام ما لا يقل عن أربعمائة ألف طائر داجني في محاولة للحد من انتشار انفلونزا الطيور — Up till now, no less than four hundred thousand chickens have been destroyed in an attempt to limit the spread of bird flu

84 | 1009 |

2404 مُحْتَمَل adj. likely, expected, probable

من المحتمل أن تحتاج بعض المال في القريب العاجل من أجل الزواج — It is possible that you will need some money soon in order to get married

84 | 1015 |

2405 مَوْج coll.n. pl. أَمْواج waves, surges

داهمني موج الغثيان وأنا أتأمل بيتي قد التهمته النيران — Waves of nausea swept over me as I watched my house being destroyed by fire

77 | 1107 |

2406 حِدَّة n. intensity, violence

عُرف الدكتور أبو زيد بين أترابه بحدة ذكائه ومحبة مرضاه له بل وتعلقهم به — Dr Abu Zayd was known among his contemporaries for the sharpness of his intelligence and his patients' love of him, indeed attachment to him

85 | 998 |

2407 ماما and مامَة (Dia.) fem.n. mom, momma, mama

لو ماما شافتني وأنا نايم على الأرض كانت تلطم — If Mama saw me sleeping on the floor, she would slap her cheeks

56 | 1503 | +spo

2408 قِطار n. train

ساعتان ونصف الساعة ويصل القطار إلى الإسكندرية، هكذا تعلم من زياراته السابقة للبهى — In two and a half hours the train will arrive in Alexandria; this is what he learned from his previous visits to Al-Bahiy

81 | 1045 |

2409 مُوجِب n. بِمُوجِب according to, in accordance with; on the basis of; by virtue of

تم عقد اتفاقيات مع عدد من الشركات تحصل بموجبها على حقوق التنقيب عن — Agreements were concluded with a number of companies by means of which these companies will obtain rights to drill for oil

75 | 1133 |

2410 مِرْفَق n. pl. مَرافِق convenience, service; facilities, installations

سيضم المشروع مرافق سكنية ومجموعة من الفنادق والمطاعم والمكاتب — The project will include housing facilities and a group of hotels and restaurants and offices

68 | 1245 | +news

2411 ضَحْك n. laughter, laughing

توفي رئيس نقابة المسرحيين في لندن بعد دخوله في نوبة ضحك توقف بعدها قلبه عن النبض — The head of the theater union died in London after falling into a laughing fit after which his heart stopped beating

83 | 1021 |

2412 صَعِدَ v. I (a) to rise, go up; to increase

يمكن لزهرة أن تصعد أى وقت تجلس مع مريم وإيفون كما تعودت — Zahra can go upstairs at any time and sit with Maryam and Yvonne, as she was wont to do

87 | 973 |

2413 أَشادَ v. IV to praise, commend بـ sth

أشاد بالاصلاحات التي اتخذتها الدولة — He praised the reforms the state has made

71 | 1191 | +news

2414 عامَّة n. populace; عامة الناس the general public; عامَّةً in general, generally

أنا ابن راع عجوز من عامة الشعب — I am the son of an old shepherd from the common people

92 | 918 |

2415 تَصْويت n. voting

تشهد بنما استفتاء حاسما يتم من خلاله التصويت حول توسعة قناة بنما — Panama is witnessing a decisive referendum through which voting will occur regarding the widening of the Panama Canal

75 | 1117 |

2416 تِلْميذ n. fem. تِلْميذَة pl. تَلاميذ student, pupil

علينا التأكد من حصول التلميذ على عدد كاف من ساعات النوم — We have to make sure the

student gets a sufficient number of hours of sleep

84 | 1007 |

2417 مَجْمُوع *adj.* gathered; *n.* total
إن وزارة الإسكان تقدم دعمًا لبناء وحدات أخرى بها — يصل مجموعه إلى ٣٤ ألف وحدة بأسعار اقتصادية The Ministry of Housing is offering support for the building of other units whose total reaches 34 thousand units at economical prices

83 | 1012 |

2418 لافِت *adj.* interesting, noteworthy; *a.p.* attracting (attention) إلى to, indicating, pointing out إلى أنَّ that
إن وضعكم لافت للنظر فعلا، وحالتكم تسترعي الانتباه — Your situation really is noteworthy, and your condition attracts attention

66 | 1271 |

2419 إضافيّ *adj.* additional, supplementary
يتحركون بضعة سنتيمترات إضافية إلى الأمام — They are moving a few additional centimeters to the front

79 | 1055 |

2420 مُصِيبة *n.* pl. مَصائِب misfortune, tragedy
عرفت يا طارق المصيبة؟! أنا حامل فى الحرام يا طارق! — Tariq, do you know what awful thing happened!? I am pregnant out of marriage, Tariq!

89 | 946 |

2421 سَقْف *n.* roof; ceiling
ظل صامتا يحدق فى السقف ما يقرب من نصف ساعة — He remained silent staring at the ceiling for about half an hour

85 | 987 |

2422 تَخَصُّص *n.* pl. -aat specialty, specialization, major field
اجتهد سنوات من أجل حلم واحد: أن يكون جرّاحا. لا يمكن أن يتحول إلى تخصص آخر — He worked diligently for years on behalf of a single dream: to become a surgeon. He can't change to another specialty

76 | 1103 |

2423 تَطَلَّع *v. V* to look, glance إلى at sth; to anticipate, look forward إلى to sth
ظل فترة واقفًا فى مكانه يتطلع إليها، ثم انصرف غاضبًا وقال لنفسه إنها مجنونة — He remained for a while standing in his place, looking at her, and then he left angrily and said to himself that she was crazy

92 | 908 |

2424 يَسار *n.* left (also political)
فى الإتيكيت يقولون إن الموائد الكاملة يجب أن تضم شوكتين على اليسار واحدة كبيرة والأخرى صغيرة وأيضا سكينين على اليمين — In etiquette they say that the complete table must include two forks on the left, one large and the other small, and also two knives on the right

85 | 983 |

2425 أَصَرَّ *v. IV* to insist on, assert على sth
بعد ما فرغ من الطعام أصر على أن يحمل الصحون بنفسه إلى المطبخ — After finishing the food, he insisted on carrying the trays by himself into the kitchen

86 | 971 |

2426 اِقْتَرَح *v. VIII* to propose, suggest sth
لا أريد أن أسبب لك المزيد من الآلام.. أقترح أن ننفصل ولو مؤقتا — I don't want to cause you more pain...I suggest we separate, even if only temporarily

85 | 980 |

2427 تَدْريس *n.* teaching, instruction, pedagogy; هَيْئَة التَّدْريس faculty
معلمات اللغة الإنجليزية في المرحلة الابتدائية بالمنطقة الشرقية اعترضن على تدريس مواد بعيدة عن تخصصهن فقط لتكملة نصاب الحصص المقررة — English language teachers in the elementary level in the eastern area objected to teaching subjects that were distant from their specialty just to complete the quota of required classes

83 | 1003 |

2428 تَراوَحَ *v. VI* to vary, fluctuate, range بَيْنَ...و between...and
هل تعرف عدد المعتقلين؟ يتراوح عددهم من ٦٠٠- ١٠٠٠ معتقل — Do you know the number of prisoners? Their number ranges from 600 to 1,000 prisoners

79 | 1048 |

2429 تَعُب *n.* trouble, inconvenience, burden

إنهم يستيقظون كالنمل بعد نوم مبكر على شمع يذوب معه تعب النهار — They wake up like ants after an early sleep to a candle with which the troubles of the day melt

78 | 1070 |

2430 حَرَمَ *v. I (i,u)* to deprive sb من of

انقطاع الكهرباء يحرمنا من النوم منذ أسبوع — The electricity cut off has kept us from sleeping for a week

85 | 979 |

2431 ثَبَّتَ *v. II* to confirm, reinforce

استطاع العالم أندريا ويل أن يثبت كيف يقوم زيت الزيتون بالتدخل في الخلية المصابة بالسرطان ويعالجها — The scientist Andrea Weil was able to confirm how olive oil intervenes in the cancer stricken cells, and heals them

87 | 956 |

2432 جُنُون *n.* madness, insanity

يا سيدي هذه كانت تحبني وما أصابها هذا الجنون إلا من أجلي — Sir, this person loved me and this craziness would not have struck her except because of me

82 | 1012 |

2433 سُور *n. pl.* أَسوار wall, fence, enclosure

تلك القلعة محور، يربط أسوار القاهرة وتحصيناتها — This fortress is a hub, connecting the walls of Cairo with its fortifications

81 | 1025 |

2434 نِسْبِيّ *adj.* relative; نِسْبِيًّا relatively

أبحث عن مكان أعيش فيه لحظات من الهدوء النسبي — I am searching for a place in which I can experience a few moments of relative peace

82 | 1007 |

2435 بَوَّابَة *n.* door, gate, entrance; (Web) portal, gateway

لا يخرج أحد من تلك البوابة حتى ولو كانت نملة صغيرة إلا بإذن شخصي منه — No one goes out that gate, not even a small ant, except with personal permission from him

86 | 959 |

2436 تَصْفِيَة *vn.* settling, solving; *n. pl.* -aat settlement, solution; (econ.) liquidation, clearing; (spo.) elimination series

حان الوقت لتصفية للحسابات.. الفقر لا يلغي الكرامة كما يعتقدون — The time has come to settle the accounts...poverty does not cancel dignity, as they believe

71 | 1161 |

2437 صامِت *adj.* silent, quiet

ظلت صامتة حتى ظننت أنها لم تسمعني — She remained silent so I thought that she hadn't heard me

81 | 1014 | +lit

2438 مَرْتَبَة *n.* level, rank; degree, class; place, position (in a competition)

يحتل الاكتئاب المرتبة الأولى بين الأمراض النفسية المشخصة لدى المنتحرين — Depression occupies first place among the diagnosed psychological diseases of people who commit suicide

84 | 981 |

2439 كائِن *adj.* existing, located; *n. pl.* -aat creature, living thing

حين نحتاج الى التعامل مع كائن بشري نحدد لغته أولا — When we need to interact with a human creature we specify his language first

85 | 966 |

2440 دَيْن *n. pl.* دُيُون debt

تتلخص الخطة التي تحظى بتأييد إفريقي كبير في أن تلقي الدول الغنية ما يصل الى ١٠٠ في المائة من ديون افريقيا للجهات متعددة الاطراف — The plan, which has a lot of African support, can be summarized in the idea that the rich states would take on what amounts to 100 percent of Africa's debts to a variety of parties

89 | 920 |

2441 سِنّ *n. pl.* أَسْنان tooth; sharp edge

برغم تقدمه في السن ظل نشطا في عدة جمعيات يسارية — Despite his old age, he stayed active in several leftist organizations

83 | 996 |

2442 اِنْتِباه *n.* attention, caution; alertness, vigilance

أطلق ضحكة عالية أثارت انتباه الناس — He let out a high laugh that attracted the attention of the people

87 | 943 |

2443 عَصْر *n.* afternoon; صَلاة العَصْر afternoon prayer

رفض طلب الزمالك بإقامة المباراة ليلا تحت الاضواء الكاشفة وسيلعبها عصرا — It refused Zamalek's request to hold the match at night under search lights, and it will play it in the afternoon

89 | 921 |

2444 الْتَزَم *v. VIII* to follow, adhere to ب (rules, laws, plans); be committed to ب sth; الْتَزَم الصَّمْت to keep quiet

قد يتأخر عمره طوال.. لم يلتزم بموعد لعودته إلى البيت — He could be a little late...His whole life, he has never adhered to a specific time for returning home

85 | 966 |

2445 دِيوان *n.* office, agency, court

تناولت اللجنة بالنقاش ما تضمنه تقرير ديوان المحاسبة من مخالفات وأوجه قصور للوقوف على أسبابها — The committee, in their discussions, dealt with the contents of the report of the Accounting Office regarding irregularities and the most prominent deficiencies to determine their causes

75 | 1097 |

2446 اِسْتَغْرَقَ *v. X* to last (an amount of time); be immersed, engrossed في in

لقد سألتهم في القنصلية.. الإجراءات بسيطة لا تستغرق نصف ساعة — I asked them in the consulate...The measures are simple, not lasting a half hour

84 | 973 |

2447 راكِب *n.* pl. رُكّاب rider, passenger; *adj.* pl. -uun riding

ما إن توقف المترو حتى انفتحت أبوابه وتدافع منها ركاب نهاية الأسبوع — Hardly had the metro stopped when its doors opened and the weekend passengers poured out of it

88 | 926 |

2448 هَنْدَسَة *n.* engineering

لقد حولوا الهندسة من علم وفن لخدمة الانسان الى اداة لتحطيم الانسان — They changed engineering from a science and art in service of mankind to a tool to destroy mankind

83 | 983 |

2449 أَوْلَوِيَّة *n.* pl. -aat priority, precedence; goal; basic principle

الرسوم الجمركية المطروحة يجب ان تنسجم مع أولويات التنمية وتأهيل وتطوير القطاعات الصناعية — The tariffs offered should be consistent with the priorities of growth and training, and developing industrial sectors

72 | 1137 |

2450 ذَوْق *n.* taste, sensitivity; good taste, refinement

أشك في أنها مهندسة ديكور لها ذوق رفيع في فهم أسرار انسجام الألوان — I doubt that she is an interior decorator who has refined taste in understanding the secrets of color harmony

75 | 1084 |

2451 وَقَّعَ *v. II* to sign على (treaty); to make sth/sb fall; to inflict, cause (damage)

أهل المدينة قد وقعوا جميعا دون استثناء رسالة رفعوها إلى فخامة الرئيس — The people of the city all signed, without exception, a letter which they sent to the president

83 | 991 |

2452 أَجْمَع *adj.* pl. -uun, fem. جَمْعاء, entire, complete; *n.* all of: أَجْمَعُهُم all of them

تذكر يا والدي أنك أصبحت اليوم ملك الأمة العربية جمعاء فحافظ على نفسك ولكن شعارك — تأدية أكبر عمل ممكن بأيسر جهد ممكن — You remember, my father, that you became King of the whole Arab Nation today, so preserve yourself, and may your slogan be performing the most work possible with the littlest effort possible

84 | 969 |

2453 صَبِيّ *n.* pl. صِبْيان, صِبْيَة young boy, youth

وقف الصبي قدام دكان الفطائر — The boy stopped in front of the fatayer (pies) shop

86 | 953 |

2454 زائد *adj.* additional, extra; exceeding, going beyond (عن/على); excessive, extravagant

لكنه على العكس يعاملها بلطف زائد ويداعبها ولا ينقطع عن المرح والضحك — On the contrary, he treated her even more nicely and kidded with her and never broke off his merriment and laughter

91 | 895 |

2455 مُبْدِع *adj.* innovative, creative; *n.* innovator, creator

نستفيد من جيل المبدعين القلائل الذين وهبوا حياتهم في الكتابة للطفل — We are benefitting from the generation of the few creative artists who have given their lives to writing for children

77 | 1063 |

2456 خَيْل *n.* pl. خُيُول horse

البدو هنا يتحدثون ويمشون كأنهم يركبون الخيل — The Bedouin here talk and walk as if they are riding horses

82 | 987 |

2457 صَوْب *n.* direction; quarter

أشار بيده صوب البيت قائلا: ذاك هو البيت — He pointed with his hand in the direction of the house, saying: That's the house

89 | 916 |

2458 صُدُور *n.* appearance; publication

ها هي الحياة تستمر بعده، والجريدة تواصل الصدور دونه — Life goes on after him, and the newspaper will continue to publish without him

80 | 1012 |

2459 حارّ *adj.* hot, fervent, passionate (kisses), warm (greetings), heartfelt (condolences), spicy (condiments)

دموع حارة تنحدر على خدي هبة — Hot tears are running down Hiba's cheeks

93 | 872 |

2460 إزاء *prep.* towards, facing; vis-à-vis, regarding

تتميز الاحزاب الكردية بموقف يكاد يكون موحدا إزاء القضايا الاساسية وخاصة مسألة الفدرالية وقانون النفط والدستور — The Kurdish parties are distinguished by a position which is almost united in regard to the basic issues, and particularly the issue of federalism and oil law and the constitution

73 | 1106 |

2461 بَرْلَمانيّ *adj.* parliamentary; *n.* parliamentarian

ألغت الحكومة نتائج انتخابات برلمانية كان الإسلاميون متقدمين فيها — The government canceled the results of parliamentary elections which the Islamists were ahead in

60 | 1354 |

2462 أَغْلَقَ *v. IV* to lock or bolt shut, to close (door)

استأذن وانصرف، وتابعته هي بنظرة لائمة حتى أغلق الباب خلفه — He excused himself and left, and she followed him with a reproachful glance until he closed the door behind him

87 | 932 |

2463 حَجّ *n.* pilgrimage, Hajj

إن أمي ستعود بعد غد من الحج.. إنني أنتظر عودتها لأسافر — My mother will return the day after tomorrow from the pilgrimage...I am waiting for her return before I leave on my trip

81 | 1003 |

2464 عَرْش *n.* throne

صارت الأميرة فوزية أخت الملك فاروق أميرة مصرية على عرش إيران — Princess Fawziya, the sister of King Faruq, became an Egyptian princess on the throne of Iran

79 | 1020 |

2465 اِسْتِشاريّ *adj.* investment

مكتب الاستثمار الكويتي في بريطانيا يعتبر من اشهر المكاتب الاستثمارية خصوصا في سوق العقار — The Kuwaiti Investment Office in Britain is considered to be one of the most famous investment offices, particularly in the real estate market

59 | 1374 |

2466 تلفزيوني /tilfizyooni, tilivizyooni/ *adj.* television, televised

في الصباح استيقظ على صوت البث التلفزيوني ـ وهو ما اعتمد عليه كمنبه — In the morning he woke up to the voice of the television broadcast which he used as an alarm clock

76 | 1061 |

2467 مُبَيِّن *adj.* clarifying, explaining, indicating (أنَّ that); (Lev.Irq.Gul.) مبين /mbayyin/ apparent, visible, showing; (invar.) it seems (أنّ that), مَبَيِّن عليها زَعْلانة she looks angry

قال وزير الأوقاف إن موسم الحج الحالي كان ناجحًا ومتميزًا بكل المقاييس مبينًا أن البعثات الإدارية والإرشادية والطبية والإعلامية قامت بمهامها — The Minister of Religious Endowments said that the current Hajj season was successful and distinguished by all standards, pointing out that the administrative, counseling,

medical and public information delegations performed their duties

66 | 1217 | +spo

2468 وُدّ *n.* affection, fondness, friendship
نصف العاملين بالورشة مسلمون والنصف الآخر مسيحيون ويجمعنا الود والمحبة في ظل الاحترام المتبادل بين الجميع — Half of the workers in the workshop are Muslim and the other half are Christian, and we are united by friendship and love under the umbrella of mutual respect among all

80 | 1009 |

2469 شَغْلَة *n.* pl. -aat (Lev.) thing, stuff; deal, matter, affair
أنا بدي اقول لك شغلة — I want to tell you something

25 | 3239 | +spo

2470 سَجين *n.* pl. سُجَناء prisoner, inmate
هناك فرق بين السجين السياسي والسجين الجنائي، ويجب أن يكون هناك أيضا فرق بين الجرم السياسي والجرم الجنائي — There is a difference between the political prisoner and the criminal prisoner, and there must also be a difference between the political crime and the criminal crime

82 | 987 |

2471 زَيْتُون *coll.n.* olives; olive tree
فلنتحد كلنا من أجل الحب والسلام، نعم لغصن الزيتون وحمام الغاب وأطفال الحياة وبراعم الفجر — Let's all unite for love and peace, yes to the olive branch and the dove of the forest and the children of life and the blossoms of dawn

80 | 1011 |

2472 ضَمير *n.* conscience; (gram.) pronoun
ألا يشعر بظل من تأنيب الضمير عندما يقترف هذا الظلم؟ — Doesn't he feel even a small prick of conscience when he commits this oppression?

84 | 960 |

2473 ميزانيّة *n.* budget
قد اعتمد مجلس الوزراء مبلغ ١٦ مليون درهم تضاف إلى الميزانية العامة تخصص لدعم العملية الانتخابية — The ministerial council

appropriated the amount of 16 million dirhams which will be added to the general budget to support the election process

72 | 1110 |

2474 فَصيلَة *n.* pl. فَصائِل faction, branch, cell; (mil.) platoon, squadron; (blood) type
من المعروف أن هناك أربعة فصائل للدم — It is known that there are four blood types

65 | 1236 |

2475 تَأَثَّر *v. V* to be affected, influenced, impressed by ب/من
يبدو أن قاسم لا يتأثر بتحذيراتنا، ترى ماذا يريد الفتى؟ — It appears that Qasim is not affected by our warnings; what do you think the young man wants?

91 | 884 |

2476 كَفّ *fem.n.* palm of the hand; *vn.* refraining, abstaining (عن from); stopping sb (عن from doing sth)
وضعت كفي على عيني لئلا أرى بشاعة المنظر — I put my palm over my eyes so I couldn't see the ugliness of the scene

79 | 1012 |

2477 جَهْل *n.* ignorance
أراد أن يهديه من ظلمة الجهل إلى نور العقل — He wanted to guide him away from the darkness of ignorance towards the light of the mind

84 | 958 |

2478 عَوْن *n.* help, assistance, aid
يجب على المرأة أن تكون عونا لزوجها، وأن لا ترهقه بمطالبها — Women must be of help to their husbands, and not wear them out with their demands

87 | 925 |

2479 آسِيَويّ *n./adj.* Asian, Asiatic
اختير أفضل لاعب في النهائيات الآسيوية — He was chosen as best player in the Asian finals

64 | 1243 |

2480 آنَذاك *adv.* then, at that time
إذا توضعت الخثرة في أحد الشرايين التاجية فإن انقطاع سير الدم آنذاك يمكن أن يسبب موت جزء من عضلة القلب — If a blood clot lodges in one

of the coronary arteries, the obstruction in the flow of blood at that time can cause the death of part of the muscles of the heart

78 | 1020 |

2481 أَحْدَث *elat.* newer/newest; more/most recent (حَدِيث)

قاعة المؤتمرات مجهزة بالكامل وفق أحدث المواصفات العالمية — The conference hall is fully equipped in accordance with the most modern international standards

82 | 976 |

2482 حَرَس *n.* guard, bodyguard

أنا مواطن عادي لا أحتاج إلى حرس خاص — I am a regular citizen; I don't need a private guard

78 | 1028 |

2483 مُعارِض *a.p.* opposing, resisting; *n.* pl. -uun adversary, opponent

اتهم حزب جبهة العمل الإسلامي الأردني المعارض الحكومة بتأزيم الأوضاع السياسية في البلاد — The opposition Jordanian Islamic Labor Front Party accused the government of aggravating the political situation in the country

78 | 1021 |

2484 نُخْبَة *n.* pl. نُخَب selection, choice item; elite

الذين يتظاهرون هم أفراد النخبة.. الجماهير المريضة لا تشغلها قضية الديمقراطية — Those who demonstrate are members of the elite...The sick masses are not concerned with the issue of democracy

79 | 1017 |

2485 نَقْدِيّ *adj.* monetary, cash; critical, criticizing

قد أثبتت أن تلك النظرية قد أصبحت تحتاج إلى رؤية نقدية جديدة — She proved that this theory had come to need a new critical view

72 | 1115 |

2486 مُتَّصِل *adj.* connected; continuous, constant

عندها خرطوم ماء متصل بحنفية — She has a water hose attached to a faucet

94 | 852 |

2487 فِقَر and فِقَرَات , فَقَرَات .n. pl فَقْرَة and فِقْرَة paragraph, clause; section, passage, part; vertebra

يمكن إلغاء كلمة أو إضافة فقرة أو إلغاء فقرة دون الإساءة إلى أي من الوفود — One can strike a word or add a paragraph or strike a paragraph without insulting any of the delegations

81 | 991 |

2488 مَذْهَب *n.* pl. مَذاهِب manner, path; ideology, doctrine; legal school

تعددت المذاهب الفقهية في الإسلام ، وبقي الإسلام هو الإسلام — The legal sects in Islam became many, and Islam stayed Islam

77 | 1033 |

2489 تَكَرَّر *v. V* to be repeated, be reiterated; to be filtered, distilled; to be refined (petroleum)

ما حدث بالأمس في الأندلس يتكرر اليوم في البوسنة والهرسك — What happened yesterday in Andalusia is being repeated today in Bosnia and Herzegovina

87 | 921 |

2490 دُفْعَة *n.* batch, shipment; class, group (graduates); instance, time

يشار إلى أن وزارة الداخلية تشترط في الدفعة الأولى من المتقدمين أن تكون متزوجة ويزيد عمرها على ٣٥ — It should be pointed out that the Ministry of the Interior stipulates for the first wave of applicants that they be married and be over 35 years old

92 | 868 |

2491 طُمُوح *n.* pl. -aat ambition, desire; wish, aspiration

من أهم أسباب النجاح هو الطموح المرفق بالجهد والقوة والعمل والإرادة — Among the most important causes of success are ambition accompanied by effort, strength, work, and desire

84 | 948 |

2492 تَخْفِيف *n.* lowering, lessening; decrease, reduction

ألا يمكن أن نقوم بعمل إنساني كهذا لتخفيف المجاعة القاسية في بلادنا؟ — Can't we do some humanistic work like this to lessen the severe famine in our country?

82 | 971 |

2493 أَطَلَّ *v. IV* to overlook, face, provide a view على of (a place); to look out مِن of (a window); to stick one's head out of (a window) بِرَأْسِهِ مِن

يمتلك شقة فاخرة مساحتها ٢٠٠ متر من مستويين — تطل على شارع فيصل بالهرم He owns a luxurious apartment whose area is 200 meters on two levels which overlooks Faisal Street in the Pyramids area
75 | 1053 |

2494 مَشْغُول *adj.* busy, occupied
جداولهم مشغولة لأسابيع قادمة، وأمامهم أبحاث علمية لا بد من إنجازها — Their schedule is busy for weeks to come, and they have scientific research which they have to accomplish
79 | 1011 |

2495 وَهْم *n. pl.* أَوْهام illusion, delusion; fantasy, imagination
مهما تكن قسوة الحقيقة فهي أرحم من الأوهام — No matter how hard the truth, it is more merciful than illusions
85 | 932 |

2496 ذَكِيّ *adj.* intelligent, clever
المسألة ليست صعبة.. أنت ذكية وستتعلمين بسرعة — The matter is not difficult...you are smart and you learn quickly
83 | 957 |

2497 خَضَعَ *v. I (a)* to submit, yield إلى to sb/sth; to be subjected إلى to sth; to undergo إلى (surgery)
رأوه يخضع للزوجة الصغيرة الجميلة، فتعجبوا من سطوة الجمال على الرجال — They saw him obeying his small beautiful wife, and they were amazed at the power of beauty over men
82 | 972 |

2498 خَصَّصَ *v. II* to specify, designate, single out sth/sb (ل for); to allocate, earmark, set aside sth (ل for)
رغم كرهه لهذا الدرس، الا انه قد خصص له ساعتين في اليوم لحفظ مادته استعدادا للا متحان الوزاري — Despite his hatred of this class, he still set aside two hours a day for memorizing its subject matter in preparation for the ministerial test
83 | 954 |

2499 اِمْتِداد *n.* extent, scope; extension, expansion
كلما أصبحت الروابط الأسرية أكثر قوة والأسرة أكثر امتدادا، فمن المتوقع أن يصبح السلوك الحسن والقيم

الحسنة أكثر انتشارا وقوة داخل المجتمع — The stronger family ties are, and the more extended the family is, the more it is expected that behavior will be good, and good values will be more widespread and strong inside the society
82 | 959 |

2500 مُواصَفَة *n. pl.* -aat description; specifications, specs
المشروع يتضمن توفير ٢٢ جهاز كمبيوتر بأعلى المواصفات متصلة بالانترنت — The project includes providing 22 high end computers, connected to the Internet
87 | 904 |

2501 بَثّ *n.* transmission, broadcast; dissemination, spreading
الهدف من هذه المنظمة هو بث روح التعاون والمودة بين اتباع الديانات المختلفة — The purpose of this organization is to spread the spirit of cooperation and friendship among the followers of the various religions
83 | 957 |

2502 اِسْتِعادَة *n.* recovering, regaining, reclaiming
لن يقنع الناخبين بأن الديموقراطيين مستعدون لاستعادة البيت الأبيض — He will never convince the voters that the Democrats are ready to reclaim the White House
83 | 956 |

2503 مُخابَرَة *n.* correspondence, communication; (Irq.Gul.) telephone call; مُخابَرات intelligence service, secret service
اعترفا بالتعامل مع جهاز المخابرات الإسرائيلي الداخلي منذ اثنى عشر عاماً — They admitted dealing with the Israeli security apparatus twelve years ago
70 | 1118 |

2504 مُنافِس *adj.* competing; *n.* competitor, rival
حاصر الاهلي منافسه في الدقائق العشر الاخيرة في منطقته بغية حسم النتيجة في الوقت الأصلي — The Ahli club besieged its competitor in the last ten minutes in its area, out of a desire to decide the score in the regular time period
78 | 1007 |

2505 جِدِّيّ *adj.* serious, earnest; جِدِّيّاً seriously, in earnest

صرت أفكر جديا بالرحيل إلى المدينة — I started to
think seriously of traveling to the city

86 | 910 |

2506 ضاقَ *v. I (i)* to be narrow or confined;
to be tight (situation)

كان قد ضاق ذرعا من كلام الرجل وثرثرته —
He was fed up with the man's words and his
chatter

81 | 968 |

2507 فارغ *adj.* unoccupied, not busy, free, idle;
empty, void

نهضت من مكانها وحملت الصينية والأكواب الفارغة
فى يديها — She got up from her place and
carried the tray and empty cups in her hands

85 | 928 |

2508 رَحيم *adj.* compassionate (God)

لقد عرف أني عشت بلا أب رحيم فقرر أن يكون أبي
— He found out that I lived without a
compassionate father, so he decided that he
would be my father

76 | 1033 |

2509 عَرَبِيَّة *n.* Arabic (language); (Egy.) pl. -aat car,
automobile

طلبت بعينيها مساعدة من ام علي لكنها لم تكترث
لها خاصة بعد ان تحدث معها الحارس بلغة عربية لم
تفهمها — She asked for help with her eyes
from Um Ali but she didn't pay attention
to her, particularly after the guard talked
with her in an Arabic language she didn't
understand

76 | 1026 |

2510 أَشْبَه *elat.* more/most similar ب to

إن مصلحة البيت وحقوق الزوج تستلزم ترتيبات
معينة تجعل المرأة أشبه بالاسير الذي لا ينفك إساره
إلا بإذن آسره — The interests of the home and
the rights of the husband require specific
arrangements which make the woman more
like a prisoner who is never released except
with the permission of the person keeping her
in prison

83 | 946 |

2511 رضا and رضّى *n.* approval, satisfaction,
pleasure

وضع العلبة في جيبه وربت عليها والاطمئنان والرضا
يستوليان على مهجته المشتاقة — He put the box in
his pocket, patted it, and tranquility and
satisfaction overcame his heart

89 | 880 |

2512 جَيْب *n.* pl. جُيُوب pocket; purse; (math.) sine;
(anat.) sinus cavity

مد رأفت يده ببطء إلى جيبه وأخرج محفظة نقوده —
Ra'fat put his hand slowly into his pocket and
pulled out his wallet

87 | 901 |

2513 تَقْسِيم *n.* partition, division; distribution

تم تقسيم الطلاب إلى ١٤ مجموعة — The students
were divided into 14 groups

82 | 954 |

2514 ناصِر *n.* pl. أنْصار partisan, supporter, follower

على عكس الكثير من السنة لم يكن مروان من أنصار
النظام العراقي السابق ولكن وبمجرد سقوطه انقلب
ضد الامريكيين — Unlike many Sunnis, Marwan
was not a supporter of the previous Iraqi
regime, but as soon as it fell he turned against
the Americans

87 | 892 |

2515 إغْلاق *n.* locking, closing; barring

قام الجيش الصهيوني بإغلاق المدخل الخارجي
للمسجد الذي كان منفذ العملية إماما له — The
Zionist army closed the outer entrance to the
mosque which the person who carried out the
operation was the Imam of

82 | 954 |

2516 صُعُود *n.* ascent, rise; take-off (aircraft)

بدأ الطلاب فى الصعود إلى شققهم، لكن شيماء ظلت
واقفة أمام مكتب الاستقبال — The students
began to go up to their apartments, but
Shimaa stayed standing in front of the
reception

85 | 914 |

2517 تَشْرِيع *n.* pl. -aat legislation, legislature

لن نتمكن من تشريع قوانين تنظم العلاقة داخل
الاسرة — We won't be able to pass laws which
organize relations inside the family

69 | 1122 |

2518 مُفاجِئ *adj.* surprising; sudden, unexpected
كان هذا الحنان المفاجئ يفوق طاقتها على التحمل،
فانخرطت فى البكاء من جديد — This sudden
compassion exceeded her ability to bear, so
she broke out in tears again
85 | 914 |

2519 اِطَّلَعَ *v. VIII* to review, examine, study على sth;
to read, peruse على sth
لا — I have وقت أمامي كي أطلع على هذه الكتب
no time to read these books
80 | 965 |

2520 اِضْطِراب *n.* pl. -aat disturbance, disorder
اجريت انتخابات في الجامعة ولم يحدث فيها اية
مشاكل او اضطرابات بين الطلبة — Elections
were held in the university and no problems
or disturbances among the students occurred
81 | 955 |

2521 نَفْطِيّ *adj.* petroleum, (mineral) oil
تلعب الشركات النفطية العالمية دورا في رفع الأسعار
— The international oil companies play a role
in raising the prices
58 | 1331 |

2522 صَلُحَ *v. I (u)* to be suitable, be fitting;
be valid
هل تعرف أحدا يصلح لهذه المهمة؟ — Do you
know anyone who would be suitable for this
duty?
87 | 894 |

2523 تَوَفَّى *v. V* (pass.) تُوُفِّيَ to die; تَوَفَّاهُ الله he died,
God took him (to Heaven)
قال مسؤول إندونيسي في مستشفى اليوم الجمعة ان
امرأة إندونيسية عمرها ٣٧ عاما توفيت بأنفلونزا
الطيور — An Indonesian official in a hospital
said today, Friday, that an Indonesian woman
aged 37 died of bird flu
94 | 822 |

2524 بِيئِيّ *adj.* environmental
التلوث الهوائي يعتبر من أكثر أشكال التلوث
البيئي انتشارا نظرا لسهولة انتقاله وانتشاره من
منطقة إلى أخرى — Air pollution is considered
to be one of the most widespread types
of environmental pollution in view of the
ease of spreading it from one area to another
65 | 1187 |

2525 عاصِفَة *n.* pl. عَواصِف storm, tempest
يتوقع أن يكون دينيس رابع عاصفة استوائية تضرب
جامايكا التي لم تكد تعافى من الاعصار القوي ايفان
الذي ضربها العام الماضي — It is expected that
Dennis will be the fourth tropical storm to hit
Jamaica, which has hardly recovered from the
strong storm, Ivan, which hit it last year
86 | 903 |

2526 تَوافُق *n.* congruence, compatibility;
agreement, conformity; consensus, concord
ان الزواج عكس ما تحكيه القصص الرومانسية، لا
يعني التوافق والتناغم الى الحد الذي يفقد كل منهما
هويته الشخصية — Marriage, as opposed to
what the romantic stories say, does not
mean mutual agreement and harmony to
the extent that each of them loses his
personal identity
71 | 1087 |

2527 اِسْتَقَرَّ *v. X* to settle down; to stabilize,
become stable
وسيبقى راغب معنا لأيام إلى أن تستقر حالته
الصحية .. وبعدها سيغادرنا — Raghib will
remain with us for a few days until his
health situation stabilizes...and after that
he will leave us
87 | 884 |

2528 حافَظَ *v. III* to preserve, protect على sth
مضى الرجل يفكر وهو يحافظ على هدوء وجهه الذى
تتطلع إليه الأبصار — The man proceeded to
think, keeping his face calm, which everyone
was looking at
92 | 837 |

2529 مَسْرَحِيّ *adj.* theatrical
أقدم عرض مسرحي في عالمنا العربي جاء بواسطة فن
شهير اسمه خيال الظل — The oldest theatrical
presentation in our Arab World came through
a famous art form called Shadow Imagination
(Shadow Puppets)
65 | 1179 |

2530 أَحْسَنَ *v. IV* to master, be good at sth
سيادة الجنرال يتقن الفرنسية ولكنه لا يحسن العربية
— His excellency the General is proficient in
French, but he is not good at Arabic
85 | 911 |

2531 حَرْبِيّ *adj.* war, military

خسرت إيطاليا سبع سفن حربية في معركة بحرية
واحدة مع البوارج البريطانية شرق البحر المتوسط —
Italy lost seven warships in a single naval
battle with British battleships in the east
of the Mediterranean

77 | 1005 |

2532 عُمْلَة *n.* pl. -aat currency, money, bills

لما أخذت تلك العملة ارتكبت ذنبا.. اختلاس شيء
من الغير حرام — When you took this currency,
you committed a sin...stealing something from
someone else is forbidden

81 | 956 |

2533 مَلِكَة *fem.n.* queen; المَلِكَة (title) Queen

ما هي مكاسب لقب ملكة جمال مصر، بالنسبة لك؟
— What are the advantages of the title of
beauty queen of Egypt, as far you are
concerned?

80 | 958 |

2534 لاقَى *v.* III to meet, encounter; to find; ملاقي
(Lev.) /mlaa'i/ *a.p.* (able) to find

كانت تلاقي شتى أنواع العنف من زوجة أبيها —
She encountered all kinds of violence from the
wife of her father

58 | 1312 | +spo

2535 عَقار *n.* pl. -aat real estate, land property

لابد من عزل ثمن الارض عن العقارات، — It is
necessary to separate the price of the land
from the real estate

68 | 1131 |

2536 كَرِهَ *v.* I (a) to hate, loathe sth/sb; to dislike,
have an aversion for sth

أنا أكره الأطفال، ولا يهمني هؤلاء الأشقياء وما
سيقولون عني — I hate children, and those
brats and what they say about me are of no
interest to me

80 | 961 |

2537 أَغْلَبِيَّة *n.* majority

ليس هذا رأي الأغلبية وإنما هو رأي حزب المؤتمر
— This is not the opinion of the majority, rather it
is the opinion of the Conference Party

78 | 985 |

2538 مُؤَكَّد *adj.* certain, confirmed, established;
guaranteed

لا نركن كثيرا إلى تاريخ الخامس والعشرين من
ديسمبر كتاريخ مؤكد لمولد المسيح عليه السلام إذ
اختلفت في ذلك الفرق المسيحية — We won't
focus much on the date of the twenty-fifth
of December as a certain date for the birth of
Christ, upon him be peace, since the Christian
factions differ in that

80 | 961 |

2539 شَوْط *n.* round, phase; game, half period;
قَطَعَ شوطاً to make headway, major progress

لقد قطعنا شوطا طويلا في المفاوضات فلا تضيعوا
علينا الفرصة — We have made a lot of progress
in the negotiations, so don't waste the
opportunity for us

55 | 1378 |

2540 مُتَوَفِّر *adj.* available, provided; ample,
abundant

ا — وعدتهم بشراء أي نوع من الحلوى متوفر لديه
promised them to buy any type of sweet he
had

87 | 877 |

2541 تَوَقُّف *n.* stopping, halting, pausing

قرر التوقف عن مزاولة مهنته في فترة دراسته —
He decided to stop practicing his profession
during the period of his studies

85 | 893 |

2542 مُحَارَبَة *n.* fight, struggle, combat

يجد الليبراليون العراقيون أنفسهم مطالبين بالذود
عن الوطن ومحاربة النزعات الطائفية والفئوية
الضيقة — The Iraqi liberals find themselves
demanded to defend the homeland and
fight against narrow factional and sectarian
tendencies

77 | 983 |

2543 فاتَ *v.* I (u) to pass by, elude sb or على sb
(time, opportunity); to enter على sth;
to stop by, visit على sb

ان ما فات فات، وما هو قادم لا بد انه آت —
That which passed has passed, and that
which is coming, it is coming for sure

76 | 1005 | +spo

2544 صَعُبَ *v. I (u)* to be difficult على for sb
(to do sth)

زوجته تجيد اللغة العربية ولكن يصعب عليها نطق
حرف الصاد و حرف الحاء — His wife speaks
Arabic well but it is hard for her to pronounce
the letter Saad and the letter Haa'

86 | 883 |

2545 ناعِم *adj.* smooth, soft; dainty

إنها جميلة جدا: شعرها أسود ناعم طويل وابتسامتها
ساحرة تبدو خلالها أسنانها الناصعة المنتظمة — She
is very beautiful: her hair is long silky black,
her smile is captivating, through which appear
her even, shiny teeth

83 | 912 |

2546 ظَنّ *n.* opinion, assumption; ظَنّي I think

وأغلب الظن أن هيرودوت على رغم كونه أجنبيا،
فهم طبيعة تدين المصريين أكثر من فهم وزير الثقافة
المصري له — It is likely that Herodotus, despite
his being a foreigner, understood the nature of
the religiosity of Egyptians more than the
Egyptian Minister of Culture does

84 | 909 |

2547 جُغْرافِيّ *adj.* geographical; *n. pl.* -uun
geographer

مدينة كركوك تقع داخل الحدود الجغرافية لاقليم
كردستان لكنها في الأساس مدينة عراقية — The
city of Kirkuk is located inside the geographic
borders of the region of Kurdistan, but at base
it is an Iraqi city

77 | 988 |

2548 عَظْم *n. pl.* عِظام bone

قد بينت بعض الدراسات الطبية أن الهورمون
الذكري مفيد لقوة العظم ورفع مستوى الرغبة
الجنسية — Some medical studies have made
it clear that the male hormone is beneficial
for bone strength and increasing the level
of sexual desire

82 | 926 |

2549 اِنْتَبَهَ *v. VIII* to be careful (إلى with); to pay
attention (إلى to); اِنْتَبِه! attention! watch out!

استغرق في أفكاره حتى انتبه على دقات الساعة المعلقة
في الصالة ، فقفز من الفراش — He got lost in his
thoughts until he became aware of the ticking

of the clock hanging in the hall, so he jumped
out of bed

81 | 933 |

2550 مُقْتَرَح *adj.* proposed, suggested; *n. pl.* -aat
proposal, suggestion

واصل الدكتور يحيى الجمل رفضه الشديد
لكافة التعديلات الدستورية المقترحة — Dr Yahya
Al-Jamal continued to repeat his strong
rejection of all the suggested constitutional
changes

73 | 1043 |

2551 أَحاطَ *v. IV* to surround, encircle ب sth

يبدو حزينا رغم هالة النور التي تحيط برأسه
— He looks sad despite the halo of light that
surrounds his head

87 | 872 |

2552 تَحْدِيث *vn.* updating, renewing; *n. pl.* -aat
update (website)

ما هي خططكم لتطوير وتحديث شبكة "فاست
لينك"؟ — What are your plans for developing
and modernizing the Fast Link network?

71 | 1070 |

2553 مُناخ and مَناخ *n.* climate, atmosphere

لم يعد هناك شك في أن مناخ الأرض يتغير —
There is no longer any doubt that the
climate of the earth is changing

76 | 998 |

2554 ثَبُتَ *v. I (u)* to be confirmed, be substantiated

بسببي أيضا قبض على حلمي حمادة، فلما ثبتت براءتي
ثبتت بالتالي براءته — Hilmy Hamada was
arrested because of me, so when my
innocence was proven, his innocence was
proven as a result of that

84 | 894 |

2555 اِنْهِيار *n.* collapse, downfall; breakdown

إن الحكومة الأمريكية أعلنت أنها ستحمي الدولار
من الانهيار الذي يتهدده — The American
government announced that it will protect the
dollar from the collapse which threatens it

82 | 919 |

2556 هاتِفِيّ *adj.* telephone, telephonic; هاتِفِيّاً by
phone

قال ان العلاقة بين رايس ووزير الدفاع دونالد رامسفيلد ساءت لدرجة أن الأخير لم يعد يرد على مكالماتها الهاتفية — He said that the relationship between Rice and the Minister of Defense Donald Rumsfeld worsened to the point that the latter no longer responds to her phone calls

81 | 932 |

2557 صِيانَة n. maintenance, preservation

هذا الدليل مهم جدا للاستخدام الأمثل للسيارة، ولعمل الصيانة المطلوبة لها — This guide is very important for the ideal use of the car and to do the necessary maintenance for it

81 | 927 |

2558 عَقيدَة n. doctrine, dogma; creed, belief, faith

ولم يكن لجمهور الناخبين الإسرائيليين أن يتخلى عن عقيدة أرض إسرائيل التوراتية إلا تحت ضغط الحقائق الجيواستراتيجية — The masses of Israeli voters are not about to relinquish the dogma of the Old Testament Land of Israel, except under the pressure of geostrategic facts

76 | 984 |

2559 مُتَطَلَّب adj. required; n. مُتَطَلَّبات requirements, demands

— ما هي المتطلبات الكاملة لتنفيذ هذا المشروع؟ What are the complete requirements for carrying out this project?

75 | 999 |

2560 صُدْفة n. surprise; coincidence, chance

ما أوجع هذه الصدفة التي تعود بي، بعد كل هذه السنوات، إلى هنا — How painful is the coincidence that brings me back here, after all these years

84 | 896 |

2561 أبْعَد elat. farther/farthest

احب ابنائي الى أبعد الحدود والطيبة اساس علاقتي بهم وهم خير نقاد لي — I love my sons to the greatest extent, and kindness is the basis of my relationship with them and they are my best critics

86 | 873 |

2562 رُعْب n. fright, panic, terror

عشرات الرصاصات خرقت هذه الجدران.. نحن نعيش في حالة رعب لا يوصف وحالة فزع لدى الاطفال — Scores of bullets penetrated the walls...we are living in a state of terror which cannot be described and a state of fear for the children

84 | 890 |

2563 مَشْهُور adj. famous, well-known

ديالى هي محافظة في العراق مشهورة بالبرتقال — Diyali is a governorate in Iraq, famous for oranges

93 | 803 |

2564 دافَعَ v. III to defend عن sth/sb

هل تختار محاميا للدفاع عنك أم أنك تدافع عن نفسك؟ — Are you choosing a lawyer to defend you, or will you be defending yourself?

85 | 884 |

2565 أقَرَّ v. IV to ratify, accept; to confess ب sth

كانت الحكومة القطرية أقرت خلال الفترة الماضية عددا كبيرا من القوانين والتشريعات — The Qatari government during the past period passed a large number of laws

80 | 931 |

2566 قَهْر n. coercion; subjugation

نحن الآن موحدون في مسعانا لإنهاء القهر والاحتلال — We are now united in our efforts to end the oppression and the occupation

79 | 945 |

2567 عايِز and عاوِز (Egy.) a.p. wanting, needing (to want, to need)

أنا مش عاوز أعمل مشاكل مع الناس — I don't want to make problems with people

42 | 1765 | +spo

2568 اسْتِطْلاع n. pl. -aat (opinion) poll; investigation; reconnaissance

تجمع عدد كبير من الناس.. دفعني حب الاستطلاع أن أتجه إليهم — A large number of people gathered...curiosity impelled me to head in their direction

71 | 1047 |

2569 سائِر n. most of, the majority of

يتفاوت الناس في إيانهم قوة وضعفا كما يتفاوتون في أجسامهم وسائر صفاتهم وشؤونهم — People differ in the strength and weakness of their

faith just as they differ in their bodies and all their characteristics and affairs

| 83 | 904 |

2570 مُوسيقيّ *adj.* musical; *n.* pl. -uun musician
الفرقة الموسيقية العسكرية تتوسط الحديقة وتعزف أغاني محمد عبد الوهاب وأم كلثوم — The military musical group was in the middle of the garden playing the songs of Muhammad Abd Al-Wahhab and Um Kalthoum

| 76 | 978 |

2571 ميناء *n.* port, harbor
عندئذ طلب منه "بونابرت" أن يذهب إلى الميناء وأن يقدم تقريرا عما يراه فعاد قائلا إنه شاهد بعض السفن في الجانب الأيمن من مدخل الميناء — At that time Bonaparte asked him to go to the port and submit a report about what he saw, and he returned saying that he saw some ships on the right side of the entrance to the port

| 77 | 969 |

2572 هٰذانِ، هٰذَيْنِ *dem.pron.* these two (masc.du.), (gen./acc.)
أقيم هذان المخيمان في العام ١٩٤٩ في محافظة بيروت — Those two (refugee) camps were set up in 1949 in the Governorate of Beirut

| 85 | 880 |

2573 حَمَى *v. I (i)* to protect sth (مِن against)
تحاول أن تحمي أمها بيديها الصغيرتين من ضربات سوط أبيها التي كانت تنزل عليها صواعق ماحقة — She is trying to protect her mother with her small hands from the blows of her father's whip which were falling upon her like destructive bolts of lightning

| 85 | 879 |

2574 كِيلُومِتر *n.* pl. -aat kilometer
يقع هذا المسجد في وسط قرية قباء على بعد ثلاثة كيلومترات عن المدينة — This mosque is located in the middle of the village of Qaba', at a distance of three kilometers from the city

| 74 | 1005 |

2575 هَبَّ *v. I (u)* to blow, rage (wind, storm); to break out (fire); to rise, take a stand; كُلُّ مَنْ everyone; every Tom, Dick and Harry; كُلُّ مَا هَبَّ وَدَبَّ anything and everything
بدأت نذر الخماسين تهب على الإسكندرية من الصحراء الغربية، واصفر الجو يوما كاملا — The Khamasin winds blew over Alexandria from the Western Desert, and the air turned yellow for a whole day

| 76 | 972 |

2576 طارِئَة *n.* pl. طَوارِئ urgent matter, emergency; حالَة طَوارِئ state of emergency
يقترح أن تقوم الولايات المتحدة بإعداد خطة طوارئ لمواجهة الفشل في العراق — He suggests that the United States prepare an emergency plan to confront failure in Iraq

| 78 | 948 |

2577 فاتِح *adj.* clear (color); (Dia.) *a.p.* opening (a window, a business), keeping open
— لا يا راجل ده ماكس فاتح اربعة و عشرين ساعة No, dude, Max is open twenty-four hours

| 77 | 961 |

2578 آمِين *interj.* amen!
وكلما دعا، قلت بيني وبين نفسي آمين، وما هي إلا خمس دقائق وإذا بكابتن الطائرة يقول لنا: نحمد الله على السلامة، لقد انفرجت الأجواء، وسوف نهبط إن شاء الله في مطار الرياض — Each time he called on God, I said "Amen" to myself, and it wasn't five minutes before the captain of the airplane said to us: Praise God for safety, the weather has cleared, we will land at Riyadh airport, God willing

| 58 | 1277 | +for

2579 اِسْتِجابَة *n.* acceptance (invitation); granting (request); complying with (demands); اِسْتِجابَةً لِـ in compliance with; in response to
طلب منهم عدم الاستجابة للرسائل الالكترونية المتطفلة (سبام) التي يبعثها قراصنة الانترنت — He requested them not to respond to the junk emails (spam) which Internet pirates send

| 83 | 889 |

2580 مُعَدّ *adj.* prepared, made; *n.* مُعَدّات equipment, material
امر جلالته بتقديم معدات طبية مساعدة للمعاقين وذوي الاحتياجات الخاصة — His majesty ordered

that medical equipment be offered as aid
to the handicapped and those with special
needs

78 | 952 |

2581 غُرْبَة *n.* exile; alienation

أترك بلادى وأعيش فى الغربة أحسن لى — I am
leaving my country and living in exile; it will
be better for me

82 | 895 |

2582 قِياسِيّ *adj.* record; analogous

البرازيل صاحبة الرقم القياسي في المشاركات في
المونديال ب ١٨ مشاركة، وصاحبة الرقم القياسي في
احراز اللقب بخمسة ألقاب — Brazil is the
holder of the record in participation in the
World Cup, with 18 times, and the record
holder in winning the title, with five titles

79 | 935 |

2583 تِكْنُولُوجِيّ *adj.* technological

اقامت العديد من المشاريع النموذجية القائمة على
احدث المواصفات التكنولوجية مثل مصانع الحرير
— They set up a number of demonstration
projects based on the most recent
technological specifications, like silk factories

71 | 1042 |

2584 نَصِيب *n.* share, portion, dividend

يجب أن يكون لي نصيب فيها تجنون من الأرباح — ا
must have my share of what you are gaining
in the way of profits

92 | 801 |

2585 ساوَى *v. III* to equalize, make equal sth; to
settle بين between; (Lev.Irq.) to do, make sth
أيش ناوية تسوي بصراحة — What do you really
intend to do?

84 | 880 | +spo

2586 حاصِل *n.* result; income; *adj.* (which)
happened, occurred; (which) was achieved,
was obtained; (who) obtained, earned
(degree, certificate)

هذا امر مخيف اذا ما ربطناه بالتطورات الكبرى
الحاصلة في المنطقة — This is a frightening
matter if we link it to the major developments
which have happened in the region

82 | 894 |

2587 إثارَة *n.* provocation, agitation

نريد ان تكون علاقاتنا مثمرة وايجابية، ولا نتمنى
اثارة مشكلات لكننا نريد ايجاد حلول وتسويات
تسمح بوقف المعاناة — We want our relationship
to be productive and positive, and we don't
want to provoke problems but we want to find
solutions and compromises which permit the
end of suffering

84 | 874 |

2588 عِشْق *n.* love, fondness

تمنت أن تتذكر آخر رواية عشق قرأتها — She was
hoping to remember the last romance novel
she had read

70 | 1039 |

2589 مَدْرَسِيّ *adj.* scholastic, school-related

يبقى ان اذكر ان ظاهرة الفشل المدرسي ظاهره قديمه
وهناك مشاهير في العالم مروا بتجارب دراسيه فاشلة
مثل نلسون روكفلر — It remains for me to
mention that the phenomenon of school
failure is an old phenomenon and there are
famous people in the world who passed
through failing school experiences like Nelson
Rockefeller

74 | 987 |

2590 عَرُوس *fem.n.* bride; (rare) *masc.n.* bridegroom;
عَرُوسَة البَحْر *fem.n.* bride; mermaid عَرُوسَة
أعلن استعداده لدفع المهر المطلوب وشراء الشبكة
التى تختارها العروس — He announced his
readiness to pay the required dowry, and to
buy the ring which the bride chose

78 | 932 |

2591 مَرْمَى *n.* goal, target; purpose; حارس المَرْمَى
goalkeeper

قد لعب الاتحاد في هذه المباراة بعناصره المعروفة ففي
حراسة المرمى تواجد الحارس لويس أغوستين — In
this match, the "Union" played its well-known
elements, so for example as goal keeper there
was the keeper Louis Augustin

69 | 1059 |

2592 إعْمار *n.* construction, building, development

فشل الغرب في تحقيق النجاح والوعود في إعادة إعمار
أفغانستان — The West failed to accomplish the
success and promises of rebuilding Afghanistan

69 | 1049 |

2593 طِراز *n.* model, class, type

يحظر القانون الجديد الترخيص بالهدم أو الاضافة للمباني والمنشآت ذات الطراز المعماري المميز أو المرتبطة بالتاريخ القومي — The new law forbids granting a demolition permit, or to add to buildings or establishments which have a unique architectural style or which are related to national history

82 | 881 |

2594 مُقاطَعَة *vn.* boycott; interruption; *n.* district, province

وأكد على أن المقاطعة الاقتصادية هي السلاح ورد الفعل الحضاري — He stressed that economic boycott is the civilized weapon and reaction

80 | 909 |

2595 صالَة *n.* hall (It., Sp. sala)

اجتمع الطلاب الاتحاديون في صالة السينما، وهي أكبر صالات المدرسة — The union students gathered in the cinema hall, and it was the biggest hall in the school

85 | 852 |

2596 مَنْظَر *n.* pl. مَناظِر view, scenery; appearance, look

وتحول المنظر إلى لوحة صيفية ينيرها القمر البهي بلون فضي — The scene changed to a summer tableau, lit by the brilliant moon with a silver light

82 | 879 |

2597 سِحْر *n.* sorcery, magic

المرأة عالم من السحر والجمال — The woman is a world of magic and beauty

77 | 935 |

2598 ذَكَر *n./adj.* pl. ذُكُور male

أصغر أبنائه الذكور طفل في الخامسة، تليه فتاة في الثالثة — His youngest son is a child of five, followed by a girl of three

90 | 806 |

2599 سَحاب *coll.n.* clouds, *un.n.* سَحابَة, pl. سُحُب

تحلقين في السحاب بعيدا عن الأرض! تكرهين الأمور العادية، الروتينية — You float in the clouds far from the earth! You hate normal, routine things

74 | 970 |

2600 مَقْصُود *n.* purpose, intent; aim, goal; *adj.* deliberate, intentional

— أقدم لكم اعتذاري عن تأخري غير المقصود I offer you my apology for my unintended lateness

90 | 806 |

2601 مُساواة *n.* equality, equal rights

إن الإسلام يقر بمبدأ الأخوة والمساواة بين البشر وانه يدين الصراع الحضاري والعرقي والديني — Islam accepts the principle of brotherhood and equality between men, and it condemns religious, ethnic, and cultural conflict

77 | 933 |

2602 اِنْضِمام *n.* joining, being added (إلى to); affiliation; annexation

رفض محمد فاروق الانضمام إلى أي حزب سياسي بريطاني المحافظين أو العمال أو الأحرار — Muhammad Faruq refused to join any British political party, the Conservatives, Labor, or the Liberals

78 | 924 |

2603 مُنْتَظَر *adj.* anticipated, expected

استطاعت هذه العصابات المجرمة ان تعرقل الانتخابات المنتظرة في العراق، وتؤخر الاستقرار هناك — These criminal gangs were able to obstruct the expected elections in Iraq, and delay stability there

85 | 854 |

2604 طُنّ *n.* ton

الخاطفون طلبوا سبعة وعشرين طنا من الوقود لإكمال رحلتهم من مرسيليا الى باريس — The kidnappers requested twenty-seven tons of fuel to complete their trip from Marseilles to Paris

71 | 1014 |

2605 نَظِير *n.* counterpart, opposite number; colleague, peer; نَظِيَر in return for, in exchange for

انهزم مساء أول أمس المنتخب المغربي لكرة الطائرة أمام نظيره المصري بثلاث جولات مقابل لا شيء — The Moroccan national volleyball team was defeated the day before yesterday by its Egyptian counterpart three rounds to nothing

81 | 890 | +news

2606 مَلِيء *adj.* full, filled

راقودة منطقة خطرة مليئة بالمخدرات والمجرمين —
Raquda is a dangerous area full of drugs and criminals

85 | 851 |

2607 عَجِزَ *v. I (a)* to be incapable, unable عن to do sth

للكلاب ألعابهم واحتفالاتهم، ويقومون بحركات وألعاب يعجز البشر عن الإتيان بها — Dogs have their games and their celebrations, and they make movements and games which people are unable come up with

82 | 878 |

2608 نُهوض *n.* promotion, advancement, furthering

يجب ترسيخ مبادئ الديمقراطية لتحقيق آمال ومتطلعات المعلمين والنهوض بمستوياتهم العلمية والمهنية، والذي سينعكس بصورة إيجابية على العملية التعليمية — The principles of democracy must be strengthened in order to achieve the hopes and aspirations of the teachers and to raise their scientific and professional level, which will reflect in a positive way on the educational process

80 | 896 |

2609 مُخْلِص *adj.* sincere; loyal

أتمنى أن يعتبرني صديقه المخلص فيبوح لي ببعض أسراره وهمومه ومشكلاته — I hope he will consider me his sincere friend, and reveal to me some of his secrets and concerns and problems

90 | 799 |

2610 جَذْر *n. pl.* جُذُور and جِذْر root, stem; جُذُور roots, origins, heritage

سأعمل على إنهاء مظاهر الفساد.. سأقلع جذور الشر المتنامية في هذا العالم — I will work on ending manifestations of corruption...I will root out the roots of evil which are growing in this world

82 | 875 |

2611 عِبْء *n. pl.* أعْباء burden, load

عليك أن تتأهب ليوم تحمل فيه وحدك أعباء أمك وزوجك وأطفالك — You need to prepare for a day in which you will bear the burden of your mother, wife, and children by yourself

84 | 851 |

2612 ظالِم *n. pl.* -uun oppressor, tyrant; *adj.* oppressive, tyrannical

يبقى السؤال من هو الظالم والمظلوم في هذه الواقعة؟ — The question remains: who is the oppressor and who the oppressed in this event?

79 | 912 |

2613 مُفَضَّل *adj.* preferred; favorite, best (friend)

ما زلت أعتبرك صديقي المفضل وسأظل كذلك — I still consider you my best friend, and I will remain like that

87 | 827 |

2614 اقْتَصَر *v. VIII* to be limited على to; to abbreviate, shorten sth

هذه الخلايا المنفلتة في زيادة العدد لا تقتصر على البقاء في مكانها حيث نشأت، بل تنتقل إلى أماكن أخرى بعيدة في الجسم عبر الدم أو الأوعية الليمفاوية — These cells of uncontrolled growth do not limit themselves to staying in their place where they were created, but rather they move to other distant parts of the body through the blood or the lymph vessels

80 | 897 |

2615 بُرْج *n.* tower; constellation; zodiac, horoscope

قرر ان يستعاض عن ذكر اسم الشهر برسم صورة البرج الفلكي الذي يشير اليه — He decided to replace the mention of the name of the month with a picture of the Zodiac sign which refers to it

89 | 801 |

2616 طَلاق *n.* divorce

بلغ بها الحنق درجة لأول مرة أن فكرت في الطلاق — Her anger reached a point that she thought for the first time about divorce

82 | 870 |

2617 لَبِسَ *v. I (a)* to put on (clothes); to wear; لابِس (Dia.) *a.p.* wearing, sporting

كانت تلبس ثوبا أبيض، وتغطي رأسها بشال من الحرير الأزرق — She was wearing a white robe, and covered her head with a shawl of blue silk

81 | 888 |

2618 مُكَوِّن *n. pl.* -aat component, constituent, element; *adj.* forming, comprising, constituting

لنبدأ من المكون الأساس للكلمة وهو الحرف..
والحرف له نوعان: حروف المباني، وحروف المعاني
— Let's start with the basic building block of
the word, and it is the letter...The letter has
two types: building letters and meaning letters
78 | 911 |

2619 إِصْبَع *n. pl.* أَصَابِع finger
يرتدي صندلا قديما تبرز منه أصابع قدميه المتسخة —
He is wearing old sandals from which his dirty
toes are protruding
82 | 876 |

2620 أَتَاحَ *v. IV* to grant, provide (opportunity)
الخجل: فرصة نادرة تتيح للفتاة أن تبدو متوردة
الوجه بدون استخدام المساحيق — Embarrassment:
a rare opportunity to allow a girl to appear
rosy-cheeked without using make-up
78 | 909 |

2621 تَعِبَ *v. I (a)* to be or become tired; to get
tired مِن of sth
لن أحاسبك على كلامك.. الواضح أن أعصابك
تعبت.. أنصحك بحمام ساخن ثم صلاة ركعتين —
I won't hold you to your words...it is clear
that your nerves are tired...I advise you to
take a hot shower and then pray a couple
of prostrations
72 | 988 |

2622 ضِياع *n.* loss; waste (esp. of time)
جاء إلَي وبكى وتوسل حتى أنقذ مستقبله من الضياع
— He came to me and cried and begged me
to save his future from disaster
82 | 869 |

2623 تَدْرِيبِيّ *adj.* practice, exercise; training,
coaching
تجرى تدريبات الفريق في المركز التدريبي للقوة البدنية
في قاعة نقابات العمال — The team practices are
taking place in the practice center for physical
strength in the hall of the labor unions
62 | 1150 |

2624 نَقْد *n. pl.* نُقُود money, cash
فرغت سيارته من الوقود وقلت في جيبه النقود —
His car was out of fuel, and his pocket had
little money in it
82 | 873 |

2625 سام *adj. (def.* سامي) lofty, exalted, sublime
لتأخذ بيدي إلى عالم الحب الجميل إلى عنفوان الحبِّ
السامي حتى نسافر أنا وأنت إلى جزيرة عشقنا
الأخاذة لتتعانق أحلامنا — Take my hand to the
beautiful world of love, to the bloom of
exalted love, so that we travel, you and I, to
the island of our captivating love, so that our
dreams can entwine
78 | 907 |

2626 أَطْوَل *elat.* longer/longest; taller/tallest
مثل هذه الأمور قد تأخذ وقتا أطول مما يعتقد البعض
— Matters such as these could take a longer
time than some believe
93 | 763 |

2627 جِدِّيَّة *n.* seriousness, earnestness
هل يمكن أن نتصور نظريا أن تسعى الولايات
المتحدة بجدية وإخلاص نحو ديمقراطية النظم
السياسية في الدول العربية؟! — Is it possible for
us to imagine, theoretically, that the United
States would strive, seriously, towards
democratizing the political regimes in the
Arab states?!
84 | 848 |

2628 تَكْرار *n.* repetition, reiteration; frequency;
تَكْراراً repeatedly, frequently
أريد كلاما يقتل فراغ النفس، أكره التكرار، أمله،
ويملني، أريد حديثا ملوَّنًا — I want words that
will kill the emptiness of soul, I hate repetition,
I am bored with it, it bores me, I want colorful
speech
85 | 840 |

2629 رايح (Dia.) *a.p.* going; *fem.* رايحة /rayHa/,
pl. رايحين /rayHiin/
والله انا رايح آكل هندى دلوقتى — Actually, I am
going to eat some Indian food now
46 | 1529 | +spo

2630 تَكَوَّنَ *v. V* to be composed, consist مِن of
كل مجتمع يتكون من طبقات فقيرة ومتوسطة وغنية
— Every society is made up of poor, middle,
and upper classes
80 | 887 |

2631 مَعْلُوم *adj.* known; مَعْلُوم *interj.* of course!
definitely! (for pl.n. مَعْلُومات see مَعْلُومَة)

ترك المهلة الزمنية مفتوحة إلى أجل غير معلوم
He left the time period open to an unknown time

97 | 733 |

2632 حِقْد *n.* hatred, resentment

لم أكد اعرفهم فقد غير الحقد ملامحهم — I didn't recognize them because hatred had altered their features

80 | 893 |

2633 مالَ *v. I (i)* to bend, incline, lean إلى towards; to have a tendency, inclination, preference إلى for; to sympathize إلى with

إن العائلات المقيمة في المناطق الحضرية أصبحت تميل إلى إنجاب عدد أقل من الأطفال — Families living in settled areas have started to tend towards producing fewer children

77 | 921 |

2634 نَشَأَ *v. I (a)* to grow, develop; to grow up, be raised; to arise, originate

يهز كتفيه ويتكلم بلكنة أهل تكساس حيث نشأ قبل مجيئه إلى شيكاجو — He shakes his shoulders and speaks with the dialect of the people of Texas, where he was raised before coming to Chicago

83 | 851 |

2635 كَرَّرَ *v. II* to repeat sth, do sth again; to filter, distill; to refine (petroleum)

يجب ألا تدعوا الفرصة تفوتكم، فالتاريخ لا يكرر نفسه أبدا — You must not let the opportunity pass you by; history never repeats itself

85 | 829 |

2636 حُلُول *vn.* advent, arrival; start, beginning; replacing, taking the place of

إني أستغل فرصة حلول العام الجديد لأتمنى لكل العالم السلام والخير والحب — I take the opportunity of the arrival of the new year to wish the whole world peace and goodness and love

80 | 886 |

2637 وَقَّفَ *v. II* to stop, detain sb; (Dia.) to stand, stand still; to stop (doing sth); to turn off, stop sth; to park (car)

نفذ العمال إضرابا شاملا يوقف عجلة الحياة تماما في البلاد — The workers carried out a

comprehensive strike which brought normal life to a complete stop in the country

93 | 759 |

2638 مُكَثَّف *adj.* intensive, heightened; thick, concentrated; compressed

الليلة قبل الأخيرة من العام شهدت غارات بريطانية مكثفة على مطاري الغزالة وطبرق — The night before the last night of the year witnessed heavy British attacks on the airports of Al-Ghazala and Tabruq

78 | 908 |

2639 تَوْصِيَة *n.* pl. -aat recommendation, advice

لذلك يجب تناول أقراص تحتوي على الفيتامينات لتعويض هذا النقص بالإضافة الى زيت السمك لفائدته العالية للجسم حسب توصيات الطبيب المختص — Therefore you need to take tablets that contain vitamins to make up for this deficiency, as well as fish oil because of its high benefit for the body according to the advice of the specialist doctor

71 | 993 |

2640 رَخيص *adj.* cheap, inexpensive

كان أول ما فعله هو أن دخل أحد الفنادق الرخيصة واستحم ونام طويلا — The first thing he did was to go in one of the cheap hotels and shower and sleep for a long time

92 | 769 |

2641 عَثَرَ *v. I (u)* to find, discover, come across على sth

ظللت أبحث عن تليفونها حتى عثرت عليها وأخبرتني عن المحل — I kept searching for her telephone until I found it and told her about the shop

83 | 848 |

2642 إِماراتِيّ *n./adj.* Emirati (of or relating to the United Arab Emirates)

اشار الدكتور نظيف إلى أن الاستثمارات الاماراتية المتدفقة إلى مصر تزداد يوما بعد يوم — Dr. Nazif pointed out that Emirati investments coming into Egypt were increasing day by day

61 | 1146 |

2643 دَمَّرَ *v. II* to destroy, demolish sth; to wreck, ruin, damage sth

— حدث زلزال رهيب دمر قرى عديدة فى تركيا
A terrible earthquake occurred which destroyed a number of villages in Turkey
82 | 863 |

2644 حَيَّ *v. I* يَحْيا to live, be alive; to experience, witness (a life of)
الیوم أنت تحيا الحياة التى كان بها يحلم أدهم — Now you live the life that Adham dreamed of
79 | 897 | +lit

2645 رَمَى *v. I (i)* to attempt, pursue, intend, aim at إلى sth (as a goal); to throw, fling sth or ب sth (at sb); to pelt, shoot at sb ب with (stones, bullets)
ظل واقفا حتى استدارت لتبتعد فركض إليها.. رمى حجرا صغيرا على النافذة، ورآها تسرع فى لهفة إليها — He stayed standing until she turned around to go off, and then he ran to her...He threw a small rock onto the window, and saw her hurrying eagerly towards it
79 | 895 |

2646 شِراكَة *n.* partnership
بحث الوزير الفرنسي مع الجانب التونسي بالخصوص تطوير الشراكة بين تونس وفرنسا من جهة وبينها وبين الاتحاد الأوروبي من جهة أخرى — The French minister discussed with the Tunisian side especially the development of the partnership between Tunis and France on the one hand, and with the European Union on the other hand
62 | 1128 |

2647 عابِر *adj.* passing by or through, crossing over; trans-, inter-; fleeting, transient, brief
كنت أتوقع أن تكون علاقتنا عابرة.. مجرد وقت ممتع — I was expecting that our relationship would be ephemeral...just a nice time
85 | 825 |

2648 خَوْض *n.* waging, embarking on, carrying out; plunging (في into)
هؤلاء القراصنة يمكنهم خوض المعارك فى البحر المتوسط ضد فرنسا فيشغلونها عنى — These pirates can plunge into the battle in the Mediterranean Sea against France, and keep it too occupied to bother us
83 | 848 |

2649 اِسْتِكْمال *n.* conclusion, termination, completion
مؤسسات إسرائيلية تحفر الأنفاق تحت مجمع عين سلوان لاستكمال تهويد القدس — Israeli organizations are digging tunnels under the Ain Salwan complex to complete the judaization of Jerusalem
78 | 900 |

2650 فَريد *adj.* unique, exceptional, singular
من سمات اللغة العربية ومیزاتها الفريدة أنها لغة اشتقاق، تعود مشتقاتها المتعددة الى جذر لغوي واحد — One of the characteristics, and unique advantages, of the Arabic language is that it is a derivational language, its various derivations going back to a single linguistic root
88 | 795 |

2651 عَسَى *adv.* perhaps, maybe; (with pron.) ماذا عَساني أن what could I possibly (do, say)?; (Irq.Gul.) hopefully; عَساك I hope (that) you
عسى أن تكرهوا شيئا وهو خير لكم وعسى أن تحبوا شيئا وهو شر لكم — Perhaps you might hate something that is good for you, and perhaps you might love something that is bad for you
66 | 1063 | +for

2652 عِقاب *n.* punishment, penalty
إن خير عقاب لمثله أن يترك حيًّا لعله يحس يومًا بتأنيب الضمير — The best punishment for such as him is to be left alive so perhaps he will feel someday a regret of conscience
86 | 816 |

2653 تَلْبِيَة *vn.* meeting (needs), fulfilling (desires, expectations); complying with (request)
الدول العربية مستعدة لتلبية كافة التزاماتها ازاء تحقيق السلام فى المنطقة — The Arab states are prepared to comply with all their obligations in regard to achieving peace in the region
84 | 836 |

2654 وَضَّحَ *v. II* to clarify, explain (ل to sb) أنَّ that
يوضح أن النرجيلة خطرة ، لأنه بالإضافة إلى النيكوتين والقطران وأكسيد الكربون الذي تحتويه، هناك البنزوبيرين، الزرنيخ، البيريليوم والرصاص وغيرها من المواد الكيميائية — He clarifies that the water pipe is dangerous, because in addition to the nicotine and tar and carbon dioxide

which it contains, there is benzopyrene, arsenic, beryllium, lead, and other chemical substances

92 | 765 |

2655 حِيَرَة and حَيْرَة *n.* confusion, bewilderment; embarrassment

سكت بيكر وراح ينظر إليه وقد تملكته حيرة حقيقية أمام هذا النوع من البشر الذى لم يره من قبل فى حياته — Baker became silent and started to look at him, having been overcome with real bewilderment in the face of this type of human being whom he had never seen before in his life

77 | 907 | +lit

2656 غُبار *n.* dust

خرج العراق من بين أنقاض الخراب والدمار نافضا عنه غبار الحرب — Iraq has emerged from the debris of destruction, shaking off the dust of war

81 | 865 |

2657 طَقْس *n.* weather, climate

انخفاض عدد الفراشات فى بريطانيا يعود الى التغير فى احوال الطقس وهو ما يهدد حياتنا — A drop in the number of butterflies in Britain can be attributed to the change in the conditions of the climate, and that is what threatens our lives

76 | 917 |

2658 فُقْدان and فِقْدان *n.* loss; bereavement

قد تتسبب فى جفاف الجلد وفقدان الشعر للمعانه وبريقه — It might cause dryness of the skin and cause the hair to lose its shine

83 | 840 |

2659 مَدار *n.* orbit, sphere; scope, range; axis, pivot; center, focus

جنودنا فى منطقة القتال يجب أن يكونوا مدار اهتمامنا الأول — Our soldiers in the war zone must be the focus of our primary concern

83 | 844 |

2660 بابا *n.* pope; البابا the Pope; بابا daddy, papa; بابا نُويِل (Fr. Papa Noël) Santa Claus; بابا غَنُّوج baba ghannouj; علي بابا Ali Baba; (eggplant dip)

إني يا سيدي أحترم قداسة البابا ولكن يجب أن تعطي ما لله لله وما لقيصر لقيصر — Sir, I respect his

Holiness, the Pope, but you must give to God what is God's and to Caesar what is Caesar's

66 | 1059 |

2661 كِيس *n.* pl. أَكْياس bag, sack

لفت الجهاز والعلبة والقرص بعناية ووضعتهم فى كيس أنيق يحمل شعار المحل — She wrapped up the device and the package and the disk carefully and put them in a nice sack that carried the logo of the shop

78 | 889 |

2662 اِحْتِجاج *n.* protest; اِحْتِجاجاً protesting, in protest (على of)

تظاهر مئات من طلاب جامعة الأزهر احتجاجا على المجزرة الإسرائيلية — Hundreds of Azhar University students demonstrated in protest of the Israeli massacre

80 | 874 |

2663 مانع *n.* obstacle, impediment; *adj.* preventing; forbidding

ثم قال: ما المانع من أن يتزوج رجل فى الخمسين فتاة فى بداية العشرينات؟ — Then he said: What is preventing a fifty-year-old man from marrying a girl in her early twenties?

90 | 776 |

2664 وَقُود *n.* fuel

تدعي إيران بفخر أنها تبني دورة وقود نووي ستمكنها من استخراج خام اليورانيوم من الأرض — Iran claims with pride that it is building a nuclear fuel centrifuge which will enable it to extract raw uranium from the ground

75 | 920 |

2665 دَجاج *coll.n.* chickens, poultry; (Lev.) جاج

تضايق السكان وانتابهم الذعر و تركوا لحوم الدجاج جانبا وأكلوا لحوم الأسماك — The inhabitants were annoyed and frightened and they avoided chicken meat and ate fish

76 | 911 |

2666 نَهْج *n.* method, procedure; way, path

إن دولة قطر سارعت بدراسة النهج الاستراتيجي للإدارة السليمة للمواد الكيئائية — The state of Qatar hurried to study the strategic procedure for the sound administration of chemical materials

77 | 904 |

2667 تَسْمِيَة *n.* naming, appellation, designation
هو شيء واحد فقط.. يمكن تسميته بمفردة واحدة:
الحب — It is just one thing: it can be called
with only one vocabulary item: love
83 | 834 |

2668 هامِش *n.* side, margin; periphery, sideline
من لم يتعلم يعش على هامش الحياة — He who is
not educated will live on the margins of life
76 | 909 |

2669 حانَ *v. I (i)* to arrive, approach (time)
ألم يحن الوقت للعمل بجدية للقضاء على اخطر آفة
تهدد المجتمع العربي؟ — Has the time not come
to work seriously to eradicate the most dangerous
scourge to threaten Arab society?
85 | 816 |

2670 تَكْريم *n.* honoring, respecting, paying tribute;
تَكْريمًا لِـ in honor of
سيجري رفع العلم السعودي على ٣٠ مبنى في البلدة
تكريما للضيوف — The Saudi flag will be raised
over 30 buildings in the town in honor of the
guests
78 | 890 |

2671 راجِع *a.p.* returning, going back إلى to; (to be)
traced back, attributed, due إلى to
إنا لله وإنا إليه راجعون — We belong to God, and
to him we are returning
77 | 903 |

2672 نَهْضَة *n.* renaissance
نهض الشعر العربي نهضة تمثلت في إقباله على التجديد
في الشكل وفي المضمون — Arab poetry experienced
a renaissance which was represented in its
accepting renewal in form and content
75 | 923 |

2673 اِعْتِقاد *vn.* belief في in sth, or أنَّ/بِأنَّ that
كان الناس يعتقدون ان الارض مسطحة.. وقد ظل
هذا الاعتقاد سائدا فترة طويلة من الزمن — People
believed that the earth is flat...and this belief
was prevalent for a long time
82 | 847 |

2674 باطِل *adj.* false, baseless; invalid; null, void;
n. falsehood; باطِل (Alg.) *adv.* in vain; *adj.*
worthless

فتحت طيبة فمها مستغربة هذا الاتهام الباطل
— Tiba opened her mouth surprised by this false
accusation
80 | 868 |

2675 اِتَّضَحَ *v. VIII* to become clear, to be clarified أنَّ
that
دلوقت اتضح لي بوضوح شديد انك تقصد تهينني..
أنا اتهنت يا عصمت — Now it has become
clear to me that you intend to insult me...
I have been insulted, Ismat
84 | 820 |

2676 تَصَدٍّ *n.* resistance, confrontation
طرح عدد من أعضاء مجلس المستشارين بعض
المقترحات العملية لتطوير الخطاب الديني وتجويده
وتيسير مضمونه على المتلقين للتصدي لما تبثه بعض
الفضائيات من فتاوى دينية خاطئة — A number
of members of the Council of Advisors put
forward some practical suggestions to develop
the religious message and improve it and to
simplify its content for the learners to resist
what some satellite channels are broadcasting
in the way of false religious edicts
76 | 905 |

2677 أَسْهَمَ *v. IV* to participate, contribute, share
كل الشكر لجميع من يسهم في العمل على محاربة
المخدرات ومكافحتها من مؤسسات رسمية وأهلية
— All thanks to everyone who is participating
in working on fighting drugs from both official
and non-governmental institutions
74 | 937 |

2678 قِيامَة *n.* resurrection; يَوْم القِيامَة Judgment
Day
قال: نحن نعيش الأيام التي تسبق مباشرة يوم
القيامة — He said: we are experiencing
the days which directly precede the
Resurrection Day
72 | 953 |

2679 مَيْدانِيّ *adj.* field (work, research), survey;
ground (troops)
توفر الدائرة فرص التدريب الميداني لطلبة كلية العلوم
الزراعية — The agency provides field training
opportunities for students in the College of
Agricultural Sciences
66 | 1037 |

2680 مُتاح *adj.* provided, available, granted
القناة سوف تكون متاحة للمشاهد العادي في مصر عبر القنوات الأرضية — The channel will be available for normal viewers in Egypt through the terrestrial channels
76 | 902 |

2681 بَرِّيّ *adj.* land, rural; by land, land-based; wild (flower, fruit, honey)
يبحث عن قبر أمه وهو يزيح الحشائش البرية عن شواهد القبور — He searches for his mother's grave, removing the weeds from the headstones
76 | 902 |

2682 وَعَدَ *v. I (i)* to promise (sb) ب sth or بِأَنْ/بِأَنَّ that
طبقت غوغل نظاما جديدا لتنقية الفيديو، كانت قد وعدت بتطبيقه منذ فترة طويلة في موقع يوتيوب التابع لها — Google applied a new system for choosing videos, which it had promised to apply for a long time in the YouTube site that belongs to it
87 | 790 |

2683 أَخْبَر *v. IV* to notify, inform, tell sb ب/عن about sth or أَنَّ/بِأَنَّ that
لقد أخبرني ياسين أنه غادر الفندق منذ مدة وأنه يعيش مختبئا لا أحد يعرف مكانه إلا هو — Yasin informed me that he left the hotel a while ago and that he is living in hiding, no one knowing where he is except him
73 | 945 |

2684 حائط *n.* wall
على الحائط صورة كبيرة للسيد رئيس الجمهورية — On the wall is a big picture of the president of the republic
90 | 767 |

2685 غامِض *adj.* obscure, vague, ambiguous; enigmatic, mysterious, inscrutable
أكد له عن فكرته عن المرأة ككائن غامض مملوء بالتناقض، يستحيل التكهن بردود أفعاله أو رغباته الدفينة — He reassured him of his concept of woman as a mysterious creature full of contradictions, whose responses or hidden desires are impossible to predict
80 | 862 |

2686 أَيْسَر *adj.* fem. يُسْرَى left, left hand
عضلات الجانب الايسر من الوجه أكثر تعبيرا من عضلات الجانب الأيمن — The muscles of the left side of the face are more expressive than the muscles of the right side
78 | 880 |

2687 خَريطَة *n.* map, chart; خَريطَة الطَّريق roadmap
هل يحقق هذا المشروع حلم الجامعات المصرية في أن تجد لها مكانا ومكانة على الخريطة العالمية؟ — Will this project accomplish the dream of Egyptian universities to find for themselves a place and position on the world map?
81 | 845 |

2688 شَكْوَى *n. pl.* شَكاوَى complaint, grievance
تم وضع آليات سهلة المنال لتلقي الشكاوى من المواطنين من خلال مكتب المظالم وحقوق الانسان — Accessible mechanisms were put in place to receive the complaints of the citizens through the Ombudsman and Human Rights office
81 | 846 |

2689 رُؤْيا *n. pl.* رُؤىً vision, dream; idea, picture
كيف يمكن التوفيق بين هذه الرؤى المختلفة؟ — How can we reconcile these differing visions?
80 | 862 |

2690 تَعَرُّض *vn.* exposure إلى to sth; encountering, running into, having to deal with إلى sth; suffering إلى (loss)
يبحث الفريق عن أول فوز له بعد تعرضه للهزيمة في ثلاث مناسبات متتالية — The team is looking for its first victory after having suffered defeat on three consecutive occasions
82 | 838 |

2691 مُحاسَبَة *n.* examination, review; accounting, bookkeeping; accountability, oversight
طالب بضرورة محاسبة من ارتكب هذه الجريمة، ومحاسبة قياداتهم — He called for holding accountable those who perpetrated this crime, and to hold their leaders accountable
84 | 817 |

2692 بَيْضَة *coll.n.* eggs, *un.n.* بَيْض
إن أول طير أصبح دجاجة وجد في البدء كجنين داخل بيضة — The first bird that became

a chicken was found in the beginning as
an embryo inside an egg

76 | 903 |

2693 عِمْلاق *adj.* gigantic, huge; super

أدخل رأسه في صدره حتى بدا كسلحفاة عملاقة..
وراح يمد عينيه وقد فتحها قليلا يرقب جموع الناس
— He put his head on his chest so that he
looked like a giant turtle, and he started to
extend his eyes, for he had opened them a
little, watching the crowds of people

83 | 826 |

2694 لُجُوء *vn.* resorting إلى to; taking refuge إلى in;
n. refuge; (political) asylum

اتفقوا أخيرا على اللجوء إلى القضاء لكي يحكم بينهم
— They finally agreed to resort to the courts
to judge between them

83 | 826 |

2695 رَقيق *adj.* gentle, delicate; slender; *coll.n.*
slaves

توقفوا لبضع دقائق للاستماع إلى صبية تغني على
المسرح بصوت رقيق حزين — They stood
still for a few minutes to listen to a young
girl singing on the stage with a sad, delicate
voice

76 | 898 |

2696 مَوْضِع *n.* place, location, position; object,
subject, focus (of interest, attention, concern)

أنت في موضع اتخاذ القرار، ولا بد من قرار عاجل
— You are in a position to make the decision,
and a quick decision is necessary

84 | 815 |

2697 تارَةً *n.* تارة once; at times, sometimes

إن حياتنا كأوراق الشجر .. تارة خضراء و تارة
صفراء — Our lives are like the leaves of the
trees...at times green and at times yellow

76 | 894 |

2698 تَفاعُل *n.* interaction, reaction; reciprocity

طريق التنمية يمر أساسا عبر التفاعل بين جميع
مكونات المجتمع — The way to growth passes,
basically, through the interaction between all
the components of society

80 | 849 |

2699 مُفَكِّر *n.* pl. -uun intellectual

إن الأمم التي تحتضن الفكر وترعى المفكرين هي
الأمم التي ستتقدم إلى الأمام — Nations that
embrace thought and care for intellectuals are
the nations that will move forward

81 | 840 |

2700 اِضْطَرَّ *v. VIII* to compel, force, oblige sb إلى to
do sth; (often pass.) اُضْطُرَّ to be compelled,
forced, obligated إلى to do sth

بعد النجاح الساحق لألبوم عمرو دياب ليلي نهاري
اضطرت شركة روتانا الى طبع عشرات الاف النسخ
الاضافية — After the overwhelming success of
Amr Diab's album Leily Nahary, the Rotana
(recording) company was forced to print tens
of thousands of extra copies

82 | 831 |

2701 وَزَّعَ *v. II* to distribute sth على among

كانت تحب الفقراء وتوزع الثياب والطعام على المياتم
— She loved the poor and distributed clothing
and food to orphanages

86 | 788 |

2702 زَلْزال *n.* pl. زَلازِل earthquake

وقبل انتهاء العام بيومين حدث زلزال رهيب دمر
قرى عديدة في تركيا — Two days before the end
of the year a terrible earthquake destroyed
a number of villages in Turkey

76 | 894 |

2703 شَرَحَ *v. I (a)* to explain sth ل to sb

من اللافت للنظر درس إمام المسجد الذي شرح فيه
— تفسيرا موجزا لكل جزء من القرآن الكريم
Imam of the mosque's lesson, in which he
explained in an abbreviated manner every
section of the Holy Qur'an, was notable

86 | 791 |

2704 اِنْتِفاضَة *n.* uprising; الانْتِفاضَة the Intifada
(Palestinian popular uprising)

لقد كرست الانتفاضة روح التعاون والتكافل بين
أبناء الشعب فكانت مدرسة تربوية نضالية
جهادية — The Intifada cemented the spirit of
cooperation and solidarity among the people,
and thus it was an educational, logistical,
militant, jihadist school

73 | 930 |

2705 ارْتَدَى *v. VIII* to wear, put on (clothes)
جاء حمدي لزيارتها، كان يرتدي ملابس جديدة غالية
الثمن، ووضع بجوارها علبة شيكولاتة — Hamdi
came to visit her, he was wearing expensive
new clothing, and he put a box of chocolates
by her side
84 | 811 |

2706 فِلْس *n. pl.* فُلُوس fils (monetary unit); فُلُوس
money
— أنا عاوز فلوس كتير.. عاوز أعيش زي الآدميين
I want a lot of money...I want to live like
a human being
61 | 1116 | +spo

2707 فارِس *n. pl.* فُرْسان horseman, rider; knight;
فُرْسان cavalry
إذا به وسط الساحة وقد أشهر فرسان القبيلة سيوفهم
في وجهه وكاد عنقه يتدحرج بينهم — He appeared
in the middle of the courtyard, and the
horsemen of the tribe waved their swords in
his face and his head almost rolled among
them
79 | 855 |

2708 نَمَط *n. pl.* أنْماط type, kind; manner, style,
form; (tech.) model, configuration
بقيت في البيت، وحافظت على نمط حياتها كما كان
— I stayed in the house, and maintained its
lifestyle as it was
78 | 864 |

2709 غِطاء *n.* cover; blanket
أحكمت حولي المعطف الثقيل وشددت غطاء الرأس
والكوفيه على وجهي — I secured the thick
overcoat around me and tightened the head
cover and the head scarf around my face
84 | 805 |

2710 شُعاع *n. pl.* أشِعَّة ray, beam
تغمرنا أشعة القمر وتحيط بنا الأشجار — We are
immersed in the rays of the moon and we are
surrounded by trees
80 | 849 |

2711 كَتيبة *n. pl.* كَتائِب squadron, brigade, regiment;
corps; الكَتائِب (Leb.) Phalangists
هذه الكتائب العظيمة من الجنود أسسها السلطان —

This great brigade of soldiers was established
by the Sultan
60 | 1129 |

2712 طَبَّق *v. II* to implement (plan, project,
decision, strategy); to apply, enforce, carry
out (law, regulation, standards)
أضاف أن العديد من الدول تطبق عقوبة الإعدام،
غير أنه شخصيا لا يؤيد عقوبة الموت — He added
that a number of states carry out capital
punishment, even though he personally does
not support capital punishment
83 | 812 |

2713 مُتَطَرِّف *n./adj.* extremist, militant, radical
المتطرفون من الفريقين هم الذين يساهمون في تبديد
هذه الفرص — The extremists from the two
teams are the ones who have a part in wasting
these opportunities
71 | 942 |

2714 أخْفَى *v. IV* to hide, conceal sth (عن from);
to lower (one's voice)
دخل راغب وقد وضع يديه خلفه كأنه يخفي شيئا
عني — Raghib entered with his hands
behind his back as if he were hiding
something from me
82 | 818 |

2715 برده and برضو /bardo/ (Egy.Lev.) *adv.* also, too
فكما كل واحد فينا يحب يخدم انا برضه احـ، اخدم
الجميع وذلك بسبب ما املكه من خبره — Just as
each of us wants to serve, I also want to serve
everyone, and that's because of the expertise
I have
35 | 1891 | +spo

2716 فائز *adj.* victorious, winning; *n. pl.* -uun
winner, victor
سيمنح الفائز جائزة ٢٥ ألف درهم لأحسن صورة
تعبر عن إمارة أبو ظبي — The winner will be
granted a 25,000 dirham prize for the best
picture which expresses the Emirate of Abu
Dhabi
78 | 856 |

2717 جَرَّب *v. II* to try out, test sth; to sample, taste
sth; to tempt, test sb

لقد جربت السلطات المصرية كل الحلول الممكنة بالحكمة والصبر ولم يبق الا التدخل المحسوب لانهاء الازمة — The Egyptian authorities tried every possible solution with wisdom and patience and there was nothing left but an intervention calculated to end the crisis

78 | 858 |

2718 مُدِيرِيَّة n. administration, management; office, department; district, province
جاءت أورطة بوليس من كوم الدكة، سحبوا الناس على المديرية وضربوهم على قفاهم — A police battalion came from Kom Al-Dakka; they dragged the people to the district office and beat them on their backs

60 | 1119 | +news

2719 عِبَادَة vn. worship, adoration, religious practice
إسرائيل أبعد ما تكون عن الحرية والديمقراطية وإعطاء حرية العبادة — Israel is as far as possible from freedom and democracy and granting religious liberty

85 | 786 |

2720 اِفْتَتَحَ v. VIII to open, inaugurate (conference, school)
احتفلت الكاتدرائية المرقسية بعيد القيامة فأقيم قداس حافل افتتح بالتضرع إلى الله أن يشمل العالم برحمته — The Marqusiyya Cathedral celebrated Easter and held a celebratory mass which opened by calling on God to encompass the world with his mercy

77 | 867 |

2721 هاذ and هذ (Lev.Irq.Gul.) /haadh/ (Lev. also /haad/) dem.pron. this (masc.sg)
لازم أروح له الأسبوع هاذ — I have to go to him this week

62 | 1076 | +spo

2722 مُعْتَمَد p.p. مُعْتَمَد عليه/عليها depended upon; adj. authorized, dependable; accredited; n. agent, representative
فهذه محمية تراث عالمي طبيعي معتمدة من اليونسكو، وهناك التزامات محلية في الإبقاء عليها — This is a natural world heritage reserve sanctioned by UNESCO, and there is a local commitment to preserving it

78 | 850 |

2723 مُظَاهَرَة n. pl. -aat demonstration, rally
ذكر نائب رئيس مجلس العمل المتحد ان المظاهرات ستستمر حتى تدرك الدول الأوروبية مدى غضب المسلمين — The vice-president of the United Labor Council mentioned that the demonstrations will continue until the European states realize the extent of Muslims' anger

70 | 955 |

2724 أَوْسَع elat. broader/broadest, wider/widest
انه يملك خبرة أوسع من خبرتي — He has a broader experience than mine

90 | 740 |

2725 اِسْتَدْعَى v. X to summon, call sb; to recall, call back sb; to invoke sth
لا أتصور أنها مريضة إلى درجة أن تستدعي طبيبًا — I don't imagine she is sick to the extent that she will summon a doctor

83 | 801 |

2726 عَقَارِيّ adj. real estate; land mortgage
ما مدى الاهتمام بالاستثمار العقاري؟ وهل لديكم اية مشاريع واهتمامات بهذا القطاع؟ — What is the extent of interest in real estate investment? Do you have any projects or interests in this sector?

55 | 1203 |

2727 سَهَّلَ v. II to facilitate, make easy, help
المصادفة تسهل للبعض طريقه وتصعب للبعض طريقه — Chance helps some on their way, and hinders others

84 | 790 |

2728 حَقَّ v. I (i) to be right; يَحِقُّ لَهُ أَنْ to have the right to do sth
هي هذه الفتاة (حتشبسوت) وهي وحدها التي يحق لها أن تخلفه بحكم القانون الكهنوتي المقدس — She is this girl "Hatshepsut", and she alone is the one who has the right to succeed him according to the holy priesthood law

85 | 781 |

2729 كَثُرَ v. I (u) to be numerous, plentiful; to be more عن than sth
سيبقى وطننا آمنا من الضياع حتى وإن كثرت الليالي الحالكة — Our nation will remain secure from loss even if the dark nights are many

89 | 747 |

2730 حِمار *n.* donkey, fem. حِمارَة she-ass, pl. حَمير؛
يا حِمار! /ya-Hmaar/ hey dummy! you idiot!
— فجأة نهق الحمار واحتج مثل كأنه يحتج مثل صاحبه
Suddenly the donkey brayed as if he were
objecting just like his master
69 | 955 |

2731 حَنين *n.* yearning, nostalgia
ترددت من جديد الأنغام العذبة التي طال حنين
الناس إليها — I played again the sweet
melodies which the people have longed for
69 | 962 | +lit

2732 حَدا /Hada/ (Lev.) *n.* anyone, somebody; (neg.)
ما حَداش and ما حَدا nobody
أهلي ما بيدخنوا يعني ما عندنا حدا في البيت بيدخن
— My family doesn't smoke, I mean, we don't
have anyone at home that smokes
28 | 2380 | +for +spo

2733 كَوْكَب *n.* pl. كَواكِب planet; star
كان يبدو بها كأنه قادم من كوكب آخر أو كأنه
شخصية خرجت من مسرحية تاريخية — He
appeared in it as if he were coming from
another planet or as if he were a person
coming out of a historical play
79 | 837 |

2734 مُتَبادَل *adj.* mutual, reciprocal; exchanged
تم التوصل الى صيغ تعاون قائمة على الاحترام
المتبادل وخدمة المصالح المشتركة — Modes
of cooperation based on mutual respect and
serving joint interests were reached
79 | 838 |

2735 اِفْتَرَض *v. VIII* to assume, suppose sth or أَنَّ
that
لقد مللت الانتظار.. كان يفترض أن يتم زواجنا منذ
سنوات — I have grown tired of waiting...Our
marriage was supposed to have taken place
years ago
76 | 869 |

2736 مُغادَرَة *n.* departure
القطار متجه نحو الموصل .. شق طريقه في المغادرة
ببطء مثل عاشق ترك حبيبته في محطة مهجورة —
The train was headed towards Mosul...
In leaving, it made its way slowly like a lover
leaving his beloved in an abandoned station
81 | 818 |

2737 اِنْطَبَق *v. VII* to be applicable (على to); to
conform (على with)
يؤمنون بأن القوانين لا تنطبق عليهم
They believe that the laws do not apply
to them
82 | 802 |

2738 عَذْب *adj.* sweet, pleasant; مِياه عَذْبَة
freshwater
وقرأ في صلاة الفجر سورة الفجر وسورة الليل
بصوته العذب، وبكى وهو يتلوهما — For dawn
prayer he read the "Dawn" Surah, and the
"Night" Surah with his sweet voice, and he
cried as he recited them
75 | 875 |

2739 اِنْسَحَب *v. VII* to withdraw, leave (مِن from); to
pull out, withdraw (armed forces)
وكان باراك قد أعلن مؤخرا ان إسرائيل لن تنسحب
من الضفة الغربية قبل ايجاد حل لهجمات الصواريخ
— Barak had announced recently that Israel
would not withdraw from the West Bank
before finding a solution to the rocket attacks
84 | 783 |

2740 عاطِفَة *n.* pl. عَواطِف emotion, sentiment;
affection
الحب الذي يأتي بعد الزواج يكون أكثر رسوخا
واحتراما من العواطف الملتهبة المتقلبة التي قد
تتلاشى فجأة أو تنتهي بمصيبة — Love which
comes after marriage can be more anchored
and more respectful than the ephemeral
burning emotions which can come to nothing
suddenly or end in a catastrophe
81 | 817 |

2741 مُعَبِّر *a.p.* expressing (عن opinion, feeling),
stating (عن position, policy)
هزت رأسها معبرة عن عدم فهم قصدها
بالضبط — She shook her head expressing
her incomprehension of her exact meaning
86 | 768 |

2742 عَقَبَة *n.* pl. -aat obstacle
ان عدم حدوث تقدم في حل النزاع يمثل عقبة أمام
التنمية الاقتصادية — Not making progress in
solving the conflict represents an obstacle
to economic growth
84 | 778 |

2743 فِراش *n.* bed

بنهاية المباراة يسقط طارق على فراشه مبهور الأنفاس والعرق يتصبب منه كأنه هو الذى خاض المصارعة — At the end of the match Tariq falls on his bed gasping for breath, sweat pouring from him, as if he was the one who had been doing the wrestling

75 | 870 | +lit

2744 سِرِّيَّة *n.* secrecy

— هذه مهمة سرية لا يعلمها أحد إلا أنا وأنت This is a secret mission, no one knows about it but you and me

83 | 786 |

2745 عَبَث *n.* joke, jest; frivolity; عَبَثاً in vain

من العبث أن نختلف الآن حول ما حدث منذ ثلاثين عاما — It is useless to disagree now about what happened thirty years ago

84 | 776 |

2746 إسْبانِيّ *n./adj.* pl. إسْبان Spanish, Spaniard

تعاونت معه في إنتاج أول ألبوم لها باللغة الأسبانية بعنوان كيف تحب المرأة — She collaborated with him in producing her first album in Spanish titled: How to love a woman

61 | 1070 |

2747 ضاحِيَة *n.* pl. ضَواحٍ (def. ضَواحِي) suburb, neighborhood, vicinity

ازداد عدد بناء المساجد الجديدة في ضواحي المدن الكبيرة كشيكاغو وواشنطن العاصمة وسان فرانسيسكو — The number of new mosques in the suburbs of the big cities like Chicago, Washington and San Francisco increased

82 | 801 |

2748 تَضامُن *n.* solidarity, cooperation

إن الوضع العربي الصعب يتطلب المزيد من التضامن والتعاون لتجاوز الظروف التي يمر بها العالم العربي — The difficult Arab situation requires more solidarity and cooperation to get beyond the circumstances which the Arab World is passing through

69 | 939 |

2749 نُفُوذ *n.* influence, effect

فشل مفاوضات السلام بين الفلسطينيين والإسرائيليين كان السبب وراء تزايد نفوذ التيار المتشدد داخل الشارع الفلسطيني — The failure of peace negotiations

between the Palestinians and Israelis was the reason behind the increase in the power of the extremist faction inside the Palestinian street

73 | 898 |

2750 مُماثِل *adj.* similar, analogous; resembling

اكدت المصادر نفسها سقوط ٤ قتلى في حادث مماثل وقع في منطقة زيونة من جانب الرصافة من العاصمة بغداد — The sources themselves confirmed the falling of 4 dead in a similar incident that happened in the Zuyuna region near Al-Rasafa in the capital Baghdad

82 | 799 |

2751 خَلِيفَة *masc.n.* successor; caliph

— هناك خلاف شديد بين الخليفة والوزير There is a strong difference of opinion between the Caliph and the minister

69 | 942 |

2752 إصْرار *n.* insistence, determination

واصلت الحكومات الإسرائيلية المتعاقبة الإصرار على أن يتنازل الفلسطينيون والعرب عن حق العودة للاجئين — Consecutive Israeli governments have continued to insist on the Palestinians and Arabs giving up the right of refugee return

82 | 793 |

2753 جَزِيل *adj.* abundant, ample; شُكْراً جَزِيلاً thank you very much! وَلَكُم مِنِّي جَزِيل الشُّكْر (in closing a letter) my sincere thanks — سَأنقذه من أجلك. I will save him for your sake. – Thank you very much

65 | 1007 | +for

2754 تَحْتِيّ *adj.* under; infra-(structure)

مجهود الدولة يتركز خصوصا في دعم البنية التحتية الأساسية بينما يوكل دور إنشاء المنتجعات والوحدات الفندقية الضخمة للخواص — The efforts of the state are concentrating particularly on supporting the infrastructure while the role of building the resorts and huge hotel units has been delegated to the private sector

60 | 1075 |

2755 خَيْط *n.* pl. خُيُوط string, thread; lead (evidence), clue

كان يجلس على سفينة آبائه، ويمد خيط سنارته إلى
الماء — He was وقد ملأ دلوه إلا البيت إلى يعود فلا
sitting on his fathers' ship, casting his fishing
line into the water, not returning home unless
his bucket was full

81 | 798 |

2756 قُبَيْلَ *prep.* shortly before
ينصح بالامتناع عن تناول اللحوم ليلا قبيل النوم —
He advises abstaining from eating meat at
night right before bed

85 | 764 |

2757 سائد *adj.* prevailing, dominant, ruling
هل تعتقد ان الظروف السياسية السائدة عطلت
العمل في هذه المشاريع الكبرى؟ — Do you
believe that the prevailing political
circumstances have stopped work on
these large projects?

75 | 860 |

2758 أَعْمَى *adj.* fem. عَمْياء blind
دلوني على رجل يقيم بالدرب الأحمر، تبين لي أنه
أعمى، ولكن أهل الحل والعقد أكدوا لي صدق
فراسته وعمق خبرته — They directed me to
a man who lives in the Darb Al-Ahmar, it
became clear to me that he was blind, but the
people in charge assured me of the accuracy
of his discernment and the depth of his
experience

78 | 831 |

2759 اِبْتِداء *n.* beginning, start; اِبْتِداءً مِن beginning
from, as of (date); starting with
سيتم فحص الحالات مجانا على مد يومين ابتداء من
غد من الثامنة صباحا بمستشفى الإيمان العام —
Cases will be examined for free for two days
starting from tomorrow at eight in the
morning in the Al-Iman General Hospital

83 | 779 |

2760 إطْلاق سَراح setting free; سَراح *n.* dismissal, release;
تم اعتقال الزوج وتقديمه إلى العدالة ليطلق سراحه
بعدما أنكر المنسوب إليه — The husband was
arrested and charged, to be released after he
denied the allegations against him

70 | 916 |

2761 مائِدَة *n.* table
كانت المائدة عامرة بشتى أنواع الطعام — The table
was loaded with various kinds of food

84 | 771 |

2762 فَرَّقَ *v. II* to differentiate, distinguish بين
between; to disperse, break up, split up
(crowd, demonstration)
لم تفرق بين المقاومة والإرهاب واعتبرت الكل إرهابا
— She made no distinction between resistance
and terrorism; she considered it all terrorism

78 | 822 |

2763 أُنْثَى *n. pl.* إناث female
اذا بشخص يقف الى جانبى بطرف عينى أدركت أنه
أنثى — Suddenly there was a person standing
beside me, and with the corner of my eye
I realized that it was female

74 | 863 |

2764 اِطِّلاع *n.* examination, inspection (على of sth);
reading, perusal (على of sth)
أغمى عليها فتهاوت أرضا، واندفع سمير وأبوه
للاطلاع عليها، لكن ممرضا قصيرا بدينا اعترضهم
— She lost consciousness and fell to the
ground, and Samir and his father rushed over
to check her out, but a short, fat nurse held
them back

82 | 785 |

2765 أَعَدَّ *v. IV* to prepare sth, make sth ready;
to set (table)
جلس يتفرج على التليفزيون حتى انتهت شيماء من
الطهى؛ أعدت المائدة ونادت عليه بصوت رن فى
سمعه مؤثرا وناعما — He sat looking at the
television until Shima finished cooking; she set
the table and called him with a voice that rang
in his ears in a sweet and affecting manner

86 | 746 |

2766 لاقَ *v. I (i)* to be proper or appropriate ب for
sb; be suitable or convenient ب for sb
فرضت على العريس احضار احدى السيارات
الفخمة التي تليق بابنتها وترضي غرورها بين النساء
— She forced the groom to bring one of the
fancy cars which would be appropriate for her
daughter and would satisfy her envy among
the women

85 | 753 |

2767 عَمَالَة *n.* workforce, employees; العَمَالة الوافِدَة foreign workers

يرغب قطاع صناعة التكنولوجيا الآن في الحصول على عِمالة رخيصة — The technology industry sector now wants to obtain a cheap workforce

68 | 939 |

2768 مَنْظُومَة *n.* system, structure; hierarchy

أشار إلى أن الرياضة المصرية منظومة متكاملة تتشكل من الجهة الإدارية والاتحادات الرياضية وغيرها — He indicated that Egyptian sport was an entire structure which is made up of an administrative side, the sport unions, etc.

66 | 974 |

2769 مُعَقَّد *adj.* complicated, complex, intricate

علينا التصرف بحكمة في مثل هذه الظروف المعقدة — We need to act wisely in complicated circumstances such as these

83 | 772 |

2770 أَوَان *n. pl.* آوِنَة time, moment

اهرب قبل فوات الأوان — Run off before it is too late!

85 | 747 |

2771 قَسْوَة *n.* harshness, severity, brutality

زوج أمها السكير كان يضربها بقسوة — Her mother's drunk husband used to beat her harshly

83 | 768 |

2772 جَدِير *adj.* worth ب (mentioning, pointing out); appropriate, proper ب for sb (to do sth); جَدِير بالذِّكْر worth mentioning

هذا الموضوع جدير بالاهتمام — This subject is worthy of interest

85 | 746 |

2773 اِسْتِيعاب *n.* comprehension, understanding; absorbing, assimilating; accommodating

حاول جاهدا لاستيعاب ثورتها، وأكد لها حرصه الشديد على استمرار العلاقة بينهما — He tried hard to accommodate her revolt, and he confirmed to her his strong insistence on continuing the relationship between them

73 | 872 |

2774 غَداء *n.* lunch; midday meal

يتناول اللاعبون وجبة الغداء اليوم في احد المطاعم بالعاصمة الاماراتية دبي لاخراجهم من جو المعسكرات التدريبية — The players ate lunch today in one of the restaurants of the Emirati capital, Dubai, to get them out of the atmosphere of the training camp

87 | 729 |

2775 ياريت /ya-reet/ (Dia.) *part.* if only, I wish; ريتك /reet-/ (with pron.) /reet-ak/ I wish you (could, would); ريتني /reet-ni/ I wish I (could)

ياريت ما تتدخل بامور اتحاد الكرة — I wish you wouldn't interfere in the affairs of the Soccer Union

38 | 1650 | +for

2776 شابَّة *n./adj.* young woman

المرأة تتمنى أن تنجب طفلا صغيرا لتثبت أنها لا تزال شابة بينما الرجل يحاول الزواج من طفلة صغيرة لنفس السبب — The woman hopes to bear a small child to prove that she is still a young woman, while the man tries to marry a young girl for the same reason

81 | 781 |

2777 ضِيق *n.* narrowness; shortness, lack of, shortage; ضِيق التَّنَفُّس difficulty in breathing

لاذ الدكتور صلاح بالصمت وبان على وجهه بعض الضيق، فأحسست بندم — Dr Salah took refuge in silence, and some annoyance showed on his face, so I felt remorse

91 | 696 |

2778 تَخَلَّى *v. V* to give up, abandon, relinquish, surrender عن sth

ماذا تسمى من يتخلى عن بلاده في محنتها ويضع نفسه في خدمة الأعداء؟ — What do you call someone who abandons his country in its trial and puts himself at the service of the enemy?

82 | 772 |

2779 مِلْكِيَّة *n.* property, ownership, possession

إذا أردنا أن يحترم الطفل ملكية غيره وجب أن نبدأ نحن باحترام ملكيته — If we want the child to respect the possessions of others, we ourselves have to begin respecting his possessions

72 | 879 |

2780 صَوَّرَ *v. II* to film, photograph sth/sb; to draw, portray, depict sth/sb

دار الحديث في هوليوود يصور فيلم صعود وسقوط "مملكة" صدام حسين — Conversation in Hollywood revolved around the shooting of a film that depicts the rise and fall of the "Kingdom" of Saddam Hussein

88 | 724 |

2781 تَحَمُّل *vn.* bearing, carrying (burden); shouldering (responsibility)

أنا مستعد لتحمل نتائج اختياري — I am prepared to bear the results of my choice

85 | 746 |

2782 تَفَاوُض *n.* negotiation, debate, discussion

الدراسات أثبتت أن دماغ المرأة مؤهل أكثر للتفاوض من دماغ الرجل — Studies have confirmed that the woman's brain is more qualified for negotiations than the man's brain

66 | 952 |

2783 مُظْلِم *adj.* dark, gloomy

كانت الحجرة مظلمة، والصمت عميقا لا يقطعه سوى تردد أنفاس زوجته — The room was dark, and the silence was deep, only broken by the repeated breathing of his wife

80 | 792 |

2784 أَكَادِيمِيّ *adj.* academic, scholarly; *n.* pl. -uun scholar, academician

إلى جانب عمله الاكاديمي عمل بين عامي ١٩٩٣ و١٩٩٩ مستشارا اقتصاديا لوزير المال اللبناني — Beside his academic work, he worked between the years 1993 and 1999 as an economic advisor to the Lebanese Minister of Finance

71 | 896 |

2785 عَزَّزَ *v. II* to strengthen, bolster, reinforce

نهنئ حركتنا النسائية بهذا المكسب الديمقراطي الهام الذي يعزز من قوة المجتمع المدني البحريني — We congratulate our women's movement on this important democratic gain which increases the strength of Bahraini civil society

76 | 837 |

2786 بَعُدَ *v. I (u)* to be located, situated (a given distance) عن from sth

وصل إلى الطريق العام الذي لا يبعد كثيرا عن منزله — He reached the main road which was not far from his house

92 | 689 |

2787 تَقْنِيّ *adj.* technical

المقابلات التي أجرتها اللجنة كانت شكلية وسطحية وليست بالمستوى التقني والعلمي المطلوب لتحديد قدرات المرشحين وكفاءاتهم للتمكن من تقييمهم — The interviews which the committee conducted were formal and superficial and not on the technical and scientific level required to determine the capabilities and qualifications of the candidates to enable one to evaluate them

69 | 915 |

2788 مُنَظَّم *adj.* organized, arranged; systematic, disciplined

ا — آسف على هذه الفوضى، فأنا شخص غير منظم am sorry for this mess, I am not an organized person

78 | 805 |

2789 مُرَكَّب *adj.* installed, assembled; composed, consisting (من) of); *n.* pl. -aat (chemical) compound; (psychological) complex

شواء اللحم بطريقة خاطئة يؤدي إلى ظهور مركبات سرطانية على اللحم — Grilling meat incorrectly can lead to the appearance of cancer-causing compounds on the meat

76 | 830 |

2790 تَنَاسَبَ *v. VI* to be compatible مع/و with, appropriate مع/و for

سيتعايش الناس مع الأسعار الجديدة، وسيضعون خيارات معينة تتناسب مع ظروفهم المالية — People will live with the new prices, and they will make specific choices which are appropriate for their economic circumstances

82 | 768 |

2791 داء *n.* sickness, disease; ailment, disorder

هي مصابة بداء في رأسها ولابد لها من عملية جراحية ستكلفنا غاليا — She is afflicted with a disease in her head and she has to have a surgical operation which will cost us a lot

82 | 767 |

2792 مُطالِب *adj.* demanding, claiming; *n.* claimant
وقف قبالتي مطالبا بصوت حاد أن أعطيه ساعتي وقلادتي وما في جيوبي — He stood in front of me demanding with a sharp voice that I give him my watch and my necklace and everything in my pockets
78 | 810 |

2793 بَرّ *n.* land, mainland; dry land, earth; بَرّاً by land
قال المصدر إن رجل الأعمال كارلو دكاش سيعود إلى لبنان برا عبر الأردن — The source said that the businessman Carlo Dakash will return to Lebanon by land through Jordan
91 | 693 |

2794 تَواجُد *n.* presence; existence
الجمهورية العربية المتحدة لا توافق على تواجد قوات تابعة للجامعة العربية في نفس الوقت الذي تتواجد فيه قوات بريطانية على أرض الكويت — The United Arab Republic does not agree to the presence of forces belonging to the Arab League at the same time that British forces are present on the land of Kuwait
72 | 870 |

2795 نَبات *coll.n.* pl. -aat plants, vegetation
الكلب يبتعد باحثا عن شيء ما في الأرض بين النباتات والشجيرات — The dog goes away searching for something on the ground between the plants and the bushes
77 | 816 |

2796 عَلّ *conj.* perhaps, maybe; (with pron.) عَلَّني perhaps I, maybe I
ثابرت على الاتصال به على مدار الأسبوع وفي أوقات مختلفة علها تنجح في الوصول إليه ولكن هاتفه النقال ظل مقفلا — She kept trying to get in touch with him throughout the week, and at various times, so that perhaps she might succeed in getting to him, but his cell phone was shut off
73 | 864 |

2797 تَحْضير *n.* pl. -aat preparation; production
افترقنا على أمل اللقاء بعد الانتهاء من تحضير الواجبات الدراسية — We parted in hope of meeting after finishing preparing our homework
80 | 779 |

2798 سَرِقَة *n.* stealing, theft
الآن ازدادت حوادث السرقة بسبب الظلام الذى شمل البلاد — Now incidents of thievery increased because of the darkness which enveloped the country
80 | 781 |

2799 دَهْر *n.* fate, fortune; lifetime, eternity
هل كتب على سيناء أن تبقى أبد الدهر وجع في قلب مصر؟ — Is it fated that Sinai will remain forever a pain in Egypt's heart?
71 | 876 | +lit

2800 تَأْخير *n.* delay, postponement
يمكن استئناف المفاوضات من دون تأخير — It is possible to resume negotiations without delay
84 | 746 |

2801 مِلْح *n.* salt
كنت أعبد صنما من ملح قذر أمطره الموت فذاب — I was worshipping an idol of dirty salt upon which death rained and it melted
76 | 822 |

2802 فَتْوى *n.* pl. فَتَاوَى fatwa (religious edict or ruling; legal opinion)
قيل يومها أن الإرهابيين هم الذين قتلوه لأنهم أرادوه أن يصدر فتوى وجوب الجهاد ضد السلطة وكل أجهزتها والمتعاملين معها لكنه أبى ذلك — It was said at the time that the terrorists were the ones who killed him, because they wanted him to issue a fatwa requiring jihad against the authority and all its agencies and those who do business with them, but he refused to do it
75 | 828 |

2803 مُكَلَّف *adj.* charged, entrusted (ب with); responsible (ب for)
ألا تعلم الهزل لا يليق برجل مثلي مكلف بمهمة دولية كلها جد — Don't you know that joking is not appropriate for a man like me who is charged with an international mission of complete seriousness?
76 | 819 |

2804 حَوْل *n.* power, might; لا حَوْلَ وَلا قُوَّةَ إلّا بِاللّه there is no power but through God (it's all in God's hands)

كيف للاموات ان تفتح لكم باب الحياة وهم لا حول ولا قوة — How can the dead open the door of life for you, they being powerless?

42 | 1472 |

2805 مُسَجِّل *n.* (audio) recorder; *a.p.* recording; scoring (point)

قطع المسافة في سباحة متواصلة دون توقف استغرقت ٤٢ ساعة مسجلا بذلك رقما قياسيا في السباحة الطويلة — He covered the distance swimming continuously without stopping for 42 hours, thereby setting a record for long distance swimming

73 | 858 |

2806 طِيلَة *n.* طِيلَة throughout, during (the entire)

لم أغادر بلادي طيلة حياتي — I have not left my country my whole life

78 | 794 |

2807 شَفَّافِيَّة *n.* transparency; clarity, openness

الانتخابات عام ٢٠٠٦ تميزت بمنتهى الشفافية، وشاركت فيها حماس في اجواء صافية — The elections in the year 2006 were characterized by the utmost transparency, and Hamas participated in them in a pure atmosphere

74 | 844 |

2808 غاضِب *adj.* angry, irate

انصرف غاضبا وقال لنفسه إنها مجنونة ولا تصلح له أبدا — He left angrily and said to himself that she was crazy and would never be a good fit for him

78 | 795 | +lit

2809 غَلَط *n.* error, mistake; (Dia.) *adj.* (invar.) wrong; (Dia.) *adv.* by mistake; incorrectly

لماذا اخبرته باسمي؟ قل له نمرة غلط وكفى — Why did you tell him my name? Tell him "wrong number" and that's it

51 | 1212 |

2810 تَأْجِيل *n.* postponement, delay; deferment, extension

زعم أن لديه أمرا هاما لا يقبل التأجيل — He claimed he had an important matter which could not be postponed

81 | 772 |

2811 اِنْعَكَسَ *v. VII* to be reflected (light, image); to have an effect on على

إلغاء الحبس بجرائم النشر في مصر انعكس إيجابيا علي الصحفيين العرب — Banning imprisonment for publication crimes in Egypt reflected positively on Arab journalists

78 | 795 |

2812 جامِع *n.* mosque

إن صلاة الموتى والغائبين قد أقيمت في جامع سيدى المرسى أبى العباس وفي الكنيسة المرقسية في وقت واحد — The prayer for the dead and departed was held in the Sidi Al-Marsa Abi Al-Abbas Mosque and in the Marqusiyya Church at the same time

87 | 717 |

2813 مُتَزايِد *adj.* growing, increasing, rising

لا يزال متمسكا بمنصبه على رغم الضغوط المتزايد لحمله على الاستقالة — He is still holding on to his position despite increasing pressure to force him to resign

74 | 837 |

2814 شِفاء *n.* cure, remedy; medication

أرجو للجرحى والمصابين الشفاء العاجل — I hope the wounded will heal quickly

83 | 748 |

2815 وَداع *n.* farewell; departure, exit; وَداعاً farewell!

رصعت أم أحمد جبين ولدها الفتى بقبلة الوداع وهي تسلمه كوفية وعقال أبيه — Um Ahmad planted a goodbye kiss on the brow of her young son, as she handed him his father's headdress and headband

75 | 826 |

2816 نَطَقَ *v. I* (u) to speak, utter, pronounce ب sth

كان اعتذاره خاليا من أى نبرة ندم.. نطق باعتذاره وكأنه يؤدى دورا فى تمثيلية — His excuse was devoid of any tone of regret...he uttered his excuse as if he were performing a role in a play

76 | 820 |

2817 مُعادَلَة *n.* equation, balance

المسرح الجيد يحافظ على المعادلة الصعبة بين الفن والجمال من جهة، والقرب من المتلقي والجاذبية التي تشده من جهة أخرى — Good theater maintains

the difficult balance between art and beauty on the one hand, and getting close to the audience and the attractiveness that moves it on the other

78 | 790 |

2818 تَسامُح *n.* tolerance, forbearance
عليكم ان تتحضروا لتنجحوا في الدفاع عن قيم التسامح والمحبة والعيش المشترك التي تشكل جميعها جوهر هذا الوطن — You need to prepare to succeed in defending the values of tolerance and love and living together all of which form the core of the nation

81 | 767 |

2819 مَسَّ *v. I (a)* to touch, handle sth; to violate, infringe upon sth
قال المحامي: إني أعترض على هذه الأسئلة التي لا تمس جوهر القضية — The lawyer said: I object to these questions which do not deal with the core of the issue

85 | 731 |

2820 رَجاً *n. pl.* أَرْجاء side wall; أَرْجاء regions, areas; في أَرْجاءِ throughout, in all corners of
كان نباح الكلاب يملأ أرجاء القرية كلها — The barking of dogs filled the corners of the whole village

86 | 723 |

2821 حالَ *v. I (u)* to prevent دُونَ sth (from happening)
كانت تحلم بالدراسة في جامعة السوربون، ولكن ظروف الأسرة حالت دون ذلك — She dreamed of studying at the Sorbonne University, but family circumstances prevented that

84 | 736 |

2822 كامِيرا *n.* camera
اعتدوا بالضرب على المصور وقاموا بتكسير الكاميرا الخاصة به — They attacked the photographer with beatings, and broke his personal camera

76 | 806 |

2823 صاحَ *v. I (i)* to scream, cry out, shout (sth, ب/على at sb)
احتضنه وقبله على جانبي وجهه، ثم صاح عاليا بلهجة ريفيه: ربنا يحفظك وينصرك ويخليك — He embraced him and kissed him on both sides of his face, and then cried out loudly in

a country dialect: May God preserve you and give you victory and keep you

66 | 937 | +lit

2824 اِشْتِباك *n. pl.* -aat skirmish, clash
وكان مصدر أمني قال إن عدد ضحايا الاشتباكات التي وقعت الثلاثاء بين قوات الأمن العراقية ومسلحين في مدينة كربلاء ارتفع إلى ٥٢ قتيلا و٢٠٦ مصابين — A security source had said that the number of victims of the clashes which took place on Tuesday between the Iraqi security forces and gunmen from the city of Karbala' rose to 52 dead and 206 wounded

62 | 988 |

2825 مَصْرَفيّ *adj.* bank, banking
يجب تطوير القطاع المصرفي ووضعه في مستوى الاداء العالمي وزيادة القدرة التنافسية في الداخل — The banking sector needs to be developed and put on a global level of performance and to increase in competitive ability internally

60 | 1018 |

2826 ناريّ *adj.* fire, fiery; gunfire
الشرطة لم تستخدم اسلحة نارية بل غازات مسيلة للدموع فحسب — The police did not use firearms, but rather tear gas only

83 | 742 |

2827 مُتَواضِع *adj.* modest, humble
بيتها الصغير المتواضع لا يحتاج إلى جهد كبير في ترتيبه وتنظيفه — Her small, humble house does not need a big effort to organize and clean

82 | 750 |

2828 عُذْر *n.* excuse; apology; عُذْراً sorry, excuse me (على for)
خطر لي أن أخفي عنها ما حدث، أن أصرفها أو أنصرف بأي عذر.. فجأة وجدتني أحكي لها كل ما حدث — It occurred to me to conceal what happened from her, to dismiss her or leave with any excuse...suddenly I found myself telling her everything that happened

74 | 824 |

2829 مُتَكَرِّر *adj.* repeated, recurring; frequent
صديقه لا يجيب على اتصالاته المتكررة منذ مدة — His friend has not been answering his repeated calls for a while

82 | 749 |

2830 مُنْطَلَق *n.* premise, principle; starting line, starting point, point of departure; launch pad
من هذا المنطلق أدعو هيئة السوق لفتح تحقيق عند حدوث هزات في السوق — From this premise, I call on the Market Organization to open an investigation when there are disturbances in the market
80 | 761 |

2831 مُكَوَّن *adj.* composed مِن of, consisting مِن of
الشقة مكونة من غرفتين وممر صغير بينهما — The apartment consists of two rooms and a small hall between them
81 | 752 |

2832 اِنْقِلاب *n.* coup, overthrow, toppling
اتهمهم بتدبير انقلاب ضد النظام الحاضر لحساب دولة أجنبية — He accused them of planning a coup against the current regime on behalf of a foreign state
78 | 784 |

2833 مُسَمَّى *n.* title, name; *adj.* called, named
لا يمكن لأي عاشق للتاريخ أن يتجاهل رحلة زاهي حواس مع قطع الفخار المتكسرة المسماة في لغة الأثريين الأوستراك — No lover of history can ignore the trip of Zahi Hawas with the broken pieces of pottery which are called in the language of archeologists: the ostraca
83 | 733 |

2834 قِياس *n.* measurement; analogy; قِياساً In comparison إلى/بِ with
لقد رأيت أن مشكلاتهم كبيرة قياسا لمشكلتي — I saw that their problems were big compared to my problems
83 | 733 |

2835 فائِق *adj.* boundless, exceeding; outstanding, excellent
أعرف أنك بقدرتك العقلية الفائقة تستطيع أن تتحكم بالأمور — I know that with your outstanding intellectual ability, you can control matters
83 | 730 |

2836 طِبْق *n.* طِبْقَ and طِبْقاً لِـ in accordance with, in conformity with; طِبْقَ الأَصْلِ faithful (copy)

يجب أن يقوم بالمطلوب طبقا للشروط — He must do what is requested according to the conditions
74 | 817 |

2837 خِرِّيج *n.* pl. -uun graduate; خِرِّيجُ سِجْنٍ former (political) prisoner
المشكلة هي مشكلة أن الخريجين عددهم كبير، ففي الأردن في السنة الواحدة يتخرج حوالي ألف أو أكثر بقليل — The problem is the problem that the number of graduates is large, so in Jordan in a single year, about one thousand, or a little more, will graduate
78 | 778 |

2838 مُؤامَرَة *n.* pl. -aat conspiracy, plot, scheme
طالب الفلسطينيين بأن يكونوا عصبة واحدة في مواجهة المؤامرات والاعتداءات الإسرائيلية — He requested the Palestinians to become a single band in facing Israeli plots and aggressions
76 | 797 |

2839 دِعاية *n.* pl. -aat advertisement, advertising; propaganda
هناك المحلات التجارية التي تصطاد الزبائن بألوان الدعاية — There are commercial shops which hunt customers with various types of propaganda
87 | 701 |

2840 كادِر *n.* pl. كَوادِر cadre, key group, staff, functionaries
جهاد شاب فلسطيني من كوادر فتح، من سكان مخيم عين الحلوة — Jihad is a Palestinian youth from the cadres of Fatah, from the inhabitants of the Ain Al-Hilwa camp
70 | 869 |

2841 مِرْآة *n.* mirror
أسرع الى الحمام، وانظر الى المرآة لاعدل من هيئتي، أمشط شعري القصير المبلل — I hurry to the bathroom and look in the mirror to adjust my appearance, I comb my short, wet hair
77 | 793 |

2842 عَوْلَمَة *n.* globalization (from عالَم world)
إن المعركة الحقيقية لا تكمن في مواجهة العولمة كعملية تاريخية، وانما ينبغي أن تكون ضد نسق القيم السائد الذي هو في الواقع إعادة إنتاج لنظام الهيمنة

القديم — The real battle does not consist of confronting globalization as a historical force, but rather it must be against the prevailing value system which in fact is a re-introduction of the old system of domination

69 | 873 |

2843 مُصالَحَة *n.* conciliation, compromise
أصبحت القضية الفلسطينية هي إجراء مصالحة بين فتح وحماس — The Palestinian issue has become a reconciliation process between Fatah and Hamas

65 | 934 |

2844 مَرارَة *n.* bitterness; gall bladder
بدأت أضحك رغم مرارة السخرية — I started to laugh despite the bitterness of the sarcasm

78 | 774 |

2845 واجد *adj.* able to find; وايد and واجد /waayid/ (Gul.) *adv.* very, a lot, really
انا اليوم زعلانه وايد — Today I am really angry

29 | 2047 | +for

2846 مَخافَة *n.* pl. مَخاوِف fear, anxiety; worry, apprehension
تصاعد النزاع بشأن الخطة الامريكية برغم جهود المسؤولين الامريكيين لتهدئة المخاوف الروسية — The conflict regarding the American plan escalated despite the efforts of the American officials to calm Russian fears

78 | 773 |

2847 مُؤْلِم *adj.* painful, aching; saddening, distressing
كيف حقا تتحمل الدنيا كل هذه القصص المؤلمة؟ — How, really, can the world bear all these painful stories

83 | 724 |

2848 مَهْما *conj.* whatever, regardless of what, no matter how
مهما قعدت هنا، ومهما حققت من نجاح، في النهاية حابقى مواطن درجة ثانية — No matter how long I have stayed here, and however much success I have accomplished, in the end I will remain a second-class citizen

89 | 681 |

2849 الحِين (Gul.) *adv.* (also دَحِّين and أَحِّين) now, right now
والله الحين ما ادري بكم تصليح الحين — Frankly, right now I don't know how much it's going to cost to fix

25 | 2358 | +spo

2850 عَشِيَّة *n.* evening; eve, night before; بَيْنَ عَشِيَّةٍ وَضُحاها overnight, suddenly
أصرّ مسؤولو إدارة بوش على أن الرئيس قد ترك الخيارات الأخرى مفتوحة حتى عشية الحرب — Officials in the Bush administration insisted that the president has left other options open until the eve of the war

78 | 769 |

2851 قارَبَ *v. III* to approach, come close to sth; to approximate sth
كانت الساعة تقارب الحادية عشرة أو الثانية عشرة عندما اقتربنا من الحدود — The time was approaching eleven or twelve when we got near the border

81 | 742 |

2852 اِسْتِئْناف *n.* resumption, renewal; (jur.) appeal
بذل مزيد من الجهود لاستئناف عملية السلام — He exerted more efforts to resume the peace process

67 | 894 |

2853 كُثْر *n.* abundance, large amount, great number; much, a lot; excessive amount
انهض فقد أقبل علينا ضيوف كثر وليس مناسبا أن تظل نائما — Get up, because many guests have arrived and it is not appropriate for you to remain sleeping

75 | 802 |

2854 غَسَلَ *v. I (i)* to wash, clean sth
هل تريد أن تغسل وجهك؟ الحمام من هنا — Do you want to wash your face? The bathroom is this way

81 | 738 |

2855 فُلان *n.* so-and-so; such-and-such
أطرق على بابه وأقول له عفوا أنا أبحث عن السيد فلان أو فلان وكان هو يقول لي إنه في الشقة المجاورة — I knock on the door and tell him: Excuse me, I am searching for Mr So-and-So, and he

told me that he was in the neighboring apartment

77 | 773 |

2856 ثَمَر *n. pl.* ثِمار fruit; result, yield, outcome
ما زال أمامنا طريق طويلة حتى تبدأ العراق بجني ثمار السلام والنجاح — We still have a long road ahead of us until Iraq can begin to reap the fruits of peace and success

83 | 721 |

2857 أَصِيل *adj.* authentic, original; native, indigenous; pure, noble; full-blooded, purebred
إننا هنا للدفاع عن حوزة أرضنا واستقلال بلادنا وهويتنا الأصيلة — We are here to defend the possession of our land and the independence of our country and our authentic identity

80 | 745 |

2858 تَغْذِيَة *n.* feeding, nutrition
ارتفعت الوفيات بين صفوفهم نتيجة الأمراض والقذارة وقلة التغذية — The number of deaths increased among their ranks as a result of diseases, filth, and malnutrition

78 | 767 |

2859 ضَمَّنَ *v. II* to guarantee, insure
المحاولة هي أصلاً فكرة نبيلة لأن لا أحد يضمن النجاح أو الفشل — Trying things out, at base, is a noble idea, because no one can guarantee success or failure

83 | 721 |

2860 طَعْم *n.* flavor, taste
— تغيرت الوجوه، البيوت، حتى طعم الأكل تغير The faces changed, the houses, even the taste of the food changed

81 | 734 |

2861 مُتْعَة *n.* pleasure, enjoyment
السفر بالقطار هو متعة حقيقية رغم الساعات الطويلة التي سنقضيها في الطريق — Travel by train is a real pleasure despite the long hours we will spend on the road

83 | 715 |

2862 مَجْرَى *n. pl.* مَجْرَيات course, path; events, happenings; مَجْرَيات الأَحْداث/الأُمُور the course of events

الخيال الخصب عندك يدفعك الى مغامرة جديدة، مشروع شخصي مهم يغير مجرى حياتك، يمكنك الاستفادة من تجاربك الشخصية السابقة — Your fertile imagination pushes you into a new adventure, an important personal project which will change the course of your life and which will allow you to benefit from your previous personal experiences

86 | 693 |

2863 عالَجَ *v. III* to treat (disease, sick person); to deal with (topic, problem); to process (data)
كان هذا الطبيب يعالج الأطفال المرضى مجانا — This doctor used to treat sick children for free

86 | 696 |

2864 مُعَلَّق *adj.* suspended, hanging, pending, outstanding
ما زال يذكر كل الصور التي كانت معلقة على جدران غرفة الجلوس — He still remembers all the pictures that were hanging on the walls of the sitting room

85 | 702 |

2865 خُصُوصِيّ *adj.* private, personal; special
كانت تعلم أبناء الحي وبناته وتعطيهم دروساً خصوصية مقابل أجر زهيد — She taught the boys and girls in the neighborhood and gave them private lessons in exchange for a paltry sum

83 | 715 |

2866 صَوْتِيّ *adj.* audio, sound, acoustic; verbal, vocal; phonetic
هذه هي المرة الاولى التي يتم فيها بث تسجيل صوتي لشاليت منذ اختطافه في ٢٥ حزيران العام الماضي — This is the first time an audio recording of Shalit has been broadcast since his kidnapping on the 25th of June last year

77 | 777 |

2867 اِسْتَعْمَلَ *v. X* to use, make use of, employ
— أرجوك لا تستعمل هذه الكلمة مرة أخرى I beg you, don't use this word again

81 | 735 |

2868 مَشْي *n.* walking, going
رحت أجول في الشوارع الخالية، جميل المشي في الهدوء والنقاء بصحبة نسائم الخريف — I started to

wander around the empty streets, it's nice to walk in calmness and purity in the company of the breezes of autumn

76 | 785 |

2869 فَخُر *n.* pride; boasting
يحق لكل الموظفين الفخر بما تم تحقيقه من إنجاز في هذا المجال — All the employees have the right to be proud of what has been accomplished in this field

80 | 743 |

2870 صَلاحِيَّة *n.* pl. -aat suitability, viability; state of being valid or active (calling card, membership); صَلاحِيّات powers, privileges
إنه مخالف للقانون، إذ ليس من صلاحيات سيادته تعيين الموظفين في وزارة التربية — It is against the law, since it is not his Excellency's prerogative to appoint the employees in the Ministry of Education

73 | 817 |

2871 مُعْتَبَر *a.p.* considering, regarding
اقترح عليه التعاون في مكافحة الإرهاب الدولي، معتبرا أنه ليس أمام روسيا سوى خيار المشاركة في التحالف — He suggested that he cooperate in fighting international terrorism, considering that Russia has no choice but to participate in the alliance

63 | 935 |

2872 مُحْتَرِف *n.* pl. -uun professional, expert
شاهد على القناة الرياضية مباراة كاملة في مصارعة المحترفين — On the sports channel he watched a complete match of professional wrestling

77 | 769 |

2873 أَدارَ *v. IV* to direct, manage sth; to conduct sth; to turn (one's face or back); to turn on or off (radio, television, car switch); to turn (key or door knob); to make spin sth
كان حزب البعث يدير كافة أوجه الحياة في العراق إلى درجة أن كل حي كان توجد فيه خلية بعثية — The Baath party used to manage all aspects of life in Iraq to the point that every neighborhood had a Baath cell in it

82 | 718 |

2874 اِشْتَرَكَ *v. VIII* to participate (مع with sb) في in sth

صارت كل جماعة من الغواصات تشترك في هجوم واحد في وقت واحد على فريسة واحدة — Each group of submarines started to participate in a single attack at the same time on a single victim

83 | 715 |

2875 تَطَرَّقَ *v. V* to broach, discuss إلى (topic, issue); to reach, get as far as إلى sth
سرعان ما تطرق الحديث إلى إمكانات تطوير الأوبرا — The conversation quickly turned to the possibilities of developing the opera

81 | 731 |

2876 إِخْراج *n.* production; extraction; removal, ousting
نزلت ديما من السيارة وبكل صعوبة استطاعت اخراج قدميها فقد كانتا مجمدتين — Dima got out of the car and with difficulty was able to extract her feet, since they had frozen

84 | 705 |

2877 سَماع *n.* hearing, listening
كنت مشتاقا جدا لسماع صوتها — I was longing to hear her voice

83 | 709 |

2878 مَدّ *n.* length, reach, extent; reaching, extending, lengthening; spreading
حذر العلماء من ان كوارث المد البحري قابلة للتكرار خلال القرن الحادي والعشرين — Scientists warned that tsunamis are likely to be repeated during the twenty-first century

85 | 696 |

2879 رِفْقَة *n.* pl. رِفاق company, group; بِرِفْقَة accompanied by, along with
كان يرى هو ورفاقه أن الطبيعة عدو يلزم قهره — He and his companions saw nature as an enemy that must be conquered

85 | 692 |

2880 اِتَّسَعَ *v. VIII* to expand, stretch, widen; to be sufficient, adequate لـ for; to be large enough لـ for
أرجو أن يتسع وقت سيادتك لبضع دقائق من أجل موضوع يخصني — I hope your excellency's time will permit some minutes for a subject that concerns me

83 | 709 |

2881 سِتّ *n.* pl. -aat lady, miss
وجدت زهرة نفسها تحملق فى الست لولا الشقراء
الملفوفة القوام المتوردة الوجه ترتدى روبا من القطن
— Zahra found herself staring at blond
Mrs Lola, round-figured, rosy-faced, wearing
a cotton robe
52 | 1113 | +spo

2882 مَهَارَة *n.* -aat capability, skill; ability,
proficiency
سيستعرض تجارب اشخاص استطاعوا محو أميتهم
وتعلم حرف واكتساب مهارات ساعدتهم على زيادة
دخلهم — It will present the experiences of
people who were able to wipe out their
illiteracy and learn professions and gain skills
which helped them to increase their income
73 | 804 |

2883 اِنْتِهاك *n.* pl. -aat violation, contravention
يحذر من أن الصمت إزاء الانتهاكات الإسرائيلية
— يتسبب في وقوع المزيد من الظلم للفلسطينيين
warns that silence in the face of Israeli
violations will cause more oppression to fall
upon the Palestinians
72 | 814 |

2884 ذِئْب *n.* pl. ذِئاب wolf, jackal
نسأل الله أن يأتي الشباب المسلم الموعود ليخلصوا
العالم من هذا الذئب المفترس — We ask God for
the promised Muslim youth to come to save
the world from this ferocious wolf
64 | 907 | +lit

2885 جَلَبَ *v. I* (i,u) to bring, provide sth; to bring
about, cause sth; to fetch, attract sth
أحدهم يفتح فمه، والآخر يجلب له قطعة من الطعام
ويضعها في فمه — One of them opens his
mouth, and the other brings him a piece
of food and puts it in his mouth
82 | 713 |

2886 كَأَنَّا *conj.* as if
ظل راكعا مغمض العينين فترة، ثم قام وفتح عينيه
وكأنما صحا من النوم — He stayed in a kneeling
position, eyes closed, for a period, and then he
stood up, opened his eyes, as if he was waking
from sleep
58 | 998 | +lit

2887 تَسَلَّمَ *v. V* to receive, accept sth; to take on,
assume (responsibility)
تسلمت اليوم نتيجة تحليل دمي — I got the results
of my blood analysis today
80 | 726 |

2888 سَلَف *coll.n.* ancestors; *n.* advance (payment);
سَلَفاً in advance; beforehand, previously
الميراث الأصيل هو ما وصلنا من السلف والقواعد
التي استند إليها كبار أساتذة الخط — The
authentic heritage is that which has come
down to us from the ancestors and the rules
which the major professors of script have
relied on
76 | 770 |

2889 تَرْحيب *n.* welcome, welcoming; greeting
تعاقبت كلمات الترحيب من السفير والقنصل
ورئيس اتحاد الدارسين — Words of welcome
from the ambassador and the consul and
the head of the student union followed in
succession
79 | 738 |

2890 تَنازُل *vn.* backing down عن from, renouncing
عن sth; *n.* pl. -aat concession
هذه قضية لا يمكن التنازل عنها — This is an
issue which we can't concede
78 | 743 |

2891 مِنْبَر *n.* pl. مَنابِر pulpit, rostrum
انتهى الخطيب من خطابه ونزل من المنبر وصفق له
الحاضرون — The speaker finished his speech
and came down from the pulpit and the
audience applauded him
79 | 735 |

2892 عِمارَة *n.* building, edifice, structure
تجمع العشرات من أبناء وصبايا الحي وصعدوا الى
سطح العمارة — Scores of the young men of
the quarter gathered and got up on the roof
of the building
84 | 688 |

2893 اِكْتَفَى *v. VIII* to be content, satisfied ب with
لم يرد على كلامهم، وإنما اكتفى بالابتسام — He
didn't respond to their words, but contented
himself with smiling
81 | 715 |

2894 مَتْحَف *n.* museum
يجري حاليا اختيار القطع الأثرية التي ستعرض في المتحف ويبلغ عددها ١٠٠ ألف قطعة تمثل مختلف العصور الفرعونية — The archeological pieces which will be displayed in the museum, and whose number reaches 100 thousand pieces which represent different eras, are currently being chosen
76 | 762 |

2895 خَفِيّ *adj.* hidden, secret; unseen, invisible
هم يعتقدون أن هناك أجندة خفية لدى الحكومة — They believe that the government has a hidden agenda
79 | 731 |

2896 اِحْتَفَظَ *v. VIII* to maintain, preserve ب sth; to keep, reserve ب sth (لِنَفْسِهِ for oneself)
لم تكن بينهما أسرار، ولكن الزوجة العجوز كانت تحتفظ بصندوق فوق أحد الأرفف، وحذرت زوجها مرارا من فتحه — They had no secrets between them, but the old wife was keeping a box on one of the shelves, and she warned her husband repeatedly not to open it
84 | 687 |

2897 عاطِفِيّ *adj.* emotional, sentimental; affectionate
أستطيع أن أؤكد من تورد وجهك أن حياتك العاطفية على ما يرام — I can confirm, from the rosiness of your face, that your emotional life is doing OK
77 | 745 |

2898 عَيْن *n.* same, exactly the same (person, thing); self (with pron.) itself, himself, etc.; (هُوَ) بِعَيْنِهِ it/him specifically, exactly
الحكاية عينها تتكرر مع كل محاولة للعيش المستقل — The same story repeats itself with each attempt at independent living
84 | 689 |

2899 كَسَبَ *v. I (i)* to win, gain sth; to earn, make (salary); to achieve, attain sth
أنا من أسرة فلسطينية فقيرة؛ والدي عامل بائس، يكسب رزقه في الفلاحة والزراعة أحيانا — I am from a poor Palestinian family; my father is a poor worker who earns his living in farming sometimes
88 | 656 |

2900 وِزارِيّ *adj.* ministerial
اكد رئيس الوزراء الأردني معروف البخيت انه بصدد اجراء تعديل وزاري «طفيف» تستدعيه ضرورات المرحلة الحالية — The Jordanian prime minister Maaruf Al-Bakit stressed that he was in the process of making a minor ministerial change which the necessities of the current stage call for
61 | 935 |

2901 سَطْر *n. pl.* سُطُور line, row
راحت ملامحه تتغير مع كل سطر يقرأه — His features began to change with every line he read
79 | 730 |

2902 كَسْب *n.* winning, gaining; earning, making (salary); achieving, attaining
لابد من عمل، لابد من وسيلة لكسب العيش — It is necessary to work, there has to be a way to earn a living
84 | 686 |

2903 أَشْرَفَ *v. IV* to supervise, manage على sth/sb; to overlook, provide a view of على sth
يا عماه هم أولادك منذ اليوم أرجو أن تشرف على تربيتهم بنفسك — Uncle, these are your children from today onward, I hope you will supervise their education yourself
83 | 687 |

2904 صَدْمَة *n.* shock, blow
السجن كان صدمة قاسية وتجربة جديدة على أولئك السجناء — Prison was a harsh shock, and a new experience for these prisoners
84 | 684 |

2905 مُحْتَرَم *adj.* honorable, respected, esteemed
وهذا يدل على إنك رجل محترم وخلوق بارك الله فيك وعليك — This indicates that you are a polite and respected man, may God bless you
85 | 676 |

2906 واثِق *adj.* confident, certain, sure
هل أنت واثق أن بمقدورك دفع ثمن هذا العشاء؟ — Are you sure of your ability to pay the price of this dinner?
83 | 688 |

2907 مِحْنَة *n.* pl. مِحَن test; trial, ordeal

لقد مرت المحنة بسلام — The ordeal passed safely

80 | 711 |

2908 مُتَطَوِّر *adj.* advanced, developed; modern, sophisticated, high-tech

بدأت إجراءات التأمين مبكرا: تم فحص المبنى بأجهزة متطورة اخترقت الجدران بأشعة إكس للتأكد من خلوها من أية أجسام غريبة مدفونة — They started security measures early: the building was searched with advanced devices which penetrated the walls with x-rays to make sure it was free of any hidden foreign objects

79 | 721 |

2909 تَبَع *n.* pl. أَتْباع follower, partisan; تَبَعاً لِ according to, pursuant to

الإسلام يقر المواطنة والمساواة مع أتباع العقائد الأخرى — Islam establishes citizenship and equality with the followers of other beliefs

82 | 698 |

2910 فاصِل *n.* pause, break; interlude, intermission; *adj.* separating, dividing; delimiting, demarcating; conclusive, decisive

كان يقرع الباب الداخلي الفاصل بين الحجرتين قرعا خفيفا — He was knocking lightly on the inside door that separates the two rooms

79 | 724 |

2911 مُهاجِم *n.* assailant, attacker; striker (soccer); *adj.* assailing, attacking

وقد قتل المهاجم بعد أن أطلق المسلحون النار عليه عند الحاجز — The attacker was killed after the gunmen opened fire on him at the barrier

65 | 873 |

2912 عُضْوِيَّة *n.* membership, affiliation

بعض الناس يرى أنه لا قيمة من وراء عضوية مصر في هذه الاتحادات — Some people are of the opinion that there is no value in Egypt's membership in these unions

69 | 824 |

2913 حَتْم *n.* necessity; حَتْماً definitely, necessarily

إن الصراحة ليست حتما هي أن تكون جافا في المعاملة مع الناس — Frankness does not necessarily mean that you have to be dry in your dealing with people

78 | 727 |

2914 عَرَبَة *n.* pl. -aat cart, wagon; vehicle

وصل القطار فركب كل منهم فى عربة مختلفة — The train arrived and everyone got on a different car

74 | 769 |

2915 أَمْثَل *elat.* fem. مُثْلَى better/best; more/most exemplary, more/most ideal

بدأ يدرس الموقف بعناية للوصول إلى الحل الأمثل — He began to study the situation carefully to reach the most ideal solution

83 | 685 |

2916 عُلْبَة *n.* pl. عُلَب can; case, box; pack

رأيت طفلا يبيع علب السجائر على مفارق الطرق — I saw a child selling cartons of cigarettes at the intersections

79 | 718 |

2917 بادَرَ *v. III* to begin, take the initiative إلى/بِ to do sth; to hasten, rush إلى/بِ to do sth; to come, occur to sb spontaneously (a feeling, thought, idea)

بهذه المناسبة "الدستور" بادرت باجراء لقاء مطول مع السفير الفرنسي لدى البلاط الملكي الهاشمي — On this occasion the "Al-Dustur" newspaper initiated an extended interview with the French ambassador to the Royal Hashemite Palace

81 | 706 |

2918 حاسِم *adj.* decisive, definitive, final; key, critical

همت بالرد عليه، ما إن فتحت شفتيها لتنطق بالجملة الحاسمة حتى اعترتها مشاعر متناقضة وغامضة أجبرتها على الصمت — She prepared to answer him, but hardly had she opened her mouth to speak the decisive sentence when mysterious, contradictory feelings swept over her, which forced her into silence

80 | 709 |

2919 بَرْميل *n.* barrel; vat; drum

الآن المملكة تنتج قرابة ١١ مليون برميل يوميا — Currently the Kingdom produces about 11 million barrels a day

64 | 891 |

2920 سِباحَة *n.* swimming

اول امبارح برضه كنت رحت جريت و نزلت حمام السباحة ولعبت تنس — The day before yesterday

I also went and ran, and I got in the swimming pool, and I played tennis

64 | 892 |

2921 حَوْض *n.* basin, sink; reservoir; aquarium
وكان يدهشني، عندما يشمر كميه ليغسل ذراعيه تحت حنفية الحوض، أن أجدهما، فوق الرسغين، بيضاوين جدا — It surprised me, when he rolled up his sleeves to wash his arms under the faucet of the sink, that I found them to be, above the wrist, very white

75 | 752 |

2922 شَرْع *n.* law; *adj.* legal
إن رؤية الهلال شرط وضعه الشرع الحنيف لتحديد أول أيام رمضان — Seeing the crescent is a condition that Islamic Law set down to designate the first of the month of Ramadan

83 | 687 |

2923 باشا *n.* pasha; (in titles) الباشا Pasha
يظن نفسه باشا.. وقد مضى عهد الباشوات — He thinks himself to be a Pasha...And the time of Pashas is long gone

70 | 811 |

2924 خِيانَة *n.* treason, treachery; betrayal; infidelity
هل يبقى القانون في صف المرأة حتى وإن كانت تمارس الخيانة بحق زوجها؟! — Does the law stay on the side of the woman, even if she has been cheating on her husband?

79 | 715 |

2925 نَيْل *n.* attainment, achievement; acquiring, gaining
الاجتهاد في التحصيل العلمي لنيل الشهادة الجامعية لا يعني ضمان المستقبل — Efforts in scientific achievement to obtain a university degree do not mean a guarantee of the future

84 | 677 |

2926 خالَة *n.* maternal aunt; (Egy.Lev.) يا خالْتي approx. ma'am (respectful form of address to an older woman)
كان زوج خالتي يمارس رقابة شديدة على ما نشاهده في التلفاز — My aunt's husband practiced an intense censorship over what we would watch on television

45 | 1249 |

2927 كاذِب *adj.* false, untrue; lying, deceitful; *n.* pl. -uun, كَذَبَة liar
أذاع أنباء كاذبة وخالية من الدقة — He broadcast false news, devoid of specificity

82 | 693 |

2928 اِسْتِفْتاء *n.* questionnaire, poll; referendum
أعتقد أن الاستفتاء لو كان أجري بعد شهرين من الهدوء لتغيرت النتيجة كثيرا — I believe that if the referendum had been held after two months of calm, the result would have been very different

71 | 791 |

2929 شُورَى *n.* consultation, deliberation; مَجْلِس الشورى Shura Council or Consultative Council
يجب عرض المشروع على مجلس الشورى — The proposal needs to be presented to the Council of Advisors

63 | 898 |

2930 حَسّاس *adj.* sensitive
الموضوع حساس، دعينا لا نتسرع ونفكر بالموضوع أكثر — The subject is sensitive, let's not hurry, rather let's think about the matter more

84 | 674 |

2931 حَقِيبة *n.* briefcase, portfolio; suitcase; bag
بدأ في إخراج محتويات الحقيبة.. ها هي ملابسه التي جاء بها من مصر — He began to extract the contents of the bag...here are his clothes with which he came to Egypt

80 | 705 |

2932 عُثُور *vn.* finding, discovering, coming across على sth
ستظل غايتك المنشودة هي العثور على ابن الحلال! — Your desired goal will remain finding a good husband

80 | 704 |

2933 اِرْتِباط *n.* bond, connection, relationship, link
لن تجد شيئين بينهما ارتباط كارتباط التربية بالتعليم — You won't find two things which have a closer relationship than the relationship of upbringing and education

80 | 708 |

2934 تَوْضِيح *n.* explanation, clarification
لم أفهم معنى كلامك، أرجو التوضيح — I didn't
understand you meant. I beg you for a
clarification
79 | 717 |

2935 هَمَّ *v. I (u)* to preoccupy, concern sb; to
matter, be important to sb; to worry, be
concerned ب about sth; to be about بأَنْ/ب
to do sth
كنت أريد أن أقول لها بأنها الشخص الوحيد الذي
يهمني فوق الأرض — I wanted to tell her that
she is the only person on earth who matters
to me
80 | 703 |

2936 سَبْعُون *num.* seventy; seventieth
أرأيت يا عمي كيف قبضوا أمس على سبعين رجلا
من وجوه المدينة، فزجوا بهم في السجون — Did
you see, my uncle, how yesterday they arrested
seventy men from the leading men of the city,
and threw them into prison?
77 | 729 |

2937 اِسْتِحْقاق *n.* pl. -aat worthiness; اِسْتِحْقاقات
claims, rights, merits
إن تشكيل الحكومة سيتم بحسب الاستحقاقات
الانتخابية وسيكون للاقليات نصيب فيها بغض النظر
عن استحقاقها الانتخابي — The government will
be formed according to the election results
and the minorities will have a part in it
without regard to their election results
62 | 900 |

2938 مَجْمَع *n.* assembly; academy
يحتفل مجمع اللغة العربية المصري في العام القادم
بعيده الماسي — The Egyptian Arab Language
Academy celebrates its diamond anniversary
next year
78 | 720 |

2939 اِنْتِقاد *n.* pl. -aat criticism, censure
كانت لا تتوقف عن كيل الانتقادات لزوجها —
She did not stop heaping criticisms on her
husband
73 | 772 |

2940 بَيْدَ *conj.* بَيْدَ أَنَّ although, however, (even)
though

عندما استيقظ بعد الظهر كان كل شيء في مجراه
الطبيعي بيد أن الحر خيم على الغرفة لإغلاقه النافذة
— When he woke up in the afternoon
everything was going normally, however heat
had settled over the room because of his
having closed the window
73 | 768 |

2941 دَلالَة *n.* pl. -aat meaning, implication,
significance, importance; دَلالات evidence,
signs
كل هذه الأرقام سندخلها إلى الحاسب لنعرف إذا
كانت لها دلالة إحصائية — We will enter all
these numbers into the computer in order to
find out whether they have statistical
significance
77 | 727 |

2942 صَحَّ *v. I (i)* to be correct, be true; to be right,
proper, appropriate (to do sth)
«الصديق وقت الضيق» في هذا الزمن يصح تعديله
ليصير «الصديق من كفاك شره وقت الضيق»
"The friend in time of trouble" nowadays
should be changed to: "the friend is the one
whose evil is enough for you in time of
trouble"
87 | 645 |

2943 يُورُو *n.* euro
ماذا يعني انخفاض الدولار أمام اليورو؟ — What
does the decline of the dollar in relation to
the Euro mean?
65 | 855 |

2944 تَوْعِيَة *n.* informing, making aware; raising
awareness, enlightening
افتتحنا مركزا مهمته تقديم التوعية والتدريب
للأطفال والأهل — We opened a center whose
mission was to offer education and training for
children and the family
75 | 745 |

2945 عَزْم *n.* firm will; determination
(على to do sth)
أكمل طريقه بكل قوة، واتخذ قراراته بكل عزم —
He completed his journey with all strength,
and he made decisions with all determination
83 | 676 |

2946 عاجِز *a.p.* incapable, unable عن to do sth; *adj.* helpless, hopeless; unable, incapacitated
لقد فقدت وظيفتها، وها هي عاجزة عن إيجاد عمل آخر — She lost her job, and she is incapable of finding another job
82 | 678 |

2947 عُطْلَة *n.* vacation, holiday, recess
أنا أعمل كثيرا للدرجة أنني فى عطلة نهاية الأسبوع أحس وكأنني طفل فى فسحة المدرسة — I work a lot to the extent that on weekends I feel like a child on school recess
85 | 657 |

2948 قاطِع *adj.* decisive, definitive, categorical; convincing, conclusive; *a.p.* interrupting, preventing; blocking; traversing (a distance); *n.* cutter (person or instrument); vendor (of tickets); incisor, canine (tooth)
نفت السفارة الإيرانية نفيا قاطعا الاتهامات بإمداد ميليشيات عراقية بالسلاح — The Iranian embassy denied categorically the accusations of supplying the Iraqi militias with arms
82 | 680 |

2949 اِبْتِدائِيّ *adj.* elementary, preparatory; initial
ترك المدرسة في سن مبكرة وهو لايزال في الصف السادس الابتدائي — He left the school at an early age when he was still in the sixth grade of elementary school
76 | 733 |

2950 جَدَّدَ *v. II* to renew, extend (permit); to renovate, modernize sth; to renew (one's efforts), to try again to do sth
لولا النوم لما استطاع الإنسان أن يجدد نشاط خلاياه الحيوية ولا أن يعيش عيش مستقرة — Were it not for sleep, people wouldn't have been able to renew the activity of their vital cells, nor to live in a stable manner
77 | 723 |

2951 عَيِّل (Egy.Gul.) *n.* pl. عيال child, kid
ربنا يسهل لو ظروفنا اتحسنت شوية يمكن أبقى أجيب العيال و نيجي نقضى معاكم أسبوع ولا عشرة أيام — May our Lord make things easy, if our situation improves a bit I might bring the children and come and spend a week or ten days with you
64 | 870 |

2952 اِسْتَغَلَّ *v. X* to exploit sth, take advantage of (an opportunity)
القوي يسيطر على الضعيف، ويعمل على سحقه واستعباده والغني يستغل الفقير — The strong controls the weak, and works to crush and enslave him, and the rich exploits the poor
83 | 667 |

2953 بَشَرِيَّة *n.* humankind, human race
يعتبر السلاح النووي مصدراً لأهم وأخطر القوى التدميرية التي عرفتها البشرية — Nuclear weapons constitute a source of the most important and most dangerous destructive forces mankind has known
82 | 677 |

2954 تَحْمِيل *vn.* downloading (files); charging sb (with responsibility); loading (cargo)
لا شك أن المسألة شائكة إزاء تحميل جهة دون أخرى مسؤولية الدمار في لبنان — There is no doubt that it's a thorny issue whether to assign responsibility to one party or the other for the destruction in Lebanon
66 | 844 | +for

2955 خَمْسِين *n.* fiftieth year; الخمسينات the Fifties
كانت ظاهرة الفقر في مصر في أواخر الخمسينات أقل مما هي عليه في منتصف السبعينات — The phenomenon of poverty in Egypt at the end of the Fifties was less than it was in the mid-Seventies
91 | 607 |

2956 مُسَجَّل *adj.* registered, recorded
عصابات مسلحة صومالية مجهولة قامت بعملية قرصنة ضد سفينة تجارية مسجلة فى دولة الإمارات العربية المتحدة كانت تبحر فى المياه الاقليمية — Unknown armed Somali gangs carried out an act of piracy against a commercial ship registered in the United Arab Emirates which was sailing in territorial waters
86 | 643 |

2957 هُنَّ *pron.* they (fem.pl.)
هؤلاء هن بنات المملكة العربية السعودية اللواتي نفخر ونفتخر بهن — These are the girls of the Kingdom of Saudi Arabia whom we are proud of
87 | 639 |

2958 عاقِل *adj.* pl. عُقَلَاء sane, rational, reasonable; *n.* sane person; كُلّ عاقِل anyone in his right mind

دعا العقلاء من ابناء بلده الى صب الماء البارد على نار التعصب — He called on reasonable citizens to pour cold water on the fire of fanaticism

85 | 650 |

2959 إلْقاء *vn.* throwing, tossing; delivering, giving (a speech); (القَبْض على) arresting sb

اشتمل الحفل على إلقاء قصائد شعرية — The celebration included the delivery of poetic odes

84 | 657 |

2960 كَثيف *adj.* intense, intensive, heavy; thick, dense, concentrated

جرى تبادل إطلاق نار كثيف بين المتطرفين وبعض عناصر القوات الحكومية — Heavy gunfire was exchanged between the extremists and some elements of the government forces

83 | 667 |

2961 كَراهِيَّة *n.* hatred, loathing; dislike, aversion

البشرية ليست بحاجة إلى مزيد من الكراهية والحروب — Mankind is not in need of more hatred and wars

79 | 697 |

2962 مُهاجِر *n.* emigrant; migrant; immigrant; *adj.* emigrating; migrating; immigrating

يبحث المهاجر عن المال أو الأمان أو عن الاثنين معا — The emigrant is looking for money or security or both of them

75 | 735 |

2963 مُنتَشِر *adj.* scattered, spread out, prevalent

يجب ممارسة بعض الحركات الرياضية البسيطة مثل التي نجدها منتشرة في عادات شعوب شرق آسيا — It is necessary to practice some simple athletic activities like those we find scattered among the customs of the peoples of East Asia

87 | 632 |

2964 تَعَوَّد *v. V* to become accustomed على to sth, to get used على to sth

اكيد كلنا تعودنا على اكلاتنا التقليدية — For sure, we've all grown accustomed to our traditional dishes

86 | 642 |

2965 مُتَمَثِّل *adj.* represented, incorporated (في in); existing, present (في in)

المشكلة التي يعاني منها التعليم العالي متمثلة في النقص الشديد في عدد الاكاديميين الذين يعملون في الجامعات — The problem higher education suffers from is represented by the severe shortage in the number of academics who work in universities

71 | 779 |

2966 أَرْوَع *elat.* more/most magnificent

نقلت القصيده .. كامله .. لانها من أروع القصائد التي قرأتها — I quoted the poem, the whole thing, because it is one of the most wonderful poems I have read

70 | 781 | +for

2967 رايَة *n.* flag, banner

يبدو انها استسلمت تماما ورفعت الراية البيضاء — It appears she has surrendered completely and raised the white flag

76 | 728 |

2968 أَخْطَر *elat.* more/most dangerous; more/most serious, critical

التدخين أخطر من أسلحة الدمار الشامل — Smoking is more dangerous than weapons of mass destruction

81 | 677 |

2969 أَكْمَل *elat.* more/most complete, more/most perfect; عَلَى أَكْمَل وَجْهِ perfectly, بِأَكْمَلِهِ entirely; to perfection; in the best possible way

نجحت في تأدية مهمتها على أكمل وأحسن وجه — She succeeded in performing her mission in the best, most perfect manner

81 | 679 |

2970 اِشْتِراك *n.* subscription; participation, partnership

اعترف بسرقة عشرة منازل بالاشتراك مع شاب آخر — He confessed to robbing ten homes with the participation of another young man

74 | 743 |

2971 تَناقُض *n.* pl. -aat contradiction; incompatibility

هذا المقال يحمل كثيرا من التناقضات — This article has a lot of contradictions

78 | 702 |

2972 مَنْدُوب *n.* delegate, representative; deputy, agent

أنا مندوب لجنة حقوق الانسان في الأمم المتحدة — I am a delegate of the human rights committee in the United Nations

71 | 776 |

2973 صِياغَة *n.* drafting, composing; formulation, wording

سمعت الأم صغيرها ، فاقتربت إليه مندهشة بجرأته وقدرته على صياغة الكلام — The mother heard her little one, so she drew near him, amazed at his daring and his ability to form the words

79 | 696 |

2974 تَطَرُّف *n.* extremism, radicalism

إنه ضد العنف والتطرف، كما أنه ضد الظلم والاستبداد — He is against violence and extremism, and he is also against oppression and slavery

71 | 770 |

2975 سَكَتَ *v. I (u)* to be quiet, be silent; اُسْكُت shut up!

تأهب عرفة لمغادرة البدروم بعد أن سكت آخر صوت في الحارة — Arafa got ready to leave the basement after the last sound in the alleyway grew silent

77 | 712 |

2976 قَذِيفَة *n. pl.* قَذائِف shell, bomb

تتابعت القذائف كمطر الشتاء — The bombs kept falling like winter rain

70 | 778 |

2977 بُقْعَة *n.* spot; stain; *pl.* بِقاع region, place, spot

كانت تحت عينه اليسرى بقعة سوداء وزرقاء — Under his left eye there was a black and blue spot

76 | 717 |

2978 إدْخال *n.* insertion, introduction, inclusion

تولي الباحث إدخال المعلومات التي تجمع من الأُسَر مباشرة في هذه الأجهزة — The use of handheld devices in the census is based on the researcher taking responsibility to enter the information which is gathered from the families directly into these devices

78 | 703 |

2979 تَطَوَّرَ *v. V* to develop, evolve, grow; to advance, make headway

الرنتيسي يؤلب المعتقلين على العصيان والاعتصام في الساحة وقد يتطور الأمر إلى إضراب عن الطعام — Rantisi incites the prisoners to rebellion and to demonstrate in the hall, and the matter could develop into a hunger strike

79 | 689 |

2980 اِعْتَذَرَ *v. VIII* to apologize إلى to sb عن for sth

طلبت منه البقاء للغداء.. اعتذر بلباقة ووعدها بزيارة قريبة — She asked him to stay for lunch...he excused himself tactfully and promised her to visit soon

79 | 695 |

2981 نِسْيان *n.* forgetfulness; oblivion

الكمبيوتر ذو ذاكرة حديدية لا تخبو ولا يعتريها النسيان — The computer has an iron memory that does not fade and that is not subject to forgetting

74 | 738 |

2982 خَمْر *fem./masc.n.* liquor, wine, alcohol

الحادث نجم عن فقدان السائق، الذي كان تحت تأثير الخمر والأدوية، السيطرة على السيارة، وهو يقود بسرعة كبيرة — The incident resulted from the driver, who was under the influence of wine and medicine, losing control over the car as he was driving very fast

69 | 785 |

2983 أَوْقَفَ *v. IV* to detain sb; to make sb stand

أرجوك أيها القاضي، أوقف تنفيذ هذه العقوبة — I beg you, judge, stop the implementation of this punishment

93 | 583 |

2984 تَخَلُّف *n.* backwardness; underdevelopment

إن معيار التقدم والتخلف والنهوض والانهيار في عالمنا الحديث لا يقاس إلا بالاقتصاد — The standard of progress and backwardness, of rising and falling, in our modern world is only measured by the economy

79 | 692 |

2985 مُسْتَهْلِك *n.* consumer; *adj.* consumer, consuming

هذه الحملة تستهدف الاعراب عن التعاطف مع المستهلكين في منطقة الشرق الأوسط ممن شعروا بالاساءة — This campaign aims to express sympathy for consumers in the Middle East who feel insulted

65 | 835 |

2986 كَلَّمَ *v. II* to speak with, talk to sb

هل فاتن تعرف أنك لا تكلم أحدا من أهلك؟ — Does Fatin know that you aren't speaking to any of your family?

44 | 1219 | +spo

2987 تَوْظِيف *n.* hiring, employment, recruitment; job appointment; usage, exercise

اكتشف القائمون على أحد مواقع التوظيف على الإنترنت أن هناك ١٥٠٠ متقدم لطلب وظيفة يحملون شهادات ودرجات علمية مزيفة — Those in charge of one of the employment sites on the Internet discovered that 1,500 applicants had forged degrees and academic qualifications

72 | 747 |

2988 إقْبال *n.* approach; concern على for; interest في

لم أصدق عيني وأنا أرى هذا الاقبال الجماهيري على مسرحيتي — I couldn't believe my eyes when I saw this popular turnout for my play

75 | 715 |

2989 تَهْنِئَة *n.* pl. تَهَانِ (def. تَهَانِي) greetings, congratulations

تبادل الجميع التهاني والقبلات والحلويات — Everyone exchanged congratulations and kisses and sweets

77 | 695 |

2990 مُدافِع *n.* defender; advocate; *adj.* defending, advocating

إنها إحدى أقوى المدافعين في الكونغرس عن ضحايا الاعتداء الجنسي في الجيش — She is one of the strongest defenders in Congress of the victims of sexual assault in the army

76 | 710 |

2991 تَحْذِير *n.* pl. -aat warning, caution

ألم تسمع تحذير الدكتور من استعمال الهاتف الجوال؟ — Didn't you hear the doctor's warning against using the cell phone?

82 | 659 |

2992 الآخِرَة *n.* الآخِرَة the hereafter (as opposed to الدُّنْيا this world)

حالات الحب لا ينالها إلا السعيد حقا في الدنيا والآخرة — Only the truly fortunate person in this life and the hereafter will experience true love (literally: Instances of love are attained only by the truly fortunate in this life and the hereafter)

69 | 775 |

2993 هُرُوب *vn.* escaping, fleeing; deserting

وأشارت الخارجية في بيان على موقعها الإلكتروني إلى حادث هروب ٢٣ سجينا بينهم عناصر من تنظيم القاعدة — The foreign ministry in a communiqué on its website referred to an incident of 23 prisoners escaping, among whom were elements of Al-Qaeda

81 | 666 |

2994 اِسْتَعَدَّ *v. X* to get ready, prepare لـ for sth

حين أواجه معضلات جديدة، يستعد عقلي للبحث عن مكان أعيش فيه لحظات من الهدوء النسبي — When I face new problems, my mind prepares to search for a place in which I can experience a few moments of relative peace

81 | 666 |

2995 جَواز *n.* permit, authorization; جَواز السَّفْر passport

الحب لا يعرف الجنسية، له لغة واحدة وليس له جواز سفر — Love doesn't know nationality; it has a single language, and it has no passport

88 | 614 |

2996 مُعْلَن *adj.* declared, announced; posted, made public

كان هدفهم غير المعلن نهب ثروات المسلمين — Their unannounced goal was to plunder the wealth of the Muslims

81 | 659 |

2997 هَدَأَ *v. I (a)* to subside, abate (storm, noise); to calm down, quiet down

أنت منفعل وغاضب . . فأرجوك أن تهدأ وتناقش الأمور بروية — You are upset and angry...I beg you to calm down and discuss matters calmly

80 | 674 |

2998 قَطُّ *adv.* (not) at all, never; nothing, no one
في حياتي لم يحدث قط أن هددت أحدا، سواء كان معي أو ضدي — In my life it has never happened that I threatened anyone, whether he was with me or against me

74 | 721 |

2999 مَطْبَخ *n.* kitchen
ارتدى ملابسه ودخل إلى المطبخ لتناول طعام الإفطار — He put on his clothes and entered the kitchen to take his breakfast

68 | 786 |

3000 رِزْق *n.* livelihood, sustenance; food, daily bread
وسعيت في طلب الرزق حتى أصبحت غنيا فوسوس إلي الشيطان أن أغريها بالمال — I attempted to earn a living until I became rich, and then Satan whispered to me that I should try to entice her with money

87 | 613 |

3001 اِحْتَمَلَ *v. VIII* to tolerate, put up with sth/sb; to expect sth; (pass.) to be likely; يُحْتَمَل أَنْ it is likely that
هو لا يحتمل أن ترتبط ابنته بعلاقة خارج الزواج — He can't bear that his daughter would be involved in a relationship outside of marriage

82 | 651 |

3002 طارئ *adj.* emergency (situation); exceptional (conditions); unscheduled, special (meeting)
أعلن السيد المدير عن اجتماع طارئ حضره جميع العمال دون استثناء — The director announced an emergency meeting which all workers without exception were to attend

79 | 679 |

3003 اِعْتَرَضَ *v. VIII* to object, be opposed على to sth
لا أحد يعترض على ما يجري على النساء يعني حتى جرائم الشرف التي تقول انها ليست من الدين لا أحد يدينها الآن — No one objects to what is happening to the women, even the honor crimes which you say are not part of religion, no one is condemning them now

83 | 645 |

3004 حِرْمان *n.* deprivation, prohibition
عاش طيلة العقود الماضية شتى انواع الحرمان والمعاناة والتشرد — He lived during the past decades through various types of deprivation, suffering, and displacement

82 | 650 |

3005 سَرَقَ *v. I (i)* to steal sth
إنه يتعلم الأرمنية والروسية من ليزا، التي صار بإمكانه أن يسرق منها بعض القبلات بين الحين والآخر — He is learning Armenian and Russian from Liza, from whom he was able to steal some kisses from time to time

80 | 664 |

3006 عار *n.* shame, disgrace, scandal
لا أريد أن أجلب العار على أهلي — I don't want to bring shame on my family

78 | 688 |

3007 سُمْعَة *n.* reputation
إن المجدلية لن تخون عيسى الناصري ولن تسيء إلى سمعته ولو أعطيتموها ملء الأرض ذهبا — The Magdalene will not betray Jesus of Nazareth and she won't insult his reputation even if you gave her the world full of gold

88 | 604 |

3008 مَلْحُوظ *adj.* noticeable, observable; remarkable, significant
إن أسعار الشقق سوف تشهد ارتفاعا ملحوظا خلال الفترة المقبلة — Apartment prices will witness a noticeable rise during the coming period

77 | 688 |

3009 آنَ *v. I (i)* to come, arrive, approach (of time)
قالت بصوت يشبه صوت الجنية: آن لك أن تنهض أيها العراقي وتفعل ما هو بانتظارك — She said in a voice resembling the voice of the Genie: The time has come for you to arise, O Iraqi, and do what is waiting for you

80 | 663 |

3010 فاكِهَة *n.* pl. فَواكِه fruit
رأيته قادما من بعيد يحمل أكياسا ورقية فيها بعض
الفاكهة والخضار — I saw him coming from afar,
carrying paper sacks in which were some fruit
and vegetables
76 | 702 |

3011 مُراعاة *n.* deference, respect; compliance,
observance; watching out for
إنه رجل متفتح، حريص على مراعاة المصالح
الفرنسية — He is an open-minded man,
intent on watching out for French interests
82 | 652 |

3012 غَلَبَ *v. I (i)* to defeat, overcome على sth/sb
ما يقوله الكتاب أن غالبية المتحدثين الرسميين
الفلسطينيين يغلب على خطابهم العاطفة والتسرع
والتشكي — What the book is saying is that
most of the official Palestinian spokesmen's
messages are dominated by emotion, haste,
and complaining
82 | 648 |

3013 تَعادُل *n.* balance, equilibrium; (sports) tie
جاءت المباراة مثيرة وانتهى شوطها الاول بالتعادل
بهدف لكل فريق — The match proceeded in an
entertaining manner, and the first half ended
with a tie with one goal for each team
56 | 954 |

3014 اِسْتِهْلاك *n.* consuming, consumption
(of consumer goods), exhaustion, depletion
(of resources)
الشركة تخطط لخفض معدل استهلاك الوقود — The
company is planning to lower the average
consumption of fuel
71 | 744 |

3015 عَمُود *n.* pl. أَعْمِدَة column, pillar
كانت على طرفي الكوبرى أربعة أعمدة معدنية، عمود
فى كل ناحية، أعلى كل منها لمبة — On both sides
of the bridge were four metal columns, a
column in each corner, on top of each of
which was a lamp
84 | 631 |

3016 سِينَمائِيّ *adj.* cinema, cinematographic
تمر الأحداث بذهنها كشريط سينمائي تستعيده
مرة بعد أخرى — The incidents pass through

her mind like a movie reel, repeating again
and again
67 | 791 |

3017 بارِحَة *n.* yesterday, yesteryear; البارحة
/l-baarHa/ (Irq.Gul.) *adv.* yesterday
لقد سكنت رصاصة رئته اليسرى وقد أجروا له
العملية البارحة — A bullet lodged in his left
lung and they performed an operation on
him yesterday
63 | 842 |

3018 عادَلَ *v. III* to be equal to sth; to make equal
to sth; (sports) to tie sb
استغفرت الله وهي تفكر بأن أحزانها هذا العام تعادل
أحزان كل البشر على وجه الأرض — She asked
God's forgiveness, feeling that her sorrows this
year were equal to the sorrows of all men on
the face of the earth
80 | 662 |

3019 سِجِلّ *n.* pl. -aat register; archive, record
كان للمرأة دور على امتداد التاريخ الإسلامي .. وان
سجلات أمانة الأوقاف تشير إلى أن المرأة كانت من
أوائل الواقفين منذ أوائل القرن التاسع عشر —
Women have had a role throughout Islamic
history. The annals of the Endowments
Secretariat indicate that women were among
the first to endow property from the
beginning of the nineteenth century
79 | 663 |

3020 اِنْتَقَدَ *v. VIII* to criticize sb/sth
لا يمكنني ان أنتقد اي مدرب لان اخلاقي لا
تسمح لي بذلك — I can't criticize any coach
because my moral values do not permit me
to do that
71 | 735 |

3021 بُورْصَة /burSa/ *n.* stock exchange, bourse
التعامل في البورصة ليس نوعا من المقامرة بل يعتمد
على دراسات اقتصادية كثيرة — Trading on the
stock exchange is not a kind of gambling,
rather it relies on many economic studies
60 | 877 |

3022 مَوْهِبَة *n.* pl. مَواهِب talent, gift
هوميروس: الشعر يا أفلاطون، يا صديقي العظيم،
موهبة إبداعية يهبها إله الشعر أبولو لمن يستحقها —

Homer: Poetry, Plato, my great friend, is a creative gift which Apollo, the God of poetry, gives to those who deserve it

79 | 666 |

3023 اِسْتِقالَة *n.* resignation

المدرب قدم استقالته وإدارة النادي رفضت الاستقالة — The coach offered his resignation and the administration of the club rejected the resignation

67 | 786 |

3024 مَخْرَج *n.* exit, outlet; escape, way out, solution

من الصعوبة وجود مخرج سريع لهذه الأزمة — It is difficult to find a quick exit from this crisis

85 | 615 |

3025 سالَ *v. I (i)* to flow, run; to leak; to melt

انفجر ضاحكا حتى سالت دموعه — He broke out laughing until his tears flowed

74 | 713 |

3026 قَفَزَ *v. I (i)* to jump, leap

رأيته يقفز من فراشه كالمجنون — I saw him jump from his bed like a madman

77 | 676 |

3027 كِفايَة *n.* sufficiency, adequacy; performance, productivity; competence; (Egy.) *adj.* (invar.) enough; *interj.* enough!

أنا عارفك، وعارف تربيتك والبيئة اللي طلعتي منها وهذا كفاية عشان أثق فيك — I know you, and I know your education and the environment you were brought up in, and this is enough for me to trust you

91 | 574 |

3028 تَوَسُّع *n.* expansion

الناس تعتقد أن هناك المزيد من فرص النمو مع توسع الشركة في اسواق جديدة — People believe that there are more growth opportunities with expanding the company into new markets

70 | 745 |

3029 عَقيد *n.* colonel; (in titles) Colonel

قال العقيد: نحن بحاجة ماسة إلى الدبابات، أين الدبابات؟ — The colonel said: We are in desperate need of tanks, where are the tanks?

64 | 817 |

3030 مُعْطٍ *adj.* given; *n.* مُعْطَيات facts, data, factors

إن الحوار المطلوب يجب أن ينطلق من معطيات القرن الحادي والعشرين — The required dialog needs to start from the "givens" of the twenty-first century

71 | 738 |

3031 زَوْجِيّ *adj.* marital; paired, coupled

الحمل هو الطريقة الأضمن لاستمرار الحياة الزوجية — Pregnancy is the most certain way to continue married life

69 | 760 |

3032 شَجَّعَ *v. II* to encourage, promote, support sb/sth

إن التعايش الإنساني يتطلب جوا من الاحترام المتبادل يشجع على السلام بين البشر والأمم — Living together as humans requires an atmosphere of mutual respect which encourages peace between men and nations

83 | 630 |

3033 حَيّا *v. II* to greet, salute sb; to praise, laud sb; حَيّاك الله (lit. may God preserve you) good for you! well done!

كيف عمي شو أخبارك؟ نعم، الله يحييك — How are you, uncle, what's your news? Yes, God greet you!

43 | 1213 |

3034 خَريف *n.* autumn, fall

كان جو الخريف رطبا مائلا للبرودة في هذه الساعة المبكرة — The air of autumn was humid, tending towards cold at this early hour

78 | 671 |

3035 جُمْهوريّ *n./adj.* republican; Republican; السَّلام الجُمْهوريّ the national anthem (in a republic)

حقق الديمقراطي جيم ويب تقدما بنحو ثمانية الاف صوت على الجمهوري المنتهية ولايته جورج الن، لكن الاخير طالب باعادة فرز الأصوات — The Democrat Jim Webb achieved a lead of about 8,000 votes over the Republican incumbent George Allen, but the latter requested a recount of the votes

64 | 819 |

3036 عَرَض *n. pl.* أَعْراض (med.) symptom; أَعْراض جانِبِيَّة side effects
مشكلة أمراض القلب التي تسبب الوفاة الفجائية للرياضيين لا تظهر لها أعراض ويوم يظهر العرض يوم يموت الرياضي — The problem of the heart disease which causes sudden death in athletes is that it doesn't show symptoms, and the day in which it shows a symptom is the day the athlete dies
66 | 785 |

3037 تَوالٍ (def. التَوالِي) *n.* consecutive or continuous succession
فاز فريق بوكا جونيور بكأس أميركا الجنوبية (كوبا أميركا) للمرة الثانية على التوالي — The Boca Juniors team won the South America Cup (the America Cup) for the second time in a row
71 | 733 |

3038 حِزْبِيّ *adj.* party-related; partisan, factional
اكد في اكثر من مناسبة على ضرورة اعادة تنظيم العمل الحزبي — On more than one occasion he has stressed the necessity of reorganizing the party work
60 | 872 |

3039 حَبْل *n.* rope, cord, cable
إن أنت قتلتني لن تفيد في شيء بالعكس سوف تلف حبل المشنقة حول رقبتك — If you kill me it won't help anything, on the contrary you'll be wrapping the hangman's noose around your neck
78 | 664 |

3040 تَوَقُّع *n. pl.* -aat expectation, anticipation; forecast
— لا يجب أن تكون عندك توقعات كبيرة في البداية You shouldn't have big expectations at first
72 | 718 |

3041 تَرْشِيح *n.* nomination, candidacy
كان المرشحون تسعة، واتفق مجلس الشورى على ترشيح ستة مرشحين آخرين — The candidates were nine, and the Advisory Council agreed on the candidacy of six other candidates
71 | 731 |

3042 قَيِّم *adj.* valuable; *n. pl.* -uun responsible (for) على)

هذا موضوع مفيد وقيم كباقي موضوعاتك الرائعة — This is a beneficial and valuable subject, just like the rest of your superb subjects
78 | 669 | +for

3043 راضٍ (def. الراضِي) *adj.* pleased, satisfied; accepting, consenting
معاناة الطفل من نقص في حاجاته الأساسية تجعله غير راض عن الواقع فلا يهتم برضى من حواليه من المربين — A child's suffering from a deficiency in his basic needs is going to make him unsatisfied with reality so that he will not be concerned with pleasing the caregivers around him
87 | 597 |

3044 كُفْر *n.* kufr (rejection of the Islamic faith), unbelief, apostasy
لقد خرج مع ذلك البكاء كل ما في قلبي من كفر ونفاق وفساد، وأحسست بأن الإيمان بدأ يسري بداخلي — With that cry, everything in my heart in the way of apostasy, hypocrisy and corruption went out, and I felt that faith began to course through me
72 | 719 |

3045 مُصْطَلَح *n. pl.* -aat technical term; مُصْطَلَحات terminology
إن مصطلح «حرية التعبير» فضفاض ينبغي تحديده — The term "freedom of expression" is loose, and needs to be defined
74 | 706 |

3046 دَهْشَة *n.* surprise, astonishment; bewilderment, confusion
كانت طاقته الجبارة على العمل تثير دهشة أساتذته وإعجابهم — His amazing ability to work incites the surprise of his professors, and their admiration
63 | 823 | +lit

3047 مَسْح *n.* survey, measure; wiping off; sweeping
مسح عرقه بطرف كم قميصه — He wiped his sweat with the end of his shirt
72 | 725 |

3048 أَسًى *n.* affliction, sorrow, grief
إن مجلس الأمة الكويتي يتابع بمزيد من الأسى والاستنكار المحنة التي حلت بلبنان الشقيق جراء

العدوان الإسرائيلي المتصاعد — The Kuwaiti National Assembly is following with increasing distress and disapproval the trials which have fallen onto "brother" Lebanon as a result of the increasing Israeli aggression

66 | 788 | +lit

3049 ظُلْمَة *n.* pl. ظُلُمات darkness

سمع – بوضوح هذه المرة – شيئا يتحرك في الظلمة بجواره — He heard, clearly this time, something moving in the darkness next to him

68 | 765 | +lit

3050 زُجاج *n.* glass; زُجاج أماميّ windshield

وفي العصر الإسلامي اشتهر فن الزجاج المعشق بالرصاص والجبس فكان يلون بألوان زاهية تخترقها أشعة الشمس — In the Islamic Age, the art of stained glass made with lead and gypsum became well known; it was colored with bright colors penetrated by the rays of the sun

75 | 689 |

3051 رَعَى *v. I (a)* to graze, take out to pasture (sheep); to care for, protect sb; to sponsor, promote sth/sb; to safeguard, look after (sb's affairs)

أنت أناني لا ترعى إلا مصلحتك الشخصية — You are selfish and only care for your own personal interests

77 | 674 |

3052 دَوَّر *v. II* (Dia.) to look, search على for sth/sb; to rotate, wind, make turn sth; to make run, operate (engine, car); to play (song on the stereo)

لو جبتي اسم الشركة ممكن ندور عليها — If you come up with the name of the company, maybe we can search for it

60 | 856 | +spo

3053 جُلُوس *n.* sitting down, being seated

نهض الضابط لمصافحتي وطلب مني الجلوس — The officer arose to shake my hand and he asked me to sit

79 | 654 |

3054 وِيّا (Irq.) *prep.* with; (with pron.) وِيّاك with you; وِيّايا and وِيّايْ with me

قلوبنا دايما ويّاك وندعيلك والله يردك انت ومريومه سالمين — Our hearts are always with you, coach, and we pray that Allah will bring you and Maryuma back safely

32 | 1601 | +spo

3055 اِسْتِعْمار *n.* colonialism; *vn.* building of settlements

حاربنا الاستعمار الفرنسي عندما كانت فرنسا على ارض لبنان وحاربنا الاستعمار البريطاني ونحارب الاستعمار الاميركي — We fought French colonialism when France was on the land of Lebanon and we fought British colonialism and we will fight American colonialism

68 | 762 |

3056 مُخالِف *adj.* divergent; against (the law); *n.* pl. -uun transgressor, offender

منع التدخين بالأماكن الصحية والمؤسسات التعليمية وفرض غرامات على المخالفين لذلك — It forbade smoking in health places (hospitals and clinics) and educational institutions, and it imposed fines of those who violated this

69 | 752 |

3057 أغْلَى *elat.* more/most expensive

كلكم أولادي وأحبكم بنفس الدرجة، فأنتم أغلى عندي من روحي التي بين جنبي — All of you are my children and I love you to the same degree, for you are more important to me than my soul in my breast

82 | 626 |

3058 مَضْمُون *n.* content; *adj.* guaranteed, insured

يقول اولمرت دون استخدام كلمة لا.. جميع اللاءات ولكن مضمون الكلام هو الرفض — Olmert says all the "noes" without using the word "no"... but the content of the talk is rejection

80 | 648 |

3059 خُطْبَة *n.* pl. خُطَب speech; sermon; خُطْبَة الجُمْعَةِ the Friday sermon

تقوم الهيئات الإسلامية بواجب التوعية والإرشاد من خلال الخطب والنشرات والحصص الإذاعية التي تسمح بها الإذاعات العربية — The Islamic organizations are performing the duty of consciousness-raising and guidance through sermons, publications and radio classes which the Arab broadcasters permit

81 | 634 |

3060 حَظْر *n.* prohibition, ban; embargo

تم تمديد الحظر على تصدير كل أنواع المنتجات الحيوانية من بريطانيا — The ban on the export of all types of animal products from Britain was extended

74 | 693 |

3061 اِقْتِراب *n.* approach, approximation; getting near

ابتعدوا عني.. من يحاول الاقتراب سأضربه بهذه العصا لأهشم رأسه — Get away from me... anyone who tries to get near me, I'll beat him with this stick to smash his head

82 | 632 |

3062 راقِي *adj.* rising, ascending; advanced; fancy, high-class

الخط العربي ليس فقط فنا من الفنون الراقية التي تسمو بالروح وتهذب النفس، بل هو صنعة وحرفة — Arabic script is not only a fine art which elevates the spirit and refines the soul, but it is also a workmanship and craft

81 | 634 |

3063 ذَكاء *n.* intelligence, cleverness

لا يحتاج هذا الأمر إلى ذكاء كبير — This matter does not need a great intelligence

77 | 668 |

3064 عُنْصُرِيّ *adj.* racist

تنتقد الرواية الجانب العنصري في أمريكا في الثلاثينيات — The novel criticizes the racist side of America in the Thirties

68 | 759 |

3065 نَبِيل *adj.* noble

الطب مهنة إنسانية نبيلة راقية لا تعدلها إلا مهنة التعليم — Medicine is a noble, refined humanistic profession, not equaled by anything except education

80 | 639 |

3066 وُدِّيّ *adj.* friendly, cordial, amicable, warm

زيارتنا الى هذا البيت الكبير زيارة ودية وطبيعية — Our visit to this large home is a friendly and natural visit

75 | 682 |

3067 جَحِيم *n.* hell, inferno; الجَحِيم Hell

كان المشهد أسطوريا مرعبا أشبه بوصف الجحيم في الكتب المقدسة — The scene was frighteningly legendary, close to the description of Hell in the scriptures

77 | 667 |

3068 نُزُول *n.* descent; reduction, losing (weight); resignation, stepping down

شهر سبتمبر كان ممطرا بشكل غير عادي وكانت نسب نزول الأمطار قياسية واستثنائية — The month of September was unusually rainy and the percent of rainfall was a record, and exceptional

82 | 625 |

3069 اِنْقَلَبَ *v. VII* to turn around; to turn over; to be reversed, be inverted

هكذا الإنسان ما بين لحظة تراه وأخرى ينقلب من حالة إلى نقيضها — From one moment to the next, you see a person going from one condition to its opposite

82 | 621 |

3070 اِحْتَرَمَ *v. VIII* to respect, revere sb/sth

لا لاضطهاد الأقليات المسلمة في الغرب ونعم لبروتوكول يحترم الخصوصية الثقافية ضمن احترام النظام العام في البلدان المضيفة — No to the persecution of Muslim minorities in the West, and yes to a protocol which respects cultural specificity along with respecting the public order in the host countries

83 | 615 |

3071 فَضائِيَّة *n.* pl. -aat satellite (broadcasting) station

بثت فضائية الجزيرة الخبر قبل أي محطة أخرى — Al-Jazeera satellite station broadcast that piece of news before any other station

80 | 643 |

3072 مَمْنُوع *adj.* forbidden, prohibited, banned

خبز السن ممنوع ان يتناوله مريض النقرس لإحتوائه على نسبة كبيرة من الردة — Coarse flour bread is forbidden for gout patients to eat since it contains a large percentage of chaff

80 | 641 |

3073 مُحَقِّق *n.* investigator; editor; *a.p.* investigating
إن تعاون المواطن مع المحقق الجنائي أمر حثت عليه الشريعة الاسلامية — The cooperation of the citizen with the criminal investigator is a matter which Islamic law encourages
59 | 869 | +lit

3074 قِيادِيّ *adj.* leading, guiding; commanding; *n.* pl. -uun commander
أنت إذن عضو قيادي في هذا الحزب — You, therefore, are a leading member of this party
68 | 752 |

3075 أَنْتَجَ *v. IV* to produce, create, yield sth; to cause, result in sth
هذا متناقض جدا لأننا نتبع سياسة في السجون تنتج مزيدا من الإرهابيين والمتطرفين — This is very contradictory because we are following a policy in the prisons which produces more terrorists and extremists
81 | 629 |

3076 رَكِبَ *v. I (a)* to get in/on (vehicle), board (ship, airplane), mount (horse, bicycle)
يحرص بعضهم على ارتداء البشت وهو يركب الدراجة ذاهبا إلى الوجهة التي يريدها — Some of them insist on wearing the robe even when riding bikes to wherever they are going
82 | 623 |

3077 رَقْص *n.* dance, dancing
الكثير من الأجنبيات يتعلمن الرقص الشرقي ويحترفن هذا الفن وينافسن حتى الراقصات المصريات — Many foreign women learn Eastern dance and become professionals of this dance and compete even with Egyptian dancers
82 | 622 |

3078 حَرَج *n.* impediment; *objection*
وإذا قيل له ارجع فليرجع ولا حرج في ذلك — And if he's told to go back then let him go back, and there's nothing wrong with that
84 | 608 |

3079 شَجاعَة *n.* courage
هناك فقهاء كثر كانت لهم مواقف شجاعة في رفض الظلم والانغلاق وفي تحرير الفكر من قيود الجمود — There are many religious scholars who had courageous positions in rejecting oppression and isolation and liberating thought from the fetters of rigidity
83 | 612 |

3080 تَوَلٍّ (def. تَوَلِّي) *n.* taking charge, assuming responsibility
مسيرة بوتين منذ توليه رئاسة روسيا يمكن تلخيصها في عبارة واحدة هي الهجوم على الهيمنة الأمريكية على العالم — Putin's path, since assumed the presidency of Russia, can be summarized in a single expression, which is: an attack on American hegemony over the world
72 | 701 |

3081 كَفِيل *adj.* guaranteeing, ensuring (ب sth); *n.* guarantor, sponsor, (person) responsible
حاول التوجه للنوم في وقت محدد يوميا، فهذا كفيل بأن يقلل الأرق وتتعود ساعة جسمك البيولوجية على وقت محدد للنوم — Try to go to bed at a set time daily, since this can guarantee a reduction of insomnia and your biological body clock will become accustomed to the set sleep time
76 | 667 |

3082 كَبِد *n.* liver (organ); center, middle
ينصح الاطباء كل من يعاني من أمراض الكبد بعدم تناول السبانخ — Doctors advise everyone suffering from liver diseases not to eat spinach
70 | 723 |

3083 عِزَّة *n.* glory, honor; power; عِزَّة النَّفْس self-esteem
أين العزة والكرامة؟؟ العزة في الاتحاد مع أبناء الوطن وليس مع الامريكان والصهاينة — Where is glory and dignity? Glory is in unity with the sons of the nation, not with the American and Zionists
73 | 694 |

3084 تَسْويق *n.* marketing
إن مصنع العطور يعتمد على السوق المحلية في تسويق منتجه — The perfume factory depends on the local market in marketing its products
68 | 745 |

3085 لَبَن *n.* (Egy.) milk; (Lev.Irq.) yoghurt
البقرة حيوان أليف تعطينا اللبن، ومن اللبن نصنع
الجبن والزبدة — The cow is a domesticated
animal that gives us milk, and from the milk
we make cheese and butter
70 | 720 |

3086 خَشَبَة *n.* pl. -aat piece of wood; board, plank;
خَشَبَات الجُول (theater) stage; خَشَبَة المَسرح
goalposts
أكبر عدد يمكن تصوره من الشباب أكبر عدد
تستطيع خشبة المسرح أن تتحمله الأرض تمتلئ تماماً
بأجسام النائمين — The biggest number of
young men you can imagine, the biggest
number that the stage of the theater can hold,
the floor is completely filled with the bodies
of the sleepers
85 | 596 |

3087 سَمّ *n.* pl. سُمُوم poison, toxin
ان شرب عصير الرمان يساعد على التخلص من
السموم في الجسم ويعالج الإسهال والتهاب المعدة
والصداع — Drinking pomegranate juice helps
in getting rid of the poisons in the body and
treats diarrhea, stomach inflammation, and
headaches
76 | 660 |

3088 فاضَ *v. I (i)* to overflow; to exceed, go beyond
عن sth
كانت الطرق في فرنسا تفيض باللاجئين الذين
تطاردهم الطائرات الألمانية — The roads in
France were overflowing with refugees who
were being pursued by German planes
70 | 714 | +lit

3089 مُستَخدِم *adj.* employing, using; *n.* pl. -uun user
يرى بعض مستخدمي الأنترنت أن هذه الأسعار
«معقولة» — Some Internet users consider this
price to be reasonable
62 | 807 |

3090 مَنطِقيّ *adj.* logical, rational
اذهب الى سوريا واجتمع مع الرئيس السوري اذ من
غير المنطقي ان نتواصل عبر الهاتف — Go to Syria
and meet with the Syrian president, since it is
not reasonable to communicate with each
other over the phone
78 | 648 |

3091 فَضِيحَة *n.* scandal; disgrace, shame
استقال الرئيس ريتشارد نيكسون وسط فضيحة
ووترجيت — President Richard Nixon
resigned in the middle of the Watergate
scandal
87 | 580 |

3092 يا تُرَى (Dia. يا تَرَى) *part.* (modal) perhaps,
maybe, I wonder
مين حيفوز ياترى؟ — Who is going to win, I
wonder?
74 | 674 |

3093 أخلاقيّ *adj.* moral, ethical
الاتجار في البشر واستغلالهم في الأعمال القسرية يمثل
مسألة غير أخلاقية وجريمة ضد الإنسانية —
Trafficking in human beings and exploiting
them in forced labor is a moral issue and a
crime against humanity
72 | 695 |

3094 لَزِمَ *v. I (a)* to be necessary (على for sb) to do
sth; to cling to; لَزِمَ الصَمْت to keep quiet;
لَزِمَ الفِراش to stay in bed
هناك متطلبات طبية رئيسية يلزم توفرها في أي متقدم
للخدمة العسكرية — There are principle medical
requirements which must be met by any
person applying for military service
83 | 604 |

3095 غَرِقَ *v. I (a)* to sink, drown, be submerged
غرقت في بحر حبك — I have drowned in the
sea of your love
74 | 674 |

3096 سوفيتي /suvyeeti/ *adj.* Soviet; also
سوفياتي /suvyaati/, سوفييتي /suvyeeti/
وفوق ذلك كان السلاح السوفيتي مازال موجودا في
المنطقة — Above and beyond that, Soviet
weapons are still present in the area
63 | 796 |

3097 تَأَمَّلَ *v. V* to reflect on, ponder (في) sth
وقف بجانب زوجته يتأمل وجهها ويفكر بها
سيقوله لها — He stood by his wife
contemplating her face and pondering
what he would tell her
75 | 667 |

3098 حِيالَ *prep.* concerning, regarding

لن يسكت حيال ما يجري في الإقليم — He will not be silent concerning what is happening in the region

72 | 694 |

3099 تَصَرَّفَ *v. V* to act, behave, proceed (مع/في with sth/sb; وَكَأَنّ as if)

لم يكن بين الموظفين أي عربي ولذلك فقد كانت تتصرف وكأنها واحدة منهم، تمازح هذا وتضحك مع ذاك — There was not a single Arab among the employees, and therefore she behaved as if she were one of them, joking with this one and laughing with that one

86 | 582 |

3100 بائِع *adj.* selling; *n. pl.* باعَة seller, vendor; merchant

دخل الزوج متجرا ليشتري ثوبا لزوجته، فسأله البائع: أي مقاس وأي لون تريد؟ فقال الزوج: لا أعرف — The husband entered to buy a robe for his wife, so the salesperson asked him: What size and what color do you want? The husband said: I don't know

75 | 670 |

3101 إحْياء *vn.* reviving, enlivening; celebrating (anniversary); commemorating; إحْياءً لِذِكْرَى in memory of

النمسا تشدد على ضرورة إحياء المفاوضات بين الفلسطينيين والإسرائيليين — Austria is stressing the necessity of reviving negotiations between the Palestinians and the Israelis

77 | 649 | +news

3102 دافِئ *adj.* warm; (Dia.) دافي

كانت أزهار الكرز بيضاء مشرقة كالفضة المتلألئة تحت أشعة الشمس الدافئة — The cherry blossoms were white, shining like glittering silver under the warm rays of the sun

71 | 705 |

3103 قِطّ *n.* cat; male cat, tomcat; قِطّة female cat; *pl.* قِطَط cats

كانت تسكن في فيلا صغيرة بشارع منشة مع عشرات من القطط — She was living in a small villa on Mansha Street with dozens of cats

63 | 793 |

3104 بَراءَة *n.* innocence; acquittal; بَراءَة اخْتِراع (invention) patent

إنني بريء من دم الذئب من دم يوسف — I am as innocent as the wolf was of the blood of Joseph

82 | 609 |

3105 ذُلّ *n.* humiliation, dishonor

من لم يذق مر التعلم ساعة تجرع ذل الجهل طول حياته — He who does not taste the bitterness of education for an hour will swallow the humiliation of ignorance throughout his life

61 | 817 | +lit

3106 حُجْرَة *n. pl.* حُجَر room, chamber; compartment, enclosure; (bio.) cell

على غير المتوقع طالب الأطباء بإخراجه من الرعاية إلى حجرة عادية — Unexpectedly the doctors requested that he be taken out of intensive care and put in a normal room

63 | 787 | +lit

3107 مُحْتَلّ *n. pl.* -uun occupier; *adj.* occupying, occupation (forces)

يجب علينا ان نطرد المحتل ونحاسبه لأنه قتل أكثر من ٣ ملايين عراقي منذ الغزو — We have to drive out the occupier and bring him to account since he killed more than 3 million Iraqis since the invasion

66 | 759 |

3108 مَبْنِيّ *adj.* built, based (على on)

وعندما رفعوا العصابة عن عيوني اكتشفت أنه مكان مبني من الطين ومهجور — When they took the blindfold off my eyes I discovered that it was a place built of clay and abandoned

79 | 633 |

3109 تَجَنُّب *n.* avoidance, avoiding

يخرجان ليلا لتجنب لقاء الناس — They go out at night to avoid meeting people

74 | 668 |

3110 كَذَبَ *v. I (i)* to lie (على to sb)

إن الحيوانات لا تكذب لأنها لا تتكلم؛ وحده الإنسان ينافق — Animals don't lie, because they don't speak; only man can be a hypocrite

78 | 637 |

3111 مَنْشُور *n.* pl. -aat publication; brochure; *adj.*
published, posted (on the Web)
وزعوا منشورات غير مرخصة وعرضوا لوحات تثير
الاستياء — They distributed unauthorized
pamphlets and displayed disgusting pictures
65 | 763 | +news

3112 خاضَ *v. I (u)* to wage (war, battle) ضِدّ
against; to embark on (a campaign);
to wade في into (water); to plunge,
dive في into (an issue)
الانتخابات الرئاسية الأخيرة في البيرو انتهت أيضا
لصالح اليسار الذي خاض المعركة الفاصلة
بمرشحين متنافسين من صفوفه — The recent
presidential elections in Peru also ended in favor
of the left which entered the decisive battle
with two competitive candidates from its ranks
73 | 673 |

3113 تَعَدَّى *v. V* to exceed, go beyond; to infringe
على on (sb's rights)
لم يتعدى اتصالي بزوجتي وأولادي غير التحية في
العودة إلى البيت — My relationship with my
wife and children didn't go beyond greeting
them upon returning to the house
78 | 634 |

3114 دَبَّابَة *n.* pl. -aat tank
ثم أدخلوا جنودهم مدججين بكل صنوف السلاح
من دبابات وطائرات ومدرعات ورشاشات،
وراحوا يدمرون البيوت فوق ساكنيها — They
brought in their soldiers, laden with every type
of weapon from tanks and airplanes and armored
cars and machine guns, and they began to
destroy the homes on top of their residents
71 | 696 |

3115 رَوْضَة *n.* pl. رياض garden; رَوْضَة الأطفال
kindergarten
تخيل صورا جميلة .. امرأة حسناء، روضة غناء ..
سماء .. صافية زرقاء — Imagine beautiful
pictures, a lovely woman, a garden of singing,
a pure blue sky
83 | 591 |

3116 صُمُود *n.* steadfastness, determination
امتدح الوزير صمود الموظفين وصبرهم — The
minister praised the steadfastness of the
employees and their patience
73 | 675 |

3117 مَضْبُوط *adj.* controlled, regulated; accurate,
precise; (Dia.) مظبوط , مزبوط /mazbuuT/ *adj.*
correct; *interj.* right!
يبقى العنوان مش مظبوط بقى — Then the
address would not be accurate
9 | 5462 | +spo

3118 نَبْض *n.* beating, palpitation, throbbing
قلبه سيتوقف عن النبض في أي لحظة إن لم تجر له
عملية جراحية سريعة — His heart will stop
beating at any moment if he doesn't have a
quick surgical operation
78 | 633 |

3119 سالِفَة *n.* pl. سَوالِف (Irq.Gul. /saalfa, swaalif/)
chat, talk, discussion; story, tale; matter, affair
اول شي مافهمت شنو السالفة بعدين فهمتها — At
the beginning I didn't understand the matter,
then I understood it
33 | 1461 | +for +spo

3120 عُمُومِيّ *adj.* general, public, common; plenary
فيها بعد.. هذه أمور لا تقال في الأماكن العمومية —
Thereafter, these are matters which are not to
be spoken of in public places
60 | 809 |

3121 قَدِمَ *v. I (a)* to arrive, come إلى to; approach
على sth
غالبية الأطباء العاملين في الولايات المتحدة قدموا من
الهند والفلبين وباكستان — Most doctors working
in the United States came from India, the
Philippines, and Pakistan
87 | 566 |

3122 عُنْق *n.* neck (person, bottle)
وضع الياقة المدورة الصلبة البيضاء حول عنقه،
وزررها بدبوس صغير لامع، ولف الكرافتة —
He put the solid round white collar around his
neck, and he fastened it with a small, shiny
pin, and then he tied the tie
79 | 624 |

3123 مُهْتَمّ *adj.* interested, concerned; *n.* pl. -uun
(person, party) interested, concerned
قرأت كتبا رائعة وجدتها عند بعض الاخوة المهتمين
بالشأن العراقي — I read a splendid book I
found at the place of some of the brothers
who are interested in Iraqi affairs
88 | 557 |

3124 عِيان *n.* eyesight, (plain) view; شاهِد عِيان eyewitness

هو لم يتجاوز الخامسة والأربعين ولكنه يظهر للعيان وكأنه قد جاوز السبعين — He is not more than forty-five years old, but to the eyes he looks like he has passed seventy

75 | 650 |

3125 مُكَرَّم *adj.* honored, revered; مَكَّة المُكَرَّمَة Mecca

وقعت أحداث هذه القصة لشاب من أبناء مكة المكرمة — The events of this story happened to a young man from Mecca

67 | 730 |

3126 انْتِماء *n.* membership, affiliation; commitment

لقد تعودت أن أحيا بلا انتماء لشيء — I got used to living without affiliating with anything

74 | 659 |

3127 قَطْرَة *n.* pl. ات drop

إنه لا يستحق قطرة واحدة من هذه الدموع التي تذرفينها عليه — He does not deserve a single drop of these tears you are shedding over him

72 | 675 |

3128 نَوَى *v. I (i)* to intend, want (to do sth)

أي إنسان ينوي ارتكاب الفاحشة لو فكر أو تذكر أن الله سوف يراه يتراجع — Any person who intends to commit adultery, if he thinks or remembers that God will see him, will back off

82 | 592 |

3129 تَرْكِيب *n.* installation, assembling; structure, construction

سيتم تركيب كاميرات داخل المدن لمتابعة حركة المرور — Cameras will be installed inside the cities to follow the traffic

69 | 702 |

3130 مُرّ *adj.* bitter

الحياة هنا مش زي مصر احنا هنا في لندن بقى لنا سنتين .. وشفنا المر قبل ما نستقر — Life here is not like Egypt, we've been here in London for two years, we saw the bitter before we settled down

73 | 665 |

3131 أنْكَرَ *v. IV* to deny, dispute (claim)

رأى المصدر أن حزب الله حقيقة سياسية لا يستطيع أحد أن ينكر وجودها — The source felt that Hizbollah was a political fact whose existence no one can deny

79 | 617 |

3132 مِشْوار *n.* walk, stroll, promenade

تعرض فريق المغرب الفاسي لأول هزيمة في مشواره ضمن محطة «البلاي أوف» — The Fez Morocco team suffered its first defeat in its journey in the Play Off station

76 | 642 |

3133 اسْتَعْرَضَ *v. X* to review, go over sth; (mil.) to review (troops); to tour (facilities)

كان يستعرض أسماء المشاركين، ففوجئ بأسماء جديدة لم يسمع بها من قبل — He reviewed the names of the participants, and was surprised at the new names he had not heard before

71 | 683 |

3134 مُرْتَفَع *n.* height, altitude, elevation; highlands

انحدرت السيارة من المرتفع الذي كانت تقف فيه إلى الخلف — The car came down from the heights on which it was parked

83 | 589 |

3135 أولِمبي /'oolimbi, 'oolumbi/ *adj.* Olympic

حقق جونسون إنجازا لم يسبقه إليه أحد لا في الألعاب الأولمبية ولا في المسابقات الأخرى — Johnson accomplished something which no one had ever done before, not in the Olympic games, and not in other races

47 | 1024 |

3136 أوْحَى *v. IV* to suggest, imply, indicate بأَنَّ that; to inspire ل sb ب to do sth

برغم كل الحزن الذي أراه في وجهك إلا أن شيئا ما يوحي لي بأنه لا يزال هناك متسع للفرح في قلبك — Despite all the sorrow which I see in your face, still something suggests to me that there is still room for joy in your heart

78 | 627 |

3137 خَجَل *n.* shame, bashfulness, shyness

قال في شيء من الخجل: أنا آسف — He said with a bit of shyness: I'm sorry

73 | 668 |

3138 حَديديّ *adj.* iron, iron-like

طارت بها الذكريات إلى منزلها في الرياض، إلى الباب الحديدي وقضبانه المذهبة الأطراف الذي طالما وقفت خلفه بعد صلاة العشاء — Memories took her back to her home in Riyadh, to the iron door and the gold-plated bars which she so often stood behind after evening prayer

70 | 697 |

3139 تَصْحِيح *n.* correction

يعتبر ابن الهيثم أول من حث على استعمال العدسات في تصحيح بعض عيوب الإبصار، كما انه ابتكر قانون انكسار الضوء — Ibn Haytham was the first to urge the use of lenses to correct some vision defects, and he also invented the law of light refraction

79 | 615 |

3140 تَبَنٍّ (def. تَبَنِّي) *n.* adoption

انه يدعو الحكومات العربية إلى تبني استراتيجية جديدة — He is calling on the Arab governments to adopt a new strategy

72 | 676 |

3141 زَرَعَ *v. I (a)* to plant (seed); to implant, transplant (organ); to set (bomb), lay (mines); to grow (plants, crops); to cultivate, farm (land)

التفاؤل من الصفات الرئيسية لأي شخصية ناجحة، فالتفاؤل يزرع الأمل، ويعمق الثقة بالنفس، ويحفز على النشاط والعمل — Optimism is one of the principle characteristics of any successful individual, since optimism breeds hope, and deepens trust in oneself, and incites one to activity and work

79 | 610 |

3142 مُلائِم *adj.* suitable, appropriate

بدأت ترتجف من البرد وقد تبللت ملابسها غير الملائمة لفصل الشتاء — She began to tremble from the cold, her clothing, inappropriate for winter, having gotten wet

77 | 632 |

3143 فَضِيلَة *n.* virtue; (in titles) فَضِيلَة الشَّيْخ His Eminence, the Sheikh

أنا على يقين أن الدين ما ترك فضيلة إلا ودعا إليها، ولا رذيلة إلا وحذر منها — I am certain that religion has not ignored any virtue without calling for it, nor any evil thing without warning against it

79 | 616 |

3144 مُنَوَّر *adj.* illuminated; honored; المَدِينة المُنَوَّرة epithet of Medina

أهلا بكل الناس الحلوة المنورة — Welcome to all the sweet, enlightened people

66 | 737 |

3145 مُشاهِد *n.* viewer, spectator

شكرا لكل المشاهدين الذين تابعوا هذه الحلقة من «من العراق» — Thanks to all the viewers who followed this episode of "From Iraq"

69 | 704 |

3146 مَعْبَر *n. pl.* مَعابِر crossing point, juncture

تفاهمنا على كثير من الأمور منها فتح المعابر — We came to a mutual understanding on many matters, among which was the opening of the crossings

71 | 684 |

3147 أَخْطَأَ *v. IV* to be wrong, make a mistake (في in doing sth); to do (في sth) incorrectly

صدام أخطأ في قراءة الخطر؛ خشي الشيعة أكثر مما خشي الأميركين — Saddam made a mistake in reading the danger; he was afraid of the Shiites more than he was afraid of the Americans

80 | 607 |

3148 أَسَد *n. pl.* أُسود lion

الان تشابكت مناطق الحروب واصبح للمدنيين نصيب الأسد من الضحايا بعد ان كانت تقتصر الضحايا علي المجندين — Now the areas of war have become intertwined and civilians have begun to have the lion's share of victims, even though previously the victims had been limited to soldiers

76 | 635 |

3149 اِشْتِراكيّ *adj.* socialist

كلها مؤشرات تستند إليها المعارضة لإلقاء اللوم على الحكومة الاشتراكية التي لم تحقق أي تقدم منذ أربع سنوات — All of them are indicators which the opposition relies on to cast blame on the socialist government which has not achieved any progress for four years

69 | 704 |

3150 عَداء *n.* aggression, hostility; enmity, animosity

المصلحة الوطنية اللبنانية تقضي ألا يكون هناك عداء بين الحكومتين والشعبين، وبالدرجة الأولى بين الشعبين — Lebanese national interest requires that there not be hostility between the two governments or the two peoples, particularly between the two peoples

78 | 618 |

3151 أَنْف *n.* nose; (fig.) pride; رَغْمَ أَنْفِهِ against his will, to spite him

انبعثت من جسدها تلك الرائحة النقية التي كانت تملأ أنفه عندما يحملها بين ذراعيه وهي طفلة — From her body emanated that pure scent that used to fill his nose when he carried her as a child in his arms

73 | 665 |

3152 قَصْر *n.* shortness, smallness; *vn.* limiting, restricting

هو دائما من حملة القضبان رغم قصر طوله عن بقية زملائه — He is always one of the ones who carry the bars despite his shortness compared to the rest of his colleagues

80 | 601 |

3153 اِخْتِصار *n.* abbreviation, shortening; بِاخْتِصار briefly, in short

الرواية، باختصار، تعكس صراع البشر الأزلي بين الجبر والاختيار — The novel, in short, reflects the eternal struggle of man between force and free will

78 | 620 |

3154 سِيجارَة /siigaara/ *n.* pl. سَجائِر /sajaa'ir, sagaa'ir/, (Dia.) سَجايِر /sagaayir/ cigarette; (Irq.Gul.) جِيگارَة /jigaara/ (Gul. also جِيگارَة /jiigaara/) pl. جَيگايِر /jigaayir/

يحتوي دخان السجائر على مواد ثبت فعلها المسرطن للخلايا — The smoke of cigarettes contains material that has been proven to cause cancer in cells

76 | 633 |

3155 بَذْل *n.* spending, expenditure; exertion, effort; donating

بدأت الولايات المتحدة تحركا مكثفا لحث باكستان على بذل مزيد من الجهود في مجال ما يسمى الحرب

— The United States has begun intensive activities to urge Pakistan to exert more efforts in the area of the so-called "war on terrorism"

80 | 598 |

3156 اِتَّسَمَ *v. VIII* to be characterized بـ by

نحن نفتقر إلى المفاهيم الأخلاقية التي تتسم بالنظام الكامل الذي يجب التفاعل معه لبناء إنسان حقيقي — We lack the moral concepts which characterize a complete system which must be dealt with to build a true human being

73 | 659 |

3157 حِلْف *n.* alliance, treaty, pact

بالنسبة لإيران أنا أريد أن أؤكد أن سوريا ليست في حلف مع إيران، سوريا ضد الأحلاف وضد الجبهات — In regard to Iran, I want to stress that Syria is not in an alliance with Iran, Syria is against alliances and against fronts

67 | 720 |

3158 حَصِيلَة *n.* result, outcome; sum, total count; revenue

كان يقدم له حصيلة تجاربه الطويلة — He presented to him the outcome of his long experience

74 | 646 |

3159 هَبَطَ *v. I (i,u)* to drop, fall, decline; (fig.) to fall (night, darkness); to land (aircraft)

عانيت قبل فترة من اختلال في ضغط الدم، فكان يهبط فجأة ومن ثم يعود للصعود المفاجئ تماما كسوق الأسهم — I suffered a while ago from a blood pressure imbalance; it would fall suddenly and then suddenly go back to rising, just like the stock market

77 | 622 |

3160 كُلْفَة *n.* cost, expenditure, overhead

من أهم اهداف القانون الجديد تقليل كلفة الخدمات الصحية — Among the most important goals of the new law is to decrease expenses of health services

65 | 738 |

3161 غُضُون *n.* interim; في غُضُون during

حصد العنف المتواصل في العراق في غضون الساعات الأربع والعشرين الماضية نحو ٣٢ عراقيا على الأقل

— Continued violence in Iraq during the last twenty-four hours claimed about 32 Iraqis, at least

73 | 651 |

3162 مَسْكَن *n.* pl. مَساكِن residence, domicile
أولادنا يكبرون ونحن بحاجة إلى مسكن خاص بنا
وحدنا — Our children are growing up, and we need a private house for us alone

76 | 630 |

3163 قُرابَة *prep.* almost, nearly
هي أكبر مدن جنوب إفريقيا، يسكنها قرابة المليونين
— It is the biggest of the South African cities, inhabited by nearly two million

76 | 627 |

3164 اِسْتَجابَ *v. X* to accept لـ (an invitation); to grant لـ (a request); to comply with لـ (sb's demands); to respond to لـ (medical treatment)
أثبتت دراسة علمية حديثة أن الأعصاب المسئولة عن الإحساس بالألم تستجيب لأحماض الكبريت الموجودة في الثوم — A recent scientific study confirmed that the nerves responsible for feeling pain respond to the sulphuric acid present in garlic

83 | 572 |

3165 رُوحِيّ *adj.* spiritual; alcoholic
غاندي هو الأب الروحي للهند المستقلة — Gandhi is the spiritual father of independent India

81 | 586 |

3166 قُدّام *prep.* (MSA) (قُدّامَ) in front of; (Egy.Lev.) /'uddaam/, (Irq.) /giddaam/, (Gul.) /jiddaam/
خرجت لقيت زحمة قدام الباب، وبوليس، وسمعت ناس بتقول أنه واحد سارق حاجة من المحل — I went out and encountered a crowd in front of the door, and police, and I heard people saying "an Egyptian"; it became clear that someone stole something from the store

47 | 1004 | +spo

3167 قَرُبَ *v. I (u)* and قَرِبَ (a) to approach, draw near
الطريق طويلة نسبيا تستغرق ما يقرب من ثلاث ساعات — The road is relatively long, lasting about three hours

81 | 586 |

3168 فاشِل *adj.* failed, failing, unsuccessful; a failure
أديسون مخترع الكهرباء قام بـ ١٨٠٠ محاولة فاشلة — Edison, the inventor of electricity, had 1,800 failed attempts before he achieved his splendid accomplishment

81 | 587 |

3169 اِبْتِعاد *n.* avoiding, moving or staying away; distancing oneself (عن from)
الخروج عن الروتين اليومي يساعد في رفع المعنويات والابتعاد عن التوتر والاكتئاب — Going outside of daily routine helps raise morale and keeps away tension and depression

80 | 587 |

3170 فَسَّر *v. II* to explain, interpret sth (لـ for sb)
لن يكون بمقدوره أن يفسر لها ما يفعله.. هو نفسه لا يفهم — He will never be able to explain to her what he did...he himself does not understand

80 | 590 |

3171 قَناعَة *n.* conviction, belief; عَن قناعة out of conviction; على قناعة convinced
في لحظة وبكل الصدق وصلت إلى درجة كبيرة من القناعة ورضا النفس بأن كل شيء قسمة ونصيب — In a moment, and with all truth, I arrived to a large degree of assurance and satisfaction of soul that everything is fate

82 | 575 |

3172 شَكا *v. I (u)* to complain إلى to sb; من about; to suffer من from
حضر ولي أمر طالبة يشكو من مدرس الفصل الذي حاول معاقبة ابنته لأنها مشاغبة — The guardian of a student came to complain to the classroom teacher who tried to punish his daughter because she was an agitator

78 | 607 |

3173 باكستانِيّ *n./adj.* Pakistani
كان الجيش الباكستاني أعلن سيطرته التامة على المسجد والمدرسة الملحقة به — The Pakistani army announced its complete control over the mosque and the school attached to it

61 | 776 |

3174 وَحْش *n. pl.* وُحُوش beast
كانت تقاتل بقوة فائقة، كأنها وحش ضار — She used to fight with superior strength as if she were a ferocious beast
74 | 634 | +lit

3175 اِسْتَيْقَظَ *v. X* to wake up; to be alert
رأيته في منتصف الليل، كنت نائمة، استيقظت على صوت بكائه، فتحت عيني فرأيته — I saw him in the middle of the night, I woke up to the sound of his crying, opened my eyes, and saw him
71 | 658 | +lit

3176 لَطِيف *adj.* kind, gentle, polite, nice; يا لَطيف oh my! wow!
إنه شاب لطيف وأنيق ومهذب — He is a nice, chic, courteous young man
79 | 591 |

3177 اِعْتِذار *n.* apology; excuse
بعض النساء يعتقدن أن في الاعتذار تقليلا من كرامتهن — Some women believe that apologizing lessens their dignity
82 | 574 |

3178 مَأْزِق *n.* impasse, predicament; dilemma, crisis
للأسف الشديد أن المواطن العربي أصبح في مأزق: إما البقاء تحت هيمنة الأنظمة الفاسده والديكتاتوريه العسكريه وإما التعاون مع أمريكا القذرة للإطاحه بتلك الأنظمه — Unfortunately the Arab citizen has come to an impasse: either stay under the domination of corrupt, dictatorial, military regimes, or cooperate with filthy America to get rid of those regimes
72 | 647 |

3179 تَدَهُوُر *n.* decline, deterioration; fall, drop
هذا التدهور الاقتصادي لم يحصل منذ زمن — This economic deterioration has not happened for a long time
73 | 637 |

3180 تَخَلِّي *n.* relinquishment, surrender, renunciation (مِن) of
أغلب هؤلاء الأطفال ليسوا أيتاما، بل تخلى ذووهم عنهم — Most of these children are not orphans, rather their families abandoned them
76 | 617 |

3181 تَزايُد *n.* (gradual) growth, increase, rise
لقد بات تزايد أعداد مرضى السرطان حقيقة ملحوظة لا تحتاج إلى من يثبتها — The increase in the number of cancer patients became a noticeable fact no one needs to prove
78 | 596 |

3182 تَواصَلَ *v. VI* to maintain, pursue (efforts); to maintain mutual contacts or intercommunication مع with
سألها عن رقم هاتفها الجوال وعن بريدها الإلكتروني ليستطيع أن يتواصل معها حين عودتها إلى بلدها — He asked her about her mobile telephone number and about her email so he could contact her when she returned to her country
76 | 616 |

3183 إنشالله and إن شالله (Dia.) /'inshaLLa/ *adv.* hopefully, Lord willing (MSA إِنْ شاءَ الله)
انشالله الفوز يكون مانشستراوي — Hopefully the victory will be to Manchester
24 | 1930 | +for

3184 تِلْوَ *prep.* after, followed by
لقد ظل يحرز النجاح تلو الآخر حتى عين مستشارا فى الخارجية — He kept achieving one success after another until he was appointed an adviser in the Foreign Ministry
79 | 589 |

3185 خَطِر *adj.* serious, grave, critical; dangerous, risky
نسب الإصابة بمرض السرطان في دول الخليج تعطي مؤشرات خطرة ولم يظهر علينا احد ليعترف بالأسباب والمسببات — The proportion of cancer cases in the Gulf countries is giving danger signals, and no one has come to acknowledge the reasons or causes
84 | 552 |

3186 تَحْكِيم *n.* arbitration; لَجْنَة تَحْكِيم jury
وقد حرصت هيئة المهرجان على أن يكون أعضاء لجنة التحكيم من الشخصيات المعروفة في مجالات اختصاصها — The festival organization has insisted on the members of the jury (the judging committee) being well known personalities in the fields of their specialization
70 | 666 |

3187 لَعْنَة *n.* curse, oath; enchantment, spell

لا يمكن أن نتخلص من تلك اللعنة الأبدية التي
تفصل الأخلاق عن السياسة — We can't rid
ourselves of this eternal curse which divides
morals from politics

62 | 743 | +lit

3188 خال *n.* maternal uncle

الفطايري أفندي متجوز بنت خال الأستاذ عبد
الحليم الدغيدي — Al-Fatayri Effendi is married
to the niece of Professor Abd Al-Halim
Al-Daghidi

61 | 754 |

3189 فاجَأَ *v. III* to surprise sb (بـ with); (frequently
pass.) فُوجِئَ to be surprised (بـ by)

عند أول محطة للوقود فوجئت أن سعر الصفيحة من
البنزين قد تضاعف منذ ليلة أمس — At the first
fueling station I was surprised that the price of
a can of gas had doubled since last night

77 | 605 |

3190 فَوْرِيّ *adj.* immediate, instant; direct

لابد من الوقف الفوري لإطلاق النار — There
needs to be an immediate cease-fire

67 | 694 |

3191 مَبيع *adj.* sold; *n.* مَبيعات sales

بلغت حصة الولايات المتحدة من مبيعات الأسلحة
إلى دول العالم الثالث نحو ٩٪ من المجموع الكلي سنة
١٩٨٦ — The share of the United States in
weapons sales to countries of the third world
reached 9% of the total in the year 1986

65 | 715 |

3192 حَريص *adj.* mindful, careful, protective على of;
eager, desirous على for, keen على on

كنت حريصة منذ صغرى على أداء فروض ديني — I
have been careful, since I was young, to fulfill
the requirements of my religion

82 | 566 |

3193 مَجَّاناً *n.* بالمَجَّان and مَجَّاناً for free, free of
charge

مازالت الدولة تقدم الخدمات العامة مجانا (الصحة،
التعليم) وتدعم أسعار العديد من السلع — The
state is still offering general services for free
(heath, education) and supports the prices
of a lot of products

85 | 544 |

3194 سَمْع *n.* hearing

يستخدم الكلب في مرافقة فاقدي السمع والبصر
وذوي الاحتياجات الخاصة — Dogs are used to
accompany those who have lost their sight or
hearing, and those who have special needs

75 | 613 |

3195 مُسْرِع *adj.* hurrying, hastening

وصل صوت الموسيقى إلى دميان في البيت، فجاء
مسرعا إلى المحطة ليروعه المشهد الجميل للجنود
السعداء العازفين — The sound of music
reached Dumyan at home, so he came quickly
to the station to be amazed at the beautiful
scene of happy soldiers playing music

63 | 734 | +lit

3196 مُغامَرَة *n.* adventure, risk

دفع شعب العراق من أطفال وعجائز ومرضى ثمن
مغامرة النظام الديكتاتوري لصدام حسين — The
people of Iraq, from children, to the aged, to
the sick, paid the price of the adventures of
the dictatorial regime of Saddam Hussein

78 | 591 |

3197 عائِليّ *adj.* family, domestic, familial

الصراع الأخوي هو بداية يعرفها كل منا في علاقته
العائلية الأولى، عندما يرزق الأهل بمولود جديد —
Sibling rivalry is a beginning which all of us
know in our first family relationships, when
the family is blessed with a new child

85 | 543 |

3198 ذَكَّرَ *v. II* to remind sb

الموقف الذي نمر به الآن يذكرني بمشاهد فلم
سينمائي سبق لي أن رأيته — The situation which
we are passing through now reminds me of
scenes from a movie which I had previously seen

83 | 555 |

3199 تَعَلُّم *n.* learning, study

الانسان في حاجة الى التعلم، والتعلم يأتي من اكتشاف
الاخطاء — People are in need of education,
and education comes from discovering errors

83 | 555 |

3200 فَرِحَ *v. I (a)* to rejoice; to be happy بـ/لـ
about sth

شكرا لكم لأنكم نشرتم اسمي في المجلة، وقد
فرحت كثيرا عندما رأيت اسمي — Thank you for

publishing my name in the magazine, I was very happy when I saw my name

78 | 588 |

3201 سَوِيّ *adj.* straight, correct; سَوِيّاً together, jointly

سنقوم بالاتصالات مع مجموعاتنا من أجل العمل — سويا لمستقبل مشترك We will get in touch with our groups in order to work together on a shared future

81 | 569 |

3202 نِضال *n.* struggle, battle

إن الديمقراطية الحقة هي نتاج نضال الشعوب — True democracy is the result of the struggle of peoples

66 | 691 |

3203 ناهِيكَ *part.* not to mention

أبو صابر محتاج إلى من يعيله ويخدمه، ناهيك عن — تحمل تكاليف العلاج الباهظة التي لا بد منها Abu Sabar needs someone to provide for him and serve him, not to mention to bear the immense costs of the treatment that he needs

72 | 637 |

3204 أَدِيب *n.* pl. أُدَباء author, writer

حسين فوزي ١٩٠٠ ـ ١٩٨٨ صديق توفيق الحكيم الدائم وأحد الأدباء والمفكرين الرواد منذ الربع الأول من القرن العشرين — Hussein Fawzi (1900–1988) was Tawfiq Al-Hakim's constant friend and one of the pioneering writers and thinkers since the first quarter of the twentieth century

72 | 638 |

3205 خَيّ (Lev.) *n.* brother; خَيِّي my brother, خَيَّك your brother, خَيُّه his brother; ياخيو /ya-xayyo/ hey buddy, hey bro'

مبارح قضينا نهار أنا وخيي رحنا عالبحر — Yesterday my brother and I spent the day and went to the beach

28 | 1648 | +for +spo

3206 عُود *n.* lute; stick, match stick; aloe plant; دُهْن العُود aloe gel; body, physique: طَرِيّ/ناعِم العُود frail, delicate

مشروع توطين اللاجئين الفلسطينيين في لبنان قد — يشكل عود الثقاب لإضرام نار الفتنة من جديد The project for settling Palestinian refugees in

Lebanon might represent the matchstick for lighting the fire of civil war once again

73 | 625 |

3207 أَعانَ *v. IV* to assist, support sb/sth

إن وقعت في ضيق لن تجد من يعينك — If you fall into problems, you won't find anyone to assist you

81 | 565 |

3208 مِيلِيشيا *n.* pl. مِلِيشيات , مِيلِيشيات and مِيلِيشيا militia

تعود الأسباب الرئيسية للعنف إلى ميليشيات مدعومة من الخارج وخصوصا من إيران وسوريا — The principle reasons for violence can be traced to the militias supported from abroad and particularly by Iran and Syria

54 | 840 |

3209 إِنْفاق *n.* spending, expenditure, disbursement; expenses

أبوه يرفض الإنفاق عليه.. يجب أن أوفر له حياة كريمة — His father refuses to spend money on him...I must provide him with a dignified life

70 | 652 |

3210 جَوْهَر *n.* pl. جَواهِر gem, jewel; (fig.) essence, substance, gist; heart, crux, core

أؤمن بأن جوهر الإنسانية الإسلامية هو العلاقة بين الخالق والمخلوق — I believe that the core of Islamic humanity is the relationship between the creator and the creature

77 | 592 |

3211 وَلاء *n.* loyalty, allegiance

الطوائف المذهبية والخصوصيات العرقية لا تقدم الولاء للوطن على الولاء للمذهب أو الخصوصية — The confessional sects and the racial groups do not put loyalty to the motherland over loyalty to the sect or group

79 | 578 |

3212 سِيناريو *n.* scenario

هو عقيد متقاعد وضع قبل عشرين عاما سيناريو غزو العراق الذي استفاد منه الجنرال تومي فرانكس — He is a retired colonel who twenty years ago laid out a scenario for the invasion of Iraq which General Tommy Franks benefitted from

70 | 651 |

3213 اِسْتَعَادَ v. X to recover, regain, reclaim sth
أتمنى أن يعود السلام للعالم وأن يستعيد الحب مكانه
ا — في القلوب لنعيش في عالم أجمل وأكثر أمانا
hope that peace will return to the world and
that love will regain its place in hearts
so that we can live in a more beautiful world,
and a safer one
79 | 579 |

3214 مَيَّزَ v. II to distinguish sth/sb, to set sth/sb
apart (عن from the rest); to differentiate,
tell the difference بين between
اللواء علاء مقلد مدير عام النادي أكد أن أهم ما
يميز الفريق الروح الجماعية بين اللاعبين والحرص
على مصلحة النادي — General Alaa Maqlid, the
general director of the club, stressed that the
most important thing that characterizes the
team is the collective spirit between the
players, and the insistence on the good of
the club
77 | 590 |

3215 تَدْرِيجِيّ adj. gradual, progressive; تَدْرِيجِيّاً
gradually
أما في المدرسة الابتدائية فيبدأ حجم النص يزداد
تدريجيا في الصفحات على حساب الصور بحسب
تقدم سن الطفل — In elementary school the
quantity of pages of text increases gradually at
the expense of pictures, according to the age
of the child
79 | 581 |

3216 خَفَّفَ v. II to lower, lessen, decrease sth; to
alleviate, mitigate مِن sth
فكر في شيء يقوله يخفف من حدة دميان وانفعاله —
He thought of something to say that would
calm Dumyan
82 | 556 |

3217 تَمَرُّد n. rebellion, insurgency, insurrection
ان كل جيل جديد من طبيعته التمرد على القديم،
وتأسيس حساسية جديدة ولغة مختلفة وكتابة مغايرة
— It is natural for every new generation to
rebel against the old, and to establish a new
sensitivity and a different language and a
different writing
74 | 614 |

3218 نَتَجَ v. I (i) to result, arise من/عن from
هذه الأزمة أثرت بشكل كبير على الاقتصاد العالمي،
حيث نتج عنها مشكلتان كبيرتان هما البطالة
والتضخم — This crisis influenced the world
economy in a big way, such that two major
problems resulted from it, unemployment and
inflation
72 | 634 |

3219 تَلَوُّث n. pollution, contamination
التلوث الهوائي يعتبر من أكثر أشكال التلوث البيئي
انتشارا — Air pollution is considered to be one
of the most widespread forms of environmental
pollution
65 | 696 |

3220 مِيثاق n. treaty, pact, charter
نص ميثاق هيئة الأمم المتحدة على تحريم الاضطهاد
العنصري والتفريق بين الأجناس — The United
Nations Charter stipulated the banning of
racial persecution or any differentiation
between the races
69 | 657 |

3221 نَظافَة n. cleanliness
مع الخميس الأول لزيارة أبى وجدت الشارع أكثر
نظافة، ولا يوجد أثر للتراب — On the first
Thursday of my father's visit I found the
street to be cleaner, with no trace of dirt
76 | 597 |

3222 هُبُوط n. drop, fall, decline; descent; landing
(aircraft); (med.) prolapse
أوروبا تمنع طائرات إسرائيلية تحمل العتاد العسكري
من الهبوط على أراضيها — Europe prevents
Israeli planes carrying military equipment from
landing on its lands
76 | 596 |

3223 مَسِيح n. messiah; المَسِيح the Messiah (Bible
and Qur'an)
الإيمان المسيحي مبني على سر الفداء أي صلب السيد
المسيح وقيامته من الموت — The Christian faith is
built on the mystery of redemption, in other
words on the crucifixion of the Lord Christ
and his resurrection from death
63 | 715 |

3224 سَتَر *v. I (u,i)* to veil, cover, hide sth

العوده للدين بتشريعاته السمحه هو الحل الوحيد
لهذه المشكله والله يستر على بنات المسلمين —
Returning to religion with its tolerant laws is
the only solution to this problem, and may
God protect the daughters of the Muslims

64 | 704 | +for

3225 عَرَق *n.* sweat, perspiration; araq (alcoholic
drink similar to ouzo)

أخذ وجهها يتقلص وتصبب منها عرق غزير،
وبدأت تشهق وكأنها تتنفس بصعوبة — Her face
began to contract and copious amounts of
sweat poured from her, and she began to
sniffle as if she was breathing with difficulty

72 | 627 |

3226 مُتَزَوِّج *adj.* married (مِن to)

أنا مولود في مصر، وابني متزوج من ثلاث زوجات
— I was born in Egypt, and my son is married
to three wives

76 | 599 |

3227 حَصْر *vn.* encirclement, containment; bounds,
limits; لا حَصْرَ لَهُ unlimited, immense

نسوق لحضرتكم – على سبيل المثال لا الحصر – ما
يلاقيه الأقباط في مصر يوميا من الازدراء بالمسيحية
— We cite for you, to give an example and not
an exhaustive list, that which the Copts in
Egypt receive daily in the way of contempt for
Christianity

73 | 620 |

3228 وِقَايَة *n.* prevention; precaution; protection

قامت وزارة الفلاحة والتنمية الريفية مؤخرا بتعزيز
إجراءات الوقاية من مرض إنفلونزا الطيور — The
Ministry of Agriculture and Rural Development
recently strengthened the protective measures
against bird flu

68 | 661 |

3229 راعِي *n.* guardian; patron, sponsor; steward

من حق الرعية أن يعدل فيها الراعي ومن حق الراعي
أن تطيعه الرعية — It is the right of the
congregation to change the pastor, and the
right of the pastor that the congregation obey
him

76 | 595 |

3230 بِئْر *fem.n.* well, spring; (Dia. بير /biir/ masc.)

ليس أمامنا إلا أن نتعاون جميعا على سحب
الماء من بئر القرية حتى ينشف — We have
no choice but to all cooperate on getting
the water from the well of the village so
it can dry

73 | 620 |

3231 مُضِيّ *n.* passing (of time); expiration
(deadline); المُضِي قُدُماً proceeding,
continuing (في with)

شدد قماطي على المضي في طريقنا للوصول الى
حكومة وحدة وطنية — Qumati stressed
going forward to reach a national unity
government

83 | 545 |

3232 تَبَنَّى *v. V* to adopt sth; to claim responsibility
for sth; to be built

يجب أن نتبنى استراتيجية أذكى — We need to
adopt a smarter strategy

70 | 640 |

3233 إقْرَار *n.* ratification, confirmation

يا آنسة.. هذا اقرار ستوقعين عليه لتكوني مسؤولة
عن اية أضرار تظهر في المستقبل — Miss...this is
a ratification you will sign to be responsible
for any damages which appear in the future

64 | 699 |

3234 صَرَفَ *v. I (i)* to spend, change (money); to
dismiss, fire sb; to divert sth (عن from)

هو كريم سخي لا يهمه أن يصرف كل ما يأتيه في يومه
— He is generous, not being concerned if he
spends everything that comes to him in a day

91 | 493 |

3235 حَشْد *vn.* (mil.) buildup, mobilization;
n. crowd, gathering

أهابت جامعة الدول العربية بالمجتمع الدولي التحرك
من أجل حشد كل القوى من أجل تجريم استخدام
القنابل العنقودية واستهداف المدنيين — The Arab
League appealed to the international
community to move to mobilize all forces
in order to criminalize the use of cluster
bombs and targeting civilians

76 | 594 |

3236 يَتِيم *n. pl.* أيْتَام orphan; *adj.* orphaned; unique, sole, only (existing)

أشكر كل من ساهموا في مسح دموع الأيتام التي أسألها طاغية القرن العشرين — I thank all those who have participated in wiping the tears of the orphans which the tyrant of the twentieth century caused to flow

76 | 590 |

3237 حَرّ *n.* warmth, heat; *adj.* warm, hot, spicy

هل يخطر ببالك أن أمواج الحر والبرد والأعاصير هي ليست من أعمال الشيطان وإنما تمثل الطقس ويمكن فهمها عقلانيا ولا دخل لله فيها؟ — Did it occur to you that the heat and cold waves, and the hurricanes, are not the works of the devil, but rather represent the weather, and it is possible to understand them intellectually, and that God has nothing to do with them?

76 | 590 |

3238 بتاع (Egy.) *poss.adj.* (fem. بتاعة /bitaa9it/, pl. بتوع) belonging to; connected to; associated with; about; (with pron.) بتاعي (fem. بتاعتي) mine; *n.* البتاع the doodad, the whatever

رحت امبارح على المركز الثقافي المصري.. قريت كل الجرايد والمجلات بتاعة الشهر اللي فات وكلت فول وطعمية وبصارة وعدس — I went to the Egyptian Cultural Center yesterday...I read all the newspapers and magazines from last month and I ate fuul and ta'miyya and bisara and lentils

33 | 1348 | +spo

3239 مَعِيشَة *n.* livelihood, subsistence; life, living

أن التنمية الصناعية ليست هدفا لذاته، ولكنها وسيلة لتحسين معيشة المواطن وتوزيع الدخل وزيادة استفادة العاملين — Industrial growth is not a goal in and of itself, but it is a means to improve the livelihood of the citizen and to distribute income and increase the benefit of the workers

84 | 536 |

3240 بَعْد (Lev.Irq.Gul.) *adv.* (with pron.) still, (not) yet; بعدها ما في البيت she's still at home, بعدها ما she hasn't arrived yet; بعدني I am still, وصلت I haven't yet

وصلتوا بغداد؟ – لأ، بعدنا في الأردن — Did you reach Baghdad? – No, we're still in Jordan

11 | 3774 |

3241 أتَمّ *v. IV* to complete, finish, conclude sth

فقد أصبح اليوم رجلا، لقد أتم عامه السابع عشر — ومع ذلك يظن أبواه أنه مازال طفلا — Today he has become a man, he finished his seventeenth year and despite this, his parents think that he is still a child

89 | 505 |

3242 نَسِيج *n.* fabric, tissue, textile

إن رحيل الأصدقاء والمقربين يمزق نسيج حياتنا، كما أن عبء الحزن لا يخف أبدا — The departure of friends and relatives tears the fabric of our lives, and the burden of sorrow never lightens

79 | 566 |

3243 مَجْهُود *adj.* expended (efforts); *n.* efforts, endeavors

تفيد الرياضة المائية من يشعرون بالتعب من جراء أقل مجهود رياضي، فهي تساعد على تنظيم التنفس وتنظيم الدورة الدموية — Water sports benefit those who feel tired from lack of physical activity, since they help regulate breathing and blood circulation

75 | 594 |

3244 تَأْييد *n.* support, assistance; approval

كانت واثقة من تأييد أبويها لها — She was certain of her parents' support of her

67 | 668 |

3245 شُهْرَة *n.* reputation, fame

الشهرة ليست مقياسا لنجاح الأديب.. هناك أدباء مشهورون بلا قيمة — Fame is not a measure of the success of the writer...There are famous writers of no value

81 | 553 |

3246 تَنافُس *n.* competition, rivalry

المباراة النهائية جرت بين الاتحادين العربي والسعودي لكرة السلة بعد اسبوعين من التنافس جمع عشرة منتخبات عربية — The final match took place between the Arab and Saudi Basketball Federations after two weeks of competition which brought together ten national Arab teams

80 | 554 |

3247 عَضَلَة *n. pl.* -aat muscle

أفضل الرياضات على الاطلاق المشي فهو يقوي العضلات كلها — The best of the sports,

absolutely, is walking, since it strengthens
all the muscles

75 | 594 |

3248 غَيْرَة and غِيرَة *n.* jealousy; zeal
الرجل الغيور قد يتفنن في اختراع طرق تعبيره عن
الغيرة، وقد يصل به الأمر أحياناً إلى حد منعها من
الخروج — The jealous man can be quite
artistic in inventing ways to express his
jealousy, and it could reach the point,
sometimes, of forbidding her to leave the
house

71 | 627 |

3249 حَدَّث *v. II* to tell sb, speak to sb (عن about);
to narrate (esp. a Hadith)
كان يجلس في المقهى يحدث الناس عن عجائب الدنيا
التي يطلع عليها في الصحف — He was sitting in
the coffee house telling the people about the
wonders of the world he was finding out about
in the newspapers

68 | 657 |

3250 عَقْلِيّ *adj.* mental, intellectual; rational
إعدام المصابين بأمراض عقلية خطيرة انتهاك
للمعايير الدولية المتبعة على نطاق واسع في هذا
الشأن — Executing people who suffer from
serious mental diseases is a violation of
international standards widely followed
in this matter

80 | 554 |

3251 أَكاديمِيَّة *n.* academy
لقد انتخب عضواً في الأكاديمية الفرنسية لمساهمته
المهمة في الأدب الفرنسي — He was elected a
member of the French Academy for his
important contributions to French literature

65 | 682 |

3252 عايِش (Dia.) *a.p.* living, alive (to live)
حتى انا عايش في بيت أبوي — Even I am living
in my father's house

52 | 855 | +spo

3253 ضَرَّ *v. I (u)* to harm, injure ب sth (one's
health)
حافظي على نظافة شعرك لأن العرق والأوساخ تضر
بالشعر وتجعله باهتاً لا حياة فيه — Maintain the

cleanliness of your hair because sweat and dirt
harm the hair and make it dull and lifeless

75 | 590 |

3254 غارَة *n.* pl. -aat raid, foray
اشتعلت المدن الإنجليزية من الغارات الألمانية
The English cities were ablaze from the
German raids

63 | 707 |

3255 خَيْمَة *n.* pl. خِيام tent
البارحة بنينا على الشاطئ خيمة قصبية للسهر
فالصيف جاء — Yesterday we built a reed tent
on the beach for late night parties, since
summer has come

78 | 569 |

3256 مُتَفَرِّق *adj.* diverse, different, separate;
dispersed, scattered, sporadic
قتل ستة جنود أميركيين في هجمات متفرقة في العراق
اليوم — Six American soldiers were killed in
separate attacks in Iraq today

77 | 579 |

3257 مُوازَنَة *n.* budget; balance, comparison
كان سعر البرميل يعادل ٣٠ دولاراً، وعندما قفز الى
الضعف تضاعفت معه ازمة الموازنة التي تعاني من
عجز اصلاً — The price of a barrel was equal
to 30 dollars, and when it jumped to double
that, the budget crisis, which was suffering
from a deficit in the first place, doubled

55 | 801 |

3258 أُسْطُورَة *n.* pl. أَساطِير myth, fable; tale, legend
عشتار ليست أهم عندي من مريم، تلك أسطورة لمن
يهوى الميثولوجيا، أما هذه فحقيقة من لحم ودم
— Ishtar is not more important to me than
Maryam, the one is a myth for those who are
into mythology, but the other is a fact of flesh
and blood

70 | 633 |

3259 مُسْتَخْدَم *adj.* used, utilized, employed
تم القبض عليه، حيث عثر بحوزته على السلاح
المستخدم في الجريمة — He was arrested, at
which point they found in his possession the
weapon used in the crime

71 | 624 |

3260 تَنْظيف *n.* cleaning
أكدت جمعية أطباء الأسنان الأمريكية مرارا على ضرورة تنظيف فم الطفل الرضيع منذ أول أيام ولادته — The American Dental Association has stressed repeatedly the importance of cleaning the mouth of the nursing baby from birth onward
74 | 594 |

3261 زَعَمَ *v. I (u)* to allege, claim أنَّ/بِأَنَّ that
هذا الرجل الطيب، كما تزعم أنت، قد قتل أبي أمام عيني وعين أمي — This good man, as you claim, killed my father before my and my mother's eyes
77 | 570 |

3262 حِضْن *n. pl.* أَحْضان bosom; arms; في/بَيْنَ أَحْضانِ amidst, in the heart of
أحاسيس الطفل تتشكل بين أحضان أمه حيث يحس بالحب والطمأنينة والأمان — The feelings of the child are formed in the arms of his mother where he feels love, confidence, and security
74 | 593 |

3263 أَقْبَلَ *v. IV* to approach, draw near على sb/sth; to engage على in
قالت صاحبة محل للهدايا إن الشباب والأطفال يقبلون على شراء الدمى ذات اللون الأحمر — The owner of the gift shop said that young men and children are coming to buy the doll with the red color
72 | 613 | +lit

3264 بَحْرَينِيّ *n./adj.* Bahraini
يجب أن تعمل الحكومة البحرينية من خلال سيطرتها على وسائل الإعلام على تغيير العقلية البحرينية — The Bahraini government, by means of its control of the media, must change the Bahraini mentality
52 | 840 | +news

3265 طين *n.* clay; mud; زادَ الطِّينَ بِلَّةً to make things worse
كانت منازل المدينة مبنية من الطين الضارب إلى الصفرة — The houses of the city were built with clay that tended towards yellow
74 | 594 |

3266 مَقْطَع *n. pl.* مَقاطِع section; selection, excerpt
أعجبت جدا بهذا المقطع من قصيدتك — I was extremely pleased with this section of your poem
74 | 590 |

3267 سُخْرِيَّة *n.* sarcasm, cynicism; ridicule
انه يتعامل معه بسخرية واضحة — He deals with him with a clear sarcasm
57 | 769 | +lit

3268 مُشابه *adj.* similar
ان الطفلين كانا يعانيان من اعراض مشابهة لتلك التى يسببها فيروس انفلونزا الطيور — The two children were suffering similar symptoms to those caused by bird flu
82 | 537 |

3269 سائِل *n. pl.* سَوائِل fluid, liquid
على المسافرين بالطائرات تناول كميات كبيرة من السوائل، خاصة الماء — Air travelers need to drink a lot of liquids, especially water
64 | 684 |

3270 سُلَّم *n.* ladder; stairs, staircase; scale
صعدنا السلم ووصلنا إلى ساحة المسجد وأقيمت الصلاة — We went up the stairs and arrived at the courtyard of the mosque, and prayer was held
84 | 518 |

3271 مُمْتَدّ *adj.* stretching, extending; spreading
عدد الذين يدرسون اللغة العربية ازداد سريعا في الفترة الممتدة بين عامي ١٩٩٨ و٢٠٠٢ — The number of those who study Arabic increased rapidly in the period extending between 1998 and 2002
74 | 587 |

3272 خَلَص (Lev.) *interj.* enough, OK, that's it, that settles it
طيب خلص سكتنا — OK...fine...we'll be quiet
14 | 2959 |

3273 اِسْتَنَدَ *v. VIII* to support, lean on, rely on إلى sth
لم تكن لك أمنية غير الإنجاب.. ولد تستند إليه في كهولتك، يرعاك في شيخوختك — Your only hope

is to give birth...a boy you will rely on in your
middle age, and who will care for you in your
old age

72 | 604 |

3274 سَرَى *v. I (i)* to flow, circulate, spread; to apply
(a law) to على

سرت الهتافات سريان النار في الهشيم وتمددت الثورة،
وانتشرت الشائعات — The cries spread like
wildfire in the straw, and the revolt extended
and the rumors spread

69 | 635 | +lit

3275 خَفْض *n.* lowering, decreasing; reduction,
diminution

يعمل على خفض نسبة الدهون والكوليسترول في
الدم — It works on decreasing the percentage
of fat and cholesterol in the blood

70 | 620 |

3276 مُفْتَرَض *adj.* assumed, presumed, supposed,
alleged

الحجرة فارغة، لأن حجرة مثلها ليس من المفترض أن
يكون فيها كرسي أو طاولة — The room is empty,
because a room like this should not have a
chair or a table in it

75 | 579 |

3277 فِراق *n.* parting, farewell, going away

هل تقدر على فراق ابنتها الوحيدة؟ — Are you
able to be separated from your only daughter?

61 | 713 |

3278 كَتِف *fem.n.* shoulder

وضعت يدها على كتفه وقالت: لا تقلق — She put
her hand on his shoulder and said: don't worry

63 | 691 | +lit

3279 مَسَكَ *v. I (u)* to grab, hold sth or ب sth

لماذا تمسك الكتاب بالمقلوب هكذا؟ — Why are
you holding the book upside down like that?

86 | 508 |

3280 تَنَوُّع *n.* variety, diversity

في تلك الصالة المدهشة تفتحت حواسكم على عوالم
بالغة التنوع والغرابة — In this surprising hall
your sensitivities are opened to extremely
diverse and strange worlds

70 | 625 |

3281 مُنْشَأَة *n.* pl. مُنْشَآت facility, installation, plant

هناك محاولات لتخريب وتدمير بعض المنشآت
النفطية — There are attempts to destroy some
oil installations

63 | 692 |

3282 عَشْوائِيّ *adj.* random, indiscriminate,
arbitrary

علينا أن نتسلح بالشجاعة فنقول لا للسلوك
العشوائي الذي يقود إلى الكوارث — We must
arm ourselves with courage and say no to
random behavior which leads to catastrophes

74 | 586 |

3283 حَدّ *vn.* limiting, curbing من (sb's freedom,
power); stopping, halting, ending من sth

إنه يساعد على تقوية الشعر والحد من تساقطه —
It helps strengthen the hair and limits it
falling out

68 | 640 |

3284 مُنَظِّم *n.* organizer, sponsor; *adj.* organizing,
sponsoring

لم أجد أي شيء يتعلق بنظام العمل والعمال يعتبر
الدستور المنظم للحياة الوظيفية — I didn't find
anything related to the work and labor system
which would be considered the organizing
constitution for working life

74 | 590 |

3285 خَشْيَة *n.* fear, anxiety; concern, worry

خاف بشكل خاص من المرايا خشية أن تعكس يوما
وجها ليس هو وجهه — He was particularly afraid
of mirrors, fearing that one day they would
reflect some face other than his

83 | 526 |

3286 ذِراع *fem./masc.n.* pl. أَذْرُع arm; lever, crank

عندما يفقد الأخطبوط إحدى أذرعه الطويلة، تنمو
ذراع بديلة لها تدريجيا فيها بعد — When the
octopus loses one of its long arms, a substitute
arm grows in its place gradually thereafter

74 | 587 |

3287 قَدِير *adj.* capable, efficient; Omnipotent (God)

أنت مدرس قدير للأدب العربي — You are
a capable teacher of Arabic literature

66 | 654 |

3288 أَقْدَمَ *v. IV* to undertake, tackle, approach على sth

أقدمت قوات الاحتلال الاسرائيلي على الاعتداء على الأسرى بالضرب والغاز والرصاص — Israeli occupation forces attacked the prisoners with beatings and gas and bullets

82 | 528 |

3289 مِثالِيّ *adj.* ideal, perfect, exemplary, model

لقد أصبح العلاج الكيميائي هو العلاج المثالي لمعظم حالات الحمل خارج الرحم — Chemical treatment has become the ideal treatment for most cases of pregnancy outside the womb

79 | 544 |

3290 نَبَوِيّ *adj.* prophetic; relating to the Prophet Muhammad

الحديث النبوي الشريف يعتمد على رواة الأحاديث — The noble prophetic Hadith depends on the narrators of the Hadith

74 | 585 |

3291 هَيْمَنَة *n.* control, power, rule; supremacy, domination

لا أرى في الأمم المتحدة إلا هيئة مشلولة أقعدتها الهيمنة الأمريكية وشلها الفيتو الأمريكي — I don't see in the United Nations anything except a paralyzed organization which American hegemony has hobbled and which the American veto has paralyzed

65 | 666 |

3292 ارْتِكاب *n.* perpetration, commission (crime, error)

الخوف من الغد يدفع بعض الناس الى ارتكاب أخطاء تصل إلى الجريمة لان حياتهم لا تسير كما يحبون — Fear of tomorrow impels some people to commit sins which can reach the point of crimes because their lives are not going as they wished

77 | 558 |

3293 نَزْع *n.* removal; elimination; deposition

اتفق الفرقاء اللبنانيون سابقا على نزع السلاح الفلسطيني خارج المخيمات، وتنظيمه داخلها — The Lebanese groups had previously agreed to remove Palestinian arms outside of the camps, and to organize them inside the camps

79 | 545 |

3294 تَخْصِيص *n.* designation, specification; allocation, appropriation; reserving, earmarking

ويجري أيضا تخصيص أراض بأنحاء المحافظة لبناء وحدات سكنية مساحتها ٤٠ مترا تخصص لمعدومي الدخل والفقراء — Lands are also being designated in various parts of the governorate to build housing units whose area is 40 meters, designated for those of no income, and for the poor

71 | 610 |

3295 اخْتِصاص *n.* specialty, area of competence; jurisdiction, domain, area of responsibility

لا يحق لمجلس الأمن ان يتدخل في ما هو من اختصاص مجلس النواب اللبناني وبقية المؤسسات الدستورية اللبنانية — It is not right for the Security Council to intervene in something that is the province of the Lebanese parliament and the rest of the Lebanese constitutional organizations

78 | 552 |

3296 نَسَمَة *n.* person, soul (in a census)

سيتطلب تهجير ١,٧ مليون نسمة يعيشون في هذه المناطق — It will require the displacement of 7.1 million people living in this region

70 | 611 |

3297 تَوّ *n.* لِلتَّوّ immediately; (with pron.) تَوّهُ he has just (done sth)

لقد نهض للتو من نومه — He immediately got up from his sleep

63 | 679 | +spo

3298 غِنِيّ *n.* wealth, affluence; لا غِنَى عَنْهُ it is indispensable; نَحْنُ في غِنِيّ عَنْهُ we can do without it

يعني باختصار الغني يزداد غنى والفقير يموت — It means, in short, that the rich will get richer, and the poor man will die

77 | 560 |

3299 غِرار *n.* manner, way; haste

ما حدث في افغانستان على يد طالبان على غرار ما يحدث في غزة الآن — What happened in Afghanistan at the hands of the Taleban is similar to what is happening in Gaza now

70 | 615 |

3300 بِسْم، بِاسْم (بِاسْمِ اللهِ) *prep.phr.* in the Name of God

بسم الله الرحمن الرحيم إن شهر رمضان شهر العبادة والغفران — In the name of God, the merciful, the compassionate...The month of Ramadan is the month of worship and forgiveness

59 | 722 |

3301 إِقْناع *n.* persuasion, convincing; conviction, firm belief

أيعقل أن يعجز رجل بقوة فراس عن إقناع أهله بزواجه من فتاة قد سبق لها الارتباط برجل قبله؟ — Does it make sense that a man with the strength of a knight would be incapable of convincing his family of his marrying a girl who had had a previous attachment to a man before him?

78 | 552 |

3302 أَسْهَل *elat.* easier/easiest

أليست هناك طريقة أسهل وأكثر أمناً؟ — Isn't there an easier and more secure method?

83 | 515 |

3303 تَقْليل *n.* diminution, reduction, decrease

كشفت دراسة حديثة بأن التفاح قادر على تقليل مخاطر سرطان القولون والبروستاتا والرئة — A modern study has revealed that apples are able to lessen the dangers of cancer of the colon and the prostate and the lung

73 | 584 |

3304 بَلَى *interj.* certainly, sure, yes indeed; (Irq.Gul.) بَلَى yes, right, of course

ألم تذهب إليها من قبل؟ بلى، وقد وجدت أنها الأفضل — Haven't you gone to it before? – Yes, and I found that it was better

53 | 810 | +lit +spo

3305 كَفَّ *v. I (u)* to give up, do without sth; to refrain, abstain عن from; to prevent, keep sb عن from doing sth

وأنا لست مع المرأة التي تضع الحجاب وهي لا تكف عن الثرثرة وعن النميمة واغتياب الآخرين — I am not with the woman who puts on the head scarf, but does not stop chatting and gossiping and talking about others behind their backs

75 | 570 |

3306 تَخْفيض *vn.* lowering, reducing; *n. pl.* -aat reduction, decrease; discount

نجح في تخفيض معدل البطالة إلى أقل من ٤٪ — He succeeded in lowering the rate of unemployment to less than 4%

78 | 549 |

3307 حِصان *n.* horse

اعتقد الباحثون لسنين طويلة ان الحصان العربي الأصيل ظهر في أفريقيا — Researchers believed for many long years that the authentic Arabian horse appeared in Africa

76 | 562 |

3308 صُراخ *n.* shouting, screaming

سلطت عليه كشافات سيارات الإطفاء. أصوات الصراخ تأتي من تحت الأنقاض وأصوات استغاثة وأصوات ألم — The emergency vehicle headlights shone on him. The sounds of screaming were coming from under the rubble, and voices calling for help, and sounds of pain

77 | 558 |

3309 شَرَعَ *v. I (a)* to start, undertake في sth

لاحظ أن تلك الابنة شرعت في قضاء أوقات طويلة مع الألعاب الالكترونية بعد دخولها مدرسة يستخدم فيها الطلاب الكومبيوتر في أداء كل شيء تقريبا — He noticed that this daughter had began to spend long periods of time with electronic games after her entrance into a school in which students use computers in performing almost everything

77 | 557 |

3310 وِفاق *n.* agreement, accord; reconciliation

من دون وفاق لا وجود للبنان — Without a reconciliation, Lebanon does not exist

69 | 619 |

3311 جِنائيّ *adj.* criminal, penal

هناك فرق بين السجين السياسي والسجين الجنائي ويجب أن يكون هناك فرق أيضاً بين الجرم السياسي والجرم الجنائي — There is a difference between a political prisoner and a criminal prisoner, and there should be a difference also between a political crime and a criminal crime

61 | 694 |

3312 حَفْر *n.* digging, drilling; excavation

وزارة البترول والثروة المعدنية وعدد من الوزارات اتخذت آلية بعدم الحفر في أي موقع في السعودية دون الرجوع إلى وكالة الآثار — The Ministry of Petroleum and Mineral Wealth and a number of ministries took the step of not digging anywhere in Saudi Arabia without checking with the Antiquities Agency

78 | 543 |

3313 اتِّحَادِيّ *adj.* unionist, federal; of or related to Ittihad/Ittehad (sports club)

قال رئيس مجلس الاحتياط المركزي (البنك المركزي الأميركي) إن البنك مستعد لتخفيض الفائدة — The president of the Federal Reserve (the central American bank) said that the bank was prepared to lower the interest rate

55 | 770 |

3314 تَجَلَّى *v. V* to become clear, evident; to appear, manifest itself

وأشادت صاحبة السمو بالمعرض وبالمستوى الفني المتميز الذي تجلى في الأعمال واللوحات المعروضة — Her majesty praised the exhibition and the distinguished artistic level which was evident in the exhibited works and canvases

78 | 542 |

3315 مِيعَاد *n.* pl. مَوَاعِيد schedule, hours; appointed time; appointment, engagement; promise

قد قدمت عدة وعود زمنية لإنهاء اعمال المحطة وآخر هذه المواعيد هو شهر آذار المقبل ونتمنى ان يكون هذا الموعد نهائيا — Several promised target dates for the completion of the station were offered, and the latest of these times is the coming March, and we hope that this time will be final

80 | 531 |

3316 أَصْعَب *elat.* more/most difficult, harder/ hardest

ففي ظل ظروف امنية صعبة وسياسية أصعب كان لرامز اسماعيل الدور الفعال في التلاقي في ما بين جارتين اسلامية ومسيحية — In light of the difficult security and more difficult political circumstances, Ramez Ismail had the effective role in bringing his Muslim and Christian neighbors together

80 | 530 |

3317 حَسَّاسِيَّة *n.* sensitivity; allergy

يهدف الوصول للحقيقة وإعداد التقرير الشامل الذي يضع النقاط على الحروف في هذا الموضوع البالغ الحساسية والأهمية — He aims to reach the truth and to prepare a comprehensive report which will "dot the i's" of this extremely important and sensitive subject

66 | 635 |

3318 حَسْم *vn.* settling (a matter, dispute)

ليس شرطا أن يكون الحسم بالقتال، إن هناك خيارات متعددة — It is not a condition that it be decided by fighting, there are many choices

69 | 608 |

3319 تَمْهِيد *n.* preparation; facilitating, paving (the way); تَمْهِيداً لِـ in preparation for, paving the way for, in order to facilitate

ظل إمام المسجد يدرس عن تعدد الزوجات وعن الطلاق تمهيدا لخطبته — The Imam of the mosque kept studying about polygamy and about divorce, in preparation for his sermon

69 | 614 |

3320 مُؤَسِّس *adj.* founding, creating; constituent; *n.* founder, creator

بيل غيتس الشريك المؤسس لشركة «مايكروسوفت» عملاق صناعة البرمجيات في العالم — Bill Gates, a founding partner of the Microsoft company, is a giant of the software industry in the world

74 | 568 |

3321 حَثَّ *v. I (u)* to encourage, urge, incite sb على to do sth

كرزاي يحث باكستان على التعاون لمواجهة طالبان والقاعدة — Karzei urges Pakistan to cooperate in confronting the Taleban and Al-Qaeda

77 | 545 |

3322 سَواد *n.* blackness; سواد الناس masses, populace

تمنح بعض القبائل الافريقية المرأة لقب جميلة كلما زاد سواد بشرتها الذي يدل عندهم على نقاء الأصل — Some African tribes call a woman "pretty" the darker her skin becomes, darkness indicating for them a purity of origin

62 | 677 |

3323 فُؤاد *n.* heart; mind

استيقظت ذات صباح مكتئب النفس مغموم الفؤاد
— I woke up one day depressed in spirit and heart

51 | 818 | +lit

3324 حَليف *n./adj.* pl. حُلَفاء ally, allied

إن النجاح دائما يكون حليف المجتهد الذي يعرف قدراته وموهبته ويستثمرها في تقديم أعمال جيدة —
Success is always an ally of the diligent person who knows his abilities
and gifts and who invests them in offering good works

70 | 603 |

3325 قَلَّل *v. II* to lessen, reduce (مِن) sth; to diminish, downplay مِن sth

المشي اليومي لمدة نصف ساعة أو ساعة يقلل من إمكانية الإصابة بمرض السرطان بنسبة ١٨٪ —
Daily walking for a period of a half hour or an hour lessens the possibility of being stricken with cancer by 18%

72 | 581 |

3326 صَواب *adj.* correct, true

الإنسان الذي يتعلم عليه أن يتعلم من الصواب وكذلك عليه ان يستفيد من الخطأ — The person who wants to become educated should learn from the right and also he must benefit from errors

75 | 556 |

3327 جَبين *n.* forehead, brow

رصعت أم أحمد جبين ولدها الفتي بقبلة الوداع وهي تسلمه كوفية وعقال أبيه — Um Ahmad adorned the forehead of her young boy with a goodbye kiss, as she handed him the headdress and headband of his father

69 | 602 | +lit

3328 شُيُوعِيّ *n./adj.* Communist

ألم يكن عضوا في قيادة الحزب الشيوعي الفرنسي مدة طويلة؟ — Wasn't he a member of the leadership of the French Communist party for a long time?

59 | 709 |

3329 ضِعْف *n.* pl. أَضْعاف double, multiple; (with num.) (عَشَرة) أَضْعاف (ten) times

صدقيني أن ما أعانيه من الألم هو أضعاف ما تعانينه أنت — Believe me, what I am suffering from in the way of pain is double what you are suffering from

82 | 512 |

3330 جَعْل *n.* making (sb/sth do sth), causing (sb/sth to be sth); appointing; beginning (to do sth)

بإمكانهم استغلال سجل كلنتون لجعل هيلاري تبدو ضعيفة في مواجهة الإرهاب — They can exploit Clinton's record to make Hilary appear weak in facing terrorism

76 | 547 |

3331 إيقاف *n.* stopping, halting, detaining

تذكروا أنه ينبغي عدم إيقاف لصوم بأطعمة كالحليب واللحم والجبن والزبد والسمك — Remember that it is necessary to not break one's fast with foods like milk and meat and cheese and butter and fish

78 | 534 |

3332 اِعْتِراض *vn.* objection, opposition على to sth

القوانين الرياضية صدرت لتطبق، ومن لديه أي اعتراض فليتقدم بالتعديل الذي يراه مناسبا ضمن الاطر الدستورية — The sports laws were issued to be applied, and anyone who has an objection can submit any amendment he finds appropriate in the constitutional framework

81 | 516 |

3333 عَبَرَ *v. I (u)* to cross (border, street)

حقا هناك من يعبد البقر في الهند، وإذا حدث وعبرت بقرة في الشارع تتوقف لها المواصلات والناس — In fact, there are those who worship cows in India, and if a cow happens to cross the street, traffic and people stop for it

75 | 554 |

3334 اِسْتِخْبار *n.* inquiry; اِسْتِخْبارات intelligence service, secret service

كشف كتاب اسرائيلي جديد ان جهاز الاستخبارات الاسرائيلي «الموساد» هو الذي اغتال القيادي — A new Israeli book revealed that the Israeli Intelligence Service (Mosad) is the one who assassinated the leader

59 | 704 |

3335 خَطَّطَ *v. II* to plan, make plans لِ to do sth; to draw lines, define (borders)

عليه أن يخطط حياته كما يريدها، لا كما تريدها أنت — He must plan out his life as he wants, not as you want

79 | 528 |

3336 سَهْرَة *n.* soiree, evening gathering

فقد أعددت لك سهرة خاصة على عشاء خاص في البلاد — I have prepared for you a special evening at a private dinner that will be attended by the most amusing clown in the country

63 | 655 |

3337 إِسْقَاط *n.* overthrowing (government); bringing down, shooting down (aircraft)

إن المرء يجد لذة وراحة نفسية في إسقاط عيبه، والتحرر من وطأة هذا العيب على نفسه — People find enjoyment and psychological contentment in getting rid of their faults, and freeing themselves from the pressure of this fault on their souls

66 | 626 |

3338 هَرَب *n.* escape, flight; desertion

الخريف في بلادنا ذو وجه عربي في معظمه وهذا الوجه العربي له احتياجات خاصة بخلاف السائح الاوروبي او الغربي عموما الذي يفضل السياحة في الشتاء هربا من صقيع بلاده في هذا الموسم — Fall in our country has an Arab flavor, mostly, and this Arab flavor has its special needs, different from those of the European or Western tourist generally who prefers to tour in the winter, fleeing from the snow of his country in that season

77 | 541 |

3339 بَقَر *coll.n.* cows, *un.n.* بَقَرَة; البَقَرَة Al-Baqara (chapter 2 of the Qurʾan)

إن والدي أحضر الطبيب البيطري وعالج البقرة وهي بخير — My father brought the veterinary doctor and he treated the cow, and it is fine

70 | 593 |

3340 مَقُولَة *n.* statement, proposition; expression

إن ما حدث في بلاد ما بين النهرين أثبت خطأ مقولة أن الحرية تؤخذ ولا تعطى — What happened in Iraq proved the error of the statement that freedom is taken, not given

75 | 553 |

3341 فَكّ *n.* dismantling, taking apart; separating, breaking up; loosening, untying; فَكّ الإشْتِباك and فَكّ الإرْتِباط disengagement of troops

منظمة الإسيسكو تدعو الدول العربية إلى فك الحصار الاقتصادي المضروب على الفلسطينيين — The ISESCO organization calls on the Arab states to lift the economic blockade imposed on the Palestinians

81 | 513 |

3342 هَرَم *n. pl.* أهْرام pyramid

في يناير ١٩٥٤ م، بدأ البحث عن مدخل الهرم أسفل الحجرات السفلية للهرم — In January 1954, the search for the entrance to the pyramid began below the lower stones of the pyramid

63 | 655 |

3343 خَطْف *n.* abduction, kidnapping; hijacking; snatch (in weightlifting)

كل عمليات خطف السياح والأجانب التي وقعت منذ عام ١٩٩٣ في اليمن انتهت بسلام — All the tourist and foreigner kidnappings which have taken place since 1993 in Yemen ended peacefully

71 | 579 |

3344 مَرْكَبَة *n.* vehicle, craft; cart, carriage; (space) shuttle

تعرضت المركبة الأمريكية التي أرسلتها ناسا عام ١٩٩٩ إلى كوكب المريخ للاختطاف — The American spaceship which NASA sent to the planet Mars in 1999 was hijacked

70 | 588 |

3345 فَلّاح *n. pl.* -uun peasant, farmer; (pl.) fellaheen

تمنى لو كان مجرد فلاح فقير يرعى شويهات، ويأكل كسرة شعير تصنعها أنامل زوجته — He wished he were a poor farmer tending sheep, eating crumbs of barley made by the fingers of his wife

67 | 614 |

3346 عَريق *adj.* deep-rooted; ancient, noble, aristocratic

في الواقع هنالك العديد من المقاهي العريقة بوسط عمان مثل السنترال والاوبرج وغيرها — The fact is that there are many ancient coffee houses in

the middle of Amman like the Central and the Auberge and others

78 | 528 |

3347 بِضاعَة n. pl. بَضائِع merchandise, goods
الناس يحبون البضائع المستوردة — People love imported goods

80 | 518 |

3348 إِثْبات n. proof, confirmation; verification
لا يزال الجيش البريطاني في حاجة إلى إثبات قُدرته على ضبط الأمن في البصرة ومحيطها — The British army is still in need of proving its ability to ensure security in Basra and its surrounding area

79 | 519 |

3349 نَوْعيّ adj. specific, characteristic; qualitative
إن البشرية مقبلة في قادم السنين على تحولات نوعية في بنياتها السياسية والاقتصادية — Mankind is approaching in the coming years a qualitative transformation in its political and economic make-up

73 | 567 |

3350 مُعَلِّق a.p. commenting; n. commentator
فقد أكد شيخ الأزهر في خطبه أمام الرئيس معلقا على الأحداث الجارية في لبنان، أن المنطقة العربية لا تتحمل مقامرين — The Sheikh of Al-Azhar confirmed in his speech in front of the president, commenting on the current events in Lebanon, that the Arab region cannot tolerate adventurers

79 | 521 |

3351 أَبَى v. I (a) to refuse, decline sth or أَنْ to do sth
الجائع السائر في الصحراء لا يأبى أكل الخبز اليابس — A starving person walking in the desert does not refuse to eat dry bread

68 | 602 |

3352 اِكْتَمَل v. VIII to be completed, finished; to be perfect, integral
وتلاشى حبي الجميل.. رأيت نهاية حلم لا يكتمل به الانسان بدونه.. ولا تسمو الحياة الا به — My beautiful love has come to nothing...I saw the end of a dream without which a person cannot be whole...and only with which life can be heavenly

81 | 507 |

3353 وَقْفَة n. stance, posture; pause, break
بينت انه لا بد من وقفة جادة من الدول الغربية وامريكا لممارسة دورها الصحيح تجاه التعامل مع معاناة الشعب الفلسطيني — She made clear that it is necessary for the Western states and America to take a serious stand to carry out their true role in regard to dealing with the suffering of the Palestinian people

80 | 510 |

3354 لُقْمَة n. morsel, bite; لُقْمَة العَيْش one's daily bread, making a living
تورط عدد كبير من المواطنين مع أجهزة الاستخبارات ركضا وراء لقمة العيش، وأحيانا لمجرد البقاء على قيد الحياة — A large number of citizens were mixed up with the intelligence agencies, running after a mouthful of bread (a living), and sometimes just to stay alive

83 | 494 |

3355 مِقْياس n. pl. مَقاييس standard, measure, measurement
أثبتت خبرة السنوات الماضية، أننا بحاجة إلى كثير من المقاييس والمعايير والضوابط لتنظيم إصلاح الأسواق، وجعلها تعمل بكفاءة — The experience of last year has proved that we need many measures and standards and controls to organize the reform of the markets and make them work more efficiently

80 | 512 |

3356 تَشْكيلَة n. assortment, group; line-up (team sports)
يجلسون على مقاعد البدلاء بعد ان انضم المحترفان المصريان الى التشكيلة الاساسية للفريق رهن اشارة المدرب — They are sitting on the bench after the two Egyptian professionals joined the basic line-up of the team following the coach's orders

63 | 645 |

3357 تَعَيَّن v. V to be incumbent على on sb أَنْ to do sth; to be appointed, be designated as sth
يتعين على المريض أخذ عقار مضاد للتجلط لفترة طويلة — The sick person should take anti-clotting medicine for a long time

73 | 562 |

3358 مائِيّ adj. watery, liquid, fluid; aquatic; hydraulic

هناك نواد رياضية بحرية فيها معدات الرياضة المائية كالسباحة والغوص والإبحار في زوارق مخصصة وفيها معدات لصيد الأسماك — There are naval sports clubs in which there is equipment for the water sports like swimming and diving and sailing in special boats, and they also have equipment for fishing

64 | 640 |

3359 أَسَاء *v. IV* to harm, offend, insult إلى sb; (with foll. *vn.*) to do sth badly, incorrectly

يُحظر نشر ما يسيء لكرامة الافراد وحرياتهم الشخصية — Things that insult the dignity of individuals and their personal freedoms are prohibited from being published

79 | 517 |

3360 تَحَكَّمَ *v. V* to control في/ب sth

— إنه يتحكم في شؤون حياتهم جميعا He controls all aspects of their lives

84 | 485 |

3361 جَرَس *n.* bell

أوجد دافينتشي علاقة ما بين صوت الجرس وبين صوت الحجر الذي يسقط في الماء — Da Vinci created a relationship between the sound of the bell and the sound of the rock which falls into the water

67 | 609 | +lit

3362 عَلِيّ *adj.* supreme, exalted, sublime; العَلِيّ the Supreme (God)

قرأ الفاتحة على روح الفقيد داعيا المولى العلي القدير أن يتغمد روح الفقيد برحمته — He read the Fatiha over the soul of the departed, calling on the high and mighty God to encompass the soul of the deceased with his mercy

66 | 614 |

3363 نَجْمَة *n.* star; female celebrity

وحيثما حلقت في طائرة آمالي رأيتك نجمة مضيئة يغار من بهائها القمر — Wherever you have flown in the plane of my hopes, I have seen you as a bright star, whose brightness the moon envies

68 | 601 |

3364 ثُلاثِيّ *adj.* three-part, tripartite, tri-; corner (shot); *n.* trio; الإسم الثُلاثِيّ one's full name (given name, middle name, surname)

أحبت الجماهير العربية جمال عبد الناصر لمواقفه القومية المعروفة، ووقوفه بوجه العدوان الثلاثي على مصر — The Arab masses loved Gamal Abd Al-Nasser because of his well-known nationalistic positions, and his standing up to the tripartite aggression against Egypt

73 | 558 |

3365 عُرُوبَة *n.* Arabism

أؤيدك فيما ذكرته بأن معنى العروبة قد ضاع و أصبح سلعة أخرى يتاجر بها السياسيون العرب — I support you in what you mentioned that the meaning of "Arabism" has been lost and it has become another commodity which Arab politicians do business with

67 | 605 |

3366 عَزاء *n.* solace, consolation, comfort; condolence(s), sympathy

وعند الدفن وقف إدريس فوق القبر يشجع أدهم بكلمات العزاء — At the burial, Idriss stood on the tomb encouraging Adham with words of consolation

74 | 548 |

3367 أَكْثَرِيَّة *n.* majority

رئيس الوزراء قد يتمكن من تحقيق الأكثرية المطلوبة — The prime minister might be able to achieve the required majority

52 | 778 |

3368 خَراب *n.* ruins, destruction

عشنا، في لبنان، حربا شرسة عاثت الخراب والدمار في كل مكان، فاتكة بالأطفال والنساء والشيوخ — In Lebanon, we lived through a vicious war which spread destruction everywhere, killing children, women, and old people

73 | 554 |

3369 مَكَّنَ *v. II* to make possible من sth (for sb)

أحب الحياة وأخلص لمهنته وعندما اقترب من المرحلة التي تمكنه من تحقيق تطلعاته وهو في عز العطاء، غدره القدر — He loved life and was loyal to his profession, and when he approached the stage which would enable him to achieve his ambitions when he was at the height of his contribution, fate betrayed him

90 | 451 |

3370 جَدُرَ *v. I (u)* (imperf.) to be worth ب (mentioning, pointing out): يَجْدُرُ بالذِّكْر/ذِكْرُهُ أَنَّ it's worth mentioning that; to be appropriate, proper for sb (to do sth); يَجْدُرُ you/we should بكَ/بنا أَنْ
تجدر الإشارة هنا إلى أن الشعوب الغربية أنتجت عشرات المنظمات الإرهابية، فلماذا الإصرار على إلصاق تهمة الإرهاب بالعرب والمسلمين دون سواهم؟ — It is worth pointing out here that the Western peoples produced scores of terrorist organizations, so why the insistence on attaching the accusation of terrorist to the Arabs and Muslims, as opposed to others?
73 | 559 |

3371 سِتار *n.* curtain; veil
أرجوك أزح لنا الستار عن النافذة لنراها — I beg you to remove the curtain from the window for us, so we can see it
78 | 522 |

3372 حَرَقَ *v. I (i)* to burn sth; to hurt sb
الشمس في الصحراء تحرق الزرع والبشر — The sun in the desert burns the vegetation and the people
82 | 493 |

3373 مُفْتِي *n.* mufti (Muslim legal scholar)
وقد أعطى فضيلة المفتي خواطره الإيمانية على بعض الآيات القرآنية المكتوبة على اللوحات — His eminence the Mufti gave his faith-promoting thoughts on some of the Qur'anic verses written on the boards
63 | 638 |

3374 حَسْبَمَا and حَسَبَمَا *conj.* according to
منعه من السفر إلى الأردن، حسبما أعلن رئيس المنظمة الوطنية لحقوق الإنسان في سوريا عمار القربي — He prevented him from traveling to Jordan, according to what the president of the National Organization for the Rights of Man in Syria, Amar Al-Qurbi, announced
67 | 603 |

3375 مَزِيَّة *n. pl.* مَزايا feature, characteristic; advantage
أظهرت الدراسات الطبية ان الرضاعة الطبيعية تقدم مزايا هائلة للاطفال فهي تحد من احتمال الاصابة بأمراض الاذن والحساسية Medical — studies have shown that natural nursing offers enormous advantages to children, since it limits the possibility of being struck with diseases of the ear, and allergies
77 | 525 |

3376 هَيْكَل *n.* framework, structure; skeleton; temple, sanctuary
قرر وزير العدل استحداث هذه المديرية، ونحن بصدد تطوير الهيكل التنظيمي لوزارة العدل وتحديد وصف وظيفي لكافة المواقع في الوزارة — The Minister of Justice decided to renew this directorate, and we are in the process of developing the organizational structure for the Ministry of Justice and defining the functional description of all the sites in the Ministry
80 | 508 |

3377 مُنْخَفِض *adj.* low; reduced
كل الأراضي التي تقع في مستوى منخفض تعرضت للتدمير — All the lands which are located at a low elevation were exposed to destruction
76 | 533 |

3378 أَحْدَثَ *v. IV* to cause, bring about (reaction, change, situation)
أشرنا الى ان القطن كمحصول نقدى أحدث تحولات كبيرة فى حياة عدد كبير من المواطنين بالاقليم — We indicated that cotton, as a cash crop, has caused big changes to the life of a large number of citizens in the region
84 | 480 |

3379 ثَوْرِيّ *adj.* revolutionary
الاستبداد السياسي واحتكار السلطة مثلت جميعا القاسم المشترك بين النظم الثورية العسكرية التي سيطرت على الحكم في البلاد العربية واستمرت فيه — Political despotism and monopolization of power represent the common denominator among the revolutionary military regimes that took power in the Arab countries and continued in power
64 | 627 |

3380 مَرْسُوم *adj.* decreed, ordered; drawn, sketched; charted (course); *n.* decree, edict, ordinance, statute
اشار الى ان مرسوم قانون الاستثمار الجديد يمنح اعفاء جمركيا كاملا لكل مستلزمات الانتاج — He

indicated that the new investment law regulation grants a complete customs exemption for all the materials needed for production

62 | 649 |

3381 عُرْضَة *n.* target, object (of criticism), exposed (to virus)

لم يتعرض للتعذيب أثناء التحقيق معه ، لكنه كان عرضة للإهانات والضغوط النفسية والتهديد — He wasn't subjected to torture during his being investigated, but he was exposed to verbal abuse, psychological pressure, and threats

80 | 506 |

3382 مُؤَهَّل *adj.* certified, qualified; competent, experienced

في اعتقادي أن إعلامنا مسير وغير مخير ورغم أنني غير مؤهل للطعن في الإعلام إلا أن إعلامنا لا يرضيني — I believe that our media is controlled and not free, and although I am not qualified to criticize the media, still, the media does not satisfy me

70 | 579 |

3383 لَبَّى *v. II* to meet (needs), fulfill (desires, expectations); to comply with (request)

ننشد بناء دولة ديمقراطية حديثة وعادلة تلبي كافة حاجات الشعب اللبناني وتحقق طموحاته في العدالة الصحية والديمقراطية — We urge the building of a modern democratic state which provides all the needs of the Lebanese people and achieves their ambitions for healthy justice and democracy

80 | 501 |

3384 حَلَّ *v. I (i)* to befall, strike ب/على sb (misfortune); to arrive, start (month, season); (Lev.) حِلّ عَنِّي leave me alone!

الكارثة التي حلت بلبنان نتيجة العدوان الأسرائيلي أصابت الجميع — The catastrophe that struck Lebanon as a result of the Israeli aggression hit everyone

81 | 495 |

3385 لافِتَة *n. pl.* -aat billboard, placard, sign

مطاعم أمريكا كانت تعلق لافتة على الباب تقول: ممنوع دخول الكلاب والزنوج واليهود — The

restaurants of America hung signs on the door saying: Entrance is forbidden for dogs, Negroes and Jews

77 | 520 |

3386 حافَّة *n.* border, edge, side; seam, hem

كنت أجلس على حافة النيل بمفردي لساعات عدة حتى منتصف الليل، أتأمل وأفكر — I was sitting at the edge of the Nile by myself for many hours until the middle of the night, pondering and thinking

73 | 550 |

3387 مُخِيف *adj.* frightful, terrifying, horrible

تزداد ظاهرة السمنة في الدول المتقدمة والدول النامية كما أنها تزداد بمعدل مخيف بين الأطفال — The phenomenon of obesity in the advanced countries and the developing countries is increasing and it is also increasing at a frightening rate among children

77 | 519 |

3388 آلِّي *adj.* mechanical, automatic; machine-

في إحدى الندوات ذكر بروفسور ياباني أن الربوت (الرجل الآلي) قد بدأ يغزو العالم في جميع التخصصات — In one of the panel discussions, a Japanese professor mentioned that the Robot (the mechanical man) has begun to invade the world in all specialties

69 | 582 |

3389 شُرْطِيّ *n.* police officer, policeman

في الموصل، أعلنت الشرطة استشهاد شرطي وإصابة ثلاثة اخرين في اشتباك مع إرهابيين مجهولين — In Mosul, the police announced the martyrdom of a policeman and the wounding of three others in clashes with unknown terrorists

71 | 563 |

3390 أَيَّدَ *v. II* to support, assist sb; to approve of sth

كان أبي رحمه الله رجلا مستنيرا يؤيد تعليم المرأة وعملها — My father, God have mercy on his soul, was an enlightened man who supported women's education and work

77 | 518 |

3391 مَرْجِعِيَّة *n.* authority; authoritative source
الحكومة هي المرجعية الوحيدة للنظر في هذا الطلب واتخاذ الموقف المناسب منه — The government is the only authority to look into this request and take an appropriate position regarding it
59 | 673 |

3392 سَلْب *n.* robbing, depriving; سَلْباً negatively
اي خروج على الدستور سينعكس سلبا على الوضع — Any departure from the constitution will reflect negatively on the situation
74 | 539 |

3393 أُسْبُوعِيّ *adj.* weekly
جلست إلى مكتبي في العاشرة صباحا، وشرعت أكتب مقالي الأسبوعي الذي سينشر في «آفاق عربية» في عدد الخميس — I sat at my desk at ten in the morning, and I started to write my weekly article which will be published in "Arabic Horizons" in its Thursday edition
77 | 522 |

3394 واجِهَة *n.* face, façade; front, forefront; (computer) interface, front end
الثقافة هي بوابة كل دولة في العالم كله وهي الواجهة الحقيقية للدول — Culture is the gateway of every country in the whole world and it is the true façade of the country
79 | 506 |

3395 مُشْرِق *adj.* splendid, shining; bright, auspicious
هذا الشعب جدير بالحياة الحرة الكريمة، وانه قادر على صنع مستقبل مشرق يضعه في مصاف الشعوب المحترمة — These people deserve an honorable, free life, and to be able to make a promising future that will put them in the ranks of respected peoples
79 | 504 |

3396 زِيّ *n.* pl. أَزْياء uniform, dress, clothing; أَزْياء fashion clothes
هنا يبيعون الأزياء الفاخرة من تصميم أكبر المصممين في العالم — Here they sell fancy clothes designed by the biggest designers in the world
83 | 481 |

3397 اللَّواتي *rel.pron.* (fem.pl.) who, whom
لا أستطيع أن أنسى الأمهات اللواتي فقدن أبناءهن في تفجيرات عمان — I can't forget the mothers who lost their sons in the Amman explosions
80 | 501 |

3398 اِدِّعاء *n.* allegation, claim; prosecution; الاِدِّعاء العامّ the public prosecutor
المجتمع الشرقي عامة قد يحرم البكاء على الرجال مع الادعاء أو الاقتناع بأن هذا البكاء يقلل من شأن الرجل — Eastern society generally might forbid crying in men with the claim or conviction that this crying would reduce a man's dignity
75 | 534 |

3399 تَقْوِية *n.* strengthening, reinforcement
الزيارة تأتي في إطار رغبة أذربيجان في تقوية العلاقات مع مصر في مختلف المجالات خاصة المجال الاقتصادي — The visit comes in the framework of the desire of Azerbaijan to strengthen its relations with Egypt in the various fields, particularly in the economic field
72 | 552 |

3400 ساحِر *n.* sorcerer, magician; *adj.* charming, enchanting
تسحب من فمها الأسرار كما يسحب الساحر حبل المناديل الملونة من قبعته بلا انقطاع — She draws secrets out of her mouth like a magician draws a rope of colored handkerchiefs out of his hat, without a break
64 | 618 |

3401 ناقِص *adj.* incomplete, defective; *a.p.* missing, lacking (sth); *n.* (math.) minus
هذه الخطوة ممتازة ولكنها ناقصة ولا بد أن تكتمل — This step is excellent but it is incomplete, and must be completed
81 | 492 |

3402 تَنْمَوِيّ *adj.* development-related
هناك برامج تنموية كثيرة للأمم المتحدة مثل اليونيسيف — The UN has many development programs like UNICEF
55 | 719 |

3403 مُباحَثَة *n.* pl. -aat discussion, debate; talk, dialog

اسفرت المباحثات في ختامها أمس عن توقيع مذكرة تفاهم بين الجانبين — The discussions, at their conclusion yesterday, resulted in the signing of a memo of understanding between the two sides

51 | 766 | +news

3404 جَذْب *n.* attraction, lure; gravitation

بعض أصحاب الشركات يؤكدون أن مصر في موقع جيد لجذب الاستثمارات الأجنبية — Some company owners confirm that Egypt is in a good position to attract foreign investments

73 | 540 |

3405 سَحْب *n.* withdrawal, pulling out; removal

هجمت الناس على البنوك لسحب أموالها — The people attacked the banks to withdraw their money

81 | 490 |

3406 إفْراج *n.* liberation; release, freeing (عن of)

كان يستقبل الزائرين بعد الإفراج عنه من الاعتقال — After his release from prison, he was receiving visitors

58 | 677 |

3407 عُزْلَة *n.* isolation, seclusion; separation

كانت تفضل أن تقضي وقتها بمفردها.. وكانت هذه العزلة هي أحب الأشياء إلى نفسها، لأنها تجعلها تفكر فيه — She preferred to spend her time by herself...and this isolation was the thing she liked best, because it made her think about him

73 | 536 |

3408 تَصْعيد *n.* escalation, intensification

كانت تصيح، وقد ظهر أنها عازمة على تصعيد الخلاف — She was screaming, and it became clear that she was determined to escalate the dispute

58 | 680 |

3409 عِماد *n.* pl. عُمُد support, base; pillar, column, mast; (mil.) major general

لا شك أن عماد الأسرة هو الفرد، كما أن عماد المجتمع هو الأسرة — There is no doubt that the pillar of the family is the individual, just like the pillar of society is the family

63 | 627 |

3410 بُطْء *n.* slowness; بِبُطْءٍ slowly

ليس العيب أن تصعد ببطء لكن العيب أن تتهاوى بسرعة — The problem is not going up slowly, the problem is in coming down too fast

68 | 577 | +lit

3411 عِبْرَة *n.* pl. عِبَر lesson, moral

عليه أن يأخذ العبرة من ذلك الخطأ وأن يتعلم من خطئه — He should take a lesson from this error and learn from his mistake

83 | 473 |

3412 رُجوع *n.* return, going back (إلى to); reversing (one's decision) عن

والله آخر شيء فكرت فيه هو الرجوع لمصر — By God, the last thing I thought about was returning to Egypt

80 | 489 |

3413 حَياء *n.* modesty, shyness, inhibition, shame

لا تخافي منها لأنها بسيطة تميل إلى اللين وشدة الحياء — Don't be afraid of her, because she is simple, and tends towards softness and extreme shyness

71 | 548 |

3414 أسْبَق *adj.* previous, former; earlier

لم يكن عملاقا سياسيا تحترمه أمته وتقدره الأمم كالرئيس الأمريكي الأسبق أيزنهاور أو جون كينيدي — There hasn't been a political giant whom his country respects and the nations esteem like the former American president Eisenhower or John Kennedy

62 | 627 |

3415 تَمَسُّك *n.* adherence, commitment (ب to)

كانت توجه أبناءها إلى ضرورة التمسك بلغتهم الأم — She guided her sons to the necessity of holding on to the mother-tongue

76 | 515 |

3416 غُروب *n.* setting; غروب الشَّمْس sunset

خرجت إلى ظهر السفينة لأشهد الغروب البديع.. كنت وحدي على ظهرها.. كان الغروب ممتعا — I went out on the deck of the ship to see the

gorgeous sunset...I was by myself on the deck, the sunset was enjoyable

71 | 549 |

3417 حافِلَة *n.* pl. -aat bus

طلب سائق الحافلة من الركاب الهدوء حتى يتمكن من السير ومواصلة الطريق — The bus driver asked the riders to be calm so that he could drive, and continue on the way

66 | 589 |

3418 مَسْعىً *n.* pl. مَساعٍ (def. مَساعِي), effort, endeavor

رابطة العالم الإسلامي تؤكد على أهمية مساعي المملكة العربية السعودية في جمع المسلمين على العقيدة الإسلامية الصحيحة — The Islamic World League affirms the importance of the efforts of the Saudi Arabian kingdom to gather Muslims to the correct Islamic doctrine

66 | 592 |

3419 حَوَى *v. I (i)* to contain, include (على) sth

عثرت يوما على حقيبة تحوي كثيرا من المال — One day I found a suitcase which contained a lot of money

80 | 489 |

3420 انْعِدام *n.* non-existence, absence, lack of

أكد تقرير صادر عن منظمة الصحة العالمية أن مليوني شخص سنويا في العالم يموتون نتيجة انعدام النشاط البدني أو الكسل — A report issued by the World Health Organization affirmed that two million people in the world die yearly as a result of lack of exercise and laziness

75 | 517 |

3421 صالُون *n.* salon, chat room, parlor, exhibit room

هذه الشقة تتألف من صالون وغرفة طعام ومطبخ وثلاث غرف نوم وحمامين — This apartment consists of a living room, a dining room, a kitchen, three bedrooms, and two baths

67 | 576 |

3422 تَصْنيف *n.* classification, categorization, sorting

وضعت معايير وامتحانات شخصية يتم على أساسها تصنيف المستخدم لنفسه إن كان من المدمنين أو لا — It put standards and personal tests on the basis of which the user can categorize himself as an addict or not

71 | 548 |

3423 مُعاهَدَة *n.* treaty, accord, pact

خسرت ألمانيا بموجب هذه المعاهدة ١٢٫٥٪ من مساحتها و ١٢٪ من سكانه — Germany lost in accordance with this treaty 12.5% of its territory and 12% of its population

61 | 639 |

3424 بُغْيَة *n.* wish; بُغْيَةَ with the purpose of

اننا وقعنا اتفاقا مع غرفة التجارة في بيروت وجبل لبنان بغية مساعدتها كي تكون اكثر فاعلية وانتاجية — We signed an agreement with the Chamber of Commerce in Beirut and Mt Lebanon with the purpose of helping them be more effective and productive

73 | 529 |

3425 سائِح *n.* pl. سُيّاح tourist

سئم السياح الغربيون من سكني ناطحات السحاب ويريدون الاستجمام في الأكواخ الخشبية — Western tourists, who live in skyscrapers, want to have their recreation in wooden shacks

66 | 584 |

3426 قافِلَة *n.* pl. قَوافِل convoy, column

خمسة صوماليين جرحوا في هجوم بالقنبلة اليدوية على قافلة كانت تنقل اسرى في منطقة حريوة المجاورة — Five Somalis were wounded in a hand grenade attack on a convoy which was transporting prisoners in the neighboring Harywa region

78 | 498 |

3427 نَشْرَة *n.* report, bulletin; publication; announcement, proclamation

في حال توقف تلك الأغنيات وحلول موعد النشرة الإخبارية فإن الكل يدير المؤشر إلى إذاعة أخرى — Whenever these songs stop and the time for the news broadcast comes, everyone turns the dial to another station

78 | 495 |

3428 جِراحِيّ *adj.* surgical

البعثة الطبية ستقوم خلال زياراتها بإجراء العديد من العمليات الجراحية للأطفال المصابين بالأمراض المعقدة والتي يصعب علاجها في اليمن — The medical missions during their visits will conduct a number of surgical operations for children afflicted with complicated diseases and which are difficult to treat in Yemen

72 | 537 |

3429 مُلِحّ adj. urgent, critical, pressing

نحن بحاجة ملحة للتضامن الداخلي — We are in desperate need of internal cohesion

74 | 522 |

3430 مُتَتالٍ (def. مُتَتالي) adj. consecutive, successive

أحرز مؤشر السوق صعودا على مدى أربعة أيام متتالية من الأحد حتى الأربعاء ربح خلالها حوالي ٢١٥ نقطة — The market indicators showed a rise over four successive days from Sunday to Wednesday during which about 215 points were gained

76 | 508 |

3431 مُعْتاد adj. accustomed, habituated على to sth; typical, usual, customary

الريح من جنود الله تعالى التي لا يقاومها شيء، فإذا خرجت عن سرعتها المعتادة – بإذن ربها – دمرت المدن وهدمت المباني — The wind is one of the soldiers of God, may He be exalted, that no one fights, and if it goes beyond its normal speed, with the permission of God, cities are destroyed, and buildings toppled

78 | 494 |

3432 حارَبَ v. III to fight, wage war against sb/sth

ان «حرب العراق» تجاوزت المدة التي حارب فيها الاميركيون اثناء الحرب العالمية الثانية — The time period of the Iraq War has exceeded the time the Americans fought during the Second World War

76 | 505 |

3433 ناسَبَ v. III to be suitable for sb

من حق العامل على الدولة والمجتمع أن ينال الأجر الذي يناسب عمله — It is the right of the worker, owed to him by the state and society, that he obtain the wage which is appropriate to his work

78 | 497 |

3434 تَجْمِيل n. embellishment, decoration

انها تؤمن كما يؤمن الجميع بأن عمليات التجميل حرام — She believes, as everyone believes, that cosmetic surgery is forbidden

68 | 563 |

3435 جَماهِيرِيَّة n. Jamahiriya (in Libya's official designation: الجماهيرية العربية الليبية الشعبية الاشتراكية العظمى Great Socialist People's Libyan Arab Jamahiriya)

سألت السفير الليبي: ما هي آخر أخبار الجماهيرية الليبية؟ — I asked the Libyan ambassador: What is the latest news of the Libyan Republic?

49 | 783 | +news

3436 لَفَّ v. I (u) to wrap sth; to turn, rotate, go around

كان صعيديا يلف على رأسه عمامة من قماش أسود He was an Upper Egyptian, wrapping a black cloth scarf around his head

76 | 503 |

3437 عَجَل n. hurry, rush, haste

أنهى المكالمة وانتفض واقفا وقال وهو يلملم أشياءه على عجل: مضطر أنصرف حالا — He ended the conversation and stood up and said, as he gathered his things quickly: I have to leave immediately

67 | 569 |

3438 راقَبَ v. III to watch, observe, monitor sth/sb; to oversee, supervise sth/sb

قرروا أن يتركوا واحدا منهم يراقب المكان وهم غائبون — They decided to leave one of them to watch the place while they were away

75 | 509 |

3439 انْقِطاع n. discontinuation, breaking off

لماذا تحدث مشكلة انقطاع الكهرباء والماء في أغنى دولة خليجية بتروليا؟ — Why is the problem of electricity and water cutoffs happening in the most oil-rich gulf state?

77 | 499 |

3440 مُحَرِّك n. motor, engine

تمكن «جون» من ركوب أول زورق يتحرك بواسطة محرك وكان عليه فقط أن يضغط على زر بسيط في جسمه — John was able to ride the first motorboat, and he only had to push a simple button on its body

72 | 534 |

3441 بَدَوِيّ n./adj. pl. بَدْو (often pronounced بَدُو) Bedouin

إن نفسية البدوي هي جزء من الصحراء التي تحيط به من كل جهة — The psychology of the Bedouin is a part of the desert that surrounds him on every side

64 | 596 |

3442 شَراب *n.* beverage, drink

لجأ الإنسان البدائي للصوم عن الطعام والشراب — كوسيلة للتداوي من الأمراض Primitive man resorted to fasting from food and drink as a means of curing diseases

69 | 558 |

3443 اِلْتِهاب *n. pl.* -aat inflammation

قضيت بضعة أيام في المستشفى للتأكد من عدم وجود الْتهاب في جروحي — I spent several days in the hospital to make sure there was no inflammation in my wounds

54 | 708 |

3444 مُجَمِّع *adj.* collecting, gathering; *n.* collector; battery; (Web) aggregator (feed reader, news reader)

وهبط مؤشر ناسداك المجمع الذي تغلب عليه اسهم التقنية ١٠,٧٥ نقطة — The Nasdaq composite index which is dominated by technical shares fell 10.75 points

73 | 527 |

3445 اِقْتَضَى *v. VIII* to demand, require sth

إن علينا جميعا أن ندرك أن الأيام المقبلة تقتضي منا جميعا مزيدا من الإيجابية والابتعاد عن السلبية — We all need to realize that the coming days will require of all of us a lot of optimism and avoiding pessimism

75 | 509 |

3446 عَدَّل *v. II* to modify, alter sth; to amend, rectify (law); to adjust, correct sth

إن البنك المركزي عدل من سياسته الاستثارية حيث سمح للمستثمر الأجنبي بالدخول في الاستثمار — The central bank modified its investment policy such that it permitted foreign investors to enter into investing

75 | 510 |

3447 قَبيل *n.* kind, sort, type

هناك سوابق لظهور مجموعات من هذا القبيل — There are precedents for the appearance of groups of that type

75 | 512 |

3448 تَفَوُّق *n.* excellence; superiority, supremacy

أتمنى لكم دوام التفوق والنجاح — I hope you have lasting excellence and success

77 | 494 |

3449 طاعَة *n.* obedience

كان سليمان الحكيم حكيما حين استثنى القلب من الطاعة في كل شيء، نعم لا سلطان على القلب — Solomon the Wise was wise when he made an exception of the heart from obeying everything; yes, there is no authority over the heart

70 | 543 |

3450 عَلَّم *v. II* to teach sb sth or أنَّ that; to mark (put a mark on) sth; to write down (phone number)

من علمني حرفا كنت له عبدا — He who teaches me a letter, I am his servant

77 | 497 |

3451 مَنْظُور *n.* perspective, point of view, angle; *adj.* anticipated, expected; foreseeable (future)

الجميع يعلم أن الإسلام هو منظور شمولي، يهتم بالمعاملات كما يهتم بالعبادات — Everyone knows that Islam is a comprehensive viewpoint, taking an interest in daily activities as much as it takes an interest in acts of worship

67 | 566 |

3452 جانِبيّ *adj.* side, lateral; marginal; secondary

زيادة تناول المشروبات التي تحتوي على الكافيين تؤدي إلى آثار جانبية على المعدة والعينين والأعصاب والكلى، وتجعل الأطفال عصبيي المزاج — Increasing the consumption of drinks that contain caffeine leads to side effects on the stomach, eyes, nerves and kidneys, and makes children nervous

77 | 493 |

3453 مُفَوَّضِيَّة *n.* delegation, legation

هذه الأرقام جاءت من مفوضية الأمم المتحدة لشؤون اللاجئين — These numbers came from the United Nations Commission for Refugee Affairs

51 | 738 | +news

3454 سُوبَر *n.* super (in سوبرماركت "supermarket" and other compound words and names)

هناك حملة بريطانية يقودها عدد من جماعات حماية البيئة لحث محلات السوبر ماركت الكبرى على تقليص حجم مخلفاتها والحد من استخدام الأغلفة — There is a British campaign led by a number of environmental protection groups to urge big

supermarkets to reduce the amount of their garbage and to limit the use of wrappers

72 | 527 |

3455 مُجْتَمِع *adj.* assembling, meeting; *n.* (meeting) participant, assemblage; مُجْتَمِعَةً combined, collectively, as a whole, as a group
كانت العائلة مجتمعة لمناقشة حالتها المضطربة — The family was gathered to discuss its troubled condition

77 | 489 |

3456 مَرْجِع *n. pl.* مَراجِع source; authority; reference work
تشير بعض المراجع إلى أنه بلغ عدد ضحايا هذه الممارسات المتطرفة أكثر من ثلاثة ملايين مسلم وأجبر — Some sources say that the number of victims of these extreme practices reached more than three million Muslims

73 | 519 |

3457 عَمَّ *v. I (u)* to become general, prevalent, commonplace; to fill up, spread throughout (a place); to be rampant, widespread (chaos, unrest)
هاهي الفرحة تعم البيت، إنه أول مولود ذكر في الأسرة — Joy filled the house, it was the first born male child in the family

78 | 484 |

3458 بَقَى /ba'a/ (Egy.) *part.* (modal with various meanings) just, then, so, exactly
خلاص بقى حايسيب العسكرية ويبقى أفندي — That's it, then, he is going to leave the military and become a white collar worker

25 | 1462 | +spo

3459 تَهْدِئَة *n.* calming, soothing; easing, relieving (tension)
ليس من المتوقع ان تلتزم الفصائل بالهدنة والتهدئة من جانب واحد بينما تطلق اسرائيل العنان لجيشها ليواصل اعتداءاته — It is not expected that the factions will stick to the truce in a one-sided manner while Israel gives free rein to its army to continue its aggression

67 | 559 |

3460 لاحَ *v. I (u)* to appear, loom (في الأُفُق on the horizon)

— أجواء الحرب قد بدأت تلوح في الأفق — The atmosphere of war has begun to appear on the horizon

71 | 530 |

3461 هَمَسَ *v. I (i)* to whisper ل to sb (في أُذُنِهِ in sb's ear)
أنا خائف عليك.. هكذا همس بجزع، فرمقته بنظرة ساخرة ثم استدارت ببطء وعادت إلى زملائها — "I am afraid for you"..Thus he whispered in fear, so she threw him a sarcastic look and then turned around slowly and returned to her colleagues

51 | 734 | +lit

3462 بَثَّ *v. I (u)* to transmit, broadcast (news, show); to disseminate, spread sth
كان الراديو يبث أغاني عاطفية — The radio was broadcasting love songs

79 | 475 |

3463 غَدا *v. I (u)* to become (acquire a quality or feature); to seem, appear
كثيرا ما أكتب، حتى غدت الكتابة هوايتي المفضلة بعد القراءة — I write a lot, until writing became my favorite hobby after reading

63 | 594 |

3464 هاجِس *n. pl.* هَواجِس worry, concern; apprehension, misgiving, premonition; fixed idea, obsessive thought
تعاني غالبية الممثلات صعوبة في ايجاد ادوار تعبر عن الهواجس النسائية — Most actresses suffer from difficulty in finding roles which express the concerns of femininity

67 | 560 |

3465 اِسْتِثْنائِيّ *adj.* exceptional, irregular; extraordinary
فقد تحقق لنا الكثير بالرغم من ظروفنا الاستثنائية وشح مواردنا — A lot was accomplished despite our exceptional circumstances, and the scarcity of our resources

67 | 553 |

3466 قُدُماً *adv.* forwards, forward
وعد أيضا بالمضي قدما في مسعى بلاده للانضمام إلى الاتحاد الأوروبي — He also promised to go

forward with his country's attempts to join the European Union

74 | 502 |

3467 عَلَم *n.* pl. أَعْلام flag, banner; badge, seal; أَعْلام celebrities, famous people

تتدفق طوابير المتظاهرين يحملون الأعلام العراقية ويرددون الهتافات الوطنية حتى يغص الميدان به — Lines of demonstrators pushed forward carrying Iraqi flags and repeating nationalistic shouts until the square was filled with them

78 | 479 |

3468 نِعْمَ *part.* (what a) wonderful

والله لا يوجد تعليق الا حسبي الله ونعم الوكيل بحكام العرب — By God there is no comment that can be made except to say: "God is all I need, he is the best guardian against the Arab rulers"

61 | 607 |

3469 مَحْمُول *adj.* portable; carried, held; *n.* mobile (phone)

كنا نقضي أوقاتا ممتعة معا وأعطيته رقم هاتفي المحمول وراح يحدثني كل ليلة — We used to spend enjoyable times together and I gave him my mobile number and he started to call me every evening

69 | 534 |

3470 صِيام *n.* fasting, abstinence

الفرح في العيد يفترض أن يأتي نتيجة لإفطار الإنسان بعد صيام طويل ونتيجة للراحة بعد كل تعب — Joy in the holiday should come as a result of the person eating after a long fast and as a result of rest after hardship and toil

65 | 574 |

3471 رَماد *n.* ashes, cinders

تكفكف رماد سجائري من على المنضده — She wipes the ashes of my cigarettes from off the table

66 | 557 |

3472 دِفاعِيّ *adj.* defensive, protective

تعمل دول المجلس لتطوير قدراته الدفاعية وفق منظور مشترك واستراتيجية موحدة — The countries of the council are working to

develop their defensive capabilities according to a shared view and a united strategy

66 | 564 |

3473 مُقَدَّمَة *n.* preface, introduction; front part; vanguard, front, head

لذا تقيم كثير من الشعوب أعيادا للضحك في مقدمتها الاحتفالات الشعبية بعيد الربيع، والأعراس، والمسارح الساخرة — Therefore many peoples hold special occasions for laughing, at the forefront of which are the popular celebrations of Spring holiday, and weddings, and sarcastic theater

65 | 567 |

3474 سُكُوت *n.* silence, calm

أليس السكوت أصعب من الكلام؟ — Isn't silence more difficult than speaking?

78 | 472 |

3475 فِقْه *n.* fiqh (Islamic jurisprudence); understanding, knowledge; science; فِقه اللُّغَة philology

إن كتب الفقه التي يرجعون إليها عادة مملوءة بالأحاديث الواهية المنكرة — The legal books they usually refer to are filled with weak and rejected Hadith

69 | 534 |

3476 اسْتَشْهَدَ *v.* X to quote, cite بـ sth; pass. أُسْتُشْهِدَ to be martyred, die in battle

هو من سكان حي التفاح الذي استشهد أثناء تصديه للاجتياح الصهيوني على شرق حي التفاح — He is among the inhabitants of the Al-Tufah quarter who were martyred during its resistance to the Zionist invasion of the eastern Al-Tufah quarter

69 | 533 |

3477 مِلْك *n.* possessions, property; land, real estate

وقتي ليس ملكي، لكنه ملك زملائي الذين منحوني المسئولية — My time is not my own, rather it belongs to my colleagues who granted me this responsibility

84 | 437 |

3478 جُلّ *n.* majority, most, main part (of)

تذكرين حين افترقنا، قبل اعوام، كنت تركزين جل اهتمامك على العمل، وتطمحين الى التقدم والتفوق — You remember when we parted, years ago,

you were concentrating all your interest in work, and you had ambitions to advance and excel

75 | 490 |

3479 دِماغ *n.* brain

دماغه تتخبط في حديد السرير.. يجيله ارتجاج في المخ — نروح في داهية His head would hit the iron of the bed, he would get a concussion and we would be ruined

75 | 495 |

3480 خَلاص *n.* liberation, deliverance, salvation; settlement

أريد الخلاص من هذه الورطة.. أريد الخلاص بأي ثمن — I want to be delivered from this mess...I want deliverance at any cost

73 | 505 |

3481 حَسّ and حِسّ *n.* sensation, feeling; sound, noise

رسمك جميل ويدل على حس فني راق — Your drawing is beautiful and indicates a refined artistic sensibility

74 | 498 |

3482 عُبُور *vn.* crossing (border, street)

بعد عبور الكوبري مباشرة ستجد محلا أبيض الواجهة — After crossing the bridge, directly, you will find a store with a white façade

78 | 474 |

3483 شَحْن *vn.* charging (battery), loading (camera); *n.* cargo, freight; transportation, shipment

كانوا يملكون باخرتي شحن تعملان على خط الإسكندرية – بيروت — They used to own two transport ships which worked the Alexandria-Beirut line

72 | 513 |

3484 مُطْرِب *adj.* delightful; *n.* pl. -uun musician, musical performer

قدمت الفرقة العديد من اللوحات الفنية المتنوعة والأغاني بمشاركة عدد من المطربين والمطربات، بالإضافة إلى العديد من القصائد الشعرية — The group presented a number of varied artistic tableaux and songs with the participation of a number of singers, in addition to a number of poetic odes

59 | 624 |

3485 نَجاة *n.* survival, deliverance, salvation; escape

صاح الرجل: أيها الناس من أراد النجاة فليتبعني — The man cried: O People, whoever wants salvation, let them follow me

76 | 482 |

3486 سُكّانِيّ *adj.* residential, population-related

أن إندونيسيا هي أكبر بلاد العالم الإسلامي من حيث التعداد السكاني — Indonesia is the biggest country in the Islamic World as far as population numbers go

62 | 589 |

3487 أَسْرَعَ *v. IV* to hurry, hasten في in doing sth

أرجوك أن تسرع بالمجيء إلينا — I beg you to hurry and come to us

64 | 576 | +lit

3488 تَحْرِيك *vn.* stimulating, activating, putting in motion, making move

جسدي لا يستجيب لرغبتي.. عجز مطبق.. أعجز عن تحريك قدمي، قدماي ليستا ملكي — My body does not respond to my desires; complete incapacity; I am unable to move my feet, my hands are not in my possession

80 | 457 |

3489 قَمْح *n.* wheat

إن مصر تعمل جاهدة على الاكتفاء الذاتي من إنتاج القمح من خلال محورين أساسيين — Egypt is working hard on self-sufficiency in wheat production through two basic axes

70 | 526 |

3490 جِراحَة *n.* surgery

فريق طبي ينجح في فصل توأمتين نيجيريتين واستغرقت الجراحة نحو ٥ ساعات — A medical team succeeded in separating Nigerian twins; the operation lasted about 5 hours

63 | 581 |

3491 مُشَرَّف *adj.* honorable, noble; honorary

نرفع له القبعة احتراما وتقديرا لمواقفه المشرفة ولاتخاذه للقرار الذي يصب في مصلحة البلد — We raise our hats to him in honor and respect for his honorable positions and for his making the decision which will be in the interest of the country

77 | 474 |

3492 أُمْنِيَّة *n.* pl. أَمَانٍ (def. أَمَانِي) wish, hope, aspiration, desire
أتقدم بأجمل التهاني وأرق الأماني للجميع بمناسبة العيد — I offer the warmest congratulations and the best wishes to all on the occasion of the holiday
74 | 494 |

3493 سِمَة *n.* pl. -aat feature, characteristic; stamp, imprint
قالوا: القسوة من سمات الذكورة — They said: Harshness is one of the characteristics of masculinity
75 | 489 |

3494 تَعْقِيد *n.* complication, complexity
ازدادت الأمور تعقيدا بين محمود وزوجته — Matters got more complicated between Mahmoud and his wife
77 | 471 |

3495 مَعْلَقَة *n.* pl. مَلاعِق (also Egy.Lev. مِلْعَقَة) spoon;
تشرب الشاي في كوب مع ثلاث ملاعق من السكر وبدون حليب — She drinks tea from a cup with three spoonfuls of sugar and without milk
41 | 873 | +for

3496 أَذًى *n.* damage, harm; injury; offense
القنابل العنقودية تنفجر بطريقة عشوائية ومحتمل تاليا أن تلحق الأذى بالمدنيين عند استعمالها في أماكن ذات كثافة سكانية عالية — Cluster bombs explode in a random fashion and may, as a result, cause damage to civilians when they are used in places with a high population density
70 | 517 |

3497 لِيرَة *n.* pl. -aat pound, lira (Leb. and Syr.)
والدي ضابط راتبه عشرة آلاف ليرة فقط لا غير — My father is an officer whose salary is ten thousand liras only
44 | 820 |

3498 فَرْعِيّ *adj.* branch, secondary, subdivision
تركنا القضية الأساسية وهي جدوى التحرك النووي لنمسك في قضية فرعية وهي الموقع المختار .. — We left the basic issue, the usefulness of nuclear activity, to grasp a side issue, which is the chosen site
65 | 562 |

3499 صانِع *n.* pl. صُنَّاع manufacturer, producer; maker
عادت نيسان إلى نقطة الصفر وأصبحت خلال سنوات قليلة صانع السيارات الأكثر ربحا في العالم — Nissan went back to point zero, and within a few years became the most profitable car maker in the world
65 | 554 |

3500 ثَلْج *n.* snow; ice
الثلج الذي هطل أثناء الليل غطى كل شيء — The snow that fell during the night covered everything
72 | 502 |

3501 عَصاً (def. عَصا) *n.* stick, baton, rod
كان يمشي متكئا على عصا ويعرج — He walked leaning on a cane, limping
75 | 481 |

3502 تَنْظِيمِيّ *adj.* organizational, planning; controlling, regulatory
يتميز مسلمو أميركا بارتفاع مستوياتهم التعليمية وقدراتهم التنظيمية، وتوحدهم من خلال منظمات رئيسة كبرى تمثلهم — The Muslims of America are characterized by a rise in their education levels and their organizational abilities, and their uniting through large, major organizations which represent them
62 | 585 |

3503 تَقَرَّر *v.* V to be decided, be resolved
لا يغيب عن هذا المؤتمر شخص نجيب محفوظ، فقد تقرر تخصيص جلسة خاصة تتضمن شهادات من اقتربوا منه بشكل شخصي — The conference did not ignore Naguib Mahfouz as a person; it was decided to designate a special session which would include the witness of those who were close to him personally
72 | 502 |

3504 طَرْد *vn.* expulsion; dismissal, firing; *n.* parcel, package
على الاردن طرد الشيعه العراقيين من الاردن فورا لانهم خطر على البلاد والعباد — Jordan needs to expel the Iraqi Shiites from Jordan immediately because they are a danger to the country and to people
76 | 476 | +news

3505 باكِر *adj.* early; (باكِراً early (*adv.*)
تعود أن يعمل منذ الصباح الباكر وحتى منتصف
الليل بغير أن يشكو أو يتذمر — He became
accustomed to working from early morning till
the middle of the night without complaining
or murmuring
73 | 494 |

3506 أَدانَ *v. IV* to condemn, denounce, censure,
disapprove of sth/sb
قالت انها تدين وتستنكر تزييف الحقائق — She said
that she condemns and rejects the falsification
of the facts
67 | 539 |

3507 ضائِع *adj.* lost; stray; wasted (time)
يقفز فرحا كطفل وجد لعبته الضائعة — He is
jumping for joy like a child who found
his lost toy
79 | 458 |

3508 قُماش *n.* pl. أَقْمِشَة fabric, cloth
اشتهرت المدن والقرى الفلسطينية بفن التطريز على
القماش منذ سنين — Palestinian cities and
villages have been famous for years for the
art of embroidery on material
66 | 546 |

3509 ساخِر *adj.* satirical; *a.p.* ridiculing
لاحظت أن عينيه تعكسان دوما تعبيرا ساخرا
وكأنه يشاهد شيئا مسليا — I noticed that his
eyes always reflect a sarcastic expression as if
he is seeing something amusing
63 | 573 | +lit

3510 وَعَى *v. I (i)* to be aware of, pay attention
to sth; (Egy.Lev.) اِوْعَى! be careful! watch out!
انه مجنون لا يعي ما يفعل — He is crazy,
he isn't aware of what he is doing
80 | 448 |

3511 شَكَّ *v. I (u)* to doubt, distrust في sth/sb
لا يجوز لأحد أن يشك في ذلك —
No one should doubt that
75 | 482 |

3512 مَعْدِنيّ *adj.* mineral, metal, metallic
تتحرك الاذرع المعدنية لالتقاط المكونات الدقيقة
للسيارة ووضعها في مكانها الصحيح بالهيكل —
Metal arms move to grasp the precise
components of the car, and put them in their
proper place in the structure
69 | 517 |

3513 اِنْعِقاد *vn.* convening, holding (meeting)
شهدت مدينة سانت جالين السويسرية اليوم السبت
مظاهرة شارك فيها المئات من معارضي العولمة وذلك
قبيل انعقاد منتدى دافوس الاقتصادي الأسبوع
القادم — The Swiss city of St Gallen witnessed
today, Saturday, a demonstration in which
hundreds of opponents of globalization
participated, and this before the opening of
the Davos Economic Forum next week
63 | 574 |

3514 مُتَبَقٍّ (def. مُتَبَقِّي) *adj.* remaining, left over; *n.*
remainder, rest
سافرت مع أسرتها لقضاء الشهر المتبقي من العطلة في
أسبانيا — She travelled with her family to spend
the remaining month of the vacation in Spain
79 | 455 |

3515 وَرْدِيّ *adj.* rose-colored, rosy, pink
كان ذلك اللون الوردي الجميل قد مزق ليتراءى من
خلفه السواد الداكن، والظلام قد عم المكان بكامله
— That beautiful rose color was ripped open
so that behind it a dark black could be seen,
and the darkness covered the entire place
67 | 531 |

3516 كَثافَة *n.* thickness, density; compactness;
intensity
أشجار الزيتون والرمان والتين انتشرت بكثافة على
شاطئ النهر — Olive, pomegranate, date and fig
trees were spread out thickly on the shores of
the river
76 | 471 |

3517 تَشْخيص *vn.* diagnosis, analysis; characterization
راجعت العديد من اطباء الاعصاب ولم يستطع اي
منهم تشخيص حالتي رغم ما دفعته من مبالغ مادية
— I consulted a number of nerve doctors and
not one of them could diagnose my condition
despite the material sums of money I paid
66 | 539 |

3518 خارِطَة *n.* map, chart; خارِطَة الطَّريق
roadmap
يجب أن نضع خارطة طريق واضحة كيف يتقدم
العراق باتجاه الاستقرار إلى الأمان — We need

to lay down a clear roadmap of how Iraq will progress in the direction of stability, and then security

72 | 495 |

3519 مِصْداقِيَّة *n.* credibility

بناء المصداقية في الأمم المتحدة يتوقف على قابليتها للإصلاح — Building credibility in the UN depends on its capacity to reform

66 | 542 |

3520 جَرَحَ *v. I (a)* to wound, injure sb; (usu. pass.) جُرِحَ to be wounded, be injured

وفي تكريت قتل عراقي وجرح آخران في انفجار سيارة مفخخة أمام مبنى حكومي — In Tikrit an Iraqi was killed and two others were wounded in a car bomb explosion in front of a government building

70 | 510 |

3521 رافِض *adj.* rejecting, refusing; *n.* rejectionist

ستجد معظمهم رافضا لهذه الفكرة جملة وتفصيلا — You will find most of them rejecting this idea both as a whole and in detail

73 | 489 |

3522 مُلَوَّن *adj.* colored, multicolored

وقف إلى جانبها مهرج في ثياب ملونة — A clown in a colored suit stood by her side

73 | 491 |

3523 حِراسَة *n.* guard, escort, protection

هيا بنا نجري من هنا قبل خروج كلب الحراسة الضخم — Let's run from here before the huge guard dog comes out

78 | 460 |

3524 مَنْشُود *adj.* pursued, desired, sought; *n.* goal, objective

أكد أنه سيساعد على الوصول الى السلام العادل المنشود — He stressed that he would help get to the desired just peace

76 | 467 |

3525 خَفِيَ *v. I (a)* to be hidden; لا يَخْفَى it's obvious, clear; لا يَخْفَى على أَحَدٍ أَنَّ as everyone knows; لا يَخْفَى عَلَيْكَ (أَنَّ) you are well aware (of the fact that)

هذه أمور عامة لا تخفى على أحد — These are general matters that are not hidden from anyone

77 | 462 |

3526 ضَبَطَ *v. I (u,i)* to regulate, control; to adjust, fix

كاد عمار أن ينفجر لولا أنه ضبط أعصابه ونظر إلى محدثه فابتسمت ابتسامة عريضة — Amar almost exploded, had he not gotten control of his nerves and looked at the one addressing him, and she smiled broadly

60 | 594 | +spo

3527 اِعْتادَ *v. VIII* to become accustomed على to sth, to get used على to sth

بعض الناس اعتاد التعامل مع هذا الزحام بشكل طبيعي — Some people got used to dealing with the crowds in a natural way

77 | 459 |

3528 صَدارَة *n.* chairmanship; precedence

يعود موضوع أسعار النفط ليحتل صدارة الأخبار الاقتصادية هذا العام، بعد أن شغل الأوساط الاقتصادية — The subject of the oil prices has returned to occupy economic news headlines this year, after it had occupied economic circles

66 | 538 |

3529 ناقِد *n.* pl. نُقَّاد critic

أرى أن هناك تربصا بالكتابة الجديدة بل إن بعض النقاد والأكاديميين تحديدا يقومون بتكسير عظام الكتاب الجدد — I see that there is a negative predisposition for new writing, in fact some critics and academics specifically break the bones of new writers

70 | 508 |

3530 تَضْحِية *n.* pl. -aat sacrifice

انه شعب عظيم قدم الكثير من التضحيات وهو جدير بالحرية — It is a great people who have offered a lot of sacrifices, and it deserves freedom

76 | 466 |

3531 مَطاف *n.* consequence, upshot; في نِهايَةِ المَطافِ in the end, finally

أعتقد أن الدين بحد ذاته بغض النظر إن كان دينا
مسيحيا أو دينا إسلاميا أو دينا آخر هو في نهاية
المطاف يسعى إلى كرامة الإنسان — I believe
that religion, in and of itself, without regard
to whether it is Christian or Islamic or another
religion, in the end, strives for the dignity
of man
77 | 457 |

3532 جَماهِيريّ *adj.* mass, throng; (of) masses
وجود مثل هذه المنتخبات الكبيرة يساعد كثيرا على
الحضور الجماهيري وعودة الروح للملاعب — The
existence of these big national teams greatly
helps fan attendance and the return of the
spirit to the arenas
66 | 532 |

3533 خَصيصَة *n. pl.* خَصائص attribute,
characteristic, feature, trait; peculiarity
فالليل لا يكون ليلا نعرف ما له من خصائص
وما فيه من جمال لو لم يعقبه صبح — If morning
did not follow it, night would not be something
whose characteristics and beauty we know
72 | 493 |

3534 تَدَفُّق *n.* flow, stream, flood; influx, invasion
منح مساعدات مالية فورية للمغرب وموريتانيا
لوقف تدفق المهاجرين — It granted immediate
monetary aid to Morocco and Mauritania to
stop the flow of emigrants
77 | 460 |

3535 بُحَيْرَة *n.* lake
انعكس النور على سطح ماء البحيرة الساكن —
The light reflected off the calm surface of the
water of the lake
73 | 484 |

3536 حَماس *n.* enthusiasm, eagerness, zeal;
fortitude, bravery
حاول أن يبعث في الجنود شيئا من الحماس والأمل
— He tried to awaken in the soldiers some
enthusiasm and hope
74 | 477 |

3537 مِنْحَة *n.* gift, donation; grant, scholarship
الجامعات الأمريكية تحتضن المواهب وترعى
الرياضيين وتمنحهم المنحة الدراسية والرعاية المالية
— American universities embrace talent and

take care of athletes and give them study
scholarships and sponsorships
69 | 511 |

3538 تَحَدُّث *n.* discussion, speaking
كان من عادته التحدث إلى نفسه بصوت عال — He
had the habit of talking to himself out loud
82 | 430 |

3539 اِسْتِضافَة *n.* hosting
يعتزم استضافة مؤتمر حول الشرق الأوسط لبحث
عدد من المبادرات — He intends to host a
conference about the Middle East to discuss
a number of initiatives
67 | 525 |

3540 غائِب *adj.* absent
قال: الشرطة في كل مكان، والعدالة غائبة —
He said: The police are everywhere, and
justice is absent
82 | 427 |

3541 تَصْدِير *n.* exporting
مصر لديها منظومة من الاتفاقيات التجارية الجيدة
التي تخدم أهداف التصدير وتساعد على جذب
الاستثمارات المحلية والأجنبية — Egypt has a
system of good trade agreements which serve
the goals of export and help attract local and
foreign investment
64 | 548 |

3542 رُباعِيّ *adj.* four-part, four-sided; *n.*
quadrangle; quartet, foursome
المبادرة تأتي غداة إنهاء مبعوث اللجنة الرباعية حول
الشرق الأوسط توني بلير زيارته الأولى للمنطقة —
The initiative comes after the envoy of the
Middle East Quartet Committee, Tony Blair,
finished his first visit to the region
56 | 625 |

3543 مَسْموح *adj.* allowed, permitted
يتم سحب رخصة كل سائق يتجاوز السرعة المسموح
بها — The permit of every driver who exceeds
the permitted speed limit is withdrawn
85 | 411 |

3544 مَكْسَب *n. pl.* مَكاسِب gain, profit, earning;
achievement, accomplishment
المرأة العاملة حصلت على مكاسب عديدة وحقوقا
وأيضا امتيازات تتلاءم وطبيعتها في كل مجالات العمل

— Working women have obtained many gains and rights, and also privileges which fit her nature in all fields of work

65 | 539 |

3545 حَصَلَ *v. I (u)* to happen, take place

حصل اتفاق على أن تحل الميليشيات وتدمج ضمن قوات الأمن — An agreement took place that the militias would be dissolved and merged into the armed forces

67 | 523 |

3546 رُمَّة *n.* entirety; (with pron.) بِرُمَّتِهِ/بِرُمَّتِها/بِرُمَّتِهم completely, all of it/them

لا يمكن لإسرائيل ولا للمنطقة برمتها أن تنعم بالأمن إذا لم ينعم الفلسطينيون بالاستقرار — Israel and the region as a whole cannot enjoy security if the Palestinians do not enjoy stability

71 | 495 |

3547 وَطَنِيَّة *n.* nationalism, patriotism

لا أريد التحدث عن الوطنية أو اللا وطنية، وإنما عن حياتي كفرد وجندي — I don't want to talk about nationalism or the opposite of nationalism, rather about my life as an individual and a soldier

70 | 499 |

3548 تَمَيُّز *n.* standing out, distinguishing oneself; distinction, excellence

قال ان حصوله على المنصب القاري يمثل علامة مهمة من التميز والتقدير — He said that obtaining the continental post represents an important sign of distinction and appreciation

61 | 570 |

3549 اِقْتِراع *n.* balloting, voting, election

قررت اربع جماعات معارضة قاطعت انتخابات ٢٠٠٢ المشاركة في هذا الاقتراع — Four opposition groups which had boycotted the 2002 elections decided to participate in this voting

54 | 645 |

3550 طاهِر *adj.* clean, pure; flawless, perfect; chaste

نحن نريد هذا الحب الطاهر في حياتنا — We want this pure love in our lives

73 | 479 |

3551 وَشْك *n.* عَلى وَشْكِ on the verge of, just about to

أحس بأنه على وشك أن يبكي — I feel that he is on the verge of crying

83 | 421 |

3552 جَنِين *n.* fetus, embryo; germ

كرومزومات الأب هي ما تحدد نوع الجنين ذكرا كان أم أنثى — The father's chromosomes are what determine the type of fetus, whether it be male or female

60 | 579 |

3553 تُرْبَة *n.* dust, ground, dirt; grave, graveyard

أنا جذوري هنا.. مغروسة في تربة هذه الدار — My roots are here...planted in the soil of this house

74 | 466 |

3554 شَبِيه *adj.* resembling, similar to

هذا العمل فريد من نوعه، لا يوجد شبيه له في تاريخ الادب — This work is unique, there is nothing like it in the history of literature

81 | 430 |

3555 مَسَحَ *v. I (a)* to rub, wipe sth; to wipe, sweep clean sth; to survey, measure sth

أخذت الأم برأس ابنتها ووضعته على حجرها وأخذت تمسح شعرها بحب وحنان — The mother took her daughter's head and put it on her lap and started to comb her hair with love and compassion

59 | 586 | +lit

3556 عَيِّنَة *n. pl.* -aat sample, specimen

وخرجت الدراسة بأن ٨٦٪ من المدرسات عينة الدراسة موافقات على زيادة مفاهيم التربية الوطنية في الكتب المدرسية — The study concluded that 86% of the teachers of the study sample were in agreement with the increase in the concepts of national education in the school books

70 | 494 |

3557 عُقْب *n. pl.* أَعْقاب consequence; في أَعْقاب immediately after

كان الجيش قد أقام معسكرا له داخل حرم الجامعة في أعقاب إعلان حالة الطوارئ على خلفية حدوث فوضى سياسية في بنجلاديش — The army had set

up camp inside the university campus
following the announcement of the state of
emergency, against a backdrop of political
chaos happening in Bangladesh
67 | 520 |

3558 جَفاف *n.* dryness, drought; dehydration,
desiccation
سبب المجاعة هو الجفاف وقلة الماء — The reason
for the famine is the drought, and the lack of
water
73 | 472 |

3559 تَقْويم *n.* rating, valuation; calendar
فمن واجب الدولة أن تعطي هذه المعلومات ليتمكن
المواطن من تقويم أداء الحكومات والإدارات — It is
the duty of the state to give this information
so that the citizens can evaluate the
performance of the government and the
administrations
66 | 520 |

3560 رَصْد *n.* observation; survey; following,
tracking, monitoring
وقد تفرقت عناصر الشرطة القضائية في مختلف
الشوارع والأزقة المعنية، ليتم رصد ومراقبة المارة —
Elements of the judicial police spread out in
the streets and alleyways of concern in order
to observe the passers-by
72 | 479 |

3561 تَشَرَّفَ *v. V* to be honored, be happy
(على to meet sb)
احنا تشرفنا إنا سمعنا صوتك، أهلا وسهلا —
We are honored that we heard your voice,
welcome
27 | 1277 | +spo

3562 وَحْشِيّ *adj.* brutal, savage
أمامنا اليوم جريمة وحشية بشعة — We have a
vicious, horrible crime in front of us today
72 | 482 |

3563 نَفَقَة *n.* pl. -aat expenditure, disbursement;
spending نَفَقات
مازالت الشركات عازفة عن تعيين موظفين جدد
وتركز على خفض النفقات لمواجهة ارتفاع قيمة
اليورو أمام الدولار — The companies are still
harping about appointing new employees and

concentrating on reducing expenses to
confront the rise in the value of the Euro
against the dollar
69 | 500 |

3564 امْتِلاك *n.* possession; control; seizure
يمكنك امتلاك بيت فخم واقتناء سيارة فاخرة —
You can own a luxurious house and own a
luxurious car
73 | 470 |

3565 مَسْبوق غَيْر *adj.* unprecedented
الشركة حققت نتائج غير مسبوقة لمعدلات الانتاج
والتصدير للمنتجات الرئيسية — The company
has achieved unprecedented results in
productivity and the export of primary
products
67 | 513 |

3566 نام (نامي .def) *adj.* developing (country)
معظم صادرات السيارات الصينية حتى الآن موجهةً
إلى الدول النامية، مثل إيران وسورية وماليزيا —
Most Chinese car exports until now are
headed for the developing countries, like Iran,
Syria and Malaysia
60 | 573 |

3567 تَلَقِّي *vn.* receiving, receipt; acquisition
تم نقلهم الى مستشفى ناصر في خان يونس لتلقي
العلاج — They were transported to the Nasir
Hospital in Khan Younis to receive treatment
75 | 459 |

3568 لُغَوِيّ *adj.* language, linguistic; pl. -uun
linguist
ان بلادنا ستقدم تقريرا مفصلا حول برنامج إعداد
المعاجم اللغوية المدرسية لمراحل التعليم العام في
الدول الأعضاء — Our countries will submit
a detailed report about the program to
prepare linguistic school dictionaries for the
stages of public education in the member
countries
65 | 525 |

3569 كِبْر *n.* pride, arrogance; greatness
إن لم يتصف الغني بالتواضع فإن جبال الكبر تنمو
في قلبه — If a rich man is not humble, the
mountains of pride start to grow in his heart
70 | 489 |

3570 تَذْكَرَة *n.* pl. تَذاكِر ticket, card

اذهب واحجز لي تذكرة في قطار الثامنة والنصف — Go and reserve a ticket for me on the 8:30 train

76 | 450 |

3571 اِسْتِماع *vn.* listening (إلى to)

كان يحسن الاستماع إلى حديثها، وكان يستمتع بما تقول — He listened to her speech very carefully, and he was enjoying what she was saying

79 | 434 |

3572 لَمَسَ *v. I* (i,u) to touch, feel, sense sth

أحسست بيد تلمس كتفي — I felt a hand touch my shoulder

76 | 446 |

3573 اِنْخَفَضَ *v. VII* to drop, fall, decrease; to be lowered, decreased, reduced

اعلنت دائرة العمل الامريكية إن طلبات البطالة قد انخفضت هذا الاسبوع لتصل الى ٣٠٨ آلاف — The American Labor Association announced that unemployment requests fell this week to reach 308,000

61 | 562 |

3574 مُشَدِّد *adj.* stressing, emphasizing; strengthening, intensifying

شيراك يعارض فرض عقوبات على حكومة تقودها حماس، مشددا على وجوب عدم الاعتراض على إرادة الشعب الفلسطيني — Chirac opposes imposing sanctions on a government which Hamas leads, stressing the necessity of not opposing the will of the Palestinian people

53 | 646 | +news

3575 نَصَحَ *v. I* (a) to advise, counsel sb (ب to do sth)

لا ينصح بغسل اللحوم بالماء قبل حفظها في الثلاجة — It is not advised that one wash meat with water before storing it in the refrigerator

61 | 556 |

3576 مَرْحُوم *adj.* deceased, late

لم أعش في الإسكندرية ولكن زرتها مرارا مع المرحوم أبي — I didn't live in Alexandria but I visited it several times with my late father

66 | 518 |

3577 اِنْفِتاح *n.* opening up, welcoming; openness, receptiveness; open-door (policy)

ان مصر في طريقها للبحث عن شركاء جدد والانفتاح بصورة أكبر على العالم من خلال شراكات واستثمارات جديدة — Egypt is on its way to search for new partners and to open up to the world more through new partnerships and investments

66 | 518 |

3578 إِنْفلَوِنْزا and إِنْفلُوِنْزا *n.* flu, influenza; (Dia. also) /'infilwanza, 'infilwinza, 'infalwinza, falwanza/

بعد ظهور حالات جديدة للإصابة بمرض أنفلونزا الطيور عاد القلق إلى جموع المواطنين من العودة الشرسة للفيروس — After the appearance of new cases of bird flu, citizens again become worried about a vicious return of the virus

54 | 622 |

3579 عَيَّنَ *v. II* to appoint, designate sb as sth; to determine, define sth

قد سجلت اللجنة التي عينها الوزير رامسفيلد ٥٥ حالة من حالات الإساءة للمعتقلين في العراق — The committee which Rumsfeld appointed recorded 55 cases of abuse of detainees in Iraq

79 | 431 |

3580 مُحَرَّم *adj.* forbidden; *n.* مُحَرَّمات forbidden things, taboos

كلما كنت قريبا من الله بكثرة العبادات والطاعات والبعد عن المحرمات كنت موفقا — The closer you get to God, with increased acts of worship and obedience and keeping away from forbidden things, the more successful you will be

80 | 424 |

3581 حُرْمَة *n.* sanctity, inviolability; taboo, prohibition; married woman, wife

كونت جمعية خيرية هدفها الحفاظ على حرمة المقابر — A philanthropic group was formed with the goal of preserving the sanctity of grave sites

73 | 463 |

3582 تَجْهِيز *vn.* preparing, putting in order; *n.* pl. -aat equipment, gear

تعاني المؤسسات التعليمية من نقص كبير في التجهيزات وتحتاج إلى كثير من الإصلاحات — The

educational establishments suffer from a huge lack of equipment and they need much reform

73 | 462 |

3583 نُكْتَة *n.* joke

— ضحك الصبية كأنهم استمعوا إلى نكتة طريفة The young men laughed as if they were listening to a funny joke

61 | 555 | +spo

3584 مُهْلَة *n.* extension, deferment; postponement, delay; break, respite; reprieve

وقد منحت مهلة اضافية من ١١ شهرا للمقاهي والمطاعم والكازينوهات والملاهي الليلية قبل ان يشملها هذا القرار — An additional period of 11 months was granted to the coffee houses, restaurants and casinos and nightclubs before this decision will apply to them

67 | 502 |

3585 فاهِم *adj.* understanding, comprehending; (Dia.) *a.p.* أنا مش فاهم/فاهمة عليك I don't understand you

دي أول مرة أشوف فيها المسرح الانجليزي.. صحيح أنا مش فاهم تلاتة أربع الكلام.. لكن حاسس كل كلمة — This is the first time I've seen English theater...It's true I don't understand three fourths of the words... But I feel every word

40 | 843 | +spo

3586 اِنْضَمَّ *v. VII* to join, become part of إلى sth

لا استطيع ان أنضم الى حزبكم.. لي ظروفي الخاصة — I can't join your party...I have my special circumstances

75 | 450 |

3587 جافّ *adj.* dry

العصر الالكتروني يقدم وسائل متقدمة تساعد في تحويل المواد العلمية الجافة الى مواضيع جذابة — The electronic age offers advanced means to help transform dry scientific material into interesting subject matter

68 | 495 |

3588 نَزِيف *n.* bleeding, hemorrhage

تمكن الأطباء من وقف النزيف — The doctors were able to stop the bleeding

75 | 446 |

3589 عارَضَ *v. III* to oppose, resist sth/sb

لا يمكن أن يعارض رغبة أخيه الأكبر — He can't oppose his older brother's desire

72 | 464 |

3590 تَهْيِئَة *n.* preparation, arrangement

لا بد من تهيئة الظروف المناسبة لذلك — We have to prepare the appropriate circumstances for that

74 | 451 |

3591 ماكو /maaku/ (Irq.Kuw.) *neg.part.* there isn't, there aren't (any); شكو ماكو /shaku maaku/ what's up? how's it going?

ازدحام فظيع أقول لك ماكو طريق سيارة كله بسطات قاعدين والناس تروح وتجي وتشتري — The traffic is horrible, I'm telling you there is almost no road for cars, everything is sidewalk, and people are going back and forth buying things

29 | 1146 | +spo

3592 اِسْتِعْراض *vn.* review, inspection; tour; parade

تم استعراض مشاكل قاطني منطقة الخالدية وعدم توفر اراض لعمل التوسعات المطلوبة — The problems of the inhabitants of the Al-Khalidiyya region, along with the problem of the non-availability of lands to make requested expansions, were reviewed

67 | 500 |

3593 أَقْسَمَ *v. IV* to swear يَمِيناً an oath, swear ب by

أنا أقسم بكل مقدس أنني لا أعرف عنها شيئا — I swear by everything holy that I don't know anything about it

66 | 507 |

3594 مِنَصَّة *n.* platform, podium

وقد أقيم هذا الحفل في الصرح البطريركي بحضور لفيف واسع من الشخصيات السياسية والدينية اللبنانية التي تتابعت على المنصة لتشيد بالبطريرك لسعة أفقه ودوره التاريخي — This ceremony was held in the Patriarchal center with the attendance of a large group of Lebanese political and religious personalities who came up one after the other to the platform to congratulate the Patriarch for the breadth of his horizons and his historic role

68 | 492 |

3595 مُوَفَّق *adj.* successful; fortunate

لم أكن موفقة في زواجي، والأكيد أن الخطأ ليس مني — I wasn't successful in my marriage, and it is certain that the fault was not mine

73 | 462 |

3596 تَظاهُرَة *n.* rally, demonstration

نقل الشاب إلى المستشفى كان مستحيلا، لأن مشاركته في التظاهرة ستنكشف، وعندها فإنه سيتعرض لغضب رجال الأمن — Transporting the young man to the hospital was impossible, because his participation in the demonstration would be discovered, and at that point he would be subject to the anger of the security men

61 | 545 |

3597 عَناء *n.* hardship, trouble; distress, preoccupation

ساءلت بعضهم عن سبب ذلك، لكنهم لم يكلفوا انفسهم عناء الرد — I asked some of them for the reason for that, but they did not bother to reply (they did not burden themselves with taking the trouble to reply)

75 | 447 |

3598 إظْهار *n.* expressing, showing, demonstrating

تم إظهار النتائج قبل الموعد المحدد لها — The results were displayed before the time appointed for them

77 | 433 |

3599 غَدْر *n.* deception; treachery, treason

رحل في صمت ووقور بعد أن تعذب وتأسى كثيرا من غدر من كان يظنهم أشقاء — He died in silence and dignity after he was tortured, and suffered a lot of treachery from those he thought were his brothers

65 | 511 |

3600 أعْلَم *elat.* more/most knowledgeable

راحوا فين؟ - الله أعلم — Where did they go? – Only God knows

69 | 480 |

3601 معليش /ma9aleesh/ and معلش /ma9alishsh/ (Egy.Lev.) *interj.* never mind, it's OK; sorry, pardon me

معليش على التأخير والتقصير — Sorry for being late, and for not doing my duty fully

37 | 883 |

3602 بَرَّرَ *v. II* to justify, warrant sth; to vindicate, acquit sth/sb

يريد ان يبرر عملا سيئا قام به — He wants to justify a bad deed he did

72 | 463 |

3603 سَدّ *n.* bridging (a gap); defrayal (of costs); paying off (a debt)

الاجور المتدنية لا تكفي لسد ادنى متطلبات الحياة — The low wages are not enough to cover even the lowest necessities of life

78 | 429 |

3604 بَلاء *n.* affliction, misfortune; tribulation

مهما طال الزمن و أشتد البلاء لابد للحق أن ينتصر ويعلو — However long it takes, and however horrible the affliction, truth will come out victorious, and will be raised on high

68 | 492 |

3605 وَظيفيّ *adj.* functional; practical; work-related, employment-related

أشار إلى دعم البنك للكفاءات الكويتية الشابة والسعي الى تطويرها ومنحها المزيد من الفرص الوظيفية — He pointed to the support of the bank of young Kuwaiti capabilities and its attempts to develop them and give them more job opportunities

65 | 512 |

3606 مُواطَنَة *n.* citizenship

نؤمن بحق المواطنة وحق المواطنة حق مكفول لكل أبناء الشعب بالمساواة والعدل والإنصاف بلا تمييز — We believe in the right of citizenship and the right of citizenship is a right guaranteed to all the sons of the people with equality and justice and equity, without distinction

62 | 535 |

3607 مَلْموس *adj.* noticeable, substantial; tangible, concrete

نجحت في تحقيق انجازات ملموسة على الأرض — She succeeded in accomplishing tangible results on the ground

72 | 460 |

3608 تَحَسُّن *n.* improvement

أحب أن أطمئنكم إلى أن أحوال المسلمين هناك في تحسن مستمر، برغم المضايقات الطائفية

I want to assure you that the conditions of the Muslims there are in a state of continual improvement, despite the sectarian problems

82 | 405 |

3609 اِسْتِشْهاد *n.* martyrdom
وكانت الغارات التي شنها الصهاينة أمس قد أدت إلى استشهاد ما يزيد على ال ٣٠ لبنانيا — The raids which the Zionists launched yesterday led to the martyrdom of more than 30 Lebanese

63 | 525 |

3610 أَبْلَغَ *v. IV* to inform, notify sb أَنَّ that; to report بـ sth or أَنَّ that
أخشى أن أبلغ رجال الأمن بعد ذلك أن ما رأيته هي أحلام — I am afraid to tell the security men, since it might become clear later that what I saw was dreams

76 | 437 |

3611 تَرْوِيج *n.* distribution; promotion, marketing
تساهم الأفلام الهندية في الترويج لأزيائنا وتقريبها من أذواق الشباب في الغرب — Indian films help promote our costumes and get them closer to the tastes of young people in the West

63 | 525 |

3612 تَعاطٍ (def. تَعاطِي) *vn.* taking (medicine, drugs); treating, handling (على a problem)
خلال العام المنصرم أوقفنا ٨٠٨ أشخاص بجرم تعاطي المخدرات و ٦٠٨ أشخاص بجرائم الاتجار والترويج وتهريب المخدرات — During the past year we arrested 808 people for the crime of taking drugs and 608 people for crimes of dealing in, advertising, and smuggling drugs

64 | 515 |

3613 تَعارَضَ *v. VI* to clash, conflict, be at odds مع/او with sth
هل تتعارض رغبتك مع رغبة والديك؟ — Is your will in opposition to your parent's will?

72 | 459 |

3614 تَبَرُّع *n.* pl. -aat donation, contribution
التبرع بالدم يعود بالكثير من الفوائد الصحية على الشخص المتبرع — Donating blood

brings a lot of health benefits to the person donating

69 | 480 |

3615 هُدْنَة *n.* truce, armistice; calm, lull
قالت الكتائب في بيان اصدرته اليوم انها لن تبادر الى هدنة مع الاحتلال الا وفق عدد من الشروط — The Brigades said in a communiqué which they issued that they would only initiate a truce with the occupation according to a number of conditions

59 | 557 |

3616 مَوْضُوعِيّ *adj.* objective
هذه كلها تفسيرات غير موضوعية وحزبية وضيقة جدا — All of these are non-objective, limited, partisan explanations

70 | 474 |

3617 جِنّ *n.* demon; jinn; genie
لم يظهر على الساحر الخوف والرعب، فنادى الجن بأعلى صوته.. ولكن دون فائدة — The magician showed no signs of fear or terror, so he called the genie at the top of his lungs, but to no avail

60 | 550 |

3618 هن and هنه /hinne/ *pron.* (Lev.) they (people)
هن عندهم معمل أحذية هون — They have a shoe factory here

8 | 3949 | +spo

3619 مُتَأَكِّد *adj.* certain, sure, convinced (من of)
هل أنت متأكد أنك لم تخطئ؟ — Are you sure that you didn't make a mistake?

72 | 457 |

3620 بَقَى *v. I (a)* /baʼa, yibʼa/ (Egy.) to become; (with imperf.) to begin to do sth; (Dia.) to remain, stay; to continue doing sth or being sth; (with neg.) to no longer do sth or be sth; (Lev.) /biʼi, yibʼa/, (Irq.) /buqa, yibqa/, (Gul.) /bigi, baga, yibga/
العصاية بقت حية.. والحية عايزة تاكل — The stick became a snake...and the snake wants to eat

12 | 2750 | +spo

3621 اِخْتَتَمَ *v. VIII* to conclude, finalize, wind up (an activity)
هذه العملية استهدفت قطع الطريق على ولادة وثيقة الوفاق الوطني التي اختتم بها الفلسطينيون جولة الحوار الوطني ما بين رام الله وغزة — This operation was intended to prevent the birth of a document of national reconciliation with which the Palestinians concluded the round of national dialog between Ramallah and Gaza
59 | 560 |

3622 تَصْنِيع *n.* manufacture, industrialization, processing
فولكسفاغن هي كبرى شركات تصنيع السيارات الاوروبية — Volkswagen is the largest European car manufacturing company
68 | 481 |

3623 تَحَرُّر *n.* (self) liberation, emancipation
العالم الثالث يمر بمرحلة التحرر الوطني من كل أشكال الاستعمار — The Third World is passing through a stage of national liberation from all types of colonialism
64 | 514 |

3624 دِرْع *n.* shield, armor; plaque (award)
لن أحتاج إلى سيف أو درع أو رمح — I won't need a sword or shield or spear
70 | 467 |

3625 شَنَّ *v. I (u)* to wage, launch sth (war, campaign)
على الحكومة ان تشن حملة جديدة لمكافحة الفساد — The government should launch a new campaign to combat corruption
65 | 503 |

3626 قَلِق *adj.* worried, concerned, uneasy
كان إنسانا قلقا تمكن من تحويل قلقه إلى إبداع — He was a stressed out person who was able to transform his stress into creativity
73 | 448 |

3627 تَبَع (Lev.) *poss.adj.* fem. تَبَعَت, pl. تَبَعُون, تاعُون belonging to; (with pron.) تَبَعِي, تَبَعَتِي for me, mine
قلت لها والأولاد تبعك وين قالت الاولاد بره — I said to her: Where are your children? She said: The children are outside
34 | 945 | +spo

3628 رادِيُو *n.* radio
كانت تفتح الراديو وتسمع الأخبار والأناشيد الوطنية والموسيقى — She used to turn on the radio and listen to the news and to national songs and music
73 | 446 |

3629 مِعْدَة and مَعِدَة *n.* stomach
ان مزج عصير الموز مع الحليب يساعد في تهدئة قرحة المعدة — Mixing banana juice with milk helps calm stomach ulcers
60 | 538 |

3630 نَعَمَ *v. I (u,a)* and نَعِمَ (a) to live in comfort; to enjoy ب sth
لم تنعم القرية بليلة هدوء واحدة — The village has not enjoyed a single night of calm
75 | 435 |

3631 حِقْبَة *n.* era, age, time period
كانت حقبة الخمسينات من القرن الماضي حقبة تحرر وطني وقومي ودعوة لتوحد أقطار وشعوب الأمة الواحدة — The period of the Fifties of the last century was a time of national liberation and an invitation to unite the regions and peoples of the single nation
65 | 501 |

3632 إِدْراك *n.* realization, awareness, comprehension; attainment
لم يكن في حالة يقظة تمكنه من إدراك ما يفعله — He wasn't awake enough to realize what he was doing
76 | 430 |

3633 فَجْوَة *n.* (mostly fig.) gap, gulf, breach
هناك فجوة كبيرة ومتسعة بين مصالح هذه الحكومات ومصالح الشعوب — There is a big, wide gap between the interests of these governments and the interests of the peoples
73 | 444 |

3634 خالَفَ *v. III* to contradict sb/sth; to conflict with, go against sth; to violate (the law); (Irq.Gul.) ما يخالِف that's OK, it doesn't matter
لا يجوز النص على ما يخالف الإسلام — It is not necessary to specify what is against Islam
73 | 442 |

3635 تَرَتَّبَ *v. V* to derive or result على from; to carry the consequence على of

قد ترتب على هذا القرار ارتفاع إيجارات المنازل وبقاء معظم سكان المدينة في الشارع — This decision could result in a rise in the rent of houses and cause most of the inhabitants to remain in the street

70 | 462 |

3636 أَرْضَى *v. IV* to satisfy, please sb

الفرصة موجودة للتوصل إلى حل وسط يرضي جميع الأطراف — The opportunity is there to reach a middle solution which will satisfy all parties

79 | 409 |

3637 حِذَاء *n.* shoe; pair of shoes

نخلع الحذاء قبل أن نخطو عتبة المسجد، ونسير بين أعمدة الرواق لصلاة العشاء — We take off our shoes before we step over the threshold of the mosque, and we walk between the columns of the colonnades for evening prayer

63 | 513 |

3638 اِسْتَوْعَبَ *v. X* to comprehend, grasp, master sth; to contain, absorb, assimilate sth

لم تستطع أن تستوعب الأفكار الجديدة — She wasn't able to grasp the new ideas

78 | 413 |

3639 وَاحَة *n.* oasis

الهدف الرئيسي لهذه الخطة الطموح هو تحويل الكويت إلى واحة خضراء — The principle goal of this ambitious plan is to transform Kuwait into a green oasis

64 | 501 |

3640 مَنْفَذ *n. pl.* مَنَافِذ exit, way out; escape, resort; gateway; port (computer)

لا يوجد أي منفذ نستطيع المرور منه — There is not any exit we can pass through

71 | 452 |

3641 طَاغٍ (def. الطَّاغِي) *n. pl.* طُغَاة tyrant, despot, oppressor; *adj.* tyrannical, oppressive (person, regime, weather)

إن مصر حكمها الطغاة أكثر من أي بلد آخر في التاريخ — Egypt has been ruled by tyrants more than any other country in history

69 | 466 |

3642 شِرْيَان *n. pl.* شَرَايِين artery

ثبت علميا أن زيت الزيتون يحمي من أمراض تصلب الشرايين — It was proven scientifically that olive oil protects from the diseases of the hardening of the arteries

69 | 464 |

3643 أَلْبُوم /'album/ *n.* album (music CD)

يجب أن يكون غلاف الألبوم سميكا حتى يتحمل الاستعمال لسنين طويلة — The album cover needs to be thick so that it can bear up under long years of use

46 | 700 | +for

3644 مِلْء *n.* filling; capacity; quantity

لا أستطيع ملء فراغ حياتك.. لا أستطيع أن أحبك — I can't fill the emptiness of your life... I can't love you

70 | 460 |

3645 تَدْبِير *vn.* managing, arranging, preparing; *n. pl.* تَدَابِير arrangement, preparation

دائما ما نقوم باتخاذ التدابير اللازمة — We always make the necessary arrangements

70 | 456 |

3646 كَافِر *n. pl.* كُفَّار kafir (person who rejects the Islamic faith), infidel, unbeliever, apostate

كل من يحمل السلاح ضد أخيه ويشارك الكافر في قتاله عقوبته النار — Everyone who bears arms against his brother and participates with the infidel in his fighting, his punishment is hell

58 | 553 |

3647 تَرْخِيص *n.* license, permission

تطوير المشروع العقاري سيبدأ بعد حوالي عام أي بعد استلام ترخيص المخطط المعدل — Developing the real estate project will begin after approximately a year, in other words after receiving a permit for the amended plan

64 | 496 |

3648 مَلَل *n.* boredom

كيف نتغلب على الملل ونحول حياتنا سهلة وبسيطة لا تغيب عنها البهجة؟ — How can we overcome boredom and transform our lives into something easy, simple, not devoid of joy?

80 | 399 |

3649 عِلاوَة *n.* increase, raise; bonus; allowance, subsidy; عِلاوَةً على in addition to فكم الخسائر التي تنتج ماديا على هذا العلاج، علاوة على الخسائر النفسية والاجتماعية — How many material losses were produced on the basis of this treatment, in addition to the psychological and social losses

64 | 495 |

3650 شُجاع *adj.* brave كان دائما يظهر بمظهر الرجل الشجاع الذي لا يخاف — He always appeared to me to be a courageous man who was not afraid

77 | 415 |

3651 سَدَّدَ *v. II* to obstruct, block (way); to settle/pay off (debt); to aim, shoot (bullet, ball) نسأل الله ان يوفقنا جميعا الى ما يحب ويرضاه، وان يسدد دروبنا على طريق الخير — We ask God to give us all success in what He desires and what satisfies Him, and to point our way in the path of goodness

64 | 495 |

3652 هَدَى *v. I (i)* to lead, guide, direct sb (إلى to); to show sb (the way) هذا هو الايمان الذي يهدي قلوبنا — This is the faith which guides our hearts

67 | 470 |

3653 طَيْف *n.* spectrum (light); pl. أطْياف ghost, apparition, phantom; vision, fantasy ذكر احد الأطفال بأنه رأى في منامه طيف أبيض — One of the children mentioned that he saw a white spectre in his sleep

61 | 521 |

3654 مُفاد *n.* meaning, content; (usu. with pron.) مُفادُها and مُفادُهُ to the effect that, implying that نريد أن نوصل إلى أهلنا وللعالم أجمع رسالة واضحة مفادها أننا لن نستسلم — We want to send a clear message to our families and to the world which says that we will never surrender

75 | 421 |

3655 خالِق *n.* creator; الخالِق the Creator; *adj.* creating, creative

جوهر الإنسانية الإسلامية هو العلاقة بين الخالق والمخلوق بمعنى أنه يوجد مسافة بينهما — The core of Islamic humanism is the relationship between the creator and the creature, meaning that there is a distance between them

66 | 476 |

3656 لَحْن *n.* melody, music, song; tone كانت المرة الأولى لي التقيت بالموسيقار حمادة النادي، وسمع اللحن وأشاد به جدًّا، وعلى الفور قام بتوزيع الأغنية — It was the first time for me to meet the musician Hamada Al-Nadi, and he listened to the tune and praised it a lot, and immediately he distributed the song

62 | 506 |

3657 مُريح *adj.* comfortable, pleasant; soothing, restful إذا كان لديك وقت كاف يمكنك الجلوس في وضع مريح للتأمل والقراءة التي تعتبر من أكثر الطرق المفيدة لإبعاد التفكير — If you have enough time you can sit in a comfortable position and contemplate or read, which is considered to be the best of the useful ways to avoid thinking

82 | 387 |

3658 خام *adj.* raw, unprocessed; crude (oil) في العام ٢٠٠٥ نمت قيمة واردات الأردن من النفط الخام ومشتقاته بشكل مذهل — In 2005 the value of imports of crude oil and its derivatives into Jordan grew at an alarming rate

57 | 552 |

3659 مُؤَدٍّ (def. مُؤَدِّي) *adj.* leading إلى to; resulting in, causing إلى sth كنا في الطريق المؤدية إلى شاطئ البحر — We were on the road leading to the beach

77 | 407 |

3660 شَمْعَة *n.* pl. شُمُوع candle تناولا العشاء على أضواء الشموع — They ate dinner by candlelight

67 | 467 |

3661 تَشَكَّلَ *v. V* to be formed, be composed كيف نشأ الكون؟ وكيف تشكلت الحياة على سطح الأرض — How was the universe created? And how was life formed on the face of the earth?

72 | 438 |

3662 مِزاج *n.* mixture; temperament; mood, feeling
صارت عصبية المزاج سريعة الانفعال — She
became nervous of temperament, quick to
get upset
77 | 408 |

3663 إسْعاف *n.* first aid, medical service; سَيَّارَة
إِسْعاف ambulance
— حضرت سيارة الإسعاف لتنقله إلى المستشفى
The ambulance came to transport him to
the hospital
71 | 444 |

3664 رَقَمِيّ *adj.* numerical; digital
نظر في الساعة الرقمية المثبتة في لوحة السيارة فكانت
تسير في الثامنة والنصف — He looked at the
digital clock fastened to the dashboard of the
car, and it was going on 8:30
53 | 596 |

3665 هِيه *interj.* uh-huh; huh?
هيه ما بغاش يديني هو راح لي قعدي أنتي هنا
— Yeah, he did not want to take me, he left
and told me to stay here
42 | 736 | +spo

3666 شَقِيقَة *n.* sister
لا ننسى ما كان للدول العربية الشقيقة من دور بناء
وكبير، في دعم لبنان ومساندته — We should not
forget the large and constructive role our sister
Arab states played in supporting Lebanon
63 | 498 |

3667 دِفْء *n.* heat, warmth
رفعت الحقيبة على ظهري وقلت: وداعا يا دفء
البيت، وأهلا بك يا برد الطريق — I put the bag
on my back and said: Goodbye to the warmth
of the home, welcome to the cold of the road
64 | 486 | +lit

3668 زلمه and زلمي /zalameh/ (Lev.) *n.* man, guy; pal,
dude
كلها توفيق من ربك يا زلمة اتركها لربك —
It is all success from your Lord, O man,
leave it to your God
28 | 1126 | +spo

3669 منيح /mniiH/ (Lev.) *adj.* pl. مناح /mnaaH/
good, fine

— مرحبا كيفك شو اخبارك؟ – الحمد لله تمام منيحة
Hello, how are you, what's new? – Praise God,
fine, good
6 | 4921 | +spo

3670 يُونانِيّ *n./adj.* Greek
كان يصفر مع إحدى الأغاني اليونانية المنبعثة من
الراديو — He was whistling along to one of the
Greek songs coming from the radio
67 | 465 |

3671 ثَبات *n.* proof, corroboration; constancy,
firmness
ضربوا أروع الأمثال في الثبات والصبر —
They gave splendid examples of reliability
and patience
75 | 415 |

3672 تَزْوير *n.* forgery; falsification (documents,
the truth); counterfeiting
قال الشيخ: هذا كذب وتزوير وخداع — The
Sheikh said: This is a lie and a falsification
and a deception
66 | 474 |

3673 عِبْرِيّ *adj.* Hebrew; الدَّوْلَة العِبْرِيَّة the Jewish
state (Israel); العِبْرِيَّة Hebrew (language)
هذه هي الاثنان والعشرون حرفا التي تشتر
ك فيها العربية مع العبرية والآرامية والسريانية
والحبشية وهكذا — These are the twenty-two
letters which Arabic and Hebrew and
Aramaic and Syriac and Ethiopic, and
the like, share
63 | 492 |

3674 صِغَر *n.* smallness; youth, infancy
تدريب اللاعبين منذ الصغر قد يؤمن لهم مستقبلا
رياضيا جيدا — Training players from a young
age might guarantee for them a good athletic
future
73 | 425 |

3675 نَفَق *n.* pl. أنْفاق tunnel; underpass, subway
اننا نرى الضوء في نهاية النفق المظلم وعلينا السير
للخروج منه — We see the light at the end of
the dark tunnel, and we need to walk to get
out of it
70 | 446 |

3676 مُتَّفَق *p.p.* مُتَّفَق عليه/عليها agreed upon
نفذت الخطة المتفق عليها تماما — She carried out
the agreed upon plan completely
| 411 | 76

3677 قُدْوَة *n.* example, role model; pattern
إنني أحاول أن أكون قدوة لأبنائي — I am trying
to be an example to my sons
| 419 | 74

3678 مُودِيل /modeel/ *n.* pl. -aat model, pattern
موديل فستانها كان كلاسيكيا جدا وغير مناسب —
The style of her dress was very classical and
not appropriate
| 692 | 45 | +spo

3679 وَطْأَة *n.* pressure, gravity; harshness, cruelty
سكت تحت وطأة نظرات زوجته — He remained
silent under the pressure of his wife's glances
| 438 | 71

3680 جَهَنَّم *n.* hell; Hell
ما الذي سيجري؟ ماذا سيحدث؟ إلى أي جهنم
سيأخذونني؟ — What is going to happen?
What will happen? To what hell are they going
to take me?
| 467 | 66

3681 خَتَم *v. I (i)* to complete, conclude sth;
to stamp, seal sth
بهذه الكلمات المؤلمة والحزينة ختم الأستاذ الجامعي
حديثه لطالباته — With these sad and painful
words, the university professor concluded his
speech to the students
| 458 | 68

3682 مُسْتَفِيد *adj.* benefiting, profiting (مِن from);
n. pl. -uun beneficiary
من هو المستفيد من هذه الأحداث وما هو الهدف
الحقيقي من كل ما حصل؟ — Who is benefitting
from these events, and what is the real
purpose of everything that has happened?
| 465 | 66

3683 وَباء *n.* epidemic, disease; scourge
جاءت من بلاد انتشر فيها وباء الكوليرا — She
came from a country in which the disease
of cholera is widespread
| 446 | 69

3684 ارْتِقاء *n.* rise, ascent; advancement,
promotion; progress; evolution
هناك خطة متكاملة لتطوير صناعة الجلود في مصر
والارتقاء بجودة المنتجات الجلدية وزيادة صادراتها
خلال المرحلة المقبلة — There is a comprehensive
plan to develop the leather industry in Egypt
and to raise the quality of the leather products
and increase their export during the coming
period
| 497 | 62

3685 اتِّباع *n.* pursuing, following; compliance
في اطار احكام التصرف في مياه الري تم اتباع عدة
مبادئ منها حماية الموائد المائية السطحية من زحف
مياه البحر أو مياه السباخ الداخلية — In the
context of the rules of behavior regarding
irrigation water, several principles were
followed, among which was the protection of
the surface water tables from the infiltration of
sea water or internal sewage water
| 418 | 74

3686 سُكُون *n.* tranquility, quietude, calm; rest, repose
انقطع الهمس فورا وساد سكون عميق قطعته
النحنحة التي تسبق كلامه — The whispering
ceased immediately and a deep silence
prevailed which was cut by the coughing
which preceded his talk
| 525 | 58 | +lit

3687 شَنّ *n.* waging, launching (a war, campaign)
كانوا يحضرون لشن هجوم على مركز للشرطة في ده
شوبان بولاية زابل — They were preparing to
launch an attack on a police center in Dah
Shoban in the State of Zabul
| 517 | 59

3688 عُقْبال (Egy.Lev.) *interj.* may it (good fortune)
be the same for
الأهل يتقدمون بأحر التهاني للابنة آمنة المأمون
بمناسبة تفوقها في امتحانات الأساس ويتمنون لها
التوفيق وعقبال الماجستير والدكتوراة — The family
offers its warmest congratulations to the girl
Amina Al-Ma'mun on the occasion of her
doing well in the basic tests, and they hope
she will have success, we look forward to the
MA and PhD
| 812 | 38 | +for +spo

3689 تَثْبِيت *n.* confirmation; stabilization

إنهم يصارعون من أجل تثبيت استقلالهم — They are wrestling to confirm their independence

76 | 404 |

3690 زَرْع *n.* planting (seed); implanting, transplanting (organ); setting (bomb), laying (mines); growing (plants, crops); cultivating, farming (land)

لقد أفلحنا في زرع الرعب في قلوبهم — We succeeded in planting terror in their hearts

77 | 400 |

3691 قَلْعَة *n.* stronghold, citadel, fort

يكفيني شرفا وفخرا ان بلدي ما تزال قلعة الصمود الباقية في وجه العدو — It is enough for me, as far as pride and dignity go, that my country is still the remaining fortress of resistance against the enemy

78 | 392 |

3692 اللَّتَان *rel.pron.* (fem.du.; gen./acc. اللَّتَيْن) who, whom; which

كتب مقالا تحدث فيه عن الوسيلتين الرئيسيتين اللتين تتبعهما الجماعات الإرهابية في العراق — He wrote an article in which he spoke about the two principal methods that terrorist groups in Iraq follow

70 | 440 |

3693 جاهِد *adj.* strenuous, vigorous; striving, endeavoring

كنت اسعى جاهدة لاوفق بين عملي والاعتناء بعائلتي — I was trying diligently to reconcile my work with taking care of my family

82 | 375 |

3694 مَتْن *n.* deck (ship); عَلَى مَتْنِ on board (ship, airplane); surface; main text, content (book, article, poem); lexicon (language); body (person, object)

هرب من فرنسا على متن طائرة أمريكية — He fled from France on board an American plane

65 | 468 |

3695 مُتَحَرِّك *adj.* moving, mobile

التلاميذ لا ينجزون واجباتهم المنزلية بسبب مشاهدة الرسوم المتحركة — The students are not doing their homework because of watching cartoons

75 | 407 |

3696 مُقَوِّم *n.* pl. -aat component, ingredient; basic element

تدعو الدولة الى تحمل مسؤولياتها في هذا الشأن وتوفير مقومات الإسكان للذين دمرت منازلهم — She is calling on the state to bear its responsibilities in this matter and provide the components of housing to those whose houses were destroyed

72 | 423 |

3697 وَهْمِي *adj.* imagined, imaginary; fake, bogus

هذه إنجازات وهمية لا أساس لها من الصحة والواقع — These are imaginary accomplishments which have no basis in truth or reality

73 | 417 |

3698 مُعْلِن *n.* announcer; advertiser; *a.p.* announcing; signaling

صادرت الحكومة البن من الأسواق، معلنة ان تجارته ستكون تابعة للحكومة نفسها لتزويد الجيوش — The government seized the coffee bean from the markets, announcing that trade in coffee would belong to the government itself in order to supply the army

81 | 374 |

3699 دُونَا *prep.* without any, without even

لا أفهم لماذا يكره بعض الناس غيرهم دونما سبب — I don't understand why some people hate others without a reason

72 | 424 |

3700 عَدْوَى *n.* infection

صار الغضب عدوى تنتقل من شخص لآخر — Anger became an infection that was transmitted from one person to another

72 | 425 |

3701 مُبالَغَة *n.* exaggeration

هذا ما حدث دون كذب أو مبالغة — This is what happened, without lie or exaggeration

76 | 398 |

3702 عاقِبَة *n.* pl. عَواقِب consequence, result, effect

لن أتخلى عن الأمر مهما تكن العواقب — I will not give up on the matter no matter what the consequences

77 | 395 |

3703 بَياض *n.* white, whiteness

ابتسم ابتسامة تظهر تفاصيل أسنانه وقال: أتلاحظون أسناني؟ بَياض — He smiled a smile that showed the details of his teeth and he said: Do you see the whiteness of my teeth?

65 | 462 |

3704 ضَمِنَ *v. I (a)* to guarantee, insure

هو سجن يكذب كل الشعارات التي تضمن حقوق السجين وإدماج السجناء — It is a prison which gives the lie to all the slogans which guarantee the rights of the prisoner and the integration of prisoners

71 | 428 |

3705 مُنْتَهىً *n.* utmost, extreme

هذا الموضوع في منتهى التعقيد وصعب جدا — This subject is of the utmost complexity, and is really difficult

73 | 415 |

3706 حُمَّى *n.* fever; heat

من أهم الأخطار الجانبية لهذا العقار هي الحمى الخبيثة والتي تتميز بارتفاع درجة الحرارة — One of the most important side effects of this drug is a malignant fever, which is characterized by a rise in temperature

63 | 480 |

3707 مَرّ *n.* passing, course (of time); going by

قال أستاذ جامعي عراقي إن الشعب العراقي على مر التاريخ كان ومازال موحدا — An Iraqi university professor said that the Iraqi people throughout history were and still are united

76 | 397 |

3708 قاوَمَ *v. III* to resist, oppose sth

ظلت طوال سنوات تقاوم المرض بتفاؤل كبير — For years she kept resisting the illness with a large degree of optimism

71 | 422 |

3709 اِئْتِلاف *n.* coalition, union

انضم التيار الصدري – وهو جزء من الائتلاف العراقي الموحد – إلى جبهة التوافق والسلطات المحلية في إقليم كردستان — The Sadrist Movement, part of the United Iraqi Coalition, has joined with the Accord Front and the local authorities in the Kurdistan region

46 | 647 |

3710 مارّ *n.* pl. مارَّة *n.* pedestrian, passerby

الشوارع خلت من المارة ولا يوجد سوى الكلاب — The streets were empty of pedestrians and there was nothing but dogs

73 | 411 |

3711 كِيمِيائيّ *adj.* chemical

طالب دول العالم بسرعة التوقيع على اتفاقية حظر الأسلحة الكياوية — He asked the nations of the world to quickly sign the agreement banning chemical weapons

66 | 452 |

3712 حَداثَة *n.* modernity, newness, novelty

ها قد جاء عصر الحداثة والرقي ليضع حدا للجهل والتخلف — Then the age of modernism and progress came to put a stop to ignorance and backwardness

53 | 570 |

3713 إيدز and أيدز /'eedz/ *n.* AIDS (usu. مَرَض الايدز)

مكاتب برنامج الأمم المتحدة الإنمائي الموجودة في ٢٠ دولة عربية تضع مكافحة الايدز في مقدمة أولوياتها — The offices of the United Nations Development Program in 20 Arab countries put the fight against AIDS at the top of their list of priorities

56 | 531 |

3714 ناخِب *n.* pl. -uun voter, elector

يجب احترام ارادة الناخبين والاستماع اليها وتطبيقها — The will of the voters must be respected and listened to and carried out

53 | 565 |

3715 اِسْتِناد *n.* dependence; اِسْتِناداً على on the basis of, according to

أكد لنا في البداية أن الرابطة لا تتخذ قراراتها استنادا الى ما يقال في الشارع — He assured us in the beginning that the organization would not make its decision depending on what was being said in the street

68 | 441 |

3716 مُجْمَل *n.* total, full amount; summary

كانت اجواء اللقاء ايجابية وتحدثنا عن مجمل الوضع في لبنان وعن المشاكل القائمة والوضع في المنطقة — The atmosphere of the talks was positive, and we spoke about the overall

situation in Lebanon and about the
outstanding problems and the situation
in the region

64 | 467 |

3717 اِحْتِفاظ *vn.* safeguarding, preservation

هل أستطيع الاحتفاظ بسيارتي القديمة؟ —
Can I keep my old car?

74 | 403 |

3718 عارٍ (def. عاري) *adj.* naked, bare

أريد الحقيقة العارية، حدثيني بها — I want the
naked truth, tell it to me

75 | 400 |

3719 سَيْل *vn.* streaming, flowing

تدفقت دموعي وكأنها سيل جارف — My tears
poured out as if they were a torrent

68 | 440 |

3720 مَفْقُود *adj.* lost, missing; *n.* missing (person)

ذلك يساعد على سريان سوائل الجسم والمخاط،
ويعوض السوائل المفقودة نتيجة لكثرة التعرق —
This helps with the secretion of body fluids
and mucus, and replaces fluids lost as a result
of heavy sweating

76 | 391 |

3721 تَفاؤُل *n.* optimism

نحن ننظر للمستقبل بعين التفاؤل — We are looking
to the future with the eye of an optimist

76 | 394 |

3722 ذَرِّيّ *adj.* atomic

الدول العظمى تعتقد ان من حقها استخدام الاسلحة
الذرية وانتاجها — The great powers believe that
it is their right to use nuclear weapons and to
produce them

54 | 550 |

3723 بَرازِيلِيّ *n./adj.* Brazilian

انتظر سيينا حتى الدقيقة ٧١ ليهدد مرمى الحارس
البرازيلي ديدا بعدما توغل توماس لوكاتيلي داخل
منطقة ميلان بمجهود فردي — Sienna waited until
the 71st minute to threaten the goal of the
Brazilian goalkeeper Dida, after Tomas Locatelli
snuck inside Milan's area on an individual effort

48 | 618 |

3724 عَتِيق *adj.* old, aged

انه صاحب محل تجاري بالمدينة العتيقة يوفر مختلف
المنتوجات التقليدية — He is the owner of
a commercial shop in the old city which
provides various traditional products

66 | 448 |

3725 مُفْرَدَة *n.* pl. -aat word, term, expression;
مُفْرَدات vocabulary

ليس لديهم الوقت لفهم مفردات لهجة لا يعرفونها
— They don't have time to understand the
vocabulary of a dialect they don't know

69 | 433 |

3726 كُورِيّ *n./adj.* Korean

يعود سبب الطلب على السيارات الكورية إلى رخص
أسعارها مقارنة بأسعار السيارات الأوروبية —
The cause of demand for Korean cars can be
attributed to the cheapness of their price
compared to the prices of European cars

52 | 566 |

3727 تَعْمِيم *n.* making general or public (education,
announcement); spreading, disseminating,
popularizing

أنا متأكدة من أنه لا يجوز التعميم في مثل هذه الأمور
— I am certain that he should not generalize
about these matters

65 | 456 |

3728 شائِعَة *n.* pl. -aat rumor

كل هذه الشائعات لا أساس لها من الصحة —
There is no basis in truth to all these
rumors

69 | 429 |

3729 طاقِم *n.* crew, staff, team

الطاقم الطبي مكون من طبيبين مكسيكيين وثلاثة
أمريكيين — The medical crew is composed of
two Mexican doctors and three Americans

69 | 429 |

3730 ثابِتَة *n.* pl. ثَوابِت principle, rule;
established norms, guiding principles

نحن ملتزمون بهذه الثوابت مهما كانت الصعوبات
— We are committed to these principles no
matter what the difficulties

65 | 458 |

3731 تَشاوُر *n.* deliberation, joint consultation

إذا كان هناك قمة ستعقد يجب التشاور حولها ويجب
الإعداد لها — If there is a summit that is going
to be held, we have got to consult about it
and we have to prepare for it

54 | 547 |

3732 عَقْليَّة *n.* mentality, attitude, way of thinking

العقلية الشرقية تفسر هذا التصرف على أنه جحود من
الأبناء — The Eastern mentality would explain
that behavior as ingratitude on the part of the
children

80 | 369 |

3733 بَلاش (Egy.Lev.) *part.* (in neg. commands or
statements) don't (do sth), forget about (sth
or doing sth); never mind, there is no need
for (sth or doing sth); (Egy.Lev.Irq.Gul.) بِبَلاش
for nothing, for free, free of charge

وحياة أبوكم يا جماعة بلاش كلام في السياسة — By
the life of your father, guys, no talking about
politics

43 | 690 | +spo

3734 صَرْخَة *n.* shout, scream

سمعت صرخة نسائية عالية قادمة من أسفل —
I heard a woman's high-pitched scream
coming from below

66 | 445 |

3735 وافِد *adj.* arriving, coming, visiting; foreign,
imported; *n.* pl. -uun visitor, newcomer;
envoy, delegate

كم عدد المرضى الوافدين على المستشفى هذه السنة؟
— What is the number of sick people coming
to the hospitals this year?

65 | 453 |

3736 لَبِثَ *v. I (a)* to stay, linger; ما لَبِثَ أَنْ
and لَمْ يَلْبَثْ أَنْ it wasn't long before

نهض وخرج من القاعة، ولم يلبث أن عاد — He got
up and left the hall, and it was not long before
he returned

61 | 484 | +lit

3737 سَراب *n.* mirage, illusion

الصراع مع العدو الصهيوني أثبت أن الاتفاقيات هي
سراب لا طائل من ورائه — The struggle with

the Zionist enemy has proven that agreements
are a mirage, with nothing to back them up

59 | 502 |

3738 لاتينيّ *adj.* Latin

تمت ترجمة الكتب العربية إلى اللغة اللاتينية —
The Arabic books were translated into Latin

66 | 446 |

3739 شَقّ *n.* splitting, opening; crack, gap

كان الآلهة الصغار هم من يقوم بالأعمال الشاقة
فيكدون في شق الانهر والقنوات والتنقيب عن المعادن
— The lesser gods are the ones who do the
hard work, so for example they labor in
digging rivers and canals and mining metals

75 | 391 |

3740 مُسانَدَة *n.* support, aid, assistance

طالب السفير الدول العربية الغنية بسرعة التبرع لدعم
ومساندة اللاجئين العراقيين — The ambassador
requested the wealthy Arab states to quickly
donate to support and help the Iraqi refugees

57 | 517 |

3741 سُكَّريّ *n.* (also مَرَض السكري) diabetes

من الأخطاء الشائعة أن يعتقد العديد من المرضى
المصابين بداء السكرى بأن السيطرة على سكر الدم
لديهم غير ممكن — One of the prevalent
mistakes is that many diabetes patients
believe that controlling their blood sugar is
not possible

59 | 498 |

3742 عُقْدَة *n.* pl. عُقَد complex (emotion, feeling);
knot (nautical)

لدي عقدة ضد أي قوة سياسية — I have
a complex against any political power

74 | 396 |

3743 مُفَخَّخ *adj.* booby-trapped; سَيَّارَة مُفَخَّخَة car
bomb; رسالة مُفَخَّخَة letter bomb

عشرات العراقيين سقطوا قتلى وجرحى بانفجار أربع
سيارات مفخخة استهدف تجمعات وقرى للطائفة
الأزيدية بالقرب من الحدود العراقية السورية
— Scores of Iraqis fell dead and wounded in an
explosion of four booby-trapped cars which
targeted communities and villages of the
Yazidiyya sect near the Iraqi Syrian border

52 | 562 | +news

3744 بَشِع *adj.* ugly, horrible, disgusting

ادان العالم كله تقريبا هذه الجريمة البشعة وطالبوا الطاغية وزمرته بالانسحاب الفوري من الاراضي الكويتية — Almost the whole world condemned this heinous crime and demanded the tyrant and his gang to withdraw immediately from Kuwaiti lands

73 | 402 |

3745 تَعْطِيل *vn.* hindering, obstructing; derailing; interrupting

توقف بعض السيارات أدى الى تعطيل بسيط لحركة السير — The stopping of some cars led to a simple traffic jam

68 | 430 |

3746 مُحْتَوًى *n. pl.* مُحْتَوَيات content

— كان علي أن أتفقد محتويات الحقيبة، لكنني لم أفعل I needed to inspect the contents of the bag, but I didn't do it

74 | 397 |

3747 منو /minu/ *interrog.* (Gul.Irq.Sud.) who

قال لي اخوي منو هذي؟ قلت له ما ادري — My brother said to me: Who is this? I told him I don't know

27 | 1073 | +spo

3748 إبّان *n.* time; إبّان during

عملت في الإدارة الأميركية إبان عهد الرئيس بيل كلينتون — I worked in the American administration during the era of Bill Clinton

69 | 425 |

3749 غَفَرَ *v. I (i)* to pardon, forgive ل sb sth

في مجتمعاتنا المرأة هي من يغفر أغلب الأحيان — In our society, it is the woman who forgives most of the time

57 | 513 |

3750 زالَ *v. I (u)* to disappear, vanish

— حرب الثقافة لن تزول لأنها لم تنته معنا بعد The culture war will not disappear, because it is not finished with us yet

65 | 451 |

3751 أيْنَما *conj.* wherever

أرحب بكم مشاهدينا الكرام أينما كنتم برفقتنا فأهلا — ا welcome you, dear viewers, wherever you are with us, welcome to you to a new episode from "The Fourth Estate"

بكم إلى حلقة جديدة من السلطة الرابعة

75 | 388 |

3752 إجْماع *n.* consensus; بالإجْماع unanimously

البرلمان أخذ قرارا بالإجماع بإقرار هذا القانون — Parliament took a decision, unanimously, to pass this law

61 | 475 |

3753 تَنَفُّس *n.* breathing, respiration; breath

اضحك بكل قوتك فإن ذلك يساعدك على التنفس وعلى امتصاص قدر أكبر من الاكسجين — Laugh with all your might, for that will help you breathe and absorb more oxygen

65 | 451 |

3754 هَدْم *n.* demolition, destruction; leveling, razing

لقد قرر المجلس البلدي هدم هذا المكان — The town council decided to destroy this place

72 | 403 |

3755 قَفَص *n.* cage; prisoner's dock

كنت أنظر من النافذة فرأيت امرأة تحمل قفص عصافير — I was looking out the window and I saw a woman carrying a bird cage

65 | 447 |

3756 جَسَّدَ *v. II* to embody, personify sth; to put sth into concrete form

وصف هذه المدينة بأنها مكان ساحر يجسد أحلامه الطفولية — He described this city as a magical place that embodies his childhood dreams

72 | 404 |

3757 خِزانَة *n.* treasury; vault, safe; خِزانَة كُتُب bookcase

أسلحة أبي في الخزانة ومفتاحها دوما معه — My father's weapons are in the safe and the key is always with him

68 | 425 |

3758 ثَمانُون *num.* eighty; eightieth

يعني شوفي الحامل إلا أنا يختلف جسمها أنا بالشهر التاسع بوصل وزني ثمانين بس مجرد ما أخلف وبتعرفي رضاعة وإشي زي هيك بينزل وزني — See, the pregnant woman, her body is different, I'm in the ninth month, my weight is close to eighty,

but as soon as I give birth, you know, nursing and such, like that, my weight will go down

56 | 520 |

3759 شَبَح *n.* ghost, specter

اليوم أصبح شبح هذه الحرب بعيد جدا، العراق ليس على حافة الحرب — Today the specter of this war is very far; Iraq is not on the verge of war

77 | 376 |

3760 يَقْظَة *n.* wakefulness; alertness

هل أنا في حلم أم في يقظة؟ — Am I in a dream or awake?

70 | 410 |

3761 حَرِج *adj.* delicate, sensitive; awkward

الجرحى في حالة حرجة جدا وتم نقلهم إلى المستشفى لتلقي العلاج — The wounded are in a very critical state and they were transferred to the hospital to receive treatment

74 | 392 |

3762 باطِن *adj.* inner, interior; hidden; *n.* inner part, inside

خبأ المال في باطن الأرض تحت حجر كبير — He hid the money inside the earth under a big stone

72 | 401 |

3763 رُخْصَة *n. pl.* رُخَص license, permit

في الدول الراقية من يريد استخراج الجواز أو الإقامة أو تجديدها، وكذلك رخص القيادة والتأمين، ليس عليه سوى إرسالها بواسطة البريد — In the advanced countries whoever wants to get a passport or a residence permit or to renew them, also a drivers license and insurance, only needs to send them by mail

69 | 417 |

3764 عالِق *adj.* pending, outstanding (issues); related, connected, relevant; caught, stranded

لماذا بقيت هناك مشاكل عالقة في دائرتك؟ — Why are there still outstanding problems in your department?

72 | 401 |

3765 جَسَدِيّ *adj.* corporeal, physical, bodily; sensual

هو يمتلك الصحة الجسدية لكنه محروم من الصحة النفسية — He possesses bodily health but he is deprived of psychological health

70 | 413 |

3766 اِشْتَدَّ *v. VIII* to intensify, grow more intense

لقد توقع ان يشتد هطول الامطار خلال ساعات الليل — It is expected that rainfall will grow more intense during the hours of the night

68 | 422 |

3767 مَعْنَوِيّ *adj.* moral, spiritual, mental; semantic

تحسنت حالتي المعنوية وانتظمت في الدراسة — My morale improved and my studies have become more organized

71 | 403 |

3768 مُزْمِن *adj.* enduring, chronic

كان مصابا بمجموعة من الأمراض المزمنة — He was stricken with a group of chronic illnesses

70 | 410 |

3769 غاز *n. pl.* غُزاة (*def.* غازي) invader, raider

قتلت جيوش الغزاة كل من وقف بوجهها — The invading armies killed everyone who stood in their way

61 | 472 |

3770 فِطْر *n.* fitr (end of the Ramadan fast); عِيد الفِطْر Eid Al-Fitr (festival of the breaking of the Ramadan fast)

سأطرح ألبومي الجديد بعد عيد الفطر — I will put out my new album after the Eid Al-Fitr

66 | 434 |

3771 فارِسِيّ *n./adj. pl.* فُرْس Persian

قد شاهدت الاهتمام الكبير تجاه اللغة الفارسية والأدب الفارسي في معظم الدول العربية — I have witnessed the big interest in Persian language and Persian literature in most of the Arab states

63 | 453 |

3772 عَلَن *n.* (the) open; عَلَناً and في العَلَن openly, publicly

كانوا يرتكبون جرائمهم علنا في الطرق ويمارسون أعمال النهب واللصوصية والفتك — They were committing their crimes openly in the streets and carrying out deeds of robbery and thieving and murder

74 | 387 |

3773 اِنْطَوَى *v. VII* to contain, include على sth; اِنْطَوَى على نَفْسِهِ to isolate oneself; to be introverted

— كان يفكر في الغد وما ينطوي عليه من مفاجآت
He was thinking about tomorrow and what it
would contain in the way of surprises
69 | 416 |

3774 اِنْقِسام *n.* fragmentation, schism; disruption
علينا ألا نختلف أو نتسبب في أي انقسام أو
انشقاق لحزبنا الجديد — We shouldn't
disagree or cause any split or break-up
of our new party
63 | 455 |

3775 كَنْز *n.* pl. كُنُوز treasure
تتكون كنوز الفرعون توت عنخ امون من ١٢٠ قطعة
— The treasures of the Pharaoh Tut Ankh Amun
consist of 120 pieces
73 | 392 |

3776 مُعادٍ (مُعادِي .def) *adj.* hostile, anti-
رفعوا اللافتات المعادية للحرب — They raised
banners opposing the war
66 | 431 |

3777 مُتْعَب *adj.* tired, weary
إنني متعب ويجب أن أذهب وأرتاح — I am tired
and I must go rest
67 | 424 |

3778 راعَى *v. III* to heed, observe sth; to respect,
show consideration for sth
أعتقد أن السيد جلال طالباني سوف يراعي
القانون وسوف يلتزم به — I believe that
Mr Jalal Talabani will respect the law and
comply with it
77 | 369 |

3779 جُزْئيّ *adj.* partial, incomplete; جُزْئيّاً partially,
in part
لا يجوز التنازل عن هذا العقد كليا او جزئيا الا بعد
الحصول على موافقة كتابية — This contract
should not be abrogated either wholly or in
part except after obtaining written agreement
65 | 437 |

3780 خَليط *n.* mixture, blend
هم خليط من الناس من مختلف الأعمار —
It is a mixture of people of various ages
71 | 402 |

3781 جانٍ (جانِي .def) *n./adj.* pl. جُناة delinquent,
criminal
وصل رجال الأمن للقبض على الجناة لكنهم لم يجدوا
أحدا — The security men arrived to arrest the
criminals, but they didn't find anyone
68 | 415 |

3782 فَقيه *n.* pl. فُقَهاء faqih (expert in Islamic
jurisprudence)
هل يقوم الفقهاء ورجال الدين بدورهم كاملا؟ —
Do the Islamic legal experts and men of
religion play their role fully?
62 | 452 |

3783 مُتَضَرِّر *adj.* damaged; injured; *n.* victim;
plaintiff
زار الوزير عددا من الأحياء و المنازل المتضررة من
هطول الأمطار خلال الأيام الماضية — The
minister visited a number of quarters and
homes damaged in the downpour during the
last few days
58 | 489 |

3784 ثَمين *adj.* costly; valuable, precious
عندي مجموعة ثمينة من الاسطوانات الموسيقية
لأعظم العباقرة — I have an expensive group of
musical records by the greatest of the geniuses
76 | 369 |

3785 اِنْتِقاليّ *adj.* transitional
لقد مرت أسواقنا جميعا بمراحل انتقالية حساسة
والذي يدعونا الى التدرج في عمليات الاصلاح بطء
— All our markets have passed through
sensitive transitional stages, which invites us to
go gradually in reform efforts
54 | 515 |

3786 بَشَرة *n.* skin, epidermis
أهم مميزات الخس أنه يحد من ظهور البقع اللونية على
البشرة خاصة الحمراء منها، كما يستخدم كمنظف —
The most important features of lettuce are
that it limits the appearance of colored spots
on the skin, particularly the red ones, and it
also used as a cleanser
52 | 542 |

3787 مُضاعَفَة *n.* doubling, compounding; pl.
مُضاعَفات complications

تعمل الجمعية على مضاعفة جهودها حتى تستطيع تقديم المزيد من البرامج والأنشطة — The club is working on doubling its efforts to be able to offer more programs and activities

70 | 399 |

3788 طُلّابيّ *adj.* student-

كان يشارك في الأنشطة الطلابية عامة، والثقافية خاصة — He participated in student activities generally, particularly the cultural ones

57 | 486 |

3789 فاضٍ (فاضِي .def) *adj.* empty; unoccupied; available, free (not busy)

يلقي نظرة سريعة عبر النافذة.. الشارع فاضي خالص — He takes a quick look out the window...The street is completely empty

33 | 836 | +spo

3790 بَنْزين *n.* gas, gasoline, petrol

أدى ارتفاع أسعار البنزين إلى تراجع مبيعات السيارات في أوروبا خلال الشهر الماضي — The rise in the price of gasoline led to a fall in auto sales in Europe during the last month

72 | 390 |

3791 اِعْتَزَم *v. VIII* to be determined, be resolute (على to do sth)

أخبرني أنه يعتزم السفر إلى الشام — He informed me that he is determined to travel to Syria

57 | 487 | +news

3792 زَهْرَة *n.* flower; (fig.) splendor

قدمت لي زهرة حمراء.. أخذتها مستغربا.. نظرت إليها — She offered me a red flower...I took it, surprised...I looked at her

58 | 485 |

3793 قَمْع *n.* oppression, repression

يناضل ويكافح ضد جميع اعمال القمع والتفرقة وانتهاكات حقوق الانسان — He struggles and fights against all acts of repression, discrimination and human rights abuses

65 | 431 |

3794 عَصْريّ *adj.* contemporary, modern

دعا الى ايجاد طريقة عصرية لفهم الدين واستيعاب مفرداته ودمجها في الحياة المعاصرة — He called for

finding a contemporary way to understand religion and to absorb and integrate its vocabulary into contemporary life

72 | 387 |

3795 عُشْب *coll.n.* grass, vegetation; عُشْبَة *un.n.* pl. أَعْشاب herb, plant

جلسنا على العشب وأسندنا ظهرنا إلى جذع الشجرة — We sat on the grass and leaned our backs against the trunk of the tree

60 | 461 |

3796 جُرْأَة *n.* boldness, audacity, courage

لم أمتلك الجرأة الكافية لفعل ذلك — I didn't possess sufficient courage to do that

70 | 396 |

3797 عَصير *n.* juice

سأعد لك كأسا من عصير البرتقال الطازج — I will prepare a cup of fresh orange juice for you

56 | 499 |

3798 أَكْثَرَ *v. IV* to do مِن sth frequently, to do a lot of مِن sth

تجنب الأماكن التي يكثر فيها التدخين والمدخنون — He avoided the places in which smoking and smokers were plentiful

73 | 382 |

3799 وَحْي *n.* inspiration

انه نبي يأتيه الوحي من السماء — He is a prophet, inspiration comes to him from heaven

64 | 438 |

3800 حَزْم *n.* determination, resoluteness

اننا نحذر هنا وبوضوح اننا سنقف بحزم ضد كل محاولة مشبوهة للنيل من وحدة شعبنا وأمنه — We warn clearly here that we will stand with determination against all suspicious attempts to undermine the unity of our people and our nation

72 | 389 |

3801 إِنْتاجِيّ *adj.* production-related; productive

القروض وفرت ٥٤٠٠ فرصة عمل مباشرة في عدد كبير من الانشطة الإنتاجية والخدمية من بينها الصناعات الغذائية وشملت ٦ مطاحن للحبوب

Loans provided 5,400 direct work opportunities in a large number of productive and service activities among which are food manufacturing and include 6 grain mills

55 | 508 |

3802 إِسَاءَة *n.* insult, affront; (with foll. *vn.*) wrong, incorrect

أنا متأسف جدا لم اقصد الإساءة — I am very sorry, I didn't mean to offend

70 | 395 |

3803 سَهُلَ *v. I (u)* to be easy, be convenient

اليمن بلاد لا يسهل حكمها — Yemen is a country which is not easy to govern

78 | 358 |

3804 رِيف *n.* country, countryside, rural area

أسرته في الأصل من الريف — His family is originally from the countryside

64 | 436 |

3805 وَضْعِيَّة *n.* situation, status; position

هذه الوضعية لا يمكن تجاوزها إلا بالقيام بثورة ديمقراطية — This situation can only be overcome through undertaking a democratic revolution

63 | 443 |

3806 طَاغِيَة *masc.n.* tyrant, despot, dictator

يسقط الطاغية! أوقفوا التعذيب! — Down with the tyrant! Stop the torture!

70 | 400 |

3807 سَرْد *n.* enumeration, listing; presentation, account

سوف تكون كاتب قصة جيدا لأن أسلوبك في سرد القصة سلس ومنتظم — You will be a good story author because your style in presenting stories is flexible and organized

67 | 412 |

3808 تِلْفَاز *n.* television set

يجب تحديد الأوقات المناسبة للأطفال لمشاهدة التلفاز — It is necessary to set the appropriate times for the children to watch television

61 | 452 |

3809 اِنْتَصَر *v. VIII* to be victorious, triumph (على over sb/sth)

الذي يطلب الموت لا يستطيع أن ينتصر على الذي يطلب الحياة — He who seeks death cannot be victorious over he who seeks life

73 | 378 |

3810 تَفَادٍ (def. تَفَادِي) *n.* avoidance, avoiding

كيف تساعدين طفلك على تفادي هذه المشكلة؟ — How do you help your child to avoid this problem?

67 | 412 |

3811 مُسْتَوْطَنَة *n.* pl. -aat settlement

إن عائلته تقيم في إحدى المستوطنات في الضفة الغربية — His family lives in one of the settlements in the West Bank

57 | 488 |

3812 عَقَلَ *v. I (i)* to be reasonable, be sensible; to make sense, be conceivable

هل يعقل أن يبعث الله لعباده بأديان مختلفة يتصارع عليها الناس — Does it make sense for God to send his people various religions people would fight about?

71 | 390 |

3813 تَرْسِيخ *n.* consolidating, reinforcing, bolstering

مصيرنا مرتبط بالبقاء هنا وترسيخ كياننا إلى الأبد — Our fate is tied up with staying here and anchoring our beings forever

61 | 455 |

3814 تَأْلِيف *vn.* authoring, compiling, composing; forming, constituting; *n.* publication, compilation, composition; formation, configuration

شارك في تأليف هذا الكتاب الجماعي الضخم ما لا يقل عن سبعين باحثا — No less than seventy researchers participated in writing this huge, collective book

65 | 427 |

3815 خَشَبِيّ *adj.* wooden, made of wood

أجلس على كرسي خشبي مدور من غير ظهر — I am sitting on a round wooden chair without a back

66 | 415 |

3816 رَكَضَ *v. I (u)* to run, race

لمحها فجأة في الشارع وظل يركض خلفها حتى أدركها — He noticed her suddenly in the

street and kept running after her until he caught up with her

62 | 441 |

3817 أَمَد *n.* period, duration, term; extent, range

التصور الآخر هو أن يبقى هذا القطر محتلا إلى أمد غير محدود — The other view is that this area will remain occupied for an undefined period of time

73 | 377 |

3818 مُخّ *n.* brain

زارنا عدد من الخبراء المتخصصين في مجال جراحة المخ والأعصاب — A number of experts specializing in the area of brain and nerve surgery visited us

57 | 480 |

3819 إيصال *n.* sending, transmitting; transporting, conveying

أصحاب المنتجات يريدون إيصال إعلاناتهم لأكبر عدد أيضا — The owners of the products also want to get their advertisement out to the largest number possible

72 | 381 |

3820 أَطْلَسِيّ *adj.* Atlantic; NATO

غادر مكتبه متجها الى قريته المطلة على المحيط الأطلسي — He left his office, heading for his village which overlooks the Atlantic Ocean

58 | 470 |

3821 مُتَشَدِّد *n./adj.* extremist, fanatic; strict, intense

إنها منغلقة على نفسها بحكم تربيتها المتشددة وعادات وتقاليد بيئتها الصغيرة — She is closed in on herself because of her extremist education and the customs and traditions of her small environment

58 | 473 |

3822 نُفاية *n.* pl. -aat waste, refuse

في كل يوم ترمى آلاف الأطنان من النفايات البشرية والصناعية والزراعية في أنهار الصين وبحيراتها — Every day thousands of tons of human, industrial, and agricultural waste are thrown into the rivers and lakes of China

62 | 438 |

3823 لَعَنَ *v. I (a)* to curse, damn sb/sth; (God) damn sb يَلْعَنَ (الله) عَلى

الشعب العراقي سوف يلعن كل من يتسبب في تأجيج الحرب الأهلية وضياع العراق — The Iraqi people will curse anyone who ignites civil war and causes the loss of Iraq

63 | 430 |

3824 مُحْتاج *n./adj.* pl. -uun needy (person); *a.p.* wanting, needing إلى sth

لم أترك العمل.. أنا سافرت لأنني محتاج للعلاج — I didn't quit work...I travelled because I need (medical) treatment

52 | 527 |

3825 تَأَكَّدَ *v. V* to ascertain من sth; to be confirmed

عندما أنظر خلفي إلى السنوات الطويلة التى مرت يتأكد لى أنني اتخذت قرارات كثيرة خاطئة — When I look behind me to the long years which passed, I become certain that I made many wrong decisions

79 | 346 |

3826 صَليب *n.* cross; crucifix

لم يقدم الصليب الاحمر او الهلال الاحمر اي مساعدة لهم — The Red Cross and the Red Crescent have not offered any aid to them

67 | 404 |

3827 ثَمَرَة *n.* fruit; result, yield, outcome

رأيت لصا يتسلل ليسرق ثمرة من هذه الثمار — I saw a thief sneak in to steal some of these fruits

74 | 365 |

3828 عَزْل *vn.* removal, dismissal, distancing; *n.* isolation, separation

لابد من عزل ثمن الارض عن العقارات — It is necessary to isolate the price of the land from the buildings on it

72 | 379 |

3829 مُسْتَقِرّ *adj.* settled, at ease; stable, permanent

كان وضعه الصحي غير مستقر — His health situation was not stable

63 | 428 |

3830 سُرُور *n.* happiness; pleasure, delight

ذهبت إلى بيتي وأنا في غاية السرور — I went to my house in a state of extreme happiness

64 | 421 |

3831 رَدَّة فِعْل *n.* echo, reverberation; رَدَّة فِعْل reaction
نعرب عن اسفنا منّ ردة فعل الحكومة التي لم تدافع عن القانون — We express our sorrow for the reaction of the government which didn't defend the law
70 | 385 |

3832 رَمْزيّ *adj.* symbolic; (data) encoded, encrypted
أدى الأمر الى التفكير بمقترح بعثة عسكرية عربية رمزية في الكويت وتتواجد لمراقبة الأوضاع فقط — The matter led to thinking about a suggestion of a symbolic Arab military mission in Kuwait, and it would be there to observe situations only
72 | 374 |

3833 أُمِّيَّة *n.* illiteracy
نجحت المرأة الاماراتية في محاربة الأمية بالتعليم والتدريب والخبرة — The Emirati woman has succeeded in battling illiteracy through education, training, and experience
69 | 391 |

3834 وَصْل *n.* link; connection, contact; receipt
أنا سأكون حلقة الوصل بين كل الموجودين — I will be the link between everyone present
62 | 435 |

3835 وَصْفَة *n.* description, portrayal; (medical) prescription; (food) recipe
كتب الطبيب المناوب لكل واحد منهم وصفة طبية — The doctor on duty wrote a medical prescription for each one of them
62 | 434 |

3836 شَرِس *adj.* vicious, savage, fierce
نحن خلف سور تطوقه كلاب شرسة — We are behind a wall surrounded by vicious dogs
74 | 366 |

3837 هاتانِ *dem.pron.* these two (fem.du.), هاتَيْنِ (gen./acc.)
يلطخ اللوحات بهذا الهراء وهاتان المرأتان الحمقاوان تعتبرانه عبقريا — He splatters the canvasses with this idiocy and these two stupid women consider it brilliant
70 | 389 |

3838 عَرِيس *n.* bridegroom
دفع الشبان صديقهم العريس أحمد ليجلس على كرسي خشبي ثقيل — The young men jostled

their friend Ahmad, the groom, into a heavy wooden chair
66 | 410 |

3839 نُصْرَة *n.* help, assistance; support, backing
فرض الله علينا أن نعمل لنصرة دينه — God has required us to work to assist His religion
64 | 422 |

3840 غَسِيل *vn.* washing; *n.* laundry, (dirty) clothes
تؤثر عمليات غسيل الأموال على حركة المبادلات المشروعة — Money laundering influences legal money exchanges
71 | 378 |

3841 عَصَفَ *v. I (i)* to be stormy, be tempestuous; to rage (wind, conflict, crisis)
هل صدفة ان الدين يقف وراء معظم التوترات التي تعصف بالعلاقات بين الشعوب والامم المختلفة؟ — Is it a coincidence that religion stands behind most of the tensions which beset the relationships between various peoples and nations?
72 | 374 |

3842 مُدَمِّر *adj.* destructive, destroying
أضاف أن عوامل كثيرة مثل فصل الشتاء البارد والأعاصير المدمرة وتراجع أسعار صرف الدولار ستؤدي حتما إلى أسعار نفط قياسية — He added that many factors like the cold winter season, destructive storms and the decline in the price of the dollar will certainly lead to record oil prices
72 | 373 |

3843 نَشِيد *n.* anthem, hymn, song
سوف نبقى هنا ونغني نشيد الحرية — We will stay here and sing the anthem of freedom
64 | 420 |

3844 عَمَّن (عَنْ مَنْ) *prep.phr.* from/about who/whom
لم يكن العرب يختلفون في ذلك عمن سبقهم أو من لحقهم — The Arabs did not disagree about that with those who preceded or followed them
71 | 377 |

3845 شَلَل *n.* paralysis, inertia; شلل الأطفال polio
أعلنت منظمة الصحة العالمية رسميا هذا العام خلو مصر من فيروس شلل الأطفال — The World

Health Organization announced officially this year that Egypt was free of the polio virus

73 | 368 |

3846 شاحِنَة *n.* pl. -aat truck, lorry, freight car
قال ان سائقي تلك الشاحنات لا يلتزمون بالقوانين المرورية — He said that the drivers of these trucks do not abide by traffic rules

62 | 429 |

3847 مَزْعُوم *adj.* so-called; alleged, claimed
قد أسقطنا أسطورة الجيش الاسرائيلي الذي لا يقهر المزعومة التي انتجتها حرب حزيران عام ١٩٦٧ — We tore down the myth of the supposedly invincible Israeli army which was formed by the June War of 1967

72 | 370 |

3848 عُبْوَة and عَبْوَة *n.* pl. عَبَوات ,عُبْوات package, pack; (explosive) charge; عبوة ناسِفَة explosive device
أعلنت الجيش البريطاني إن ثلاثة من جنوده قتلوا وأصيب آخر في انفجار عبوة ناسفة لدى مرور دوريتهم جنوبي شرقي البصرة — The British army announced that three of its soldiers were killed and another was wounded by a roadside bomb that detonated while their patrol was passing through south-east of Basra

50 | 534 | +news

3849 أَمَّنَ *v. II* to secure, safeguard, protect sth/sb; to insure, underwrite (ضد against) على sth/sb
نحن الآن لا نؤمن على الإنسان فقط وإنا نؤمن على أجزاء منه — We don't insure just people now, but we insure parts of people (people's body parts)

69 | 390 |

3850 شُرْفَة *n.* balcony
وليس يدري ما الذي دعاه أن يرفع بصره إلى تلك الشرفة المستديرة.. كانت بفستانها الأحمر المطرز، وشعرها الفاحم — He doesn't know what called him to raise his eyes to that round balcony... She was in her red, embroidered dress, and her charcoal hair

51 | 520 | +lit

3851 نَفْع *n.* benefit, advantage; use
ما نفع العيش بلا دين؟ — What is the benefit of living without religion?

74 | 364 |

3852 قُصُور *n.* shortcoming, insufficiency; negligence
اشار ايضا الى ان اسباب قصور القلب النهائي تعود الى امراض مكتسبة تصيب عضلات القلب — He also pointed out that the causes of terminal heart failure can be traced to inherited diseases which strike the muscles of the heart

70 | 382 |

3853 إحْداث *n.* effectuation, implementation; bringing about
كيف يقومون بتدريبهم على إحداث ذلك التغير؟ — How are they training them to put this change into effect?

69 | 389 |

3854 مُنْتَظِم *adj.* regular, systematic; orderly
واصل الطرفان إتاحة الفرصة بصورة منتظمة لممثلي اللجنة الدولية للصليب الأحمر لتفقد سجونها — The two sides continued to give the opportunity in a regular manner to the representatives of the international committees of the Red Cross to visit their prisons

70 | 381 |

3855 مانيش /ma-nii-sh/ *neg.part.* (Egy. with predicate *n./adj.*) I am not; (Alg. مانيش and ماني /maani/, Gul. only) I am not, I don't, I haven't, I can't
قلت لك مانيش جاي — I told you I'm not coming

32 | 817 | +spo

3856 نَبَعَ *v. I (u)* to emerge, originate; to emanate, flow
هذه الصورة لسياسة ايرانية شديدة المكيافيلية تنبع من قلق العراقيين العميق الدائم ازاء جارتهم إيران — This depiction of a strongly Machiavellian Iranian policy flows from Iraqis' deep and constant anxiety towards their neighbor, Iran

77 | 347 |

3857 مُقاتِل *n.* pl. -uun combatant, warrior
بعض المقاتلين يعودون من الجبهة فى أجازة قصيرة — Some of the fighters are returning from the front on a short vacation

61 | 441 |

3858 راوٍ (راوِي def.) *n.* narrator, storyteller;
reciter (of poetry)
الراوي الرئيسي في الجزء الأول من الرواية هو أستاذ
جامعي — The main narrator in the first part
of the novel is a university professor
39 | 688 | +lit

3859 رَقَبَة *n.* neck; في رَقَبَتِهِ his responsibility
— يحس ألما في رقبته وصداعا خفيفا في رأسه
He feels a pain in his neck and a slight
headache in his head
64 | 414 |

3860 عُصْفُور *n.* pl. عَصَافِير bird, sparrow
ابتدأت العصافير بالزقزقة استعدادا لنهار آخر —
The birds began to chirp in preparation for
another day
59 | 454 |

3861 اِحْتَفَل *v. VIII* to celebrate بـ (anniversary,
graduation)
لبنان يحتفل بذكرى تحرير الجنوب — Lebanon
is celebrating the anniversary of the liberation
of the South
76 | 352 |

3862 قَوِيَ *v. I (a)* to be strong (enough)
إنه الآن لا يقوى على الحركة إلا بصعوبة —
He is now not able to move except with
difficulty
62 | 426 | +lit

3863 مُعْتَدِل *adj.* moderate (weather, policy),
restrained; balanced
تتميز المنطقة بالطقس المعتدل طوال العام —
The area is characterized by moderate
weather all year round
63 | 418 |

3864 تَمْدِيد *n.* lengthening; extension, prolongation
قرر تمديد المدة لتسعة شهور أخرى — He decided
to extend the period for another nine months
59 | 449 |

3865 اِنْتِحار *n.* suicide
لا يستبعد أن يقدم في يوم من الأيام على
الانتحار — He doesn't dismiss the idea
that he may one day proceed to commit
suicide
69 | 382 |

3866 خَصْم *n.* adversary
يمتلك الخصم سلاحا يخفيه عن علم خصمه، ليمنعه
من اتخاذ التدابير — The enemy owns a weapon
which he hides from his enemy, to prevent
him from taking (preventive) measures
69 | 385 |

3867 تَقْصِير *n.* deficiency, inadequacy
التقصير في أداء الأمانة وظلم الناس يضيع حقوقهم
— Inadequate performance of duties and
treating people unjustly will cause the loss
of their rights
73 | 363 |

3868 فَرَج *n.* relief, relaxation, happiness
الصبر مفتاح الفرج — Patience is the key to
happiness
64 | 416 |

3869 إعْجاب *vn.* admiration, amazement; wonder,
surprise
لقد كنت دائما شديد الإعجاب بالثقافة الغربية
وبرسالتها التنويرية — I always admired Western
culture and its Enlightenment message
69 | 381 |

3870 إبْعاد *n.* removal; distancing; banishment,
deportation, exile
يجب إبعاد أحواض الأسماك المكشوفة عن القطط
وكذلك أقفاص العصافير — It is necessary to
keep open fish bowls away from cats, also
bird cages
73 | 361 |

3871 هسة (also هسه and هسا) /hassa/ (Irq.Gul.Lev.)
adv. now, right away, just now; also هسع and
هساع /hassa9/ (Lev.Irq.), and إسه /'issa/ (Lev.)
أنا في الرياض هسا — I'm in Riyadh now
8 | 3168 | +spo

3872 سَدَّ *v. I (u)* to close, barricade (door); to turn
off (electricity, water); to pay, settle (a debt);
to fill (gap), provide (need)
وإذا سد أخوكم حاجة بعض فقراء القرية فمن يسد
حاجة البقية؟ — So if your brother takes care of
the needs of some of the poor in the village,
who will take care of the needs of the rest?
72 | 368 |

3873 حَلَّقَ *v. II* to fly, soar, hover; to circle (the skies)

كانت الطائرة تحلق على علو منخفض جدا — The plane was hovering at a very low altitude

67 | 394 |

3874 مُرْتاح *adj.* relaxed; at ease, resting; happy, satisfied

لقد سافر لأنه غير مرتاح في هذا البلد.. يريد أن يجرب حظه في الخارج مثله مثل الآخرين — He traveled because he was not comfortable in this country...he wants to try his luck abroad, just like the others

56 | 472 | +spo

3875 هيـ /hay-/ and هيا /hayyaa-/ (Lev.) *part.* (with pron.) there (he is), here (I am); approx. voilà; هيو /hayyo/ there he/it is; هيني /hayni/ here I am; هيانا /hayyaana/ here we are

رجع يوسف ولا بعده؟ هيو موجود هون — Has Yusuf returned yet? There he is, present here

42 | 616 |

3876 أَبْسَط *elat.* simpler/simplest; more/most basic (بَسيط)

الفلسطينيون محرومون من أبسط الخدمات — Palestinians are deprived of the most basic services

72 | 365 |

3877 نَقيب *n.* leader, head; union boss; (mil.) captain

بقي أن نذكر أن المرشحين لمنصب النقيب ولعضوية مجلس النقابة عدد غير قليل من المحامين — It remains to be said that the candidates for the position of Union leader and for membership in the union council are a not small number of lawyers

50 | 525 |

3878 يُورانيُوم *n.* uranium

أعلنت نيتها أنها ستقوم بعمليات تطوير وبحث فيما يتعلق بتخصيب اليورانيوم — It announced its intention to undertake development operations and research regarding the enrichment of uranium

48 | 548 |

3879 نَسَب *n.* lineage; kinship

هناك ١٤ ألف طفل من مجهولي النسب هم نتاج هذا النوع من الزواج — There are 14 thousand children of unknown ancestry who are the result of this type of marriage

67 | 387 |

3880 سامع *a.p.* listening, hearing, able to hear; having heard

ده احنا سامعين إن انتو كنتوا عايزين تيجوا — We've heard that you wanted to come

9 | 2703 | +spo

3881 تَداع *n.* pl. -aat (تَداعي .def) breakdown, collapse; تَداعيات reflections, thoughts; repercussions

هناك تداعيات خطيرة لهذا الحادث — There are serious repercussions of this incident

65 | 399 |

3882 خَيْرَة *n.* pl. -aat good deed; خَيْرات resources, wealth, treasures

كل تأخيرة وفيها خيرة — Every delay has a silver lining

78 | 333 |

3883 حُفْرَة *n.* pl. حُفَر pit, hole

لا تيأس إذا تعثرت أقدامك.. وسقطت في حفرة واسعة.. فسوف تخرج منها وأنت أكثر تماسكا — Don't despair if your feet stumble...and fall into a big hole...for you will get out of it more "together"

72 | 357 |

3884 قديش /'addeesh/ and قديه /'addeeh/ (Lev.) *interrog.* how many, how much; what (number)

قديش بدك أعطيكي؟ — How much do you want me to give you?

7 | 3388 | +spo

3885 اِسْتَأْهَلَ *v. X* to deserve, merit sth; (Dia.) يستاهل ,istaahal/ استاهل/ /yistaahil, yistaahal/

مصر -كلها- تستاهل أن ينظر ناسها إليها ويحبوها ويشعروا بأنها تحبهم — Egypt, all of it, deserves that its people look to it and love it and feel that it loves them

37 | 697 | +for

3886 مُقَدِّم *n.* person presenting or submitting; *a.p.* offering, presenting, submitting (request, complaint), applying على for

لا يستطيعون الاستغناء عن الجنس الناعم والدليل هو أن مقدم البرنامج هي مذيعة جديدة اسمها ليلى

— They can't do without the fair sex, and the evidence is that the presenter of the program is a new (female) broadcaster whose name is Layla

76 | 337 |

3887 تَوَاجَدَ *v. VI* to exist, live; to be found, be located; to be present
أعلنت حرصها على الامن والاستقرار في المناطق التي — تتواجد فيها القوات الدولية It announced its insistence on security and stability in the areas in which international forces are found

68 | 378 |

3888 بَسْمَة *n.* smile
هذا المشروع يستهدف ادخال البسمة والفرحة والسرور على الاطفال — This project aims to bring smiles, joy, and happiness to the children

63 | 405 |

3889 إسْرَاع *n.* hurrying, speeding up; acceleration
أرجوك سيدي، عليك الإسراع لأنني لا أستطيع الانتظار أكثر — I beg you, sir, you must hurry because I can't wait any more

69 | 370 |

3890 لَفْظ *vn.* uttering, saying; *n.* pl. ألفاظ word, term, expression
هناك كثير من الألفاظ العربية في اللغات الأوروبية — There are a lot of Arabic expressions in European languages

62 | 409 |

3891 خَبِيث *adj.* malicious, evil; malignant, pernicious; جَمْرَة خَبِيثَة anthrax
لا استطيع ان أمنع نفسي من التفكير في هذه الفكرة الخبيثة — I am not able to prevent myself from thinking about this malicious idea

65 | 393 |

3892 طابق *n.* floor, story
سقطت نقود بخيل من الطابق الرابع فهب مسرعا إلى أسفل لإحضارها إلا أنه لم يجدها — A stingy man's money fell from the fourth floor, so he rushed down to get it, but he did not find it

65 | 390 |

3893 وُجُوب *n.* necessity, obligation, duty
لذلك فاننا نرى وجوب الاستمرار في الاتصال بالدول العربية جميعها حتى تكون على معرفة تامة بوجهة نظر الكويت — Therefore, we see the

necessity of continuing to contact all the Arab states so they will have a complete knowledge of Kuwait's point of view

68 | 374 |

3894 خَبَّر *v. II* to tell sb sth or عن about sth or أَنَّ that
شو في أخبار جديدة عندك؟ خبرينا؟ — What's new with you? Tell us?

46 | 556 | +spo

3895 اِنْتِقام *n.* revenge; retaliation, reprisal
العمدة فجأة قرر الانتقام مما فعله به البهي زمان، فأحيا حكاية الثأر — The mayor suddenly decided to take revenge on what Bahiy had done to him years ago, so he revived the story of the revenge

72 | 352 |

3896 جامع *adj.* comprehensive, extensive; gathering, collecting; *n.* pl. -uun collector (stamps, etc.)
سيبويه وضع أول كتاب جامع في النحو — Sibawaih wrote the first comprehensive book on grammar

60 | 426 |

3897 خالِد *adj.* immortal, eternal; glorious
ان اعماله الخالدة ستكون بلا ريب اكبر فوز له بعد الممات — His eternal deeds will be, no doubt, his greatest victory after death

66 | 385 |

3898 صَحَابَة *pl.n.* Sahaba (companions of the Prophet)
كتب السيرة مليئة بأسماء الصحابة وعددهم وقصصهم — The biography books are full of the names of the companions and their number and their stories

56 | 449 |

3899 تَصَاعُد *n.* rise, ascent; escalation
كان صعود حماس للسلطة نقطة حاسمة في تصاعد حدة الخلاف بين الحكومة الفلسطينية المنتخبة والرئيس الفلسطيني — The rise of Hamas to power was a critical point in the rise in the sharpness of the disagreements between the elected Palestinian government and the Palestinian president

68 | 373 |

3900 لَوْم *n.* blame, fault; disapproval, reproach

يؤكد التقرير أن بريطانيا وجهت اللوم إلى طهران بسبب وصول مثل هذه الأسلحة إلى أيدي المتمردين — The report stresses that Britain has directed censure towards Tehran because of the arrival of weapons such as these into the hands of the rebels

72 | 350 |

3901 مَنْزِلِيّ *adj.* domestic, household

قال: الأعمال المنزلية من اختصاص النساء، وأنا رجل مثل أبي، والرجال لا يقومون بالأعمال المنزلية — He said: Housework is the specialty of women, and I am a man like my father, and men do not do housework

63 | 404 |

3902 صُحْبَة *n.* friendship; بصحبة accompanied by

بعد نصف ساعة خرجت بصحبة الطبيب الشاب — After a half hour she went out in the company of the young doctor

68 | 373 |

3903 اِفْتَقَرَ *v. VIII* إلى to lack, be in need of sth

إن مربي الدواجن والعاملين في مزارع الطيور الداجنة التي تفتقر إلى تطبيق الاشتراطات الصحية والبيئية فيها هم الفئة الأكثر تعرضا لأنفلونزا الطيور — Chicken growers and workers in chicken farms which have not yet carried out the preventative health precautions are the group most exposed to bird flu

71 | 357 |

3904 دَفْتَر *n.* notebook; ledger

امرأتك خضرة أتت إلى هنا في الصباح، وتركت دفتر الحساب عند سويسي أفندي، وراحت لأم مسعد بائعة الجرائد — Your wife Khadra came here in the morning, and left the account book with Suweesi Effendi, and then went to Um Masad, the newspaper saleslady

70 | 362 |

3905 تَعْبِئَة *n.* (mil.) mobilization, alert; (manufacture) packaging, canning, bottling

أعلنت بلجيكا التعبئة العامة وأجريت مناورات مشتركة — Belgium announced a general mobilization and joint maneuvers were held

67 | 374 |

3906 مِظَلَّة *n.* umbrella

القبيلة يجب ألا تتجاوز كونها كيانا اجتماعيا تحت مظلة هذا الوطن الذي يساوي دستوره بين مواطنيه جميعا بلا استثناء — The tribe must not go beyond being a social entity under the umbrella of the homeland whose constitution makes all its citizens equal, without exception

68 | 373 |

3907 مُطَّلِع *adj.* well-informed (على about sth)

وذكرت مصادر مطلعة أن المتهم هدد كذلك بتفجير مستشفى الشيخ زايد — Informed sources mentioned that the accused also threatened to blow up the Sheikh Zayd Hospital

61 | 414 |

3908 لِمَ *interrog.* why

فلم السكوت على القادة المتهورين الذين تبعوا أمثال فرعون وهتلر وموسيليني؟ — Why the silence about the irresponsible leaders who followed the likes of Pharaoh, Hitler, and Mussolini?

41 | 605 |

3909 مُراد *n.* object, goal, intention; (what is) desired, intended

اعلم ضرورة فهم الشيء المراد حفظه أولا؛ لأن الفهم يحقق حفظا سريعا ويسيرا — Know the necessity of understanding the thing which one desires to memorize first; because understanding makes for quick and easy memorization

68 | 373 |

3910 رَصَدَ *v. I (u)* to observe, watch sth; to follow, track, monitor (weather); to earmark, set aside (funds)

هو أحد أبرز المطلوبين من قبل الولايات المتحدة التي رصدت 5 ملايين دولار مقابل رأسه — He is one of the most prominent wanted men by the United States which has allocated a fund of 5 million dollars for his arrest

68 | 369 |

3911 جالِيَة *n.* expatriate community, colony

بعض الأطفال الصغار من أبناء الجالية الإسلامية في جنيف يدرسون اللغة العربية — Some small children from among the children of the Islamic expatriate community in Geneva are studying the Arabic language

61 | 415 |

3912 اِخْتَرَقَ *v. VIII* to exceed, break (barrier); to pierce, penetrate sth; to hack into (computer, network); to traverse, cross (region)
العالم مكان ضيق والحب وحده يخترق الجدران — The world is a narrow place, and only love can break through the walls
70 | 358 |

3913 أَلْغَى *v. IV* to cancel, terminate; abrogate
تمكن من القيام بذلك من دون ان يلغي السرية المصرفية وهي من العناصر الاساسية للقطاع المصرفي — He was able to do that without abrogating bank secrecy, and that is one of the basic elements of the banking sector
76 | 330 |

3914 مَثِيل *n.* equal, match; peer; لا مَثِيلَ لَهُ beyond comparison
اشتعل مجلس الشعب في جدل ساخن لم يسبق له مثيل — The people's assembly ignited into a debate, the likes of which had not happened before
77 | 327 |

3915 وِجْدان *n.* feeling, emotion; conscience
شعبنا العراقي يدفع ثمنا غاليا لتلك الحروب الهوجاء التي لا يرضى بها ضمير او وجدان — Our Iraqi people are paying a high price for these reckless wars which no conscience can be satisfied with
72 | 349 |

3916 مُرْتَقَب *adj.* expected, anticipated
قال ان المباراة المرتقبة ستكون حافلة بالاثارة والمتعة وعلى الجماهير عدم تفويت الفرصة هذه بمتابعة نجوم برازيل — He said that the expected match will be very exciting and enjoyable, and that the fans should not let this opportunity to follow Brazil's stars pass
64 | 389 |

3917 أَكْرَمَ *v. IV* to honor, respect sb; to venerate, pay tribute to sb; (Egy.) الله يِكْرَمَك thanks! (for a service or compliment)
الله يحفظك تكرم عينك الله يخليكي — God keep you, thanks, God keep you
61 | 410 | +spo

3918 مُسْتَهْدَف *adj.* targeted, aimed at, intended
كنت داخل الملجأ المستهدف، استيقظت على صراخ الناس — I was inside the targeted refuge; I woke to the screams of the people
65 | 383 |

3919 صَحْراوِيّ *adj.* desert; Saharan
يريد أن يحول هذه المنطقة الصحراوية إلى بساتين خضراء — He wants to transform this desert area into green orchards
60 | 419 |

3920 اِنْدَرَجَ *v. VII* to be inserted, included; to be classified, categorized, filed
لو راجعنا أغلب حالات النزاع المعروضة على دوائر الأحوال الشخصية في مصر لوجدنا أغلبها يندرج تحت بند واحد هو زواج الصدفة — If we review most of the cases of conflict that came before the Social Services agencies in Egypt, we find that most of them can be classified under a single heading: temporary marriages
69 | 364 |

3921 لِباس *n.* clothes, dress, attire
أنا فيلسوف في لباس راهب — I am a philosopher in monks' clothing
68 | 369 |

3922 أَضاعَ *v. IV* to lose sth; to waste (time); to miss, let go by (opportunity)
نتمنى أن لا يضيع دم الحريري في سلة المصالح الدولية المتقلبة — We hope that Al-Hariri's blood will not be lost in the basket of volatile international interests
67 | 370 |

3923 حَراك *n.* movement, motion
كان المريض ضعيفا سقيما لا يقدر على الحراك — The patient was weak and sick, not able to move
68 | 367 |

3924 أَنْزَلَ *v. IV* to bring or send down, lower sth
انزل قدميه على الأرض وجلس على حافة الفراش — He dangled his legs onto the ground and sat on the edge of the mattress
68 | 367 |

3925 جامِد *adj.* frozen; rigid
هي إنسانة جامدة المشاعر، لا تعرف شيئا عن الرومانسية — She is a person with rigid feelings, not knowing anything about romance
54 | 462 |

3926 بَهْجَة *n.* splendor, magnificence; delight
وجدت أن الخروج إلى السوق لم تعد له البهجة القديمة — I found that going to the market no longer carried the old delight
67 | 373 |

3927 ذابَ *v. I (u)* to dissolve, melt
بدأ الجليد يذوب من فوق الجبال — The ice started to melt from off the mountains
60 | 416 |

3928 ساحِليّ *adj.* coastal, seaside
بعد لحظات من الآن سيكون في الطريق الساحلي الملاصق للبحر — A few moments from now he will be on the coastal road that follows the coast
52 | 476 |

3929 ضَجيج *n.* noise; commotion
أجد في الليل هروبا من ضجيج النهار، وفرصة ألتقي فيها مع نفسي — I find in the night an escape from the commotion of the day, and an opportunity to meet with myself
62 | 402 |

3930 مَوْضُوعِيَّة *n.* objectivity
الموضوعية بالنسبة له ليست هي الدور الحقيقي للصحافة، وإنما ما يميز الصحافة حقا هي مراقبتها للسلطة ومراكز القوى — Objectivity, for him, is not the true role of the press, but rather what distinguishes the press truly is watching over the centers of power
66 | 379 |

3931 نِتاج *n.* result, outcome; production; offspring
يعتقدون أن النصر هو نتاج الجهاد الذي لا يتطلب معرفة عميقة بالحياة ولا تجارب عدة فيها — They believe that victory is the result of struggle/jihad, which does not require a deep knowledge of life nor a lot of experiences in it
71 | 352 |

3932 مُزارِع *n. pl.* -uun farmer
وقع حصان أحد المزارعين في بئر مياه عميقة ولكنها جافة — A horse of one of the farmers fell into a deep water well but it was dry
55 | 447 |

3933 مَرَضِيّ *adj.* pathological; diseased; medical
انتهت اليوم إجازتي المرضية واستعددت لأعود إلى مهنتي — My sick vacation ended today, and I prepared to return to my profession
73 | 339 |

3934 حَنيف *adj.* orthodox; الدِّين الحَنيف Islam
إن ديننا الحنيف يحث على العمل.. والجهد.. والانتاج — Our true religion encourages work, diligence, and productivity
70 | 356 |

3935 سارَعَ *v. III* to hurry, hasten إلى to a place, or to do sth
كانت إيران من أول الدول التي سارعت إلى الاعتراف بالنظام الجديد في أفغانستان وإلى تقديم المساعدات — Iran was one of the first countries that hurried to recognize the new regime in Afghanistan and to offer aid
71 | 346 |

3936 خِلافَة *n.* succession; caliphate
كانت بغداد هي عاصمة الخلافة في الدولة العباسية — Baghdad was the capital of the Caliphate in the Abbasid state
54 | 454 |

3937 ناسِف *adj.* explosive, exploding
في الجنوب اللبناني انفجرت عبوة ناسفة صغيرة الحجم قرب مركز لقوات حفظ السلام الدولية التابعة للأمم المتحدة — In the Lebanese south, a small-sized package bomb exploded near a center for the international peace-keeping forces belonging to the UN
44 | 565 | +news

3938 بُلُوغ *n.* reaching, attaining
غالب الإصابات تحصل بعد بلوغ الستين من العمر — Most of the cases occur after reaching sixty years of age
72 | 344 |

3939 تَرَكَّزَ *v. V* to be centered, concentrated في/عَلَى/حَوْلَ in/on/around sth; to be focused عَلَى on sth

يتوقع أن يجري مباحثات تتركز على التعاون بين واشنطن وإسلام آباد في مكافحة الإرهاب — He expects that discussions will center on cooperation between Washington and Islamabad in fighting terrorism

65 | 379 |

3940 حَلا *v. I (u)* to be sweet; يَحْلُو لَهُ أَنْ to enjoy doing sth; كَمَا يَحْلُو لَهُ as he pleases

الطقس أخذ يحلو ويطيب، بعد أيام من اشتداد الحرارة — The weather has started to become nicer, after days of extreme heat

69 | 357 |

3941 تَوافَقَ *v. VI* to agree, concur

لا نقبل الدعم المشروط إن لم يتوافق مع أولوياتنا — We will not accept conditional support if it does not agree with our priorities

69 | 355 |

3942 اِسْتَضافَ *v. X* to host, invite sb

دولة قطر هي أول دولة عربية تستضيف الألعاب الأسيوية التي تقام كل أربع سنوات — The state of Qatar is the first Arab state to host the Asian Games which are held every four years

58 | 421 |

3943 مَصْرَع *n.* death, fatality

لقي عشرات الأشخاص مصرعهم في حادث تصادم قطار للركاب بشاحنة — Scores of people met their deaths in the collision of a passenger train with a truck

54 | 453 | +news

3944 مُتَظاهِر *n.* pl. -uun demonstrator; *a.p.* demonstrating

انصرف المتظاهرون بعد انتهاء المظاهرة في هدوء — The demonstrators left calmly after the end of the demonstration

58 | 426 |

3945 مَفْعُول *n.* impact, effect; result; ساري المَفْعُول valid (permit)

نحن أول المطالبين بأن تكون هدنة المئة يوم سارية المفعول على كل الجبهات — We are the first of those who demand that the 100-day truce be in effect on all fronts

71 | 346 |

3946 خَيالِيّ *adj.* imaginary, fantastic; fictitious

هذه قصة خيالية، ولكنها ليست خرافة، فوقائعها محتملة الحدوث — This is an imaginary story, but it is not a fable, since its events are likely to happen

76 | 323 |

3947 كَمّ *n.* amount, quantity

استغربت لوجود هذا الكم الهائل من الطيور خلف الباب — I was surprised at finding this huge amount of birds behind the door

76 | 322 |

3948 تَشْكِيلِيّ *adj.* visual, graphic

كنت الطفل الوحيد داخل أسرتي الذي يميل إلى الفن التشكيلي وتوقعوا لي أن أكون فنانا مشهورا — I was the only child in my family who tended towards visual arts and they expected me to become a famous artist

49 | 496 |

3949 اِزْدِياد *n.* growth, increase, rise

ازدياد حوادث السير يعود الى ارتفاع اعداد المركبات والسائقين في المملكة — The increase in the number of traffic accidents can be attributed to the rise in the number of vehicles and drivers in the Kingdom

71 | 346 |

3950 اِسْتِعانة *vn.* seeking help ب from sb, resorting ب to sth, making use ب of sth

سوف اضطر إلى الاستعانة بحبوب المهدئ التي أعطانيها الطبيب لعلها تمكنني من نوم هادئ — I will be forced to rely on the tranquilizer pills the doctor gave me, perhaps they will allow me to have a calm sleep

73 | 334 |

3951 مُحَلِّل *n.* pl. -uun analyst

لم يكن المحلل المالي مفرطا في التفاؤل — The financial analyst was not excessively positive

61 | 399 |

3952 مُنْصَرِم *adj.* gone by, elapsed (time period)

لا وجود لاختراع من اختراعات القرن المنصرم نالَ ما حازه التلفزيون من إقبال وتنويع وتطوير

وإضافات — There is no invention of the last century that got as much acceptance, diversification, development, and additions as the television did

67 | 364 |

3953 عِنْدَئِذٍ *adv.* then, at that time

سيفهم الجميع.. ولكن عندئذ سيكون الوقت قد فات — Everyone will understand...but at that point the time will have passed

60 | 409 |

3954 صِنْف *n.* pl. أَصْناف type, class, kind, category

معظم النمل الذي نراه هو من صنف الشغالات وكلهن من الإناث — Most of the ants we see are of the "worker" type, and all of them are female

68 | 359 |

3955 اِسْتَبْعَدَ *v. X* to rule out (regard as unlikely) sth

لا استبعد ان يكون الرئيس السوري فعلا يريد السلام ولكن الطريق لذلك هي مفاوضات مباشرة — I don't rule out the idea that the Syrian president in fact wants peace, but the way to that is through direct negotiations

68 | 357 |

3956 أَضْحَى *v. IV* to become; (with imperf.) to begin, start (doing)

كرامة الإنسان أضحت في مهب الريح — The dignity of man has begun to blow in the wind

51 | 476 | +lit

3957 حِبْر *n.* ink

وصفت بنود الاتفاق بأنها حبر على ورق — He described the points of the agreement as ink on paper

62 | 390 |

3958 زِينَة *n.* embellishment, adornment, decoration

ينبغي أن يكون هذا الحجاب خاليا من كل زينة، ومن كل تطريز — This veil needs to be free of all decoration, and from any needlework

70 | 347 |

3959 اِسْتِشارِيّ *adj.* advisory, consultative, consulting; *n.* advisor, consultant

أصبحنا نعمل معا في مكتب استشاري هندسي — We have started to work together in an engineering consulting office

55 | 438 |

3960 جَلِيل *adj.* venerable, eminent; glorious, great

هذا هو العالم الجليل سعيد بن جبير — This is the important scholar Said bin Jabir

65 | 372 |

3961 هاتِ *part.* (imperative, fem. هاتِ, pl. هاتُوا) to bring, fetch, get sth; to give, hand over sth

قال لي أبي هات مخدة لأضع رأسي عليها — My father said to me: Bring a pillow so I can put my head on it

50 | 483 |

3962 تَبْرِير *n.* justification, pretext; vindication, exoneration

حاول تبرير ما فعله بأنه كان بسبب الانفعال — He tried to justify what he did in that it was because of being so upset

68 | 354 |

3963 جِذْرِيّ *adj.* radical, fundamental, basic

الحلول يجب أن تكون جذرية وليس مؤقتة، لأن الحلول المؤقتة تتكرر معها المشكلات — The solutions need to be radical and not temporary because problems recur with temporary solutions

67 | 362 |

3964 تَوالَى *v. VI* to follow in succession, come one after the other

لا زالت الأسئلة تتوالى — The questions are still coming one after another

70 | 347 |

3965 خُضار *coll.n.* vegetables, greens

ركزت تفاصيل الهرم الغذائي الحديث على دور الخضار والفاكهة في المحافظة على الصحة وتحسين مقاومة الجسم للأمراض الحادة — The details of the modern food pyramid concentrate on the role of vegetables and fruits in maintaining health and improving the resistance of the body to acute illness

63 | 382 |

3966 حَرَّمَ *v. II* to outlaw, ban sth; to forbid على sb to do sth; to prevent على sb from doing sth

فعلا مشكلتها ليس لها حل في ظل شريعة تحرم الطلاق كما تحرم الزواج بثانية — Her problem

indeed does not have a solution in light of a law that forbids divorce and also forbids marrying a second wife

73 | 333 |

3967 مُحاوِل *a.p.* attempting, trying (to do sth)

ابتلع فيصل ريقه محاولا البقاء ثابتا أمام الضابط — Faisal swallowed his spit, trying to stand firm in front of the officer

63 | 383 | +lit

3968 فَلَك *n.* celestial body, orbit; عِلْم الفَلَك astronomy

خواني ما هي إلا أيام قلائل حتى تكتمل دورة الفلك ويشرق على الدنيا هلال شهر رمضان المبارك — My brothers, it is only a few days until the celestial orbit completes its round and the advent of the month of blessed Ramadan will break upon the world

67 | 360 |

3969 جَمَل *n. pl.* جِمال camel

صبرت عليه صبر الجمل، والجمل حيوان بري يصبر على الجوع والعطش أياما — I waited as patiently as a camel for him, and the camel is a wild animal that can be patient with hunger and thirst for days

67 | 361 |

3970 مُؤَلَّف *adj.* composed (مِن of); compiled; *n.* publication, book; compilation, composition; أُلُوف مُؤَلَّفَة thousands and thousands

كل الذين ترجموا لوالدنا كانوا يذكرون بأن أول مؤلف كان يشتغل به هو (مراكش في عصرها الذهبي) — All those who wrote biographies of my father mentioned that the first publication he worked on was "Marrakesh in its Golden age"

66 | 363 |

3971 مَعْرُوض *adj.* on display, shown; offered, available; *n.* offering, proposal

دائما نصدر المنتج الأجود من المعروض في الداخل — We always export the better product than what is offered in the interior

67 | 360 |

3972 ذَرَّة *n.* atom, particle

هل هناك ذرة من الحقيقة في هذا القول؟ — Is there a particle of truth in this statement?

68 | 353 |

3973 جَمْر *n.* embers

يتقلب على فراشه كأنه يتقلب على الجمر — He is turning over on his bed as if turning over in embers

56 | 431 |

3974 تَسَلَّلَ *v. V* to infiltrate إلى sth

يقف عند الباب سادا الضوء الذي كان يتسلل إلى الداخل من الفناء — He stands at the door blocking the light which was infiltrating into the inside from the courtyard

63 | 381 | +lit

3975 مُرْض (مُرْضِي .def) *adj.* satisfactory, satisfying, pleasing; adequate, sufficient

اعتبر أن التقدم الذي تم تحقيقه في العراق غير مرض — He felt that the progress that has been achieved in Iraq is not satisfactory

73 | 328 |

3976 مُصَلٍّ (مُصَلِّي .def) *a.p.* praying, worshipping; *n. pl.* -uun person praying or worshipping

مع انبثاق اللحظات الأولى من نهار اليوم بدأت جموع المصلين تتجه صوب بيوت الله لاداء صلاة العيد — With the breaking forth of the first moments of daylight today, masses of worshippers began to head toward mosques to perform the Eid prayer

67 | 359 |

3977 هاجَمَ *v. III* to attack, assault sth/sb; to raid, launch a strike against sth

الصحف القومية تهاجم الوزير وصحف المعارضة تؤيده — The state-owned press is attacking the minister and the opposition press is supporting him

71 | 339 |

3978 زَبُون *n. pl.* زَبائِن customer, client

غير مسموح لنا أن نشرب مع الزبائن — We are not permitted to drink with the customers

61 | 390 |

3979 مُقَرَّب *adj.* close, near; *n. pl.* -uun close companion, protégé

واكدت مصادر مقربة من رئيس الوزراء ان الحكومة لن تقبل بتكرار تجربة التدوير — Sources close to the prime minister said that the government would not accept a repetition of the experience of recycling

66 | 365 |

3980 طائِفِيَّة *n.* sectarianism, factionalism

دعا الى نبذ العنف والطائفية والعشائرية والقبلية — He called for renouncing violence, sectarianism, and tribalism.

50 | 475 |

3981 طُمَأْنِينَة *n.* calm, tranquility, serenity; rest, repose

الأب يعطي الأمن والطمأنينة لأسرته والأم تمنحهم الحب والعطف — The father gives security and confidence to his family and the mother gives them love and emotion

71 | 335 |

3982 تَهْريب *n.* smuggling (goods or persons)

كانوا متخصصين في تهريب المخدرات — They were specialists in smuggling drugs

59 | 403 |

3983 إِتْمام *n.* completion; realization

أحزنه هذا الاختلاف الذي منع الرجلين من إتمام هذا العمل العظيم — This disagreement that prevented the two men from completing this great work made him sad

72 | 330 |

3984 صَحْوَة *n.* awakening, revival; resurgence

من إيجابيات الصحوة الإسلامية أنها تركز في خطابها على رصيد الفصحى — One of the positive things about the Islamic revival is that it concentrates, in its message, on the classical language

65 | 369 |

3985 وِقائِيّ *adj.* protective; preservative; preventive

الحكومة لم تتخذ الاجراءات الوقائية الضرورية لحمايتهم — The government has not taken the necessary preventive measures to protect them

59 | 405 |

3986 خَطَرَ *v. I (u,i)* to occur ل to sb; to come على/ب to sb's mind

هذه نافذة مفتوحة للرد على أي تساؤل يخطر على بالك وتريد له إجابة — This is an open window to respond to any question that occurs to your mind and you want an answer to

69 | 347 |

3987 دائِر *adj.* taking place, happening; ongoing, current

ما هو تعليقك على الجدل الدائر حاليا بين دومينيك وهيفاء وهبي على أغنية واوا؟ — What is your comment on the controversy currently going on between Dominique and Haifa Wahbi concerning the song "Wawa"?

62 | 382 |

3988 وَيْل *n.* woe, distress; يا وَيْلي! woe is me!

يا ويل الوطن من العسكر — Woe to the country from the military

58 | 412 |

3989 أَجْدَى *v. IV* to be useful, helpful; يُجْدِي نَفْعاً it's useful

دعي التفكير بما لا يجدي وتابعي التقدم في تغيير حياتك ولا تيأسي — Let go of thinking about things that aren't useful, and continue progressing in changing your life, and don't despair

65 | 368 |

3990 عَتْمَة *n.* dark, darkness, gloom

في العتمة يبدو الضوء قريبا، لكنك تمشي طويلا قبل أن تصل إليه — In the darkness the light looks close, but you walk a long time before you reach it

53 | 444 | +lit

3991 شَقَّ *v. I (u)* to split, cut through sth; شق طريقه to make one's way (إلى towards)

ارتفع آذان الفجر يشق السماء — The dawn call to prayer cut through the sky

64 | 370 | +lit

3992 مَعْمَل *n. pl.* مَعامِل laboratory; factory, installation, (production) facility

يقضي عمره في معمل مغلق بارد، منكفئا على الميكروسكوب لساعات طويلة — He is spending his life in a cold, closed-up laboratory, bent over a microscope for long hours

65 | 362 |

3993 دِبْلُوماسِيَّة *n.* diplomacy

أكد البرادعي أن الدبلوماسية هي السبيل الوحيد لعلاج النزاع — Al-Baradaie stressed that diplomacy was the only way to deal with the conflict

58 | 408 |

3994 دُهْن *n.* pl. دُهُون oil, grease, fat (esp. in food)
الأطعمة السريعة والجاهزة تحتوي على نسبة عالية من
الدهون والملح والسكريات — Fast and prepared
foods contain high proportions of fats, salt,
and sugars
54 | 437 |

3995 فيتامين *n.* pl. -aat vitamin
الفيتامينات مهمة جدا للجسم والمعروف أن معظم
الفيتامينات يتم الحصول عليها عن طريق الغذاء
وخاصة الخضراوات — Vitimins are very
important for the body, and it is known that
most vitamins are obtained from food,
particularly vegetables
41 | 579 |

3996 اِخْتِراق *n.* breaking (barrier); incursion,
penetration; traversing, crossing (region);
hacking into (computer, network)
لقد نجح "حزب الله" في اختراق دفاعات خصومه
السياسيين وكسر محاولات عزله — Hizbollah
succeeded in penetrating the defenses of its
political adversaries and breaking attempts to
isolate it
69 | 341 |

3997 فَخامَة *n.* excellence, eminence; (in titles)
فَخامَة الرَّئيس His Excellency, the President
كان صاحب الجلالة السلطان قابوس بن سعيد
المعظم على رأس مستقبلي فخامة رئيس جمهورية
بيلاروس والوفد المرافق له لدى وصوله — His
majesty Sultan Qabus bin Saed, the great, was
at the head of those greeting his excellency
the president of the Republic of Belarus and
the delegation accompanying him upon his
arrival
42 | 557 | +news

3998 نَحْل *coll.n.* bees, *un.n.* نَحْلَة
كانا اكثر نشاطا من خلية النحل — They were
more active than a hive of bees
59 | 400 |

3999 نِقاب *n.* niqab (full-face veil), veil; كَشَفَ النِّقاب
عن to disclose, reveal sth
أضاف أن ارتداء النقاب لا يمنع التأكد من شخصية
من ترتديه — He added that wearing the

full-veil does not prevent ascertaining the
identity of the one wearing it
67 | 351 |

4000 مُنْفَصِل *adj.* separate, disconnected; detached,
loose
بلغ ضيقه من ذلك أنه بدأ يحس بيده اليمنى وكأنها
منفصلة عن جسده — His annoyance with that
reached the point that he began to feel as if
his right hand was separated from his body
69 | 341 |

4001 اِزْدِهار *n.* blossoming, prosperity, boom,
expansion
المسرح هو أبو الفنون فقد ساهم في ازدهار العديد
من الفنون الأخرى — The theater is the father
of the arts, for it participated in the flourishing
of a number of the other arts
63 | 373 |

4002 مَخْزُون *adj.* stored; in stock; *n.* store, storage;
supplies, reserves, deposits
وحذرت (الفاو) من الاتجاه إلى انخفاض المخزون
العالمي من الحبوب رغم الزيادة الكبيرة في الإنتاج
— The FAO warned against the trend towards a
reduction in the worldwide stocks of seeds
despite the big increase in production
70 | 339 |

4003 حَيِّز *n.* sphere, scope; field, domain, area
دخل الاتفاق، حيز التنفيذ في ٣ ايلول ١٩٨١ بعدما
صادق عليه ٢٠ بلدا — The agreement went into
effect on 3 September 1981 after 20 countries
ratified it
64 | 367 |

4004 رَبْع *n.* pl. رُبُوع housing, lodging; residence,
home; territory, inhabited area
مسكنا مكون من حجرة وحيدة في فناء ربع —
Our dwelling is made up of a single room
in the courtyard of a house
66 | 355 |

4005 مالِك *n.* proprietor, owner; *adj.* possessing,
owning; having, holding
ما من مالك يستطيع إزاحة جدار من مكانه، دون
هدم الدار المجاورة — No owner can tear down

the walls of his place without destroying the neighboring home

67 | 353 |

4006 زَكاة *n.* zakat (almsgiving in Islam); charity
الهدف من وراء دفع الزكاة هو تحقيق العدالة الاجتماعية — The goal of paying the Zakat tax is to accomplish social justice

56 | 416 |

4007 مُصادَرة *n.* confiscation, seizure; expropriation; impounding
يشتكي بعض المثقفين من مصادرة كتبهم في الجمارك والحدود — Some authors are complaining about the confiscation of their books at Customs and Borders

64 | 364 |

4008 مَظلُوم *adj.* oppressed, treated unjustly
حينما لا يستثمر المظلوم فرصة التحرر واستعادة الحق المسلوب لنفسه، يصبح ظالما لنفسه — When the victim does not invest in the opportunity to liberate himself or to retrieve lost rights, he becomes an oppressor of himself

65 | 362 |

4009 طَيَّبَ *v. II* to make pleasant; to enhance, make delicious (food); to perfume, scent sth; طَيَّبَ خاطِرَهُ to appease sb
أحسنتم وطيب الله أنفاسكم — You did well, and may God make your breath sweet

70 | 333 |

4010 خِتامِيّ *adj.* concluding, closing, final
انا حضرت الحفل الختامي للسنة الماضية وكان اكثر من رائع — I attended the final party for last year, and it was more than splendid

57 | 409 |

4011 هادِف *adj.* purposeful, directed; (plans, efforts) aimed at
دعم الجهود والتحركات الشعبية الهادفة إلى إغلاق السفارات والمكاتب الصهيونية الموجودة في بعض الدول العربية — He supported the efforts and popular movements which aim to close the Zionist embassies and offices which are present in some Arab countries

67 | 348 |

4012 رِيفِيّ *adj.* rural, countryside; rustic
الولاية تحتاج الى جهود كبيرة لتوفير الخدمات في المناطق الريفية — The state needs great efforts to provide services in rural areas

56 | 417 |

4013 اِحْتِواء *vn.* containing, including; controlling, holding back, curbing; *n.* inclusion, content
هناك عدة وسائل يمكن أن تعين الأزواج على احتواء الخلافات الزوجية في لحظاتها الأولى — There are several means which can help couples contain marital disagreements when they first appear

59 | 393 |

4014 إِسْكان *n.* housing
نهدف الى حل مشكلة الإسكان على المدى القصير والبعيد — We aim to solve the housing problem in the short and long terms

50 | 462 |

4015 رُزّ and أَرُزّ *n.* rice
وزاد محصول الأرز بنسب 9-24.6٪ عند تنمية الأسماك في حقول الأرز — The rice harvest increased by a percentage of 9–24.6% when fish were grown in the rice fields

64 | 362 |

4016 مُقاوِم *n.* antagonist, adversary; *a.p.* resisting, opposing
وقعت اشتباكات عنيفة بين المقاومين وقوات الاحتلال — Violent confrontations broke out between the resistance and the occupation forces

56 | 416 |

4017 نَزَفَ *v. I (i)* to bleed, hemorrhage; drain
لا تزال دماء الشهداء تنزف بفعل القنابل العنقودية الاميركية — The blood of martyrs is still flowing as a result of American cluster bombs

63 | 367 |

4018 غَمْرَة *n.* inundation, flood; *pl.* غِمار heat, passion (of conflict)
هل قرر القائد سليمان خوض غمار المعركة الرئاسية بعد مرحلة اظهر فيها الكثير من التردد؟ — Did the leader Sulayman decide to plunge into the heat of the presidential battle after a period in which he showed a lot of hesitation?

71 | 326 |

4019 قَبْضَة *n.* grip; fistful; seizure

وقد أدت هذه السياسة الى تشديد قبضة اسرائيل على الارض المحتلة — This policy lead to a strengthening of Israel's grip on the Occupied land

63 | 365 |

4020 أَقْدَم *elat.* older/oldest, more/most ancient

يعتبر هذا التل أقدم مستوطنة بشرية في العالم — This tel is the oldest human settlement in the world

75 | 309 |

4021 نَخِيل *n.* date palms

وقف شوقي ينظر إلى النخيل، ثم قال لسكرتيره اكتب، فأخرج السكرتير قلما وورقة — Shawqi stood looking at the palm trees, then he said to his secretary: write! So the secretary took out a pen and paper

60 | 382 |

4022 مُعَوِّق *n. pl.* -aat obstacle, hurdle, impediment

سيعرض على القمة العربية المقبلة في الخرطوم معوقات حركة التجارة العربية — He will present to the Arab Summit in Khartoum the impediments to Arab trade

63 | 369 |

4023 عامَلَ *v. III* to treat, deal with sth/sb (ب in a manner)

كانت امرأة ابوه تعامله بحقد ورغم ذلك فهو لا يكرهها يعاملها بكل احترام — His father's wife used to treat him with hatred and despite that he did not hate her, treating her with all respect

73 | 315 |

4024 تَرْكِيبَة *n.* structure, composition; arrangement, configuration

تؤكد الدراسات أن عمل المرأة سيحدث أثرا إيجابيا على التركيبة الاجتماعية والاقتصادية في المملكة العربية السعودية — The studies affirm that women working would cause a positive effect on the social and economic structure of the Kingdom of Saudi Arabia

64 | 358 |

4025 حَنُون *adj.* affectionate, compassionate; loving, dear

عطف الدنيا وحنانها لا يعادلان ضمة إلى صدر أمه الدافئ الحنون — The affection and sympathy of the world are not equal to the warm, affectionate embrace of his mother

60 | 384 |

4026 مَذْهَبِيّ *adj.* doctrinal, sectarian

هذه المنطقة مميزة بتنوعها المذهبي والديني — This area is distinguished by its religious and sectarian diversity

51 | 449 |

4027 لَوَّحَ *v. II* to wave ب with (hand) إلى at sb; to allude to, hint at ب sth

ما زالت تلوح بيدها في اتجاه نافذته — She continued to wave in the direction of his window

71 | 323 |

4028 مُفْرَد *adj.* individual, separate; بِمُفْرَدِه alone, by itself/himself

في سنواته الأخيرة كان يجلس بمفرده، حزينا لفقد ابنه الوحيد إسماعيل — In his last years he would sit by himself, saddened by the loss of his only son Ismael

72 | 318 |

4029 رُوَيْد *n.* رُوَيْداً رُوَيْداً slowly, gradually; (with pron.) رُوَيْدَك slow down!

أخذت أصواتهم تخف رويدا رويدا حتى ساد الصمت — Their voices started to quiet down bit by bit until silence reigned

54 | 420 |

4030 قاتَلَ *v. III* to fight (sb)

من غير المعقول ان نقول أن حزب الله يقاتل ويخوض هذه الحرب بسبب ايران او بسبب سوريا — It is not reasonable for us to say that Hizbollah is fighting and plunging into this war because of Iran or because of Syria

63 | 361 |

4031 مِيزَة *n.* characteristic, distinguishing feature; merit, distinction, advantage, asset

لهذه المقبرة ميزة جليلة وهى أنها لا يمكن أن تسرق — This graveyard has a wonderful characteristic, and that is that it cannot be robbed

75 | 303 |

4032 بَحْرِيَّة *n.* navy

توفي جندي من مشاة البحرية بعد أن أصيب بجروح في مواجهات مع مسلحين بالفلوجة — A Marine

died after he was wounded in a confrontation with gunmen in Faluja

56 | 404 |

4033 نَزْعَة *n.* inclination, tendency; trend

سرعان ما تحول إعجابه كالعادة إلى نزعة عدوانية، وحاول جاهدا أن يسيطر عليها — His admiration quickly changed, as usual, to a hostile tendency, and he tried hard to control it

64 | 355 |

4034 رَأَسَ *v. I (a)* to head, lead, direct sth; to chair (meeting)

ومارس الرجل العمل الصحفي فترة من الزمن، وهو الآن يرأس تحرير مجلة "بانقيا" ويشغل موقع رئيس الاتحاد العام — The man practiced journalism for a period of time, and he is now the editor-in-chief of the magazine "Panqia" and he occupies the position of head of the general union

61 | 371 |

4035 نَدًى *n.* dew; generosity; قَطَر النَّدَى dew drop

تبادل الحب بين عينيه وعينيها، كقطر الندى حين يداعب الورود، وكالقمر حين ينافس سكون الليل — Love was exchanged between his eyes and her eyes, like dewdrops touching the roses, like the moon when it competes with the silence of the night

46 | 493 | +lit

4036 طَرَأَ *v. I (a)* to happen (unexpectedly) على to sb; to occur على to sb (an idea)

تعتبر واشنطن ان تغييرا حقيقيا طرأ على السياسة السورية — Washington considers that a real change has happened in Syrian policies

71 | 321 |

4037 أُفّ and أُوف (Lev.Irq.Gul.) *interj.* (dismay) ugh!; (disgust) phew!

لا تقل لهما أف ولا تنهرهما و قل لهما قولا كريما — Don't tell them "ugh!" and don't scold them; say nice things to them

42 | 543 | +spo

4038 خُلاصَة *n.* gist; synopsis, abstract, summary; خُلاصَة القَوْل in brief, in short

كان في بيته يحضر لجامعته، يقرأ خلاصة المحاضرة التي سمعها بالأمس — He was in his house

preparing for his university, reading the summary of the lecture which he had heard yesterday

70 | 325 |

4039 مَعْرِفيّ *adj.* knowledge-related, information-related; cognitive

كان هو أول من فكر في إصدار القاموس المعرفي المبسط — He was the first one who thought of publishing the simplified knowledge encyclopedia

60 | 379 |

4040 شَيْخَة *n.* matron, elderly woman, elderly female; يا شَيْخَة my dear lady, ma'am

لا يا شيخة بلاش قرف — No, ma'am, don't be disgusting

41 | 555 |

4041 حَراريّ *adj.* thermal, caloric, heat-related; الإِحْتِباس الحَراريّ greenhouse effect, global warming

عملية بناء المفاعل النووي الحراري ستستغرق ١٠ سنوات — The operation of building thermo-nuclear reactors will last 10 years

58 | 389 |

4042 لُعْبَة *n. pl.* لُعَب game, sport; toy, play thing; (fig.) deal, trick; (sports) move

تحمل بين يديها لعبة لصالح تحثه بها على المشي نحوها — She carries in her hands a toy for Salih to encourage him to walk towards her

51 | 444 |

4043 مُتَغَيِّر *adj.* changing, alternating; *n.* مُتَغَيِّرات variables

حاسة صوتك متغير كتير تعبانة شي؟ — I feel like your voice has changed a lot, are you a bit sick?

67 | 339 |

4044 قُطْر *n. pl.* أَقْطار region, district; countries

لقد تمكنت مختلف الأقطار العربية من تنفيذ برامج تتصل بتوفير الخدمات الأساسية للمواطنين — Various Arab regions were able to carry out programs related to providing basic services to the citizens

64 | 350 |

4045 مُلْتَزِم *adj.* committed (ب) to); involved, loyal

تظاهر بأنه مسلم ملتزم ومؤمن صالح، فكان يحرص على حضور صلاة الجمعة — He pretended that

he was a practicing Muslim and a good believer, so he insisted on attending Friday prayer

71 | 318 |

4046 طالِب *adj.* requesting, demanding

تلقت اتصالات هاتفية مكثفة من أسر سعودية طالبة خادمات سعوديات لمعرفتهن بالمجتمع وعاداته وتقاليده — She received a lot of phone calls from Saudi families requesting Saudi maids because of their knowledge of the society and its customs and traditions

65 | 349 |

4047 كليب *n.* pl. -aat (film, video) clip

كانت راضية تماما عن تجربتها الأولى بتصوير الفيديو كليب — She was perfectly satisfied with her first experience of filming a video clip

50 | 446 |

4048 زَحْمَة *n.* (traffic) congestion, jam, bottleneck; crowd, throng

ما في زحمة هناك الواحد يرتاح — There is no crowding there, a person can relax

57 | 394 |

4049 فِداء *n.* sacrifice; self-sacrifice

كان زينة الابطال الذين فتحوا صدورهم لنار الفداء ليبقى وطنهم عزيزا — He was the most beautiful of the heroes who opened their breasts to the fire of self-sacrifice so their homeland would remain dear

60 | 376 |

4050 اِجْتِياح *n.* strike, invasion

تجاهلت الولايات المتحدة اعتراضات روسيا على اجتياح العراق — America ignored Russia's objections to the invasion of Iraq

62 | 363 |

4051 حَيَوِيَّة *n.* vigor, vitality; liveliness

كان بجانبه شاب نضر الوجه مفتول العضل كله حيوية ونشاط — Beside him was a fresh-faced, sinewy young man, who was all vitality and activity

72 | 311 |

4052 بِرّ *n.* charity; piety, righteousness

ثقي بالله ولا تفقدي الرجاء في بره وكرمه — Trust in God and don't lose hope in his righteousness and his generosity

61 | 365 |

4053 حامِل *fem.adj.* pregnant

كانت حاملا في شهرها الثامن — She was pregnant, in her eighth month

61 | 369 |

4054 إِنْسانِيَّة *n.* humanity, humankind; humaneness

اتمنى لحزبنا كل النجاح في اخطر معركة تواجه شعبنا بل والانسانية عموما — I wish our party all success in the most serious battle which faces our people, indeed mankind generally

63 | 353 |

4055 اِقْتِحام *n.* incursion, assault; storming into, breaching

أدانت اللجنة انسحاب المراقبين الامريكيين والبريطانيين قبل اقتحام السجن — The committee condemned the withdrawal of the American and British observers before the assault on the prison

67 | 337 |

4056 تَلا *v. I (u)* to follow, come after sth/sb; to recite (Qur'an)

ثم جاء عام ١٩٥٢ وما تلاه من العدوان على الحياة المدنية — Then came the year 1952, and what followed it in the way of attacks on civilian life

67 | 333 |

4057 مِئَوِيّ *adj.* one-hundred, hundredth; percent; Celsius, centigrade

من الممكن تخفيض هذه النسبة سنويا بحوالي اربع نقاط مئوية — It is possible to lower this ratio yearly by about four percent

49 | 455 |

4058 نَوَّهَ *v. II* to point out, mention بـ/إلى أَنَّ that

ونوه سموه بالدور الكبير الذي تبذله منظمة المؤتمر الإسلامي — His majesty mentioned the huge role which the Organization of the Islamic Conference has played

45 | 497 | +news

4059 روائِيّ *n.* pl. -uun novelist, narrator; *adj.* narrative, novelistic

وقع الاختيار على اسم الروائي المصري العالمي الراحل نجيب محفوظ ليمثل شخصية المعرض هذا العام — The name of the world-class late

Egyptian novelist Naguib Mahfouz was chosen to represent the "personality of the exhibition" this year

43 | 516 |

4060 اِنْعِكاس *n.* pl. -aat repercussion; reflection
يكتشف ان جمال العالم المادي ما هو الا انعكاس للجمال الالهي — He is discovering that the beauty of the physical world is only a reflection of divine beauty

68 | 330 |

4061 حِدَة *n.* عَلى حِدَةٍ separately, individually
لا بد من دراسة كل حالة على حدة — Each case needs to be studied separately

74 | 300 |

4062 دَوّامَة *n.* spiral, cycle; whirlpool, vortex; dizziness, confusion
ما هي رؤيتكم لإخراج العراق من دوامة العنف؟ — What is your vision for extracting Iraq from the cycle of violence?

71 | 316 |

4063 إهْمال *n.* neglect, negligence, carelessness
الأبحاث التي أشرف عليها أتحمل مسؤوليتها.. أى إهمال فيها يمسني شخصيا — The research I supervise, I bear the responsibility for...Any neglect in them harms me personally

70 | 320 |

4064 فائِت *adj.* past, expired, elapsed, gone by; (Dia.) *a.p.* entering (على sth); stopping by to visit (على sb)
متوسط السكان لكل طبيب وصل إلى ٦٤٧ مواطنا العام الفائت بعد أن كان ٧١٧ في عام ٢٠٠٣ — The average number of inhabitants per doctor reached 647 citizens last year after it had been 717 in 2003

60 | 372 |

4065 رَصيف *n.* sidewalk; platform
كانوا يضعون المصابين بعيدا على الرصيف متجاورين حتى تحملهم عربات الإسعاف بنظام — They placed the wounded far from the platform, side by side in rows, so that the ambulances could transport them in an orderly fashion

57 | 389 |

4066 صَبِيَّة *n.* pl. صَبايا girl, young girl, young (unmarried) woman
أعرف ليلى منذ أن كانت طفلة، ثم صبية ثم طالبة جامعية، والآن مدرسة — I have known Laila since she was a child, then as a young woman, then as a university student, and now as a teacher

54 | 413 |

4067 هِبَة *n.* gift, grant
اسبانيا قدمت هبة من المعدات لمعالجة التلوث البيئي في لبنان — Spain offered a gift of equipment to treat environmental pollution in Lebanon

69 | 320 | +lit

4068 مَعْدُود *adj.* limited in number, countable
النظام الفاسد يهتز بشدة، واعتقد أن أيامه معدودة — The corrupt regime is badly shaken, and I believe that its days are numbered

71 | 311 |

4069 رَكْب *n.* procession, cavalcade; entourage, retinue
عاهد على البذل والعطاء لبناء "الأردن أولا" ليكون في طليعة الركب لخدمة الامة واهدافها — He pledged that they would exert efforts and give what they could to build "Jordan First" so it would be in the forefront of service to the nation and its goals

65 | 339 |

4070 تَقارُب *n.* mutual affinity; rapprochement
حدث تقارب ملحوظ بين البلدين عقب الاحتلال الأميركي للعراق — A noticeable rapprochement occurred between the two countries after the American occupation of Iraq

66 | 334 |

4071 رافِد *n.* tributary; الرّافِدان Tigris and Euphrates; بلاد الرّافِدَيْن Mesopotamia
أعلن زعيم تنظيم القاعدة في بلاد الرافدين أبو حمزة المهاجر إطلاق حملة جديدة سماها الفتح المبين — The leader of the Al-Qaeda organization in Iraq Abu Hamza Al-Muhajir announced the launching of a new campaign he called The Clear Conquest

57 | 384 |

4072 حَـ (Egy.) *part.* (future marker, with imperf.) will

سمعت انه حياخد الشقة دي من النهارده — I heard that he was going to take this apartment starting today

13 | 1669 | +spo +for

4073 طَوَّل *v. II* to lengthen, extend, prolong sth; to take (a long) time; to stay, linger; to last

آسف إذا طولت عليكم — I'm sorry if I've kept you too long

43 | 512 |

4074 هُوَّة *n.* abyss, chasm; gulf, gap

لميس مصرة على انتشال صديقاتها من هوة الحزن التي غرقن فيها — Lamis is insistent on snatching her girlfriends from the gulf of sadness they have sunk into

70 | 313 |

4075 مُشاوَرَة *n.* pl. -aat consultation, deliberation, discussion

كان يتردد على القاهرة لإجراء بعض المشاورات السياسية — He used to go to Cairo frequently to carry out some political consultations

51 | 430 | +news

4076 مُطْمَئِنّ *adj.* calm, at ease; relieved, reassured; certain, sure, confident (إلى about)

استرخى ونام هادئا مطمئنا في عالمه الجديد — He sprawled out and slept calmly in his new world

65 | 340 |

4077 نَظَرِيّ *adj.* theoretical

كثير من جامعاتنا عمدت إلى إغلاق كثير من التخصصات النظرية مثل الجغرافيا والتاريخ والدراسات الإسلامية — Many of our universities intend to close many of the theoretical specialties like geography, history, and Islamic studies

71 | 312 |

4078 وِدّ (Gul.) *n.* desire, wish; (with pron.) وِدِّي I would like; وِدِّج /widdich/ would you (fem.sg.) like?

والله ودي أعرف أهل هؤلاء الشباب أين هم من أبنائهم؟ — I really want to know why the families of these youths do not care for their children?

32 | 692 | +for +spo

4079 تَدَفَّق *v. V* to flow, stream; to drip, drop

عندما يتدفق الدم نحو الجلد يتوجب على القلب حينذاك أن ينبض بسرعة — When the blood rushes towards the skin, the heart at that time must beat quickly

66 | 335 |

4080 أَبْعَد *v. IV* to remove, eliminate sb عن from; to expel, banish sb; to distance نَفْسَهُ عن oneself from sth

أعلن رئيس وزراء مصر أن حياد إيطاليا هو الذى يبعد الخطر عن مصر — The prime minister of Egypt announced that Italy's neutrality was the thing which would keep danger away from Egypt

66 | 334 |

4081 حَكَم *n.* pl. حُكَّام (sports) arbiter, referee

طرد من مقاعد الاحتياط بسبب اعتراضه على قرارات الحكم — He was expelled from the reserves bench because of his objection to the decisions of the referee

64 | 343 |

4082 تَضَخُّم *n.* (econ.) inflation

ترتفع معدلات التضخم في جميع دول الخليج العربية — The rate of inflation is rising in all the gulf countries

47 | 465 |

4083 رَشِيد *adj.* rational, sensible, wise, mature

منظمة العفو الدولية أرسلت إلى حكومتنا الرشيدة مذكرة تعرض فيها مأساتي — Amnesty International sent our "wise" government a note presenting my tragedy

60 | 367 |

4084 جَبان *adj.* coward, cowardly; *n.* coward

يقول عنترة: إني لأضرب الجبان ضربة ينخلع لها قلب الشجاع — Antar says: I will strike the coward so hard that the heart of the courageous man will be ripped out

62 | 355 |

4085 تَقاعُد *n.* retirement

هو عربي الأصل، أحيل إلى التقاعد ولكن أسندت إليه الحكومة الكندية مسئولية هيئة لتنشيط السياحة — He is of Arab origin, and was retired, but the Canadian government assigned him the

responsibility of an organization to revive tourism

64 | 343 |

4086 عَجَبَ *v. I (i)* (Egy.Lev.) to please, satisfy sb; to be pleasing to sb; *a.p.* عاجِب عاجِبني I like it (it pleases me)

شكرا كثير على القصة الحلوة عن جد كثير عجبتني — Many thanks for the nice story, really, I really liked it

29 | 760 |

4087 مَوْطِن *n.* pl. مَواطِن home country; residence; locality, area

هذه البلدة المتواضعة على شاطئ النيل تدرى أنها ستكون يوما موطن شخصية يتحدث عنها العالم بأسره — This humble village on the banks of the Nile knows that it will one day be the home town of someone the whole world will talk about

69 | 316 |

4088 عَجَلَة *n.* wheel, tire

اهتمت محافظة قنا بدفع عجلة التنمية الصناعية وتشجيع الاستثمار الصناعي — The Qina Governorate took an interest in pushing the wheel of industrial growth forward, and in encouraging industrial investment

69 | 317 |

4089 ضَئِيل *adj.* small, meager, sparse

هذه الشركات لا تعطي للعراق سوى نسبة ضئيلة من الارباح لا تسد الاحتياجات الأمنية والعسكرية These companies only give Iraq a small portion of profits which don't meet the military and security needs

72 | 302 |

4090 مُرُورِيّ *adj.* traffic-related

الحوادث المرورية تعتبر احدى المشكلات التي تواجه كافة دول العالم — Traffic accidents are considered one of the problems which faces all countries of the world

51 | 427 |

4091 فَسِيح *adj.* wide, extensive; lengthy, extended; ample, roomy

تحدث عن مزايا الراحل املا من الله ان يتغمده فسيح جنانه وان يلهم العائلة الصبر والسلوان — He

spoke about the good points of the deceased, praying to God that he would shelter him in his wide paradise and inspire the family with patience and comfort

59 | 369 |

4092 مَرْئِيّ *adj.* visual; visible

بدأت الدعاية للمشروع في وسائل الإعلام المقروءة والمسموعة والمرئية في الظهور، محليا و عبر الفضائيات — Advertising for the project began to appear on the written, oral, and visual media, locally and by satellite

67 | 324 |

4093 مُرُونَة *n.* flexibility

لقد شجعني على ان أكون أكثر مرونة في التعامل مع الوسط الفني، وفي كتابة السيناريوهات — He encouraged me to be more flexible in dealing with the artistic milieu, and in writing scenarios

66 | 329 |

4094 رافَقَ *v. III* to accompany, escort sb

ابنه الشاب يرافقه إلى المستشفى ذهابا وإيابا — His young son is accompanying him to the hospital, both going and coming

63 | 343 |

4095 عُمْرانِيّ *adj.* building, construction, architectural; civilized, populated

هذه المنطقة كانت مزدهرة بالنشاط العمراني خلال العصور القديمة — This area was flourishing with building activity in the Middle Ages

52 | 416 |

4096 شُبْهَة *n.* pl. -aat suspicion, doubt

قبض على لصلتي المعروفة باسماعيل، ولم تكن توجد شبهة ضدي — I was arrested because of my known relationship with Ismael, and there was no suspicion against me

68 | 316 |

4097 سِحْرِيّ *adj.* magical, magic; enchanting

أخذت تتلو عليه كلمات سحرية اريد منها اعادته الى الحياة — She started to recite magic words over him which were meant to restore him to life

72 | 301 |

4098 تَعَدُّد *n.* pluralism, multi-

— قبض على سيدة تسمى بدرية بتهمة تعدد الأزواج
A woman named Badrayya was arrested accused of having plural husbands

60 | 363 |

4099 عِرْقيّ *adj.* ethnic, racial

تضمن ان لا تتعرض هذه الاقليات الى التطهير العرقي او التكريد — He guaranteed that these minorities would not be exposed to ethnic cleansing or Kurdification

57 | 380 |

4100 إكْمال *n.* completion, conclusion; perfection

يبدأ خلال الأيام القليلة المقبلة إكمال المشاورات وتحديد المعالم الرئيسية لحكومة الوحدة الوطنية — In the coming few days, he will begin to complete the consultations and to define the principle features of the national unity government

72 | 300 |

4101 ذِمَّة *n.* protection, security; conscience

لا ذمة له ولا ضمير — He has no conscience

73 | 296 |

4102 تَواضُع *n.* modesty, humility

ينظر إلى الأرض متصنعا التواضع ثم يرفع رأسه ناظرا للملك المنصور — He looks at the ground, faking humility, and then he lifts his head looking at the victorious king

71 | 305 |

4103 مَبْعُوث *n.* envoy; delegate; representative

يعرف أيضا ان تعيين مبعوث اميركي للعالم الاسلامي لن يغير آراء المسلمين تجاه العمليات التي تقوم بها القوات الحليفة في افغانستان والعراق — He also knows that appointing an American delegate to the Islamic World will not change the views of Muslims towards the operations which the Allied forces are carrying out in Afghanistan and Iraq

56 | 381 |

4104 مَشْرِق *n.* East, Levant

انتهى وجود الصليبيين في المشرق العربي بعد قرنين من الحروب — The presence of Crusaders ended in the Arab East after two centuries of wars

68 | 318 |

4105 رَحْمَن and رَحْمان *adj.* merciful (God)

باسم الله الرحمن الرحيم اولا شكرا للاخ الاستاذ عبد الباري على ما قاله — In the name of God the merciful, the compassionate, first thanks to brother professor Abd Al-Bari for what he said

52 | 411 |

4106 دُكْتُوراه *n.* doctorate

ودرست أيضا أثناء إعداد رسالة الدكتوراه في إنجلترا (كمبردج) — I also studied, during the preparation of the doctoral dissertation, in England (Cambridge)

68 | 314 |

4107 تَنْشيط *n.* stimulation, encouragement, energizing

السوق المالية لم تلعب بعد الدور المرتقب منها في تنشيط البورصة — The money market has not yet played the role expected of it in bringing the stock market to life

62 | 346 |

4108 قَصَّرَ *v. II* to shorten, curtail sth; (Gul.) to fall short, fail; to be stingy

قال البعض إن الشرطة قصرت في أداء واجبها — Some said that the police failed to do their duty

49 | 431 | +for

4109 زِمام *n.* reins

الجماعة الإسلامية تمتلك زمام المبادرة في الشمال حيث الأغلبية السنية — The Islamic Group holds the reins of the initiative (they are in charge) in the north, where there is a Sunni majority

71 | 300 |

4110 طَبَق *n.* dish, course, meal

هناك العديد من الأشخاص الذين إذا لم يجدوا طبق الأرز أمامهم لا يعتبرون أنفسهم أكلوا على الإطلاق — There are a lot of people who, if they don't find a plate of rice in front of them, don't consider themselves as having eaten at all

62 | 343 |

4111 اِسْتَغْرَبَ *v. X* to be surprised (مِن at), regard sth as strange

انتبه فجأة على جرس الباب، استغرب ولم يصدق تماما حتى سمع رنة أخرى — He suddenly noticed the doorbell; he was surprised and

didn't completely believe it until he heard another ring

70 | 306 |

4112 كَسْر *vn.* breaking; violating, defying (tradition, the law); *n.* fracture, crack; (math.) fraction

للأسف لم يستمر نشاطها لتعرضها لكسر في كتفها الأيمن مما أدى إلى تعطل كل ذراعها اليمنى — Unfortunately she did not continue her activity because of her undergoing the breaking of her right shoulder which led to the disuse of her right arm

77 | 278 |

4113 اللَّاتي *rel.pron.* (fem.pl.) who, whom

من المسئول عن هذه الصورة غير الصحيحة لنساء الريف اللاتي يشكلن ٨٠٪ من المصريات؟ — Who is responsible for this false depiction of the women of the countryside who represent 80% of Egyptian women?

60 | 357 |

4114 حَلْوَى *n.* pastry, dessert

كنت أنا وأصحابي من الأطفال نذهب إلى بيتها للحصول على الحلوى والشيكولاتة — My friends and I, as children, used to go to her house to get sweets and chocolate

73 | 290 |

4115 حَدَّ *v. I (u)* to limit, curb من (sb's freedom, power); to halt, stop مِن sth

هذا الاكتشاف يمكن أن يحد من انتشار هذا المرض الخطير — This discovery could limit the spread of this dangerous disease

71 | 297 |

4116 مُتَسَائِل *adj.* asking oneself, wondering, pondering

صادفه مرة فحدجه بنظرة قاسية، ثم اعترض سبيله متسائلا: أين كانت غيبتك؟ — He happened upon him once, and stared at him with a harsh look, and then blocked his way wondering: Where have you been?

69 | 309 |

4117 مَوْلِد *n.* birthday, anniversary; birthplace; المَوْلِد النَّبَوِيّ Mawlid (the Prophet's birthday)

هى سنغالية المولد نشأت بالقرب من باريس ودخلت غمار السياسة في سن مبكرة — She is Senegalese by birth, raised near Paris, and she entered into politics at an early age

60 | 353 |

4118 آسِف *adj.* sorry, regretful, remorseful

آسف يافندم.. آسف جدا، لا مؤاخذة أصلي افتكرتك واحد زميلنا دايماً يهزر معانا — I'm sorry sir...very sorry, no offense, you see I thought you were one of our colleagues who always likes to joke with us

53 | 398 |

4119 حَرْق *vn.* burning, incineration; *n.* burn (wound)

أقدم متطرفون على حرق دار «ريكس» للعرض السينمائي بمن فيها — Extremists came to burn the Rex House for Cinematic Production with whoever was in it

76 | 277 |

4120 ناجِم *a.p.* arising, originating, resulting عن from

قد عالجنا حالات من السعال وصعوبات التنفس الناجمة عن الازدحام في الأماكن الضيقة — We have treated cases of coughing and difficulties breathing resulting from crowding in narrow places

61 | 347 |

4121 عائِق *n. pl.* عَوائِق obstacle, hurdle, impediment

الحريات الدينية في العالم ما زالت أسيرة العديد من العوائق والحواجز — Religious freedoms in the world are still held prisoner to a number of obstacles and barriers

72 | 293 |

4122 رامِي *adj.* aimed (إلى) at), attempting (إلى) to do sth); *n.* (person) throwing; rifleman; archer

تهدد بانهاء المحاولات الرامية للتوصل الى تسوية سلمية للخلافات العربية الاسرائيلية — He threatened to end the attempts which aim to reach a peaceful settlement of the Arab-Israeli differences

51 | 413 |

4123 قُبَّة *n.* dome, cupola

ينبغى علينا جميعا ان نعرف الفرق بين مسجد قبة الصخرة والمسجد الاقصى — We should all know

the difference between the Dome of the Rock and the Al-Aqsa Mosque

65 | 323 |

4124 حُزْمَة *n. pl.* حُزَم package, bundle; set, collection

أخرجت من حقيبتها حزمة من عيدان البخور وعلبة كبريت — She got out of her bag a bundle of incense sticks and a package of matches

67 | 314 |

4125 رَقَصَ *v. I (u)* to dance

الواحد لما يحب يرقص مع واحدة.. يقول لها أيه؟ — A guy, when he wants to dance with a girl, what does he say to her?

54 | 389 | +lit

4126 اِرْتِداء *n.* wearing, putting on (clothes)

أعلنت تأييدها حق المرأة المسلمة في ارتداء النقاب — She announced her support for the right of Muslim women to wear the full-face veil

69 | 304 |

4127 تَزْوِيد *n.* providing, supplying (ب with)

يمكن تزويد الكمبيوتر بوحدة نسخ اقراص فيديو رقمية مقابل مائة دولار اخرى — The computer can be supplied with a digital video disk copying unit for another hundred dollars

59 | 354 |

4128 أُسَرِيّ *adj.* family, domestic

كانت تشتاق لدفء والحياة الأسرية وتشتاق للزواج والانجاب — She used to long for the warmth of family and family life and to long for marriage and having children

62 | 336 |

4129 ذُهُول *n.* numbness, indifference, confusion

الأصدقاء يتبادلون النظرات وهم في حالة ذهول — The friends exchange glances, in confusion

57 | 365 | +lit

4130 إِلهِيّ *adj.* divine, heavenly, holy; theological

فقد شاءت الإرادة الإلهية أن تحرمه من الولد فوهبته ثلاث بنات تباعًا — Divine will decided to prevent him from having a boy, and granted him three girls in a row

63 | 335 |

4131 هَذاك (Lev.Irq.Gul.; Magh.Lev. هَذاك) *dem.pron.* that, that one; fem. هَذِيك (Magh.Lev.), هَذِيج /hadhiich/ (Irq.Gul.); pl. هَذُوك (Magh.; Alg. هَذُوك); Lev. also with masc.: هذيك اليوم

والله حكيت معاه هذاك اليوم — By God I talked to him that day

9 | 2342 | +spo

4132 مُراسِل *n.* correspondent, reporter

روبرت فيسك هو أشهر مراسل صحفي بريطاني في الشرق الأوسط — Robert Fisk is the most famous British newspaper correspondent in the Middle East

62 | 339 |

4133 تَجَمَّعَ *v. V* to gather together, assemble, rally

السحابات يجب أن تتجمع قبل أن تنهمر — The clouds have to gather before it can start raining

66 | 317 |

4134 عِنَب *coll.n.* grapes, *un.n.* عِنَبَة

لا يوجد اي دليل قاطع على ان تناول عصير العنب الأحمر له تأثير على الأمور التي تهم صحتنا — There is no sure proof that drinking red grape juice has an effect on health matters

60 | 348 |

4135 غَزِير *adj.* abundant, plentiful; substantial, generous

وقد شهدت البلاد عواصف رعدية وامطارا غزيرة — The country witnessed thunderstorms and copious rain

64 | 325 |

4136 اِجْتاحَ *v. VIII* to strike, invade (country, region)

عندما اجتاحت جيوش هتلر فرنسا كانت هناك مقاومة فرنسية سرية مخلصة — When Hitler's armies swept over France, there was a sincere, secret French resistance

70 | 297 |

4137 ماجِسْتِير *n.* master's degree, MA

سيعلق شهادة الماجستير على عيادته فى القاهرة ليقنع المرضى بأنه قادر على شفائهم — He will hang the MA diploma on (the wall of) his clinic in Cairo to convince the sick that he is able to heal them

63 | 329 |

4138 سَبَحَ *v. I (a)* to swim
قرر أن يسبح وحيدا إلى أقرب سفينة — He decided to swim by himself to the nearest ship
62 | 332 |

4139 فَوَات *n.* expiration, passing (time, deadline)
يجب ان نستغل الوقت ونتحرك بسرعة قبل فوات الأوان — We must exploit the time and move quickly before it's too late
71 | 291 |

4140 تَخَيَّلَ *v. V* to imagine, suppose sth or أنَّ that; (imperat.) تَخَيَّل ! just imagine! fancy that!
تخيل كم من الوقت تحتاجه لتطل على التلفزيون Imagine how much time you need to watch television
50 | 417 | +spo

4141 خانَة *n.* compartment, partition; square (chessboard); field (form, questionnaire); cell (spreadsheet)
سوف تشاهده هكذا وسوف ترى خانة الإجابة فارغة، عند ذلك عليك كتابة الإجابة السرية — You will see it like this, and you will see the answer box empty, at that point you should type the password
65 | 319 |

4142 مُحَمَّل *adj.* loaded, burdened, charged
في بغداد احترقت شاحنة عسكرية أمريكية محملة بالعتاد على الطريق الرئيسية لمنطقة النهضة وسط العاصمة العراقية — In Baghdad an American military transport carrying equipment burned on the main road of the Al-Nahda area in the middle of the Iraqi capital
72 | 289 |

4143 جَرُؤَ *v. I (u)* to dare على to do sth
لا يجرؤ أي رئيس تحرير أو رسام على ارتكاب مثل هذا الأمر — No editor or cartoonist would dare commit such an act
58 | 355 |

4144 عَشِقَ *v. I (a)* to love, be fond of sth/sb
إنه لا يطيق فكرة أن تعشق ابنته رجلا آخر، ولذلك يشعر بغيرة قاتلة من جيف — He couldn't bear the idea that his daughter would love another man, and therefore he felt a fatal jealousy against Jeff
62 | 334 |

4145 حَطَّ *v. I (u)* to descend, land (على on)
عاد النائب سعد الحريري إلى بيروت أمس على متن مروحية عسكرية فرنسية حطت في بيروت — The deputy, Saad Hariri, returned to Beirut yesterday on board a French military helicopter which landed in Beirut
63 | 327 |

4146 فِنْجان *n.* cup, coffee cup
تسمح لي أن أدعوك إلى فنجان قهوة في أى مكان — Allow me to invite you for a cup of coffee anywhere
57 | 362 |

4147 ثانَوِيَّة *n.* secondary school, high-school
وجاء تعييني في مدرسة ثانوية عفرين، وتركت زوجتي في بيتنا المستأجر في حي الجميلية — I was appointed to the Afrin Secondary School, and I left my wife in our rented house in the Al-Jamiliyya quarter
51 | 404 |

4148 شُبَّاك *n.* window
قال لي ادخل البيت وابقى بقرب الشباك فذهبت الى الشباك فنظرت الى ان الشمس تشرق من الغرب — He told me to come into the house and to stay near the window, so I went to the window and watched the sun rise from the west
65 | 318 |

4149 إكْتَسَبَ *v. VIII* to earn, gain, win sth
عندما يضحك يكتسب وجهه طابعا ودودا — When he laughs, his face takes on a friendly cast
69 | 299 |

4150 مَخْلُوق *adj.* created; *n.* pl. -aat creature
انني أسعد مخلوق على سطح الارض — I am the happiest creature on the face of the earth
49 | 415 |

4151 سُدّ *n.* dam
بدأ الرئيس جمال عبد الناصر في بناء مشروع السد العالي ١٩٦٠ — President Gamal Abd Al-Nasser began to build the High Dam project in 1960
56 | 369 |

4152 مَناعَة *n.* resistance, immunity

إن الأطعمة الملوثة بالبكتيريا تشكل خطورة كبيرة على كبار السن بالذات، لضعف جهاز المناعة لديهم — Food contaminated with bacteria represents a big danger to the elderly specifically, because of the weakness of their immune system

59 | 350 |

4153 عَقّار *n.* pl. عَقاقِير drug, medicine

للأسف فإن تناول العقاقير المشابهة لهذا العقار عن طريق الفم لم تؤد الى نتيجة — Unfortunately, taking drugs like this one through the mouth did not lead to any result

58 | 351 |

4154 غَضِبَ *v. I (a)* to become angry

لا تغضب من كلامي.. لكن الصراحة أساس علاجك — Don't get angry with my words... but frankness is the basis of your treatment

58 | 354 |

4155 مَيْل *n.* inclination, tendency; leaning, sympathy

لا اعتقد ان احدا يرغب بمخالفة القانون، او لديه ميلا لذلك — I don't believe that anyone wants to break the law, or has an inclination to do so

65 | 316 |

4156 تَجاهُل *n.* disregard; feigned ignorance; mutual disregard

في الحقيقة كنت قد قررت تجاهل موضوع أمينة ووالدها.. قلت ما دخلي في قضايا الناس — In fact I had decided to ignore the matter of Amina and her father...I said: why should I interfere in the affairs of the people?

67 | 306 |

4157 اِسْتِجْواب *n.* interrogation, questioning

يتم استخدام أساليب استجواب قاسية مع المعتقلين — Harsh interrogation methods are used with the prisoners

44 | 464 |

4158 تَعاقُد *n.* contract, mutual agreement

طلب وزارة الزراعة الموافقة على التعاقد مع العاملين في مشروع مكافحة التصحر — He asked the Ministry of Agriculture to agree to the contract with the workers in the anti-desertification project

54 | 377 |

4159 فاسِد *adj.* spoiled, rotten; corrupt, immoral

ليس بمقدوره أن يتحمل مسئولية إحضار أطفال إلى هذا العالم الفاسد — He is not able to bear the responsibility of bringing children into this corrupt world

62 | 328 |

4160 تَأَثُّر *n.* being influenced, affected (ب by); emotion, sensitivity

إنها مريضة بالضغط وقد تتعب في أي وقت من شدة التأثر والانفعال — She is sick from high blood pressure, and she could tire at any time from being too excited or getting upset

70 | 291 |

4161 عَلّامَة *masc.n.* eminent scholar, erudite person

سأل عن تمثال أمام مدخل الجامعة فقلت هذا تمثال المرحوم العلامة قدري طوقان — He asked about the statue in front of the entrance of the university, and I told him that it was the statue of the late great scholar Qadri Tuqan

68 | 300 |

4162 أَفْلَحَ *v. IV* to succeed, prosper, thrive في in sth

أصيب بالصمم وفقدان البصر على إثر إصابة عينيه بمرض لم يفلح معه العلاج، وكان عمره آنذاك تسع سنوات — He was struck deaf and lost his sight as a result of his eyes getting an incurable disease, and his age at the time was nine years

66 | 309 |

4163 مَوْكِب *n.* parade, procession

شيعت جنازة الضابط في موكب رسمي، ثم نقل إلى بلده حيث دفن — The funeral of the officer was held with an official procession, and then he was transferred to his village, where he was buried

64 | 316 |

4164 بُنِّيّ *adj.* brown

كان يرتدي قميصا بني اللون وفوقه سترة ذخيرة سوداء — He was wearing a brown-colored shirt, and above it a black ammunition vest

58 | 350 |

4165 خَشَب *n.* wood; خَشَب مُعاكِس plywood

تقف الممثلة الفرنسية ايملي دوكين أول مرة على خشبة المسرح للقيام ببطولة مسرحية الآنسة جولي للكاتب السويدي الراحل — The French actress Emily

Dequenne is standing for the first time on the stage of the theater to play the leading role in the play of "Miss Julie" by the late Swedish author

86 | 236 |

4166 طَرَق *v. I (u)* to knock on (door)
قبض حمدان على المطرقة النحاسية وطرق الباب ففتح بعد قليل عن البواب بوجهه الكئيب — Hamdan grabbed the brass knocker and knocked on the door; it opened after a while onto the concierge, with his gloomy face

60 | 339 | +lit

4167 تَرَدُّد *n.* repetition; frequenting (على a place); hesitation (في to do sth); frequency (of waves)
كل صوت له تردد معين — Every sound has a particular frequency

67 | 302 |

4168 مُنَسِّق *n.* coordinator
أما جورج إسحاق المنسق العام لحركة "كفاية" فقد قرر هذا العام عدم الذهاب إلى المصيف لانشغاله بأمور داخل الحركة — George Ishaq, the general coordinator of the Kifaya Movement, decided this year not to go on his summer vacation because of being busy with the affairs of the movement

54 | 375 | +news

4169 مُنْكَر *adj.* reprehensible; *n.* vice; النَّهِي عَن المُنْكَر the prevention of vice
اطمئنوا.. أنا لم، ولن أقرب هذا المنكر في حياتي — Have confidence...I did not, and will not even come close to this reprehensible thing in my life

59 | 341 |

4170 نَسِيم *n.* breeze, wind; شَمّ النَّسِيم Egyptian spring festival
كان نسيم الليل قد بدا باردا نوعا ما — The night breeze appeared a bit cold

49 | 412 | +lit

4171 تَغَلُّب *n.* surmounting, overcoming على (challenges)
حاول إياد التغلب على وحدته بأن جعل من ضريح أسامة محجا يوميا — Iyad tried to overcome his

loneliness by making Usama's grave a place of daily pilgrimage

71 | 284 |

4172 تَوَجَّب *v. V* to be necessary على for sb أَنْ to do sth
وبموجب بروتوكول كيوتو يتوجب على الدول الصناعية ان تقلص انبعاث ثاني اوكسيد الكربون بمعدل ٥ بالمئة على الاقل — According to the Kyoto Protocol, the industrial states have to reduce carbon dioxide emissions by 5 percent at least

61 | 327 |

4173 غَيْب *n.* (what is) invisible, concealed
أعطني نورا استضيء به في هذا الغيب المجهول، فإنني حائر — Give me light with which I can illuminate this unknown darkness, since I am confused

55 | 361 |

4174 فاعِلِيَّة *n.* effectiveness; activity
الاتحاد الأوروبي ينتظر من مصر دورا أكثر فاعلية في مساندة الدعم الزراعي الأوروبي في مفاوضات منظمة التجارة العالمية — The European Union expects Egypt to play a more effective role in giving European agricultural support in the World Trade Organization's negotiations

64 | 315 |

4175 مَحْض *adj.* (invar.) pure, mere, complete (fantasy, lies, coincidence)
أصبح المضي في هذه الطريقة والإصرار عليها محض شر — Going on in this way and insisting on it became pure evil

63 | 316 |

4176 سَعَة *n.* volume, capacity
كلفة بناء مستشفى واحد سعة ٢٠٠ سرير تبلغ ٧٥ مليار دينار — The cost of building a single hospital with 200 beds reaches 75 billion dinar

68 | 294 |

4177 رَجْعَة *n.* return, going back, turning back
هذا الزمن قد ولى الى غير رجعة والامور ستوضع في نصابها الصحيح — That time has passed, never to return, and things will be put back into their proper places

75 | 265 |

4178 خَصْخَصَة *n.* privatization

أعتقد أنه حان الوقت لتطبيق الخصخصة، فلا مجال للتأخير — I believe that the time has come to apply privatization, since there is no room for delay

48 | 414 |

4179 حاسُوب *n.* computer

هل يحل الحاسوب محل المعلم ويؤدي جميع الأدوار المطلوبة من المعلم؟ — Will the computer take the place of the teacher and perform all the required roles of the teacher?

56 | 356 |

4180 تَخَرُّج *n.* graduation

درس إدارة الأعمال في إحدى الجامعات البريطانية، وبعد التخرج عمل في إدارة مؤسسة حكومية في مدينة لندن — He studied business administration in one of the British universities, and after graduation he worked in the administration of a government agency in the City of London

64 | 311 |

4181 كُريم *n.* cream (food, cosmetic)

عليها ان تعرف ان كريم الحماية مهم جدا حتى لا تتكون بقع داكنة على بشرتها — She needs to know that protective cream is very important so that dark spots don't form on her skin

41 | 489 | +for

4182 مَحالَة *n.* لا مَحالَة without fail, without a doubt

من لم يتعلم من أخطائه، فالتاريخ سيعيد نفسه لا محالة — He who does not learn from his mistakes, history will repeat itself, for sure

64 | 309 |

4183 مِيل *n.* mile

خلال صيف ١٩٤١ تقدم الجيش الالماني مسافة اربعمائة ميل باتجاه موسكو وذلك خلال ثلاثة اسابيع فقط — During the summer of 1941, the German army advanced a distance of 400 miles in the direction of Moscow, and they did it in only three weeks

66 | 303 |

4184 سَبْق *n.* precedence, antecedence

قام بعض الصحفيين بالتصوير حرصا على السبق الصحفي — Some journalists made their

photographs paying close attention to journalistic precedence

87 | 229 |

4185 مَدْعُوم *adj.* supported, bolstered, promoted

وأضاف البيان أن المعارك اندلعت بينما كانت قوات أفغانية مدعومة بوحدات من قوات التحالف الدولي تقوم بدوريات في المنطقة — The statement added that battles broke out while Afghani forces supported by units from the forces of the Allied states were undertaking patrols in the region

65 | 307 |

4186 أمامِيّ *adj.* front, forward

كانت كل الكراسي الأمامية محجوزة مسبقاً — All the front chairs were previously reserved

61 | 323 |

4187 ضَحْكَة *n.* laugh, laughter

راح يبتسم ثم تحولت ابتسامته إلى ضحكة عريضة — He started to smile and then his smile changed to a broad laugh

47 | 423 | +lit

4188 عاقَبَ *v. III* to punish sb ب (with a sentence) على for (a crime)

يجب أن يعاقب هذا الصبي السارق كي لا يعتاد على السرقة — This thieving boy must be punished so that he does not get used to stealing

68 | 293 |

4189 مُساهِم *n.* shareholder, stockholder; participant

أود أن أشكر جميع المساهمين للثقة التي منحوها إيانا — I want to thank all the participants for the trust they have granted us

47 | 422 |

4190 اِنْهارَ *v. VII* to collapse, fall down; to break down, fall apart

تبذل مجهودا خارقا للتحكم في نفسها، لكنها في النهاية انهارت وأجهشت بالبكاء — She exerted miraculous efforts to control herself, but in the end she collapsed and broke down crying

67 | 295 |

4191 اِخْتِطاف *n.* abduction, kidnapping; hijacking

تتهمه الادارة الامريكية بالضلوع في اختطاف طائرة عام ١٩٨٥ قتل بحار أمريكي كان على متنها — The

American Administration accuses him of being involved with the hijacking of a plane in 1985, on board of which an American sailor was killed

62 | 320 |

4192 تَأَخُّر *n.* delay, slowness; backwardness, lack of development

تأجلت مباراة ليسوثو مع اوغندا الى يوم الثلاثاء — بسبب تأخر وصول الحكام The Lesotho/Uganda match was postponed until Tuesday because of the referees arriving late

66 | 297 |

4193 حافِز *n.* pl. حَوافِز incentive, stimulus, motive

وقال ان ذلك يمثل أيضا حافزا كبيرا للاعب عمرو في البطولات القادمة — And he said that this would also represent a big incentive for the player Amr in the coming championships

59 | 336 |

4194 قِبْلَة *n.* qiblah (direction faced in prayer, i.e. the Kaaba in Mecca); (fig.) onus, focus of attention

فحتى في النظم الديمقراطية الراسخة والقوية التي تعد قبلة أنظار المنادين بالديمقراطية مثل أوروبا وأميركا ما زال الرجل هو صاحب السيطرة — Even in the strong and stable democratic regimes which are considered to be the focus of attention of those who call for democracy, like Europe and America, men are still in control

66 | 299 |

4195 رَهْن *n.* mortgage, security; رَهْنَ subject/liable to, dependent/conditional on

ستجدني رهن إشارتك في كل ما أستطيع — You will find me doing your bidding whenever I can

65 | 301 |

4196 را (Alg.) *part.* (with pron., to indicate present continuous) واش راك تدير /wash rak tdir/ what are you (masc.sg.) doing? what's up?; راني في الخِدْمَة/الدّار I'm at work/home

قلتي لي راني صابرة، قلت لكي علاش راكي صابرة — You said to me: I am being patient; so I said to you: Why are you being patient?

5 | 3962 | +spo

4197 تَمْرين *n.* pl. تَمَارِين exercise, drill, practice, training

الضحك مثل التمارين البدنية يجعل الاوعية الدموية — تعمل بشكل أكثر كفاءة Laughing, like physical exercise, makes the blood vessels work more efficiently

50 | 393 |

4198 إغاثَة *n.* aid, relief assistance

ذكرت وكالات الإغاثة التابعة للأمم المتحدة أن — وصول قوافل الإغاثة إلى مناطق الجنوب تم أخيرا The Aid agency belonging to the United Nations mentioned that the arrival of aid caravans to the south region recently took place

53 | 370 |

4199 زَوال *n.* ending, cessation; disappearance, vanishing; noon, noontime; زَوالًا at noon

كان جبل طارق وقناة السويس وميناء عدن أهم ثلاث نقاط ترتكز عليها الإمبراطورية البريطانية في طريقها إلى الهند، ورغم زوال هذه الإمبراطورية — فلم تزل سطوتها على جبل طارق Gibraltar, the Suez Canal and the port of Aden were the three most important points the British Empire depended on on their way to India, and despite the disappearance of this empire, its control over Gibraltar has not ceased

69 | 283 |

4200 تَوْبَة *n.* repentance, penance

ما الدوافع التي جعلتك تطلب المغفرة وتعلن التوبة؟ — What are the motivations which caused you to seek forgiveness and announce your repentance?

55 | 354 |

4201 حَلاوَة *n.* sweetness, pleasantness; sweets, candy; confectionery; (Dia.) يا حَلاوَة! how nice! sweet!

بيعت كميات رهيبة من حلاوة المولد ومن الأحصنة — والعرائس الحلاوة Huge quantities of Mulid sweets and sugar horses and dolls were sold

66 | 298 |

4202 حِيلَة *n.* pl. حِيَل trick, ruse, stratagem

لقد اتفقنا نحن الثلاثة على أن ندبر حيلة للقضاء على — الساحر الأزرق We three agreed that we would plan out a stratagem to get rid of the blue magician

62 | 318 | +lit

4203 جَوْهَرِيّ *adj.* fundamental, essential; core, central

لا توجد فروق جوهرية بينهما — There are no fundamental differences between them

60 | 325 |

4204 حُدُودِيّ *adj.* frontier, border

هناك دراسة لإنشاء شركة مشتركة لاستغلال خامات الفوسفات المتوافرة في المناطق الحدودية بين سوريا وتركيا لانتاج الفوسفات والأسمدة للتصدير — There is a study to set up a joint company to exploit the raw phosphate which is plentiful in the border regions between Syria and Turkey in order to produce phosphate and fertilizer for export

58 | 336 |

4205 نُطْق *n.* pronunciation; utterance

يساعد الجهاز المحمول الاشخاص الذين يعانون مشاكل في نطق الكلمات بوضوح — The mobile device aids people who suffer problems pronouncing words clearly

67 | 290 |

4206 ضَجَّة *n.* noise; commotion

استيقظت الحارة في باكر الصباح على ضجة صارخة مفزعة.. فتحت النوافذ وأطلت الرءوس — The alley awoke early in the morning to a frightening, loud commotion...windows opened and heads leaned out

65 | 298 |

4207 حَمَام *coll.n.* dove, pigeon

أنت تضع القط بين الحمام بحسب القول المأثور — You put the cat among the pigeons as the saying goes

54 | 359 |

4208 حَسَنَة *n.* pl. -aat good deed, merit

هل حاولت يوما أن تعد سيئاتك كما تعد حسناتك؟ — Have you ever tried counting your bad deeds like you count your good deeds?

34 | 568 | +for

4209 مُشار *p.p.* المُشار إليه/إليها the aforementioned

الاستثمارات الاجنبية المباشرة المشار اليها نمت ب ٢١,٧٪ عن نفس الفترة من السنة الماضية — The direct foreign investments referred to grew by 21.7% compared to the same period of last year

57 | 341 |

4210 إسْتِهْداف *vn.* targeting, aiming at, intending; *n.* allergy

صواريخ حماس هي رد فعل على استهداف اسرائيل للمدنيين الفلسطينيين — Hamas' rockets are a response to Israel's targeting of Palestinian civilians

51 | 383 |

4211 رُومِيّ *n./adj.* pl. رُوم Byzantine; الرُّوم الأُرْثُوذُكْس Greek Orthodox; الرُّوم الكاثُوليك Roman Catholics

وقف الجيش المسلم في ثلاثة آلاف جندي يواجه جيش الروم في مائتي ألف عند «مؤتة» بالشام — The Muslim army with three thousand soldiers stood facing the Byzantine army with two hundred thousand at Mu'ta in the Levant

52 | 374 |

4212 خِضَمّ *n.* (fig.) sea, ocean; في خِضَمّ in the middle of, in the thick of

تنحدر من عائلة ثرية ولكن في خضم جو عائلي لا يطاق — She descends from a rich family, but in the midst of a family atmosphere which could not be born

62 | 315 |

4213 كَنَّ *v. I (i)* to conceal, hide sth; to harbor (feelings) ل towards sb; to hold, maintain (respect) ل for sb

صار القارئ يكن احتراما اكثر للمطبوع خارج البلد — The reader started to harbor more respect for that which is printed outside of the country

68 | 283 |

4214 أَضاء *v. IV* to illuminate, shine upon sth

كان نور القمر يضيء كل شيء.. المباني والسيارات وأشجار النخيل — The light of the moon illuminated everything...the buildings and the cars and the palm trees

60 | 324 |

4215 ناشِئ *adj.* growing, emerging; resulting عن/من from; النّاشِئة *pl.n.* youth, adolescents

كل الدول الغربية وأكثرية الدول الناشئة تعتمد سياسة سعر الصرف الحر «الذكية» — All the Western states and most of the developing states adopt a "smart" free-market currency pricing policy

62 | 311 |

4216 غُمُوض *n.* vagueness, obscurity, lack of clarity
انها بحاجة الى حوار اكاديمي يزيل الغموض واللبس
وضعف المعرفة المتوافرة عن الاسلام — It needs
an academic dialog to eliminate the mystery
and ambiguity and the inadequacy of
knowledge available about Islam

66 | 290 |

4217 مُعْجِزَة *n.* miracle
إن تصدي رجال المقاومة اللبنانية للجيش الصهيوني
وقدرتهم على تدمير أحدث أنواع الدبابات في العالم
معجزة بكل المقاييس العسكرية — The resistance
of the men of the Lebanese Resistance to the
Zionist army and their ability to destroy the
most modern types of tanks in the world is
a miracle by any military measure

67 | 287 |

4218 تَجْمِيع *n.* gathering, assembling
المحامي بصدد إعداد ملفه وننتظر فقط تجميع
الوثائق، إنها مسألة وقت فقط — The lawyer
is in the process of preparing his file, and
we are only waiting to gather the documents,
it is just a matter of time

66 | 289 |

4219 حاسِب *n.* calculator; الحاسِب الآلِّي computer
كل هذه الأرقام سندخلها إلى الحاسب لنعرف إذا
كانت لها دلالة إحصائية — We will enter all of
these numbers into the computer to find out
if they have statistical significance

48 | 401 |

4220 طابَ *v. I (i)* to be good or pleasant; to heal,
get well; to be cured
يطيب له التنهد «والله زمان يا زمان» — He likes
sighing the phrase: "by God, the old days, O
the old days!"

53 | 360 | +lit

4221 مُبِين *adj.* plain, clear, obvious
أعلن كلمة العدل وقضى لنا بالحق ونجانا من الهلاك
المبين — He announced the word of justice and
judged us rightly and saved us from a certain
destruction

59 | 321 |

4222 تَعايُش *n.* coexistence, living together
طوائف لبنان تستطيع التعايش وعاشت على التعايش
— The sects of Lebanon are able to live

together, and they have experienced living
together

58 | 326 |

4223 صَوْم *n.* fasting, abstinence
يهملون المتابعة الطبية خلال شهر الصوم مما يعرضهم
لمضاعفات المرض — They neglect medical
follow-up care during the month of fasting
which exposes them to complications of the
disease

57 | 337 |

4224 رَوَّجَ *v. II* to promote, market sth; to circulate,
spread sth
ينبغي الوقوف بصراحة ووضوح ضد الحرب التي
تروج لها الآن بعض الأوساط فالمنطقة شبعت حروب
— It is necessary to stand frankly and clearly
against the war which is being politicked for
now in some circles, since the region is sick of
wars

67 | 285 |

4225 نِفاق *n.* hypocrisy
أعترض على إرسال برقية مبايعة للرئيس.. هذا نفاق
لا يليق بنا كمبعوثين — I am opposed to sending
a telegraph of loyalty to the president...this is
hypocrisy which is not appropriate for us as
delegation members

59 | 323 |

4226 شَمْل *n.* inclusion, containing
نجحتم مؤخرا في لم شمل الاحزاب الأردنية التي
عقدت عدة اجتماعات موسعة في مقر حزبكم —
You succeeded recently in bringing together
the Jordanian parties which held a number
of wide-ranging meetings in the headquarters
of your party

72 | 265 |

4227 مُواكَبة *n.* accompanying, keeping pace with;
escorting
يهدف هذا المشروع إلى مواكبة التطورات الاقتصادية
الحديثة — This project aims to keep pace with
modern economic developments

48 | 397 |

4228 قاع *n.* bottom, floor
أدخلت إلى صفوفها فئات واسعة جديدة صعدت من
قاع المجتمع وطبقاته الفقيرة — It enrolled in its

ranks broad new groups which have risen up from the depths of society and from its poor classes

65 | 292 |

4229 اِسْتِبْدال *n.* substitution, replacement; exchange
سجن رجال العلم وأجبر الأتراك على استبدال (البرنيطة) بالطربوش — He imprisoned scholars and forced the Turks to exchange (the hat) for the tarboosh

67 | 281 |

4230 مال (Irq.Gul.) *part.* fem. مالْت (genitive marker) of, for, with, belonging to; about, concerning
المنطقة مالتنا تبعد تقريبا نص ساعة بالسيارة — Our area is about a half hour away by car

12 | 1467 | +spo

4231 غَلَقَ *v. I (i)* to lock or bolt shut, to close (door)
خرجت لأشتري حاجيات للأكل قبل أن تغلق المحلات الغذائية ظهر الأحد — I went out to buy something to eat before the food stores close at noon on Sunday

69 | 273 |

4232 خَلْفِيّ *adj.* back, rear, end; background
دس أبو أسامة القطعة النقدية ذات العشرين دينارا في جيبه الأمامي وأخرج محفظته من جيبه الخلفي ودفع إليها بخمسة دنانير — Abu Usama put the twenty dinar coin into his front pocket and took out his wallet from his back pocket and paid her five dinar

61 | 307 |

4233 مُرَتَّب *adj.* organized, in order; neat, tidy, trim; arranged, prepared; regulated; *n.* salary, wage, pay
لمست شعري، قد يكون غير مرتب، فرددته خلف أذني — I touched my hair, it might be out of order, so I put it behind my ear

55 | 344 |

4234 حَيَوانِيّ *adj.* animal, animal-like, zoological
وما إن أشبع غريزته الحيوانية حتى أطلق سراحها — Hardly had he satiated his large animal appetite when he let her go

54 | 350 |

4235 نُصْب *n.* monument, memorial; نُصْب *prep.* in front of

ضاؤوا الشموع عند النصب التذكاري لشهداء صور — They lit candles at the memorial for the martyrs of Tyre

59 | 321 |

4236 جاهِل *adj.* ignorant, foolish; (Irq.Yem.) جاهِل, بَيّال, child, kid (pl. Irq. جُهّال, Gul. ياهِل, Yem. جِهّال)
أنت تعلمين أن يدي لم تمتد إلى الحرام وأنا صغير — جاهل، فكيف تمتد الآن وقد كبرت وتعلمت You know that my hand has not extended to thievery (I was never a thief) when I was young and ignorant, so why would I do so now that I have grown up and become educated?

55 | 343 | +spo

4237 تَكامُل *n.* integration
قد اتخذت خطوات لعقد قمة عربية دورية ولتحقيق التكامل الاقتصادي العربي — Steps have been taken to hold a regular Arab summit and to achieve Arab economic integration

61 | 306 |

4238 تَبارَكَ *v. VI* to be blessed, praised (of God); الله تَبارَكَ وَتَعالَى approx. God the Blessed and Exalted
فإن الله تبارك وتعالى اصطفى محمدا صلى الله عليه وسلم بنبوته — For God, may He be blessed and exalted, chose Muhammad, the peace and prayers of God be upon him, for his prophecy

49 | 379 |

4239 نَمَّ *v. I (u,i)* to slander, gossip على about sb; to reveal, disclose, show, manifest عن sth
ثيابه أنيقة متناسقة تنم عن ذوق راق — His clothes are chic and harmonious, indicating a refined taste

60 | 312 |

4240 عاذَ *v. I (u)* to take refuge, seek protection بالله in God
اللهم إني أعوذ بك من الكسل وأعوذ بك من الجبن — God, I seek refuge in thee from laziness, and I seek refuge in thee from cowardice

49 | 381 |

4241 أَقَلِّيَّة *n.* pl. -aat minority
إن الحكم الديمقراطي يعطي الأكثرية الحق في حكم الأقلية — Democratic rule gives the majority the right to rule the minority

51 | 363 |

4242 مُعْضِلَة *n.* dilemma, problem, difficulty
هنا يرقد البلسم الحنون الذي كان يلجأ إليه كلما أَلَمَّت
به مشكلة أو ضاقت به معضلة — Here
lies the compassionate balm he would resort
to whenever he had a problem: here was his
mother
65 | 288 |

4243 بَلاغ *n.* report, communiqué; notice,
notification; بَلاغ كاذِب false statement
أوضحت الوزارة في بلاغ لها أن هذا المنع جاء بقرار
من وزير الاتصال — The ministry clarified in a
communiqué that this ban came in a decision
from the Minister of Communications
56 | 330 |

4244 خِصِّيصاً *adv.* especially, specifically
يرش الجو بزجاجة عطر اشتراها خصيصا للمناسبة
— He is spraying the air with a bottle of
perfume he bought specifically for the
occasion
69 | 272 |

4245 بُنْدُقِيَّة *n.* rifle; gun, weapon
هذه ملفات لا يمكن ان تحسمها البندقية وانما تحتاج
الى مشروع سياسي — These are issues which
cannot be decided by the gun, but rather they
need a political project
64 | 292 |

4246 جَبَّار *adj.* mighty, powerful; huge, gigantic
للقبلة وقعها الجبار والكبير على قلب المرأة بالتحديد
— A kiss has a large, amazing effect on the
hearts of women, specifically
61 | 304 |

4247 اِقْتِتال *n.* fighting (each other)
اسوأ الاحتمالات هو العودة الى الحرب واستئناف
الاقتتال — The worst-case scenario would be to
return to the war and resume the fighting
53 | 352 |

4248 تِلْقائِيّ *adj.* automatic, spontaneous; تِلْقائِيّاً
automatically, spontaneously
قطع الكهرباء يؤدي تلقائيا لقطع الماء لان ماتورات
الماء تعمل بالكهرباء — Cutting off the electricity
leads automatically to cutting off the water
because the water motors work with electricity
67 | 278 |

4249 اِحْتِياطِيّ *n.* reserves (economic, geological,
military, sports); *adj.* precautionary,
contingency, reserve
ظل نفط العراق الذي يعتقد انه يمثل أكبر ثاني
احتياطي في العالم دوما في اعلى قائمة مطامع
الشركات العالمية — Iraq's oil, which is believed
to represent the second largest reserve in the
world, has always remained at the top of the
list of the ambitions of global companies
50 | 370 |

4250 اِسْتِسْلام *n.* surrender, capitulation; resignation
فاجأهم من خلف الجدران صوت غليظ يدعوهم إلى
الاستسلام لرجال الشرطة — A rough voice
surprised them from behind the walls, calling
on them to surrender to the policemen
65 | 284 |

4251 ثارَ *v. I (u)* to revolt, arise
يبدو أنك لم تقرأ التاريخ جيدا.. لقد ثار المصريون
ضد الحملة الفرنسية مرتين خلال ثلاثة أعوام
It appears that you have not read history
well...the Egyptians revolted against the French
campaign twice during three years
59 | 314 |

4252 وَتِيرة *n.* way, manner, style; method, approach
المهم هو اننا سنواصل العمل على وتيرة اسرع من
الاشهر الماضية — The important thing is that
we will continue working at a faster pace than
the past months
65 | 287 |

4253 اِنْدِماج *n.* integration, assimilation; absorption,
fusion
لست أدري لماذا لم أستطع الاندماج مع مجتمع غير
مجتمعي الأصلي، رغم انطلاقي وتحرري
I don't know why I was not able to fit into a
society other than my original society, despite
my being such a liberated person
63 | 296 |

4254 قابَلَ *v. III* to meet, encounter, face sb
حاولي ان تجعلي طفلك يقابل المعلمة قبل بدء الدراسة
— حتى يشعر بمزيد من التقارب معها — Try to make
your child meet the teacher before classes
start so that he will feel more closeness with
her
67 | 276 |

4255 بُرْهَة *n.* moment, instant

وقف فجأة وأغمض عينيه وظل ساكنا في مكانه برهة — He suddenly stood up, closed his eyes and remained silent in his place for a moment

41 | 449 | +lit

4256 ضِياء *n.* light, glow

كان الجو صحوا والشمس مشرقة تملأ الكون ضياء — The weather was clear and the sun was shining filling the world with light

44 | 419 | +lit

4257 نَدَم *n.* remorse, regret

وبفضل هذه النظريات الحكيمة، أصبح بمقدور المستعمرين أن يقتلوا ما شاءوا من الهنود بلا أدنى ظل من الندم أو الشعور بالذنب — Thanks to these wise theories, the colonialists have become able to kill whatever Indians they wanted without the slightest shadow of regret or feeling of guilt

60 | 310 |

4258 راغِب *adj.* (person) wanting, wishing for, desiring (في sth)

طالب الحكومة بإنشاء صندوق لمساعدة الراغبين في الزواج حيث استشرى الزواج السري في مصر — He demanded that the government set up a fund to help those who want to marry, since secret marriage has become rampant in Egypt

57 | 323 |

4259 انْدِلاع *n.* breaking out, flaring up (fire, war)

هذه أول مرة يشاهدون الألمان الذين ظلوا لغزا منذ اندلاع الحرب — This is the first time they see the Germans who have remained a riddle since the outbreak of the war

59 | 313 |

4260 نَعِيم *n.* comfort, luxury, happiness

ظننتك تقول إن شخصا مات وانتقل إلى جنة النعيم — I thought you said that someone died and was transported to the heaven of happiness (Paradise)

57 | 323 |

4261 مُسْتَجِدّ *adj.* new, recent; *n.* مُسْتَجِدّات recent events or incidents, latest developments

تبادلوا وجهات النظر في المستجدات في المنطقة، بما في ذلك تطورات الأوضاع الخطيرة في فلسطين — They exchanged points of view about recent events in the region, including developments in the dangerous situation in Palestine

57 | 320 |

4262 تَشْويه *n.* distortion

كل ذلك أدى الى تشويه صورة الآخر وتشكيل صورة شيطانية عن الغرب في العالم الاسلامي — All of this led to a distortion of the image of the "other", and the formation of a Satanic image of the West in the Islamic World

68 | 270 |

4263 امْتِياز *n.* distinction, excellence; special right, privilege

تعتبر مقاهي الضاحية الجنوبية لبيروت من المقاهي الشعبية بامتياز، فهي حكر على الرجال وحدهم لا تقربها النساء — The coffee houses of the southern suburbs of Beirut are considered to be distinctly "popular", since they are the exclusive domain of men, no women approaching them

58 | 313 |

4264 بَدَنِيّ *adj.* bodily, physical

تعتبر تمارين اللياقة البدنية أهم التمارين الرياضية التي تفيد مرضى ضغط الدم — Physical fitness exercises are considered the most important sports exercises which benefit those with high blood pressure

54 | 338 |

4265 مُصَوِّر *n.* photographer; illustrator

يبدو أن المصور لم يكن ذكيا بما يكفي لملاحظة ما حدث — It appears that the photographer was not smart enough to notice what happened

62 | 294 |

4266 قُبْلَة *n.* kiss

ان المرأة تعتبر القبلة غاية في حد ذاتها، فهي تعشق القبلة التي من خلالها تحس بأنها محبوبة ومرغوبة — Women consider the kiss to be a goal in and of itself, and they love the kiss by means of which they feel that they are loved and desired

53 | 340 | +lit

4267 مَحْفِل *n.* pl. مَحافِل gathering, assembly; circles, groups

أوقف البوليس واحدا منهم سائلا: أتعرف السباحة؟ — The police stopped one of them, asking: Do you know how to swim?

61 | 294 |

4274 رَنَّ *v. I (i)* to ring, sound (phone, bell); (Lev.) to call ل sb (on the phone); رنيتلك امبارح /ranneet-lak imbaariH/ I called you yesterday

رن جرس تلفوني الخلوي فإذا به رقم والدي فتركت كل ما بين يدي من أعمال وبادرت للرد عليه — My cell phone rang, and it was the number of my father, so I left all the work I was doing and proceeded to answer it

43 | 415 | +spo

4275 جُغْرافيا *n.* geography

تغير اسرائيل الجغرافيا والديموغرافيا في الاراضي المحتلة — Israel is changing the geography and demographics of the occupied territories

64 | 281 |

4276 كَثَب *n.* nearness, closeness; عَن كَثَب closely

قد قمنا بزيارات ميدانية لمجموعة من هذه المصانع لنطلع عن كثب على ما تنتجه هذه المصانع — We made a field visit to a group of these factories to find out "up close" about what these factories produce

69 | 262 |

4277 جُنْد *n.* army, soldiers; جُنْد الشّام Jund Al-Sham ("Soldiers of Greater Syria")

المسلمون كلهم جند في جيش المسلمين — All Muslims are soldiers in the army of Muslims

55 | 327 |

4278 تَسَرُّب *n.* leak, escape; infiltration

تم احتجازها بموجب توجيهات مباشرة ومشددة من قبل وزير الداخلية اليمني عقب تسرب معلومات عن محاولات للإفراج عن الشحنة — It was seized on the direct and firm order from the Yemeni Minister of the Interior, after the leakage of information about an attempt to release the shipment

65 | 277 |

4279 مُتَرَتِّب *adj.* derived or resulting على from; associated or connected على with; arranged, organized, regulated

---

إننا حريصون على الدفاع عن مصالحها في كل المحافل الدولية — We are intent on defending its interests in all international venues

61 | 298 |

4268 ضاحِك *adj.* laughing

قال لها ضاحكا إن الطلاب الآن يتحدثون عن ضرورة جلاء الإنجليز بعد الحرب — He told her laughingly that the students now speak about the necessity of evacuating the English after the war

47 | 386 | +lit

4269 تارِك *adj.* leaving (behind), quitting, abandoning

رحل في عام ٩٠٩ ميلادي عن عمر يناهز مائة وتسعة أعوام، تاركا وراءه ما لا يقل عن مائة كتاب مفيد — He died in 909 AD at an age of more than a hundred and nine years, leaving behind him no fewer than one hundred useful books

63 | 286 |

4270 اِشْتَمَل *v. VIII* to include, comprise, contain على sth

أما الغرف فكان يرسم على جدرانها نقوشاً كثيرة، تشتمل على رسوم الحيوانات والطيور والنباتات وأوراق الأشجار — As for the rooms, he drew many engravings onto their walls, including drawings of animals, birds, plants, and leaves

57 | 315 |

4271 ساكِن *adj.* quiet, calm; motionless; لَمْ يُحَرِّك ساكِناً he didn't do a thing, he didn't lift a finger

كان جسمها ساكنا، لكن نبرة صوتها كانت تنم عن الغضب — Her body was still, but her tone of voice revealed anger

55 | 327 | +lit

4272 قَلَبَ *v. I (i)* to turn around; to turn (one's face, a page); to overthrow, topple (a regime)

يتوقع لهذه العقاقير أن تقلب الموازين في المعركة ضد الفيروس — These drugs are expected to tip the scales in the battle against the virus

60 | 300 |

4273 سائِل *adj.* asking, inquiring; requesting; *n.* person asking; beggar

لقد أدرك القادة العسكريون المخاطر المترتبة على نشر القوات الأمريكية بأعداد قليلة نسبيا وعلى مساحات شاسعة — The military leaders realized the dangers stemming from

deploying the American forces in relatively small numbers over vast distances

63 | 284 |

4280 تَقْلِيص *n.* reducing, shrinking, cutting back

نجحوا في العام الفائت وحده في تقليص معدل الفقر بنسبة ١٠٪ — They succeeded last year alone in reducing the poverty percentage by 10%

62 | 289 |

4281 خَلَّفَ *v. II* to give birth to (a child); to appoint sb as successor; to leave sth behind

أطلقت الطائرات الحربية صاروخا واحدا باتجاه المنجرة مما ادى الى تدميرها بالكامل دون ان يخلف القصف اصابات في صفوف المدنيين — The warplanes launched a single rocket towards Al-Manjara which led to its complete destruction without the bombing resulting in any wound in the ranks of civilians

70 | 256 |

4282 عَمْد *n.* intent; *adj.* deliberate, premeditated; عَمْداً deliberately, voluntarily

اتهمت منظمة العفو الدولية إسرائيل بأنها استهدفت عن عمد قصف المدنيين في لبنان خلال حربها مع حزب الله — Amnesty International accused Israel of purposely targeting civilians with bombs in Lebanon during its war with Hizbollah

67 | 267 |

4283 تاع and مُتاع (Magh.) *poss.adj.* of, belonging to; (with pron.) تاعك/متاعك your/yours, تاعي/متاعي my/mine

شحال النوميرو تاع داركم باش نعيط لكي العشية؟ — What's your home number so I can call you this evening?

8 | 1988 | +spo

4284 شَغّال *adj.* busy, occupied; in operation, running, functioning; working, employed

أنا شغال في بلدي مش محتاج بسبور — I am working in my country, I don't need a passport

33 | 539 | +spo

4285 مُبْتَسِم *adj.* smiling

حاول أن تبدو مبتسما دائما فهذا يجعلك مقبولا لدى الناس — Try to appear smiling always, for this makes you acceptable to people

45 | 394 | +lit

4286 إيقاع *vn.* imposition (of a punishment); causing (discord); *n.* rhythm, beat

تدور في ذلك الثوب نصف استدارة على إيقاع الموسيقى — She revolves, in that dress, a half turn to the beat of the music

57 | 307 |

4287 مُهَدَّد *adj.* threatened, intimidated; in danger, at risk

هل صحيح ما يقال ان التركيبة السياسية في لبنان مهددة بالزوال؟ — Is it true what is being said that the political framework in Lebanon is threatened with extinction?

63 | 278 |

4288 عَلْمانِيّ *adj.* secular

إن أتاتورك هو الذي أسقط الخلافة الإسلامية بتركيا وأقام الدولة العلمانية — Ataturk is the one who got rid of the Islamic caliphate in Turkey and set up a secular state

49 | 358 |

4289 مَصْرُوف *n.* pl. مَصاريف expenditure, expense; allowance

كنت أطرد من المدرسة أمام زملائي لأنني لا أستطيع دفع مصاريف الدراسة — I was expelled from school in front of my colleagues because I could not pay the school expenses

61 | 289 |

4290 تَسَلُّل *n.* infiltration

السنيورة دعا إلى الحذر من تسلل مقاتلي فتح الإسلام إلى خارج نهر البارد — Siniora called for caution against Fath Al-Islam fighters infiltrating outside Nahr Al-Barid

64 | 276 |

4291 شابَهَ *v. III* to resemble, be similar to sth/sb

قلنا لهم بأنك مريض، أو جائع، أو ما شابه ذلك — We told them you were sick, or hungry, or something like that

66 | 266 |

4292 سَماوِيّ *adj.* heavenly, celestial

دعا إلى احترام المعتقدات والأديان السماوية الأخرى ومراعاة مشاعر المؤمنين بها — He called for respect for other heavenly beliefs and religions and to watch out for the feelings of those who believe in them

61 | 286 |

4293 رَبِحَ *v. I (a)* to profit مِن from sth; to gain sth; to win (money, sporting event); to prevail (truth)

ماذا يفيد المرء إذا ربح العالم وخسر نفسه؟ — What shall it profit a man if he shall gain the whole world and lose his own soul?

32 | 542 | +spo

4294 مُدَّعٍ *(def.* المُدَّعِي*) n.* plaintiff, prosecutor; *a.p.* claiming, alleging

إن المدعي العام يعمل بحرية كاملة وباستقلال كامل — The public prosecutor works with complete freedom and total independence

49 | 357 |

4295 مَزِيج *n.* combination, mixture, blend

لا تعرف سوى بعض الكلمات العربية بلهجة هي مزيج من المصرية والتركية — She only knows a few Arabic words in a dialect which is a mix of Egyptian and Turkish

65 | 269 |

4296 سَبْعِين *n.* seventieth year; السبعينات the Seventies

قد تعرفت عليه منذ منتصف السبعينات واجريت له في الثمانينات حوارين نشرتها جريدة الصباح — I got to know him in the mid-Seventies, and during the Eighties I conducted two interviews with him which the newspaper "Al-Sabah" published

57 | 307 |

4297 تِباعاً *adv.* in succession, consecutively, one after the other

ظهر أعضاء الفرقة تباعا، وبعد برهة ظهرت فتاة رشيقة ترتدي ثوبا أبيض طويلا — The members of the group appeared one after the other, and after few moments an elegant girl appeared wearing a long white robe

68 | 257 |

4298 اِنْفِصال *n.* separation, break-up; secession

اخترت أن أذهب للإقامة في مازفران تأجيلا لقرار الانفصال عن زوجتي — I chose to go to live in Mazafran in order to put off the decision to separate from my wife

58 | 303 |

4299 جاهِلِيَّة *n.* ignorance (esp. of divine guidance); Jahiliyah (pre-Islam)

في الجاهلية وقبل الاسلام كانوا يئدون البنات فجاء الاسلام وقضى على هذه العادة الآثمة — In the Jahiliyya period and before Islam, they used to bury young girls alive; Islam came and did away with this abominable custom

57 | 306 |

4300 بَصَل *coll.n.* onions

شوربة البصل من الأطباق الفرنسية الشهيرة وتقدم مع الخبز المحمص — Onion soup is one of the famous French dishes, and is served with toasted bread

48 | 365 |

4301 اِسْتِقْطاب *n.* polarization, attraction

حرصنا على استقطاب أفضل الكفاءات الطبية للعمل بهذا المستشفى — We were intent on attracting the best medical skills to work in this hospital

58 | 299 |

4302 دَمْج *n.* inclusion, incorporation, integration; consolidation, merger

يجب دمج هذه الميليشيات في الاجهزة الامنية وقبل ذلك يجب تدريبهم — These militias need to be merged with the Security Forces, and before that they must be trained

62 | 282 |

4303 غَفْلَة *n.* negligence, lack of attention

مرة واحدة فقط استطعت أن أقترب منك في غفلة من عيون والديك — Only once have I been able to get near you away from the eyes of your parents

57 | 306 |

4304 مُذِيع *n.* broadcaster, announcer

عليك ألا تعتقد ان المذيع هو كل شيء، فهناك كادر كبير يعمل خلفه — You shouldn't think that the

announcer is everything, since there is a large cadre which works behind him

47 | 371 |

4305 طَوْر *n.* stage, phase; period, time

العراق في طور اعادة بناء نفسه رغم المرحلة الاستثنائية والانتقالية التي يمر بها — Iraq is in a stage of rebuilding itself despite the exceptional, transitional period it is passing through

65 | 267 |

4306 بَذْر *n.* pl. بُذُور seed

ثمانون في المائة من بذور القطن تنتج في حقول البلدان النامية — Eighty percent of cotton seeds are produced in the fields of developing countries

68 | 254 |

4307 أَثَرِيّ *adj.* archeological; historical

قد دلت الاكتشافات الأثرية على أن أول مظاهر الدين كانت مرتبطة بالأنوثة — The archeological discoveries have shown that the first evidences of religion were related to femininity

56 | 311 |

4308 لِصّ *n.* pl. لُصُوص thief

خد بالك من اللصوص في الزحام — Be careful of thieves in the crowd

54 | 322 |

4309 تَقْوَى *n.* piety, religiousness, devoutness

الأزمات تذكر المؤمنين بضرورة اللجوء الى الله بكل التقوى والخشوع والدعاء — Crises remind believers of the necessity of seeking refuge in God in all righteousness and modesty and prayer

56 | 306 |

4310 تَأَهُّل *n.* qualification, competency; marriage, getting married

يجب ان نفوز اذا اردنا التأهل الى النهائيات — We have to win if we want to qualify for the finals

42 | 407 |

4311 كِلِّش and كُلِّش (Irq.Gul.) *adv.* very, very much, a lot

يعني موديل حلو كلش حلو — Well, it's a nice model, really nice

30 | 579 | +spo

4312 لِبْس *n.* clothing, dress, attire

يتوسط كل هذه الأشياء رجل في الستين من عمره يرتدي لبس الشيوخ والقضاة العرب — In the middle of all these things was a man in his sixties wearing the dress of Arab sheikhs and judges

60 | 286 |

4313 بَوْل *n.* urination; urine

انسياب البول من الكلية إلى المثانة هي عملية مستمرة على مدار ٢٤ ساعة — The flow of urine from the kidney to the bladder is an ongoing process 24 hours a day

44 | 387 |

4314 مُوَزَّع *adj.* distributed, scattered (على among)

بينت المؤشرات أن عدد المصارف الوطنية بلغ ٢٢ مصرفا موزعة على ٣٦٢ فرعا في مختلف مناطق الدولة — The indicators clarified that the number of national banks has reached 22 banks, distributed through 362 branches in various areas of the country

65 | 266 |

4315 حَذِرَ *v. I (a)* to be cautious, beware (من of)

يحذر ما استطاع الحذر إيقاظ جماعات الذباب الهاجعة — He was careful as he could be not to stir up the swarms of sleeping flies

64 | 269 |

4316 تَوافُر *n.* availability

المهم هو كيفية تطبيق الديمقراطية ومدى توافر الشروط الملائمة للتحول الديمقراطي الحقيقي من الفكر إلى السلوك والممارسة — The important thing is how democracy is put into effect, and the extent to which are provided appropriate conditions for real democratic change from (just) ideas to (actual) behavior and practice

53 | 322 |

4317 هَوْل *n.* fright, shock

كأن هذه البقعة المتأججة من الأرض تكاد تتفجر من هول الأحداث المتعاقبة على مسرحها ...As if this fiery piece of land was about to explode from the shock of the series of events which had played out on its stage

59 | 290 |

4318 جُمْرُك *n.* pl. جَمارِك customs; customs house; الجَمارِك customs; customs duties, tariffs

طلبت الوكالة من سلطات الجمارك الأميركية منع دخول العدسات اللاصقة التجميلية إلى الولايات المتحدة — The agency requested from the American Customs authorities to forbid the entrance of cosmetic contact lenses into the United States

51 | 336 |

4319 إِنْجاح *vn.* granting success, making successful; *n.* success

هناك قواعد محددة لإنجاح التغيير يمكن تعلمها واكتسابها — There are defined rules for success in making changes which can be learned and acquired

56 | 307 |

4320 عُثْمانيّ *n./adj.* Ottoman

كانت الدولة العثمانية في صراع مع بريطانيا للحفاظ على وجودها في العراق — The Ottoman State was in conflict with Britain to maintain its existence in Iraq

54 | 318 |

4321 مُتَمَنّي *a.p.* wishing, desiring; hoping for

كان ممددا على السرير متمنيا أن ينام إلى الأبد — He was stretched out on the bed wishing to sleep forever

53 | 320 |

4322 بادِيَة *n.* desert, wilderness

لقد خرج الإسلام من البادية العربية — Islam emerged from the Arabian wilderness

46 | 366 |

4323 بَوْح *n.* uncovering, revealing (a secret); disclosure, confession

أحسست أنها تحمل في أعماقها أسرارا كثيرة تود البوح بها — I felt that she was holding in her depths many secrets she wanted to reveal

57 | 296 |

4324 صَلَّحَ *v. II* to fix, repair, mend sth; to put sth in order

يجب عليه أن يصلح نفسه ثم يدعو غيره إلى ما آمن به — He needs to fix himself and then invite others to what he has come to believe in

62 | 276 |

4325 غَرام *n.* love, infatuation

كان محبا لأكل اللحوم، إلا أنه وقع في غرام وجبات دجاج الكنتاكي — He had been a lover of eating (red) meat, but (then) he fell in love with Kentucky (Fried) Chicken meals

50 | 336 |

4326 قَوْمِيَّة *n.* nationalism

يرى أن فكرة القومية العربية قد انتهت وتلاشت تحديدا بعد احتلال صدام حسين للكويت — He is of the opinion that the idea of Arab Nationalism has ended and come to nothing, particularly after Saddam Hussein's occupation of Kuwait

49 | 345 |

4327 إِرْتاحَ *v. VIII* to relax, rest; to be satisfied, pleased ب with sth; to delight, find pleasure ب in sth

هذا يعني أن لاعبنا لن يرتاح خلال الفترة الصيفية مع أنه بحاجة ماسة إلى استراحة معقولة — This means that our player will not rest during the summer period despite the fact that he is in critical need of a reasonable rest

62 | 274 |

4328 إِلْتِحاق *n.* entering; joining; affiliation

فشل في الالتحاق بأكاديمية الفنون في فيينا، مما جعله يترك النمسا — He failed to be accepted to the Academy of Arts in Vienna, which made him leave Austria

62 | 275 |

4329 شِمال *n./adj.* left

أما أهل الغرب فهم يكتبون بالعكس من الشمال إلى اليمين — As for the people of the West, well they write the opposite, from left to right

58 | 292 |

4330 عَلَنِيّ *adj.* public, open

لا يقوم بهذا الدور العلني والمؤثر ويكتفي باتصالات شخصية محدودة لا تأثير لها — He does not play this effective, public role; he makes do with limited personal contacts which have no effect

60 | 282 |

4331 هُولانْدِيّ and هُولَنْدِيّ *n./adj.* Dutch, of or relating to Holland

أصبح طبيبا في الجيش الملكي الهولندي، وتيسر له
السفر إلى جاوا — He became a doctor in the
Royal Dutch Army, and it became possible for
him to travel to Java

50 | 334 |

4332 كَرَم *n.* generosity, magnanimity
أرجو ألا تقاطعني يا صديقي.. فمنك تعلمت
الكرم.. ومنك تعلمت الشجاعة الأدبية — I beg
you not to cut me off, my friend...for from
you I have learned generosity...from you
I have learned literary courage

67 | 251 |

4333 مَفْصِل *n.* pl. مَفاصِل (anat.) joint; articulation;
juncture, turning point, crossroads
قامت الوزارة بتوفير هذه المفاصل الصناعية المتقدمة
إضافة إلى كافة أدوات ولوازم جراحة العظام — The
ministry provided these advanced artificial
joints in addition to all the equipment and the
requirements for bone surgery

55 | 307 |

4334 تَنَقُّل *n.* transfer; movement; transportation
يصعب على المريض التنقل بين المدن الفلسطينية
والوصول إلى المشافي المختصة وتلقي العلاج المطلوب
— It is hard for a sick person to be
transported between Palestinian cities to reach
the specialized hospitals to receive the
necessary treatment

67 | 250 |

4335 إفْطار *n.* iftar (evening meal, usu. of dates,
that breaks the daily fast during Ramadan);
breakfast
كان يتناول الإفطار وحده ويتغدى فى الخارج — He
used to eat breakfast by himself, and would
take lunch outside the house

55 | 304 |

4336 شَوْك *coll.n.* thorns, *un.n.* شَوْكَة; *n.* شَوْكَة fork
إذا كان وجود الشوك في الورود يحزننا فإن وجود
الورود وسط الشوك يفرحنا — If the presence of
thorns in the roses saddens us, the presence
of roses amidst the thorns brings us joy

49 | 339 | +lit

4337 ذَريعَة *n.* means; pretext, excuse
يبدو الأمر واضحا ان قضية دارفور اصلا ذريعة
للتدخل تحت الفصل السابع وليس الفصل السادس

It appears to be clear that the issue of
Darfur was originally a pretext for interference
under Article 7 and not Article 6

56 | 298 |

4338 صارم *adj.* severe, strict; ruthless
لقد وضعت الرقابة حدودا صارمة للصراحة ، في
الأمور المتعلقة بالدين والجنس والسياسة — The
censors placed strict limits on expression, in
matters pertaining to religion, sex, and politics

65 | 257 |

4339 مَبْذُول *adj.* exerted, expended; *n.* expenditure;
exertion, effort
أعرب عن امله بان تنضم ايران للجهود المبذولة
لتحقيق الاستقرار في المنطقة — He expressed his
hope that Iran would join efforts being exerted
to achieve stability in the region

53 | 313 | +news

4340 حينَئِذ *adv.* then, at the time
كانوا يطلقون علينا حينئذ اسم القوات الخاصة
They used to call us, at that time, by the name
"Special Forces"

57 | 291 |

4341 كَيْفَما *conj.* however, whatever, whichever
أريد أن ابرم معك عقدا، وإلا سنطبع جميع أعمالك
من دون موافقتك، وتصرف كيفما تريد أو تشاء — I
want to make a contract with you, and if not,
we will print all of your works without your
permission, do whatever you may want

63 | 265 |

4342 عَلِقَ *v. I (a)* to hang, be suspended; to be
pending or outstanding; to be attached ب to
sth; to latch on ب to sb
إذا بكعب حذائي يعلق بطرف فستاني وأقع على
وجهي.. حاولت الوقوف عبثا — There was the
heel of my shoe hanging from the end of my
dress, and I fell on the floor...I tried to stand
up in vain

65 | 258 |

4343 نَقْلَة *n.* move, shift; advance, progress;
نَقْلَة نَوْعِيَّة quantum leap
هذا المؤتمر سوف يحقق نقلة نوعية للخطاب
الاسلامي ومنهجيات الافتاء — This conference
will achieve a qualitative shift in the Islamic
message and the approaches of legal rulings

55 | 303 |

4344 أَسْعَد *elat.* happier/happiest; luckier/luckiest
سأجعلك أسعد إنسانة في الدنيا — I will make you
the happiest person in the world
| 60 | 276 |

4345 فِرار *n.* escape (من from); desertion, defection
(من from)
يطاردون العصابات ويشتبكون معها حتى قتلوا أفرادها
أو أجبروهم على الفرار — They pursue the gangs
and fight with them until their members were
killed or until they forced them to flee
| 64 | 258 |

4346 مُتَمَرِّد *n.* pl. -uun rebel, insurgent
وجه العلماء نداء إلى المتمردين يمنحونهم فيه فرصة
أخيرة لإلقاء السلاح وترك التمرد — The scholars
sent out a call to the rebels granting them a
last opportunity to give up their arms and
leave the rebellion
| 51 | 323 |

4347 قَوْس *n.* bow, arch; vault, arc; بَيْنَ قَوْسَيْنِ
between (two) parentheses
ربطت الفتحات الثلاث بصريا بفتحة رابعة فوقها
على شكل قوس — The three openings were
connected visually by a fourth opening above
them in the form of an arch
| 49 | 339 |

4348 مُذ *prep.* since, ago
تابعت المشروع مذ كان فكرة على الورق —
I have followed the project since it was an
idea on paper
| 41 | 403 | +lit

4349 فاتِحَة *n.* opening, preface; الفاتِحَة Al-Fatiha, the
first surah (chapter) in the Qurʾan
اتجهت إلى قبر والدتها.. قرأت سورة الفاتحة أمام
قدميها ووضعت الزهور عند الرأس — She headed
for the grave of her mother...she read the
Fatiha surah (the opening verses of the Qurʾan)
at her feet, and she put flowers at her head
| 57 | 289 |

4350 شَيْخُوخَة *n.* old age, seniority
مرض الزهايمر هو أحد أمراض الشيخوخة التي قد
تصيب المسنين — Alzheimer's disease is one of
the diseases of old age which can strike old
people
| 57 | 287 |

4351 جَوْف *n.* belly, abdomen; cavity, hollow; في
جَوْف in the middle of
وقد مكث سيدنا يونس – عليه السلام – في جوف
الحوت المظلم فترة طويلة كان خلالها ملازما لذكر الله
— Our master, Jonah – may peace be upon
him – stayed in the dark belly of the whale
for a long time, during which he continually
praised God
| 53 | 311 | +lit

4352 حَذْف *n.* deletion, omission
طلبت حذف اسمي من عناوين المسلسل قبل بث
المسلسل — I requested the deletion of my
name from the titles of the series before the
series was broadcast
| 58 | 282 | +for

4353 زِرّ *n.* button; (push) button, switch button
بعدها اضغط زر «طلب اتصال» (وهو الزر الاخضر)
— After that, press the "connect" button (and
it is the green button)
| 47 | 348 |

4354 داجِن *adj.* pl. دَواجِن tame, domesticated; *n.*
دَواجِن chickens, poultry
يعمل في مزرعة لتربية الدواجن — He works on a
poultry farm
| 40 | 409 |

4355 دِيوان *n.* anthology or collection of poems
تفتح أمامي ديوان شعر جديد كتبه أحمد — She
opens in front of me a new poetry collection
written by Ahmad
| 50 | 325 |

4356 رِجْل *fem.n.* leg; رِجْلَيْهِ his (two) legs; (Gul.)
ريل /riil/
يقيس طول رجليه الى بعضهما فيجدها متساويتين
تماما — He measures the length of his legs
compared to each other, and finds them
exactly equal
| 57 | 286 |

4357 صَميم *n.* depth, innermost part; *adj.* true,
genuine
اعترف بأنني أكره والدي من صميم قلبي لأنه
ليس أبا عادلا أو رحيما — I admit that I hate my
father from the depths of my heart because
he is not a just or merciful father
| 67 | 243 |

4358 ثَمَانِين *n.* eightieth year; الثَّمَانِينَات the Eighties
لم يكن لدينا الفاكس الذي لم نعرفه الا في بداية الثمانينات — We didn't have a fax machine, which we weren't aware of until the beginning of the Eighties

56 | 294 |

4359 تَفَاقُم *n.* aggravation, exacerbation; worsening
ان الشركات «الأمنية» تلعب الدور الرئيسي في تفاقم هذه المشكلة — The "Al-Umniyyah" companies are playing the principle role in exacerbating this problem

62 | 262 |

4360 جَالَ *v. I (u)* to wander, roam about (ب/في a place); ما يُجولُ بخاطرِه/بباله what's on his mind, what he's worried about
ماذا كان يجول في عقولنا الصغيرة في تلك الأيام البعيدة — What was going through our small minds in those distant days?

57 | 289 |

4361 قُبالة *prep.* facing, in front of
جلست قبالة نافورة يتدفق منها الماء أتأمل حركتها إلى أن تأتي — I sat in frontn of a fountain from which water was flowing, contemplating its movement, until you came

57 | 286 |

4362 تَكْثِيف *vn.* increasing, heightening, intensifying; thickening (hair); *n.* compression, condensation
تضطر كذلك إلى تكثيف حراسة الحدود والسواحل — It is also forced to beef up its border and coastal security

56 | 292 |

4363 أهو /'ahu/ (Egy.) *part.* here he is; fem. أهي /'ahiyya/ here she is
الله يرحمها وماتت فى المستشفى برضه اهي النهارده — God rest her soul, she died in the hospital also here today

35 | 459 |

4364 لَيْمُون *n.* lemon; also /lamuun/ (Egy.Lev.) and /leemuun/ (Lev.Irq.)
إذا شرب عصير الليمون المركز على الريق ساعد على إنقاص الوزن — If he drinks concentrated

lemon juice on an empty stomach, it will help in losing weight

46 | 356 |

4365 عَظَمَة *n.* majesty, greatness, grandeur
جمع بين عظمة العلم وتواضع العلماء — He combined the greatness of science with the humility of the scientists

67 | 244 |

4366 مَفَرّ *n.* escape, avoiding; لا مَفَرَّ مِنْهُ (it's) inevitable
وجد نفسه مضطرا اضطرارا لا مفر منه للسفر — He found himself forced, unavoidably, to travel

67 | 243 |

4367 تَجَاوُب *n.* response, responsiveness (to need); rapport
ناشد الجميع التجاوب مع المبادرة العربية — He appealed to everyone to respond to the Arab initiative

62 | 263 |

4368 اِحْتَضَنَ *v. VIII* to embrace, welcome sb; to comprise, encompass, include sth
ظهرت في المشهد الأول وهي تحتضن طفلها في سعادة — She appeared in the first scene, as she joyfully embraced her child

63 | 259 |

4369 عِيادَة *n.* clinic, outpatient clinic
وجد نفسه ممددا على المقعد الطويل فى عيادة الطبيب النفسى — He found himself stretched out on the couch in the psychiatrist's clinic

64 | 255 |

4370 غارق *adj.* drowned; immersed, engrossed (في in)
المكان غارق فى الهدوء، وثمة موسيقى خافتة تنبعث من الإذاعة — The place is drowning in calm (is in a deep calm), and there is light music coming from the radio

56 | 289 |

4371 مَرْكَب *n.* ship, vessel
غرقت المركب وغرق من فيها إلا القلة ممن يجيدون السباحة — The boat sank and everyone in it drowned except a few who were good at swimming

61 | 266 |

4372 مِنين /mineen/ (Egy.) *interrog.* (prep.phr.) from where

انا كنت لسه حاسألك بتتكلم منين؟ — I was just going to ask you: where are you speaking from?

9 | 1681 | +spo

4373 كُلْيَة *n.* pl. كُلَى and كُلْوَة kidney

أشار الى ان المملكة تعد من الدول الرائدة فى زراعة الكلى وعمليات الغسيل الكلوى — He indicated that the Kingdom is considered one of the pioneering states in kidney transplants, and dialysis procedures

51 | 315 |

4374 باكٍ (def. الباكي) *adj.* crying, weeping (على over sth/sb); mourning, weeping (for sb)

عادت الابنة إلى بيت أبيها باكية تشتكي من ضرب زوجها لها — The girl returned to her father's home crying, complaining about her husband hitting her

48 | 338 | +lit

4375 إِيَّاكَ *part.* (with 2nd pers. pron.) و/من إِيَّا be careful with, watch out for!

إياك أن تتجاهل مهاجمك، وإياك أن تقاومه، من يسرقك بالإكراه غالبا لا يعى من فرط السكر أو التخدير، وقد يقتلك فى أية لحظة — Don't ignore your attacker, and don't resist him; someone who forcibly steals from you would usually be somewhat out of it (not be aware) from too much drink or drugs, and he may kill you at any moment

46 | 351 | +lit

4376 رام *v. I* (u) to desire, crave sth; عَلَى ما يُرامُ fine, okay; in order

كانت الزيارة بهدف الاطمئنان على ان الامور تسير على ما يرام — The visit was to make sure everything was going as it should

58 | 280 |

4377 فَرْط *n.* excess, excessive amount, hyper-

فقدت صوابها من فرط الغضب وبدأت فى مطاردته كنمرة هائجة — She lost her mind from an excess of anger, and began to chase him like an enraged tiger

57 | 285 |

4378 جَلِيّ *adj.* clear, evident, obvious

يظهر التمايز جليا بين هذا المقهى والمقاهي الاخرى ويبدأ من لحظة دخولك اليه — The distinction between this coffee house and the other coffee houses appears clearly, and begins the moment you enter

65 | 247 |

4379 خُلُود *n.* immortality; perpetuity; *vn.* remaining, staying (في at a place); repairing إلى to (rest, sleep)

كنت أسير صباحا في الحقول وأرى في يقظة الطبيعة رمز الخلود — I was walking in the morning in the fields and I saw in the awakening of nature the symbol of eternity

49 | 325 | +lit

4380 عَلْمانِيَّة *n.* secularism

إن العلمانية تؤكد على وحدة الشعب على قاعدتي الحرية والمساواة بين الأفراد — Secularism stresses the unity of the people over the principles of freedom and equality between individuals

45 | 357 |

4381 عُلْوِيّ *adj.* upper, top; superior

لاحظت أن جارتنا في الدور العلوي قد أكثرت الزيارات لأهلي — I noticed that our neighbor in the upper floor had started visiting our family a lot

60 | 269 |

4382 لَمَحَ *v. I* (a) to see, notice sth

بينما كنت جالسة في السيارة، لمحت شيئا ما يخرج من بين مجموعة البيوت الصغيرة المحيطة — When I was sitting in the car, I noticed something come out from among the group of surrounding small houses

48 | 331 | +lit

4383 اِكْتِمال *n.* completion; perfection

نحتفل اليوم بافتتاح العام الدراسي بعد اكتمال اعمال البناء والترميم في المدارس المتضررة من العدوان الاسرائيلي — We are celebrating today the opening of the academic year after completing the work of building and renovating in the schools which were damaged by the Israeli aggression

61 | 265 |

4384 سَماحَة *n.* magnanimity; (honorific) His Eminence

استنكر سماحة المفتي بشدة تصوير الفواحش والموبقات وإرسال الصور عبر الانترنت — His eminence, the Mufti, strongly denounced taking pictures of obscene and shameful things and sending the pictures over the Internet

55 | 289 |

4385 انْطِلاقَة *n.* start, launch, outset

أعتقد أن هذه الانطلاقة في هذا المساء انطلاقة جيدة وتبشر إن شاء الله بالخير — I believe that this beginning, tonight, is a good beginning and bodes well, God willing

58 | 276 |

4386 أَنْجَزَ *v. IV* to implement, carry out (project); to accomplish, perform sth

أنجز الشاب أشغاله المنزلية، رأيته يكنس مربط البقرات أمام الدار — The young man did his housework; I saw him sweeping the cow stall in front of the house

58 | 274 |

4387 ماسّ *adj.* urgent, pressing; touching

لابد وأن يعود إلى وطنه، فأسرته في حاجة ماسة إليه — He needs to return to his homeland, his family needs him

64 | 250 |

4388 عَصَب *n. pl.* أَعْصاب nerve

أوجزت لها أخباري المتضمنة عذري، وكانت قلقة متوترة الأعصاب فأكثرت من التدخين — I summarized my news for her, including my excuse, and she was worried and tense, so she smoked a lot

55 | 289 |

4389 كَهْف *n.* cave, cavern; hole, cavity

بنوا حائطا ليسدوا به مدخل الكهف — They built a wall to block up the entrance of the cave

53 | 302 |

4390 مُتَفاوت *adj.* different, diverse

من جهة أخرى أصيب ستة مدنيين بجروح متفاوتة جراء انفجار عبوة ناسفة بالقرب من طوز خورماتو بمحافظة صلاح الدين — On the other hand, six civilians were wounded with a variety of wounds as a result of a package bomb explosion near Tuz Khurmatu in the Salah Al-Din province

63 | 252 |

4391 نَوَّرَ *v. II* to illuminate; to enlighten; (fig.) to brighten (a home, a Web forum, by one's visit)

أهلا بك.. نورت بيتنا — Hello...You have lit up our home

36 | 435 | +for

4392 بَرْق *n.* lightning; telegraph

يستل خنجره بسرعة البرق ويغرزه في صدر الخوري — He unsheathes his dagger as quick as lightning and buries it in the chest of the priest

54 | 297 |

4393 بَديع *adj.* wonderful, magnificent, marvelous

لقد دخلت كاميليا البيت ذلك اليوم كعصفور طليق في فضاء بديع — Camelia entered the house that day like a freed bird in the marvelous sky

55 | 288 |

4394 تَأَمُّل *n.* contemplation, reflection; pondering

كان هتلر يدور حول مبنى المستشارية في برلين في حالة من التأمل العميق — Hitler was going around the Chancellery building in Berlin in a state of deep contemplation

62 | 255 |

4395 فِرْدَوْس *n.* paradise; الفِرْدَوْس Paradise

جزاك الله خيراً وإن شاء الله تنالي الفردوس الأعلى — May God reward you good things and hopefully you will attain the highest paradise

48 | 331 |

4396 تِمْثال *n.* statue

ولأمر غير مفهوم فكرت زهرة فجأة في تمثال محمد علي باشا فوق جواده بالمنشية — For some incomprehensible reason Zahra suddenly thought about the statue of Muhammad Ali Pasha on his horse in Manshiya

55 | 288 |

4397 عَتَبَة *n.* step, stair; threshold; عَتَبَة دارِه sb's front door, sb's doorsteps

يموت المريض على عتبة المستشفى ولا يجد من يعالجه — The sick person dies on the doorstep of

the hospital, and doesn't find anyone to treat him

60 | 264 |

4398 مُصَمِّم *adj.* determined, resolute (على to do sth); *n.* designer, stylist

إن الشعب اللبناني مصمم على بناء دولة قوية: دولة تستطيع أن تستعيد موقع لبنان كواحة للاعتدال — The Lebanese people are determined to build a strong state: a state that can restore Lebanon's position as an oasis of moderation

55 | 286 |

4399 تَجَدَّدَ *v. V* to be renewed, to be revived; to come up again, to repeat itself

تجدد الجدل حول الاجهاض في بريطانيا — The conflict about abortion was revived in Britain

65 | 242 |

4400 نَهْب *n.* looting, plundering; stealing, robbing

اتهمت الولايات المتحدة ومسؤولون أميركيون السودان بتسليح ميليشيا عربية قامت بأعمال اغتصاب ونهب وقتل — The US and American officials accused the Sudan of arming an Arab militia which proceeded to rape, plunder, and kill

56 | 280 |

4401 فاتُورَة *n.* invoice, bill

تلك في ظني هي المشكلة الكبرى التي نعاني منها وندفع فاتورة غالية ثمنا لها بسبب العشوائية في القرار والارتجال في التفكير — This, in my way of thinking, is the major problem from which we are suffering, and we are paying a heavy price for it because of the randomness of the decision making and the improvisational nature of the thinking

66 | 239 |

4402 عِوَض *n.* replacement; compensation, restitution; عِوَضاً عَن and عِوَضَ instead of, in compensation for

لقد شاء كاتبو التقرير أن يستخدموا تعبير التنمية الانسانية عوضا عن التنمية البشرية الذي يستخدمه برنامج الأمم المتحدة للتنمية — The authors of the report wanted to use the expression "humanistic development" instead of the expression "human development" that the UN program for development uses

60 | 264 |

4403 مُتَّبَع *adj.* followed, observed, adhered to

ابدت موافقتها على العرض رغم تحفظها على الوسائل المتبعة خاصة وأنها ومنذ سنوات كانت تسعى للحصول على طفل بغرض التبني — She expressed her agreement for the offer despite her reservation about the means followed, particularly since for many years she has been trying to obtain a child for the purpose of adoption

57 | 274 |

4404 وَجَع *n.* ache, pain

تناول حبة مسكن آلام لتهدأ وجع أسنانه على معدة خاوية — He took a painkiller on an empty stomach to calm his tooth pain

53 | 294 |

4405 تَوافَرَ *v. VI* to be abundantly available

في هذه المدن تتوافر أشهر الفنادق العالمية التي تناسب جميع المستويات — In these cities there are many international hotels available which are appropriate for all levels

58 | 270 |

4406 اِسْتِغْناء *n.* dispensing with, doing without sth عن

التعليم والتدريب يعتبران ضرورة لا يمكن الاستغناء عنها في بناء الفرد والمجتمع — Education and training are considered to be a necessity that cannot be done without in building the individual and society

62 | 252 |

4407 أَعَزّ *elat.* stronger/strongest; dearer/dearest

أنتم أعز الأصدقاء ولا أدري لولا وقوفكم الى جانبنا ماذا كنا فاعلين — You are the dearest of friends and I don't know what we would have done were it not for your standing by us

58 | 268 |

4408 ذُرْوَة *n.* peak, summit, height

تنبأ وقتها بأن العالم سيصل في عام ١٩٩٥ إلى ذروة الإنتاج النفطي — At the time he predicted that the world would reach the peak of oil production in 1995

61 | 254 |

4409 قَدّ *n.* amount; ما قد as much as; هالقد
(Lev. /ha-l-'add/, Irq. /ha-l-gadd/) *adv.* so
much, this much, this amount; (Lev. also
هالقدة
/ha-l-'adde/)
— قديه عمرك يا محمد؟ يعني إنت قد أولادي
How old are you Muhammad? I mean, you
are the age of my children
9 | 1618 | +spo

4410 كَنَديّ *n./adj.* Canadian
ارتفع عدد الشركات الكندية العاملة في مصر في مجال
أنشطة البحث والاستكشاف عن البترول — The
number of Canadian companies working in
Egypt in the area of the exploration and
discovery of oil has increased
53 | 296 |

4411 تَذْكير *n.* reminding
ويجب التذكير على هذا المستوى أن اللاعب يوسف
رابح تألق بشكل جيد في مباريات كأس العالم
للشبان — It should be remembered at this
level that the player Yusuf Rabih really shone
in the World Cup for Youth matches
62 | 253 |

4412 لَهَب *n.* flame
فوجئت بأن محل سوبر ماركت أسفل العمارة تخرج
منه ألسنة اللهب، فقمت بكسر الباب وفصل
الكهرباء — I was surprised that (tongues of)
flames were coming out of a supermarket in
the bottom of the building, so I broke down
the door and cut off the electricity
54 | 287 | +lit

4413 مُنَوِّه *a.p.* pointing out, mentioning بـ/إلى أنَّ
that
رحب فخامة الرئيس الباكستاني بسمو ولي العهد
— منوها بالعلاقات الطيبة التي تجمع بين البلدين
His excellency the Pakistani president
welcomed his majesty the Crown Prince,
alluding to the good relations which bring
the two countries together
38 | 408 | +news

4414 اِسْتِبْداد *n.* despotism, absolutism, tyranny
اعلنت السيدة كونداليزا رايس ان الاستبداد العربي
أثار حالة من اليأس والاحباط اللذين صنعا
الارهابيين — Mrs Condoleezza Rice

announced that Arab totalitarianism had
incited a condition of despair and depression
which created terrorists
49 | 315 |

4415 رَيّ *n.* irrigation
هناك تلازم بين شبكة الري وبين ارتفاع ملوحة
الأرض — There is a correlation between the
irrigation network and the rise in the salinity
of the ground
52 | 298 |

4416 كَمال *n.* perfection, completeness
علينا ألا نتوقع أبدا الكمال في أي شيء له علاقة
بالإنسان — We need to not ever expect
perfection in anything which has a relationship
to people
63 | 247 |

4417 تَفْكيك *n.* dismantling, taking apart;
separating, breaking up; fragmentation,
dissolution
رجاله مختصون في تفكيك القنابل — His men are
experts in disarming bombs
56 | 277 |

4418 هَنْدَسيّ *adj.* engineering; technical
ليلى مهندسة معمارية وتعمل في احدى الشركات
الهندسية — Laila is an architectural engineer
and works in one of the engineering
companies
50 | 307 |

4419 عاهِل *n.* monarch, king
تلك عينها هي اللحظة التي قطع فيها العاهل
السعودي الملك فيصل علاقاته مع الأميركيين —
That is the exact moment in which the Saudi
monarch King Faisal cut off his relations with
the Americans
43 | 355 | +news

4420 فُرْن *n.* oven; furnace; bakery
انبعثت في أنفه رائحة العجين في الفرن — The
smell of the dough in the oven awakened in
his nose
47 | 327 |

4421 زِحام *n.* crowd, throng; (traffic) congestion
لم تتمكن من العودة لنقل بقية الحجاج بسبب
الزحام — You won't be able to return to

transport the rest of the pilgrims because
of the crowds

55 | 278 |

4422 أُسْوَة *n.* model, example; pattern; concept;
أُسْوَةً بِـ based on the model of
فلم لم تشاركي بعمل، إسوة بزملائك؟ — Why
didn't you participate in the work, the same
as your colleagues?

62 | 249 |

4423 مَقْرَبَة and مَقْرُبَة *n.* vicinity, proximity;
على مَقْرُبَةٍ من close to, near
كان آخر لقاء لي بعباس في مقهى صغيرة تقع على
مقربة من مبنى كليته — The last meeting I had
with Abbas was in a small coffeehouse that is
located near the building of his college

59 | 260 |

4424 هَيْبَة *n.* reverence, respect; dignity, prestige;
fear, awe
كانت هيبة اسمه حاضرة في ذهني دائما — The
prestige of his name is always present in my
mind

61 | 253 |

4425 بَصَرِيّ *adj.* visual; optical
يرمي إلى إحداث نوع من الخداع البصري لدى
الحاضرين — He is trying to cause a kind of
visual deception for the audience

54 | 285 |

4426 جَرَّ *v. I (u)* to drag, pull sth
حرام عليك ان تجر لبنان الى الهاوية بحثا عن
موقع تريده، فلبنان لأبنائه — Shame on you
for dragging Lebanon into hell, searching for
a place you want, because Lebanon is for its
people

59 | 260 |

4427 خَفَّ *v. I (i)* to become lighter (weight);
to decrease in intensity; to quicken (one's
pace); to rush, hurry إلى to do sth
بدأ المطر يخف من فوق سماء المدينة والسحب السوداء
تقف بعيدا — The rain began to lighten up
above the sky of the city, and the black clouds
stood far off

64 | 237 |

4428 اِتِّساع *n.* expansion, extension, stretching,
widening
أغلقت التلفاز وبصقت ثانية وهي تراقب اتساع
عيون الأطفال والدهشة التي اعترتهم — She
turned off the television and spat once again,
watching the eyes of the children grow wide,
and observing the surprise which overcame
them

65 | 232 |

4429 قُدُوم *n.* arrival, coming; entering (a chat
room)
تنبأ بقرب قدوم المعركة الأخيرة — He predicted
the imminent arrival of the final battle

64 | 237 |

4430 بَرْقِيَّة *n.* telegram
كما أرسل موسى برقية للسلطات الأميركية أعرب
فيها عن الأسى البالغ لكارثة الإعصار —
Musa sent a telegram to the American
authorities in which he expressed his extreme
sorrow for the catastrophe of the hurricane

47 | 321 | +news

4431 هَيْهاتُ *interj.* how impossible! not even close!
(it was) in vain!
يطوفون بالأسواق عساهم يعثرون على قمصان
بيضاء، لكن هيهات، على ما يبدو — They go
around the markets to perhaps find white
shirts, but in vain, as it appears

46 | 331 | +lit

4432 جَنَّنَ *v. II* to infuriate sb; to drive sb insane;
(Dia.) to be fantastic (insanely great)
المحلات هنا فيها حاجات تجنن — The shops here
have fantastic things

25 | 604 |

4433 تِسْعِين *n.* ninetieth year; التسعينات the Nineties
قامت روسيا بتطوير الصاروخ في أواخر التسعينات
وزادت من مداه ليصل حتى ١٥٠ كلم — Russia
developed the missile at the end of the Nineties
and increased its range to reach 150 km

54 | 278 |

4434 مُقام *adj.* raised, erected; installed, established,
set up; held, hosted (event, party)
جلسنا تحت مظلات مقاهي الميدان المفتوحة،
وشاهدنا الحفلات الموسيقية المقامة في الهواء الطلق

— We sat under the umbrellas of the open air cafés in the square, and we watched the concerts being held in the open air

56 | 269 |

4435 مُعْرِب *a.p.* expressing, indicating, manifesting (opinion, sentiment) عن

اشاد المبعوث الأممي بالموقف الحكيم لدولة الامارات فى الوصول لحل سلمى للجزر الثلاث معربا عن أمله — The UN فى تحقيق الامن والسلام بالمنطقة delegate praised the wise position of the Emirati state in reaching a peaceful solution to the three islands, expressing his hope for the achievement of security and peace in the region

41 | 371 | +news

4436 ما *interrog.* (with لـ and pron.) what is wrong with...?; (Lev.) (شُو) مالَك؟ what's wrong with you? what's bothering you?

كان شكلها عسول اوى دلوقتى مش عارفة مالها — She used to look really nice, but now I don't know what's wrong with her

44 | 344 |

4437 هاوُن *n.* mortar (weapon)

يقول عسكريون أمريكيون إن قذائف الهاون أصبحت السلاح المفضل لدى المقاتلين بسبب سهولة إطلاقها — American military men say that mortar shells have become the preferred weapon for the fighters because of the ease of launching them

42 | 357 | +news

4438 فَقِيد *n./adj.* deceased

المجلس يتقدم إلى أسرة الفقيد بخالص العزاء والمواساة لهذا المصاب الجلل — The assembly offers the family of the deceased the most sincere consolation for this significant shock

53 | 285 |

4439 حَدّ (Lev.) *prep.* next to, beside; (alone) with

بالشتا ما بحب أقعد غير حدى الدفاية — In the winter I don't like sitting unless it's next to the heater

12 | 1209 | +spo

4440 اِسْتيراد *n.* importing, importation

قررت الحكومة البولندية استيراد الغاز الطبيعي من مصر فى حدود ٥ مليارات متر مكعب — The

Polish government decided to import natural gas from Egypt in the range of 5 billion cubic meters

52 | 287 |

4441 مِساس *n.* violation, infringement (of ب)

وضح كيفية الاستفادة من الفرص التي توفرها هذه المنظمة دون المساس بالمصالح الوطنية أو الاعتبارات المحلية — He clarified how to benefit from the opportunities which this organization was providing without violating national interests or local considerations

61 | 247 |

4442 اِكْتِفاء *n.* contentment, satisfaction; sufficiency, adequacy

يشدد على ضروره نيل الاستقلال وتحقيق الاكتفاء الذاتي وعدم التبعيه للاجنبي — He stresses the necessity of obtaining independence and achieving self-sufficiency and not being dependent on foreigners

59 | 255 |

4443 أجادَ *v. IV* to be proficient, be an expert at sth; to do sth well

يجيد خمس لغات غير العربية — He is proficient in five languages, besides Arabic

63 | 238 |

4444 نِسْوَة *pl. n.* women

نسي التلاميذ دروسهم.. وأهملت النسوة أشغال المنازل.. وتعطل الرجال عن العمل — The students forgot their lessons...the women neglected the household chores...the men stopped working

50 | 298 | +lit

4445 لَذَّة *n.* pleasure, joy, delight, enjoyment

يفتح الزجاجة ويبدأ بشربها في لذة — He opens the bottle and begins to drink it in pleasure

52 | 287 |

4446 وِساطة *n.* mediation, intercession

قال دبلوماسيون عرب أمس الأربعاء إن جهود الوساطة المصرية لعقد لقاء قمة بين العاهل السعودي الملك عبدالله والزعيم الليبي معمر القذافي وصلت إلى طريق مسدود — Arab diplomats said yesterday, Wednesday, that the Egyptian mediation efforts to hold

a summit meeting between the Saudi
monarch King Abdallah and the Libyan
leader Moammar Al-Qadhafi, have reached
an impasse

51 | 291 |

4447 حَجْز *n.* reservation (seat, room); seizure,
confiscation, impounding
لذلك سأطلب منكِ أن توافقا على طلبي في حجز
غرفة في بيت الطالبات — Therefore I will request
from you to agree to my request to reserve
a room in the girl's dorm

60 | 248 |

4448 مُخَلَّف *adj.* left behind; *n.* مُخَلَّفات leftovers
تنتج الأعلاف غير التقليدية من مخلفات قش الأرز،
لتقليل استيراد الذرة الصفراء والأعلاف المركزة —
The non-conventional feed is produced
from remnants of rice straw, to reduce the
importation of maize and concentrated feed

60 | 248 |

4449 وَهَبَ *v. I (a)* to donate, grant sth ل to sb;
to give, dedicate (one's life) ل to
وهب حياته فداء للوطن واستشهد وهو يقارع
الاستعمار الإيطالي البغيض — He gave his
life a ransom for his homeland and he died
a martyr fighting the hateful Italian
colonialism

52 | 286 |

4450 مُجيب *adj.* responding, answering; responsive;
n. person answering, person able or willing
to answer
جعل عيدنا سعيدا إنه قريب مجيب، وكل عام وأنتم
بخير — May He make our holiday happy;
He is near, and He answers us, may you be
well every year

60 | 248 |

4451 مُضْطَرّ *adj.* compelled, forced, obligated
(إلى to do sth)
غبت مضطرا، لا أعرف كم غبت، لكنني عدت —
I was forced to be absent, I don't know how
long I was gone, but I have returned

62 | 240 |

4452 أَشْمَر *adj.* fem. سَمْراء, pl. سُمْر brown, tanned,
brown-skinned

ملامح وجهه تقول بصراحة متناهية: أنا فلسطيني..
البشرة السمراء.. الشعر الأسود والعينان السوداوان
غير الواسعتين — The features of his face say
with an excessive frankness: I am a
Palestinian...The dark skin...the black hair,
the black eyes, not wide

61 | 242 |

4453 غَبيّ *adj.* stupid, ignorant
انه غبي يصدق كل ما يقال له — He is stupid,
believing everything that is said to him

50 | 298 |

4454 سَوَى and سَوا *adv.* (Dia.) together, all;
(adj.) equal, the same; (Irq.) /suwa/
مروان ابني ٦ سنوات زملكاوي فظيع، بنروح
الماتشات سوا — Marwan, my son, 6 years old,
is a fanatic Zamalkawi, we go to the matches
together

34 | 429 | +spo

4455 مَشْرَف *n.* pl. مَشارِف view; مَشارِف heights,
elevations
أنت بالكاد على مشارف العشرين من العمر والحياة
بكل ما فيها من سعادة لازالت أمامك — You are
almost (within view of) twenty years old, and
life with all that is in it in the way of happiness
is still in front of you

60 | 246 |

4456 حَميد *adj.* praiseworthy, laudable; positive,
good; (med.) benign
نتمنى له النجاح والتوفيق في هذا المسعى الحميد —
We wish him success in this admirable
endeavor

63 | 232 |

4457 أذان *n.* adhan (Islamic call to prayer)
وقتها سمعت الأذان فتهدج قلبي وردد: لاحول ولا
قوة الا بالله — At that time I heard the call
to prayer; my heart trembled and repeated
(the phrase): there is no power except
in God

52 | 280 |

4458 هَمْس *n.* whispering; هَمْساً in whispers,
by whispering
انقطع الهمس فورا وساد سكون عميق قطعته
النحنحة التى تسبق كلامه — The whispering

ceased immediately and a deep silence reigned, broken by the cough which preceded his speech

47 | 310 |

4459 قُطْب *n.* axis, pole; leader, top figure
ظروف الجو في القطب الجنوبي تختلف عنها في أي مكان آخر على الأرض — The weather conditions in the South Pole differ from those in any other place on earth

59 | 248 |

4460 مُكَعَّب *adj.* cubic (foot, meter); cube-shaped
رفع سعر الغاز الروسي الى ٢٣٠ دولارا لكل ألف متر مكعب تماشيا مع الأسعار العالمية — He raised the price of Russian gas to 230 dollars for every thousand cubic meters, in accord with world prices

43 | 336 |

4461 عافَى *v. III* to heal, cure sb; (Lev.Irq.Gul.) الله يعافيك God grant you good health! (used primarily to express gratitude; approx.: God bless you!)
أسأل المولى عز وجل أن يعافيك من هذه العادة الذميمة والمدمرة — I ask God, may He be exalted, to cure you of this reprehensible and destructive habit

25 | 572 |

4462 لين /leen/ *conj.* (Gul.) when, whenever; *prep.* until; لين ما /leen-ma/ as soon as
باصبر لين ما يجي — I will be patient until he comes

27 | 529 | +for +spo

4463 أَشْرَقَ *v. IV* to rise, shine
هل يرضيك يا صديقي أن تشرق شمس العيد على أولادك هؤلاء دون أن يفرحوا بملابس جديدة — Are you satisfied, my friend, for the sun of the Holiday to rise on these children of yours without them having the joy of new clothes?

54 | 268 |

4464 أَنْشَأ *v. IV* to establish, found; to install, set up
هذه البلدة ليس لديها إلا مدرسة ابتدائية للبنات، لم تنشأ إلا مؤخراً، ولا يوجد مدرسة متوسطة — This village has only an elementary school for girls,

and it was only recently built, and there is no middle school

63 | 233 |

4465 ضَباب *n.* fog, mist; vapor
الشمس تعوم في زرقة السماء وتشكل طبقة من الضباب فوق سطح البحر البعيد — The sun swims in the blue of the sky and forms a layer of fog above the surface of the distant sea

55 | 263 |

4466 بَشَّرَ *v. II* to give good news; to evangelize; يُبَشِّر بالخَيْر to augur well, to be a good omen
هناك عدة ملاحظات على أداء الفريق.. فالأداء لا يبشر بالخير.. وكان المستوى ضعيف — There are several observations about the performance of the team...the performance does not bode well...the level was weak

59 | 248 |

4467 مَجِيد *adj.* glorious, exalted
يمضون قدما بعزم لا يلين نحو هدفهم المجيد، فيدمرون إسرائيل وأمريكا ، ولا بأس أوروبا أيضا — They are going forward, with a determination that does not soften, towards their glorious goal, to destroy Israel and America, and probably Europe too

55 | 263 |

4468 وَجِيز *adj.* brief, short; summarized
تحسب أن الأمور ستعود إلى ما كانت عليه بعد فترة وجيزة — She figures that things will return to how they were after a short period

64 | 225 |

4469 مَكْرُوه *adj.* detested, loathsome; *n.* accident, misfortune, mishap
حفظ الله الكويت واهلها من كل مكروه — May God keep Kuwait and its people from all misfortune

57 | 255 |

4470 نَقَصَ *v. I* (u) to lack sth; to be less (عن than); to be reduced
خذ مالك كاملا لم ينقص منه شيء — Take all of your money, nothing is missing from it

64 | 225 |

4471 راجِل /raagil/ (Egy.) *n.* man
البنت من سن أربعتاشر قابلة للزواج من أي راجل — ولو كان زي جنابك في الستين — A fourteen-year-old girl is ready for marriage to any man, even if it be to an old geezer of sixty like you
31 | 461 |

4472 لِئَلّا *conj.* (= لِـ أَنْ لا) in order not to
يفر منه لئلا يصيبه منه أذى — He flees from him so that he will not do him any harm
54 | 267 |

4473 صَهْيُونِيّة *n.* Zionism
ثيودور هرتسل مؤسس الصهيونية السياسية اعتقد أن اليهود يجب أن يجتمعوا في دولة — Theodor Herzl, the founder of political Zionism, believed that the Jews needed to gather together into a state
48 | 299 |

4474 كِفاح *n.* struggle, fight
دعا الطاهر كوادر الجبهة لمواصلة الكفاح، مؤكدا أن إسرائيل تريد فرض الاستسلام — Al-Tahir called on the cadres of the Front to continue the struggle, stressing that Israel wants to impose a surrender
58 | 248 |

4475 مُكافأة *n.* compensation, remuneration; reward
قرر مكافأة نفسه بالتهام قطعة بسبوسة يتناسب حجمها مع ما تم إنجازه — He decided to reward himself by devouring a piece of basbusa whose size would be appropriate for what he had achieved
59 | 246 |

4476 مُتَداوَل *adj.* in circulation, in common, prevailing
عرفت بورصة بيروت أمس ارتفاعا باهرا في نسبة الأسهم المتداولة في ردهاتها لم يسبق لها مثيل منذ وقت بعيد — The Beirut Stock Exchange yesterday witnessed a dazzling rise in the percentage of shares circulated in its halls, to an extent which has not been seen in a long time
48 | 300 |

4477 قَفْز *n.* jumping, leaping
— كانت في حفرة واسعة، لا تستطيع القفز منها It was in a wide hole, and couldn't jump out of it
60 | 239 |

4478 قامَة *n.* stature, status; height
كان أحب إخوته إلى أمه، طويل القامة، أسمر اللون، في ملامحه ملاحة ووسامة — He was the most beloved of his siblings to his mother; (he was) tall of stature, dark of color, in his features were a beauty and handsomeness
48 | 299 | +lit

4479 رَيْب *n.* doubt, suspicion; لا رَيْبَ فيهِ/فيها there is no doubt about it; بِلا رَيْب without a doubt
لا ريب أنه يطمح للثأر، وهذا يدعو لليقظة والانتباه — There is no doubt he is aspiring for revenge, and that calls for watchfulness and alertness
49 | 294 | +lit

4480 حَزِنَ *v. I (a)* to be sad, grieve لـ/على for
أمي تشعر بمعاناتي، لكني لا أخبرها بشيء حتى لا تحزن وتمرض — My mother feels for my suffering, but I don't tell her anything so she won't become sad and get sick
50 | 286 |

4481 امبارح and مبارح /mbaariH/ (Lev.) *adv.* yesterday; also امبيرح /mbeeriH/
خلصت الامتحانات امبارح — I finished the tests yesterday
9 | 1497 | +spo

4482 عُدْوانِيّ *adj.* hostile, aggressive
اضافت الوكالة ان اللقاء تناول تطورات الحرب العدوانية الاسرائيلية على لبنان — The agency added that the meeting dealt with the developments of the Israeli aggressive war against Lebanon
53 | 269 |

4483 اِسْتِدْعاء *n.* summons, call, appeal, petition; recall, calling back
طلب محامي الدفاع استدعاء خبراء عالميين لاعداد تقرير حول اسباب انتشار المرض في ليبيا — The defense attorney requested the summoning of world experts to prepare a report about the causes of the spread of the disease in Libya
61 | 235 |

4484 أَجَنْدَة *n.* agenda, schedule, program; roadmap, blueprint

لابد من تحديد أجندة لهذا الحوار يوافق عليها الطرفان — An agenda needs to be defined for this dialog which the two sides agree on

50 | 284 |

4485 جَفَّ *v. I (i)* to dry, become dry; (fig.) to freeze, run cold (blood)

هل جف نهر الحب يا مليكتي؟ — Has the river of love dried up, my queen?

49 | 292 | +lit

4486 وَلَّدَ *v. II* to generate, produce (energy)

الصحيح يولد الصحيح والخطيئة تولد الخطيئة — Truth produces truth, and error produces error

65 | 222 |

4487 مُتَعاقِب *adj.* consecutive, successive, alternating

وهل الرئيس السنيورة هوالذي أدخل البلاد في هذه الحروب المتعاقبة؟ — Is it President Siniora who threw the country into these consecutive wars?

57 | 251 |

4488 أَرْضِيَّة *n.* floor, basis, groundwork; background

شدد على ضرورة إيجاد أرضية تفاهم مع بكين وسيول — He stressed the importance of finding some ground of mutual understanding with Beijing and Seoul

53 | 270 |

4489 مُبالَغ مُبالَغ فيه/فيها *p.p.* exaggerated

استخدمت العنف المبالغ فيه لإخضاع السكان — It used exaggerated force to bring the inhabitants into line

66 | 217 |

4490 زُجاجَة *n.* bottle; (piece of) glass

جلس دنانه إلى المائدة أمام صفوت الذي فتح حقيبته وأخرج زجاجة ويسكي صغيرة مينياتور — Danana sat at the table in front of Safwat who opened his briefcase and pulled out a small "miniature" bottle of whiskey

53 | 268 |

4491 اِقْتَحَمَ *v. VIII* to invade sth; to storm, burst into sth

قال مراسل الجزيرة إن قوات كبيرة اقتحمت المدينة وتمركزت في البلدة القديمة — The Al-Jazeera

reporter said that large forces had stormed into the city and concentrated in the old city

44 | 327 | +news

4492 خَيْبَة خَيْبَة أَمَل *n.* failure, frustration; disappointment

لديك ما يكفيك من خيبة الأمل بسببي — You have had enough disappointment on my account

64 | 224 |

4493 تَنازَلَ *v. VI* to back down عن from; to renounce, waive, forego عن sth

اليس من حقها حماية الفلسطينيين هناك؟ هل يتنازل العرب عن حق العودة للفلسطينيين؟ — Isn't it her right to protect the Palestinians there? Are the Arabs giving up the right of return for the Palestinians?

66 | 216 |

4494 اِنْدَلَعَ *v. VII* to break out, flare up (fire, war)

أود أن أضيف هنا أنه عندما اندلعت الحرب في لبنان، أرسل خالد مشعل أسرته إلى عمان — I want to add here that when the war broke out in Lebanon, Khalid Mashal sent his family to Amman

54 | 264 |

4495 مُشْتَبَه مشتبه فيه/فيها/فيهم *p.p.* suspicious, suspected

يخول للجنود سلطات كاملة لقتل المتمردين المشتبه بهم في ظل حصانة من الملاحقة القانونية — He grants the soldiers full powers to kill the suspected rebels under the protection of immunity from legal prosecution

49 | 291 | +news

4496 اِخْتِفاء *n.* disappearance; absence

أدى إدخال الأغنام من صنف «دوبر» إلى اختفاء الأغنام الحمراء من صنف «معاساي» اختفاء تاما — The introduction of sheep of the "Douber" variety led to the complete disappearance of red sheep of the "Masawi" variety

65 | 219 |

4497 مُوَجِّه *adj.* sending, guiding, directing

ثم استدار في عزم موجها بصره نحو بيت الناظر فاتجهت الرءوس إليه — Then he turned around determinedly directing his gaze towards the house of the supervisor, and all the heads turned towards him

58 | 244 |

4498 سَكَّر v. II (Lev.Gul.) to close, shut (window, door)

بدي اسكر الخط لإنه ما اني بالبيت وما عندي بطارية الخط — بدي أسكر الخط — I want to hang up because I'm not at home and I don't have a battery, I want to hang up

11 | 1223 | +spo

4499 تَرْمِيم n. restoration, renovation

ويذكر ان مشروع اعادة ترميم المدارس يتم بالتنسيق مع المنطقة التربوية في الجنوب — He mentions that the school renovation project is taking place in coordination with the educational region in the south

54 | 261 |

4500 واخِد (Lev.Irq.Gul.) ماخِذ (.Egy) a.p. (fem. واخدة /waxda/, ماخذة /maxdha/, pl. واخدين /waxdiin/, ماخذين /maxdhiin/) taking, having taken (also, taking sb in marriage, getting married); واخد باله to be aware of

هو اساسا كان مسافر وقت طويل فيعني مكانش واخد باله قوي إن انا مش موجودة لإن هو كمان مش موجود — He basically was away for a long time, so he was not paying attention to the fact that I wasn't there since he also wasn't there

28 | 510 | +spo

4501 سَهَر n. sleeplessness, night without sleep; watchfulness, vigilance

لا بد أن يتوافر في البلد عدد من رجال الشرطة والأمن المكلفين بحماية الامن عن طريق السهر على تطبيق القانون ومنع انتهاكه — There needs be a number of security and police men provided in the country tasked with protecting security by carefully watching over the implementation of the law and preventing its being violated

51 | 278 |

4502 اِخْتِراع n. invention

أشهر ما اقترن باسم عباس ابن فرناس هي محاولته اختراع آلة يستطيع الإنسان أن يطير بها في الفضاء — The most famous thing associated with the name of Abbas Ibn Firnas is his attempt to invent a device with which a person can fly in space

57 | 248 |

4503 سَعِدَ v. I (a) to be happy, delight ب in sth

سعدت كثيرا بنشر قصتي في «البيان» — I was really happy about the publication of my story in "Al-Bayan"

57 | 248 |

4504 نازِح n. pl. -uun displaced person; emigrant

أشارت الحركة في بيان لها إلى أنها افتتحت مكتبا لتسجيل النازحين وتنسيق الخدمات الإغاثية لهم — The movement indicated in one of its communiqués that it has opened an office to record the displaced persons and coordinate aid services for them

41 | 345 |

4505 تَعَصُّب n. fanaticism, extremism; intolerance

الإسلام دين رحمة وعدل ولا مكان فيه للعنف أو التعصب — Islam is a religion of mercy and justice and there is no place in it for violence and intolerance

56 | 251 |

4506 مَبْدَئِيّ adj. fundamental, basic; مَبْدَئِيّاً in principle

وقعت إيران وتركيا اتفاقا مبدئيا لضخ الغاز الإيراني الى أوروبا عبر تركيا — Iran and Turkey signed an agreement in principle to pump Iranian gas to Europe through Turkey

56 | 252 |

4507 مُخْتار n. mukhtar (village chief); elder; mayor; adj. chosen, selected; elected; favorite, preferred

لدى إحدى القرى سأل الزائر عن منزل المختار فقيل له إنه بجوار منزل معلم المدرسة — In one of the villages, the visitor asked about the house of the mayor, and he was told that it was next to the house of the school teacher

40 | 348 | +lit

4508 دَرَج n. step, stairs; route, course

ظل ينصت إلى وقع قدميها على الدرج الخشبي وهو يخفت مبتعدا — He kept listening to the sound of her feet on the wooden stairs, as it dimmed and got further away

52 | 272 |

4509 إِجْمال n. sum, whole; إِجْمالاً in general, on the whole

الجو العام إجمالا ما انه كثير منيح بالبلد — The general atmosphere as a whole was very good in the country

51 | 274 |

4510 مَعْمُول *adj.* in use, applied, carried out, effected

القوانين المعمول بها في معظم الدول العربية تحد من طموح المرأة في مختلف الاطر المهنية والسياسية والاجتماعي — The laws in effect in most Arab states limit the ambitions of women in various occupational, political and social contexts

58 | 241 |

4511 نِفْس (Egy.; Lev. نَفْس) *n.* appetite; desire, wish; نِفْسِي (Egy.) I wish, I'd like; فَتَح النفس to stimulate the appetite

يا ترى هوه ده الحب؟ نفسي أمد أيدي والمس أيدها — I wonder is this love? I want to reach out my hand and touch her hand

33 | 426 |

4512 تَسَنَّى *v. V* to be feasible, be possible

نأمل أن يتسنى لك دائما مراسلتنا والمشاركة في مسابقاتنا الثقافية المفيدة — We hope you will always be able to correspond with us and participate in our useful cultural competitions

61 | 228 |

4513 عَرَّفَ *v. II* to introduce sb ب to sb else; to let sb know sth

انت ايش عرفك إن انا حاكون فى المحل؟ — Who told you I would be at the shop?

36 | 385 | +spo

4514 مُوضَة /mooDa/ *n.* fashion, style (It. moda)

لا يتبع الموضة، زيه ثابت — He doesn't follow fashion, his clothing is fixed

54 | 256 |

4515 مَرْسَم *n.* pl. مَرَاسِم art studio, shop; ceremonies, rituals; conventions, protocol

سيجرى مراسم افتتاح رسمية لمركز الحاسوب والمكتبة خلال الأسبوع القادم — Official opening ceremonies for the Computing Center and the Library will be held during the next week

59 | 235 |

4516 حَمَّلَ *v. II* to load (cargo); حَمَّلَهُ المَسْؤُوليَّةَ to put sb in charge; to blame sb; to download (files)

حملوا مؤسساتهم التعليمية مسؤولية ضعف المشاركة الشبابية في مختلف الجامعات — They blamed their educational institutions for the weak youth participation in the various universities

63 | 219 |

4517 أها and أَهَه /'ahaa/ (Dia.) *interj.* yes, right, yeah, uh-huh

من كاليفورنيا بتحكي؟ أها من كاليفورنيا — You're speaking from California? Ah, from California

9 | 1552 | +spo

4518 صَحْن *n.* bowl, plate; courtyard (of a mosque)

قرعت رجاء الباب ودخلت حاملة صحن كبة مشوية — Raja' knocked on the door and entered carrying a plate of roasted kibbeh

46 | 298 |

4519 ذِهْنِيّ *adj.* mental, intellectual

تنبأ له معلموه بمستقبل باهر بسبب قوة شخصيته وانضباطه وكفاءته الذهنية والجسمانية — His teachers predicted a bright future for him because of the strength of his personality, his discipline, and his mental and physical efficiency

60 | 230 |

4520 فَيْض *n.* abundance; flood, stream

يركز البرنامج على ضخ فيض من المعلومات في ذهن المشاهد حول المواضيع التي يعرضها — The program concentrates on pumping a flood of information into the brain of the viewer concerning the subjects it is presenting

48 | 287 |

4521 نَشْوَة *n.* intoxication, rapture, elation

خرجنا إلى الشارع ونحن في نشوة الشراب — We went out into the street in a state of intoxication

49 | 282 | +lit

4522 شُعْبَة *n.* pl. شُعَب branch, subdivision, department

يمكن لتلاميذ الاعلامية الصناعية الانتقال الى شعبة العلوم التقنية — Industrial media students can transfer to the branch of technical sciences

57 | 242 |

4523 مُقْتَنِع *adj.* satisfied, content; convinced

الراجل مقتنع بيه مية فى المية دلوقتى — The man is satisfied with him a hundred percent now

| 224 | 62

4524 رِئَة *n.* lung

التفاح يقي أيضا من سرطان الرئة، فعندما تتناول تفاحة طازجة واحدة، تحصل على أكثر من ثلاثة جرامات من الألياف الغذائية — Apples also protect from lung cancer, and when you eat a single fresh apple, you get over three grams of food fiber

| 229 | 60

4525 بادِرَة *n.* pl. بَوادِر gesture, sign, indication; early signs, first indications

ان العراق يعيش فى الواقع بوادر حرب طائفية مريرة — Iraq is actually experiencing the first signs of a bitter sectarian war

| 226 | 61

4526 إخْفاء *n.* hiding, concealing, keeping secret; lowering (one's voice)

لم يستطع إخفاء سعادته — He was not able to conceal his happiness

| 234 | 59

4527 أرْحَم *elat.* more/most merciful

ألم يقل اغلب العراقيين ان الجنود الامريكان هم أرحم من جنود الحرس الوطني وشرطة وزارة الداخلية؟ — Didn't most Iraqis say that the American soldiers are more merciful than the soldiers of the National Guard or the Ministry of the Interior policemen?

| 289 | 47

4528 تَحْصيل *n.* acquisition, attainment; تَحْصيل حاصِل foregone conclusion; self-evident (fact, truth)

تمكن من تحصيل ٦٠ الف دولار خلال "حرب عون" وحدها، ما ساعده على بناء منزله الصيفي في قريته آنذاك — He was able to obtain 60 thousand dollars during the "Aun war" alone, which helped him build his summer home in his village at that time

| 231 | 59

4529 مَقْدِرَة *n.* ability, potential, capacity

كان له مقدرة مذهلة على الغفران — He had an amazing ability to forgive

| 227 | 60

4530 تَكْريس *n.* dedication, devotion; consecration

يدعو العلماء والمتخصصين في هذا المجال الى تكريس جهودهم في إيجاد وسائل حديثة لعلاج هذا المرض — Scholars and specialists in this field are calling for consecrating their efforts on finding modern means to treat these diseases

| 259 | 53

4531 نَجا *v. I (u)* to survive, come out alive; to escape, be rescued من from

معظم من نجا من عمليات القتل قال إن المسلحين ينطقون بلهجة عراقية صافية — Most of those who survived the killing operations said that the gunmen were speaking in a pure Iraqi dialect

| 221 | 62

4532 قُطْن *n.* cotton

يعتمد جمع القطن على الأطفال وهي مهمة ليست شاقة — The gathering of cotton depends on children, and it is a task that is not difficult

| 279 | 49

4533 أعْمَق *elat.* deeper/deepest

إن الأمر أعمق بكثير مما يتصوره العامة — The matter is a lot deeper than the general public imagines

| 220 | 62

4534 البروفسور /brofisoor/ بروفسور *n.* professor; Prof.

نشرت مقالات البروفسور يوست في الواشنطن بوست — Professor Yost's articles were published in the "Washington Post"

| 277 | 49

4535 صُنْع *n.* manufacture, industry

إيران تكشف طائرة حربية محلية الصنع — Iran is revealing a locally manufactured warplane

| 220 | 62

4536 مُراهَقَة *n.* adolescence; puberty

ينظر كثير من الباحثين الى المراهقة باعتبارها فترة عاصفة في حياة الانسان يسودها التوتر — Many researchers looking at adolescence consider it to be a turbulent stage in the life of a person, filled with stress

| 236 | 58

4537 تَعاوَنَ *v. VI* to cooperate, collaborate
with sb مع
— ما دمت تعرف أنهم هكذا فكيف تتعاون معهم؟
As long as you know that they are that way,
how can you cooperate with them?

62 | 218 |

4538 مَلِيّ *n.* long time; مَلِيًّا for a long time,
for quite some time
تطلعت إليه مليا كأنها تختبر صدقه — She looked at
him for quite a while, as if she was testing his
truthfulness

46 | 295 | +lit

4539 تَوْلِيد *n.* producing, generating (energy,
electricity)
الحكومة تعمل على جذب بعض الاستثمارات بغض النظر
عن جنسيتها بهدف توليد مزيد من فرص العمل
لابناء مصر — The government is working on
attracting investment without regard to its
nationality, with the goal of generating more
job opportunities for the sons of Egypt

55 | 245 |

4540 عُنْصُرِيَّة *n.* racism
إن تجارب الحرب العالمية الأولى والثانية أثبتت أن
العنصرية والقومية لا تأتي إلا بالدمار والحروب
وسكب المزيد من الدماء — The experiences
of the First and Second World Wars proved
that racism and nationalism only come
with destruction and wars, and spilling a lot
of blood

51 | 264 |

4541 شائِع *adj.* widespread, well-known
من الأخطاء الشائعة بين الطلبة السهر طويلا في ليالي
الامتحانات — One of the common mistakes
students make is to stay up late the night
before exams

56 | 243 |

4542 مُرْفَق *adj.* attached, appended; enclosed
كنا هنا نقدم تمثيلية عن حياة المسيح في المسرح المرفق
بالمستشفى ، وأنا أمثل هنا دور يوسف النجار — We
were here presenting a play about the life of
Christ in the theater attached to the hospital,
and I was playing here the part of Joseph the
carpenter

50 | 268 |

4543 مِسْتَر *n.* Mr/Mister
— وأنت يا مستر كروسمان ماذا تعتقد؟ And you,
Mr Crossman, what do you believe?

35 | 380 | +lit

4544 خاطَبَ *v. III* to address, speak to sb
العيب فيك لأنك لم تتغير.. الرئيس لا يخاطب
أمثالك بل يخاطب الشباب المتعلم بلغة التقدم —
The fault is in you, since you did not change...
The president is not addressing the likes of
you, but rather is addressing the educated
youths in the language of progress

58 | 232 |

4545 مُتَناوَل *n.* في مُتَناوَل اليَد within reach, available
ألقوا على المتظاهرين بكل ما وجدوه في متناول
أيديهم، بدءا من البيض النيء والطماطم الفاسدة
وحتى الحجارة والهراوات — They threw onto
the demonstrators everything they could get
their hands on, beginning with raw eggs and
rotten tomatoes, and even stones and sticks

61 | 221 |

4546 تَخَرَّجَ *v. V* to graduate من from
درس في ثانوية الشويخ وتخرج فيها عام ١٩٦٨ —
He studied at the Al-Shuyukh Secondary
School and graduated there in 1968

61 | 221 |

4547 كابْتِن *n.* captain; (title) Captain
حصل الكابتن أحمد الغيلاني على كأس أفضل مدرب
— Captain Ahmad Al-Ghilani got the cup for
best trainer

39 | 339 |

4548 غَيْمَة *n.* pl. غُيُوم cloud
طقس: جو مشمس إلى قليل الغيوم بالشمال هذه
الظهيرة وصحو خلال الليلة القادمة — Weather:
sunny skies to a few clouds in the north
this afternoon, and clear during the coming
night

47 | 286 | +lit

4549 دِراما *n.* drama
الأوبريت الغنائي يمزج بين الدراما والشعر والغناء
— The (singing) operetta mixes between
drama, poetry, and singing

41 | 323 |

4550 مَسِيحِيَّة *n.* Christianity

هناك أمر آخر هو أن تعاليم المسيحية لم ينفذها أحد ، وبقيت مجرد كلمات مقروءة أو مكتوبة — There's another thing, and that is that no one has ever put Christianity into practice, it has remained mere written or read words

50 | 268 |

4551 دِيانَة *n.* pl. -aat religion, creed

جميع الديانات، على ما أعلم، تعالج الأمر بنفس المنظار — All the religions, as far as I know, treat the matter from the same point of view (with the same lens)

52 | 258 |

4552 هَيْكَلَة *vn.* structuring, framing; organizing, composing; *n.* framework, structure, make-up

لقد سارعت الحكومة إلى إعادة هيكلة صناعة الدواجن، وذلك بإعداد تشريع ينظم هذه الصناعة المهمة — The government hastened to prepare a structure for the poultry industry, and that by preparing legislation which organizes this important industry

44 | 303 |

4553 تَعْمِيق *vn.* deepening; broadening, strengthening (collaboration, partnership)

قالت مديرة المركز كاملة عبيدات ان المركز يهدف الى تعميق وعي الطلبة — The director of the center, Kamila Ubeidat, said that the center aims to deepen the consciousness of the students

52 | 256 |

4554 مُعَظَّم *adj.* glorified, venerated; majesty

أشترط قبل كل شيء أن يوافق جلالة الملك المعظم على هذا الرأي — I would stipulate, before everything, that His Majesty the King must agree with this view

31 | 429 | +news

4555 عَوَّض *v. II* to repay, compensate, reward sb; to replace, substitute for sth/sb

اجعلي من كلماته بلسما لجراحك وعسى أن يعوض صبرك خيرا — Make his words a salve to your wounds and perhaps your patience will be rewarded with good

74 | 182 |

4556 هاوِيَة *n.* cliff, precipice; abyss, chasm

علمتنا التجارب أن الولايات المتحدة تستخدم سياسة حافة الهاوية دائما لتحقيق مقاصد في سياستها الخارجية — Experiences have taught us that the United States always uses the policy of "the edge of the cliff" to accomplish aims in its foreign policy

58 | 232 |

4557 أَدَقّ *elat.* more/most accurate, precise

يبدو أن الحفيدين قادمان.. ما أدق مواعيدهما — It looks like the two grandkids are coming... How precise their appointments are

65 | 204 |

4558 باي (Dia.) *interj.* bye! goodbye!

مع السلامة باي باي وداعا — Goodbye, bye bye, goodbye

32 | 418 | +spo

4559 مِسْك *n.* musk

يا رب اجعل ذكرك في قلبي كازهار المسك والريحان — Lord, make your remembrance in my heart like the musk and basil flowers

48 | 276 |

4560 رُقْعَة *n.* patch, plot of land, area; range, scope; (chess) board, (checkers) board; coupon, ticket; (computer) board or card

استخدام الانترنت وسع إلى حد بعيد رقعة حركة حقوق الإنسان في مصر وعزز فعاليتها — Use of the Internet has expanded to a great extent the scope of the Human Rights movement in Egypt and has strengthened its effectiveness

60 | 223 |

4561 اِسْتِعْمارِيّ *adj.* colonialist; (related to) building of settlements

معظم المتاحف الجزائرية إما أنها بنيت في الحقبة الاستعمارية أو أثناء التواجد التركي بالجزائر — Most of the Algerian museums were either built in the colonial period or during the Turkish presence in Algeria

49 | 273 |

4562 تَعَدُّدِيَّة *n.* multiplicity, pluralism, plurality

تدعو إلى نوع من الوفاق الثقافي وإلى قبول التعددية الثقافية ووقف حملات الإبادة والتصفية — She is calling for a type of cultural harmony and for

accepting cultural pluralism and stopping the campaigns of destruction and elimination

50 | 265 |

4563 وَثِيق *adj.* secure, firm, solid; steady, reliable
أكدت على العلاقات الوثيقة التي تربط أبو مازن بالبيت الأبيض — She stressed the firm relationship that binds Abu Mazin with the White House

63 | 212 |

4564 اِسْتِبْعاد *n.* ruling out, regarding as unlikely; excluding
لماذا تم استبعاد الأحزاب الوطنية اللبنانية من المشاركة في المؤتمر؟ — Why was the Lebanese National Party excluded from participation in the conference?

57 | 233 |

4565 باقَة *n.* bouquet (flowers); packet (computer, satellite communications, etc.)
اقدم لك شكري واعتزازي لردك الكريم.. مع باقة ا — من الزهور الصيفية.. متمنيا بأن تنال اعجابك offer you my thanks and appreciation for your kind response...with a bouquet of summer flowers...hoping that you will like them

56 | 236 |

4566 كُرْه and كَرْه *n.* hatred, loathing; عَلى كُرْهٍ and كُرْهاً unwillingly, reluctantly, forcibly
من أسباب كره المعلم للمدرسة تسلط المدير وتهميش دور المعلم — One of the reasons the teacher hates the school is the control of the director and the marginalization of the role of the teacher

53 | 249 |

4567 شَهِيَّة *n.* appetite
لم أجع بعد.. لا أجد شهية للطعام — I didn't get hungry yet...I can't find an appetite for the food

56 | 238 |

4568 مُرْشِد *n.* guide, instructor; adviser, aide
حينما دلفت إلى معبد الكرنك، أخذ المرشد يشرح، قائلا: هذا ليس معبد، هذه مدينة — When I walked around the Karnak Temple, the guide began to explain, saying: This is not a temple, this is a city

51 | 257 |

4569 قابِض *adj.* holding (company, bank)
قال إن من أبرز المشاريع التي حددتها الشركة الكويتية الأردنية القابضة إنشاء منتجع سياحي ومركز تجاري في مدينة العقبة — He said that among the most prominent of the projects which the Kuwait Jordan Holding Company was planning was the building of a tourist resort and commercial center in the city of Aqaba

37 | 360 |

4570 تَمْكِين *n.* enabling, making possible
تعمل الحكومة على تمكين المرأة للاستفادة من فرص التعليم — The government is working on enabling women to benefit from educational opportunities

55 | 241 |

4571 رَصاصَة *n.* bullet; shot
العالم يعرف ان الليبي السجين سياسيا، لا يساوي ثمن رصاصة — The world knows that a Libyan who is imprisoned for political reasons is not worth the price of a bullet

59 | 224 |

4572 مَحْو *n.* eradication, elimination; erasing, wiping out
المؤتمر السنوي الخامس سيستعرض تجارب اشخاص استطاعوا محو أميتهم وتعلم حرف واكتساب مهارات ساعدتهم على زيادة دخلهم — The fifth annual conference will display the experiences of people who were able to overcome their illiteracy and learn trades and gain skills which helped them increase their income

57 | 232 |

4573 تَوْصِيل *n.* connection, contact
دخلوا في قوائم انتظار في انتظار توصيل الكهرباء إلى بناياتهم — They put their names on waiting lists in anticipation of electricity being connected to their buildings

52 | 251 |

4574 بَحْت *adj.* pure, exclusive
قد حول الجمهورية إلى نظام ديمقراطي بحت — He transformed the republic into a purely democratic system

52 | 252 |

4575 حَشَرة *n.* pl. -aat insect

أولا: ينظف مكان لدغة الحشرات ثم يدلك بالثوم المفروم حيث يعمل على تطهير المكان المصاب — First: the site of the insect bite is cleaned, and then it is massaged with chopped garlic which works to purify the affected region

53 | 245 |

4576 رَيْثَا *conj.* as long as; until

اعتبرت الأمر خطوة بالاتجاه الصحيح، وعليها الصبر قليلا ريثا تصل إلى قرار، ومن بعده ستصبح أحسن — She considered the matter to be a step in the right direction, and that she needed to have a bit of patience until she reached a decision, and after that she would be better

46 | 281 | +lit

4577 قامُوس *n.* dictionary, lexicon; vocabulary

كلمة أصدقائنا في قاموس المؤسسة الأميركية فتعني الاسرائيليين لا أي طرف آخر — The word "our friends" in the dictionary of the American establishment means the Israelis and not any other party

62 | 211 |

4578 بنَاية *n.* building, edifice; structure

كانت عائلته تمتلك بناية كبيرة جنوب طريق ستانتون، قرب شارع الملوك — His family owned a big building south of Stanton Road, near Kings Street

54 | 241 |

4579 سُيُولَة *n.* liquid state, liquidity

تمكن أصحاب تلك المصارف من تحقيق أرباح ضخمة عبر السيولة التي يملكونها بتصريفها إلى دولارات وتهريبها إلى خارج البلاد — The owners of these banks were able to achieve huge earnings through the liquidity which they possess by changing them to dollars and smuggling them out of the country

43 | 301 |

4580 تَلاعُب *n.* manipulation, tampering

تعيش وتسترزق عن طريق استغلال اموال صغار المستثمرين من خلال التلاعب بالسوق — She is living and earning her living by exploiting the money of small investors by manipulating the market

60 | 216 |

4581 تَخْصِيب *n.* fertilization; enrichment (uranium)

تنتهي اليوم المهلة التي حددها مجلس الامن لوقف طهران تخصيب اليورانيوم — Today is the end of the period set by the Security Council for Tehran to stop the enrichment of uranium

41 | 316 | +news

4582 شِلْو *n.* pl. أَشْلاء corpse; body part, limb; piece, fragment

تناثرت أشلاء الجثث داخل الحافلات التي كانت تستعد لمغادرة المحطة — Body parts were scattered about inside the buses which were preparing to leave the station

49 | 263 | +lit

4583 شَبابِيّ *adj.* youthful, juvenile; of or relating to youths

لا حديث داخل الأوساط الشبابية في مصر هذه الأيام سوى عن قضية التزوير — There is no talk in youthful circles of Egypt these days except about the issue of counterfeiting

48 | 268 |

4584 رَكْلَة *n.* kick, shot (in sports)

سجل العمري هدفا ثانيا للكرمل من ركلة جزاء في الدقيقة ٥٧ — Al-Amry scored a second goal for Karmel off of a penalty kick in the 57th minute

37 | 346 |

4585 مَرْجُوّ *adj.* requested, desired, wished for

فشلت زيادة عدد القوات في اعطاء النتائج المرجوة — The increase in the number of troops failed to give desired for results

58 | 224 |

4586 صُلْح *n.* peace, reconciliation

عرض الصلح على صلاح الدين، فقبل بشرط ألّا يبقى في يد الصليبيين سوى الساحل من يافا إلى عكا — He offered Salah Al-Din a truce, and he accepted on condition that nothing would remain in the hands of the Crusaders except the coast from Jaffa to Akka

52 | 248 |

4587 عاطِل *adj.* pl. -uun (عَن العَمَل) unemployed, jobless; broken, non-functioning, out of order; useless, worthless, no-good; (Dia.) حَظّ عاطِل bad luck

— الوقت ليست بالأمور الهامة لدى العاطلين
Time is not one of the important things for
the unemployed

55 | 234 |

4588 سَرِيَّة *n.* pl. سَرايا (military) company,
squadron

قد أكد لهم قائد السرية أنهم جاءوا لأسرها وليس
قتلها — The leader of the squadron assured
them that they came to capture her, not to
kill her

36 | 352 |

4589 أَنَّ *v. I (i)* to complain, moan

شعر بألم شديد في إحدى قدميه، وبقي ممددا يئن
ويستغيث حتى مرت سيارة الإسعاف فحملته
وانطلقت — He felt a sharp pain in one of his
feet, and he stayed on the ground, moaning
and calling for help until an ambulance came
by, picked him up and set off

44 | 294 | +lit

4590 دلوقتي/دلوقت (Egy.) /dilwa'ti/ *adv.* now

قالت لهم ده أنا ساكنة هنا دلوقتى — She told
them: I live here now

19 | 685 | +spo

4591 مُحال *adj.* impossible, absurd; *p.p.* referred,
assigned على to; transferred, passed on
إلى to

القوى العظمى تحارب لتنتصر، لكن اذا وجدت ان
النصر محال فإنها ستعيد حساباتها وترى حربها فاشلة،
بل عبثية — The great powers fight to win, but
if they find that victory is impossible, they
re-evaluate and view their war as a failure,
indeed a waste of time

50 | 256 |

4592 لـ *part.* (with jussive) لِيَكُنْ let there be;
وَلْيَكُنْ/ فَلْيَكُنْ (فَ and وَ after) let there be
لا تضيع هذه الفرصة واختر وقتا يقل فيه الزحام
وليكن أول الشهر — Don't waste this
opportunity; choose a time in which it is less
crowded, and let it be the beginning of the
month

57 | 227 |

4593 هَنِيء *adj.* healthful, beneficial; good,
pleasant; هَنِيئاً bon appétit! cheers!

— هنيئا لوالديك ولزوجتك ولجميع عائلة الغنام
Congratulations to your parents and to your
wife and to all the Al-Ghanam family

47 | 274 | +lit +for

4594 شاكِر *adj.* thankful, grateful

انحنيت شاكرا واعدا بتتميم ما يجب على الابن نحو
صديق أبيه — I bowed in thanks, promising
to do what a son owes to the friend of his
father

52 | 245 |

4595 ياسُمين *n.* jasmine

نستطيع تشبيه الحب بشجيرة الياسمين الصغيرة التي
تحتاج للرعاية لتكبر وتزهر وتبدأ جذورها بالتشبث
بالأرض — We can compare love to a small
jasmine bush which needs care to grow and
flower and for its roots to cling to the earth

44 | 294 |

4596 أَرْجَح *elat.* more/most likely, probable

نجحوا في التهرب من العدالة، وإنه من الأرجح ألا
تجري محاكمتهم على ما اقترفت أيديهم — They
succeeded in fleeing from justice, and it is likely
that they will not be tried for what they did

54 | 239 |

4597 مُلاحَقَة *n.* pursuit, chase; legal prosecution

— الجيش يواصل ملاحقة المعتدين في مخيم نهر البارد
The army is continuing to pursue the
aggressors in Camp Nahr Al-Barid

58 | 223 |

4598 كَرْبُون *n.* carbon

كان جوها مشحونا بكميات من ثاني اكسيد الكربون
والامونيا والميثان — Its air was laden with
quantities of CO_2 and ammonia and methane

49 | 262 |

4599 زفاف *n.* wedding

يصر عمها على سفره من باريس الى قسنطينة لحضور
الزفاف ومباركة الزيجة — Her uncle insists on
traveling from Paris to Constantine to attend
the wedding and bless the couple

51 | 250 |

4600 لَذيذ *adj.* delicious; delightful, marvelous

نظرت إلى الخروفين وأنا أشعر بالجوع ممنيا معدتي
بطعام شهي لذيذ — I looked at the two sheep,

feeling hungry, my stomach hoping for some delicious, wonderful food

47 | 270 |

4601 تُفَّاح *coll.n.* apples
اظهرت الدراسات الطبية تركيزا شديدا على فوائد تناول التفاح في منع نشوء السرطان — Medical studies have shown a strong focus on the benefits of eating apples in preventing the growth of cancer

46 | 279 |

4602 حَياتِيّ *adj.* biological, living; daily life related
التجربة الشعرية ليست بالضرورة هي التجربة الحياتية للشاعر، فالشاعر انتقائي في إبداعه — The poetic experience is not, of necessity, the life experience of the poet, since the poet is selective in his creativity

58 | 222 |

4603 تَبِعَة *n.* pl. -aat consequence; responsibility
أنا مستعد لتحمل كافة تبعات منصبي السياسية والقانونية — I am prepared to bear all the political and legal responsibilities of my office

62 | 206 |

4604 خُضُوع *n.* submission, subjection; undergoing (surgery)
إن اثنين من إخوته يتمردان عليه، ويرفضان الخضوع لزعامته — Two of his brothers are rebelling against him, and they refuse to be subject to his leadership

61 | 210 |

4605 مُهَاجَمة *n.* attack, assault; raid, strike
جدد الجيش التركي التأكيد على ضرورة مهاجمة المتمردين الأكراد داخل الأراضي العراقية — The Turkish army renewed its affirmation of the necessity of attacking the Kurdish rebels inside Iraqi lands

60 | 213 |

4606 مُوب and مُب (Gul.) *neg.part.* not
أظن الحياه بدون ألم وأمل مب حلوه — I think that life without pain and hope is not sweet

17 | 744 | +for

4607 أَضْحَى *n.* sacrifice, immolation; عِيد الأضحى Feast of the Sacrifice
يعود أبناؤنا وبناتنا هذا الأسبوع إلى مدارسهم بعد إجازة عيد الأضحى المبارك — Our sons and daughters are returning this week to their schools after the Blessed Feast of the Sacrifice vacation

50 | 255 |

4608 إِمْسَاك *vn.* holding (sth); refraining (عن from); *n.* restraint; (med.) constipation; imsak (start of Ramadan fast)
ولم يتشاجرا حول من يحق له الإمساك بالريموت — كونترول أمام التلفاز — They didn't fight over who had the right to hold the remote control for the TV

53 | 240 |

4609 هول /hool/ (Lev.) *dem.pron.* these (contraction of هذول /hadhool/)
ما كملوا معي المسابقة هول — Those guys didn't finish the race with me

28 | 458 | +spo

4610 تَنْبِيه *n.* warning, alarm
يستعمل الكلام كما يستعمل قائد السيارة آلة التنبيه — He uses words like a car driver uses the horn

55 | 230 |

4611 تَنَام (تَنَامِي .def) *n.* gradual growth, steady increase
الأطراف الثلاثة متخوفون من تنامي التشدد والتطرف من باكستان مرورا بأفغانستان وإيران وفلسطين — The three parties are afraid of the growth of extremism from Pakistan passing through Afghanistan, Iran, and Palestine

55 | 233 |

4612 غَيْبُوبَة *n.* unconsciousness; trance; coma
أصيب بمرض حاد في الأوعية الدموية، فرقد في غيبوبة تامة — He was smitten with a serious disease in the cardiovascular system, so he has been lying in a complete coma

60 | 212 |

4613 بَدَّل *v. II* to change, modify sth; to substitute sth ب for sth else
أخذ نسخة جديدة وبدل الستايل اللي عندك بالستايل الموجود والملفات اللي عندك بالملفات الموجودة

He took a new copy and changed the style you have with the style that was there, and the files you have with the files that were there

63 | 203 |

4614 مُحَذِّر *a.p.* warning, cautioning

أشار بيده اليسرى إلى جهة الباب الحديدي، محذرا من قدوم الحارس — He pointed with his left hand in the direction of the iron door, warning of the coming of the guard

54 | 235 |

4615 إِزَّاي (Egy.) *adv.* how, just how; how come, why

ازاي هو مردش علينا ده احنا مرتين كلمناه — How could he not respond to us, we spoke to him twice!

35 | 365 | +spo

4616 يُسْر *n.* ease, facility; affluence, prosperity

لقد اخترنا ان نقوم بهذه الجولة لكي نوضح للراغبين كيفية عمل ذلك بكل سهولة ويسر — We chose to make this trip to clarify to those who want to know how to do this with ease

59 | 214 |

4617 كَامِن *adj.* hidden, concealed, secret; latent, dormant

كان ألبانيا أصيلا ولكنه فجر الكثير من الطاقات الكامنة في نفوس الفلاحين المصريين العرب — He was pure Albanian, but he expanded many of the hidden powers in the souls of the Arab Egyptian farmers

59 | 214 |

4618 مَدْعُوّ *adj.* invited, called; named

هذا الرجل المدعو الرنتيسي خطر علي وعليك وعلى كل يهودي — This man who is called Al-Rantisi is a danger to me and to you and to every Jew

50 | 251 |

4619 غَرَابَة *n.* strangeness, oddness

قلت لمريم إن النهاية قد تكون أكثر غرابة.. هذه بيروت — I told Miryam that the end could be even more strange...this is Beirut

55 | 231 |

4620 طَمُوح *adj.* ambitious, desirous

لدينا الآن مشروع طموح جدا وهو مشروع الحوار الاجتماعي — We now have a very ambitious project, and it is the social dialog project

74 | 170 |

4621 ثَأْر *n.* revenge, retaliation

من المحرم لدى العشائر ارتكاب عملية الثأر في حق المرأة او الطفل او المسن — It is forbidden among the clans to commit an act of revenge against a woman, child, or elderly person

52 | 242 |

4622 خَلْط *n.* mixing, blending; mixture, blend

كان عرفة منهمكا في خلط بعض المواد وعجنها في وعاء من الفخار كبير — Arafa was engrossed in mixing some materials and kneading them together in a big ceramic vessel

61 | 207 |

4623 غِشّ *n.* cheating, swindling

إنها أحدث طريقة ابتكرناها لمنع الغش والتزوير، كما أنها أسهل طريقة وأكثرها دقة وتوفيرا للوقت — It is the latest way we have invented to prevent cheating and fraud, and it is also the easiest and most precise way to save time

55 | 230 |

4624 عَدا *v. I (u)* to run, race; to gallop; لا يَعْدُو أَنْ and لا يَعْدُو كَوْنَ it is nothing but, it is merely

الوعل ذو القرون الطويلة هو أسرع المخلوقات على وجه هذه الأرض، انه يستطيع أن يعدو بسرعة ثابتة قدرها ٣٥ ميلا في الساعة لعدد كبير من الأميال — The long-horned ibex is one of the fastest creatures on earth; it can run at a fixed speed estimated at 35 miles an hour for a number of miles

56 | 226 |

4625 تُرَاثِيّ *adj.* heritage-based, historical; inherited

تعد الاثار والمواقع الاثرية والبنى التراثية من الثروات الوطنية — The ruins and archeological sites and the heritage buildings are considered to be part of the national wealth

51 | 248 |

4626 حَلْبَة *n.* arena, ring, circuit, track
أولئك الذين لا يشاركون فسيبقون خارج حلبة النقاش — Those who don't participate will remain outside the arena of discussion
53 | 239 |

4627 أَسْمَى *elat.* higher/highest, loftier/loftiest
تفضلوا حضرة القائد وأخي العزيز بقبول أسمى عبارات التقدير والمودة — Mr Leader, my dear brother, please accept our highest expressions of esteem and love
55 | 229 |

4628 أَصْدَق *elat.* truer/truest; more/most reliable
ليس ثمة عمل أدبي في البرازيل يرسم صورة أصدق عن الروابط العاطفية بين المهاجرين الذين غادروا البلاد ومواطنيهم الذين ظلوا فيها، من الرواية المؤثرة التي أصدرها اميل فرحات في عنوان «مال على الطريق» — There is not a literary work in Brazil which paints a truer picture of the emotional ties between the emigrants who left the country, and citizens who stayed in it, than the affecting novel which Emile Farahat published with the title "Money on the Road"
59 | 213 |

4629 تَراكُم *n.* build-up, accumulation; backlog
تعطل عمل المستشفيات والنقل الجوي والبري بسبب تراكم الثلوج التي غطت مناطق واسعة من اليابان اليوم الخميس — The work of the hospitals was interrupted, as well as air and land transport, because of the build-up of snow which covered wide areas of Japan today, Thursday
60 | 208 |

4630 قَميص *n.* pl. قُمْصان shirt
نفسي اتمشى على النيل في أكتوبر وأنا لابس قميص بكم قصير — I would like to take a stroll along the Nile in October, wearing a short-sleeved shirt
57 | 219 |

4631 حَمِدَ *v. I (a)* to praise, extol, glorify sb; to applaud (sb's position)
وأحمد الله أنني حضرت هذا الحفل — I praise God that I was able to attend this ceremony
54 | 231 |

4632 سِمْنَة *n.* fat; obesity
مكافحة السمنة تساعد على تقليل احتمالات الإصابة بأمراض القلب — Fighting obesity helps reduce the possibility of being struck with heart diseases
43 | 290 |

4633 مُسْوَدَّة *n.* rough draft
لقد انتحر همنغواي أيضا صيف ١٩٦١ تاركا خلفه مسودة روايته الأخيرة «الصيف الخطر» — Hemingway committed suicide also in the summer of 1961 leaving behind a rough draft of his last novel "The Dangerous Summer"
47 | 263 |

4634 فَتْحَة *n.* opening; porthole; fatha (Arabic short vowel "a")
وقعا في الحب عبر فتحة صغيرة في باب حديدي — They fell in love through a small opening in an iron door
48 | 259 |

4635 اِعْتِصام *vn.* adhering, holding on (ب to); taking refuge (ب in); *n.* sit-in strike
قد أعرب العديد من المشاركين في الاعتصام عن استيائهم من الأزمة الاقتصادية التي يعاني منها المواطنون — Many of the participants in the sit-in expressed their disgust at the economic crisis which the citizens are suffering from
46 | 274 |

4636 لَعِين *adj.* accursed, damned; hateful
تمنيت لو قدرت على مد أصابعي وخنقت هذا الفأر اللعين الذي غدا يطاردني في كل مكان — I hoped I would be able to stretch my fingers and strangle that cursed mouse which has started to pursue me everywhere
44 | 281 | +lit

4637 اِسْتِلام *n.* receiving, accepting
لم يتردد من استلام كأسه، لكنه فكر قليلا قبل الشرب — He did not hesitate to accept the cup, but he thought a bit before drinking
55 | 225 |

4638 حام *n.* pl. حُماة (def. حامِي) *n.* protector, guardian; patron; *adj.* hot, burning; fierce, passionate

ستبقى فتح حامية المشروع الوطني وستعود إلى قيادة الشعب الفلسطيني — Fatah will remain the protector of the national project and it will return to the leadership of the Palestinian people

47 | 266 |

4639 فَنَاء *n.* extinction, doom, end
تدرك القوى الكبرى أن استخدام الأسلحة النووية يعني فناء الجميع — The major powers realize that using nuclear arms means the annihilation of everyone

46 | 271 | +lit

4640 أَهْوَن *adj.* easy, simple; comfortable, convenient; unimportant, insignificant; *elat.* easier/easiest; lesser/least; lower/lowest
قال ان التعامل مع الميليشيات أهون على الحكومة من التعامل مع المسلحين — He said that dealing with the militias was easier for the government than dealing with the gunmen

57 | 216 |

4641 قَوَّى *v. II* to strengthen, fortify
نظام الغذاء ونمط الحياة المناسب لتركيبة الفرد، يقوي الجسم والعقل والوعي — Diet and a lifestyle appropriate for the composition of the individual strengthen the body, the mind, and the consciousness

60 | 207 |

4642 مَعِيشِيّ *adj.* livelihood-related; living (conditions, circumstances)
أقيمت مشروعات صغيرة بهدف توفير فرص عمل للشباب وتحسين المستويات المعيشية للفئات غير القادرة في المجتمع — Small projects were set up with the goal of providing job opportunities to youths and improving the living standard of the less able groups in society

53 | 235 |

4643 عَشِيرَة *n.* pl. عَشَائِر clan, tribe
إن أغلب العشائر البدوية التي تمتلك الجمال لا تأكل لحمها إلا عند الضرورة — Most Bedouin clans that own camels don't eat their meat except when necessary

45 | 275 |

4644 عِشاء *n.* evening; صَلَاة العِشاءِ evening prayer

قال صلى الله عليه و سلم: من صلى العشاء في جماعة فكأنما قام نصف الليل — (Muhammad), peace be upon him, said: He who prays the evening prayer in the mosque with a group, it is as if he stood praying half the night

51 | 243 |

4645 آلَ *v. I (u)* to become, turn into, come to be إلى sth (to reach a certain state)
يؤسفني ما آلت اليه التداعيات في العلاقات السورية السعودية — I feel bad for what the degeneration in Syrian-Saudi relations has come to

42 | 291 |

4646 عنان *n.* bridle, reins
استلقيت على فراشي بعد تعب اليوم المضني مطلقا عنان الذاكرة لاحدى رحلاتي اليومية — I threw myself onto my bed after the tiredness of the difficult day, loosing the reins to memory of one of my daily trips

59 | 209 |

4647 عَذْراء *fem.n./adj.* virgin; العَذْراء (مَرْيَم) The Virgin Mary; العَذْراء (بُرْج) Virgo
كانت فقط تنتظره وتدعو له العذراء أن تحفظه من أى مكروه — She was only waiting for him and calling on the Virgin to protect him from any harm

48 | 256 |

4648 بَطِيء *adj.* slow
ساروا بخطى بطيئة وعيون فاحصة إلى مسرح الجريمة — They walked with slow steps and searching eyes to the scene of the crime

57 | 218 |

4649 مُذْهِل *adj.* amazing, startling
يعمل الدكتور بدرجة مذهلة من التركيز — The doctor works with an amazing degree of concentration

58 | 212 |

4650 أَدْلَى *v. IV* to give, express ب (opinion); to provide, grant ب sth
وقال الإدريسي في تصريح أدلى به: لا يمكن تزوير التاريخ بهذا الشكل — Idrissi said in a statement he gave: It is not possible to falsify history in this manner

54 | 227 |

4651 مُدْرَج *adj.* registered, listed; included, incorporated

عدد الشركات المدرجة حاليا في سوق الأوراق المالية السعودي يقل عن ٩٠ شركة — The number of companies currently listed in the Saudi Money Exchange Market is less than 90

40 | 303 |

4652 صَرْح *n.* building, structure, edifice; institution

يسرني في هذا الظرف ان اكون بينكم في هذا الصرح الثقافي العريق الذي كان ولا يزال منارة للروح واشعاعا للفكر — It gives me pleasure in this circumstance to be among you in this deep-rooted cultural institution which was and still is a lighthouse for the spirit and radiation for thought

55 | 224 |

4653 بَريق *n.* sparkle, glitter; luster, shine

يمعن النظر إلى وجهها ويتأمل بريق الدموع التي اغرورقت في عينيها — He stares at her face and contemplates the shimmer of the tears which filled her eyes

53 | 231 |

4654 مَبْسوط *adj.* happy, cheerful; satisfied, content

ايوه يا حاج والله العظيم انا مبسوطة دا إن انا سمعت صوتكو — Yes, Hajj, by God (really) I am fine, (especially since) I heard your voice

28 | 441 | +spo

4655 إِنْذار *n.* warning, caution, alarm

تأتي المقاطعة من المذيع من دون سابق إنذار، ويكتفي الضيف بالوقوف على آخر حرف قاله قبل مقاطعة المذيع — The cut-off comes from the announcer without prior warning, and the guest has to be satisfied with standing on the last letter he said before the announcer cut him off

58 | 209 |

4656 قُرْآنِي *adj.* Qurʾanic

منهم من دعا إلى التعامل مع الآيات القرآنية كنصوص تاريخية تخضع للنقد — Among them are those who call for treating Qurʾanic verses like historical texts which are subject to criticism

58 | 209 |

4657 إِبْراز *n.* highlighting, emphasizing, accentuating

وقد تم إبراز هذه المسألة في العديد من فصول هذا الكتاب — This issue has been highlighted in a number of chapters of this book

57 | 213 |

4658 جَليد *n.* ice

يمكن أيضا تذويب الجليد في الماء البارد في أكياس عازلة للماء وتغيير الماء كل ٣٠ دقيقة إلى أن يذوب الجليد — The ice can also be melted in cold water in sacks that protect it from the water, and changing the water every 30 minutes until the ice melts

56 | 217 |

4659 عَجيبَة *n.* pl. عَجائِب marvel, wonder

تبدو مسابقة التصويت لاختيار عجائب الدنيا السبع الجديدة محكومة بالكثير من العوامل غير الثقافية — The competition for voting on choosing the seven new wonders of the world appears to be governed by a lot of non-cultural factors

54 | 225 |

4660 خوش /khoosh/ (Irq.) *adj.* good, fine, great

والله خوش لاعب. صاحب تمريرات حلوه وصاحب اخلاق عاليه — Really, he's a great player. He makes good passes and is a man of high moral character

23 | 519 | +spo

4661 بَتَّة *n.* البَتَّة (not) at all; (none) whatsoever; in (no) way, shape, or form

لن نعترف البتة بشرعية الكيان الصهيوني على ارضنا بهدف التكفير عن خطايا سوانا — We will never admit the legality of the Zionist entity on our land in order to atone for the sins of someone else

55 | 222 |

4662 أَشْهَر *elat.* more/most famous

أصبح جورج سوروس، المهاجر من المجر، واحدا من أشهر البليونيرات في اميركا — George Soros, the emigrant from Hungary, became one of the most famous billionaires in America

58 | 210 |

4663 تَمْر *coll.n.* dates (fruit)

يجب البدء بتناول عدد من ثمار التمر لانه يحتوي على نسبة كبيرة من السكريات سريعة الهضم — One

should begin by eating a number of dates, because they contain a high percentage of easily digested sugars

49 | 250 |

4664 اِشْتَرَطَ *v. VIII* to stipulate sth
يشترط لقبول المتقدمين الحصول على شهادة الثانوية العامة — For applicants to be accepted, it is stipulated that they obtain a General Secondary Certificate

59 | 205 |

4665 كُرْدِسْتانِيّ *n./adj.* Kurdistani
فرت مع اسرتها من العراق في ديسمبر ٢٠٠٤ عبر الشمال الكردستاني الى سوريا ومن ثم الى لبنان — She fled with her family from Iraq in December 2004 through Northern Kurdistan to Syria, and from there to Lebanon

36 | 335 |

4666 أَفْضَى *v. IV* to lead إلى to (solution, agreement); to communicate, disclose ب sth
الكاتب لا يفضي بآرائه الشخصية في الرواية — The author does not disclose his personal opinions in the novel

58 | 208 |

4667 مُتَلَقٍّ (مُتَلَقِّي .def) *n.* recipient, (person) receiving
اللافت في ثلاثيته انه يتلاعب مع المتلقي مرجحا اياه بين الشك واليقين، باستمرار — What is noticeable in his trilogy is that he plays with the recipient (the reader), constantly swinging him between doubt and certainty

48 | 251 |

4668 عَيَّطَ *v. II* to scream, shout; (Magh.) to call ل sb (on the phone), to call على for sb
يعطوا لي، أنا ما نعيطش — They need to call me, I won't call (them)

7 | 1670 | +spo

4669 طَبْخ *n.* cooking, cuisine
الحمد لله أنها تعلمت الطبخ من أمها فانتزعت إعجابه — Praise God, she learned to cook from her mother, so she got his admiration

55 | 218 |

4670 بَعْثِيّ *n./adj.* pl. -uun Baathist
قررت قوات التحالف فصل كافة الموظفين البعثيين الذين كانوا يعملون في مختلف إدارات الدولة العراقية — The allied forces decided to fire all the Baathist employees who had worked in the various administrations of the Iraqi state

35 | 341 |

4671 يَدَوِيّ *adj.* manual, by hand
تكثر في هذا الحي متاجر الصناعات اليدوية لانتاج وبيع التذكارات التقليدية — There are a lot of handicraft shops in this quarter for producing and selling traditional souvenirs

57 | 211 |

4672 ثَدْي *n.* breast; udder
اتباع نظام غذائي صحي بعد الاصابة بسرطان الثدي يعد عاملا أساسيا لتحقيق الشفاء وتنشيط الجهاز المناعي — Following a healthy diet after being stricken with breast cancer is considered a basic factor in achieving healing and reactivating the immune system

39 | 307 |

4673 واصِف *adj.* describing, portraying, depicting, characterizing
كان شيراك قد انتقد التصعيد ضد اللبنانيين، واصفا العدوان الصهيوني بأنه «غير متكافئ ولا متناسب» — Chirac had criticized the escalation against the Lebanese, describing the Zionist aggression as "disproportionate and inappropriate"

51 | 236 |

4674 بائِن (باين .Dia) *adj.* clear, plain; evident, obvious; (Dia.) باين (invar.) apparently, it seems أنّ that), باين عليها زَعْلانة she looks angry
باين عليك وعليه مش خايفين من بعض — It is clear that you and he do not fear each other

34 | 353 |

4675 مُؤْسِف *adj.* regrettable, unfortunate; sorry, sad
من المؤسف أن ينقطع انسان عن دراسته العليا — It is regrettable that a person would be cut off from his higher studies

57 | 211 |

4676 سِتِّين *n.* sixtieth year; الستينات the Sixties انا عمري ستين الحين تعبانة — I'm sixty years old now and I'm tired

53 | 224 |

4677 عَمَدَ *v. I (i)* to do sth deliberately في منتصف الخمسينيات عمد إلى محاولة الكتابة للسينما في هوليوود — In the middle of the Fifties, he set out deliberately to write for the cinema in Hollywood

58 | 206 |

4678 شَرِيطَة *n.* condition; شَرِيطَةَ أَنْ on condition that لدي ٥٠ نسخة من أعداد قديمة وحديثة من العربي أود أن أهديها لمن يرغب، شريطة أن يتحمل نفقتها البريدية — I have 50 copies of old and new issues of Al-Arabi, which I want to give to whoever wants them, on condition that he bear the postal expense

58 | 207 |

4679 اِعْتِدال *n.* moderation, restraint مشاركة حماس في الانتخابات دليل على اتجاه نحو الاعتدال لدى الحركة — Hamas' participation in the elections is evidence of a tendency towards moderation in the movement

50 | 238 |

4680 اِسْتَحالَ *v. X* to be impossible (على for sb) أَنْ to do sth; to be transformed (إلى into) يستحيل التكهن بردود أفعاله أو رغباته الدفينة — It is impossible to predict his reactions or his hidden desires

57 | 209 |

4681 عَسْكَر *coll.n.* army, troops أرجو أن يتكرم السادة العسكر بإعطائنا فكرة عن آخر تطورات الحرب — I hope that the soldiers will do us the favor of giving us an idea of the latest developments of the war

47 | 254 |

4682 اِسْتيلاء *n.* appropriation, seizure تمكن الجيش الإنجليزي من الاستيلاء على الساحل بين صور وحيفا، تمهيدا لاحتلال بيت المقدس — The English army was able to take control of the coast between Tyre and Haifa, in preparation for seizing Jerusalem

60 | 200 |

4683 كَفَلَ *v. I (u)* to guarantee sth لِ for sb; to support, maintain, provide for sb الجسد السليم قد يكفل للإنسان سعادة الدنيا فحسب، أما الأخلاق السليمة الصالحة فتكفل له سعادة الدارين الدنيا والآخرة — A sound body might guarantee a man happiness in this world only, but good, sound morals guarantee him happiness both in this world and the hereafter

56 | 214 |

4684 فَريضَة *n.* religious duty يريد أداء فريضة الصلاة ولكنه مريض ولا يستطيع الجلوس إلا على كرسي — He wants to perform the duty of prayer, but he is ill and can only sit on a chair

59 | 202 |

4685 مَنْقُول *adj.* conveyed, transferred; quoted, copied (عن from); mobile هذا خبر منقول من احد الصحف الصينيه — This is news quoted from one of the Chinese newspapers

27 | 446 | +for

4686 أَوْصَى *v. IV* to advise sb (ب to do sth); to make a will هذه الحجرة بالذات كانت في الزمن البعيد قبرا لصاحبها الذي أوصى قبل مماته بأن يدفن فيها — This room, specifically, was in the old days a tomb for its owner who stipulated in his will before his death that he be buried in it

57 | 210 |

4687 جذي /chidhi/ (Gul.) and كذي *adv.* thus, this way, like this انا ما انكر اني بعض الأوقات اصير جذي وهذا غلط طبعا — I don't deny that I sometimes get (become) like that, and this is wrong, of course

14 | 817 | +spo

4688 تَعادَلَ *v. VI* to be balanced, be equitable; to tie (each other, in sports) فاز على مسقط ٢-١ وتعادل مع السيب ٢-٢ — It beat Musqat 2-1, and tied with Al-Sib 2-2

37 | 322 |

4689 أَقْسَى *elat.* harsher/harshest, more/most cruel

ما أقسى الحياة هنا! ما ذنب هؤلاء الأطفال المساكين؟
— How harsh life is here! What is the sin of
these poor children?

52 | 228 |

4690 وَهَج *n.* blaze, fire; glare, glow
كان يسير في وهج الشمس — He was walking
in the glare of the sun

55 | 219 |

4691 كُرَوِيّ *adj.* round, spherical, ball-shaped;
of or relating to football (soccer)
افتتح فريق برشلونة الموسم الكروي الإسباني بفوز
كبير على مضيفه ريال بيتيس بثلاثية نظيفة — The
Barcelona team opened the Spanish soccer
season with a big victory over its host Real
Betis, with a clean triple

35 | 342 |

4692 شَمْسِيّ *adj.* solar, sun-
تعتبر ألمانيا في طليعة الدول التي تنتج أنواع الطاقة
الشمسية — Germany is considered to be in the
vanguard of countries which produce types
of solar power

45 | 266 |

4693 تَسْيِير *n.* propulsion; steering, guidance
لا صحة لما يقال عن سطوة الأحزاب الدينية الشيعية
في تسيير أمور المحافظة بعيدا من سيطرة الدولة
There is no truth to what is being said about
the ascendency of the Shiite religious parties
in steering the affairs of the province far from
the control of the state

50 | 236 |

4694 واقِعِيّة *n.* realism, reality
يقول دعاة الواقعية في العلاقات الدولية أن على
الدولة عدم التدخل في شؤون الغير — Proponents
of realism in international relations say that a
state should not interfere in the affairs of
another

53 | 225 |

4695 مَعْلُوماتِيّ *adj.* informatics, information
technology, information science
نضيف صوتنا إلى صوته منبهين إلى أننا ندخل عصر
الثورة المعلوماتية، وهي ثورة أخطر من كل الثورات
السياسية — We add our voice to his voice
warning that we are entering the age of the
Information Revolution, and it is a more

dangerous revolution than all the political
revolutions

47 | 254 |

4696 وَثِقَ *v. I (i)* to trust ب in sth/sb; to rely,
depend ب on sth/sb
يقول نور الشريف إنه يثق بقدراتها كمخرجة —
Nur Al-Sharif says that he trusts her abilities
as a producer

63 | 190 |

4697 إسْتاد *n.* stadium
يلتقي طنطا مع الترسانة في استاد طنطا في الساعة
الثالثة عصرا — Tanta will meet Tarsana in the
Tanta stadium at three in the afternoon

39 | 301 |

4698 إسْتِهْلاكِيّ *adj.* consumer (goods)
ارتفع مؤشر أسعار السلع الاستهلاكية بنسبة ١,٠ في
المائة في شهر تشرين اول مقارنة بالمتوقع — The
index of consumer prices rose 1.0 percent in
the month of October compared to what was
expected

49 | 244 |

4699 ناشِر *n.* publisher
يفترض أن الكتاب ينشر قبل الرقابة وقبل أي شيء
من الكاتب إلى الناشر ومن الناشر إلى السوق — The
book is supposed to be published before
censorship, and before anything from the
author to the publisher and from the publisher
to the market

31 | 381 |

4700 مَنْفًى *n.* exile, banishment
الظروف صارت أصعب الآن لأنني أصبحت في
المنفى بعد ٥٠ سنة من النضال في الداخل — Things
have gotten more difficult lately because I've
gone into exile after 50 years of struggle
inside the country

49 | 240 |

4701 هَوَى *v. I (i)* to drop, fall down, collapse
كانت دهشته كبيرة عندما رأت رجلا من سقف
المنزل قد هوى على المقعد التي كانت تجلس عليه منذ
دقائق — Her surprise was great when she saw
from the roof of the house a man collapsing
onto the chair on which she had been sitting
minutes before

44 | 268 | +lit

4702 مَكْشُوف *adj.* open, public, candid; exposed, uncovered; open-air
ليس تلك، في تقديري، سوى محاولة مكشوفة من جانب إسرائيل لتطبيع العلاقات مع الدول العربية قبل التوصل إلى اتفاق — This is not, in my estimation, anything but a transparent attempt on the part of Israel to normalize relations with the Arab states before reaching an agreement
59 | 201 |

4703 ثَنِيَّة *n. pl.* ثَنايا incisor; في/بَيْنَ ثَنايا inside, within, among
كم من أمة طاغية ذهبت في ثنايا التاريخ بسبب نكرانها للحقوق — How many oppressive nations have disappeared into history because of their having denied (people) their rights
54 | 217 |

4704 تَحَقُّق *vn.* ascertainment, verification مِن of sth
بدأ التحقق من هوية الرجلين وبدأ في مراجعة أرقامهما الهاتفية — He began to verify the identity of the two men, and to review their telephone numbers
59 | 201 |

4705 وَقْع *n.* impact, effect; impression, imprint; beat (music); fall, falling
للقبلة وقعها الجبار على قلب المرأة بالتحديد — A kiss makes a big impression particularly on the heart of the woman
47 | 251 | +lit

4706 مُشْكِل *n.* problem, difficulty
أعتقد أن المشكل هنا لا يرتبط فقط بزوجي، لكن أيضا بطريقة تطبيق القانون — I believe that the problem here is not only related to my husband, but also to the way the law is applied
44 | 266 |

4707 مَقْطُوع *adj.* cut off, severed; blocked; interrupted; disconnected
الاتصالات مقطوعة بيننا منذ حوالي الشهرين عندما أعلمتني حينها بنتها بالزواج — Communications between us have been cut off for about two months since she informed me at the time of her intention to marry
54 | 217 |

4708 مُفْتَرَق *n.* intersection, junction, crossroads
اليوم الشعب اللبناني يقف عند فترق طرق وهذا من شأنه أن يقرر مستقبل لبنان — Today the Lebanese people are standing at a crossroads and this is likely to decide the future of Lebanon
61 | 192 |

4709 مَعْدِن *n. pl.* مَعادِن mineral, metal
انعكس ضعف الدولار الاميركي ازاء الاورو ايجابا على المعادن الثمينة الاسبوع الماضي — The weakness of the American dollar compared to the Euro reflected positively on precious metals last week
52 | 225 |

4710 مُسْتَدام *adj.* sustainable (development); sustained
ولعل أهمية هذه المشروعات تكمن في انها تأتي منسجمة مع اهداف التنمية الاقتصادية المستدامة التي يسعى الاردن حثيثا لتحقيقها — Perhaps the importance of these projects lies in the fact that they come in coordination with the goals of sustained economic growth which Jordan is diligently trying to achieve
41 | 282 | +news

4711 لِحاق *vn.* catching up ب with; enrollment ب in; meeting, joining up ب with
العرض لا بد له من اللحاق بالطلب — Supply must catch up with the demand
60 | 195 |

4712 مُزْمَع *adj.* imminent, expected; scheduled, planned, intended
اعتقد ان الموقف الاميركي شديد الوضوح بخصوص المؤتمر المزمع عقده — I believe that the American position is extremely clear regarding the conference that is intended to be held
52 | 225 |

4713 خَلَف *n.* substitute; successor; descendant; recompense, compensation
كان بوتين قد وصل إلى السلطة خلفا للرئيس السابق بوريس يلتسي — Putin came to power in succession to the former president Boris Yeltsin
53 | 219 |

4714 خَرَقَ *v. I (i,u)* to pierce, perforate sth; to violate (the law); to exceed, break (barrier)

خرق عشرات الشبان حظر التجول ونظموا مسيرات حاشدة — Scores of youths broke the curfew and organized mass marches

54 | 217 |

4715 فَقْرِيّ and فِقْرِيّ *adj.* spinal, vertebral

شعرت بهذا الانحراف في العمود الفقري منذ ١٥ سنة حتى وصل الى مرحلة الألم — I have felt this curvature in the spine for 15 years, until it reached the level of pain

57 | 205 |

4716 مُمَرِّض *n. pl.* -uun (male) nurse; مُمَرِّضَة *pl.* -aat (female) nurse

التفتت تنظر إلى ممرات المستشفى، لم يكن هناك سوى الممرضات — She turned to look at the halls of the hospital, there was no one there but nurses

43 | 267 |

4717 عِرْض *n. pl.* أَعْراض honor, dignity

أجبرنا برفع السلاح دفاعا عن الأهل والأرض والعرض، ومازال الكفاح المسلح مستمر — It forced us to raise our weapons in defense of family, land and honor, and the armed struggle is continuing

57 | 203 |

4718 أَمْضَى *v. IV* to complete, finalize sth; to spend, pass (time)

ظهر أنه قد أمضى طفولته فى مصر — It appeared that he spent his childhood in Egypt

55 | 210 | +lit

4719 مُرَكَّز *adj.* concentrated, intensive; centralized; condensed; *n.* concentrate

مكثت في العناية المركزة ستة أشهر لا ادري من زارني خلالها — I stayed in intensive care for six months; I don't know who visited me during that time

53 | 219 |

4720 أَحْرَى *elat.* more/most adequate; بالأحرى rather, to be more precise

تلك القصة لم تكن قصتي، أو بالأحرى، حتى الآن لم تكن كذلك — That story was not my story, or more explicitly, until now it wasn't

53 | 218 |

4721 عُمْرِيّ *adj.* age-related, age-based, age group

الفئة العمرية من ٢٣ حتى ٣٠ عام ظهر في زيارتها للموقع الاهتمام الشديد بزيارة مواقع التوظيف — The age group from 23–30 years showed, in their visits to the site, a strong interest in visiting employment sites

49 | 234 |

4722 إخْلاص *n.* sincerity; loyalty

إن الله عز وجل لا يقبل عملا بغير الإخلاص — God, may He be glorified, does not accept an action done without sincerity

49 | 236 |

4723 تَدْقيق *n.* investigation, audit, probe; verification, check; accuracy, precision

أرجأ وفد الخبراء الدوليين إعلان نتائج التدقيق في الانتخابات التشريعية التي جرت في البلاد قبل شهر — The international experts put off the announcement of the results of the investigation of the legislative elections which took place in the country a month ago

55 | 210 |

4724 اجْتِهاد *n.* effort; independent thinking; reinterpretation of the Qurʾan (in light of changing circumstances)

طموحي بلا حدود، وما زالت أمامي سنوات أخرى من الاجتهاد في الجامعة فلن أتنازل عن الاستمرار في تفوقي — My ambition is unbounded, and there are still years of effort in the university ahead of me, so I won't give up continuing to excel

51 | 226 |

4725 الْتِقاط *vn.* obtaining, receiving; taking (photographs)

خلال بضع سنوات ستكون أجهزة التصوير قادرة على التقاط الفيديو العالي الوضوح وبثه لاسلكيا إلى جهاز كومبيوتر لغرض تحريره — In the next few years photographic devices will be able to take high-definition video and send it wirelessly to a computer for editing purposes

58 | 199 |

4726 طَيّ *n.* fold, crease; turn (the page); في طَيّ within, inside

كم نحن في أمس الحاجة الى طي صفحة الماضي البغيض، ومواجهة الأوضاع المستجدة بجدية — We

are in so much need of turning the page of
the hated past, and facing the new situations
with seriousness

53 | 216 |

4727 تَوْقِيف *n.* detention; stopping, halting
اعلنت الشرطة الالمانية توقيف ١١ شخصا امس في
روستوك على هامش تظاهرات معادية لقمة مجموعة
الثاني — German police announced the arrest
of 11 persons yesterday in Rostock on the
sidelines of demonstrations opposed to the
Group of Eight Summit

48 | 238 |

4728 صُومالِيّ *n./adj.* Somali
شهدت العاصمة الصومالية مقديشو تجددا
للاشتباكات بين المقاومة الصومالية وقوات الاحتلال
الإثيوبية — The Somali capital Mogadishu
witnessed a renewal of fighting between the
Somali resistance and the Ethiopian
occupation forces

31 | 363 | +news

4729 عُمّالِيّ *adj.* labor (party); workers
الاضرابات العمالية لا تحدث في العادة الا بعد سلسلة
من المطالبات الودية — Workers strikes don't
usually happen except after a series of friendly
demands

47 | 245 |

4730 اِحْتِقان *n.* congestion; (political) tension
تم اللجوء لمجموعة من الإجراءات التي ساعدت
على الحد من الاحتقان السياسي — Refuge was
taken in a group of measures which helped
to limit political tension

53 | 215 |

4731 بَطْرِيَرْك *n.* (Chr.) patriarch; البطريرك Patriarch
البطريرك هو أعلى مرجعية مسيحية في لبنان —
The patriarch is the highest Christian
authority in Lebanon

29 | 392 |

4732 رَمْي *n.* throwing, tossing, pelting;
shooting (bullets)
يجب على الفلسطينيين في لبنان رمي السلاح كما في
الأردن — The Palestinians in Lebanon
need to throw away their weapons as in
Jordan

58 | 197 |

4733 مَلَأ *n.* crowd; audience, assembly;
على الملأ in public
كيف يستطيع إنسان أن يهين بلاده على الملأ بهذه
البساطة؟ — How can a person insult his
country in public with this ease?

56 | 203 |

4734 اِسْتَوْجَبَ *v. X* to require sth, make sth necessary
لقد أدرك الآن فقط أنه لم يكن هناك ما يستوجب
حضوره ولا هذه العجلة — He just now realized
that there was nothing that required his
coming, nor this urgency

62 | 184 |

4735 مَوَدَّة *n.* friendship, affection
تتابعت اللقاءات وتراكمت الأحاديث وتوثقت المودة
— The meetings continued, and they had
more and more conversations, and the
friendship became strong

57 | 198 |

4736 سالم *adj.* safe, secure, sound, intact
الله يشفيهم ويعافيهم إن شاء الله ويرجعهم لأهلهم
سالمين — May God heal them and give them
health, God-willing, and return them safe to
their families

59 | 190 |

4737 رَقِيب *n.* observer, inspector; censor; (mil.)
sergeant
ولولا لباسه العسكري ورتبته رقيب لظن من يراه
لأول وهلة أنه رجل رياضي — Were it not for his
military clothing and his rank of sergeant,
anyone who saw him at first glance would
think that he was a sportsman

55 | 206 |

4738 نَمْل *coll.n.* ants
سرعان ما توافد عليها آلاف المستعمرين كما يتدافع
النمل على إناء العسل — Quickly, thousands of
colonists poured into it, as ants stream over a
pot of honey

44 | 253 |

4739 كَوْنِيّ *adj.* cosmic, relating to the universe
اكد المؤلفان أن علماء ناسا يعرفون جيدا أن
المخلوقات الكونية هي التي استولت على المركبة
الفضائية قبل أن تهبط — The two authors
confirmed that NASA scientists knew full

well that space creatures had taken over the spaceship before it fell

54 | 210 |

4740 تَجَزَّأَ *v. V* to be divided, be partitioned; to be separated, be detached

صحة الفم هي جزء لا يتجزأ من الصحة العامة — Oral health is an integral part of general health

56 | 202 |

4741 مُخَاطِب *n.* speaker, interlocutor; *adj.* addressing, speaking to

قالت مخاطبة الصحفيين باللهجة اللبنانية «أنا ما بعرف احكي كتير» — She said, addressing the reporters in the Lebanese dialect: "I don't know how to speak much"

52 | 216 |

4742 قَلْبِيّ *adj.* cardiac, heart-related

هذه الحالة هي المسئولة عن نصف عدد الوفيات في الأزمات القلبية، ولا سبيل معها لإسعاف الضحية إلا بإعادة تشغيل القلب — This condition is what is responsible for half of the deaths in heart attacks, and there is no way to save the victim except by restarting the heart

49 | 228 |

4743 حُسْبان *n.* consideration, estimation, calculation

لن تدنو إلى الإجابة الصحيحة ما لم تأخذ في الحسبان السياسة والشؤون الجيوسياسية — You will not get close to the right answer as long as you don't take politics and geopolitical matters into consideration

62 | 180 |

4744 فَضِيل *adj.* excellent, splendid; commendable; virtuous; distinguished, eminent

أحرص كثيرا خلال الشهر الفضيل على التقليل من فترة الدوام في العيادة — I try hard, during Ramadan (the splendid month), to reduce the time I have to spend in the clinic

50 | 225 |

4745 قَصَر *v. I (i)* to shorten, curtail sth; قَصُر (u) to be insufficient; قَصَر (u) to fall short عن of sth, to fail عن to do sth

لم أقصر في شيء نحو أطفالي — I was not at all negligent with my children

52 | 217 |

4746 مُسْتَلْزَم *adj.* required; *n.* مُسْتَلْزَمات requirements

تذهب مع أختها الكبرى لشراء مستلزمات الطفلة بعد الولادة — She is going with her older sister to buy the things the child will need after she is born

57 | 196 |

4747 تَصاعَدَ *v. VI* to climb, increase, rise

شوهد دخان كثيف يتصاعد من المقر — Thick smoke was seen rising from the place

55 | 201 |

4748 أَرْقَى *elat.* higher/highest; more/most advanced; *adj.* top, finest

كانوا يحتلون أرقى المناصب السياسية والعسكرية والإدارية وأكثرها حساسية — They occupied the highest political, military, and administrative positions, and the most sensitive of them

58 | 191 |

4749 تَدْعِيم *n.* supporting, backing, propping up

اتفقنا جميعا على أن فكرة تدعيم الفريق بلاعبين بارزين هي الطريق نحو الدفع ببايرن إلى الأمام ليعود إلى تحقيق النجاح — We all agreed that the idea of propping up the team with prominent players was the way to push Bayern ahead to return to achieving success

49 | 226 |

4750 عَنْوَة *n.* force, violence; عَنْوَةً forcibly, by force

يقول الطبيب إنه في مثل هذه الأحوال يجب أن ننقله إلى المستشفى عنوة — The doctor says that in such cases it is necessary to transport him to the hospital by force

53 | 209 |

4751 خخخ *interj.* (laughter) ha-ha-ha, he-he-he (written in varying lengths: خخخخ, خخخخخ, etc.)

فاهم غلط خخ ماستوعب — He understood it wrong, he-he, he didn't get it

14 | 751 | +for

4752 تَطَرَّق *n.* broaching, discussing إلى (a topic)
اكتشفنا أنه من الضروري التطرق إلى هذا الموضوع
— We discovered that it is necessary to broach this subject
54 | 206 |

4753 رَحْبَة *n.* pl. رحاب open area; public square; رحاب vastness; generosity, protection; (university) campus
سيكون له الحق من جديد في الدخول إلى رحاب الجامعة — He will again have the right to enter into the campus of the university
51 | 217 |

4754 غازِيّ *adj.* gaseous; soft (drinks)
تكونت وجبة العشاء من قطع الدجاج والبطاطس المقلية والمشروبات الغازية والعصائر — Dinner consisted of pieces of chicken and fried potatoes and carbonated drinks and juices
54 | 206 |

4755 مَأْلُوف *adj.* familiar, typical, usual; customary, conventional
تأملت لحيته التي غيرت من شكله المألوف لديها — She contemplated his beard which had changed the way she was accustomed to seeing him
58 | 190 |

4756 تَسْدِيد *n.* payment, settlement; aiming, shooting
لم تتخلف مرة عن تسديد أي فاتورة — She was never late in paying any bill
53 | 209 |

4757 إدانَة *n.* condemnation, denunciation, censure
لقد أوصى محققون عسكريون بأن يغلق الملف دون إدانة مرتكبي الجريمة — Military analysts recommend that the file be closed without condemning the perpetrators of the crime
50 | 222 |

4758 عِداد *n.* number, quantity
أطلب من الله تعالى أن يكتب لك النجاة، وأن يجعلك في عداد الفائزين — I ask God, may He be exalted, to give you success and make you among the number of winners
58 | 192 |

4759 شَفّاف *adj.* transparent, translucent
جاءت إلى السلطة من خلال انتخابات شفافة وديمقراطية — She came to power through transparent and democratic elections
61 | 182 |

4760 بُرُوز *n.* emergence, appearance; prominence
كشفت مصادر عشائرية بروز خلافات بين تنظيم القاعدة وعشائر الانبار — Clan sources revealed the emergence of disagreements between the Al-Qaeda organization and the clans of Anbar
53 | 208 |

4761 قَصَفَ *v. I (i)* to bomb, shell sth
وردا على العدوان الإسرائيلي قصفت المقاومة صباح الجمعة سديروت وعسقلان بعدد من الصواريخ والقذائف — In response to the Israeli aggression, on Friday morning the resistance bombarded Sedarot and Askelon with a number of rockets and shells
44 | 252 |

4762 نَبْذ *n.* discarding; rejection, renunciation
يريدون تقطيع أوصال الإسلام، ونبذ تعاليمه — They want to cut off the arms and legs of Islam, and renounce its teachings
53 | 206 |

4763 خاتَم *n.* ring; seal, stamp; خاتَم الأَنْبِياء/النَّبِيِّين the Seal of the Prophets (Muhammad)
لماذا لا تلبس خاتم الزواج؟ — Why don't you wear your wedding ring?
55 | 201 |

4764 وِراثِيّ *adj.* hereditary; genetic, congenital; وِراثِيّاً genetically
يلي ذلك استخلاص المادة الوراثية «دنا» من هذه الخلايا، وتحليلها للتأكد من أنها تنتمي إلى أغشية البطانة — After that is the extraction of the hereditary matter, the DNA, from these cells, and analyzing them to make sure that they belong to the membrane lining
42 | 259 |

4765 تَحْطِيم *n.* demolition, destruction
لم يتمكن أحد من تحطيم هذا الرقم القياسي — No one has been able to break this record
61 | 180 |

4766 جوز *n.* Egy. /gooz/, Lev. /jooz/ husband
هي مبسوطة مع جوزها، جوزها ظريف بصراحة
مش زي اجوازنا — She is happy with her
husband, her husband is nice, frankly, not like
our husbands
20 | 552 | +spo

4767 رواق *n.* pl. أَرْوِقَة corridor, hall; porch,
portico
القضية الآن يدور النقاش حولها في أروقة مجلس
الشورى — The issue is now being discussed
in the halls of the Upper House of Parliament
58 | 189 |

4768 مَلَّ *v. I (a)* to get bored, fed up (من with sth)
مل الانتظار فترك السفينة ولجأ إلى حصن الشيخ —
He got tired of waiting so he left the ship and
took refuge in the fortress of the Sheikh
51 | 215 |

4769 حَرِير *n.* silk
هي تصنع من مواد مختلفة، من الحرير والصوف
وأنواع أخرى من الأقمشة ، تختلف باختلاف
الفصول — It is made of various materials,
from silk and wool and other types of cloth,
which differ with the change of seasons
51 | 215 |

4770 قَبَلِيّ *adj.* tribal
الحسابات الطائفية والقبلية لن تعطي المرشحتين أي
فرصة للفوز الذي من المرجح ان يكون من نصيب
مرشح قبيلة «العوازم» — Sectarian and tribal
considerations do not give the two female
candidates any opportunity for victory, which
would likely go to the candidate from the
Awazim tribe
55 | 200 |

4771 رُجُولَة *n.* masculinity, manhood, virility
ما هي الرجولة يا ولدي؟ أجاب ابنه الصغير قائلاً:
الرجولة يا أبي هي: الصبر في الرخا والبلا، وتقوى
الله في العلا والخلا — What is manhood, my
son? The small son answered, saying: Manhood, my
father, is: patience in good and bad fortune,
and piety towards God in good times and bad
47 | 233 |

4772 غُرُور *n.* deception, delusion; vanity
إن هذا يؤول به إلى الهلاك، وهذا حال أهل الغرور،
يغمض عينيه عن العواقب — That is going to

lead to destruction, and this is the state of the
people of deception, closing their eyes to the
consequences
52 | 211 |

4773 بِلْيُون /bilyoon/ *num.* billion
لقد انفق الجيش الاميركي ما يزيد عن نصف بليون
دولار على تطوير انواع مختلفة من الطائرات غير
المأهولة — The American army spent more
than a half billion dollars on developing
various types of unmanned aircraft
35 | 311 |

4774 تَخْرِيب *n.* destruction; sabotage, terrorism
يساهم في تخريب هذه البلاد التي مات من أجلها
الشرفاء — He is helping to destroy this country
for which the noble ones have died
56 | 193 |

4775 تَبْدِيل *n.* replacement, substitution, exchange
لديه قدرة كبيرة على تبديل شكله ونمطه الوراثي
بطريقة تجعل من الصعب تطوير لقاح ضده — It
has a great ability to change its form and its
genetic type in a way that makes it difficult
to develop a vaccination against it
57 | 192 |

4776 مَرْفُوض *adj.* rejected, refused; intolerable,
unacceptable
قتل الأبرياء مرفوض بكل الأشكال — Killing
innocent people is rejected in every form
57 | 190 |

4777 زَعَامَة *n.* leadership
حركة مجتمع السلم بزعامة أبو جرة سلطاني فضلت
هذه المرة ترشيح وجوه جديدة على رأس قوائمها
— The Peace Society movement under the
leadership of Abu Jarra Sultani preferred this
time to nominate new faces at the head
of its lists
44 | 248 |

4778 فادِح *adj.* serious, grave; heavy
إن حرب تموز أدت ومن دون شك إلى خسائر فادحة
وعلى الصعد كافة — The July War led, without a
doubt, to terrible losses, on every level
57 | 190 |

4779 أَخَصّ *elat.* more/most specific; بِالأَخَصّ
particularly, especially

أساعدها في أعمال المنزل وبالأخص إن كان عندها وليمة — I help her with the housework, particularly if she has a banquet

55 | 197 |

4780 قِتالِيّ *adj.* fighting, battle

جدير بالذكر أنه شارك في العمليات القتالية العنيفة في مدينة جرديز العاصمة الإقليمية لولاية باكتيا جنوب كابول — It is worth mentioning that he participated in violent fighting operations in the city of Gardez, the regional capital of the state of Paktia to the south of Kabul

52 | 207 |

4781 أَزالَ *v. IV* to remove, eliminate; to uninstall (software)

ثبت علميا أن الصوم يزيل العناصر المضرة بالجسم — It has been scientifically proven that fasting removes harmful substances from the body

56 | 192 |

4782 كابُوس *n.* nightmare

هل سيختفي على الأقل كابوس واحد من حياة العراقيين، كابوس اسمه الدكتاتور؟ — Will one nightmare, at least, disappear from the lives of the Iraqis, the nightmare called "the dictator"?

55 | 198 |

4783 مَلْجَأ *n.* shelter, refuge

قلنا إن المخيم لن يكون ملجأ للهاربين من وجه العدالة — We said that the camp will not be a refuge for those who are fleeing from justice

59 | 185 |

4784 هَيْدِي (Lev.) *dem.pron.* this (fem.sg.)

شو هيدي اللي عاملينها معنا؟ — What's this you are doing with us?

8 | 1364 | +spo

4785 فَحْم *n.* coal

قال مسؤولون إن سبب الانفجار مزيج من مسحوق الفحم وغاز الميثان — Officials said that the reason for the explosion was a mixture of coal dust and methane gas

52 | 206 |

4786 فَريسَة *n.* victim, prey

نترك أولادنا فريسة للتليفزيون والمسلسلات والأفلام التي تبث فيهم القيم الهابطة — We leave our children

to be victims of television, serials, and films which spread degraded values

57 | 190 |

4787 شَغَب *n.* unrest, disturbance

انتشرت شرطة مكافحة الشغب أمام مبنى الأوبرا قبل ساعات من رفع الستار — The anti-riot police spread out in front of the Opera building hours before the curtain rose

54 | 199 |

4788 نَقّال *adj.* portable, mobile

يعد الهاتف النقال من أهم المقتنيات التكنولوجية التي أفرزتها التطورات العلمية الحديثة — The mobile phone is one of the most important technological possessions which modern scientific developments have produced

46 | 232 |

4789 تِسْعينيّ *adj.* ninetieth; ninety-year; *n.* التِسْعينيّات the Nineties

منذ أواخر التسعينيات ظهر تحسن بالعلاقات العسكرية اليمنية الأميركية — Since the end of the Nineties an improvement in Yemeni-American military relations has become apparent

46 | 236 |

4790 تَساقَطَ *v. VI* to collapse; to fall gradually

بدأت دموعه تتساقط فوق لحيته البيضاء — His tears started to fall onto his white beard

50 | 217 |

4791 رُطُوبَة *n.* moisture, dampness, humidity

يقل نمو البكتريا كلما قلت نسبة الرطوبة في الثلاجات وزاد توزيع الهواء البارد على أسطح الذبائح — The growth of bacteria is lessened the less humidity there is in the refrigerator and the more cold air is circulated over the surface of the carcass

47 | 229 |

4792 واع (واعِي) (def.) *adj.* conscious, awake; aware, informed; alert

هل هي واعية بالمخاطر التي يمكن أن تقع فيها وهي تقوم بمهمتها؟ — Is she aware of the dangers she can fall into as she undertakes her mission?

56 | 191 |

4793 اِنْتِظام *n.* order, regularity

القانون الألماني يلزم أصحاب الكلاب بإخراجها
للتمشي بانتظام كي لا تنبح وتزعج السكان —
German law requires dog owners to take
them out for a walk regularly so that they
don't bark and bother the neighbors

57 | 188 |

4794 سِكِّين *n.* knife

ألقى السكين جانبا واتصل بالإسعاف وصار يصرخ
كالمجنون — He threw the knife aside and
contacted emergency services and began to
scream like a madman

51 | 212 |

4795 وَسيط *n.* mediator, intermediary, go-between;
adj. middle, medium

عرضنا لكم سابقا أن القرص الصلب بالكمبيوتر هو
الوسيط الأساسي لتخزين البرامج والملفات —
We previously presented to you the fact that
the hard drive on the computer is the basic
means for storing programs and files

52 | 207 |

4796 فَخّ *n.* trap, snare

يجب أن لا نقع في فخ استعمالنا من قبل الأحزاب
السياسية كمجرد رموز للتعدد العرقي والثقافي —
We should fall into the trap of being used by
the political parties as merely symbols of
cultural and ethnic diversity

55 | 193 |

4797 مَعْشَر *n.* assembly, community, group,
society

أيها الناس يا معشر المسلمين أصغوا إلي يرحمكم الله
— O people, O camp of the Muslims, listen to
me, may God have mercy on you

48 | 222 | +lit

4798 مُلّا *n.* mullah (Muslim cleric); المُلّا (title)
Mullah

تعلم في الكتاب عند الملا زكريا بن محمد؛ زكريا والد
الشاعر الأديب الاستاذ عبدالله زكريا — He was
educated in the Qurʾan School with Mullah
Zakaria bin Muhammad; Zakaria is the father
of the poet and man of letters, Professor
Abdallah Zakaria

44 | 242 |

4799 مُصادَفَة *n.* coincidence

من قال إن هذه مصادفة؟ إن الرب لا يصنع شيئا على
صدفة — Who said that this is a coincidence?
The Lord doesn't do anything by chance

48 | 220 |

4800 مِرْصاد *n.* lookout, ambush; بالمِرْصاد (lying)
in wait

عيون الوطن الساهرة من رجال الأمن كانوا لهم
بالمرصاد دائما — The watchful eyes of the
nation in the form of the security men
were always lying in wait for them

59 | 181 |

4801 شُرُوع *vn.* embarking في on, engaging في in

يفضل فصل التيار الكهربائي عن الجهاز قبل
الشروع في عملية التنظيف — He prefers to
unplug the electrical current from the device
before beginning the cleaning operation

51 | 210 |

4802 جُرْعَة *n.* dosage, dose; vaccine; gulp

يعتبر تطعيم الإنفلونزا واقيا وهو جرعة واحدة
تعطي في شهر أكتوبر أو نوفمبر — The
influenza vaccine is considered to be
protective, and it is a single dose given
in the month of October or November

43 | 246 |

4803 أَسِفَ *v. I (a)* to be or feel sorry على/لـ
about/for sth/sb

انا اسف جدا جدا على التأخير في الرد بسبب
ظروفي الصعبة — I am very, very sorry for
being late in responding because of my
difficult situation

38 | 277 | +for

4804 نَصْرانيّ *n./adj.* pl. نَصارى Christian

يوم الاحد هو معظم ايضا عند النصارى وكثير من
النصوص النصرانية تقول عنه انه يوم بهجة —
Sunday is also venerated by the Christians,
and many of the Christian texts say about
it that it is a day of joy

42 | 251 |

4805 صِباً *n.* youth, childhood (def. الصِبا)

ما كاد البهى يبلغ مرحلة الصبا حتى راح يخرج من
الدار مع الصباح ، ولا يعود إلا في المساء —
Bahiy had hardly reached the stage of young

manhood when he started leaving the house
as soon as it was morning and not returning
until evening

42 | 254 | +lit

4806 صارخ *adj.* shouting, screaming, crying out
ثم أخذ يركض صارخا: يا أمي، هناك لص! — He
began to run, crying: Mother, there is a thief!

49 | 218 |

4807 بُرْتُقال *coll.n.* oranges
بالنسبة لزهرة البرتقال فهي غنية بالزيوت الأساسية
المهدئة الأعصاب — In regard to the flower
of the orange tree, it is rich in essential
nerve-calming oils

45 | 236 |

4808 مَدْرُوس *adj.* studied, planned, investigated;
calculated, deliberate
هذه العمليات مدروسة ومخطط لها — These
operations are deliberate and planned out

55 | 193 |

4809 إيميل /'iimeel/ *n.* pl. -aat email
هذه المعلومات وصلت لي عبر الايميل، ورأيت أن
أنقلها — This information reached me by
email, and I thought I would pass it on

29 | 361 | +for

4810 مُسْتَوْرَد *adj.* imported
لا نستطيع اضافة رسوم جمركية على المنتجات النفطية
المستوردة من الخارج لان القانون والاتفاقيات
الدولية الغت جميعها معظم الرسوم الجمركية على
المواد الاولية — We cannot add customs duties
to imported oil products from the outside
because the law and international agreements
have all banned most customs duties on raw
materials

50 | 212 |

4811 مُسْتَطاع *n.* (what is) possible, feasible
نريد أن تكون عائلتنا كبيرة قدر المستطاع — We
want our families to be as big as possible

60 | 178 |

4812 حِزام *n.* belt, band; cordon, barrier
لم يستطع أن يغلق حزام البنطلون على بطنه — He
wasn't able to fasten the belt of his pants
around his belly

57 | 187 |

4813 مُتَطَوِّع *n./adj.* pl. -uun volunteer
إنها كواحدة من آلاف المتطوعين تنتظر بفارغ الصبر
دورة الألعاب الآسيوية الدوحة ٢٠٠٦ — As one
of thousands of volunteers, she is waiting
impatiently for the Doha Asian Games of 2006

52 | 202 |

4814 تَزايَدَ *v. VI* to increase, grow in number
يتوقع البعض أن تتزايد الأهمية الاعلامية للخلوي
— Some expect that the media importance
of the cell phone will increase

58 | 182 |

4815 مُسْتَعْمَل *adj.* used, in use, employed
السيارات المستعملة كانت ومازالت مصدر حيرة
للتجار ومصدر خشية للمستهلكين — Used cars
were and still are a source of confusion for
businessmen, and a source of fear for the
consumers

51 | 209 |

4816 مَغْرِب *n.* sunset; evening, time of sunset
يمضي الوقت ويكاد وقت المغرب ينتهي — Time is
passing and the evening is almost over

48 | 220 |

4817 مانح *adj.* granting, donating; *n.* donor
طالبوا الدول المانحة العمل لفك اسر هذه الاموال
وتقديمها مباشرة الى مستحقيها — They asked the
donor states to work on freeing up this money
and offering it directly to the intended
recipients

40 | 262 |

4818 مَمَرّ *n.* passageway, corridor
اجتاز الرئيس الممر، وخلفه بخطوتين مشى السفير
بخشوع، يتبعهما بقية المستقبلين — The president
passed through the hallway, with the
ambassador two steps behind him,
submissively, with the rest of the welcoming
party following

40 | 261 | +lit

4819 تَمَتُّع *n.* enjoyment
تؤكد على حق كل فرد في التمتع بجنسية ما ولا يجوز
حرمان شخص من جنسيته — She stresses the
right of each individual to enjoy some
citizenship, and a person should not be
denied his citizenship

58 | 183 |

4820 أَسْلَمَ *v. IV* to hand over, surrender sth إلى to sb; to become a Muslim, embrace Islam

كل الأمور كانت عادية وهادئة إلى حدود الحادية عشرة من تلك الليلة، عندما أسلم الجميع للنوم في كامل الطمأنينة — Everything was normal and quiet up until eleven o'clock that night, when everyone surrendered to sleep in complete confidence

29 | 360 |

4821 اِمْتِصاص *n.* absorption, suction

الرياضة تؤدي إلى سرعة امتصاص الأنسولين من تحت الجلد — Participating in sports leads to a quick absorption of the insulin from under the skin

54 | 194 |

4822 أَفْسَدَ *v. IV* to spoil, ruin sth; to corrupt sb

شخصيا، أعتقد أن استعمال الدين في السياسة يفسد السياسة — Personally, I believe that using religion in politics spoils the politics

58 | 180 |

4823 نُبُوَّة *n.* prophethood; prophecy

يزعم الكاتب أن تاريخ الإسلام في مرحلة ما بعد النبوة شهد نوعا من الفصل بين الشأن الديني والشأن السياسي — The author claims that the history of Islam in the post-prophetic stage witnessed a kind of separation between religious and political matters

45 | 235 |

4824 مَنْزِلَة *n.* grade, rank, position

أراك تنتهز كل فرصة لتظهر نفسك في منزلة مساوية لمنزلتي — I see you grab every opportunity to show yourself to be in a position equal to my position

54 | 193 |

4825 لُغْز *n. pl.* أَلْغاز mystery, enigma; puzzle, riddle

— كما أن المرأة لغز، فالرجل لغز آخر، وعلى المرأة حله Just like the woman is a riddle, so also the man is a riddle, and the woman must solve him

58 | 181 |

4826 مُجْتَمَعِيّ *adj.* societal

يحقق مفهوم الشرطة المجتمعية بهدف توثيق العلاقة بين رجل الأمن العام والمواطن — The concept of social policing achieves the goal of

strengthening the relationship between the policeman and the citizen

43 | 241 |

4827 زَعْلان *adj. fem.* زَعْلانَة angry (من/على with/at), mad (at), annoyed (with)

أنا زعلان منك لانك كان يجب ان تنزل عندي وليس في الدير — I am angry with you because you were supposed to stay at my house, and not at the monastery

36 | 292 |

4828 أَحْصَى *v. IV* to count, calculate; لا يُحْصَى innumerable

نلاحظ كذلك أن بيد الحزاب ومؤسسات التيار ملايين لا تحصى من الدنانير والدراهم والدولارات والريالات — We note that the parties and political organizations have in their hands uncounted millions of dinars, dirhams, dollars, and riyals

58 | 182 |

4829 عيلة /9eele/ (Lev.) *n.* family; عيلتي /9eelti/ my family

I — أنا بحب العيلة الصغيرة وبفضل ثلاثة أولاد like small families, and I prefer three children

8 | 1267 | +spo

4830 لَهِيب *n.* flame

رأيي لن يحرمه الجنة أو يدفع عنه لهيب جهنم — My opinion will not keep him out of heaven or protect him from the flames of hell

44 | 235 | +lit

4831 هذول /hadhool/ (Lev.Irq.Gul.; Lev. also /hadool/) *dem.pron.* these, those

طبعا أنا بحب الدجاج والسمك واللحمة كل هذول الأكلات — Of course I love chicken and fish and meat and all those foods

10 | 1055 | +spo

4832 حَريم *coll.n.* women, harem

ما رأيك فى فنجان قهوة، نعطى الحريم فرصة للسهر؟ — What do you think about a cup of coffee, we'll give the women a chance to stay up?

42 | 246 |

4833 لَهْو *n.* entertainment, amusement

نعوذ بالله أن يكون ديننا دين لهو وغناء كما يفعل سامي يوسف — We take refuge in God that our

religion becomes a religion of entertainment and singing, as Sami Yusuf is doing

52 | 202 |

4834 عَطَى *v. I (i)* (Magh.Lev.Gul.) to give sth to sb

نروح عند خياط أوكي عشان نعطي الموديل صح مو بكل خياط يفهم الموديل — We'll go to the tailor, OK, so we can give him the style correctly, not every tailor understands style

9 | 1168 | +spo

4835 واش (Magh.) *interrog.* what; واش مِن (Alg.) which; واش عليه /wash 9aleh/ (Alg.) OK, no problem

نهار الإثنين نتلاقوا وتحكي لنا واش كاين في قلبك — We'll meet on Monday and you'll tell us what is in your heart

3 | 3503 | +spo

4836 طَقْس *n.* pl. طُقُوس ritual, rite

لم أعد أحس بالتعب وأنا أمارس طقوس العمل في هذه الأرض — I no longer feel tired when I carry out the rites of work in this land

50 | 210 |

4837 رُكُوب *vn.* getting in/on, riding in/on (vehicle); boarding, traveling by (ship, airplane); mounting, riding (horse, bicycle)

أكبر مشكلة تواجهني في السفر هي ركوب الطائرة، فأنا أخافها جدا — The biggest problem that I face in traveling is flying, since I am really afraid of airplanes

57 | 182 |

4838 وعاء *n.* container, receptacle; vessel

يقوم البعض بملء نصف وعاء من الزيت، وكلما وجد عقربا وضعه في هذا الوعاء — Some fill a container half-full of oil, and whenever they find a scorpion they put it in this container

48 | 215 |

4839 تَطَلُّع *n.* pl. -aat aspiration, hope

أكد أن خطة خارطة الطريق هي السبيل الوحيد لتحقيق تطلعات الفلسطينيين للاستقلال والإسرائيليين للأمن — He stressed that the Roadmap plan was the only way to accomplish the aspirations of the Palestinians for independence, and of the Israelis for security

47 | 219 |

4840 دَقَّة *n.* pl. -aat knock, stroke, tick, beat

تسارعت دقات قلبها واضطربت أنفاسها، وكادت تفقد الوعي — Her heart beat sped up and her breathing became troubled, and she almost lost consciousness

45 | 232 |

4841 تَأْشِيرَة *n.* visa (travel, entrance, exit)

أبلغ المسؤولون أن إجراءات الحصول على تأشيرة لدخول العراق ستتغير — Officials announced that the procedures for obtaining a visa for entering Iraq were going to change

51 | 201 |

4842 سَبْعِينيّ *adj.* seventieth; 70-year; *n.* السبعينيات the Seventies

ازداد الطلب على المياه المعدنية كشراب منذ أواسط عقد السبعينيات من هذا القرن — The demand for mineral water as a drink has increased since the middle of the Seventies in this century

43 | 237 |

4843 حَجْب *vn.* hiding, veiling; covering, shielding; withholding, restraining, holding back

تضم تلك المزايا القدرة على حجب الإعلانات غير المرغوب فيها التي تظهر على الشاشة — These advantages include the ability to hide undesirable advertisements that appear on the screen

53 | 195 |

4844 فَرَّ *v. I (i)* to escape, flee; to defect, desert

بعد الحادثة فر أكثر من عشرين ألف عراقي إلى إيران — After the incident, more than twenty thousand Iraqis fled to Iran

54 | 190 |

4845 تَدَنٍّ (def. التَّدَنِّي) *n.* fall, decline; sinking

حمل مدير التربية في العقبة أولياء الأمور مسؤولية تدني مستوى التحصيل الدراسي لبعض الطلبة — The director of education in Aqaba held the parents (guardians) responsible for the low level of academic achievement by some students

53 | 195 |

4846 حَلْق *n.* throat; chasm, gorge

لآلام الحلق يستعمل خل التفاح لعمل غرغرة بنسبة ملعقة صغيرة من الخل في كوب ماء — For a sore

throat you can use apple cider vinegar to make a gargling solution of one teaspoon of vinegar per cup of water
49 | 210 |

4847 تَأَسَّسَ *v. V* to be established, be founded
لقد تأسست الفيدرالية العامة لمسلمي فرنسا منذ عام ١٩٨٥ ميلادية — The General Federation for the Muslims of France was established in 1985 AD
53 | 193 |

4848 كاد *n.* بالكاد almost
المعونات التي حصلت عليها السلطة بالكاد تكفي لدفع رواتب الشرطة — The aid which the Authority received is almost enough to pay the salaries of the policemen
51 | 202 |

4849 امتى (Egy.) /'eemta/, and ايمتا and امتا (Lev.) /'imta/ *interrog.* when
حتكلمونا إمتى بقى المرة الجاية؟ — When will you call again next?
11 | 945 | +spo

4850 رهان *n.* bet, wager; contest
وأصبح الرهان الآن: مين الصادق ومين الكاذب — The bet has now become: who is the truthful one, and who is the liar
54 | 190 |

4851 عَزِيمَة *n.* determination, (firm) resolve, (strong) will; incantation; (Lev.Irq.) invitation; (Irq.) dinner party
أختي رند بها عزيمة وإصرار ورغبة صادقة في التغيير — My sister Rand has determination and perseverance, and a sincere desire to change
53 | 193 | +spo

4852 العُمْرَة *n.* "lesser" pilgrimage to Mecca: Al-Umra
في أواخر ديسمبر سنة ١٩٨٧ تركت إسلام آباد لأداء العمرة وزيارة أبنائي في القاهرة — At the end of December 1987, I left Islamabad to perform the minor Hajj and to visit my sons in Cairo
52 | 197 |

4853 كَفَلَ *v. II* to support, maintain, provide for sb
طريق الخلاص هو العودة إلى الحياة الديمقراطية التي تكفل للمواطن حقوقه الإنسانية — The road to

salvation is a return to democratic life which provides for the citizen his human rights
53 | 194 |

4854 بَنَّاء *adj.* constructive, positive
هذا البرنامج يعتبر نتاجا للتعاون المثمر والبناء مع وزارة الصحة — This program is considered a result of fruitful and constructive cooperation with the Ministry of Health
57 | 180 |

4855 شُعْلَة *n.* torch, flame, fire
كي لا تنطفئ شعلة الحب من المفيد القيام بإجازة كل فتره كأنها شهر عسل — So that the flame of love won't be extinguished it is useful to take a vacation every so often, as if it were a honeymoon
52 | 198 |

4856 طَمْأَنَ *v. QI* to pacify, assuage, reassure sb
حتى قبل الإفراج كان حريصا على أن يطمئن على تأدية العبادات بشكل صحيح — Even before being released he was insistent on reassuring himself that he was performing his acts of worship in a correct manner
58 | 177 |

4857 تَنافُسِيّ *adj.* competitive; antagonistic
إنها احد العوامل الاساسية المؤثرة في زيادة معدلات الاستثمار ورفع القدرات التنافسية والتمويلية للشركات — It is one of the basic factors affecting the increase in the rates of investment and raising the competitive and financing abilities of the companies
44 | 230 |

4858 عَبَاية and عَبَاءَة *n.* abaya (traditional black robe worn by Muslim women)
كانوا ينشرون عباءة قيمة على بركة ماء لكي لا يتلوث حذاء سيدتهم — They used to spread out their expensive cloaks over a pool of water so that the shoes of their wives would not get dirty
53 | 193 |

4859 بُؤْرَة *n.* center, focus
إن المنطقة العربية أصبحت بؤرة للصراعات منذ نشأة الدولة العبرية — The Arab region has become a focus of conflict ever since the foundation of the Hebrew state
56 | 183 |

4860 بُرْكان *n.* volcano

رأيت بركان الدموع يتفجر في عينيه وينهمر على خديه — I saw a volcano of tears explode in his eyes and pour down his cheeks

51 | 199 |

4861 غَلا (Gul.) *adj.* dear, precious; *n.* dearness, preciousness; يا هَلا وغَلا approx.: welcome dear friend(s)

هلا وغلا والفين وغلا هلا فيك يالغالي — Welcome, two thousand welcomes to you, dear

14 | 704 | +for

4862 تَحْريض *n.* incitement, provocation; induction

منظمة التحرير تواصل التحريض ضد حماس — The PLO is continuing its incitement against Hamas

49 | 208 |

4863 مِنْشان and مِنْشان (Lev.) *prep.* for, for the sake of; *conj.* so that, in order to; (مِن شأن from)

لو سمحت تعلي صوتك شوي مشان أسمع صوتك — Please raise your voice a bit so I can hear your voice

11 | 936 | +spo

4864 شكُون (Magh.) *interrog.* who

شكون هذه يا اللي عندك؟ — What's this you've got?

13 | 792 | +spo

4865 اِفْتِتاحِيّ *adj.* opening, leading, introductory; inaugural

وزير الدولة للتطوير الإداري سيقوم بإلقاء الكلمة الافتتاحية للمؤتمر — The minister of state for administrative development will deliver the opening remarks of the conference

48 | 213 |

4866 مَغْفُور لَهُ/لَها *p.p.* the late, deceased

إنها لا تنسى عطف المغفور له الملك فؤاد الأول على والدها — She won't forget the kindness of the late King Fuad I towards her father

45 | 226 |

4867 والٍ (الوالي .def) *n.* ruler, governor

وصل رؤوف بيك وهو مبعوث عسكري من والي البصرة محسن باشا إلى الشيخ مبارك للتأكد من سلامته — Rauf Bey, the military emissary of the governor of Basra, Muhsin Pasha, arrived to Sheikh Mubarak to make sure he was well

41 | 246 |

4868 قَلَّ *adv.* rarely, seldom; hardly, barely

هذا الجانب بالذات قلما يتنبه له الكثيرون — This aspect, specifically, how seldom do many pay any attention to it

56 | 183 |

4869 نَقِيّ *adj.* pure, clean; undiluted

كانت حدائقه متنفسا لمن يبحث عن الهدوء والهواء الصحي النقي — Its gardens were refreshing for those searching for calm and pure, healthy air

59 | 172 |

4870 مُفَدَّى *adj.* beloved, cherished, greatly esteemed; (in official titles) المَلِك المُفَدَّى His Majesty the King

بفضل من الله سبحانه وتعالى ومن ثم حكمة جلالة السلطان المفدى أمكن لبلادنا أن تعيش هذه الأجواء من الاستقرار والأمان — Thanks to God, may He be praised and exalted, and also thanks to the wisdom of His Majesty the beloved Sultan, our country was able to experience this period of stability and security

28 | 356 |

4871 مُرَجَّح *adj.* probable, likely

عندما تكون هذه الأعراض مصحوبة بغثيان، تقيّؤ، تعرّق، ضيق تنفّس أو الإحساس بالإغماء، فمن المرجح أن تكون الحالة نوبة قلبية — When these symptoms are accompanied by nausea, vomiting, sweating, shortness of breath, or a fainting sensation, it is likely that the situation is a heart attack

49 | 207 |

4872 مَحْضَر *n.* report, minutes; attendance

جاء في محضر النيابة أن المتهم عاطل عن العمل — According to the court records of the prosecution the accused was unemployed

52 | 196 |

4873 عُبُودِيَّة *n.* slavery, servitude; veneration
إنني أركه الظلم لأن الظلم يوصل إلى العبودية
للإنسان — I hate oppression, because
oppression leads to slavery for mankind
55 | 185 |

4874 نَصْح *n.* advice, counsel
للمعلمة دور مهم جدا في هذا الأمر بتوجيه النصح
للطالبة بالطرق المباشرة وغير المباشرة — The
teacher has a very important role in this
matter by giving direct and indirect advice to
the student
58 | 175 |

4875 تَمْرِير *n.* passing, transfer
بعد شد وجذب استطاع الحزب الوطني الحاكم أن
يحشد غالبيته لتمرير القانون — After some
pushing and pulling, the ruling National
Party was able to amass its majority to pass
the law
51 | 200 |

4876 شَتَات *n.* scattering; diaspora
ترك الحرية لكل فلسطيني في العودة أو البقاء في
الشتات — It left to each Palestinian the
freedom to return or to stay in the diaspora
45 | 225 |

4877 مَنَام *n.* sleep; sleeping place
لقد زارها أبوها في المنام حتى يشجعها على إكمال
البعثة — Her father visited her in a dream to
encourage her to finish the mission
44 | 228 |

4878 نَفَر *n.* group, party; soldier, private; person,
individual (in a population)
حين كان طفلا في المرحلة الابتدائية، هرب مع نفر من
زملائه من المدرسة إلى ظاهر المدينة — When he
was a child in the elementary stage, he ran
away with a number of his colleagues from
school to the outskirts of the city
47 | 213 |

4879 أَبْقَى *v. IV* to maintain, preserve (على) sth/sb;
to keep sth/sb (على) in a state)
أبقى الأبواب مفتوحة على إمكان التلاقي والتحاور
— He left the doors open for the possibility
of meeting and conversing
49 | 207 |

4880 حَسَّنَ *v. II* to improve sth, make sth better;
to decorate sth, make sth nice
التدخين يحسن علاقتك بزوجتك — Smoking
improves your relationship with your wife
59 | 170 |

4881 ثَلَّاجَة *n.* refrigerator, cooler; freezer, ice-box
يمكن حفظ اللحوم الطازجة في الثلاجة لمدة ٣ – ٥
أيام — Fresh meat can be kept in the
refrigerator for 3–5 days
45 | 222 |

4882 أَبْلَغ *elat.* more/most eloquent
صورة أبلغ من ألف كلمة — A picture is more
eloquent than a thousand words
58 | 173 |

4883 فِضِّيّ *adj.* silver
توجت قطر بذهبية هذه المسابقة، بينما نالت اليابان
الفضية — Qatar was crowned with the gold in
this competition, while Japan got the silver
51 | 196 |

4884 فِيزِياء *n.* physics
حصل على شهادة بكالوريوس في الفيزياء
والرياضيات من الجامعة العبرية — He received
a BA degree in Physics and Math from the
Hebrew University
54 | 188 |

4885 حَيْثُما *conj.* wherever
اتق الله حيثما كنت — Fear God wherever you are
51 | 199 |

4886 اِسْتِرَاحَة *n.* intermission, recess; time-out,
(fig.) truce; rest, relaxation; lodge, hostel, rest
house; rest area, waiting room, visitors
lounge; shrine (esp. martyr); refuge, shelter
(animal protection)
اكد على ضرورة توفير استراحة للمسافرين في حالة
الازدحام — He stressed the necessity of providing
rest to the travelers in case of crowding
37 | 274 | +spo

4887 حَفْنَة *n.* handful
بعض المقتنيات تكلف حفنة من الدولارات فقط..
أما النادر منها فيتكلف الآلاف — Some possessions
cost only a handful of dollars...rare ones cost
thousands
53 | 188 |

4888 مُعاقَبَة *n.* punishment, sanction

بكاء الطفل وقت الخوف أمر متوقع فلا يمكن معاقبة الطفل على ما هو طبيعي أن يصدر عنه — A child's crying when he is scared is expected; one shouldn't punish a child for what is natural for him to do

57 | 175 |

4889 شِبْر *n.* span of the hand or foot; وَلا شِبْر not (even) an inch

إني لست على استعداد أن أتخلى عن شبر واحد من هذه البلاد لتذهب إلى غير أهلها — I am not prepared to give up a single inch of this country so that it would go to other than its people

50 | 202 |

4890 اِسْتَغْفَرَ *v. X* to beg (God) for forgiveness

استغفر ربنا عن وقتك فراغك اللي ضاع على الفاضي — Beg forgiveness from God for your free time which was wasted on nothing

36 | 281 |

4891 حَسْرَة *n.* grief, pain, sorrow; regret

سالت دموعي حسرة وندامة — My tears flowed, from loss and regret

42 | 237 | +lit

4892 تَسَوُّق *n.* shopping

يرافقه ابن شقيقه غالبا في جولات التسوق أو في الزيارات الاجتماعية — His brother's son usually accompanies him on his shopping trips and on social visits

51 | 195 |

4893 نزين and انزين (Gul.) /nzeen/ *interj.* good, fine; OK

ما دام إنكم لايقين على بعض وتحبوا بعض خلاص انزين تزوجوا — Since you complete each other and love each other, then fine, go ahead and get married

12 | 840 | +spo

4894 مَشْروب *n.* pl. -aat beverage, drink

الاكتئاب أيضا بذاته يؤثر على مدى اتباع تطبيق إرشادات سلوكيات نمط الحياة الصحية من التغذية والرياضة وعدم التدخين أو تناول المشروبات الكحولية، وعلى مدى الالتزام بتناول الأدوية — Depression, also, by itself, influences the extent of carrying out the behavioral prescriptions of a healthy life style in terms of nutrition, sports, not smoking or drinking alcoholic beverages, and also influences the degree of compliance in taking medication

47 | 210 |

4895 مُخاطَبَة *vn.* speaking to, addressing sb; *n.* conversation

من الضروري استغلال شبكة الانترنت تقديم مواقع قادرة على مخاطبة الشباب بالعالم العربي — It is necessary to exploit the Internet to offer sites able to address the youth of the Arab World

55 | 183 |

4896 اِمْتَلَأَ *v. VIII* to be filled, to become full

ساروا رافعين المصاحف ومعهم سجاد الصلاة، حتى امتلأت بهم ساحة نادي المحامين — They walked along, raising their Qurʾans and carrying their prayer rugs, until the courtyard of the lawyer's club was filled with them

50 | 199 |

4897 عاتق *n.* shoulder

هذا الواجب يقع على عاتق الأمم المتحدق والأسرة الدولية من أجل وقف هذه الانتهاكات — This duty falls on the shoulders of the United Nations and the International Community in order to bring a stop to these encroachments

54 | 184 |

4898 ضُحىً *n.* forenoon; morning

القديسة الشابة تخرج ساعتين في الضحى وساعتين بعد الظهر والناس تتقاتل في الاندفاع إليها — The young saint emerges for two hours in the morning and two hours in the afternoon, and the people fight with each other while rushing towards her

35 | 284 | +lit

4899 تِسْعُون *num.* ninety; ninetieth

عليك ان ترسل نسخاً من هذه الرسالة بعد ستة وتسعون ساعة من قراءتك لها — You should send copies of this letter ninety-six hours after reading it

15 | 671 |

4900 مَرْأىً *n.* sight, view

كانت عملية الفرز علنية وعلى مرأى ومسمع من الجميع — The selection process happened

in public, within the sight and hearing of everyone

56 | 178 |

4901 قالِب *n.* form, model; mold

اختار أهم جوانب محتوى الدروس ووضعها في قالب معلوماتي «الإعلام الآلي» — He chose the most important aspects of the content of the lessons and put them in the information form of "automatic instruction" (computer assisted instruction)

55 | 182 |

4902 باكِر and باجِر /baachir/ (Irq.Gul.; UAE also / baakir/) *adv.* tomorrow; عقب باجِر /9ugub baachir/ the day after tomorrow

لا باكر الثلاثا لا اليوم الثلاثا صح باكر الاربعا — No, tomorrow is Tuesday, no, today is Tuesday, right, tomorrow is Wednesday

17 | 591 |

4903 اِسْتِخْراج *n.* extraction; removal

قد تم استخراج جثث نحو ٤٠٠ تلميذ من تحت أنقاض المدرستين — About 400 student corpses were extracted from under the remains of the two schools

51 | 195 |

4904 بِتْرُولِيّ *adj.* petroleum-, oil-based or related

بلغ اجمالي مبيعات القطاع العام من المنتجات البترولية ١٧ مليار جنيه — The total sales of the public sector of petroleum products is 17 billion pounds

38 | 261 |

4905 علاش /9laash/ (Magh.) *interrog.* why; علاه /9laah/ (Alg.) variant of علاش

قالت له أنا نحبك وعلاش دير لي هكذا؟ — She said to him: I love you, so why do you do this to me?

12 | 836 | +spo

4906 فَرَقَ *v. I (i)* to differ, be different; to make a difference; (Egy.Lev.) ما بْتِفْرِق it doesn't matter (مع to sb)

لن يفرق بيننا إلا الموت — Only death will separate us

78 | 127 |

4907 هَيْدا (Lev.) *dem.pron.* this (masc.sg.)

طيب بس ليش هيك عم بيعمل؟ شو هيدا؟ — OK, but why is he doing this? What is this?

7 | 1430 | +spo

4908 ثَناء *n.* praise, commendation; appreciation

أخذ يشكر ذلك الطيب المخلص، ويكيل له عبارات الثناء والمدح — He began to thank that sincere doctor, and to offer him expressions of praise

56 | 178 |

4909 حَلَوِيّات *pl.n.* sweets, candy; confectionery; pastries, desserts; (Lev.) /Hilwiyyaat/

اللحوم الحمراء مسؤولة عن ١١ في المائة من هذه التسممات، والحلويات والسمك عن حوالي ٨ في المائة منها — Red meat is responsible for 11 percent of these poisonings, and sweets and fish for approximately 8 percent of them

50 | 200 |

4910 وِصاية *n.* trusteeship, guardianship; care, custody, tutelage

اكد رئيس الحكومة فؤاد السنيورة اننا لن نقبل الوصاية ولا التبعية — The president of the government Fuad Siniora stressed that we will never accept guardianship or dependency

40 | 248 |

4911 أَلْحَقَ *v. IV* to attach, append ب sth; to enroll, register sb ب in (a school)

حتى لو نظرت إلى الشمس لفترة قصيرة فيمكن أن تلحق الضرر بعينك وتفقد جزءا من بصرك — Even if you look at the sun for a short period, it can cause damage to the eye and you could lose part of your eyesight

55 | 180 |

4912 مَأْوىً *n.* refuge, shelter

أخيرا وجدت مأوى يحميها وأطفالها من مخاطر زوجها وعائلته — Finally she found a refuge that would protect her and her children from the dangers of her husband and his family

54 | 185 |

4913 بِرْكَة *n.* pool, puddle; (swimming) pool

قام بتمارين اقتصرت على المشي حول بركة السباحة بفندق الانتر عقب تناول طعام الإفطار مباشرة

He did some exercises which were limited to walking around the swimming pool of the Inter Hotel directly after eating breakfast

46 | 215 |

4914 أَجَل *interj.* yes, of course; عَيَل (Gul.) and أَجَل *conj.* so, then, therefore

عيل شو رايك؟ — So, what do you think?

21 | 458 | +spo +for

4915 تَخْزِين *n.* storage, safekeeping

بدا واضحا أن المجتمع الدولي لن يمنع حزب الله من تخزين الصواريخ ومهاجمة إسرائيل — It became clear that international society would not prevent Hizbollah from storing rockets and attacking Israel

50 | 196 |

4916 صُغَيَّر (Egy.) *adj.* small, young

همّ لسه صغيرين — They're still young (kids)

15 | 665 | +spo

4917 تَمَسَّكَ *v. V* to clutch, adhere to ب sth

لابد للمؤمن أن يتمسك بدينه — The believer must adhere to his religion

60 | 166 |

4918 تَجَسُّس *n.* espionage, spying

كان يحمل على متنه قمرين مهمتهما التجسس على كوريا الشمالية — It carried on board two satellites whose mission was to spy on North Korea

50 | 199 |

4919 أَبْرَزَ *v. IV* to highlight, expose sth

تقدم نحوي وهو يبرز بطاقة من جيبه الداخلي: «مكتب التحقيقات الفيدرالي» — He came towards me, showing a card from his inner pocket: "The Federal Bureau of Investigations"

71 | 140 |

4920 مَنال *n.* attainment, achievement; reach, capacity

تبدو الديمقراطية حلما صعب المنال — Democracy seems to be a dream that is difficult to obtain

57 | 173 |

4921 مليح /mliiH/ (Lev.Alg.) *adj.* good, nice; *adv.* well

يا ستي خيرها في غيرها ان شا الله مليح اللي ما اجيت مبارح كان يعني ما لقيتش حد — Madame, good

can pop up unexpectedly, if God wills it; it is good you didn't come yesterday, you would not have found anyone

9 | 1104 | +spo +for

4922 هاجَرَ *v. III* to emigrate

عندما هاجر يهود سوريا إلى فلسطين وجدوا أنفسهم في أسفل السلم الاجتماعي — When the Jews of Syria emigrated to Palestine they found themselves at the bottom of the social ladder

54 | 183 |

4923 تَنْقِيب *n.* drilling, excavation; exploration

أصدر مجلس الوزراء قرارا في أيلول من العام ٢٠٠٥ — يقضي بمنع التنقيب عن المعادن في محمية ضانا The Council of Ministers issued a decree in September of 2005 which stipulates the forbidding of excavating for minerals in the Dana Reserve

49 | 200 |

4924 عُضْوِيّ *adj.* organic; أَمْراض عُضْوِيَّة organic diseases

اليوم يستخدم السماد الطبيعي البقري على نطاق كبير في الزراعة العضوية — Today natural cow manure is used widely in organic agriculture

48 | 206 |

4925 ظَهِيرة *n.* noon, midday

ينام حتى ما بعد الظهيرة — He sleeps even after noon

47 | 210 |

4926 نقابيّ *adj.* union, syndicate

تبدأ اليوم انتخابات المرحلة الأولى للجان النقابية في نقابات الغزل والنسيج والمرافق العامة والصناعات الغذائية والصناعات المعدنية — First stage elections for the union committees in the textile, public utilities, food industries, and metal industries unions begin today

40 | 247 |

4927 مُتَساو (def. مُتَساوي) *adj.* equivalent, similar

حظوظ الجميع متساوية في القبول في جامعة الكويت — Everyone has an equal chance of getting accepted into the University of Kuwait

52 | 188 |

4928 فتبول futbool and فوتبول /futbool/ *n.* football, soccer
يالله شوف قول لي عن الملاعب عندكوا يا زلمة قول لي — عن الفتبول انا باحب الفوتبول Look, tell me about the stadiums where you are, man, tell me about soccer, I love soccer
22 | 452 | +spo

4929 فَدّ (Irq.) *part.* (indefinite article) one, a; فد شي /fadd shi/ something
انتظرني فد لحظة. دأحاكي هذا صديقي — Wait for me just a moment. I'm talking to this (person), my friend
23 | 432 | +spo

4930 مَعْمُورَة *adj.* populated, inhabited; *n.* الْمَعْمُورَة the world
تعمل قوات حفظ السلام الأردنية والفرنسية جنبا إلى جنب على امتداد المعمورة — Jordanian and French peace-keeping forces work side by side throughout the world
56 | 175 |

4931 مَرْدُود *n.* returns, revenue, yield
غالبية المبدعين لا يعيشون من مردود إنتاجهم الأدبي لأن المقابل محدود جدا — Most authors do not live off of the revenue of their literary works because what they get is very limited
54 | 181 |

4932 تَحَسُّب *n.* expectation, anticipation; تَحَسُّباً لِـ in anticipation of
ما هي الاحياطات الواجب اتخاذها على الدولة الآن تحسبا للسيول والفيضانات؟ — What are the precautions that the state should take now in anticipation of torrential rains and floods?
50 | 197 |

4933 وَجْد *n.* love, affection, intimacy; passion, ecstasy; contentment, well-being
أنت يا هذا.. ألم تحرقك نار الوجد بعد؟ — Hey you, hasn't the fire of love burned you yet?
31 | 316 | +lit

4934 ضَخّ *n.* pumping; injecting
يركز البرنامج على ضخ فيض من المعلومات في ذهن المشاهد حول المواضيع التي يعرضها — The program concentrates on pumping a flood of information into the minds of the viewer concerning the subjects which it presents
55 | 180 |

4935 مِتْجَوِّز (Lev.) *adj.* married
حارجع الاقيك متجوز ومخلف عيال يعني — I'll return and find you married and having fathered kids, you know
26 | 381 | +spo

4936 جنازَة *n.* funeral; funeral procession
نزل من سيارته دون تفكير ومشى في جنازة هذا الميت — He got out of his car without thinking and walked in the funeral procession of that deceased person
52 | 188 |

4937 خاطِرَة *n. pl.* خَواطِر idea, thought
أكتب ما يجول بقلبي من مشاعر وخواطر — I am writing what was going around in my heart in the way of feelings and thoughts
51 | 192 |

4938 لاشَيْء *n.* nothingness, non-existence; (sports) zero, nil
كان المنتخب الاولمبي الأثيوبي تفوق على المنتخب المصري بهدفين مقابل لاشيء في مباراة الذهاب يوم ٢٥ النوار الماضي بملعب أديس أبابا — The Ethiopian Olympic team had beaten the Egyptian national team by two goals to nothing in an away match this past 25th of Nuwwar in the Addis Ababa stadium
43 | 226 | +lit

4939 اِطْمِئْنان *n.* peace of mind, serenity; calm, tranquility
البحث عن الاطمئنان المادي هو شيء خادع — Searching for material reassurance is a deceptive thing
53 | 185 |

4940 تَقَيُّد *vn.* being bound ب to sth; *n.* restriction, limitation
أكد أن التقيد بالتعليمات فيه ضمان للجميع للعيش في مجتمع آمن — He stressed that obeying the instructions would be a guarantee to everyone of living in a secure society
56 | 174 |

4941 كيفاش and كيفاه (Magh.) *interrog.* how, how come; what
كيفاش تروح بلا ما تقول لي؟ — How could you go without telling me?
10 | 986 | +spo

4942 مُسْتَقِيم *adj.* straight, correct; righteous
الواجب يقضي أن يحكم نواب الأمة ضميرهم المستقيم
— Duty dictates that the deputies of the
nation be governed by their strict conscience
49 | 199 |

4943 مُشْتاق *adj.* yearning, longing إلى for sth/sb
(= to miss sth/sb)
والله إني مشتاقة لك ما نسمع صوتك عساك طيب —
By God I miss you. We rarely hear your voice. I
hope you're OK
28 | 352 | +spo

4944 قُرْص *n.* disk, tablet
انسخ المعلومات على قرص صلب خارجي — Copy
the information onto an external hard drive
46 | 214 |

4945 عِلاجِيّ *adj.* therapeutic, healing, curative
غادرت الطفلة المدينة الطبية بعد انتهاء الفترة
العلاجية — The child left the medical city
after finishing her treatment period
44 | 219 |

4946 مُثَلَّث *n.* triangle; *adj.* triangle-shaped
يحتوي مثلث برمودا على أكثر من ٣٠٠ جزيرة —
The Bermuda Triangle contains more than
300 islands
54 | 180 |

4947 مُوبايل *n.* pl. -aat mobile phone, cell phone
الرقم تبعي تبع الموبايل كان خالص حطيت رقم
جديد — My number, my mobile number,
expired, I got a new number
20 | 492 | +spo

4948 جَهَلَ *v. I (a)* to ignore, not know sth
إنه كان يجهل تماما عمق المأزق الذي وضع فيه
الولايات المتحدة — He was completely ignorant
of the depth of the predicament into which he
placed the United States
54 | 181 |

4949 اِحْتِراف *n.* professionalism
تقرر تشكيل ٤ لجان داخل نادي الجزيرة من أجل
تطبيق الاحتراف على باقي لاعبي الفريق الكروي —
It was decided to form 4 committees inside
the Gezira Club in order to carry out the
professionalization of the rest of the players
of the soccer team
35 | 279 |

4950 أَحْضَر *v. IV* to bring, supply sth; to prepare
(food)
أحضر له كأسا من الماء أو العصير إن كان عطشانا
— Bring him a cup of water or juice if he
is thirsty
50 | 195 |

4951 فَضّ *vn.* resolving, settling (conflict, disputes);
breaking up, dispersing, dissolving
أوضح لأبنائك أنك لست ضد محاولتهم فض
الخلاف بأنفسهم — Make it clear to your
children that you are not against them trying
to solve the dispute by themselves
55 | 176 |

4952 مَطْبُوع *adj.* printed; *n.* مَطْبُوعات publications,
printed materials
قد تم توزيع جميع المطبوعات والبالغ عددها ٢ مليون
نسخة على ٦٤ مركز اعلام — All the publications,
whose number reached 2 million copies, were
distributed over 64 media centers
46 | 213 |

4953 شاكو and شكو /shaku/ (Irq.Kuw.) *interrog.*
what? what is there? شكو ماكو؟ /shaku
maaku/ what's up? how's it going?
وانتي؟ شكو ماكو؟ شدتسوين؟ — And you?
How's it going? What are you doing?
35 | 280 | +spo

4954 غَلْطان (Dia.) *adj.* fem. -a wrong, mistaken
أعذرني لو كنت غلطان — Excuse me if I am
wrong
41 | 239 |

4955 صَلِيبِيّ *adj.* cross-shaped; Crusader
حتى عصر الحروب الصليبية كانت أكثرية السكان
ببلاد الشام ومصر لا تزال مسيحية — Until the
age of the Crusader wars, most of the
inhabitants of Greater Syria and Egypt
were still Christians
48 | 204 |

4956 تَوْجِيهِيّ *adj.* directing, guiding; instructional;
n. التَّوْجِيهِيّ tawjihi (secondary school exam
and diploma, Jor. and Pal.)
بس انجح بالتوجيهي باجي عندك — Just pass the
General Secondary Exam, and I'll come and
stay with you
36 | 272 | +spo

4957 جُوّا /guwwa/ (Lev.Irq.) and جوه /guwwa/ (Egy.) *prep./ adv.* inside; (Irq.) also: *prep.* underneath; *adv.* downstairs

حتى لو غبتي عنا رح تبقي جوا قلوبنا اختي العزيزه — Even when you are far from us you will remain inside our hearts, dear sister

26 | 376 | +spo

4958 مُصاحِب *adj.* accompanying

مثل هؤلاء الأطفال يكونون عرضة للإصابة بالأمراض المصاحبة للسمنة كأمراض القلب والسكري — Children like these are subject to being stricken with diseases that accompany obesity like heart diseases and diabetes

51 | 189 |

4959 تَعَهَّدَ *v. V* to commit oneself, pledge ب to do sth

تعهد رئيس الوزراء البريطاني بالعمل على دعم قوى الأمن اللبنانية — The British Prime Minister pledged to work to support the Lebanese security forces

49 | 196 |

4960 كَبَسَ *v. I (i)* to press (button, key); to dial (phone number); to click (mouse)

اكبس على الموس باليمين واختار فتح بستخدام — Right-click with the mouse and choose Open With

26 | 375 | +for +spo

4961 مُتَوَجِّه *a.p.* going, heading إلى to; turning, facing إلى towards

خرج من منزله في حي البحيرات متوجها إلى السوق لشراء احتياجات العيد لأبنائه — He left his house in the Al-Buhayrat quarter, heading for the market to buy holiday things for his children

52 | 184 |

4962 البارح /l-bareH/ (Magh.) *adv.* yesterday

البارح جابوا العرايس بصح ما رحناش البارح اليوم نروحوا — Yesterday they brought the arayes (food dish), but we didn't go yesterday. We're going to go today

21 | 464 | +spo

4963 هوايا /hwaaya/ (Irq.) *adv.* a lot, very much

تعبنا هوايا تعبنا بها — We got really tired, we got tired of it

31 | 314 | +spo

4964 خِيَرَة *n.* choice, best, pick, elite

عرض عليه خيرة بنات قريش فأبى — He was offered the best girls of Quraish, and he refused

53 | 182 |

4965 أَسْمَى *v. IV* to name, designate, call

طالب بتوفير الأمن، محذرا في الوقت نفسه ما أسماه السقوط في الهاوية — He demanded the provision of security, warning at the same time against what he called "falling into the pit"

73 | 133 |

4966 مُخْتَلِط *adj.* mixed, co-ed (schools); hybrid, blended (forces)

زمان كان ما في إلا سباحة مختلطة ومفتوحة — In the old days, the only thing there was, was mixed and open swimming

41 | 237 | +spo

4967 مُعْتَدٍ (def. مُعْتَدِي) *n. pl.* -uun aggressor, assailant

الجيش يواصل ملاحقة المعتدين في مخيم نهر البارد — The army is continuing to pursue the aggressors in the Nahr Al-Barid camp

52 | 184 |

4968 قَبَضَ *v. I (i)* to arrest, apprehend, seize على sb

سرق أول محفظه وفورا قبض عليه رجل وسيم يرتدي لبس فاخر — He stole his first wallet and immediately a handsome man wearing expensive clothing arrested him

50 | 193 |

4969 النهارده (Egy.) /in-nahaar-da/ *adv.* today

كلنا كويسين بابا بس كان تعبان شوية النهارده — We're all fine, it's just dad is a little sick today

42 | 231 | +spo

4970 دَقِيق *n.* flour

اشترى جحا كيسا من الدقيق وأعطاه لرجل حتى يحمله إلى المنزل — Juha bought a sack of flour and gave it to a man, so that he would carry it to the house

41 | 233 |

4971 مُتَفائِل *adj.* optimistic; *n.* optimist

إن شاء الله أنا متفائل بإذن الله أن يكون الحل قريبا — God willing, I am optimistic, with God's permission, that the solution is near

54 | 178 |

4972 عَدّ *n.* counting, calculating

فرغ الهواء ببطء من الفم حتى العد ٥ — Exhale through the mouth for a count of 5

55 | 176 |

4973 اِسْتَنَّى / بِسْتَنَّى *v.* (Dia. form X+II, from اِسْتَنَّى) to wait for sth/sb; (Alg.) تْسَنَّى (from إِسْتَنَّى) to wait في for sth/sb

إستنى حابقى أتصل انا بيك، حاتصل بيك بعدين — Wait and I'll get in touch with you, I'll call you later

20 | 484 | +spo

4974 نِطَى *v. I (i)* يِنْطِي (Irq.) to give, provide sth; to allow sth; اِنْطِيني خَالِد (in telephone speech) give me Khaled

الله يساعدك ينطيك الصحة والعافية — May God help you, may God give you health and strength

41 | 236 | +spo

4975 مُصْحَف *n.* manuscript, copy (esp. of the Qurʾan)

يتكون هذا المصحف الذهبي من ١٦٣ صحيفة يبلغ طول كل واحدة منها ١٣٦ ملم، وعرضها ٩٦ ملم — This golden copy of the Qurʾan is composed of 163 pages each of which is 136 mm long and 96 mm wide

46 | 209 |

4976 ناو (def. ناوِي) *a.p.* intending, wanting (to do sth)

طب انتى ناوية ترجعي إمتى القاهرة — OK, when do you intend to return to Cairo?

22 | 439 | +spo

4977 عارِم *adj.* tempestuous, frenzied

جميع أرجاء البلاد سوف تشهد مظاهرات احتجاجية عارمة — All parts of the country will witness violent protest demonstrations

56 | 172 |

4978 نَطَر *v. I (u)* to wait for sth/sb; to watch, guard sth/sb; ناطِر *a.p.* (Lev.Gul.) waiting for sth/sb

لو سمحت انطري ما بعرف قديه — Please wait, I don't know how long

17 | 567 | +spo

4979 شْگَد and شْگَد /shgadd/ (Irq.) *interrog.* how many, how much

شقد ياخذ الوقت من بيتنا؟ — How long does it take from our house?

33 | 292 | +spo

4980 أكو /ʾaku/ (Irq.Kuw.Bah.) *part.* there is, there are; (see also شكو /shaku/ and ماكو /maaku/)

أكو برامج إسلامية. أكو برامج كل شي — There are Islamic (television) shows. There are shows about everything

18 | 535 | +spo

4981 بُرْتُغالِيّ *n./adj.* Portuguese

شدد بيان صادر عن مكتب الرئيس البرتغالي على أنّ الاتحاد الأوروبي يدين استهداف بينظير بوتو — A communiqué issued by the office of the Portuguese president stressed that the European Union condemns the targeting of Benazir Bhutto

37 | 258 |

4982 تَعَدَّدَ *v. V* to be numerous; to be diverse or varied

هي المقالة التي تعددت عليها اردود سواء في الأهرام أو في الصحف الأخرى — It is the article to which there were many responses whether in the "Ahram" or the other newspapers

59 | 161 |

4983 وَفِيّ *adj.* loyal, faithful

أنا صديقك الوفي الذي من المستحيل أن يتخلى عنك — I am your faithful friend who could not abandon you

53 | 178 |

4984 كَيْد *n.* trick, ruse, plot, scheme

حفظك الله من كل شر وحفظك من كيد الأعداء وخياناتهم — May God keep you from all evil, and may He keep you from the schemes and betrayals of the enemies

48 | 197 |

4985 أَشْرَف *elat.* nobler/noblest; more/most honorable

الحمد لله رب العالمين والصلاة والسلام على أشرف المرسلين وبعد — Praise be to God, Lord of the Worlds, and prayers and peace be upon the most noble of messengers

53 | 179 |

4986 بَلْكِي (Lev.Irq.) *adv.* maybe, perhaps; بَلْكِن ،بَرْكِن ،بَرْكِي also (Irq.) ;بَلْكَت also (Lev.) بلكي حققوا لك أمنيتك — Perhaps they fulfilled your wish

9 | 1061 | +spo

4987 وُسْع *n.* capability, capacity ما كان في وسع أحد أن يقتله — No one was able to kill him

53 | 180 |

4988 تَوَرُّط *n.* involvement, entanglement حماس تعثر على مستندات تكشف تورط دحلان في مقتل عرفات — Hamas found documents which revealed Dahlan's being mixed up in the killing of Arafat

50 | 191 |

4989 شاطِر (Dia.) *adj.* pl. -iin clever, smart; handy, skilful; cute, sweet الناس هنا شاطرين قوى فى عمايل الحلويات — The people here are really clever in making sweets

35 | 273 | +spo

4990 مَصاري (Lev.) *pl.n.* money, cash أيوا بدي أعطيك مصاري واوصيك على شوية أغراض — Yes, I want to give you money and advise you on some things (to buy)

17 | 562 | +spo

4991 جابَ *v. I (u)* to explore, traverse, pass through مئات المظاهرات تجوب العالم تقف في وجه أمريكا — Hundreds of demonstrations are taking place throughout the world, standing in the face of America

52 | 182 |

4992 مَتِين *adj.* firm, solid, strong, unshakable الزواج لبنة متينة في جدار الأمة لابد من مراعاتها وطرد ما يؤذيها — Marriage is a firm brick in the wall of the nation which it is necessary to care for and drive out whatever harms it

53 | 177 |

4993 مُوَقَّع *adj.* signed, bearing signature لم تخالف إيران حتى الآن الاتفاقات الموقعة مع الوكالة الدولية للطاقة الذرية فيما يتعلق بأنشطة تخصيب اليورانيوم — Iran has not yet broken the signed agreements with the International

Agency for Nuclear Power, in regard to its activities enriching uranium

43 | 221 |

4994 اِرْتَكَزَ *v. VIII* to be centered, focused على around/on sth إذا قلنا نحن إن دولتنا ترتكز على تعاليم وقيم الإسلام فيكون ذلك غير مقبول — If we said that our state concentrates on the teachings and values of Islam, that would be unreasonable

52 | 181 |

4995 بيه ،بك and بيه بيك /bee, beeh/ *n.* Bey (title); (Egy.) (used informally as a sign of respect) تشرب أيه يا بيه؟ — What will you have to drink, sir?

39 | 242 |

4996 مَلْحَمَة *n.* fierce battle; epic اليوم يكتب الجيش اللبناني ملحمة جديدة بالدم ضد شكل آخر من أشكال الإرهاب — Today the Lebanese army is writing a new epic in blood against another type of terrorism

50 | 189 |

4997 اِحْتِكار *n.* monopoly, hoarding ليس من حق أي فئة أو تيار أن يزعم احتكار هذا الحق — It is not the right of any group or tendency to claim a monopoly on this right

50 | 188 |

4998 فاحَ *v. I (u)* to be fragrant; to emanate من from sb (scent, perfume) كان أنيقا كالعادة تفوح منه رائحة عطر فاخر — He was elegant, as usual, the scent of expensive perfume emanating from him

46 | 203 |

4999 أَضْعَف *elat.* weaker/weakest التمثال الضخم كسر في أضعف نقطته.. الركبة — The huge statue broke at its weakest point... the knee

58 | 163 |

5000 ضَمّ *n.* joining; addition, annexation لم يدخل الطب الحديث البلاد إلا بعد ضم الحجاز عام ١٩٢٥ — Modern medicine did not enter the country until after the annexation of the Hejaz in 1925

56 | 167 |

Alphabetical index

Format of entries

headword, *part of speech*, English equivalent, rank frequency

ا

أ *part.* (interrog.) ألا doesn't; ألَمْ didn't 372

ابد

أبَد *n.* eternity, forever; أبَداً never 584

ابن

اِبْن *n.* pl. أبْناء son; أبْناء children 145

اِبْنَة *n.* daughter (pl. بَنات, cf. بِنْت) 1386

إبّان *n.* time; إبّانَ during 3748

ابو

أب *n.* pl. آباء father; (in idafa) nom. أبو 76

ابي

أبَى *v. I (a)* to refuse sth or أنْ to do sth 3351

اتي

أتَى *v. I (i)* to come إلى to; to bring ب sth 343

آتٍ *adj.* coming; following, next 2245

اثر

أثَّر *v. II* to affect على sth/sb 1336

تأثَّر *v. V* to be affected ب/مِن by 2475

أثَر *n.* pl. آثار trace; sign; effect 554

أثَرِيّ *adj.* archeological; historical 4307

إثْر *prep.* and في إثْرِ right after 2257

تأثير *n.* pl. -aat effect, impression (في/على on) 1020

تأثُّر *n.* being influenced (ب by); emotion 4160

مُؤَثِّر *adj.* effective; *n.* effect 2360

اجر

أجْر *n.* pl. أجُور wage; fee; recompense 2304

اجل

أجْل *n.* مِن أجْلِ because of 300

أجَل *n.* time, period, term 1652

أجَل *interj.* yes, of course 4914

تأجيل *n.* postponement; deferment 2810

اجند

أجَنْدَة *n.* agenda, program; roadmap 4484

احد

أحَد *n.* fem. إحْدَى one (of) 63

حَدا *n.* (Lev.) anyone, somebody 2732

حَدّ *n.* (Egy.Lev.) someone, anyone 2042

الأحَد *n.* (يَوْم) Sunday 1174

اخذ

أخَذَ *v. I (u)* to take sth; to begin to do sth 198

اتَّخَذَ *v. VIII* to adopt, pass (a resolution) 1475

أخْذ *n.* taking; seizure 1785

واخِد *a.p.* (Egy.), ماخِذ (Lev.Irq.Gul.) taking 4500

اتِّخاذ *n.* adopting, passing (a resolution) 1355

اخر

تأخَّر *v. V* to be late, fall behind 2221

آخَر *adj.* fem. أخْرَى other, another 38

آخِر *adj.* pl. أواخِر last, final 474

الآخِرَة *n.* the hereafter 2992

أخير *adj.* last; latest, recent 206

تأخير *n.* delay, postponement 2800

مُؤَخَّر *n.* rear; مُؤَخَّراً recently 1565

تأخُّر *n.* slowness; backwardness 4192

مُتَأخِّر *adj.* pl. -uun late, delayed 2016

اخو

أخ *n.* pl. إخْوَة, إخْوان brother 66

خَيّ *n.* (Lev.) brother; خَيِّي my brother 3205

أخْت *n.* pl. أخَوات sister 226

ادب

أدَب *n.* pl. آداب literature; etiquette 1195

أدَبِيّ *adj.* literary; ethical, moral 2030

أديب *n.* pl. أدَباء author, writer 3204

ادو

أداة *n.* pl. أدَوات tool; appliance 1665

ادي

أدَّى *v. II* to cause إلى sth; to lead إلى to 429

أداء *n.* performance; rendering; fulfillment 946

مُؤَدٍّ *adj.* (def. مُؤَدِّي) leading إلى to 3659

اذ

إِذ **conj.** since; while; given that 421

اذا

إِذا **conj.** when, if; whether 43

إِذَن/إِذاً **adv.** therefore, consequently 655

اذن

أَذان **n.** adhan (call to prayer) 4457

أُذُن/أُذْن **fem.n.** pl. آذان ear 1853

إِذْن **n.** permission, authorization 1290

اذي

أَذىً **n.** harm; injury; offense 3496

ارخ

تاريخ **n.** date; history 286

تاريخيّ **adj.** historical 1013

اردن

أُرْدُنّيّ **n./adj.** Jordanian 878

ارض

أَرْض **fem.n.** pl. أراضٍ earth; land 116

أَرْضيّ **adj.** ground; land-based 1955

أَرْضيّة **n.** floor, basis; background 4488

ازاي

إِزّاي **adv.** (Egy.) how's come, why 4615

ازق

مَأْزِق **n.** impasse; dilemma, crisis 3178

ازم

أَزْمَة **n.** pl. أَزَمات crisis, crunch 675

ازي

إِزاءَ **prep.** towards; vis-à-vis, regarding 2460

اسبانيا

إِسْبانيّ **n./adj.** pl. إِسْبان Spanish, Spaniard 2746

استاد

إِسْتاد **n.** stadium 4697

استاذ

أُسْتاذ **n.** pl. أَساتِذة professor 562

استراتيجي

إِسْتراتيجيّ **adj.** strategic; **n.** strategist 1691

إِسْتراتيجيّة **n.** pl. -aat strategy 1696

اسد

أَسَد **n.** pl. أُسود lion 3148

اسر

أَسْر **n.** captivity; بِأَسْرِه completely 2268

أُسْرَة **n.** pl. أُسَر family, community 664

أُسَريّ **adj.** family, domestic 4128

أَسِير **n.** pl. أَسْرَى prisoner, captive 1292

اسرائيل

إِسْرائيليّ **n./adj.** pl. -uun Israeli 233

اسس

تَأَسَّسَ **v. V** to be established, be founded 4847

أَساس **n.** pl. أُسُس foundation; basis 485

أَساسيّ **adj.** basic, fundamental 557

تَأْسيس **n.** foundation; creation; installation 1920

مُؤَسِّس **adj.** founding; **n.** founder 3320

مُؤَسَّسَة **n.** pl. -aat institution 290

اسطورة

أُسْطورَة **n.** pl. أَساطير myth, fable 3258

اسف

أَسِفَ **v. I (a)** to feel sorry على about 4803

أَسَف **n.** regret; pity, sympathy 1116

آسِف **adj.** sorry, regretful 4118

مُؤْسِف **adj.** unfortunate; sorry, sad 4675

اسو

أَسىً **n.** affliction, sorrow, grief 3048

أُسْوَة **n.** model; pattern; concept 4422

مَأْساة **n.** pl. مَآسٍ tragedy 2262

اسيا

آسِيَويّ **n./adj.** Asian, Asiatic 2479

اشر

تَأْشيرَة **n.** visa (travel, exit) 4841

مُؤَشِّر **n.** pl. -aat indicator; measure 1467

اصل

أَصْل **n.** pl. أُصول source; lineage 547

أَصْليّ **adj.** original; real, true 1630

أَصيل **adj.** authentic; native; pure 2857

اطر

إِطار **n.** framework, context 697

اطلس

أَطْلَسيّ **adj.** Atlantic; NATO 3820

افريقيا

إِفْريقيّ **n./adj.** pl. أَفارِقة African 1087

افق

أُفُق **n.** pl. آفاق horizon; perspective 1481

اقت

مُؤَقَّت **adj.** temporary, interim 1944

اقلم

إِقْليم **n.** pl. أَقاليم region, district 1813

إِقْليميّ **adj.** regional; provincial 1230

أكاديمي

أَكاديميّ **adj.** academic; **n.** scholar 2784

أَكاديميَّة **n.** academy 3251

اكد

أَكَّد **v. II** to confirm أَنَّ that; to emphasize 187

تَأَكَّد **v. V** to ascertain مِن sth 3825

أَكيد **adj.** sure, certain, definite 632

تَأْكيد **n.** confirmation; certainty 1033

مُؤَكِّد **adj.** confirming; emphasizing 1060

مُؤَكَّد **adj.** certain; guaranteed 2538

تَأَكُّد **n.** assurance (مِن of); certainty 1935

مُتَأَكِّد **adj.** sure, convinced (مِن of) 3619

اكل

أَكَل **v. I (u)** to eat sth; to consume sb 1338

أَكْل **vn.** eating; **n.** food, meal 1495

اكو

أَكو **part.** /'aku/ (Irq.Kuw.Bah.) there is 4980

شَكو/شاكو **interrog.** (Irq.Kuw.) is there? 4953

ماكو **neg.part.** (Irq.Kuw.) there isn't 3591

ال

الـ **part.** (definite article) the 1

الا

أَلَّا **conj.** (= أَنْ لا) not to 1189

لِئَلَّا **conj.** (= لـ أَنْ لا) in order not to 4472

إِلَّا **part.** (exception) except (for) 53

وَلَّا/وِلَّا/واﻻ **conj.** or; otherwise, or else 712

البوم

أَلْبوم **n.** /'album/ album 3643

الذي

الَّذي **rel.pron.** (masc.sg.) who, whom; which 24

اللَّذانِ **rel.pron.** (masc.du.) who, whom 2073

الَّتي **rel.pron.** (fem.sg.) who, whom; which 18

اللَّتانِ **rel.pron.** (fem.du.) who, whom; which 3692

الَّذينَ **rel.pron.** (masc.pl.) who, whom 131

اللَّواتي **rel.pron.** (fem.pl.) who, whom 3397

اللَّاتي **rel.pron.** (fem.pl.) who, whom 4113

الف

أَلْف **num.** pl. آلاف thousand 111

تَأْليف **vn.** authoring; **n.** publication 3814

ائْتِلاف **n.** coalition, union 3709

مَأْلوف **adj.** familiar, typical; customary 4755

مُؤَلِّف **n.** author, composer 2062

مُؤَلَّف **adj.** composed (مِن of); **n.** publication 3970

الكترون

إِلِكْتْرونيّ **adj.** electronic; e-(mail) 1399

اللي

اللي **rel.pron.** /illi/ (Dia.) that, which, who 112

الم

أَلَم **n.** pl. آلام pain, hurt; suffering 929

مُؤْلِم **adj.** painful; distressing 2847

المانيا

أَلْمانيّ **n./adj.** pl. أَلْمان German 1166

اله

إِله **n.** god, deity; God 1326

إِلهيّ **adj.** divine, holy; theological 4130

الله **n.** God, Allah 12

اللَّهُمَّ **interj.** oh God! dear God! 784

يالله/يللا/يلا **interj.** /yaLLa/ (Dia.) c'mon! 1257

إِنشالله **adv.** /'inshaLLa/ (Dia.) hopefully 3183

الو

ألُو/آلو **interj.** /'aloo/ (Dia.) hello! 1378

الي

إِلَى **prep.** to, towards; till, until 9

ام

أَم **conj.** or (in questions) 273

اما

أَمّا **part.** .. فَ .. أَمّا as for... 134

إِمّا **conj.** إِمّا .. أَوْ/إِمّا either...or 1234

امد

أَمَد **n.** period, term; extent, range 3817

امر

أَمَر **v. I (u)** to order sb بـ to do sth 2205

أَمْر **n.** pl. أُمور matter, issue 70

أَمْر **n.** pl. أَوامِر order, command 1667

إِمارَة **n.** pl. -aat Emirate 810

إِماراتيّ **n./adj.** Emirati, UAE 2642

أَمير **n.** prince; Emir 589

مُؤامَرَة **n.** pl. -aat conspiracy, plot 2838

مُؤْتَمَر **n.** pl. -aat conference 394

امرك
أَمْريكيّ **n./adj.** pl. -uun, أَمْريكان American 85

امس
أَمْس **adv.** yesterday 237

امل
أَمَلَ **v. I (u)** to hope for, expect (في/ب) sth 1779

تَأَمَّلَ **v. V** to ponder (في) sth 3097

أَمَل **n.** pl. آمال hope, wish 648

تَأَمُّل **n.** reflection; pondering 4394

امم
أُمّ **n.** pl. أُمَّهات mother 163

أُمِّيَّة **n.** illiteracy 3833

أَمام **n.** front; أَمامَ in front of 153

أَماميّ **adj.** front, forward 4186

إمام **n.** prayer leader; Imam 1102

أُمَّة **n.** pl. أُمَم nation; people 248

امن
أَمَّنَ **v. II** to safeguard; to insure 3849

آمَنَ **v. IV** to believe ب in 1411

أَمْن **n.** security; order, control 238

أَمْنيّ **adj.** safety, security 549

أَمان **n.** safety, security 1494

أَمانة **n.** loyalty; honesty; secretariat 1681

أَمين **n.** pl. أُمَناء trustee; **adj.** loyal 710

آمِن **adj.** secure, safe 2241

تَأْمين **n.** protecting; insuring 1320

إيمان **n.** faith, belief (ب in) 1302

مُؤْمِن **adj.** believing; **n.** believer 1144

امين
آمين **interj.** amen! 2578

ان
أَنْ **conj.** (with subjunctive) to 13

أَنَّ **conj.** that (with foll. **n.** in acc.) 8

كَأَنَّ/وَكَأَنَّ **conj.** as if 318

كَأَنَّما **conj.** as if 2886

لِأَنَّ **conj.** because 57

إِنْ **conj.** if; whether 61

إِنَّ **conj.** that 29

إِنَّ **part.** indeed 127

إِنَّما **conj.** but rather; but also 483

انا
أَنا **pron.** I 25

آني **pron.** (Irq.Alg.) I 1972

مانيش **neg.part.** /ma-nii-sh/ (Egy.) I am not 3855

انت
أَنْتَ **pron.** you (masc.sg.) 54

أَنْتِ/إِنْتِي **pron.** (Dia.) you (fem.sg.) 544

انتم
أَنْتُم **pron.** you (masc.pl.) 1106

إِنْتو/إِنْتوا **pron.** (Dia.) you (pl.) 1906

انث
أُنْثى **n.** pl. إِناث female 2763

انجلز
إنجليزي/إنكليزي **n./adj.** /'ingliizi/ English 1462

انزين
انزين/نزين **interj.** /nzeen/ (Gul.) good; OK 4893

انس
إِنْسان **n.** pl. أُناس human being 204

إِنْسانيّ **adj.** human; humane 747

إِنْسانيَّة **n.** humanity, humankind 4054

انف
أَنْف **n.** nose; (fig.) pride 3151

اِسْتِئْناف **n.** resumption; appeal 2852

انفلونزا
إِنْفلوَنْزا/إِنْفلُوَنْزا **n.** flu, influenza 3578

انما
إِنَّما **conj.** but rather; but also 483

انن
أَنَّ **v. I (i)** to complain, moan 4589

اني
اِسْتَنَّى **v. X+II** بِسْتَنَّى (Dia.) to wait 4973

آني **pron.** (Irq.Alg.) I 1972

اه
آه **interj.** (Dia.) yes, right 142

آه **interj.** ah! ouch! 1340

أَها/أَهَه **interj.** (Dia.) /'ahaa/ yeah, uh-huh 4517

اهل
اِسْتَأْهَلَ **v. X** to deserve sth 3885

أَهْل **coll.n.** pl. أَهالي family; people 128

هَلا/ياهَلا **interj.** (Lev.Irq.Gul.) welcome! 900

أَهْليّ **adj.** civil; family; private (school) 1410

تَأْيِيد **n.** support, assistance 3244

ايدز

إيدز/أيدز **n.** /ʾeedz/ AIDS 3713

ايران

إيرانيّ **n./adj.** pl. -uun Iranian 944

ايش

أيش **interrog.** /ʾeesh/ (Lev.Gul.) what 1053

وِش/ويش **interrog.** /weesh/ (Gul.Sau.) what 1695

ايض

أيْضاً **n.** also; besides 146

ايطاليا

إيطاليّ **n./adj.** Italian 1954

ايميل

إيميل **n.** /ʾiimeel/ pl. -aat email 4809

اين

أيْنَ **interrog.** where 461

أيْنَما **conj.** wherever 3751

وين **interrog.** /ween/ (Lev.Irq.Gul.) where 406

فين **interrog.** /feen/ (Egy.Lev.) where 2177

ايوه

أيوا/أيْوه **interj.** /ʾaywa, ʿaywah/ (Dia.) yes 1927

ايه

إيه **interrog.** /ʾee/ (Egy.) what 405

إيه/إي **interj.** /ʾiih, ʾii/ (Dia.) yeah, uh-huh 164

ايها

أيُّها **voc.part.** fem. أيَّتُها oh! 853

ب

بِـ **prep.** with, by 6

بيـ **prep.** (Dia.) with, by 1345

بِـ **part.** (Egy.Lev.) /bi-/ **imperf.** verb prefix 31

بابا

بابا **n.** pope; daddy; (Ali) Baba 2660

بأر

بِئْر **fem.n.** well, spring; (Dia. بير /biir/ masc.) 3230

بُؤْرة **n.** center, focus 4859

بأس

بأْس **n.** لا بأْسَ بِه not a bad ... at all 1795

باشا

باشا **n.** pasha; الباشا Pasha 2923

باكستان

باكِستانيّ **n./adj.** Pakistani 3173

تَأْهِيل **n.** certification; training 2352

مُؤَهَّل **adj.** qualified; competent 3382

تَأَهُّل **n.** qualification; marriage 4310

اهو

أهو **part.** /ʾahu/ (Egy.) here he is 4363

او

أَو **conj.** or 23

اوروبا

أُورُوبّيّ/أُورُبّيّ **n./adj.** /ʾurubbi/ European 603

اوف

أُوف/أُفّ **interj.** (Lev.Irq.Gul.) ugh! phew! 4037

اوكي

أوكي/أوكيه **interj.** /ʾokey/ (Dia.) OK 1540

اول

آلَ **v. I (u)** to come to إلى sth 4645

أَوَّل **adj.** fem. أُولَى first 41

أَوَّليّ **adj.** first, primary, chief 2289

آل **n.** family, clan 1914

آلة **n.** pl. -aat instrument; machine 1988

آليّ **adj.** mechanical, automatic 3388

آليّة **n.** pl. -aat mechanism; vehicle 1515

أَوْلَوِيّة **n.** pl. -aat priority; goal 2449

اولمبي

أولمبي **adj.** /ʾoolimbi/ Olympic 3135

اولئك

أُولئِكَ/أُولائِكَ **dem.pron.** those (human) 1876

اون

آنَ **v. I (i)** to arrive (of time) 3009

آن **n.** time, moment; الآنَ now 125

آنَذاك **adv.** then, at that time 2480

أوان **n.** pl. آوِنة time, moment 2770

اوي

مَأْوًى **n.** refuge, shelter 4912

اي

أيْ **part.** in other words, i.e. 1259

أيّ **n.** fem. أيّة any; which 46

آيَة **n.** pl. -aat verse (Qurʾan); sign 1436

ايا

إيّا **part.** إيّاها to her/it 614

إيّا **part.** إيّاكَ و/من be careful with! 4375

ايد

أَيَّدَ **v. II** to support, assist sb 3390

بال

بال **n.** mind, attention 771

باي

باي **interj.** (Dia.) bye! goodbye! 4558

بتت

بَتَّة **n.** البَتَّة (not) at all 4661

بتاع

بِتاع **poss.adj.** (Egy.) belonging to; of 3238

بترول

بِتْرُول **n.** petroleum, oil 2264

بِتْرُولِيّ **adj.** petroleum-, oil-based 4904

بث

بَثَّ **v. I (u)** to broadcast; to disseminate 3462

بَثّ **n.** transmission; dissemination 2501

بحت

بَحْت **adj.** pure, exclusive 4574

بحث

بَحَثَ **v. I (a)** to look عن for; to discuss في 676

بَحْث **n.** pl. بُحُوث , أبحاث search (عن for) 332

مُباحَثَة **n.** pl. -aat discussion, dialog 3403

باحِث **adj.** searching (عن for); **n.** researcher 1282

بحر

بَحْر **n.** pl. بِحار sea 507

بَحْرِيّ **adj.** maritime; naval, navy 1874

بَحْرِيَّة **n.** navy 4032

بَحْرَيْنِيّ **n./adj.** Bahraini 3264

بُحَيْرَة **n.** lake 3535

بد

بِدّ/بَد **part.** (Lev.) to wish, want, need 344

بدأ

بَدَأَ **v. I (a)** to start, begin (في) sth 172

بَدْء **n.** start, beginning 1023

بِدايَة **n.** pl. -aat beginning, start 415

مَبْدَأ **n.** pl. مَبادِئ principle, basis 1099

مَبْدَئِيّ **adj.** fundamental, basic 4506

اِبْتِداء **n.** beginning, start 2759

اِبْتِدائِيّ **adj.** elementary; initial 2949

بدد

بُدّ **n.** avoidance, escape 455

اِسْتِبْداد **n.** despotism, tyranny 4414

بدر

بادَرَ **v. III** to begin; to hasten 2917

مُبادَرَة **n.** pl. -aat initiative; proposal 1105

بادِرَة **n.** pl. بَوادِر gesture, sign 4525

بدع

بَدِيع **adj.** wonderful, magnificent 4393

إبْداع **n.** creativity, originality 1642

مُبْدِع **adj.** creative; **n.** innovator 2455

بدل

بَدَّلَ **v. II** to change, substitute sth 4613

بَدَل **n.** بَدَلاً مِن instead of 864

بَدِيل **n.** pl. بَدائِل alternative; **adj.** substitute 1434

تَبْدِيل **n.** replacement, substitution 4775

تَبادُل **n.** exchange, interchange 1602

اِسْتِبْدال **n.** substitution; exchange 4229

مُتَبادَل **adj.** mutual, reciprocal; exchanged 2734

بدن

بَدَنِيّ **adj.** bodily, physical 4264

بدو

بَدا **v. I (u)** to appear (أَنَّ that); to seem 329

أبْدى **v. IV** to demonstrate, express sth 2091

بَدَوِيّ **n./adj.** pl. بَدْو/بَدُو Bedouin 3441

بادِيَة **n.** desert, wilderness 4322

بذر

بَذْر **n.** pl. بُذُور seed 4306

بذل

بَذَلَ **v. I (u,i)** to exert, expend (effort) 2197

بَذْل **n.** spending; donating; effort 3155

مَبْذُول **adj.** exerted; **n.** expenditure; effort 4339

برأ

بَرِيء **adj.** pl. أبْرِياء innocent; naive; exempt 1673

بَراءَة **n.** innocence; acquittal 3104

برازيل

بَرازِيلِيّ **n./adj.** Brazilian 3723

برتغال

بُرْتُغالِيّ **n./adj.** Portuguese 4981

برتقال

بُرْتُقال **coll.n.** oranges 4807

برج

بُرْج **n.** tower; constellation; horoscope 2615

برح

الْبَارِح **adv.** /l-bareH/ (Magh.) yesterday 4962

بَارِحَة **n.** yesterday, yesteryear 3017

امبارح/امبیرح **adv.** (Lev.) yesterday 4481

برد

بَرْد **n.** cold, coldness 2242

بَارِد **adj.** cold; bland (food) 1380

بَرِيد **n.** mail; post office 1812

برر

بَرَّرَ **v. II** to justify; to vindicate 3602

بِرّ **n.** charity; piety, righteousness 4052

برا/بره **prep.** /barra/ (Dia.) outside 2054

بَرّ **n.** land; earth 2793

بَرّيّ **adj.** rural; land-based; wild 2681

تَبْرِير **n.** pretext; vindication 3962

مُبَرِّر **adj.** justifying; **n.** pl. -aat excuse 2363

برز

بَرَزَ **v. I** (u) to emerge; to stand out 2313

أَبْرَزَ **v. IV** to highlight, expose sth 4919

بُرُوز **n.** emergence; prominence 4760

أَبْرَز **elat.** more/most prominent 1557

إِبْرَاز **n.** highlighting, emphasizing 4657

بَارِز **adj.** outstanding, distinguished 2130

برضو

برضو/بَرْدَه **adv.** /bardo/ (Egy.Lev.) also, too 2715

برع

تَبَرُّع **n.** pl. -aat donation, contribution 3614

برق

بَرْق **n.** lightning; telegraph 4392

بَرْقِيّة **n.** telegram 4430

بَرِيق **n.** sparkle, glitter; shine 4653

برك

بَارَكَ **v. III** to bless في sb (of God) 971

تَبَارَكَ **v. VI** to be praised (of God) 4238

بَرَكَة **n.** pl. -aat blessing 1928

بِرْكَة **n.** puddle; (swimming) pool 4913

مَبْرُوك **adj.** blessed, happy 1535

مُبَارَك **adj.** blessed; lucky, fortunate 1803

بركن

بُرْكان **n.** volcano 4860

برلمان

بَرْلَمَان **n.** parliament 1413

بَرْلَمَانِيّ **adj.** parliamentary; **n.** parliamentarian 2461

برمل

بَرْمِيل **n.** barrel; vat; drum 2919

برنامج

بَرْنَامَج **n.** pl. بَرَامِج program 161

بره

بُرْهَة **n.** moment, instant 4255

بروفسور

بروفسور **n.** /brofisoor/ professor; Prof. 4534

بري

مُبَاراة **n.** pl. مُبَارَيات game; competition 419

بريطانيا

بِرِيطَانِيّ **n./adj.** pl. -uun British 907

بسس

بَس **adv.** (Egy.Lev.Irq.Gul.) only, just 156

بسط

بَسِيط **adj.** pl. بُسَطَاء simple; easy; trifle 849

بَسَاطَة **n.** simplicity; بِبَسَاطَة simply 2210

أَبْسَط **elat.** simpler/simplest; more/most basic 3876

مَبْسُوط **adj.** happy; satisfied, content 4654

بسم

إِبْتَسَمَ **v. VIII** to smile (ل at sb) 1802

بَسْمَة **n.** smile 3888

إِبْتِسَامَة **n.** smile 2031

مُبْتَسِم **adj.** smiling 4285

بشر

بَشَّرَ **v. II** to give good news 4466

بَشَر **coll.n.** humankind, humans 1068

بَشَرِيّ **adj.** human 1120

بَشَرِيَّة **n.** humankind, human race 2953

بَشَرَة **n.** skin, epidermis 3786

مُبَاشَرَة **n.** pursuit; مُبَاشَرَةً directly 1150

مُبَاشِر **adj.** direct; live (broadcast) 912

بشع

بَشِيع **adj.** horrible, disgusting 3744

بصر

بَصَر **n.** perception; sight; view 2385

بَصَرِيّ **adj.** visual; optical 4425

بصل
بَصَل **coll.n.** onions 4300

بضع
بِضْعَة **n.** fem. بِضْع some, several 2098

بِضاعَة **n.** pl. بَضائِع merchandise, goods 3347

بطأ
بُطْء **n.** slowness; بِبُطْء slowly 3410

بَطيء **adj.** slow 4648

بطريرك
بَطْرِيَرْك **n.** (Chr.) patriarch 4731

بطق
بِطاقة **n.** pl. -aat card; tag; ticket 1486

بطل
بِطالة/بَطالة **n.** unemployment; inactivity 2357

باطِل **adj.** false; invalid; **n.** falsehood 2674

بَطَل **n.** pl. أَبْطال hero; champion; star 871

بُطولة **n.** heroism; pl. -aat championship 616

بطن
بَطْن **n.** stomach; interior; depth 2080

باطِن **adj.** inner; hidden; **n.** inside 3762

بعث
بَعَثَ **v. I (a)** to send, mail sth إلى to sb 1441

بَعْثِيّ **n./adj.** pl. -uun Baathist 4670

بَعْثة/بِعْثة **n.** pl. بَعَثات delegation; mission 2325

مَبْعوث **n.** envoy; delegate; representative 4103

بعد
بَعُدَ **v. I (u)** to be located, situated, found 2786

أَبْعَدَ **v. IV** to remove, eliminate, expel 4080

اِبْتَعَدَ **v. VIII** to move away, distance oneself 2332

اِسْتَبْعَدَ **v. X** to rule out (regard as unlikely) 3955

بَعْدَ **prep.** after 34

بَعْدُ **adv.** afterward; still; (not) yet 789

بَعَد **adv.** (Lev.Irq.Gul.) still, (not) yet 3240

بَعْدَما **conj.** after 1305

بعدين **adv.** /ba9deen/ (Egy.Lev.) later 1032

بُعْد **n.** pl. أَبْعاد dimension; distance 1358

بَعيد **adj.** pl. بِعاد distant, remote 355

أَبْعَد **elat.** farther/farthest 2561

إِبْعاد **n.** removal; banishment, exile 3870

اِبْتِعاد **n.** avoiding; distancing oneself 3169

اِسْتِبْعاد **n.** ruling out, regarding as unlikely 4564

بعض
بَعْض **n.** some, several 50

بغي
بَغى **v. I (i)** to pursue, strive for sth 1006

اِنْبَغى **v. VII** to be necessary (= must, should) 1331

بُغْية **n.** wish; purpose 3424

بقر
بَقَر **coll.n.** cows; بَقَرة (one) cow 3339

بقع
بُقْعة **n.** spot; pl. بِقاع region 2977

بقي
بَقِيَ **v. I (a)** to remain; to endure; to continue 257

بَقى **v. I (a)** /ba'a, yib'a/ (Egy.) to become 3620

بَقى **part.** /ba'a/ (Egy.) just, then, so 3458

أَبْقى **v. IV** to keep sth/sb على in a state) 4879

تَبَقّى **v. V** to be left over; to stay 2084

بَقِيّة **n.** pl. بَقايا remainder; end 928

بَقاء **n.** survival; **vn.** remaining, staying 1555

باقٍ **adj.** pl. باقُون remaining; **n.** remainder 919

مُتَبَقٍّ **adj.** remaining; **n.** rest 3514

بك
بك/بيه/بيك **n.** /bee, beeh/ Bey 4995

بكر
بُكْرة/بُكْرا **adv.** (Egy.Lev.Gul.) tomorrow 1810

باكِر **adj.** early 3505

باكِر/باچِر **adv.** /baachir/ (Irq.Gul.) tomorrow 4902

مُبَكِّر **adj.** early; مُبَكِّراً early 1424

بكي
بَكى **v. I (i)** to weep; to mourn 1238

بُكاء **n.** crying, weeping 1945

باكٍ **adj.** weeping; mourning 4374

بل
بَل **conj.** but, rather; in fact 160

بلا
بِلا **prep.** without 581

بلاش
بَلاش **part.** (Egy.Lev.Irq.Gul.) بِبَلاش for free 3733

بلد
بَلَد **n.** pl. بُلْدان, بِلاد country, nation 99

بَلْدة **n.** town, township, community 1458

بَلَدِيّ **adj.** indigenous; popular; municipal 2236

بَلَدِيّة **n.** pl. -aat municipality, township 1243

بهج

بَهْجَة **n.** magnificence; delight 3926

بوأ

بِيئَة **n.** environment; milieu 1039

بِيئِيّ **adj.** environmental 2524

بوب

باب **n.** pl. أَبْواب door; category; chapter 298

بَوّابَة **n.** door; portal, gateway 2435

بوح

بَوْح **n.** uncovering; disclosure, confession 4323

بورصة

بُورْصَة **n.** /burSa/ stock exchange, bourse 3021

بوق

باقَة **n.** bouquet; packet (data) 4565

بول

بَوْل **n.** urination; urine 4313

بيت

باتَ **v. I (i)** to become, begin, stay overnight 1079

بَيْت **n.** pl. بُيُوت house; pl. أَبْيات verse 104

بيد

بَيْدَ **conj.** بَيْدَ أَنَّ although 2940

بيض

بَيْض **coll.n.** eggs, un.n. بَيْضَة 2692

بَيَاض **n.** white, whiteness 3703

أَبْيَض **adj.** fem. بَيْضاء pl. بِيض white 564

بيع

باعَ **v. I (i)** to sell sth 1620

بَيْع **n.** sale; selling 1078

بائِع **adj.** selling; **n.** pl. باعَة seller 3100

مَبِيع **adj.** sold; **n.** مَبِيعات sales 3191

بين

بَيَّنَ **v. II** to clarify; to show; to seem 1616

تَبَيَّنَ **v. V** to become clear; to appear 1755

بَيْنَ **prep.** between; among 32

بَيْنَما **conj.** while 546

بَيان **n.** declaration; communiqué 552

بائِن **adj.** (Dia. بايِن) clear; obvious 4674

مُبَيِّن **adj.** explaining; /mbayyin/ it seems 2467

مُبِين **adj.** plain, clear, obvious 4221

بيه

n. بك/بيه/بيك /bee, beeh/ Bey 4995

بلغ

بَلَغَ **v. I (u)** to reach, attain; to come to sb 443

أَبْلَغَ **v. IV** to inform sb; to report 3610

بَلاغ **n.** communiqué; notice 4243

بُلُوغ **n.** reaching, attaining 3938

أَبْلَغ **elat.** more/most eloquent 4882

مَبْلَغ **n.** pl. مَبالِغ amount; extent; scope 962

مُبالَغَة **n.** exaggeration 3701

بالِغ **adj.** extreme; **a.p.** reaching; **n.** adult 1318

مُبالَغ **p.p.** مُبالَغ فيه/فيها exaggerated 4489

بلكي

بَلْكي **adv.** (Lev.Irq.) maybe, perhaps 4986

بلي

بَلَى **interj.** certainly, sure, yes 3304

بَلاء **n.** affliction, misfortune 3604

بليون

بِلْيُون **num.** /bilyoon/ billion 4773

بما

بِما **part.** بِما في ذلِكَ including 234

بن

بِنْت **n.** pl. بَنات daughter, girl 252

بَنُو **pl.n.** (sg. ابْن cf. بِن) sons, children 1151

بند

بَنْد **n.** pl. بُنُود article, clause 2248

بندق

بُنْدُقِيَّة **n.** rifle; gun, weapon 4245

بنزين

بَنْزِين **n.** gas, gasoline, petrol 3790

بنك

بَنْك **n.** pl. بُنُوك bank (fin.) 625

بنن

بُنِّيّ **adj.** brown 4164

بني

بَنَى **v. I (i)** to build, construct sth 1881

تَبَنَّى **v. V** to adopt sth; to be built 3232

تَبَنٍّ **n.** adoption 3140

بِناء **vn.** constructing; **n.** building 400

بِنْيَة **n.** pl. بِنًى/بُنًى structure; physique 1522

بَنَّاء **adj.** constructive, positive 4854

بِنايَة **n.** building, edifice; structure 4578

مَبْنًى **n.** pl. مَبانٍ building; structure 1524

مَبْنِيّ **adj.** built, based (على on) 3108

تبع

تَبِعَ *v. I (a)* to follow, pursue sth/sb 1699

تَابَعَ *v. III* to follow, monitor sth/sb 887

تَبَع *n. pl.* أَتْبَاع follower 2909

تَبَع *poss.adj.* (Lev.) belonging to 3627

تَبِعَة *n. pl.* -aat consequence; responsibility 4603

تِبَاعاً *adv.* in succession, consecutively 4297

مُتَابَعَة *n.* pursuing, following; continuation 1077

اِتِّبَاع *n.* pursuing, following; compliance 3685

تَابِع *adj.* belonging ل to; *n. pl.* -uun follower 957

مُتَّبَع *adj.* followed, observed 4403

تجر

تِجَارَة *n.* commerce, business 886

تِجَارِيّ *adj.* commercial, business 836

تَاجِر *n. pl.* تُجَّار merchant; *adj.* trading 1662

تحف

مَتْحَف *n.* museum 2894

تحت

تَحْت *n.* bottom; تَحْتَ *prep.* below 216

تَحْتِيّ *adj.* under; infra-(structure) 2754

ترب

تُرْبَة *n.* dust, dirt; grave 3553

تُرَاب *n.* dirt, soil 1833

ترث

تُرَاث *n.* heritage; inheritance 1821

تُرَاثِيّ *adj.* historical; inherited 4625

ترجم

تَرْجَمَة *n.* translation; biography 2228

ترك

تَرَكَ *v. I (u)* to leave (behind), abandon sth 472

تَارِك *adj.* leaving (behind), quitting 4269

تُرْكِيّ *n./adj. pl.* تُرْك, أَتْرَاك Turk; Turkish 1480

تسع

تِسْعَة *num. fem.* تِسْع nine 1140

تِسْعُون *num.* ninety; ninetieth 4899

التسعينات *n.* the Nineties 4433

تِسْعِينِيّ *adj.* ninetieth; *n.* التِسْعِينِيّات the Nineties 4789

تَاسِع *adj.* ninth (ordinal) 1655

تعب

تَعِبَ *v. I (a)* to get tired من of sth 2621

تَعْب *n.* trouble, inconvenience 2429

مُتْعَب *adj.* tired, weary 3777

تفح

تُفَّاح *coll.n.* apples 4601

تقن

تَقْنِيّ *adj.* technical 2787

تَقْنِيَّة *n. pl.* -aat technology, technique 1414

تقي

تَقْوَى *n.* piety, devoutness 4309

تكنولوجيا

تِكْنُولُوجِيا *n.* technology 1868

تِكْنُولُوجِيّ *adj.* technological 2583

تلفز

تِلْفَاز *n.* television set 3808

تلفزيون

تلفزيون *n.* /tilfizyoon/ television 1067

تلفزيوني *adj.* /tilfizyooni/ television, televised 2466

تلفن

تليفون/تلفون *n. pl.* -aat telephone 1562

تلك

تِلْكَ *dem.pron.* that (fem.sg.); those 129

تلمذ

تِلْمِيذ *n. pl.* تَلامِيذ student, pupil 2416

تلو

تَلا *v. I (u)* to come after; to recite (Qur'an) 4056

تالٍ *adj.* following; بالتالي therefore 466

مُتَالٍ *adj.* consecutive, successive 3430

تِلْوَ *prep.* after, followed by 3184

تمر

تَمْر *coll.n.* dates (fruit) 4663

تمم

تَمَّ *v. I (i)* to finish; to take place 78

أَتَمَّ *v. IV* to complete, finish, conclude sth 3241

تَمَام *adj.* exact; complete; good, fine 448

إِتْمَام *n.* completion; realization 3983

تَامّ *adj.* complete, concluded 1675

توب

تَوْبَة *n.* repentance, penance 4200

تور

تَارَةً *n.* once; sometimes 2697

تونس

تُونِسِيّ *n./adj.* Tunisian 2052

توو

تَوّ *n.* لِلتَّوِّ immediately 3297

تيح

أَتاحَ *v. IV* to provide (opportunity) 2620

مُتاح *adj.* provided, available, granted 2680

تير

تَيّار *n.* pl. -aat current, stream 1298

ثأر

ثَأْر *n.* revenge, retaliation 4621

ثبت

ثَبَتَ *v. I (u)* to be confirmed 2554

ثَبَّتَ *v. II* to confirm, reinforce 2431

أَثْبَتَ *v. IV* to prove, ascertain sth 1511

ثَبات *n.* proof; constancy, firmness 3671

تَثْبيت *n.* confirmation; stabilization 3689

إِثْبات *n.* proof; verification 3348

ثابِت *adj.* established; stable, steady 1466

ثابِتة *n.* pl. ثَوابِت principle, rule 3730

ثدي

ثَدْي *n.* breast; udder 4672

ثرو

ثَرْوة *n.* pl. ثَروات wealth; abundance 1743

ثقف

ثَقافة *n.* pl. -aat culture, civilization 519

ثَقافي *adj.* cultural, intellectual 629

مُثَقَّف *n.* pl. -uun intellectual; *adj.* educated 1973

ثقل

ثَقيل *adj.* heavy, cumbersome 1568

ثلث

ثُلُث *n.* one third 2359

ثَلاثة *num.* fem. ثَلاث three 151

ثَلاثون *num.* thirty; thirtieth 1108

ثُلاثاء *n.* (يَوْم) الثُلاثاء Tuesday 1504

ثُلاثي *adj.* three-part, tri-; *n.* trio 3364

ثالِث *adj.* third (ordinal) 367

مُثَلَّث *n.* triangle; *adj.* triangle-like 4946

ثلج

ثَلْج *n.* snow; ice 3500

ثَلاجة *n.* refrigerator; freezer 4881

ثمر

ثَمَر *n.* pl. ثِمار fruit; yield 2856

ثَمَرة *n.* fruit; result, outcome 3827

استِثْمار *vn.* investing; *n.* pl. -aat investment 803

استِثْماري *adj.* investment 2465

مُسْتَثْمِر *n.* pl. -uun investor; *adj.* investing 2263

ثمم

ثَمَّ *adv.* there (is/are); مِن ثَمَّ therefore 1310

ثَمَّة *adv.* there (is/are) 1350

ثُمَّ *conj.* then, afterwards; besides, furthermore 108

ثمن

ثَمَن *n.* price, cost; value, worth 1101

ثَمين *adj.* costly; valuable, precious 3784

ثَمانية *num.* fem. ثَمانٍ eight 875

ثَمانون *num.* eighty; Eighties 3758

الثَّمانينات *n.* the Eighties 4358

ثامِن *adj.* eighth (ordinal) 1585

ثني

اثْنانِ *num.* fem. اثْنَتانِ two; اثْنا عَشَر twelve 653

الاثْنَيْن *n.* (يَوْم) Monday 1347

ثانَوي *adj.* secondary; subordinate 1455

ثانَوية *n.* secondary school, high-school 4147

أَثْناء *prep.* during; في هٰذِهِ الأَثْناء meanwhile 706

ثَنِيّة *n.* pl. ثَنايا incisor; في/بَيْنَ ثَنايا within 4703

ثَناء *n.* praise, commendation; appreciation 4908

ثُنائي *adj.* dual, bilateral 2152

ثانٍ *adj.* second, additional; next, following 80

ثانية *n.* pl. ثَوانٍ second (time span) 2303

اسْتِثْناء *n.* باسْتِثْناء with the exception (of) 2093

اسْتِثْنائي *adj.* exceptional, irregular 3465

ثوب

ثَوْب *n.* pl. ثِياب robe, tunic; ثِياب clothes 1433

مَثابة *n.* بِمَثابة virtually, tantamount to 2135

ثور

ثارَ *v. I (u)* to revolt, arise 4251

أَثارَ *v. IV* to stir up sth; to bring up (a subject) 1198

ثَوْرة *n.* revolution, uprising 1031

ثَوْري *adj.* revolutionary 3379

إِثارة *n.* provocation, agitation 2587

مُثير *adj.* influential; *a.p.* provoking, agitating 2193

جبر

جَبّار *adj.* mighty, powerful; huge, gigantic 4246

جبل

جَبَل *n.* pl. جِبال mountain 830

جبن

جَبان **adj.** coward, cowardly; **n.** coward 4084

جَبين **n.** forehead, brow 3327

جبه

جَبْهَة **n.** (military, political, weather) front 1447

جثث

جُثَّة **n.** pl. جُثَث corpse, body 1482

جحم

جَحِيم **n.** hell, inferno; الجَحِيم Hell 3067

جدد

جَدَّدَ **v. II** to renew, renovate; to try again 2950

تَجَدَّدَ **v. V** to be renewed; to repeat itself 4399

جَدّ **n.** grandfather, fem. جَدَّة grandmother 1226

جِدّ **n.** seriousness; جِدّاً very much 171

جِدِّيّ **adj.** serious, earnest; جِدِّيّاً in earnest 2505

جِدِّيَّة **n.** seriousness, earnestness 2627

جَدِيد **adj.** pl. جُدُد new; مِن جَدِيد again 60

تَجْدِيد **n.** renovation, renewal 2076

جادّ **adj.** earnest, serious 1808

مُجَدَّد **adj.** renewed, renovated; مُجَدَّداً again 2074

مُسْتَجِدّ **adj.** new; **n.** مُسْتَجِدّات recent events 4261

جدر

جَدُرَ **v. I (u)** to be worth ب (mentioning) 3370

جَدِير **adj.** worth ب (mentioning) 2772

جِدار **n.** pl. جُدْران wall 1131

جدل

جَدَل **n.** controversy, dispute; debate 2186

جدو

أَجْدَى **v. IV** to be useful, helpful 3989

جَدْوَى **n.** benefit, advantage, utility 2266

جدول

جَدْوَل **n.** pl. جَداوِل table, chart; schedule 1889

جذب

جَذْب **n.** attraction, lure; gravitation 3404

جذر

جِذْر/جَذْر **n.** pl. جُذُور root, stem 2610

جِذْرِيّ **adj.** radical, fundamental, basic 3963

جرأ

جَرُؤَ **v. I (u)** to dare على to do sth 4143

جُرْأَة **n.** boldness, audacity, courage 3796

جرب

جَرَّبَ **v. II** to test, sample sth; to tempt sb 2717

تَجْرِبَة **n.** pl. تَجارِب test; experience; trial, ordeal 587

جرح

جَرَحَ **v. I (a)** (pass.) جُرِحَ to be injured 3520

جُرْح **n.** pl. جِراح ,جُرُوح wound, injury 1011

جِراحَة **n.** surgery 3490

جِراحِيّ **adj.** surgical 3428

جَرِيح **n./adj.** pl. جَرْحَى wounded, injured 1977

جرد

جَرِيدَة **n.** pl. جَرائِد newspaper, periodical 1339

مُجَرَّد **adj.** bare; **n.** mere, nothing but 766

جرر

جَرَّ **v. I (u)** to drag, pull sth 4426

جرس

جَرَس **n.** bell 3361

جرع

جُرْعَة **n.** dosage, dose; vaccine; gulp 4802

جرم

جَرِيمَة **n.** pl. جَرائِم crime 740

مُجْرِم **n./adj.** criminal 2250

جري

جَرَى **v. I (i)** to happen; to flow, run 353

أَجْرَى **v. IV** to conduct, carry out, perform sth 1397

مَجْرَى **n.** pl. مَجْرَيات course, path; events 2862

إِجْراء **vn.** conducting; **n.** pl. -aat procedure 492

جار **adj.** present; occurring; flowing 1088

جَرَّاء **n.** مِن جَرَّاء and جَرَّاءَ as a result of 1770

جزأ

تَجَزَّأ **v. V** to be divided, partitioned, detached 4740

جُزْء **n.** pl. أَجْزاء section, part, piece; portion 524

جُزْئِيّ **adj.** partial, incomplete; جُزْئِيّاً in part 3779

جزر

جَزِيرَة **n.** pl. جُزُر island; شِبْه جَزِيرَة peninsula 1733

جَزائِرِيّ **n./adj.** Algerian 1663

مَجْزَرَة **n.** pl. مَجازِر massacre, slaughter 2347

جزل

جَزِيل **adj.** abundant 2753

جزي

جَزَى **v. I (i)** to repay, reward sb 1846

جَزاء **n.** reward; punishment; penalty 2075

جسد

جَسَّدَ **v. II** to embody, personify sth 3756

جَسَد **n.** pl. أَجْساد body 963

جَسَدِيّ **adj.** physical, bodily; sensual 3765

جسر

جِسْر **n.** pl. جُسُور bridge; beam, bar 1456

جسس

تَجَسُّس **n.** espionage, spying 4918

جسم

جِسْم **n.** pl. أَجْسام body; form, mass; organism 745

جعل

جَعَلَ **v. I (a)** to make sb/sth do sth 323

جَعْل **n.** making (sb/sth do sth) 3330

جغرافيا

جُغْرافِيا **n.** geography 4275

جُغْرافِيّ **adj.** geographical 2547

جفف

جَفَّ **v. I (i)** to become dry 4485

جَفاف **n.** dryness, drought; dehydration 3558

جافّ **adj.** dry 3587

جلب

جَلَبَ **v. I (i,u)** to bring about, cause sth 2885

جلد

جِلْد **n.** skin; leather 2178

جَلِيد **n.** ice 4658

جلس

جَلَسَ **v. I (i)** to sit (down); to sit إلى at (a table) 924

جَلْسَة **n.** pl. جَلَسات session, meeting 832

جُلُوس **n.** sitting down, being seated 3053

جالِس **adj.** seated, sitting 2399

مَجْلِس **n.** pl. مَجالِس council, board 101

جلل

جَلَّ **v. I (i)** to be majestic, exalted (of God) 1950

جُلّ **n.** majority, most, main part (of) 3478

جَلِيل **adj.** venerable, eminent; glorious, great 3960

جَلالَة **n.** majesty 1521

مَجَلَّة **n.** pl. -aat magazine, journal 1132

جلو

تَجَلَّى **v. V** to become evident 3314

جَلِيّ **adj.** clear, evident, obvious 4378

جالِيَة **n.** expatriate community, colony 3911

جمد

جامِد **adj.** frozen; rigid 3925

جمر

جَمْر **n.** embers 3973

جمرك

جُمْرُك **n.** pl. جَمارِك customs; الجَمارِك tariffs 4318

جمع

جَمَعَ **v. I (a)** to gather, assemble sth 1107

تَجَمَّعَ **v. V** to gather together, assemble, rally 4133

اِجْتَمَعَ **v. VIII** to meet مع/ب with 1974

جَمْع **n.** gathering, assembling 1471

جَمْع **n.** pl. جُمُوع crowd, gathering; collection 2158

جُمعة **n.** (يَوْم) الجُمْعَة Friday 955

جَمْعِيَّة **n.** pl. -aat association, society 560

جَمِيع **n.** all (of); every one (of); جَمِيعاً all 82

أَجْمَع **adj.** pl. -uun, fem. جَمْعاء, entire; **n.** all of 2452

جَماعَة **n.** pl. -aat group, party; gang 609

جَماعِيّ **adj.** group, collective; common 1654

مَجْمَع **n.** assembly; academy 2938

تَجْمِيع **n.** gathering, assembling 4218

إِجْماع **n.** consensus; بالإجْماع unanimously 3752

تَجَمُّع **n.** pl. -aat gathering, assembly; grouping 1985

اِجْتِماع **n.** pl. -aat meeting 475

اِجْتِماعِيّ **adj.** social 368

جامِع **n.** mosque 2812

جامِع **adj.** comprehensive; **n.** collector 3896

جامِعَة **n.** pl. -aat university; league 210

جامِعِيّ **adj.** university 1570

مَجْمُوع **adj.** gathered; **n.** total 2417

مَجْمُوعَة **n.** pl. -aat collection, group 293

مُجَمِّع **adj.** collecting, gathering; **n.** collector 3444

مُجْتَمِع **adj.** meeting; **n.** (meeting) participant 3455

مُجْتَمَع **n.** pl. -aat society 222

مُجْتَمَعِيّ **adj.** societal 4826

جمل

جُمْلَة **n.** pl. جُمَل sentence, clause; group 1422

جَمَل **n.** pl. جِمال camel 3969

جَمال **n.** beauty 1169

جَمِيل **adj.** beautiful, nice; الفُنُون الجَمِيلَة fine arts 304

أَجْمَل **elat.** more/most beautiful 1183

تَجْمِيل **n.** embellishment, decoration 3434

إِجْمَال **n.** sum, whole; إِجْمَالًا in general 4509

إِجْمَالِيّ **adj.** comprehensive, full; total, gross 1931

مُجْمَل **n.** total, full amount; summary 3716

جمهر

جُمْهُور **n.** pl. جَمَاهِير multitude, masses 724

جُمْهُورِيّ **n./adj.** republican; Republican 3035

جُمْهُورِيَّة **n.** republic 824

جَمَاهِيرِيّ **adj.** mass, throng; (of the) masses 3532

جَمَاهِيرِيَّة **n.** Jamahiriya (Libya) 3435

جنب

جَنْب **n.** side; جَنْبَ next to 1984

جَنُوب **n.** south; جَنُوبًا southward 416

جَنُوبِيّ **adj.** southern, south 1279

جَانِب **n.** pl. جَوَانِب side; إِلَى جَانِبِ next to 208

جَانِبِيّ **adj.** side, lateral; marginal; secondary 3452

أَجْنَبِيّ **n./adj.** pl. أَجَانِب foreign, foreigner 723

تَجَنُّب **n.** avoidance, avoiding 3109

جنح

جَنَاح **n.** pl. أَجْنِحَة wing; flank 2000

جند

جُنْد **n.** army, soldiers 4277

جُنْدِيّ **n.** pl. جُنُود soldier 654

جنرال

جِنِرَال **n.** (mil.) general; الجِنِرَال General 2160

جنز

جِنَازَة **n.** funeral 4936

جنس

جِنْس **n.** gender, sex; type, kind 1980

جِنْسِيّ **adj.** sexual 2290

جِنْسِيَّة **n.** nationality, citizenship 1635

جنن

جَنَّنَ **v. II** to drive sb insane 4432

جِنّ **n.** demon; jinn; genie 3617

جَنَّة **n.** pl. جَنَّات , جِنان paradise; garden 984

جَنِين **n.** fetus, embryo; germ 3552

جُنُون **n.** madness, insanity 2432

مَجْنُون **n./adj.** pl. مَجَانِين crazy, insane 2308

جني

جِنَائِيّ **adj.** criminal, penal 3311

جَانٍ **n./adj.** pl. جُنَاة delinquent, criminal 3781

جنيه

جُنَيْه **n.** pl. -aat pound (currency) 1676

جهد

جَهْد **n.** pl. جُهُود effort; endeavor 731

جُهْد **n.** effort, exertion, strain 1415

جِهَاد **n.** jihad (struggle in the way of God) 1443

اِجْتِهَاد **n.** effort; independent thinking 4724

جَاهِد **adj.** strenuous, vigorous; striving 3693

مَجْهُود **adj.** expended (efforts); **n.** efforts 3243

مُجَاهِد **adj.** fighting; **n.** pl. -uun warrior 2039

جهز

جِهَاز **n.** pl. أَجْهِزَة apparatus; appliance; agency 338

تَجْهِيز **vn.** preparing; **n.** pl. -aat equipment 3582

جَاهِز **adj.** ready, prepared; equipped 1775

جهل

جَهِلَ **v. I (a)** to ignore, not know sth 4948

جَهْل **n.** ignorance 2477

تَجَاهُل **n.** feigned ignorance; disregard 4156

جَاهِل **adj.** ignorant; (Irq.Yem.Gul.) child 4236

جَاهِلِيَّة **n.** ignorance; Jahiliyah (pre-Islam) 4299

مَجْهُول **adj.** unknown; **n.** unidentified 1741

جهنم

جَهَنَّم **n.** hell; Hell 3680

جوب

جَابَ **v. I (u)** to explore, traverse 4991

أَجَابَ **v. IV** to respond, reply (إِلَى to) 1110

اِسْتَجَابَ **v. X** to accept; to comply with 3164

جَوَاب **n.** answer; (Egy.) pl. -aat letter 1391

إِجَابَة **n.** pl. -aat answer, reply, response 1716

تَجَاوُب **n.** responsiveness (to need); rapport 4367

اِسْتِجَابَة **n.** acceptance; complying with 2579

اِسْتِجْوَاب **n.** interrogation, questioning 4157

مُجِيب **adj.** responding; **n.** person answering 4450

جوح

اِجْتَاحَ **v. VIII** to strike, invade (country) 4136

اِجْتِيَاح **n.** strike, invasion 4050

جود

أَجَادَ **v. IV** to be proficient, do sth well 4443

جَوْدَة **n.** excellence, good quality 2378

جَيِّد **adj.** good; جَيِّدًا adv. well 488

جور

جَار **n.** pl. جِيرَان neighbor 1550

جِوَار **n.** proximity, vicinity; بِجِوَارِ near 1721

مُجَاوِر **adj.** neighboring, adjacent 1793

جوز

جازَ **v. I (u)** to be allowed, be possible ل for sb 1299

تَجاوَزَ **v. VI** to surmount, go beyond sth 1135

جوز **n.** (Egy.) /gooz/, (Lev.) /jooz/ husband 4766

جَواز **n.** permit; جَواز السَّفَر passport 2995

إجازَة **n.** holiday; permit; pass; certificate 2114

تَجاوُز **vn.** surmounting; **n.** -aat violations 1753

جائِزَة **n.** pl. جَوائِز prize, award, reward 1086

مِتْجَوِّز **adj.** (Lev.) married 4935

جوع

جُوع **n.** hunger; starvation 2187

جوف

جَوْف **n.** belly, abdomen; cavity, hollow 4351

جول

جالَ **v. I (u)** to wander, roam about 4360

جَوْلَة **n.** pl. -aat tour; round; session; patrol 1207

جَوّال **n.** mobile (phone); **adj.** itinerant 2396

مَجال **n.** pl. -aat area; domain; sector; arena 262

جوهر

جَوْهَر **n.** pl. جَواهِر gem, jewel; essence 3210

جَوْهَرِيّ **adj.** essential; core, central 4203

جو

جَوّ **n.** pl. أَجْواء air; weather, climate 667

جَوِّيّ **adj.** air; atmospheric; weather-related 1492

جوا

جُوّا **prep./adv.** (Lev.Irq.) and جوه (Egy.) inside 4957

جيأ

جاء **v. I (i)** to come, arrive; to show up 109

جاي **a.p.** (Dia.) coming, arriving; **adj.** next 1982

جيب

جاب **v. I (i)** (Dia.) to bring sth 1046

جَيْب **n.** pl. جُيُوب pocket; purse 2512

جيش

جَيْش **n.** pl. جُيُوش army; armed forces; troops 337

جيل

جِيل **n.** pl. أَجْيال generation, age 1103

ح

حَ **part.** (Egy., future, with imperf.) will 4072

حبب

حَبَّ **v. I (i)** to love, like sb; to want, like sth 495

أَحَبَّ **v. IV** to love, like sth/sb; to want sth 342

حُبّ **n.** love, affection 209

حَبّ **coll.n.** grain; pl. حُبُوب seed; pill 1575

حَبِيب **n./adj.** pl. أَحْباب, أَحِبَّة dear 347

مَحَبَّة **n.** love, affection 2327

مُحِبّ **adj.** affectionate; **n.** fan, enthusiast 2351

حبر

حِبْر **n.** ink 3957

حبل

حَبْل **n.** rope, cord, cable 3039

حتم

حَتْم **n.** necessity; حَتْمًا definitely, necessarily 2913

حتي

حَتَّى **prep.** until, up to; لحتى (Lev.) /la-Hatta/ 81

حَتَّى **conj.** (with subjunctive) in order to 279

حَتَّى **adv.** even, including; even though 378

حثث

حَثَّ **v. I (u)** to urge, incite sb على to do sth 3321

حجب

حَجْب **vn.** veiling; covering; holding back 4843

حِجاب **n.** hijab (Islamic head scarf), veil 2373

حجج

حَجّ **n.** pilgrimage, Hajj 2463

حُجَّة **n.** pretext, excuse; proof, evidence 1851

اِحْتِجاج **n.** protest; اِحْتِجاجاً protesting 2662

حاجّ **n.** fem. حاجَّة pl. حُجّاج pilgrim 1155

حجر

حَجَر **n.** pl. حِجارَة stone 1363

حُجْرَة **n.** pl. حُجَر room, chamber; cell 3106

حجز

حَجْز **n.** reservation (seat, room); confiscation 4447

حاجِز **n.** pl. حَواجِز obstacle; **adj.** blocking 1836

حجم

حَجْم **n.** volume, size 778

حدث

حَدَثَ **v. I (u)** to happen, occur, take place 408

حَدَّثَ **v. II** to tell sb (عن about); to narrate sth 3249

أَحْدَثَ **v. IV** to cause (reaction, change) 3378

تَحَدَّثَ **v. V** to speak to/with sb; to discuss 453

حَدَث **n.** pl. أَحْداث event, incident 599

حَدِيث **n.** pl. أَحادِيث discussion; interview 369

حَدِيث **adj.** new, recent; modern; حَدِيثاً lately 769

حُدُوث **n.** happening, taking place 2113

حَدَاثَة *n.* modernity, newness, novelty 3712

أَحْدَث *elat.* newer/newest 2481

تَحْدِيث *vn.* renewing; *n.* pl. -aat update 2552

مُحَادَثَة *n.* pl. -aat discussion, talk; negotiation 2219

إِحْدَاث *n.* implementation; bringing about 3853

تَحَدُّث *n.* discussion, speaking 3538

حَادِث *n.* pl. حَوَادِث incident, accident 1431

حَادِثَة *n.* pl. حَوَادِث incident, accident 1270

مُتَحَدِّث *n.* fem. -a, spokesperson, speaker 1759

حدد

حَدَّ *v. I (u)* to limit مِن sth; to halt, stop مِن sth 4115

حَدَّدَ *v. II* to specify sth; to define sth 1275

حَدّ *vn.* limiting مِن sth; stopping مِن sth 3283

حَدّ *n.* pl. حُدُود extent, limit; edge; حُدُود border 197

حَدّ *prep.* (Lev.) next to, beside; (alone) with 4439

حُدُودِيّ *adj.* frontier, border 4204

حِدَّة *n.* intensity, violence 2406

حَدِيد *n.* iron 1720

حَدِيدِيّ *adj.* iron, iron-like 3138

تَحْدِيد *n.* specification; definition 684

حَادّ *adj.* sharp, intense 1643

مَحْدُود *adj.* limited; determined 1600

مُحَدَّد *adj.* defined, determined, set 1139

حدق

حَدِيقَة *n.* pl. حَدَائِق garden 1624

حدو

تَحَدٍّ *n.* pl. -aat challenge 1129

حَادِي *adj.* first; الحَادِي عَشَر eleventh 2249

حذر

حَذِرَ *v. I (a)* to be cautious, beware مِن of 4315

حَذَّرَ *v. II* to warn, caution sb مِن of 2025

حِذْر/حَذَر *n.* care, caution, vigilance 2234

تَحْذِير *n.* pl. -aat warning, caution 2991

مُحَذِّر *a.p.* warning, cautioning 4614

حذف

حَذْف *n.* deletion, omission 4352

حذو

حِذَاء *n.* shoe; pair of shoes 3637

حرب

حَارَبَ *v. III* to fight, wage war against sb/sth 3432

حَرْب *fem.n.* pl. حُرُوب war, warfare 165

حَرْبِيّ *adj.* war, military 2531

مُحَارَبَة *n.* fight, struggle, combat 2542

حرج

حَرَج *n.* impediment, difficulty 3078

حَرِج *adj.* delicate, sensitive; awkward 3761

حرر

حَرّ *n.* warmth, heat; *adj.* warm, hot, spicy 3237

حُرّ *adj.* pl. أَحْرَار free; *n.* أَحْرَار liberals 793

حُرِّيَّة *n.* pl. -aat freedom 529

حَرِير *n.* silk 4769

حَرَارَة *n.* temperature, heat; fever 1370

حَرَارِيّ *adj.* thermal, caloric, heat-related 4041

تَحْرِير *n.* liberation; editorship, editing 906

تَحَرُّر *n.* (self) liberation, emancipation 3623

حَارّ *adj.* hot; fervent; warm, heartfelt; spicy 2459

حرس

حَرَس *n.* guard, bodyguard 2482

حِرَاسَة *n.* guard, escort, protection 3523

حَارِس *n.* pl. حُرَّاس guard; keeper; goalie 1417

حرص

حَرَصَ *v. I (a)* to desire, be eager عَلَى for sth 2348

حِرْص *n.* desire, eagerness; concern 1516

حَرِيص *adj.* mindful, protective; eager 3192

حرض

تَحْرِيض *n.* incitement, provocation; induction 4862

حرف

حَرْف *n.* pl. حُرُوف letter (of the alphabet) 1143

اِحْتِرَاف *n.* professionalism 4949

مُحْتَرِف *n.* pl. -uun professional, expert 2872

حرق

حَرَقَ *v. I (i)* to burn sth; to hurt sb 3372

حَرْق *vn.* burning; *n.* burn (wound) 4119

حَرِيق *n.* pl. حَرَائِق fire 2391

حرك

حَرَّكَ *v. II* to make move, activate sth/sb 2279

تَحَرَّكَ *v. V* to move, get moving 1381

حَرَكَة *n.* pl. -aat movement, activity 193

حَرَاك *n.* movement, motion 3923

تَحْرِيك *vn.* stimulating, activating 3488

تَحَرُّك *n.* pl. -aat movement, activity, motion 1921

مُحَرِّك *n.* motor, engine 3440

مُتَحَرِّك *adj.* moving, mobile 3695

حرم

حَرَمَ **v. I (i,u)** to deprive sb مِن of 2430

حَرَّمَ **v. II** to outlaw, ban, forbid sth 3966

اِحْتَرَمَ **v. VIII** to respect, revere sb/sth 3070

حَرَم **n.** holy site; (university) campus 1688

حُرْمَة **n.** sanctity; taboo; married woman, wife 3581

حَرام **adj.** forbidden; sacred, holy 1261

حَرِيم **coll.n.** women, harem 4832

حِرْمان **n.** deprivation, prohibition 3004

اِحْتِرام **n.** respect, honor 1044

مُحَرَّم **adj.** forbidden; **n.** مُحَرَّمات taboos 3580

مُحْتَرَم **adj.** honorable, respected, esteemed 2905

حري

أَحْرَى **elat.** بِالأحْرَى rather, to be more precise 4720

حزب

حِزْب **n.** pl. أَحْزاب (political) party 289

حِزْبِيّ **adj.** party-related; partisan, factional 3038

حزم

حَزْم **n.** determination, resoluteness 3800

حُزْمَة **n.** pl. حُزَم bundle; set, collection 4124

حِزام **n.** belt, band; cordon, barrier 4812

حزن

حَزِنَ **v. I (a)** to be sad, grieve على/ل for 4480

حُزْن **n.** pl. أَحْزان sadness, grief; anguish 821

حَزِين **adj.** sad, unhappy, sorrowful 1766

حسب

حَسِبَ **v. I (a,i)** to consider sb/sth to be 2190

حَسْب **n.** enough; فَحَسْب/وَحَسْب **adv.** only 1538

حَسَب **n.** حَسَب/بِحَسَب according to 423

حَسْبَما/حَسَبَما **conj.** according to 3374

حُسْبان **n.** consideration, estimation 4743

حِساب **n.** pl. -aat calculation; account 746

حاسُوب **n.** computer 4179

مُحاسَبَة **n.** examination; accounting; oversight 2691

تَحَسُّب **n.** expectation, anticipation 4932

حاسِب **n.** calculator; الحاسِب الآلِيّ computer 4219

حسر

حَسْرَة **n.** grief, sorrow 4891

حسس

حَسَّ **v. I (i,a)** to feel, sense ب sth; **a.p.** حاسّ 1294

أَحَسَّ **v. IV** to feel, sense ب sth or أَنَّ that 1477

حِسّ/حَسّ **n.** sensation, feeling; sound, noise 3481

حَسّاس **adj.** sensitive 2930

حَسّاسِيَّة **n.** sensitivity; allergy 3317

إِحْساس **n.** feeling, sensation; sensitivity 1622

حسم

حَسْم **vn.** settling (a matter, dispute) 3318

حاسِم **adj.** decisive, final; key, critical 2918

حسن

حَسَّنَ **v. II** to improve sth; to decorate sth 4880

أَحْسَنَ **v. IV** to master, be good at sth 2530

حُسْن **n.** good, goodness; beauty 1723

حَسَن **adj.** good; حَسَناً well; **interj.** OK 1729

أَحْسَن **elat.** better/best 776

حَسَنَة **n.** pl. -aat good deed, merit 4208

تَحْسِين **vn.** improving; **n.** improvement 1523

تَحَسُّن **n.** improvement 3608

حشد

حَشْد **vn.** (mil.) build-up; **n.** crowd 3235

حشر

حَشَرَة **n.** pl. -aat insect 4575

حصر

حَصْر **vn.** containment; bounds, limits 3227

حِصار **n.** siege, blockade 1744

حصص

حِصَّة **n.** pl. حِصَص share, quota 1864

حصل

حَصَلَ **v. I (u)** to get, obtain, acquire على sth 445

حَصَلَ **v. I (u)** to happen, take place 3545

حُصُول **vn.** obtaining; occurring 846

حَصِيلَة **n.** result, outcome; sum; revenue 3158

تَحْصِيل **n.** acquisition, attainment 4528

حاصِل **n.** result; **adj.** (what) happened 2586

حصن

حِصان **n.** horse 3307

حصو

أَحْصَى **v. IV** to count, calculate sth 4828

حضر

حَضَرَ **v. I (u)** to attend sth; to view (show) 809

أَحْضَرَ **v. IV** to bring sth; to prepare (food) 4950

حَضْرَة **n.** (polite term of address) حَضْرَتَك you 1091

حُضُور **vn.** arrival; attending; viewing 700

حَضارَة **n.** pl. -aat civilization; culture 1412

حَضارِيّ **adj.** cultural; civilized 1969

مَحْضَر *n.* report, minutes; attendance 4872

تَحْضِير *n.* pl. -aat preparation; production 2797

مُحَاضَرَة *n.* pl. -aat lecture 1961

حَاضِر *adj.* present; *n.* person present 1094

حضن

اِحْتَضَنَ *v. VIII* to embrace; to include 4368

حِضْن *n.* pl. أَحْضَان bosom; arms 3262

حطط

حَطَّ *v. I (u)* to descend, land (على on) 4145

حَطَّ *v. I (u)* to put, place, set down; *a.p.* حَاطّ 1574

مَحَطَّة *n.* pl. -aat station; stop, layover 941

حطم

تَحْطِيم *n.* demolition, destruction 4765

حظر

حَظْر *n.* prohibition, ban; embargo 3060

حظظ

حَظّ *n.* luck, fortune 1453

حظي

حَظِيَ *v. I (a)* to enjoy ب (respect, support) 2246

حفر

حَفْر *n.* digging, drilling; excavation 3312

حُفْرَة *n.* pl. حُفَر pit, hole 3883

حفز

حَافِز *n.* pl. حَوَافِز incentive, stimulus, motive 4193

حفظ

حَفِظَ *v. I (a)* to preserve; to memorize 1228

حَافَظَ *v. III* to preserve, protect على sth 2528

اِحْتَفَظَ *v. VIII* to preserve, keep ب sth 2896

حِفْظ *vn.* saving, preserving; memorizing 1597

حِفَاظ *vn.* guarding; memorizing; *n.* diaper 1446

مُحَافَظَة *vn.* preservation; *n.* conservatism 1885

مُحَافَظَة *n.* pl. -aat province, governorate 660

اِحْتِفَاظ *vn.* safeguarding, preservation 3717

مُحَافِظ *n.* governor; *adj.* conservative 1615

حفل

اِحْتَفَلَ *v. VIII* to celebrate ب sth 3861

حَفْل *n.* ceremony, celebration 1303

حَفْلَة *n.* pl. حَفَلَات party, ceremony 1732

مَحْفِل *n.* pl. مَحَافِل gathering, assembly 4267

اِحْتِفَال *vn.* celebrating; *n.* pl. -aat celebration 1556

حَافِلَة *n.* pl. -aat bus 3417

حفن

حَفْنَة *n.* handful 4887

حقب

حِقْبَة *n.* era, age, time period 3631

حَقِيبَة *n.* briefcase, portfolio; suitcase; bag 2931

حقد

حِقْد *n.* hatred, resentment 2632

حقق

حَقَّ *v. I (i)* to be right, have the right 2728

حَقَّقَ *v. II* to achieve sth; to investigate في sth 707

تَحَقَّقَ *v. V* to become reality; to verify مِن sth 1313

اِسْتَحَقَّ *v. X* to deserve, merit sth 1459

حَقّ *n.* truth; pl. حُقُوق right; *adj.* true 84

حَقِيقَة *n.* pl. حَقَائِق truth, reality; fact 322

حَقِيقِيّ *adj.* true, real, factual, authentic 537

تَحْقِيق *vn.* and *n.* pl. -aat achievement 302

تَحَقُّق *vn.* ascertainment, verification مِن of sth 4704

اِسْتِحْقَاق *n.* pl. -aat worthiness; claim, right 2937

مُحَقِّق *n.* investigator; editor; *a.p.* investigating 3073

حقل

حَقْل *n.* pl. حُقُول field 1806

حقن

اِحْتِقَان *n.* congestion; (political) tension 4730

حكر

اِحْتِكَار *n.* monopoly, hoarding 4997

حكم

حَكَمَ *v. I (u)* to govern; to sentence على sb 1694

تَحَكَّمَ *v. V* to control ب/في sth 3360

حُكْم *n.* government; pl. أَحْكَام verdict 311

حَكَم *n.* pl. حُكَّام (sports) arbiter, referee 4081

حِكْمَة *n.* wisdom; pl. حِكَم wise saying 1559

حَكِيم *adj.* wise; *n.* sage; philosopher 1948

حُكُومَة *n.* pl. -aat government, administration 103

حُكُومِيّ *adj.* governmental; *n.* officer 884

مَحْكَمَة *n.* pl. مَحَاكِم court, tribunal 540

تَحْكِيم *n.* arbitration; لَجْنَة تَحْكِيم jury 3186

مُحَاكَمَة *n.* trial, legal proceeding 2302

تَحَكُّم *vn.* control (في of) 2191

حَاكِم *n.* pl. حُكَّام ruler; *adj.* ruling 828

حكي

حَكَى *v. I (i)* to report; (Lev.Irq.) to speak 224

حِكَايَة *n.* pl. -aat story, tale, account, narrative 1296

حلب

حَلْبَة **n.** arena, ring, circuit, track 4626

حَليب **n.** milk 2272

حلف

حِلْف **n.** alliance, treaty, pact 3157

حَليف **n./adj.** pl. حُلَفاء ally, allied 3324

تَحالُف **n.** alliance 2112

حلق

حَلَّق **v. II** to hover; to circle (the skies) 3873

حَلْق **n.** throat; chasm, gorge 4846

حَلْقَة/حَلَقَة **n.** pl. حَلَقات ring; program, show 1213

حلل

حَلَّ **v. I (u)** to dissolve sth; to solve 1651

حَلَّ **v. I (i)** to befall ب/على sb; to start 3384

اِحْتَلَّ **v. VIII** to occupy (land); to fill (post) 2261

حَلّ **vn.** solving; **n.** pl. حُلول solution 269

حَلال **adj.** permissible, legitimate; Halal 2397

حُلول **vn.** arrival; beginning; replacing 2636

مَحَلّ **n.** pl. -aat, مَحالّ place, location; shop, store 701

مَحَلِّيّ **adj.** local; مَحَلِّيّاً locally 569

تَحْليل **vn.** dissolving; **n.** pl. تَحاليل analysis 1610

اِحْتِلال **vn.** occupation (of land); filling (a post) 563

مُحَلِّل **n.** pl. -uun analyst 3951

مُحْتَلّ **adj.** occupied (land); filled (post) 1965

مُحْتَلّ **n.** pl. -uun occupier; **adj.** occupying 3107

حلم

حَلَمَ **v. I (u)** to dream ب of sth/sb 1895

حُلْم **n.** pl. أَحْلام dream 637

حلو

حَلا **v. I (u)** to be sweet; to enjoy doing sth 3940

حُلْو **adj.** sweet, nice, pleasant 255

حَلْوَى **n.** pastry, dessert 4114

حَلَوِيّات **pl.n.** sweets, candy; pastries, desserts 4909

حَلاوَة **n.** pleasantness; sweets, candy 4201

أَحْلَى **elat.** sweeter/sweetest 1309

حمد

حَمِدَ **v. I (a)** to praise, glorify sb; to applaud sth 4631

حَمْد **n.** praise; الحَمْدُ لله praise God! 296

حَميد **adj.** laudable; positive; (med.) benign 4456

حمر

حِمار **n.** donkey, fem. حِمارَة she-ass, pl. حَمير 2730

أَحْمَر **adj.** fem. حَمْراء, pl. حُمْر red 927

حمس

حَماس **n.** enthusiasm, zeal; fortitude, bravery 3536

حمل

حَمَلَ **v. I (i)** to carry sth; to become pregnant 334

حَمَّلَ **v. II** to load (cargo); to blame sb 4516

تَحَمَّلَ **v. V** to bear (burden, responsibility) 1844

اِحْتَمَلَ **v. VIII** to tolerate; to expect 3001

حَمْل **n.** carrying; pregnancy 1256

حَمْلَة **n.** pl. حَمَلات campaign; attack, raid 918

تَحْميل **vn.** loading; downloading 2954

تَحَمُّل **vn.** bearing (burden, responsibility) 2781

اِحْتِمال **n.** probability, likelihood 1406

حامِل **adj.** bearing; **n.** pl. حَمَلَة carrier 1817

حامِل **fem.adj.** pregnant 4053

مَحْمُول **adj.** portable; **n.** mobile (phone) 3469

مُحَمَّل **adj.** loaded, burdened, charged 4142

مُحْتَمَل **adj.** likely, expected, probable 2404

حمم

حُمَّى **n.** fever; heat 3706

حَمام **coll.n.** dove, pigeon 4207

حَمّام **n.** bath, bathroom 2309

حمي

حَمَى **v. I (i)** to protect sth (مِن against) 2573

حِمايَة **n.** protection, protecting 757

حامٍ **n.** pl. حُماة n. protector, guardian; **adj.** hot 4638

مُحامٍ **n.** pl. مُحامُون lawyer, defense counsel 1826

حنف

حَنيف **adj.** orthodox; الدّين الحَنيف Islam 3934

حنن

حَنان **n.** affection, love; sympathy 2384

حَنين **n.** yearning, nostalgia 2731

حَنُون **adj.** affectionate; loving, dear 4025

حوج

اِحْتاجَ **v. VIII** to need, want إلى sth/sb 538

حاجَة **n.** pl. -aat need, want; wish; goal 621

حاجَة **n.** pl. -aat thing; Magh. حَوايج clothes 669

اِحْتِياج **n.** pl. -aat need, requirement 2233

مُحْتاج **n./adj.** pl. -uun needy; **a.p.** wanting 3824

حور

حِوار **n.** pl. -aat discussion, dialog, talk 439

حارَة **n.** quarter; neighborhood; alley 2379

مِحْوَر **n.** pl. مَحاوِر axle; axis, pivot 1645

حوز

حَيِّز **n.** sphere, scope; field, domain, area 4003

حوض

حَوْض **n.** basin, reservoir; aquarium 2921

حوط

أحاطَ **v. IV** to surround, encircle ب sth 2551

اِحْتِياطِيّ **n.** reserves; **adj.** precautionary 4249

حائِط **n.** wall 2684

مُحيط **adj.** surrounding; **n.** milieu; ocean 1435

حوف

حافَة **n.** border, edge, side; seam, hem 3386

حول

حالَ **v. I (u)** to prevent دُونَ sth 2821

حَوَّلَ **v. II** to convert sth (إلى) 2306

حاوَلَ **v. III** to attempt, try to do sth 319

تَحَوَّلَ **v. V** to be changed, be transformed 1047

اِسْتَحالَ **v. X** to be impossible 4680

حال **n.** (rare as fem.) pl. أحْوال situation 157

حالَة **n.** pl. -aat condition, state; case 205

حالِيّ **adj.** present, current; حالِيّاً currently 310

حَوْل **n.** power, might; لا حَوْلَ وَلا قُوَّةَ إلّا بِالله 2804

حَوْل **prep.** around; about, concerning 136

حِيلَة **n.** pl. حِيَل trick, ruse, stratagem 4202

حِيالَ **prep.** concerning, regarding 3098

حَوالَيْ/حَوالَيْ **prep.** approximately, about 808

لا مَحالَة **n.** without fail, without a doubt 4182

تَحْويل **n.** conversion, transfer 1687

مُحاوَلَة **n.** pl. -aat attempt, effort 680

تَحَوُّل **n.** pl. -aat change, conversion 1490

مُحاوِل **a.p.** attempting, trying (to do sth) 3967

مُحال **adj.** impossible; **p.p.** assigned على to 4591

مُسْتَحيل **adj.** impossible 1614

حوي

حَوَى **v. I (i)** to contain, include (على) sth 3419

اِحْتَوَى **v. VIII** to contain, include على sth 1797

اِحْتِواء **vn.** controlling; **n.** content 4013

مُحْتَوَى **n.** pl. مُحْتَوَيات content 3746

حيث

حَيْثُ **adv.** where; **conj.** so that 79

حَيْثُما **conj.** wherever 4885

حير

حَيْرَة/حِيرَة **n.** bewilderment; embarrassment 2655

حين

حانَ **v. I (i)** to arrive, approach (time) 2669

حِين **n.** pl. أحْيان time; أحْياناً sometimes 358

الحِين **adv.** (Gul., also دَحِّين and أحِّين) now 2849

حِينَ **prep.** when 245

حِينَئِذٍ **adv.** then, at the time 4340

حِينَما **conj.** when, while 1517

حيي

حَيَّ **v. I** to live; to experience (a life of) 2644

حَيّا **v. II** to greet, salute sb; to praise, laud sb 3033

حَيّ **adj.** pl. أحْياء alive; **n.** pl. أحْياء creature 1071

حَيّ **n.** pl. أحْياء quarter, district 833

حَياء **n.** modesty, shyness, inhibition, shame 3413

حَياة **n.** life 94

حَياتِيّ **adj.** biological, living; daily life related 4602

حَيَوِيّ **adj.** vital; lively; biological 2100

حَيَوِيَّة **n.** vigor, vitality; liveliness 4051

حَيَوان **n.** pl. -aat animal, creature 1314

حَيَوانِيّ **adj.** animal, animal-like, zoological 4234

تَحِيَّة **n.** pl. -aat, تَحايا greeting, salute, salutation 812

إحْياء **vn.** reviving; commemorating 3101

خام

خام **adj.** raw, unprocessed; crude (oil) 3658

خان

خانَة **n.** field, block; cell (spreadsheet) 4141

خبث

خَبيث **adj.** malicious, evil; malignant 3891

خبر

خَبَّرَ **v. II** to tell sb sth or عن about sth 3894

أخْبَرَ **v. IV** to notify, tell sb ب/عن about sth 2683

خَبَر **n.** news, report; الأخْبار the news 285

خِبْرَة **n.** pl. -aat, خِبَرات experience, expertise 1125

خَبير **n./adj.** pl. خُبَراء expert, specialist 1247

مُخابَرَة **n.** correspondence; telephone call 2503

اِخْتِبار **vn.** testing; **n.** pl. -aat test, experiment 2032

اِسْتِخْبار **n.** inquiry; اِسْتِخْبارات secret service 3334

خبز

خُبْز **n.** bread 2153

ختم

خَتَمَ **v. I (i)** to conclude sth; to seal sth 3681

اِخْتَتَمَ **v. VIII** to finalize (an activity) 3621

خاتَم *n.* ring; seal, stamp 4763

خِتام *n.* conclusion, closure, end 1971

خِتامِيّ *adj.* concluding, closing, final 4010

خجل

خَجَل *n.* shame, bashfulness, shyness 3137

خخخ

خخخ *interj.* (laughter) ha-ha-ha! 4751

خدر

مُخَدِّر *n.* anesthetic: مُخَدِّرات narcotics, drugs 2291

خدم

خَدَمَ *v. I (i,u)* to serve, assist sb 1768

اِسْتَخْدَمَ *v. X* to use, employ, utilize sth 1055

خِدْمَة *n.* pl. خَدَمات service; (Magh.) work 307

اِسْتِخْدام *n.* usage, using, utilization 645

خادِم *adj.* serving, assisting; *n.* servant 2129

مُسْتَخْدِم *adj.* using; *n.* pl. -uun user 3089

مُسْتَخْدَم *adj.* used, utilized, employed 3259

خرب

خَراب *n.* ruins, destruction 3368

تَخْرِيب *n.* destruction; sabotage, terrorism 4774

خرج

خَرَجَ *v. I (u)* to go out; to deviate عن from 345

أَخْرَجَ *v. IV* to expel sb; to publish sth 2020

تَخَرَّجَ *v. V* to graduate من from 4546

خُرُوج *n.* departure; exit; deviation (عن from) 872

خِرِّيج *n.* pl. -uun graduate 2837

مَخْرَج *n.* exit, outlet; escape, way out, solution 3024

إِخْراج *n.* production; extraction; removal 2876

تَخَرُّج *n.* graduation 4180

اِسْتِخْراج *n.* extraction; removal 4903

خارِج *n.* outside, exterior; بالخارِج overseas 349

خارِجِيّ *adj.* foreign; outer, exterior, outside 765

خارِجِيَّة *n.* foreign ministry, foreign office 649

مُخْرِج *n.* (screen, stage) director; *adj.* directing 2319

خرط

خَرِيطَة *n.* map, chart; خَرِيطَة الطَّرِيق roadmap 2687

خارِطَة *n.* map, chart; خارِطَة الطَّرِيق roadmap 3518

خرع

اِخْتِراع *n.* invention 4502

خرف

خَرِيف *n.* autumn, fall 3034

خرق

خَرَقَ *v. I (i,u)* to violate (law) 4714

اِخْتَرَقَ *v. VIII* to break into; to traverse 3912

اِخْتِراق *n.* incursion; traversing 3996

خزن

خِزانَة *n.* treasury; vault, safe; (book)case 3757

تَخْزِين *n.* storage, safekeeping 4915

مَخْزُون *adj.* stored; in stock; *n.* supplies 4002

خسر

خَسِرَ *v. I (a)* to fail; to lose (game, time) 1762

خَسارَة *n.* pl. خَسائِر failure; casualty 1123

خشب

خَشَب *n.* wood; خَشَب مُعاكِس plywood 4165

خَشَبَة *n.* pl. -aat piece of wood; board, plank 3086

خَشَبِيّ *adj.* wooden, made of wood 3815

خشي

خَشِيَ *v. I (a)* to fear sth/sb; to be anxious 1679

خَشْيَة *n.* fear, anxiety; concern, worry 3285

خصب

تَخْصِيب *n.* fertilization; enrichment 4581

خصخص

خَصْخَصَة *n.* privatization 4178

خصر

اِخْتِصار *n.* abbreviation; باِخْتِصار briefly 3153

خصص

خَصَّ *v. I (u)* to concern sb/sth 1801

خَصَّصَ *v. II* to specify, designate 2498

خُصُوص *n.* (in this) regard; خُصُوصاً especially 482

خُصُوصِيّ *adj.* private, personal; special 2865

خَصِيصَة *n.* pl. خَصائِص characteristic 3533

خِصِّيصاً *adv.* especially, specifically 4244

أَخَصّ *elat.* more/most specific 4779

تَخْصِيص *n.* specification; allocation 3294

تَخَصُّص *n.* pl. -aat specialty, specialization 2422

اِخْتِصاص *n.* specialty; jurisdiction, domain 3295

خاصّ *adj.* special; private, personal; exclusive 135

خاصَّة *n.* خاصَّةً especially 361

مُخَصَّص *adj.* designated; allocated, set aside 2045

مُتَخَصِّص *adj.* specialized; *n.* specialist 1519

مُخْتَصّ *adj.* responsible; *n.* specialist 2026

خصم

خَصْم **n.** adversary 3866

خضر

خُضار **coll.n.** vegetables, greens 3965

أخْضَر **adj.** fem. خَضْراء, pl. خُضْر green 987

خضع

خَضَعَ **v. I (a)** to submit إلى to sb/sth 2497

خُضُوع **n.** submission, subjection 4604

خضم

خِضَمّ **n.** في خِضَمِّ in the middle of 4212

خطأ

أخْطَأَ **v. IV** to make a mistake 3147

خَطَأ **n.** pl. أخْطاء mistake; **adj.** (invar.) wrong 811

خاطِئ **adj.** mistaken, at fault 2380

خطب

خاطَبَ **v. III** to address, speak to sb 4544

خُطْبة **n.** pl. خُطَب speech; sermon 3059

خِطاب **n.** speech; message, letter 1203

مُخاطَبة **vn.** speaking to; **n.** conversation 4895

مُخاطِب **n.** speaker; **adj.** speaking to 4741

خطر

خَطَرَ **v. I (u,i)** to occur ل to sb 3986

خَطَر **n.** pl. أخْطار danger; risk; alarm (signal) 911

خَطِر **adj.** serious, grave; dangerous 3185

خَطير **adj.** significant; serious; dangerous 1153

خُطُورة **n.** importance; seriousness; danger 1996

أخْطَر **elat.** more/most dangerous/serious 2968

مَخاطِر **pl.n.** dangers, perils; adventures 2019

خاطِر **n.** pl. خَواطِر idea, thought; mind; wish 1970

خاطِرة **n.** pl. خَواطِر idea, thought 4937

خطط

خَطَّطَ **v. II** to make plans; to define (borders) 3335

خَطّ **n.** pl. خُطوط line; airline; writing 431

خُطّة/خِطّة **n.** pl. خِطَط، خُطَط plan, project 670

تَخْطيط **n.** planning, preparation; sketch 1756

مُخَطَّط **n.** pl. -aat plan; **adj.** planned; patterned 2068

خطف

خَطْف **n.** abduction, kidnapping; hijacking 3343

اخْتِطاف **n.** abduction, kidnapping; hijacking 4191

خطو

خَطْوة/خُطْوة **n.** pl. خَطَوات step, stride 583

خفض

انْخَفَضَ **v. VII** to decrease, be reduced 3573

خَفْض **n.** lowering; reduction 3275

تَخْفيض **vn.** lowering; **n.** pl. -aat reduction 3306

انْخِفاض **n.** reduction, decrease, drop 2276

مُنْخَفِض **adj.** low; reduced 3377

خفف

خَفَّ **v. I (i)** to become lighter 4427

خَفَّفَ **v. II** to lower, lessen sth 3216

خَفيف **adj.** light; slight, minor; sparse 1420

تَخْفيف **n.** lowering; decrease, reduction 2492

خفي

خَفِيَ **v. I (a)** to be hidden; لا يُخْفَى obvious 3525

أخْفَى **v. IV** to hide sth; to lower (one's voice) 2714

اخْتَفَى **v. VIII** to disappear; to hide 2057

خَفِيّ **adj.** hidden, secret; unseen, invisible 2895

إخْفاء **n.** concealing; lowering (one's voice) 4526

اخْتِفاء **n.** disappearance; absence 4496

خلج

خَليج **n.** gulf 993

خَليجيّ **adj.** of the Persian Gulf (الخَليج العَرَبيّ) 1371

خلد

خُلود **n.** immortality; **vn.** remaining 4379

خالِد **adj.** immortal, eternal; glorious 3897

خلص

خَلَصَ **v. I (u)** to arrive إلى at (a result) 1315

خَلَّصَ **v. II** (Dia.) to finish sth 2168

خَلَص **interj.** (Lev.) enough, OK 3272

خَلاص **n.** liberation, salvation 3480

خَلاص **interj.** (Egy.Gul.Alg.) OK, that's it 1244

خُلاصة **n.** gist; synopsis, abstract, summary 4038

إخْلاص **n.** sincerity; loyalty 4722

تَخَلُّص **n.** escape, freedom (مِن from) 2024

خالِص **adj.** sincere; pure; (Egy.) totally 1929

مُخْلِص **adj.** sincere; loyal 2609

خلط

خَلْط **n.** mixing, blending; mixture, blend 4622

خَليط **n.** mixture, blend 3780

مُخْتَلِط **adj.** mixed, co-ed (schools); hybrid 4966

خلف

خَلَّفَ **v. II** to give birth; to leave sth behind 4281

خالَفَ **v. III** to violate (the law) 3634

اِخْتَلَفَ **v. VIII** to be different عن from 1109

خَلْف **n.** back, rear part; خَلْفَ **prep.** behind 685

خَلْفِيّ **adj.** back, rear, end; background 4232

خَلْفِيَّة **n.** background, history 2173

خَلَف **n.** successor; descendant 4713

خِلاف **n.** pl. -aat dispute; disagreement 958

خِلافَة **n.** succession; caliphate 3936

خَلِيفَة **masc.n.** successor; caliph 2751

مُخالَفَة **n.** pl. -aat infraction; (sports) foul 2151

تَخَلُّف **n.** backwardness; underdevelopment 2984

اِخْتِلاف **n.** difference, disagreement; conflict 1682

مُخَلَّف **adj.** left behind; **n.** مُخَلَّفات leftovers 4448

مُخالِف **adj.** against (the law); **n.** offender 3056

مُخْتَلِف **adj.** different, divergent; various 259

خلق

خَلَقَ **v. I (u)** to create, form sth 1717

خَلْق **vn.** creating, forming; **n.** creation 1096

خُلُق **n.** أَخْلاق personality; أَخْلاق morals 1807

أَخْلاقيّ **adj.** moral, ethical 3093

خالِق **n.** الخالِق the Creator; **adj.** creative 3655

مَخْلُوق **adj.** created; **n.** pl. -aat creature 4150

خلل

خَلَل **n.** malfunction; flaw; deficiency 2305

خِلال **prep.** during; مِن خِلالِ by means of 73

خلو

خَلا **v. I (u)** to be free مِن of sth; to be alone 2136

خَلَّى **v. II** (Dia.) to preserve, keep sb safe 763

تَخَلَّى **v. V** to relinquish, surrender عن sth 2778

خَلِيَّة **n.** pl. خَلايا cell; beehive 1893

تَخَلِّي **n.** surrender, renunciation (مِن of) 3180

خالي **adj.** empty, devoid, free (مِن of) 2050

خمر

خَمْر **fem./masc.n.** liquor, wine, alcohol 2982

خمس

خَمْسَة **num.** fem. خَمْس five; خَمْسَة عَشَر fifteen 330

خَمْسُون **num.** fifty; fiftieth 1526

خَمْسِين **n.** fiftieth year; الخمسينات the Fifties 2955

(يَوْم) الخَمِيس **n.** خَمِيس Thursday 1115

خامِس **adj.** fifth (ordinal) 1012

خوش

خوش **adj.** /khoosh/ (Irq.) good, fine, great 4660

خوض

خاضَ **v. I (u)** to wage (war, campaign) 3112

خَوْض **n.** waging, embarking on, carrying out 2648

خوف

خافَ **v. I (a)** to fear sth/sb 1042

خَوْف **n.** fear; خَوْفاً for fear (مِن of) 862

مَخافَة **n.** pl. مَخاوِف fear, anxiety; worry 2846

خائِف **adj.** afraid, fearful, frightened 1503

مُخِيف **adj.** frightful, terrifying, horrible 3387

خول

خال **n.** maternal uncle 3188

خالَة **n.** maternal aunt 2926

خون

خِيانَة **n.** treason, treachery; betrayal; infidelity 2924

خيب

خَيْبَة **n.** failure; خَيْبَة أَمَلٍ disappointment 4492

خير

اِخْتارَ **v. VIII** to select, pick sth/sb 1205

خَيْر **n.** goodness, good; **adj.** better مِن than 140

خَيْريّ **adj.** charitable, philanthropic 2256

خَيْرَة **n.** pl. -aat good deed; خَيْرات wealth 3882

خِيَرَة **n.** choice, best, pick, elite 4964

خِيار **n.** pl. -aat choice; preference 1321

اِخْتِيار **n.** choice, selection; election; preference 959

مُخْتار **n.** mukhtar; elder; **adj.** chosen 4507

خيط

خَيْط **n.** pl. خُيُوط string, thread; clue 2755

خيل

تَخَيَّلَ **v. V** to imagine, suppose sth or أَنَّ that 4140

خَيْل **n.** pl. خُيُول horse 2456

خَيال **n.** imagination, fantasy 1975

خَيالِيّ **adj.** imaginary, fantastic; fictitious 3946

خيم

خَيْمَة **n.** pl. خِيام tent 3255

مُخَيَّم **n.** pl. -aat camp; refugee camp 1249

خيي

خَيّ **n.** (Lev.) brother; خَيِّي my brother 3205

دا

دا/ده **dem.pron.** /da/ (Egy.) this (masc.) 826

دِي **dem.pron.** (Egy.) this (fem.), these 1232

دبب

دَبّابَة **n.** pl. -aat tank 3114

دبر

تَدْبِير *vn.* arranging; *n.* pl. تَدابِير preparation 3645

دبلوماسي

دِبْلُوماسِيّ *adj.* diplomatic; *n.* diplomat 2147

دِبْلُوماسِيَّة *n.* diplomacy 3993

دجج

دَجاج *coll.n.* chickens, poultry; (Lev.) جاج 2665

دجن

داجِن *adj.* pl. دَواجِن domesticated 4354

دخل

دَخَلَ *v. I (u)* to enter (إلى sth) 297

أَدْخَلَ *v. IV* to insert, include sth إلى/في in 1601

تَدَخَّلَ *v. V* to intervene, interfere, meddle 1715

دَخْل *n.* income; دَخْلَك! (Lev.) please! 2040

دُخُول *n.* entering, entrance 595

مَدْخَل *n.* pl. مَداخِل entrance; introduction 1960

إِدْخال *n.* insertion, introduction, inclusion 2978

تَدَخُّل *n.* intervention, interference 1666

داخِل *n.* interior; داخِلَ *prep.* inside (of) 246

داخِلِيّ *adj.* internal; domestic 520

داخِلِيَّة *n.* (ministry) interior, of state 1548

دخن

دُخان *n.* smoke; smoking 2269

تَدْخِين *n.* smoking; fumigating 2333

دراما

دِراما *n.* drama 4549

درب

دَرْب *n.* pl. دُرُوب path, pathway, trail, road 1590

تَدْرِيب *vn.* training; *n.* pl. -aat exercise 922

تَدْرِيبِيّ *adj.* practice; training, coaching 2623

مُدَرِّب *n.* trainer, coach; instructor 1255

درج

اِنْدَرَجَ *v. VII* to be included; to be categorized 3920

دَرَج *n.* step, stairs; route, course 4508

دَرَجَة *n.* pl. -aat degree, grade, level; class, rank 473

تَدْرِيجِيّ *adj.* gradual; تَدْرِيجِيّاً gradually 3215

مُدْرَج *adj.* registered, listed; included 4651

درس

دَرَسَ *v. I (u)* to study, learn sth 1066

دَرْس *vn.* studying; *n.* pl. دُرُوس lesson 1272

دِراسَة *n.* pl. -aat study, research, examination 287

دِراسِيّ *adj.* school-; instructional, pedagogical 1718

مَدْرَسَة *n.* pl. مَدارِس school 303

مَدْرَسِيّ *adj.* scholastic, school-related 2589

تَدْرِيس *n.* teaching, instruction, pedagogy 2427

مَدْرُوس *adj.* studied, planned; calculated 4808

مُدَرِّس *n.* teacher, instructor 2196

درع

دِرْع *n.* shield, armor; plaque (award) 3624

درك

أَدْرَكَ *v. IV* to grasp; to reach, attain 1084

إِدْراك *n.* realization, awareness; attainment 3632

درهم

دِرْهَم *n.* pl. دَراهِم dirham 1886

دري

دَرَى *v. I (i)* to know, be aware of sth 417

دستر

دُسْتُور *n.* constitution 1287

دُسْتُورِيّ *adj.* constitutional 1777

دعم

دَعَمَ *v. I (a)* to support, promote sth/sb 2103

دَعْم *n.* support, assistance, promotion 404

مَدْعُوم *adj.* supported, bolstered, promoted 4185

تَدْعِيم *n.* supporting, backing, propping up 4749

دعو

دَعا *v. I (u)* to call إلى for sth; to invite sb إلى to 418

اِدَّعَى *v. VIII* to allege, claim أَنَّ/بِأَنَّ that 2107

اِسْتَدْعَى *v. X* to summon sb; to invoke sth 2725

دَعْوَة *n.* pl. دَعَوات call; invitation; propaganda 582

دَعْوَى *n.* lawsuit; claim; (Egy.Lev.) right 2295

دُعاء *n.* call, appeal, request; invocation 1591

دِعايَة *n.* pl. -aat advertisement; propaganda 2839

تَداع *n.* pl. -aat breakdown; repercussion 3881

اِدِّعاء *n.* allegation, claim; prosecution 3398

اِسْتِدْعاء *n.* summons, call, appeal; recall 4483

داع *n.* reason; *n.* pl. دُعاة (person) calling 1222

مَدْعُوّ *adj.* invited, called; named 4618

مُدَّعٍ *n.* plaintiff, prosecutor; *a.p.* alleging 4294

دفا

دِفْء *n.* heat, warmth 3667

دافِئ *adj.* warm; (Dia.) دافي 3102

دفتر

دَفْتَر *n.* notebook; ledger 3904

دفع

دَفَعَ *v. I (a)* to push; to pay; to compel 650

دافَعَ *v. III* to defend عن sth/sb 2564

دَفْع *vn.* pushing; compelling; payment 1178

دُفْعَة *n.* batch; class (graduates); instance 2490

دِفاع *n.* defense (military, legal, sports) 542

دِفاعِيّ *adj.* defensive, protective 3472

دافِع *n. pl.* دَوافِع motive; *adj.* pushing 2184

مُدافِع *n.* defender; *adj.* defending 2990

دفق

تَدَفَّقَ *v. V* to flow, stream; to drip, drop 4079

تَدَفُّق *n.* flow, stream, flood; influx, invasion 3534

دقق

دَقَّ *v. I (u)* to strike; to knock; to ring (bell) 1176

دَقَّة *n. pl.* -aat knock, stroke, tick, beat 4840

دِقَّة *n.* accuracy, precision; minuteness 1941

دَقِيق *adj.* accurate; minute; delicate 1577

دَقِيق *n.* flour 4970

دَقِيقَة *n. pl.* دَقائِق minute 424

أَدَقّ *elat.* more/most accurate, precise (دَقِيق) 4557

تَدْقِيق *n.* investigation; verification; accuracy 4723

دكتر

دُكْتُور *n. pl.* دَكاتِرَة doctor (physician, PhD) 253

دُكْتُوراه *n.* doctorate 4106

دلع

انْدَلَعَ *v. VII* to break out, flare up (fire, war) 4494

انْدِلاع *n.* breaking out, flaring up (fire, war) 4259

دلل

دَلَّ *v. I (u)* to point at, indicate that 1513

دَلِيل *n. pl.* دَلائِل, أَدِلَّة sign, clue; pl. أَدِلَّة guide 934

دَلالَة *n. pl.* -aat meaning, significance 2941

دلوقتي

دلوقتي/دلوقت *adv.* (Egy.) /dilwa'ti/ now 4590

دلي

أَدْلَى *v. IV* to give, provide ب sth 4650

دمج

دَمْج *n.* inclusion; merger 4302

انْدِماج *n.* integration; absorption 4253

دمر

دَمَّرَ *v. II* to destroy sth; to wreck, ruin sth 2643

دَمار *n.* destruction, devastation, ruin 1816

تَدْمِير *n.* destruction; wrecking, ruining 1609

مُدَمِّر *adj.* destructive, destroying 3842

دمع

دَمْع *coll.n.* tears, *un.n.* دَمْعَة, pl. دُمُوع 975

دمغ

دِماغ *n.* brain 3479

دمي

دَم *n. pl.* دِماء blood; (Dia.) دَم 363

دَمَوِيّ *adj.* bloody; blood- 2362

دنو

أَدْنَى *elat.* lower/lowest, nearer/nearest 1792

دُنْيا *n.* world 494

تَدَنٍّ *n.* fall, decline; sinking 4845

دهر

دَهْر *n.* fate, fortune; lifetime, eternity 2799

دهش

دَهْشَة *n.* surprise; bewilderment, confusion 3046

دهن

دُهْن *n. pl.* دُهُون oil, grease, fat (esp. in food) 3994

دهور

تَدَهْوُر *n.* decline, deterioration; fall, drop 3179

دوي

داء *n.* sickness, disease; ailment, disorder 2791

دور

دارَ *v. I (u)* to revolve; to go around حَوْلَ sth 1034

دَوَّرَ *v. II* (Dia.) to look على for 3052

أَدارَ *v. IV* to direct, manage sth; to turn 2873

دار *fem.n. pl.* دُور, دِيار house, home 594

دَوْر *n. pl.* أَدْوار role; floor; round; turn 169

دَوْرَة *n. pl.* -aat tournament; cycle; round; tour 600

دَوْرِيّ *n. pl.* -aat tournament; *adj.* regular 1018

دَوْرِيَّة *n. pl.* -aat patrol, squad; periodical 2175

مَدار *n.* orbit, sphere; scope, range; axis, pivot 2659

إدارَة *n. pl.* -aat management; bureau, office 228

إدارِيّ *adj.* administrative, management 1161

دائِر *adj.* taking place, happening; ongoing 3987

دائِرَة *n. pl.* دَوائِر bureau; district; circle 866

مُدِير *n.* director, manager; (office) boss, chief 379

مُدِيرِيَّة *n.* office; district, province 2718

دول

دَوْلَة *n. pl.* دُوَل state, country 51

دُوَلِيّ/دَوْلِيّ *adj.* international, world, global 121

تَداوُل **n.** circulation; alternation; deliberation 2043

مُتَداوَل **adj.** in circulation, prevailing 4476

دولار

دُولار **n.** pl. -aat dollar 399

دوم

دامَ **v. I (u)** to last, continue; ما دامَ as long as 982

دَوْم **n.** continuance, continuation; دَوْماً always 1611

دَوام **n.** business hours, work schedule 1761

دَوّامَة **n.** spiral; dizziness, confusion 4062

دائِم **adj.** lasting; permanent; دائِماً always 283

مُسْتَدام **adj.** sustainable (development) 4710

دون

دُونَ **prep.** without; under, below; بِدُونِ without 105

دُونَما **prep.** without any, without even 3699

دِيوان **n.** office, agency, court 2445

دِيوان **n.** anthology or collection of poems 4355

دَواء **n.** pl. أَدْوِيَة remedy, medication 1239

دير

دار **v. I (i)** (Egy.Lev.Irq.Gul.) to turn 1629

ديمقراطي

دِيمُقراطِيّ/دِيمُوقراطِيّ **adj.** democratic 943

دِيمُقراطِيَّة/دِيمُوقراطِيَّة **n.** democracy 1003

دين

أَدانَ **v. IV** to denounce, censure sth/sb 3506

دَيْن **n.** pl. دُيُون debt 2440

إدانَة **n.** condemnation, denunciation, censure 4757

دِين **n.** pl. أَدْيان religion 333

دِينِيّ **adj.** religious; spiritual 691

دِيانَة **n.** pl. -aat religion, creed 4551

دينار

دِينار **n.** pl. دَنانِير dinar 1036

ذا

ذا **dem.pron.** fem. ذِي this, that 2389

ذاكَ **dem.pron.** that, that (other) one 1004

لِذا **conj.** therefore, that's why, because of that 1156

كَذا **adv.** thus, like that, in this way 715

هُكَذا **adv.** like this, this way, thus 530

ذأب

ذِئْب **n.** pl. ذِئاب wolf, jackal 2884

ذات

ذات **fem.n.** pl. ذَوات ego; ذات same, -self 200

ذاتِيّ **adj.** autonomous, self-, auto- 1702

ذرر

ذَرَّة **n.** atom, particle 3972

ذَرِّيّ **adj.** atomic 3722

ذرع

ذِراع **fem./masc.n.** pl. أَذْرُع arm; lever, crank 3286

ذَرِيعَة **n.** means; pretext, excuse 4337

ذرو

ذُرْوَة **n.** peak, summit, height 4408

ذكر

ذَكَرَ **v. I (u)** to mention, remember sth/sb 266

ذَكَّرَ **v. II** to remind sb 3198

تَذَكَّرَ **v. V** to remember sth/sb 1217

ذِكْر **n.** mention, citation; memory 1002

ذَكَر **n./adj.** pl. ذُكُور male 2598

ذِكْرَى **n.** pl. ذِكْرَيات memory; anniversary 960

تَذْكِرَة **n.** pl. تَذاكِر ticket, card 3570

تَذْكِير **n.** reminding 4411

ذاكِرَة **n.** memory (human and computer) 1306

مَذْكُور **adj.** mentioned, cited 2003

مُذَكِّرَة **n.** pl. -aat note; notebook 2270

ذكو

ذَكاء **n.** intelligence, cleverness 3063

ذَكِيّ **adj.** intelligent, clever 2496

ذلك

ذٰلِكَ **dem.pron.** that (masc.sg.) 36

تِلْكَ **dem.pron.** that (fem.sg.); those 129

أُولٰئِكَ/أُولائِكَ **dem.pron.** those (human) 1876

لِذٰلِكَ **conj.** therefore 465

كَذٰلِكَ **adv.** likewise, also 317

هَذاكَ **dem.pron.** (Lev.Irq.Gul.) that, that one 4131

ذلل

ذُلّ **n.** humiliation, dishonor 3105

ذمم

ذِمَّة **n.** protection, security; conscience 4101

ذنب

ذَنْب **n.** pl. ذُنُوب fault, offense, misdeed 1998

ذهب

ذَهَبَ **v. I (a)** to go, leave, depart 489

ذَهَب **n.** gold 1904

ذَهَبِيّ **adj.** golden, gilded 1692

ذَهاب **n.** going; leaving; first half (game) 1594

ذهب

مَذْهَب **n.** pl. مَذاهِب path; ideology 2488

مَذْهَبِيّ **adj.** doctrinal, sectarian 4026

ذهل

ذُهُول **n.** numbness, indifference, confusion 4129

مُذْهِل **adj.** amazing, startling 4649

ذهن

ذِهْن **n.** pl. أَذْهان mind, thought, intellect 1875

ذِهْنِيّ **adj.** mental, intellectual 4519

ذو

ذو **n.** pl. أُولُو, ذَوُو, fem. ذات, pl. ذَوات having 773

ذوب

ذابَ **v. I (u)** to dissolve, melt 3927

ذوق

ذَوْق **n.** taste, good taste; refinement 2450

ذيب

ذِئْب **n.** pl. ذِئاب wolf, jackal 2884

ذيع

إذاعَة **vn.** broadcasting; **n.** pl. -aat broadcast 1919

مُذيع **n.** broadcaster, announcer 4304

را

را **part.** (Alg., indicates present continuous) 4196

رئة

رِئَة **n.** lung 4524

راديو

رادِيُو **n.** radio 3628

رأس

رَأَسَ **v. I (a)** to lead sth; to chair (meeting) 4034

رَأْس **n.** (Dia. راس) pl. رُؤُوس head; tip 215

رَئِيس **n.** pl. رُؤَساء president, leader; chief, head 47

رَئِيسِيّ **adj.** main, chief, principal 839

رِئاسَة **n.** presidency, leadership, direction 867

رِئاسِيّ **adj.** presidential; executive 2204

رأي

رَأى **v. I** يَرَى to see sth/sb; to think أَنَّ that 75

يا تُرَى **part.** Dia. (modal) perhaps 3092

رَأْي **n.** pl. آراء opinion, view; idea 227

رايَة **n.** flag, banner 2967

رُؤْيَة **n.** vision, sight; view; perspective 885

رُؤْيا **n.** pl. رُؤىً vision, dream; idea, picture 2689

مَرْأى **n.** sight, view 4900

مَرْئِيّ **adj.** visual; visible 4092

مِرْآة **n.** mirror 2841

ربب

رَبّ **n.** pl. أَرْباب lord, master; owner 194

رُبَّا/لَرُبَّا **adv.** perhaps, maybe 374

ربح

رَبَحَ **v. I (a)** to profit; to win (game) 4293

رِبْح **vn.** winning; **n.** pl. أَرْباح profit, gain 1877

ربط

رَبَطَ **v. I (i,u)** to tie, connect sth 2213

إرْتَبَطَ **v. VIII** to be tied ب to sth 2278

رَبْط **vn.** connecting, linking; **n.** connection 2146

إرْتِباط **n.** bond, connection, link 2933

رابِط **adj.** linking; **n.** link (website) 2258

رابِطَة **n.** pl. رَوابِط union, league; tie, link 1815

مُرْتَبِط **adj.** connected, linked ب to 1731

ربع

رَبْع **n.** pl. رُبُوع housing; residence; territory 4004

رُبْع **n.** pl. أَرْباع quarter, fourth 1319

رَبِيع **n.** spring (season) 1943

أَرْبَعَة **num.** fem. أَرْبَع four; أَرْبَعَة عَشَر fourteen 356

أَرْبَعُون **num.** forty; fortieth 1650

رُباعِيّ **adj.** four-part; **n.** quadrangle; quartet 3542

الأَرْبِعاء **n.** (يَوْم) الأَرْبِعاء Wednesday 1291

رابِع **adj.** fourth (ordinal) 714

مُرَبَّع **adj.** quadruple; square; **n.** square 2393

ربو

تَرْبِيَة **n.** education; child-rearing; breeding 829

تَرْبَوِيّ **adj.** pedagogical; child-rearing 1964

رتب

تَرَتَّبَ **v. V** to derive or result على from 3635

مَرْتَبَة **n.** level, rank; degree; position 2438

تَرْتِيب **n.** pl. -aat preparation; planning 1534

راتِب **n.** pl. رَواتِب salary, wage, pay 1778

مُرَتَّب **adj.** organized; regulated; **n.** salary 4233

مُتَرَتِّب **adj.** derived على from 4279

رجح

أَرْجَح **elat.** more/most likely, probable 4596

مُرَجَّح **adj.** probable, likely 4871

رجع

رَجَعَ **v. I (i)** to return إلى to 613

تَراجَعَ **v. VI** to retreat; to decrease 1869

رَجْعَة **n.** return, going back, turning back 4177

رُجُوع **n.** return; reversing عن (one's decision) 3412

مَرْجِع **n.** pl. مَراجِع source; authority 3456

مَرْجِعِيَّة **n.** authority; authoritative source 3391

مُراجَعَة **n.** review, inspection; checking 1878

تَراجُع **n.** retreat, backing down/off; decrease 1736

راجِع **a.p.** returning إلى to; traced back إلى to 2671

رجل

رَجُل **n.** pl. رِجال n. man 92

رِجْل **fem.n.** leg; (Gul.) ريل /riil/ 4356

رُجُولَة **n.** masculinity, manhood, virility 4771

راجِل **n.** /raagil/ (Egy.) man 4471

رجو

رَجا **v. I (u)** to hope for, request sth 964

رَجاً **n.** pl. أرْجاء side wall; أرْجاء regions, areas 2820

رَجاء **n.** hope, expectation; رَجاءً please 2388

مَرْجُوّ **adj.** requested, desired, wished for 4585

رحب

رَحَّب **v. II** to welcome, receive ب sth/sb 2022

رَحْبَة **n.** pl. رِحاب open area; vastness 4753

مَرْحَباً **interj.** (usu. مَرْحَبا) hello! welcome! 1072

تَرْحِيب **n.** welcome, welcoming; greeting 2889

رحل

رَحَل **v. I (a)** to depart; to pass away; to travel 2203

رِحْلَة **n.** pl. -aat trip, excursion; career 1009

رَحِيل **n.** departure; death, demise 2015

مَرْحَلَة **n.** pl. مَراحِل phase; (sports) round 366

راحِل **adj.** deceased, late 2271

رحم

رَحَم **v. I (a)** to have mercy (God) on sb 1154

رَحِم **n.** uterus, womb; bosom; inside 2372

رَحْمَة **n.** mercy, compassion 972

رَحْمن/رَحْمان **adj.** merciful (God) 4105

رَحِيم **adj.** compassionate (God) 2508

أرْحَم **elat.** more/most merciful 4527

مَرْحُوم **adj.** deceased, late 3576

رخص

رُخْصَة **n.** pl. رُخَص license, permit 3763

رَخِيص **adj.** cheap, inexpensive 2640

تَرْخِيص **n.** license, permission 3647

ردد

رَدَّ **v. I (u)** to respond على to 396

رَدَّدَ **v. II** to repeat, reiterate sth 1918

تَرَدَّدَ **v. V** to hesitate; to frequent على (a place) 1738

رَدّ **n.** pl. رُدُود response, reply; رَدّ فِعْل reaction 440

رَدَّة **n.** echo, reverberation; رَدَّة فِعْل reaction 3831

تَرَدُّد **n.** repetition; hesitation; frequency 4167

مَرْدُود **n.** returns, revenue, yield 4931

ردي

اِرْتَدَى **v. VIII** to wear, put on (clothes) 2705

اِرْتِداء **n.** wearing, putting on (clothes) 4126

رزز

أرُزّ/رُزّ **n.** rice 4015

رزق

رِزْق **n.** livelihood; food, daily bread 3000

رسخ

تَرْسِيخ **n.** reinforcing, bolstering 3813

رسل

أرْسَلَ **v. IV** to send, transmit (ب) sth إلى to sb 1592

رَسُول **n.** pl. رُسُل messenger, apostle 523

رِسالة **n.** pl. رَسائِل letter; thesis; pl. -aat mission 433

إرْسال **vn.** sending; deploying; **n.** broadcast 1748

مُراسِل **n.** correspondent, reporter 4132

رسم

رَسَم **v. I (u)** to draw (picture); to outline sth 1387

رَسْم **vn.** illustrating; **n.** pl. رُسُوم picture; fee 1569

رَسْمِيّ **adj.** official, formal; رَسْمِيّاً officially 561

مَرْسَم **n.** pl. مَراسِم art studio 4515

مَرْسُوم **adj.** decreed; drawn; charted; **n.** decree 3380

رشح

تَرْشِيح **n.** nomination, candidacy 3041

مُرَشَّح **adj.** nominated; **n.** pl. -uun candidate 1496

رشد

رَشِيد **adj.** rational, sensible, wise, mature 4083

مُرْشِد **n.** guide, instructor; adviser, aide 4568

رصد

رَصَدَ **v. I (u)** to observe, track, monitor sth 3910

رَصْد **n.** observation; survey; tracking 3560

رَصِيد **n.** balance; funds; stock, inventory 2013

مِرْصاد **n.** lookout, ambush; lying in wait 4800

رصص

رَصاص **n.** lead (metal); **coll.n.** bullets 1946

رَصاصَة **n.** bullet; shot 4571

رصف

رَصِيف **n.** sidewalk; platform 4065

رضي

رَضِيَ **v. I (a)** to be pleased ب/عن/على with 1191

أَرْضَى **v. IV** to satisfy, please sb 3636

رِضا/رِضًى **n.** approval, satisfaction, pleasure 2511

راضٍ **adj.** pleased, satisfied; accepting 3043

مُرْضٍ **adj.** satisfying, pleasing; adequate 3975

رطب

رُطُوبَة **n.** moisture, dampness, humidity 4791

رعب

رُعْب **n.** fright, panic, terror 2562

رعي

رَعَى **v. I (a)** to protect sb; to sponsor sth/sb 3051

راعَى **v. III** to heed, observe sth; to respect sth 3778

رِعايَة **n.** custody; patronage; (social) welfare 1041

مُراعاة **n.** deference, respect; compliance 3011

راعِي **n.** guardian; patron, sponsor; steward 3229

رغب

رَغِبَ **v. I (a)** to wish for, desire, want في sth 1838

رَغْبَة **n.** pl. رَغَبات wish, desire 935

راغِب **adj.** (person) wanting, desiring (في sth) 4258

رغم

عَلَى الرَّغْمِ مِن and رَغْمَ **n.** رَغْم/رُغْم despite 207

رفد

رافِد **n.** tributary; الرّافِدانِ Tigris and Euphrates 4071

رفض

رَفَضَ **v. I (u)** to reject, refuse sth 708

رَفْض **n.** rejection, refusal 1208

رافِض **adj.** rejecting, refusing; **n.** rejectionist 3521

مَرْفُوض **adj.** rejected; unacceptable 4776

رفع

رَفَعَ **v. I (a)** to raise sth; to increase sth 733

اِرْتَفَعَ **v. VIII** to rise, ascend; to increase, grow 1095

رَفْع **n.** raising, lifting; increasing, boosting 848

رَفيع **adj.** lofty; high-ranking; thin; fine 2194

اِرْتِفاع **n.** rise, increase; height, elevation 868

مُرْتَفِع **adj.** high, elevated; rising, soaring 2350

مُرْتَفَع **n.** height, altitude, elevation; highlands 3134

رفق

رافَقَ **v. III** to accompany, escort sb 4094

رِفْقَة **n.** pl. رِفاق company, group 2879

رَفيق **n.** pl. رِفاق companion, partner 1990

مِرْفَق **n.** pl. مَرافِق convenience, service 2410

مُرْفَق **adj.** attached, appended; enclosed 4542

رقب

راقَبَ **v. III** to monitor, supervise sth/sb 3438

رَقَبَة **n.** neck; في رَقَبَتِهِ his responsibility 3859

رَقيب **n.** observer; censor; (mil.) sergeant 4737

رَقابَة **n.** censorship; surveillance; supervision 2011

مُراقَبَة **n.** censorship; inspection; supervision 1617

مُراقِب **n.** observer; supervisor, monitor 2401

مُرْتَقَب **adj.** expected, anticipated 3916

رقص

رَقَصَ **v. I (u)** to dance 4125

رَقْص **n.** dance, dancing 3077

رقع

رُقْعَة **n.** plot of land; (chess) board 4560

رقق

رَقيق **adj.** delicate; slender; **coll.n.** slaves 2695

رقم

رَقْم **n.** number, numeral, figure; rate; record 351

رَقَمِيّ **adj.** numerical; digital 3664

رقي

أَرْقَى **elat.** higher/highest; **adj.** top, finest 4748

اِرْتِقاء **n.** ascent; promotion; evolution 3684

راقِي **adj.** ascending; advanced; high-class 3062

ركب

رَكِبَ **v. I (a)** to get in, get on board 3076

اِرْتَكَبَ **v. VIII** to commit (crime, error) 2141

رَكْب **n.** procession; entourage, retinue 4069

رُكُوب **vn.** getting in, boarding 4837

مَرْكَب **n.** ship, vessel 4371

مَرْكَبَة **n.** vehicle; cart; (space) shuttle 3344

تَرْكيب **n.** installation; structure, construction 3129

تَرْكيبَة **n.** structure, composition 4024

اِرْتِكاب **n.** commission (crime, error) 3292

راكِب **n.** pl. رُكّاب passenger; **adj.** riding 2447

مُرَكَّب **adj.** installed; composed مِن of 2789

ركز

رَكَّزَ **v. II** to focus على on sth 2102

تَرَكَّزَ **v. V** to be centered في on sth 3939

اِرْتَكَزَ **v. VIII** to be centered, focused على on 4994

مَرْكَز **n.** pl. مَراكِز center; station; ranking 223

مَرْكَزِيّ **adj.** central 1311

تَرْكيز **n.** emphasis, focus (علی on) 1684

مُرَكَّز **adj.** concentrated; centralized 4719

رکض

رَكَضَ **v. I (u)** to run, race 3816

رکل

رَكْلة **n.** kick, shot (in sports) 4584

رکم

تَراكُم **n.** build-up, accumulation; backlog 4629

رکن

رُكْن **n.** pl. أرْكان pillar; (mil.) chief of staff 1487

رمد

رَماد **n.** ashes, cinders 3471

رمز

رَمْز **n.** pl. رُمُوز symbol; **vn.** symbolizing 1604

رَمْزِيّ **adj.** symbolic; encoded (data) 3832

رمل

رَمْل **n.** pl. رِمال sand 2095

رمم

رُمَّة **n.** entirety; بِرُمَّتِه completely 3546

تَرْميم **n.** restoration, renovation 4499

رمي

رَمَی **v. I (i)** to aim at (إلی) sth; to throw sth 2645

رَمْي **n.** throwing; shooting (bullets) 4732

مَرْمَی **n.** target; حارِس المَرْمَی goalkeeper 2591

رامي **adj.** aimed (إلی) at); **n.** archer 4122

رنن

رَنَّ **v. I (i)** to ring, sound (phone, bell) 4274

رهب

رَهيب **adj.** awful, horrible, gruesome 2192

إرْهاب **n.** terrorism; **vn.** terrorizing 741

إرْهابِيّ **n./adj.** terrorist 1162

رهق

مُراهَقة **n.** adolescence; puberty 4536

رهن

رَهْن **n.** mortgage, security 4195

رِهان **n.** bet, wager; contest 4850

راهِن **adj.** present, current 1776

روج

رَوَّجَ **v. II** to promote sth; to spread sth 4224

تَرْويج **n.** distribution; promotion, marketing 3611

روح

راح **v. I (u)** (Dia.) to go; راح (future marker) 113

تَراوَحَ **v. VI** to vary, range بَيْن..و between...and 2428

إرْتاحَ **v. VIII** to relax; to be pleased 4327

راحة **n.** rest, relaxation; palm (of the hand) 1476

رُوح **fem./masc.n.** pl. أرْواح spirit, soul; life 389

رُوحِيّ **adj.** spiritual; alcoholic 3165

ريح **n.** pl. رِياح wind; odor 1235

إسْتِراحة **n.** intermission; rest area; shrine 4886

رايِح **a.p.** (Dia.) going; pl. رايحين /rayHiin/ 2629

رائِحة **n.** pl. رَوائِح scent, odor, perfume 1546

مُريح **adj.** pleasant; soothing, restful 3657

مُرْتاح **adj.** relaxed; at ease; happy 3874

رود

أرادَ **v. IV** to want, desire sth or أنْ to do sth 126

رُوَيْد **n.** رُوَيْداً رُوَيْداً slowly, gradually 4029

إرادة **n.** desire, will 1757

رائِد **n.** pl. رُوّاد pioneer; leader; **adj.** leading 1771

مُراد **n.** goal, intention; (what is) desired 3909

روس

رُوسِيّ **n./adj.** pl. رُوس Russian 1491

روض

رَوْضة **n.** pl. رِياض garden 3115

رِياضة **n.** sports; physical education; math 704

رِياضِيّ **adj.** sports; math; **n.** mathematician 721

روع

رَوْعة **n.** magnificence, splendor 1800

أرْوَع **elat.** more/most magnificent 2966

رائِع **adj.** fantastic, amazing, awesome 491

روق

رِواق **n.** pl. أرْوِقة corridor, hall; porch, portico 4767

روم

رامَ **v. I (u)** to crave sth; عَلی ما يُرامُ in order 4376

رُومِيّ **n./adj.** pl. رُوم Byzantine 4211

روي

رَوَی **v. I (i)** to narrate; to provide an account 1994

رِواية **n.** pl. -aat novel, story; report, account 1182

رِوائِيّ **n.** pl. -uun novelist; **adj.** narrative 4059

راوٍ **n.** storyteller; reciter (of poetry) 3858

ریال

ريال **n.** riyal (currency) 1074

ريب

رَيْب **n.** doubt; بِلا رَيْب without a doubt 4479

ريت

ياريت **part.** /ya-reet/ (Dia.) if only, I wish 2775

ريث

رَيْثَما **conj.** as long as; until 4576

ريد

راد **v. I (i)** (Irq.Gul.) to want, need sth 1937

ريف

رِيف **n.** country, countryside, rural area 3804

رِيفيّ **adj.** rural, countryside; rustic 4012

ريي

رَيّ **n.** irrigation 4415

زبن

زَبُون **n.** pl. زَبائِن customer, client 3978

زجج

زُجاج **n.** glass; زُجاج أَماميّ windshield 3050

زُجاجة **n.** bottle; (piece of) glass 4490

زحم

زَحْمة **n.** (traffic) congestion; crowd 4048

زِحام **n.** crowd, throng; (traffic) congestion 4421

زرر

زِرّ **n.** button; (push) button, switch button 4353

زرع

زَرَعَ **v. I (a)** to plant; to cultivate (land) 3141

زَرْع **n.** planting; growing; farming 3690

زِراعة **n.** agriculture; transplanting (organ) 1508

زِراعيّ **adj.** agricultural, farming 1579

مَزْرَع **n.** pl. مَزارِع farm, plantation 1769

مُزارِع **n.** pl. -uun farmer 3932

زرق

أَزْرَق **adj.** fem. زَرْقاء blue 1754

زعل

زَعْلان **adj.** fem. زَعْلانة angry (على/من with/at) 4827

زعم

زَعَمَ **v. I (u)** to allege, claim أَنَّ/بِأَنَّ that 3261

زَعيم **n.** pl. زُعَماء leader, head of state 1173

زَعامة **n.** leadership 4777

مَزْعُوم **adj.** so-called; alleged, claimed 3847

زفف

زِفاف **n.** wedding 4599

زكو

زَكاة **n.** zakat (almsgiving in Islam); charity 4006

زلزل

زِلْزال **n.** pl. زَلازِل earthquake 2702

زلم

زلمه/زلمي **n.** /zalameh/ (Lev.) man, guy 3668

زمع

مُزْمَع **adj.** imminent; scheduled, intended 4712

زمل

زَميل **n.** pl. زُمَلاء colleague, associate 1428

زمم

زِمام **n.** reins 4109

زمن

زَمَن **n.** time, period, duration 551

زَمَنيّ **adj.** chronological; transitory 2275

زَمان **n.** time, period; مِن زَمانٍ long time ago 737

مُزْمِن **adj.** enduring, chronic 3768

زهر

زَهْر **coll.n.** pl. زُهُور , أَزْهار flowers 1879

زَهْرة **n.** flower; (fig.) splendor 3792

اِزْدِهار **n.** blossoming, prosperity 4001

زوج

تَزَوَّج **v. V** to marry sb; to get married 1700

زَوْج **n.** pl. أَزْواج spouse; husband 464

زَوْجة **n.** pl. -aat wife 496

زَوْجيّ **adj.** marital; paired, coupled 3031

زَواج **n.** marriage; wedding 764

مُتَزَوِّج **adj.** married (مِن to) 3226

زود

تَزْويد **n.** providing, supplying (ب with) 4127

زور

زارَ **v. I (u)** to visit sb or a place 1563

زِيارة **vn.** visiting; **n.** pl. -aat visit 490

تَزْوير **n.** forgery; falsification 3672

زائر **n.** pl. زُوَّار visitor, guest; tourist 2123

زول

زالَ **v. I (a)** لا/ما زالَ/يَزالُ to continue to be/do 214

زالَ **v. I (u)** to disappear, vanish 3750

أَزالَ **v. IV** to remove; to uninstall (software) 4781

زَوال **n.** ending; disappearance; noon 4199

إِزالة **n.** removal; uninstalling (software) 2169

زوي
زاوِيَة *n.* pl. زَوايا corner; section; angle 1656

زيت
زَيْت *n.* oil (food, mineral) 1745

زيتن
زَيْتُون *coll.n.* olives; olive tree 2471

زيد
زادَ *v. I (i)* to increase; to exceed 502

تَزايَدَ *v. VI* to increase, grow in number 4814

اِزْدادَ *v. VIII* to grow, increase, rise 1367

زِيادَة *n.* increase, rise, growth; addition 533

مَزيد *n.* addition, added amount; additional 687

تَزايُد *n.* (gradual) growth, increase, rise 3181

اِزْدِياد *n.* growth, increase, rise 3949

زائِد *adj.* extra; exceeding; excessive 2454

مُتَزايِد *adj.* growing, increasing, rising 2813

زين
زَيْن *adj.* lovely, pretty; (Irq.Gul.) good, fine 961

زِينَة *n.* embellishment, adornment 3958

زيي
زَيّ *prep.* (Egy.Lev.) like, similar to; زَيِّي like me 897

زِيّ *n.* pl. أَزْياء uniform; أَزْياء fashion clothes 3396

س
سَـ *part.* (future marker, from سَوْفَ) will 149

سأل
سَأَلَ *v. I (a)* to ask; to request; to pray to (God) 325

تَساءَلَ *v. VI* to ask oneself, wonder, ponder 1764

سُؤال *n.* pl. أَسْئِلَة question, inquiry 267

مَسْأَلَة *n.* pl. مَسائِل issue, affair; matter, question 738

تَساؤُل *n.* pl. -aat questions, doubts 2176

سائِل *adj.* asking; requesting; *n.* beggar 4273

مَسْؤُول/مَسْئُول *n.* official; *adj.* responsible 354

مَسْؤُولِيَّة/مَسْئُولِيَّة *n.* pl. -aat responsibility, duty 794

مُتَسائِل *adj.* asking oneself, wondering 4116

سبب
سَبَّبَ *v. II* to cause, produce, provoke sth 1668

تَسَبَّبَ *v. V* to cause, result in بـ/في sth 2044

سَبَب *n.* pl. أَسْباب reason; بِسَبَب because of 117

سبت
سَبْت *n.* (يَوْم) السَّبْت Saturday 1148

سبح
سَبَحَ *v. I (a)* to swim 4138

سُبْحان *n.* praise; سُبْحان الله praise God! 1059

سِباحَة *n.* swimming 2920

سبع
سَبْعَة *num.* fem. سَبْع seven; سَبْعَةَ عَشَر seventeen 689

سَبْعُون *num.* seventy; seventieth 2936

سَبْعين *n.* seventieth year; السبعينات the Seventies 4296

سَبْعِينِيّ *adj.* seventieth; *n.* السبعينيات the Seventies 4842

أُسْبُوع *n.* pl. أَسابيع week 393

أُسْبُوعِيّ *adj.* weekly 3393

سابِع *adj.* seventh (ordinal) 1333

سبق
سَبَقَ *v. I (i,u)* to precede, do previously 1025

سَبْق *n.* precedence, antecedence 4184

أَسْبَق *adj.* previous, former; earlier 3414

سِباق *n.* pl. -aat race; competition 1884

مُسابَقَة *n.* pl. -aat contest, competition; race 1040

سابِق *adj.* pl. -uun former; سابِقاً previously 284

مَسْبُوق *adj.* غَيْر مَسْبُوق unprecedented 3565

مُسْبَق *adj.* previous; مُسْبَقاً in advance 2235

سبل
سَبيل *n.* pl. سُبُل way, road; means 543

ستت
سِتّ *n.* pl. -aat lady, miss 2881

سِتَّة *num.* fem. سِتّ six; سِتَّةَ عَشَر sixteen 591

سِتُّون *num.* sixty; sixtieth 2185

سِتّين *n.* sixtieth year; الستينات the Sixties 4676

ستر
سَتَرَ *v. I (u,i)* to veil, cover, hide sth 3224

سِتار *n.* veil, curtain 3371

سجد
مَسْجِد *n.* pl. مَساجِد mosque 852

سجل
سَجَّلَ *v. II* to register, record; to score 877

سِجِلّ *n.* pl. -aat register; archive, record 3019

تَسْجيل *n.* registration; recording 1297

مُسَجِّل *n.* recorder; *a.p.* recording 2805

مُسَجَّل *adj.* registered, recorded 2956

سجن
سِجْن *n.* pl. سُجُون prison 790

سَجين *n.* pl. سُجَناء prisoner, inmate 2470

سحب

سَحَبَ ***v. I (a)*** to withdraw, take out sth 1746

اِنْسَحَبَ ***v. VII*** to withdraw, leave (مِن from) 2739

سَحْب ***n.*** withdrawal, pulling out; removal 3405

سَحاب ***coll.n.*** clouds, ***un.n.*** سَحابَة, pl. سُحُب 2599

اِنْسِحاب ***n.*** withdrawal; evacuation 1698

سحر

سِحْر ***n.*** sorcery, magic 2597

سِحْرِيّ ***adj.*** magical, magic; enchanting 4097

ساحِر ***n.*** sorcerer, magician; ***adj.*** charming 3400

سحل

ساحِل ***n.*** pl. سَواحِل coast, seashore, beach 2199

ساحِلِيّ ***adj.*** coastal, seaside 3928

سخر

سُخْرِيَّة ***n.*** sarcasm, cynicism; ridicule 3267

ساخِر ***adj.*** satirical; ***a.p.*** ridiculing 3509

سخن

ساخِن ***adj.*** hot, heated 2355

سدد

سَدَّ ***v. I (u)*** to close; to turn off; to pay; to fill 3872

سَدَّدَ ***v. II*** to obstruct; to pay off; to aim, shoot 3651

سَدّ ***n.*** bridging; defrayal; paying off 3603

سُدّ ***n.*** dam 4151

تَسْدِيد ***n.*** payment; aiming, shooting 4756

سدس

سادِس ***adj.*** sixth (ordinal) 1237

سرب

سَراب ***n.*** mirage, illusion 3737

تَسَرُّب ***n.*** leak, escape; infiltration 4278

سرح

سَراح ***n.*** release; إطْلاق سَراح setting free 2760

مَسْرَح ***n.*** theater, stage 1211

مَسْرَحِيّ ***adj.*** theatrical 2529

مَسْرَحِيَّة ***n.*** play (theater) 2208

سرد

سَرْد ***n.*** listing; presentation, account 3807

سرر

سِرّ ***n.*** pl. أَسْرار secret; أَمِين السِّر secretary 792

سِرِّيّ ***adj.*** secret; private 1848

سِرِّيَّة ***n.*** secrecy 2744

سُرُور ***n.*** happiness; pleasure, delight 3830

سَرِير ***n.*** pl. أَسِرَّة bed, couch 1951

سرطن

سَرْطان ***n.*** cancer 2134

سرع

سارَعَ ***v. III*** to hurry, hasten إلى to a place 3935

أَسْرَعَ ***v. IV*** to hurry, hasten في in doing sth 3487

سُرْعَة ***n.*** speed; بِسرعة quickly 640

سَرْعان ***n.*** سُرْعانَ ما it didn't take long for 2334

سَرِيع ***adj.*** quick, prompt; سَرِيعاً quickly 854

أَسْرَع ***elat.*** faster/fastest; sooner/soonest 2230

إِسْراع ***n.*** hurrying, speeding up; acceleration 3889

مُسْرِع ***adj.*** hurrying, hastening 3195

سرق

سَرَقَ ***v. I (i)*** to steal sth 3005

سَرِقَة ***n.*** stealing, theft 2798

سري

سَرَى ***v. I (i)*** to flow; to apply (a law) على to 3274

سَرِيَّة ***n.*** pl. سَرايا (mil.) company, squadron 4588

سطح

سَطْح ***n.*** surface 1796

سطر

سَطْر ***n.*** pl. سُطُور line, row 2901

سعد

سَعِدَ ***v. I (a)*** to be happy, delight ب in sth 4503

ساعَدَ ***v. III*** to help, assist, support sb 1056

أَسْعَدَ ***v. IV*** to make happy 2161

سَعِيد ***adj.*** pl. سُعَداء happy, content 1295

سَعادَة ***n.*** happiness; (honorific) His Excellency 753

سَعُودِيّ ***n./adj.*** pl. -uun Saudi 479

أَسْعَد ***elat.*** happier/happiest; luckier/luckiest 4344

مُساعَدَة ***n.*** pl. -aat help, support; مساعدات aid 692

مُساعِد ***n.*** aide; ***adj.*** helping, assisting 1658

سعر

سِعْر ***n.*** pl. أَسْعار price, cost, rate 444

سعف

إِسْعاف ***n.*** first aid; سَيّارَة إِسْعاف ambulance 3663

سعي

سَعَى ***v. I (a)*** to strive إلى for (a goal) 860

سَعْي ***n.*** endeavor, pursuit; striving 1987

مَسْعًى ***n.*** pl. مَساعٍ effort, endeavor 3418

سفر

سافَرَ ***v. III*** to travel إلى to; to depart (on a trip) 1672

أَسْفَرَ ***v. IV*** to result عن in, cause عن sth 2283

سَفَر **vn.** traveling; **n.** journey, trip 1027

سَفِير **n.** pl. سُفَراء ambassador 1015

سِفارَة/سَفارَة **n.** pl. -aat embassy 1892

مُسافِر **n.** pl. -uun passenger; **a.p.** traveling 2082

سفل

أَسْفَل **elat.** lower/lowest; **n.** bottom part 2267

سفن

سَفِينَة **n.** pl. سُفُن ship, vessel 1781

سقط

سَقَطَ **v. I (u)** to fall; drop, decline 1058

تَساقَطَ **v. VI** to collapse 4790

سُقُوط **n.** fall, collapse; crash (aircraft) 1545

إِسْقاط **n.** overthrowing; shooting down 3337

سقف

سَقْف **n.** roof; ceiling 2421

سكت

سَكَتَ **v. I (u)** to be quiet, be silent 2975

سُكُوت **n.** silence, calm 3474

سكر

سَكَّرَ **v. II** (Lev.Gul.) to close, shut (door) 4498

سُكَّر **n.** sugar; مَرَض السكر diabetes 1683

سُكَّرِيّ **n.** (also مَرَض السكري) diabetes 3741

سكن

سَكَنَ **v. I (u)** to live في at/in; **a.p.** ساكِن 1328

سَكَن **n.** housing 2342

سَكَنِيّ **adj.** housing, residential 2400

سُكُون **n.** quiet, calm; rest, repose 3686

سِكِّين **n.** knife 4794

مَسْكَن **n.** pl. مَساكِن residence, domicile 3162

إِسْكان **n.** housing 4014

ساكِن **n.** pl. سُكَّان resident, inhabitant 748

ساكِن **adj.** motionless 4271

سُكَّانِيّ **adj.** residential, population-related 3486

سلب

سَلْب **n.** robbing, depriving; سَلْبًا negatively 3392

سَلْبِيّ **adj.** negative; passive 1236

أُسْلُوب **n.** pl. أَساليب style, manner; method 1017

سلح

سِلاح **n.** pl. أَسْلِحَة weapon; (mil.) branch 514

مُسَلَّح **n.** pl. -uun gunman; **adj.** armed 917

سلسل

سِلْسِلَة **n.** chain, series 1719

مُسَلْسَل **n.** pl. -aat serial show, soap opera 1704

سلط

سُلْطَة **n.** pl. سُلُطات power, authority 328

سلطن

سَلْطَنَة **n.** sultanate 2252

سُلْطان **n.** Sultan; power, authority (على over) 950

سلع

سِلْعَة **n.** pl. سِلَع commodity; pl. سِلَع goods 2381

سلف

سَلَف **coll.n.** ancestors; **n.** advance (payment) 2888

سلك

سُلُوك **n.** behavior, conduct 1727

سلل

تَسَلَّلَ **v. V** to infiltrate إلى sth 3974

سَلَّة **n.** basket 2188

تَسَلُّل **n.** infiltration 4290

سلم

سَلِمَ **v. I (a)** to be safe; تَسْلَم thanks! 531

سَلَّمَ **v. II** to hand over sth; to greet sb 294

أَسْلَمَ **v. IV** to surrender, hand over sth 4820

تَسَلَّمَ **v. V** to receive sth; to take on sth 2887

سِلْم **n.** peace 2310

سِلْمِيّ **adj.** peaceful 1983

سُلَّم **n.** ladder; stairs, staircase; scale 3270

سَلام **n.** peace; pl. -aat greeting, salute 188

سَلامَة **n.** security, safety; integrity 855

سَلِيم **adj.** correct, sound; flawless; safe 1533

تَسْلِيم **n.** delivery, handing over; surrender 1991

إِسْلام **n.** Islam 365

إِسْلامِيّ **adj.** Islamic; **n./adj.** Islamist 184

اِسْتِلام **n.** receiving, accepting 4637

اِسْتِسْلام **n.** surrender; resignation 4250

سالِم **adj.** safe, secure, sound, intact 4736

مُسْلِم **n./adj.** pl. -uun Muslim 229

سمح

سَمَحَ **v. I (a)** to allow, permit لـ sb (to do sth) 787

سَماح **n.** permission; magnanimity 2320

سَماحَة **n.** magnanimity; His Eminence 4384

تَسامُح **n.** tolerance, forbearance 2818

مَسْمُوح **adj.** allowed, permitted 3543

سمر

أَسْمَر *adj.* fem. سَمْراء, pl. سُمْر brown, tanned 4452

سمع

سَمِعَ *v. I (a)* to hear sb, listen إلى to sb 154

إِسْتَمَعَ *v. VIII* to listen إلى to 2143

سَمْع *n.* hearing 3194

سُمْعَة *n.* reputation 3007

سَماع *n.* hearing, listening 2877

إِسْتِماع *vn.* listening (إلى to) 3571

سامِع *a.p.* listening, hearing, able to hear 3880

سمك

سَمَك *coll.n.* fish, *un.n.* سَمَكَة, pl. أَسْماك 1916

سمم

سَمّ *n.* pl. سُمُوم poison, toxin 3087

سمن

سِمْنَة *n.* fat; obesity 4632

سمو

سَمَّى *v. II* to name, designate, call 896

أَسْمَى *v. IV* to name, designate, call 4965

سُمُوّ *n.* loftiness; His/Her Highness 909

سَماء *n.* pl. سَمَوات, سَماوات sky, heaven 728

سَماوِيّ *adj.* heavenly, celestial 4292

إِسْم *n.* pl. أَسْماء, أَسام (def. أَسامي) name 89

بِسْم *prep.phr.* بِسْم الله in the Name of God 3300

أَسْمَى *elat.* higher/highest, loftier/loftiest 4627

تَسْمِيَة *n.* naming, appellation, designation 2667

سام *adj.* (def. سامِي) lofty, exalted, sublime 2625

مُسَمَّى *n.* title, name; *adj.* called, named 2833

سند

إِسْتَنَدَ *v. VIII* to lean on, rely on إلى sth 3273

مُساندَة *n.* support, aid, assistance 3740

إِسْتِناد *n.* dependence; إِسْتِناداً على on the basis of 3715

سنن

سِنّ *n.* age (of a person) 1083

سِنّ *n.* pl. أَسْنان tooth; sharp edge 2441

سُنَّة *n.* sunna (orthodox Islam) 1725

سُنِّيّ *n./adj.* pl. سُنَّة Sunni 1811

سنو

تَسَنَّى *v. V* to be feasible, be possible 4512

سَنَة *n.* pl. سَنَوات, سِنُون (gen./acc. سِنِين) year 69

سَنَوِيّ *adj.* annual, yearly; سَنَوِيّاً yearly 1192

سهر

سَهَر *n.* sleeplessness; watchfulness, vigilance 4501

سَهْرَة *n.* soiree, evening gathering 3336

سهل

سَهُلَ *v. I (u)* to be easy, be convenient 3803

سَهَّلَ *v. II* to facilitate, make easy 2727

سَهْل *adj.* easy, simple 1147

سَهْلَ *n.* أَهْلاً وَسَهْلاً *interj.* hello! welcome! 1728

سُهُولَة *n.* ease, facility 1824

أَسْهَل *elat.* easier/easiest 3302

تَسْهِيل *n.* pl. -aat facilitation, assistance 2115

سهم

ساهَمَ *v. III* to participate in, contribute to 1474

أَسْهَمَ *v. IV* to participate, contribute, share 2677

سَهْم *n.* pl. أَسْهُم (econ.) share; pl. سِهام arrow 736

مُساهَمَة *vn.* participation, contribution 1871

مُساهِم *n.* shareholder, stockholder 4189

سوء

أَساء *v. IV* to offend إلى sb; to do sth badly 3359

سُوء *n.* offense; bad, ill; miss- 1263

أَسْوَأ *elat.* worse/worst 2265

إِساءَة *n.* insult, affront 3802

سَيِّء *adj.* bad 1493

سوبر

سُوبَر *n.* super (in سوبرماركت "supermarket") 3454

سوح

ساحَة *n.* pl. -aat scene; field, arena 879

سود

سادَ *v. I (u)* to prevail; to rule, govern 2171

سائِد *adj.* prevailing, dominant, ruling 2757

سَواد *n.* blackness; سواد الناس masses 3322

أَسْوَد *adj.* fem. سَوْداء, pl. سُود black 682

سُودانِيّ *n./adj.* Sudanese 1266

مُسَوَّدَة *n.* rough draft 4633

سَيِّد *n.* pl. سادة Sir, Mr; lord, master, boss 189

سَيِّدَة *n.* pl. -aat lady 968

سِيادَة *n.* sovereignty, supremacy 1603

سور

سُور *n.* pl. أَسْوار wall, fence, enclosure 2433

سُورَة *n.* pl. سُوَر Surah (Qurʾanic chapter) 2238

سوريا

سُوريّ **n./adj.** Syrian 578

سوس

سِياسَة **n.** politics; pl. -aat policy 370

سِياسيّ **adj.** political; **n.** politician 106

سوع

ساعَة **n.** pl. -aat hour, time; watch 185

سوف

سَوْفَ **part.** (future) will, shall 460

مَسافَة **n.** pl. -aat distance, interval 1500

سوفيت

سوفييتي/سوفيتي/سوفياتي **adj.** Soviet 3096

سوق

سُوق **fem.n.** (rarely masc.) pl. أَسْواق market 295

سِياق **n.** context, course 1589

تَسْويق **n.** marketing 3084

تَسَوُّق **n.** shopping 4892

سائق **n.** pl. -uun chauffeur, driver 1959

سولف

سالِفَة **n.** pl. سَوالِف (Irq.Gul.) chat; story 3119

سوي

سَوّى **v. II** (Lev.Irq.Gul.) to do, make 1070

ساوى **v. III** to equalize sth 2585

سِوى **neg.part.** other than, except for 506

سَواء **conj.** whether (or not), either (or) 633

سَوا/سَوى **adv.** (Dia.) together; **adj.** equal 4454

سَويّ **adj.** straight, correct; سَويّاً together 3201

سِيّا **adv.** (usu. لاسِيّا) especially 1245

تَسْوِيَة **n.** settlement, solution 2140

مُساواة **n.** equality, equal rights 2601

مُتَساوٍ **adj.** equivalent, similar 4927

مُسْتَوىً **n.** pl. مُسْتَوَيات level, standard 271

سيجارة

سِيجارَة **n.** pl. سَجائِر (سَجايِر .Dia) cigarette 3154

سيح

سِياحَة **n.** tourism 1566

سِياحيّ **adj.** tourist, tourism 1711

سائِح **n.** pl. سُيّاح tourist 3425

سير

سارَ **v. I (i)** to move, march; (Gul.) to go, walk 819

سَيْر **n.** course, motion, march; going, walking 1372

سيرَة **n.** pl. سِيَر biography; epic 2079

سَيّارَة **n.** pl. -aat car, automobile, vehicle 251

مَسار **n.** pl. -aat path, route; trajectory, orbit 1891

مَسيرَة **n.** march, parade; movement, course 1366

تَسْيير **n.** propulsion; steering, guidance 4693

سائِر **n.** most of, the majority of 2569

سيطر

سَيْطَرَ **v. QI** to control, dominate على sth 2259

سَيْطَرَة **n.** control, dominion 1288

سيف

سَيْف **n.** sword 2345

سيل

سالَ **v. I (i)** to flow, run; to leak; to melt 3025

سَيْل **vn.** streaming, flowing 3719

سُيُولَة **n.** liquid state, liquidity 4579

سائِل **n.** pl. سَوائِل fluid, liquid 3269

سيناريو

سِيناريو **n.** scenario 3212

سينما

سِينَما **n.** cinema 1730

سِينَمائيّ **adj.** cinema, cinematographic 3016

ش

ـشـ **interrog.** (Irq., shortened form of شُو) what 1364

ـش **part.** (Dia. suffix, negative marker) not 965

شأن

شَأْن **n.** pl. شُؤُون matter case; situation 265

مِشان/مِنْشان **prep.** (Lev.) for; **conj.** so that 4863

عَشان/عَلَشان **conj.** (Egy.Lev.Gul.) because 933

شاي

شاي **n.** tea 2070

شبب

شَبّ **n./adj.** young man, pl. شَباب youths 264

شَبابيّ **adj.** youthful, juvenile 4583

شابّ **n.** pl. شُبّان young man; **adj.** youthful 576

شابّة **n./adj.** young woman 2776

شبح

شَبَح **n.** ghost, specter 3759

شبر

شِبْر **n.** span of the hand or foot 4889

شبك

شَبَكَة **n.** pl. -aat، شِباك net; web, network 762

شُبّاك **n.** window 4148

اِشْتِباك **n.** pl. -aat skirmish, clash 2824

شبه

شابَهَ *v. III* to resemble, be similar to sth/sb 4291

أَشْبَهَ *v. IV* to resemble, look like sth/sb 1571

شِبْه *n.* semi-, almost, like 1483

شُبْهَة *n.* pl. -aat suspicion, doubt 4096

شَبيه *adj.* resembling, similar to 3554

أَشْبَه *elat.* more/most similar ب to 2510

مُشابِه *adj.* similar 3268

مُشْتَبَه *p.p.* مشتبه فيه/فيها/فيهم suspected 4495

شتت

شَتَّى *n.* all, many, diverse 2131

شَتات *n.* scattering; diaspora 4876

شتو

شِتاء *n.* winter 1722

شجر

شَجَر *coll.n.* trees, *un.n.* شَجَرَة, pl. أَشْجار 1001

شجع

شَجَّعَ *v. II* to encourage, support sb/sth 3032

شُجاع *adj.* brave 3650

شَجاعَة *n.* courage 3079

تَشْجيع *vn.* encouragement, support 1922

شحن

شَحْن *vn.* charging, loading; *n.* cargo 3483

شاحِنَة *n.* pl. -aat truck, lorry, freight car 3846

شخص

شَخْص *n.* pl. أَشْخاص person, individual 241

شَخْصِيّ *adj.* personal, private; شَخْصِيّاً in person 760

شَخْصِيَّة *n.* pl. -aat personality; individual 709

تَشْخيص *vn.* diagnosis, analysis 3517

شدد

شَدَّ *v. I (i,u)* to make sth tight or strong 2227

شَدَّدَ *v. II* to strengthen, emphasize sth 2041

اِشْتَدَّ *v. VIII* to intensify, grow more intense 3766

شِدَّة *n.* intensity; بِشِدَّة forcefully 1384

شَديد *adj.* intense, strong, severe 658

أَشَدّ *elat.* stronger/strongest 1798

مُشَدِّد *adj.* emphasizing; strengthening 3574

مُتَشَدِّد *n./adj.* extremist, fanatic; strict, intense 3821

شرب

شَرِبَ *v. I (a)* to drink; (Dia.) to smoke 2081

شُرْب *vn.* drinking; (Dia.) smoking 2369

شَراب *n.* beverage, drink 3442

مَشْرُوب *n.* pl. -aat beverage, drink 4894

شرح

شَرَحَ *v. I (a)* to explain sth ل to sb 2703

شَرْح *n.* explanation, commentary 2121

شَريحَة *n.* pl. شَرائِح slice, cross-section; slide 2145

شرر

شَرّ *n.* evil, malice 1199

شرس

شَرِس *adj.* vicious, savage, fierce 3836

شرط

اِشْتَرَطَ *v. VIII* to stipulate sth 4664

شَرْط *n.* pl. شُروط precondition, stipulation 779

شُرْطَة *n.* police 618

شُرْطِيّ *n.* police officer, policeman 3389

شَريط *n.* tape, strip, ribbon 1613

شَريطَة *n.* condition 4678

شرع

شَرَعَ *v. I (a)* to start, undertake في sth 3309

شَرْع *n.* law; *adj.* legal 2922

شَرْعِيّ *adj.* legitimate, lawful; legislative 1308

شَرْعِيَّة *n.* legitimacy, legality 2154

شُروع *vn.* embarking في on, engaging في in 4801

شَريعَة *n.* law; Sharia (Islamic law) 2317

تَشْريع *n.* pl. -aat legislation, legislature 2517

تَشْريعِيّ *adj.* legislative 1913

شارِع *n.* pl. شَوارِع street; (fig.) الشارع the public 467

مَشْروع *n.* pl. -aat, مَشاريع project; *adj.* lawful 150

شرف

أَشْرَفَ *v. IV* to supervise, manage على sth/sb 2903

تَشَرَّفَ *v. V* to be honored (على to meet sb) 3561

شَرَف *n.* honor, distinction 1484

شُرْفَة *n.* balcony 3850

شَريف *adj.* pl. شُرَفاء noble, honorable 1220

أَشْرَف *elat.* nobler/noblest 4985

مَشْرَف *n.* pl. مَشارِف view; heights 4455

إِشْراف *n.* supervision, direction 2280

مُشَرِّف *adj.* honorable, noble; honorary 3491

مُشْرِف *n.* supervisor; *adj.* supervising 1842

شرق

أَشْرَقَ *v. IV* to rise, shine 4463

شَرْق *n.* east; شَرْقاً eastward, in the east 386

شَرْقِيّ *adj.* Eastern; *n.* east, eastern region 1114

مَشْرِق **n.** East, Levant 4104

مُشْرِق **adj.** splendid; bright, auspicious 3395

شرك

شارَكَ **v. III** to participate (with sb) في in 672

اِشْتَرَكَ **v. VIII** to participate (with sb) في in 2874

شَرِكَة **n.** pl. -aat company, corporation 118

شِراكَة **n.** partnership 2646

شَرِيك **n.** pl. شُرَكاء partner, associate 1599

مُشارَكَة **n.** pl. -aat participation, association 339

اِشْتِراك **n.** subscription; participation 2970

اِشْتِراكِيّ **adj.** socialist 3149

مُشارِك **n.** participant; **adj.** participating 1076

مُشْتَرِك **n.** participant; **adj.** participating 1351

مُشْتَرَك **adj.** shared, common, joint, collective 823

شري

اِشْتَرَى **v. VIII** to buy, purchase sth 1265

شِراء **n.** buying, purchasing; purchase 1210

شرين

شِرْيان **n.** pl. شَرايين artery 3642

شطأ

شاطِئ **n.** pl. شَواطِئ shore, coast, beach 2220

شطر

شاطِر **adj.** (Dia.) pl. -iin clever; handy; cute 4989

شعب

شَعْب **n.** pl. شُعُوب people, nation 122

شَعْبِيّ **adj.** popular; national, of the people 659

شَعْبِيّة **n.** popularity, mass appeal 2339

شُعْبَة **n.** pl. شُعَب branch, department 4522

شعر

شَعَرَ **v. I (u)** to feel, be aware of ب sth 508

شُعُور **n.** feeling, sentiment, awareness 1111

شِعْر **n.** poetry 568

شِعْرِيّ **adj.** poetic 1932

شِعار **n.** pl. -aat slogan, motto; emblem 1329

شاعِر **n.** pl. شُعَراء poet 636

مَشْعَر **n.** pl. مَشاعِر feeling, sense, emotion 1104

شَعْر **coll.n.** hair, **un.n.** شَعْرَة, pl. شُعُور 947

شعع

شُعاع **n.** pl. أَشِعَّة ray, beam 2710

شعل

شُعْلَة **n.** torch, flame, fire 4855

شغب

شَغَب **n.** unrest, disturbance 4787

شغل

شَغَلَ **v. I (a)** to occupy (a post or position) 2104

اِشْتَغَلَ **v. VIII** to work, be employed 1092

شُغْل **n.** pl. أَشْغال work, labor; occupation 749

شَغْلَة **n.** pl. -aat (Lev.) thing, deal, matter 2469

شَغّال **adj.** busy, occupied; in operation 4284

تَشْغِيل **n.** operation, activation; employment 1849

مَشْغُول **adj.** busy, occupied 2494

شفف

شَفّاف **adj.** transparent, translucent 4759

شَفافِيّة **n.** transparency; clarity, openness 2807

شفه

شَفَة **n.** pl. شِفاه lip; edge, ridge, margin 2089

شفي

شِفاء **n.** cure, remedy; medication 2814

مُسْتَشْفَى **n.** pl. مُسْتَشْفَيات hospital 711

شقق

شَقَّ **v. I (u)** to split, cut through sth 3991

شَقّ **n.** splitting, opening; crack, gap 3739

شَقَّة **n.** apartment, flat 2321

شَقِيق **n.** pl. أَشِقّاء brother, full brother 1767

شَقِيقَة **n.** sister 3666

شكر

شَكَرَ **v. I (u)** to thank, give thanks to sb 920

شُكْر **n.** thankfulness; شُكْرًا **interj.** thank you 220

شاكِر **adj.** thankful, grateful 4594

مَشْكُور **adj.** thankful, grateful; **interj.** thanks! 699

شكك

شَكَّ **v. I (u)** to doubt, distrust في sth/sb 3511

شَكّ **n.** pl. شُكُوك doubt 842

شكل

شَكَّلَ **v. II** to constitute, form, compose sth 780

تَشَكَّلَ **v. V** to be formed, be composed 3661

شَكْل **n.** pl. أَشْكال manner; shape; look 132

تَشْكِيل **n.** formation, composition, constitution 998

تَشْكِيلَة **n.** assortment, group; lineup 3356

تَشْكِيلِيّ **adj.** visual, graphic 3948

مُشْكِل **n.** problem, difficulty 4706

مُشْكِلَة **n.** pl. -aat, مَشاكِل problem, issue 181

شكو
شَكا **v. I (u)** to complain إلى to sb 3172

شَكْوَى **n.** pl. شَكاوَى complaint, grievance 2688

شَكو/شاكو **interrog.** (Irq.Kuw.) is there? 4953

شكون
شكُون **interrog.** (Magh.) who 4864

شلل
شَلَل **n.** paralysis, inertia 3845

شلو
شِلْو **n.** pl. أَشْلاء corpse; limb; piece 4582

شلون
شلون **interrog.** /shloon/ (Bah.Irq.Qat.) how 2277

شمس
شَمْس **fem.n.** sun 686

شَمْسِيّ **adj.** solar, sun- 4692

شمع
شَمْعَة **n.** pl. شُمُوع candle 3660

شمل
شَمِلَ **v. I (a)** and شَمَلَ (u) to include sth 1029

اِشْتَمَلَ **v. VIII** to include, contain على sth 4270

شَمْل **n.** inclusion, containing 4226

شَمال **n.** north; **adj.** northern 624

شَمالِيّ **adj.** northern, north 1225

شِمال **n./adj.** left 4329

شامِل **adj.** comprehensive; extensive; full 953

شنن
شَنَّ **v. I (u)** to wage (a war, campaign) 3625

شَنّ **n.** waging, launching (a war, campaign) 3687

شنو
شنو **interrog.** /shinu/ (Gul.Irq.) what 1390

شهد
شَهِدَ **v. I (a)** to witness, see sth/sb; to testify 513

شاهَدَ **v. III** to see, watch, observe sth/sb 1789

اِسْتُشْهِدَ **v. X** pass. to be martyred 3476

شَهادَة **n.** pl. -aat certificate; testimony 956

شَهيد **n.** pl. شُهَداء martyr 732

شاهِد **n.** pl. شُهُود witness; **adj.** witnessing 1653

مَشْهَد **n.** pl. مَشاهِد scene, view, spectacle, sight 1127

مُشاهَدَة **n.** observation, viewing; inspection 2090

مُشاهِد **n.** viewer, spectator 3145

اِسْتِشْهاد **n.** martyrdom 3609

شهر
شَهْر **n.** pl. أَشْهُر , شُهُور month 158

شَهْرِيّ **adj.** monthly; شَهْرِيّاً **adv.** monthly 2343

شُهْرَة **n.** reputation, fame 3245

شَهير **adj.** famous, well-known 2142

أَشْهَر **elat.** more/most famous 4662

مَشْهُور **adj.** famous, well-known 2563

شهي
شَهِيّة **n.** appetite 4567

شو
شو **interrog.** /shu/ (Lev.Kuw.UAE) what 141

شور
أَشارَ **v. IV** to indicate, cite, refer to إلى sth 312

شُورَى **n.** consultation, deliberation; Shura 2929

مِشْوار **n.** walk, stroll, promenade 3132

مُشاوَرَة **n.** pl. -aat consultation, discussion 4075

إشارَة **vn.** mentioning; **n.** pl. -aat sign 1037

تَشاوُر **n.** deliberation, joint consultation 3731

اِسْتِشاريّ **adj.** advisory, consultative; **n.** advisor 3959

مُثير **a.p.** pointing out; **adj.** indicative 761

مُشار إليه/إليها **p.p.** the aforementioned 4209

مُسْتَشار **n.** counselor, adviser 1978

شوش
شاشَة **n.** pl. -aat screen; computer monitor 1598

شوط
شَوْط **n.** round, phase; game, half period 2539

شوف
شاف **v. I (u)** (Dia.) to see sth/sb; **a.p.** شايف 282

شوق
شَوْق **n.** desire, yearning 1576

مُشْتاق **adj.** yearning, longing إلى for sth/sb 4943

شوك
شَوْك **coll.n.** thorns, **un.n.** شَوْكَة; **n.** fork 4336

شوه
تَشْويه **n.** distortion 4262

شيأ
شاء **v. I (a)** to want, desire sth; إن شاء الله 124

شَيْء **n.** pl. أَشْياء thing, something 39

لاشَيْء **n.** nothingness, non-existence 4938

شوي **adv.** /shway/ (Lev.Gul.Irq.) a little bit 742

شيخ

شَيْخ *n.* pl. مَشايخ, شُيُوخ sheikh, elder 186

شَيْخَة *n.* matron, elderly woman 4040

شَيْخُوخَة *n.* old age, seniority 4350

شيد

أَشادَ *v. IV* to praise, commend ب sth 2413

شيطن

شَيْطان *n.* pl. شَياطِين devil; الشيطان Satan 1580

شيع

شِيعَة *n.* Shiites; partisans, followers 1713

شِيعِيّ *n./adj.* Shiite 1872

شُيُوعِيّ *n./adj.* Communist 3328

شائِع *adj.* widespread, well-known 4541

شائِعَة *n.* pl. -aat rumor 3728

صال

صالَة *n.* hall (It., Sp. sala) 2595

صالون

صالُون *n.* salon, chat room, parlor 3421

صبب

صَبَّ *v. I (u)* to flow; to rain; to pour (tea) 2298

صبح

أَصْبَحَ *v. IV* to become; to begin to do sth 178

صُبْح *n.* morning, daybreak 1967

صَباح *n.* morning; صَباحاً in the morning 449

صبر

صَبْر *n.* patience, endurance 1163

صبع

إِصْبَع *n.* pl. أَصابِع finger 2619

صبو

صِبا *n.* youth, childhood 4805

صَبِيّ *n.* pl. صِبْيان, صِبْيَة young boy, youth 2453

صَبِيَّة *n.* pl. صَبايا girl, young girl 4066

صحب

صُحْبَة *n.* friendship; بِصحبة accompanied by 3902

صَحابَة *pl.n.* Sahaba (companions) 3898

صاحِب *n.* pl. أَصْحاب owner; originator; friend 190

مُصاحِب *adj.* accompanying 4958

صحح

صَحَّ *v. I (i)* to be true; to be proper 2942

صَحّ *adj.* right, correct; true 674

صِحَّة *n.* health, wellness; authenticity, truth 458

صِحِّيّ *adj.* health-related, sanitary 698

صَحيح *adj.* true, correct; sound; authentic 364

تَصْحيح *n.* correction 3139

صحر

صَحْراء *n.* desert 1693

صَحْراوِيّ *adj.* desert; Saharan 3919

صحف

صَحيفَة *n.* pl. صُحُف newspaper 486

صُحُفِيّ *adj.* journalistic; *n.* reporter 939

صَحافَة *n.* journalism, press 1418

صَحافِيّ *adj.* journalistic; *n.* reporter 1751

مُصْحَف *n.* manuscript, copy (Qurʾan) 4975

صحن

صَحْن *n.* bowl, plate; courtyard (of a mosque) 4518

صحو

صَحْوَة *n.* awakening, revival; resurgence 3984

صخر

صَخْر pl. صُخُور, *un.n.* صَخْرَة, *coll.n.* rocks 2155

صدد

صَدَد *n.* في صَدَدِ in/with regard to 2058

صدر

صَدَرَ *v. I (u)* to be published; to emerge 1050

أَصْدَرَ *v. IV* to publish; to issue; to emit 1359

صَدْر *n.* pl. صُدُور chest; bosom 786

صَدارَة *n.* chairmanship; precedence 3528

صُدُور *n.* appearance; publication 2458

مَصْدَر *n.* pl. مَصادِر source 407

تَصْدير *n.* exporting 3541

مُصادَرَة *n.* confiscation, seizure; expropriation 4007

إِصْدار *n.* exporting; issuing, publication 1647

صادِر *adj.* issued; *n.* صادِرات exports 1170

صدف

صُدْفَة *n.* surprise; coincidence, chance 2560

مُصادَفَة *n.* coincidence 4799

صدق

صَدَقَ *v. I (u)* to be truthful; to be correct 2301

صَدَّقَ *v. II* to believe sb/sth; to ratify على sth 989

صِدْق *n.* sincerity, candor 1637

صَداقَة *n.* friendship 2206

صَديق *n.* pl. أَصْدِقاء friend 398

أَصْدَق *elat.* truer/truest; more/most reliable 4628

مِصْداقِيَّة *n.* credibility 3519

صادِق *adj.* truthful, veracious 1392

صدم

صَدْمَة **n.** shock, blow 2904

صدي

صَدَىً **n.** pl. أَصْداء echo; effect; repercussion 2157

تَصَدِّي **n.** resistance, confrontation 2676

صرح

صَرَّحَ **v. II** to declare, announce بِأَنَّ that 1671

صَرْح **n.** building, structure, edifice 4652

صَرِيح **adj.** candid, sincere 2376

صَرَاحَة **n.** sincerity, candor; بِصَرَاحَة frankly 608

تَصْرِيح **n.** pl. -aat declaration, statement 888

صرر

أَصَرَّ **v. IV** to insist on, assert عَلى sth 2425

إِصْرار **n.** insistence, determination 2752

صرخ

صَرَخَ **v. I (u)** to shout, scream 1894

صَرْخَة **n.** shout, scream 3734

صُرَاخ **n.** shouting, screaming 3308

صارُوخ **n.** pl. صَوارِيخ missile, rocket 1489

صارِخ **adj.** shouting, screaming 4806

صرع

مَصْرَع **n.** death, fatality 3943

صِراع **n.** pl. -aat struggle, conflict, fight 890

صرف

صَرَفَ **v. I (i)** to spend (money), dismiss sb 3234

تَصَرَّفَ **v. V** to act, behave (في/مع) with sth/sb 3099

صَرْف **n.** spending, changing (money) 1908

مَصْرَف **n.** pl. مَصارِف bank 2255

مَصْرَفِيّ **adj.** bank, banking 2825

تَصَرُّف **n.** pl. -aat behavior, conduct 1657

مَصْرُوف **n.** pl. مَصارِيف expense; allowance 4289

صرم

صارِم **adj.** severe, strict; ruthless 4338

مُنْصَرِم **adj.** gone by, elapsed (time period) 3952

صعب

صَعُبَ **v. I (u)** to be difficult عَلى for sb 2544

صَعْب **adj.** difficult, hard 597

أَصْعَب **elat.** more/most difficult 3316

صُعُوبَة **n.** pl. -aat difficulty 1283

صعد

صَعِدَ **v. I (a)** to rise, go up; to increase 2412

تَصاعَدَ **v. VI** to climb, increase 4747

صُعُود **n.** ascent, rise; take-off (aircraft) 2516

صَعِيد **n.** pl. أَصْعِدَة level, plane 1252

تَصْعِيد **n.** escalation, intensification 3408

تَصاعُد **n.** rise, ascent; escalation 3899

صغر

صِغَر **n.** smallness; youth, infancy 3674

صَغِير **adj.** pl. صِغار small; young 230

صُغَيَّر **adj.** (Egy.) small, young 4916

أَصْغَر **elat.** fem. صُغْرَى smaller/smallest 1860

صفح

صَفْحَة **n.** pl. صَفَحات page; leaf 916

صفر

صِفْر **n.** pl. أَصْفار zero; **adj.** empty 1093

أَصْفَر **adj.** fem. صَفْراء, pl. صُفْر yellow 2099

صفف

صَفّ **n.** pl. صُفُوف row, rank; classroom 905

صفق

صَفْقَة **n.** pl. صَفَقات deal, transaction 1632

صفو

تَصْفِيَة **vn.** settling, solving; **n.** settlement 2436

صافٍ **adj.** pure, clear; sincere 2387

صلب

صُلْب **adj.** hard, solid; steel; **n.** core 2323

صَلِيب **n.** cross; crucifix 3826

صَلِيبِيّ **adj.** cross-shaped; Crusader 4955

صلح

صَلُحَ **v. I (u)** to be suitable, be fitting; be valid 2522

صَلَّحَ **v. II** to repair sth; to put sth in order 4324

صُلْح **n.** peace, reconciliation 4586

صَلاحِيَّة **n.** pl. -aat suitability, viability; validity 2870

مَصْلَحَة **n.** pl. مَصالِح interest, favor; department 484

مُصالَحَة **n.** conciliation, compromise 2843

إِصْلاح **n.** pl. -aat reform, restoration 945

صالِح **n.** advantage; **adj.** suitable; pious 949

مُصْطَلَح **n.** pl. -aat technical term 3045

صلو

صَلَّى **v. II** to pray, worship; to say a prayer 470

صَلاة **n.** pl. صَلَوات prayer 635

مُصَلٍّ **a.p.** praying; **n.** pl. -uun person praying 3976

صمت

صَمْت **n.** silence 859

صامِت **adj.** silent, quiet 2437

صمد

صُمُود *n.* steadfastness, determination 3116

صمم

صَمِيم *n.* depth; *adj.* true, genuine 4357

تَصْمِيم *n.* determination; pl. تَصامِيم design 1325

مُصَمَّم *adj.* determined; *n.* designer 4398

صندق

صُنْدُوق *n.* pl. صَنادِيق box; treasury; trunk 1069

صنع

صَنَعَ *v. I (a)* to design, build; fabricate 1742

صُنْع *n.* making, building 2118

صُنْع *n.* manufacture, industry 4535

صِناعَة *n.* industry; pl. -aat trade, craft 797

صِناعِيّ *adj.* industrial; manufacturing 1136

مَصْنَع *n.* pl. مَصانِع factory, industrial plant 1859

تَصْنِيع *n.* manufacture, processing 3622

صانِع *n.* pl. صُنّاع manufacturer; maker 3499

صنف

صِنْف *n.* pl. أَصْناف type, class, kind, category 3954

تَصْنِيف *n.* classification; sorting 3422

صهين

صَهْيُونِيّ *n./adj.* Zionist 940

صَهْيُونِيَّة *n.* Zionism 4473

صوب

أَصابَ *v. IV* أُصِيبَ ب to suffer (injuries) 755

صَوْب *n.* direction; quarter 2457

صَواب *adj.* correct, true 3326

إِصابَة *n.* illness; pl. -aat casualty; score 816

مُصِيبَة *n.* pl. مَصائِب misfortune, tragedy 2420

مُصاب *n./adj.* injured, wounded; afflicted 1488

صوت

صَوْت *n.* pl. أَصْوات voice, sound; vote 152

صَوْتِيّ *adj.* verbal, vocal; acoustic, phonetic 2866

تَصْوِيت *n.* voting 2415

صور

صَوَّرَ *v. II* to film, photograph; to portray 2780

تَصَوَّرَ *v. V* to imagine, envision, ponder sth 2337

صُورَة *n.* pl. صُوَر picture, photo; manner, way 120

تَصْوِير *n.* photography; illustration 1880

مُصَوِّر *n.* photographer; illustrator 4265

تَصَوُّر *n.* depiction, conception, imagination 2349

صوغ

صِيغَة *n.* pl. صِيَغ form, shape; formula 2244

صِياغَة *n.* drafting, composing; formulation 2973

صوم

صَوْم *n.* fasting, abstinence 4223

صِيام *n.* fasting, abstinence 3470

صومل

صُومالِيّ *n./adj.* Somali 4728

صون

صِيانَة *n.* maintenance, preservation 2557

صيح

صاحَ *v. I (i)* to shout (sth, ب/على at sb) 2823

صيد

صَيْد *n.* hunting, fishing 2281

صير

صارَ *v. I (i)* to become; to happen 180

مَصِير *n.* path, destiny, fate 1532

صيف

صَيْف *n.* summer 1121

صَيْفِيّ *adj.* summer, summery 2377

صين

صِينِيّ *n./adj.* Chinese 1763

ضأل

ضَئِيل *adj.* small, meager, sparse 4089

ضبب

ضَباب *n.* fog, mist; vapor 4465

ضبط

ضَبَطَ *v. I (u,i)* to regulate, control; adjust, fix 3526

ضَبْط *n.* adjusting; regulating; seizure 895

ضابِط *n.* pl. ضُبّاط officer; pl. ضَوابِط controller 1008

مَضْبُوط *adj.* controlled, regulated; accurate 3117

ضجج

ضَجَّة *n.* noise; commotion 4206

ضَجِيج *n.* noise; commotion 3929

ضحك

ضَحِكَ *v. I (a)* to laugh (على at) 1054

ضَحْك *n.* laughter, laughing 2411

ضَحْكَة *n.* laugh, laughter 4187

ضاحِك *adj.* laughing 4268

ضحو

أَضْحَى *v. IV* to become; to start (doing) 3956

ضُحًى *n.* forenoon 4898

ضَحِيّة *n.* pl. ضَحايا victim 1164

أُضْحَى *n.* sacrifice, immolation 4607

تَضْحِيّة *n.* pl. -aat sacrifice 3530

ضاحِيّة *n.* pl. ضَواحٍ suburb, neighborhood 2747

ضخخ

ضَخّ *n.* pumping; injecting 4934

ضخم

ضَخْم *adj.* large, voluminous 1403

تَضَخُّم *n.* (econ.) inflation 4082

ضدد

ضِدّ *n.* opposite; ضِدّ *prep.* against 352

مُضادّ *adj.* anti-, counter-; *n.* anti(biotic) 2284

ضرب

ضَرَبَ *v. I (i)* to strike, hit; to give an example 1089

ضَرْب *vn.* beating; *n.* strike; type, kind 1843

ضَرْبَة *n.* pl. -aat blow, strike; shot 1605

ضَريبة *n.* pl. ضَرائِب tax, levy 1900

اِضْطِراب *n.* pl. -aat disturbance, disorder 2520

ضرر

ضَرَّ *v. I (u)* to harm ب (one's health) 3253

اِضْطَرَّ *v. VIII* to compel, force sb إلى to do sth 2700

ضَرَر *n.* pl. أُضرار damage; harm; *n.* evil 1724

ضَرُورَة *n.* necessity, need; بالضرورة necessarily 555

ضَرُوريّ *adj.* necessary, required 1214

مُضْطَرّ *adj.* forced, obligated إلى to do sth 4451

مُتَضَرِّر *adj.* damaged; injured; *n.* victim 3783

ضعف

ضُعْف *n.* weakness 1229

ضَعيف *adj.* pl. ضُعَفاء weak; powerless 1285

أَضْعَف *elat.* weaker/weakest 4999

ضِعْف *n.* pl. أَضْعاف double, multiple 3329

مُضاعَفة *n.* doubling; (pl.) complications 3787

ضغط

ضَغَطَ *v. I (u)* to press, click on على sth 2311

ضَغْط *vn.* pressing; *n.* pl. ضُغُوط pressure 735

ضفف

ضِفّة *n.* pl. ضِفاف shore, bank 1361

ضمر

ضَمير *n.* conscience; (gram.) pronoun 2472

ضمم

ضَمَّ *v. I (u)* to include, incorporate sth 931

اِنْضَمَّ *v. VII* to join, become part of إلى sth 3586

ضَمّ *n.* joining; addition, annexation 5000

اِنْضِمام *n.* joining; affiliation; annexation 2602

ضمن

ضَمِنَ *v. I (a)* to guarantee, insure 3704

ضَمَّنَ *v. II* to guarantee, insure 2859

تَضَمَّنَ *v. V* to guarantee; comprise, include 1274

ضِمْنَ *prep.* within, inside; among 602

ضَمان *n.* pl. -aat guarantee, insurance 1246

تَضامُن *n.* solidarity, cooperation 2748

مَضْمُون *n.* content; *adj.* guaranteed, insured 3058

ضوء

أَضاء *v. IV* to illuminate, shine upon sth 4214

ضَوْء *n.* pl. أَضْواء light, lamp 863

ضِياء *n.* light, glow 4256

ضيع

ضاعَ *v. I (i)* to disappear, vanish 2007

أَضاعَ *v. IV* to lose sth; to waste (time) 3922

ضِياع *n.* loss; waste (esp. of time) 2622

ضائِع *adj.* lost; stray; wasted (time) 3507

ضيف

أَضافَ *v. IV* to add sth 291

اِسْتَضافَ *v. X* to host, invite sb 3942

ضَيْف *n.* pl. ضُيُوف guest, visitor 1454

إضافة *n.* addition; بالإضافة إلى in addition to 382

إضافيّ *adj.* additional, supplementary 2419

اِسْتِضافة *n.* hosting 3539

مُضيف *n.* host; *a.p.* adding; *adj.* hosting 1956

ضيق

ضاقَ *v. I (i)* to be narrow, tight (situation) 2506

ضيق *n.* narrowness; lack of, shortage 2777

ضَيِّق *adj.* narrow, restricted, tight 1784

طاولة

طاوِلة *n.* table; لَعْبة الطّاوِلة backgammon 1857

طبب

طِبّ *n.* medicine, medical treatment 1529

طِبِّيّ *adj.* medical 865

طَبيب *n.* pl. أَطِبّاء physician, doctor 644

طبخ

طَبْخ *n.* cooking, cuisine 4669

مَطْبَخ *n.* kitchen 2999

طبع

طَبْع **n.** nature, character; طَبْعاً of course 340

طَبِيعَة **n.** nature; normal, natural (state) 902

طَبِيعيّ **adj.** natural, normal 574

طابِع/طَبْع **n.** pl. طَوابِع stamp, mark; feature 2133

مَطْبُوع **adj.** printed; **n.** مَطْبُوعات publications 4952

طبق

طَبَّق **v. II** to implement (a plan) 2712

انْطَبَق **v. VII** to be applicable; to conform with 2737

طِبْق **n.** طِبْقاً لِـ and طِبْقَ in accordance with 2836

طَبَق **n.** dish, course, meal 4110

طَبَقَة **n.** pl. -aat class, rank; level, layer 1750

تَطْبِيق **n.** implementation (of a plan) 986

طابِق **n.** floor, story 3892

طرأ

طَرَأ **v. I (a)** to happen, occur عَلى to sb 4036

طارِئ **adj.** emergency; exceptional 3002

طارِئَة **n.** pl. طَوارِئ emergency 2576

طرب

مُطْرِب **adj.** delightful; **n.** pl. -uun musician 3484

طرح

طَرَح **v. I (a)** to suggest, propose; to offer 1224

طَرْح **n.** suggestion, proposal; offering, offer 1278

مَطْرُوح **adj.** proposed, offered; prostrate 2364

طرد

طَرْد **vn.** expulsion; firing; **n.** parcel 3504

طرز

طِراز **n.** model, class, type 2593

طرف

طَرَف **n.** pl. أَطْراف edge; tip; extremity 371

تَطَرُّف **n.** extremism, radicalism 2974

مُتَطَرِّف **n./adj.** extremist, militant, radical 2713

طرق

طَرَق **v. I (u)** to knock on (door) 4166

تَطَرَّق **v. V** to broach, discuss إِلى (topic, issue) 2875

تَطَرُّق **n.** broaching, discussing إِلى (a topic) 4752

طَريق **fem./masc.n.** pl. طُرُقات ,طُرُق road; way 115

طَريقَة **n.** method, procedure, way 401

طعم

طَعْم **n.** flavor, taste 2860

طَعام **n.** pl. أَطْعِمَة food 1051

مَطْعَم **n.** pl. مَطاعِم restaurant 1823

طغو

طاغ **n.** pl. طُغاة tyrant; **adj.** tyrannical 3641

طاغِيَة **masc.n.** tyrant, despot, dictator 3806

طفل

طِفْل **n.** child; fem. طِفْلَة girl, pl. أَطْفال children 174

طُفُولَة **n.** childhood, infancy; youth 1949

طقس

طَقْس **n.** weather, climate 2657

طَقْس **n.** pl. طُقُوس ritual, rite 4836

طقم

طاقِم **n.** crew, staff, team 3729

طلب

طَلَب **v. I (u)** to request sth; to order sth 457

طالَب **v. III** to demand بِ sth (from sb) 774

تَطَلَّب **v. V** to require sth (from sb) 1572

طَلَب **n.** pl. -aat request; demand; application 575

مَطْلَب **n.** pl. مَطالِب request; demand 1841

مُطالَبَة **n.** demand; requirement 2324

طالِب **n.** pl. طَلَبَة ,طُلّاب student 270

طُلّابيّ **adj.** student-related 3788

طالِب **adj.** requesting, demanding 4046

مَطْلُوب **adj.** wanted, needed; required 802

مُطالِب **adj.** demanding, claiming; **n.** claimant 2792

مُتَطَلِّب **adj.** required; **n.** مُتَطَلَّبات demands 2559

طلع

طَلَع **v. I (u)** to appear, emerge; to go out 306

تَطَلَّع **v. V** to look إِلى at sth; to anticipate 2423

اطَّلَع **v. VIII** to examine, peruse عَلى sth 2519

مَطْلَع **n.** beginning, dawn (of an era) 2382

تَطَلُّع **n.** pl. -aat aspiration, hope 4839

اطِّلاع **n.** inspection, perusal عَلى of sth 2764

اسْتِطْلاع **n.** pl. -aat (opinion) poll 2568

مُطَّلِع **adj.** well-informed (عَلى about sth) 3907

طلق

أَطْلَق **v. IV** to release, set free; to fire, shoot 831

انْطَلَق **v. VII** to depart, take off; to begin 1175

طَلاق **n.** divorce 2616

إِطْلاق **n.** releasing; shooting; إِطْلاقاً (not) at all 678

انْطِلاق **n.** start, departure 1674

انْطِلاقَة **n.** start, launch, outset 4385

مُطْلَق **adj.** absolute, unlimited 1536

مُنْطَلَق **n.** premise; starting point; launch pad 2830

طلل

أَطَلَّ **v. IV** to overlook, provide a view على of 2493

طمأن

طَمْأَنَ **v. QI** to pacify, assuage, reassure sb 4856

طُمَأْنِينَة **n.** calm, serenity; rest, repose 3981

اِطْمِئْنان **n.** peace of mind, serenity; calm 4939

مُطْمَئِنّ **adj.** calm; relieved; certain (إلى about) 4076

طمح

طُمُوح **n.** pl. -aat ambition, desire; wish 2491

طَمُوح **adj.** ambitious, desirous 4620

طنن

طُنّ **n.** ton 2604

طهر

طاهِر **adj.** clean, pure; flawless, perfect; chaste 3550

طور

تَطَوَّرَ **v. V** to develop, grow; to advance 2979

طَوْر **n.** stage, phase; period, time 4305

تَطْوِير **n.** development, advancement 623

تَطَوُّر **n.** pl. -aat progress; تَطَوُّرات events 814

مُتَطَوِّر **adj.** advanced, developed; modern 2908

طوع

اِسْتَطاعَ **v. X** to be able أَنْ/**v.n.** to do sth 235

طاعَة **n.** obedience 3449

مُتَطَوِّع **n./adj.** pl. -uun volunteer 4813

مُسْتَطاع **n.** (what is) possible, feasible 4811

طوف

طائِفَة **n.** pl. طَوائِف faction, sect 1907

طائِفِيّ **adj.** sectarian, factional 1646

طائِفِيَّة **n.** sectarianism, factionalism 3980

مَطاف **n.** consequence; في نِهايَةِ المَطاف finally 3531

طوق

طاقَة **n.** energy, power; potential, ability 716

طول

طالَ **v. I (u)** to be lengthy; to take a while 1284

طَوَّلَ **v. II** to prolong sth; to take (a long) time 4073

طالَما/لَطالَما **conj.** as long as; how often! 1419

طُول **n.** length; height; طُولَ throughout 713

طَوالَ/طِوالَ **n.** طَوال/طِوال throughout 1343

طِيلَة **n.** طِيلَةَ throughout, during (the entire) 2806

طَوِيل **adj.** pl. طِوال long; tall 316

أَطْوَل **elat.** longer/longest; taller/tallest 2626

طوي

اِنْطَوَى **v. VII** to contain, include على sth 3773

طَيّ **n.** fold, crease; في طَيّ within, inside 4726

طيب

طابَ **v. I (i)** to be good or pleasant 4220

طَيَّبَ **v. II** to make pleasant; to enhance 4009

طَيِّب **adj.** nice; pleasant; delicious; **interj.** OK 147

طير

طارَ **v. I (i)** to fly; طارَ عَقْلُهُ to lose one's mind 2395

طَيْر **n.** pl. طُيُور bird 1233

طَيَران **n.** aviation, flying; airline 1463

مَطار **n.** pl. -aat airport, airfield 1349

طائِر **n.** bird; **adj.** flying, airborne 2403

طائِرَة **n.** pl. -aat aircraft, airplane 973

طيف

طَيْف **n.** spectrum (light); pl. أَطْياف ghost 3653

طين

طِين **n.** clay; mud; زادَ الطِّينَ بِلَّةً 3265

ظرف

ظَرْف **n.** pl. ظُرُوف condition, situation 663

ظلل

ظَلَّ **v. I (a)** to stay; to keep on doing 387

ظِلّ **n.** pl. ظِلال shade; patronage 876

مِظَلَّة **n.** umbrella 3906

ظلم

ظُلْم **n.** injustice; ظُلْمًا wrongly, unjustly 1404

ظُلْمَة **n.** pl. ظُلُمات darkness 3049

ظَلام **n.** darkness; injustice 1587

ظالِم **n.** pl. -uun tyrant; **adj.** oppressive 2612

مَظْلُوم **adj.** oppressed, treated unjustly 4008

مُظْلِم **adj.** dark, gloomy 2783

ظنن

ظَنَّ **v. I (u)** to think, believe, presume أَنَّ that 1038

ظَنّ **n.** opinion, assumption; ظَنِّي I think 2546

ظهر

ظَهَرَ **v. I (a)** to appear; seem كَأَنَّ as if 611

أَظْهَرَ **v. IV** to show, manifest, demonstrate 1024

ظَهْر **n.** back; rear; deck (ship) 1373

ظُهْر **n.** noon, afternoon 1425

ظَهِيرَة **n.** noon, midday 4925

ظُهُور **n.** appearance, emergence; advent 1507

مَظْهَر **n.** pl. مَظاهِر view; appearance, looks 1831

مُظاهَرة **n.** pl. -aat demonstration, rally 2723

إظْهار **n.** expressing, showing, demonstrating 3598

تَظاهُرة **n.** rally, demonstration 3596

ظاهِر **adj.** evident, apparent; **n.** obvious 1832

ظاهِرة **n.** pl. ظَواهِر phenomenon 1057

مُتَظاهِر **n.** pl. -uun demonstrator 3944

ع

عَـ **prep.** also عَ (Dia., short form of عَلَى) on 280

عبأ

عِبْء **n.** pl. أَعْباء burden, load 2611

عَباية/عَباءة **n.** abaya (traditional black robe) 4858

تَعْبِئَة **n.** (mil.) mobilization; packaging 3905

عبث

عَبَث **n.** joke, jest; frivolity; عَبَثًا in vain 2745

عبد

عَبْد **n.** pl. عَبيد servant, slave 694

عِبادة **vn.** worship, religious practice 2719

عُبُودِيَّة **n.** slavery, servitude; veneration 4873

عبر

عَبَر **v. I (u)** to cross (border, street) 3333

عَبَّر **v. II** to express (opinion), state (policy) 1168

اِعْتَبَر **v. VIII** to regard as; to believe that 341

عَبْر **prep.** across, over, via; be means of 385

عِبْرة **n.** pl. عِبَر lesson, moral 3411

عِبْري **adj.** Hebrew; Jewish (state) 3673

عِبارة **n.** pl. -aat expression; phrase, word 904

عُبُور **vn.** crossing (border, street) 3482

مَعْبَر **n.** pl. مَعابِر crossing point, juncture 3146

تَعْبير **vn.** expressing; **n.** expression 1062

اِعْتِبار **vn.** regarding; **n.** pl. -aat consideration 758

عابِر **adj.** passing, crossing; transient, brief 2647

مُعَبِّر **a.p.** expressing, stating 2741

مُعْتَبَر **a.p.** considering, regarding 2871

عبو

عُبُوّة/عَبْوة **n.** pl. -aat package, pack; charge 3848

عتب

عَتَبة **n.** step, stair; threshold 4397

عتق

عَتيق **adj.** old, aged 3724

عاتِق **n.** shoulder 4897

عتم

عَتْمة **n.** dark, darkness, gloom 3990

عثر

عَثَر **v. I (u)** to find, come across على sth 2641

عُثُور **vn.** finding, coming across على sth 2932

عثمان

عُثْماني **n./adj.** Ottoman 4320

عجب

عَجَب **v. I (i)** (Egy.Lev.) to be pleasing to sb 4086

أَعْجَب **v. IV** to please sb (يُعْجِبُني I like it) 2035

عَجَب **n.** pl. أَعْجاب admiration, amazement 2117

عَجيب **adj.** wonderful; astonishing 1787

عَجيبة **n.** pl. عَجائِب marvel, wonder 4659

إعْجاب **vn.** admiration, amazement 3869

عجز

عَجَز **v. I (a)** to be unable عن to do sth 2607

عَجْز **n.** weakness, inability; (econ.) deficit 2159

عَجُوز **n./adj.** old person, elderly 1952

عاجِز **a.p.** unable عن to do sth; **adj.** helpless 2946

مُعْجِزة **n.** miracle 4217

عجل

عَجَل **n.** hurry, rush, haste 3437

عَجَلة **n.** wheel, tire 4088

عاجِل **adj.** urgent, speedy 1855

عدد

عَدّ **v. I (u)** to regard sth/sb as; لا يُعَدُّ countless 834

أَعَدَّ **v. IV** to prepare, make ready sth 2765

تَعَدَّدَ **v. V** to be numerous or diverse 4982

اِسْتَعَدَّ **v. X** to get ready لـ for sth 2994

عَدّ **n.** counting, calculating 4972

عِدّة **n.** a number of; **adj.** several 503

عَدَد **n.** pl. أَعْداد number; issue, edition 119

عَديد **n.** large quantity; **adj.** numerous 469

عِداد **n.** number, quantity 4758

إعْداد **vn.** preparation 1113

تَعَدُّد **n.** pluralism, multi- 4098

تَعَدُّدِيَّة **n.** multiplicity, pluralism, plurality 4562

اِسْتِعْداد **vn.** preparation; **n.** readiness 1177

مَعْدُود **adj.** limited in number, countable 4068

مُعَدّ **adj.** made; **n.** مُعَدّات equipment 2580

مُتَعَدِّد **adj.** diverse, numerous, multi-, poly- 1375

مُسْتَعِدّ **a.p.** preparing لـ for; **adj.** ready 1852

عدل

عَدَّلَ *v. II* to modify, amend, adjust sth 3446

عادَلَ *v. III* to be equal to sth; (sports) to tie sb 3018

تَعادَلَ *v. VI* to be balanced, tie each other 4688

عَدْل *n.* justice, fairness 1223

عَدالَة *n.* justice, fairness 1549

تَعْديل *pl.* -aat adjustment; amendment 1141

مُعادَلَة *n.* equation, balance 2817

تَعادُل *n.* balance, equilibrium; (sports) tie 3013

اِعْتِدال *n.* moderation, restraint 4679

عادِل *adj.* fair, just, honest, equitable 2046

مُعَدَّل *n.* pl. -aat average; *adj.* amended 1122

مُعْتَدِل *adj.* moderate (weather, policy) 3863

عدم

عَدَم *n.* (in idafa) absence of, lack of; non-, not 191

إِعْدام *n.* execution, capital punishment 2139

اِنْعِدام *n.* non-existence, absence, lack of 3420

عدن

مَعْدِن *n.* pl. مَعادِن mineral, metal 4709

مَعْدِنيّ *adj.* mineral, metal, metallic 3512

عدو

عَدا *v. I (u)* to run, race 4624

تَعَدَّى *v. V* to go beyond; to infringe على on 3113

عَدا (ما) عَدا فيما *part.* and عَدا except for 2124

عَدُوّ *n./adj.* pl. أعْداء enemy 799

عَداء *n.* aggression, hostility; enmity 3150

عَدْوَى *n.* infection 3700

عُدْوان *n.* aggression, hostility; enmity 1202

عُدْوانيّ *adj.* hostile, aggressive 4482

اِعْتِداء *n.* pl. -aat assault, attack, aggression 1660

مُعادٍ *adj.* hostile, anti- 3776

مُعْتَدٍ *n.* pl. -uun aggressor, assailant 4967

عذب

عَذْب *adj.* sweet, pleasant; مِياه عَذْبَة freshwater 2738

عَذاب *n.* punishment, torture; pain, suffering 2127

تَعْذيب *n.* torture; punishment 2179

عذر

اِعْتَذَرَ *v. VIII* to apologize إلى to sb عن for sth 2980

عُذْر *n.* excuse; apology; عُذْراً excuse me 2828

عَذْراء *fem.n./adj.* virgin 4647

اِعْتِذار *n.* apology; excuse 3177

عرب

أعْرَبَ *v. IV* to express عن (one's opinion) 2018

عَرَبيّ *n./adj.* pl. عَرَب Arab; Arabian; Arabic 45

عَرَبيّة *n.* Arabic (language); (Egy.) pl. -aat car 2509

عَرَبَة *n.* pl. -aat cart, wagon; vehicle 2914

عُروبَة *n.* Arabism 3365

مُعْرِب *a.p.* expressing عن (opinion) 4435

عرس

عُرْس *n.* pl. أعْراس wedding 2120

عَروس *fem.n.* bride; *masc.n.* bridegroom 2590

عَريس *n.* bridegroom 3838

عرش

عَرْش *n.* throne 2464

عرض

عَرَضَ *v. I (i)* to exhibit sth; to inspect sth 1280

عارَضَ *v. III* to oppose, resist sth/sb 3589

تَعَرَّضَ *v. V* to be exposed إلى to sth 688

تَعارَضَ *v. VI* to clash, conflict مع/و with sth 3613

اِعْتَرَضَ *v. VIII* to object على to sth 3003

اِسْتَعْرَضَ *v. X* to review sth; to tour (facilities) 3133

عَرْض *n.* pl. عُروض display; offer; width 432

عِرْض *n.* pl. أعْراض honor, dignity 4717

عَرَض *n.* pl. أعْراض (med.) symptom 3036

عُرْضَة *n.* target, object (of criticism) 3381

عَريض *adj.* wide, broad; bold (line) 1989

مَعْرِض *n.* pl. مَعارِض exhibit, exhibition, show 1010

مُعارَضَة *n.* opposition, resistance 1200

تَعَرُّض *vn.* being exposed إلى to sth 2690

اِعْتِراض *vn.* objection, opposition على to sth 3332

اِسْتِعْراض *vn.* review, inspection; tour; parade 3592

مَعْروض *adj.* on display; offered; *n.* proposal 3971

مُعارِض *a.p.* opposing; *n.* pl. -uun opponent 2483

عرف

عَرَفَ *v. I (i)* to know sth/sb; to learn, find out 49

عَرَّفَ *v. II* to introduce sb ب to sb else 4513

تَعَرَّفَ *v. V* to get to know على sb 1634

اِعْتَرَفَ *v. VIII* to admit ب (doing) sth 1335

مَعْرِفَة *vn.* knowing; *n.* pl. مَعارِف knowledge 610

مَعْرِفيّ *adj.* knowledge-related; cognitive 4039

تَعْريف *vn.* defining; *n.* definition 2083

تَعَرُّف *vn.* getting to know على sb 1966

اِعْتِراف **vn.** admission ب of sth 1626

عارِف **a.p.** (Egy.Lev.Gul.) (= to know) 851

مَعْرُوف **adj.** well-known; **n.** favor, good deed 720

عرق

عِرْقِيّ **adj.** ethnic, racial 4099

عَرَق **n.** sweat; araq (alcoholic drink) 3225

عَرِيق **adj.** deep-rooted; noble, aristocratic 3346

عِراقِيّ **n./adj.** Iraqi 177

عرك

مَعْرَكَة **n.** pl. مَعارِك battle, campaign 970

عرم

عارِم **adj.** tempestuous, frenzied 4977

عري

عارٍ **adj.** naked, bare 3718

عزز

عَزَّ **v. I (i)** to be strong; اللهُ عَزَّ وَجَلَّ 2055

عَزَّزَ **v. II** to strengthen, bolster, reinforce 2785

عِزّ **n.** prime, peak, height 2356

عِزَّة **n.** glory, honor; power; (self-)esteem 3083

عَزِيز **adj.** pl. أَعِزّاء dear, precious 641

أَعَزّ **elat.** stronger/strongest; dearer/dearest 4407

تَعْزِيز **vn.** strengthening; **n.** reinforcement 1194

عزل

عَزْل **vn.** removal, dismissal; **n.** isolation 3828

عُزْلَة **n.** isolation, seclusion; separation 3407

عزم

اِعْتَزَم **v. VIII** to be determined على to do sth 3791

عَزْم **n.** will, determination على to do sth 2945

عَزِيمَة **n.** determination, will; invitation 4851

عزو

عَزاء **n.** consolation, comfort; condolence(s) 3366

عسكر

عَسْكَر **coll.n.** army, troops 4681

عَسْكَرِيّ **adj.** pl. -uun military; **n.** soldier 335

مُعَسْكَر **n.** pl. -aat camp, encampment 2287

عسل

عَسَل **n.** honey 2051

عسي

عَسَى **adv.** perhaps; (Irq.Gul.) hopefully 2651

عشان

عَشان/عَلَشان **conj.** (Egy.Lev.Gul.) because 933

عشب

عُشْب **coll.n.** grass; pl. أَعْشاب herb, plant 3795

عشر

عَشَرَة **num.** fem. عَشْر ten; **n.** عَشَرات scores 182

عِشْرُون **num.** twenty; twentieth 615

العِشْرِينات **n.** twentieth year; the 20s 1997

عَشِيرَة **n.** pl. عَشائِر clan, tribe 4643

مَعْشَر **n.** assembly, community, group, society 4797

عاشِر **adj.** tenth (ordinal) 1865

عشق

عَشِقَ **v. I (a)** to love, be fond of sth/sb 4144

عِشْق **n.** love, fondness 2588

عاشِق **n.** pl. -uun, عُشّاق lover; admirer, fan 1638

عشو

عَشْوائِيّ **adj.** random, indiscriminate, arbitrary 3282

عَشاء **n.** dinner, supper, evening meal 2239

عِشاء **n.** evening; صَلاة العِشاء evening prayer 4644

عَشِيَّة **n.** evening; eve, night before 2850

عصب

عَصَب **n.** pl. أَعْصاب nerve 4388

عَصَبِيّ **adj.** nervous, irritable; neural 2335

عِصابَة **n.** pl. -aat gang, band, group 2300

تَعَصُّب **n.** fanaticism, extremism; intolerance 4505

عصر

عَصْر **n.** pl. عُصُور age, period, time, epoch 880

عَصْر **n.** afternoon 2443

عَصْرِي **adj.** contemporary, modern 3794

عَصِير **n.** juice 3797

مُعاصِر **adj.** contemporary; modern 2370

عصف

عَصَفَ **v. I (i)** to rage (wind, conflict) 3841

عاصِفَة **n.** pl. عَواصِف storm, tempest 2525

عصفر

عُصْفُور **n.** pl. عَصافِير bird, sparrow 3860

عصم

عاصِمَة **n.** pl. عَواصِم capital city 696

اِعْتِصام **vn.** adhering (ب to); **n.** sit-in strike 4635

عصو

عَصاً **n.** stick, baton, rod 3501

عضل

عَضَلَة **n.** pl. -aat muscle 3247

مُعْضِلَة **n.** dilemma, problem, difficulty 4242

عضو

عُضْو *n.* pl. أَعْضاء member, associate; organ 278

عُضْويّ *adj.* organic 4924

عُضْوِيَّة *n.* membership, affiliation 2912

عطر

عِطْر *n.* pl. عُطُور perfume 2315

عطف

عاطِفَة *n.* pl. عَواطِف emotion; affection 2740

عاطِفيّ *adj.* emotional; affectionate 2897

عطل

عُطْلَة *n.* vacation, holiday, recess 2947

تَعْطيل *vn.* hindering; derailing 3745

عاطِل *adj.* pl. -uun (عَن العَمَل) unemployed 4587

عطي

عَطى *v. I (i)* (Magh.Lev.Gul.) to give sth to sb 4834

أَعْطى *v. IV* to give, provide sth to sb, or لـ to sb 346

عَطاء *vn.* giving, offering; *n.* gift, present 2149

إعْطاء *vn.* giving, donating; *n.* offer, donation 2215

تَعاطٍ *vn.* taking (medicine); handling 3612

مُعْطىً *adj.* given; *n.* مُعْطَيات facts, data, factors 3030

عظم

عَظْم *n.* pl. عِظام bone 2548

عَظَمَة *n.* majesty, greatness, grandeur 4365

عَظيم *adj.* pl. عِظام great, mighty, powerful 570

أَعْظَم *elat.* fem. عُظْمى greater/greatest 1209

مُعَظَّم *adj.* glorified, venerated 4554

مُعْظَم *n.* (in idafa) most of, the majority of 841

عفو

عافى *v. III* to heal, cure sb 4461

عَفْو *n.* pardon, amnesty; عَفْواً excuse me! 1379

عافِيَة *n.* good health, vigor 835

عقب

عاقَبَ *v. III* to punish sb على for (a crime) 4188

عَقِب *fem.n.* pl. أَعْقاب heel; عَقِبَ after 1423

عُقْب *n.* pl. أَعْقاب consequence 3557

عَقَبَة *n.* pl. -aat obstacle 2742

عُقُوبَة *n.* pl. -aat penalty, sanction 1464

مُعاقَبَة *n.* punishment, sanction 4888

عِقاب *n.* punishment, penalty 2652

عاقِبَة *n.* pl. عَواقِب consequence, result, effect 3702

مُتَعاقِب *adj.* consecutive, alternating 4487

عقبال

عُقْبال *interj.* (Egy.Lev.) may it be the same for 3688

عقد

عَقَدَ *v. I (i)* to hold, convene (meeting) 874

اِعْتَقَدَ *v. VIII* to believe في in sth, or أَنْ/بِأَنَّ that 422

عَقْد *vn.* holding, convening (meeting) 1118

عَقْد *n.* pl. عُقُود contract, agreement 1197

عَقْد *n.* pl. عُقُود decade 2253

عُقْدَة *n.* pl. عُقَد complex (emotion); knot 3742

عَقيد *n.* colonel; (in titles) Colonel 3029

عَقيدَة *n.* doctrine, dogma; creed, belief, faith 2558

تَعْقيد *n.* complication, complexity 3494

تَعاقُد *n.* contract, mutual agreement 4158

اِنْعِقاد *vn.* convening, holding (meeting) 3513

اِعْتِقاد *vn.* belief في in sth, or أَنْ/بِأَنَّ that 2673

مُعَقَّد *adj.* complicated, complex, intricate 2769

عقر

عَقار *n.* pl. -aat real estate, land property 2535

عَقاريّ *adj.* real estate; land mortgage 2726

عَقار *n.* pl. عَقاقير drug, medicine 4153

عقل

عَقَلَ *v. I (i)* to be reasonable; to make sense 3812

اِعْتَقَلَ *v. VIII* to arrest, detain sb 2202

عَقْل *n.* pl. عُقُول mind, intellect 646

عَقْليّ *adj.* mental, intellectual; rational 3250

عَقْليَّة *n.* mentality, attitude, way of thinking 3732

اِعْتِقال *n.* pl. -aat arrest, detention 1782

عاقِل *adj.* pl. عُقَلاء rational; *n.* sane person 2958

مَعْقُول *adj.* reasonable, plausible, logical 1348

مُعْتَقَل *n.* prison; *n.* prisoner; *adj.* detained 1858

عكس

عَكَسَ *v. I (i)* to reflect; to contradict 1993

اِنْعَكَسَ *v. VII* to be reflected; to have an effect 2811

عَكْس *n.* opposite, reverse, contrary 995

اِنْعِكاس *n.* pl. -aat repercussion; effect 4060

علاش

علاش *interrog.* /9laash/ (Magh.) why 4905

علب

عُلْبَة *n.* pl. عُلَب can; case, box; pack 2916

علج

عالَجَ *v. III* to treat; to deal with; to process 2863

مُعالَجَة *vn.* treatment; dealing with 1322

علاج **n.** treatment, therapy 750

عِلاجِيّ **adj.** therapeutic, healing, curative 4945

علق

عَلِقَ **v. I (a)** to be pending; to be attached 4342

عَلَّقَ **v. II** to comment on; to postpone 2096

تَعَلَّقَ **v. V** to be connected ب with sth/sb 756

عَلاقَة **n.** pl. -aat relation, link, tie, connection 219

تَعْلِيق **vn.** commenting; suspending 1324

عالِق **adj.** pending; related; stranded 3764

مُعَلِّق **a.p.** commenting; **n.** commentator 3350

مُعَلَّق **adj.** suspended, pending, outstanding 2864

مُتَعَلِّق **adj.** attached to, concerning ب sth/sb 1427

علل

عَلَّ **conj.** perhaps, maybe; عَلَّنِي maybe I 2796

لَعَلَّ **conj.** perhaps, maybe; لَعَلِّي maybe I 921

علم

عَلِمَ **v. I (a)** to know sth, find out أَنَّ that 377

عَلَّمَ **v. II** to teach sb sth; to mark sth 3450

تَعَلَّمَ **v. V** to learn, study sth 1179

عِلْم **vn.** knowing; **n.** knowledge, information 515

عِلْم **n.** pl. عُلُوم science, the study of 548

عِلْمِيّ **adj.** scientific, scholarly, academic 545

عَلَم **n.** pl. أَعْلام flag; celebrities 3467

عَلّامَة **masc.n.** eminent scholar 4161

عَلامَة **n.** pl. -aat mark, indication, sign; point 1552

عالَم **n.** pl. -uun, عَوالِم world 93

عالَمِيّ **adj.** international, global 308

مَعْلَم **n.** pl. مَعالِم sign, mark; مَعالِم landmarks 2288

تَعْلِيم **n.** pl. -aat, تَعالِيم education, teaching 388

تَعْلِيمِيّ **adj.** educational, pedagogical 1400

إِعْلام **n.** information, media; **vn.** informing 571

إِعْلامِيّ **adj.** media, information; **n.** journalist 1075

تَعَلُّم **n.** learning, study 3199

عالِم **n.** pl. عُلَماء scientist, scholar; **a.p.** knowing 869

أَعْلَم **elat.** more/most knowledgeable 3600

مَعْلُوم **adj.** known; مَعْلُوم **interj.** of course! 2631

مَعْلُومَة **n.** item of information; pl. مَعْلُومات data 412

مَعْلُوماتِيّ **adj.** informatics, information science 4695

مُعَلِّم **n.** pl. -uun teacher; master; boss 899

علمن

عَلْمانِيّ **adj.** secular 4288

عَلْمانِيَّة **n.** secularism 4380

علن

أَعْلَنَ **v. IV** to announce (عن) sth or أَنَّ that 426

عَلَن **n.** (the) open; عَلَناً openly, publicly 3772

عَلَنِيّ **adj.** public, open 4330

إِعْلان **vn.** declaring; **n.** pl. -aat announcement 873

مُعْلِن **n.** announcer; **a.p.** announcing 3698

مُعْلَن **adj.** declared, announced; posted 2996

علو

عَلا **v. I (u)** to rise, ascend, loom 1901

تَعالَى **v. VI** to be exalted (God) 420

عَلَى **prep.** on, above; (with pron.) عَلَيْـ 7

عَلِيّ **adj.** supreme, exalted; العَلِيّ (God) 3362

عِلاوَة **n.** increase; bonus 3649

عُلْوِيّ **adj.** upper, top; superior 4381

أَعْلَى **elat.** fem. عُلْيا higher/highest 402

مَعْلاة **n.** pl. مَعالِي greatness, nobility; glory 2282

عالٍ **adj.** high, elevated 505

عم

عَم **part.** (Lev., for present continuous) 517

عما

عَمّا **prep.phr.** (عَنْ ما) regarding 1130

عمد

عَمَدَ **v. I (i)** to do sth deliberately 4677

اِعْتَمَدَ **v. VIII** to depend, rely على on sth/sb 1145

عَمْد **n.** intent; **adj.** deliberate 4282

عِماد **n.** pl. عُمُد pillar; (mil.) major general 3409

عَمِيد **n.** dean; chief; (mil.) brigadier general 2383

عَمُود **n.** pl. أَعْمِدَة column, pillar 3015

اِعْتِماد **vn.** reliance, dependence على on 1362

مُعْتَمَد **p.p.** مُعْتَمَد عليه depended upon 2722

عمر

عُمْر **n.** pl. أَعْمار age (of a person); life, lifetime 281

عُمْرِيّ **adj.** age-related, age-based, age group 4721

عُمْرَة **n.** "lesser" pilgrimage to Mecca 4852

عِمارة **n.** building, edifice, structure 2892

عُمْرانِيّ **adj.** architectural; civilized, populated 4095

إِعْمار **n.** construction, building, development 2592

اِسْتِعْمار **n.** colonialism 3055

اِسْتِعْمارِيّ **adj.** colonialist 4561

مَعْمُور **adj.** inhabited; **n.** المَعْمُورَة the world 4930

عمق

عُمْق **n.** pl. أَعْماق depth, deep, bottom 1241

عَميق **adj.** deep, profound 1242

أَعْمَق **elat.** deeper/deepest 4533

تَعْميق **vn.** deepening; broadening 4553

عمل

عَمِلَ **v. I (a)** to work, function; to make sth 137

عامَلَ **v. III** to treat sth/sb 4023

تَعامَلَ **v. VI** to deal with مع sth/sb 1873

اِسْتَعْمَلَ **v. X** to use, make use of, employ 2867

عَمَل **vn.** working; **n.** pl. أَعْمال work, activity 48

عَمَليّ **adj.** practical, pragmatic 2077

عَمَليَّة **n.** pl. -aat operation, process 133

عُمْلة **n.** pl. -aat currency, money, bills 2532

عَميل **n.** pl. عُمَلاء agent; lackey; client 2049

عَمالة **n.** workforce, employees 2767

مَعْمَل **n.** pl. مَعامِل laboratory; facility 3992

مُعامَلَة **n.** pl. -aat treatment, procedure 2006

تَعامُل **n.** pl. -aat working (مع with) 891

اِسْتِعْمال **n.** use, usage; handling; application 1992

عامِل **adj.** working; active 1064

عامِل **n.** pl. -uun employee; staff 628

عامِل **n.** pl. عَوامِل factor, element, agent 1160

عُمّاليّ **adj.** labor (party); workers 4729

مَعْمُول **adj.** in use, applied, carried out 4510

مُسْتَعْمَل **adj.** used, in use, employed 4815

عملق

عِمْلاق **adj.** gigantic, huge; super 2693

عمم

عَمَّ **v. I (u)** to become prevalent 3457

عَمّ **n.** pl. عُمُوم paternal uncle 770

عُمُوم **n.** generality, totality, whole 1204

عُمُوميّ **adj.** general, public, common; plenary 3120

تَعْميم **n.** making general or public; spreading 3727

عامّ **adj.** general, common, public 88

عامّة **n.** populace; عامّةً in general 2414

عمن

عُمانيّ **n./adj.** Omani 2017

عمي

أَعْمَى **adj.** fem. عَمْياء blind 2758

عن

عَن **prep.** from, about; عَن طَريقِ by way of, via 14

عَمّا **prep.phr.** (عَنْ ما) regarding 1130

عَمَّن **prep.phr.** (عَنْ مَنْ) from whom 3844

عنب

عِنَب **coll.n.** grapes, **un.n.** عِنَبَة 4134

عند

عِنْدَ **prep.** with, next to; at (time, location) 40

عِنْدَما **conj.** when, as soon as 166

عِنْدَئِذٍ **adv.** then, at that time 3953

عنصر

عُنْصُر **n.** pl. عَناصِر factor; (pl.) individuals 782

عُنْصُريّ **adj.** racist 3064

عُنْصُريَّة **n.** racism 4540

عنف

عُنْف **n.** violence, force 901

عَنيف **adj.** violent, forceful, fierce 2138

عنق

عُنْق **n.** neck (person, bottle) 3122

عنن

عِنان **n.** bridle, reins 4646

عنو

عَنْوة **n.** force, violence; عَنْوةً forcibly, by force 4750

عنون

عُنْوان **n.** pl. عَناوين address; title, headline 643

عني

عَنَى **v. I (i)** to mean, imply sth or أَنَّ that 138

يَعْني **part.** (used as a filler) I mean, y'know 751

عانَى **v. III** to suffer sth or مِن from sth 898

عَناء **n.** hardship, trouble; distress 3597

عِنايَة **n.** care, concern, attention, regard 1902

مَعْنًى **n.** pl. مَعانٍ sense, meaning, significance 436

مُعاناة **n.** effort; hardship, suffering 1934

مَعْنيّ **adj.** affected; concerned ب with 1389

مَعْنَويّ **adj.** moral, spiritual, mental; semantic 3767

عهد

تَعَهَّدَ **v. V** to pledge ب to do sth 4959

عَهْد **n.** pl. عُهُود age; tenure; treaty; oath 892

مَعْهَد **n.** pl. مَعاهِد institute, academy, school 1231

مُعاهَدة **n.** treaty, accord, pact 3423

عهل

عاهِل **n.** monarch, king 4419

عود

عادَ **v. I (u)** to return, go back إلى to sth 123

عاد **adv.** (Lev.Gul.) so; (Irq.) **adv.** already 1369

أعادَ **v. IV** to repeat sth, do sth again 1082

تَعَوَّدَ **v. V** to get accustomed على to sth 2964

اعْتادَ **v. VIII** to get used على to sth 3527

اِسْتَعادَ **v. X** to recover, regain, reclaim sth 3213

عُود **n.** lute; stick, match stick; aloe plant 3206

عَوْدَة **n.** return, going back; return trip 504

عادَة **n.** pl. -aat habit, practice; عادَةً usually 734

عادِيّ **adj.** regular, normal; ordinary 631

عِيادَة **n.** clinic, outpatient clinic 4369

إعادَة **n.** repeating, doing sth again 516

اِسْتِعادَة **n.** recovering, regaining, reclaiming 2502

عائِد **a.p.** returning إلى to; **n.** pl. -aat revenue 2061

مُعْتاد **adj.** accustomed على to sth; typical, usual 3431

عوذ

عاذَ **v. I (u)** to take refuge بالله in God 4240

عوز

عايِز/عاوِز **a.p.** (Egy.) wanting (= to want) 2567

عوض

عَوَّضَ **v. II** to repay, reward sb 4555

عِوَض **n.** replacement; compensation 4402

تَعْويض **n.** pl. -aat restitution 2237

عوق

عائِق **n.** pl. عَوائِق obstacle, hurdle 4121

مُعَوَّق **n.** pl. -aat obstacle, hurdle, impediment 4022

عول

عائِلَة **n.** pl. -aat family, household, clan 850

عائِلِيّ **adj.** family, domestic, familial 3197

عولم

عَوْلَمَة **n.** globalization (from عالَم world) 2842

عوم

عام **n.** pl. أعْوام year 62

عون

أعانَ **v. IV** to assist, support sb/sth 3207

تَعاوَنَ **v. VI** to cooperate مع with sb 4537

عَوْن **n.** help, assistance, aid 2478

تَعاوُن **n.** cooperation 463

اِسْتِعانَة **vn.** seeking help ب from 3950

عيب

عَيْب **n.** pl. عُيُوب fault; shame, disgrace 1670

عيد

عيد **n.** pl. أعْياد holiday, festival, feast 647

عير

عار **n.** shame, disgrace, scandal 3006

مِعْيار **n.** pl. مَعايير standard, norm; gauge 1677

عيش

عاشَ **v. I (i)** to live, be alive; to experience sth 326

عَيْش **n.** life, living; (Egy.) bread; (Gul.) rice 1408

مَعيشَة **n.** livelihood, subsistence; life, living 3239

مَعيشِيّ **adj.** living (conditions) 4642

تَعايُش **n.** coexistence, living together 4222

عايِش **a.p.** (Dia.) living, alive (= to live) 3252

عيط

عَيَّطَ **v. II** to scream; (Magh.) to phone ل sb 4668

عيل

عَيِّل **n.** (Egy.Gul.) pl. عِيال child, kid 2951

عيلة **n.** /9eele/ (Lev.) family 4829

عين

عَيَّنَ **v. II** to appoint sb; to define sth 3579

تَعَيَّنَ **v. V** to be incumbent على on sb 3357

عَيْن **fem.n.** pl. أعْيُن, عُيُون eye; water spring 130

عَيْن **n.** same (person, thing); -self 2898

عَيِّنَة **n.** pl. -aat sample, specimen 3556

عِيان **n.** eyesight, (plain) view 3124

تَعْيين **n.** appointing, designating 2125

مُعَيَّن **adj.** specific, determined; set; designated 847

غاز

غاز **n.** pl. -aat natural gas 1307

غازِيّ **adj.** gaseous; soft (drinks) 4754

غبر

غُبار **n.** dust 2656

غبي

غَبِيّ **adj.** stupid, ignorant 4453

غدر

غادَرَ **v. III** to leave (a place), depart (on a trip) 1706

غَدْر **n.** deception; treachery, treason 3599

مُغادَرَة **n.** departure 2736

غدو

غَدا *v. I (u)* to become; to seem, appear 3463

غَداء *n.* lunch; midday meal 2774

غَد *n.* tomorrow; غَداً tomorrow 775

غذو

غِذاء *n.* pl. أَغْذِيَة food, nourishment 1981

غِذائِيّ *adj.* nutritional, food-related 1827

تَغْذِيَة *n.* feeding, nutrition 2858

غرب

اِسْتَغْرَبَ *v. X* to be surprised (مِن at) 4111

غَرْب *n.* west; West; غَرْباً westward, in the west 695

غَرْبِيّ *adj.* Western; *prep.* west of 553

غُرْبَة *n.* exile; alienation 2581

غَرابَة *n.* strangeness, oddness 4619

غُرُوب *n.* setting; غروب الشَّمْس sunset 3416

غَريب *adj.* strange; *n.* pl. غُرَباء stranger 526

مَغْرِب *n.* sunset 4816

مَغْرِبِيّ *n./adj.* pl. مَغارِبَة Moroccan; Maghrebi 1405

غرر

غُرُور *n.* deception, delusion; vanity 4772

غِرار *n.* manner, way; haste 3299

غرض

غَرَض *n.* pl. أَغْراض goal, purpose, intent 1509

غرف

غُرْفَة *n.* pl. غُرَف room, chamber 527

غرق

غَرِقَ *v. I (a)* to sink, drown, be submerged 3095

اِسْتَغْرَقَ *v. X* to last (time); be engrossed في in 2446

غارِق *adj.* drowned; engrossed في in 4370

غرم

غَرام *n.* love, infatuation 4325

غزر

غَزير *adj.* abundant, plentiful; substantial 4135

غزو

غَزْو *n.* invasion, raid 2094

غازٍ *n.* pl. غُزاة invader, raider 3769

غسل

غَسَلَ *v. I (i)* to wash, clean sth 2854

غَسيل *vn.* washing; *n.* laundry, (dirty) clothes 3840

غشش

غِشّ *n.* cheating, swindling 4623

غضب

غَضِبَ *v. I (a)* to become angry 4154

غَضَب *n.* anger, rage; غَضَباً in anger, angrily 1165

غاضِب *adj.* angry, irate 2808

غضض

غَضّ *n.* lowering (one's gaze) 2307

غضن

غُضُون *n.* interim; في غُضُون during 3161

غطو

غَطَّى *v. II* to cover; conceal 2207

غِطاء *n.* cover; blanket 2709

تَغْطِيَة *n.* covering; (news) coverage 2316

غفر

غَفَرَ *v. I (i)* to pardon, forgive لـ sb sth 3749

اِسْتَغْفَرَ *v. X* to beg (God) for forgiveness 4890

مَغْفُور *p.p.* المغفور لَهُ/لَها the late, deceased 4866

غفل

غَفْلَة *n.* negligence, lack of attention 4303

غلب

غَلَبَ *v. I (i)* to defeat, overcome على sth/sb 3012

أَغْلَب *elat.* most, majority 1804

أَغْلَبِيَّة *n.* majority 2537

تَغَلُّب *n.* overcoming على (challenges) 4171

غالِب *n.* winner; majority; غالِباً mostly 1398

غالِبِيَّة *n.* majority 2216

غلط

غَلَط *n.* error, mistake; (Dia.) *adj.* wrong 2809

غَلْطان *adj.* (Dia.) fem. -a wrong, mistaken 4954

غلق

غَلَقَ *v. I (i)* to bolt shut, to close (door) 4231

أَغْلَقَ *v. IV* to lock or bolt shut, to close (door) 2462

إِغْلاق *n.* locking, closing; barring 2515

مُغْلَق *adj.* closed, locked 2223

غلل

اِسْتَغَلَّ *v. X* to take advantage of sth/sb 2952

اِسْتِغْلال *n.* exploitation, taking advantage 1957

غلو

غَلا *adj.* (Gul.) dear, precious; *n.* preciousness 4861

أَغْلَى *elat.* more/most expensive 3057

غالٍ *adj.* expensive; dear, precious, beloved 785

غمر

غَمْرَة **n.** flood; pl. غِمار heat (of conflict) 4018

مُغامَرَة **n.** adventure, risk 3196

غمض

غُمُوض **n.** vagueness, obscurity, lack of clarity 4216

غامِض **adj.** obscure, vague, ambiguous 2685

غني

غَنَّى **v. II** to sing (sth) 2328

غِنِيّ **n.** wealth, affluence 3298

غَنِيّ **adj.** pl. أغْنِيا rich, wealthy 1799

غِناء **n.** singing 2212

أغْنِية/أُغْنِيَّة **n.** pl. أغانٍ, أغْنِيات song, melody 838

اسْتِغْناء **n.** doing without عن sth 4406

غوث

إغاثَة **n.** aid, relief assistance 4198

غور

غارَة **n.** pl. -aat raid, foray 3254

غول

اغْتِيال **n.** pl. -aat assassination 1659

غي

غايَة **n.** utmost, extreme; pl. -aat goal 1028

غيب

غابَ **v. I (i)** to be absent; to set (sun) 1607

غَيْب **n.** (what is) invisible, concealed 4173

غابَة **n.** pl. -aat forest, jungle; (fig.) haze 2144

غِياب **n.** absence; disappearance 1212

غَيْبُوبَة **n.** unconsciousness; trance; coma 4612

غائِب **adj.** absent 3540

غير

غَيْر **n.** other (than), different (than) 42

غَيَّر **v. II** to modify sth; to replace sth 1648

تَغَيَّر **v. V** to change, be modified 952

غَيْرَة/غِيرَة **n.** jealousy; zeal 3248

تَغْيِير **n.** pl. -aat change; replacement 592

تَغَيُّر **n.** pl. -aat change, variation 1896

مُتَغَيِّر **adj.** changing; **n.** مُتَغَيِّرات variables 4043

غيم

غَيْمَة **n.** pl. غُيُوم cloud 4548

ف

فَـ **conj.** and, so; (Dia.) sometimes written فا 21

فئة

فِئَة **n.** pl. -aat faction, party; group, sector 1171

فاتورة

فاتُورَة **n.** invoice, bill 4401

فأد

فُؤاد **n.** heart; mind 3323

فأل

تَفاؤُل **n.** optimism 3721

مُتَفائِل **adj.** optimistic; **n.** optimist 4971

فتح

فَتَحَ **v. I (a)** to open sth; to turn on (lights, TV) 512

افْتَتَحَ **v. VIII** to open, inaugurate sth 2720

فَتْح **n.** opening; beginning; conquest 910

فَتْحَة **n.** opening; porthole 4634

مِفْتاح **n.** pl. مَفاتِيح key; switch; wrench 1845

انْفِتاح **n.** opening up, welcoming; openness 3577

افْتِتاح **n.** opening, inauguration 1780

افْتِتاحِيّ **adj.** opening; introductory 4865

فاتِح **adj.** clear (color); (Dia.) **a.p.** opening 2577

فاتِحَة **n.** opening, preface 4349

مَفْتُوح **adj.** open, opened 1045

فتر

فَتْرَة **n.** pl. فَتَرات time period, phase, interval 263

فتش

تَفْتِيش **n.** search, inspection; (security) check 2367

فتن

فِتْنَة **n.** pl. فِتَن charm, allure; dissent, unrest 1560

فتو

فَتَى **n.** pl. فِتْيَة young man, adolescent, youth 2065

فَتاة **n.** pl. فَتَيات young woman, girl 791

فَتْوَى **n.** pl. فَتاوَى fatwa (legal opinion) 2802

اسْتِفْتاء **n.** questionnaire, poll; referendum 2928

مُفْتِي **n.** mufti (Muslim legal scholar) 3373

فجأ

فاجَأ **v. III** to surprise sb (ب) with 3189

فَجْأة/فُجْأة **n.** surprise; suddenly 1146

مُفاجَأة **n.** pl. مُفاجَآت surprise 1854

مُفاجِئ **adj.** surprising; sudden 2518

فجر

انْفَجَرَ **v. VII** to explode; to burst, erupt 2358

فَجْر **n.** dawn 1048

تَفْجِير **vn.** detonating; **n.** pl. -aat explosion 1820

انْفِجار **n.** pl. -aat explosion, detonation 1623

فجو

فَجْوَة **n.** (mostly fig.) gap, gulf, breach 3633

فحص

فَحْص **n.** pl. فُحُوصات , فُحُوص exam 1986

فحم

فَحْم **n.** coal 4785

فخخ

فَخّ **n.** trap, snare 4796

مُفَخَّخ **adj.** booby-trapped 3743

فخر

فَخْر **n.** pride; boasting 2869

فخم

فَخامَة **n.** excellence, eminence 3997

فدح

فادِح **adj.** serious, grave; heavy 4778

فدد

فَدّ **part.** (Irq., indef. article) one, a 4929

فدي

فِداء **n.** sacrifice; self-sacrifice 4049

تَفادٍ **n.** (def. التَفادي) avoidance, avoiding 3810

مُفَدًّى **adj.** beloved, cherished 4870

فرج

فَرَج **n.** relief, relaxation, happiness 3868

إفْراج **n.** liberation; release, freeing (عن of) 3406

فرح

فَرِحَ **v. I (a)** to be happy ب/ل about sth 3200

فَرَح **n.** joy, happiness; pl. أفْراح party 1181

فَرْحَة **n.** joy, happiness 2109

فرد

فَرْد **n.** pl. أفْراد individual, person 626

فَرْدِيّ **adj.** personal, private; individual, single 2251

فَريد **adj.** unique, exceptional, singular 2650

مُفْرَد **adj.** individual, separate 4028

مُفْرَدَة **n.** pl. -aat word; مُفْرَدات vocabulary 3725

فردس

فِرْدَوْس **n.** paradise; الفِرْدَوْس Paradise 4395

فرر

فَرّ **v. I (i)** to escape, flee; to defect, desert 4844

فِرار **n.** escape, desertion (من from) 4345

مَفَرّ **n.** escape; لا مَفَرَّ مِنْهُ (it's) inevitable 4366

فرس

فَريسَة **n.** victim, prey 4786

فارِس **n.** pl. فُرْسان horseman; knight 2707

فارِسيّ **n./adj.** pl. فُرْس Persian 3771

فرش

فِراش **n.** bed 2743

فرص

فُرْصَة **n.** pl. فُرَص chance, opportunity 410

فرض

فَرَضَ **v. I (i)** to impose sth على on 1554

إفْتَرَضَ **v. VIII** to suppose sth or أنَّ that 2735

فَرْض **vn.** imposing; **n.** (religious) duty 1254

فَريضَة **n.** religious duty 4684

مَفْروض **adj.** necessary, required; **n.** duty 1469

مُفْتَرَض **adj.** assumed, presumed 3276

فرط

فَرْط **n.** excess, excessive amount, hyper- 4377

فرع

فَرْع **n.** pl. فُروع branch, department 1531

فَرْعِيّ **adj.** branch, secondary, subdivision 3498

فرغ

فَراغ **n.** vacuum, empty space; free time 1912

فارِغ **adj.** unoccupied, free, idle; empty 2507

فرق

فَرَقَ **v. I (i)** to be different, make a difference 4906

فَرَّقَ **v. II** to distinguish بين between 2762

فَرْق **n.** difference, distinction; discrepancy 1445

فِرْقَة **n.** pl. فِرَق group, team; band; squad 882

فِراق **n.** parting, farewell, going away 3277

فَريق **n.** team, group, band; faction, party 256

فارِق **n.** difference; distinctive feature 2119

مُتَفَرِّق **adj.** diverse, different; scattered 3256

مُفْتَرَق **n.** intersection, junction 4708

فرن

فُرْن **n.** oven; furnace; bakery 4420

فرنسا

فَرَنْسِيّ **n./adj.** pl. -uun French 572

فسح

فَسيح **adj.** wide; lengthy; ample, roomy 4091

فسد

أَفْسَدَ **v. IV** to spoil, ruin sth; to corrupt sb 4822

فَساد **n.** corruption; deterioration 1215

فاسِد **adj.** spoiled, rotten; corrupt, immoral 4159

فسر

فَسَّرَ **v. II** to explain, interpret sth (ل for sb) 3170

تَفْسِير **n.** explanation, commentary; Tafsir 1999

فشل

فَشِلَ **v. I (a)** to fail, be unsuccessful في in sth 1452

فَشَل **n.** failure 2247

فاشِل **adj.** failed, failing; a failure 3168

فصل

فَصَلَ **v. I (i)** to detach sth; to dismiss sb 1915

فَصْل **vn.** detaching, separating; firing 1377

فَصْل **n.** pl. فُصُول chapter; season; class 1856

فَصِيلَة **n.** pl. فَصائِل faction; (mil.) platoon 2474

مَفْصِل **n.** pl. مَفاصِل (anat.) joint; juncture 4333

تَفْصِيل **n.** pl. تَفاصِيل detail, elaboration 1112

انْفِصال **n.** separation, break-up; secession 4298

فاصِل **n.** pause, break; **adj.** separating 2910

مُنْفَصِل **adj.** separate, disconnected 4000

فضح

فَضِيحَة **n.** scandal; disgrace, shame 3091

فضض

فَضّ **vn.** settling (disputes); breaking up 4951

فِضّيّ **adj.** silver 4883

فضل

فَضَّلَ **v. II** to prefer sth (على to sth else) 1470

تَفَضَّلَ **v. V** please (come in, sit down, etc.) 1618

فَضْل **n.** favor; kindness; merit; بِفَضْل due to 705

فَضِيل **adj.** excellent; virtuous; eminent 4744

فَضِيلَة **n.** virtue; فَضِيلَة الشَّيْخ His Eminence 3143

أَفْضَل **elat.** better/best 390

فاضِل **adj.** eminent; **n.** leftover 2314

مُفَضَّل **adj.** preferred; favorite, best (friend) 2613

فضو

أَفْضَى **v. IV** to lead إلى to; to disclose ب sth 4666

فَضاء **n.** space; cosmos; vacant (land) 1478

فَضائيّ **adj.** (outer) space, satellite 2122

فَضائيّة **n.** pl. -aat satellite station 3071

فاضٍ **adj.** empty; unoccupied; free (not busy) 3789

فطر

فِطْر **n.** fitr (end of the Ramadan fast) 3770

إفْطار **n.** iftar (Ramadan evening meal) 4335

فعل

فَعَلَ **v. I (a)** to do sth 456

فِعْل **vn.** doing; **n.** pl. أَفْعال act, action 254

فِعْليّ **adj.** actual, real; فِعْليّاً really 2002

فَعّال **adj.** effective, efficient; active 2231

فَعّاليّة **n.** effectiveness; فَعّاليّات events 1547

تَفْعِيل **n.** putting into effect, activating 2027

تَفاعُل **n.** interaction, reaction; reciprocity 2698

فاعِل **adj.** active; **n.** pl. -uun doer, agent 1926

فاعِليّة **n.** effectiveness; activity 4174

مَفْعُول **n.** impact, effect; result 3945

فقد

فَقَدَ **v. I (i)** to lose sth; to lack, be missing sth 1264

فَقِيد **n./adj.** deceased 4438

فِقْدان/فُقْدان **n.** loss; bereavement 2658

مَفْقُود **adj.** lost, missing; **n.** missing (person) 3720

فقر

افْتَقَرَ **v. VIII** to lack, be in need إلى of sth 3903

فَقْر **n.** poverty, lack of; فَقْر الدَّم anemia 1501

فِقْرات/فَقَرات/فِقَر **n.** pl. فِقْرَة/فَقْرَة paragraph 2487

فِقْريّ/فَقْريّ **adj.** spinal, vertebral 4715

فَقِير **adj.** poor; destitute; **n.** poor (person) 1357

فقط

فَقَط **part.** only, just, solely; (with neg.) not just 274

فقم

تَفاقُم **n.** aggravation, exacerbation; worsening 4359

فقه

فِقْه **n.** fiqh (Islamic jurisprudence); science 3475

فَقِيه **n.** pl. فُقَهاء faqih (legal expert) 3782

فكر

فَكَّرَ **v. II** to think في/ب about, believe أنَّ that 622

فِكْر **n.** pl. أَفْكار thinking; idea, concept 522

فِكْرَة **n.** idea, concept, notion (عن about) 471

فِكْريّ **adj.** intellectual, mental 1356

تَفْكِير **n.** thinking, reflection 1065

مُفَكِّر **n.** pl. -uun intellectual 2699

فكك

فَكّ **n.** dismantling; breaking up; untying 3341

تَفْكِيك **n.** taking apart; separating; dissolution 4417

فكه

فاكِهَة **n.** pl. فَواكِه fruit 3010

فلح

أَفْلَحَ **v. IV** to succeed, prosper, thrive في in sth 4162

فَلّاح **n.** pl. -uun peasant, farmer 3345

فلس

فِلْس **n.** pl. فُلُوس fils; فُلُوس money 2706

فلسف

فَلْسَفَة **n.** philosophy 2365

فلسطين

فِلَسْطِينِيّ **n./adj.** Palestinian 107

فلك

فَلَك **n.** orbit; عِلْم الفَلَكِ astronomy 3968

فلم

فِيلم **n.** /film/ pl. أَفْلام film, movie 573

فلان

فُلان **n.** so-and-so; such-and-such 2855

فم

فَم **n.** pl. أفواه mouth 1525

فنجان

فِنْجان **n.** cup, coffee cup 4146

فندق

فُنْدُق **n.** pl. فَنادِق hotel 1352

فنن

فَنّ **n.** pl. فُنُون art; specialty; type, variety 817

فَنّيّ **adj.** artistic; technical; **n.** technician 604

فَنّان **n.** fem. -a, pl. -uun artist 925

فني

فَناء **n.** extinction, doom, end 4639

فهم

فَهِمَ **v. I (a)** to understand sth/sb or أَنّ that 580

فَهْم **n.** understanding, comprehension 1388

تَفاهُم **n.** mutual understanding 1947

فاهِم **adj.** understanding, comprehending 3585

مَفْهُوم **adj.** understood; **n.** pl. مَفاهِيم concept 1286

فوت

فاتَ **v. I (u)** to elude sb; to stop by على sb 2543

فَوات **n.** expiration, passing (time, deadline) 4139

فائِت **adj.** past, expired, elapsed, gone by 4064

مُتَفاوِت **adj.** different, diverse 4390

فوتبول

فتبول/فوتبول **n.** /futbool/ football, soccer 4928

فوح

فاحَ **v. I (u)** to emanate (scent, perfume) 4998

فور

فَوْر **n.** عَلى الفَوْر and فَوْراً immediately, at once 1253

فَوْرِيّ **adj.** immediate, instant; direct 3190

فوز

فازَ **v. I (u)** to win (ب sth); to defeat على sb 1432

فَوْز **n.** victory 788

فائِز **adj.** victorious; **n.** pl. -uun winner 2716

فوض

فَوْضَى **n.** chaos, anarchy 1897

مُفاوَضة **n.** pl. -aat negotiation, talk 1608

تَفاوُض **n.** negotiation, debate, discussion 2782

مُفَوَّضِيّة **n.** delegation, legation 3453

فوق

فاقَ **v. I (u)** to surpass sth/sb 1953

فَوْق **n.** top, upper part; فَوْقَ above, over 348

تَفَوُّق **n.** excellence; superiority, supremacy 3448

فائِق **adj.** exceeding; outstanding 2835

في

في **prep.** in; on (date); at (time); about (topic) 3

فيه **part.** (Egy.Lev.Gul.) there is, there are 315

فيها **conj.** while, meanwhile; فِيما بَعْدُ later 309

فيتامين

فِيتامِين **n.** pl. -aat vitamin 3995

فيد

أَفادَ **v. IV** to report أَنّ/بِأَنّ that 1117

اِسْتَفادَ **v. X** to benefit, profit مِن from 1734

اِسْتِفادة **n.** benefiting مِن from 1582

فائِدة **n.** pl. فَوائِد benefit, usefulness 1124

مُفِيد **adj.** useful, beneficial 1385

مُفاد **n.** content; مُفادُها to the effect (that) 3654

مُسْتَفِيد **adj.** benefiting; **n.** pl. -uun beneficiary 3682

فيديو

فيديو **n.** /viidiyo, vidyo/ video 2111

فيروس

فَيْروس **n.** pl. -aat virus 2211

فيزي

فِيزياء **n.** physics 4884

فيض
فاضَ *v. I (i)* to overflow; to exceed عن sth 3088

فَيْض *n.* abundance; flood, stream 4520

فين
فين *interrog.* /feen/ (Egy.Lev.) where 2177

فئة
فِئَة *n.* pl. -aat faction, party; group, sector 1171

قبب
قُبَّة *n.* dome, cupola 4123

قبر
قَبْر *n.* pl. قُبُور tomb, sepulcher 1786

مَقْبَرة *n.* pl. مَقابِر grave, tomb; graveyard 2286

قبض
قَبَضَ *v. I (i)* to arrest, apprehend, seize على sb 4968

قَبْض *n.* arrest, seizure, capture 2053

قَبْضَة *n.* grip; fistful; seizure 4019

قابِض *adj.* holding (company, bank) 4569

قبل
قَبِلَ *v. I (a)* to accept, receive; approve 1097

قابَلَ *v. III* to meet, encounter, face sb 4254

أَقْبَلَ *v. IV* to approach على sb/sth 3263

تَقَبَّل *v. V* to receive, accept 1883

اِسْتَقْبَلَ *v. X* to meet, welcome, greet sb 1726

قَبْل *prep.* before; قَبْلُ *adv.* previously 68

قِبَل *n.* مِن قِبَل on the part of 1747

قِبْلَة *n.* qiblah (direction faced in prayer) 4194

قُبْلَة *n.* kiss 4266

قَبَلِيّ *adj.* tribal 4770

قُبالة *prep.* facing, in front of 4361

قَبُول *n.* reception; acceptance, approval 1300

قَبِيل *n.* kind, sort, type 3447

قُبَيْل *prep.* shortly before 2756

قَبِيلة *n.* pl. قَبائِل tribe 1539

مُقابَلة *n.* pl. -aat encounter; interview 1818

إِقْبال *n.* approach; concern على for 2988

اِسْتِقْبال *n.* reception; receiving, welcoming 1583

قابِل *adj.* capable, able 2224

مَقْبُول *adj.* acceptable; welcome 1963

مُقابِل *n.* opposite (to), corresponding (to) 666

مُقْبِل *adj.* next, coming, approaching, nearing 598

مُسْتَقْبَل *n.* future; مُسْتَقْبَلًا in the future 539

مُسْتَقْبَلِي *adj.* future 2167

قتل
قَتَلَ *v. I (u)* to kill sb; (pass.) قُتِلَ to be killed 639

قاتَلَ *v. III* to fight (sb) 4030

قَتْل *n.* murder, killing 818

قَتِيل *n.* pl. قَتْلَى casualty, dead/killed person 1581

مَقْتَل *n.* murder, killing 1473

قِتال *n.* fighting, combat 2078

قِتالِيّ *adj.* fighting, battle 4780

اِقْتِتال *n.* fighting (each other) 4247

قاتِل *n.* pl. قَتَلَة murderer; *adj.* deadly; fatal 1710

مُقاتِل *n.* pl. -uun combatant, warrior 3857

قحم
اِقْتَحَمَ *v. VIII* to invade, burst into sth 4491

اِقْتِحام *n.* incursion, assault; storming into 4055

قد
قَدْ *part.* (with perf.) has/have already 37

لَقَدْ *part.* (with perf.) has/have already 213

قَدْ *part.* (with imperf.) may, might 277

قدد
قَدّ *n.* amount; هالقد (Lev.Irq.) *adv.* so much 4409

شقد/شگد *interrog.* (Irq.) how many/much 4979

قديش/قديه *interrog.* (Lev.) how many/much 3884

قدر
قَدَرَ *v. I (i)* and قَدِرَ (a) to be capable of 681

قَدَّرَ *v. II* to estimate, value sth 1260

قَدْر *n.* extent; amount, value; ability, capacity 743

قَدَر *n.* fate, destiny 1939

قُدْرة *n.* pl. -aat, قُدُرات capacity, ability 606

قَدِير *adj.* capable, efficient 3287

مَقْدِرة *n.* ability, potential, capacity 4529

مِقْدار *n.* extent; value; dosage 1862

تَقْدِير *vn.* appreciation; *n.* pl. -aat estimate 992

قادِر *adj.* pl. -uun capable, able 827

قدس
مُقَدَّس *adj.* holy; *n.* مُقَدَّسات sacred sites 1639

قدم
قَدِمَ *v. I (a)* to arrive, come إلى to 3121

قَدَّمَ *v. II* to offer, submit sth 240

أَقْدَمَ *v. IV* to undertake, tackle على sth 3288

تَقَدَّمَ *v. V* to present sth; to advance 1100

قَدَم *fem.n.* pl. أَقْدام foot 627

قُدُمًا *adv.* forwards, forward 3466

قَدِيم *adj.* pl. قُدَماء ,قُدَامَى old, ancient 499

قُدُوم *n.* arrival; entering (a room) 4429

قُدَّام *prep.* (MSA قُدَّامَ) in front of 3166

أَقْدَم *elat.* older/oldest, more/most ancient 4020

تَقْدِيم *n.* offering, presenting, submitting 585

تَقَدُّم *n.* progress; *vn.* coming forward 759

قَادِم *adj.* next, following; *a.p.* arriving, coming 500

مُقَدِّم *n.* person presenting; *a.p.* offering 3886

مُقَدِّمَة *n.* pl. -aat preface; front part 1530

مُقَدَّم *adj.* offered; advanced 1887

مُقَدَّمَة *n.* preface, introduction; front part 3473

مُتَقَدِّم *adj.* advanced; *n.* applicant 1578

قدو

قُدْوَة *n.* example, role model; pattern 3677

قذف

قَذِيفَة *n.* pl. قَذائِف shell, bomb 2976

قرأ

قَرَأ *v. I (a)* and (Dia.) قَرَى (a) to read sth 727

قِراءَة *n.* reading; recitation; interpretation 923

القُرْآن *n.* the Qurʾan 837

قُرْآنِيّ *adj.* Qurʾanic 4656

قارِئ *n.* pl. قُرَّاء reader; Qurʾanic reciter 2201

قرب

قَرُب *v. I (u)* and قَرِبَ (a) to approach 3167

قارَبَ *v. III* to come close to sth 2851

اقْتَرَبَ *v. VIII* to get close مِن to sth 1383

قُرْب *n.* proximity, nearness; بِالقُرْبِ مِن near 977

قَرِيب *adj.* near; related; *n.* pl. قَرائِب relative 476

قُرابَةَ *prep.* almost, nearly 3163

أَقْرَب *elat.* nearer/nearest; *n.* pl. أَقارِب relatives 1354

مَقْرُبَة/مَقْرَبَة *n.* vicinity; على مَقْرُبَةٍ مِن near 4423

تَقْرِيب *n.* approximation; تَقْرِيباً approximately 913

تَقارُب *n.* mutual affinity; rapprochement 4070

اقْتِراب *n.* approach; getting near 3061

مُقَرَّب *adj.* near; *n.* close companion 3979

قرح

اقْتَرَحَ *v. VIII* to propose, suggest sth 2426

اقْتِراح *n.* proposal, suggestion 2029

مُقْتَرَح *adj.* proposed; *n.* pl. -aat proposal 2550

قرر

قَرَّرَ *v. II* to decide, resolve أن to do sth 767

أَقَرَّ *v. IV* to ratify, accept; to confess بـ sth 2565

تَقَرَّرَ *v. V* to be decided, be resolved 3503

اسْتَقَرَّ *v. X* to settle down, become stable 2527

قَرار *n.* pl. -aat decision, resolution 211

مَقَرّ *n.* center, headquarters, main residence 1281

تَقْرِير *n.* pl. تَقارِير report, account 509

إقْرار *n.* ratification, confirmation 3233

اسْتِقْرار *n.* stability; setting down 997

قارَّة *n.* pl. -aat continent 2390

مُقَرَّر *adj.* decided upon; *n.* agenda, plan 1697

مُسْتَقِرّ *adj.* settled, at ease; stable, permanent 3829

قرص

قُرْص *n.* disk, tablet 4944

قرض

قَرْض *n.* pl. قُرُوض (bank) loan 2386

قرع

اقْتِراع *n.* balloting, voting, election 3549

قرن

قَرْن *n.* pl. قُرُون century, age; horn 883

مُقارَنَة *n.* comparison 1401

قري

قَرْيَة *n.* pl. قُرَى village 665

قسم

أَقْسَمَ *v. IV* to swear يَمِينا an oath 3593

قِسْم *n.* pl. أَقْسام section; department 683

تَقْسِيم *n.* partition, division; distribution 2513

انْقِسام *n.* fragmentation, schism; disruption 3774

قسو

قَسْوَة *n.* harshness, severity, brutality 2771

أَقْسَى *elat.* harsher/harshest, more/most cruel 4689

قاسِي *adj.* (def. قاسِي) harsh, cruel, severe 1905

قصد

قَصَدَ *v. I (i)* to mean sth; to pursue sth 1337

قَصْد *n.* intent, purpose, goal 1330

قَصِيدَة *n.* pl. قَصائِد poem, ode 996

اقْتِصاد *n.* economy; saving 969

اقْتِصادِيّ *adj.* economic, economical; thrifty 331

مَقْصُود *n.* purpose, intent; *adj.* deliberate 2600

قصر

قَصَرَ *v. I (i)* to shorten; قَصُرَ (u) to fall short 4745

قَصَّرَ *v. II* to shorten; (Gul.) to fall short 4108

اقْتَصَرَ *v. VIII* to be limited على to 2614

قَصْر *n.* pl. قُصُور castle, palace 1269

قَصْر *n.* shortness; *vn.* restricting 3152

قُصُور *n.* shortcoming; negligence 3852

قَصِير *adj.* short, small (of stature) 1061

تَقْصِير *n.* deficiency, inadequacy 3867

قصص

قِصَّة *n.* pl. قِصَص story, tale 414

قصف

قَصَفَ *v. I (i)* to bomb, shell sth 4761

قَصْف *n.* bombardment, shelling 2064

قصو

أَقْصَى *adj.* fem. قُصْوَى farthest, most remote 1073

قضي

قَضَى *v. I (i)* to pass, spend (time) 1138

اِقْتَضَى *v. VIII* to demand, require sth 3445

قَضَاء *n.* justice; court; district; judgment; fate 1090

قَضَاء *vn.* extermination على of 2240

قَضَائِيّ *adj.* judicial, legal 2005

قَضِيَّة *n.* pl. قَضايا problem, issue; lawsuit 202

قَاضٍ *n.* (def. قَاضِي) pl. قُضَاة judge, magistrate 1221

قطب

قُطْب *n.* axis, pole; leader, top figure 4459

اِسْتِقْطاب *n.* polarization, attraction 4301

قطر

قَطَرِيّ *n./adj.* Qatari 1847

قَطْرَة *n.* pl. قَطَرات drop 3127

قُطْر *n.* pl. أَقْطار region; أَقْطار countries 4044

قِطار *n.* train 2408

قطط

قَطُّ *adv.* (not) at all, never; nothing, noone 2998

قِطّ *n.* cat; قِطَّة female cat; pl. قِطَط cats 3103

قطع

قَطَعَ *v. I (a)* to cut off sth; to cover (distance) 1030

اِنْقَطَعَ *v. VII* to break, be cut off 2170

قَطْع *vn.* breaking off, interrupting 1543

قِطْعَة *n.* pl. قِطَع piece, portion, segment 2072

قُطْعَة *n.* parcel (of land), plot, lot 2001

قِطاع *n.* pl. -aat sector, section 292

مَقْطَع *n.* pl. مَقَاطِع section; selection, excerpt 3266

مُقَاطَعَة *vn.* boycott; *n.* district 2594

اِنْقِطاع *n.* discontinuation, breaking off 3439

قاطِع *adj.* decisive; *a.p.* blocking 2948

مَقْطُوع *adj.* cut off; interrupted; blocked 4707

قطن

قُطْن *n.* cotton 4532

قعد

قَعَدَ *v. I (u)* to sit down, be seated 2036

مَقْعَد *n.* pl. مَقَاعِد seat; place 1472

تَقَاعُد *n.* retirement 4085

قاعِد *a.p.* sitting; (Dia.) staying, remaining 1439

قَاعِدَة *n.* pl. قَوَاعِد rule; (military) base 630

قفز

قَفَزَ *v. I (i)* to jump, leap 3026

قَفْز *n.* jumping, leaping 4477

قفص

قَفَص *n.* cage; prisoner's dock 3755

قفل

قَافِلَة *n.* pl. قَوَافِل convoy, column 3426

قلب

قَلَبَ *v. I (i)* to turn (face, page); to topple sth 4272

اِنْقَلَبَ *v. VII* to turn around/over 3069

قَلْب *n.* pl. قُلُوب heart; *vn.* toppling 110

قَلْبِيّ *adj.* cardiac, heart-related 4742

قالِب *n.* form, model; mold 4901

اِنْقِلاب *n.* coup, overthrow, toppling 2832

قلد

تَقْلِيد *n.* pl. تَقَالِيد tradition, custom 2023

تَقْلِيدِيّ *adj.* traditional, conventional 1680

قلص

تَقْلِيص *n.* reducing, shrinking, cutting back 4280

قلع

قَلْعَة *n.* stronghold, citadel, fort 3691

قلق

قَلَق *n.* unrest, unease; concern, anxiety 1365

قَلِق *adj.* worried, concerned, uneasy 3626

قلل

قَلَّ *v. I (i)* to be less; to decrease 447

قَلَّلَ *v. II* to reduce sth; to downplay sth 3325

قَلَّما *adv.* rarely, seldom; hardly, barely 4868

قِلَّة *n.* scarcity; small number/amount 1772

قَلِيل *adj.* few, small amount; قَلِيلًا *adv.* a little 376

أَقَلّ *elat.* less/least, lower/lowest; *n.* minimum 446

أَقَلِّيَّة *n.* pl. -aat minority 4241

تَقْلِيل *n.* diminution, reduction, decrease 3303

اِسْتِقْلال *n.* independence 1898

مُسْتَقِلّ *adj.* independent, autonomous 1479

قلم

قَلَم *n.* pl. أَقْلام pencil, pen; بِقَلَم written by 1021

قمح

قَمْح *n.* wheat 3489

قمر

قَمَر *n.* pl. أَقْمار moon; قَمَر صِناعِيّ satellite 1081

قمس

قامُوس *n.* dictionary, lexicon; vocabulary 4577

قمش

قُماش *n.* pl. أَقْمِشَة fabric, cloth 3508

قمص

قَمِيص *n.* pl. قُمْصان shirt 4630

قمع

قَمْع *n.* oppression, repression 3793

قمم

قِمَّة *n.* pl. قِمَم summit 798

قنبل

قُنْبُلَة *n.* pl. قَنابِل bomb, shell; grenade 1822

قنع

قَناعَة *n.* conviction, belief 3171

إِقْناع *n.* persuasion; conviction 3301

مُقْتَنِع *adj.* satisfied, content; convinced 4523

قنن

قانُون *n.* pl. قَوانِين law, statutes, regulations 232

قانُونِيّ *adj.* legal, law-related; legitimate 1158

قنو

قَناة *n.* pl. قَنَوات canal; channel (broadcasting) 844

قهر

قَهْر *n.* coercion; subjugation 2566

قهو

قَهْوَة *n.* coffee; café, coffeehouse 1840

مَقْهَى *n.* pl. مَقاهٍ (def. مَقاهِي) café, coffeehouse 2218

قود

قادَ *v. I (u)* to guide sb; to drive, pilot sth 1289

قِيادَة *n.* leadership; driving; قِيادات leaders 541

قِيادِيّ *adj.* leading; *n.* pl. -uun commander 3074

قائِد *n.* pl. قادَة leader, commander 534

قوس

قَوْس *n.* bow, arc; قَوْسانِ parentheses 4347

قوع

قاع *n.* bottom, floor 4228

قاعَة *n.* pl. -aat hall, large room 1444

قول

قالَ *v. I (u)* to say إِنَّ that, to tell لـ sb إِنَّ that 15

قَوْل *n.* pl. أَقْوال statement; saying 320

مَقال/مَقالَة *n.* pl. -aat article, essay 1022

قائِل *a.p.* saying; *n.* (person) saying 718

مَقُولَة *n.* statement, proposition; expression 3340

قوم

قامَ *v. I (u)* to stand; to carry out بـ (task) 102

قاوَمَ *v. III* to resist, oppose sth 3708

أَقامَ *v. IV* to install, set up sth; to reside في at 861

قَوْم *n.* people, nation 1402

قَوْمِيّ *adj.* national, state; nationalist 1085

قَوْمِيَّة *n.* nationalism 4326

قامَة *n.* stature, status; height 4478

قِيمَة *n.* pl. قِيَم value, worth; قِيَم morals, ethics 427

قَيِّم *adj.* valuable; *n.* responsible على for 3042

قِيام *vn.* carrying out بـ (task) 651

قِيامَة *n.* resurrection; يَوْم القِيامَة Judgment Day 2678

مَقام *n.* place, position, rank 2189

تَقْوِيم *n.* rating, valuation; calendar 3559

مُقاوَمَة *n.* resistance, opposition 567

إِقامَة *n.* residency; setting up, establishing 752

قائِم *a.p.* carrying out بـ (task); *adj.* ongoing 937

قائِمَة *n.* pl. قَوائِم list, index; قَوائِم legs (chair) 1098

مُقَوِّم *n.* pl. -aat component, ingredient 3696

مُقاوِم *n.* antagonist; *a.p.* resisting 4016

مُقِيم *n.* resident; *a.p.* residing 2037

مُقام *adj.* installed, set up; held, hosted 4434

مُسْتَقِيم *adj.* straight, correct; righteous 4942

قوي

قَوِيَ *v. I (a)* to be strong 3862

قَوَّى *v. II* to strengthen, fortify 4641

قُوَّة *n.* pl. -aat, قُوىً force; قُوّات armed forces 71

قَوِيّ *adj.* strong, powerful; great 438

أَقْوَى *elat.* stronger/strongest 1685

تَقْوِيَة *n.* strengthening, reinforcement 3399

قيد

قَيْد **n.** pl. قُيُود restriction; فِي قَيْد in the process of 1558

تَقَيُّد **vn.** being bound بـ to; **n.** restriction 4940

قيس

قِياس **n.** measurement; analogy; comparison 2834

قِياسِيّ **adj.** record; analogous 2582

مِقْياس **n.** pl. مَقايِيس standard, measure 3355

قيل

اِسْتِقالَة **n.** resignation 3023

قيم

تَقْيِيم **n.** evaluation, assessment; rating 2106

ك

كَـ **prep.** as, like; كَالتّالِي as follows 870

كابتن

كابْتِن **n.** captain; (title) Captain 4547

كاد

كادَ **v. I (a)** (with imperf.) to almost do sth 985

كاد **n.** بالكاد almost 4848

كأس

كَأْس/كاس **n.** pl. كُؤُوس cup; Cup (prize) 840

كاميرا

كامِيرا **n.** camera 2822

كأن

كَأَنّ/وَكَأَنّ **conj.** as if 318

كَأَنَّما **conj.** as if 2886

كبد

كَبِد **n.** liver (organ); center, middle 3082

كبر

كَبُرَ **v. I (u)** to grow up; to get bigger 1925

كِبْر **n.** pride, arrogance; greatness 3569

كَبِير **adj.** pl. كِبار large; important; adult 65

أَكْبَر **elat.** fem. كُبْرَى larger/largest; **adj.** senior 195

كبس

كَبَسَ **v. I (i)** to press; to dial, click 4960

كابُوس **n.** nightmare 4782

كتب

كَتَبَ **v. I (u)** to write, author sth 357

كِتاب **n.** pl. كُتُب book 196

كِتابَة **n.** pl. -aat writing; script; essay 966

كَتِيبَة **n.** pl. كَتائِب squadron, brigade 2711

مَكْتَب **n.** pl. مَكاتِب office, bureau, department 565

مَكْتَبَة **n.** pl. -aat library; bookstore 1830

كاتِب **n.** pl. كُتّاب author; pl. كَتَبَة clerk 719

مَكْتُوب **adj.** written; **n.** pl. مَكاتِيب letter 1835

كتف

كَتِف **fem.n.** shoulder 3278

كتل

كُتْلَة **n.** pl. كُتَل bloc, group; mass, bulk 1619

كثب

كَثَب **n.** nearness, closeness; عَن كَثَب closely 4276

كثر

كَثُرَ **v. I (u)** to be plentiful 2729

أَكْثَرَ **v. IV** to do مِن sth frequently 3798

كُثْر **n.** abundance; great number; much, a lot 2853

كَثْرَة **n.** abundance, large number/amount 1595

كَثِير **adj.** pl. -uun many, much; كَثِيراً ما often 55

أَكْثَر **elat.** more/most, greater/greatest in number 64

أَكْثَرِيَّة **n.** majority 3367

كثف

كَثِيف **adj.** intense, intensive; thick, dense 2960

كَثافَة **n.** thickness, density; intensity 3516

تَكْثِيف **vn.** intensifying; **n.** compression 4362

مُكَثَّف **adj.** intensive; thick; compressed 2638

كدر

كادِر **n.** pl. كَوادِر cadre, key group, staff 2840

كده

كده/كدا **adv.** /kida/ (Egy.) thus, this way 1000

كذا

كَذا **adv.** thus, like that, in this way 715

كذب

كَذَبَ **v. I (i)** to lie (عَلى to sb) 3110

كِذْب **n.** lying; deceit 2166

كاذِب **adj.** false; deceitful; **n.** pl. -uun، كَذَبَة liar 2927

كذي

كذي/چذي **adv.** (Gul.) /chidhi/ thus, this way 4687

كربون

كَرْبُون **n.** carbon 4598

كرث

كارِثَة **n.** pl. كَوارِث catastrophe, tragedy 1707

كرد

كُرْدِيّ **n./adj.** pl. أَكْراد Kurd, Kurdish 2296

كردستان

كُرْدِستانِيّ **n./adj.** Kurdistani 4665

كرر

كَرَّرَ **v. II** to repeat sth; to filter, refine sth 2635

تَكَرَّرَ **v. V** to be reiterated; to be filtered 2489

تَكْرار **n.** repetition; تَكْراراً repeatedly 2628

مُتَكَرِّر **adj.** repeated, recurring; frequent 2829

كرس

تَكْريس **n.** dedication, devotion; consecration 4530

كرسي

كُرْسيّ **n.** pl. كَراسٍ (def. الكَراسِي) chair, seat 1749

كرم

أَكْرَمَ **v. IV** to honor, respect sb; to venerate sb 3917

كَرَم **n.** generosity, magnanimity 4332

كَرامَة **n.** dignity, honor; generosity 1882

كَريم **adj.** pl. كِرام noble; generous; precious 556

تَكْريم **n.** honoring, respecting 2670

مُكَرَّم **adj.** honored, revered; مَكَّة المُكَرَّمَة Mecca 3125

كره

كَرِهَ **v. I (a)** to hate sth/sb; to dislike sth 2536

كُرْه **n.** hatred; عَلَى كُرْهٍ/كُرْه unwillingly 4566

كَراهِيَّة **n.** hatred, loathing; dislike, aversion 2961

مَكْروه **adj.** detested; **n.** accident, mishap 4469

كرو

كُرَة **n.** pl. -aat ball; globe; كورة football 501

كُرَويّ **adj.** round; relating to football (soccer) 4691

كريم

كُريم **n.** cream (food, cosmetic) 4181

كسب

كَسَبَ **v. I (i)** to gain, achieve, earn sth 2899

اِكْتَسَبَ **v. VIII** to earn, gain, win sth 4149

كَسْب **n.** gaining; earning; achieving, attaining 2902

مَكْسَب **n.** pl. مَكاسِب gain, profit 3544

كسر

كَسَرَ **v. I (i)** to break sth; to violate (law) 2163

كَسْر **vn.** breaking; violating; **n.** fracture, crack 4112

كشف

كَشَفَ **v. I (i)** to reveal عن sth; to examine على sb 772

اِكْتَشَفَ **v. VIII** to discover, uncover sth 1737

كَشْف **n.** revelation, disclosure, report 1995

اِكْتِشاف **n.** discovery; detection, uncovering 2183

مَكْشوف **adj.** open, public; exposed; open-air 4702

كعب

مُكَعَّب **adj.** cubic (foot, meter); cube-shaped 4460

كفأ

كَفاءَة **n.** pl. -aat qualification; talent 2085

مُكافَأَة **n.** compensation; reward 4475

كفح

كِفاح **n.** struggle, fight 4474

مُكافَحَة **n.** fight, battle, confrontation 1451

كفر

كُفْر **n.** kufr (rejection of the Islamic faith) 3044

كافِر **n.** pl. كُفّار kafir (non-believer) 3646

كفف

كَفَّ **v. I (u)** to abstain عن from sth 3305

كَفّ **fem.n.** palm (hand); **vn.** abstaining 2476

كافَّة **n.** all of; كافَّة all together 693

كفل

كَفَلَ **v. I (u)** to guarantee sth; to support sb 4683

كَفَّلَ **v. II** to support, maintain, provide for sb 4853

كَفيل **adj.** ensuring (ب sth); **n.** sponsor 3081

كفي

كَفَى **v. I (i)** to be enough (for sth/sb) 976

اِكْتَفَى **v. VIII** to be content, satisfied ب with 2893

كِفايَة **n.** adequacy; performance; competence 3027

اِكْتِفاء **n.** satisfaction; sufficiency, adequacy 4442

كافٍ **adj.** sufficient, adequate; competent 1301

كلا

كِلا **part.** fem. كِلْتا both of; كِلاهُما both of them 2260

كَلّا **interj.** not at all, definitely not 2105

كلب

كَلْب **n.** pl. كِلاب dog 1267

كلش

كُلِّش/كِلِّش **adv.** (Irq.Gul.) very, a lot 4311

كلف

كَلَّفَ **v. II** to cost; to charge sb ب with (a task) 2148

كُلْفَة **n.** cost, expenditure, overhead 3160

تَكْليف **vn.** charging, entrusting sb ب with 2209

تَكْلِفَة **n.** cost, expense, charge 2392

مُكَلَّف **adj.** charged, entrusted; responsible 2803

كلل

كُلّ **n.** each; every; all (of); الكُلّ everyone 19

كُلَّما **conj.** (with perf. verb) whenever 974

كُلِّيّ **adj.** complete, total; كُلِّيّاً completely 2004

كُلِّيَّة **n.** pl. -aat college; entirety, totality 893

كلم

كَلَّمَ **v. II** to speak with, talk to sb 2986

تَكَلَّمَ **v. V** to speak (مع with sb) 926

كَلِمَة **n.** pl. -aat word; remark; speech 173

كَلام **n.** speech, talk; remark; saying 242

مُكالَمة **n.** pl. -aat discussion; (phone) call 2226

كلو

كُلْيَة **n.** pl. كُلًى/كُلْوَة kidney 4373

كليب

كليب **n.** pl. -aat (film, video) clip 4047

كم

كَم **interrog.** how many/much; (Egy.) كام /kaam/ 336

كما

كَما **conj.** and, also, as well 52

كمان

كَمان **adv.** (Egy.Lev.) also; كَمان مَرّة once more 768

كمبيوتر

كمبيوتر/كومبيوتر **n.** /kumbyuutar/ computer 1016

كمل

أَكْمَلَ **v. IV** to complete, finish sth 1752

اِكْتَمَلَ **v. VIII** to be finished, be perfect 3352

كَمال **n.** perfection, completeness 4416

أَكْمَل **elat.** more/most complete 2969

إِكْمال **n.** completion, conclusion; perfection 4100

تَكامُل **n.** integration 4237

اِكْتِمال **n.** completion; perfection 4383

اِسْتِكْمال **n.** conclusion, completion 2649

كامِل **adj.** complete; perfect; بالكامِل completely 384

مُتَكامِل **adj.** integral, comprehensive 2394

كمم

كَم **n.** amount, quantity 3947

كَمِّيَّة **n.** pl. -aat quantity, amount 1258

كمن

كَمَنَ **v. I (u)** and كَمِنَ (a) to be hidden في in 2059

كامِن **adj.** hidden; latent, dormant 4617

كندا

كَنَدِيّ **n./adj.** Canadian 4410

كنز

كَنْز **n.** pl. كُنُوز treasure 3775

كنس

كَنِيسة **n.** pl. كَنائِس church; temple 2056

كنن

كَنَّ **v. I (i)** to harbor (feelings) ل for sb 4213

كهرب

كَهْرَباء/كَهْرُباء **n.** electricity 1185

كَهْرَبائِيّ **adj.** electrical; **n.** electrician 2048

كهف

كَهْف **n.** cave, cavern; hole, cavity 4389

كوت

كُوَيْتِيّ **n./adj.** Kuwaiti 1063

كود

كادَ **v. I (a)** (with imperf.) to almost do sth 985

كاد **n.** بالكاد almost 4848

كوريا

كُورِيّ **n./adj.** Korean 3726

كوكب

كَوْكَب **n.** pl. كَواكِب planet; star 2733

كون

كانَ **v. I (u)** to be; (Irq.Gul.) چان /chaan/ 10

تَكَوَّنَ **v. V** to be composed, consist مِن of 2630

كَوْن **vn.** being; **n.** الكَوْن the universe 739

كَوْنِيّ **adj.** cosmic, relating to the universe 4739

كِيان **n.** entity; essence, being; structure 1942

مَكان **n.** pl. أَمْكِنَة، أَماكِن place; position 179

مَكانة **n.** position, standing, status, reputation 2116

تَكْوين **vn.** creating; educating; **n.** structure 1936

كائِن **adj.** existing, located; **n.** pl. -aat creature 2439

مُكَوِّن **n.** pl. -aat component; **adj.** forming 2618

مُكَوَّن **adj.** composed مِن of, consisting مِن of 2831

كويت

كُوَيْتِيّ **n./adj.** Kuwaiti 1063

كي

كَيْ/لِكَيْ **conj.** (with subjunctive) in order to 397

كيد

كَيْد **n.** trick, ruse, plot, scheme 4984

كيس

كِيس **n.** pl. أَكْياس bag, sack 2661

كُوَيِّس **adj.** (Egy.Lev.) pl. -iin good, nice 1888

كيف

كَيْفَ **interrog.** how; (Gul.) چيف /cheef/ 67

كَيْفَما **conj.** however, whatever, whichever 4341

كَيْفِيَّة **n.** manner, mode; way; how 1429

كيفاش
كِيفاش/كِيفاه **interrog.** (Magh.) how 4941

كيلو
كِيلُو **n.** kilo, kilogram; (Dia.) kilometer 2028

كيلومتر
كِيلُومتر **n.** pl. -aat kilometer 2574

كيميا
كِيميائيّ **adj.** chemical 3711

ل
لِ **prep.** for, to; (with pron.) لَهُ/لَها and لِي/لِّي 5

لِ **conj.** (with subjunctive) in order to, so that 442

لِ **part.** (with jussive) لِيَكُنْ let there be 4592

لَ **part.** (conditional) لَوْ ... لَ if ... then 1149

لَ **part.** (emphatic) indeed, truly 2162

لا
لا **neg.part.** no; not, non-; (Dia.) لأ 11

لاتين
لاتِينيّ **adj.** Latin 3738

لأم
مُلائِم **adj.** suitable, appropriate 3142

لأن
لِأَنَّ **conj.** because 57

لبث
لَبِثَ **v. I (a)** to linger; ما لَبِثَ أَنْ it wasn't long 3736

لبس
لَبَسَ **v. I (a)** to put on, wear 2617

لِبْس **n.** clothing, dress, attire 4312

لِباس **n.** clothes, dress, attire 3921

مَلْبَس **n.** pl. مَلابِس clothes, dress, attire 1709

لبن
لَبَن **n.** (Egy.) milk; (Lev.Irq.) yoghurt 3085

لُبْنانيّ **n./adj.** Lebanese 212

لبي
لَبَّى **v. II** to meet (needs); to comply with 3383

تَلْبِية **vn.** meeting (needs); complying with 2653

لجأ
لَجَأَ **v. I (a)** to resort إلى to, take refuge إلى in 2398

لُجُوء **vn.** resorting إلى to; **n.** refuge; asylum 2694

مَلْجَأ **n.** shelter, refuge 4783

لاجِئ **n.** refugee; **adj.** seeking refuge 2312

لجن
لَجْنة **n.** pl. لِجان committee, commission 258

لحح
مُلِحّ **adj.** urgent, critical, pressing 3429

لحظ
لاحَظَ **v. III** to notice, observe sth or أَنَّ that 1353

لَحْظة **n.** pl. لَحَظات moment, instant 409

مُلاحَظة **vn.** noticing; **n.** pl. -aat note 1498

مَلْحُوظ **adj.** noticeable, observable; significant 3008

لحق
لَحِقَ **v. I (a)** to follow, be attached to 2033

أَلْحَقَ **v. IV** to append بِ sth 4911

لِحاق **vn.** catching up بِ with 4711

مُلاحَقة **n.** pursuit, chase; legal prosecution 4597

الْتِحاق **n.** entering; joining; affiliation 4328

لاحِق **adj.** later; next; لاحِقًا shortly, soon 1783

لحم
لَحْم **n.** pl. لُحُوم meat, flesh 1518

مَلْحَمة **n.** fierce battle; epic 4996

لحن
لَحْن **n.** melody, music, song; tone 3656

لدي
لَدَى **prep.** with, by, at; لَدَيْهِ he/it has, لَدَيَّ I have 176

لذا
لِذا **conj.** therefore, that's why, because of that 1156

لذذ
لَذّة **n.** pleasure, joy, delight, enjoyment 4445

لَذِيذ **adj.** delicious; delightful, marvelous 4600

لزم
لَزِمَ **v. I (a)** to be necessary; to cling to 3094

الْتَزَم **v. VIII** to adhere to, be committed to بِ 2444

الْتِزام **vn.** adhering to; **n.** commitment 1342

لازِم **adj.** necessary; (Dia.) must, should 462

مُلْتَزِم **adj.** committed (بِ to); involved, loyal 4045

مُسْتَلْزَم **adj.** required; **n.** -aat requirements 4746

لسس
لِسّه/لِسّا/لِسّة **adv.** (Egy.Lev.Gul.) yet, still 2069

لسن
لِسان **n.** pl. أَلْسِنة tongue; language 1026

لصص
لِصّ **n.** pl. لُصُوص thief 4308

لطف
لَطِيف **adj.** kind, gentle, polite, nice 3176

لعب

لَعِبَ **v. I (a)** to play (game, role) 619

لَعْب **vn.** playing; **n.** pl. أَلْعاب game 843

لَعْبَة **n.** competition; **un.n.** game 1196

لُعْبَة **n.** pl. لُعَب game, sport; toy, play thing 4042

مَلْعَب **n.** pl. مَلاعِب playground; stadium 1304

تَلاعُب **n.** manipulation, tampering 4580

لاعِب **n.** pl. -uun player, athlete; **a.p.** playing 428

لعق

مِلْعَقَة **n.** pl. مَلاعِق spoon; (also Egy.Lev.) مَعْلَقَة 3495

لعن

لَعَنَ **v. I (a)** to curse, damn sb/sth 3823

لَعْنَة **n.** curse, oath; enchantment, spell 3187

لَعِين **adj.** accursed, damned; hateful 4636

لغز

لُغْز **n.** pl. أَلْغاز mystery, enigma; puzzle, riddle 4825

لغو

أَلْغَى **v. IV** to cancel, terminate; abrogate 3913

لُغَة **n.** pl. -aat language 441

لُغَوِيّ **adj.** linguistic; pl. -uun linguist 3568

إِلْغاء **vn.** cancellation; abrogation, repeal 2108

لفت

لَفَتَ **v. I (i)** to turn sb's attention إلى to 1701

الْتَفَتَ **v. VIII** to turn around 2366

لافِت **adj.** interesting; **a.p.** getting (attention) 2418

لافِتَة **n.** pl. -aat billboard, placard, sign 3385

لفف

لَفَّ **v. I (u)** to wrap sth; to turn, rotate 3436

مِلَفّ/مَلَفّ **n.** pl. -aat file; dossier 777

لفظ

لَفْظ **vn.** uttering; **n.** pl. أَلْفاظ word 3890

لقب

لَقَب **n.** title; nickname 1499

لقط

الْتِقاط **vn.** receiving; taking (photos) 4725

لقم

لُقْمَة **n.** morsel, bite 3354

لقي

لَقِيَ **v. I (a)** to find; meet, encounter sb/sth 1128

لاقَى **v. III** to meet, encounter; to find 2534

أَلْقَى **v. IV** to throw sth; to deliver (a speech) 1043

تَلَقَّى **v. V** to receive, get 1520

الْتَقَى **v. VIII** to meet, encounter ب/مع sb 1049

لِقاء **n.** pl. -aat meeting, encounter; interview 395

تِلْقائِيّ **adj.** automatic; تِلْقائِيّاً automatically 4248

إِلْقاء **vn.** throwing; giving (a speech) 2959

تَلَقِّي **vn.** receiving, receipt; acquisition 3567

مُتَلَقٍّ **n.** recipient, (person) receiving 4667

مُلْتَقَى **n.** meeting place; forum, conference 2243

لكن

لٰكِن **conj.** however, but; (also لاكن informally) 91

لٰكِنَّ **conj.** however, but 58

لكي

كَيْ/لِكَيْ **conj.** (with subjunctive) in order to 397

لم

لَمْ **neg.part.** (with jussive) did not; أَلَمْ didn't...? 27

لِمَ **interrog.** why 3908

لما

لَمّا **conj.** when, after 324

لِما **prep.phr.** to what, for what 938

لماذا

لِماذا **interrog.** why 375

لمح

لَمَحَ **v. I (a)** to see, notice sth 4382

مَلامِح **pl.n.** features, characteristics 1606

لمس

لَمَسَ **v. I (i,u)** to touch, feel, sense sth 3572

مَلْموس **adj.** noticeable; tangible 3607

لن

لَنْ **neg.part.** (with subjunctive) will never 162

لهب

لَهَب **n.** flame 4412

لَهِيب **n.** flame 4830

الْتِهاب **n.** pl. -aat inflammation 3443

لهج

لَهْجَة **n.** tone, voice; pl. لَهَجات dialect 2086

لهو

لَهْو **n.** entertainment, amusement 4833

لو

لَوْ **conj.** if; وَلَوْ even if; لَوْلا if not for 87

لوث

تَلَوُّث **n.** pollution, contamination 3219

لوح

لاحَ **v. I (u)** to appear, loom 3460

لَوَّحَ **v. II** to wave إلى at sb; to hint at ب sth 4027

لَوْحَة **n.** pl. -aat painting, picture; panel, board 1276

لائِحَة **n.** pl. لَوائِح list, table; schedule 2361

لوم

لَوْم **n.** blame, fault; censure 3900

لون

لَوْن **n.** pl. أَلْوان color, tint, hue; type, sort, kind 498

مُلَوَّن **adj.** colored, multicolored 3522

لوي

لِواء **n.** district; banner; (mil.) brigade 1805

ليبيا

لِيبِيّ **n./adj.** pl. -uun Libyan 1739

لَيت

لَيْتَ **part.** (and يا لَيْتَ) if only; I wish 2060

ياريت **part.** /ya-reet/ (Dia.) if only, I wish 2775

لير

لِيرَة **n.** pl. -aat pound, lira (Leb. Syr.) 3497

ليس

لَيْسَ **v. I** he/it is not; أَلَيْسَ isn't...? 59

ليش

ليش **interrog.** /leesh/ (Lev.Irq.Gul.) why 1119

ليق

لاقَ **v. I (i)** to be proper, suitable ب for sb 2766

ليل

لَيْل **n.** night, night-time; لَيْلًا by night 392

لَيْلَة **n.** pl. لَيالٍ night, evening; اللَّيْلَة tonight 518

ليمون

لَيْمُون **n.** lemon; also /lamuun/ (Egy.Lev.) 4364

لين

لين **conj.** /leen/ (Gul.) whenever; **prep.** until 4462

ليه

ليه **interrog.** /leeh/ (Egy.Lev.Gul.) why 1271

ما

ما **neg.part.** not; أما don't/doesn't/didn't ...? 28

مانِيش **neg.part.** /ma-nii-sh/ (Egy.) I am not 3855

ما **rel.pron.** what, whatever, that which 30

ما **rel.pron.** (in apposition) a certain, any 951

ما **interrog.** what, which 231

ما **interrog.** مالـ what's wrong with? 4436

ما **part.** (durative) ما دامَ as long as 932

ما **part.** (exclamatory) ما أَجْمَلَ how beautiful...! 1505

ما **part.** (nominalizing) بَعْدَ ذَهابِهِ = بَعْدَ ما ذَهَبَ 1187

ما **part.** (redundant) إذا ما if, whether 1837

ماجستير

ماجِسْتِير **n.** master's degree, MA 4137

ماذا

ماذا **interrog.** what 275

لِماذا **interrog.** why 375

ماما

ماما/مامَة **fem.n.** (Dia.) mom, mama 2407

مائة

مِئَة/مائة **num.** hundred, pl. مِئات hundreds 244

مِئَوِيّ **adj.** hundredth; percent; centigrade 4057

مب

مُب/مُوب **neg.part.** (Gul.) not 4606

متاع

تاع/مُتاع **poss.adj.** (Magh.) of, belonging to 4283

متر

مِتْر **n.** pl. أَمْتار meter 1262

متع

تَمَتَّعَ **v. V** to enjoy, be blessed ب with 1542

مُتْعَة **n.** pleasure, enjoyment 2861

تَمَتُّع **n.** enjoyment 4819

متن

مَتْن **n.** عَلى مَتْنِ on board (ship, airplane) 3694

مَتِين **adj.** firm, solid, strong, unshakable 4992

متي

مَتَى **interrog.** when 815

ايمتى/ايمتا/امتى **interrog.** (Lev.Egy.) when 4849

مثل

مَثَّلَ **v. II** to represent sb; to act as sb 662

تَمَثَّلَ **v. V** to be represented; to be seen في in 1788

مِثْل **n.** pl. أَمْثال (someone, something) similar 86

مِثْلَما **conj.** like, as, just as 1631

مَثَل **n.** pl. أَمْثال example; proverb 350

مِثال **n.** pl. مُثُل, أَمْثِلَة example, model, ideal 1180

مِثالِيّ **adj.** ideal, perfect, exemplary, model 3289

مَثِيل **n.** equal, match; peer 3914

أَمْثَل **elat.** fem. مُثْلَى more/most ideal 2915

تِمْثال **n.** statue 4396

تَمْثِيل **n.** representation; acting 2338

مُمَثِّل **adj.** representing; **n.** pl. -uun actor 903

مُماثِل **adj.** similar, analogous; resembling 2750

مُتَمَثِّل **adj.** represented (في in); present (في in) 2965

مجد

مَجْد **n.** glory, magnificence, splendor 2326

مَجِيد **adj.** glorious, exalted 4467

مجن

مَجَّان **n.** بالمَجّان and مَجّاناً for free, free of charge 3193

مَجَّانِيّ **adj.** free, free of charge 2368

محض

مَحْض **adj.** (invar.) pure, mere (fantasy) 4175

محن

مِحْنَة **n.** pl. مِحَن test; trial, ordeal 2907

اِمْتِحان **n.** pl. -aat examination, test; trial 1528

محو

مَحْو **n.** eradication; wiping out 4572

مخخ

مُخّ **n.** brain 3818

مدد

مَدَّ **v. I (u)** to extend sth; to stretch out sth 1586

اِمْتَدَّ **v. VIII** to extend, reach, spread إلى to 1644

مَدّ **n.** length, reach; extending; spreading 2878

مُدَّة **n.** time period, length of time, interval 590

تَمْدِيد **n.** lengthening; extension, prolongation 3864

اِمْتِداد **n.** extent, scope; extension, expansion 2499

مادَّة **n.** pl. مَوادّ substance; subject; paragraph 430

مادِّيّ **adj.** material; materialistic; financial 1250

مُمْتَدّ **adj.** stretching, extending; spreading 3271

مدن

مَدَنِيّ **adj.** civil, civilian; **n.** pl. -uun civilian 671

مَدِينَة **n.** pl. مُدُن city 144

مدي

مَدىً **n.** range, extent; time period 586

مذ

مُذ **prep.** since, ago 4348

مرأ

مَرْء **n.** man; person; المَرْء people 2137

مَرْأَة **n.** woman, wife; (without def. article) اِمْرَأَة 321

اِمْرَأَة **n.** woman; (with def. article) المَرْأَة 1052

مرد

تَمَرُّد **n.** rebellion, insurgency, insurrection 3217

مُتَمَرِّد **n.** pl. -uun rebel, insurgent 4346

مرر

مَرَّ **v. I (u)** to go past; to stop by على (sb's place) 510

اِسْتَمَرَّ **v. X** to last; to continue في doing 726

مَرّ **n.** passing, course (of time); going by 3707

مَرَّة **n.** pl. -aat, مِرار time, moment, occasion 74

مُرُور **vn.** passing; stopping by; **n.** traffic 528

مُرُورِيّ **adj.** traffic-related 4090

مَمَرّ **n.** passageway, corridor 4818

تَمْرِير **n.** passing, transfer 4875

اِسْتِمْرار **n.** continuation, continuity 806

مارّ **n.** pl. مارّة **n.** pedestrian, passerby 3710

مُسْتَمِرّ **adj.** continuous, incessant; continuing 999

مُرّ **adj.** bitter 3130

مَرارَة **n.** bitterness; gall bladder 2844

مرس

مارَسَ **v. III** to practice (profession, hobby) 1393

مُمارَسَة **vn.** practice, pursuit; **n.** pl. -aat activity 988

مرض

مَرَض **n.** pl. أمْراض illness, disease 452

مَرَضِيّ **adj.** pathological; diseased; medical 3933

مَرِيض **n.** pl. مَرْضَى patient; **adj.** ill, sick 822

مُمَرِّض **n.** pl. -uun (male) nurse 4716

مرن

مُرُونَة **n.** flexibility 4093

تَمْرِين **n.** pl. تَمارِين exercise, drill, training 4197

مزج

مِزاج **n.** mixture; mood, feeling 3662

مَزِيج **n.** combination, mixture, blend 4295

مزن

مَزِيَّة **n.** pl. مَزايا feature; advantage 3375

مستر

مِسْتَر **n.** Mr, Mister 4543

مسح

مَسَحَ **v. I (a)** to wipe sth clean; to survey 3555

مَسْح **n.** survey; wiping; sweeping 3047

مِساحَة **n.** pl. -aat surface; space; land, terrain 1137

مَسِيح **n.** المَسِيح Christ, the Messiah 3223

مَسِيحِيّ **n./adj.** Christian 1561

مَسِيحِيَّة **n.** Christianity 4550

مسس

مَسَّ **v. I (a)** to touch sth; to violate sth 2819

مِساس **n.** violation, infringement (ب of) 4441

ماسّ **adj.** urgent, pressing; touching 4387

مسك

مَسَكَ **v. I (u)** to grab, hold sth or ب sth 3279

أَمْسَكَ **v. IV** to hold sth; to refrain from 2344

تَمَسَّكَ **v. V** to clutch, adhere to ب sth 4917

مِسْك **n.** musk 4559

إِمْساك **vn.** holding; refraining from 4608

تَمَسُّك **n.** adherence, commitment (ب to) 3415

مسكن

مِسْكِين **n.** pl. مَساكِين poor soul; **adj.** poor 1828

مسو

مَساء **n.** evening 642

مش

مِش/مُش **neg.part.** (Egy.Lev.Gul.) not 239

مشان

مِشان/مِنْشان **prep.** (Lev.) for; **conj.** so that 4863

مشي

مَشَى **v. I (i)** to walk, go; to leave, go away 1248

مَشْي **n.** walking, going 2868

ماشي **adj.** (Dia.) going, walking; **interj.** OK 1621

مصر

مِصْرِيّ **n./adj.** pl. -uun Egyptian 381

مَصاري **pl.n.** (Lev.) money, cash 4990

مصص

اِمْتِصاص **n.** absorption, suction 4821

مضي

مَضَى **v. I (i)** to go by, elapse (time) 908

أَمْضَى **v. IV** to finalize sth; to spend (time) 4718

مُضِيّ **n.** passing (of time); expiration 3231

ماضي **adj.** last, previous; **n.** الماضي the past 203

مطر

مَطَر **n.** pl. أَمْطار rain 1468

مع

مَعَ **prep.** with; مَعاً together 17

معد

مَعِدة/مِعْدة **n.** stomach 3629

معليش

معليش/معلش **interj.** (Egy.Lev.) never mind 3601

مكن

مَكَّنَ **v. II** to make possible مِن sth (for sb) 3369

أَمْكَنَ **v. IV** to be possible (ل for sb) to do sth 90

تَمَكَّنَ **v. V** to be able مِن to do sth 981

تَمْكين **n.** enabling, making possible 4570

إِمْكان **n.** pl. -aat capability, ability 1510

إِمْكانِيّة **n.** pl. -aat possibility; capability 1409

مُمْكِن **adj.** possible 403

ملا

مُلّا **n.** mullah (Muslim cleric); Mullah 4798

ملأ

مَلَأَ **v. I (a)** to fill sth up; to occupy 2067

اِمْتَلَأَ **v. VIII** to be filled, to become full 4896

مِلْء **n.** filling; capacity; quantity 3644

مَلَأ **n.** crowd; audience, assembly 4733

مَلِيء **adj.** full, filled 2606

ملح

مِلْح **n.** salt 2801

مَلِيح **adj.** (Lev.Alg.) good, nice; **adv.** well 4921

ملك

مَلَكَ **v. I (i)** to own, possess sth; to control sth 800

اِمْتَلَكَ **v. VIII** to possess, own sth 1979

مِلْك **n.** possessions, property; land, real estate 3477

مَلِك **n.** pl. مُلُوك king; الْمَلِك (title) King 425

مَلِكة **fem.n.** queen; الْمَلِكة (title) Queen 2533

مَلَكِيّ **adj.** royal; of or relating to a kingdom 1773

مِلْكِيّة **n.** property, ownership, possession 2779

مَلاك **n.** pl. مَلائِكة angel 2292

مَمْلَكة **n.** kingdom 677

اِمْتِلاك **n.** possession; control; seizure 3564

مالِك **n.** owner; **adj.** possessing; having 4005

ملل

مَلَّ **v. I (a)** to get bored, fed up (مِن with sth) 4768

مَلَل **n.** boredom 3648

ملو

مَلِيّ **n.** long time; مَلِيّاً for a long time 4538

مليار

مِلْيار **num.** pl. -aat billion (Fr. milliard) 942

مليون

مِلْيُون **num.** pl. مَلايين million 250

من

مِنْ **prep.** from; (with verb) since 4

منين **interrog.** (Egy.) from where 4372

مِمّا **rel.pron.** (مِنْ ما) which; a fact that 299

مِمَّنْ **prep.phr.** (مِنْ مَنْ) from whom 1277

مَنْ **rel.pron.** who, whom 100

مَنْ **interrog.** who, whom 795

منو **interrog.** /minu/ (Gul.Irq.Sud.) who 3747

منح

مَنَحَ **v. I (a)** to award sth ل to sb 1924

مَنْح **n.** granting, bestowing; awarding 2008

مِنْحَة **n.** gift, donation; grant, scholarship 3537

مانِح **adj.** granting, donating; **n.** donor 4817

مْنِيح **adj.** (Lev.) pl. مْناح good, fine 3669

منذ

مُنْذُ **prep.** since, ago; **conj.** starting from 175

مُذ **prep.** since, ago 4348

منشان

مِشان/مِنْشان **prep.** (Lev.) for; **conj.** so that 4863

منع

مَنَعَ **v. I (a)** to forbid sth; to prevent sb from 1421

مَنْع **n.** prohibition; depriving 1152

مَناعَة **n.** resistance, immunity 4152

مانِع **n.** obstacle; **adj.** preventing; forbidding 2663

مَمْنُوع **adj.** forbidden, prohibited, banned 3072

منو

منو **interrog.** /minu/ (Gul.Irq.Sud.) who 3747

مني

تَمَنَّى **v. V** to wish ل sb sth; to hope أَنْ that 451

أُمْنِيَّة **n.** pl. (def. أَماني) أَمانِ wish, hope 3492

مُتَمَنِّي **a.p.** wishing, desiring; hoping for 4321

مهد

تَمْهِيد **n.** preparation; facilitating 3319

مهر

مَهارَة **n.** -aat capability, skill; ability 2882

مهرج

مَهْرَجان/مِهْرَجان **n.** pl. -aat festival 1188

مهل

مُهْلَة **n.** deferment; delay; break 3584

مهما

مَهْما **conj.** whatever, no matter how 2848

مهن

مِهْنَة **n.** pl. مِهَن vocation, trade 1829

مِهْنِيّ **adj.** professional, vocational 1863

مو

مُو **neg.part.** (Irq.Gul.Lev.) not 754

مُب/مُوب **neg.part.** (Gul.) not 4606

موبايل

مُوبايِل **n.** pl. -aat mobile phone, cell phone 4947

موت

ماتَ **v. I (u)** to die 593

مَوْت **n.** death 481

مَيِّت **n./adj.** pl. أَمْوات, مَوْتَى dead, deceased 1395

موج

مَوْج **coll.n.** pl. أَمْواج waves, surges 2405

مَوْجَة **n.** pl. -aat wave 2172

موديل

مُوديل **n.** /modeel/ pl. -aat model, pattern 3678

موسيقى

مُوسِيقَى **fem.n.** music 1440

مُوسِيقِيّ **adj.** musical; **n.** pl. -uun musician 2570

موض

مُوضَة **n.** /mooDa/ fashion, style (It. moda) 4514

مول

مال **n.** pl. أَمْوال money; رَأْس مال capital 391

مال **part.** (Irq.Gul.) fem. مالْت of, for, about 4230

مالِيّ **adj.** financial, monetary, fiscal 979

مالِيَّة **n.** finance 856

تَمْوِيل **n.** financing, funding, backing 1678

مون

مِيناء **n.** port, harbor 2571

موه

ماء **n.** pl. مِياه water; liquid; juice 236

مائِيّ **adj.** liquid, fluid; aquatic; hydraulic 3358

ميد

مَيْدان **n.** pl. مَيادِين arena; city square, plaza 1661

مَيْدانِيّ **adj.** field, ground; survey 2679

مائِدَة **n.** table 2761

ميز

مَيَّزَ **v. II** to differentiate بين between 3214

تَمَيَّزَ **v. V** to distinguish oneself; to be different 1938

مِيزَة **n.** characteristic, feature; merit 4031

تَمْييز **n.** distinction; discrimination 2354

تَمَيُّز **n.** distinguishing oneself; excellence 3548

اِمْتِياز **n.** distinction, excellence; privilege 4263

مُمَيَّز **adj.** distinguished; special 1344

مُتَمَيِّز **adj.** distinguished; different from 1457

مُمْتاز **adj.** excellent, superior; privileged 1449

ميل

مالَ **v. I (i)** to bend, lean إلى towards 2633

مَيْل **n.** tendency; leaning, sympathy 4155

مِيل **n.** mile 4183

ميليشيا

مِيليشيا/مِليشيا **n.** pl. -aat militia 3208

مين

مين **interrog.** (Egy.Lev.) who; لَمِين (Lev.) whose 717

نبأ

نَبَأ **n.** news item, report; pl. أنْباء news 1201

نبت

نَبات **coll.n.** pl. -aat plants, vegetation 2795

نبذ

نَبْذ **n.** discarding; rejection, renunciation 4762

نبر

مِنْبَر **n.** pl. مَنابِر pulpit, rostrum 2891

نبض

نَبْض **n.** beating, palpitation, throbbing 3118

نبع

نَبَعَ **v. I (u)** to emerge; to emanate, flow 3856

نبل

نَبِيل **adj.** noble 3065

نبه

اِنْتَبَهَ **v. VIII** to be careful; to pay attention 2549

تَنْبِيه **n.** warning, alarm 4610

اِنْتِباه **n.** attention, caution; alertness, vigilance 2442

نبو

نَبِيّ **n.** pl. أنْبِياء prophet 813

نَبَوِيّ **adj.** prophetic 3290

نُبُوَّة **n.** prophethood; prophecy 4823

نتج

نَتَجَ **v. I (i)** to result, arise من/عن from 3218

أنْتَجَ **v. IV** to produce, result in 3075

نِتاج **n.** result, outcome; production 3931

نَتِيجَة **n.** pl. نَتائِج result, outcome; consequence 225

إنْتاج **n.** production, output 845

إنْتاجِيّ **adj.** production-related; productive 3801

ناتِج **a.p.** resulting from; **n.** product 2063

مُنْتِج **adj.** productive; **n.** manufacturer 2165

مُنْتَج **adj.** produced; **n.** pl. -aat product 1814

نجح

نَجَحَ **v. I (a)** to succeed 954

نَجاح **n.** pl. -aat success 617

إنْجاح **vn.** granting success; **n.** success 4319

ناجِح **adj.** successful, winning; **n.** winner 1765

نجز

أنْجَزَ **v. IV** to implement, accomplish sth 4386

إنْجاز **vn.** implementation; **n.** achievement 1167

نجم

نَجْم **n.** pl. نُجُوم star, constellation; celebrity 1019

نَجْمَة **n.** star; female celebrity 3363

ناجِم **a.p.** originating, resulting عن from 4120

نجو

نَجا **v. I (u)** to escape, be rescued من from 4531

نَجاة **n.** survival, deliverance, salvation; escape 3485

نحر

اِنْتِحار **n.** suicide 3865

نحل

نَحْل **coll.n.** bees, **un.n.** نَحْلَة 3998

نحن

نَحْنُ **pron.** we; Dia. إحْنا , Lev. نِحْنا 97

نحو

نَحْوَ **prep.** towards; approximately 314

نَحْو **n.** way, method; pl. أنْحاء areas, regions 1080

ناحِيَة **n.** pl. نَواحٍ side, perspective; area, region 801

نخب

نُخْبَة **n.** pl. نُخَب selection, choice item; elite 2484

اِنْتِخاب **n.** pl. -aat election; selection 434

اِنْتِخابِيّ **adj.** electoral, election; selection 1690

ناخِب **n.** pl. -uun voter, elector 3714

مُنْتَخَب **adj.** elected; **n.** -aat (spo.) national team 652

نخل

نَخِيل **n.** date palms 4021

ندب

مَنْدُوب **n.** delegate, deputy, agent 2972

ندر

نادِر **adj.** rare, unusual; نادِراً seldom 1861

ندم

ندَم *n.* remorse, regret 4257

ندو

نادَى *v. III* to call ﺏ for sth/sb 1923

نَدْوَة *n.* pl. -aat seminar, symposium 1442

نَدىً *n.* dew; generosity 4035

نِداء *n.* call, appeal; invitation, summons 2318

نادِي *n.* pl. أَنْدِيَة club, association 411

مُنْتَدىً *n.* pl. مُنْتَدَيات gathering place; forum 566

نذر

إِنْذار *n.* warning, caution, alarm 4655

نزح

نازِح *n.* pl. -uun displaced person; emigrant 4504

نزع

نَزْع *n.* removal; elimination; deposition 3293

نَزْعَة *n.* inclination, tendency; trend 4033

نِزاع *n.* conflict, struggle 2110

نزف

نَزَفَ *v. I (i)* to bleed, hemorrhage; drain 4017

نَزيف *n.* bleeding, hemorrhage 3588

نزل

نَزَلَ *v. I (i)* and نَزِلَ *(a)* to descend; stay فِي at 673

أَنْزَلَ *v. IV* to bring or send down, lower sth 3924

تَنازَلَ *v. VI* to back down عَن from 4493

نُزُول *n.* descent; losing (weight); resignation 3068

مَنْزِل *n.* pl. مَنازِل house, residence 550

مَنْزِلِيّ *adj.* domestic, household 3901

مَنْزِلَة *n.* grade, rank, position 4824

تَنازُل *vn.* backing down; *n.* concession 2890

نسب

ناسَبَ *v. III* to be suitable for sb 3433

تَناسَبَ *v. VI* to be compatible مع/و with 2790

نَسَب *n.* lineage; kinship 3879

نِسْبَة *n.* pl. نِسَب ratio, rate, percentage figure 155

نِسْبِيّ *adj.* relative, نِسْبِيّاً relatively 2434

مُناسَبَة *n.* pl. -aat occasion, opportunity 783

مُناسِب *adj.* suitable, appropriate 807

نسج

نَسيج *n.* fabric, tissue, textile 3242

نسخ

نُسْخَة *n.* pl. نُسَخ copy, replica 1323

نسف

ناسِف *adj.* explosive, exploding 3937

نسق

تَنْسيق *n.* coordination, collaboration 1553

مُنَسِّق *n.* coordinator 4168

نسم

نَسَمَة *n.* person, soul (in a census) 3296

نَسيم *n.* breeze, wind 4170

نسو

نِساء *pl.n.* women (sg. اِمْرَأَة – see under مرأ) 511

نِسائِيّ *adj.* women-related; feminine 2353

نِسْوَة *pl.n.* women 4444

نسي

نَسِيَ *v. I (a)* to forget sth/sb 730

نِسْيان *n.* forgetfulness; oblivion 2981

نشأ

نَشَأَ *v. I (a)* to grow up; to originate 2634

أَنْشَأَ *v. IV* to establish, found; to install, set up 4464

إِنْشاء *vn.* establishing, setting up, founding 967

ناشِئ *adj.* growing; resulting from 4215

مُنْشَأَة *n.* pl. مُنْشَآت facility, installation, plant 3281

نشد

نَشيد *n.* anthem, hymn, song 3843

مَنْشود *adj.* pursued, sought; *n.* goal 3524

نشر

نَشَرَ *v. I (u)* to publish, announce sth 1035

اِنْتَشَرَ *v. VIII* to spread out; to be publicized 1968

نَشْر *n.* spreading, propagation; publication 796

نَشْرَة *n.* report, bulletin; publication 3427

اِنْتِشار *n.* spreading, diffusion 1502

ناشِر *n.* publisher 4699

مَنْشور *n.* pl. -aat brochure; *adj.* published 3111

مُنْتَشِر *adj.* scattered, spread out, prevalent 2963

نشط

نَشاط *n.* pl. -aat, أَنْشِطَة activity, action 601

تَنْشيط *n.* stimulation, energizing 4107

نشو

نَشْوَة *n.* intoxication, rapture, elation 4521

نصب

نُصْب *n.* monument; نُصْبَ in front of 4235

نَصيب *n.* share, portion, dividend 2584

مَنْصِب *n.* pl. مَناصِب post, position, office 1346

نصح

نَصَحَ **v. I (a)** to advise sb (ب to do sth) 3575

نُصْح **n.** advice, counsel 4874

نَصِيحَة **n.** pl. نَصائِح advice, counsel 1866

نصر

اِنْتَصَر **v. VIII** to be victorious (على over sb/sth) 3809

نَصْر **n.** victory, triumph 1193

نُصْرَة **n.** help, assistance; support, backing 3839

نَصْرانِيّ **n./adj.** pl. نَصارَى Christian 4804

اِنْتِصار **n.** pl. -aat victory, triumph 1790

ناصِر **n.** pl. أَنْصار partisan, supporter, follower 2514

نصص

نَصَّ **v. I (u)** to stipulate, specify على sth 2294

نَصّ **n.** pl. نُصوص text; wording 914

مِنَصَّة **n.** platform, podium 3594

نصف

نِصْف **n.** half, middle, semi- 607

نُصّ **n.** (Dia.) half, middle, semi- 2195

مُنْتَصَف **n.** middle, halfway 1649

نضل

نِضال **n.** struggle, battle 3202

نطر

نَطَرَ **v. I (u)** to wait for sth/sb 4978

نطق

نَطَقَ **v. I (u)** to speak, utter, pronounce ب sth 2816

نُطْق **n.** pronunciation; utterance 4205

نِطاق **n.** scope, range, extent 1933

مَنْطِق **n.** logic, mentality 1627

مَنْطِقِيّ **adj.** logical, rational 3090

مِنْطَقَة **n.** pl. مَناطِق region, area, zone, territory 83

ناطِق **n.** speaker, spokesperson; (fig.) voice 2274

نطي

نِطَى **v. I (i)** يِنْطِي (Irq.) to give, provide sth 4974

نظر

نَظَرَ **v. I (u)** to look إلى at, في into sth/sb 478

اِنْتَظَر **v. VIII** to expect, wait for sth/sb 661

نَظَر **vn.** looking إلى at; **n.** pl. أَنْظار view; opinion 261

نَظْرَة **n.** pl. -aat look, glance, view 994

نَظَرِيّ **adj.** theoretical 4077

نَظَرِيَّة **n.** pl. -aat theory 2087

نَظِير **n.** counterpart; colleague, peer 2605

مَنْظَر **n.** pl. مَناظِر view, scenery; look 2596

اِنْتِظار **vn.** waiting, anticipating 1190

مَنْظُور **n.** perspective; **adj.** expected 3451

مُنْتَظَر **adj.** anticipated, expected 2603

نظف

نَظافَة **n.** cleanliness 3221

نَظِيف **adj.** clean, tidy 2336

تَنْظِيف **n.** cleaning 3260

نظم

نَظَّمَ **v. II** to organize, arrange; regulate 1360

نِظام **n.** pl. نُظُم, أَنْظِمَة regime; system 199

تَنْظِيم **vn.** organizing; **n.** pl. -aat organization 703

تَنْظِيمِيّ **adj.** controlling, regulatory 3502

اِنْتِظام **n.** order, regularity 4793

مَنْظُومَة **n.** system, structure; hierarchy 2768

مُنَظِّم **n.** organizer; **adj.** organizing 3284

مُنَظَّم **adj.** organized; disciplined 2788

مُنَظَّمَة **n.** pl. -aat organization 521

مُنْتَظِم **adj.** regular, systematic; orderly 3854

نعم

نَعَمَ **v. I (u,a)** and نَعِمَ **(a)** to live in comfort 3630

نَعَم **interj.** yes 201

نِعْمَ **part.** (what a) wonderful 3468

نِعْمَة **n.** pl. نِعَم blessing, grace 1794

نَعِيم **n.** comfort, luxury, happiness 4260

ناعِم **adj.** smooth, soft; dainty 2545

نفذ

نَفَّذَ **v. II** to implement, carry out, execute 1537

نُفُوذ **n.** influence, effect 2749

مَنْفَذ **n.** pl. مَنافِذ exit; escape; gateway 3640

تَنْفِيذ **n.** execution, implementation 497

تَنْفِيذِيّ **adj.** executive, implementing 1460

نافِذَة **n.** pl. نَوافِذ window 1407

نفر

نَفَر **n.** soldier, private; person, individual 4878

نفس

نَفْس **n.** pl. أَنْفُس (with pron.) same, self 44

نَفْس **fem.n.** pl. نُفُوس soul, spirit 805

نَفَس **n.** pl. أَنْفاس breath 2164

نَفْس **n.** (Egy.; Lev. نَفَس) appetite; desire, wish 4511

نَفْسِيّ **adj.** mental, spiritual; psychological 991

مُنافَسَة **n.** pl. -aat competition, rivalry 1890

تَنَفُّس **n.** breathing, respiration; breath 3753

نقص

نَقَصَ **v. I (u)** to lack sth; to be less (عن than) 4470

نَقْص **n.** lack; decrease; deficit; deficiency 1714

ناقِص **adj.** incomplete; **a.p.** lacking (sth) 3401

نقض

تَناقُض **n.** pl. -aat contradiction 2971

نقط

نُقْطَة **n.** pl. نِقاط point, dot; location, position 437

نقل

نَقَلَ **v. I (u)** to transfer sth; to translate sth 858

اِنْتَقَلَ **v. VIII** to move, transfer 1512

نَقْل **n.** transportation, transfer; transmission 536

نَقْلَة **n.** move, shift; advance, progress 4343

نَقّال **adj.** portable 4788

تَنَقُّل **n.** transfer; movement; transportation 4334

اِنْتِقال **n.** transfer; transition 2180

اِنْتِقاليّ **adj.** transitional 3785

مَنْقُول **adj.** conveyed; quoted; mobile 4685

نقم

اِنْتِقام **n.** revenge; retaliation, reprisal 3895

نقو

نَقِيّ **adj.** pure, clean; undiluted 4869

نكت

نُكْتَة **n.** joke 3583

نكر

أَنْكَرَ **v. IV** to deny, dispute (claim) 3131

مُنْكَر **adj.** reprehensible; **n.** vice 4169

نمط

نَمَط **n.** pl. أَنْماط type; form; model 2708

نمل

نَمْل **coll.n.** ants 4738

نمم

نَمَّ **v. I (u,i)** to slander, gossip على about sb 4239

نمو

نَما **v. I (u)** to grow, develop; rise, increase 2330

اِنْتَمَى **v. VIII** to be affiliated إلى with 2066

نُمُوّ **n.** development, growth; progress 1142

تَنْمِية **n.** development, growth; progress 620

تَنْمَويّ **adj.** development-related 3402

تَنامٍ **n.** gradual growth, steady increase 4611

اِنْتِماء **n.** membership, affiliation; commitment 3126

نامٍ **adj.** developing (country) 3566

تَنافُس **n.** competition, rivalry 3246

تَنافُسِيّ **adj.** competitive; antagonistic 4857

مُنافِس **adj.** competing; **n.** competitor, rival 2504

نفض

اِنْتِفاضة **n.** uprising; الانْتِفاضة the Intifada 2704

نفط

نَفْط/نِفْط **n.** petroleum, (mineral) oil 948

نَفْطِيّ **adj.** petroleum, (mineral) oil 2521

نفع

نَفَعَ **v. I (a)** to be useful ل to/for sb 2097

نَفْع **n.** benefit, advantage; use 3851

نفق

نَفَق **n.** pl. أَنْفاق tunnel; underpass, subway 3675

نَفَقة **n.** pl. -aat expenditure; نَفَقات spending 3563

نِفاق **n.** hypocrisy 4225

إِنْفاق **n.** spending, expenditure; expenses 3209

نفي

نَفَى **v. I (i)** to deny, disavow; reject 2101

نُفاية **n.** pl. -aat waste, refuse 3822

مَنْفِيّ **n.** exile, banishment 4700

نقب

نِقاب **n.** veil; كَشَفَ النِّقاب عن to disclose 3999

نِقابة **n.** pl. -aat union, syndicate 2150

نِقابِيّ **adj.** union, syndicate 4926

نَقِيب **n.** union boss; (mil.) captain 3877

تَنْقِيب **n.** drilling, excavation; exploration 4923

نقد

اِنْتَقَدَ **v. VIII** to criticize sb/sth 3020

نَقْد **n.** criticism, critique 1740

نَقْد **n.** pl. نُقُود money, cash 2624

نَقْدِيّ **adj.** monetary, cash; critical, criticizing 2485

اِنْتِقاد **n.** pl. -aat criticism, censure 2939

ناقِد **n.** pl. نُقّاد critic 3529

نقذ

إِنْقاذ **n.** rescue, saving; relief, bailout 1819

نقش

ناقَشَ **v. III** to debate, argue (an issue, topic) 2092

مُناقَشة **n.** pl. -aat argument, debate 1316

نِقاش **n.** argument, debate 1758

نمذج

نَمُوذَج **n.** pl. نَمَاذِج sample; model, example 1430

نهب

نَهْب **n.** looting, plundering; stealing, robbing 4400

نهج

نَهْج **n.** method, procedure; way, path 2666

مَنْهَج **n.** pl. مَنَاهِج method, approach; program 1633

نهر

نَهْر **n.** pl. أَنْهَار river 1184

نَهَار **n.** daytime, day; نَهَاراً by day 980

النهارده **adv.** (Egy.) /in-nahaar-da/ today 4969

نهض

نَهَض **v. I (a)** to rise; to stand على upon 2088

نَهْضَة **n.** renaissance 2672

نُهُوض **n.** promotion, advancement 2608

نهك

اِنْتِهاك **n.** pl. -aat violation, contravention 2883

نهو

أَنْهَى **v. IV** to complete, finish 2273

اِنْتَهَى **v. VIII** to end, finish, conclude sth 525

نِهَايَة **n.** end, finish; termination, ending 380

نِهائِيّ **adj.** final; **n.** final (in sports) 744

إِنْهَاء **n.** termination, completion, ending 1911

اِنْتِهاء **n.** finish, completion, conclusion 1273

ناهِيكَ **part.** not to mention 3203

مُنْتَهَى **n.** utmost, extreme 3705

نوب

نِيابَة **n.** proxy; نِيابَةً عَن on behalf of 2182

نِيابِيّ **adj.** representative; parliamentary 2232

نائِب **n.** pl. نُوّاب deputy, delegate; vice- 360

نوخ

مَناخ/مُناخ **n.** climate, atmosphere 2553

نور

نَوَّر **v. II** to illuminate, brighten; to enlighten 4391

نار **fem.n.** pl. نِيران fire; gunfire; hellfire 468

نارِيّ **adj.** fire, fiery; gunfire 2826

نُور **n.** pl. أَنْوار light; lamp 657

مُنَوَّر **adj.** illuminated; honored 3144

نوس

ناس **pl.n.** (also fem.sg.) people; persons 114

نوع

نَوْع **n.** pl. أَنْوَاع type, kind, form 305

نَوْعِيّ **adj.** specific, characteristic; qualitative 3349

نَوْعِيَّة **n.** peculiarity, characteristic 2331

تَنَوُّع **n.** variety, diversity 3280

مُتَنَوِّع **adj.** diverse; sundry, various 2375

نول

تَنَاوَل **v. VI** to deal with; to eat (meal) 1218

تَنَاوُل **vn.** dealing with; eating 1686

مُتَنَاوَل **n.** (فِي مُتَنَاوَل اليَد) within reach 4545

نوم

نامَ **v. I (a)** to sleep; lie down 1268

نَوْم **n.** sleep 930

مَنام **n.** sleep; sleeping place 4877

نائِم **a.p.** (Dia. نايِم) sleeping, asleep 2214

نوه

نَوَّهَ **v. II** to point out, mention ب/إِلى أَنَّ that 4058

مُنَوِّه **a.p.** pointing out ب/إِلى أَنَّ that 4413

نوي

نَوَى **v. I (i)** to intend, want (to do sth) 3128

نَوَوِيّ **adj.** nuclear, atomic; nucleic 881

ناوٍ **a.p.** intending, wanting (to do sth) 4976

نِيَّة **n.** pl. نَوايا intention, purpose; desire 1712

نيل

نالَ **v. I (a)** to win sth; to gain (fame) 1825

نَيْل **n.** attainment; acquiring, gaining 2925

مَنال **n.** attainment; reach, capacity 4920

هـ

هَـ **dem.pron.** هال (Lev.Irq.Gul.) this 1909

ها

ها **interj.** look! here (he/she is, they are) 192

هات

هاتِ **part.** (fem. هاتِي, pl. هاتُوا) give! 3961

هاون

هاوُن **n.** mortar (weapon) 4437

هبب

هَبَّ **v. I (u)** to rage (wind, storm) 2575

هبط

هَبَطَ **v. I (i,u)** to fall, drop; to land (aircraft) 3159

هُبُوط **n.** drop, fall; descent; landing 3222

هتف

هاتِف *n.* pl. هَواتِف telephone 1227

هاتِفِيّ *adj.* telephone; هاتِفِيّاً by phone 2556

هجر

هاجَرَ *v. III* to emigrate 4922

هِجْرَة *n.* emigration; الهِجْرَة the Hijrah 1760

مُهاجِر *n.* emigrant; immigrant; *adj.* migrating 2962

هجس

هاجِس *n.* pl. هَواجِس worry; apprehension 3464

هجم

هاجَمَ *v. III* to assault sth/sb; to raid sth 3977

هَجْمَة *n.* pl. -aat attack, assault; raid, strike 1664

هُجُوم *n.* attack, assault; charge, raid 1133

مُهاجَمة *n.* attack, assault; raid, strike 4605

مُهاجِم *n.* assailant; striker (soccer) 2911

هدأ

هَدَأ *v. I (a)* to subside, abate; to calm down 2997

هُدُوء *n.* calmness, quiet, peace 1312

تَهْدِئَة *n.* calming; easing, relieving (tension) 3459

هادِئ *adj.* calm, quiet, peaceful 1596

هدد

هَدَّدَ *v. II* to threaten sb ب with 1867

تَهْدِيد *vn.* threatening; *n.* pl. -aat threat 1437

مُهَدَّد *adj.* threatened; in danger, at risk 4287

هدف

هَدَفَ *v. I (i)* to aim at إلى sth 1374

اِسْتَهْدَفَ *v. X* to target, aim at sth/sb 1708

هَدَف *n.* pl. أهْداف goal, target; objective 218

اِسْتِهْداف *vn.* targeting, intending; *n.* allergy 4210

هادِف *adj.* purposeful; aimed at 4011

مُسْتَهْدَف *adj.* targeted, aimed at, intended 3918

هدم

هَدْم *n.* demolition; leveling, razing 3754

هدن

هُدْنَة *n.* truce, armistice; calm, lull 3615

هدي

هَدَى *v. I (i)* to lead, guide sb 3652

هُدًى *n.* guidance; الهُدَى the right path 2341

هَدِيَّة *n.* pl. هَدايا gift, present; هَدِيَّةً as a gift 1438

هذا

هٰذا *dem.pron.* this (masc.) 16

هٰذانِ *dem.pron.* these two (masc.) 2572

هٰذِهِ *dem.pron.* this (fem.), these (things) 22

هاتانِ *dem.pron.* these two (fem.) 3837

هٰؤُلاءِ *dem.pron.* these (people) 435

دا/ده *dem.pron.* /da/ (Egy.) this (masc.) 826

دِي *dem.pron.* (Egy.) this (fem.), these 1232

هاذ *dem.pron.* (Lev.Irq.Gul.) this (masc.) 2721

هٰذِي *dem.pron.* (also هاذي) this (fem.), these 729

هاي *dem.pron.* (Lev.Irq.Gul.) this (fem.) 725

هذول *dem.pron.* (Lev.Irq.Gul.) these 4831

هول *dem.pron.* /hool/ (Lev.) these 4609

هَيْدا *dem.pron.* (Lev.) this (masc.) 4907

هَيْدِي *dem.pron.* (Lev.) this (fem.) 4784

هرب

هَرَبَ *v. I (u)* to flee, escape مِن from sth/sb 2200

هَرَب *n.* escape, flight; desertion 3338

هُرُوب *vn.* escaping, fleeing; deserting 2993

تَهْرِيب *n.* smuggling (goods or persons) 3982

هرم

هَرَم *n.* pl. أهْرام pyramid 3342

هزز

هَزَّ *v. I (u)* to shake, jolt, rock sth 2128

هزم

هَزِيمَة *n.* defeat 2071

هسا

هسة/هسه/هسا *adv.* /hassa/ (Irq.Gul.Lev.) now, right away 3871

هكذا

هٰكَذا *adv.* like this, this way, thus 530

هل

هَل *interrog.* هَل هُناك is there any ...? 72

هلق

هلق *adv.* /halla'/ (Lev.) now 1703

هلك

اِسْتِهْلاك *n.* consuming; exhaustion, depletion 3014

اِسْتِهْلاكِيّ *adj.* consumer (goods) 4698

مُسْتَهْلِك *n.* consumer; *adj.* consuming 2985

هم

هُم *pron.* they (masc.); همه /humma/ (Egy.Irq.Gul.) 168

هما

هُما *pron.* they both 1159

همس

هَمَسَ **v. I (i)** to whisper ل to sb 3461

هَمْس **n.** whispering; هَمْساً in whispers 4458

همش

هامِش **n.** side, margin; periphery, sideline 2668

همل

إهْمال **n.** neglect, negligence, carelessness 4063

همم

هَمَّ **v. I (u)** to preoccupy, concern sb 2935

أَهَمَّ **v. IV** to concern sb; to be important to sb 1527

اهْتَمَّ **v. VIII** to be interested ب in sth 1625

هَمَّ **n.** pl. هُموم worry; anxiety; care, interest 1450

أَهَمَّ **elat.** more/most important 454

أَهَمِّيَّة **n.** importance, significance 596

اهْتِمام **n.** interest, attention; care, concern 690

هامّ **adj.** important, significant 1368

مُهِمّ **adj.** important, serious 249

مُهِمَّة/مَهَمَّة **n.** pl. -aat, مَهامّ task, mission 820

مُهْتَمّ **adj.** concerned; **n.** pl. -uun (person) 3123

هنا

هُنا **adv.** here 159

هُناكَ **adv.** over there; there is, there are 77

هُنالِكَ **adv.** over there; there is, there are 1791

هنأ

هَنيء **adj.** healthful; good; هَنيئاً bon appétit 4593

تَهْنِئَة **n.** pl. تَهاني (def. تَهانِ) greetings 2989

هند

هِنْدِيّ **n./adj.** pl. هُنود Indian 1640

هندس

هَنْدَسَة **n.** engineering 2448

هَنْدَسِيّ **adj.** engineering; technical 4418

مُهَنْدِس **n.** engineer, technician 1134

هنن

هُنَّ **pron.** they (fem.pl.) 2957

هن/هنه **pron.** /hinne/ (Lev.) they (people) 3618

هه/هه

ههه **interj.** (laughter) ha-ha-ha, he-he-he 2021

هو

هُوَ **pron.** he, it; /huwwa/ (Dia.), /huwwe/ (Lev.) 20

أهو **part.** /'ahu/ (Egy.) here he is 4363

هُوِيَّة **n.** identity; identity card 1485

هور

انْهارَ **v. VII** to collapse; to break down 4190

انْهِيار **n.** collapse, downfall; breakdown 2555

هول

هَوْل **n.** fright, shock 4317

هائِل **adj.** great, huge; frightful 1564

هولندا

هُولَنْدِيّ/هُولانْدِيّ **n./adj.** Dutch 4331

هون

هون **adv.** /hoon/ (Lev.) here 1465

أَهْوَن **adj.** easy, simple; **elat.** easier/easiest 4640

هوي

هَوَى **v. I (i)** to drop, fall down, collapse 4701

هُوَّة **n.** abyss, chasm; gulf, gap 4074

هوايا **adv.** /hwaaya/ (Irq.) a lot, very much 4963

هَوَىً **n.** love, affection; desire, wish 1593

هَواء **n.** air; climate; عَلى الهَواء live (broadcast) 1219

هاوِيَة **n.** cliff, precipice; abyss, chasm 4556

هي

هِيَ **pron.** she; it (fem.sg.); they (things) 33

هيـ/هيا **part.** (Lev.) هيو /hayy-o/ there he/it is 3875

هيا

هَيّا **interj.** let's go! 1962

هيأ

هَيْئَة **n.** pl. -aat agency; appearance, look 413

تَهْيِئَة **n.** preparation, arrangement 3590

هيب

هَيْبَة **n.** reverence; dignity; fear, awe 4424

هيدا

هَيْدا **dem.pron.** (Lev.) this (masc.) 4907

هَيْدِي **dem.pron.** (Lev.) this (fem.) 4784

هيك

هيك **adv.** /heek/ (Lev.), (Irq.) هيچ /hiich/ like this 532

هيكل

هَيْكَل **n.** framework; skeleton; temple 3376

هَيْكَلَة **vn.** structuring; **n.** framework 4552

هيمن

هَيْمَنَة **n.** control, power; domination 3291

هيه

هيه **interj.** uh-huh 3665

هيهات

هَيْهاتُ **interj.** not even close! 4431

و

وَ **conj.** and; **prep.** with 2

وَ **part.** (oath) وَالله by God! (I swear!) 272

واح

واحَة **n.** oasis 3639

واش

واش **interrog.** (Magh.) what 4835

وبأ

وَباء **n.** epidemic, disease; scourge 3683

وتر

وَتيرَة **n.** way, manner, style; method 4252

تَوَتُّر **n.** pl. -aat tension, strain, unrest 1940

وثق

وَثِقَ **v. I (i)** to trust ب in sth/sb 4696

ثِقَة **n.** confidence, trust 894

وَثيق **adj.** secure, firm, solid; steady, reliable 4563

وَثيقَة **n.** pl. وَثائِق document; deed 1551

ميثاق **n.** treaty, pact, charter 3220

واثِق **adj.** confident, certain, sure 2906

وجب

وَجَبَ **v. I (i)** to be necessary عَلى for sb 260

تَوَجَّبَ **v. V** to be necessary عَلى for sb 4172

اِسْتَوْجَبَ **v. X** to require sth 4734

وَجْبَة **n.** pl. وَجَبات meal; menu 2340

وُجوب **n.** necessity, obligation, duty 3893

إيجابيّ **adj.** good, positive; affirmative 1206

واجِب **adj.** necesssary; **n.** pl. -aat duty 1382

مُوجِب **n.** بِمُوجِب in accordance with 2409

وجد

وَجَدَ **v. I (i)** to find sth/sb; يوجَدُ there is/are 139

تَواجَدَ **v. VI** to be located; to be present 3887

وَجْد **n.** affection; well-being 4933

وِجْدان **n.** feeling, emotion; conscience 3915

وُجود **n.** existence; presence, being present 268

إيجاد **n.** discovery, finding 1376

واجِد **adj.** and وايد (Gul.) **adv.** very, a lot 2845

مَوْجود **adj.** existing, found, located; present 450

تَواجُد **n.** presence; existence 2794

وجز

وَجيز **adj.** brief, short; summarized 4468

وجع

وَجَع **n.** ache, pain 4404

وجه

وَجَّهَ **v. II** to send, direct sth إلى to 983

واجَهَ **v. III** to face sth; to confront sb 1007

تَوَجَّهَ **v. V** to face إلى towards sth/sb 2374

اِتَّجَهَ **v. VIII** to face إلى/نحو towards 2009

جِهَة **n.** pl. -aat side; direction; sector; entity 313

وَجْه **n.** pl. وُجوه face; pl. أوْجُه aspect 170

وِجْهَة/وُجْهَة **n.** pl. -aat direction, angle 1240

تُجاه/اِتِّجاه **prep.** towards; facing 1293

تَوْجيه **vn.** sending; **n.** pl. -aat instruction 1573

تَوْجيهيّ **adj.** directing, guiding; instructional 4956

مُواجَهَة **vn.** facing; **n.** pl. -aat confrontation 612

تَوَجُّه **n.** pl. -aat attitude, orientation 1917

اِتِّجاه **n.** pl. -aat direction; course; trend 857

واجِهَة **n.** façade; front; (computer) interface 3394

مُوَجِّه **adj.** sending, guiding, directing 4497

مُوَجَّه **adj.** directed, aimed 1903

مُتَوَجِّه **a.p.** heading إلى to 4961

وحد

حِدَة **n.** عَلى حِدَةٍ separately, individually 4061

وَحْد **n.** (with pron.) وَحْدَهُ by himself 579

وَحْدَة **n.** unity; solitude; pl. -aat unit, item 247

وَحيد **adj.** only, sole, exclusive; alone 588

تَوْحيد **n.** unity; standardization; monotheism 2297

اِتِّحاد **vn.** unification, unifying; **n.** pl. -aat union 301

اِتِّحاديّ **adj.** unionist, federal 3313

واحِد **num.** one; **adj.** one, single 56

مُوَحَّد **adj.** united, unified 1774

مُتَّحِد **adj.** united 221

وحش

وَحْش **n.** pl. وُحوش beast 3174

وَحْشيّ **adj.** brutal, savage 3562

وحي

أوْحَى **v. IV** to suggest بأنّ that 3136

وَحْي **n.** inspiration 3799

ودد

وَدَّ **v. I (a)** to want, like sth or أنْ to do sth 1899

وِدّ **n.** (Gul.) desire, wish 4078

وُدّ **n.** affection, fondness, friendship 2468

وُدّيّ **adj.** friendly, cordial, amicable, warm 3066

مَوَدَّة **n.** friendship, affection 4735

ودع

وَدَعَ **v. I (a)** to let, allow sb to do sth 1850

وَداع **n.** departure, exit; وَداعاً farewell! 2815

ودي

وادٍ **n.** (def. وادي) wadi (dry riverbed), valley 1396

ورث

وِراثيّ **adj.** hereditary; genetic, congenital 4764

ورد

وَرَدَ **v. I (i)** to show up; to appear في in (a text) 1870

مَوْرِد **n.** pl. مَوارِد source, resource 1839

اِسْتيراد **n.** importing, importation 4440

وارد **adj.** imported; **n.** الوارِدات imports 2010

مُسْتَوْرَد **adj.** imported 4810

وَرْد **coll.n.** roses, flowers; **un.n.** وَرْدَة 1584

وَرْديّ **adj.** rose-colored, rosy, pink 3515

ورش

وَرْشَة **n.** pl. وِرَش workshop 2371

ورط

تَوَرُّط **n.** involvement, entanglement 4988

ورق

وَرَق **coll.n.** paper; leaves; cards; **un.n.** وَرَقَة 558

وري

وَراء **n.** وَراءَ behind, past, beyond 577

وزر

وَزير **n.** pl. وُزَراء minister 96

وِزارَة **n.** pl. -aat ministry 217

وِزاريّ **adj.** ministerial 2900

وزع

وَزَّعَ **v. II** to distribute sth على among 2701

تَوْزيع **n.** distribution (على among) 1317

مُوَزَّع **adj.** distributed, scattered (على among) 4314

وزن

وَزْن **vn.** weighing; **n.** pl. أَوْزان weight 1461

ميزان **n.** pl. مَوازين weight scales; standard 1958

ميزانيَّة **n.** budget 2473

مُوازَنَة **n.** budget; balance, comparison 3257

تَوازُن **n.** balance, equilibrium; balancing 2329

وسط

وَسَط **n.** pl. أَوْساط middle, center 477

وِساطَة **n.** mediation, intercession 4446

وَسيط **n.** mediator; **adj.** middle, medium 4795

أَوْسَط **adj.** fem. وُسْطى middle, central 679

واسِطَة

بِواسِطَة **n.** by means of, by using 1669

مُتَوَسِّط **adj.** middle, central; medium, average 1172

وسع

اِتَّسَعَ **v. VIII** to be large enough لـ for 2880

سَعَة **n.** volume, capacity 4176

وُسْع **n.** capability, capacity 4987

أَوْسَع **elat.** broader/broadest, wider/widest 2724

تَوْسيع **n.** expanding, widening, augmenting 2174

تَوَسُّع **n.** expansion 3028

اِتِّساع **n.** expansion, extension, widening 4428

واسِع **adj.** wide, broad, extensive, widespread 825

وسل

وَسيلَة **n.** pl. وَسائِل device, means 535

وسم

اِتَّسَمَ **v. VIII** to be characterized بـ by 3156

سِمَة **n.** pl. -aat feature, imprint 3493

مَوْسِم **n.** pl. مَواسِم season, festival 978

وش

وِشّ/ويش **interrog.** /weesh/ (Gul.Sau.) what 1695

وشك

وَشْك **n.** عَلى وَشْك on the verge of 3551

وصف

وَصَفَ **v. I (i)** to describe; to prescribe 1186

صِفَة **n.** pl. -aat feature; trait 1126

وَصْف **n.** description; **n.** pl. أَوْصاف trait 1497

وَصْفَة **n.** description; prescription; recipe 3835

واصِف **adj.** describing, characterizing 4673

مُواصَفَة **n.** pl. -aat description; مُواصَفات specs 2500

وصل

وَصَلَ **v. I (i)** to arrive إلى at; to link بَيْن between 183

واصَلَ **v. III** to continue doing sth 1334

تَوَصَّلَ **v. V** to reach بـ (an agreement) 2299

تَواصَلَ **v. VI** to pursue (efforts) 3182

اِتَّصَلَ **v. VIII** to get in touch بـ with sb 722

صِلَة **n.** pl. -aat link, connection; contact 1735

وَصْل **n.** link; connection, contact; receipt 3834

وُصول **n.** arrival; attainment, achievement 638

تَوْصيل **n.** connection, contact 4573

مُواصَلَة **vn.** continuation 1910

إيصال **n.** sending; transporting 3819

تَوَصُّل **n.** arrival; attainment, achievement 2038

تَواصُل **n.** continuation; mutual contact 1506

اِتِّصال **n.** pl. -aat contact; connection 493

مُتَواصِل **adj.** continuous; connected 1976

مُتَّصِل **adj.** connected; continuous, constant 2486

وصي

أَوْصَى **v. IV** to advise sb (ب to do sth) 4686

وِصايَة **n.** guardianship; care, custody, tutelage 4910

تَوْصِيَة **n.** pl. -aat recommendation, advice 2639

وضح

وَضَّحَ **v. II** to clarify, explain (ل to sb) أَنَّ that 2654

أَوْضَحَ **v. IV** to clarify, explain (ل to sb) أَنَّ that 605

اِتَّضَحَ **v. VIII** to become clear أَنَّ that 2675

وُضُوح **n.** clarity; بِوُضُوح clearly 1834

تَوْضِيح **n.** explanation, clarification 2934

واضِح **adj.** clear, explicit; obvious, visible 480

مُوَضِّح **adj.** clarifying, explaining 2156

وضع

وَضَعَ **v. I (a)** to put, place sth; to lay down 359

وَضْع **vn.** laying down; **n.** pl. أَوْضاع situation 167

وَضْعِيَّة **n.** situation, status; position 3805

مَوْضِع **n.** location, position 2696

تَواضُع **n.** modesty, humility 4102

مَوْضُوع **n.** pl. مَواضيع subject; **adj.** placed 95

مَوْضُوعِيّ **adj.** objective 3616

مَوْضُوعِيَّة **n.** objectivity 3930

مُتَواضِع **adj.** modest, humble 2827

وطأ

وَطْأَة **n.** pressure, gravity; harshness, cruelty 3679

وطن

وَطَن **n.** pl. أَوْطان nation, homeland 373

وَطَنِيّ **adj.** national; **n.** pl. -uun nationalist 143

وَطَنِيَّة **n.** nationalism, patriotism 3547

مَوْطِن **n.** pl. مَواطِن home country; area 4087

مُواطَنَة **n.** citizenship 3606

مُواطِن **n.** pl. -uun citizen; fellow citizen 327

مُسْتَوْطَنَة **n.** pl. -aat settlement 3811

وظف

وَظِيفَة **n.** pl. وَظائِف job, position; work; task 1157

وَظِيفِيّ **adj.** functional; practical; work-related 3605

تَوْظِيف **n.** hiring, recruitment; usage, exercise 2987

مُوَظَّف **n.** pl. -uun employee 915

وعب

اِسْتَوْعَبَ **v. X** to grasp sth; to absorb sth 3638

اِسْتيعاب **n.** comprehension; absorbing 2773

وعد

وَعَدَ **v. I (i)** to promise (sb) ب sth 2682

وَعْد **n.** pl. وُعُود promise, pledge 1809

مَوْعِد **n.** pl. مَواعِد appointed time; deadline 1005

ميعاد **n.** pl. مَواعيد appointment; promise 3315

وعي

وَعَى **v. I (i)** to be aware of sth 3510

وَعْي **n.** consciousness; awareness, attention 1416

وِعاء **n.** container, receptacle; vessel 4838

تَوْعِيَة **n.** informing, making aware 2944

واعٍ **adj.** (def. واعِي) conscious; alert 4792

وفد

وَفْد **n.** pl. وُفُود delegation 990

وافِد **adj.** imported; **n.** pl. -uun newcomer 3735

وفر

وَفَّرَ **v. II** to fulfill sth; to save (time) 2181

تَوَفَّرَ **v. V** to be met, fulfilled في in sth/sb 1541

تَوافَرَ **v. VI** to be abundantly available 4405

تَوْفير **n.** fulfillment; saving (time) 1014

تَوافُر **n.** availability 4316

مُتَوَفِّر **adj.** provided; abundant 2540

وفق

وَفَّقَ **v. II** to grant success (God) to sb 2198

وافَقَ **v. III** to agree with sb 1426

تَوافَقَ **v. VI** to agree, concur 3941

اِتَّفَقَ **v. VIII** to agree (مع with sb) 1332

وَفْق **n.** وِفْقاً لـِ and according to 781

تَوْفيق **n.** success; reconciliation, mediation 1251

وِفاق **n.** agreement, accord; reconciliation 3310

مُوافَقَة **n.** agreement; approval 1588

تَوافُق **n.** compatibility; conformity; consensus 2526

اِتِّفاق **n.** pl. -aat agreement; accord. treaty 656

اِتِّفاقِيَّة **n.** pl. -aat treaty, accord 1216

مُوَفَّق **adj.** successful; fortunate 3595

مُوافِق **adj.** agreeing; coinciding with (date) 2217

مُتَّفَق **p.p.** مُتَّفَق عليه/عليها agreed upon 3676

وفي

تَوَفَّى **v. V** (pass.) تُوُفِّيَ to die 2523

وَفاء **n.** loyalty; **vn.** fulfillment 2047

وَفاة **n.** pl. وَفَيات death; الوفيات obituaries 1544

وَفِيّ **adj.** loyal, faithful 4983

وقت

وَقْت **n.** pl. أَوْقات time, moment, period 98

تَوْقِيت **n.** (standard) time; timing 2229

وقد

وَقُود **n.** fuel 2664

وقع

وَقَعَ **v. I (a)** to fall down; to take place 459

وَقَّعَ **v. II** to sign (treaty) على 2451

تَوَقَّعَ **v. V** to anticipate sth 804

وَقْع **n.** impact; impression, imprint 4705

وُقُوع **n.** occurrence, happening; falling 2132

مَوْقِع **n.** pl. مَواقِع position, site; website 243

تَوْقِيع **n.** signing; signature 1448

إيقاع **vn.** imposition; **n.** rhythm 4286

تَوَقُّع **n.** pl. -aat expectation; forecast 3040

واقِع **n.** reality, fact; **adj.** located, situated 383

واقِعَة **n.** pl. وَقائِع incident, event 2222

واقِعِيّ **adj.** realistic; actual 2293

واقِعِيَّة **n.** realism, reality 4694

مُوَقَّع **adj.** signed, bearing signature 4993

مُتَوَقَّع **adj.** expected, anticipated 1341

وقف

وَقَفَ **v. I (i)** to stop; to stand; to support 487

وَقَّفَ **v. II** to stop sb; to stop doing sth 2637

أَوْقَفَ **v. IV** to detain sb; to make sb stand 2983

تَوَقَّفَ **v. V** to stop; to be dependent on 936

وَقْف **vn.** stopping, ceasing; **n.** pl. أَوْقاف waqf 889

وَقْفَة **n.** stance, posture; pause, break 3353

وُقُوف **n.** standing, stopping, halting 1567

مَوْقِف **n.** pl. مَواقِف position 288

تَوْقِيف **n.** detention; stopping, halting 4727

إيقاف **n.** stopping, halting, detaining 3331

تَوَقُّف **n.** stopping, halting, pausing 2541

واقِف **adj.** standing; stopped 2034

وقي

وِقايَة **n.** prevention; precaution; protection 3228

وِقائِيّ **adj.** protective; preservative; preventive 3985

وكب

مَوْكِب **n.** parade, procession 4163

مُواكَبَة **n.** accompanying; escorting 4227

وكل

وَكِيل **n.** representative, agent 1514

وِكالَة **n.** pl. وِكالات/وَكالات agency; proxy 668

ولد

وَلَدَ **v. I (i)** (pass.) وُلِدَ to be born 1612

وَلَّدَ **v. II** to generate, produce (energy) 4486

وَلَد **n.** pl. أَوْلاد, وِلاد (Egy.) child, son, boy 362

وِلادَة **n.** birth; childbearing, parturition 2012

مَوْلِد **n.** birthday, anniversary; birthplace 4117

مِيلاد **n.** birthday; birth 1930

تَوْلِيد **n.** producing, generating (energy) 4539

والِد **n.** father; fem. والِدَة mother 559

مَوْلُود **n.** pl. مَوالِيد newborn infant 2402

ولي

وَلِيَ **v. I (i)** to follow, come after (sth/sb) 1705

تَوَلَّى **v. V** to seize control of sth 2014

تَوالَى **v. VI** to follow in succession 3964

وَلِيّ **n.** pl. أَوْلِياء patron 1394

وَلاء **n.** loyalty, allegiance 3211

وِلايَة **n.** mandate, term of office; pl. -aat state 276

مَوْلًى **n.** master, lord, patron 2225

تَوَلٍّ **n.** taking charge 3080

تَوالٍ **n.** consecutive succession 3037

اِسْتِيلاء **n.** appropriation, seizure 4682

والٍ **n.** (def. الوالي) ruler, governor 4867

وهب

وَهَبَ **v. I (a)** to dedicate (one's life) ل to 4449

هِبَة **n.** gift, grant 4067

مَوْهِبَة **n.** pl. مَواهِب talent, gift 3022

وهج

وَهَج **n.** blaze, fire; glare, glow 4690

وهم

اِتَّهَمَ **v. VIII** to accuse sb ب of 2126

تُهَمَة **n.** pl. تُهَم accusation, charge 1641

وَهْم **n.** pl. أَوْهام illusion; fantasy 2495

وَهْمِيّ **adj.** imagined, imaginary; fake, bogus 3697

اِتِّهام **n.** pl. -aat accusation, charge, indictment 1636

مُتَّهَم **adj.** accused ب of; **n.** pl. -uun accused 1628

ويا

ويّا **prep.** (Irq.) with; ويّاك with you 3054

ويش

وشّ/ويش **interrog.** /weesh/ (Gul.Sau.) what 1695

ويل

وَيْل **n.** woe, distress; يا وَيْلي! woe is me! 3988

وين

وين **interrog.** /ween/ (Lev.Irq.Gul.) where 406

يا

يا **voc.part.** يا سَلام! wow! يا أُسْتاذ! Sir! 35

يابان

يابانيّ **n./adj.** Japanese 2346

يأس

يَأْس **n.** despair, hopelessness 2254

ياسمين

ياسْمين **n.** jasmine 4595

ياريت

ياريت **part.** /ya-reet/ (Dia.) if only, I wish 2775

يتم

يَتيم **n.** pl. أَيْتام orphan; **adj.** orphaned 3236

يد

يَد **fem.n.** pl. أَيْدٍ (def. الأَيْدي) hand 148

يَدَويّ **adj.** manual, by hand 4671

يسر

يُسْر **n.** ease, facility; affluence, prosperity 4616

يَسار **n.** left (also political) 2424

أَيْسَر **adj.** fem. يُسْرَى left, left hand 2686

يقظ

اِسْتَيْقَظَ **v. X** to wake up; to be alert 3175

يَقْظَة **n.** wakefulness; alertness 3760

يقن

يَقين **n.** certainty; conviction 2285

يمن

يَمَنيّ **n./adj.** Yemeni 1689

يَمين **n.** right side; **fem.n.** right hand; oath 1327

أَيْمَن **adj.** fem. يُمْنَى right, right hand 2322

يهود

يَهُوديّ **n./adj.** pl. يَهُود Jew, Jewish 702

يورانيوم

يُورانْيُوم **n.** uranium 3878

يورو

يُورُو **n.** euro 2943

يوم

يَوْم **n.** pl. أَيّام day; اليَوْمَ today 26

يَوْميّ **adj.** daily; يَوْمِياً adv. every day 634

يونان

يُونانيّ **n./adj.** Greek 3670

Part of speech index

Format of entries

rank frequency, **headword**, [dialect(s)], English equivalent

---

Function words

Conjunction

2 وَ and; *prep.* with

8 أَنَّ that (with foll. n. in acc.)

13 أَنْ (with subjunctive) to

21 فَـ and, so; (Dia.) sometimes written فا

23 أَو or

29 إِنَّ that

43 إِذا when, if; whether

52 كَما and, also, as well

57 لِأَنَّ because

58 لٰكِنَّ however, but

61 إِنْ if; whether

87 لَوْ if; وَلَوْ even if; لَوْلا if not for

91 لٰكِن however, but; (also لاكن informally)

108 ثُمَّ then, afterwards; besides, furthermore

160 بَل but, rather; in fact

166 عِنْدَما when, as soon as

273 أَم or (in questions)

279 حَتَّى (with subjunctive) in order to

309 فيما while, meanwhile; فيما بَعْدُ later

318 كَأَنَّ/وَكَأَنَّ as if

324 لَمَّا when, after

397 كَيْ/لِكَيْ (with subjunctive) in order to

421 إِذ since; while; given that

442 لِـ (with subjunctive) in order to, so that

465 لِذٰلِكَ therefore

483 إِنَّما but rather; but also

546 بَيْنَما while

633 سَواء whether (or not), either (or)

712 وَلّا/وِالّا or; otherwise, or else

921 لَعَلَّ perhaps, maybe; لَعَلِّي maybe I

933 عَشان/عَلَشان (Egy.Lev.Gul.) because

974 كُلَّما (with perf. verb) whenever

1156 لِذا therefore, that's why, because of that

1189 أَلّا (= أَنْ لا) not to

1234 إِمّا .. أَوْ/إِمّا : إِمّا either...or

1305 بَعْدَما after

1419 طالَما/لَطالَما as long as; how often!

1517 حينَما when, while

1631 مِثْلَما like, as, just as

2796 عَلَّ perhaps, maybe; عَلَّني maybe I

2848 مَهْما whatever, no matter how

2886 كَأَنَّما as if

2940 بَيْدَ أَنَّ : بَيْدَ although

3374 حَسْبَما/حَسَبَما according to

3751 أَيْنَما wherever

4341 كَيْفَما however, whatever, whichever

4462 لين /leen/ (Gul.) whenever; *prep.* until

4472 لِئَلّا (= لِـ أَنْ لا) in order not to

4576 رَيْثَما as long as; until

4885 حَيْثُما wherever

Interjection

142 آه (Dia.) yes, right

164 إيه/إي /'iih, 'ii/ (Dia.) yeah, uh-huh

192 ها look! here (he/she is, they are)

201 نَعَم yes

784 اللّٰهُمَّ oh God! dear God!

900 هَلا/ياهَلا (Lev.Irq.Gul.) welcome!

1072 مَرْحَباً (usu. مَرْحَبا) hello! welcome!

1244 خَلاص (Egy.Gul.Alg.) OK, that's it

1257 يالله/يللا/يلا /yaLLa/ (Dia.) c'mon!

1340 آه ah! ouch!

1378 ألو/آلو /'aloo/ (Dia.) hello!

1540 أوكي/أوكيه /'okey/ (Dia.) OK

1927 أَيوا/أَيوه /'aywa, 'aywah/ (Dia.) yes

1962 هَيّا let's go!

2021 هههه (laughter) ha-ha-ha, he-he-he

2105 كَلّا not at all, definitely not

2578 آمين amen!

3272 خَلَص (Lev.) enough, OK

3304 بَلَى certainly, sure, yes

3601 معليش/معلش (Egy.Lev.) never mind

3665 هيه uh-huh

3688 عُقْبال (Egy.Lev.) may it be the same for

4037 أُوف/أُفّ (Lev.Irq.Gul.) ugh! phew!

4431 هَيْهات not even close!

4517 أَها/أَهَه /'ahaa/ (Dia.) yeah, uh-huh

4558 باي (Dia.) bye! goodbye!

4751 خخخخ (laughter) ha-ha-ha!

4893 انزين/نزين /nzeen/ (Gul.) good; OK

4914 أَجَل yes, of course

Interrogative

67 كَيْفَ how; (Gul.) چيف /cheef/

72 هَل : هَل هُناك is there any...?

141 شو /shu/ (Lev.Kuw.UAE) what

231 ما what, which

275 ماذا what

336 كَم how many/much; (Egy.) كام /kaam/

375 لِماذا why

405 إيه /'ee/ (Egy.) what

406 وين /ween/ (Lev.Irq.Gul.) where

461 أَيْنَ where

717 مين (Egy.Lev.) who; لَين (Lev.) whose

795 مَنْ who, whom

815 مَتَى when

1053 أيش /'eesh/ (Lev.Gul.) what

1119 ليش /leesh/ (Lev.Irq.Gul.) why

1271 ليه /leeh/ (Egy.Lev.Gul.) why

1364 شـ (Irq., shortened form of شُو) what

1390 شنو /shinu/ (Gul.Irq.) what

1695 وش/ويش /weesh/ (Gul.Sau.) what

2177 فين /feen/ (Egy.Lev.) where

2277 شلون /shloon/ (Bah.Irq.Qat.) how

3747 منو /minu/ (Gul.Irq.Sud.) who

3884 قديش/قديه (Lev.) how many/much

3908 لِمَ why

4372 منين (Egy.) from where

4436 ما لـ : what's wrong with?

4835 واش (Magh.) what

4849 ايمتى/ايمتا/امتى (Lev.Egy.) when

4864 شكُون (Magh.) who

4905 علاش /9laash/ (Magh.) why

4941 كيفاش/كيفاه (Magh.) how

4953 شَكو/شاكو (Irq.Kuw.) is there?

4979 شقد/شگد (Irq.) how many/much

Number

56 واحِد one; adj. one, single

111 أَلْف pl. آلاف thousand

151 ثَلاث fem. ثَلاثَة three

182 عَشَر fem. عَشَرَة ten; n. عَشَرات scores

244 مِئَة/مائَة hundred, pl. مِئات hundreds

250 مِلْيُون pl. مَلايين million

330 خَمْس fem. خَمْسَة five; خَمْسَة عَشَر fifteen

356 أَرْبَعَة fem. أَرْبَع four; أَرْبَعَةَ عَشَر fourteen

591 سِتّ fem. سِتَّة six; سِتَّة عَشَر sixteen

615 عِشْرُون twenty; twentieth

653 اِثْنان fem. اِثْنَتان two; اِثْنا عَشَر twelve

689 سَبْعَة fem. سَبْع seven; سَبْعَة عَشَر seventeen

875 ثَمانِيَة fem. ثَمانِ eight

942 مِلْيار pl. -aat billion (Fr. milliard)

1108 ثَلاثُون thirty; thirtieth

1140 تِسْعَة fem. تِسْع nine

1526 خَمْسُون fifty; fiftieth

1650 أَرْبَعُون forty; fortieth

2185 سِتُّون sixty; sixtieth

2936 سَبْعُون seventy; seventieth

3758 ثَمانُون eighty; eightieth

4773 بِلْيُون /bilyoon/ billion

4899 تِسْعُون ninety; ninetieth

Particle

1 الـ (definite article) the

11 لا neg.part. no; not, non-; (Dia.) لأ

27 لَم neg.part. (with jussive) did not; أَلَم didn't...?

28 ما neg.part. not; أَما don't/doesn't/didn't...?

31 بـ /bi-/ (Egy.Lev.) imperf. verb prefix

35 يا voc.part. يا أُسْتاذ! Sir! يا سَلام! wow!

37 قَدْ (with perf.) has/have already

53 إِلّا (exception) except (for)

127 إِنَّ indeed

134 أَمّا : أَمّا .. فَ as for...

149 سَـ (future marker, from سَوْفَ) will

162 لَن neg.part. (with subjunctive) will never

213 لَقَدْ (with perf.) has/have already

234 بِما including بِما في ذلِكَ

239 مِش/مُش neg.part. (Egy.Lev.Gul.) not

272 وَ (oath) by God! وَالله (I swear!)

274 فَقَط only, just, solely; (with neg.) not just

277 قَدْ (with imperf.) may, might

315 فيه (Egy.Lev.Gul.) there is, there are

2756 قُبَيْلَ shortly before

3054 وِيّا (Irq.) with; وِيّاك with you

3098 حِيالَ concerning, regarding

3163 قُرابَةَ almost, nearly

3166 قُدَّام (MSA قُدَّامَ) in front of

3184 تِلْوَ after, followed by

3300 بِسْمِ prep.phr. بِسْمِ اللهِ in the Name of God

3699 دُونَا without any, without even

3844 عَمَّن prep.phr. (عَن مَن) from whom

4348 مُذ since, ago

4361 قُبالَة facing, in front of

4439 حَدّ (Lev.) next to, beside; (alone) with

4863 مِشان/مِنْشان (Lev.) for; conj. so that

4957 جُوّا prep./adv. (Lev.Irq.) and جوه (Egy.) inside

Pronoun

16 هٰذا dem.pron. this (masc.)

18 الّتي rel.pron. (fem.sg.) who, whom; which

20 هُوَ he, it; /huwwa/ (Dia.), /huwwe/ (Lev.)

22 هٰذِه dem.pron. this (fem.), these (things)

24 الّذي rel.pron. (masc.sg.) who, whom; which

25 أَنا I

30 ما rel.pron. what, whatever, that which

33 هِيَ she; it (fem.sg.); they (things)

36 ذٰلِكَ dem.pron. that (masc.sg.)

54 أَنْتَ you (masc.sg.)

97 نِحْنا we; (Dia.) إحْنا, (Lev.) نَحْنُ

100 مَنْ rel.pron. who, whom

112 اللي rel.pron. /illi/ (Dia.) that, which, who

129 تِلْكَ dem.pron. that (fem.sg.); those

131 الّذينَ rel.pron. (masc.pl.) who, whom

168 هُم they (masc.); همه /humma/ (Egy.Irq.Gul.)

299 مِمّا rel.pron. (مِن ما) which; a fact that

435 هٰؤُلاءِ dem.pron. these (people)

544 أَنْتِي/إِنْتِي (Dia.) you (fem.sg.)

725 هاي dem.pron. (Lev.Irq.Gul.) this (fem.)

729 هٰذِي dem.pron. (also هاذي) this (fem.), these

826 دَه/دا dem.pron. /da/ (Egy.) this (masc.)

951 ما rel.pron. (in apposition) a certain, any

1004 ذاكَ dem.pron. that, that (other) one

1106 أَنْتُم you (masc.pl.)

1159 هُما they both

1232 دِي dem.pron. (Egy.) this (fem.), these

1876 أُولٰئِكَ/أُولائِكَ dem.pron. those (human)

1906 إِنْتو/إِنْتوا (Dia.) you (pl.)

1909 هَـ ... هالـ dem.pron. (Lev.Irq.Gul.) this

1972 آني (Irq.Alg.) I

2073 اللَّذانِ rel.pron. (masc.du.) who, whom

2389 ذا dem.pron. fem. ذِي this, that

2572 هٰذانِ dem.pron. these two (masc.)

2721 هاذ dem.pron. (Lev.Irq.Gul.) this (masc.)

2957 هُنَّ they (fem.pl.)

3397 اللَّواتي rel.pron. (fem.pl.) who, whom

3618 هِن/هِنه /hinne/ (Lev.) they (people)

3692 اللَّتانِ rel.pron. (fem.du.) who, whom; which

3837 هاتانِ dem.pron. these two (fem.)

4113 اللّاتي rel.pron. (fem.pl.) who, whom

4131 هَذاك dem.pron. (Lev.Irq.Gul.) that, that one

4609 هول dem.pron. /hool/ (Lev.) these

4784 هَيْدي dem.pron. (Lev.) this (fem.)

4831 هذول dem.pron. (Lev.Irq.Gul.) these

4907 هَيْدا dem.pron. (Lev.) this (masc.)

Lexical words

Adjective (includes Active/ Passive Participle)

38 آخَر fem. أُخْرى other, another

41 أَوَّل fem. أُولى first

45 عَرَبيّ n./adj. pl. عَرَب Arab; Arabian; Arabic

55 كَثير pl. -uun many, much; كَثيراً ما often

60 جَديد pl. جُدُد new; مِن جَديد again

65 كَبير pl. كِبار large; important; adult

80 ثانٍ second, additional; next, following

85 أَمْريكيّ n./adj. pl. -uun, أَمْريكان American

88 عامّ general, common, public

106 سِياسيّ political; n. politician

107 فِلَسْطينيّ n./adj. Palestinian

121 دُوَليّ/دَوْليّ international, world, global

135 خاصّ special; private, personal; exclusive

143 وَطَنيّ national; n. pl. -uun nationalist

147 طَيِّب nice; pleasant; delicious; interj. OK

177 عِراقيّ n./adj. Iraqi

184 إِسْلاميّ Islamic; n./adj. Islamist

203 ماضي last, previous; n. the past

206 أَخِير last; latest, recent

212 لُبْنانيّ n./adj. Lebanese

221 مُتَّحِد united

229 مُسْلِم n./adj. pl. -uun Muslim

230 صِغار .pl small; young

233 إِسْرائيليّ n./adj. pl. -uun Israeli

249 مُهِمّ important, serious

255 حُلْو sweet, nice, pleasant

259 مُخْتَلَف different, divergent; various

264 شَبّ n./adj. young man, pl. شَباب youths

283 دائِم lasting; permanent; دائِمًا always

284 سابِق pl. -uun former; سابقاً previously

304 جَمِيل beautiful, nice; الفُنُون الجَمِيلَة fine arts

308 عالَميّ international, global

310 حاليّ present, current; حاليًّا currently

316 طَوِيل pl. طِوال long; tall

331 اِقْتِصاديّ economic, economical; thrifty

335 عَسْكَريّ pl. -uun military; n. soldier

347 حَبِيب n./adj. pl. أَحِبَّة , أَحْباب dear

355 بَعِيد pl. بِعاد distant, remote

364 صَحِيح true, correct; sound; authentic

367 ثالِث third (ordinal)

368 اِجْتِماعيّ social

376 قَلِيل few, small amount; قَلِيلًا adv. a little

381 مِصْريّ n./adj. pl. -uun Egyptian

384 كامِل complete; perfect; بالكامِل completely

403 مُمْكِن possible

438 قَويّ strong, powerful; great

448 تَمام exact; complete; good, fine

450 مَوْجُود existing, found, located; present

462 لازِم necessary; (Dia.) must, should

466 تال following; بالتالي therefore

474 آخِر pl. أَواخِر last, final

476 قَرِيب near; related; n. pl. قَرائِب relative

479 سَعُوديّ n./adj. pl. -uun Saudi

480 واضِح clear, explicit; obvious, visible

488 جَيِّد good; جَيِّدًا adv. well

491 رائِع fantastic, amazing, awesome

499 قَدِيم pl. قُدَماَى , قُدَماء old, ancient

500 قادِم next, following; a.p. arriving, coming

505 عال high, elevated

520 داخِليّ internal; domestic

526 غَرِيب strange; n. pl. غُرَباء stranger

537 حَقِيقيّ true, real, factual, authentic

545 عِلْميّ scientific, scholarly, academic

549 أَمْنيّ safety, security

553 غَرْبيّ Western; prep. west of

556 كَرِيم pl. كِرام noble; generous; precious

557 أَساسيّ basic, fundamental

561 رَسْميّ official, formal; رَسْميًّا officially

564 أَبْيَض fem. بَيْضاء, pl. بِيض white

569 مَحَلّيّ local; locally

570 عَظِيم pl. عِظام great, mighty, powerful

572 فَرَنْسيّ n./adj. pl. -uun French

574 طَبِيعيّ natural, normal

578 سُوريّ n./adj. Syrian

588 وَحِيد only, sole, exclusive; alone

597 صَعْب difficult, hard

598 مُقْبِل next, coming, approaching, nearing

603 أُورُوبّيّ/أُورُبّيّ n./adj. /'urubbi/ European

604 فَنّيّ artistic; technical; n. technician

629 ثَقافيّ cultural, intellectual

631 عاديّ regular, normal; ordinary

632 أَكِيد sure, certain, definite

634 يَوْميّ daily; يَوْميًّا adv. every day

641 عَزِيز pl. أَعِزّاء dear, precious

652 مُنْتَخَب elected; n. -aat (spo.) national team

658 شَدِيد intense, strong, severe

659 شَعْبيّ popular; national, of the people

671 مَدَنيّ civil, civilian; n. pl. -uun civilian

674 صَحّ right, correct; true

679 أَوْسَط middle, central; fem. وُسْطَى

682 أَسْوَد black; fem. سَوْداء, pl. سُود

691 دِينيّ religious; spiritual

698 صِحّيّ health-related, sanitary

699 مَشْكُور thankful, grateful; interj. thanks!

702 يَهُوديّ n./adj. pl. يَهُود Jew, Jewish

714 رابِع fourth (ordinal)

718 قائِل a.p. saying; n. (person) saying

720 مَعْرُوف well-known; *n.* favor, good deed

721 رِياضِيّ sports; math; *n.* mathematician

723 أَجْنَبِيّ *n./adj.* pl. أَجانِب foreign, foreigner

744 نِهائِيّ final; *n.* final (in sports)

747 إِنْسانِيّ human; humane

760 شَخْصِيّ personal, private; شَخْصِيّاً in person

761 مُثِير *a.p.* pointing out; *adj.* indicative

765 خارِجِيّ foreign; outer, exterior, outside

766 مُجَرَّد bare; *n.* mere, nothing but

769 حَدِيث new, recent; modern; حَدِيثاً lately

785 غالٍ expensive; dear, precious, beloved

793 حُرّ free; *n.* pl. أَحْرار liberals

799 عَدُوّ *n./adj.* pl. أَعْداء enemy

802 مَطْلُوب wanted, needed; required

807 مُناسِب suitable, appropriate

823 مُشْتَرَك shared, common, joint, collective

825 واسِع wide, broad, extensive, widespread

827 قادِر pl. -uun capable, able

836 تِجارِيّ commercial, business

839 رَئِيسِيّ main, chief, principal

847 مُعَيَّن specific, determined; set; designated

849 بَسِيط pl. بُسَطاء simple; easy; trifle

851 عارِف *a.p.* (Egy.Lev.Gul.) (= to know)

854 سَرِيع quick, prompt; سَرِيعاً quickly

865 طِبِّيّ medical

878 أُرْدُنِّيّ *n./adj.* Jordanian

881 نَوَوِيّ nuclear, atomic; nucleic

884 حُكُومِيّ governmental; *n.* officer

903 مُمَثِّل representing; *n.* pl. -uun actor

907 بِرِيطانِيّ *n./adj.* pl. -uun British

912 مُباشِر direct; live (broadcast)

919 باقٍ pl. باقُون remaining; *n.* remainder

927 أَحْمَر fem. حَمْراء, pl. حُمْر red

937 قائِم *a.p.* carrying out بِ (task); *adj.* ongoing

939 صُحُفِيّ journalistic; *n.* reporter

940 صَهْيُونِيّ *n./adj.* Zionist

943 دِيمُقراطِيّ/دِيمُوقراطِيّ democratic

944 إِيرانِيّ *n./adj.* pl. -uun Iranian

953 شامِل comprehensive; extensive; full

957 تابِع belonging to لِ; *n.* pl. -uun follower

961 زَيْن lovely, pretty; (Irq.Gul.) good, fine

979 مالِيّ financial, monetary, fiscal

987 أَخْضَر fem. خَضْراء, pl. خُضْر green

991 نَفْسِيّ mental, spiritual; psychological

999 مُسْتَمِرّ continuous, incessant; continuing

1012 خامِس fifth (ordinal)

1013 تارِيخِيّ historical

1045 مَفْتُوح open, opened

1060 مُؤَكِّد confirming; emphasizing

1061 قَصِير short, small (of stature)

1063 كُوَيْتِيّ *n./adj.* Kuwaiti

1064 عامِل working; active

1071 حَيّ pl. أَحْياء alive; *n.* pl. أَحْياء creature

1073 أَقْصَى fem. قُصْوَى farthest, most remote

1075 إِعْلامِيّ media, information; *n.* journalist

1085 قَوْمِيّ national, state; nationalist

1087 إِفْرِيقِيّ *n./adj.* pl. أَفارِقَة African

1088 جارٍ present; occurring; flowing

1094 حاضِر present; *n.* person present

1114 شَرْقِيّ Eastern; *n.* east, eastern region

1120 بَشَرِيّ human

1136 صِناعِيّ industrial; manufacturing

1139 مُحَدَّد defined, determined, set

1144 مُؤْمِن believing; *n.* believer

1147 سَهْل easy, simple

1153 خَطِير significant; serious; dangerous

1158 قانُونِيّ legal, law-related; legitimate

1161 إِدارِيّ administrative, management

1162 إِرْهابِيّ *n./adj.* terrorist

1166 أَلْمانِيّ *n./adj.* pl. أَلْمان German

1170 صادِر issued; *n.* صادِرات exports

1172 مُتَوَسِّط middle, central; medium, average

1192 سَنَوِيّ annual, yearly; سَنَوِيّاً yearly

1206 إِيجابِيّ good, positive; affirmative

1214 ضَرُورِيّ necessary, required

1220 شَرِيف pl. شُرَفاء noble, honorable

1225 شَمالِيّ northern, north

1230 إِقْلِيمِيّ regional; provincial

1236 سَلْبِيّ negative; passive

1237 سادِس sixth (ordinal)

1242 عَمِيق deep, profound

1247 خَبِير *n./adj.* pl. خُبَراء expert, specialist

1250 مادِّيّ material; materialistic; financial

1261 حَرام forbidden; sacred, holy

1266 سُودانِيّ n./adj. Sudanese

1279 جَنُوبِيّ southern, south

1282 باحِث searching (عن for); n. researcher

1285 ضَعِيف pl. ضُعَفاء weak; powerless

1286 مَفْهُوم understood; n. pl. مَفاهِيم concept

1295 سَعِيد pl. سُعَداء happy, content

1301 كافٍ sufficient, adequate; competent

1308 شَرْعِيّ legitimate, lawful; legislative

1311 مَرْكَزِيّ central

1318 بالِغ extreme; a.p. reaching; n. adult

1333 سابِع seventh (ordinal)

1341 مُتَوَقَّع expected, anticipated

1344 مُمَيَّز distinguished; special

1348 مَعْقُول reasonable, plausible, logical

1356 فِكْرِيّ intellectual, mental

1357 فَقِير poor; destitute; n. poor (person)

1368 هامّ important, significant

1371 خَلِيجِيّ of the Persian Gulf (الخَلِيج العَرَبِيّ)

1375 مُتَعَدِّد diverse, numerous, multi-, poly-

1380 بارِد cold; bland (food)

1382 واجِب necesssary; n. pl. -aat duty

1385 مُفِيد useful, beneficial

1389 مَعْنِيّ affected; concerned ب with

1392 صادِق truthful, veracious

1395 مَيِّت n./adj. pl. مَوْتَى , أَمْوات dead, deceased

1399 إلِكْتْرونِيّ electronic; e-(mail)

1400 تَعْلِيمِيّ educational, pedagogical

1403 ضَخْم large, voluminous

1405 مَغْرِبِيّ n./adj. pl. مَغارِبَة Moroccan; Maghrebi

1410 أَهْلِيّ civil; family; private (school)

1420 خَفِيف light; slight, minor; sparse

1424 مُبَكِّر early, مُبَكِّراً early

1427 مُتَعَلِّق attached to, concerning ب sth/sb

1435 مُحِيط surrounding; n. milieu; ocean

1439 قاعِد a.p. sitting; (Dia.) staying, remaining

1449 مُمْتاز excellent, superior; privileged

1455 ثانَوِيّ secondary; subordinate

1457 مُتَمَيِّز distinguished; different from

1460 تَنْفِيذِيّ executive, implementing

1462 إنجليزي/إنكليزي n./adj. /'ingliizi/ English

1466 ثابِت established; stable, steady

1469 مَفْرُوض necessary, required; n. duty

1479 مُسْتَقِلّ independent, autonomous

1480 تُرْكِيّ n./adj. pl. أَتْراك , تُرْك Turk; Turkish

1488 مُصاب n./adj. injured, wounded; afflicted

1491 رُوسِيّ n./adj. pl. رُوس Russian

1492 جَوِّيّ air; atmospheric; weather-related

1493 سَيِّء bad

1496 مُرَشَّح nominated; n. pl. -uun candidate

1503 خائِف afraid, fearful, frightened

1519 مُتَخَصِّص specialized; n. specialist

1533 سَلِيم correct, sound; flawless; safe

1535 مَبْرُوك blessed, happy

1536 مُطْلَق absolute, unlimited

1561 مَسِيحِيّ n./adj. Christian

1564 هائِل great, huge; frightful

1568 ثَقِيل heavy, cumbersome

1570 جامِعِيّ university

1577 دَقِيق accurate; minute; delicate

1578 مُتَقَدِّم advanced; n. applicant

1579 زِراعِيّ agricultural, farming

1585 ثامِن eighth (ordinal)

1596 هادِئ calm, quiet, peaceful

1600 مَحْدُود limited; determined

1614 مُسْتَحِيل impossible

1621 ماشِي (Dia.) going, walking; interj. OK

1628 مُتَّهَم accused ب of; n. pl. -uun accused

1630 أَصْلِيّ original; real, true

1639 مُقَدَّس holy; n. مُقَدَّسات sacred sites

1640 هِنْدِيّ n./adj. pl. هُنُود Indian

1643 حادّ sharp, intense

1646 طائِفِيّ sectarian, factional

1654 جَماعِيّ group, collective; common

1655 تاسِع ninth (ordinal)

1663 جَزائِرِيّ n./adj. Algerian

1673 بَرِيء pl. أَبْرِياء innocent; naive; exempt

1675 تامّ complete, concluded

1680 تَقْلِيدِيّ traditional, conventional

1689 يَمَنِيّ n./adj. Yemeni

1690 إنْتِخابِيّ electoral, election; selection

1691 إسْتْراتِيجِيّ strategic; n. strategist

1692 ذَهَبِيّ golden, gilded

1697 مُقَرَّر decided upon; n. agenda, plan

1702 ذاتيّ autonomous, self-, auto-

1711 سِياحيّ tourist, tourism

1718 دِراسيّ school-; instructional, pedagogical

1729 حَسَن good; حَسَناً well; interj. OK

1731 مُرْتَبِط connected, linked ب to

1739 لِيبيّ n./adj. pl. -uun Libyan

1741 مَجْهُول unknown; n. unidentified

1751 صَحافيّ journalistic; n. reporter

1754 أَزْرَق blue; fem. زَرْقاء

1763 صينيّ n./adj. Chinese

1765 ناجِح successful, winning; n. winner

1766 حَزين sad, unhappy, sorrowful

1773 مَلَكيّ royal; of or relating to a kingdom

1774 مُوَحَّد united, unified

1775 جاهِز ready, prepared; equipped

1776 راهِن present, current

1777 دُسْتوريّ constitutional

1783 لاحِق later; next; لاحِقاً shortly, soon

1784 ضَيِّق narrow, restricted, tight

1787 عَجيب wonderful; astonishing

1793 مُجاوِر neighboring, adjacent

1799 غَنيّ pl. أَغْنِيا rich, wealthy

1803 مُبارَك blessed; lucky, fortunate

1808 جادّ earnest, serious

1811 سُنّيّ n./adj. pl. سُنَّة Sunni

1814 مُنْتَج produced; n. pl. -aat product

1817 حامِل bearing; n. pl. حَمَلة carrier

1827 غِذائيّ nutritional, food-related

1832 ظاهِر evident, apparent; n. obvious

1835 مَكْتُوب written; n. pl. مَكاتيب letter

1847 قَطَريّ n./adj. Qatari

1848 سِرّيّ secret; private

1852 مُسْتَعِدّ a.p. preparing ل for; adj. ready

1855 عاجِل urgent, speedy

1861 نادِر rare, unusual; نادِراً seldom

1863 مِهْنيّ professional, vocational

1865 عاشِر tenth (ordinal)

1872 شيعيّ n./adj. Shiite

1874 بَحْريّ maritime; naval, navy

1887 مُقَدَّم offered; advanced

1888 كُوَيِّس (Egy.Lev.) pl. -iin good, nice

1903 مُوَجَّه directed, aimed

1905 قاس (def. قاسِي) harsh, cruel, severe

1913 تَشْريعيّ legislative

1926 فاعِل active; n. pl. -uun doer, agent

1929 خالِص sincere; pure; (Egy.) totally

1931 إِجْماليّ comprehensive, full; total, gross

1932 شِعْريّ poetic

1944 مُؤَقَّت temporary, interim

1948 حَكيم wise; n. sage; philosopher

1952 عَجُوز n./adj. old person, elderly

1954 إيطاليّ n./adj. Italian

1955 أَرْضيّ ground; land-based

1963 مَقْبُول acceptable; welcome

1964 تَرْبَويّ pedagogical; child-rearing

1965 مُحْتَلّ occupied (land); filled (post)

1969 حَضاريّ cultural; civilized

1976 مُتَواصِل continuous; connected

1977 جَريح n./adj. pl. جَرْحَى wounded, injured

1982 جاي a.p. (Dia.) coming, arriving; adj. next

1983 سِلْميّ peaceful

1989 عَريض wide, broad; bold (line)

2002 فِعْليّ actual, real; فِعْلِيّاً really

2003 مَذْكُور mentioned, cited

2004 كُلّيّ complete, total; كُلِّيّاً completely

2005 قَضائيّ judicial, legal

2010 وارِد imported; n. الوارِدات imports

2016 مُتَأَخِّر pl. -uun late, delayed

2017 عُمانيّ n./adj. Omani

2026 مُخْتَصّ responsible; n. specialist

2030 أَدَبيّ literary; ethical, moral

2034 واقِف standing; stopped

2039 مُجاهِد fighting; n. pl. -uun warrior

2045 مُخَصَّص designated; allocated, set aside

2046 عادِل fair, just, honest, equitable

2048 كَهْرَبائيّ electrical; n. electrician

2050 خالٍ empty, devoid, free (من of)

2052 تونِسيّ n./adj. Tunisian

2061 عائِد a.p. returning إلى to; n. pl. -aat revenue

2063 ناتِج a.p. resulting from; n. product

2074 مُجَدَّد renewed, renovated; مُجَدَّداً again

2077 عَمَليّ practical, pragmatic

2099 أَصْفَر fem. صَفْراء, pl. صُفْر yellow

2100 حَيَويّ vital; lively; biological

2122 فَضائيّ (outer) space, satellite

2129 خادِم serving, assisting; n. servant

2130 بارِز outstanding, distinguished

2138 عَنِيف violent, forceful, fierce

2142 شَهِير famous, well-known

2147 دِيبْلُوماسِيّ diplomatic; *n.* diplomat

2152 ثُنائِيّ dual, bilateral

2156 مُوَضِّح clarifying, explaining

2165 مُنْتِج productive; *n.* manufacturer

2167 مُسْتَقْبَلِيّ future

2192 رَهِيب awful, horrible, gruesome

2193 مُثِير influential; *a.p.* provoking, agitating

2194 رَفِيع lofty; high-ranking; thin; fine

2204 رِئاسِيّ presidential; executive

2214 نائِم *a.p.* (Dia. نايِم) sleeping, asleep

2217 مُوافِق agreeing; coinciding with (date)

2223 مُغْلَق closed, locked

2224 قابِل capable, able

2231 فَعّال effective, efficient; active

2232 نِيابِيّ representative; parliamentary

2235 مُسْبَق previous; مُسْبَقاً in advance

2236 بَلَدِيّ indigenous; popular; municipal

2241 آمِن secure, safe

2245 آتٍ coming; following, next

2249 حادِي first; الحادِيَ عَشَر eleventh

2250 مُجْرِم *n./adj.* criminal

2251 فَرْدِيّ personal, private; individual, single

2256 خَيْرِيّ charitable, philanthropic

2258 رابِط linking; *n.* link (website)

2271 راحِل deceased, late

2275 زَمَنِيّ chronological; transitory

2284 مُضادّ anti-, counter-; *n.* anti(biotic)

2289 أَوَّلِيّ first, primary, chief

2290 جِنْسِيّ sexual

2293 واقِعِيّ realistic; actual

2296 كُرْدِيّ *n./adj.* pl. أَكْراد Kurd, Kurdish

2308 مَجْنُون *n./adj.* pl. مَجانِين crazy, insane

2314 فاضِل eminent; *n.* leftover

2322 أَيْمَن fem. يُمْنَى right, right hand

2323 صُلْب hard, solid; steel; *n.* core

2335 عَصَبِيّ nervous, irritable; neural

2336 نَظِيف clean, tidy

2343 شَهْرِيّ monthly; شَهْرِيّاً *adv.* monthly

2346 يابانِيّ *n./adj.* Japanese

2350 مُرْتَفِع high, elevated; rising, soaring

2351 مُحِبّ affectionate; *n.* fan, enthusiast

2353 نِسائِيّ women-related; feminine

2355 ساخِن hot, heated

2360 مُؤَثِّر effective; *n.* effect

2362 دَمَوِيّ bloody; blood-

2363 مُبَرِّر justifying; *n.* pl. -aat excuse

2364 مَطْرُوح proposed, offered; prostrate

2368 مَجّانِيّ free, free of charge

2370 مُعاصِر contemporary; modern

2375 مُتَنَوِّع diverse; sundry, various

2376 صَرِيح candid, sincere

2377 صَيْفِيّ summer, summery

2380 خاطِئ mistaken, at fault

2387 صافٍ pure, clear; sincere

2393 مُرَبَّع quadruple; square; *n.* square

2394 مُتَكامِل integral, comprehensive

2397 حَلال permissible, legitimate; Halal

2399 جالِس seated, sitting

2400 سَكَنِيّ housing, residential

2404 مُحْتَمَل likely, expected, probable

2417 مَجْمُوع gathered; *n.* total

2418 لافِت interesting; *a.p.* getting (attention)

2419 إِضافِيّ additional, supplementary

2434 نِسْبِيّ relative; نِسْبِيّاً relatively

2437 صامِت silent, quiet

2439 كائِن existing, located; *n.* pl. -aat creature

2452 أَجْمَع pl. -uun, fem. جَمْعاء, entire; *n.* all of

2454 زائِد extra; exceeding; excessive

2455 مُبْدِع creative; *n.* innovator

2459 حارّ hot; fervent; warm, heartfelt; spicy

2461 بَرْلَمانِيّ parliamentary; *n.* parliamentarian

2465 اِسْتِثْمارِيّ investment

2466 تِلْفِزْيونِي /tilfizyooni/ television, televised

2467 مُبَيِّن explaining; /mbayyin/ it seems

2479 آسِيَوِيّ *n./adj.* Asian, Asiatic

2483 مُعارِض *a.p.* opposing; *n.* pl. -uun opponent

2485 نَقْدِيّ monetary, cash; critical, criticizing

2486 مُتَّصِل connected; continuous, constant

2494 مَشْغُول busy, occupied

2496 ذَكِيّ intelligent, clever

2504 مُنافِس competing; *n.* competitor, rival

2505 جِدِّيّ serious, earnest; جِدِّيّاً in earnest

2507 فارغ unoccupied, free, idle; empty

2508 رَحِيم compassionate (God)

2518 مُفاجِئ surprising; sudden

2521 نَفْطِيّ petroleum, (mineral) oil

2524 بيئيّ environmental

2529 مَسْرَحِيّ theatrical

2531 حَرْبِيّ war, military

2538 مُؤَكَّد certain; guaranteed

2540 مُتَوَفِّر provided; abundant

2545 ناعِم smooth, soft; dainty

2547 جُغْرافِيّ geographical

2550 مُقْتَرَح proposed; n. pl. -aat proposal

2556 هاتِفِيّ telephone; هاتِفِيّاً by phone

2559 مُتَطَلَّب required; n. مُتَطَلَّبات demands

2563 مَشْهُور famous, well-known

2567 عايِز/عاوِز a.p. (Egy.) wanting (= to want)

2570 مُوسِيقِيّ musical; n. pl. -uun musician

2577 فاتِح clear (color); (Dia.) a.p. opening

2580 مُعَدّ made; n. مُعَدّات equipment

2582 قِياسِيّ record; analogous

2583 تِكْنُولُوجِيّ technological

2589 مَدْرَسِيّ scholastic, school-related

2598 ذَكَر n./adj. pl. ذُكُور male

2603 مُنْتَظَر anticipated, expected

2606 مَلِيء full, filled

2609 مُخْلِص sincere; loyal

2613 مُفَضَّل preferred; favorite, best (friend)

2623 تَدْرِيبِيّ practice; training, coaching

2625 سامٍ (def. سامِي) lofty, exalted, sublime

2629 رايِح a.p. (Dia.) going; pl. رايِحين /rayHiin/

2631 مَعْلُوم known; مَعْلُوم interj. of course!

2638 مُكَثَّف intensive; thick; compressed

2640 رَخِيص cheap, inexpensive

2642 إماراتِيّ n./adj. Emirati, UAE

2647 عابِر passing, crossing; transient, brief

2650 فَرِيد unique, exceptional, singular

2671 راجِع a.p. returning إلى to; traced back إلى to

2674 باطِل false; invalid; n. falsehood

2679 مَيْدانِي field, ground; survey

2680 مُتاح provided, available, granted

2681 بَرِّيّ rural; land-based; wild

2685 غامِض obscure, vague, ambiguous

2686 أَيْسَر fem. يُسْرَى left, left hand

2693 عِمْلاق gigantic, huge; super

2695 رَقِيق delicate; slender; coll.n. slaves

2713 مُتَطَرِّف n./adj. extremist, militant, radical

2716 فائِز victorious; n. pl. -uun winner

2722 مُعْتَمَد p.p. مُعْتَمَد عليه depended upon

2726 عَقارِيّ real estate; land mortgage

2734 مُتَبادَل mutual, reciprocal; exchanged

2738 عَذْب sweet, pleasant; مِياه عَذْبة freshwater

2741 مُعَبِّر a.p. expressing, stating

2746 إسْبانِي n./adj. pl. إسْبان Spanish, Spaniard

2750 مُماثِل similar, analogous; resembling

2753 جَزِيل abundant

2754 تَحْتِيّ under; infra-(structure)

2757 سائِد prevailing, dominant, ruling

2758 أَعْمَى fem. عَمْياء blind

2769 مُعَقَّد complicated, complex, intricate

2772 جَدِير worth ب (mentioning)

2776 شابّة n./adj. young woman

2783 مُظْلِم dark, gloomy

2784 أَكادِيمِي academic; n. scholar

2787 تَقْنِيّ technical

2788 مُنَظَّم organized; disciplined

2789 مُرَكَّب installed; composed of مِن

2792 مُطالِب demanding, claiming; n. claimant

2803 مُكَلَّف charged, entrusted; responsible

2808 غاضِب angry, irate

2813 مُتَزايِد growing, increasing, rising

2825 مَصْرَفِيّ bank, banking

2826 نارِيّ fire, fiery; gunfire

2827 مُتَواضِع modest, humble

2829 مُتَكَرِّر repeated, recurring; frequent

2831 مُكَوَّن composed مِن of, consisting مِن of

2835 فائِق exceeding; outstanding

2845 واجِد (Gul.) adv. very, a lot وايد and

2847 مُؤْلِم painful; distressing

2857 أَصِيل authentic; native; pure

2864 مُعَلَّق suspended, pending, outstanding

2865 خُصُوصِيّ private, personal; special

2866 صَوْتِيّ verbal, vocal; acoustic, phonetic

2871 مُعْتَبِر a.p. considering, regarding

2895 خَفِيّ hidden, secret; unseen, invisible

2897 عاطِفِيّ emotional; affectionate

2900 وِزارِيّ ministerial

2905 مُحْتَرَم honorable, respected, esteemed

2906 واثِق confident, certain, sure

2908 مُتَطَوِّر advanced, developed; modern

2918 حاسِم decisive, final; key, critical

2927 كاذِب false; deceitful; n. pl. -uun كَذَبَة liar

2930 حَسّاس sensitive

2946 عاجِز a.p. unable عن to do sth; adj. helpless

2948 قاطِع decisive; a.p. blocking

2949 اِبْتِدائِيّ elementary; initial

2956 مُسَجَّل registered, recorded

2958 عاقِل pl. عُقَلاء rational; n. sane person

2960 كَثِيف intense, intensive; thick, dense

2963 مُنْتَشِر scattered, spread out, prevalent

2965 مُمَثَّل represented (في in); present (في in)

2996 مُعْلَن declared, announced; posted

3002 طارِئ emergency; exceptional

3008 مَلْحُوظ noticeable, observable; significant

3016 سِينَمائِيّ cinema, cinematographic

3030 مُعْطى given; n. مُعْطَيات facts, data, factors

3031 زَوْجِيّ marital; paired, coupled

3035 جُمْهُورِيّ n./adj. republican; Republican

3038 حِزْبِيّ party-related; partisan, factional

3042 قَيِّم valuable; n. responsible على for

3043 راضٍ pleased, satisfied; accepting

3056 مُخالِف against (the law); n. offender

3062 راقٍ ascending; advanced; high-class

3064 عُنْصُرِيّ racist

3065 نَبِيل noble

3066 وُدِّيّ friendly, cordial, amicable, warm

3072 مَمْنُوع forbidden, prohibited, banned

3074 قِيادِيّ leading; n. pl. -uun commander

3081 كَفِيل ensuring (ب sth); n. sponsor

3089 مُسْتَخْدِم using; n. pl. -uun user

3090 مَنْطِقِيّ logical, rational

3093 أَخْلاقِيّ moral, ethical

3096 سوفييتي/سوفيتي/سوفياتي Soviet

3100 بائِع selling; n. pl. باعَة seller

3102 دافِئ warm; (Dia.)

3108 مَبْنِيّ built, based (على on)

3117 مَضْبُوط controlled, regulated; accurate

3120 عُمُومِيّ general, public, common; plenary

3123 مُهْتَمّ concerned; n. pl. -uun (person)

3125 مُكَرَّم honored, revered; مَكَّة المُكَرَّمَة Mecca

3130 مُرّ bitter

3135 أولِمبي /'oolimbi/ Olympic

3138 حَدِيدِيّ iron, iron-like

3142 مُلائِم suitable, appropriate

3144 مُنَوَّر illuminated; honored

3149 اِشْتِراكِيّ socialist

3165 رُوحِيّ spiritual; alcoholic

3168 فاشِل failed, failing; a failure

3173 باكِستانِيّ n./adj. Pakistani

3176 لَطِيف kind, gentle, polite, nice

3185 خَطِر serious, grave; dangerous

3190 فَوْرِيّ immediate, instant; direct

3191 مَبِيع sold; n. مَبِيعات sales

3192 حَرِيص mindful, protective; eager

3195 مُسْرِع hurrying, hastening

3197 عائِلِيّ family, domestic, familial

3201 سَوِيّ straight, correct; سَوِيّاً together

3215 تَدْرِيجِيّ gradual; تَدْرِيجِيّاً gradually

3226 مُتَزَوِّج married (مِن to)

3243 مَجْهُود expended (efforts); n. efforts

3250 عَقْلِيّ mental, intellectual; rational

3252 عايِش a.p. (Dia.) living, alive (= to live)

3256 مُتَفَرِّق diverse, different; scattered

3259 مُسْتَخْدَم used, utilized, employed

3264 بَحْرَيْنِيّ n./adj. Bahraini

3268 مُشابِه similar

3271 مُمْتَدّ stretching, extending; spreading

3276 مُفْتَرَض assumed, presumed

3282 عَشْوائِيّ random, indiscriminate, arbitrary

3287 قَدِير capable, efficient

3289 مِثالِيّ ideal, perfect, exemplary, model

3290 نَبَوِيّ prophetic

3311 جِنائِيّ criminal, penal

3313 اِتِّحادِيّ unionist, federal

3320 مُؤَسِّس founding; n. founder

3324 حَلِيف n./adj. pl. حُلَفاء ally, allied

3326 صَواب correct, true

3328 شُيُوعِيّ n./adj. Communist

3346 عَرِيق deep-rooted; noble, aristocratic

3349 نَوْعِيّ specific, characteristic; qualitative

3350 مُعَلِّق *a.p.* commenting; *n.* commentator

3358 مائِيّ liquid, fluid; aquatic; hydraulic

3362 عَلِيّ supreme, exalted; العَلِيّ (God)

3364 ثُلاثِيّ three-part, tri-; *n.* trio

3377 مُنْخَفِض low; reduced

3379 ثَوْرِيّ revolutionary

3380 مَرْسُوم decreed; drawn; charted; *n.* decree

3382 مُؤَهَّل qualified; competent

3387 مُخِيف frightful, terrifying, horrible

3388 آلِيّ mechanical, automatic

3393 أُسْبُوعِيّ weekly

3395 مُشْرِق splendid; bright, auspicious

3401 ناقِص incomplete; *a.p.* lacking (sth)

3402 تَنْمَوِيّ development-related

3414 أَسْبَق previous, former; earlier

3428 جِراحِيّ surgical

3429 مُلِحّ urgent, critical, pressing

3430 مُتَتالٍ consecutive, successive

3431 مُعْتاد accustomed على to sth; typical, usual

3441 بَدَوِيّ *n./adj.* pl. بَدْو/بُدُو Bedouin

3444 مُجَمِّع collecting, gathering; *n.* collector

3452 جانِبِيّ side, lateral; marginal; secondary

3455 مُجْتَمِع meeting; *n.* (meeting) participant

3465 اِسْتِثْنائِيّ exceptional, irregular

3469 مَحْمُول portable; *n.* mobile (phone)

3472 دِفاعِيّ defensive, protective

3484 مُطْرِب delightful; *n.* pl. -uun musician

3486 سُكَّانِيّ residential, population-related

3491 مُشَرَّف honorable, noble; honorary

3498 فَرْعِيّ branch, secondary, subdivision

3502 تَنْظِيمِيّ controlling, regulatory

3505 باكِر early

3507 ضائِع lost; stray; wasted (time)

3509 ساخِر satirical; *a.p.* ridiculing

3512 مَعْدِنِيّ mineral, metal, metallic

3514 مُتَبَقٍّ remaining; *n.* rest

3515 وَرْدِيّ rose-colored, rosy, pink

3521 رافِض rejecting, refusing; *n.* rejectionist

3522 مُلَوَّن colored, multicolored

3524 مَنْشُود pursued, sought; *n.* goal

3532 جَماهِيرِيّ mass, throng; (of the) masses

3540 غائِب absent

3542 رُباعِيّ four-part; *n.* quadrangle; quartet

3543 مَسْمُوح allowed, permitted

3550 طاهِر clean, pure; flawless, perfect; chaste

3554 شَبِيه resembling, similar to

3562 وَحْشِيّ brutal, savage

3565 غَيْر مَسْبُوق : مَسْبُوق unprecedented

3566 نامٍ developing (country)

3568 لُغَوِيّ linguistic; pl. -uun linguist

3574 مُشَدِّد emphasizing; strengthening

3576 مَرْحُوم deceased, late

3580 مُحَرَّم forbidden; *n.* مُحَرَّمات taboos

3585 فاهِم understanding, comprehending

3587 جافّ dry

3595 مُوَفَّق successful; fortunate

3605 وَظِيفِيّ functional; practical; work-related

3607 مَلْمُوس noticeable; tangible

3616 مَوْضُوعِيّ objective

3619 مُتَأَكِّد sure, convinced (مِن of)

3626 قَلِق worried, concerned, uneasy

3650 شُجاع brave

3657 مُرِيح pleasant; soothing, restful

3658 خام raw, unprocessed; crude (oil)

3659 مُؤَدٍّ (def. مُؤَدِّي) leading إلى to

3664 رَقَمِيّ numerical; digital

3669 مُنِيح (Lev.) pl. مُناح good, fine

3670 يُونانِيّ *n./adj.* Greek

3673 عِبْرِيّ Hebrew; Jewish (state)

3676 مُتَّفَق *p.p.* مُتَّفَق عليه/عليها agreed upon

3682 مُسْتَفِيد benefiting; *n.* pl. -uun beneficiary

3693 جاهِد strenuous, vigorous; striving

3695 مُتَحَرِّك moving, mobile

3697 وَهْمِيّ imagined, imaginary; fake, bogus

3711 كِيمِيائِيّ chemical

3718 عارٍ naked, bare

3720 مَفْقُود lost, missing; *n.* missing (person)

3722 ذَرِّيّ atomic

3723 بَرازِيلِيّ *n./adj.* Brazilian

3724 عَتِيق old, aged

3726 كُورِيّ *n./adj.* Korean

3735 وافِد imported; *n.* pl. -uun newcomer

3738 لاتِينِيّ Latin

3743 مُفَخَّخ booby-trapped

3744 بَشِع horrible, disgusting

3761 حَرِج delicate, sensitive; awkward

3762 باطِن inner; hidden; n. inside

3764 عالِق pending; related; stranded

3765 جَسَدِيّ physical, bodily; sensual

3767 مَعْنَوِيّ moral, spiritual, mental; semantic

3768 مُزْمِن enduring, chronic

3771 فارِسِيّ n./adj. pl. فُرْس Persian

3776 مُعادٍ hostile, anti-

3777 مُتْعَب tired, weary

3779 جُزْئِيّ partial, incomplete; جُزْئِيّاً in part

3781 جانٍ n./adj. pl. جُناة delinquent, criminal

3783 مُتَضَرِّر damaged; injured; n. victim

3784 ثَمِين costly; valuable, precious

3785 اِنْتِقالِيّ transitional

3788 طُلّابِيّ student-related

3789 فاضٍ empty; unoccupied; free (not busy)

3794 عَصْرِيّ contemporary, modern

3801 إِنْتاجِيّ production-related; productive

3815 خَشَبِيّ wooden, made of wood

3820 أَطْلَسِيّ Atlantic; NATO

3821 مُتَشَدِّد n./adj. extremist, fanatic; strict, intense

3824 مُحْتاج n./adj. pl. -uun needy; a.p. wanting

3829 مُسْتَقِرّ settled, at ease; stable, permanent

3832 رَمْزِيّ symbolic; encoded (data)

3836 شَرِس vicious, savage, fierce

3842 مُدَمِّر destructive, destroying

3847 مَزْعُوم so-called; alleged, claimed

3854 مُنْتَظِم regular, systematic; orderly

3863 مُعْتَدِل moderate (weather, policy)

3874 مُرْتاح relaxed; at ease; happy

3880 سامِع a.p. listening, hearing, able to hear

3891 خَبِيث malicious, evil; malignant

3896 جامِع comprehensive; n. collector

3897 خالِد immortal, eternal; glorious

3901 مَنْزِلِيّ domestic, household

3907 مُطَّلِع well-informed (على about sth)

3916 مُرْتَقَب expected, anticipated

3918 مُسْتَهْدَف targeted, aimed at, intended

3919 صَحْراوِيّ desert; Saharan

3925 جامِد frozen; rigid

3928 ساحِلِيّ coastal, seaside

3933 مَرَضِيّ pathological; diseased; medical

3934 حَنِيف orthodox; الدِّين الحَنِيف Islam

3937 ناسِف explosive, exploding

3946 خَيالِيّ imaginary, fantastic; fictitious

3948 تَشْكِيلِيّ visual, graphic

3952 مُنْصَرِم gone by, elapsed (time period)

3959 اِسْتِشارِيّ advisory, consultative; n. advisor

3960 جَلِيل venerable, eminent; glorious, great

3963 جِذْرِيّ radical, fundamental, basic

3967 مُحاوِل a.p. attempting, trying (to do sth)

3970 مُؤَلَّف composed (من of); n. publication

3971 مَعْرُوض on display; offered; n. proposal

3975 مُرْضٍ satisfying, pleasing; adequate

3976 مُصَلٍّ a.p. praying; n. pl. -uun person praying

3979 مُقَرَّب near; n. close companion

3985 وِقائِيّ protective; preservative; preventive

3987 دائِر taking place, happening; ongoing

4000 مُنْفَصِل separate, disconnected

4002 مَخْزُون stored; in stock; n. supplies

4008 مَظْلُوم oppressed, treated unjustly

4010 خِتامِيّ concluding, closing, final

4011 هادِف purposeful; aimed at

4012 رِيفِيّ rural, countryside; rustic

4025 حَنُون affectionate; loving, dear

4026 مَذْهَبِيّ doctrinal, sectarian

4028 مُفْرَد individual, separate

4039 مَعْرِفِيّ knowledge-related; cognitive

4041 حَرارِيّ thermal, caloric, heat-related

4043 مُتَغَيِّر changing; n. مُتَغَيِّرات variables

4045 مُلْتَزِم committed (ب to); involved, loyal

4046 طالِب requesting, demanding

4053 حامِل fem.adj. pregnant

4057 مِئَوِيّ hundredth; percent; centigrade

4064 فائِت past, expired, elapsed, gone by

4068 مَعْدُود limited in number, countable

4076 مُطْمَئِنّ calm; relieved; certain (إلى about)

4077 نَظَرِيّ theoretical

4083 رَشِيد rational, sensible, wise, mature

4084 جَبان coward, cowardly; n. coward

4089 ضَئِيل small, meager, sparse

4090 مُرُورِيّ traffic-related

4091 فَسِيح wide; lengthy; ample, roomy

4092 مَرْئِيّ visual; visible

4095 عُمْرانِيّ architectural; civilized, populated

4097 سِحْرِيّ magical, magic; enchanting

4099 عِرْقِيّ ethnic, racial

4105 رَحْمن/رَحْمان merciful (God)

4116 مُتَسائِل asking oneself, wondering

4118 آسِف sorry, regretful

4120 ناجِم a.p. originating, resulting from (عن)

4122 رامِي aimed (إلى at); n. archer

4128 أُسَرِيّ family, domestic

4130 إلهِيّ divine, holy; theological

4135 غَزِير abundant, plentiful; substantial

4142 مُحَمَّل loaded, burdened, charged

4150 مَخْلُوق created; n. pl. -aat creature

4159 فاسِد spoiled, rotten; corrupt, immoral

4164 بُنِّيّ brown

4169 مُنْكَر reprehensible; n. vice

4175 مَحْض (invar.) pure, mere (fantasy)

4185 مَدْعُوم supported, bolstered, promoted

4186 أمامِيّ front, forward

4203 جَوْهَرِيّ essential; core, central

4204 حُدُودِيّ frontier, border

4209 مُشار المُشار إليه/إليها p.p. the aforementioned

4211 رُومِيّ n./adj. pl. رُوم Byzantine

4215 ناشِئ growing; resulting from

4221 مُبِين plain, clear, obvious

4232 خَلْفِيّ back, rear, end; background

4233 مُرَتَّب organized; regulated; n. salary

4234 حَيَوانِيّ animal, animal-like, zoological

4236 جاهِل ignorant; (Irq.Yem.Gul.) child

4246 جَبّار mighty, powerful; huge, gigantic

4248 تِلْقائِيّ automatic; تِلْقائِياً automatically

4258 راغِب (person) wanting, desiring (في sth)

4261 مُسْتَجِدّ new; n. مُسْتَجِدّات recent events

4264 بَدَنِيّ bodily, physical

4268 ضاحِك laughing

4269 تارِك leaving (behind), quitting

4271 ساكِن motionless

4273 سائِل asking; requesting; n. beggar

4279 مُتَرَتِّب derived (على from)

4284 شَغّال busy, occupied; in operation

4285 مُبْتَسِم smiling

4287 مُهَدَّد threatened; in danger, at risk

4288 عَلْمانِيّ secular

4292 سَماوِيّ heavenly, celestial

4307 أثَرِيّ archeological; historical

4314 مُوَزَّع distributed, scattered (على among)

4320 عُثْمانِيّ n./adj. Ottoman

4321 مُتَمَنِّي a.p. wishing, desiring; hoping for

4329 شِمال n./adj. left

4330 عَلَنِيّ public, open

4331 هُولَنْدِيّ/هُولانْدِيّ n./adj. Dutch

4338 صارِم severe, strict; ruthless

4339 مَبْذُول exerted; n. expenditure; effort

4354 داجِن pl. دَواجِن domesticated

4370 غارِق drowned; engrossed في in

4374 باكٍ weeping; mourning

4378 جَلِيّ clear, evident, obvious

4381 عُلْوِيّ upper, top; superior

4387 ماسّ urgent, pressing; touching

4390 مُتَفاوِت different, diverse

4393 بَدِيع wonderful, magnificent

4398 مُصَمِّم determined; n. designer

4403 مُتَّبَع followed, observed

4410 كَنَدِيّ n./adj. Canadian

4413 مُنَوِّه a.p. pointing out ب/إلى أنّ that

4418 هَنْدَسِيّ engineering; technical

4425 بَصَرِيّ visual; optical

4434 مُقام installed, set up; held, hosted

4435 مُعْرِب a.p. expressing عن (opinion)

4438 فَقِيد n./adj. deceased

4448 مُخَلَّف n. left behind; مُخَلَّفات leftovers

4450 مُجِيب responding; n. person answering

4451 مُضْطَرّ forced, obligated إلى to do sth

4452 أسْمَر fem. سَمْراء, pl. سُمْر brown, tanned

4453 غَبِيّ stupid, ignorant

4456 حَمِيد laudable; positive; (med.) benign

4813 مُتَطَوِّع n./adj. pl. -uun volunteer

4815 مُسْتَعْمَل used, in use, employed

4817 مانِح granting, donating; n. donor

4826 مُجْتَمَعِيّ societal

4827 زَغْلان fem. زَغْلانَة angry (على/من with/at)

4842 سَبْعِينِيّ seventieth; n. السبعينيات the 70s

4854 بَنّاء constructive, positive

4857 تَنافُسِيّ competitive; antagonistic

4861 غَلا (Gul.) dear, precious; n. preciousness

4865 افْتِتاحِيّ opening; introductory

4866 مَغْفُور p.p. لَهُ/لَها المغفور the late, deceased

4869 نَقِيّ pure, clean; undiluted

4870 مُفَدَّى beloved, cherished

4871 مُرَجَّح probable, likely

4883 فِضِّيّ silver

4904 بِتْرُولِيّ petroleum-, oil-based

4916 صُغَيَّر (Egy.) small, young

4921 مُلِيح (Lev.Alg.) good, nice; adv. well

4924 عُضْوِيّ organic

4926 نِقابِيّ union, syndicate

4927 مُتَساوٍ equivalent, similar

4930 مَعْمُور inhabited; n. المَعْمُورَة the world

4935 مِتْجَوِّز (Lev.) married

4942 مُسْتَقِيم straight, correct; righteous

4943 مُشْتاق yearning, longing إلى for sth/sb

4945 عِلاجِيّ therapeutic, healing, curative

4952 مَطْبُوع printed; n. مَطْبُوعات publications

4954 غَلْطان (Dia.) fem. -a wrong, mistaken

4955 صَلِيبِيّ cross-shaped; Crusader

4956 تَوْجِيهِيّ directing, guiding; instructional

4958 مُصاحِب accompanying

4961 مُتَوَجِّه a.p. heading إلى to

4966 مُخْتَلِط mixed, co-ed (schools); hybrid

4971 مُتَفائِل optimistic; n. optimist

4976 ناوٍ a.p. intending, wanting (to do sth)

4977 عارِم tempestuous, frenzied

4981 بُرْتُغالِيّ n./adj. Portuguese

4983 وَفِيّ loyal, faithful

4989 شاطِر (Dia.) pl. -iin clever; handy; cute

4992 مَتِين firm, solid, strong, unshakable

4993 مُوَقَّع signed, bearing signature

Adverb

77 هُناكَ over there; there is, there are

79 حَيْثُ where; conj. so that

156 بَس (Egy.Lev.Irq.Gul.) only, just

159 هُنا here

237 أَمْس yesterday

317 كَذلِكَ likewise, also

374 رُبَّا/لَرُبَّا perhaps, maybe

378 حَتَّى even, including; even though

530 هٰكَذا like this, this way, thus

532 هيك /heek/, (Lev.) هيج (Irq.) /hiich/ like this

655 إِذَنْ/إِذاً therefore, consequently

715 كَذا thus, like that, in this way

742 شوي /shway/ (Lev.Gul.Irq.) a little bit

768 كَمان (Egy.Lev.) also; كَمان مَرّة once more

789 بَعْدُ afterward; still; (not) yet

1000 كده/كدا /kida/ (Egy.) thus, this way

1032 بعدين /ba9deen/ (Egy.Lev.) later

1245 سِيَّا (لاسِيَّا usu.) especially

1310 مِن ثَمَّ there (is/are); ثَمَّ therefore

1350 ثَمَّة there (is/are)

1369 عاد (Lev.Gul.) so; (Irq.) adv. already

1465 هون /hoon/ (Lev.) here

1703 هلق /halla'/ (Lev.) now

1791 هُنالِكَ over there; there is, there are

1810 بُكْرَة/بُكْرا (Egy.Lev.Gul.) tomorrow

2069 لِسَّه/لِسّا/لِسّة (Egy.Lev.Gul.) yet, still

2480 آنَذاك then, at that time

2651 عَسَى perhaps; (Irq.Gul.) hopefully

2715 برضو/برده /bardo/ (Egy.Lev.) also, too

2849 الحِين (Gul., also دَحِّين and أَحِّين) now

2998 قَطّ (not) at all, never; nothing, noone

3183 إنشالله /'inshaLLa/ (Dia.) hopefully

3240 بَعْد (Lev.Irq.Gul.) still, (not) yet

3466 قُدُماً forwards, forward

3871 هسة/هسه/هسا /hassa/ (Irq.Gul.Lev.) now, right away

3953 عِنْدَئِذ then, at that time

4244 خِصِّيصاً especially, specifically

4297 تِباعاً in succession, consecutively

4311 كُلِّش/كِلِّش (Irq.Gul.) very, a lot

4340 حِينَئِذٍ then, at the time

4454 سَوا/سَوَى (Dia.) together; adj. equal

4481 امبارح/امبيرح (Lev.) yesterday

4590 دلوقتي/دلوقت /dilwa'ti/ (Egy.) now

4615 إزّاي (Egy.) how's come, why

4687 كذي/چذي /chidhi/ (Gul.) thus, this way

4868 قَلَّما rarely, seldom; hardly, barely

4902 باكِر/باچر /baachir/ (Irq.Gul.) tomorrow

4962 البارح /l-bareH/ (Magh.) yesterday

4963 هوايا /hwaaya/ (Irq.) a lot, very much

4969 النهارده /in-nahaar-da/ (Egy.) today

4986 بَلْكِي (Lev.Irq.) maybe, perhaps

Elative

64 أكْثَر more/most, greater/greatest in number

195 أكْبَر fem. كُبْرَى larger/largest; adj. senior

390 أفْضَل better/best

402 أعْلَى fem. عُلْيا higher/highest

446 أقَلّ less/least, lower/lowest; n. minimum

454 أهَمّ more/most important

776 أحْسَن better/best

1183 أجْمَل more/most beautiful

1209 أعْظَم fem. عُظْمَى greater/greatest

1309 أحْلَى sweeter/sweetest

1354 أقْرَب nearer/nearest; n. pl. أقارِب relatives

1557 أبْرَز more/most prominent

1685 أقْوَى stronger/strongest

1792 أدْنَى lower/lowest, nearer/nearest

1798 أشَدّ stronger/strongest

1804 أغْلَب most, majority

1860 أصْغَر fem. صُغْرَى smaller/smallest

2230 أسْرَع faster/fastest; sooner/soonest

2265 أسْوَأ worse/worst

2267 أسْفَل lower/lowest; n. bottom part

2481 أحْدَث newer/newest

2510 أشْبَه more/most similar ب to

2561 أبْعَد farther/farthest

2626 أطْوَل longer/longest; taller/tallest

2724 أوْسَع broader/broadest, wider/widest

2915 أمْثَل fem. مُثْلَى more/most ideal

2966 أرْوَع more/most magnificent

2968 أخْطَر more/most dangerous/serious

2969 أكْمَل more/most complete

3057 أغْلَى more/most expensive

3302 أسْهَل easier/easiest

3316 أصْعَب more/most difficult

3600 أعْلَم more/most knowledgeable

3876 أبْسَط simpler/simplest; more/most basic

4020 أقْدَم older/oldest, more/most ancient

4344 أسْعَد happier/happiest; luckier/luckiest

4407 أعَزّ stronger/strongest; dearer/dearest

4527 أرْحَم more/most merciful

4533 أعْمَق deeper/deepest

4557 أدَقّ more/most accurate, precise (دَقيق)

4596 أرْجَح more/most likely, probable

4627 أسْمَى higher/highest, loftier/loftiest

4628 أصْدَق truer/truest; more/most reliable

4662 أشْهَر more/most famous

4689 أقْسَى harsher/harshest, more/most cruel

4720 أحْرَى : بالأحرى rather, to be more precise

4748 أرْقَى higher/highest; adj. top, finest

4779 أخَصّ more/most specific

4882 أبْلَغ more/most eloquent

4985 أشْرَف nobler/noblest

4999 أضْعَف weaker/weakest

Noun

12 الله God, Allah

19 كُلّ الكُلّ each; every; all (of); everyone

26 يَوْم pl. أيّام day; اليَوْم today

39 شَيْء pl. أشْياء thing, something

42 غَيْر other (than), different (than)

44 نَفْس pl. أنْفُس (with pron.) same, self

46 أيّ fem. أيّة any; which

47 رَئيس pl. رُؤَساء president, leader; chief, head

48 عَمَل vn. working; n. pl. أعْمال work, activity

50 بَعْض some, several

51 دَوْلَة pl. دُوَل state, country

62 عام pl أعْوام year

63 أحَد fem. إحْدَى one (of)

66 أخ brother pl. إخْوَة, إخْوان

69 سَنَة pl. سَنَوات, سِنون year (سِنين gen./acc.)

70 أمْر pl. أمُور matter, issue

71 قُوّة force; pl. قُوَى قُوّات, -aat armed forces

74 مَرَّة pl. -aat, مِرار time, moment, occasion

76 أَب pl. آبَاء father; (in idafa) nom. أَبُو

82 جَمِيع all (of); every one (of); جَمِيعاً all

83 مِنْطَقَة pl. مَنَاطِق region, area, zone, territory

84 حَقّ truth; pl. حُقُوق right; adj. true

86 مِثْل pl. أَمْثَال (someone, something) similar

89 اِسْم pl. أَسْمَاء , أَسَامٍ (def. أَسَامِي) name

92 رَجُل n. man pl. رِجَال

93 عَالَم pl. -uun, عَوَالِم world

94 حَيَاة life

95 مَوْضُوع pl. مَوَاضِيع subject; adj. placed

96 وَزِير vizier وُزَرَاء minister

98 وَقْت pl. أَوْقَات time, moment, period

99 بَلَد pl. بِلاد , بُلْدان country, nation

101 مَجْلِس pl. مَجَالِس council, board

103 حُكُومَة pl. -aat government, administration

104 بَيْت house; pl. بُيُوت أَبْيَات verse

110 قَلْب pl. قُلُوب heart; vn. toppling

114 نَاس pl.n. (also fem.sg.) people; persons

115 طَرِيق fem./masc.n. pl. طُرُق , طُرُقَات road; way

116 أَرْض fem.n. pl. أَرَاضِي earth; land

117 سَبَب pl. أَسْبَاب reason; بِسَبَب because of

118 شَرِكَة pl. -aat company, corporation

119 عَدَد pl. أَعْدَاد number; issue, edition

120 صُورَة pl. صُوَر picture, photo; manner, way

122 شَعْب pl. شُعُوب people, nation

125 آن time, moment; الآنَ now

128 أَهْل coll.n. pl. أَهَالٍ family; people

130 عَيْن fem.n. pl. أَعْيُن , عُيُون eye; water spring

132 شَكْل pl. أَشْكَال manner; shape; look

133 عَمَلِيَّة pl. -aat operation, process

140 خَيْر goodness, good; adj. better مِن than

144 مَدِينَة pl. مُدُن city

145 اِبْن pl. أَبْنَاء son; children

146 أَيْض : أَيْضاً also; besides

148 يَد fem.n. pl. أَيْدٍ (def. أَيْدِي) hand

150 مَشْرُوع pl. -aat, مَشَارِيع project; adj. lawful

152 صَوْت pl. أَصْوات voice, sound; vote

153 أَمَام front; أَمَامَ in front of

155 نِسْبَة pl. نِسَب ratio, rate, percentage figure

157 حَال (rare as fem.) pl. أَحْوَال situation

158 شَهْر pl. شُهُور , أَشْهُر month

161 بَرْنامَج pl. بَرامِج program

163 أُمّ pl. أُمَّهَات mother

165 حَرْب fem.n. pl. حُرُوب war, warfare

167 وَضْع vn. laying down; n. pl. أَوْضَاع situation

169 دَوْر pl. أَدْوار role; floor; round; turn

170 وَجْه pl. وُجُوه , أَوْجُه face; pl. aspect

171 جِدّ seriousness; جِدّاً very much

173 كَلِمَة pl. -aat word; remark; speech

174 طِفْل child; fem. طِفْلَة girl, pl. أَطْفَال children

179 مَكَان pl. أَمْكِنَة , أَماكِن place; position

181 مُشْكِلَة pl. -aat, مَشَاكِل problem, issue

185 سَاعَة pl. -aat hour, time; watch

186 شَيْخ pl. شُيُوخ , مَشَايِخ sheikh, elder

188 سَلام peace; pl. -aat greeting, salute

189 سَيِّد pl. سَادَة Sir, Mr; lord, master, boss

190 صَاحِب pl. أَصْحاب owner; originator; friend

191 عَدَم (in idafa) absence of, lack of; non-, not

193 حَرَكَة pl. -aat movement, activity

194 رَبّ pl. أَرْباب lord, master; owner

196 كِتَاب pl. كُتُب book

197 حَدّ pl. حُدُود extent, limit; edge; حُدُود border

199 نِظَام pl. نُظُم , أَنْظِمَة regime; system

200 ذات fem.n. pl. ذَوَات ego; same, -self

202 قَضِيَّة pl. قَضَايا problem, issue; lawsuit

204 إِنْسَان pl. أُنَاس human being

205 حَالَة pl. -aat condition, state; case

207 رَغْم : رَغْمَ and رَغْم/رُغْم despite عَلَى الرَّغْم مِن

208 جَانِب pl. جَوَانِب side; إِلَى جَانِب next to

209 حُبّ love, affection

210 جَامِعَة pl. -aat university; league

211 قَرار pl. -aat decision, resolution

215 رَأْس (Dia. راس) pl. رُؤُوس head; tip

216 تَحْت bottom; تَحْتَ prep. below

217 وِزارَة pl. -aat ministry

218 هَدَف pl. أَهْداف goal, target; objective

219 عَلاقَة pl. -aat relation, link, tie, connection

220 شُكْراً thankfulness; interj. thank you

222 مُجْتَمَع pl. -aat society

223 مَرْكَز pl. مَراكِز center; station; ranking

225 نَتِيجَة pl. نَتائِج result, outcome; consequence

226 أُخْت pl. أَخَوات sister

227 رَأْي pl. آراء opinion, view; idea

228 إِدارَة pl. -aat management; bureau, office

232 قانُون pl. قَوانِين law, statutes, regulations

236 ماء pl. مِياه water; liquid; juice

238 أَمْن security; order, control

241 شَخْص pl. أَشْخاص person, individual

242 كَلام speech, talk; remark; saying

243 مَوْقِع pl. مَواقِع position, site; website

246 داخِل interior; داخِلَ prep. inside (of)

247 وَحْدَة unity; solitude; pl. -aat unit, item

248 أُمَّة pl. أُمَم nation; people

251 سَيّارَة pl. -aat car, automobile, vehicle

252 بِنْت pl. بَنات daughter, girl

253 دُكْتُور pl. دَكاتِرَة doctor (physician, PhD)

254 فِعْل vn. doing; n. pl. أَفْعال act, action

256 فَرِيق team, group, band; faction, party

258 لَجْنَة pl. لِجان committee, commission

261 نَظَر vn. looking إلى at; n. pl. أَنْظار view; opinion

262 مَجال pl. -aat area; domain; sector; arena

263 فَتْرَة pl. فَتَرات time period, phase, interval

265 شَأْن pl. شُؤُون matter case; situation

267 سُؤال pl. أَسْئِلَة question, inquiry

268 وُجُود existence; presence, being present

269 حَلّ vn. solving; n. pl. حُلُول solution

270 طالِب pl. طُلّاب , طَلَبَة student

271 مُسْتَوًى pl. مُسْتَوَيات level, standard

276 وِلايَة mandate, term of office; pl. -aat state

278 عُضْو pl. أَعْضاء member, associate; organ

281 عُمْر pl. أَعْمار age (of a person); life, lifetime

285 خَبَر : أَخْبار news, report; الأَخْبار the news

286 تارِيخ date; history

287 دِراسَة pl. -aat study, research, examination

288 مَوْقِف pl. مَواقِف position

289 حِزْب pl. أَحْزاب (political) party

290 مُؤَسَّسَة pl. -aat institution

292 قِطاع pl. -aat sector, section

293 مَجْمُوعَة pl. -aat collection, group

295 سُوق fem.n. (rarely masc.) pl. أَسْواق market

296 حَمْد praise; الحَمْدُ لله praise God!

298 باب pl. أَبْواب door; category; chapter

300 مِنْ أَجْلِ : أَجْل because of

301 اتِّحاد vn. unification, unifying; n. pl. -aat union

302 تَحْقِيق vn. and n. pl. -aat achievement

303 مَدْرَسَة pl. مَدارِس school

305 نَوْع pl. أَنْواع type, kind, form

307 خِدْمَة pl. خَدَمات service; (Magh.) work

311 حُكْم government; pl. أَحْكام verdict

313 جِهَة pl. -aat side; direction; sector; entity

320 قَوْل pl. أَقْوال statement; saying

321 مَرْأَة woman, wife; (without def. article) اِمْرَأَة

322 حَقِيقَة pl. حَقائِق truth, reality; fact

327 مُواطِن pl. -uun citizen; fellow citizen

328 سُلْطَة pl. سُلْطات power, authority

332 بَحْث pl. بُحُوث , أَبْحاث search (for عن)

333 دِين pl. أَدْيان religion

337 جَيْش pl. جُيُوش army; armed forces; troops

338 جِهاز pl. أَجْهِزَة apparatus; appliance; agency

339 مُشارَكَة pl. -aat participation, association

340 طَبْع nature, character; طَبْعاً of course

348 فَوْق top, upper part; فَوْق above, over

349 خارِج outside, exterior; بِالخارِج overseas

350 مَثَل pl. أَمْثال example; proverb

351 رَقْم number, numeral, figure; rate; record

352 ضِدَّ opposite; ضِدَّ prep. against

354 مَسْؤُول/مَسْئُول official; adj. responsible

358 حِين pl. أَحْيان time; أَحْياناً sometimes

360 نائِب pl. نُوَّاب deputy, delegate; vice-

361 خاصَّةً : خاصَّة especially

362 وَلَد pl. أَوْلاد (Egy.) وِلاد), child, son, boy

363 دَم pl. دِماء blood; (Dia.) دَم

365 إسْلام Islam

366 مَرْحَلَة pl. مَراحِل phase; (sports) round

369 حَدِيث pl. أحادِيث discussion; interview

370 سِياسَة politics; pl. -aat policy

371 طَرَف pl. أطْراف edge; tip; extremity

373 وَطَن pl. أَوْطان nation, homeland

379 مُدِير director, manager; (office) boss, chief

380 نِهايَة end, finish; termination, ending

382 إضافَة addition; بِالإضافَة إلى in addition to

383 واقِع reality, fact; adj. located, situated

386 شَرْق east; شَرْقاً eastward, in the East

388 تَعْلِيم pl. -aat, تَعالِيم education, teaching

389 رُوح fem./masc.n. pl. أَرْواح spirit, soul; life

391 مال money; pl. أَمْوال money; رَأْس مال capital

392 لَيْل night, night-time; لَيْلاً by night

393 أُسْبُوع pl. أَسابِيع week

394 مُؤْتَمَر pl. -aat conference

395 لِقاء pl. -aat meeting, encounter; interview

398 صَدِيق pl. أَصْدِقاء friend

399 دُولار pl. -aat dollar

400 بِناء vn. constructing; n. building

401 طَرِيقَة method, procedure, way

404 دَعْم support, assistance, promotion

407 مَصْدَر pl. مَصادِر source

409 لَحْظَة pl. لَحَظات moment, instant

410 فُرْصَة pl. فُرَص chance, opportunity

411 نادِي pl. أَنْدِيَة club, association

412 مَعْلُومَة item of information; pl. مَعْلُومات data

413 هَيْئَة pl. -aat agency; appearance, look

414 قِصَّة pl. قِصَص story, tale

415 بِدايَة pl. -aat beginning, start

416 جَنُوب south; جَنُوباً southward

419 مُباراة pl. مُبارَيات game; competition

423 حَسَب : حَسَب/بِحَسَب according to

424 دَقِيقَة pl. دَقائِق minute

425 مَلِك pl. مُلُوك king; الَمَلِك (title) King

427 قِيمَة pl. قِيَم value, worth; morals, ethics

428 لاعِب pl. -uun player, athlete; a.p. playing

430 مادَّة pl. مَوادّ substance; subject; paragraph

431 خَطّ pl. خُطُوط line; airline; writing

432 عَرْض pl. عُرُوض display; offer; width

433 رِسالَة pl. رَسائِل letter; thesis; pl. -aat mission

434 إنْتِخاب pl. -aat election; selection

436 مَعْنىً pl. مَعانٍ sense, meaning, significance

437 نُقْطَة pl. نِقاط point, dot; location, position

439 حِوار pl. -aat discussion, dialog, talk

440 رَدّ pl. رُدُود response, reply; رَدّ فِعْل reaction

441 لُغَة pl. -aat language

444 سِعْر pl. أَسْعار price, cost, rate

449 صَباح morning; صَباحاً in the morning

452 مَرَض pl. أَمْراض illness, disease

455 بُدّ avoidance, escape

458 صِحَّة health, wellness; authenticity, truth

463 تَعاوُن cooperation

464 زَوْج pl. أَزْواج spouse; husband

467 شارِع pl. شَوارِع street; (fig.) الشارِع the public

468 نار fem.n. pl. نِيران fire; gunfire; hellfire

469 عَدِيد large quantity; adj. numerous

471 فِكْرَة idea, concept, notion (عن about)

473 دَرَجَة pl. -aat degree, grade, level; class, rank

475 إجْتِماع pl. -aat meeting

477 وَسَط pl. أَوْساط middle, center

601 نَشاط pl. -aat, أَنْشِطَة activity, action

606 قُدْرَة pl. -aat, قُدُرات capacity, ability

607 نِصْف half, middle, semi-

608 صَراحَة sincerity, candor; بِصَراحَة frankly

609 جَماعَة pl. -aat group, party; gang

610 مَعْرِفَة vn. knowing; n. pl. مَعارِف knowledge

612 مُواجَهَة vn. facing; n. pl. -aat confrontation

616 بُطُولَة heroism; pl. -aat championship

617 نَجاح pl. -aat success

618 شُرْطَة police

620 تَنْمِيَة development, growth; progress

621 حاجَة pl. -aat need, want; wish; goal

623 تَطْوِير development, advancement

624 شَمال north; adj. northern

625 بَنْك pl. بُنُوك bank (fin.)

626 فَرْد pl. أَفْراد individual, person

627 قَدَم fem.n. pl. أَقْدام foot

628 عامِل pl. -uun employee; staff

630 قاعِدَة pl. قَواعِد rule; (military) base

635 صَلاة pl. صَلَوات prayer

636 شاعِر pl. شُعَراء poet

637 حُلْم pl. أَحْلام dream

638 وُصُول arrival; attainment, achievement

640 سُرْعَة speed; بِسرعة quickly

642 مَساء evening

643 عُنْوان pl. عَناوين address; title, headline

644 طَبِيب pl. أَطِبّاء physician, doctor

645 اِسْتِخْدام usage, using, utilization

646 عَقْل pl. عُقُول mind, intellect

647 عِيد pl. أَعْياد holiday, festival, feast

648 أَمَل pl. آمال hope, wish

649 خارِجِيّة foreign ministry, foreign office

651 قِيام vn. carrying out ب (task)

654 جُنْدِيّ pl. جُنُود soldier

656 اِتِّفاق pl. -aat agreement; accord, treaty

657 نُور pl. أَنْوار light; lamp

660 مُحافَظَة pl. -aat province, governorate

663 ظَرْف pl. ظُرُوف condition, situation

664 أُسْرَة pl. أُسَر family, community

665 قَرْيَة pl. قُرىً village

666 مُقابِل opposite (to), corresponding (to)

667 جَوّ pl. أَجْواء air; weather, climate

668 وِكالَة/وَكالَة pl. -aat agency; proxy

669 حاجَة pl. -aat thing; (Magh.) حوايج clothes

670 خُطَّة pl. خُطَط/خِطَط , خِطَط , خُطَط plan, project

675 أَزْمَة pl. أَزْمات crisis, crunch

677 مَمْلَكَة kingdom

678 إِطْلاق releasing; shooting; إِطْلاقاً (not) at all

680 مُحاوَلَة pl. -aat attempt, effort

683 قِسْم pl. أَقْسام section; department

684 تَحْدِيد specification; definition

685 خَلْف back, rear part; خَلْفَ prep. behind

686 شَمْس fem.n. sun

687 مَزِيد addition, added amount; additional

690 اِهْتِمام interest, attention; care, concern

692 مُساعَدَة pl. -aat help, support; مساعدات aid

693 كافَّة all of; كافَّةً all together

694 عَبْد pl. عَبِيد servant, slave

695 غَرْب west; West; غَرْباً westward, in the West

696 عاصِمَة pl. عَواصِم capital city

697 إِطار framework, context

700 حُضُور vn. arrival; attending; viewing

701 مَحَلّ pl. -aat, مَحالّ place, location; shop, store

703 تَنْظِيم vn. organizing; n. pl. -aat organization

704 رياضَة sports; physical education; math

705 فَضْل favor; kindness; merit; بِفَضْل due to

709 شَخْصِيَّة pl. -aat personality; individual

710 أَمِين pl. أُمَناء trustee; adj. loyal

711 مُسْتَشْفىً pl. مُسْتَشْفَيات hospital

713 طُول length; height; طُولَ throughout

716 طاقَة energy, power; potential, ability

719 كاتِب pl. كُتّاب author; pl. كَتَبَة clerk

724 جُمْهُور pl. جَماهِير multitude, masses

728 سَماء pl. سَماوات , سَمَوات sky, heaven

731 جَهْد/جُهْد pl. جُهُود effort; endeavor

732 شَهِيد pl. شُهَداء martyr

734 عادَة pl. -aat habit, practice; عادَةً usually

735 ضَغْط vn. pressing; n. pl.
ضُغُوط pressure

736 سَهْم pl. أَسْهُم (econ.) share;
pl. سِهام arrow

737 زَمان time, period; مِن زَمانٍ
a long time ago

738 مَسْألَة pl. مَسائِل issue, affair;
matter, question

739 كَوْن vn. being; n. الكَوْن the
universe

740 جَرِيمَة pl. جَرائِم crime

741 إِرْهاب terrorism;
vn. terrorizing

743 قَدْر extent; amount, value;
ability, capacity

745 جِسْم pl. أَجْسام body; form,
mass; organism

746 حِساب pl. -aat calculation;
account

748 ساكِن pl. سُكّان resident,
inhabitant

749 شُغْل pl. أَشْغال work, labor;
occupation

750 عِلاج treatment, therapy

752 إِقامَة residency; setting up,
establishing

753 سَعادَة happiness; (honorific)
His Excellency

757 حِمايَة protection, protecting

758 اِعْتِبار vn. regarding; n. pl. -aat
consideration

759 تَقَدُّم progress; vn. coming
forward

762 شَبَكَة pl. -aat, شِباك net; web,
network

764 زَواج marriage; wedding

770 عَمّ pl. عُمُوم paternal uncle

771 بال mind, attention

773 ذُو pl. أُولُو، ذَوُو، fem. ذات، pl.
ذَوات having

775 غَد tomorrow; غَدًا
tomorrow

777 مِلَفّ/مَلَفّ pl. -aat file;
dossier

778 حَجْم volume, size

779 شَرْط pl. شُرُوط precondition,
stipulation

781 وَفْقَ : and وِفْقًا لِ
according to

782 عُنْصُر pl. عَناصِر factor; (pl.)
individuals

783 مُناسَبَة pl. -aat occasion,
opportunity

786 صَدْر pl. صُدُور chest;
bosom

788 فَوْز victory

790 سِجْن pl. سُجُون prison

791 فَتاة pl. فَتَيات young woman,
girl

792 سِرّ pl. أَسْرار secret; أَمِين السِّرّ
secretary

794 مَسْؤُولِيَّة/مَسْئُولِيَّة pl. -aat
responsibility, duty

796 نَشْر spreading, propagation;
publication

797 صِناعَة industry; pl. -aat trade,
craft

798 قِمَّة pl. قِمَم summit

801 ناحِيَة pl. نَواحٍ side,
perspective; area, region

803 اِسْتِثْمار vn. investing; n. pl. -aat
investment

805 نَفْس fem.n. pl. نُفُوس soul,
spirit

806 اِسْتِمْرار continuation,
continuity

810 إِمارَة pl. -aat Emirate

811 خَطَأ pl. أَخْطاء mistake; adj.
(invar.) wrong

812 تَحِيَّة pl. -aat, تَحايا greeting,
salute, salutation

813 نَبِيّ pl. أَنْبِياء prophet

814 تَطَوُّر pl. -aat progress; تَطَوُّرات
events

816 إِصابَة illness; pl. -aat casualty;
score

817 فَنّ pl. فُنُون art; specialty; type,
variety

818 قَتْل murder, killing

820 مُهِمَّة/مَهَمَّة pl. -aat, مَهامّ task,
mission

821 حُزْن pl. أَحْزان sadness, grief;
anguish

822 مَرِيض pl. مَرْضَى patient; adj.
ill, sick

824 جُمْهُورِيَّة republic

828 حاكِم pl. حُكّام ruler; adj.
ruling

829 تَرْبِيَة education; child-rearing;
breeding

830 جَبَل pl. جِبال mountain

832 جَلْسَة pl. جَلَسات session,
meeting

833 حَيّ pl. أَحْياء quarter, district

835 عافِيَة good health, vigor

837 القُرْآن the Qurʾan

838 أُغْنِيَة/أُغْنِيَّة pl. أَغانٍ، أُغْنِيات
song, melody

840 كَأْس/كاس pl. كُؤُوس cup;
Cup (prize)

841 مُعْظَم (in idafa) most of, the
majority of

842 شَكّ pl. شُكُوك doubt

843 لَعْب vn. playing; n. pl. أَلْعاب
game

844 قَناة pl. قَنَوات canal; channel
(broadcasting)

845 إِنْتاج production, output

846 حُصُول vn. obtaining;
occurring

848 رَفْع raising, lifting; increasing,
boosting

850 عائِلَة pl. -aat family,
household, clan

852 مَسْجِد pl. مَساجِد mosque

855 سَلامَة security, safety; integrity

856 ماليّة finance

857 اتِّجاه pl. -aat direction; course; trend

859 صَمْت silence

862 خَوْف fear; خَوْفاً for fear (مِن of)

863 ضَوْء pl. أضواء light, lamp

864 بَدَل instead of : بَدَلاً مِن

866 دائِرة pl. دَوائِر bureau; district; circle

867 رِئاسَة presidency, leadership, direction

868 ارْتِفاع rise, increase; height, elevation

869 عالِم pl. عُلَماء scientist, scholar; a.p. knowing

871 بَطَل pl. أبْطال hero; champion; star

872 خُروج departure; exit; deviation (عن from)

873 إعْلان vn. declaring; n. pl. -aat announcement

876 ظِلّ pl. ظِلال shade; patronage

879 ساحَة pl. -aat scene; field, arena

880 عَصْر pl. عُصُور age, period, time, epoch

882 فِرْقة pl. فِرَق group, team; band; squad

883 قَرْن pl. قُرون century, age; horn

885 رُؤْية vision, sight; view; perspective

886 تِجارة commerce, business

888 تَصْريح pl. -aat declaration, statement

889 وَقْف /waqf/ vn. stopping, ceasing; n. pl. أوْقاف

890 صِراع pl. -aat struggle, conflict, fight

891 تَعامُل pl. -aat working (مع with)

892 عَهْد pl. عُهود age; tenure; treaty; oath

893 كُلِّيّة pl. -aat college; entirety, totality

894 ثِقة confidence, trust

895 ضَبْط adjusting; regulating; seizure

899 مُعَلِّم pl. -uun teacher; master; boss

901 عُنْف violence, force

902 طَبيعة nature; normal, natural (state)

904 عِبارة pl. -aat expression; phrase, word

905 صَفّ pl. صُفوف row, rank; classroom

906 تَحْرير liberation; editorship, editing

909 سُمُوّ loftiness; His/Her Highness

910 فَتْح opening; beginning; conquest

911 خَطَر pl. أخْطار danger; risk; alarm (signal)

913 تَقْريب approximation; تَقْريباً approximately

914 نَصّ pl. نُصوص text; wording

915 مُوَظَّف pl. -uun employee

916 صَفْحة pl. صَفَحات page; leaf

917 مُسَلَّح pl. -uun gunman; adj. armed

918 حَمْلة pl. حَمَلات campaign; attack, raid

922 تَدْريب vn. training; n. pl. -aat exercise

923 قِراءة reading; recitation; interpretation

925 فَنّان fem. -a, pl. -uun artist

928 بَقِيّة pl. بَقايا remainder; end

929 ألَم pl. آلام pain, hurt; suffering

930 نَوْم sleep

934 دَليل pl. دَلائِل , أدِلّة sign, clue; pl. أدِلّة guide

935 رَغْبة pl. رَغَبات wish, desire

941 مَحَطّة pl. -aat station; stop, layover

945 إصْلاح pl. -aat reform, restoration

946 أداء performance; rendering; fulfillment

947 شَعْر coll.n. hair, un.n. شَعْرة, pl. شُعور

948 نَفْط/نِفْط petroleum, (mineral) oil

949 صالِح advantage; adj. suitable; pious

950 سُلْطان Sultan; power, authority (على over)

955 جُمْعة (يَوْم) الجُمْعة Friday

956 شَهادة pl. -aat certificate; testimony

958 خِلاف pl. -aat dispute; disagreement

959 اخْتِيار choice, selection; election; preference

960 ذِكْرى pl. ذِكْرَيات memory; anniversary

962 مَبْلَغ pl. مَبالِغ amount; extent; scope

963 جَسَد pl. أجْساد body

966 كِتابة pl. -aat writing; script; essay

967 إنْشاء vn. establishing, setting up, founding

968 سَيِّدة pl. -aat lady

969 اقْتِصاد economy; saving

970 مَعْرَكة pl. مَعارِك battle, campaign

972 رَحْمة mercy, compassion

973 طائِرة pl. -aat aircraft, airplane

975 دَمْع coll.n. tears, un.n. دَمْعة, pl. دُموع

977 قُرْب proximity, nearness;
بالقُرْبِ مِن near

978 مَوْسِم pl. مَواسِم season,
festival

980 نَهار daytime, day; نَهاراً by day

984 جَنَّة pl. جَنّات, جِنان paradise;
garden

986 تَطْبيق implementation (of a
plan)

988 مُمارَسة vn. practice, pursuit;
n. pl. -aat activity

990 وَفْد pl. وُفود delegation

992 تَقْدير vn. appreciation;
n. pl. -aat estimate

993 خَليج gulf

994 نَظْرة pl. -aat look, glance, view

995 عَكْس opposite, reverse,
contrary

996 قَصيدة pl. قَصائد poem, ode

997 اِسْتِقْرار stability; setting down

998 تَشْكيل formation,
composition, constitution

1001 شَجَر coll.n. trees, un.n. شَجَرة,
pl. أَشْجار

1002 ذِكْر mention, citation;
memory

1003 ديمُقراطِيّة/ديمُقراطِيّة
democracy

1005 مَوْعِد pl. مَواعِد appointed
time; deadline

1008 ضابط pl. ضُبّاط officer;
pl. ضَوابِط controller

1009 رِحْلة pl. -aat trip, excursion;
career

1010 مَعْرِض pl. مَعارِض exhibit,
exhibition, show

1011 جُرْح pl. جِراح, جُروح wound,
injury

1014 تَوْفير fulfillment; saving (time)

1015 سَفير pl. سُفَراء ambassador

1016 كمبيوتر/كومبيوتر
/kumbyuutar/ computer

1017 أُسْلوب pl. أَساليب style,
manner; method

1018 دَوْرِيّ pl. -aat tournament;
adj. regular

1019 نَجْم pl. نُجوم star,
constellation; celebrity

1020 تَأْثير pl. -aat effect, impression
(on في/على)

1021 قَلَم pl. أَقْلام pencil, pen;
بقَلَم written by

1022 مَقال/مَقالة pl. -aat article,
essay

1023 بَدْء start, beginning

1026 لِسان pl. أَلْسِنة tongue;
language

1027 سَفَر vn. traveling; n. journey,
trip

1028 غاية utmost, extreme; pl. -aat
goal

1031 ثَوْرة revolution, uprising

1033 تَأْكيد confirmation; certainty

1036 دينار pl. دَنانير dinar

1037 إشارة vn. mentioning;
n. pl. -aat sign

1039 بيئة environment; milieu

1040 مُسابَقة pl. -aat contest,
competition; race

1041 رِعاية custody; patronage;
(social) welfare

1044 اِحْترام respect, honor

1048 فَجْر dawn

1051 طَعام pl. أَطْعِمة food

1052 اِمْرَأة woman; (with def. article)
المَرْأة

1057 ظاهِرة pl. ظَواهِر phenomenon

1059 سُبْحان praise; سُبْحانَ الله
praise God!

1062 تَعْبير vn. expressing;
n. expression

1065 تَفْكير thinking, reflection

1067 تلفزيون/تليفزيون /tilfizyoon/
television

1068 بَشَر coll.n. humankind,
humans

1069 صُنْدوق pl. صَناديق box;
treasury; trunk

1074 ريال riyal (currency)

1076 مُشارِك participant; adj.
participating

1077 مُتابَعة pursuing, following;
continuation

1078 بَيْع sale; selling

1080 نَحْو way, method; pl. أَنْحاء
areas, regions

1081 قَمَر pl. أَقْمار moon; قَمَر صِناعِيّ
satellite

1083 سِنّ age (of a person)

1086 جائِزة pl. جَوائِز prize, award,
reward

1090 قَضاء justice; court; district;
judgment; fate

1091 حَضْرة (polite term of address)
حضرتك you

1093 صِفْر pl. أَصْفار zero; adj.
empty

1096 خَلْق vn. creating, forming; n.
creation

1098 قائِمة pl. قَوائِم list, index; قَوائِم
legs (chair)

1099 مَبْدَأ pl. مَبادِئ principle, basis

1101 ثَمَن price, cost; value, worth

1102 إمام prayer leader; Imam

1103 جيل pl. أَجْيال generation, age

1104 مَشْعَر pl. مَشاعِر feeling, sense,
emotion

1105 مُبادَرة pl. -aat initiative;
proposal

1111 شُعور feeling, sentiment,
awareness

1112 تَفْصيل pl. تَفاصيل detail,
elaboration

1113 إعْداد vn. preparation

1115 خَميس (يَوْم) الخَميس Thursday

1116 أَسَف regret; pity, sympathy

1118 عَقْد vn. holding, convening (meeting)

1121 صَيْف summer

1122 مُعَدَّل pl. -aat average; adj. amended

1123 خَسَارَة pl. خَسَائِر failure; casualty

1124 فائِدَة pl. فَوائِد benefit, usefulness

1125 خِبْرَة pl. -aat, خِبَرات experience, expertise

1126 صِفَة pl. -aat feature; trait

1127 مَشْهَد pl. مَشَاهِد scene, view, spectacle, sight

1129 تَحَدّ pl. -aat challenge

1131 جِدَار pl. جُدْران wall

1132 مَجَلَّة pl. -aat magazine, journal

1133 هُجُوم attack, assault; charge, raid

1134 مُهَنْدِس engineer, technician

1137 مِسَاحَة pl. -aat surface; space; land, terrain

1141 تَعْدِيل pl. -aat adjustment; amendment

1142 نُمُوّ development, growth; progress

1143 حَرْف pl. حُرُوف letter (of the alphabet)

1146 فَجْأَة surprise; فَجْأَةً/فُجْأَةً suddenly

1148 سَبْت (يَوْم) السَّبْت Saturday

1150 مُبَاشَرَة pursuit; directly

1151 بَنُو pl.n. (sg. اِبْن cf. اِبْن) sons, children

1152 مَنْع prohibition; depriving

1155 حاجّ fem. حاجّة pl. حُجّاج pilgrim

1157 وَظِيفَة pl. وَظائِف job, position; work; task

1160 عامِل pl. عَوامِل factor, element, agent

1163 صَبْر patience, endurance

1164 ضَحِيَّة pl. ضَحايا victim

1165 غَضَب anger, rage; غَضَباً in anger, angrily

1167 إِنْجاز vn. implementation; n. achievement

1169 جَمال beauty

1171 فِئَة pl. -aat faction, party; group, sector

1173 زَعِيم pl. زُعَماء leader, head of state

1174 أَحَد (يَوْم) الأَحَد Sunday

1177 اِسْتِعْداد vn. preparation; n. readiness

1178 دَفْع vn. pushing; compelling; payment

1180 مِثال pl. مُثُل, أَمْثِلَة example, model, ideal

1181 فَرَح joy, happiness; pl. أَفْراح party

1182 رِواية pl. -aat novel, story; report, account

1184 نَهْر pl. أَنْهار river

1185 كَهْرَباء/كَهْرُباء electricity

1188 مَهْرَجان/مِهْرَجان pl. -aat festival

1190 اِنْتِظار vn. waiting, anticipating

1193 نَصْر victory, triumph

1194 تَعْزِيز vn. strengthening; n. reinforcement

1195 أَدَب pl. آداب literature; etiquette

1196 لَعْبَة competition; un.n. game

1197 عَقْد pl. عُقُود contract, agreement

1199 شَرّ evil, malice

1200 مُعَارَضَة opposition, resistance

1201 نَبَأ news item, report; pl. أَنْباء news

1202 عُدْوان aggression, hostility; enmity

1203 خِطاب speech; message, letter

1204 عُمُوم generality, totality, whole

1207 جَوْلَة pl. -aat tour; round; session; patrol

1208 رَفْض rejection, refusal

1210 شِراء buying, purchasing; purchase

1211 مَسْرَح theater, stage

1212 غِياب absence; disappearance

1213 حَلْقَة pl. حَلَقات ring; حَلْقَة/حَلَقَة program, show

1215 فَساد corruption; deterioration

1216 اِتِّفاقِيَّة pl. -aat treaty, accord

1219 هَواء air; climate; عَلَى الهَواء live (broadcast)

1221 قاضٍ (قاضِي def.) pl. قُضاة judge, magistrate

1222 داعٍ reason; n. pl. دُعاة (person) calling

1223 عَدْل justice, fairness

1226 جَدّ grandfather, fem. جَدَّة grandmother

1227 هاتِف pl. هَواتِف telephone

1229 ضُعْف weakness

1231 مَعْهَد pl. مَعاهِد institute, academy, school

1233 طَيْر pl. طُيُور bird

1235 رِيح pl. رِياح wind; odor

1239 دَواء pl. أَدْوِيَة remedy, medication

1240 وِجْهَة/وُجْهَة pl. -aat direction, angle

1241 عُمْق pl. أَعْماق depth, deep, bottom

1243 بَلَدِيَّة pl. -aat municipality, township

1246 ضَمان pl. -aat guarantee, insurance

1249 مُخَيَّم pl. -aat camp; refugee camp

1251 تَوْفِيق success; reconciliation, mediation

1252 صَعِيد pl. أَصْعِدَة level, plane

1253 فَوْر : عَلى الفَوْر and فَوْراً immediately, at once

1254 فَرْض vn. imposing; n. (religious) duty

1255 مُدَرِّب trainer, coach; instructor

1256 حَمْل carrying; pregnancy

1258 كَمِّيَّة pl. -aat quantity, amount

1262 مِتْر pl. أَمْتار meter

1263 سُوء offense; bad, ill; miss-

1267 كَلْب pl. كِلاب dog

1269 قَصْر pl. قُصُور castle, palace

1270 حادِثَة pl. حَوادِث incident, accident

1272 دَرْس vn. studying; n. pl. دُرُوس lesson

1273 اِنْتِهاء finish, completion, conclusion

1276 لَوْحَة pl. -aat painting, picture; panel, board

1278 طَرْح suggestion, proposal; offering, offer

1281 مَقَرّ center, headquarters, main residence

1283 صُعُوبَة pl. -aat difficulty

1287 دُسْتُور constitution

1288 سَيْطَرَة control, dominion

1290 إِذْن permission, authorization

1291 الأَرْبِعاء (يَوْم) أَرْبِعاء Wednesday

1292 أَسِير pl. أَسْرَى prisoner, captive

1296 حِكايَة pl. -aat story, tale, account, narrative

1297 تَسْجِيل registration; recording

1298 تَيّار pl. -aat current, stream

1300 قَبُول reception; acceptance, approval

1302 إِيمان faith, belief (ب in)

1303 حَفْل ceremony, celebration

1304 مَلْعَب pl. مَلاعِب playground; stadium

1306 ذاكِرَة memory (human and computer)

1307 غاز pl. -aat natural gas

1312 هُدُوء calmness, quiet, peace

1314 حَيَوان pl. -aat animal, creature

1316 مُناقَشَة pl. -aat argument, debate

1317 تَوْزِيع distribution (على among)

1319 رُبْع pl. أَرْباع quarter, fourth

1320 تَأْمِين protecting; insuring

1321 خِيار pl. -aat choice; preference

1322 مُعالَجَة vn. treatment; dealing with

1323 نُسْخَة pl. نُسَخ copy, replica

1324 تَعْلِيق vn. commenting; suspending

1325 تَصْمِيم determination; pl. تَصامِيم design

1326 إِله god, deity; God

1327 يَمِين right side; fem.n. right hand; oath

1329 شِعار pl. -aat slogan, motto; emblem

1330 قَصْد intent, purpose, goal

1339 جَرِيدَة pl. جَرائِد newspaper, periodical

1342 اِلْتِزام vn. adhering to; n. commitment

1343 طَوال/طِوالَ : طَوالَ/طِوال throughout

1346 مَنْصِب pl. مَناصِب post, position, office

1347 الاِثْنَيْن (يَوْم) اِثْنَيْن Monday

1349 مَطار pl. -aat airport, airfield

1351 مُشْتَرَك participant; adj. participating

1352 فُنْدُق pl. فَنادِق hotel

1355 اِتِّخاذ adopting, passing (a resolution)

1358 بُعْد pl. أَبْعاد dimension; distance

1361 ضِفَّة pl. ضِفاف shore, bank

1362 اِعْتِماد vn. reliance, dependence على on

1363 حَجَر pl. حِجارَة stone

1365 قَلَق unrest, unease; concern, anxiety

1366 مَسِيرَة march, parade; movement, course

1370 حَرارَة temperature, heat; fever

1372 سَيْر course, motion, march; going, walking

1373 ظَهْر back; rear; deck (ship)

1376 إِيجاد discovery, finding

1377 فَصْل vn. detaching, separating; firing

1379 عَفْو pardon, amnesty; عَفْواً excuse me!

1384 شِدَّة intensity; بِشِدَّة forcefully

1386 اِبْنَة daughter (pl. بَنات, cf. بِنْت)

1388 فَهْم understanding, comprehension

1391 جَواب answer; (Egy.) pl. -aat letter

1394 وَلِيّ pl. أَوْلِياء patron

1396 وادٍ (def. الوادِي) wadi (dry riverbed), valley

1398 غالِب winner; majority; غالِباً mostly

1401 مُقارَنَة comparison

1402 قَوْم people, nation

1404 ظُلْم injustice; ظُلْماً wrongly, unjustly

1406 اِحْتِمال probability, likelihood

1407 نافِذَة pl. نَوافِذ window

1408 عَيْش life, living; (Egy.) bread; (Gul.) rice

1409 إِمْكانِيَّة pl. -aat possibility; capability

1412 حَضارَة pl. -aat civilization; culture

1413 بَرْلَمَان parliament

1414 تَقْنِيَّة pl. -aat technology, technique

1415 جُهْد effort, exertion, strain

1416 وَعْي consciousness; awareness, attention

1417 حَارِس pl. حُرَّاس guard; keeper; goalie

1418 صَحَافَة journalism, press

1422 جُمْلَة pl. جُمَل sentence, clause; group

1423 عَقِب fem.n. pl. أَعْقَاب heel; عَقِبَ after

1425 ظُهْر noon, afternoon

1428 زَمِيل pl. زُمَلَاء colleague, associate

1429 كَيْفِيَّة manner, mode; way; how

1430 نَمُوذَج pl. نَمَاذِج sample; model, example

1431 حَادِث pl. حَوَادِث incident, accident

1433 ثَوْب pl. ثِيَاب robe, tunic; ثِيَاب clothes

1434 بَدِيل pl. بَدَائِل alternative; adj. substitute

1436 آيَة pl. -aat verse (Qurʾan); sign

1437 تَهْدِيد vn. threatening; n. pl. -aat threat

1438 هَدِيَّة pl. هَدَايَا gift, present; هَدِيَّةً as a gift

1440 مُوسِيقَى fem.n. music

1442 نَدْوَة pl. -aat seminar, symposium

1443 جِهَاد jihad (struggle in the way of God)

1444 قَاعَة pl. -aat hall, large room

1445 فَرْق difference, distinction; discrepancy

1446 حِفَاظ vn. guarding; memorizing; n. diaper

1447 جَبْهَة (military, political, weather) front

1448 تَوْقِيع signing; signature

1450 هَمّ pl. هُمُوم worry; anxiety; care, interest

1451 مُكَافَحَة fight, battle, confrontation

1453 حَظّ luck, fortune

1454 ضَيْف pl. ضُيُوف guest, visitor

1456 جِسْر pl. جُسُور bridge; beam, bar

1458 بَلْدَة town, township, community

1461 وَزْن vn. weighing; n. pl. أَوْزَان weight

1463 طَيَرَان aviation, flying; airline

1464 عُقُوبَة pl. -aat penalty, sanction

1467 مُؤَشِّر pl. -aat indicator; measure

1468 مَطَر pl. أَمْطَار rain

1471 جَمْع gathering, assembling

1472 مَقْعَد pl. مَقَاعِد seat; place

1473 مَقْتَل murder, killing

1476 رَاحَة rest, relaxation; palm (of the hand)

1478 فَضَاء space; cosmos; vacant (land)

1481 أُفُق pl. آفَاق horizon; perspective

1482 جُثَّة pl. جُثَث corpse, body

1483 شِبْه semi-, almost, like

1484 شَرَف honor, distinction

1485 هُوِيَّة identity; identity card

1486 بِطَاقَة pl. -aat card; tag; ticket

1487 رُكْن pl. أَرْكَان pillar; (mil.) chief of staff

1489 صَارُوخ pl. صَوَارِيخ missile, rocket

1490 تَحَوُّل pl. -aat change, conversion

1494 أَمَان safety, security

1495 أَكْل vn. eating; n. food, meal

1497 وَصْف description; n. pl. أَوْصَاف trait

1498 مُلَاحَظَة vn. noticing; n. pl. -aat note

1499 لَقَب title; nickname

1500 مَسَافَة pl. -aat distance, interval

1501 فَقْر poverty, lack of; فَقْر الدَم anemia

1502 اِنْتِشَار spreading, diffusion

1504 ثُلَاثَاء (يَوْم) الثُّلَاثَاء Tuesday

1506 تَوَاصُل continuation; mutual contact

1507 ظُهُور appearance, emergence; advent

1508 زِرَاعَة agriculture; transplanting (organ)

1509 غَرَض pl. أَغْرَاض goal, purpose, intent

1510 إِمْكَان pl. -aat capability, ability

1514 وَكِيل representative, agent

1515 آلِيَّة pl. -aat mechanism; vehicle

1516 حِرْص desire, eagerness; concern

1518 لَحْم pl. لُحُوم meat, flesh

1521 جَلَالَة majesty

1522 بِنْيَة/بُنْيَة pl. بِنَى/بُنَى structure; physique

1523 تَحْسِين vn. improving; n. improvement

1524 مَبْنَى pl. مَبَانٍ building; structure

1525 فَم pl. أَفْوَاه mouth

1528 اِمْتِحَان pl. -aat examination, test; trial

1529 طِبّ medicine, medical treatment

1530 مُقَدِّمَة pl. -aat preface; front part

1531 فَرْع pl. فُرُوع branch, department

1653 شاهِد pl. شُهُود witness; *adj.* witnessing

1656 زاوِية pl. زَوايا corner; section; angle

1657 تَصَرُّف pl. -aat behavior, conduct

1658 مُساعِد aide; *adj.* helping, assisting

1659 اِغْتِيال pl. -aat assassination

1660 اِعْتِداء pl. -aat assault, attack, aggression

1661 مَيْدان pl. مَيادِين arena; city square, plaza

1662 تاجِر pl. تُجّار merchant; *adj.* trading

1664 هَجْمة pl. -aat attack, assault; raid, strike

1665 أداة pl. أدَوات tool; appliance

1666 تَدَخُّل intervention, interference

1667 أَمْر pl. أوامِر order, command

1669 واسِطة : بِواسِطة by means of, by using

1670 عَيْب pl. عُيُوب fault; shame, disgrace

1674 اِنْطِلاق start, departure

1676 جُنَيْه pl. -aat pound (currency)

1677 مِعْيار pl. مَعايِير standard, norm; gauge

1678 تَمْوِيل financing, funding, backing

1681 أمانة loyalty; honesty; secretariat

1682 اِخْتِلاف difference, disagreement; conflict

1683 سُكَّر sugar; مَرَض السكر diabetes

1684 تَرْكِيز emphasis, focus (على)

1686 تَناوُل *vn.* dealing with; eating

1687 تَحْوِيل conversion, transfer

1688 حَرَم holy site; (university) campus

1693 صَحْراء desert

1696 إِسْتِراتِيجِيّة pl. -aat strategy

1698 اِنْسِحاب withdrawal; evacuation

1704 مُسَلْسَل pl. -aat serial show, soap opera

1707 كارِثة pl. كَوارِث catastrophe, tragedy

1709 مَلْبَس pl. مَلابِس clothes, dress, attire

1710 قاتِل pl. قَتَلة murderer; *adj.* deadly; fatal

1712 نِيّة pl. نَوايا intention, purpose; desire

1713 شِيعة Shiites; partisans, followers

1714 نَقْص lack; decrease; deficit; deficiency

1716 إِجابة pl. -aat answer, reply, response

1719 سِلْسِلة chain, series

1720 حَدِيد iron

1721 جِوار proximity, vicinity; بِجِوار near

1722 شِتاء winter

1723 حُسْن good, goodness; beauty

1724 ضَرَر pl. أضْرار damage; harm; *n.* evil

1725 سُنّة Sunna (orthodox Islam)

1727 سُلُوك behavior, conduct

1728 سَهْل : أهْلًا وَسَهْلًا *interj.* hello! welcome!

1730 سِينَما cinema

1732 حَفْلة pl. حَفَلات party, ceremony

1733 جَزِيرة pl. جُزُر island; شِبه جَزِيرة peninsula

1735 صِلة pl. -aat link, connection; contact

1736 تَراجُع retreat, backing down/ off; decrease

1740 نَقْد criticism, critique

1743 ثَرْوة pl. ثَرَوات wealth; abundance

1744 حِصار siege, blockade

1745 زَيْت oil (food, mineral)

1747 قِبَل : مِن قِبَل on the part of

1748 إِرْسال *vn.* sending; deploying; *n.* broadcast

1749 كُرْسِيّ pl. كَراسٍ (def. كَراسِي) chair, seat

1750 طَبَقة pl. -aat class, rank; level, layer

1753 تَجاوُز *vn.* surmounting; *n.* -aat violations

1756 تَخْطِيط planning, preparation; sketch

1757 إِرادة desire, will

1758 نِقاش argument, debate

1759 مُتَحَدِّث fem. -a, spokesperson, speaker

1760 هِجْرة emigration; الهِجْرة the Hijrah

1761 دَوام business hours, work schedule

1767 شَقِيق pl. أشِقّاء brother, full brother

1769 مَزْرَع pl. مَزارِع farm, plantation

1770 جَرّاء : مِن جَرّاء and جَرّاءَ as a result of

1771 رائِد pl. رُوّاد pioneer; leader; *adj.* leading

1772 قِلّة scarcity; small number/ amount

1778 راتِب pl. رَواتِب salary, wage, pay

1780 اِفْتِتاح opening, inauguration

1781 سَفِينة pl. سُفُن ship, vessel

1782 اِعْتِقال pl. -aat arrest, detention

1785 أخْذ taking; seizure

1922 تَشْجِيع vn. encouragement, support

1928 بَرَكَة pl. -aat blessing

1930 مِيلاد birthday; birth

1933 نِطاق scope, range, extent

1934 مُعاناة effort; hardship, suffering

1935 تَأَكُّد assurance (مِن of); certainty

1936 تَكْوِين vn. creating; educating; n. structure

1939 قَدَر fate, destiny

1940 تَوَتُّر pl. -aat tension, strain, unrest

1941 دِقَّة accuracy, precision; minuteness

1942 كِيان entity; essence, being; structure

1943 رَبِيع spring (season)

1945 بُكاء crying, weeping

1946 رَصاص lead (metal); coll.n. bullets

1947 تَفاهُم mutual understanding

1949 طُفُولَة childhood, infancy; youth

1951 سَرِير pl. أَسِرَّة bed, couch

1956 مُضِيف host; a.p. adding; adj. hosting

1957 اِسْتِغْلال exploitation, taking advantage

1958 مِيزان pl. مَوازِين weight scales; standard

1959 سائِق pl. -uun chauffeur, driver

1960 مَدْخَل pl. مَداخِل entrance; introduction

1961 مُحاضَرة pl. -aat lecture

1966 تَعَرُّف vn. getting to know على sb

1967 صُبْح morning, daybreak

1970 خاطِر pl. خَواطِر idea, thought; mind; wish

1971 خِتام conclusion, closure, end

1973 مُثَقَّف pl. -uun intellectual; adj. educated

1975 خَيال imagination, fantasy

1978 مُسْتَشار counselor, adviser

1980 جِنْس gender, sex; type, kind

1981 غِذاء pl. أَغْذِية food, nourishment

1984 جَنْب side; جَنْبَ next to

1985 تَجَمُّع pl. -aat gathering, assembly; grouping

1986 فَحْص pl. فُحُوص , فُحُوصات exam

1987 سَعْي endeavor, pursuit; striving

1988 آلَة pl. -aat instrument; machine

1990 رَفِيق pl. رِفاق companion, partner; comrade

1991 تَسْلِيم delivery, handing over; surrender

1992 اِسْتِعْمال use, usage; handling; application

1995 كَشْف revelation, disclosure, report

1996 خُطُورَة importance; seriousness; danger

1997 عِشْرِين twentieth year; العِشْرِينات the 20s

1998 ذَنْب pl. ذُنُوب fault, offense, misdeed

1999 تَفْسِير explanation, commentary; Tafsir

2000 جَناح pl. أَجْنِحَة wing; flank

2001 قِطْعَة parcel (of land), plot, lot

2006 مُعامَلَة pl. -aat treatment, procedure

2008 مَنْح granting, bestowing, awarding

2011 رَقابَة censorship; surveillance; supervision

2012 وِلادَة birth; childbearing, parturition

2013 رَصِيد balance; funds; stock, inventory

2015 رَحِيل departure; death, demise

2019 مَخاطِر pl.n. dangers, perils; adventures

2023 تَقْلِيد pl. تَقالِيد tradition, custom

2024 تَخَلُّص escape, freedom (مِن from)

2027 تَفْعِيل putting into effect, activating

2028 كِيلُو kilo, kilogram; (Dia.) kilometer

2029 اِقْتِراح proposal, suggestion

2031 اِبْتِسامَة smile

2032 اِخْتِبار vn. testing; n. pl. -aat test, experiment

2037 مُقِيم resident; a.p. residing

2038 تَوَصُّل arrival; attainment, achievement

2040 دَخْل income; (Lev.) دَخْلَك! please!

2042 حَدّ (Egy.Lev.) someone, anyone

2043 تَداوُل circulation; alternation; deliberation

2047 وَفاء loyalty; vn. fulfillment

2049 عَمِيل pl. عُمَلاء agent; lackey; client

2051 عَسَل honey

2053 قَبْض arrest, seizure, capture

2056 كَنِيسَة pl. كَنائِس church; temple

2058 في صَدَدِ : in/with regard to

2062 مُؤَلِّف author, composer

2064 قَصْف bombardment, shelling

2065 فَتَى pl. فِتْية young man, adolescent, youth

2068 مُخَطَّط pl. -aat plan; adj. planned; patterned

2070 شاي tea

2071 هَزِيمَة defeat

2072 قِطْعَة pl. قِطَع piece, portion, segment

2075 جَزَاء reward; punishment; penalty

2076 تَجْدِيد renovation, renewal

2078 قِتَال fighting, combat

2079 سِيرَة pl. سِيَر biography; epic

2080 بَطْن stomach; interior; depth

2082 مُسَافِر pl. -uun passenger; a.p. traveling

2083 تَعْرِيف vn. defining; n. definition

2085 كَفَاءَة pl. -aat qualification; talent

2086 لَهْجَة tone, voice; pl. لَهَجَات dialect

2087 نَظَرِيَّة pl. -aat theory

2089 شَفَة pl. شِفَاه lip; edge, ridge, margin

2090 مُشَاهَدَة observation, viewing; inspection

2093 اِسْتِثْنَاء : بِاسْتِثْنَاء with the exception (of)

2094 غَزْو invasion, raid

2095 رَمْل pl. رِمَال sand

2098 بِضْعَة fem. بِضْع some, several

2106 تَقْيِيم evaluation, assessment; rating

2108 إِلْغَاء vn. cancellation; abrogation, repeal

2109 فَرْحَة joy, happiness

2110 نِزَاع conflict, struggle

2111 فِيدِيو /viidiyo, vidyo/ video

2112 تَحَالُف alliance

2113 حُدُوث happening, taking place

2114 إِجَازَة holiday; permit; pass; certificate

2115 تَسْهِيل pl. -aat facilitation, assistance

2116 مَكَانَة position, standing, status, reputation

2117 عَجَب pl. أَعْجَاب admiration, amazement

2118 صَنْع making, building

2119 فَارِق difference; distinctive feature

2120 عُرْس pl. أَعْرَاس wedding

2121 شَرْح explanation, commentary

2123 زَائِر pl. زُوَّار visitor, guest; tourist

2125 تَعْيِين appointing, designating

2127 عَذَاب punishment, torture; pain, suffering

2131 شَتَّى all, many, diverse

2132 وُقُوع occurrence, happening; falling

2133 طَابِع pl. طَوَابِع طَابَع/طَبَع stamp, mark; feature

2134 سَرْطَان cancer

2135 مَثَابَة : بِمَثَابَة virtually, tantamount to

2137 مَرْء man; person; الْمَرْء people

2139 إِعْدَام execution, capital punishment

2140 تَسْوِيَة settlement, solution

2144 غَابَة pl. -aat forest, jungle; (fig.) haze

2145 شَرِيحَة pl. شَرَائِح slice, cross-section; slide

2146 رَبْط vn. connecting, linking; n. connection

2149 عَطَاء vn. giving, offering; n. gift, present

2150 نِقَابَة pl. -aat union, syndicate

2151 مُخَالَفَة pl. -aat infraction; (sports) foul

2153 خُبْز bread

2154 شَرْعِيَّة legitimacy, legality

2155 صَخْر coll.n. rocks, un.n. صَخْرَة, pl. صُخُور

2157 صَدًى pl. أَصْدَاء echo; effect; repercussion

2158 جَمْع pl. جُمُوع crowd, gathering; collection

2159 عَجْز weakness, inability; (econ.) deficit

2160 جِنِرَال (mil.) general; الْجِنِرَال General

2164 نَفَس pl. أَنْفَاس breath

2166 كِذْب lying; deceit

2169 إِزَالَة removal; uninstalling (software)

2172 مَوْجَة pl. -aat wave

2173 خَلْفِيَّة background, history

2174 تَوْسِيع expanding, widening, augmenting

2175 دَوْرِيَّة pl. -aat patrol, squad; periodical

2176 تَسَاؤُل pl. -aat questions, doubts

2178 جِلْد skin; leather

2179 تَعْذِيب torture; punishment

2180 اِنْتِقَال transfer; transition

2182 نِيَابَة عَن : نِيَابَة proxy; on behalf of

2183 اِكْتِشَاف discovery; detection, uncovering

2184 دَافِع pl. دَوَافِع motive; adj. pushing

2186 جَدَل controversy, dispute; debate

2187 جُوع hunger; starvation

2188 سَلَّة basket

2189 مَقَام place, position, rank

2191 تَحَكُّم vn. control (فِي of)

2195 نُصّ (Dia.) half, middle, semi-

2196 مُدَرِّس teacher, instructor

2199 سَاحِل pl. سَوَاحِل coast, seashore, beach

2201 قَارِئ pl. قُرَّاء reader; Qur'anic reciter

2206 صَدَاقَة friendship

2208 مَسْرَحِيَّة play (theater)

2209 تَكْلِيف vn. charging, entrusting sb ب with

2210 بَساطَة simplicity; بِبَساطَة simply

2211 فَيْرُوس/فِيرُوس pl. -aat virus

2212 غِناء singing

2215 إعْطاء vn. giving, donating; n. offer, donation

2216 غالِبيَّة majority

2218 مَقْهَى pl. مَقاهٍ (def. مَقاهِي) café, coffeehouse

2219 مُحادَثَة pl. -aat discussion, talk; negotiation

2220 شاطِئ pl. شَواطِئ shore, coast, beach

2222 واقِعَة pl. وَقائِع incident, event

2225 مَوْلًى master, lord, patron

2226 مُكالَمَة pl. -aat discussion; (phone) call

2228 تَرْجَمة translation; biography

2229 تَوْقيت (standard) time; timing

2233 اِحْتِياج pl. -aat need, requirement

2234 حِذْر/حَذَر care, caution, vigilance

2237 تَعْويض pl. -aat restitution

2238 سُورَة pl. سُوَر Surah (Qurʾanic chapter)

2239 عَشاء dinner, supper, evening meal

2240 قَضاء vn. extermination على of

2242 بَرْد cold, coldness

2243 مُلْتَقًى meeting place; forum, conference

2244 صيغَة pl. صِيَغ form, shape; formula

2247 فَشَل failure

2248 بَنْد pl. بُنود article, clause

2252 سَلْطَنَة sultanate

2253 عَقْد pl. عُقود decade

2254 يَأْس despair, hopelessness

2255 مَصْرَف pl. مَصارِف bank

2262 مَأْساة pl. مَآسٍ tragedy

2263 مُسْتَثْمِر pl. -uun investor; adj. investing

2264 بِتْرُول petroleum, oil

2266 جَدْوَى benefit, advantage, utility

2268 أَسْر captivity; بِأَسْرِه completely

2269 دُخان smoke; smoking

2270 مُذَكِّرَة pl. -aat note; notebook

2272 حَليب milk

2274 ناطِق speaker, spokesperson; (fig.) voice

2276 اِنْخِفاض reduction, decrease, drop

2280 إشْراف supervision, direction

2281 صَيْد hunting, fishing

2282 مَعْلاة pl. مَعالي greatness, nobility; glory

2285 يَقين certainty; conviction

2286 مَقْبَرَة pl. مَقابِر grave, tomb; graveyard

2287 مُعَسْكَر pl. -aat camp, encampment

2288 مَعْلَم pl. مَعالِم sign, mark; landmarks

2291 مُخَدِّر anesthetic: مُخَدِّرات narcotics, drugs

2292 مَلاك pl. مَلائِكَة angel

2295 دَعْوَى lawsuit; claim; (Egy.Lev.) right

2297 تَوْحيد unity; standardization; monotheism

2300 عِصابَة pl. -aat gang, band, group

2302 مُحاكَمَة trial, legal proceeding

2303 ثانِيَة pl. ذَوانٍ second (time span)

2304 أَجْر pl. أُجور wage; fee; recompense

2305 خَلَل malfunction; flaw; deficiency

2307 غَضّ lowering (one's gaze)

2309 حَمّام bath, bathroom

2310 سِلْم peace

2312 لاجِئ refugee; adj. seeking refuge

2315 عِطْر pl. عُطور perfume

2316 تَغْطِيَة covering; (news) coverage

2317 شَريعَة law; Sharia (Islamic law)

2318 نِداء call, appeal; invitation, summons

2319 مُخْرِج (screen, stage) director; adj. directing

2320 سَماح permission; magnanimity

2321 شَقَّة apartment, flat

2324 مُطالَبَة demand; requirement

2325 بَعْثَة/بِعْثَة pl. بَعَثات delegation; mission

2326 مَجْد glory, magnificence, splendor

2327 مَحَبَّة love, affection

2329 تَوازُن balance, equilibrium; balancing

2331 نَوْعيَّة peculiarity, characteristic

2333 تَدْخين smoking; fumigating

2334 سُرْعانَ ما it didn't take long for

2338 تَمْثيل representation; acting

2339 شَعْبيَّة popularity, mass appeal

2340 وَجْبَة pl. وَجَبات meal; menu

2341 هُدًى guidance; الهُدَى the right path

2342 سَكَن housing

2345 سَيْف sword

2347 مَجْزَرَة pl. مَجازِر massacre, slaughter

2349 تَصَوُّر depiction, conception, imagination

2352 تَأْهِيل certification; training

2354 تَمْيِيز distinction; discrimination

2356 عِزّ prime, peak, height

2357 بِطالة/بَطالة unemployment; inactivity

2359 ثُلْث one third

2361 لائِحَة pl. لَوائِح list, table; schedule

2365 فَلْسَفَة philosophy

2367 تَفْتِيش search, inspection; (security) check

2369 شُرْب vn. drinking; (Dia.) smoking

2371 وَرْشَة pl. وِرَش workshop

2372 رَحِم uterus, womb; bosom; inside

2373 حِجاب hijab (Islamic head scarf), veil

2378 جَوْدَة excellence, good quality

2379 حارَة quarter; neighborhood; alley

2381 سِلْعَة pl. سِلَع commodity; pl. سِلَع goods

2382 مَطْلَع beginning, dawn (of an era)

2383 عَمِيد dean; chief; (mil.) brigadier general

2384 حَنان affection, love; sympathy

2385 بَصَر perception; sight; view

2386 قَرْض pl. قُرُوض (bank) loan

2388 رَجاء hope, expectation; رَجاءً please

2390 قارَّة pl. -aat continent

2391 حَرِيق pl. حَرائِق fire

2392 تَكْلِفَة cost, expense, charge

2396 جَوّال mobile (phone); adj. itinerant

2401 مُراقِب observer; supervisor, monitor

2402 مَوْلُود pl. مَوالِيد newborn infant

2403 طائِر bird; adj. flying, airborne

2405 مَوْج coll.n. pl. أَمْواج waves, surges

2406 حِدَّة intensity, violence

2407 ماما/مامَة fem.n. (Dia.) mom, mama

2408 قِطار train

2409 مُوجِب in بِمُوجِب : accordance with

2410 مِرْفَق pl. مَرافِق convenience, service

2411 ضَحْك laughter, laughing

2414 عامَّة populace; عامَّةً in general

2415 تَصْوِيت voting

2416 تِلْمِيذ pl. تَلامِيذ student, pupil

2420 مُصِيبَة pl. مَصائِب misfortune, tragedy

2421 سَقْف roof; ceiling

2422 تَخَصُّص pl. -aat specialty, specialization

2424 يَسار left (also political)

2427 تَدْرِيس teaching, instruction, pedagogy

2429 تَعَب trouble, inconvenience

2432 جُنُون madness, insanity

2433 سُور pl. أَسْوار wall, fence, enclosure

2435 بَوّابَة door; portal, gateway

2436 تَصْفِيَة vn. settling, solving; n. settlement

2438 مَرْتَبَة level, rank; degree; position

2440 دَيْن pl. دُيُون debt

2441 سِنّ pl. أَسْنان tooth; sharp edge

2442 اِنْتِباه attention, caution; alertness, vigilance

2443 عَصْر afternoon

2445 دِيوان office, agency, court

2447 راكِب pl. رُكّاب passenger; adj. riding

2448 هَنْدَسَة engineering

2449 أَوْلَوِيَّة pl. -aat priority; goal

2450 ذَوْق taste, good taste; refinement

2453 صَبِيّ pl. صِبْيَة , صِبْيان young boy, youth

2456 خَيْل pl. خُيُول horse

2457 صَوْب direction; quarter

2458 صُدُور appearance; publication

2463 حَجّ pilgrimage, Hajj

2464 عَرْش throne

2468 وُدّ affection, fondness, friendship

2469 شَغْلَة pl. -aat (Lev.) thing, deal, matter

2470 سَجِين pl. سُجَناء prisoner, inmate

2471 زَيْتُون coll.n. olives; olive tree

2472 ضَمِير conscience; (gram.) pronoun

2473 مِيزانِيَّة budget

2474 فَصِيلَة pl. فَصائِل faction; (mil.) platoon

2476 كَفّ fem.n. palm (hand); vn. abstaining

2477 جَهْل ignorance

2478 عَوْن help, assistance, aid

2482 حَرَس guard, bodyguard

2484 نُخْبَة pl. نُخَب selection, choice item; elite

2487 فِقْرَة pl. فِقْرَة/فِقَر/فَقَرات/فِقَرات paragraph

2488 مَذْهَب pl. مَذاهِب path; ideology

2490 دُفْعَة batch; class (graduates); instance

2491 طُمُوح pl. -aat ambition, desire; wish

2492 تَخْفِيف lowering; decrease, reduction

2495 وَهْم pl. أَوْهام illusion; fantasy

2499 اِمْتِداد extent, scope; extension, expansion

2500 مُواصَفَة pl. -aat description; مُواصَفات specs

2501 بَثّ transmission; dissemination

2502 اِسْتِعادَة recovering, regaining, reclaiming

2503 مُخابَرَة correspondence; telephone call

2509 عَرَبِيَّة Arabic (language); (Egy.) pl. -aat car

2511 رِضا/رِضًى approval, satisfaction, pleasure

2512 جَيْب pl. جُيُوب pocket; purse

2513 تَقْسِيم partition, division; distribution

2514 ناصِر pl. أَنْصار partisan, supporter, follower

2515 إِغْلاق locking, closing; barring

2516 صُعُود ascent, rise; take-off (aircraft)

2517 تَشْرِيع pl. -aat legislation, legislature

2520 اِضْطِراب pl. -aat disturbance, disorder

2525 عاصِفَة pl. عَواصِف storm, tempest

2526 تَوافُق compatibility; conformity; consensus

2532 عُمْلَة pl. -aat currency, money, bills

2533 مَلِكَة fem.n. queen; الْمَلِكَة (title) Queen

2535 عَقار pl. -aat real estate, land property

2537 أَغْلَبِيَّة majority

2539 شَوْط round, phase; game, half period

2541 تَوَقُّف stopping, halting, pausing

2542 مُحارَبَة fight, struggle, combat

2546 ظَنّ opinion, assumption; أَظُنِّي I think

2548 عَظْم pl. عِظام bone

2552 تَحْدِيث vn. renewing; n. pl. -aat update

2553 مَناخ/مُناخ climate, atmosphere

2555 اِنْهِيار collapse, downfall; breakdown

2557 صِيانَة maintenance, preservation

2558 عَقِيدَة doctrine, dogma; creed, belief, faith

2560 صُدْفَة surprise; coincidence, chance

2562 رُعْب fright, panic, terror

2566 قَهْر coercion; subjugation

2568 اِسْتِطْلاع pl. -aat (opinion) poll

2569 سائِر most of, the majority of

2571 مِيناء port, harbor

2574 كِيلُومِتر pl. -aat kilometer

2576 طارِئَة pl. طَوارِئ emergency

2579 اِسْتِجابَة acceptance; complying with

2581 غُرْبَة exile; alienation

2584 نَصِيب. share, portion, dividend

2586 حاصِل result; adj. (what) happened

2587 إِثارَة provocation, agitation

2588 عِشْق love, fondness

2590 عَرُوس fem.n. bride; masc.n. bridegroom

2591 حارِس الْمَرْمَى target; مَرْمًى goalkeeper

2592 إِعْمار construction, building, development

2593 طِراز model, class, type

2594 مُقاطَعَة vn. boycott; n. district

2595 صالَة hall (It., Sp. sala)

2596 مَنْظَر pl. مَناظِر view, scenery; look

2597 سِحْر sorcery, magic

2599 سَحاب coll.n. clouds, un.n. سَحابَة, pl. سُحُب

2600 مَقْصُود purpose, intent; adj. deliberate

2601 مُساواة equality, equal rights

2602 اِنْضِمام joining; affiliation; annexation

2604 طُنّ ton

2605 نَظِير counterpart; colleague, peer

2608 نُهُوض promotion, advancement

2610 جُذُور pl. جِذْر/جَذْر root, stem

2611 عِبْء pl. أَعْباء burden, load

2612 ظالِم pl. -uun tyrant; adj. oppressive

2615 بُرْج tower; constellation; horoscope

2616 طَلاق divorce

2618 مُكَوِّن pl. -aat component; adj. forming

2619 إِصْبَع pl. أَصابِع finger

2622 ضِياع loss; waste (esp. of time)

2624 نَقْد pl. نُقُود money, cash

2627 جِدِّيَّة seriousness, earnestness

2628 تَكْرار repetition; تَكْراراً repeatedly

2632 حِقْد hatred, resentment

2636 حُلُول vn. arrival; beginning; replacing

2639 تَوْصِيَة pl. -aat recommendation, advice

2646 شِراكَة partnership

2648 خَوْض waging, embarking on, carrying out

2649 اِسْتِكْمال conclusion, completion

2652 عِقاب punishment, penalty

2653 تَلْبِيَة vn. meeting (needs); complying with

2655 حَيْرَة/حِيرَة bewilderment; embarrassment

2656 غُبار dust

2657 طَقْس weather, climate

2658 فِقْدان/فُقْدان loss; bereavement

2659 مَدار orbit, sphere; scope, range; axis, pivot

2660 بابا pope; daddy; (Ali) Baba

2661 كِيس pl. أَكْياس bag, sack

2662 اِحْتِجاج protest; اِحْتِجاجاً protesting

2663 مانِع obstacle; adj. preventing; forbidding

2664 وَقُود fuel

2665 دَجاج coll.n. chickens, poultry; (Lev.) جاج

2666 نَهْج method, procedure; way, path

2667 تَسْمِية naming, appellation, designation

2668 هامِش side, margin; periphery, sideline

2670 تَكْريم honoring, respecting

2672 نَهْضة renaissance

2673 اِعْتِقاد vn. belief في in sth, or أَنَّ/بِأَنَّ that

2676 تَصَدِّي resistance, confrontation

2678 يَوْم القِيامة resurrection; قِيامة Judgment Day

2684 حائِط wall

2687 خَريطة map, chart; خَريطة الطَّريق roadmap

2688 شَكْوى pl. شَكاوى complaint, grievance

2689 رُؤْيا pl. رُؤى vision, dream; idea, picture

2690 تَعَرُّض vn. being exposed إلى to sth

2691 مُحاسَبة examination; accounting; oversight

2692 بَيْض coll.n. eggs, un.n. بَيْضة

2694 لُجُوء vn. resorting إلى to; n. refuge; asylum

2696 مَوْضِع location, position

2697 تارَة : تارَةً once; sometimes

2698 تَفاعُل interaction, reaction; reciprocity

2699 مُفَكِّر pl. -uun intellectual

2702 زِلْزال pl. زَلازِل earthquake

2704 اِنْتِفاضة uprising; الاِنْتِفاضة the Intifada

2706 فِلْس pl. فُلُوس fils; فُلُوس money

2707 فارِس pl. فُرْسان horseman; knight

2708 نَمَط pl. أَنْماط type; form; model

2709 غِطاء cover; blanket

2710 شُعاع pl. أَشِعَّة ray, beam

2711 كَتيبة pl. كَتائِب squadron, brigade

2718 مُديرِيَّة office; district, province

2719 عِبادة vn. worship, religious practice

2723 مُظاهَرة pl. -aat demonstration, rally

2730 حِمار donkey, fem. حِمارة she-ass, pl. حَمير

2731 حَنين yearning, nostalgia

2732 حَدا (Lev.) anyone, somebody

2733 كَوْكَب pl. كَواكِب planet; star

2736 مُغادَرة departure

2740 عاطِفة pl. عَواطِف emotion; affection

2742 عَقَبة pl. -aat obstacle

2743 فِراش bed

2744 سِرِّيَّة secrecy

2745 عَبَث joke, jest; frivolity; عَبَثاً in vain

2747 ضاحِية pl. ضَواح suburb, neighborhood

2748 تَضامُن solidarity, cooperation

2749 نُفُوذ influence, effect

2751 خَليفة masc.n. successor; caliph

2752 إِصْرار insistence, determination

2755 خَيْط pl. خُيُوط string, thread; clue

2759 اِبْتِداء beginning, start

2760 سَراح release; إِطْلاق سَراح setting free

2761 مائِدة table

2763 أُنْثى pl. إِناث female

2764 اِطِّلاع inspection, perusal على of sth

2767 عَمالة workforce, employees

2768 مَنْظُومة system, structure; hierarchy

2770 أَوان pl. آوِنة time, moment

2771 قَسْوة harshness, severity, brutality

2773 اِسْتيعاب comprehension; absorbing

2774 غَداء lunch; midday meal

2777 ضيق narrowness; lack of, shortage

2779 مِلْكِيَّة property, ownership, possession

2781 تَحَمُّل vn. bearing (burden, responsibility)

2782 تَفاوُض negotiation, debate, discussion

2791 داء sickness, disease; ailment, disorder

2793 بَرّ land; earth

2794 تَواجُد presence; existence

2795 نَبات coll.n. pl. -aat plants, vegetation

2797 تَحْضير pl. -aat preparation; production

2798 سَرِقة stealing, theft

2799 دَهْر fate, fortune; lifetime, eternity

2800 تَأْخير delay, postponement

2801 مِلْح salt

2802 فَتْوَى pl. فَتَاوَى fatwa (legal opinion)

2804 حَوْل power, might; لا حَوْلَ وَلا قُوَّةَ إِلّا بِاللَّه

2805 مُسَجِّل recorder; a.p. recording

2806 طِيلَة : طِيلَة throughout, during (the entire)

2807 شَفَّافِيَّة transparency; clarity, openness

2809 غَلَط error, mistake; (Dia.) adj. wrong

2810 تَأْجِيل postponement; deferment

2812 جَامِع mosque

2814 شِفَاء cure, remedy; medication

2815 وَدَاع departure, exit; وَدَاعاً farewell!

2817 مُعَادَلَة equation, balance

2818 تَسَامُح tolerance, forbearance

2820 رَجَا pl. أَرْجَاء side wall; أَرْجَاء regions, areas

2822 كَامِيرا camera

2824 اشْتِبَاك pl. -aat skirmish, clash

2828 عُذْر excuse; apology; عُذْراً excuse me

2830 مُنْطَلَق premise; starting point; launch pad

2832 انْقِلاب coup, overthrow, toppling

2833 مُسَمَّى title, name; adj. called, named

2834 قِيَاس measurement; analogy; comparison

2836 طِبْق : طِبْقَ and طِبْقاً لِـ in accordance with

2837 خِرِّيج pl. -uun graduate

2838 مُؤَامَرَة pl. -aat conspiracy, plot

2839 دِعَايَة pl. -aat advertisement; propaganda

2840 كَادِر pl. كَوَادِر cadre, key group, staff

2841 مِرْآة mirror

2842 عَوْلَمَة globalization (from عَالَم world)

2843 مُصَالَحَة conciliation, compromise

2844 مَرَارَة bitterness; gall bladder

2846 مَخَافَة pl. مَخَاوِف fear, anxiety; worry

2850 عَشِيَّة evening; eve, night before

2852 اسْتِئْنَاف resumption; appeal

2853 كُثْر abundance; great number; much, a lot

2855 فُلان so-and-so; such-and-such

2856 ثَمَر pl. ثِمَار fruit; yield

2858 تَغْذِيَة feeding, nutrition

2860 طَعْم flavor, taste

2861 مُتْعَة pleasure, enjoyment

2862 مَجْرَى pl. مَجْرَيَات course, path; مَجْرَيَات events

2868 مَشْي walking, going

2869 فَخْر pride; boasting

2870 صَلاحِيَّة pl. -aat suitability, viability; validity

2872 مُحْتَرَف pl. -uun professional, expert

2876 إِخْرَاج production; extraction; removal

2877 سَمَاع hearing, listening

2878 مَدّ length, reach; extending; spreading

2879 رِفْقَة pl. رِفَاق company, group

2881 سِتّ pl. -aat lady, miss

2882 مَهَارَة -aat capability, skill; ability

2883 انْتِهَاك pl. -aat violation, contravention

2884 ذِئْب pl. ذِئَاب wolf, jackal

2888 سَلَف coll.n. ancestors; n. advance (payment)

2889 تَرْحِيب welcome, welcoming; greeting

2890 تَنَازُل vn. backing down; n. concession

2891 مِنْبَر pl. مَنَابِر pulpit, rostrum

2892 عِمَارَة building, edifice, structure

2894 مَتْحَف museum

2898 عَيْن same (person, thing); -self

2901 سَطْر pl. سُطُور line, row

2902 كَسْب gaining; earning; achieving, attaining

2904 صَدْمَة shock, blow

2907 مِحْنَة pl. مِحَن test; trial, ordeal

2909 تَبَع pl. أَتْبَاع follower

2910 فَاصِل pause, break; adj. separating

2911 مُهَاجِم assailant; striker (soccer)

2912 عُضْوِيَّة membership, affiliation

2913 خَتْم necessity; حَتْماً definitely, necessarily

2914 عَرَبَة pl. -aat cart, wagon; vehicle

2916 عُلْبَة pl. عُلَب can; case, box; pack

2919 بَرْمِيل barrel; vat; drum

2920 سِبَاحَة swimming

2921 حَوْض basin, reservoir; aquarium

2922 شَرْع law; adj. legal

2923 بَاشا pasha; الباشا Pasha

2924 خِيَانَة treason, treachery; betrayal; infidelity

2925 نَيْل attainment; acquiring, gaining

2926 خَالَة maternal aunt

2928 اسْتِفْتَاء questionnaire, poll; referendum

2929 شُورَى consultation, deliberation; Shura

2931 حَقِيبَة briefcase, portfolio; suitcase; bag

2932 عُثُور vn. finding, coming across على sth

2933 إِرْتِباط bond, connection, link

2934 تَوْضِيح explanation, clarification

2937 اِسْتِحْقاق pl. -aat worthiness; claim, right

2938 مَجْمَع assembly; academy

2939 اِنْتِقاد pl. -aat criticism, censure

2941 دَلالة pl. -aat meaning, significance

2943 يُورُو euro

2944 تَوْعِيَة informing, making aware

2945 عَزْم will, determination على to do sth

2947 عُطْلَة vacation, holiday, recess

2951 عَيِّل (Egy.Gul.) pl. عِيال child, kid

2953 بَشَرِيَّة humankind, human race

2954 تَحْمِيل vn. loading; downloading

2955 الخمسينات fiftieth year; خَمْسِين the Fifties

2959 إِلْقاء vn. throwing; giving (a speech)

2961 كَراهِيَّة hatred, loathing; dislike, aversion

2962 مُهاجِر emigrant; immigrant; adj. migrating

2967 رايَة flag, banner

2970 اِشْتِراك subscription; participation

2971 تَناقُض pl. -aat contradiction

2972 مَنْدُوب delegate, deputy, agent

2973 صِياغة drafting, composing; formulation

2974 تَطَرُّف extremism, radicalism

2976 قَذِيفة pl. قَذائِف shell, bomb

2977 بُقْعَة spot; pl. بِقاع region

2978 إِدْخال insertion, introduction, inclusion

2981 نِسْيان forgetfulness; oblivion

2982 خَمْر fem./masc.n. liquor, wine, alcohol

2984 تَخَلُّف backwardness; underdevelopment

2985 مُسْتَهْلِك consumer; adj. consuming

2987 تَوْظِيف hiring, recruitment; usage, exercise

2988 إِقْبال approach; concern على for

2989 تَهْنِئَة pl. تَهانٍ (def. تَهاني) greetings

2990 مُدافِع defender; adj. defending

2991 تَحْذِير pl. -aat warning, caution

2992 الآخِرَة the hereafter

2993 هُرُوب vn. escaping, fleeing; deserting

2995 جَواز permit; جَواز السَّفَر passport

2999 مَطْبَخ kitchen

3000 رِزْق livelihood; food, daily bread

3004 حِرْمان deprivation, prohibition

3006 عار shame, disgrace, scandal

3007 سُمْعَة reputation

3010 فاكِهَة pl. فَواكِه fruit

3011 مُراعاة deference, respect; compliance

3013 تَعادُل balance, equilibrium; (sports) tie

3014 اِسْتِهْلاك consuming; exhaustion, depletion

3015 عَمُود pl. أَعْمِدَة column, pillar

3017 بارِحَة yesterday, yesteryear

3019 سِجِلّ pl. -aat register; archive, record

3021 بُورْصَة /burSa/ stock exchange, bourse

3022 مَوْهِبَة pl. مَواهِب talent, gift

3023 اِسْتِقالة resignation

3024 مَخْرَج exit, outlet; escape, way out, solution

3027 كِفايَة adequacy; performance; competence

3028 تَوَسُّع expansion

3029 عَقِيد colonel; (in titles) Colonel

3034 خَرِيف autumn, fall

3036 عَرَض pl. أَعْراض (med.) symptom

3037 تَوالٍ consecutive succession

3039 حَبْل rope, cord, cable

3040 تَوَقُّع pl. -aat expectation; forecast

3041 تَرْشِيح nomination, candidacy

3044 كُفْر kufr (rejection of the Islamic faith)

3045 مُصْطَلَح pl. -aat technical term

3046 دَهْشَة surprise; bewilderment, confusion

3047 مَسْح survey; wiping; sweeping

3048 أَسًى affliction, sorrow, grief

3049 ظُلْمَة pl. ظُلُمات darkness

3050 زُجاج glass; زُجاج أَمامِيّ windshield

3053 جُلُوس sitting down, being seated

3055 اِسْتِعْمار colonialism

3058 مَضْمُون content; adj. guaranteed, insured

3059 خُطْبَة pl. خُطَب speech; sermon

3060 حَظْر prohibition, ban; embargo

3061 اِقْتِراب approach; getting near

3063 ذَكاء intelligence, cleverness

3067 جَحِيم hell, inferno; الجَحِيم Hell

3068 نُزُول descent; losing (weight); resignation

3071 فَضائِيَّة pl. -aat satellite station

3073 مُحَقِّق investigator; editor; a.p. investigating

3077 رَقْص dance, dancing

3078 حَرَج impediment, difficulty

3079 شَجَاعَة courage

3080 تَوَلٍّ taking charge

3082 كَبِد liver (organ); center, middle

3083 عِزَّة glory, honor; power; (self-) esteem

3084 تَسْوِيق marketing

3085 لَبَن (Egy.) milk; (Lev.Irq.) yoghurt

3086 خَشَبَة pl. -aat piece of wood; board, plank

3087 سَمّ pl. سُمُوم poison, toxin

3091 فَضِيحَة scandal; disgrace, shame

3101 إِحْيَاء vn. reviving; commemorating

3103 قِطّ cat; قِطّة female cat; pl. قِطَط cats

3104 بَرَاءَة innocence; acquittal

3105 ذُلّ humiliation, dishonor

3106 حُجْرَة pl. حُجَر room, chamber; cell

3107 مُحْتَلّ pl. -uun occupier; adj. occupying

3109 تَجَنُّب avoidance, avoiding

3111 مَنْشُور pl. -aat brochure; adj. published

3114 دَبَّابَة pl. -aat tank

3115 رَوْضَة pl. رِياض garden

3116 صُمُود steadfastness, determination

3118 نَبْض beating, palpitation, throbbing

3119 سَالِفَة pl. سَوَالِف (Irq.Gul.) chat; story

3122 عُنْق neck (person, bottle)

3124 عِيَان eyesight, (plain) view

3126 اِنْتِماء membership, affiliation; commitment

3127 قَطْرَة pl. قَطَرَات drop

3129 تَرْكِيب installation; structure, construction

3132 مِشْوَار walk, stroll, promenade

3134 مُرْتَفَع height, altitude, elevation; highlands

3137 خَجَل shame, bashfulness, shyness

3139 تَصْحِيح correction

3140 تَبَنٍّ adoption

3143 فَضِيلَة virtue; فَضِيلَة الشَّيْخ His Eminence

3145 مُشَاهِد viewer, spectator

3146 مَعْبَر pl. مَعَابِر crossing point, juncture

3148 أَسَد pl. أُسُود lion

3150 عَدَاء aggression, hostility; enmity

3151 أَنْف nose; (fig.) pride

3152 قَصْر shortness; vn. restricting

3153 اِخْتِصار abbreviation; بِاخْتِصار briefly

3154 سِيجَارَة pl. سَجَائِر (Dia. سَجاير) cigarette

3155 بَذْل spending; donating; effort

3157 حِلْف alliance, treaty, pact

3158 حَصِيلَة result, outcome; sum; revenue

3160 كُلْفَة cost, expenditure, overhead

3161 غُضُون interim; فِي غُضُون during

3162 مَسْكَن pl. مَسَاكِن residence, domicile

3169 اِبْتِعاد avoiding; distancing oneself

3171 قَنَاعَة conviction, belief

3174 وَحْش pl. وُحُوش beast

3177 اِعْتِذار apology; excuse

3178 مَأْزِق impasse; dilemma, crisis

3179 تَدَهْوُر decline, deterioration; fall, drop

3180 تَخَلٍّ surrender, renunciation (of مِن)

3181 تَزَايُد (gradual) growth, increase, rise

3186 تَحْكِيم arbitration; لَجْنَة تَحْكِيم jury

3187 لَعْنَة curse, oath; enchantment, spell

3188 خال maternal uncle

3193 مَجَّان and بِالمَجَّان for free, free of charge

3194 سَمْع hearing

3196 مُغامَرَة adventure, risk

3199 تَعَلُّم learning, study

3202 نِضال struggle, battle

3204 أَدِيب pl. أُدَبَاء author, writer

3205 خَيّ (Lev.) brother; خَيِّي my brother

3206 عُود lute; stick, match stick; aloe plant

3208 مِيلِيشِيا/مِلِيشِيا pl. -aat militia

3209 إِنْفاق spending, expenditure; expenses

3210 جَوْهَر pl. جَوَاهِر gem, jewel; essence

3211 وَلَاء loyalty, allegiance

3212 سِينارِيو scenario

3217 تَمَرُّد rebellion, insurgency, insurrection

3219 تَلَوُّث pollution, contamination

3220 مِيثاق treaty, pact, charter

3221 نَظَافَة cleanliness

3222 هُبُوط drop, fall; descent; landing

3223 المَسِيح : مَسِيح Christ, the Messiah

3225 عَرَق sweat; araq (alcoholic drink)

3227 حَصْر vn. containment; bounds, limits

3365 عُرُوبَة Arabism

3366 عَزَاء consolation, comfort; condolence(s)

3367 أَكْثَرِيَّة majority

3368 خَرَاب ruins, destruction

3371 سِتَار veil, curtain

3373 مُفْتِي mufti (Muslim legal scholar)

3375 مَزِيَّة pl. مَزَايا feature; advantage

3376 هَيْكَل framework; skeleton; temple

3381 عُرْضَة target, object (of criticism)

3385 لافِتَة pl. -aat billboard, placard, sign

3386 حافَة border, edge, side; seam, hem

3389 شُرْطِيّ police officer, policeman

3391 مَرْجِعِيَّة authority; authoritative source

3392 سَلْب robbing, depriving; سَلْباً negatively

3394 واجِهَة façade; front; (computer) interface

3396 زِيّ pl. أَزْياء uniform; أَزْياء fashion clothes

3398 ادِّعاء allegation, claim; prosecution

3399 تَقْوِيَة strengthening, reinforcement

3400 ساحِر sorcerer, magician; adj. charming

3403 مُباحَثَة pl. -aat discussion, dialog

3404 جَذْب attraction, lure; gravitation

3405 سَحْب withdrawal, pulling out; removal

3406 إفْراج liberation; release, freeing (عن of)

3407 عُزْلَة isolation, seclusion; separation

3408 تَصْعِيد escalation, intensification

3409 عِماد pl. عُمُد pillar; (mil.) major general

3410 بُطْء slowness; بِبُطْءٍ slowly

3411 عِبْرَة pl. عِبَر lesson, moral

3412 رُجُوع return; reversing (one's decision) عن

3413 حَياء modesty, shyness, inhibition, shame

3415 تَمَسُّك adherence, commitment (ب to)

3416 غُرُوب setting; غروب الشَّمْس sunset

3417 حافِلَة pl. -aat bus

3418 مَسْعىً pl. مَساع effort, endeavor

3420 انْعِدام non-existence, absence, lack of

3421 صالُون salon, chat room, parlor

3422 تَصْنِيف classification; sorting

3423 مُعاهَدَة treaty, accord, pact

3424 بُغْيَة wish; purpose

3425 سائِح pl. سُيَّاح tourist

3426 قافِلَة pl. قَوافِل convoy, column

3427 نَشْرَة report, bulletin; publication

3434 تَجْمِيل embellishment, decoration

3435 جَماهِيرِيَّة Jamahiriya (Libya)

3437 عَجَل hurry, rush, haste

3439 انْقِطاع discontinuation, breaking off

3440 مُحَرِّك motor, engine

3442 شَراب beverage, drink

3443 الْتِهاب pl. -aat inflammation

3447 قَبِيل kind, sort, type

3448 تَفَوُّق excellence; superiority, supremacy

3449 طاعَة obedience

3451 مَنْظُور perspective; adj. expected

3453 مُفَوَّضِيَّة delegation, legation

3454 سُوبَر ماركت super (in سُوبَر "supermarket")

3456 مَرْجِع pl. مَراجِع source; authority

3459 تَهْدِئَة calming; easing, relieving (tension)

3464 هاجِس pl. هَواجِس worry; apprehension

3467 عَلَم pl. أَعْلام flag; أَعْلام celebrities

3470 صِيام fasting, abstinence

3471 رَماد ashes, cinders

3473 مُقَدَّمَة preface, introduction; front part

3474 سُكُوت silence, calm

3475 فِقْه fiqh (Islamic jurisprudence); science

3477 مِلْك possessions, property; land, real estate

3478 جُلّ majority, most, main part (of)

3479 دِماغ brain

3480 خَلاص liberation, salvation

3481 حِسّ/حَسّ sensation, feeling; sound, noise

3482 عُبُور vn. crossing (border, street)

3483 شَحْن vn. charging, loading; n. cargo

3485 نَجاة survival, deliverance, salvation; escape

3488 تَحْرِيك vn. stimulating, activating

3489 قَمْح wheat

3490 جِراحَة surgery

3492 أُمْنِيَّة pl. أَمانٍ (def. أَماني) wish, hope

3493 سِمَة pl. -aat feature, imprint

3494 تَعْقِيد complication, complexity

3495 مِلْعَقَة pl. مَلاعِق spoon; (also مَعْلَقَة Egy.Lev.)

3496 أَذًى harm; injury; offense

3497 لِيرَة pl. -aat pound, lira (Leb.Syr.)

3499 صانِع pl. صُنَّاع manufacturer; maker

3500 ثَلْج snow; ice

3501 عَصاً stick, baton, rod

3504 طَرْد vn. expulsion; firing; n. parcel

3508 قُماش pl. أَقْمِشَة fabric, cloth

3513 اِنْعِقاد vn. convening, holding (meeting)

3516 كَثافَة thickness, density; intensity

3517 تَشْخِيص vn. diagnosis, analysis

3518 خارِطَة map, chart; خارِطَة الطَّرِيق roadmap

3519 مِصْداقِيَّة credibility

3523 حِراسَة guard, escort, protection

3528 صَدارَة chairmanship; precedence

3529 ناقِد pl. نُقّاد critic

3530 تَضْحِيَة pl. -aat sacrifice

3531 مَطاف consequence; في نِهايَة المَطاف finally

3533 خَصِيصَة pl. خَصائِص characteristic

3534 تَدَفُّق flow, stream, flood; influx, invasion

3535 بُحَيْرَة lake

3536 حَماس enthusiasm, zeal; fortitude, bravery

3537 مِنْحَة gift, donation; grant, scholarship

3538 تَحَدُّث discussion, speaking

3539 اِسْتِضافَة hosting

3541 تَصْدِير exporting

3544 مَكْسَب pl. مَكاسِب gain, profit

3546 رُمَّة entirety; بِرُمَّتِه completely

3547 وَطَنِيَّة nationalism, patriotism

3548 تَمَيُّز distinguishing oneself; excellence

3549 اِقْتِراع balloting, voting, election

3551 وَشْك : عَلى وَشْكِ on the verge of

3552 جَنِين fetus, embryo; germ

3553 تُرْبَة dust, dirt; grave

3556 عَيِّنَة pl. -aat sample, specimen

3557 عُقْب pl. أَعْقاب consequence

3558 جَفاف dryness, drought; dehydration

3559 تَقْوِيم rating, valuation; calendar

3560 رَصْد observation; survey; tracking

3563 نَفَقَة pl. -aat expenditure; نَفَقات spending

3564 اِمْتِلاك possession; control; seizure

3567 تَلَقِّي vn. receiving, receipt; acquisition

3569 كِبْر pride, arrogance; greatness

3570 تَذْكَرَة pl. تَذاكِر ticket, card

3571 اِسْتِماع vn. listening (إلى to)

3577 اِنْفِتاح opening up, welcoming; openness

3578 إِنْفَلْوَنْزا/إِنْفَلُوَنْزا flu, influenza

3581 حُرْمَة sanctity; taboo; married woman, wife

3582 تَجْهِيز vn. preparing; n. pl. -aat equipment

3583 نُكْتَة joke

3584 مُهْلَة deferment; delay; break

3588 نَزِيف bleeding, hemorrhage

3590 تَهْيِئَة preparation, arrangement

3592 اِسْتِعْراض vn. review, inspection; tour; parade

3594 مِنَصَّة platform, podium

3596 تَظاهُرَة rally, demonstration

3597 عَناء hardship, trouble; distress

3598 إِظْهار expressing, showing, demonstrating

3599 غَدْر deception; treachery, treason

3603 سَدّ bridging; defrayal; paying off

3604 بَلاء affliction, misfortune

3606 مُواطَنَة citizenship

3608 تَحَسُّن improvement

3609 اِسْتِشْهاد martyrdom

3611 تَرْوِيج distribution; promotion, marketing

3612 تَعاطٍ vn. taking (medicine); handling

3614 تَبَرُّع pl. -aat donation, contribution

3615 هُدْنَة truce, armistice; calm, lull

3617 جِنّ demon; jinn; genie

3622 تَصْنِيع manufacture, processing

3623 تَحَرُّر (self) liberation, emancipation

3624 دِرْع shield, armor; plaque (award)

3628 رادِيُو radio

3629 مَعِدَة/مِعْدَة stomach

3631 حِقْبَة era, age, time period

3632 إِدْراك realization, awareness; attainment

3633 فَجْوَة (mostly fig.) gap, gulf, breach

3637 حِذاء shoe; pair of shoes

3639 واحَة oasis

3640 مَنْفَذ pl. مَنافِذ exit; escape; gateway

3641 طاغٍ pl. طُغاة tyrant; adj. tyrannical

3642 شِرْيان pl. شَرايِين artery

3643 أَلْبوم /album/ album

3644 مِلْء filling; capacity; quantity

3645 تَدْبِير vn. arranging; n. pl. تَدابِير preparation

3646 كافِر pl. كُفّار kafir (non-believer)

3647 تَرْخِيص license, permission

3648 مَلَل boredom

3649 عِلاوَة increase; bonus

3653 طَيْف spectrum (light); pl. أَطْياف ghost

3654 مُفاد content; مُفادُها to the effect (that)

3655 الخالِق : الخالِق the Creator; adj. creative

3656 لَحْن melody, music, song; tone

3660 شَمْعَة pl. شُمُوع candle

3662 مِزاج mixture; mood, feeling

3663 إِسْعاف first aid; سَيّارَة إِسْعاف ambulance

3666 شَقِيقَة sister

3667 دِفْء heat, warmth

3668 زلمه/زلمي /zalameh/ (Lev.) man, guy

3671 ثَبات proof; constancy, firmness

3672 تَزْوِير forgery; falsification

3674 صِغَر smallness; youth, infancy

3675 نَفَق pl. أَنْفاق tunnel; underpass, subway

3677 قُدْوَة example, role model; pattern

3678 مُودِيل /modeel/ pl. -aat model, pattern

3679 وَطْأَة pressure, gravity; harshness, cruelty

3680 جَهَنَّم hell; Hell

3683 وَباء epidemic, disease; scourge

3684 إِرْتِقاء ascent; promotion; evolution

3685 اِتِّباع pursuing, following; compliance

3686 سُكُون quiet, calm; rest, repose

3687 شَنّ waging, launching (a war, campaign)

3689 تَثْبِيت confirmation; stabilization

3690 زَرْع planting; growing; farming

3691 قَلْعَة stronghold, citadel, fort

3694 عَلى مَتْنِ : مَتْن on board (ship, airplane)

3696 مُقَوِّم pl. -aat component, ingredient

3698 مُعْلِن announcer; a.p. announcing

3700 عَدْوى infection

3701 مُبالَغَة exaggeration

3702 عاقِبة pl. عَواقِب consequence, result, effect

3703 بَياض white, whiteness

3705 مُنْتَهى utmost, extreme

3706 حُمّى fever; heat

3707 مَرّ passing, course (of time); going by

3709 اِئْتِلاف coalition, union

3710 مارّة n. pl. مارّة n. pedestrian, passerby

3712 حَداثَة modernity, newness, novelty

3713 إيدز/أيدز /'eedz/ AIDS

3714 ناخِب pl. -uun voter, elector

3715 اِسْتِناد dependence; اِسْتِناداً على on the basis of

3716 مُجْمَل total, full amount; summary

3717 اِحْتِفاظ vn. safeguarding, preservation

3719 سَيْل vn. streaming, flowing

3721 تَفاؤُل optimism

3725 مُفْرَدَة pl. -aat word; مُفْرَدات vocabulary

3727 تَعْمِيم making general or public; spreading

3728 شائِعَة pl. -aat rumor

3729 طاقِم crew, staff, team

3730 ثابِتَة pl. ثَوابِت principle, rule

3731 تَشاوُر deliberation, joint consultation

3732 عَقْلِيَّة mentality, attitude, way of thinking

3734 صَرْخَة shout, scream

3737 سَراب mirage, illusion

3739 شَقّ splitting, opening; crack, gap

3740 مُساندَة support, aid, assistance

3741 سُكَّرِيّ (also مَرَض السكري) diabetes

3742 عُقْدَة pl. عُقَد complex (emotion); knot

3745 تَعْطِيل vn. hindering; derailing

3746 مُحْتَوى pl. مُحْتَوَيات content

3748 إِبّان time; إِبّانَ during

3752 إِجْماع consensus; بالإِجْماع unanimously

3753 تَنَفُّس breathing, respiration; breath

3754 هَدْم demolition; leveling, razing

3755 قَفَص cage; prisoner's dock

3757 خِزانَة treasury; vault, safe; (book)case

3759 شَبَح ghost, specter

3760 يَقْظَة wakefulness; alertness

3763 رُخْصَة pl. رُخَص license, permit

3769 غاز pl. غُزاة invader, raider

3770 فِطْر fitr (end of the Ramadan fast)

3772 عَلَن (the) open; عَلَناً openly, publicly

3915 وِجْدان feeling, emotion; conscience

3921 لِباس clothes, dress, attire

3923 حَراك movement, motion

3926 بَهْجَة magnificence; delight

3929 ضَجِيج noise; commotion

3930 مَوْضُوعِيَّة objectivity

3931 نِتاج result, outcome; production

3932 مُزارِع pl. -uun farmer

3936 خِلافَة succession; caliphate

3938 بُلُوغ reaching, attaining

3943 مَصْرَع death, fatality

3944 مُتَظاهِر pl. -uun demonstrator

3945 مَفْعُول impact, effect; result

3947 كَمّ amount, quantity

3949 اِزْدِياد growth, increase, rise

3950 اِسْتِعانَة ب vn. seeking help from

3951 مُحَلِّل pl. -uun analyst

3954 صِنْف pl. أَصْناف type, class, kind, category

3957 حِبْر ink

3958 زِينَة embellishment, adornment

3962 تَبْرِير pretext; vindication

3965 خُضار coll.n. vegetables, greens

3968 فَلَك orbit; عِلْم الفَلَك astronomy

3969 جَمَل pl. جِمال camel

3972 ذَرَّة atom, particle

3973 جَمْر embers

3978 زَبُون pl. زَبائِن customer, client

3980 طائِفِيَّة sectarianism, factionalism

3981 طُمَأْنِينَة calm, serenity; rest, repose

3982 تَهْرِيب smuggling (goods or persons)

3983 إِتْمام completion; realization

3984 صَحْوَة awakening, revival; resurgence

3988 وَيْل woe, distress; يا وَيْلِي! woe is me!

3990 عَتْمَة dark, darkness, gloom

3992 مَعْمَل pl. مَعامِل laboratory; facility

3993 دِبْلُوماسِيَّة diplomacy

3994 دُهْن pl. دُهُون oil, grease, fat (esp. in food)

3995 فِيتامِين pl. -aat vitamin

3996 اِخْتِراق incursion; traversing

3997 فَخامَة excellence, eminence

3998 نَحْل coll.n. bees, un.n. نَحْلَة

3999 نِقاب veil; كَشَفَ النِّقاب عن to disclose

4001 اِزْدِهار blossoming, prosperity

4003 حَيِّز sphere, scope; field, domain, area

4004 رُبُوع pl. رَبْع housing; residence; territory

4005 مالِك owner; adj. possessing; having

4006 زَكاة zakat (almsgiving in Islam); charity

4007 مُصادَرَة confiscation, seizure; expropriation

4013 اِحْتِواء vn. controlling; n. content

4014 إِسْكان housing

4015 أَرُزّ/رُزّ rice

4016 مُقاوِم antagonist a.p. resisting

4018 غَمْرَة flood; pl. غِمار heat (of conflict)

4019 قَبْضَة grip; fistful; seizure

4021 نَخِيل date palms

4022 مُعَوِّق pl. -aat obstacle, hurdle, impediment

4024 تَرْكِيبَة structure, composition

4029 رُوَيْد slowly, gradually رُوَيْداً رُوَيْداً

4031 مِيزَة characteristic, feature; merit

4032 بَحْرِيَّة navy

4033 نَزْعَة inclination, tendency; trend

4035 نَدًى dew; generosity

4038 خُلاصَة gist; synopsis, abstract, summary

4040 شَيْخَة matron, elderly woman

4042 لُعْبَة pl. لُعَب game, sport; toy, play thing

4044 قُطْر pl. أَقْطار region; countries

4047 كَلِيب pl. -aat (film, video) clip

4048 زَحْمَة (traffic) congestion; crowd

4049 فِداء sacrifice; self-sacrifice

4050 اِجْتِياح strike, invasion

4051 حَيَوِيَّة vigor, vitality; liveliness

4052 بِرّ charity; piety, righteousness

4054 إِنْسانِيَّة humanity, humankind

4055 اِقْتِحام incursion, assault; storming into

4059 رِوائِيّ pl. -uun novelist; adj. narrative

4060 اِنْعِكاس pl. -aat repercussion; effect

4061 حِدَة : عَلَى حِدَةٍ separately, individually

4062 دَوَّامَة spiral; dizziness, confusion

4063 إِهْمال neglect, negligence, carelessness

4065 رَصِيف sidewalk; platform

4066 صَبِيَّة pl. صَبايا girl, young girl

4067 هِبَة gift, grant

4069 رَكْب procession; entourage, retinue

4070 تَقارُب mutual affinity; rapprochement

4071 رافِد tributary; الرّافِدانِ Tigris and Euphrates

4219 حاسِب calculator; الحاسِب الآلِيّ computer

4222 تَعايُش coexistence, living together

4223 صَوْم fasting, abstinence

4225 نِفاق hypocrisy

4226 شَمْل inclusion, containing

4227 مُواكَبة accompanying; escorting

4228 قاع bottom, floor

4229 اِسْتِبْدال substitution; exchange

4235 نُصْب monument; نُصْبَ in front of

4237 تَكامُل integration

4241 أَقَلِّيّة pl. -aat minority

4242 مُعْضِلة dilemma, problem, difficulty

4243 بَلاغ communiqué; notice

4245 بُنْدُقِيّة rifle; gun, weapon

4247 اِقْتِتال fighting (each other)

4249 اِحْتِياطِيّ reserves; adj. precautionary

4250 اِسْتِسْلام surrender; resignation

4252 وَتيرة way, manner, style; method

4253 اِنْدِماج integration; absorption

4255 بُرْهة moment, instant

4256 ضِياء light, glow

4257 نَدَم remorse, regret

4259 اِنْدِلاع breaking out, flaring up (fire, war)

4260 نَعيم comfort, luxury, happiness

4262 تَشْويه distortion

4263 اِمْتِياز distinction, excellence; privilege

4265 مُصَوِّر photographer; illustrator

4266 قُبْلة kiss

4267 مَحْفِل pl. مَحافِل gathering, assembly

4275 جُغْرافِيا geography

4276 كَثَب nearness, closeness; عَن كَثَب closely

4277 جُنْد army, soldiers

4278 تَسَرُّب leak, escape; infiltration

4280 تَقْليص reducing, shrinking, cutting back

4282 عَمْد intent; adj. deliberate

4286 إيقاع vn. imposition; n. rhythm

4289 مَصْروف pl. مَصاريف expense; allowance

4290 تَسَلُّل infiltration

4294 مُدَّع plaintiff, prosecutor; a.p. alleging

4295 مَزيج combination, mixture, blend

4296 سَبْعين seventieth year; السبعينات the Seventies

4298 اِنْفِصال separation, break-up; secession

4299 جاهِلِيّة ignorance; Jahiliyah (pre-Islam)

4300 بَصَل coll.n. onions

4301 اِسْتِقْطاب polarization, attraction

4302 دَمْج inclusion; merger

4303 غَفْلة negligence, lack of attention

4304 مُذيع broadcaster, announcer

4305 طَوْر stage, phase; period, time

4306 بَذْر pl. بُذُور seed

4308 لِصّ pl. لُصُوص thief

4309 تَقْوى piety, devoutness

4310 تَأَهُّل qualification; marriage

4312 لِبْس clothing, dress, attire

4313 بَوْل urination; urine

4316 تَوافُر availability

4317 هَوْل fright, shock

4318 جُمْرُك pl. جَمارِك customs; الجَمارِك tariffs

4319 إنْجاح vn. granting success; n. success

4322 بادِية desert, wilderness

4323 بَوْح uncovering; disclosure, confession

4325 غَرام love, infatuation

4326 قَوْمِيّة nationalism

4328 اِلْتِحاق entering; joining; affiliation

4332 كَرَم generosity, magnanimity

4333 مَفْصِل pl. مَفاصِل (anat.) joint; juncture

4334 تَنَقُّل transfer; movement; transportation

4335 إفْطار iftar (Ramadan evening meal)

4336 شَوْك coll.n. thorns, un.n. شَوْكة; n. fork

4337 ذَريعة means; pretext, excuse

4343 نَقْلة move, shift; advance, progress

4345 فِرار escape, desertion (مِن from)

4346 مُتَمَرِّد pl. -uun rebel, insurgent

4347 قَوْس bow, arc; قَوْسانِ parentheses

4349 فاتِحة opening, preface

4350 شَيْخُوخة old age, seniority

4351 جَوْف belly, abdomen; cavity, hollow

4352 حَذْف deletion, omission

4353 زِرّ button; (push) button, switch button

4355 ديوان anthology or collection of poems

4356 رِجْل fem.n. leg; (Gul.) ريل /riil/

4357 صَميم depth; adj. true, genuine

4358 ثَمانين : الثَّمانينات the Eighties

4359 تَفاقُم aggravation, exacerbation; worsening

4362 تَكْثيف vn. intensifying; n. compression

4528 تَحْصِيل acquisition, attainment

4529 مَقْدِرَة ability, potential, capacity

4530 تَكْرِيس dedication, devotion; consecration

4532 قُطْن cotton

4534 بروفيسور /brofisoor/ professor; Prof.

4535 صُنْع manufacture, industry

4536 مُراهَقَة adolescence; puberty

4538 مَلِيّاً long time; for a long time

4539 تَوْلِيد producing, generating (energy)

4540 عُنْصُرِيَّة racism

4543 مِسْتَر Mr, Mister

4545 مُتَناوَل (في مُتَناوَل اليَد) within reach

4547 كابْتِن captain; (title) Captain

4548 غُيُوم .pl غَيْمَة cloud

4549 دِراما drama

4550 مَسِيحِيَّة Christianity

4551 دِيانة pl. -aat religion, creed

4552 هَيْكَلَة vn. structuring; n. framework

4553 تَعْمِيق vn. deepening; broadening

4556 هاوِية cliff, precipice; abyss, chasm

4559 مِسْك musk

4560 رُقْعَة plot of land; (chess) board

4562 تَعَدُّدِيَّة multiplicity, pluralism, plurality

4564 اِسْتِبْعاد ruling out, regarding as unlikely

4565 باقَة bouquet; packet (data)

4566 كُرْه/كَرْه hatred; عَلى كُرْه unwillingly

4567 شَهِيَّة appetite

4568 مُرْشِد guide, instructor; adviser, aide

4570 تَمْكِين enabling, making possible

4571 رَصاصَة bullet; shot

4572 مَحْو eradication; wiping out

4573 تَوْصِيل connection, contact

4575 حَشَرَة pl. -aat insect

4577 قامُوس dictionary, lexicon; vocabulary

4578 بِنايَة building, edifice; structure

4579 سُيُولَة liquid state, liquidity

4580 تَلاعُب manipulation, tampering

4581 تَخْصِيب fertilization; enrichment

4582 شِلْو pl. أَشْلاء corpse; limb; piece

4584 رَكْلَة kick, shot (in sports)

4586 صُلْح peace, reconciliation

4588 سَرِيَّة pl. سَرايا (mil.) company, squadron

4595 ياسْمِين jasmine

4597 مُلاحَقَة pursuit, chase; legal prosecution

4598 كَرْبُون carbon

4599 زِفاف wedding

4601 تُفّاح coll.n. apples

4603 تَبِعَة pl. -aat consequence; responsibility

4604 خُضُوع submission, subjection

4605 مُهاجَمة attack, assault; raid, strike

4607 أَضْحى sacrifice, immolation

4608 إِمْساك vn. holding; refraining from

4610 تَنْبِيه warning, alarm

4611 تَنام gradual growth, steady increase

4612 غَيْبُوبَة unconsciousness; trance; coma

4616 يُسْر ease, facility; affluence, prosperity

4619 غَرابَة strangeness, oddness

4621 ثَأْر revenge, retaliation

4622 خَلْط mixing, blending; mixture, blend

4623 غِشّ cheating, swindling

4626 حَلْبَة arena, ring, circuit, track

4629 تَراكُم build-up, accumulation; backlog

4630 قَمِيص pl. قُمْصان shirt

4632 سِمْنَة fat; obesity

4633 مُسْوَدَة rough draft

4634 فَتْحَة opening; porthole

4635 اِعْتِصام vn. adhering (ب to); n. sit-in strike

4637 اِسْتِلام receiving, accepting

4638 حام pl. حُماة n. protector, guardian; adj. hot

4639 فَناء extinction, doom, end

4643 عَشِيرَة pl. عَشائِر clan, tribe

4644 عِشاء evening; صَلاة العِشاء evening prayer

4646 عِنان bridle, reins

4652 صَرْح building, structure, edifice

4653 بَرِيق sparkle, glitter; shine

4655 إِنْذار warning, caution, alarm

4657 إِبْراز highlighting, emphasizing

4658 جَلِيد ice

4659 عَجِيبَة pl. عَجائِب marvel, wonder

4661 بَتَّة : البَتَّة (not) at all

4663 تَمْر coll.n. dates (fruit)

4667 مُتَلَقٍّ recipient, (person) receiving

4669 طَبْخ cooking, cuisine

4672 ثَدْي breast; udder

4676 سِتِّين sixtieth year; الستينات the Sixties

4678 شَرِيطَة condition

4679 اِعْتِدال moderation, restraint

4681 عَسْكَر coll.n. army, troops

4682 اِسْتِيلاء appropriation, seizure

4684 فَرِيضَة religious duty

4690 وَهَج blaze, fire; glare, glow

4693 تَسْيِير propulsion; steering, guidance

4694 واقِعِيَّة realism, reality

4697 إِسْتاد stadium

4699 ناشِر publisher

4700 مَنْفَى exile, banishment

4703 ثَنِيَّة pl. ثَنايا incisor; في/بَيْنَ ثَنايا within

4704 تَحَقُّق vn. ascertainment, verification مِن of sth

4705 وَقْع impact; impression, imprint

4706 مُشْكِل problem, difficulty

4708 مُفْتَرَق intersection, junction

4709 مَعْدِن pl. مَعادِن mineral, metal

4711 لَحاق vn. catching up ب with

4713 خَلَف successor; descendant

4716 مُمَرِّض pl. -uun (male) nurse

4717 عِرْض pl. أَعْراض honor, dignity

4722 إِخْلاص sincerity; loyalty

4723 تَدْقِيق investigation; verification; accuracy

4724 اِجْتِهاد effort; independent thinking

4725 اِلْتِقاط vn. receiving; taking (photos)

4726 طَيّ fold, crease; في طَيّ within, inside

4727 تَوْقِيف detention; stopping, halting

4730 اِحْتِقان congestion; (political) tension

4731 بَطْرِيَرْك (Chr.) patriarch

4732 رَمْي throwing; shooting (bullets)

4733 مَلَأ crowd; audience, assembly

4735 مَوَدَّة friendship, affection

4737 رَقِيب observer; censor; (mil.) sergeant

4738 نَمْل coll.n. ants

4741 مُخاطِب speaker; adj. addressing, speaking to

4743 حُسْبان consideration, estimation

4749 تَدْعِيم supporting, backing, propping up

4750 عَنْوَة force, violence; عَنْوَةً forcibly, by force

4752 تَطَرُّق broaching, discussing إلى (a topic)

4753 رَحْبَة pl. رِحاب open area; vastness

4756 تَسْدِيد payment; aiming, shooting

4757 إِدانَة condemnation, denunciation, censure

4758 عِداد number, quantity

4760 بُرُوز emergence; prominence

4762 نَبْذ discarding; rejection, renunciation

4763 خاتَم ring; seal, stamp

4765 تَحْطِيم demolition, destruction

4766 جوز (Egy.) /gooz/, (Lev.) /jooz/ husband

4767 رِواق pl. أَرْوِقَة corridor, hall; porch, portico

4769 حَرِير silk

4771 رُجُولَة masculinity, manhood, virility

4772 غُرُور deception, delusion; vanity

4774 تَخْرِيب destruction; sabotage, terrorism

4775 تَبْدِيل replacement, substitution

4777 زَعامَة leadership

4782 كابُوس nightmare

4783 مَلْجَأ shelter, refuge

4785 فَحْم coal

4786 فَرِيسَة victim, prey

4787 شَغَب unrest, disturbance

4791 رُطُوبَة moisture, dampness, humidity

4793 اِنْتِظام order, regularity

4794 سِكِّين knife

4795 وَسِيط mediator; adj. middle, medium

4796 فَخّ trap, snare

4797 مَعْشَر assembly, community, group, society

4798 مُلّا mullah (Muslim cleric); Mullah

4799 مُصادَفَة coincidence

4800 مِرْصاد lookout, ambush; lying in wait

4801 شُرُوع vn. embarking في on, engaging في in

4802 جُرْعَة dosage, dose; vaccine; gulp

4805 صِبا youth, childhood

4807 بُرْتُقال coll.n. oranges

4809 إيميل /'iimeel/ pl. -aat email

4811 مُسْتَطاع (what is) possible, feasible

4812 حِزام belt, band; cordon, barrier

4816 مَغْرِب sunset

4818 مَمَرّ passageway, corridor

4819 تَمَتُّع enjoyment

4821 اِمْتِصاص absorption, suction

4823 نُبُوَّة prophethood; prophecy

4824 مَنْزِلَة grade, rank, position

4825 لُغْز pl. أَلْغاز mystery, enigma; puzzle, riddle

4829 عِيلة /9eele/ (Lev.) n. family

4830 لَهِيب flame

4832 حَرِيم coll.n. women, harem

4833 لَهْو entertainment, amusement

4836 طَقْس pl. طُقُوس ritual, rite

4837 رُكُوب vn. getting in, boarding

4838 وِعاء container, receptacle; vessel

4839 تَطَلُّع pl. -aat aspiration, hope

4840 دَقَّة pl. -aat knock, stroke, tick, beat

4841 تَأْشِيرَة visa (travel, exit)

4843 حَجْب vn. veiling; covering; holding back

4845 تَدَنٍّ fall, decline; sinking

4846 حَلْق throat; chasm, gorge

4848 بالكاد : كاد almost

4850 رِهان bet, wager; contest

4851 عَزِيمَة determination, will; invitation

4852 عُمْرَة "lesser" pilgrimage to Mecca

4855 شُعْلَة torch, flame, fire

4858 عَبايَة/عَباءَة abaya (traditional black robe)

4859 بُؤْرَة center, focus

4860 بُرْكان volcano

4862 تَحْريض incitement, provocation; induction

4867 والٍ (def. والي) ruler, governor

4872 مَحْضَر report, minutes; attendance

4873 عُبُودِيَّة slavery, servitude; veneration

4874 نَصْح advice, counsel

4875 تَمْرير passing, transfer

4876 شَتات scattering; diaspora

4877 مَنام sleep; sleeping place

4878 نَفَر soldier, private; person, individual

4881 ثَلَّاجَة refrigerator; freezer

4884 فِيزِياء physics

4886 اِسْتِراحَة intermission; rest area; shrine

4887 حَفْنَة handful

4888 مُعاقَبَة punishment, sanction

4889 شِبْر span of the hand or foot

4891 حَسْرَة grief, sorrow

4892 تَسَوُّق shopping

4894 مَشْروب pl. -aat beverage, drink

4895 مُخاطَبَة vn. speaking to; n. conversation

4897 عاتِق shoulder

4898 ضُحًى forenoon

4900 مَرْأى sight, view

4901 قالِب form, model; mold

4903 اِسْتِخْراج extraction; removal

4908 ثَناء praise, commendation; appreciation

4909 حَلَوِيّات pl.n. sweets, candy; pastries, desserts

4910 وِصايَة guardianship; care, custody, tutelage

4912 مَأْوًى refuge, shelter

4913 بِرْكَة puddle; (swimming) pool

4915 تَخْزين storage, safekeeping

4918 تَجَسُّس espionage, spying

4920 مَنال attainment; reach, capacity

4923 تَنْقيب drilling, excavation; exploration

4925 ظَهيرَة noon, midday

4928 فتبول/فوتبول /futbool/ football, soccer

4931 مَرْدود returns, revenue, yield

4932 تَحَسُّب expectation, anticipation

4933 وَجْد affection; well-being

4934 ضَخّ pumping; injecting

4936 جِنازَة funeral

4937 خاطِرَة pl. خَواطِر idea, thought

4938 لاشَيْء nothingness, non-existence

4939 اِطْمِئْنان peace of mind, serenity; calm

4940 تَقَيُّد vn. being bound ب to; n. restriction

4944 قُرْص disk, tablet

4946 مُثَلَّث triangle; adj. triangle-like

4947 موبايِل pl. -aat mobile phone, cell phone

4949 اِحْتِراف professionalism

4951 فَضّ vn. settling (disputes); breaking up

4964 خِيرَة choice, best, pick, elite

4967 مُعْتَدٍ pl. -uun aggressor, assailant

4970 دَقيق flour

4972 عَدّ counting, calculating

4975 مُصْحَف manuscript, copy (Qur'an)

4984 كَيْد trick, ruse, plot, scheme

4987 وُسْع capability, capacity

4988 تَوَرُّط involvement, entanglement

4990 مَصاري pl.n. (Lev.) money, cash

4995 بك/بيه/بيك /bee, beeh/ Bey

4996 مَلْحَمَة fierce battle; epic

4997 اِحْتِكار monopoly, hoarding

5000 ضَمّ joining; addition, annexation

Verb

10 كانَ I (u) to be; (Irq.Gul.) جان /chaan/

15 قالَ I (u) to say إنَّ that, to tell ل sb إنَّ that

49 عَرَفَ I (i) to know sth/sb; to learn, find out

59 أَلَيْسَ I لَيْسَ he/it is not; لَيْسَ isn't ...?

75 يَرى ا رَأى I to see sth/sb; to think أنَّ that

78 تَمَّ I (i) to finish; to take place

90 أَمْكَنَ IV to be possible (ل for sb) to do sth

102 قامَ I (u) to stand; to carry out ب (task)

109 جاءَ I (i) to come, arrive; to show up

113 راحَ I (u) (Dia.) to go; (future marker)

123 عادَ I (u) to return, go back إلى to sth

124 شاء I (a) to want, desire sth; إن شاءَ الله

126 أرادَ IV to want, desire sth or أنْ to do sth

137 عَمِلَ I (a) to work, function; to make sth

138 عَنَى I (i) to mean, imply sth or أنَّ that

139 وَجَدَ I (i) to find sth/sb; يُوجَدُ there is/are

154 سَمِعَ I (a) to hear sb, listen إلى to sb

172 بَدَأَ I (a) to start, begin (في) sth

178 أصْبَحَ IV to become; to begin to do sth

180 صارَ I (i) to become; to happen

183 وَصَلَ I (i) to arrive إلى at; to link بَينَ between

187 أكَّدَ II to confirm أنَّ that; to emphasize

198 أخَذَ I (u) to take sth; to begin to do sth

214 زالَ (a) ما زالَ/يَزالُ ما/لا to continue to be/do

224 حَكَى I (i) to report; (Lev.Irq.) to speak

235 اِسْتَطاعَ X to be able أنْ; v.n. to do sth

240 قَدَّمَ II to offer, submit sth

257 بَقِيَ I (a) to remain; to endure; to continue

260 وَجَبَ I (i) to be necessary على for sb

266 ذَكَرَ I (u) to mention, remember sth/sb

282 شاف I (u) (Dia.) to see sth/sb; شايف a.p.

291 أضافَ IV to add sth

294 سَلَّمَ II to hand over sth; to greet sb

297 دَخَلَ I (u) to enter (إلى sth)

306 طَلَعَ I (u) to appear, emerge; to go out

312 أشارَ IV to indicate, cite, refer إلى to sth

319 حاوَلَ III to attempt, try to do sth

323 جَعَلَ I (a) to make sb/sth do sth

325 سَألَ I (a) to ask; request; to pray to (God)

326 عاشَ I (i) to live, be alive; to experience sth

329 بَدا I (u) to appear (أنَّ that); to seem

334 حَمَلَ I (i) to carry sth; to become pregnant

341 اِعْتَبَر VIII to regard as; to believe that

342 أحَبَّ IV to love, like sth/sb; to want sth

343 أتَى I (i) to come إلى to; to bring ب sth

345 خَرَجَ I (u) to go out; to deviate عن from

346 أعْطَى IV to give, provide sth to sb, or ل to sb

353 جَرَى I (i) to happen; to flow, run

357 كَتَبَ I (u) to write, author sth

359 وَضَعَ I (a) to put, place sth; to lay down

377 عَلِمَ I (a) to know sth, find out أنَّ that

387 ظَلَّ I (a) to stay; to keep on doing

396 رَدَّ I (u) to respond على to

408 حَدَثَ I (u) to happen, occur, take place

417 دَرَى I (i) to know, be aware of sth

418 دَعا I (u) to call إلى for sth; to invite sb إلى to

420 تَعالَى VI to be exalted (God)

422 اِعْتَقَد VIII to believe في in sth, or أنَّ/بأنَّ that

426 أعْلَنَ IV to announce (عن) sth or أنَّ that

429 أدَّى II to cause إلى sth; to lead إلى

443 بَلَغَ I (u) to reach, attain; to come to sb

445 حَصَلَ I (u) to get, obtain, acquire على sth

447 قَلَّ I (i) to be less; to decrease

451 تَمَنَّى V to wish ل sb sth; to hope أنْ that

453 تَحَدَّثَ V to speak to/with sb; to discuss

456 فَعَلَ I (a) to do sth

457 طَلَبَ I (u) to request sth; to order sth

459 وَقَعَ I (a) to fall down; to take place

470 صَلَّى II to pray, worship; to say a prayer

472 تَرَكَ I (u) to leave (behind), abandon sth

478 نَظَرَ I (u) to look إلى at, في into sth/sb

487 وَقَفَ I (i) to stop; to stand; to support

489 ذَهَبَ I (a) to go, leave, depart

495 حَبَّ I (i) to love, like sb; to want, like sth

502 زادَ I (i) to increase; to exceed; to add to sth

508 شَعَرَ I (u) to feel, be aware of ب sth

510 مَرَّ I (u) to go past; to stop by على (sb's place)

512 فَتَحَ I (a) to open sth; to turn on (lights, TV)

513   شَهِدَ I (a) to witness, see sth/sb; to testify

525   اِنْتَهَى VIII to end, finish, conclude sth

531   سَلِمَ I (a) to be safe; تَسْلَم thanks!

538   اِحْتاجَ VIII to need, want إلى sth/sb

580   فَهِمَ I (a) to understand sth/sb or أَنَّ that

593   ماتَ I (u) to die

605   أَوْضَحَ IV to clarify, explain (ل to sb) أَنَّ that

611   ظَهَرَ I (a) to appear; seem كَأَنَّ as if

613   رَجَعَ I (i) to return إلى to

619   لَعِبَ I (a) to play (game, role)

622   فَكَّرَ II to think في/ب about, believe أَنَّ that

639   قَتَلَ I (u) to kill sb; (pass.) قُتِلَ to be killed

650   دَفَعَ I (a) to push; to pay; to compel

661   اِنْتَظَرَ VIII to expect, wait for sth/sb

662   مَثَّلَ II to represent sb; to act as sb

672   شارَكَ III to participate (with sb) في in

673   نَزَلَ I (i) and نَزِلَ (a) to descend; stay في at

676   بَحَثَ I (a) to look عن for; to discuss في

681   قَدَرَ I (i) and قَدِرَ (a) to be capable of

688   تَعَرَّضَ V to be exposed إلى to sth

707   حَقَّقَ II to achieve sth; to investigate في sth

708   رَفَضَ I (u) to reject, refuse sth

722   اِتَّصَلَ VIII to get in touch ب with sb

726   اِسْتَمَرَّ X to last; to continue في doing

727   قَرَأَ I (a) and (Dia.) قَرَى (a) to read sth

730   نَسِيَ I (a) to forget sth/sb

733   رَفَعَ I (a) to raise sth; to increase sth

755   أَصابَ IV أُصِيبَ to suffer ب (injuries)

756   تَعَلَّقَ V to be connected ب with sth/sb

763   خَلَّى II (Dia.) to preserve, keep sb safe

767   قَرَّرَ II to decide, resolve أَنْ to do sth

772   كَشَفَ I (i) to reveal عن sth; to examine على sb

774   طالَبَ III to demand ب sth (from sb)

780   شَكَّلَ II to constitute, form, compose sth

787   سَمَحَ I (a) to allow, permit ل sb (to do sth)

800   مَلَكَ I (i) to own, possess sth; to control sth

804   تَوَقَّعَ V to anticipate sth

809   حَضَرَ I (u) to attend sth; to view (show)

819   سارَ I (i) to move, march; (Gul.) to go, walk

831   أَطْلَقَ IV to release, set free; to fire, shoot

834   عَدَّ I (u) to regard sth/sb as; لا يُعَدُّ countless

858   نَقَلَ I (u) to transfer sth; to translate sth

860   سَعَى I (a) to strive إلى for (a goal)

861   أَقامَ IV to install, set up sth; to reside في at

874   عَقَدَ I (i) to hold, convene (meeting)

877   سَجَّلَ II to register, record; to score

887   تابَعَ III to follow, monitor sth/sb

896   سَمَّى II to name, designate, call

898   عانَى III to suffer sth or من from sth

908   مَضَى I (i) to go by, elapse (time)

920   شَكَرَ I (u) to thank, give thanks to sb

924   جَلَسَ I (i) to sit (down); to sit إلى at (a table)

926   تَكَلَّمَ V to speak (مع with sb)

931   ضَمَّ I (u) to include, incorporate sth

936   تَوَقَّفَ V to stop; to be dependent on

952   تَغَيَّرَ V to change, be modified

954   نَجَحَ I (a) to succeed

964   رَجا I (u) to hope for, request sth

971   بارَكَ III to bless في sb (of God)

976   كَفَى I (i) to be enough (for sth/sb)

981   تَمَكَّنَ V to be able مِن to do sth

982   دامَ I (u) to last, continue; ما دامَ as long as

983   وَجَّهَ II to send, direct sth إلى to

985   كادَ I (a) (with imperf.) to almost do sth

989   صَدَّقَ II to believe sb/sth; to ratify على sth

1006   بَغَى I (i) to pursue, strive for sth

1007   واجَهَ III to face sth; to confront sb

1024 أَظْهَرَ *IV* to show, manifest, demonstrate

1025 سَبَقَ *I (i,u)* to precede, do previously

1029 شَمِلَ *I (a)* and شَمَلَ *(u)* to include sth

1030 قَطَعَ *I (a)* to cut off sth; to cover (distance)

1034 دَارَ *I (u)* to revolve; to go around حَوْلَ sth

1035 نَشَرَ *I (u)* to publish, announce sth

1038 ظَنَّ *I (u)* to think, believe, presume أَنَّ that

1042 خَافَ *I (a)* to fear sth/sb

1043 أَلْقَى *IV* to throw sth; to deliver (a speech)

1046 جَاب *I (i)* (Dia.) to bring sth

1047 تَحَوَّلَ *V* to be changed, be transformed

1049 الْتَقَى *VIII* to meet, encounter ب/مع sb

1050 صَدَرَ *I (u)* to be published; to emerge

1054 ضَحِكَ *I (a)* to laugh (على at)

1055 اِسْتَخْدَمَ *X* to use, employ, utilize sth

1056 سَاعَدَ *III* to help, assist, support sb

1058 سَقَطَ *I (u)* to fall; drop, decline

1066 دَرَسَ *I (u)* to study, learn sth

1070 سَوَّى *I* (Lev.Irq.Gul.) to do, make

1079 بَاتَ *I (i)* to become, begin, stay overnight

1082 أَعَادَ *IV* to repeat sth, do sth again

1084 أَدْرَكَ *IV* to grasp; to reach, attain

1089 ضَرَبَ *I (i)* to strike, hit; to give an example

1092 اِشْتَغَلَ *VIII* to work, be employed

1095 اِرْتَفَعَ *VIII* to rise, ascend; to increase, grow

1097 قَبِلَ *I (a)* to accept, receive; approve

1100 تَقَدَّمَ *V* to present sth; to advance

1107 جَمَعَ *I (a)* to gather, assemble sth

1109 اِخْتَلَفَ *VIII* to be different عن from

1110 أَجَابَ *IV* to respond, reply (إلى to)

1117 أَفَادَ *IV* to report أَنَّ/بِأَنَّ that

1128 لَقِيَ *I (a)* to find; meet, encounter sb/sth

1135 تَجَاوَزَ *VI* to surmount, go beyond sth

1138 قَضَى *I (i)* to pass, spend (time)

1145 اِعْتَمَدَ *VIII* to depend, rely على on sth/sb

1154 رَحِمَ *I (a)* to have mercy (God) on sb

1168 عَبَّرَ *II* to express (opinion), state (policy)

1175 اِنْطَلَقَ *VII* to depart, take off; to begin

1176 دَقَّ *I (u)* to strike; to knock; to ring (bell)

1179 تَعَلَّمَ *V* to learn, study sth

1186 وَصَفَ *I (i)* to describe; to prescribe

1191 رَضِيَ *I (a)* to be pleased ب/عن/على with

1198 أَثَارَ *IV* to stir up sth; to bring up (a subject)

1205 اِخْتَارَ *VIII* to select, pick sth/sb

1217 تَذَكَّرَ *V* to remember sth/sb

1218 تَنَاوَلَ *VI* to deal with; to eat (meal)

1224 طَرَحَ *I (a)* to suggest, propose; to offer

1228 حَفِظَ *I (a)* to preserve; to memorize

1238 بَكَى *I (i)* to weep; to mourn

1248 مَشَى *I (i)* to walk, go; to leave, go away

1260 قَدَّرَ *II* to estimate, value sth

1264 فَقَدَ *I (i)* to lose sth; to lack, be missing sth

1265 اِشْتَرَى *VIII* to buy, purchase sth

1268 نَامَ *I (a)* to sleep; lie down

1274 تَضَمَّنَ *V* to guarantee; comprise, include

1275 حَدَّدَ *II* to specify sth; to define sth

1280 عَرَضَ *I (i)* to exhibit sth; to inspect sth

1284 طَالَ *I (u)* to be lengthy; to take a while

1289 قَادَ *I (u)* to guide sb; to drive, pilot sth

1294 حَسَّ *I (i,a)* to feel, sense ب sth; a.p. حاسّ

1299 جَازَ *I (u)* to be allowed, be possible ل for sb

1313 تَحَقَّقَ *V* to become reality; to verify من sth

1315 خَلَصَ *I (u)* to arrive إلى at (a result)

1328 سَكَنَ *I (u)* to live في at/in; a.p. ساكِن residing

1331 اِنْبَغَى *VII* to be necessary (= must, should)

1332 اِتَّفَقَ *VIII* to agree (مع with sb)

1334 وَاصَلَ *III* to continue doing sth

1335 اِعْتَرَفَ *VIII* to admit ب (doing) sth

1336 أَثَّرَ *II* to affect على sth/sb

1337 قَصَدَ *I (i)* to mean sth; to pursue sth

1338 أَكَلَ *I (u)* to eat sth; to consume sb

1353 لاَحَظَ *III* to notice, observe sth or أَنَّ that

1359 أَصْدَرَ *IV* to publish; to issue; to emit

1360 نَظَّمَ *II* to organize, arrange; regulate

1367 اِزْدَادَ *VIII* to grow, increase, rise

1374 هَدَفَ *I (i)* to aim at إلى sth

1381 تَحَرَّكَ *V* to move, get moving

1383 اِقْتَرَبَ *VIII* to get close من to sth

1387 رَسَمَ *I (u)* to draw (picture); to outline sth

1393 مَارَسَ *III* to practice (profession, hobby)

1397 أَجْرَى *IV* to conduct, carry out, perform sth

1411 آمَنَ *IV* to believe ب in

1421 مَنَعَ *I (a)* to forbid sth; to prevent sb from

1426 وَافَقَ *III* to agree with sb

1432 فَازَ *I (u)* to win (ب sth); to defeat على sb

1441 بَعَثَ *I (a)* to send, mail sth إلى to sb

1452 فَشِلَ *I (a)* to fail, be unsuccessful في in sth

1459 اِسْتَحَقَّ *X* to deserve, merit sth

1470 فَضَّلَ *II* to prefer sth (على to sth else)

1474 سَاهَمَ *III* to participate in, contribute to

1475 اِتَّخَذَ *VIII* to adopt, pass (a resolution)

1477 أَحَسَّ *IV* to feel, sense ب sth or أَنَّ that

1511 أَثْبَتَ *IV* to prove, ascertain sth

1512 اِنْتَقَلَ *VIII* to move, transfer

1513 دَلَّ *I (u)* to point at, indicate that

1520 تَلَقَّى *V* to receive, get

1527 أَهَمَّ *IV* to concern sb; to be important to sb

1537 نَفَّذَ *II* to implement, carry out, execute

1541 تَوَفَّرَ *V* to be met, fulfilled في in sth/sb

1542 تَمَتَّعَ *V* to enjoy, be blessed ب with

1554 فَرَضَ *I (i)* to impose sth على on

1563 زَارَ *I (u)* to visit sb or a place

1571 أَشْبَهَ *IV* to resemble, look like sth/sb

1572 تَطَلَّبَ *V* to require sth (from sb)

1574 حَطَّ *I (u)* to put, place, set down; *a.p.* حَاطّ

1586 مَدَّ *I (u)* to extend sth; to stretch out sth

1592 أَرْسَلَ *IV* to send, transmit (ب) sth إلى to sb

1601 أَدْخَلَ *IV* to insert, include sth إلى/في in

1607 غَابَ *I (i)* to be absent; to set (sun)

1612 وَلَدَ *I (i)* (pass.) وُلِدَ to be born

1616 بَيَّنَ *II* to clarify; to show; to seem

1618 تَفَضَّلَ *V* please (come in, sit down, etc.)

1620 بَاعَ *I (i)* to sell sth

1625 اِهْتَمَّ *VIII* to be interested ب in sth

1629 دَار *I (i)* (Egy.Lev.Irq.Gul.) to turn

1634 تَعَرَّفَ *V* to get to know على sb

1644 اِمْتَدَّ *VIII* to extend, reach, spread إلى to

1648 غَيَّرَ *II* to modify sth; to replace sth

1651 حَلَّ *I (u)* to dissolve sth; to solve; to replace

1668 سَبَّبَ *II* to cause, produce, provoke sth

1671 صَرَّحَ *II* to declare, announce بِأَنَّ that

1672 سَافَرَ *III* to travel إلى to; to depart (on a trip)

1679 خَشِيَ *I (a)* to fear sth/sb; to be anxious

1694 حَكَمَ *I (u)* to govern; to sentence على sb

1699 تَبِعَ *I (a)* to follow, pursue sth/sb

1700 تَزَوَّجَ *V* to marry sb; to get married

1701 لَفَتَ *I (i)* to turn sb's attention إلى to

1705 وَلِيَ *I (i)* to follow, come after (sth/sb)

1706 غَادَرَ *III* to leave (a place), depart (on a trip)

1708 اِسْتَهْدَفَ *X* to target, aim at sth/sb

1715 تَدَخَّلَ *V* to intervene, interfere, meddle

1717 خَلَقَ *I (u)* to create, form sth

1726 اِسْتَقْبَلَ *X* to meet, welcome, greet sb

1734 اِسْتَفَادَ *X* to benefit, profit من from

1737 اِكْتَشَفَ *VIII* to discover, uncover sth

1738 تَرَدَّدَ *V* to hesitate; to frequent على (a place)

1742 صَنَعَ *I (a)* to design, build; fabricate

1746 سَحَبَ *I (a)* to withdraw, take out sth

1752 أَكْمَلَ *IV* to complete, finish sth

1755 تَبَيَّنَ *V* to become clear; to appear

1762 خَسِرَ I (a) to fail; to lose (game, time)

1764 تَساءَلَ VI to ask oneself, wonder, ponder

1768 خَدَمَ I (i,u) to serve, assist sb

1779 أَمَلَ I (u) to hope for, expect (ب/في) sth

1788 تَمَثَّلَ V to be represented; to be seen في in

1789 شاهَدَ III to see, watch, observe sth/sb

1797 اِحْتَوَى VIII to contain, include على sth

1801 خَصَّ I (u) to concern sb/sth

1802 اِبْتَسَمَ VIII to smile (ل at sb)

1825 نالَ I (a) to win sth; to gain (fame)

1838 رَغِبَ I (a) to wish for, desire, want في sth

1844 تَحَمَّلَ V to bear (burden, responsibility)

1846 جَزَى I (i) to repay, reward sb

1850 وَدَعَ I (a) to let, allow sb to do sth

1867 هَدَّدَ II to threaten sb ب with

1869 تَراجَعَ VI to retreat; to decrease

1870 وَرَدَ I (i) to show up; to appear في in (a text)

1873 تَعامَلَ VI to deal with مع sth/sb

1881 بَنَى I (i) to build, construct sth

1883 تَقَبَّلَ V to receive, accept

1894 صَرَخَ I (u) to shout, scream

1895 حَلَمَ I (u) to dream ب of sth/sb

1899 وَدَّ I (a) to want, like sth or أَنْ to do sth

1901 عَلا I (u) to rise, ascend, loom

1915 فَصَلَ I (i) to detach sth; to dismiss sb

1918 رَدَّدَ II to repeat, reiterate sth

1923 نادَى III to call ب for sth/sb

1924 مَنَحَ I (a) to award sth ل to sb

1925 كَبُرَ I (u) to grow up; to get bigger

1937 راد I (i) (Irq.Gul.) to want, need sth

1938 تَمَيَّزَ V to distinguish oneself; to be different

1950 جَلَّ I (i) to be majestic, exalted (of God)

1953 فاقَ I (u) to surpass sth/sb

1968 اِنْتَشَرَ VIII to spread out; to be publicized

1974 اِجْتَمَعَ VIII to meet مع/ب with

1979 اِمْتَلَكَ VIII to possess, own sth

1993 عَكَسَ I (i) to reflect; to contradict

1994 رَوَى I (i) to narrate; to provide an account

2007 ضاعَ I (i) to disappear, vanish

2009 اِتَّجَهَ VIII to face إلى/نحو towards

2014 تَوَلَّى V to seize control of sth

2018 أَعْرَبَ IV to express عن (one's opinion)

2020 أَخْرَجَ IV to expel sb; to publish sth

2022 رَحَّبَ II to welcome, receive ب sth/sb

2025 حَذَّرَ II to warn, caution sb من of

2033 لَحِقَ I (a) to follow, be attached to

2035 أَعْجَبَ IV to please sb (يُعْجِبُني I like it)

2036 قَعَدَ I (u) to sit down, be seated

2041 شَدَّدَ II to strengthen, emphasize sth

2044 تَسَبَّبَ V to cause, result in ب/في sth

2055 عَزَّ I (i) to be strong; الله عَزَّ وَجَلَّ

2057 اِخْتَفَى VIII to disappear; to hide

2059 كَمَنَ I (u) and كَمِنَ (a) to be hidden في in

2066 اِنْتَمَى VIII to be affiliated إلى with

2067 مَلَأَ I (a) to fill sth up; to occupy

2081 شَرِبَ I (a) to drink; (Dia.) to smoke

2084 تَبَقَّى V to be left over; to stay

2088 نَهَضَ I (a) to rise; to stand على upon

2091 أَبْدَى IV to demonstrate, express sth

2092 ناقَشَ III to debate, argue (an issue, topic)

2096 عَلَّقَ II to comment on; to postpone

2097 نَفَعَ I (a) to be useful ل to/for sb

2101 نَفَى I (i) to deny, disavow; reject

2102 رَكَّزَ II to focus على on sth

2103 دَعَمَ I (a) to support, promote sth/sb

2104 شَغَلَ I (a) to occupy (a post or position)

2107 اِدَّعَى VIII to allege, claim أَنَّ/بِأَنَّ that

2126 اِتَّهَمَ VIII to accuse sb ب of

2128 هَزَّ I (u) to shake, jolt, rock sth

2136 خَلا I (u) to be free مِن of sth; to be alone

2141 اِرْتَكَبَ VIII to commit (crime, error)

2143 اِسْتَمَعَ VIII to listen إلى to

2148 كَلَّفَ II to cost; to charge sb ب with (a task)

2161 أَسْعَدَ IV to make happy

2163 كَسَرَ *I (i)* to break sth; to violate (law)

2168 خَلَّصَ *II* (Dia.) to finish sth

2170 اِنْقَطَعَ *VII* to break, be cut off

2171 سَادَ *I (u)* to prevail; to rule, govern

2181 وَفَّرَ *II* to fulfill sth; to save (time)

2190 حَسِبَ *I (a,i)* to consider sb/sth to be

2197 بَذَلَ *I (u,i)* to exert, expend (effort)

2198 وَفَّقَ *II* to grant success (God) to sb

2200 هَرَبَ *I (u)* to flee, escape مِن from sth/sb

2202 اِعْتَقَلَ *VIII* to arrest, detain sb

2203 رَحَلَ *I (a)* to depart; to pass away; to travel

2205 أَمَرَ *I (u)* to order sb ب to do sth

2207 غَطَّى *II* to cover; conceal

2213 رَبَطَ *I (i,u)* to tie, connect sth

2221 تَأَخَّرَ *V* to be late, fall behind

2227 شَدَّ *I (i,u)* to make sth tight or strong

2246 حَظِيَ *I (a)* to enjoy ب (respect, support)

2259 سَيْطَرَ *QI* to control, dominate عَلَى sth

2261 اِحْتَلَّ *VIII* to occupy (land); to fill (post)

2273 أَنْهَى *IV* to complete, finish

2278 اِرْتَبَطَ *VIII* to be tied ب to sth

2279 حَرَّكَ *II* to make move, activate sth/sb

2283 أَسْفَرَ *IV* to result عن in, cause عن sth

2294 نَصَّ *I (u)* to stipulate, specify عَلَى sth

2298 صَبَّ *I (u)* to flow; to rain; to pour (tea)

2299 تَوَصَّلَ *V* to reach ب (an agreement)

2301 صَدَقَ *I (u)* to be truthful; to be correct

2306 حَوَّلَ *II* to convert sth (إلى)

2311 ضَغَطَ *I (u)* to press, click on عَلَى sth

2313 بَرَزَ *I (u)* to emerge; to stand out

2328 غَنَّى *II* to sing (sth)

2330 نَمَا *I (u)* to grow, develop; rise, increase

2332 اِبْتَعَدَ *VIII* to move away, distance oneself

2337 تَصَوَّرَ *V* to imagine, envision, ponder sth

2344 أَمْسَكَ *IV* to hold sth; to refrain from

2348 حَرَصَ *I (a)* to desire, be eager عَلَى for sth

2358 اِنْفَجَرَ *VII* to explode; to burst, erupt

2366 اِلْتَفَتَ *VIII* to turn around

2374 تَوَجَّهَ *V* to face إلى towards sth/sb

2395 طَارَ *I (i)* to fly; طارَ عَقْلُهُ to lose one's mind

2398 لَجَأَ *I (a)* to resort إلى to, take refuge إلى in

2412 صَعِدَ *I (a)* to rise, go up; to increase

2413 أَشَادَ *IV* to praise, commend ب sth

2423 تَطَلَّعَ *V* to look إلى at sth; to anticipate إلى sth

2425 أَصَرَّ *IV* to insist on, assert عَلَى sth

2426 اِقْتَرَحَ *VIII* to propose, suggest sth

2428 تَرَاوَحَ *VI* to vary, range بَيْن...و between ... and

2430 حَرَمَ *I (i,u)* to deprive sb مِن of

2431 ثَبَّتَ *II* to confirm, reinforce

2444 اِلْتَزَمَ *VIII* to adhere to, be committed to ب

2446 اِسْتَغْرَقَ *X* to last (time); be engrossed فِي in

2451 وَقَّعَ *II* to sign عَلَى (treaty)

2462 أَغْلَقَ *IV* to lock or bolt shut, to close (door)

2475 تَأَثَّرَ *V* to be affected ب/مِن by

2489 تَكَرَّرَ *V* to be reiterated; to be filtered

2493 أَطَلَّ *IV* to overlook, provide a view عَلَى of

2497 خَضَعَ *I (a)* to submit إلى to sb/sth

2498 خَصَّصَ *II* to specify, designate

2506 ضَاقَ *I (i)* to be narrow, tight (situation)

2519 اِطَّلَعَ *VIII* to examine, peruse عَلَى sth

2522 صَلُحَ *I (u)* to be suitable, be fitting; be valid

2523 تَوَفَّى *V* (pass.) تُوُفِّيَ to die

2527 اِسْتَقَرَّ *X* to settle down, become stable

2528 حَافَظَ *III* to preserve, protect عَلَى sth

2530 أَحْسَنَ *IV* to master, be good at sth

2534 لاقَى *III* to meet, encounter; to find

2536 كَرِهَ *I (a)* to hate sth/sb; to dislike sth

2543 فَاتَ *I (u)* to elude sb; to stop by عَلَى sb

2544 صَعُبَ *I (u)* to be difficult عَلَى for sb

2549 اِنْتَبَهَ *VIII* to be careful; to pay attention

2551 أَحَاطَ *IV* to surround, encircle ب sth

2554 ثَبُتَ *I (u)* to be confirmed

2564 دافَعَ III to defend عن sth/sb

2565 أَقَرَّ IV to ratify, accept; to confess ب sth

2573 حَمَى I (i) to protect sth (من against)

2575 هَبَّ I (u) to rage (wind, storm)

2585 ساوَى III to equalize sth

2607 عَجِزَ I (a) to be unable عن to do sth

2614 اِقْتَصَر VIII to be limited على to

2617 لَبِسَ I (a) to put on, wear

2620 أَتاحَ IV to provide (opportunity)

2621 تَعِبَ I (a) to get tired من of sth

2630 تَكَوَّنَ V to be composed, consist من of

2633 مالَ I (i) to bend, lean إلى towards

2634 نَشَأَ I (a) to grow up; to originate

2635 كَرَّرَ II to repeat sth; to filter, refine sth

2637 وَقَّفَ II to stop sb; to stop doing sth

2641 عَثَرَ I (u) to find, come across على sth

2643 دَمَّرَ II to destroy sth; to wreck, ruin sth

2644 حَيَّ يَحْيا to live; to experience (a life of)

2645 رَمَى I (i) to aim at إلى sth; to throw sth

2654 وَضَّحَ II to clarify, explain (ل to sb) أَنَّ that

2669 حانَ I (i) to arrive, approach (time)

2675 اِتَّضَحَ VIII to become clear أَنَّ that

2677 أَسْهَمَ IV to participate, contribute, share

2682 وَعَدَ I (i) to promise (sb) ب sth

2683 أَخْبَرَ IV to notify, tell sb ب/عن about sth

2700 اِضْطَرَّ VIII to compel, force sb إلى to do sth

2701 وَزَّعَ II to distribute sth على among

2703 شَرَحَ I (a) to explain sth ل to sb

2705 اِرْتَدَى VIII to wear, put on (clothes)

2712 طَبَّقَ II to implement (a plan)

2714 أَخْفَى IV to hide sth; to lower (one's voice)

2717 جَرَّبَ II to test, sample sth; to tempt sb

2720 اِفْتَتَحَ VIII to open, inaugurate sth

2725 اِسْتَدْعَى X to summon sb; to invoke sth

2727 سَهَّلَ II to facilitate, make easy

2728 حَقَّ I (i) to be right, have the right

2729 كَثُرَ I (u) to be plentiful

2735 اِفْتَرَضَ VIII to suppose sth or أَنَّ that

2737 اِنْطَبَقَ VII to be applicable; to conform with

2739 اِنْسَحَبَ VII to withdraw, leave (من from)

2762 فَرَّقَ II to distinguish بين between

2765 أَعَدَّ IV to prepare, make ready sth

2766 لاقَ I (i) to be proper, suitable ب for sb

2778 تَخَلَّى V to relinquish, surrender عن sth

2780 صَوَّرَ II to film, photograph; to portray

2785 عَزَّزَ II to strengthen, bolster, reinforce

2786 بَعُدَ I (u) to be located, situated, found

2790 تَناسَبَ VI to be compatible مع/و with

2811 اِنْعَكَسَ VII to be reflected; to have an effect

2816 نَطَقَ I (u) to speak, utter, pronounce ب sth

2819 مَسَّ I (a) to touch sth; to violate sth

2821 حالَ I (u) to prevent دونَ sth

2823 صاحَ I (i) to shout (sth, ب/على at sb)

2851 قارَبَ III to come close to sth

2854 غَسَلَ I (i) to wash, clean sth

2859 ضَمَّنَ II to guarantee, insure

2863 عالَجَ III to treat; to deal with; to process

2867 اِسْتَعْمَلَ X to use, make use of, employ

2873 أَدارَ IV to direct, manage sth; to turn

2874 اِشْتَرَكَ VIII to participate (with sb) في in

2875 تَطَرَّقَ V to broach, discuss إلى (topic, issue)

2880 اِتَّسَعَ VIII to be large enough ل for

2885 جَلَبَ I (i,u) to bring about, cause sth

2887 تَسَلَّمَ V to receive sth; to take on sth

2893 اِكْتَفَى VIII to be content, satisfied ب with

2896 اِحْتَفَظَ VIII to preserve, keep ب sth

2899 كَسَبَ I (i) to gain, achieve, earn sth

2903 أَشْرَفَ IV to supervise, manage على sth/sb

2917 بادَرَ *III* to begin; to hasten

2935 هَمَّ *I* (u) to preoccupy, concern sb

2942 صَحَّ *I* (i) to be true; to be proper

2950 جَدَّدَ *II* to renew, renovate; to try again

2952 اِسْتَغَلَّ *X* to take advantage of sth/sb

2964 تَعَوَّدَ *V* to get accustomed على to sth

2975 سَكَتَ *I* (u) to be quiet, be silent

2979 تَطَوَّرَ *V* to develop, grow; to advance

2980 اِعْتَذَرَ *VIII* to apologize إلى to sb عن for sth

2983 أَوْقَفَ *IV* to detain sb; to make sb stand

2986 كَلَّمَ *II* to speak with, talk to sb

2994 اِسْتَعَدَّ *X* to get ready ل for sth

2997 هَدَأَ *I* (a) to subside, abate; to calm down

3001 اِحْتَمَلَ *VIII* to tolerate; to expect

3003 اِعْتَرَضَ *VIII* to object على to sth

3005 سَرَقَ *I* (i) to steal sth

3009 آنَ *I* (i) to arrive (of time)

3012 غَلَبَ *I* (i) to defeat, overcome على sth/sb

3018 عادَلَ *III* to be equal to sth; (sports) to tie sb

3020 اِنْتَقَدَ *VIII* to criticize sb/sth

3025 سالَ *I* (i) to flow, run; to leak; to melt

3026 قَفَزَ *I* (i) to jump, leap

3032 شَجَّعَ *II* to encourage, support sb/sth

3033 حَيَّا *II* to greet, salute sb; to praise, laud sb

3051 رَعَى *I* (a) to protect sb; to sponsor sth/sb

3052 دَوَّرَ *II* (Dia.) to look على for

3069 اِنْقَلَبَ *VII* to turn around/over

3070 اِحْتَرَمَ *VIII* to respect, revere sb/sth

3075 أَنْتَجَ *IV* to produce, result in

3076 رَكِبَ *I* (a) to get in, get on board

3088 فاضَ *I* (i) to overflow; to exceed عن sth

3094 لَزِمَ *I* (a) to be necessary; to cling to

3095 غَرِقَ *I* (a) to sink, drown, be submerged

3097 تَأَمَّلَ *V* to ponder (في) sth

3099 تَصَرَّفَ *V* to act, behave في/مع with sth/sb

3110 كَذَبَ *I* (i) to lie على to sb)

3112 خاضَ *I* (u) to wage (war, campaign)

3113 تَعَدَّى *V* to go beyond; to infringe على on

3121 قَدِمَ *I* (a) to arrive, come إلى to

3128 نَوَى *I* (i) to intend, want (to do sth)

3131 أَنْكَرَ *IV* to deny, dispute (claim)

3133 اِسْتَعْرَضَ *X* to review sth; to tour (facilities)

3136 أَوْحَى *IV* to suggest بِأَنَّ that

3141 زَرَعَ *I* (a) to plant; to cultivate (land)

3147 أَخْطَأَ *IV* to make a mistake

3156 اِتَّسَمَ *VIII* to be characterized ب by

3159 هَبَطَ *I* (i,u) to fall, drop; to land (aircraft)

3164 اِسْتَجابَ *X* to accept; to comply with

3167 قَرُبَ *I* (u) and قَرِبَ (a) to approach

3170 فَسَّرَ *II* to explain, interpret sth (ل for sb)

3172 شَكا *I* (u) to complain إلى to sb

3175 اِسْتَيْقَظَ *X* to wake up; to be alert

3182 تَواصَلَ *VI* to pursue (efforts)

3189 فاجَأَ *III* to surprise sb (ب with)

3198 ذَكَّرَ *II* to remind sb

3200 فَرِحَ *I* (a) to be happy ب/ل about sth

3207 أَعانَ *IV* to assist, support sb/sth

3213 اِسْتَعادَ *X* to recover, regain, reclaim sth

3214 مَيَّزَ *II* to differentiate بين between

3216 خَفَّفَ *II* to lower, lessen sth

3218 نَتَجَ *I* (i) to result, arise من/عن from

3224 سَتَرَ *I* (u,i) to veil, cover, hide sth

3232 تَبَنَّى *V* to adopt sth; to be built

3234 صَرَفَ *I* (i) to spend (money), dismiss sb

3241 أَتَمَّ *IV* to complete, finish, conclude sth

3249 حَدَّثَ *II* to tell sb (عن about); to narrate sth

3253 ضَرَّ *I* (u) to harm ب (one's health)

3261 زَعَمَ *I* (u) to allege, claim أَنَّ/بِأَنَّ that

3263 أَقْبَلَ *IV* to approach على sb/sth

3273 اِسْتَنَدَ *VIII* to lean on, rely on إلى sth

3274 سَرَى *I* (i) to flow; to apply على to (a law)

3279 مَسَكَ *I* (u) to grab, hold sth or ب sth

3288 أَقْدَمَ IV to undertake, tackle على sth

3305 كَفَّ I (u) to abstain عن from sth

3309 شَرَعَ I (a) to start, undertake في sth

3314 تَجَلَّى V to become evident; to manifest itself

3321 حَثَّ I (u) to urge, incite sb على to do sth

3325 قَلَّلَ II to reduce sth; to downplay sth

3333 عَبَرَ I (u) to cross (border, street)

3335 خَطَّطَ II to make plans; to define (borders)

3351 أَبَى I (a) to refuse sth or أَنْ to do sth

3352 اِكْتَمَلَ VIII to be finished, be perfect

3357 تَعَيَّنَ V to be incumbent على on sb

3359 أَسَاءَ IV to offend إلى sb; to do sth badly

3360 تَحَكَّمَ V to control ب/في sth

3369 مَكَّنَ II to make possible مِن sth (for sb)

3370 جَدُرَ I (u) to be worth ب (mentioning)

3372 حَرَقَ I (i) to burn sth; to hurt sb

3378 أَحْدَثَ IV to cause (reaction, change)

3383 لَبَّى II to meet (needs); to comply with

3384 حَلَّ I (i) to befall ب/على sb; to start

3390 أَيَّدَ II to support, assist sb

3419 حَوَى I (i) to contain, include (على) sth

3432 حَارَبَ III to fight, wage war against sb/sth

3433 نَاسَبَ III to be suitable for sb

3436 لَفَّ I (u) to wrap sth; to turn, rotate

3438 رَاقَبَ III to monitor, supervise sth/sb

3445 اِقْتَضَى VIII to demand, require sth

3446 عَدَّلَ II to modify, amend, adjust sth

3450 عَلَّمَ II to teach sb sth; to put a mark on sth

3457 عَمَّ I (u) to become prevalent

3460 لاَحَ I (u) to appear, loom

3461 هَمَسَ I (i) to whisper ل to sb

3462 بَثَّ I (u) to broadcast; to disseminate

3463 غَدَا I (u) to become; to seem, appear

3476 اِسْتَشْهَدَ X (pass.) اُسْتُشْهِدَ to be martyred

3487 أَسْرَعَ IV to hurry, hasten في in doing sth

3503 تَقَرَّرَ V to be decided, be resolved

3506 أَدَانَ IV to denounce, censure sth/sb

3510 وَعَى I (i) to be aware of sth

3511 شَكَّ I (u) to doubt, distrust في sth/sb

3520 جَرَحَ I (a) (pass.) جُرِحَ to be injured

3525 خَفِيَ I (a) to be hidden; لا يُخْفَى obvious

3526 ضَبَطَ I (u,i) to regulate, control; adjust, fix

3527 اِعْتَادَ VIII to get used على to sth

3545 حَصَلَ I (u) to happen, take place

3555 مَسَحَ I (a) to wipe sth clean; to survey

3561 تَشَرَّفَ V to be honored (على to meet sb)

3572 لَمَسَ I (i,u) to touch, feel, sense sth

3573 اِنْخَفَضَ VII to decrease, be reduced

3575 نَصَحَ I (a) to advise sb (ب to do sth)

3579 عَيَّنَ II to appoint sb; to define sth

3586 اِنْضَمَّ VII to join, become part of إلى sth

3589 عَارَضَ III to oppose, resist sth/sb

3593 أَقْسَمَ IV to swear يَمِيناً an oath, swear ب by

3602 بَرَّرَ II to justify; to vindicate

3610 أَبْلَغَ IV to inform sb; to report

3613 تَعَارَضَ VI to clash, conflict مع/و with sth

3620 بَقَى I (a) /ba'a, yib'a/ (Egy.) to become

3621 اِخْتَتَمَ VIII to finalize (an activity)

3625 شَنَّ I (u) to wage (a war, campaign)

3630 نَعَمَ I (u,a) and نَعِمَ I (a) to live in comfort

3634 خَالَفَ III to violate (the law)

3635 تَرَتَّبَ V to derive or result على from

3636 أَرْضَى IV to satisfy, please sb

3638 اِسْتَوْعَبَ X to grasp sth; to absorb sth

3651 سَدَّدَ II to obstruct; to pay off; to aim, shoot

3652 هَدَى I (i) to lead, guide sb

3661 تَشَكَّلَ V to be formed, be composed

3681 خَتَمَ I (i) to conclude sth; to seal sth

3704 ضَمِنَ I (a) to guarantee, insure

3708 قَاوَمَ III to resist, oppose sth

3736 لَبِثَ I (a) to linger; ما لَبِثَ أَنْ it wasn't long

3749 غَفَرَ I (i) to pardon, forgive لِ sb sth

3750 زَالَ I (u) to disappear, vanish

3756 جَسَّدَ II to embody, personify sth

3766 اِشْتَدَّ VIII to intensify, grow more intense

3773 اِنْطَوَى VII to contain, include على sth

3778 رَاعَى III to heed, observe sth; to respect sth

3791 اِعْتَزَمَ VIII to be determined على to do sth

3798 أَكْثَرَ IV to do مِن sth frequently

3803 سَهُلَ I (u) to be easy, be convenient

3809 اِنْتَصَرَ VIII to be victorious (على) over sb/sth

3812 عَقَلَ I (i) to be reasonable; to make sense

3816 رَكَضَ I (u) to run, race

3823 لَعَنَ I (a) to curse, damn sb/sth

3825 تَأَكَّدَ V to ascertain مِن sth

3841 عَصَفَ I (i) to rage (wind, conflict)

3849 أَمَّنَ II to safeguard; to insure

3856 نَبَعَ I (u) to emerge; to emanate, flow

3861 اِحْتَفَلَ VIII to celebrate بِ sth

3862 قَوِيَ I (a) to be strong

3872 سَدَّ I (u) to close; to turn off; to pay; to fill

3873 حَلَّقَ II to hover; to circle (the skies)

3885 اِسْتَأْهَلَ X to deserve sth

3887 تَوَاجَدَ VI to be located; to be present

3894 خَبَّرَ II to tell sb sth or عن about sth

3903 اِفْتَقَرَ VIII to lack, be in need إلى of sth

3910 رَصَدَ I (u) to observe, track, monitor sth

3912 اِخْتَرَقَ VIII to break into; to traverse

3913 أَلْغَى IV to cancel, terminate; abrogate

3917 أَكْرَمَ IV to honor, respect sb; to venerate sb

3920 اِنْدَرَجَ VII to be included; to be categorized

3922 أَضَاعَ IV to lose sth; to waste (time)

3924 أَنْزَلَ IV to bring or send down, lower sth

3927 ذَابَ I (u) to dissolve, melt

3935 سَارَعَ III to hurry, hasten إلى to a place

3939 تَرَكَّزَ V to be centered في on sth

3940 حَلَا I (u) to be sweet; to enjoy doing sth

3941 تَوَافَقَ VI to agree, concur

3942 اِسْتَضَافَ X to host, invite sb

3955 اِسْتَبْعَدَ X to rule out (regard as unlikely)

3956 أَضْحَى IV to become; to start (doing)

3964 تَوَالَى VI to follow in succession

3966 حَرَّمَ II to outlaw, ban, forbid sth

3974 تَسَلَّلَ V to infiltrate إلى sth

3977 هَاجَمَ III to assault sth/sb; to raid sth

3986 خَطَرَ I (u,i) to occur لِ to sb

3989 أَجْدَى IV to be useful, helpful

3991 شَقَّ I (u) to split, cut through sth

4009 طَيَّبَ II to make pleasant; to enhance

4017 نَزَفَ I (i) to bleed, hemorrhage; drain

4023 عَامَلَ III to treat sth/sb

4027 لَوَّحَ II to wave إلى at sb; to hint at بِ sth

4030 قَاتَلَ III to fight (sb)

4034 رَأَسَ I (a) to lead sth; to chair (meeting)

4036 طَرَأَ I (a) to happen, occur على to sb

4056 تَلَا I (u) to come after; to recite (Qurʾan)

4058 نَوَّهَ II to point out, mention بِ/إلى أَنَّ that

4073 طَوَّلَ II to prolong sth; to take (a long) time

4079 تَدَفَّقَ V to flow, stream; to drip, drop

4080 أَبْعَدَ IV to remove, eliminate, expel

4086 عَجَبَ I (i) (Egy.Lev.) to be pleasing to sb

4094 رَافَقَ III to accompany, escort sb

4108 قَصَّرَ II to shorten; (Gul.) to fall short

4111 اِسْتَغْرَبَ X to be surprised (مِن at)

4115 حَدَّ I (u) to limit مِن sth; to halt, stop مِن sth

4125 رَقَصَ I (u) to dance

4133 تَجَمَّعَ V to gather together, assemble, rally

4136 اِجْتَاحَ VIII to strike, invade (country)

4138 سَبَحَ I (a) to swim

4140 تَخَيَّلَ V to imagine, suppose sth or أَنَّ that

4143 جَرُؤَ I (u) to dare على to do sth

4680 اِسْتَحَالَ X to be impossible

4683 كَفَلَ I (u) to guarantee sth; to support sb

4686 أَوْصَى IV to advise sb (ب to do sth)

4688 تَعَادَلَ VI to be balanced, tie each other

4696 وَثِقَ I (i) to trust ب in sth/sb

4701 هَوَى I (i) to drop, fall down, collapse

4714 خَرَقَ I (i,u) to violate (law); to break (barrier)

4718 أَمْضَى IV to finalize sth; to spend (time)

4734 اِسْتَوْجَبَ X to require sth

4740 تَجَزَّأَ V to be divided, partitioned, detached

4745 قَصَرَ I (i) to shorten; قَصَر (u) to fall short

4747 تَصَاعَدَ VI to climb, increase

4761 قَصَفَ I (i) to bomb, shell sth

4768 مَلَّ I (a) to get bored, fed up (من with sth)

4781 أَزَالَ IV to remove; to uninstall (software)

4790 تَسَاقَطَ VI to collapse

4803 أَسِفَ I (a) to feel sorry على about

4814 تَزَايَدَ VI to increase, grow in number

4820 أَسْلَمَ IV to surrender, hand over sth

4822 أَفْسَدَ IV to spoil, ruin sth; to corrupt sb

4828 أَحْصَى IV to count, calculate sth

4834 عَطَى I (i) (Magh.Lev.Gul.) to give sth to sb

4844 فَرَّ I (i) to escape, flee; to defect, desert

4847 تَأَسَّسَ V to be established, be founded

4853 كَفَّلَ II to support, maintain, provide for sb

4856 طَمْأَنَ QI to pacify, assuage, reassure sb

4879 أَبْقَى IV to keep sth/sb (على in a state)

4880 حَسَّنَ II to improve sth; to decorate sth

4890 اِسْتَغْفَرَ X to beg (God) for forgiveness

4896 اِمْتَلَأَ VIII to be filled, to become full

4906 فَرَقَ I (i) to be different, make a difference

4911 أَلْحَقَ IV to append ب sth

4917 تَمَسَّكَ V to clutch, adhere to ب sth

4919 أَبْرَزَ IV to highlight, expose sth

4922 هَاجَرَ III to emigrate

4948 جَهِلَ I (a) to ignore, not know sth

4950 أَحْضَرَ IV to bring sth; to prepare (food)

4959 تَعَهَّدَ V to pledge ب to do sth

4960 كَبَسَ I (i) to press; to dial, click

4965 أَسْمَى IV to name, designate, call

4968 قَبَضَ I (i) to arrest, apprehend, seize على sb

4973 اِسْتَنَّى X+II بِسْتَنَّى (Dia.) to wait

4974 نِطَى I (i) يِنْطِي (Irq.) to give, provide sth

4978 نَطَرَ I (u) to wait for sth/sb

4982 تَعَدَّدَ V to be numerous or diverse

4991 جَابَ I (u) to explore, traverse

4994 اِرْتَكَزَ VIII to be centered, focused على on

4998 فَاحَ I (u) to emanate (scent, perfume)